Child and Adolescent Development

Child and Adolescent Development

LAWRENCE B. SCHIAMBERG

MICHIGAN STATE UNIVERSITY

edited and researched by GALE SPIRTAS SCHIAMBERG

MACMILLAN PUBLISHING COMPANY
NEW YORK

Collier Macmillan Publishers
LONDON

Dedication

For a book that deals, in part, with the vital contributions of the family to child and adolescent development, it is fitting that this book be dedicated to my family—Gale, Scott, Bruce, Elizabeth, and Miriam Schiamberg, and to the memory of Louis Schiamberg and Elizabeth and Abe Spirtas.

Complete reference citation for quoted material or for pictures not original to *Child and Adolescent Development* can be found in the ''References'' section on pp. A-25–A-56. Furthermore, exact wording of credit lines, as stipulated by certain copyright holders, appears on pp. A-22–A-24, which constitute a continuation of the copyright page.

Copyright © 1988, Macmillan Publishing Company, a division of Macmillan, Inc.

PRINTED IN THE UNITED STATES OF AMERICA

Macmillan Publishing Company
866 Third Avenue, New York, New York 10022

Collier Macmillan Canada, Inc.

LIBRARY OF CONGRESS CATALOGING-IN-PUBLICATION DATA

Schiamberg, Lawrence B.
  Child and adolescent development.

  Bibliography
  Includes index.
  1. Child development. 2. Adolescence. I. Title.
RJ131.S27 1988   155.4   87-20245
ISBN 0-02-406820-9

Printing: 3 4 5 6 7   Year: 9 0 1 2 3 4

Preface

The study of child and adolescent development is nothing less than the study of fascinating and vital parts of life—the years before adulthood. This book, designed for introductory courses in child and adolescent development, has a threefold purpose: (1) to introduce the beginning student to the challenge and excitement of studying the infant, the child, and the adolescent from a lifespan perspective; (2) to demonstrate a framework for considering the developing child and adolescent in relation to the significant social environments of life; and (3) to present the theories, research, and principles of child and adolescent development in such a manner as to capture something of the day-to-day reality of children's and adolescents' relationships with their families, teachers, and friends. Some of the fascination of studying child and adolescent development lies in the recognition that it deals with our own lives; that is, what we are and what may have contributed to our own development.

Child and Adolescent Development is arranged to reflect the aim of the study: to examine the qualitative and quantitative changes in human beings over time. Following the first three introductory chapters, the book is organized chronologically, examining the changes from the prenatal period through late adolescence. Chapter 1 introduces the major concepts and principles of child and adolescent development; Chapter 2 surveys more closely the main theories introduced in Chapter 1; and Chapter 3 describes the specific factors that influence the development of human beings and the methods by which we study it. Chapters 4–17 proceed chronologically: Chapters 4 and 5 review the prenatal period and birth; Chapters 6, 7, and 8 examine infancy and toddlerhood; Chapters 9, 10, and 11 focus on the preschooler; Chapters 12, 13, and 14 discuss middle childhood; and Chapters 15, 16, and 17 conclude the text's lifespan perspective with a detailed coverage of adolescence.

The book's approach throughout is to treat child and adolescent development as a process that involves the *mutual*, *reciprocal*, and *dynamic* interaction of the individual with the significant social environments of his or her life. These social environments include the family, the community/neighborhood, the peer group, and the school, as well as "significant others"—parents, siblings, friends, and teachers. We call this approach to child development the *systems* or *ecological perspective*. In its simplest form, the systems approach is a way to understand the holistic and interactive dimensions of child behavior and development. It provides beginning students with a useful technique for approaching the significant issues and problems of child and adolescent development by: calling attention to the mutual adaptation between the developing child and the significant contexts of life, the systems perspective does *not* ask students to rely on simplistic, overly general, or convenient solutions, but rather it helps students to ask the right questions about child development.

A significant aspect of this book is its complete and comprehensive consideration of the role of the family throughout the lifespan. The book gives credence to the relatively new concept of the family as a system: current research on the family is presented in a way that clearly shows how the family relates to the development of the individual at each stage of childhood and adolescence. The family-systems approach allows students to examine the contributions of the family to child growth and development. Further, attention is given to the impact of alternative family forms and of working mothers on child and adolescent development.

An effort has been made to balance necessary depth with a breadth of subjects that introduce students to important and unique perspectives in child development. Many pedagogical devices and special features are included in the text to aid students in their study. For example, each chapter includes the following basic aids:

· Chapter-opening outline.
· Drawings, charts, and photographs that complement and expand on the text.
· End-of-chapter summaries that highlight major points and concepts.
· Key terms. (A complete glossary is included at the end of the book.)
· Questions for discussion or self-study.
· Suggested readings (annotated lists of selected key books).

In addition, each chapter features application boxes that focus and expand on a specific topic, theory, or issue. The application boxes and the many real-life examples used throughout the book are designed to encourage students to reflect on their own experiences and opinions and to generate group discussion.

Four full-color photo essays beautifully depict the infant, the child, and the adolescent in key social environments that contribute to development: the family, the community/neighborhood, the school, and the peer group. The photo essays enhance and complement the key theories and concepts of child and adolescent development presented in the book.

The text is accompanied by an extensive package of supplementary materials for instructors and students. The *Study Guide*, developed by Pamela E. Chibucos and Thomas R. Chibucos of Northern Illinois University, contains a full range of material to aid students in better understanding the text. Each chapter in the guide includes a list of objectives, important terms and concepts, study questions, discussion questions, self-tests, practice exercises, and suggested activities. A *Test Bank*, also prepared by Pamela E. Chibucos and Thomas R. Chibucos, contains over 2,000 test items and essay questions for each chapter, as well as two midterm and two final exams. The *Test Bank* is available in booklet form and in computerized versions for Apple II and IBM-PC. A comprehensive *Instructor's Manual*, written by Phyllis Click of Moorpark College, is also available. It contains a section of general information to aid in planning and conducting a course: included are sample syllabi, suggestions for group discussion and role playing, study projects, the use and sources of audio-visual material, and other information to assist in creating an exciting course. A second section is arranged by chapter and includes teaching goals, chapter summaries, ideas for classroom discussion, and suggested audio-visual materials.

Acknowledgments

There have been many individuals—family members, professional colleagues, reviewers, friends, photographers, students, typists, and staff of Macmillan Publishing Company—who have provided invaluable assistance in the writing of this book. In particular, I would like to thank my family, Gale, Scott, Bruce, and Elizabeth, for their endless cooperation and patience in an effort that took many years to complete. Appreciation is also exended to my mother, Mrs. Louis Schiamberg, and my sisters, brothers, and their families for their longstanding support. My wife, Gale, deserves special recognition for her numerous contributions to the project: for obtaining many of the excellent photographs in the book, updating vital census information, gathering research, and carefully reading the manuscript and typeset proofs. Readers will appreciate her insistence on accuracy, detail, and clear writing.

My appreciation is also extended to my students and colleagues at the College of Human Ecology, Michigan State University, who provided invaluable contributions to the formulation of ideas central to this book, as well as for creating an atmosphere in which the book could be written. Among them are Lois Lund, Robert Griffore, the late Beatrice Paolucci, Robert Boger, Donald Melcer, and Verna Hildebrand. Many of the excellent photographs in this book are the professional work of Sylvia Byers, Darryl Jacobson, Jerrold Jacobson, David Kostelnik, Hope and Jeffrey Morris, Irving Rader, Gary Rowe, and Gene Tamashiro.

I am indebted as well to the many reviewers of the text, whose valuable contributions, suggestions, and criticisms were instrumental in its development: Curt Acredolo, University of California at Davis; Lee Ross, Frostburg State University; John Bonvillian, University of Virginia; Virginia Monroe, University of South Dakota; Hurts Hall, Northwestern State University; David V. Williams, Ithaca College; Roberta Corrigan, University of Wisconsin, Milwaukee; Gary B. Verna, Children's Hospital, Boston; Afred Stone, Edinboro University; Thomas Hannain, Auburn University; Michael Ash, Texas A & M University; James Davidson, Bowling Green State University; Doris Williams, University of Idaho; Bill Meredith, University of Nebraska at Omaha; Ann Mills, Oklahoma State University; Jo Rosauer, Iowa State University; Beverly Sulley, Southern Illinois University at Carbondale; and Thomasita Chandler, University of Akron.

I wish to thank Dr. Dorothy McKeekin of the Department of Natural Science at Michigan State University, for her helpful review, suggestions, and critique of genetic factors in Chapter 4. My appreciation also goes to Professor Jacqueline Wright of the College of Nursing at Michigan State University, for her helpful review of and suggestions for Chapter 5; to the staff of Lansing Public Library, especially Joseph Brooks and Judy Forrester; to the staff of East Lansing Public Library, especially Sylvia Marabate and John Gleason; and to the staff of Michigan State University, Library of Michigan Documents Division, especially Eleanor Boyles, Marilyn Owens, and Jon Harrison. The help of Michigan State University reference librarians Lori Goetsch, Denise Forro, and Kimberly Ginther-Webster is much appreciated. For their assistance in obtaining infant photographs, I thank the staffs of Lansing General, St. Lawrence, and Sparrow hospitals. For her assistance in typing the manuscript, I am grateful to Martha West. I also want to thank the staff of the Okemos High School, including Dr. Mary Carew, Ms.

Eleanor Keating, Dr. John Lanzetta, and Mr. Scott Purvis, for their assistance with the manuscript and photographs.

Finally, the editorial, production, and design staff of the College Division of Macmillan Publishing Company provided invaluable assistance, guidance, and advice. In particular, I am thankful to the college division editor, Julie Alexander; the project editor, Herb Kirk; the production editor, Aliza Greenblatt; the designer, Bob Freese, and the dummier, Holly Reid McLaughlin, who were ever ready with professional advice and personal support.

Lawrence B. Schiamberg

Brief Contents

Detailed Contents

3 Determinants of Child Development   63

4 The Beginning: Genetic Factors and Prenatal Development   107

5   Birth: An Emerging Family Relationship   153

6   Infancy and Toddlerhood: Contexts of Development   191

7 Infancy and Toddlerhood: Physical and Cognitive Development 221

8 Infancy and Toddlerhood: Social and Personality Development 271

Child and Adolescent Development

1 Child Development: Concepts and Principles

Sweet childish days, that were as long
As twenty days are now.
                    —Wordsworth, To a Butterfly

Heaven lies about us in our infancy!
Shades of the prison-house begin to close
Upon the growing boy,
But he beholds the light, and whence it flows,
He sees it in his joy;
The Youth, who daily farther from the East
Must travel, still is Nature's priest,
And by the vision splendid
Is on his way attended;
At length, the man perceives it die away,
And fade into the light of common day.
                    —Wordsworth, Intimations of Immortality

This book has three purposes:

1. To introduce the beginning student to the challenge and excitement of studying the individual through the childhood and adolescent years from a *lifespan perspective*. We thus consider childhood and adolescence in relation to the events and developments that both precede and follow these phases of life. Often these phases are approached as relatively isolated periods; in contrast, we emphasize that in order to understand the child and the adolescent fully, we must be aware of:
   - An individual's *developmental history*, or what has occurred prior to a given point in time.
   - An individual's *developmental trajectory*, or *predicted future*—how events at a given point in time may relate to and influence the tasks and experiences of later (yet-to-be-experienced) life phases.
2. To present a framework for thinking about the developing child and adolescent in relation to the significant social environments of his or her life. These social environments include the family, the school, the peer group, the community, the neighborhood, the media, and the world of work. We call this approach to child development—which emphasizes the *reciprocal and dynamic interaction* of person and environment—the *systems* or *ecological perspective* (Fig. 1.1).
   - The relationships are *reciprocal:* One source of influence (a parent) has an effect on another source of influence (a child) that in turn has an effect back on the first influence, and so on.
   - The relationships are *dynamic* because they are continually changing.

2

The course of human development is influenced by many people and experiences.

One important aspect of this perspective is its *multidisciplinary* nature. Information from many disciplines, including psychology, sociology, family studies, anthropology, biology and physiology, history, child development, medicine, and education is applied to the study of the child and the adolescent.

3. To present the theory, research, and principles of child and adolescent development in a way that captures something of the *reality of children and their families,* teachers, and friends. In other words, the approach to child development taken here is a holistic one that examines living, breathing, feeling, thinking human beings. The study of child and adolescent development is nothing less than the study of a fascinating and vital time of life—the years before adulthood. Some of this fascination lies in the recognition that the content of this book deals with *our lives:* what we are and what may have contributed to our own development.

Why Examine Child Development from a Lifespan Perspective?

The strength of a lifespan view of child development is the recognition that the period from the prenatal years through adolescence is only one part of human development. Since many child-development textbooks cover development only through the adolescent years, there is a very real danger that some readers may

FIGURE 1.1
The systems or ecological perspective to child and adolescent development emphasizes the reciprocal *and* dynamic *interaction of person and environment.*

assume that many of the important dimensions of the life process are over—or at least well on their way to completion—by the end of adolescence. Major developmental events and processes do indeed take place between conception and adolescence, but human beings continue to change after adolescence and throughout the lifespan.

Further, there is some evidence that many such changes cannot be readily predicted from knowledge about childhood or adolescent development alone. For example, lifespan research on intellectual development has demonstrated several pertinent findings in support of this point (Schaie, Labouvie, and Buech, 1973; Schaie, 1983; Baltes, Dittman-Kohli, and Dixon, 1984), including the following:

- There is *considerable diversity in the pattern of intellectual development and change* throughout adulthood and the aging period. For example, from young adulthood (age twenty-five) through the aging years (eighty-one), intellectual performance for some individuals declined, for others it increased, and for still others it remained virtually unchanged (Schaie, 1983).
- *Differences between individuals* on intellectual performance became *greater* as they progressed through the adult years (compared with differences between these same individuals as children or adolescents).
- Emergent differences between individuals cannot be completely understood by a simple knowledge of the differences between individuals in intellectual development as children and adolescents.
- *Changes in intellectual performance* over the adult years were found to be *more related to the birth cohort* (the group composed of all individuals born at a given time in history, such as in a specific year) of an individual *than to the chronological age* of that individual. For example, a group of fifty-nine-year-olds born in 1904 (thus, a 1904 cohort) showed higher intellectual performance (when tested in 1963, at the age of fifty-nine) than another group of fifty-nine-year-olds born in 1897 (an 1897 cohort) and tested in 1956. Further, a similar pattern of higher intellectual performance was found when the fifty-nine-year-olds from the 1904 cohort reached sixty-six and seventy-three years of age respectively (compared with sixty-six- and seventy-three-year-olds from the 1897 cohort) (Schaie, 1983).

With reference to the last point, it was suggested that individuals in different birth cohorts were likely to have experienced different or unique historical circumstances that resulted in differing paths of development. That is, a group of people or a birth cohort may develop in a particular way because they were born at a specific time in history and therefore experienced events unlike those of people born at other times. There is reason to believe that individuals who were adolescents at the time of the Watergate political scandal in the United States, or the Vietnam War or the Great American Depression, were influenced by events unlike those of adolescents in other birth cohorts (Elder, Nguyen, and Caspi, 1985). There is increasing evidence that such "cohort effects" may have a greater impact on adolescent development than do factors sometimes associated with age alone (Nesselroade and Baltes, 1974; Schaie, 1983; Baltes, Dittman-Kohli, and Dixon, 1984). A full understanding of the historical background of an individual is thus a vital dimension of the lifespan perspective.

Likewise, the lifespan perspective includes the influence of significant life events. Many such life events are **normative** (occur for most individuals at a specific time or range of times) and include the development of language in infancy, entering school at the beginning of middle childhood, the onset of puberty, and leaving home during adolescence. Other life events are **nonnormative** (occur for some but not all individuals at almost any time) such as divorce, the death of a parent, or the onset of a serious illness or handicapping condition. A number of such events that can influence developmental change across the lifespan are discussed in this book.

Why Examine Child Development from a Systems Perspective?

Whereas a **lifespan perspective** helps us understand and appreciate the long-term nature and characteristics of human development, a **systems or ecological perspective** of development emphasizes the mutual interaction of the person and the significant contexts of development. Many of the important events of the lifespan, including childhood and adolescence, are the results of the *reciprocal* and *dynamic interactions* or the *relationships* between the person and the significant, enduring contexts of life (family, school, peer group, community, and so on) (Bronfenbrenner, Moen, and Garbarino, 1984; Schiamberg, 1985). Examples include the following:

- The growth and development of the prenatal child can be viewed as a reciprocal and dynamic exchange between the embryo or fetus and the pregnant mother. (Chapter 4 discusses the ecology of prenatal development in detail.)
- The birth of the child can be viewed from a systems (or ecological) perspective as the reciprocal interaction of the new parents (their personal characteristics, developmental histories, and so on) and the organized environment for childbirth (hospital organization and delivery practices). (Chapter 5 contains a detailed discussion of the childbirth system.)

David Kostelnik

Children learn to organize their behavior in relation to the world of family and play.

- The growth and development of the infant and toddler can be viewed as the reciprocal interaction and adaptation of the child and family or caretakers (see Chapters 6, 7, and 8).
- The success of the child in the elementary school can be viewed as a reciprocal and dynamic interaction and adaptation between the characteristics of the child and the characteristics of the school. Some children seem to do very well in traditional, teacher-structured classrooms, for example, whereas other children do better in a less-structured or open arrangement (see Chapter 12).
- The ability of the later adolescent or young adult to successfully leave home for work or schooling is, in part, a function of the reciprocal and dynamic relationship between the characteristics of the adolescent and the functioning of the family as a healthy unit or system in its own right (see Chapter 15).

A major feature of this book is its emphasis on the critical role of the social contexts of development (such as work, family, school, and neighborhood) on the development of the child and adolescent. This is both a unique and a necessary perspective since the study of child development is much more than simply describing the changes in the individual over time. The more complete understanding and practical application of the concepts of child and adolescent development requires serious attention to the *progressive interaction* and *mutual adaptation* of human beings and the significant social contexts of the lifespan. In much the same manner that biologists and zoologists have successfully described and studied the *ecology* or mutual relationships between plant and animal life and their environments or habitats, the study of child development becomes much richer, more accurate, and more practically useful by focusing on a systems perspective (Ricklefs, 1973; Mitchell and Shively, 1984). However, it is important to note that in contrast to the ecological analysis of plant and animal life, the ecological (systems) perspective to child development includes a major focus on the widely diverse man-made or culturally evolved environment (including schools, computers, television, and world organizations) that dramatically influences child and adolescent development (Ambrose, 1977; Bronfenbrenner, Moen, and Garbarino, 1984). Remember that throughout this book we examine development from an ecological perspective.

The Nature of Child Development

In its simplest definition, *development* is *change*. Human development, however, is a particular type of change:

- Development is *cumulative* over time. New modes of behavior are organized and built on the foundation of existing behaviors, skills, and resources. Using this criterion, random or temporary changes in behavior are not considered developmental.
- Development occurs in the *context* of the significant social environments of the life process (e.g., the family, the school, the peer group, and the community).

Three general conditions or criteria must be met to classify a given behavioral change as a **developmental change.**

1. The change is *orderly* or *sequential*, part of an organized pattern that appears over time.
2. The change results in a *permanent* alteration of a behavior.
3. The change results in a new behavior or mode of functioning that is *more advanced, adaptive,* or *useful* than prior behaviors.

An example will help clarify both the meaning of development and the criteria for developmental change. The development of locomotion or movement is an important event for both infant and parents. The infant is then capable of a higher level of control or self-regulation by being able to move toward—or away from—objects in the environment, including other infants, parent(s), and toys.

Newborns, of course, cannot perfectly regulate their locomotion movements in such a way as to move from one place to another efficiently. During the first two years of life, the infant learns to coordinate balance, vision, and body movements in going from one place to another, from one object to another, or from one person to another.

These critical components of physical, intellectual, and social development do not occur all at once, of course. Rather, the infant gradually develops improved control over the components of locomotion (including postural balance, visual guidance of movement, and strength in individual muscles of the arms, legs, and neck) during the first two years of life. In brief, the progression involves crawling movements, head orientation movements, sitting alone, standing, walking, and more complex locomotor movements (including climbing stairs and jumping).

During the first year of life infants develop crawling skills that enable them to be mobile, although at a rather slow rate. Beginning at approximately 1½ months, infants develop head orientation skills, which includes the ability to hold the head erect and steady for at least fifteen seconds. As vision improves, head orientation skills enable the infant to survey the terrain. Between approximately two and six or seven months, the infant gradually acquires the skill of sitting upright without support. This skill allows the infant to use hands freely to grasp and manipulate objects. Soon the infant can crawl toward objects such as tables or chairs, grasp them, and pull up to a standing position (at approximately eight months). Between eight months and about one year, the infant is able to stand alone and begin to walk independently. Between one year and twenty-four months, these walking skills are further refined, perfected, and expanded to include such activities as stair climbing and jumping (Bayley, 1969).

These changes in locomotion skill are *developmental* in terms of our criteria. First, they are *orderly* and *sequential*. Each new skill is integrated with prior skills in an organized fashion. For example, the head orientation skills of one and a half months are perfected and integrated with the skill of sitting alone (around six months) and then with the skill of pulling oneself to a standing position around eight months. New acquisitions are not haphazard; they fit in with those that came before. Second, locomotion skills represent *permanent changes* in a normal infant's behavior. After about six months a normal child will always be able to sit upright. After twelve to thirteen months the infant will always be able to walk. Throughout the remainder of childhood and adulthood, the individual continues to coordinate and refine locomotion skills. Each of the achievements of locomotion is *more advanced* than the preceding skill. For example, rapid crawling with head erect and guiding direction is more advanced than the limited crawling movements of the first two months of life. Walking up or down stairs is more complicated than standing alone for the first time (Bayley, 1969).

In addition to locomotion skills, there are numerous ways human beings develop during infancy, childhood, and adolescence. Such developments include the ability to think, speak, write, read, draw, play, interact with others, create original ideas and objects, control feelings, and so on. Changes in each of these areas of human behavior are developmental—orderly and sequential, permanent and more advanced, adaptive or more useful than prior behaviors.

The study of infants, children, and adolescents is concerned with two primary types of change over time: quantitative and qualitative.

- **Quantitative change** refers to the easily measurable and sometimes obvious aspects of development, including physical growth (height and weight) and years of education.
- **Qualitative change** refers to variations and modifications in *functioning*. The progression of locomotion skills, intellectual skills, and the development of grasping behavior from inaccurate whole-hand swiping motions to the precise pincerlike grasp of the year-old infant are all examples of qualitative changes in development.

Principles of Child Growth and Development

Several general patterns or principles of growth hold true in describing the way human beings develop. The processes of human growth and development relate to changes in the psychological, social, emotional, physical, intellectual, and moral domains throughout life. Growth and development operate in accordance with several principles:

1. **Growth Gradients.** Growth gradients or axes of growth refer to the various *directions* physiological changes take in the human body. There are three directions for such growth:

- **Cephalocaudal.** Physical growth occurs from the top (head) of the body downward: the cephalocaudal direction. This principle of growth can be illustrated in many ways. During prenatal development (conception to birth), the brain and the central nervous system develop first, followed by developmental changes in the lower body (Fig. 1.2). From an evolutionary perspective, the development of the head and the central nervous system probably occurs first because of their importance to the regulation of all behavior (Fig. 1.3).

  After birth (the postnatal years), infants first gain control over total head movements as well as movements of the eyes and the mouth. Then they gain control over trunk movements and, finally, over leg movements. Babies can move their heads in several directions before they can sit up; they can sit up before they can stand; and, of course, they can stand before they can walk.
- **Proximodistal.** In accordance with the proximodistal (Latin: near-to-far) growth gradient, growth and development proceeds outward from the center of the body to the periphery or extremities (Fig. 1.2). During prenatal development, this gradient is apparent in the growth of arms from the trunk and in the later emergence of hands and fingers from these arms. During postnatal development, the infant first gains control of its body, then its arms, then its hands, and finally its finger movements.

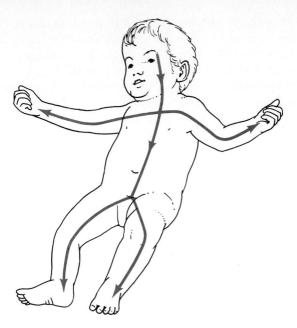

FIGURE 1.2
The axes of human growth.

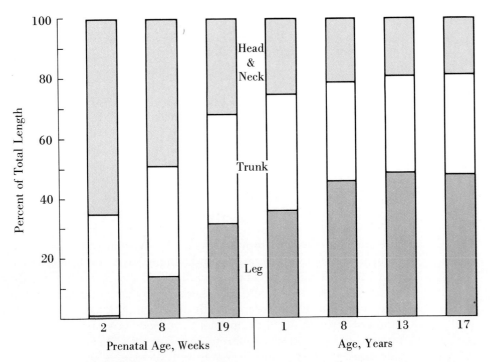

FIGURE 1.3
Percentage of total body length—head-and-neck, trunk, and legs—in boys at various stages of prenatal and postnatal growth. From Meredith, 1939, p. 141.

· **Differentiation.** This principle suggests that the direction of growth and development is from gross to specific or from simple to complex. During prenatal development, the brain, as a differentiated structure, appears approximately two to three weeks after conception. Parts of the brain such as the *cerebellum* (the part of the brain concerned with the smooth and even performance of voluntary movements) and the *cerebral cortex* (the part of the brain that contains the most highly developed centers of the nervous system including intelligence, memory, and sight) do not become differentiated until approximately six to eight weeks after conception. During postnatal development, infants are able to move their arms (a "gross" or "simple" movement) sooner than being able to oppose the thumb and index finger in grasping a toy (a "specific" or "complex" movement).

2. **Orderly and Sequential Development.** As noted above, human growth and development are orderly processes rather than simply random or totally unpredictable events—and throughout this book we will be examining current theory and research on the nature and extent of predictable patterns of growth and development. The sequence of physical *growth* is a fairly well established phenomenon, although the ages at which various events occur can only be specified within a range of ages. For example, the adolescent growth spurt occurs in all normal adolescents; however, the timing of the spurt can range from approximately ten to thirteen years of age in girls and from thirteen to sixteen years of age in boys (see Fig. 1.4). The sequence of *development* is, however, clearer for the development of physically based functions such as locomotion or grasping than for cognitive or socially based functions such as thinking, moral development, play, and

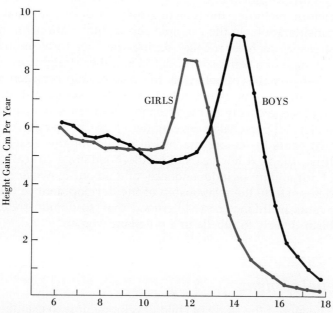

FIGURE 1.4
The adolescent growth spurt. From Tanner, 1962.

so on. As we can see later in this chapter, there is disagreement about the existence and validity of stages of development in such domains as cognitive and moral behavior.

3. **Individual Variation.** While individuals follow patterns of sequential change in dimensions of growth and development, there is considerable variation among individuals in the rate of growth and development. Children and adolescents vary markedly in height, weight, and other dimensions of physical growth, such as length of legs and arms and size of hands and feet. Many factors influence these variations, including genetic endowment and environmental factors such as nutrition and illnesses.

As a result of these variations in growth and development, a concern that frequently arises among children and parents, has to do with "normality." Children or parents may ask themselves or others, "Is it 'normal' for ten-year-old Johnny to be only four feet tall?" or "Is it 'normal' for my fourteen-month-old infant not to be talking yet?" Appropriate responses to such questions vary considerably—depending on the child, the parents, and the specific situation.

4. **Sensitive (Critical) Periods.** The critical period hypothesis suggests that there are specific time periods when the potential for growth and development (as well as damage from the environment) is maximal. In prenatal development, an example of such a period is the first three months of pregnancy. If a woman takes certain drugs, receives X rays or contracts certain diseases during the first three months of pregnancy, the impact on the unborn child is likely to be far more severe than if these environmental stresses occur later in the pregnancy. If a woman has rubella (German measles) during this critical period, her baby will be far more likely to be born with serious birth defects than if she has rubella at a later time in the pregnancy.

The usefulness of the concept of critical or sensitive periods depends on several factors, including the type of growth or developmental event and outcome under consideration. In the example above, the relationship between an environmental stressor, such as rubella, during the first three months of pregnancy and the outcome of a serious birth defect is rather straightforward and clear. However, in other domains of behavior, the relationship between a presumed critical period and an outcome is much less clear. For example, Erik Erikson has proposed an eight-stage theory of the lifespan with each stage constituting a critical period in social and personality development (see Chapter 2). According to Erikson, the first two years of life are the critical period for the development of a basic sense of trust, the next few years of toddlerhood are a critical period for the development of autommomy or independence, and so on. However, it is much more difficult to demonstrate the relationship of the development of trust or autonomy to specific events in infancy or toddlerhood than to demonstrate the relationship of infant birth defects to rubella in a pregnant woman.

Periods of Child Development

The aim of the study of child development is to examine the qualitative and quantitative changes over time, and in this book we examine these changes from the prenatal period through later adolescence (Table 1.1).

TABLE 1.1
The Periods of Child Development

LIFE STAGE	APPROXIMATE AGES
Prenatal period	Conception to birth.
Infancy (includes toddler period from 2–3 years)	0–3 years.
Preschool years	3–5 years of age.
Middle childhood	5–12 or 13 years of age (the onset of puberty).
Early adolescence	Approximately 12 or 13 (the onset of puberty) until 17 or 18 years of age (the high school years).
Later adolescence	Approximately 17–18 years of age (the completion of high school) until the person attains a sense of social status or social identity in the early 20s.

Child Development Themes and Issues

Several themes and issues recur in the study of child development and raise fundamental questions about the nature of human development. Such issues have been discussed for centuries by philosophers, educators, theologians, and social thinkers and remain a source of controversy and debate. We examine a few of them briefly here and in more detail throughout the book.

Are There Stages of Development?

We have seen that a fundamental principle of child development is that behavior is orderly and sequential. We have also suggested that these orderly patterns or sequences seem clearer for physically based functions such as locomotion than for socially based functions such as cognitive development.

The concept of stage has frequently been used to clarify such orderly and sequential processes. A stage represents a particular grouping of abilities or behaviors and has the following characteristics:

• Each stage is qualitatively different and more mature than the preceding stage.
• Each stage is universal in that everyone passes through the same stage.
• Each stage is part of an invariant (fixed) sequence of stages.

An alternative conception to stage theories is the notion that the course of development is *continuous*, that changes in development occur in gradual increments in such a way that stages of functioning are either not present or not easy to identify.

Can Later Development be Predicted from Child and Adolescent Development?

Long-term predictability depends on several factors, including the specific characteristic under consideration, the age of the individual, and the sex of the individual. The answer to this question is therefore a loud and unqualified "maybe."

In the case of physical growth, height in middle childhood is an accurate predictor of early adult height (Petersen, Tobin-Richards, and Boxer, 1983; Boxer and Petersen, 1986). That is, height of a child prior to the adolescent growth spurt is a good indicator of height following the growth spurt.

On the other hand, infant intellectual performance tends to be a rather poor predictor of intellectual performance later in childhood (McCall, 1979; Honzik, 1983). However, some studies demonstrate moderate predictability of intellectual performance from childhood through adulthood (McCall, 1979; Kopp and McCall, 1982). The general findings are that between about two and five years of age intelligence test scores become better predictors of later intelligence test scores. Therefore, the score of a ten or twelve-year-old child will tend to be similar to the score of that child when he or she was a three or four-year-old. Although such scores may be relatively stable over time, there were some exceptions. About one-third of all the children in the McCall study showed major shifts in I.Q. scores during childhood. The inadequacy of using infant intelligence test scores (particularly those for infants below eighteen months of age) to predict childhood and adult intelligence may be due, in part, to the difference between intelligence measures for infants and those for children, adolescents, and adults. Intelligence measures or tests for infants are based almost entirely on infant motor (or movement) skills. Intelligence tests used in childhood and beyond rely much more on the measurement of conceptual and verbal skills. Therefore, intelligence test scores may be more reliably predictable from childhood and beyond, in part, because they are measuring similar things.

Concerns about predictability have also arisen with reference to such personality dimensions as temperament, distractibility, activity level, and independence, to name only a few. The available evidence provides some limited support for the stability of some personality characteristics over time. For example, boys who were rated as highly aggressive in early childhood were also aggressive as adults (Kagan and Moss, 1983; Kagan, 1984); that is, boys who were physically aggressive as preschoolers tended to become verbally aggressive adults. Aggressiveness in girls was not found to be as stable over time as in boys. On the other hand, girls' dependency behavior was more stable than boys' dependency behavior (Kagan and Moss, 1983). For example, dependency behavior as manifested by clinging to parents and teachers, seeking unnecessary help, or seeking recognition from peers was more stable for girls than for boys from ages three through fourteen.

Is Development the Result of Heredity or Environment?

The well-known *nature versus nurture* controversy has generated considerable debate throughout history. The debate has centered around the relative contribution of inherited or genetic factors and environmental factors. Most current research suggests that *both* genetic and environmental factors are responsible for development, although the genetic factors contribute more to some aspects of development

Continuity and Change in Human Development

One of the most perplexing yet stimulating questions in the study of lifespan development is that of continuity and change. To what extent do individuals remain the same personalities throughout their lives and to what extent do they change? Such concerns are particularly pertinent to our investigation of child and adolescent development since it is at these times that personality is initially forged and developed.

In general, such child behaviors as aggression toward peers, dominance with peers, dependence on parents, and shyness or sociability with unfamiliar people are rather stable from ages five or six through adolescence (Olweus, 1981; Kagan and Moss, 1983). The extremely shy or timid five-year-old child will most likely grow up to become an adolescent who may be quiet and nervous in the company of strangers. When a group of extremely withdrawn and shy boys (three to eight years old) was interviewed as adults (approximately twenty years later), the majority had taken jobs with minimized risk and competitiveness and had focused on job security (Kagan and Moss, 1983).

Such results demonstrate some level of constancy throughout the lifespan, but there is considerable debate about such findings. Research on the stability over time of psychological characteristics must be treated with caution for at least two reasons:

· Few reliable longitudinal studies have followed individuals from childhood well into the adult years (Kagan, 1984).

· The traditional assumption that early experiences and early development shape or even predict later life has been challenged by some studies (Runyan, 1982; Skolnick, 1986). For example, no clear relationship exists between traumatic losses or family tension early in life and an unhappy or unsuccessful adulthood. Many individuals survive less-than-ideal childhood circumstances to become successful adults, among them outstanding artists, authors, political leaders, entertainers, and scientists. Nor does every child from a comfortable home turn out to be a successful or happy adult (Skolnick, 1986). According to Orville Brim and Jerome Kagan (1980), "Humans have a capacity for change across the entire life span" (p. 1).

While the entire matter of continuity or change in lifespan development is far from settled, one point is clear: there are *multiple paths* of development. Two children who start out from seemingly similar circumstances can end up to be quite different personalities. For example, John Hinckley, who shot President Ronald Reagan in 1981, came from a comfortable and respected upper-middle-class family. His older brother was an athlete, a scholar, and a social leader who became a successful engineer (Elkind, 1981).

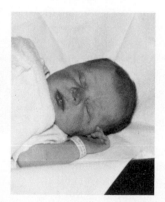   

The Same Child at Several Different Ages.

Courtesy Ann and Greg Gessert

than to others. For example, eye color and hair color are determined exclusively by genetic factors, whereas personality traits such as concern for others and social responsibility appear to be largely influenced or nurtured by the environment. Many important human traits such as intelligence, aggressiveness, independence, and temperament involve complex interactions between genetic or biological factors and a social environment. In Chapters 3 and 4 we examine current theory and research on this fascinating interplay of heredity and environment.

Can Social Policies be Guided by Knowledge of Child Development?

To a large extent we consider ourselves a society that cares about children and families. However, many policies at every level of our society indicate a subtle and perhaps unintentional bias against both. The adversarial nature of the legal system in divorce proceedings often results in actions that are disruptive to families and to child development. Many urban renewal projects and neighborhood redevelopment programs have resulted in the virtual destruction of the neighborhood social networks that had traditionally provided support for families and children. Corporate and business policies sometimes require middle-level managers to relocate their families frequently, disrupting both family life and developing children. Other corporate or business policies of inflexible working hours make it difficult for families in which both parents work to have a parent at home when

---

Social Policies and Children: An Ecological Perspective

The ecology of human development involves the study of the "progressive and mutual accommodation" between the developing human being and the significant contexts of life (including family, school, peer group, community-neighborhood, and the broad culture) (Bronfenbrenner, 1979). Public policy constitutes one of the primary contexts for children and families:

What are the implications of mass societal changes from the development of children? To address this issue, it is necessary to know what the environmental and social conditions are that are most crucial for the development of human beings from early childhood on. Bronfenbrenner (1979) has sought to bring together available knowledge on this topic and found it sobering to discover that the principal conclusions from these data could be summarized in two tentative propositions. Shorn of their technical terminology, the two propositions do not sound very earthshaking. But when applied to our present world, they may shake us up nevertheless.

Proposition 1: In order to develop normally, a child needs the enduring, irrational involvement of one or more adults in care and joint activity with that child. In short, somebody has to be crazy about that kid. But that is not all the proposition stipulates. Someone has to *be there* and to be *doing something*—not alone, but together *with* the child. This brings us to the next proposition, which defines a second environmental condition equally essential if development is to occur.

Proposition 2: The involvement of one or more adults in joint activity with the child requires public policies and practices that provide opportunity, status, resources, encouragement, stability, example, and above all, *time* for parenthood, primarily by parents, but also by other adults in the child's environment, both within and outside the home. (Bronfenbrenner and Weiss, 1983, pp. 393–414)

children return from school or at other times when children need them, such as during illness. The frequently limited range of choices in quality child care and the related absence of a formal social/governmental policy toward day care may make working problematic for parents of infants and young children.

Such policies and practices, as well as many others, make it difficult for families to carry out their child-rearing functions. For the most part, these policies were not intended to threaten or weaken families; in most instances, the potential impact on families or child development was not even considered (Zigler, Kagan, and Klugman, 1983; Stevenson and Siegel, 1984). One of the purposes of this book is to increase the awareness and sensitivity of those who now work with—or who will work with—children and families to the need for informed social policies and practices that positively enhance the lives of children and families.

Summary

1. The purposes of this book are threefold: (a) to introduce the beginning student to the challenge and excitement of studying the infant, the child, and the adolescent from a lifespan perspective; (b) to present a framework for thinking about the developing infant, child, and adolescent in relation to the significant social environments of his or her life; (c) to present the theory, research, and principles of child development in such a manner as to capture something of the reality of children and their families, teachers, and friends.

2. The importance of a lifespan view of child development is the recognition that the period from the prenatal years through adolescence is only one part of human development. There is some evidence that many life changes that occur in the adulthood and aging years cannot be readily predicted from knowledge about childhood or adolescent development. An understanding of the historical context of an individual's background (a war, an economic depression, or the like) is an important consideration in a lifespan perspective. Likewise, the lifespan perspective examines the significance of life events— *normative age-graded events* (e.g., entering the school at the beginning of middle childhood, the onset of puberty, and so on), *nonnormative events* (e.g., death of a parent, onset of a serious illness, divorce of parents, and so on).

3. A systems (or ecological) perspective to child development focuses on the *reciprocal* and *dynamic* interaction of the individual child and the significant contexts of development (e.g., the family, the school, the peer group, and the neighborhood/community). Many events of childhood and adolescence are the result of such reciprocal and dynamic interactions between the individual and the contexts of development, including the birth of a child, the success of the child in school, and so on).

4. *Development* in simplest terms is *change*. However, development is a particular type of change that is *cumulative* and *occurs in contexts* or environments such as family, school, and the like. In order for a given behavioral change to be classified as developmental, three criteria must be met: the change is *orderly* or *sequential*, the change results in permanent modification of a behavior, and the change results in a behavior that is more *advanced* or *adaptive* than a prior behavior.

The study of child development involves two types of changes in human beings over time: *quantitative* and *qualitative.*

5. There are several general patterns or principles of growth and development. The principle of *growth gradients* or directions of growth involves the following features: the *cephalocaudal* direction, the *proximodistal* direction, and *differentiation.* Development is *orderly* and *sequential.* It involves *individual variation.* It involves *sensitive* or *critical periods.*

6. Several important themes or issues in the study of child development include the following: (a) Are there really stages of development? (b) Is it possible to predict later development based on child and adolescent development? (c) Is development the result of heredity or environment or some combination of both? (d) Can social policies be guided by knowledge of child development?

Key Terms

Cephalocaudal
Critical periods
Developmental change
Differentiation
Growth gradients
Individual variation
Lifespan perspective

Nonnormative life events
Normative life events
Proximodistal
Qualitative change
Quantitative change
Systems (or Ecological) perspective

Questions

1. Define the meaning of a lifespan perspective. Why are historical events an important part of such a perspective? What are normative age-graded events and why are they important? Discuss the role of nonnormative events in the lifespan perspective.
2. Define a systems (or ecological) perspective to child and adolescent development. Why is it important to consider the contribution of significant social contexts to development? Discuss the meaning of reciprocal and dynamic interactions.
3. Give examples of quantitative and qualitative changes in development.
4. Distinguish between the cephalocaudal and proximodistal directions of developmental growth. Give an example of each.
5. What is meant by a sensitive or critical period of development?
6. What is meant by "multiple paths" of development, mentioned in the box on continuity and change in development?
7. Give one example of a social policy related to child development. Discuss your view of the policy.

Suggested Readings

BELSKY, J., LERNER, R. M., and SPANIER, G. B. *The Child in the Family*. Reading, Mass.: Addison-Wesley, 1984. The authors provide an excellent overview of the lifespan and the human ecological perspectives. The book is divided into four sections: conceptual foundations, parent-child relations, families in conflict, and contemporary issues.

KAGAN, J. *The Nature of the Child*. New York: Basic Books, 1984. Kagan argues that early experience does not inevitably shape the lives of children. Instead, individuals have a life-long capacity for change and development. Likewise, the influence of the family on the child is less deterministic than previously thought.

LASCH, C. *Haven in a Heartless World*. New York: Basic Books, 1977. This book provides an interesting and well-documented description of how the roles of the family have changed over time. Lasch suggests that the traditional functions of the family have been gradually assumed by other institutions, such as schools and health organizations. He argues that the survival of the family may be at stake.

SMUTS, A. B., and HAGEN, J. W. (eds). *History and Research in Child Development*. Chicago: University of Chicago Press, 1985. This book offers a provocative discussion in which both professional historians and child developmentalists discuss the history of child development.

SOMMERVILLE, J. *The Rise and Fall of Childhood*. Beverly Hills, Calif.: Sage, 1982. Sommerville gives a concise review of the role of childhood throughout civilization.

2 Theories of Child Development

There is nothing so practical as a good theory.
                                    —*Kurt Lewin*

The primary purpose of reviewing theories of child development is to demonstrate how such theories help us formulate questions and answers about the basic processes of growth and development:

· Is child behavior self-regulated or is it determined largely by external factors?
· Are children rational creatures who address life with thought and logic or are they driven by uncontrollable passions and desires?
· Do children have an inborn sense of what is best for them or must they be guided and controlled to ensure positive outcomes?
· Can we describe a child's life by simply knowing that the child has previously been rewarded or punished?
· Is adolescence a period with inevitable stress and personal difficulty?

To help us deal with these and other important questions, theories of child development provide formulations or assumptions about child development that can then be used to develop testable hypotheses.

Maturation Theories

During the early years of the twentieth century, considerable interest was generated in the United States in describing how individual patterns of growth and development differ with age. These **maturation theories** were based on the idea that human development is the result of the unfolding of the human being's genetic inheritance. Therefore, behavior becomes more complex as the individual matures, both physically and mentally. Perhaps the major influence on the development of such theories was.Charles Darwin's *On the Origin of Species*, originally published in 1859. Darwin was interested in demonstrating the general evolution of humans from lower animals. In Darwin's scheme of things, infants were considered evolutionary links between lower animal life and mature humans. (Infant behaviors such as object manipulation seemed to Darwin an evolutionary link between similar activities in such lower animals as monkeys and the tool-using skills of mature humans.) He considered the behavior of lower animals primarily instinctual and inflexible. On the other hand, Darwin viewed the behavior of the human species as largely trainable and learned from adults. He emphasized the evolutionary significance of the lengthy period of helplessness in human infancy (compared with the shorter time for the infants of other species). During this period, parents and adults ensured the physical survival of infants by teaching them appropriate information and skills. It followed from Darwin's notion of the evolution of species that human behavior could also be understood by studying its origins in the infant and child.

Major Contributors

One of the leaders of this movement in the United States was G. Stanley Hall, who is often cited as the founder of the field of child and adolescent development. Hall believed that development through adolescence was primarily the result of biological and genetic factors. Having been heavily influenced by the work of Charles Darwin, Hall also speculated that the development of the individual human being reflected or recapitulated the evolution of the human species. For example, the infant and toddler's developing skill in using tools "recapitulated" the tool-using discoveries of the cave dwellers. According to Judith Gallatin (1975), Hall believed that

> Rather than reflecting the entire sweep of evolution, childhood was supposed to proceed in stages, each of which mirrored a primitive stage of the human species. Very early childhood might correspond, Hall speculated, to a monkey-like ancestor

G. Stanley Hall (1844–1924)

G. Stanley Hall was an articulate leader who founded the field of child study in the United States at the turn of the century. In 1889, Hall went from being a professor of psychology at Johns Hopkins University to the presidency of Clark University. Like most of his contemporaries, Hall knew rather little about children's development, their behavior, their interests, and their abilities. Hall's interests were largely educational: He wanted to incorporate the study of child development into educational training. He began by developing summer workshops for schoolteachers and school administrators.

Hall's method of investigating child behavior was a questionnaire. He and his students developed questions on a wide range of child behaviors (play, fear, anger, dreams, and reading habits). The questionnaires were given to teachers, who, in turn, gave them to thousands of children. The results were sent to Hall for his analysis. Hall published many of the findings in a journal he founded: *Pedagogical Seminary* (later to become the *Journal of Genetic Psychology*). Although many of Hall's results were interesting, his questionnaire method gradually fell into disfavor as a reliable technique for collecting unbiased information about children. The results of Hall's research may have been questionable, but his idea of studying the normal development of children profoundly influenced educators and psychologists.

Hall's influence was not confined to childhood. In 1904, he wrote *Adolescence*, which initiated the modern study of adolescence in the United States. Hall was also a key figure in introducing Sigmund Freud to American psychologists. (Freud's theories of personality development had a significant influence on American psychologists.) In 1909, Hall celebrated the twentieth anniversary of Clark University by inviting Freud to deliver a series of influential and controversial lectures. G. Stanley Hall was truly a monumental figure in the study of human development.

of the human race that had reached sexual maturity around the age of six. The years between eight and twelve allegedly represented a reenactment of a more advanced, but still prehistoric form of mankind, possibly a species that had managed to survive by hunting and fishing. (pp. 26–27)

Hall's theory of recapitulation came under criticism for several reasons, including the observation that by two or three years of age a human child has gone well beyond the abilities of monkeys, apes, and prehistoric humanlike creatures such as Neanderthal Man. That is, the verbal, social, and movement skills of human three-year-olds are typically far more advanced than the adults among these other species.

Although Hall's recapitulation theory was never accepted as a *specific* approach to human development, his *general* emphasis on a *genetic basis* for the unfolding of development had a marked influence on the study of child development. Because of his influential position as a major figure in the establishment of human development as a scientific study, Hall exerted considerable influence on his students to adopt a "nature" or genetic perspective to human development. Two of his students—Arnold Gesell and Lewis Terman—turned out to be among the most prominent developmentalists of the early twentieth century.

ARNOLD GESELL. Gesell founded the Clinic of Child Development at Yale University in 1911. Hall was fascinated with the stages of development that children demonstrated as they matured, and as his student, Gesell emphasized that growth and development were determined primarily by a fixed timetable of maturation. Gesell was a strong believer in the notion that innate, built-in, or genetic tenden-

Arnold Gesell (1880–1961)

Arnold Gesell was born in Alma, Wisconsin, on June 21, 1880. He obtained his Ph.D. from Clark University in 1906 and his M.D. from Yale University in 1915. As a physician and psychologist, Gesell was a leading proponent of the maturational perspective to child development. He stressed the idea that growth and development occur in an orderly and predictable sequence. Among Gesell's notable contributions to the field of child development was the establishment of the Institute of Child Development at Yale University in the 1930s.

As director of the Institute of Child Development, Gesell was called upon to diagnose developmental problems in hundreds of infants, experiences that helped focus his research. Using the most advanced techniques of photography and observation available in the 1930s, Gesell documented the behavior of infants and children at many different ages. The documentation of such behavior led to the formulation of developmental standards in a broad range of areas that included motor skills, language development, and social behavior. Gesell's standards have been refined and are still in use in such well-known diagnostic tests as the Denver Development Screening Test and the Bayley Tests of Mental and Motor Development.

Gesell was considered a leading authority on child development during the 1930s and 1940s. His most influential books include *The First Five Years of Life* (1940), *Infant and Child in the Culture of Today* (1943), *The Child from Five to Ten* (1946), and *Youth: The Years from Ten to Sixteen* (1956).

cies toward optimal development control the rate of child growth and learning in each individual. Environmental factors had a minimal impact.

> Acceleration of development . . . is typically an inherent biological characteristic of the individual, most probably hereditary in nature. There is no convincing evidence that fundamental acceleration of development can be readily induced by either pernicious or enlightened methods of stimulation. (Gesell, 1928, pp. 363–64)

Gesell believed that this innate or programmed process of development could be documented through detailed observations and photographs of the behavior of infants and children at varying ages. Such documentation would not only show the course of physical and mental development but would also provide, for Gesell, a basis for the construction of diagnostic measurements or tests.

As a result of these detailed observations, Gesell developed schedules or standards for motor, visual-adaptive, personal-social, and language behavior. These standards described the sequences of development throughout childhood (see Table 2.1).

On the basis of these observations of the sequences of behavior during development (e.g., the unvarying and predictable appearance of creeping and crawling prior to standing and walking), two principles of Gesell's theory became popular during the 1930s and 1940s: *maturational readiness* and *behavioral stages* (such as the "terrible twos").

Maturational readiness meant that a given child had matured to an appropriate point at which he or she could benefit from a specific type of training. In other words, the child who was ready could attain competence at a given activity. The immature child would need to spend more time and effort on that same activity and still might not perform at a comparable level. Gesell demonstrated the principle of readiness in a series of classic experiments involving identical twins. For example, one twin of a pair was given practice in stair climbing well before stair-climbing skill would be expected to occur in infants. The other twin was given no specific training in stair climbing. Gesell and his colleagues found that the twin who had received no training in stair climbing later attained stair-climbing skill at

TABLE 2.1
Gesell's Developmental Sequences for Infant Communication (15–24 months)

15 months— 1. Uses massive, total-response gestures.
              2. Indicates refusal by bodily protest.
              3. Responds to a few key and catch words.
18 months— 1. Communicates both by gestures and words, but words are beginning to replace gestures.
              2. Responds to simple commands.
              3. Verbalizes ends of actions such as "bye-bye," "thank you," "all gone."
              4. Refusals may be expressed by "no" but more usually by bodily response.
21 months— 1. Asks for food, toilet, drink.
              2. Repeats single words said to him, or last word or two of a phrase.
24 months— 1. Speech accompaniment of activity.
              2. Asks questions such as "What's that?"
              3. Verbalizes immediate experiences.
              4. Much vocalization in a group, but little conversation.
              5. Refers to himself by his name.
              6. Refusals expressed by "no."

Adapted from Gesell, 1940, p. 249.

The "terrible twos."

only a slightly slower pace than the trained twin. Furthermore, there was no ultimate difference between the twins in stair-climbing ability. These types of experimental results were taken as evidence that the critical determinant of development was the notion of maturational readiness. Experience and training made no difference unless the child was at the appropriate maturational level. This idea of maturational readiness was adapted to school learning by educators. The notion was that there were optimal times in the development of children when they were *ready* to learn such skills as reading or writing.

The concept of **behavioral stages** emerged from Gesell's notion that maturation, in fact, represented the unfolding of interweaving growth forces. Gesell referred to this as the principle of *reciprocal interweaving*:

> Development in the human infant is orderly; it is, however, not necessarily so orderly that he achieves one function in its perfection and then develops another which he appends to the first. Two functions which are to be integrated tend to develop almost simultaneously, at first apparently unrelated to each other, first one than the other taking lead and precedence. They seem to weave in and about each other as they develop, until they finally merge, synergize, coordinate. It is a reciprocal kind of interweaving. So it is with the development of upright posture and locomotion. (Gesell and Amatruda, 1947, p. 192.)

Gesell applied this notion of reciprocal interweaving to personality development by suggesting that the "terrible twos" (a stage during which the infant demonstrates improving locomotion and grasping combined with a seeming indifference to the verbal requests of parents or caretakers) is inevitably followed by the "conforming threes" and the "inquisitive fours." These stages of child personality were popular ideas with many parents in the 1940s and 1950s, who were looking for some explanation of children's seemingly negative behavior. The notion of stages of personality based on maturity was, of course, a comforting idea to nervous parents since Gesell indicated that the more trying stages were always followed by stages that were easier to cope with.

LEWIS TERMAN.   Terman was a professor at Stanford University whose primary interest was mental measurement. Terman was one of the first to translate into English the first intelligence test developed by Alfred Binet in Paris (Binet and Simon, 1905a, 1905b). He published the test in 1916 as the Stanford-Binet Intelligence Test.

Terman believed that intelligence was primarily a genetic or hereditary characteristic. Terman's work on mental measurement was based on two assumptions about intelligence: Older children (because they are more mature) should perform better on tests of intelligence than younger children, and smarter children should do better than average children. In keeping with the influence of his mentor, G. Stanley Hall, Terman assumed that intelligence gradually unfolded with maturation, like other forms of growth and development. Although intelligence was expected to increase with age, differences between children were presumed to remain stable over time. Individual differences among people of similar age or between groups of people from varied social or family background were presumed to reflect genetic or hereditary differences in intelligence. (We examine this highly controversial notion of intelligence as well as some of the issues in intelligence measurement in Chapters 7, 10, and 13.)

In addition to developing an instrument for measuring intelligence, Terman was very much interested in doing research to determine the genetic component of intelligence. His monumental project, *Genetic Studies of Genius,* begun in 1921, was a study of the development of gifted children over time (Terman, 1925; Terman and Oden, 1959). Although his research did not establish that intelligence was genetically determined, it was important for several reasons. It was one of the first major longitudinal studies (the same persons are repeatedly measured over time) conducted in the United States (Sears, 1975). (We discuss research methods in human development, including longitudinal research, in Chapter 3.) As such, Terman's study of the intellectually gifted, which spanned almost fifty years, encouraged the development of other longitudinal studies. It provided useful information on a wide variety of developmental dimensions. Terman's work also did much to dispel stereotypes and myths about the intellectually gifted. For example, Terman's data showed that, as a group, intellectually gifted individuals were *not* physically weak, socially maladjusted, or sickly; they tended to be just as healthy, physically fit, and socially adept as nongifted individuals. In addition, Terman's research contributed to the emergence of human development as a *normative science.* (A **norm** is a statement of typical characteristics or behaviors for a specific group.) His research on gifted individuals, as well as his work with I.Q. tests, involved the development of normative descriptions about individuals. As we shall see throughout this book, much of the research, theory, and application in human development involves, in part, the careful development, evaluation, and application of normative statements about children and adolescents.

Evaluation of Traditional Maturation Theories

The work of Gesell and Terman reached a peak of popularity during the late 1940s. The major problem with such an exclusively maturational perspective was that it ignored the significant role of the environment in development. In essence, both Terman and Gesell were suggesting that since human development was nature-based (rather than nurture-based), a full understanding of the individual required only that typical or normative changes in development be described. In the case of Terman, these norms of development could be determined through the use of intelligence tests. Both the use of psychological tests to measure intelligence and the notion that intelligence is primarily an innate or nature-based phenomenon have come under serious criticism. For Gesell, growth norms were determined through systematic and careful observation, and cataloging of child behavior. Today the extreme maturational theory that Gesell advocated has been almost totally rejected. By the mid-1960s, research was beginning to accumulate that demonstrated the importance of environmental experience and human maturation in human development (Lazar et al., 1982; Bronfenbrenner and Weiss, 1983). It became clear that both maturation and experience interact to influence the development of the individual. Many programs such as Project Head Start were launched on the assumption that experience—particularly early experience—can make a substantial difference in developmental outcomes.

Behavior and Learning Theories

In contrast to maturational theories, **behavior and learning theories** portray human behavior as primarily the result of environmental stimulation. Much of what an individual becomes is the result of what he or she has experienced or *learned*. This emphasis on the role of experience in human development is not new. (Philosophers such as Aristotle and John Locke had long ago developed notions of the importance of experience.) However, it was not until the early part of the twentieth century that formal theories of learning were developed in psychology. Until that time, the prevailing emphases in psychology had been on:

- **Nativism.** The belief that individual differences in children were the result of genetic or constitutional factors. In other words, if one child was shy and introverted and another was aggressive and outgoing, these differences were considered due entirely to the children's inborn temperaments.
- **Subjectivism.** The belief that the main activity of psychologists and others interested in human development was a type of *introspectionism*. Introspection involved the study of the contexts of the human mind through self-analysis that was virtually unrelated to real issues of human development, including the growth and maturation of children, mental illness, and so on.

The Beginnings of Behaviorism and Learning Theories

In the 1920s John B. Watson challenged both the prevailing nativism and the subjectivism of his time with an approach that he called *behaviorism*. In contrast to the nativists or maturationists, Watson insisted that children are not born with innate characteristics. Rather, they enter the world as *tabula rasa* (blank slates) to be shaped and influenced entirely by the environment. For example, if a child strikes another child, it is because such aggressiveness is in some fashion *rewarding* for the child. Likewise, a child who shows fear of cats has had a frightening experience with cats.

Thus Watson placed a strong emphasis on the *environment* as the primary force in influencing the development of children. In fact, he wrote this testimonial to his behaviorist perspective:

> Give me a dozen healthy infants, well-formed and my own specified world to bring them up in, and I'll guarantee to take any one at random and train him to be any type of specialist I might—doctor, lawyer, artist, merchant, chief and yes, even beggar man and thief! (1950, p. 104)

Not only did Watson dismiss the nativist perspective, he also rejected the idea that the study of human development should deal with "mentalistic" concepts such as feelings, thoughts, intentions, and so on. Rather, he suggested that the focus move away from the study of the mind to the scientific study of *behavior*. Watson argued that psychologists should be examining *observable or overt* behavior and explaining such behavior with terms such as stimulus, response, and reinforcement. Given their focus on observable behavior, behaviorists such as Watson could promise not only to explain the origins of behavior but also to change behavior.

The behaviorism of Watson and his followers was composed of several core assumptions:

- *All behavior is learned.*
- *All behavior is learned in small units or bits* rather than in large wholes. Watson believed that the complex behaviors of adults are built on the elementary foundation of the simple inborn reflexes of infants continually refined through experiences with the environment. He described this process as being composed of chains of S–R (stimulus-response) units that become associated with one another through learning. For example, the complex activity of riding a bicycle can presumably be reduced to a series of elementary behaviors such as balancing the bicycle and pedaling. These individual behaviors are then combined in the act of bicycle riding.
- The basic principles of learning are thought to be applicable for all species— animals and human beings. For example, the chaining together of S–R units into complex behaviors would be as applicable for rats and pigeons as for human beings.

Watson was extraordinarily enthusiastic about behaviorism. "The behaviorist asks for nothing to start with in building a human being but the squirmings everyone can see in the new-born infant" (1924). His general idea was that these "squirmings" or infant reflex units could be linked in almost random sequences through conditioning. Watson's contemporary E. L. Thorndike suggested much the same thing when he said that it is possible to "get any response of which a learner is capable associated with any situation to which he is sensitive" (1913–1914).

Watson's general notion of human development has been challenged by research on infant development (see Chapter 6). The following ideas of Watson have been discredited: (1) that inborn responses or reflexes are simple and initially disorganzied and (2) that learning through conditioning occurs largely by chance. For example, rather than having simple and unorganized responses, the infant has the visual ability, at birth, to follow a moving light with its eyes. In addition, it turns its mouth in the direction of a touch on the cheek. Contrary to the notion

A bull moose cannot play the bassoon. Contrary to the behaviorist idea that individuals can learn virtually any response if they happen to be reinforced for the response, behavior patterns are defined and limited in all organisms.

of the chance learning of responses, the general pattern of behavior is both defined and limited in people and in animals. For example, the ability to use the hands and fingers for operating precision tools or playing musical instruments is a characteristic of only some animal species (including humans). A bull moose cannot play the bassoon.

Conditioning

Learning theorists have generally agreed on two processes or types of conditioning that are important to human learning and development. The first process is called *classical conditioning*, the type of learning that Watson and Pavlov stressed. The second process—*operant conditioning*—was identified by Edward Thorndike (1911) and B. F. Skinner (1938).

CLASSICAL CONDITIONING.   Pavlov's experiment is an excellent example of **classical conditioning** (Fig. 2.1). In that experiment, the sight or smell of food produced salivating behavior, an *unconditioned reflex*, in the dog. *Unconditioned reflexes* are responses that—prior to any learning—are naturally combined with specific unconditioned stimuli. For example, a dog salivates when it sees or smells food, and an infant is startled at the sound of a loud noise.

In Pavlov's experiment, because the sound of a bell (originally a neutral stimulus) was repeatedly heard just before food was presented, the dog associated the bell ringing with food and began to salivate when it heard the bell. The dog now salivated at the sound of the bell whether food was presented or not. Thus a *conditioned reflex* was established. *Conditioned reflexes* are formed when one asso-

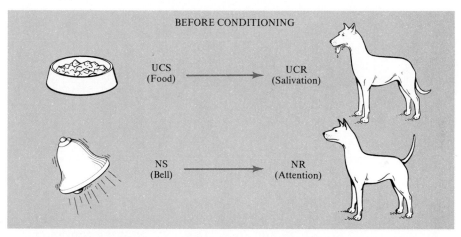
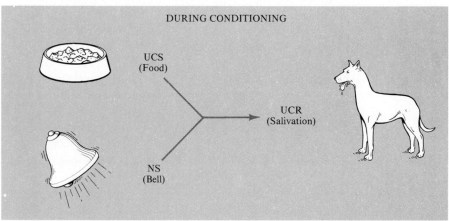
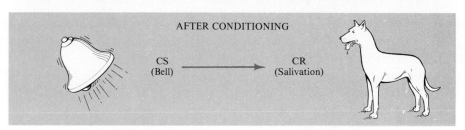

UCS = Unconditioned Stimulus   NR = Neutral Response
UCR = Unconditioned Responses   CS = Conditioned Stimulus
NS = Neutral Stimulus   CR = Conditioned Response

FIGURE 2.1
Classical conditioning.

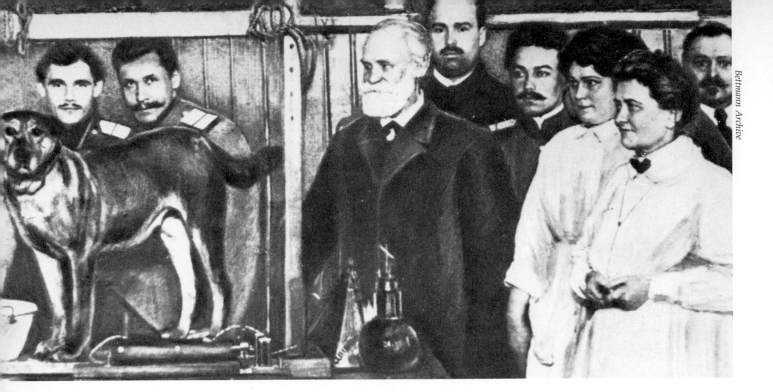

Ivan Pavlov conducting classical conditioning experiment.

ciates a previously neutral stimulus (e.g., the sound of a bell) with an unconditioned stimulus (e.g., food). Because the conditioned stimulus (the sound of the bell) was repeatedly presented just before the unconditioned stimulus (food), the dog began to respond to the conditioned stimulus just as it had originally responded to the unconditioned stimulus.

OPERANT CONDITIONING. **Operant conditioning** is a learning process that depends on rewards and punishments. The major difference between classical conditioning and operant conditioning is that behavior in the latter cannot be automatically or naturally produced. This means that the behavior must first occur before any learning can take place. In other words, the behavior to be conditioned must first occur so that it can be strengthened or reinforced. For example, a child

---

The Learning Theory Point of View: A Summary

Sheldon White, one of the leading authorities on the learning theory approach to child development, has indicated the following as the primary assumptions of such a viewpoint:

1. The environment may be unambiguously characterized in terms of *stimuli.*
2. Behavior may be unambiguously characterized in terms of *responses.*
3. A class of stimuli exist which, applied contingently and immediately following a response, increase it or decrease it in some measurable fashion. These stimuli may be treated as *reinforcers.*
4. *Learning* may be completely characterized in terms of various possible couplings among stimuli, responses, and reinforcers.
5. Unless there is definite evidence to the contrary, classes of behavior may be assumed to be learned, manipulable by the environment, extinguishable, and trainable. (1970, pp. 665–66)

John Dewey (1859–1952).

John Dewey: An Early Critic of Behaviorism

John Dewey (1896) criticized what he considered the unrealistic and overly simplistic views of behaviorism. Dewey's criticism was the forerunner of what today might be called a *systems perspective to learning and development.* Dewey argued that the parts of the S–R model (stimulus, brain activity, or neural connections, and response) are *not* separate units. Rather, they exist only as functioning units in the *unified* activities of behavior. Dewey regarded the reflex as an artificial concept because the reflex never exists alone. He suggested that the nature of a stimulus is determined by the makeup of the organism and the activities going on inside it. In addition, he pointed out that every response produces additional stimulating properties, which themselves produce behavior. Dewey suggested that the entire process was a *dynamic* and *continuous* one that could not realistically be reduced to S–R units. For example, walking or speaking involves a continuous pattern of behavior that can be broken up into S–R units only at the risk of gross oversimplification.

goes to the bathroom alone, and the behavior is then reinforced with candy. Another example would be when a child hits a baseball, and this accomplishment is reinforced by a big smile and words of approval from mom and dad. *Reinforcement,* or the perceived consequences of behavior, influences the frequency with which that behavior occurs. For example, if a child is positively rewarded for mowing the lawn, then he or she will do it again in the future. On the other hand, if a child is punished or gets no reward for a behavior, he or she will do it less frequently or not at all. (The behavior is then said to be *extinguished*.) One of the primary proponents of operant conditioning has been the psychologist B. F. Skinner.

Evaluation of Traditional Behaviorism and Learning Theory

Several general remarks are in order after our brief review of behaviorism and learning theory in human development:

1. *Behaviorism and learning theory tend to portray humans as reactive organisms.* People are shaped or molded by the nature of the associations in their environment and the rewards, punishments, and reinforcements to which they are subjected. This approach tends to emphasize a *mechanistic* interpretation of human life. People are set in motion by stimuli. Little need is seen for analyzing the structure of the human "machine" (the nature of the human body, the interaction of physiology and behavior, or the nature of the self and the mind) in relation to human behavior.
2. *Behaviorism and learning theory tend to be reductionistic.* The general thrust of learning theory is that complex behavior can be derived from simple stimuli and responses, or S–R units. The result of this reductionistic emphasis is the general failure of learning theory to address the broad—and more important—questions of how the human being organizes, controls, and regulates behavior.

3. *Behaviorism and learning theory tend to be deterministic. Determinism* means that everything about the individual and his or her behavior is the result of past or present experiences. Philosophers have long debated whether human beings are free to control their behavior or whether they are the product of their environment. This long-standing debate (free will versus determinism) is resolved very neatly by learning theorists. They simply state there is no such thing as free will. All human behavior, including values, attitudes, emotional responses, and moral precepts, are determined by the external environment (past or present). B. F. Skinner, in *Beyond Freedom and Dignity* (1971), suggested that concepts such as respect, dignity, and freedom are irrelevant because an individual is simply the product of his or her previous learning history.

Social Learning Theory

OBSERVATION AND IMITATION.   **Social learning theory** is one of the major extensions of and variations on traditional behaviorism. This approach examines the broad range of learning that is accomplished by means of **observation** and **imitation (modeling).** Social learning theorists have maintained that much of what we learn is learned by watching the behavior of others rather than through the direct shaping or "conditioning" of responses (Bandura, 1973, 1977; Bandura and Walters, 1963). The social learning perspective deals with the ways human beings learn such behaviors as aggression, generosity, and affiliation by observing those behaviors in such significant others as parents, peers, teachers, and friends.

SYMBOLIC ACTIVITY.   Another important component of social learning theory is **symbolic activity:** the individual's ability to *process information* by using words and concepts that may serve as a guide for organizing future behavior. For example, a child's experiences are stored in memory, from which they can later be retrieved for guidance of future action. The child who observes two peers fighting with one another develops a symbolic, or conceptual, notion of fighting. This "concept" of fighting depends on several factors, including the child's prior experiences with fighting and the impact of the current observational experience. What has this child learned about fighting from earlier experiences? What were the consequences for the two peers who had been fighting? Did they appear to have fun without seriously injuring one another? Did one or both suffer cuts or bruises and begin crying? Did significant adults look on with seeming approval at displays of aggression or self-defense? These factors all contribute to the development of a "concept" of fighting that will guide future behavior.

SELF-REGULATION.   A third component of social learning theory as advanced by Albert Bandura is *self-regulatory activity.* **Self-regulation** refers to the ability to monitor one's behavior in relation to *antecedents* (informative environmental cues that create expectations based on past experiences) and *consequents* (the results or consequences of actions). However, Bandura indicates that because the likelihood of behavior may be increased or decreased by the consequences of what follows, this does *not* mean that its control resides with consequences: ". . . response consequences influence behavior antecedently by creating expectations of similar outcomes on future occasions. The likelihood of particular actions is increased by anticipated reward and reduced by anticipated punishment" (1977, p. 96).

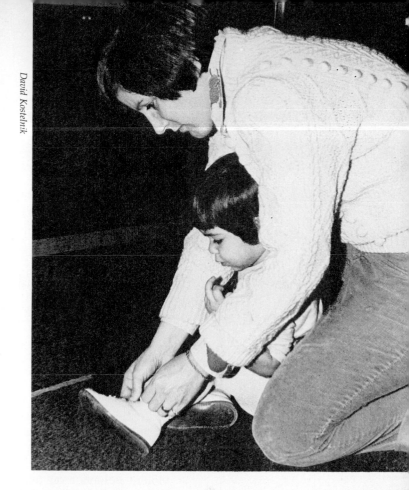

Social learning theory suggests that human beings can learn a broad range of skills by observing and following the behavior of significant others.

Albert Bandura

SOCIAL LEARNING AND TELEVISION.   An example of the application of social learning theory to child development is the impact of television on children's behavior. How are children affected by the portrayal of violence on television? A considerable body of research has demonstrated that the viewing of aggressive or violent behavior on television can have a significant impact on the subsequent performance of such behavior by children (Bandura, 1973, 1977). According to social learning theory, the *modeling* of aggressive behavior depends on several factors (Parke and Slaby, 1983):

- Does the child *identify* with the aggressive model? For example, is the model someone whose behavior the child is likely to imitate (such as another child who is popular or athletically skilled, or a successful adult)?
- What are the *consequences* of aggression to the model? For example, is the model praised or treated positively by others or punished as a result of the aggression?
- What is the *age* of the child? Is the child old enough to distinguish between *reality* (a real child or adult actually performing an act of aggression) and *fantasy* (a cartoon or a dramatized act of violence)?
- What do *parents* or significant others say to the child about the aggression of the model? If necessary, do parents clarify the distinction between make-believe aggression in cartoons and real-life violence?

Evaluation of Social Learning Theory

In summary, social learning theory has made several important contributions to our understanding of child development, among them:

1. Modifying and correcting the traditional learning theory idea that "stimuli" are simply *external* entities. According to social learning theory, stimuli can be *internal* processes such as symbols that help human beings make decisions and exercise control over their lives.

2. Suggesting that other people (including family members, peers, and adults in the community) are significant in human learning and development. The fact that human beings can learn from one another is an important theme of human development throughout the entire lifespan. In this book we shall see the importance of the interaction of children and adolescents with the significant others in their lives as a primary aspect of growth and development.

Although these contributions are important, several criticisms of social learning theory have been made, including the following two:

1. Although some social learning theorists have emphasized the importance of internal cognitive processes in learning, they have not described these processes in sufficient detail. For example, although social learning theorists indicate the involvement of such cognitive processes as memory or perception in such behaviors as imitation or modeling, no detailed analysis is provided beyond their role as mediators of external events.
2. Social learning theorists do not use the concept of stages of development. Instead, they imply that new behaviors that are learned through imitation do not involve new levels of psychological functioning. However, some critics argue that the ability of the child to imitate the behavior of a model is based on the child's *stage* of cognitive functioning. For example, a three-month-old infant cannot imitate the lengthy verbal utterance of a caretaker. Such imitation depends, in part, on the level or stage of the infant's speech and language development.

Cognitive Theory: Piaget

Although its roots in the traditions of European thinking are very old, **cognitive theory** has appeared relatively recently on the American scene. A *cognitive* approach to learning and human development emphasizes mental or internal factors as contrasted with the environmental or external factors of the traditional behaviorists. (Many social learning theorists, such as Bandura, incorporate cognitive processes into their theories.) Perhaps the major breakthrough for cognitive psychology occurred with the gradual recognition of the work of the Swiss biologist and philosopher Jean Piaget. Although a good deal of Piaget's work was done before 1950, not until the mid-1960s was his work seriously considered by American developmentalists. In contrast to the behaviorists and traditional learning theorists, Piaget viewed the mind as central to the understanding of how human beings develop. According to Piaget, the mind is not simply a passive receiver of information but an active processor of experience. The mind is like other living and growing structures because it does not simply respond or react to experience but actively changes and adapts to the world.

Intellectual Organization and Adaptation

As a result of his early work in biology, Piaget came to believe that biological activities (including animal and plant behaviors) are the result of **adaptation** to the physical environment. This idea led him to think of human cognitive development in the same way. In other words, thinking involves adaptation to an environment and results in the **organization** of the mind. The organized patterns of behavior and perception are called **schemas** (*schemas* [or *schemata*], plural; *schema*, singular). Infant schemas are usually action-oriented (sucking, grasping, looking), whereas adult schemas are abstractions (concepts of justice and the concept of the conservation of matter). The cognitive schemas of the adult are derived from the motor schemas of the child (Kagan, 1984; Piaget, 1963).

Assimilation and Accommodation

The processes responsible for the adaptation of schemas are complementary processes called *assimilation* and *accommodation*. As long as a person learns (which happens from birth to death), these processes remain important.

> *SOME DEFINITIONS*
>
> **Assimilation.** The process of using the same schema in more than one way—of applying existing habits and existing ideas to new objects. An infant sucks on a nipple, its thumb, its hand, and even its blanket.
>
> **Accommodation.** The process of changing a schema to fit a new situation—of modifying an action to fit a new object. An infant sucks on a nipple but has to adjust its sucking action in order to drink from a cup.

The processes of assimilation and accommodation work together and are necessary for cognitive growth. Of equal importance are the comparative amounts of assimilation or accommodation that occur. A balance between assimilation and accommodation is important and is referred to by Piaget as *equilibrium*. The absence of equilibrium provides the motivation for seeking a new state of balance or equi-

The Jean Piaget Society

Jean Piaget (1896–1980)

Piaget was born in 1896 in Neuchâtel, Switzerland. Intellectually precocious, he published his first article at age eleven—a description of an albino sparrow. This early interest in biology was reflected in all his later work. In 1915, at eighteen, Piaget received his baccalaureate degree from the University of Neuchâtel. He received his doctoral degree in the natural sciences from the same institution in 1918, by which time he had published twenty-one papers, mostly on mollusks, and was considered an expert in this area of biology.

Piaget's primary interest then turned to psychology. His work in biology had led him to the conclusion that biological development was the result not only of maturation (and heredity) but also of features of the environment. Piaget's observations of structural changes in successive generations of mollusks led him to the notion that biological development was a process of *adaptation* to the environment, a concept that led to his later view of human mental development as likewise a process of adaptation to the environment. He also viewed mental development as an extension of biological development. Beginning in 1921, Piaget launched a career of research that focused on the mental development of children. Piaget's first books in psychology were *The Language and Thought of the Child* (1923) and *Judgment and Reasoning in the Child* (1924).

Piaget's method of determining the child's level of cognitive development involved asking the child questions about problem solving.

librium. The interaction of assimilation and accommodation in the process of attaining equilibrium accounts for cognitive development.

Stages of Cognitive Development

According to Piaget, cognitive development proceeds through a series of stages, each qualitatively different from the prior stage. Cognitive development can be divided into four broad periods (Piaget, 1963):

1. **Sensori-motor intelligence** (0–2 years). During this period, behavior is primarily motor. Infant schemas involve action, movement, and perceptual activity (looking, hearing, and touching).
2. **Preoperational thought** (2–7 years). This period is characterized by the development of symbolic functions such as language or imaginative play. During this stage the child evolves from an organism that functions primarily in a sensori-motor mode to one that functions primarily in a conceptual or symbolic mode. The child is increasingly able to internally represent events (to "think") while becoming less dependent on motor activities for the direction of behavior.
3. **Concrete operations** (7–11 years). In this period, the child is able to use operations or logical thought processes that can be applied to concrete (actual or real) objects or experiences. The concrete operational child cannot yet apply logic to abstract or hypothetical problems.

4. **Formal operations** (11–15 years). In this stage, the child's thinking reaches its greatest level of development. The child is able to apply logic to all types of problems including the abstract and the hypothetical. The child is no longer dependent on the concrete or the real.

Evaluation of Piaget's Cognitive Theory

Cognitive theorists such as Piaget have generally rejected the mechanistic theories of development and learning that reduce development to S–R associations and reinforcements. R. W. White (1959) suggested that S–R theory does not explain the commonly observed phenomenon of individuals (including animals) who work or engage in any activity without any apparent reward. White seems to be saying that when people engage in some activities, such as play, they may well be motivated by their own basic "competence" rather than by a mere reinforcement.

The contributions of Piaget's cognitive theory include:

· The recognition that the child is *actively* involved in interpreting the environment. The child does not simply respond to the world as a "tabula rasa" or blank state, waiting to be influenced by the external world, as the behaviorists had claimed. Nor does the child simply unfold his or her inborn or innate characteristics, as the maturationists had claimed. Rather, Piaget suggested that the child actively explores the environment in a manner similar to scientists, manipulating objects, testing out ideas, modifying concepts or theories in light of experience, and so on.

· The recognition that at each stage of cognitive development the same objective experience can lead to different—and equally real—views of the world. For example, the infant in the sensori-motor stage (birth to approximately two years of age) will not recognize that objects have a permanent existence in the world. If shown a familiar toy, which is then covered with a cloth, the infant will make no attempt to search for the toy or to reach for it. Such behavior indicates that the infant has not yet attained the concept of object permanence. On the other hand, a seven-year-old in the stage of concrete operations will immediately remove the cloth covering the toy, indicating an understanding of object permanence.

· Piaget's theories have been widely applied to educational design. Curricula can be planned to fit the needs of children. It is possible to determine the stage of thinking of a child and to design educational experiences in accordance with that stage. For example, in learning mathematics, the concrete-operational child would benefit more from the use of actual objects (blocks and marbles) than from a presentation using symbols and abstractions.

In addition to the important contributions of the Piagetian viewpoint, his theory of cognitive development has not been immune to criticism, including these points:

· *Concerns about Piaget's methodology and the validity of his concepts.* Some critics have argued that Piaget's interview format of examining child thinking processes leads to unrealistic and unverifiable findings.

> Although Piaget's popularity has increased dramatically in recent years, there is a great deal of concern . . . that the terms and concepts invoked by his theory more closely reflect Piaget's own cognitive structures and unique methodological approach

than they do the real world of mental and behavioral phenomena. Many . . . believe that his constructs have not yet been sufficiently validated by the results of empirical investigation, and they fear that the nature of the system is such that its components may not even be subject to such validation. (Diamond, 1982, p. 21)

- *Overemphasis on intellectual or mental processes in development.* Another problem with Piaget's cognitive theory, in general, is that it tends to emphasize intellectual or mental processes as the primary organizing features of human development. Whereas traditional behaviorists have made it a point to ignore cognitive characteristics of the organism or person in explaining development, it can be argued that some cognitive theorists have overemphasized the role of mental activities in governing human behavior. While Piaget did not completely ignore social, moral, or emotional contributions to development, he pays minimal attention to the role of social and cultural variations in child thinking. Some critics have argued that his conclusions about stages of cognitive development are valid only for modern Western cultures.
- *Piaget does not provide an adequate explanation for movement of the child from one stage of cognitive development to another.* Critics have suggested that Piaget's theory does not deal with the important question of why or how a child moves from one stage to the next.
- *Piaget tends to underestimate the cognitive ability of young children and to overestimate the cognitive ability of adolescents and adults.* Piaget argued that young children tend to be embedded in their own point of view to the extent that they have difficulty understanding an alternative perspective (that is, they are *egocentric*). In addition, he suggested that very young children have extremely limited number skills. There is evidence that young children are far less egocentric and more numerically skilled than Piaget had given them credit for (Borke, 1978; Gelman, 1978).

  In addition, Piaget believed that most adolescents and certainly all adults will have attained the final stage of cognitive development. However, there is evidence that only 30 to 40 percent of adolescents and adults have attained this level of thinking (Grinder, 1975).

The Psychoanalytic Tradition

The theories of Sigmund Freud, the neo-Freudians (Otto Rank, Carl Jung, Alfred Adler, Karen Horney, and Erik Erikson) and the so-called ego psychologists constitute the *psychoanalytic tradition.* The focus of these theories is on aspects of human development not addressed in any detail in the maturational, behaviorist/learning, and cognitive theories discussed so far. Specifically, the psychoanalytic tradition focuses on emotional factors and personality development.

Freud

Like that of the learning theorists, Freud's notion of humans was essentially deterministic. Unlike the learning theorists, he believed that the source of determinism was not the environment but powerful forces within the person. **Psychoanalytic theory** pictures humans as creatures driven by inner forces that often remain at the level of the unconscious. Human development represents the effort of the individual to channel or redirect these potentially self-destructive forces of sex and aggression in socially constructive directions. Much of Freud's theory points to the development of personality in childhood as the critical clue to understanding adult personality.

In contrast to Piaget, Freud formulated a stage theory of development relating to the development of emotions and personality. The driving force in Freud's theory is his concept of *libido*. **Libido** (or sexual energy) presumably occurs in a fixed amount at birth in each individual. The libido is centered in certain areas of the body at certain periods in life. At each location site of the libido, the individual could be gratified with the release of tensions (associated with the accumulation of libido at a specific site) or be frustrated if the appropriate stimulation did not occur. Frustration (or the absence of gratification) was associated with the development of emotional or psychological problems later in life.

The movement of libido to different parts of the body determined not only the method of gratification or frustration but also the progression from one developmental stage to the next. Freud believed that the location of the libido followed a sequence of unvarying or universal stages. He postulated that personality develops in a relatively predictable pattern of **psychosexual stages** (see Table 2.2):

1. *The* **oral stage.** The first location of libido is centered in the oral region for approximately the first eighteen months of the child's life. Accordingly, the infant is either stimulated (gratified) or frustrated by being able—or unable—to suck on things (e.g., mother's nipple, bottle nipple, or thumb) or, when teeth erupt, to bite on things.

   When the infant's oral needs are blocked or frustrated, problems in the infant's development may occur. If frustration is severe enough, *fixation* may occur and some of the infant's libido will remain (presumably for the rest of

TABLE 2.2
Freud's Stages of Development

STAGE	APPROXIMATE AGE	CHARACTERISTICS
Oral	0–18 months	The sources of pleasure include sucking, biting, and swallowing. Preoccupation with immediate gratification of impulses.
Anal	18 months–3 years	The sources of gratification include urination and the explusion or retention of feces.
Phallic	3–6 years	The child becomes concerned with the genitals. Source of sexual pleasure involves manipulating genitals. Period of Oedipus or Electra complex.
Latency	6 years–onset of puberty (approximately 12 years)	Loss of interest in sexual gratification. Identification with like-sexed parent.
Genital	puberty–the adolescent years	Concern with adult modes of sexual pleasure, barring fixations or regressions (movement to an earlier pattern of behavior).

Sigmund Freud (1856–1939)

Sigmund Freud was born in Freiberg, Moravia (now Czechoslovakia) in 1856 but lived most of his life in Vienna, where he obtained a medical degree in 1881. He pursued an academic career instead of practicing medicine immediately and produced excellent research on the nervous system. Unable to support his family on a limited university-faculty income and kept from promotion by the widespread anti-Semitism in Vienna at the time, Freud began full-time practice as a physician.

In Freud's medical practice, which involved work with patients who had emotional and psychological problems, he used the *free association* method, an approach that allowed his patients to talk freely about whatever was on their minds. Through the use of free association and another method he called dream interpretation, Freud laid the foundations and developed major tools of a method of treatment for emotional or neurotic disorders called *psychoanalysis*.

Through psychoanalysis Freud determined that most of his adult patients repressed memories of childhood experiences and consequently he formulated an influential *psychoanalytic theory of development*.

Freud's writings were voluminous; his books include *Psychical Mechanism of Hysterical Phenomena* (1893), *The Interpretation of Dreams* (1899), *The Future of an Illusion* (1927), *The Ego and the Id* (1927), *Civilization and Its Discontents* (1930), and *The Problem of Anxiety* (1936).

Freud's last years were spent in London, where he died in 1939.

one's life) at the oral zone. When such an oral fixation occurs, the individual will attempt to gain the gratification missed earlier in life. Thus, the emotional or psychological problems that a person has as an adult may be based on fixations at early ages (Erikson, 1963).

2. *The* **anal stage.** This stage extends from approximately eighteen months to three years while, according to Freud, the libido is located in the anal region of the body. The primary gratification in this stage occurs with the use of the anal muscles that control the opening or closing of the anal sphincters. The child is stimulated either by the expulsion or retention of feces.

   Anal fixations result from frustrations during this period. Since the anal stage coincides in our culture with the period of toilet training, some children may have *anal expulsive* fixations (the result of overly severe toilet training).

3. *The* **phallic stage.** This stage involves the movement of the libido to the genital areas. The phallic stage extends from ages three to six. Because of the structural differences in male and female genitalia, it is appropriate to discuss both a male and female phallic stage (Erikson, 1963).

   The male phallic stage. For the male, gratification is obtained by the stimulation of the genitals during routine care. Freud believed that it was the boy's mother who provides some of this stimulation and that, therefore, the boy would sexually *desire* his mother. However, since the father stands in the way of attaining his goal, the boy develops negative feelings toward the father. Freud labeled this entire complex of feelings the *Oedipus complex*.

   As the boy comes to recognize his father as a rival for his mother's love, he gradually comes to fear the potential retaliation of the father. Thus, as a result of the Oedipus complex, the boy experiences *castration anxiety*. Because of the strength of this anxiety, the boy ultimately gives up his desire for his mother. He replaces it with an *identification* with his father. The identification with the father is an important development because the boy models himself after the father. In so doing, he internalizes characteristics required for becoming an adult male in society (Erickson, 1963).

The female phallic stage. As with the male phallic stage, the libido moves to the genital zone. However, in this case the girl desires to sexually possess her father. Since the mother stands in the way of the girl's goal, the girl at first has negative feelings toward the mother and fears punishment from her. Gradually, however, the girl transforms her dislike of the mother into a positive identification and adopts the characteristics of the mother. Freud identified this entire complex of feelings in the female as the female Oedipus complex, sometimes called the Electra complex (Erikson, 1963).

4. *The* **latency stage.** During this stage, which extends from six years of age until the onset of puberty, the libido submerges and is not localized in a specific body zone. Freud uses the term *latency* to describe this absence or inactivity of libido.

5. *The* **genital stage.** With the onset of puberty, the libido emerges once again. If the individual has been largely gratified—rather than frustrated from birth until age six—he or she is now prepared for full adult sexuality. This means that the individual's sexuality can now be directed to reproductive functions (Erikson, 1963).

Freud discussed additional concepts and principles in his voluminous writing, and Freudian theory continues to be reinterpreted today (Greenberg and Mitchell, 1983; Eagle, 1984). Our purpose here has been to provide the core concepts of his developmental theory, which have served as the historical basis for considerable research and theory in human development.

Erikson

Erikson's theory of development has much in common with Freud's. In fact, he referred to Freud's work as the rock on which all significant improvements in personality theory would be based. However, Erikson's theory differs from Freud's approach in three major ways (Maier, 1969):

1. Erickson emphasized the concept of the *ego* or the self whereas Freud emphasized the importance of feelings. That is, Freud was primarily concerned with the biologically based libido and the emerging feelings of gratification or frustration, and Erikson emphasized development of the self or ego in relation to the social environment. For this reason, it has been suggested that Freud's theory is *psychosexual,* whereas Erikson's theory is **psychosocial.**

2. Erikson introduced a *social complex* or *framework* to replace the classical Freudian notion of individual dynamics in the context of the child-mother-father triangle. The Eriksonian social context in which the ego or self operates is quite broad and includes the following elements:
   • The individual and his or her parents within the context of the family.
   • The family setting in relation to the wider social-cultural setting (including the historical-cultural heritage of the family).

3. Whereas Freud was primarily concerned with *pathological development,* Erikson

Erik Erikson (b. 1902)

Erik Erikson, born in Germany, as a young adult met Freud in Vienna and became interested in the psychoanalytic approach to the study of personality development. That approach had a pronounced influence on the direction of his career and his writings.

Erikson came to the United States when the Nazis came to power in Germany. He held several positions at major universities and child guidance centers. He was on the senior staff of the Austen Riggs Center and participated in research on the Sioux Indians while at the Harvard Psychological Clinic. He also worked and did research at the Yale Institute of Human Relations, the Institute of Child Welfare at the University of California, and the Western Psychiatric Institute in Pittsburgh. Most recently he has been professor of human development and lecturer on psychiatry at Harvard University.

Erikson's books include *Young Man Luther* (1958), *Insight and Responsibility* (1964), *Identity: Youth and Crisis* (1968), *Gandhi's Truth* (1969), and *Toys and Reasons* (1976). He has been a winner of both the Pulitzer Prize and the National Book Award.

focused on the *successful* or *positive solution* of developmental crises. Freud had concentrated on proving the existence and functioning of the unconscious in controlling one's fate. Erikson was trying to show that there were *developmental opportunities* that allowed one the chance to triumph over the hazards of living.

According to Erikson, the ego or the self develops as new demands are continually being placed on it by the social environment. Each new social demand produces an emotional crisis which, in turn, carries with it the opportunity for a positive resolution and healthy development. Erikson proposed a stage theory of psychosocial development based on a maturational principle—the *epigenetic principle*.

> The **epigenetic principle** . . . states that anything that grows has a *ground plan*, and that out of this ground plan the parts arise, each having its *time* of special ascendancy, until all parts have arisen to form a *functioning whole*. (1959, p. 52)

According to this principle, various capabilities compose the fully developed ego. These capabilities are not fully developed early in life. Rather, each part of the ego has a specific stage in the life cycle when it is the focus or center of development. Because the entire process is based on a maturational timetable, a person must successfully negotiate each stage at its appointed time. Development will move on to the next stage whether or not the necessary capability has been established. For this reason, Erikson views each stage of development as a critical period (Lerner, 1986).

Erikson's major idea is that the stages of development require the individual to *adapt* to the *social environment* in terms of changes in the *ego* or *self*. Erikson first discussed his model of development—the eight stages of development—in his book *Childhood and Society*. In that book, he suggested that every human being experiences eight stages or crises during the course of the lifespan. Erikson identified the following stages of development—each of which may be described as a point where individual adaptation may lean in one of two directions (see Tables 2.3 and 2.4):

1. *Stage 1:* **Trust versus mistrust.** This stage corresponds to Freud's oral stage and occurs from birth to approximately eighteen months. If the infant develops a feeling or general expectancy of physical comfort rather than of fear or uncertainty, it will develop a sense of *trust.* If the infant comes to expect that its needs will be met with some regularity (that the world is a somewhat predictable and friendly place: food is available when one is hungry, attention is available when one is distressed, and so on), a basic foundation of trust will be established. This trust can then be extended to new experiences. If, on the other hand, a sense of fear or uncertainty is created in the infant, adaptation will lean in the direction of *mistrust.*

   Although feeding or oral interaction is surely important, it is only one mode of sensory interaction that can reassure the infant. Thus, the parent or

TABLE 2.3
Erikson's Stages of Development: Positive and Negative Resolutions

CENTRAL LIFE CRISIS	POSITIVE RESOLUTION	NEGATIVE RESOLUTION
Trust versus mistrust (0–18 mos)	Reliance on caregiver leads to development of trust in the environment.	Fear, anxiety, and suspicion. Lack of care, both physical and psychological, by caregiver leads to mistrust of environment (e.g., fear, anxiety, or suspicion).
Autonomy versus shame and doubt (18 mos–3 years)	Sense of self as worthy. Assertion of choice and will. Environment encourages independence, leading to sense of pride.	Loss of self-esteem. Sense of external control may produce self-doubt and doubt about others.
Initiative versus guilt (3–6 years)	The ability to learn, to initiate activities, to enjoy achievement and competence.	The inability to control newly developed power. Realization of potential failure leads to fear of punishment and guilt.
Industry versus inferiority (6 years–puberty)	Learning the value of work; acquiring skills and tools of technology. Competence helps to order life and to make things work.	Repeated frustration and failure lead to feelings of inadequacy and inferiority that may affect view of life.
Identity versus role confusion (adolescence)	Experiments with various roles in developing mature individuality.	Pressure and demands may lead to confusion about self.
Intimacy versus isolation (young adulthood)	A commitment to others. Close heterosexual relationship and procreation.	Withdrawal from such intimacy; isolation, self-absorption, and alienation from others.
Generativity versus stagnation (middle age)	The care and concern for the next generation. Widening interest in work and ideas.	Self-indulgence and resulting psychological impoverishment.
Ego integrity versus despair (old age)	Acceptance of one's life. Realization of the inevitability of death. Feeling of dignity and meaning in one's existence.	Disappointment with one's life and desperate fear of death.

Adapted from Erikson, 1963.

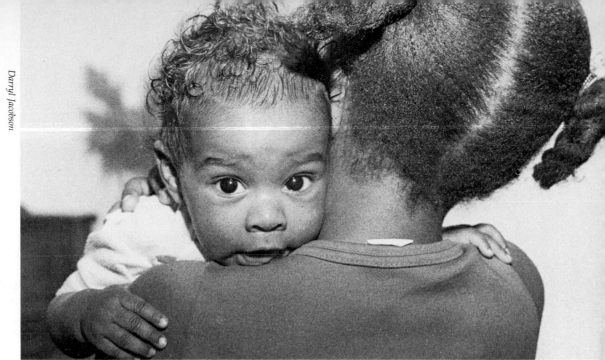

According to Erikson, infant reliance on a caregiver leads to the development of trust.

TABLE 2.4

Erikson's Eight Stages of Development

Stage	1	2	3	4	5	6	7	8
Maturity								Ego integrity vs. despair
Adulthood							Generativity vs. stagnation	
Young adulthood						Intimacy vs. isolation		
Puberty and adolescence					Identity vs. diffusion			
Latency				Industry vs. inferiority				
Locomotor genital			Initiative vs. guilt					
Muscular anal		Autonomy vs. shame						
Oral sensory	Trust vs. mistrust							

Erikson's first four stages are similar to Freud's stages—the anal, oral, phallic, and latency stages, respectively. The remaining four represent Erikson's application of interpersonal and social factors to adolescent and adult development.

Adapted from Erikson, 1963.

caretaker can also develop trust through various other methods, including touching, holding, or looking at the infant.

2. *Stage 2:* **Autonomy versus shame and doubt.** This stage corresponds to Freud's anal stage and extends from approximately eighteen months to three years of age. Whereas Freud limited his concern in the anal stage to gratification or frustration through control of the anal musculature, Erikson expanded his approach to include the other muscles of the body. Just as the infant and toddler learns to control anal muscles, likewise he or she learns when to "hold on" or "let go" with reference to all the body muscles.

    If the infant or toddler feels in control of its own body, a sense of autonomy will develop. On the other hand, if the infant is incapable of controlling his or her own body movements in relation to the environment, then he or she will develop a sense of shame or doubt.

3. *Stage 3:* **Initiative versus guilt.** According to Erikson, the three-to-six-year-old child is faced with the developmental dilemma of initiative versus guilt. This period corresponds to Freud's phallic stage, in which exploration and manipulation of the genitals becomes a source of pleasure for the young child. Although Erikson does not ignore Freud's notion of the Oedipus complex, his conceptualization of the conflict has broader psychosocial application than Freud's approach. That is, if the child is to resolve the Oedipus complex, he or she must be independent of parental figures. Erikson suggested that the child must now employ the previously developed skills of autonomy and motor control by moving out into the world, thereby breaking the Oedipal "apron strings."

    If the child is able to step out into this new world of experience without the prodding of the parent, a sense of *initiative* will develop. On the other hand, if the child is overly dependent on the parent for permission to move out into the world, he or she will experience a sense of *guilt*. According to Erikson, guilt will arise when the relatively immature Oedipal attachments prevent the child from doing what society now expects him or her to be able to do—independently experience the world.

4. *Stage 4:* **Industry versus inferiority.** This stage occurs from six years to the onset of puberty and corresponds to Freud's latency stage. Since Freud believed that the libido was submerged during this stage, he did not think that any significant *psychosexual* development was occurring in the latency phase. On the other hand, Erikson believed that this period was filled with *psychosocial* developments of considerable importance.

    According to Erikson, children begin to learn the basic skills necessary for independent functioning in adult society during this phase of life. This

Exploring and searching the environment are a part of the "initiative versus guilt" stage of development.

The development of a sense of industry means that children apply their skills to make things happen.

learning ordinarily occurs, in part, in the setting of the formal school and includes such skills as reading, writing, and reasoning. *Industry* refers to the sense of accomplishment the child gets from applying these skills to life situations, tasks, or problems. *Inferiority* refers to the sense of *helplessness* or lack of control that occurs when children feel that their existing skill level is no match for the tasks at hand. The role of the parent or caretaker and the teacher is of prime importance during this stage, because the child who develops academic and social skills will likely emerge from this period with a sense of competence and productivity.

5. *Stage 5:* **Identity versus identity diffusion** *or role confusion.* This phase corresponds to the genital stage of Freud's psychosexual stages of development. The crisis of identity versus diffusion occurs during adolescence—the period that extends from the onset of puberty until the development of a tentative "stance toward the world" (an identity). During this phase, the adolescent begins to ask crucial psychosocial questions such as

   · Who am I in relation to society?
   · What vocation or career do I wish to pursue?
   · What set of values or beliefs will guide my life?
   · What type of a general lifestyle do I prefer?
   · Over what elements in my life can I now exercise some choice?

   Two significant changes occur during this period that influence the adolescent's resolution of identity questions.

   a. The first change is *physical*. The onset of puberty results in bodily changes that may encourage adolescents to view themselves, at least physically, as adults.
   b. The second change is the development of abstract reasoning (Piaget's final stage of cognitive functioning) that enables the adolescent to deal with the concepts or ingredients of identity: values, views of self, and views of society (e.g., notions of justice, truth, and equality).

Thus, Erikson views this period of the life cycle as involving much more than the psychosexual development in Freud's genital phase. For example, adolescent maturity may make possible a new way of understanding the complexities of reality through the use of abstractions. The adolescent can now think about the vast array of possible life roles (student, mother, father, brother, teacher, lawyer, mechanic, pharmacist) in a logical, abstract fashion such that he or she can now begin to fashion (from this vast array of possible roles) a reasonably organized description of the self or an identity. Thinking about such roles is usually accompanied by some role experimentation on the part of the adolescent. If this normal process of testing and trying out roles results in a tentative commitment to a role and an accompanying set of values, the adolescent has successfully completed this stage. On the other hand, if adolescents cannot find a role that suits them, they may remain in a state of continual experimentation, moving from one role to another without making a permanent commitment to any role. According to Erikson, such an individual who is not able to successfully resolve the identity crisis may have a sense of *role confusion* or *identity diffusion*.

6. *Stage 6:* **Intimacy versus isolation.** At this point Erikson departs from Freud's psychosexual model by discussing the psychosocial implications beyond adolescence—and therefore beyond our detailed concern in this book. Erikson's last three developmental stages are nevertheless noted below and included in Tables 2.3 and 2.4 because they are important elements of his lifespan approach to development.

7. *Stage 7:* **Generativity versus stagnation.** The developmental crisis of middle age has to do with the dimensions of "generativity versus stagnation" or "self-absorption."

8. *Stage 8:* **Ego integrity versus despair.** The eighth and final stage of development occurs in old age, when the individual looks back on his or her life.

Evaluation of the Psychoanalytic Approach

The strengths of the psychoanalytic perspective are at least twofold:

1. It takes a holistic view of human development. Unlike other cognitive theories or behaviorism, which focuses on specific dimensions of human functioning such as thinking or overt behavior, the psychoanalytic tradition treats the broad range of development, including topics such as emotions, motivation, and the broad sweep of human behavior.
2. It attempts to understand problems of human behavior in developmental terms.

A major and serious weakness of psychoanalytic theory is its inadequate attention to proving or demonstrating principles of development in a scientifically valid manner. (**Scientific validity** refers to the clear statement of objective procedures, methods of measurement, and findings such that other scientists can independently replicate these procedures, methods, and findings.) How, for example, did Freud prove the existence or validity of the concept of psychic energy or *libido*? Further, much of the so-called evidence for psychoanalytic theory comes from case studies of adults and therefore has relatively minor bearing on our detailed study of human development only through adolescence.

Ecological or Systems Theories

Systems theories emphasize the necessary interaction between the developing person and the environment. According to this perspective, human development is the result of three major factors:

1. The *person* and what he or she brings to a particular situation or stage of development. This includes the results of experience as well as of motivation.
2. The *environment,* or what is available to the individual in a particular situation or stage of life. This includes the significant *contexts* of life such as family, school, and neighborhood/community.
3. The reciprocal nature of the *interaction* between the person and the environment.

PERSON ⇆ ENVIRONMENT

European Origins

The **ecological or systems perspective** has its origins in the work of the European *gestalt* psychologists. (*Gestalt* means "pattern" in German.) The gestalt perspective emphasizes the unity and the integration of the whole person. Whereas behaviorists are concerned with the "parts" of human behavior (stimuli and responses), the gestaltists view human behavior as a patterned or unified whole (a *gestalt*), which has to be studied as such. For gestalt theorists, the human being cannot simply be reduced to the sum of its parts (as the behaviorists imply). This tradition of looking at the whole person adapting to the environment was carried to the United States by the German psychologist Kurt Lewin. Lewin extended the gestalt approach by developing a closely related view known as *field theory.*

The Kansas Tradition

In the late 1940s at the University of Kansas, Roger Barker and Herbert Wright began investigations of child life in a small midwestern town. Their research was influenced by the work of Kurt Lewin because it emphasized the adaptation of children in specific environments. Furthermore, their research was "naturalistic" because it occurred in real-life settings rather than in the laboratory. In their early studies (Barker and Wright, 1955) they described a small midwestern town of 700 people (120 of the total number were children) as it functioned over a year. Later research (Barker and Schoggen, 1973; Schoggen, 1983) measured the environments of two towns in different countries: Midwest, Kansas, and Yoredale, England (real cities with fictitious names). What made Barker and Schoggen's research unique was that they did not simply examine beliefs expressed by children or adults, or specific actions by caretakers or children; they looked at how *total environments* influenced children and how children participated in these environments. Barker and Schoggen found many interesting differences between the cities. American children (Midwest, Kansas) were presented with more situations where they were free to come and go than English (Yoredale) children. When these researchers looked at adolescents, they found that the English Yoredale system tended to delay significant participation in community life until adulthood. On the other hand, the American Midwest system involved children in community activities earlier. Barker and his colleagues concluded that the behavior of their subjects was more situation-oriented than person-oriented. Barker referred to this general process as one of "behavior settings."

Although we have looked at only one study of person-environment interaction, considerable research has been done in the area, including the following:

1. *Children and housing*. Housing provides the immediate environment of the child's early years. As children become more mobile, they first enter the environment fairly close to the house. Opportunities for children's activities are determined, to some extent, by how much space is available both inside and outside the home, as well as by how this space is structured (Walter, 1981, 1982).
2. *Environments for preschoolers*. Research has been done in *day-care* settings, including the conditions and future needs in this area (Belsky, 1984; Ainslie, 1984; Weikert, 1984).
3. *Public school environments*. Considerable research has been directed at the examination of school environments, including the degree of involvement of pupils in school activities, the physical structure of schools, and high school environments (Rutter et al., 1979; Stigler et al., 1982; Csikszentmihalyi and Larson, 1984; Hess and Holloway, 1984).

The Ethologists

In addition to the work of the Kansas group, a relatively small group of naturalists (called *ethologists*) have attempted to describe development in real-life or natural settings. Although ethologists have been primarily concerned with the study of animal behavior, their research has been applied to human development. They view development as a process of adaptation to the environment in which the survival of a species depends on successful organism-environment interaction (Immelmann, 1980).

Cornell University

Urie Bronfenbrenner

Urie Bronfenbrenner (b. 1917)

Urie Bronfenbrenner, a professor in the Department of Human Development and Family Studies, College of Human Ecology, Cornell University, received his Ph.D. in psychology from the University of Michigan in 1942. He is recognized as one of the world's foremost developmental psychologists.

Bronfenbrenner has maintained that laboratory studies of child behavior (the most common mode of developmental research; the subject under investigation is usually removed from a real-life setting and placed in a psychological testing room or laboratory) sacrifice too much in order to gain experimental data. He has argued that laboratory studies have led to "the science of the strange behavior of children in strange situations with strange adults for the briefest possible periods of time." If we are to understand the way human beings develop, Bronfenbrenner feels, behavior and development should be observed in natural settings. Such natural settings involve interactions with familiar people over long periods of time.

Bronfenbrenner and the Ecology of Human Development

A relatively recent statement of an adaptation or systems theory is the work of the developmental psychologist Urie Bronfenbrenner (1979, 1986). Bronfenbrenner uses the word *ecology* to refer to the interaction of the person and his or her social and physical setting (environment).

Bronfenbrenner defined the ecology of human development as follows:

> The ecology of human development involves the scientific study of the progressive, mutual accommodation between an active growing human being and . . . the settings in which the developing person lives . . . [Development is also influenced] by the relations between these settings and by the larger contexts in which the settings are embedded. (1979, p. 21)

The three significant features of this definition according to Bronfenbrenner appear on p. 54 (see also Figure 2.2).

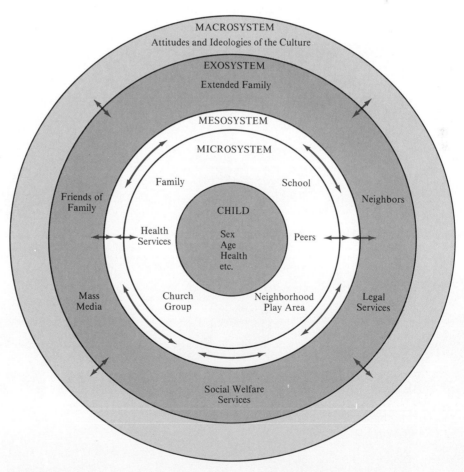

FIGURE 2.2
Bronfenbrenner's model of the ecology of human development. From Garbarino, 1982b, p. 648.

1. The *developing person* is viewed as a growing, active individual.
2. The *interaction* between the developing person and the environment is viewed as a two-directional or *reciprocal* relationship. In other words, there is a process of mutual accommodation to which both person *and* environment make contributions.
3. The *environment* that is relevant to human development is not limited to a single, immediate setting (home, school, or work). Rather, the *ecological environment* is much broader and includes immediate settings and interaction between immediate settings (the relationship between home and school or home and workplace) and larger settings, including the culture (which influences specific settings).

    The **ecological environment** is composed of four structural levels:

    a. *The* **microsystem.** This system involves the interaction between the developing person in an *immediate* setting or context. For example, the relationship between a child and teachers or peers in the *school* and the relationship between an adolescent and his employer in a *work* setting are topics of microsystem analysis.

The ecology of human development is the study of the mutual interaction between the developing person and the settings or contexts of development.

Guy Gillette/Photo Researchers, Inc.

Some Examples of Ecological Interactions

1. *Interactions between the individual and an immediate environment.* When the child enters the formal school for the first time, there is an interaction between the child and the environments of the school. In states with compulsory kindergartens, children usually go to school only a half day during their first year because it is recognized that the child may still require some resting or napping and may need a gradual daily separation from mother and home.

2. *Interactions between immediate environments.* In the example cited above, the success of the child's adaptation to school is dependent not simply on the child's immediate relationship to the school. It is also a function of the interaction of at least two immediate environments—the school and the family—that influence the child's relationship to the school. For example, a child's initial performance and adjustment to the formal school is largely the result of the preparation of the child in the family context (Hess and Holloway, 1984; Laosa and Sigel, 1982).

3. *Interactions between immediate environments and larger social contexts* (in which the immediate environments are embedded). Immediate environments such as school and family are embedded in larger or cultural contexts, such as economic, social, or political systems. For example, the immediate environment of the school is contained in—or exists in the context of—an economic system. The economic system determines, among other things, the method of school financing—the property tax. The property tax provides funds for schools based on the value of the property in a given neighborhood. The value of the property is, in turn, directly related to the income levels of the neighborhood residents. Under this system, lower-income neighborhoods generate fewer funds for school through the property tax than more affluent communities. This is an example of how the economic system—an overarching cultural pattern—influences the quality of educational experiences for each child.

---

b. *The* **mesosystem.** This system involves the relationships among the various settings or contexts in which the developing person finds himself or herself. For example, for a nine-year-old child, the mesosystem would involve the relationship between the school and the family or the relationship between the family and the peer group.

c. *The* **exosystem.** This system includes the primary social structures that influence the developing person. The exosystem would be the formal and informal institutions such as political/governmental structures, neighborhood and community organizations, transportation networks, and the informal communication networks within neighborhoods, communities, and workplaces.

d. *The* **macrosystem.** This system is the *overarching institutional patterns of a culture* (e.g., the economic educational, legal, social, and political systems of which the micro-, meso-, and exosystems are specific and *concrete manifestations* [1979, pp. 6–8, 258–91]). The macrosystem consists of the most general values, beliefs, or ideologies that influence the ways in which special institutions are organized and, therefore, the way in which human development occurs. For example, the value that a particular culture or society places on the child or the family will influence how individual children and families are treated in specific situations.

A Closer Look at the Ecological/Systems Perspective

Ecology, as defined by ecologists, is the scientific study of the relationships of living organisms with each other and with their environments (Ambrose, 1977). In biology, ecological studies of the relationship between *living communities* and their nonliving environments are known as the science of *ecosystems.* These interactions are studied at a biological level with special interest in the exchange of materials between the living and nonliving parts of the total ecosystem. The ecological study of various biological species requires the description of species habitat, way of life, population characteristics, social organization, and relationship with other species.

The application of an ecosystems perspective to human development poses several initial problems:

1. On the one hand human beings have a large diversity of habitats, styles of life, population, characteristics, and forms of social organization.
2. Unlike other animal species whose capacities for adaptation are determined primarily by biological evolution, humans have adaptive skills that are broadly extended by cultural evolution.
3. Human beings have significant power to alter their environment both by intentional control and through the unplanned effects of intervention. Some have suggested that man is an "intervening animal." (McGurk, 1977)

Before discussing the principles of the systems approach to human development, it is necessary to define a system. A *system* is an organized sustained pattern of interaction between two or more units or components and their attributes or characteristics resulting in an integrated, self-governed adaptation of these units or components (Ambrose, 1977).

To reduce the generality of this definition, we will discuss its significant terms.

1. *Components.* These are the parts of the total system. Components are almost unlimited in their variety. In the physical world these parts might be genes, neurons, bones, and so on. Abstractions such as rules, laws, morality, and justice can also be components. Components in human development systems might include a whole range of both physical and social entities (family, child, neighborhood, community, language, gene, body build) as well as derived abstractions (self-concept, morality, cognitive processes).
2. *Attributes* or *human factors.* These are the properties of the components. For example, the components listed below have the following attributes:
   Family—number of total members, emotional and physical state of the members, number of children (if any), "rules" of behavior, level of activity, and so on.
   Adult—family of origin, age, occupation, emotional/psychological state, physical attributes, friendship groups, self-concept, and so on.
   Child—age, physical/body structure (hair color, height, weight), self-concept, neighborhood and community of residence, race, and so on.
   School—location and physical setting, number of students, number of teachers.
3. *Interactions.* These are the relationships that "tie the system together." The relationships to be considered in any given situation depend on the problem or pertinent issue under consideration. The following example illustrates the concept of relationships:
   Sample issue: "Why do some children from some ethnic or minority families (e.g., black, Hispanic) have difficulty succeeding in school?
   Applying the tools of systems theory to this problem, we first begin by identifying the "components" of the system and their significant "attributes." In the above example, relevant components might include at least the following: middle-class school; black or Hispanic child; black or Hispanic family; and the community support system. Relevant "attributes" might include the economic status and values of the family; the interests, skills, attitudes, and abilities of the child; the programmatic emphasis of the school (e.g., college preparation, vocational training, etc.); and the attitudes of teachers and administrators toward children and their families.

Note that the process of accurate determination of components and their attributes is the *beginning* of the systems analysis of any significant problem or issue in human development. The next step, the specification of the *relationships* between components, is also vital. It is at the level of relationships that the complexity of many human development issues becomes apparent. In the above example, the systems nature of the problem becomes clear when one examines the interaction between components. Specifically, one can raise the following *relationship* questions: What is the relationship between the school and the family? Is the relationship characterized by mutual support? Are there open and meaningful channels of communication between home and school? What is the nature of the relationship between the child and his family vis-à-vis the school? Assuming that the school and the family are at least cordial, what are the features of parent-child interaction that promote or hinder successful school experiences? What is the relationship between the child and the school? What is the nature of teacher attitudes toward the child? Are textbooks and school materials designed to maximize success in school?

These relationship questions are simply examples of the large variety of questions that could be asked. The significant contribution of the systems perspective is that it provides a framework for critically examining and raising such important questions. The assumption is that at least half the battle in dealing with issues and problems of human development is asking the "right" questions!

4. *Environment.* As Ambrose suggests:

> The most significant parts of the environment with which man interacts are his social environment and those aspects of his physical environment that have been brought about or changed by his technologies. Because the human way of life is now based upon individual participation in a multiplicity of groups, its ecological analysis is concerned not just with the biotic community and its physical environment, but, to a large extent, with the community in the sociological sense and its cultural environment. Thus, in the ecological study of the dynamic interactions of human beings within a given ecosystem, the man-made environment figures very large. This includes not only the buildings and equipment required for reproduction, child rearing, education, production, transport and communication, and servicing of all kinds, but also the many kinds of social groups which directly or indirectly affect the individual in his daily life, with their group aims and norms, social procedures and institutions. (1977, p. 5)

5. *Feedback.* Feedback is the reciprocal or mutual interaction among the components of the system. Feedback allows the system, as a whole, to self-regulate itself. Some examples of feedback will help to clarify the concept:
   a. *Household Thermostat.* The common thermostat used to monitor the heating and/or cooling of a home is a good example of a system that uses feedback to self-regulate its activity. If the occupant wishes to increase the heat on a cold winter day, he or she will set the thermostat at the desired tempera-

ture. The thermostat will then send a signal to the heater, which will then generate enough heat to attain the desired goal or temperature. Throughout this process, information or feedback indicating the present temperature in the house is continuously monitored by the thermostat. This temperature is compared with the goal of the system or the temperature desired by a resident. If the desired temperature has been attained (i.e., a perfect match between the desired goal or thermostat setting and the actual temperature of the house), the system shuts itself off. If the desired temperature has not been reached, signals will continue to the heater until sufficient heat is generated to attain the desired room temperature.

The critical feature of this system is the fact that it is *feedback-regulated*. This means that the total heating system is regulated by the continual exchange of information among the components of the system. This exchange process is a circular one in which the components of the system both send and receive information.

   b. *Human Motor Skills.* A child (or even a professional baseball player) catching a baseball illustrates how human motor-performance can be viewed as a feedback-regulated system. When the ball is tossed to the child by a parent, the child's goal is to catch it. The child receives feedback from his or her eyes as the ball approaches. How large is the ball? How fast is it coming? This feedback information goes to the brain, which sends signals to the muscles of the body, particularly in the arms. These signals result in specific body movements designed to catch the oncoming baseball. The child's eyes continue to monitor the oncoming baseball in relation to motor movements such as extended arms and bending knees. Visual observation of his or her own movements and the approaching ball will result in continual feedback signals to the brain which will, in turn, result in continual adjustments in limb position and body posture. This process of observation and body movement and vice versa is both continuous and circular in much the same way as the previous example of the household thermostat. The system is *feedback-regulated* because it depends on the continuous exchange of information necessary to catch the baseball.

Evaluation of the Ecological/Systems Perspective

A major contribution of the ecological or systems perspective on human development is its focus of attention on defining issues and formulating questions relating to *social policy matters*. For example, the ecological research on child abuse and adolescent maltreatment emphasizes the necessity of moving beyond a simple cause-effect relationship for explaining child abuse (parents with particular characteristics are *the cause* of child abuse) (Belsky, 1980; Garbarino, 1982b; Goldberg and DiVitto, 1983; Garbarino, Schellenbach, and Sebes, 1986). Rather, Garbarino and Sherman (1980) have focused on neighborhood-community characteristics as a context for child abuse. *Neighborhoods* were assessed as high or low risks for child maltreatment. The environment and its support systems can thus be a contributing influence to child maltreatment.

Summary

1. The primary reason for examining theories of child development is to demonstrate the resulting variation in posing and answering important questions relating to human development (e.g., What is the basic nature of man?). In addition, theories of human development are ways of organizing the "facts" (or presumed facts) of human behavior into formulations or assumptions that can then be tested.
2. *Maturation* theory is based on the idea or assumption that human development is the result of the timed unfolding of a human being's genetic inheritance. Major contributors to this approach included G. Stanley Hall, Arnold Gesell, and Lewis Terman. Extensive research in human growth and development now supports the idea that *both* maturation and experience (or the environment) interact to influence the course of the human lifespan.
3. *Behavior* and *learning* theories contrast with maturation theory by portraying human behavior as primarily the result of environmental stimulation. Important contributors to this approach included J. B. Watson, Ivan Pavlov, and B. F. Skinner. This "traditional" behavior and learning theory had several problems. Human beings were frequently portrayed as primarily *reactive organisms*. These theories tended to be *reductionistic*. (Complex processes of human interaction and behavior were frequently and erroneously "broken down" or reduced to simplistic stimulus-response-reinforcement units.) Traditional behavior and learning theory promoted an unwarranted *deterministic* view of human development. *Social learning theory* as developed by Albert Bandura represented a significant modification of traditional learning theory.
4. A *cognitive* approach to child development emphasizes mental or internal factors as contrasted with the environmental or external emphasis of the traditional behaviorists. One of the foremost cognitive theorists was Jean Piaget (1896–1980). Piaget emphasized that the human mind was similar to other living and growing structures because it actively changed and adapted to the world rather than simply responding or reacting to experience. According to Piaget, cognitive development proceeds through a series of stages, each of which is qualitatively different from, yet dependent on, the prior

stage. Cognitive theorists such as Piaget have rejected mechanistic approaches that reduce human development and learning to simple associations and reinforcements. Cognitive theories (in particular, Piaget's ideas) have been widely applied to educational design. A problem with cognitive theory is that it tends to overemphasize the mentalistic or thinking components of human functioning.

5. The *psychoanalytic* approach to development has focused largely on those dimensions of human functioning omitted by cognitive theorists—the emotional, personal, or "irrational" forces of behavior. Psychoanalytic theories include those of Freud and his followers Rank, Jung, Adler, and Erikson. Freud's view of human behavior was, like the behaviorists, a deterministic one. Unlike the behaviorists, however, the source of determinism was not the environment but the powerful forces within the person. Human development was the effort of the individual to channel or redirect these potentially self-destructive forces of sex and aggression in socially and personally constructive directions.

   Erik Erikson's theory of human development has much in common with Freud's theory although there are some major differences. Erikson's model of development is *psychosocial*, whereas Freud's model is *psychosexual*. Erikson's theory goes beyond Freud's stages by including adulthood and aging. A strength of psychoanalytic theory is that it does attempt—albeit with limited scientific evidence—to deal with such important aspects of human development as emotion, feelings, and motivation. A major weakness of psychoanalytic theory is its insufficient attention to the scientific testing of principles of development.

6. *Systems* theories of human development emphasize the necessary and mutual interaction between the developing person and the environment or contexts of life. In this perspective, three major factors are involved: the person, the environment, and the interaction between both person and environment. A relatively recent and important statement of an adaptation or systems theory is contained in the work of the developmental psychologist Urie Bronfenbrenner, who has identified the "ecology of human development."

Key Terms

Accommodation	Exosystem
Adaptation	Formal operations
Anal stage	Generativity versus stagnation
Assimilation	Genital stage
Autonomy versus shame and doubt	Identity versus identity diffusion
Behavioral stages	Imitation (Modeling)
Behavior and learning theories	Industry versus inferiority
Classical conditioning	Initiative versus guilt
Cognitive theory	Intimacy versus isolation
Concrete operations	Latency stage
Ecological environment	Libido
Ecological or systems theories	Macrosystem
Ego Integrity versus despair	Maturational readiness
Epigenetic principle	Maturation theories

Mesosystem   Psychoanalytic theory
Microsystem   Psychosexual stages
Nativism   Psychosocial
Norm   Schemas
Observation   Scientific validity
Operant conditioning   Self-regulation
Oral stage   Sensori-motor intelligence
Organization   Social learning theory
Phallic stage   Subjectivism
Preoperational thought   Trust versus mistrust

Questions

1. How would you describe your current view or "theory" of human development? Is it similar to one or more of the theories discussed in this chapter? If so, identify the similarities.
2. Is your approach, view, or theory of human development similar to that of your parents, friends, or instructors?
3. Make a chart of the theories discussed in this chapter. Include the following in your chart: the name of the theory, central ideas, several proponents of the theory, and your evaluation of each theory.
4. Indicate several examples of the practical relationships between several of the theories of human development and applications in the family, community, world of work, or in public policy. In terms of your planned or current line of work or activity, cite several examples of the relationship of a theory of human development to a practical issue.

Suggested Readings

BRONFENBRENNER, U. *The Ecology of Human Development*. Cambridge, Mass.: Harvard U.P., 1979. This book is a challenge to the traditional way in which psychologists have studied human development—through "laboratory" studies. Bronfenbrenner argues that such studies lead to "the science of the strange behavior of children in strange situations with strange adults." Bronfenbrenner suggests that to really understand human behavior, it is necessary to observe human behavior in natural settings with familiar people over prolonged periods of time.

ERIKSON, E. H. *Childhood and Society*. New York: Norton, 1963. This book presents a readable introduction to Erikson's theory, including the eight stages of human development.

GESELL, A. *The First Five Years of Life*. New York: Harper & Row, 1940. Gesell and his colleagues wrote several books, including this one, that represent a maturational view of human development. The book contains much interesting, highly readable, and accurate information on the development of infants, toddlers, and preschoolers. Gesell's charts and sequential lists of age-related behaviors make interesting reading.

LERNER, R. M. *Concepts and Theories of Human Development* (2nd ed.). Reading, Mass.: Addison-Wesley, 1986. An excellent review and analysis of major theories of concepts of human development.

PIAGET, J., and INHELDER, B. *The Psychology of the Child*. New York: Basic Books, 1969. A brief book that summarizes many of Piaget's major ideas.

SKINNER, B. F. *Beyond Freedom and Dignity*. New York: Knopf, 1971. In this book, Skinner applies his learning theories to such considerations as the meaning of freedom, the origin of values, and the design of culture.

SKINNER, B. F. *Reflections on Behaviorism and Society*. Englewood

Cliffs, N.J.: Prentice-Hall, 1978. Skinner is a pioneer in the development of operant conditioning. The book explores applications of his theories to social organization, the science of behavior, and education. The book is a collection of occasional papers.

WADSWORTH, B. J. *Piaget's Theory of Cognitive and Affective Development* (3rd ed.). New York: McKay, 1984. This is an introductory overview of Piaget's theory of cognitive development for students of psychology and education. Piaget's central and major concepts are presented in a simple and readable fashion.

WATSON, J. B. *Behaviorism*. New York: Norton, 1924. This book will provide interesting reading for those who wish to explore the history of behaviorism, as written by one of its founding fathers. The book covers such topics as definitions of behaviorism and methods for studying the behavior and the emotional development of human beings.

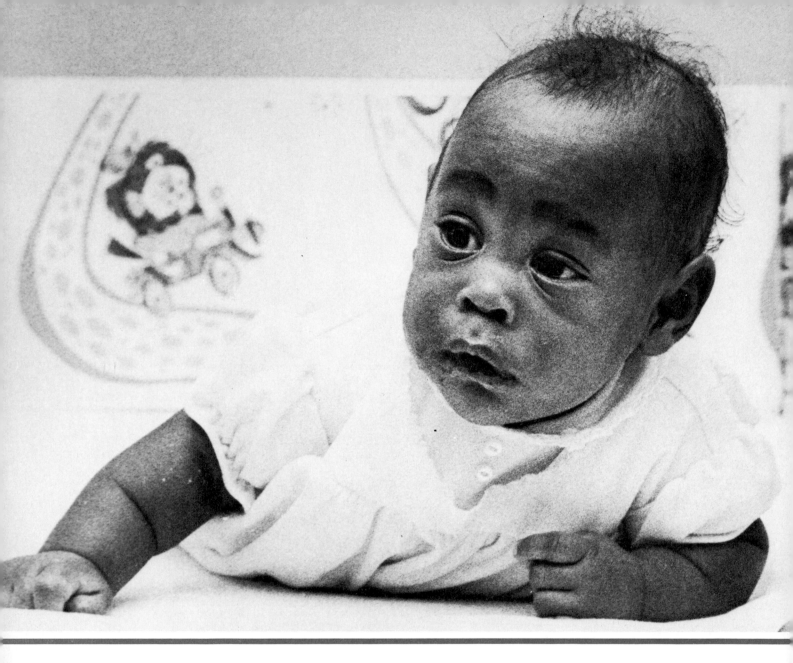

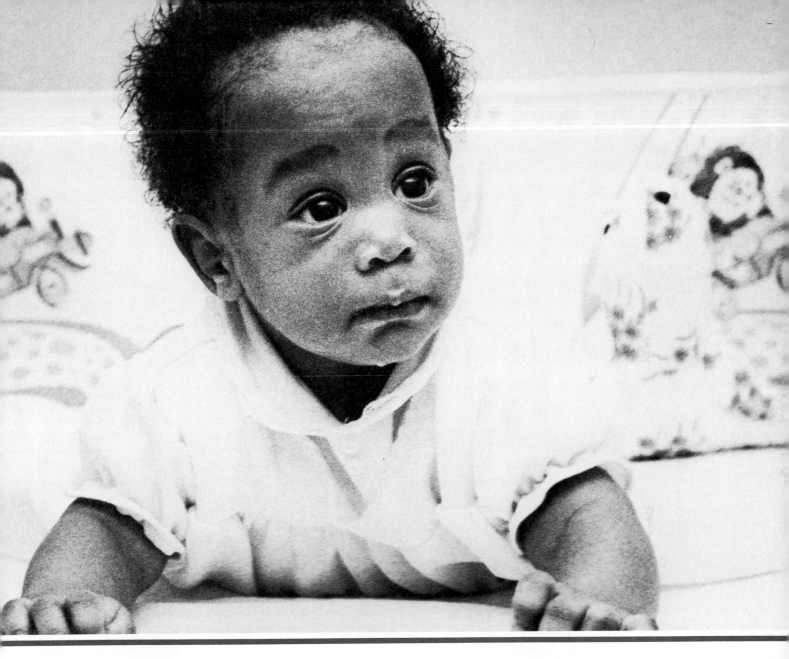

3 Determinants of Child Development

In every child who is born,
under no matter what circumstances,
and of no matter what parents,
the potentiality of the human race is born again.
                                    —James Agee

Types of Determinants

In this chapter we discuss the primary determinants of child development, the contexts and stages of child development, and the research methods used to study child development. The determinants or primary components of development can be divided into three major categories:

1. The *biological foundations* of development—the hereditary or genetic basis for growth and change.
2. The *social environments* or *contexts* of development, which include family, peer group, community/neighborhood, and school.
3. The *interaction* between biological foundations and social contexts in the form of an active, growing, and changing human being who is influenced by—as well as exerts influence on—the social environment and biological processes. Examples include the child who both is influenced by parental discipline and influences parent choice of disciplinary technique because of temperament or personality and the child whose genetic predisposition for certain risk factors (such as heart disease) is addressed by active controls of diet and exercise.

These factors are the essential elements of an *ecological* or *systems* perspective to child and human development.

Some basic principles of the ecological perspective are:

1. Development is characterized by *quantitative* changes in height, weight, and individual biology and by *qualitative* changes in such processes as memory, thinking, motivation, and perception.
2. The explanations or theories that describe these quantitative and qualitative changes involve *both* **heredity** (genetic factors) and the **environment.** In other words, human development is the result of the *interaction* of both heredity and environment.
3. The interaction between heredity and environment is *reciprocal* or *bidirectional.*

| HEREDITY | ⇄ | ENVIRONMENT |

Biological Factors

These are the genetic or inherited aspects of development, including physical features and physiological organs:

- *Cardiovascular system* (lungs and heart).
- *Central nervous system* (brain and spinal cord).
- *Musculoskeletal system* (bones and attached muscles).
- *Endocrine system* (ductless glands such as the pituitary, the thyroid, and the adrenals, which secrete hormones directly into the blood or lymph system).
- *Skin.*

The environment or contexts of life act on the individual child's characteristics (such as temperament or disposition and maturational processes) and individuals act on their environment—parents, siblings, peers, and teachers. In other words, the individual plays an active role in contributing to his or her development (Lerner and Busch-Rossnagel, 1981; Belsky, Lerner, and Spanier, 1984; Lerner, 1984, 1986).

Biological Foundations of Development

HEREDITY.   Every human being inherits a general biological code from his or her parents by means of biochemical agents called *genes* and *chromosomes.* (Our focus here is on the general process of heredity. In Chapter 4 we deal with the operation of genes, chromosomes, and the specific mechanisms of heredity in more detail.)
    There are two primary hereditary codes:

1. *General heredity.* The **general hereditary code** includes the attributes that make individuals of any species, including human beings, similar to other members of that species. For example, all normal children have a brain, one heart, two kidneys, and two eyes. A bird's egg cannot develop into an elephant—except, of course, in the imaginary world of children's literature.
2. *Specific heredity.* The **specific hereditary code** is composed of the attributes (including physical and psychological characteristics) that distinguish one member of a species from another member of the same species. Human beings, for example, differ from each other in terms of height, weight, eye color, sex, and temperament.

Psychosocial Factors

These factors are the *physical environment* (e.g., home, school, neighborhood) and the *social environment* (e.g., parents, teachers, peers) as well as the individual's personal or psychological "interpretations" of these environments, including:

- *Cognitive development* (the development of thinking and language).
- *Personality development* (the development of the self-concept, including behavior patterns and values).
- *Social development* (the lifelong process by which individuals develop attitudes, beliefs, knowledge, the awareness of expectations, and appropriate role behaviors).

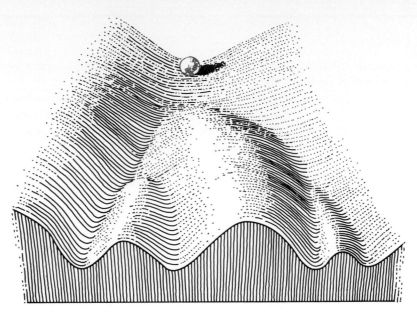

FIGURE 3.1
Waddington's model of genetic canalization. Adapted from Waddington, 1957.

INTERACTION OF HEREDITY AND ENVIRONMENT.   Heredity and environment are both completely intertwined in determining the organization and development of human beings. One way to understand this interaction of nature and nurture is by examining several models that have been proposed for interpreting that relationship. We will examine three: *canalization, norm of reaction,* and *niche picking.* These models have marked similarities and each illustrates the complexity of the nature-nurture interaction.

1. **Canalization.** Conrad Waddington (1966) proposed that the development of genetic traits could be conceptualized using an analogy of a ball rolling down a valley or a canal (Fig. 3.1). The ball represents an individual trait such as height or intelligence. The contour of the landscape represents the extent to which given traits are under the control of genetic factors. If the valley floor of a canal is wide with shallow slopes, the rolling ball (or trait) is subject to greater environmental influence (and, therefore, is under less strict genetic control). For example, individual traits of personality such as aggressiveness or sociability are subject to considerable environmental influence (Moss and Susman, 1980; Skolnick, 1986). On the other hand, if the canal is narrow with steep slopes, the rolling ball or trait is subject to much less environmental influence (and is therefore under more strict genetic control). For example, an individual's height is subject primarily to genetic factors (although extreme environmental deviations such as chronic malnutrition or disease may alter ultimate height).

   During periods of rapid growth (sometimes called *sensitive* or *critical periods*), even some traits that are under more direct genetic control may be subject to environmental influence (Fishbein, 1984). For example, during a critical period, the rolling ball may arrive at a point where several shallow canals meet. In human beings and in some mammals, vision develops rapidly just before and in the months following birth. Research has shown that kittens deprived of light until three months after birth will never be capable of vision (Hubel and

Wiesel, 1963). Deprivation of light after this sensitive period has no impact on their vision. Likewise, in human beings, a pregnant woman who has rubella (German measles) early in pregnancy (the critical or sensitive period) may give birth to a child with such serious birth handicaps as blindness, deafness, or heart abnormalities.

A remarkable feature of child development is the tendency of children apparently to "catch up" or recover from environmental stress to fulfill their genetic program. For example, a five-year-old child whose growth was slowed for about six months due to malnutrition will rebound or "catch up" during the next year or so provided that the environment is supportive (in this case, if the child receives adequate nutrition).

The principle of canalization also illustrates the concept of gene expression. Simply because an individual possesses a given genetic endowment (*genotype*) for a particular trait does not mean that the trait will automatically be translated into a physical characteristic (*phenotype*). In other words, whether or not genetic factors are "expressed" depends in part on the modifying influence of the environment. For example, the expression of height in human beings (which has a strong genetic basis) depends on a variety of growth hormones, good nutrition, and a healthy childhood.

2. *The* **Norm of Reaction.** We cannot simply determine an individual's phenotype by knowledge of his or her genotype. Rather, the phenotype represents the product or result of the complex interaction of the environment and one's genetic endowment. Our genetic inheritance is therefore really a range of potential outcomes rather than a blueprint for what will occur (see Figs. 3.2

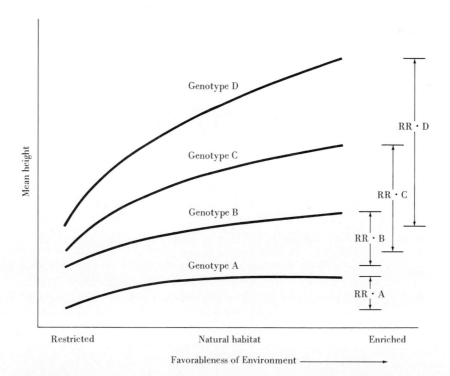

FIGURE 3.2

Several genotypes for adolescent height—A, B, C, and D—can vary in expression in relation to the environment. For example, a person with genotype D would have a wider range or norm of reaction for the expression of height than a person with genotype A. From Gottesman, 1974, p. 60.

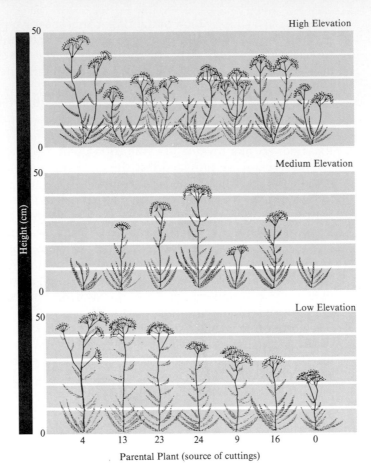

FIGURE 3.3
*The norm of reaction in plants. Growth of cuttings
from genetically different Achillea plants when
grown at three different elevation levels. From
Lewontin, 1982, p. 23.*

and 3.3). This leads us to a definition of the concept of the *norm of reaction:*
"The same genotype can give rise to a wide array of phenotypes depending
upon the environment in which it develops" (Hirsch, 1970, p. 73).

In actuality, the norm of reaction is almost completely unknown in most
cases (Hirsch, 1970; McGuire and Hirsch, 1982). The reason for this is that, in
order to be able to specify or predict the norm of reaction for any given
genotype, one would have to be able to reproduce that genotype exactly
numerous times and then expose those identical genotypes to a diverse array
of environments. The phenotypes that develop from such interactions would
then provide an estimate of the norm of reaction for a given genotype. In
reality, both the development of numerous identical genotypes as well as the
exposure of these genotypes to a totally inclusive set of all possible environments would be extraordinarily difficult, if not impossible. As Hirsch indicated:

Even in the most favorable materials only an approximate estimate can be obtained
for the norm of reaction when, as in plants and some animals, an individual genotype
can be replicated many times and its development studied over a range of environmental conditions. The more varied the conditions, the more diverse might be the
phenotypes developed from any one genotype. (1970, pp. 69-70)

Therefore the limits set for our genetic endowment can never be accurately specified or predicted in advance. We cannot know any individual's range of genetic potential.

To further complicate the situation, even if we could know that several individuals have the same genotype, the norm of reaction would be expected to be unique for each individual. This means that the range of phenotypes that would develop from a given genotype in varying environments would be different for each individual. Such individual phenotypic uniqueness would make it almost impossible to accurately predict in advance the likely outcome of any genetic potential.

The concept of the norm of reaction emphasizes the importance of viewing the development of human behavior as an *interaction* between hereditary and environmental factors. As Hirsch has suggested, "extreme environmentalists were wrong to hope that one law or set of laws described universal features of modifiability. Extreme hereditarians were wrong to ignore the norm of reaction" (1970, p. 73).

3. **Niche Picking.** A third model that helps us understand the interaction of heredity and environment in human development is called *niche picking* (Scarr and McCartney, 1983) and deals with the question "How do genetic and environmental factors combine to produce individual differences in development?" According to this model, the answer is that individuals *actively* seek out environments, situations, or "niches" that are stimulating and compatible with their personal characteristics. These niche selections are presumably related to the intellectual, personality, and motivational aspects of our genetic inheritance or genotypes. From a niche-picking perspective, sociable or affiliative children become so not only by being exposed (by adults) to social/group experiences but also because these children *actively seek out* the company of other children in social group activities. Children who are by temperament or genotype outgoing and active become involved in a wider range of activities than children who are bashful and retiring. In turn, these variables in social experiences serve to further enhance the expression of the genotypic factors associated with sociability for some children and shyness for others.

Sylvia Byers

Individuals actively seek out environments, situations, or "niches" that are stimulating and compatible with their personal characteristics.

Nature-Nurture Interaction and Behavior: Intelligence and Personality

As we have seen, explanation of the interaction of heredity and environment is not a simple matter. Here we examine two complex human processes—intelligence and personality—as they are discussed in research that has dealt with the contributions of both nature and nurture.

Hereditary factors operate from the moment of conception in determining some features of human growth and development. For example, heredity determines eye color, hair color and texture, and susceptibility to some diseases (e.g., diabetes and some types of cancer).

In discussing the interaction of heredity and environment, it is much easier to examine genetic effects in some plants or lower animals than in human beings. The reason is that it is possible to create, in some cases, through plant or animal breeding, "pure strains" (or genotypes) for a specific trait. As a result of this control of genetic factors, many experiments have demonstrated the important role of heredity in animals (Lewontin, 1982; Lewontin, Rose, and Kamin, 1984). Such precise control of genetic factors is much less common in studies of human beings except in the relatively few instances where specific genes have been shown to be directly related to abnormal physical traits or diseases. For example, Huntington's chorea, a degenerative disease of the nervous system, is the direct result of a single gene. There is also evidence that certain genes—*oncogenes*—may be directly associated with specific types of human cancer (Blair et al., 1982; Marx, 1982).

Given this basic limitation in the study of human genetics (serious *ethical* problems would arise if there were to be genetic manipulation of human breeding), we still can say some things about human heredity. Our current understanding of human genetics makes it fairly clear that many human physical traits are inherited. The physical resemblance of members of the same family provides some support for this view. We know that genetic factors are involved in the development of the human body from the time of conception. However, we do not yet fully understand the scientific mechanisms of the interaction of genetic and environmental factors in controlling human growth and development. The relationship of this nature-nurture interaction to *human behavior* is even less clear. This is particularly true for our understanding of human *intelligence* and human *personality.*

DEFINITION

Correlation coefficient. A number that indicates how similar two sets of measurements are to each other. In research in human development, correlation coefficients range from -1.00 to $+1.00$.

−1.00	0.00	+1.00

$+1.00$ shows a perfectly similar relationship between pairs of measurements (i.e., both measurements are in the same direction); 0.00 shows no relationship between measurements; -1.00 shows a perfectly opposite relationship between measurements (i.e., when one measurement is very high, the other is very low).

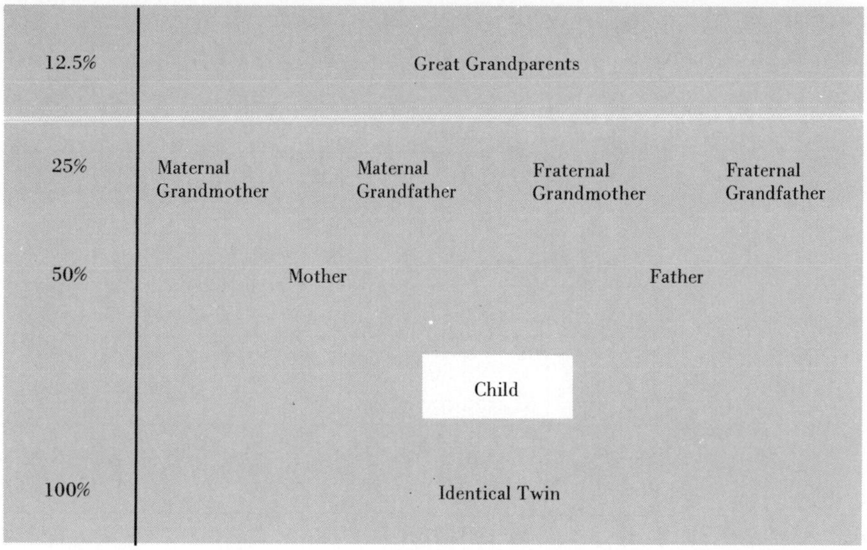

12.5%		Great Grandparents		
25%	Maternal Grandmother	Maternal Grandfather	Fraternal Grandmother	Fraternal Grandfather
50%		Mother	Father	
		Child		
100%		Identical Twin		

FIGURE 3.4

Shared heredity among family members. The percentages in the left-hand column indicate the amount of heredity shared between the child and the individuals on the right.

INTELLIGENCE.   The study and measurement of intelligence in children is a subject of considerable controversy and debate. Not only is there disagreement about the nature and degree of the contributions of heredity and environment, but there is also some debate about the meaning and measurement of intelligence. Exactly what is intelligence? What does it mean to behave in an intelligent fashion? Do so-called intelligence tests, as used in school and vocational settings, actually measure intelligence? (At this point, we will simply acknowledge these important controversies and return to a more detailed discussion of them when we discuss intelligence in later chapters. For purposes of our discussion here, we *assume* that the abilities that constitute intelligence reflect some traditional characteristics such as verbal fluency, comprehension, reasoning, memory, spatial perception, and numerical skills.) It is a fairly common observation that the more closely related people are, the more they resemble one another in physical traits such as height and facial features (see Fig. 3.4 and Table 3.1). There is evidence that as relatedness between two people increases, the similarity of their intelligence (in this case, IQ scores) increases. In Table 3.1 we can see that correlation coefficients for intelligence scores between individuals who are more closely related are larger than for those who are less closely related. For example, the correlation of intelligence scores for identical twins, reared together ($r = +.87$), is much higher than for unrelated individuals reared apart ($r = -.01$). Such evidence shows that there is a relationship between intelligence and genetic factors.

Does this mean that genetic contributions are the most important factor in a person's intelligence? Not necessarily. The data in Table 3.1 can also be interpreted in another way. For example, as "relatedness" between individuals increases, environmental similarities also increase. Thus identical twins, reared together, have more similar environments and shared experiences than two unrelated individuals reared apart. Therefore it could be argued that Table 3.1, in fact, shows that intelligence scores of more related people are similar because their environments are more similar.

TABLE 3.1

Observed Correlations in IQ Between People of Different Degrees of Relationship

CATEGORY		0.00 0.10 0.20 0.30 0.40 0.50 0.60 0.70 0.80 0.90	GROUPS INCLUDED
Unrelated persons	Reared apart	●●● ●	4
	Reared together	●● ●● ●	5
Foster-parent child		●● ●	3
Parent child		● ● ●● ● ●●●● ● ●	13
Siblings	Reared apart	● ●	2
	Reared together	●● ●●●●●● ●●●●●●●●● ●● ●	35
Twins: two-egg	Opposite sex	● ●●● ●●●●●	9
	Same sex	●●●●● ●●●● ●	10
Twins: one-egg	Reared apart	● ●●●	3
	Reared together	●●●●●●●●● ●●●●	13

Each point is a separate study and each vertical line shows the median (average) value for each degree of relationship.

From Lewontin, 1982, p. 99.

    The debate about heredity and environment continues. Following are several ways of studying the question.

Research on Twins. Studies of the intelligence of twins usually involve comparisons of *identical twins* (identical genetic endowment) and *fraternal twins* (different genetic endowment). Identical twins are called **monozygotic twins** (a single sperm fertilizes a single ovum [egg] and early in its embryonic development an extra split occurs). Fraternal twins are called **dizygotic twins** (two separate sperm fertilize two separate eggs). (Twins are either identical or fraternal only because of these developmental processes—no matter how much alike or unalike they may appear later in life.) Although both monozygotic and dizygotic twins are *assumed* to share

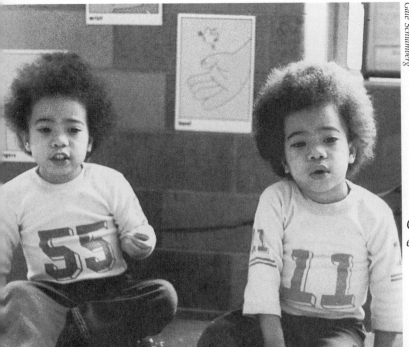

Gale Schiamberg

One way of studying the interaction of heredity and environment is with identical twins.

similar childhood experiences and, therefore, to share similar environments, dizygotic twins do not have similar genetic makeup. Furthermore, dizygotic twins do not have to be the same sex nor need they physically resemble one another. In fact, they are no more genetically alike than ordinary siblings. (They are siblings with the same birth date.)

Given this natural laboratory of twins for studying the interaction of heredity and environment, we might derive the following hypotheses:

1. If *genetic factors* play a more significant role in the determination of intelligence than environment, we would expect the IQ scores of monozygotic twins reared together to be more similar (more highly correlated) than the IQ scores of either dizygotic twins reared together or nontwin siblings reared in the same home.
2. On the other hand, if *environment* plays a more significant role than heredity in the determination of intelligence, we might expect that the IQ scores of identical twins reared together (same genes and similar environment) would be more similar (more highly correlated) than those of identical twins reared apart (same genes and different environments).

Both hypotheses have, in fact, been confirmed in research. In a review of fifty studies extending over a period of approximately fifty years, Erlenmeyer-Kimling and Jarvik (1963) found that individuals who were more genetically related were also more similar in intelligence to one another. In fact, the similarity in intelligence increased in direct proportion to the degree of relatedness. Furthermore, the genetic contribution to intelligence is demonstrated by the fact that the degree of similarity or correlation between IQ scores increases (for individuals reared together and reared apart), as one goes from unrelated individuals to siblings, to dizygotic twins, to monozygotic twins (Figure 3.5).

Additional evidence for the important role of heredity suggests that even *variations over time* in measured intelligence may have a genetic component (Wilson,

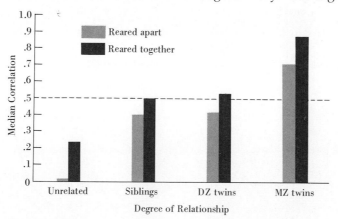

FIGURE 3.5

The contributions of heredity and environment to intelligence. Shown are the mean values for the correlation of IQ scores for monozygotic (identical) twins, dizygotal (fraternal) twins, ordinary siblings, and unrelated individuals reared apart or reared together. Based on Erlenmeyer-Kimling and Jarvik, 1963.

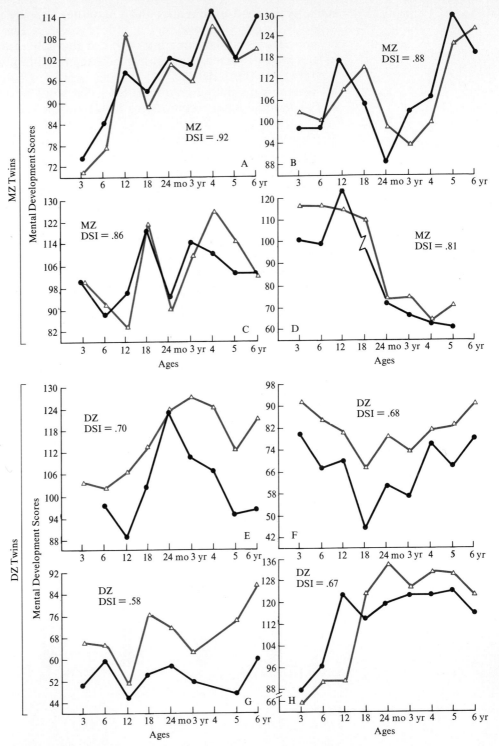

FIGURE 3.6

Intelligence score profiles indicating the similarity in development status of four pairs of identical (monozygotic) twins and four fraternal (dizygotic) twins. The similarity is greater for MZ twins than for DZ twins. From Wilson, 1978.

1978, 1983). Repeated measurements of intelligence for 261 identical and fraternal twins indicated a more similar developmental profile (e.g., spurts and lags in measured intelligence over time) for identical twins than for fraternal twins (see Figs. 3.6 and 3.7). Further, when one hundred pairs of these twins were tested again at ages four, five, and six, the intelligence-test scores of the identical twins were more similar than those of the fraternal twins (Wilson, 1978, 1983). Such similar developmental sequences in twins were taken as evidence of timed-gene action producing similar spurts and lags (Wilson, 1983).

Additional follow-up studies of the same twins from the preschool years through adolescence found a comparable pattern of similar scores for the twins reared apart: "[T]he message from these results seems clear: there is a strong developmental thrust in the growth of intelligence that continues through adolescence that . . . is guided by [a] ground plan rooted in genetic processes" (Wilson, 1983, p. 311).

However, support for the strength of environmental contributions to intelligence can also be seen in Fig. 3.5. That is, IQ scores of identical twins reared together (same genes and similar environment) are more highly correlated than IQ scores for identical twins reared apart (same genes and different environments). (The correlation between IQ scores in the figure is always greater within each category for those reared together than for those reared apart.)

Ironically, another reason for an environmental perspective comes from the studies that have compared IQ scores of identical twins reared together with IQ scores of fraternal twins reared together. These studies consistently report a higher IQ correlation for identical twins than for fraternal twins (Bouchard and McGue, 1981; Wilson, 1983). This result has typically been taken as supporting a hereditary perspective because it has been assumed that both identical twins reared together and fraternal twins reared together have similar environments. (Therefore, any differences may be attributed to hereditary factors). This hereditary viewpoint is misleading in light of the large body of evidence that identical twins reared to-

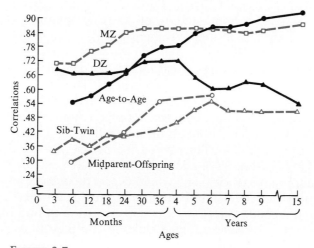

FIGURE 3.7

Mental development correlations for monozygotic twins (MZ), dizygotic twins (DZ), each child with itself, over time (age-to-age), a sibling with a twin · (sib-twin) and a parent with an offspring (midparent-offspring). From Wilson, 1983, pp. 298–316.

Fraternal twins are no more genetically alike than ordinary siblings.

gether, in fact, have much more similar environments than fraternal twins reared together (Lewontin, Rose, and Kamin, 1984). This may happen because identical twins are often treated as "one" by teachers and peers who cannot tell them apart or determine which one did what behavior. Furthermore, identical twins spend more time together and are more likely to sleep in the same room and dress alike than fraternal twins (especially when the fraternal twins are opposite-sex). Therefore, the higher IQ correlations for identical twins reared together must be attributed, at least in part, to greater similarity of environment. There is still no way of knowing the exact contribution of environment or heredity to this difference between identical and fraternal twins (Lewontin, Rose, and Kamin, 1984).

Studies of Adopted Children. Further evidence regarding the nature-nurture controversy comes from studies of adopted children (Horn, 1983; Plomin and De Fries, 1983; Scarr and Weinberg, 1983):

- *Comparisons of IQ scores of adopted children with the IQ scores of their adoptive parents and the IQ scores of their biological parents.* The findings of these studies indicate a higher correlation between adopted children's and their biological parents' intellectual level than between adopted children's and their adoptive parents' intellectual level. Although these results may appear to support a genetic interpretation of intelligence, such a perspective would be misleading for one primary reason. Since adoptive parents have usually been rigorously screened by adoption agencies, one would expect them to be a very special and intelligent group who would almost uniformly provide an excellent environment for the adopted child. Therefore, it is not surprising to find higher correlations or similarities between adopted children and their biological parents than between adopted children and their adoptive parents. One would surely expect to find a greater similarity between the IQs of a randomly selected group of adopted children (who would represent a range of IQs) and their biological parents (who would also represent a range of IQs) than between those same adopted children and a uniformly special (and probably highly intelligent) group of adoptive parents (Horn, 1983).
- *Comparisons of the adoptive parent with the adopted child and with a biological child of the adoptive parent.* Many adoptive families contain not only an adopted child

but also a biological child of the same parents. Such families would appear to be useful for examining the relationship between heredity and environment. That is, in each of these families the biological child has received *both* genes and environment from the parents, whereas the adopted child received *only* the environment from these same parents. To the extent that IQ is a primary result of heredity, one would expect the similarity or correlation between parent IQ and biological child IQ to be greater than that between these same parents and the adopted child. Some studies have demonstrated significant differences between the IQs of the mothers and their biological children compared with the IQs of the same mothers and their adopted children (the IQ scores of the mothers and their biological children were much more similar than those of the same mothers and their adopted children) (Horn, 1983; Scarr and Weinberg, 1983). As stated above, such results must be viewed cautiously in light of the highly selective character of adoptive families. Other adoption studies have failed to show any significant differences between the IQ of the mother and the IQ of the biological child compared with the IQ of the same mother and the IQ of the adopted child (Horn, Loehlin, and Willerman, 1979; Scarr and Weinberg, 1980).

· *Comparisons between adopted children and biological children in adoptive families.* From Fig. 3.5 we can see that for each type of kinship relationship (e.g., unrelated persons, siblings, DZ twins, MZ twins), there is greater intellectual similarity for persons reared together than for persons reared apart (suggesting an important environmental contribution to intelligence). This relationship is

Both hereditary and environmental contributions are intimately involved in the development of human beings.

Erika Stone

strikingly illustrated in the case of individuals who are biologically unrelated to one another. For example, children who share no genes in common (are biologically unrelated) and who live in different environments (are reared apart) display virtually no intellectual similarity. On the other hand, biologically unrelated children who are reared together (an adopted child and a biological child) show a definite intellectual similarity. (The actual correlation is $r = .23$.) This similarity can only be the result of their shared environment.

Such environmental contributions have, in fact, been demonstrated in some adoption studies. Sandra Scarr and Richard Weinberg (1983) found that black children adopted into white families demonstrated a definite intellectual resemblance to their white siblings ($r = .30$). Since these interracial siblings had no hereditary factors in common, their intellectual similarity must be attributed to the similarity of their environments. Scarr and Weinberg also found that their sample of black adoptees averaged 20 IQ points higher than comparable children raised in the black community. Since the adoptive parents in the study were highly educated, they probably provided a very stimulating home experience for their adoptees. Perhaps the best summary of the relationship of adoption studies to the question of heredity and environment is that they do *not* support the notion of a simple hereditary or environmental contribution to intelligence. In addition, Horn (1983) suggested that the impact of environment may be greater for children adopted at younger ages than for children adopted as older children or adolescents (see box).

Intervention Studies. Although the purpose of intervention studies has been to improve the lives of human beings, they have shed some light on the question of heredity and environment. As might be expected in such helping programs, intervention research studies usually support an environmental position (Scarr, 1982). Many of these studies involve preschool children and suggest that IQ scores can be dramatically increased when young children experience enriched environments (Lazar and Darlington, 1982; MacPhee, Ramey, and Yeates, 1984; Ramey et al., 1985; Bronfenbrenner, 1986). Successful intervention programs frequently in-

---

The Texas Adoption Project: Intellectual Similarity of Adopted Children to Their Biological and Adoptive Parents

Adoption studies are important because they provide one of the few methods available for separating the effects of heredity and environment in studies of development. . . . [In the Texas study] . . . intelligence scores were obtained from parents and children in 300 adoptive families and compared with similar measures available for the biological mothers of the same adopted children. Results supported the hypothesis that genetic variability is an important influence in the development of individual differences for intelligence. The most [obvious] finding was [that] the adopted children resemble their biological mothers more than they resemble the adoptive parents who reared them from birth. . . .

A word is in order concerning the meaning of these results for intervention programs. Far from negating the utility of intervention, per se, adoption studies actually demonstrate that *radical* (adoption at a very early age) interventions succeed in permanently raising the average IQ of adopted children over what it would have been if the children were raised by their natural parents. Such results are found in Scarr and Weinberg (1980) and Skodak and Skeels (1949), as well as the Texas Adoption Project. What remains problematical is the success of programs with interventions milder than being adopted at an early age (Horn, 1981). It should also be noted that, at the same time the IQs are being raised through environmental enrichment (adoptive placement), the genes are at work in the individual differences. Even after receiving the benefits of the adoptive environment, the brighter children are those from the brighter biological parents.

From Horn, 1983, p. 268–75.

volve home visits with young children and their mothers. That is, where the value of the family as a support system was recognized, significant improvements and long-term effects were more likely (Garbarino, 1982a; Bronfenbrenner, 1986). (We return to the discussion of intervention programs in Chapter 9 when we examine the impact of preschool programs on child development.)

PERSONALITY.   Personality refers to the relatively consistent and unique characteristics of an individual including temperament, values, attitudes, and distinctive behavioral patterns (aggressive, quiet, boisterous, shy, outgoing, and so on). Unlike some physical traits in which characteristics are specific and easily identified, personality characteristics are both more general and more difficult to measure. For example, hair color, eye color, or other physical characteristics are readily apparent to an observer. On the other hand, friendliness, aggressiveness, shyness, or other personality characteristics may appear in individuals in varying degrees and in varied situations. In this section we review several studies that have examined the relationship of hereditary and environmental factors in the development of personality.

> *DEFINITIONS*
>
> **Personality.** Personality refers to the relatively consistent and unique characteristics of an individual, including temperament, values, attitudes, and distinctive behavioral patterns (such as aggressive, shy, outgoing, and so on).
> **Temperament.** Temperament refers to the *natural disposition* of an infant, including such characteristics as activity level, irritability, calmness, social responsiveness, and emotionality. This natural disposition is presumably the basis of childhood personality.

Where do differences in personality or temperament come from? Friends or relatives are frequently quick to comment that an infant has a temper "like his father" or is easygoing "like his mother," suggesting that such differences are inherited. In fact, there is accumulating evidence to support the heritability or genetic basis of temperamental differences (Goldsmith and Gottesman, 1981; Kagan, 1984; Kagan et al., 1984). For example, there is evidence of greater similarity between identical twins than between fraternal twins in such temperament characteristics as sociability, emotionality, and activity level (Goldsmith and Gottesman, 1981). Such evidence suggests the impact of genetic factors on temperament and personality development.

Does this mean that infant temperament is genetically determined? Not necessarily, since the environment plays an important role in the expression of temperament. According to Kagan (1984), temperament is best viewed as a natural bias toward a given behavioral direction (difficult, easygoing, introverted, extroverted, and so on). The expression of this bias depends on one's environment or experience: the child with a temperamental "bias" for a high activity level may in fact be easygoing and mild mannered in a relaxed family environment. The bias for high activity levels may appear only in stressful or competitive situations.

Additional insight into the joint role of heredity and environment comes from the New York Longitudinal Study (NYLS) (Thomas and Chess, 1977; Thomas, Chess, and Korn, 1982; Thomas et al., 1983)—one of the most extensive examinations of the development of temperament from infancy through early childhood to date. This research has led to several major findings about the development of personality:

1. *Extremely early in life children appear to possess characteristic patterns of temperament that are maintained throughout the childhood years.* According to the NYLS investigators, most infants appear to fit into one of three temperamental categories (Thomas and Chess, 1977; Thomas et al., 1983):

- *The easy child.* Easygoing children are usually positive, even-tempered, and generally adaptable to new experiences. Their behavior patterns are relatively predictable.
- *The difficult child.* Difficult children have relatively irregular behavior patterns and are active and irritable. They are slow to adapt to new experiences or people and frequently react negatively to changes in routine.
- *The slow-to-warm-up child.* These children are moody and inactive. They are typically slow to adapt to new situations or to changes in routine. Unlike "difficult" children, however, they react to new people or novel situations with mild resistance (e.g., looking away in response to cuddling rather than kicking or crying as the difficult child might do).

2. *The source of individuality of childhood personality has its origins in the interaction of both hereditary and environmental factors.* Because infants and children show individually unique temperaments and reaction styles, it follows that children may react differently to what are objectively the same environmental circumstances; the same environmental factors—whether intentionally designed or not—will not have the same impact on different children. The child's personality is the result of this complex interaction of heredity and environment.

3. *The child should be viewed as playing an active and participatory role in his or her development.* The results of the New York Longitudinal Study support this conclusion. That is, the characteristics of individuality (which develop from the individually unique interaction of heredity and environment) result in a differential selection of environmental settings by the individual and differential responses to the individual by significant others (parents, teachers, friends, and so on) in that environment (Scarr and McCartney, 1983). These differential selections of environments and differential responses to the individual provide an arena for the *direct participation* of the individual in the self-organization of personality development (Lerner and Busch-Rossnagel, 1981).

The evidence reviewed in this section demonstrates that child personality and temperament depend on the joint contributions of heredity, environment, and the individual. We turn to a more detailed discussion of the determinants of infant personality development in Chapter 8.

Environments or Contexts of Development

The environments or "contexts" of life play a major role in the development of human beings throughout the lifespan. Even the most ardent genetically oriented theorists acknowledge that the environment contributes to human development. However, it is not enough simply to state that environment is important. Rather, it is necessary to be more specific about what is *meant* by environment and how it interacts with and influences human beings. In this section we define some of the environments that are important to human development. In order to facilitate our discussion, we divide environments into two broad categories. "Immediate" environments are those that the human being interacts with *directly* (e.g., the infant interacts with the family, and the adult interacts with the work setting) and "larger" environments are those that the human being interacts with *indirectly*, usually through the medium of an immediate environment. For example, the child may interact with the values of his or her culture through the medium of the family or the school, or the adult may interact with cultural expectations of job performance in the work setting. In other words, the *culture* of a society is a significant context that the individual experiences indirectly through the medium of other direct contexts (Bronfenbrenner, 1986).

THE FAMILY.   The majority of children grow up in a family context that usually includes a father and/or a mother and, in many instances, brothers and sisters. The family has been shown to have an impact on important processes, including the development of self-concept, sex roles, language, intellectual abilities, and interpersonal skills (Parke, 1984; Bronfenbrenner, 1986).

The Developmental Stages of Family Life. Although developmental theories have emerged to describe the growth and maturation of the individual, a parallel trend has been to describe the changing pattern of the family life cycle as a series of developmental stages (Duvall and Miller, 1985) (see Fig. 3.8 and Table 3.2). Family

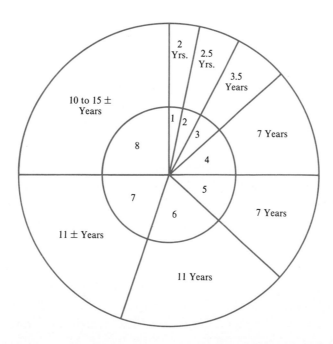

1. Married Couples (without children)

2. Childbearing Families (oldest child birth to 30 months)

3. Families with Preschool Children (oldest child 30 months to 6 years)

4. Families with Schoolchildren (oldest child 6 to 13 years)

5. Families with Teenagers (oldest child 13 to 20 years)

6. Families Launching Young Adults (first child gone to last child leaving home)

7. Middle-aged Parents (empty nest to retirement)

8. Aging Family Members (retire- ment to death of both spouses)

*General marital satisfaction, positive companionship; satisfaction with present stage in the life cycle; and absence of negative feeling.

FIGURE 3.8

The family life cycle by length of time in each of eight stages. From Duvall and Miller, 1985, p. 28.

TABLE 3.2

Stage-Sensitive Family Developmental Tasks Through the Family Life Cycle

STAGE OF THE FAMILY LIFE CYCLE	POSITIONS IN THE FAMILY	STAGE-SENSITIVE FAMILY DEVELOPMENTAL TASKS
1. Married couple	Wife Husband	Establishing a mutually satisfying marriage Adjusting to pregnancy and the promise of parenthood Fitting into the kin network
2. Childbearing	Wife-mother Husband-father Infant daughter or son or both	Having, adjusting to, and encouraging the development of infants Establishing a satisfying home for both parents and infant(s)
3. Preschool-age	Wife-mother Husband-father Daughter-sister Son-brother	Adapting to the critical needs and interests of preschool children in stimulating, growth-promoting ways Coping with energy depletion and lack of privacy as parents
4. School-age	Wife-mother Husband-father Daughter-sister Son-brother	Fitting into the community of school-age families in constructive ways Encouraging children's educational achievement
5. Teenage	Wife-mother Husband-father Daughter-sister Son-brother	Balancing freedom with responsibility as teenagers mature and emancipate themselves Establishing postparental interests and careers as growing parents
6. Launching center	Wife-mother-grandmother Husband-father-grandfather Daughter-sister-aunt Son-brother-uncle	Releasing young adults into work, military service, college, marriage, and so on, with appropriate rituals and assistance Maintaining a supportive home base
7. Middle-aged parents	Wife-mother-grandmother Husband-father-grandfather	Refocusing on the marriage relationship Maintaining kin ties with older and younger generations
8. Aging family members	Widow or widower Wife-mother-grandmother Husband-father-grandfather	Coping with bereavement and living alone Closing the family home or adapting it to aging Adjusting to retirement

From Duvall and Miller, 1985, p. 62.

developmentalists view the family, like the individual, as having certain primary functions at certain points in the life cycle (see the discussion of Erik Erikson's theory in Chapter 2). Families, like individuals, have developmental tasks or stages.

> *DEFINITION*
>
> **Family Developmental Tasks.** Family developmental tasks are "growth responsibilities that must be accomplished by a family at a given stage of its development in a way that satisfies (1) its members' biological requirements, (2) society's cultural imperatives, and (3) its members' aspirations and values—if the family is to continue functioning as a unit" (Duvall and Miller, 1985, pp. 60-61).

The Developing Child and the Marital Relationship. Given this family development task framework, we can now deal in more detail with the relationship of the developing child and the marital relationship. Specifically, how does parenthood or raising children influence the marriage relationship across the entire family life course? Summing up the many investigations on the transition to parenthood (the period of family life from the first pregnancy through the first two years of the child's life), four primary problems have been identified by Donna Sollie and Brent Miller (1980):

- *Physical demands of caring for children.* First-time parents commonly report some stress due to fatigue and loss of sleep resulting from care of a newborn. This stress appears to be particularly common for the mothers who experience the "role strain" of being the primary caregiver in addition to their preparenthood roles of homemaker, spouse, employee, and so on.
- *Strains in the marital relationship.* New parents frequently complain about the reduction in time spent together as a couple, and fatigue due to caring for the infant may reduce interest in sexual interaction.
- *Emotional strain.* Some parents experience stress with the responsibilities of complete care for the infant. Parents may also experience some doubts about their parenting competence.
- *Opportunity costs and restrictions.* Some parents complain about the limitation on social life brought on by responsibility for a newborn. They may no longer be able to do things on short notice, particularly if a babysitter must be located. When an infant is included on a long excursion or even on a short shopping trip, strollers, diapers, a change of clothes, blankets, and other equipment must be brought along.

Although most studies agree that some parents experience some stress during the transition to parenthood, there is no apparent agreement that such stress inevitably results in disruption of the marital relationship or a decline in marital satisfaction (Belsky, Lerner, and Spanier, 1984). Other factors that appear to influence marital satisfaction in addition to the possible stresses and strains listed above include:

- *Infant characteristics.* Infant temperament and personality depend for their expression on the joint contributions of heredity, environment (parenting strategies), and individual behavior (through the active selection of environments, particularly as the child grows older). There is also some evidence that the quality of the marital relationship may be influenced by infant temperament and infant health (Belsky, Lerner, and Spanier, 1984). The quality of the marital relationship is adversely affected, particularly if the infant has a "difficult" temperament or has a serious physical problem (e.g., Down syndrome infants).
- *Unfulfilled parental expectations.* Some couples tend to romanticize the way in which a new infant will change their lives and their marital relationship. There is evidence that mothers, in particular, who underestimated the impact of a newborn (e.g., reduced sleep, less time for husband-wife relationship, reduced sense of freedom, and so on) were likely to experience stress and a reduced quality of marital life (Kach and McGhee, 1982). In addition, some individuals may be disappointed with a traditional division of labor along sex-stereotyped lines for parenting responsibilities (i.e., the female becomes the primary caregiver). Such a division of labor may be particularly distressing when the couple had endorsed liberated or egalitarian sex-role beliefs before parenthood. Likewise, a traditional division of labor for parenting responsibilities may be upsetting to families in which the transition to parenthood simply adds to a

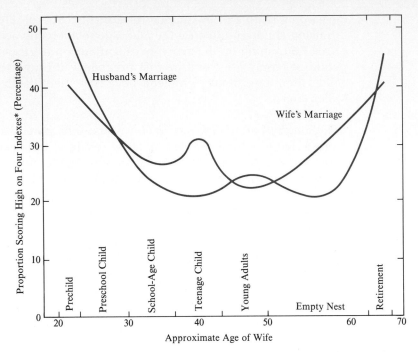

*General marital satisfaction, positive companionship; satisfaction with present stage in the life cycle; and absence
of negative feeling.

FIGURE 3.9

Marital-parental satisfaction over the family development cycle. Rollins and Feldman (1970) and other investigators have found that reported satisfaction is initially high but declines during the middle years of marriage and returns to its previously high level in the postparental years. Adapted from Rollins and Feldman, 1970.

mother's already burdensome household responsibilities (Dickie, 1981; Feldman, Biringer, and Nash, 1981). In such families, the sharing of caregiving responsibilities contributes substantially to improved marital satisfaction.

Having mentioned the influence of the first two years of parenthood on the marriage relationship, we can now deal with the effects of children across the family life course. Generally, the evidence indicates that a common (although not the only) pattern is that marital satisfaction reaches its highest level prior to parenthood, with a drop in satisfaction throughout the childbearing and child-rearing years (Rollins and Feldman, 1970; Glenn and McLanahan, 1982) (see Fig. 3.9). The low point in marital satisfaction occurs for husbands when the children are adolescents and for wives when the children are young adults. Marital satisfaction begins to increase when the children are gone (during the "empty nest" and retirement years).

Although the evidence points to the pattern shown in Figure 3.9, such results must be viewed cautiously (Skolnick, 1981). One reason is that the outcomes of such studies are frequently confounded by factors such as divorce that eliminate unhappy couples during the course of the family life cycle, leaving only the more happily married for study in the later years. This selective elimination of unhappy couples may help explain why marital evaluations during the empty nest phase begin to increase. Furthermore, some couples may wait until after children grow up and leave home to end a dissatisfying marriage. Such a delay of divorce may

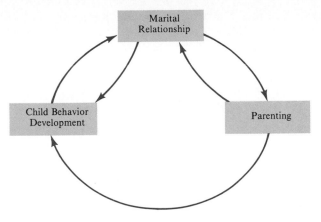

FIGURE 3.10
*The family as a system involving the mutual
interaction of the marital relationship, parenting,
and child behavior development. From Belsky, 1981.*

tend to increase the apparently negative effect on marriage of children as well as to increase the presumed positive effect on marriage of children departing.

The family, then, provides an important context for child and adolescent development. Specifically, as we have seen, the quality of marital relationships is influenced by parenting responsibilities which, in turn, influence the development of children and adolescence in the family. These relationships between the marital relationship, parenting, and child behavior development can be thought of as components or parts of a *family system* (Fig. 3.10).

THE NEIGHBORHOOD/COMMUNITY. Every child and adult lives in some type of neighborhood or community. Children grow up and develop surrounded by various arrangements of buildings, people, open space, and roadways. This **neighborhood/community** provides both a setting for human growth and development and a potential resource and support system for the development of human beings (Bronfenbrenner, Moen, and Garbarino, 1984).

From the preschool years through adulthood, the human being uses the neighborhood and community setting as a primary arena for the use of unstructured time. The neighborhood provides the setting for the child's development of competence in naturally occurring social and physical experiences. Can fences be

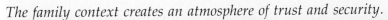

The family context creates an atmosphere of trust and security.

Gale Schiamberg

climbed? Are the children on the next block going to fight if someone enters their territory? Can children get the wood necessary for their treehouse? Are there safe places to play basketball, baseball, soccer? Is there a community center or some place where community people of all ages can meet to share ideas and skills? These concerns and comparable challenges are the kinds of experience that take place in neighborhoods and communities. Through exploration of the neighborhood, children gain an understanding of the social and physical characteristics of the community, as well as its characteristics as a setting for play. And when individuals reach adult status, they are often, to some degree, in a position to reorganize or further develop their community as a setting for both children and adults.

The neighborhood has a more sophisticated psychological meaning as one proceeds through the lifespan. As children grow and become more mobile, they have increasing experiences with the physical and social features of the neighborhood. Also, as the cognitive skills for representing or thinking about the community develop throughout childhood, children's appreciation of the community also changes.

The impact of the community on children and families remains an understudied dimension of child development (Bronfenbrenner, Moen, Garbarino, 1984). The influence of the community on the developing child is largely through the medium of the family. Community factors exert their influence through both **formal community structures** (health services, welfare and social services, religious institutions, and so on) and informal community structures. An example of **informal community structures** is **social networks**—the informal relations of family members, friends, relatives, and neighbors that contribute to the well-being of families and child development. Such interpersonal relationships can be a source of emotional support, actual services for family members, or information about access to formal community structures.

To what extent do such social support networks influence the development of children? There is some evidence that the presence of a social network in the form of dependable friends to whom a parent can turn in times of need is associated with child achievement and positive feelings toward peers (Homel, Burns, and Goodnow, 1984).

THE SCHOOL.   As the child moves from the preschool period to the early childhood years (five or six), the formal school emerges as a major institution in the transfer of cultural traditions and skills from society to the developing child and young person (Hess and Holloway, 1984). As cultures become more complex and more technological, they produce a more sophisticated, elaborate, and abundant collection of skills, knowledge, and information. These must be transmitted to the developing individual as necessary prerequisites for effective participation in the culture. Historically the role of the school in industrialized and technological societies has been to serve this function of cultural transfer and transmission.

The formal school provides the growing child an environment that has four major features: (1) the *curriculum*, or what is taught; (2) the *physical setting*, or the design of space—the arrangement of classrooms, hallways, and play areas; (3) the *methods of instruction*; and (4) the *characteristics of the classroom group*—the size of the group, the patterns of interactions, and the teacher's style of leadership.

The School and the Family. Both the school and the family are systems in their own right that interact in the process of educating the child and the adolescent (Hess and Holloway, 1984; Cochran, 1987). The school and the family are interdependent. Schools depend on parents to support the school, its activities, and its programs and to encourage the child to participate. Families depend on the school to teach their children not only how to read, write, and work with numbers but also how to develop their physical skills, communication skills, social skills, and so on. The ability of the child to take full advantage of the school program is, in part, a function of family encouragement and support of the child and the school.

What family behaviors or activities are associated with children's school achievement? Several types of parent activities appear repeatedly in the research literature:

- *Verbal interaction between parents and children.* There is considerable evidence indicating a link between verbal communication between parent and child and school achievement (Marjoribanks, 1980; Laosa, 1982a; Norman-Jackson, 1982; Bradley and Caldwell, 1984; Hess et al., 1984). For example, such activities as parental requests for verbal rather than nonverbal child responses, direct parental teaching of language behavior to children, and parents' reading to children have been linked to school achievement.
- *Parental expectations for achievement.* Child performance in school has been associated with parental aspirations for a child's educational or occupational attainment (Laosa, 1982a; Seginer, 1983; Hess et al., 1984; Schiamberg and Chin, 1986) and with parent achievement orientation toward specific schoolwork activities (Marjoribanks, 1980).
- *A warm relationship between parent and child.* The evidence suggests that parental warmth and nurturance are related to child success in school (Sigel, 1982; Hess and Holloway, 1984).
- *Control and discipline.* Parental use of control strategies and disciplinary techniques are associated with school achievement (Epstein, 1983; Hess et al., 1984; Hess and McDevitt, 1984). For example, the similarity or "degree of fit" between the type of authority structures at home (i.e., democratic, authoritarian, or permissive parent behavior) and those at school is related to child achievement (Epstein, 1983).
- *Parental beliefs.* There is evidence that parents' beliefs about their child's self-concept and potential performance in mathematics have a greater influence on the child's self-concept and mathematics achievement than the child's *actual* performance in mathematics (Parsons, Adler, and Kaczala, 1982). In addition, parental beliefs about child potential for mathematics achievement influence parental responses to their child's high or low performance (Hess et al., 1986). For example, a parent who expects or believes that his or her child is capable of competent performance will be less likely to accept low achievement than if the parent believes the child has limited potential.

The School and the World of Work. One of the problems adolescents in our society face is the need to make some commitment to a vocation or a career in the face of little or no direct experience in the world of work or knowledge about occupations. It has been suggested that the young are systematically excluded from the working world of adults as a function of the inherent age segregation in American society and of the American school in particular (Carnegie Commission on Policy Studies in Higher Education, 1980). Systematic attempts have been made to overcome this problem by the reorganizing and rethinking of the relationship between the school and the world of work. Such efforts include programs designed to inform high-school and grade-school students about occupations and types of jobs, as well as by providing experiential opportunities (Hamilton, 1981).

The number of adolescents who work in part-time (after-school) jobs has increased since World War II (Greenberger and Steinberg, 1986). However, such work activities guarantee neither a valuable learning experience nor integration into the adult world. For example, the range of jobs open to adolescents is limited and includes work in such areas as retail sales and fast-food restaurants. Such work may neither be challenging nor involve substantial interaction with adults (Greenberger and Steinberg, 1986). (We consider these matters in greater detail in Chapter 15).

THE WORLD OF WORK.   One of the first things adults want to know on first meeting is each other's occupation. This is understandable since occupation generally defines one's life-style, interpersonal relationships, and, to some extent, further potential for development. The world of work becomes a central life focus for many people because it represents the primary basis for scheduling human activities on a daily, weekly, or yearly basis over the lifespan. Because of its economic and social significance, the world of work provides the material resources for behavior, for family life, and for development itself (Kamerman and Hayes, 1982; Hayes and Kamerman, 1983; Voydanoff, 1984; Neff, 1985).

If the opportunity to work is absent, or if the nature of the work is not sufficiently rewarding, repercussions are likely to be experienced by the individual worker and his or her family (Allan, 1985), and there is evidence that unemployment among breadwinners is a primary factor leading to marital instability (Neff, 1985). The absence of work or work that fails to fulfill the functions of economic security, self-esteem, identity, and a sense of mastery over one's environment prevents one from finding the stable basis required to build supportive family relationships.

It is particularly important to recognize and emphasize the relationship between work and the *family as a system*. The influence of work on families (and, likewise, the impact of family life on work) cannot be understood without examining the *larger context* in which both the worlds of family and work occur:

> The most critical aspect of this larger context has to do with the availability of both formal and informal support systems for the family in such forms as child care, health and social services, necessary financial resources, and assistance and support from relatives, friends, neighbors, and co-workers. It is in this broader area that the richest opportunities lie . . . for . . . social policy. (Bronfenbrenner and Crouter, 1982, p. 78).

PEER GROUP AND FRIENDS.   Peer-group and friendship relationships influence development throughout the lifespan. From the preschool years through the years of adulthood, peer groups serve as a source of information for the individual about social expectations and behavioral roles as well as a source of mutual support (Hartup, 1983).

Sylvia Byers

Peer group relationships provide valuable feedback to the developing individual.

During the preschool and early school years, the peer group offers an environment that helps the child to move out of the family. The peer group has its own values and expectations of behavior. Peer relations during these early years are marked by informality and the absence of formal roles for group membership. Participation in preschool peer groups is largely the result of the physical closeness of the other children. In other words, children play together because they happen to live near one another or to be in the same class (preschool class, swim class, and so on).

Peer relations during middle childhood are characterized by same-sex groups. Children learn such things as appropriate behaviors and the roles they may be expected to play in later life—what is expected of males and females in society. Peer groups also provide the opportunity for the child to learn about competition and cooperation.

Peer relations during adolescence provide several critical experiences (Hartup, 1983):

· The individual develops a greater sensitivity to the needs of the "best friend." These early intimate relationships provide a valuable training ground for later interpersonal relationships.
· The peer group further develops and supports appropriate sex-role behaviors and expectations.
· Interpersonal relationships with the opposite sex often occur through support of the peer group.
· The peer group helps the adolescent to break away from the home.
· The peer group helps the adolescent to develop an identity by providing an arena for testing ideas and behaviors.

A LARGER CONTEXT: CULTURE. The "immediate" environments we have just described do not exist in a vacuum; they occur in a larger context: the culture (see Fig. 3.11). The *culture* of a society is the collection of principles, beliefs, norms,

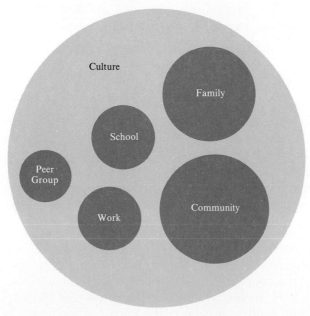

FIGURE 3.11
Culture: The larger context.

rules, and expected behaviors that govern the organization of that society. Culture shapes our behavior, how we dress, what we eat, how we solve problems, what we value as important, and how our institutions (government, work and business, schools, and families) are organized. Our cultural patterns for organizing social institutions such as work and family exert a considerable influence on the conditions of human development.

For example, the family in America (and in most industrialized societies) is organized in a *nuclear* form (a husband, a wife, and their children, if any). This form of family organization is different from family organization in other cultures (a common family form in other cultures is the *extended* family, which includes the immediate family plus other relatives). The implications of family form for human development are significant. For example, the nuclear family form provides considerable independence for the family unit (i.e., the family unit is relatively free of the influence of other relatives). On the other hand, this freedom is not without its price, as young children and their parents (in an increasingly mobile society where families may move frequently) may not benefit from the advice and support of grandparents and other relatives.

The Contexts of Life and the Stages of Child Development

The contexts of life that we have just described interact with the developing human being in a somewhat predictable pattern. That is, some contexts, such as family and school, are more prominent during the early phases of the lifespan, whereas other contexts, such as work, perform a primary role in adulthood. In this book, we will be looking at the total human being. Table 3.3 summarizes how the child and adolescent interact with the significant people of his or her life and the significant social institutions of the social system. This approach is both developmental and interactional, and it constitutes what we mean by a *systems perspective* for the following reasons.

1. It involves the *mutual interaction* of the developing person or self with the significant contexts of development.
2. It involves the *changing and evolving nature of the significant contexts of development* in the various periods of life. For example, the family is the central context of development during infancy; the school emerges as a significant context during middle childhood and adolescence; and the world of work is a primary context during adulthood.
3. It involves the *cumulative impact of each context of development* as the individual proceeds through the lifespan. This means that although a given context such as the family may have a more central or primary influence during certain stages of life, its influence does not disappear in later phases of life. For example, the family has a primary influence on development throughout the early years of life. That "primary" influence is shared with the social and the peer group as the individual proceeds through childhood and adolescence. However, when the individual is ready to leave the home and establish an independent existence, the impact of the family is still present. In fact, the influence of the family of origin continues to have an impact on many features of the adult's life (including how the adult raises his or her children).

TABLE 3.3
Child Development as an Ecosystem

PERIOD OF DEVELOPMENT (THE INDIVIDUAL)	←——→ MUTUAL ACCOMMODATION	PRIMARY CONTEXTS OF HUMAN DEVELOPMENT
The fetus and neonate: This period begins with conception and ends shortly after birth, extending to about the first few days of life.		The *intrauterine environment* before birth. The *extrauterine environment* during the first few days after birth.
The infant: This period extends from birth to about 3 years of age (this includes the toddler period from approximately 2 to 3 years of age).		The *family* and the emerging relationship (attachment) between infant, parent(s), and other family members. The world of the "household" is a significant learning laboratory.
The preschooler: This period extends from about 3 years of age until entrance into formal school at 5 or 6 years of age.		The *family*. The *neighborhood*, particularly in the immediate vicinity of the child's residence, and peer friendships within this limited range.
Middle childhood: This period begins with entrance into the formal school and continues to the beginning of adolescence with the onset of puberty (from about 5 or 6 years of age to approximately the age of 12 or 13).		The impact of the *family* is important particularly as it now contributes to the self-definition of the child in relation to the school. The *school* assumes a primary role during middle childhood as the major source of transmission of the culture (e.g., reading and writing). The *neighborhood and local community* includes the immediate vicinity as well as the larger community. The child becomes familiar with major community resources such as the school, the library, the supermarket, and the post office. The *peer group*. Peer interactions and friendships become more formalized as organized clubs and grade-level friendships emerge. Peer relations also serve as a valuable "bridge" to negotiating newly discovered community resources.
Early adolescence: This period begins with the onset of puberty and extends through the high-school years to about 17 or 18 years of age. The organizing feature of this stage is the development of a sense of "group" identity relative to the world of high-school peer organization. Thus the central task is to come to grips with the pressure to join groups.		The *family* serves as a base from which the adolescent begins to establish his or her identity in relation to the high school and peers. In addition, the self-development skills that the adolescent has learned up to this point (reading, writing, thinking, etc.) serve as the basis for the emerging "adult-to-adult" relationship (replacing the "parent-child" relationship). From a social perspective, the *high school* and its staff tend to support the peer emphasis and orientation of early adolescence. The types of groupings that are formed in the high school (e.g., student council, service groups, athletic boosters) reinforce the peer groupings of early adolescence. The high-school student expands his or her understanding of resources in the *community* to include local, state, and national institutions.

(Continued)

TABLE 3.3
Child Development as an Ecosystem (Continued)

PERIOD OF DEVELOPMENT (THE INDIVIDUAL)	⟷ MUTUAL ACCOMMODATION	PRIMARY CONTEXTS OF HUMAN DEVELOPMENT

Later adolescence and youth: This period of development begins with completion of high school (17–18 years of age) and extends until the person attains a sense of social status or social identity and a control of resources in the adult community (early 20s). In summary, this period deals with the post–high school years and the development of the skills that the individual now uses to develop a "stance toward the world." (Erikson, 1974)

The family. A common feature of later adolescence is independent living coupled with the crystallization of autonomy from parents. Although the independence from the parents has been forming prior to this period (i.e., the skills of independent living, including reading, writing, thinking, and social cooperation, have been developing throughout childhood and early adolescence), the crystallization of these activities during later adolescence creates a situation of potential parent-adolescent conflict. The adolescent learns to resolve prior patterns of childhood dependence with the emerging needs for autonomy. The result is the development of an adult-adult relationship, which replaces the parent-adolescent relationship.

The world of work and/or postsecondary education. The end of the high school years may lead the adolescent in one of at least three directions: full-time work; additional education (college, university, or community college), which may lead to full-time employment at a later date; or a combination of both work and education. The development of an identity or stance toward the world necessitates a beginning choice of occupation during this period.

Peers. During later adolescence, peer relationships are integrated with work and/or postsecondary education, as well as with residential patterns. Peer relationships may continue to serve as a buffer between the adolescent and his or her family in the process of identity formation. Later adolescent living arrangements, school experience, and work settings represent social selection processes in the determination of associates or peers. When these selection processes become too rigid, members of ethnic, economic, and racial minorities may be excluded from advanced developmental experiences.

The community. In contrast to the early adolescent, who may have an "understanding" of the community and its resources, the later adolescent probably has some actual experience with significant community institutions and resources.

Methods of Studying Child Development

Now we will look briefly at how the primary determinants of child development are studied. What research methods are used, for example, to determine what human beings are like at various stages of development?

Naturalistic Observation

Naturalistic observations view people in their real-life settings with no attempt made to alter what people do in these settings. Naturalistic studies result in *normative* (typical) information about people and their settings. For example, we could use naturalistic studies to examine the social development of children in the actual settings or contexts in which such behavior occurs. Using observational methods, researchers might examine the interaction of family members during dinner or how friendships are formed on middle-school playgrounds.

Recent years have seen a renewed interest in the use of naturalistic research methods. This resurgence of interest is in part due to the limitations of other research strategies, such as laboratory experiments (which we discuss in more detail below). It has been argued that laboratory experiments remove the experiment from "real life" by setting up artificial conditions (in the laboratory) that do not demonstrate how children actually behave in their natural environments (Bronfenbrenner, 1974, 1979). For example, the results of a laboratory experiment in which children watch a violent television program and then are placed in a free-play situation to determine the impact of the program on the expression of child aggression may not help us answer the question of how violent programming actually affects behavior in natural family or peer-group settings. In fact, Bronfenbrenner (1974, 1979) has argued that many such laboratory studies lack what he calls **ecological validity** (i.e., the ability to generalize or apply the results of a research study to real-life circumstances). That is, many laboratory experiments

---

Are Laboratory Experiments "Real?"

In questions of public policy, the focus is on the enduring (and thereby familiar) social contexts in which the child lives, or might live, and in which the participants occupy enduring (and thereby familiar) roles and engage in activities that have social meaning in that setting. Such an orientation stands in contrast to many, but I hasten to add not all, laboratory situations in which the situation is of short duration and unfamiliar, the task is not only unfamiliar but artificial (in the sense that its social significance is at best unclear), and the other participants are strangers. In fact, usually there is only one other participant—a graduate student, whose prior relationship with the child is nonexistent, or, if existent, trivial in character. Indeed, it can be said that "much of American developmental psychology is the science of the behavior of children in strange situations with strange adults. . . ."

More correctly, we should say the behavior of a child with "one" strange adult. . . .

These features so common in our research are hardly characteristic of the situations in which chil-

dren actually live and develop. Thus, in the family, the day-care center, preschool, play group, school classroom or neighborhood, (a) there are usually more than two people; (b) the child invariably influences those who influence him; (c) the other participants are not strangers but persons who have enduring roles and relationships vis-à-vis the child; (d) finally, the behavior of all these persons is profoundly affected by other social systems [e.g., work, school] in which these same persons participate in significant roles and relationships, both toward the child and each other. . . .

By removing the child from the environment in which he ordinarily finds himself and placing him in another setting [laboratory] which is typically unfamiliar, short-lived, and devoid of the persons, objects and experiences that have been central in his life, we are getting only a partial picture both of the child and of his environment.

From Bronfenbrenner, 1974, pp. 1–5.

involve children interacting with strangers (i.e., "experimenters") in strange situations (i.e., the laboratory). The intent of naturalistic studies is to examine child behavior in the context of "real" circumstances, such as families, day-care centers, and schools. Such real contexts have several important characteristics:

- The children in such contexts have *enduring* or long-lasting relationships with others in such settings (e.g., parents, teachers, and peers).
- The interaction between children and others is *reciprocal* or mutual (others influence the child *and* the child influences them).
- The behavior of the child and others is influenced by the physical and social contexts (e.g., the neighborhood, parents' work, mass media, and so on).

An example of a naturalistic study is the observational research by Gerald Patterson and his associates on children's aggression in families (Patterson, 1982). This study demonstrated that boys acted more aggressively toward their young brothers before dinner time than at other times during the day. It was apparent to the investigators that the boys' behavior escalated to aggressiveness as the only way to gain their parents' attention. The boys' milder efforts to gain parental attention were ignored by the parents, who were busy preparing dinner. Unfortunately, only when they began hitting their younger brothers did they receive their parents' complete and undivided attention. Patterson and his associates concluded that parents were unintentionally supporting the very behaviors of child aggression that were undesirable.

Although naturalistic observation has many advantages, it nonetheless has one major drawback: The presence of an observer may influence what is going on. For example, there is some evidence that people behave very differently when they are being observed than when they are not being observed (or think they are not being observed). In one study, a group of middle-class mothers who knew they were being observed interacted with their children in a very positive manner (i.e., displayed "good" parenting techniques such as talking to their children, playing with them, and encouraging them to display skills) compared with how they behaved when they thought they were not being observed but really were (Graves and Glick, 1978). In the latter case the mothers were much less attentive to their children and appeared to be busy with their own activities or preoccupied with their own thoughts. In fact, the middle-class mothers in the "unobserved" session behaved in ways that had previously been attributed to lower-class mothers. Such evidence suggests the very real possibility that people frequently behave differently when they know they are being observed. Furthermore, a situation in which subjects believe they are not being observed but are in reality being observed raises *ethical* questions about intruding into the lives of children and families without their permission. (We discuss ethical issues in research later in this chapter).

The Case Study

The **case study** method is an intensive study of one individual. Early case studies were, in fact, detailed observations of single individuals. For example, Darwin's observations of infant development were detailed case studies (see box). The case study usually involves a researcher and one individual or subject at a time, and it combines observation with careful questioning. The case study has the advantage of being flexible. Tasks or questioning can be individualized for each person.

Charles Darwin and the Infant Case Study

Charles Darwin (1809–1882) is best known for his theories of evolution (especially his book *On the Origin of Species*, 1859). These theories made a considerable impact on the study of human development. If species develop or "evolve," then societies and, indeed, human beings develop. Darwin was one of the first scientists to call attention to this development through the careful observation of infants. In the selection that follows Darwin discusses anger in infants. (By modern standards, he had some curiously humorous ideas about sex differences in the expression of anger.)

It was difficult to decide at how early an age anger was felt; on his eighth day he frowned and wrinkled the skin around his eyes before a crying fit, but this may have been due to pain or distress, and not to anger. . . . When eleven months old, if a wrong plaything was given him, he would push it away and beat it; I presume that the beating was an instinctive sign of anger, like the snapping of the jaws by a young crocodile just out of the egg. . . . When two years old and three months old, he became adept at throwing books or sticks . . . at anyone who offended him; and so it was with some of my other sons. On the other hand, I could never see a trace of such aptitude in my infant daughters; and this makes me think that a tendency to throw objects is inherited in boys.

From Darwin, 1877, p. 286.

A more recent example of the use of the case study occurs in the research of Piaget (1952). In studying the development of thinking in children, Piaget was very much interested in the reasons some children were able to accomplish certain tasks and other children were not. In order to understand this, he used a combination of tests or tasks and individualized questions.

Although the case study method has the advantage of flexibility (allowing Piaget, for example, to probe the thought processes of young children), it has the disadvantage of producing conclusions that are highly dependent on an interviewer's ability to ask the right questions. Results that are produced in this fashion may need to be confirmed by others using the same or different methods before any faith can be placed in them. In the case of Piaget's work, many of his findings about children's thinking processes have, in fact, been supported by other investigators using similar as well as other methods.

Experimental Research

In recent years, as we have already noted, there has been a renewed emphasis on research in natural settings (Bronfenbrenner, 1979, 1986). Many investigators now use films and elaborate videotaping equipment to study behavior and development as it occurs in real life. Although naturalistic studies have the advantage of describing behavior that can be "generalized" to people in "natural" settings, they permit the experimenter little control over the experimental conditions (e.g., con-

FIGURE 3.12
The settings that experimenters use can range from the most "controlled" laboratory settings to the most "uncontrolled" natural settings. Based on Gage, 1963.

trol of specific individuals in the study or of other events going on at the time of the experiment) (see Fig. 3.12).

The **experimental method** is designed to provide an investigator with control over the subjects and the conditions in a study. The advantage of an experimental study is that this control allows the researcher to be more certain of the experimental results. In other words, the findings reflect what the experimenter says they reflect rather than some "uncontrolled" event. If, for example, an experiment is done for the purpose of demonstrating the relationship between parental attitudes and motor-skill development, then the findings of the experiment should demonstrate that relationship only. If they are to do that, it is necessary for the experimenter to "control" such factors as the age of the child (e.g., older children may be better at motor skills and also more responsive to parental attitudes than younger children). If the age of the children in the experiment is not controlled in some way (such as by having all of the children at the same age), then an experimental finding could be demonstrating a relationship between age and motor skills rather than parental attitude and motor skills.

Another primary advantage of experimental research compared with naturalistic studies is that the standardized procedures of experiments ensure that the study can be repeated or *replicated* by other investigators. Replication provides a test for the reliability of the experimental findings. If others get similar results using the same procedures with different subjects, then the findings have greater strength and status. A major disadvantage of the experimental method is that the precise

Variables of an Experiment

INDEPENDENT VARIABLES. The **independent variables** are the factors in an experiment that the researcher can systematically control or change. In the example of the experiment on parental attitude and motor skills, the independent variable is parental attitude. An experimenter might wish to group parents into three categories:

1. Parents who have a positive attitude toward motor skills.

2. Parents who have a negative attitude toward motor skills.

3. Parents who are neutral or indifferent toward motor skills.

DEPENDENT VARIABLES. A **dependent variable** is the resulting behavior that is of interest to the researcher. In the experimental example, the dependent variable is the child's motor skills (e.g., running and throwing).

control of experimental conditions results in findings that have limited application (except to other children in laboratory settings). Some developmentalists have argued, therefore, that the results of many laboratory studies provide unreal pictures of human development (Bronfenbrenner, 1979).

Correlational Research

In situations where the use of experimental methods is difficult or impossible, experimenters can still examine the relationships between certain events or variables. The term **correlational study** is often used to describe such studies of factors or variables that are not manipulated per se. For example, if one wished to study the association between newborn birth weight and maternal smoking, it would be unethical to select 300 pregnant women randomly and ask half of them to smoke two packs of cigarettes a day (and the other half to abstain from smoking) to determine the impact of smoking on babies. Instead, an investigator could conduct an "after-the-fact" correlational study comparing the various birth weights of a group of newborns born to mothers who smoked varying amounts during pregnancy. In addition, every attempt could be made to match both groups of mothers (smokers and nonsmokers) on such factors as maternal age, educational level, social class, and so on, to ensure that the computed correlation will reflect as much as possible *only* the association between smoking and birth weight (i.e., one could not argue that newborn birth weight may be related to the young age of mothers if both smoking and nonsmoking mothers were matched for age).

A **correlation coefficient** is a numerical value that can be calculated to represent the *degree of association between two variables* or factors. The relationship between height and weight, for example, could be expressed as a correlation. Typically, taller people weigh more than shorter people. Likewise, there is a relationship between education and occupational attainment. The higher the level of education, the more likely one is to be found at a higher occupational level.

There are two important points to understand regarding correlational relationships that affect the degree of relationship measured:

- The fact that two variables (e.g., height and weight or education and occupational attainment) are generally related for large numbers of people does not mean that they are related in every instance. For example, there are tall, slender individuals who weigh much less than shorter, stockier individuals. Relationships can vary in degree from no relationship (expressed as 0.0) to very strong relationships (see Fig. 3.13).
- *Correlation does not indicate causation.* For example, the correlation between education and occupational attainment does not necessarily mean that level of education is the primary explanation or *cause* for occupational attainment. It may mean that better-educated people are more likely to make the "right connections" or meet the "right" people in educational settings (relationships that facilitate career development). Therefore, interpersonal skills may be more important than educational achievement in explaining occupational success. Or it may be that a third factor such as intelligence is, in reality, responsible for *both* educational success and occupational attainment.

Furthermore, a correlation coefficient indicates the *direction* and *magnitude* of a relationship between two variables. There are two types (or directions) of correlation—*positive* and *negative*.

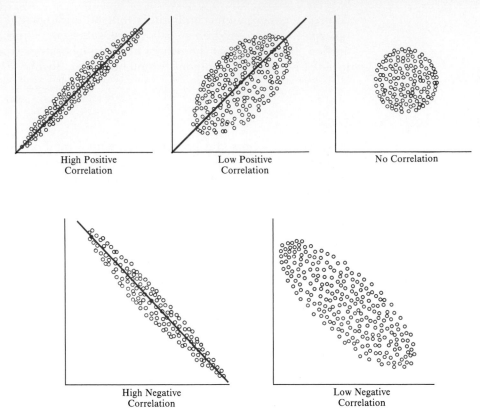

FIGURE 3.13

A correlation coefficient (r = #) expresses the relationship or degree of association between two variables. (Each dot in the scatter plots above represents the score of one child on each variable, x and y). The strength of a correlation can be seen as a function of the form or shape of an ellipse of points. The higher the correlation the more elongated the ellipse.

- *Positive.* Whenever two variables or factors change in the *same* direction, there is a **positive correlation.** For example, when height increases, weight also increases.
- *Negative.* When two variables are *inversely* related (i.e., when one variable increases, the other one decreases), there is a **negative correlation** (Fig. 3.13). For example, when the amount of calories consumed decreases, the number of pounds lost increases.

The *magnitude* of a correlation coefficient refers to the *degree* of the relationship between two variables. Correlation coefficients are reported as numbers that range from $r = -1.00$ (a perfect inverse or negative relationship) to $r = +1.00$ (a perfectly direct or positive relationship) (see Table 3.4). The closer the number is to $+1.00$ or to -1.00, the stronger the relationship—either positive or negative. For example, a correlation coefficient $r = +.80$ or $r = -.80$ indicates a high but not perfect association between two variables. A correlation coefficient of $r = 0.00$ indicates that there is no discernible relationship (either positive or negative) between two variables. For example, there is no evidence that eye color has anything to do with level of intelligence.

TABLE 3.4
Perfect Correlations

+1.00 CORRELATION BETWEEN SCORES ON TWO VARIABLES		−1.00 CORRELATION BETWEEN SCORES ON TWO VARIABLES	
Variable A (height)	*Variable B (weight)*	*Variable A (approximate daily caloric consumption*)*	*Variable B (monthly weight loss)*
5 ft. 1 in.	110 lb.	1,925	0
5 ft. 2 in.	120 lb.	1,800	1
5 ft. 3 in.	125 lb.	1,700	2
5 ft. 4 in.	130 lb.	1,575	3
5 ft. 5 in.	135 lb.	1,425	4
5 ft. 6 in.	140 lb.		
5 ft. 7 in.	145 lb.		
5 ft. 8 in.	150 lb.		
5 ft. 9 in.	160 lb.		
5 ft. 10 in.	170 lb.		

*For inactive men, aged 40.

Another way of thinking about the magnitude or degree of relationship between two variables is graphically, using Figure 3.13. When the relationship between two variables is zero, the pattern of the dots representing each individual's score on variables X and Y is a *circle*. Such a circular pattern means that we cannot know the outcome of one variable based on the performance of another variable. However, when the pattern of dots approaches the form of an *ellipse*, it becomes possible to predict the performance of one variable based on what happens to another variable. The more *elongated* the ellipse (i.e., the more it approaches a straight line), the higher or stronger the correlation between the two variables.

Correlational studies use data from existing groups and describe the differences between these groups. For example, an investigator who wished to examine the relationship between child exposure to lead and behavior problems or low IQ score would begin by identifying a group of children who had been exposed to lead and a group who had not. The results of many such studies indicate that exposure to lead *is positively correlated* with child behavior patterns. Does this mean that exposure to lead *causes* behavior problems? No. Simply because two variables are associated or occur together does not mean that one variable causes the other. In the case of lead exposure, poor and minority children are more likely than middle-class children to live in older buildings with walls covered with lead paint. However, poor and minority children are also more likely than middle-class children to suffer from poor nutrition, child abuse, absent fathers, and poorly educated parents. There is some evidence that each of these factors is also correlated with child behavior problems. Therefore, using only correlational evidence, it is not possible to isolate the effects of lead exposure from all of these other possible causes of behavior problems (Scarr, 1985).

Cross-Sectional and Longitudinal Designs

Studies that deal with human development are usually concerned with one major aim: the description of how human beings change over time. There are two pri-

100

mary methods of data collection that serve this goal: *longitudinal* research and *cross-sectional* designs.

1. **Longitudinal designs.** The experimenter identifies a group of people and then measures them on some variable(s) of interest (e.g., behavior, attitudes, or feelings) at two or more moments in time. By examining the same people, the researcher can see the changes that occur as a result of development over a time period.

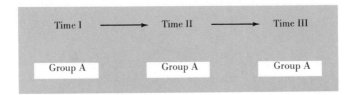

2. **Cross-sectional designs.** The experimenter compares groups of different individuals who are themselves at different ages at one time.

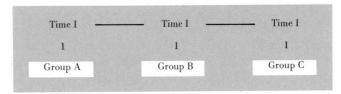

The settings that experimenters use can range from the most "controlled" laboratory settings to the most "uncontrolled" natural settings. Based on Gage, 1963.

Longitudinal designs measure the changes that occur in single individuals over a period of time. Cross-sectional designs measure differences at one time among different groups of individuals. Each approach has its strengths and weaknesses.

3. **Cross-sequential designs:** *Combinations of longitudinal and cross-sectional designs.* In order to overcome some of the limitations of both the longitudinal and

Longitudinal Research

ADVANTAGE	DISADVANTAGES
• Is more sensitive to changes in individual behavior than cross-sectional research.	• Requires several years (sometimes several decades) to collect data. • Is usually expensive. • Subjects may drop out of the study because of death, illness, moving, and so on.

Cross-Sectional Research

ADVANTAGE

· A sizable amount of information can be gathered in a relatively short time.

DISADVANTAGES

· Generational or cohort effects may be present (effects that are the result of factors associated with being born at different times).
· Does not reflect individual changes over time.

cross-sectional designs, the cross-sequential design was developed (Schaie, 1983). This design combines both the longitudinal and cross-sectional approaches by initially doing a cross-sectional sample of subjects and then following these same subjects longitudinally over time. The cross-sequential approach avoids the drawbacks and biases of both traditional designs. Research utilizing cross-sequential designs in the study of cognitive functioning in adulthood illustrates the value of this design in providing a more accurate and careful description of adult intelligence than either the longitudinal or cross-sectional designs (Schaie, 1983). This is so because cross-sectional designs typically give an *overestimate* in the drop in intellectual performance because of generational or cohort effects. For example, if we compared twenty-, forty-, and sixty-year-olds on a test of intellectual functioning, we would likely find a drop in performance with age. This drop would probably be due more to generational or cohort effects (e.g., given that educational experiences would have improved for the twenty-year-olds compared with that of the two older groups, we might expect to find a drop in intellectual functioning as a result of such a cohort effect), than to age, per se. On the other hand, the longitudinal design tends to *underestimate* any drop in intellectual functioning with age primarily because *dropouts* from the original sample of twenty-year-olds might make the sample at age sixty a much more able group of individuals than the original group. *Dropouts* from longitudinal research studies are rarely random in their characteristics. (That is, those with poor health, lower occupational status, lower economic status, or, in this case, lower intelligence are far more likely to drop out of such a study.) The cross-sequential design will presumably provide a more realistic picture of the variation of intellectual functioning by avoiding either an underestimation or an overestimation.

The cross-sequential design is not without its disadvantages. As is the case with longitudinal designs, additional time and expense are required for cross-sequential designs compared with cross-sectional research.

Ethical Considerations in Research

In recent years increased attention has been paid to the impact of research on human beings. Although it is not a common occurrence for participation in research to result in abusive practices, it is nonetheless a distinct possibility. For example, ethically questionable practices could include the involvement of people in research without their knowledge or consent, coercing or forcing individuals to participate in research, invading a subject's privacy, exposing people to potential physical or psychological harm, failing to maintain the confidentiality of subject

Standards for the Ethical Conduct of Research

The researcher must ensure that children and families who are the subjects of research investigations are not harmed by the research. The Society for Research in Child Development suggests several precautions:

· No matter how young, the child has rights that supersede the rights of the investigator.
· The investigator must respect the right of the child to choose to participate in a study and to withdraw from that same study at any time without penalty.

· The investigator should obtain the informed consent of parents or those who act on behalf of the child's interests (teachers, school superintendents, and so on). Such informed consent must be in writing. Informed consent requires that the parent or other responsible adult be told of all the aspects of the research that may affect the child.
· The investigator should use no research operation that will physically or psychologically harm the child.

performance, and so on. As a result, the federal government and various scientific and professional organizations have formulated ethical guidelines for the conduct of research. In addition, most institutions that engage in or sponsor research have research ethics advisory committees that evaluate proposed research and monitor ongoing projects to ensure conformity to ethical guidelines by avoiding the abuses discussed above, as well as other potentially unethical behavior (see box).

Summary

1. This chapter described the *primary determinants* of child development, the *contexts* and *stages* of child development, and the *research methods* used to study children and adolescents. There are *three primary determinants of development:* (a) biological foundations, (b) *social environments* or *contexts*, and (c) the interaction of biological and social factors. These three factors constitute the essential parts of a *human ecological* or *systems perspective* to child and human development.

   The basic principles of the ecological perspective are (a) development is characterized by *quantitative* and *qualitative* changes; (b) the explanation of these changes involves *both* hereditary and environmental factors; (c) the interaction between heredity and environment is *reciprocal*.

2. The biochemical agents that carry an individual's general biological code are *genes* and *chromosomes*. There are two primary types of heredity: *general heredity* and *specific heredity*. One way of better understanding the relationship between heredity and environment is by examining several models that address the relationship—*canalization*, the *norm of reaction*, and *niche picking*.

   The explanation of the interaction of heredity and environment is complex. Such complexity becomes apparent in our discussions of the contributions of hereditary and environmental factors to *intelligence* and *personality*. We know that genetic factors are involved in the development of the human body from the moment of conception. However, we do not yet fully understand the scientific mechanisms of interaction of genetic and environmental factors in controlling growth and development. The relationship of this nature-nurture interaction to *human behavior* is even less clear, particularly for such characteristics as *intelligence* and *personality*.

The research on the joint contributions of heredity and environment to intelligence includes studies of *twins, adopted children,* and *intervention research.* The evidence for personality development suggests that there is a genetic basis for infant temperament, with an important role accorded to the environment in the expression of such personality dispositions.

3. The environments or "contexts" of the life process play a large role in the development of human beings throughout the lifespan. It is not enough to simply state that heredity and environment interact. It is necessary to be more specific about what we mean by "environment." For our purposes, there are two broad categories of environments: *immediate* and *larger* environments.

4. The *family* is a significant immediate context throughout the lifespan. The influence of the family in childhood is critical in the development of self-concept, sex roles, language, intellectual abilities, and interpersonal skills. Duvall and Miller (1985) have described the changing pattern of the family life cycle as a series of developmental stages with primary functions at each point in the life cycle.

   Using this family developmental framework, we can examine the relationship of the developing child and the marital relationship. The quality of the marital relationship is influenced by parenting responsibilities which, in turn, influence the development of children and adolescents in families.

5. The *neighborhood/community* is another significant context for child and adolescent development. The impact of the neighborhood/community on children and families is an understudied and underemphasized dimension of child development. The influence of the community/neighborhood on the developing child is largely through the medium of the family. Such influence occurs through both *formal community structures* and *informal community structures* such as *social networks.*

6. The *school* as a context of development emerges as a major institution for the formal transfer of cultural traditions and skills from society to the developing child and young person. Both the school and the family are systems in their own right that interact in the process of educating the child and the adolescent. The relationship between the school and the world of work has been the subject of some debate. Earlier emphasis on work experience for high-school students has been modified by recent evidence that such experiences guarantee neither a valuable learning experience nor integration or involvement in the adult world.

7. *Peers and friends* are a vital source of feedback and support during childhood and more prominently during adolescence.

8. The *culture* serves as a "larger," more indirect context of development. The immediate environments of family, school, neighborhood/community, and peers do not exist in a vacuum. Rather, they occur in the context of the culture. The *culture* of a society is the collection of principles, beliefs, norms, rules, and ranges of behaviors that govern the organization of society. For example, our broad culture provides the framework for the organization of family, work, neighborhood/community, and peer contexts.

9. The "contexts" or environments just described interact with the developing human beings in a somewhat predictable pattern. That is, some contexts such as family are usually more prominent during the infancy and the

preschool years, whereas others such as school and work emerge in child-hood, adolescence, and young adulthood. In this book we focus on this changing interactional or "systems" pattern between person and contexts from the prenatal period through adolescence. This developmental-interactional pattern is what we mean by a *systems* or an *ecological* approach and has the following major characteristics: (a) it involves the *mutual interaction* of the developing person or self with the significant contexts of development; (b) it involves the *changing or evolving nature of these contexts* of development in each stage of development; (c) it involves the *cumulative impact of each context of development* as the individual moves through life.

10. Methods for studying child and adolescent development include *naturalistic observations*, the *case study, experimental research, correlational research,* and *cross-sectional* or *longitudinal designs. (Cross-sequential designs* combine both the cross-sectional and longitudinal approaches.)

11. It is the *ethical responsibility* of a researcher to ensure that children and families who are the subjects of research investigations are not harmed or put at risk by the research.

Key Terms

Canalization	Heredity
Case study	Independent variables
Correlational study	Informal community structures
Correlation coefficient	Longitudinal designs
Cross-sectional designs	Monozygotic (identical) twins
Cross-sequential design	Naturalistic observations
Dependent variable	Negative correlation
Dizygotic (fraternal) twins	Neighborhood/community
Ecological validity	Niche picking
Environment	Norm of reaction
Experimental method	Positive correlation
Family developmental tasks	Social networks
Formal community structures	Specific hereditary code
General hereditary code	

Questions

1. Based on your own experiences, can you cite significant physical similarities between parents and children or grandparents and grandchildren?
2. Indicate the reasons that the relationship between intelligence and heredity is unclear. If you heard someone say that a given group of people tend to do poorly in school because they are "genetically inferior," how would you counter the argument?
3. Briefly describe some of the significant "contexts" of, or settings for, human development. Do some contexts or settings play a greater or lesser role during various stages of life? Give several examples.
4. Define the following terms: naturalistic study, independent variable, dependent variable, cross-sectional study, longitudinal study.

Suggested Readings

BRIM, O. G., and KAGAN, J. (eds.). *Constancy and Change in Human Development*. Cambridge, Mass.: Harvard University Press, 1980. An excellent collection of essays on the question of continuity in development. A broad range of domains are covered including physical health, cognitive development, and personality.

LERNER, R. *On the Nature of Human Plasticity*. Cambridge: Cambridge University Press, 1984. An excellent review of the emerging viewpoint that the potential for change in development exists across the lifespan.

LEWONTIN, R. *Human Diversity*. New York: Scientific American Books, 1982. A readable synthesis of molecular biology, genetics, physiology, and social science applied to explanation of human diversity.

NEFF, W. S. *Work and Human Behavior* (3rd ed.). New York: Aldine, 1985. The book develops a general theory of work behavior that is then applied to practical issues such as female employment and minority and handicapped workers.

PARKE, R. D. (ed.). *Review of Child Development Research*, Vol. 7: *The Family*. Chicago: The University of Chicago Press, 1984. An entire volume in the distinguished series produced by the Society for Research in Child Development devoted to studies of the family. The volume underscores the growing recognition that child development cannot be fully understood unless the family context is explored.

4 The Beginning: Genetic Factors and Prenatal Development

Yes—*the history of a man for the nine months preceding his birth would probably be far more interesting and contain events of greater moment than all three score years that follow it.*
        —*Samuel Taylor Coleridge, 1885*

The science of genetics has made extraordinary gains in the last two decades. As a result, we are beginning to accumulate a great deal of information about the mechanisms of heredity. In addition, genetic research has introduced such innovations as genetic screening and **amniocentesis** (the withdrawal of amniotic fluid surrounding the unborn child in order to examine skin cells and other substances in the fluid for abnormality), which have led to the possibility of treating some problems before or immediately after birth and the possibility of terminating the life of the fetus early in pregnancy. Genetic advances that have made possible the treatment of some problems before or immediately after birth have received wide acceptance and support; the termination of pregnancy through abortion has created much debate and discussion. As is often the case with scientific and technological advances, the implications for human values and human decision making became apparent only after the innovations were discovered.

This chapter deals with current knowledge about genetic factors in development and about the prenatal development of the unborn child.

Life Begins

Conception

The process of **conception** occurs when fertilization takes place. **Fertilization** occurs when a *sperm* cell from a male unites with an *egg* from a female and forms a single cell. This single cell is called a *zygote* (Figs. 4.1–4.3). (Both egg and sperm are called **gametes**.) Although we may casually state that life begins with the process of fertilization, this biological fact does not fully answer the question of when life begins.

> *DEFINITIONS*
> **Zygote.** The fertilized ovum formed by the union of the male sperm and the female ovum.
> **Embryo.** The name given to the developing organism during the six-week period from about the end of the second week after conception (when the egg becomes well implanted in the uterine wall) until the developing organism takes on a humanlike appearance as the result of cell differentiation (about the end of the second month after conception).
> **Fetus.** The term used to describe the developing human organism from the end of the second month after conception (end of the embryonic period) until birth.

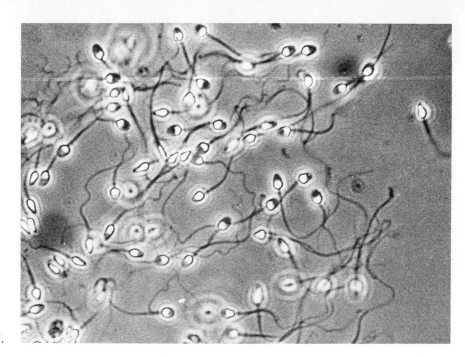

FIGURE 4.1
Human sperm. From Rahn, 1980.

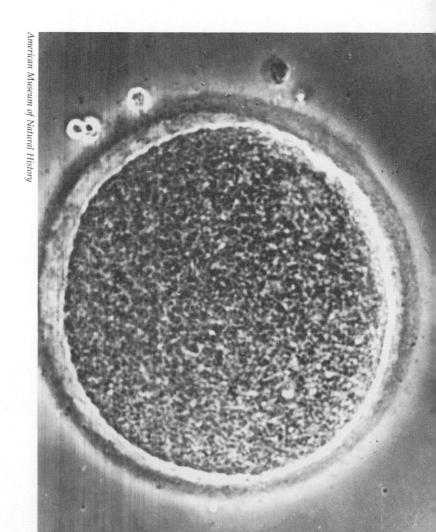

FIGURE 4.2
Human egg. A highly magnified human egg or
ovum. The nucleus of the egg carries the mother's
chromosomes.

American Museum of Natural History

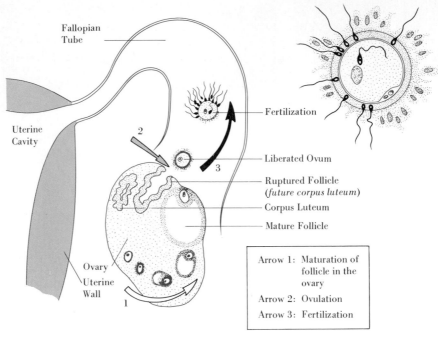

Arrow 1:	Maturation of follicle in the ovary
Arrow 2:	Ovulation
Arrow 3:	Fertilization

FIGURE 4.3

Fertilization. Conception or fertilization occurs when the sperm cell from the father unites with the egg cell (ovum) from the mother. Fertilization marks the beginning of pregnancy. The diagram at the top right shows the union of egg and sperm. The diagram at the left center shows the location of fertilization in the female reproductive system. Adapted from Tuchmann-Duplessis, David, and Haegel, 1972, 1975.

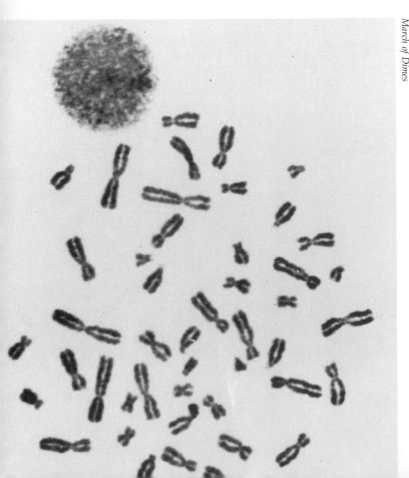

March of Dimes

FIGURE 4.4

Human chromosomes. The photograph is of a magnified cell nucleus (top) and forty-six chromosomes of a normal human male. The chromosomes shown here are from a cell that is in the middle of cell division.

Indeed, the question of an abortion of an *embryo* or a *fetus* hinges, in part, on a definition on the beginning of life. Does life begin with conception? Or does life begin sometime later in pregnancy when the full assortment of human systems becomes differentiated? The notion of when life begins remains controversial among both scientists and the lay public.

Chromosomes and Genes

At the moment of conception there is a union of twenty-three small particles called *chromosomes* from the sperm with twenty-three chromosomes from the ovum. This process of combining chromosomes from father and mother is of particular interest because these chromosomes carry *genes*.

> *DEFINITIONS*
>
> **Chromosomes.** These rod-shaped structures (Fig. 4.4) containing genes are present in every cell. Genes contain the mechanisms for directing the activity of every cell. All normal human cells have forty-six chromosomes, or twenty-three chromosome pairs, except the germ cells (sperm and ovum), which each have twenty-three chromosomes (Figs. 4.4 and 4.5).
>
> **Genes.** The basic units of heredity that are carried on the chromosomes.

When the fertilized ovum divides, each new cell contains the same number of chromosomes and genes. Genes are composed of DNA (deoxyribonucleic acid).

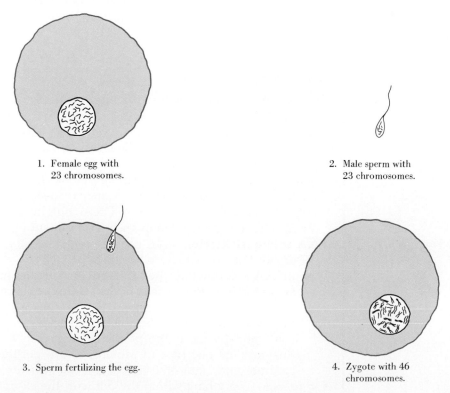

1. Female egg with 23 chromosomes.

2. Male sperm with 23 chromosomes.

3. Sperm fertilizing the egg.

4. Zygote with 46 chromosomes.

FIGURE 4.5
The pattern of chromosomes before and after fertilization.

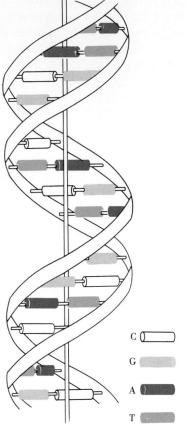

C ▭
G ▭
A ▭
T ▭

FIGURE 4.6

Model of a DNA molecule. The drawing is a theoretical representation, as DNA has never been observed. Each level of the spiral is composed of chemicals (see definition of DNA). The arrangement of these chemicals in the nucleus of each cell constitutes the genetic blueprint for the synthesis of proteins outside the nucleus of each cell. From Lucille F. Whaley, Understanding Inherited Disorders. *St. Louis: The C. V. Mosby Company, 1974, p. 16.*

DEFINITIONS

Protein. A molecule containing amino acids (the basic building blocks of protein).

Enzyme. A protein that promotes reactions in a living system.

DNA (deoxyribonucleic acid). The chemical substance (composed of sugar, phosphate, and four bases—adenine, guanine, cytosine, and thymine) that makes up genes. The structure of DNA looks like a spiral ladder. The DNA molecule consists of two chains, which are coiled around each other in the form of a double helix (Fig. 4.6). DNA contains the genetic blueprint (genetic code) for the regulation and development of the human organism.

RNA (ribonucleic acid). RNA can be either messenger (mRNA) or transfer (+RNA). Both are structurally similar to DNA.

1. mRNA is formed on the DNA and carries the instructions for protein synthesis from the nucleus of the cell to the ribosome in the cytoplasm.

2. +RNA is also formed on the DNA. +RNA is coded to pick up one of the twenty naturally occurring amino acids, which it takes to the ribosome and places in the proper sequence to form a specific protein. Enzymes are one type of protein, as are portions of cell membranes, chromosomes, and other important cell structures.

Cytoplasm. Everything within the cell with the exception of the nucleus.

Ribosome. Small spherical bodies in the cytoplasm; the cite of protein synthesis; composed of protein and RNA.

The elements of human heredity involve complex processes. Some of the characteristics that involve hereditary processes include physical traits (e.g., height, hair color, eye color), the timing of the onset of puberty, and susceptibility to diseases such as diabetes. These inherited characteristics are subject to the influence of genes and their complex constituents including DNA and RNA. DNA is the "genetic code" or "genetic blueprint" for the transmission of inherited human characteristics. DNA indicates which human traits will be transmitted and expressed in the offspring. In addition, DNA guides growth and development through the lifespan (e.g., rate of growth in childhood, the onset of puberty in adolescence, the onset and duration of the female menopause in adulthood, and the loss in hair in males in adulthood). DNA is composed of molecules of sugar, phosphate, and four bases (cytosine, adenine, guanine, and thymine), which combine in varying patterns with genes. The DNA molecule is in the shape of a double helix resembling a twisted ladder (Fig. 4.6). The strands of the DNA molecule that make up the "sides" of the "ladder" are composed of alternating sugar and phosphate molecules. The "rungs" of the ladder are made up of combinations of adenine and thymine or cytosine and guanine. The *order* of the chemical combinations of these bases on the rungs of the ladder determine the genetic code for a given characteristic to be inherited. Specifically, this order determines the types of proteins that will be synthesized in each human cell. Different patterns of DNA are different genes which, in turn, direct the production of different enzymes. The activity of different genes in different cells directs some cells to become bones, others to become body organs, and so on.

Since DNA is found within the nucleus of a given cell, it is necessary for the "message" of DNA to be transmitted outside the nucleus to the site of cell growth (cytoplasm). This DNA information is carried by RNA (ribonucleic acid). There are two types of RNA molecules that accomplish this transfer function, messenger RNA and transfer RNA.

Production of Body Cells and Sex (Germ) Cells

After conception, the growth and development of the human being proceeds as a result of cell division. It is important to note that there are two different types of cells in the human body: **body (somatic) cells** and **sex (germ) cells,** from which sperm and ova develop. Body cells are reproduced through the process of cell division called *mitosis* (Fig. 4.7). Through mitosis, cells divide and make exact copies of themselves. The "directions" for the development of these new cells come from the DNA molecule in the genes.

> *DEFINITIONS*
>
> **Mitosis.** The process in which a single body cell divides into two exactly equal parts. Each of the duplicate parts has exactly the same twenty-three pairs of chromosomes as in the original cell.
> **Meiosis.** A type of cell division that occurs only during the production of sex or germ cells (ova and sperm). During this process, each chromosome pair splits and separates so that the resulting ovum or sperm contains only twenty-three single chromosomes.

In contrast, sex or germ cells are produced by a process called *meiosis*. At the time of the final cell division during meiosis, the germ cells split, but the chromosomes do not (Fig. 4.8). Chromosome pairs separate during the formation of

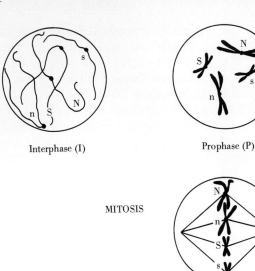

Interphase (I)   Prophase (P)

MITOSIS

Metaphase (M)

Anaphase (A)

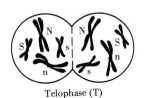

Telophase (T)

FIGURE 4.7
Cell division or mitosis. The diagram shows only two pairs of chromosomes per cell instead of the twenty-three pairs usually present in humans. Diagram drawn by Dr. Dorothy McKeekin, Michigan State University.

male and female sex cells so that each egg or sperm cell carries *half* of the total number of chromosomes. When fertilization occurs, twenty-three chromosomes from the sperm and twenty-three from the ovum unite to define the genetic potential of a new human being.

Because the reproductive cells formed during meiosis have only a random half of the genetic materials of the parent cell, the chance of any two siblings' receiving the same random assortment of chromosomes is virtually nonexistent (except for identical twins, identical triplets, and so on). Or, put another way, the chances of two people having identical chromosomal arrangements are about 1 in 64 trillion! In addition, the process called **crossing over** further increases the likelihood that each sperm and ovum will be unique (and therefore that each child will be unique). The process of crossing over is the exchange of DNA material between chromosomes in a pair during Metaphase I of meiosis (Fig. 4.9).

FIGURE 4.8

Meosis. During both mitosis and meiosis the chromosome containing DNA duplicates. The two processes differ: (1) After mitosis the chromosome number is the same as the original cell; after meiosis the chromosome number is half the original number. (2) In mitosis genes/chromosomes duplicate with each of the two new cells receiving identical genotypes—NnSs. In meiosis genes/chromosomes assort or segregate independently at metaphase 1, leading to only two possible gamete (sperm or egg) genotypes in Telephase II—Ns and nS or NS and ns represent the genes for two characteristics. With 23 chromosomes, each carrying a different expression of the gene (N/n, S/s or Brown/blue eyes, Norman/affected), the number of gamete types will be 2^{23} or $2 \times 2 \times 2. . . .23$ times or 8,388,608. When a sperm fertilizes an egg the chances of two identical independently fertilized eggs ever occurring is $8,388, 698^2$ or 64 trillion to one.

In the female, only one of the four cells produced by meiosis matures into an egg. In the male, all four cells mature.

Interphase in both mitosis and meiosis is not a resting cell. The very elongated chromosomal material with great surface area contains the DNA code controlling the RNA which in turn directs enzyme synthesis and all cellular reactions. Diagram drawn by Dr. Dorothy McKeekin, Michigan State University.

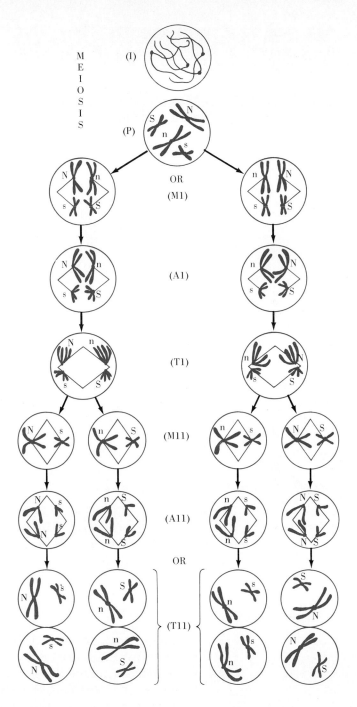

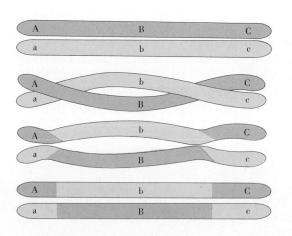

FIGURE 4.9

Crossing over. The diagram shows how the process of crossing over can result in a new organization or grouping of genes on chromosomes. Crossing over sometimes occurs during meiosis. Adapted from Otto and Towle, 1977, p. 628.

Darryl Jacobson

Courtesy Cynthia, Jennifer, and Jill Carmichael

Because the reproductive cells formed during meiosis have only a random half of the genetic materials of the parent cell, the chance of any two siblings receiving the same random assortment of chromosomes is virtually nonexistent (except for identical twins, identical triplets, and so on). Only two of the triplets shown in the photo on the left are identical—the one on the left and the one on the right.

Simple Genetic Transmission

A common observation is that children may or may not resemble their parents. For example, both parents may have brown eyes, and one of their children may have blue eyes. How are characteristics passed on—or not passed on—from parent to offspring?

DOMINANT AND RECESSIVE GENES.   The genetic transmission of most traits (including eye color) is dependent not on a single gene but on several genes. To illustrate genetic transmission more easily, we will discuss a trait or characteristic that is, in fact, dependent on a single pair of genes: phenylketonuria (PKU). **PKU** is an inherited disease that results in the inability to metabolize phenylalanine, which is a component of many foods. If not treated, PKU can result in moderate to severe retardation, as well as other physical problems. (Most states require the testing of newborn children for PKU). In order to explain the transmission of PKU, we use N to symbolize the gene for normal metabolic activity and n to represent the gene for PKU. Related genes, such as N and n, are called *alleles*. In this case, N is the *dominant* gene and n is the *recessive* gene. Individuals can have *three* possible genetic expressions (genotypes) with reference to PKU: *NN, Nn,* or *nn.*

DEFINITIONS

Dominant gene. A gene that always expresses its hereditary characteristic. When paired with a different or subordinate gene for a given trait, the "dominant" gene will prevail in manifesting its hereditary characteristic.

Recessive gene. A gene that expresses its hereditary characteristic *only* when paired with a similar (recessive) gene. When paired with a dominant gene for a given trait, the expression of the hereditary characteristic of the recessive gene is masked. For example, blue-eyed genes are recessive to brown-eyed genes (dominant) and expressed only when pure or exclusively blue-eyed genes are present.

Allele. Any of several alternative or possible genes for a given trait that might be found at the appropriate location on a chromosome.

Genotype. The fundamental hereditary constitution (assortment of genes) of an individual contained in the cells of the human body.

Phenotype. The expressed or observable characteristics of human beings that result from both a particular genotype and a particular environment.

If a mother is *Nn* and a father is *Nn* (see Fig. 4.10), one of three possible *genotypes* can occur at conception: *NN, Nn,* or *nn.* At conception, *each child* of these parents has a 50 percent chance of being an *Nn* genotype, a 25 percent chance of being an *NN* genotype, and a 25 percent chance of being an *nn* genotype.

Which genotype would have normal metabolism, and which would have inherited PKU? An *NN* baby would be normal, as it has two normal genes. The *Nn* babies would also be normal because the *N* gene is *dominant* over the *n* gene, which is *recessive.* The *nn* baby would inherit PKU. It should be noted that the *Nn* offspring are considered *carriers* of the PKU trait (*n*). In other words, they have the trait in their genotypes (genetic formulas) but not in their phenotypes (actual physical characteristics).

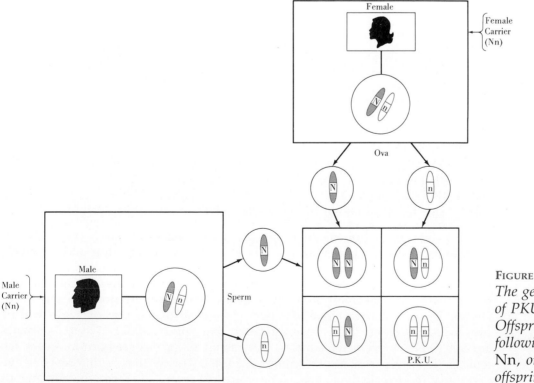

FIGURE 4.10
The genetic transmission of PKU. (Nn *genotype*). *Offspring may have the following genotypes:* NN, Nn, *or* nn. *Only* nn *offspring will have PKU.*

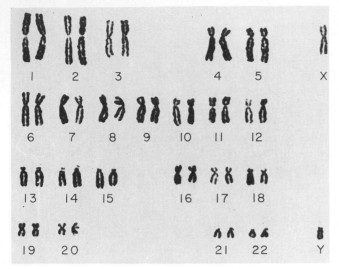

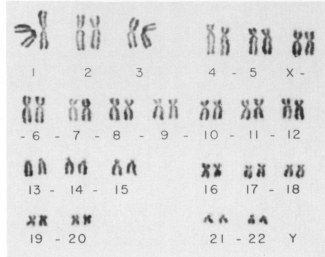

FIGURE 4.11

Male sex chromosomes. The picture shows a karyotype arrangement of normal male chromosomes. The twenty-two paired chromosomes (the autosomes) are arranged in descending order according to size and shape. The X and Y chromosomes, which determine the sex of the individual, are set apart from the autosomes. From the March of Dimes.

FIGURE 4.12

Female sex chromosomes. The diagram shows a karyotype of the chromosomes of a normal female lined up in descending order by size. You may note that the paired autosomes (1–22) are not recognizably different from those of the male (Figure 4.11). There is, however, no Y chromosome (lower right hand corner). Instead there are two XX chromosomes (in the upper right corner). From the March of Dimes

TRANSMISSION OF SEX TYPE.   One of the significant human traits passed on from the adult is the sex of the offspring. As we indicated earlier, each human cell contains twenty-three pairs of chromosomes (with the exception of sex cells, which contain twenty-three single chromosomes). Of the twenty-three pairs of chromosomes, twenty-two pairs are called *autosomes,* and the twenty-third pair is the *sex chromosome* (Figs. 4.11 and 4.12).

> *DEFINITIONS*
>
> **Autosomes.** The first twenty-two pairs of chromosomes of the total twenty-three pairs of chromosomes. Autosomes are responsible for determining the physical characteristics of the child other than the sex.
>
> **Sex chromosome.** The twenty-third pair of chromosomes which is responsible for determining the sex of the child.

In the female, both members of the sex chromosome pair are X chromosomes (XX). In the male, one chromosome of the pair is an X chromosome and the other, much smaller chromosome is a Y chromosome (XY). Each male sperm cell therefore contains either an X or a Y chromosome. Because both female sex-cell chromosomes are X chromosomes, each ovum always has an X chromosome (Fig. 4.13). On the basis of chance alone, the odds are 50–50 that a boy or a girl will be conceived. However, it has been estimated that approximately 130 to 150 males are conceived for every 100 females. Only about 105 males are born for every 100 females (U.S. Department of Commerce, 1985c). This birth-rate difference is evidence that more male than female fetuses are lost prenatally through spontaneous abortions. This higher prenatal fatality rate for males is consistent with postnatal

FIGURE 4.13

Sex determination of offspring. On the basis of chance alone, the odds are 50-50 that either a boy (XY) or a girl (XX) will be conceived.

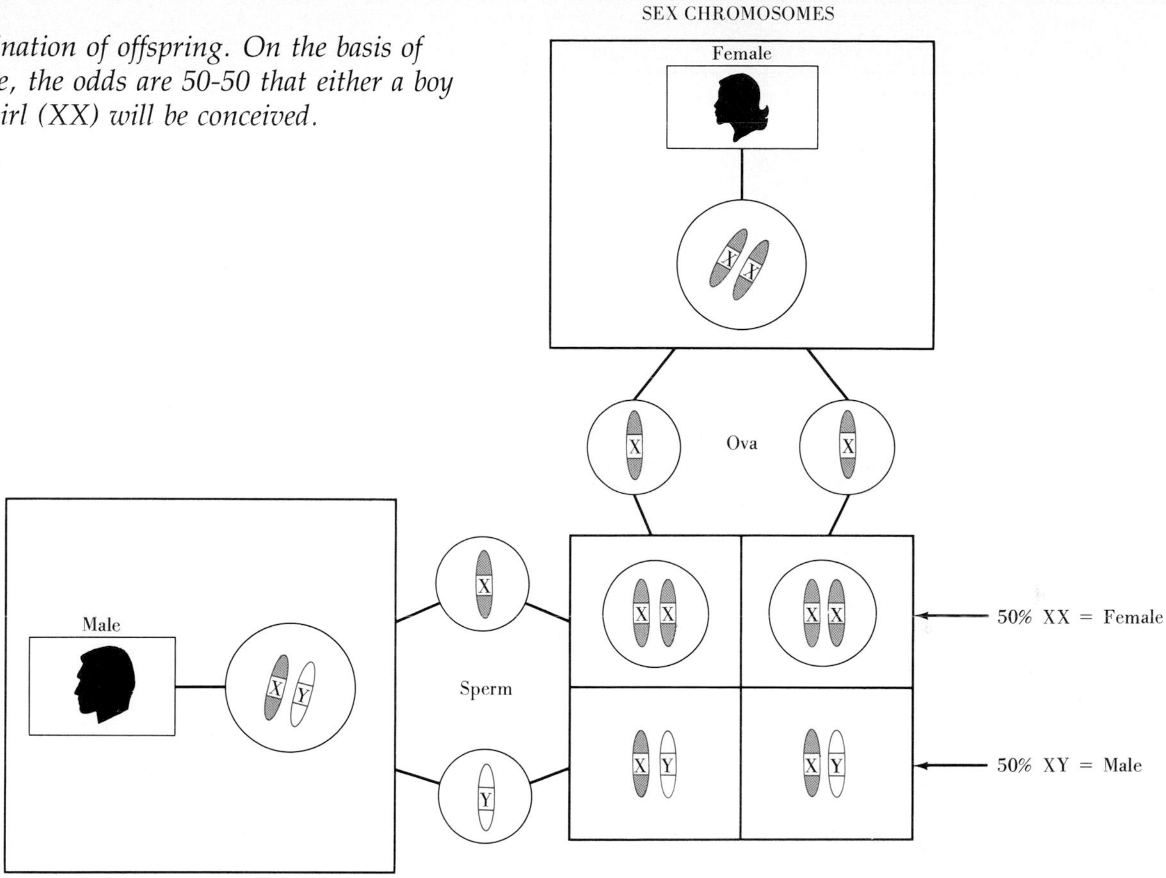

SEX CHROMOSOMES

Female

Ova

Male

Sperm

50% XX = Female

50% XY = Male

survival statistics. For example, males have a higher death rate during infancy than females (U.S. Department of Commerce, 1985c) and have a shorter life expectancy than females. At birth, the life expectancy for males is 70.11 years and for females is 77.62 years (National Center for Health Statistics, 1985). Male babies have more congenital malformations (both major malformations and multiple malformations) than female babies. The reasons for this marked sex difference are not known (Goodman, 1986).

TRANSMISSION OF BIRTH DEFECTS.   Included, unfortunately, in the vast array of traits that some offspring may have are birth defects.

Of all the many hundreds of potentially serious birth defects, only about 25 percent have been clearly identified as genetic "errors." Most of the remaining 75 percent are usually attributed either to *congenital* defects (caused by something going wrong in the womb or in the birth process) or to some "complex" or unknown causes. It is highly probable that a good number of the currently identified unknown causes may yet turn out to be of genetic origin.

Where there is some genetic basis for a birth defect, it usually involves one of the following methods of transmission (see Table 4.1).

1. Dominant inheritance of genetic defects (see Fig. 4.14).
2. Recessive inheritance of genetic defects (see Fig. 4.15).
3. X-linked (sometimes called sex-linked) inheritance of genetic defects (see Fig. 4.16).
4. Chromosomal abnormalities (see Fig. 4.17).

TABLE 4.1

Selected Birth Defects, USA

BIRTH DEFECT	TYPE	CAUSE	DETECTION	TREATMENT	PREVENTION
Down syndrome	functional/ structural: retardation often associated with physical defects	chromosomal abnormality	amniocentesis, chromosome analysis	corrective surgery, special physical training and schooling	genetic services
Markedly low birthweight (prematurity)	structural/ functional: organs often immature	hereditary and/or environmental: maternal disorder or malnutrition	prenatal monitoring, visual inspection at birth	intensive care of newborn, high-nutrient diet	proper prenatal care, genetic services, maternal nutrition
Muscular dystrophy	functional: impaired voluntary muscular function	hereditary: often recessive inheritance	apparent at onset	physical therapy	genetic services
Congenital heart malformations	structural	hereditary and/or environmental	examination at birth and later	corrective surgery, medication	genetic services
Clubfoot	structural: misshapen foot	hereditary and/or environmental	examination at birth	corrective surgery, corrective splints, physical training	genetic services
Polydactyly	structural: multiple fingers or toes	hereditary: dominant inheritance	visual inspection at birth	corrective surgery, physical training	genetic services
Spina bifida and/ or hydrocephalus	structural/ functional: incompletely formed spinal canal; "water on the brain"	hereditary and environmental	amniocentesis, prenatal X ray, ultrasound, maternal blood test, examination at birth	corrective surgery, prostheses, physical training, special schooling for any mental impairment	genetic services
Cleft lip and/or cleft palate	structural	hereditary and/or environmental	visual inspection at birth	corrective surgery	genetic services
Diabetes mellitus	metabolic: inability to metabolize carbohydrates	hereditary and/or environmental	appears in childhood or later; blood and urine tests	oral medication, special diet, insulin injections	genetic services
Cystic fibrosis	functional: respiratory and digestive system malfunction	hereditary; recessive inheritance	sweat and blood tests	treat respiratory and digestive complications	genetic services
Sickle-cell anemia	blood disease: malformed red blood cells	hereditary: incomplete recessive—most frequent among blacks	blood test	transfusions	genetic services

TABLE 4.1
Selected Birth Defects, USA (continued)

BIRTH DEFECT	TYPE	CAUSE	DETECTION	TREATMENT	PREVENTION
Hemophilia (classic)	blood disease: poor clotting ability	hereditary: sex-linked recessive inheritance	blood test	clotting factor	genetic services
Congenital syphilis	structural: multiple abnormalities	environmental: acquired from infected mother	blood test, examination at birth	medication	proper prenatal care
Phenylketonuria (PKU)	metabolic: inability to metabolize a specific amino acid	hereditary: recessive inheritance	blood test at birth	special diet	carrier identification, genetic services
Tay Sachs disease	metabolic: inability to metabolize fats in nervous system	hereditary: recessive inheritance—most frequent among Ashkenazic Jews	blood and tear tests, amniocentesis	none	carrier identification, genetic services
Thalassemia	blood disease: anemia	hereditary: incomplete recessive inheritance	blood test	transfusions	carrier identification, genetic services
Galactosemia	metabolic: inability to metabolize milk sugar galactose	hereditary: recessive inheritance	blood and urine tests, amniocentesis	special diet	carrier identification, genetic services
Erythroblastosis (Rh disease)	blood disease: destruction of red blood cells	hereditary and environmental: Rh− mother has Rh+ child	blood tests	transfusion: intrauterine or postnatal	Rh vaccine, blood tests to identify women at risk, genetic services
Turner syndrome	structural/ functional	chromosomal abnormality	amniocentesis, chromosome analysis	corrective surgery, medication	genetic services
Congenital rubella syndrome	structural/ functional: multiple defects	environmental maternal infection	antibody tests and viral culture	corrective surgery, prostheses, physical therapy and training	rubella vaccine

DOMINANT INHERITANCE

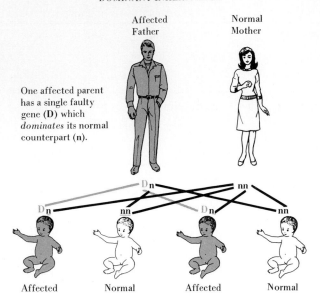

Affected Father / Normal Mother

One affected parent has a single faulty gene (**D**) which *dominates* its normal counterpart (**n**).

D n / nn

D n — Affected; nn — Normal; D n — Affected; nn — Normal

Each child's chances of inheriting either the **D** or the **n** from the affected parent are 50%.

Currently, close to 2,000 confirmed or suspected autosomal dominant disorders have been catalogued. Examples include:

- achondroplasia—*a form of dwarfism*
- chronic simple glaucoma (some forms)—*a major cause of blindness if untreated*
- Huntington's disease—*progressive nervous system degeneration*
- hypercholesterolemia—*high blood cholesterol levels, propensity to heart disease*
- polydactyly—*extra fingers or toes*

FIGURE 4.14
Dominant inheritance of genetic defects. An affected child must have one parent with the same disorder. In such a family, there is a 50 percent risk that each child will have the disorder, even though it may not be apparent at birth. There is an equal likelihood that a child will not receive this defect. Therefore, both this child and his or her own children will be free of the disorder and will not carry any gene for the disorder. Figures 4.14–4.17 courtesy March of Dimes.

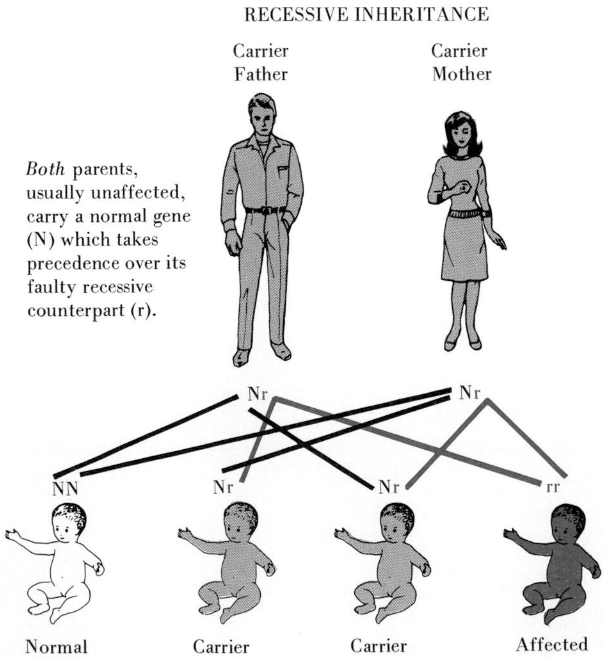

RECESSIVE INHERITANCE

Carrier Father / Carrier Mother

Both parents, usually unaffected, carry a normal gene (**N**) which takes precedence over its faulty recessive counterpart (**r**).

Nr / Nr

NN — Normal; Nr — Carrier; Nr — Carrier; rr — Affected

The odds for each child are:
1. A 25% risk of inheriting a "double dose" of r genes which may cause a serious birth defect.
2. A 25% chance of inheriting two Ns, thus being unaffected.
3. A 50% chance of being a carrier as both parents are.

Among more than 1,000 confirmed or suspected autosomal recessive disorders are:

- cystic fibrosis—*affects function of mucus and sweat glands*
- galactosemia—*inability to metabolize milk sugar*
- phenylketonuria—*essential liver enzyme deficiency*
- sickle cell disease—*blood disorder primarily affecting blacks*
- thalassemia—*blood disorder primarily affecting persons of Mediterranean ancestry*
- Tay-Sachs disease—*fatal brain damage primarily affecting infants of East European Jewish ancestry*
- Gaucher disease—*most commonly a chronic disorder affecting liver, spleen, bones, and blood, primarily in Jews of East European descent*

FIGURE 4.15
Recessive inheritence of genetic defects. Both parents of an affected child appear normal. However, both carry the harmful gene although neither may be aware of it. Unfortunately, recessive abnormalities tend to be more severe than dominant ones.

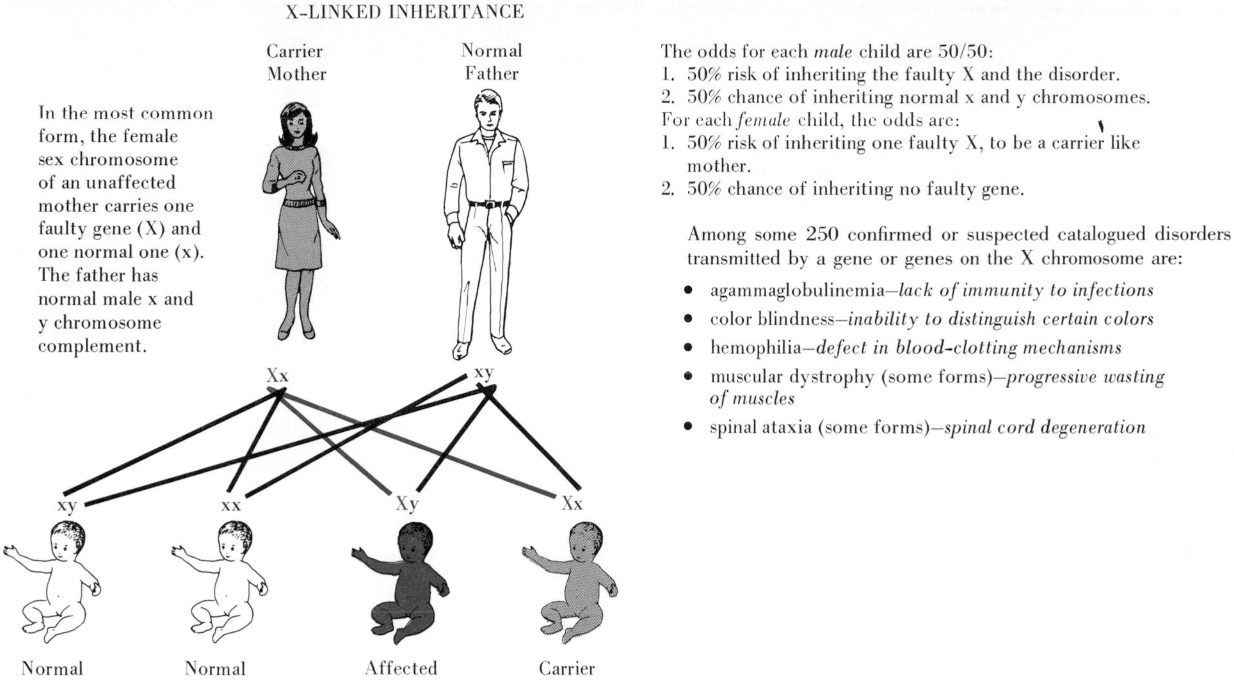

X-LINKED INHERITANCE
Carrier Mother
Normal Father
In the most common form, the female sex chromosome of an unaffected mother carries one faulty gene (X) and one normal one (x). The father has normal male x and y chromosome complement.
Xx
xy
xy
xx
Xy
Xx
Normal
Normal
Affected
Carrier
The odds for each *male* child are 50/50:
1. 50% risk of inheriting the faulty X and the disorder.
2. 50% chance of inheriting normal x and y chromosomes.
For each *female* child, the odds are:
1. 50% risk of inheriting one faulty X, to be a carrier like mother.
2. 50% chance of inheriting no faulty gene.
Among some 250 confirmed or suspected catalogued disorders transmitted by a gene or genes on the X chromosome are:
• agammaglobulinemia—*lack of immunity to infections*
• color blindness—*inability to distinguish certain colors*
• hemophilia—*defect in blood-clotting mechanisms*
• muscular dystrophy (some forms)—*progressive wasting of muscles*
• spinal ataxia (some forms)—*spinal cord degeneration*

FIGURE 4.16
Sex-linked inheritance of genetic defects.

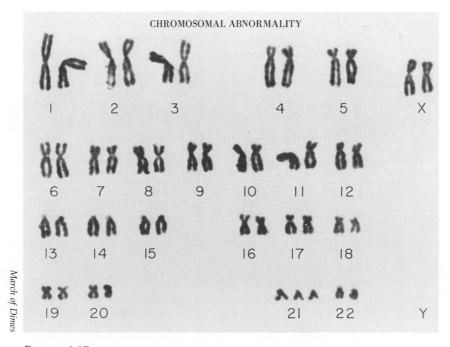

CHROMOSOMAL ABNORMALITY
1
2
3
4
5
X
6
7
8
9
10
11
12
13
14
15
16
17
18
19
20
21
22
Y

March of Dimes

FIGURE 4.17
Down syndrome, a chromosomal abnormality. The karyotype in the diagram is that of a female with an extra chromosome, Number 21. This extra chromosome is responsible for the set of symptoms known as Down syndrome (i.e., mental retardation and abnormal physical features).

Genetic Counseling

Genetic counseling provides and interprets medical information based on expanding knowledge of human genetics, the branch of science concerned with heredity. Its major goal is to convey understanding of birth defects to affected families, and enable prospective parents to make informed decisions about childbearing.

Birth defects may be inherited or may result from environmental factors—unfavorable "living conditions" for the fetus—during prenatal development. Often they reflect a combination of the effects of heredity and environment.

Although specific birth defects may seem relatively uncommon, together they occur in about 7 percent of all births and the total number of affected families is well in the millions. Each year more than 250,000 American babies are born with physical or mental defects of varying severity. Some of these defects, though present at birth, do not become apparent until months or years later.

Using as tools the basic laws governing heredity, plus knowledge of the frequency of specific birth defects in the population, the genetic counselor can often predict the probability of recurrence of a given abnormality in the same family. Sophisticated new techniques are being rapidly developed and refined to translate statistical estimates into accurate forecasts, using tests before pregnancy and before birth to determine the chance of bearing a child with a defect, and presence or absence of a growing list of inherited defects.

Genetic counseling is concerned with all factors causing birth defects. A counselor must first determine whether the defect in question is transmitted by the genes passed from parents to children or due to infection or other influence during life in the womb. Appropriate information can enable families and physicians to prevent defects or, in some cases, to reverse or at least reduce their damaging effects.

From March of Dimes, 1987, p. 5.

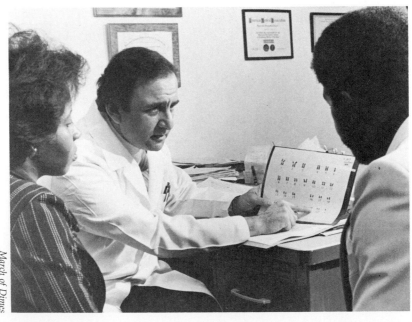

March of Dimes

Genetic counseling helps prospective parents know the risk of having a baby with a birth defect, and often alleviates their concern.

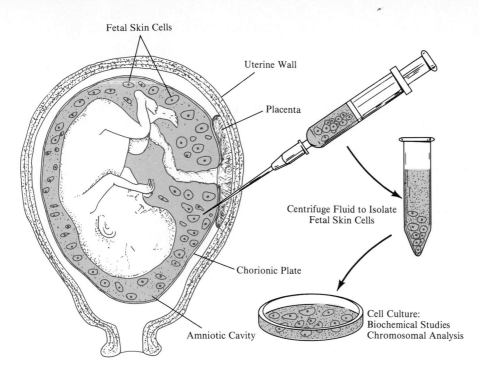

Fetal Skin Cells
Uterine Wall
Placenta
Centrifuge Fluid to Isolate Fetal Skin Cells
Chorionic Plate
Amniotic Cavity
Cell Culture: Biochemical Studies Chromosomal Analysis

Fetal screening and amniocentesis. After 14 weeks of fetal development, an ultrasonic scan will reveal the location of the fetus and placenta in the uterus. The physician can then guide a hypodermic needle into the amniotic sac and withdraw a sample of amniotic fluid containing fetal cells. These cells can then be grown in tissue culture for chromosome and biochemical analysis. Several serious hereditary diseases can be detected in this way, allowing the woman to consider the option of continuing the pregnancy or having an abortion.

DEFINITION

Congenital defects. These are abnormalities that are present at birth. They may be influenced by genetic factors or they may be due to the effect of environmental factors on the unborn child.

Figures 4.14, 4.15, and 4.16 show the first three methods of transmitting birth defects. We now turn to chromosome abnormalities. These abnormalities are not specifically genetic in origin; they result from accidents that occur to a sperm or an egg cell, producing an abnormal assortment of chromosomes. The phenomenon of physical abnormalities and mental retardation called *Down syndrome* is an example. This abnormality occurs in one of every two thousand newborns. In **Down syndrome,** the child is born with *three* rather than *two* of the chromosomes numbered 21 (Fig. 4.17). The mother and father of such a child are normal except in the rare case of a woman with Down syndrome who gives birth to a child; the copying or replication error occurs either in the germ cell or in the initial cell division of the embryo.

Complex Genetic Transmission

If all traits followed the pattern of inheritance described for PKU (controlled by one gene pair), there would be a limited number of categories of height, or pigmentation, or intelligence in humans. The fact that there is great variation in these traits means that more gene pairs are involved (polygenic)—the more genes, the more diversity.

Two blue-eyed people can produce a child with brown eyes; a modifying gene has suppressed the gene for brown in one parent. It is very rare, but a child can have two genes for PKU and be normal. For some unknown reason the PKU gene is not expressed completely.

There are several kinds of epilepsy. The type induced by physical injury is not inherited. Another form of epilepsy is inherited and is expressed. (It is a genetic-dominant trait.) Another inherited type is expressed—only if one has a predisposition—when the person is subjected to stress, high temperature, hypoglycemia (low blood sugar), or photic stimulation (e.g., flashing lights).

A PARADOX.   Persons with one gene for sickle-cell anemia or thalassemia do not have these diseases, but they do have the trait. These people are resistant to malaria. On the other hand, people with two of these genes are debilitated by the respective diseases. There is a high frequency of sickle-cell anemia only in those parts of Africa and the Mediterranean where the incidence of malaria is high. Likewise, there is a high frequency of thalassemia only in those parts of the Middle East, southern Asia, and Africa where the incidence of malaria is high. This leads to the question of whether those *populations* that have a high frequency of PKU, cystic fibrosis, or Tay Sachs disease may also be more vigorous (have more surviving offspring) in a particular environment if they have the *trait* (one recessive gene for the disease and one normal gene) rather than the disease itself (two recessive genes). This, of course, is only speculation based on the *assumption* that the relatively high frequency of the disease and the trait in their populations might serve a positive evolutionary or adaptive function.

WHAT IS NORMALCY?   Most of the examples given in the preceding sections deal with what have been called genetic "defects." Actually there is evidence from detailed studies of the amino acids in protein molecules (i.e., hemoglobin, which is the iron-containing protein compound in blood) that most genes, and even the changes in them (mutations), are neutral. They do not reduce or enhance one's chances for survival under present conditions. These genes have not received much attention because they are not harmful. They are not very conspicuous (Volpe, 1981).

An example of such a neutral gene is the one for the production of the enzyme *lactase* that helps human beings digest milk. The largest single nutrient in milk is a natural sugar called *lactose*. In order for individuals to digest milk, it is necessary to produce *lactase*. Almost all infants are born with the ability to produce lactase and thus are able to digest lactose. Most infants continue to produce enough lactase at least until five years of age. When the human body ceases to produce lactase in sufficient quantity, the digestion of milk or milk products becomes difficult. This condition (called *lactase deficiency*) typically appears in the first two decades of life and is characterized by such symptoms as cramps, gas, diarrhea, and bloating. There is evidence that only in those populations descended from northern Europeans does the production of this enzyme persist throughout adulthood (Kolars et al., 1984). In fact, a surprisingly high proportion of the world adult population (almost 75 percent) has a lactase deficiency (Kolars et al., 1984). Groups that are particularly vulnerable include American Indians, Central and South Americans, Asians, blacks, Ashkenazic Jews, and Mediterraneans (Lact Aid, 1985). These people, which includes many of us, are all considered *normal*. The genetic circumstance resulting in such widespread lactase deficiency is considered relatively neutral because such individuals can deal with the problem through dietary substitutions or supplements (e.g., eating dairy products that are low in lactose, such as cheese and yogurt, or getting calcium through vitamin supplements).

Prenatal Development

The months from conception to the birth of the child are marked by significant developments that have a profound impact on the rest of the individual's life.

> DEFINITION: THE TRIMESTERS OF PREGNANCY
>
> **First trimester**—conception until the end of the third month of pregnancy.
> **Second trimester**—the fourth, fifth, and sixth months of pregnancy.
> **Third trimester**—the seventh, eighth, and ninth months of pregnancy.

Germinal Stage

When fertilization occurs, the sets of twenty-three chromosomes contributed by the reproductive cell of each parent line up to form twenty-three pairs of chromosomes. This paired arrangement will be repeated in each new cell that is developed from this first cell, or fertilized egg. Although the chromosomes and the genes on the chromosomes contain the individual's genetic potential, they are not the only determinant of development. From the very beginning—indeed, from the moment of conception—the development of the individual is a product of *both* heredity and environment.

> DEFINITION
>
> **Blastocyst (blastula).** A hollow ball of cells that has developed from the fertilized egg. This stage of development lasts for about a week after conception, until the sphere is implanted in the uterine wall. During the blastocyst period, cells begin to differentiate.

As the fertilized zygote or egg travels down the Fallopian tube, it continues to divide. First it divides into two cells; then the two cells divide into four in a geometric progression (2, 4, 8, 16, 32 . . .). This process of division continues as the zygote floats in the uterus and becomes embedded in the uterine wall. About five days after conception, a hollow cluster of cells has been formed. This cluster is called a *blastocyst* (see Figs. 4.18 and 4.19). The cells of the blastocyst have begun to differentiate according to future functions. Two layers of cells are forming:

Three Stages of Prenatal Growth

1. **Germinal stage.** This is the period of development from fertilization until approximately the end of the second week after conception. This period ends when the fertilized egg (ovum), or *blastocyst*, is implanted in the wall of the uterus.
2. **The embryonic stage.** This stage covers the six-week period from about the end of the second week until about the conclusion of the second month after conception. At the end of this period, the first bone cell is developed and the embryo appears to be a miniature human being. In other words, the embryo has all of its essential parts.
3. **The fetal stage.** This period lasts from about the end of the second month until birth.

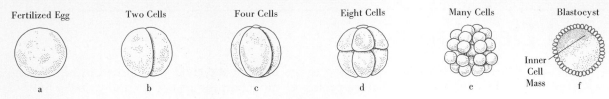

Fertilized Egg   Two Cells   Four Cells   Eight Cells   Many Cells   Blastocyst

FIGURE 4.18

The blastocyst. As the fertilized egg travels down the Fallopian tube, it divides.
After about one week, a hollow cluster (blastocyst) of 1,000 cells is formed. From
Otto and Towle, 1977, p. 627.

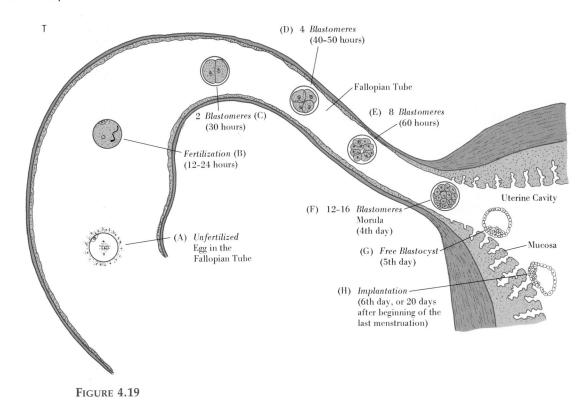

FIGURE 4.19

From ovulation to implantation. (A) The ovary releases one egg (more eggs could
result in multiple births); (B) the egg is fertilized; (C) the fertilized egg or zygote
divides into two cells or blastomeres *as it travels down the Fallopian tube; (D)*
4 blastomeres at 40-50 hours; (E) 8 blastomeres at 60 hours; (F) 12–16
blastomeres at 4 days (called morula*); (G) by the fifth day the fertilized egg*
forms a central cavity and is called a blastocyst*; (H) the blastocyst implants*
itself on the uterine lining or mucosa *on the sixth day. Based on Tuchmann-*
Duplessis, David, and Haegel, 1972, 1975.

(1) an outer layer that serves nourishing and protective functions and will become
the *placenta* (the organ through which the baby is attached to the mother), the
umbilical cord (which attaches the baby to the placenta), and the amniotic sac (the
membrane filled with amniotic fluid that completely surrounds the embryo by the
eighth week after conception); (2) an inner cell cluster that becomes the embryo.
At the end of the germinal period, the unborn infant is about the *size of the period*
at the end of this sentence. The first prenatal stage, or the germinal stage, ends
when the blastocyst is embedded in the uterine wall.

Embryonic Stage

After implantation in the uterine wall, the second (embryonic) stage begins. The embryo now receives nourishment from the mother by means of the umbilical cord, which is attached to the placenta. The embryo (and later, the fetus) receives oxygen, water, immunities to some disease (e.g., measles, polio, and hepatitis), and nutrients (e.g., sugars, fats, and proteins) from the mother across membranes in the placenta. The mother's and infant's bloodstreams are not directly connected. Waste products from the embryo also pass through these membranes to the mother. Unfortunately, some diseases and drugs from the mother (e.g., rubella, mumps, thalidomide, and heroin) also pass through these membranes.

During this period, the embryo is growing rapidly. At the end of the first month, three differentiated cell layers have developed in the embryo (Fig. 4.20):

1. The **ectoderm** (outer layer) produces the skin, the sense organs, and the nervous system.
2. The **mesoderm** (middle layer) produces the muscles, the circulatory system, and the excretory system.
3. The **endoderm** (inner layer) produces the gland systems and lungs (see Table 4.2).

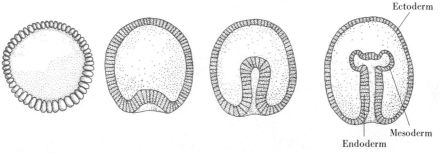

FIGURE 4.20

The differentiation of the embryo. After implantation in the uterine wall, the embryo grows rapidly. By the end of the first month, three cell layers have been differentiated. These cell layers, in turn, give rise to the tissues and organs of the human body. Adapted from Moon, Otto, and Towle, 1963, p. 616.

TABLE 4.2

Structures Formed from Specific Primitive Germ Layers

ECTODERM	MESODERM	ENDODERM
Skin and skin glands	Connective tissue	Lining of alimentary canal from pharynx to rectum
Hair	Bone	
Most cartilage	Most muscles	Thyroid and parathyroids
Nervous system	Kidneys and ducts	Trachea and lungs
Pituitary gland	Gonads and ducts	Bladder
Lining of mouth to the pharynx	Blood, blood vessels, heart, and lymphatics	
Part of the lining of rectum		
Adrenal medulla		

From Otto and Towle, 1977, p. 627.

Actual Size:
¼ inch

Heart pulsating and pumping blood.

Backbone and spinal canal forming.

No eyes, nose or external ears visible.

Digestive system beginning to form.

Small buds which will eventually
become arms and legs are present.

At End of Four Weeks

FIGURE 4.21

The embryo at four weeks. Courtesy Carnation Company.

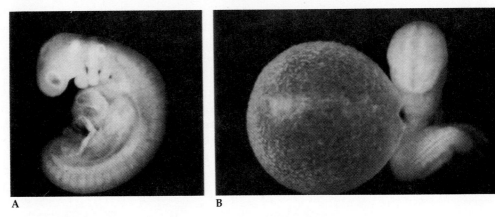

A   B

FIGURE 4.22

(A) Side view of a 28-day-old human embryo. (B) Photograph of the same embryo taken at a different angle, showing the size of the yolk sac. From Streeter. Courtesy Carnegie Institution of Washington.

At End of Eight Weeks

About 1 1/8 inches long.

Weighs about 1/30 ounce.

Face and features forming: eyelids fused.

Limbs beginning to show distinct divisions
into arms, elbows, forearm and hand,
thigh, knee, lower leg and foot.

Distinct umbilical cord formed.

Long bones and internal organs developing.

Tail-like process disappears.

FIGURE 4.23

Human fetus at eight weeks. Carnation Company.

At this point, the embryo is ten thousand times larger than the original zygote. The embryo is crescent-shaped and about three-sixteenths of an inch long. By this time, a beating heart has appeared in the embryo. Blood is flowing through very tiny veins and arteries. In addition to a heart, the embryo also has a very tiny brain, kidney, liver, and digestive tract (Figs. 4.21 and 4.22). At the end of the second month, the embryo is about one and one-eighth inches long. Virtually all of the body systems that will be found in the newborn have developed, at least to a somewhat primitive level. The head of the embryo is virtually one-half of the

TABLE 4.3

Approximate Periods of Critical Differentiation for Some Organs

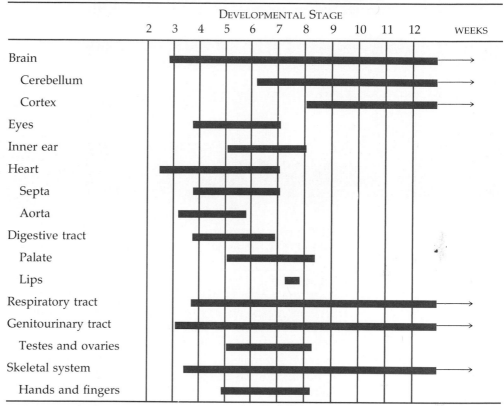

From Whaley, 1974, p. 16.

total body length. The forehead is conspicuous because of the early development of the brain. Facial features, including eyes, ears, nose, lips, and tongue, are present (Fig. 4.23).

Thus, the first two months of embryo development are particularly crucial. By the end of the embryonic period, at around eight weeks, about 95 percent of all body parts have been developed (see Table 4.3), and the fetus has increased in size by 2 million percent. Much growth and development remain; however, they will be an extension of what already exists. Because foundational development is so rapid and critical during this period, the unborn child is extremely vulnerable to disruptions of normal growth, including influences from the environment. We discuss some of these influences later in this chapter.

Fetal Stage

Around the end of the second month after conception, the term *fetus* is applied to the unborn child. Technically, an embryo is called a fetus when the first bone cell appears. The fetal stage lasts about seven months. It is the longest of the prenatal stages. At the end of the third month, the fetus is about three inches long and weighs about one ounce. During this stage, the fetus is capable of breathing movements, sucking movements when the mouth area is stimulated, kicking movements, and head turning. Because the fetus is so small, fetal kicking and

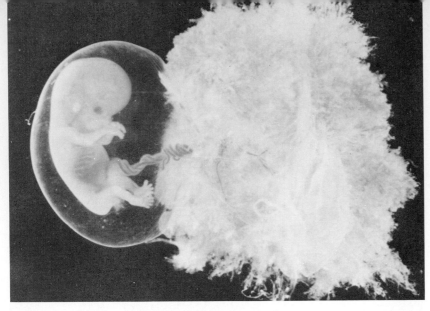

FIGURE 4.24
The fetus at two months. Robert Rugh and Landrum B. Shettles, M.D. Reprinted by permission of Mrs. Robert Rugh. Copyright © 1971.

head turning are not felt by the mother. During this stage, fingers and toes are formed, and fingernails are in the process of forming (Figs. 4.24, 4.25, 4.26, and 4.27).

One of the most interesting events that occurs during the second and early part of the third months is sex differentiation. During this period, the external genitals develop. Up to about five weeks, the fetus has undifferentiated sex gonads (the female ovaries or the male testes; germ-cell producing organs). In the case of the male, genetic action on the Y male sex chromosome causes the fetal gonads to produce the male sex hormone androgen. As a result, the previously undifferentiated sex gonads become male testes. In the case of the female, as there is no Y chromosome (females are XX), there is no production of androgen by the undifferentiated sex gonads. At about the tenth week, the gonads become ovaries.

During the fourth month, the fetus makes considerable gains in growth. The fetus is now more than six inches in length. At this time, we find the continued development of movements, including sucking, head turning, and a variety of limb, foot, and hand movements. It is during the fourth month that the mother

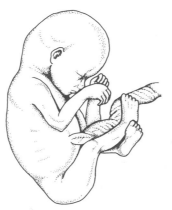

About 3 inches long.

Weighs about 1 ounce.

Arms, hands, fingers and legs, feet, toes fully formed.

Nails on digits beginning to develop.

External ears are present.

Tooth sockets and buds forming in the jawbones.

Eyes almost fully developed, but lids still fused.

Heartbeat can be detected with special instruments.

At End of Twelve Weeks

FIGURE 4.25
The fetus at twelve weeks. "Pregnancy in Anatomical Illustrations," appear courtesy of the copyright owner © Carnation Company, Los Angeles, Ca., 1962.

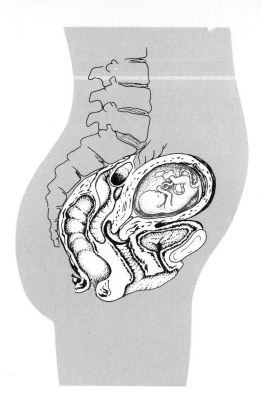

Your baby is now about 3 inches long and weighs about 1 ounce. It may continue to develop in the position shown or may turn or rotate frequently. The uterus begins to enlarge with the growing fetus and can now be felt extending about half-way up to the umbilicus.

Baby's hands are fully formed even at 12 weeks with fingers and nails all distinctly present.

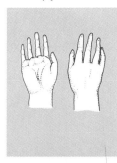

FIGURE 4.26

The fetus at three months. Carnation Company.

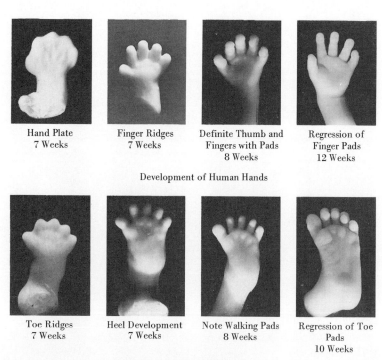

Hand Plate
7 Weeks

Finger Ridges
7 Weeks

Definite Thumb and
Fingers with Pads
8 Weeks

Regression of
Finger Pads
12 Weeks

Development of Human Hands

Toe Ridges
7 Weeks

Heel Development
7 Weeks

Note Walking Pads
8 Weeks

Regression of Toe
Pads
10 Weeks

Development of Human Feet

FIGURE 4.27

The development of embryonic and fetal hands and feet through twelve weeks. Carnegie Institute of Washington.

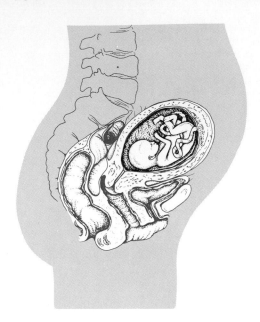

Your baby is now about 6½–7 inches long and weighs about 4 ounces. It has a strong heartbeat, fair digestion and active muscles. Its skin is bright pink and transparent and is covered with a fine down-like hair. Most bones are distinctly indicated throughout the body.

Head is disproportionately large at this stage. Eyes, ears, nose and mouth approach typical appearance. Eyebrows appear.

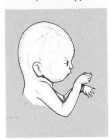

FIGURE 4.28
The fetus at four months. Carnation Company.

FIGURE 4.29
Photograph of a seventeen-week-old fetus. Slightly larger than actual size. Note that the ears stand out from the head and that no hair is visible. Because there is no subcutaneous fat and the skin is thin, the blood vessels of the scalp are visible. Fetuses of this age are unable to survive if born prematurely, mainly because their respiratory system is immature. The alveolar surface area is insufficient, and the vascularity of the lungs is underdeveloped. From K. L. Moore, The Developing Human: Clinically Oriented Embryology. *3rd edition, 1982. Courtesy W. B. Saunders Company.*

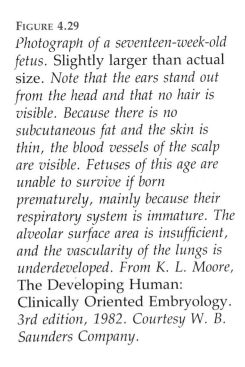

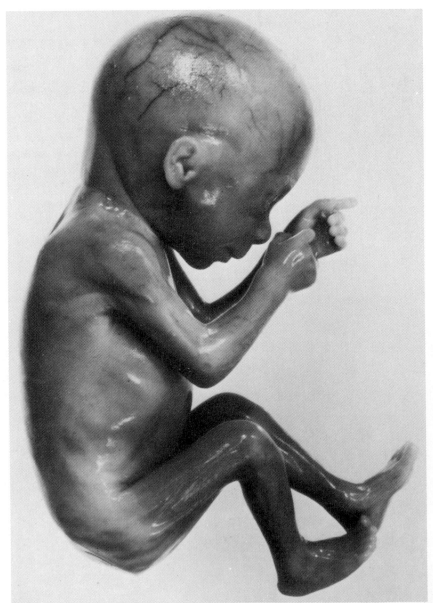

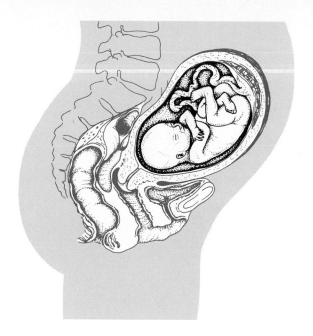

Your baby measures about 10–12 inches long and weighs from ½ to 1 pound. It is still bright red. Its increased size now brings the dome of the uterus to the level of the umbilicus. The internal organs are maturing at astonishing speed but the lungs are insufficiently developed to cope with conditions outside of the uterus.

The eyelids are still completely fused at the end of five months. Some hair may be present on the head.

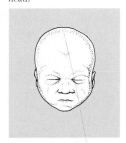

FIGURE 4.30
The fetus at five months. Carnation Company.

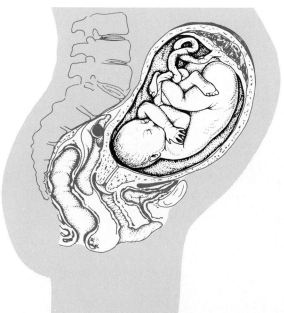

At the end of the 6th month your baby measures 11–14 inches and may weigh from 1¼–1½ pounds. The skin is quite wrinkled and still somewhat red and is covered with a heavy protective creamy coating. The eyelids are finally separated and eyelashes are formed.

Fingernails now extend to the end of the fingers.

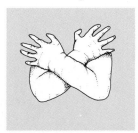

FIGURE 4.31
The fetus at six months. Carnation Company.

begins actually to feel fetal movement. Usually this is a significant milestone for the father as well as for the mother (Figs. 4.28 and 4.29).

The fifth month is the midpoint of the pregnancy. The baby has grown considerably, weighs from one-half to one pound, and is about one foot in length. Evidence suggests that the fetus develops differentiated rhythms of sleeping and waking during the fifth month (Fig. 4.30).

During the sixth month, the fetus ordinarily grows another inch or two and gains another one-half to one pound in weight. Several interesting changes occur during this month: Fetal eyes open for the first time (previously the eyelids had been fused shut); the fetus can make irregular breathing movements; and it has a fairly well developed grasping reflex. Relating to the breathing movement, mothers often report feeling fetal hiccups (Fig. 4.31).

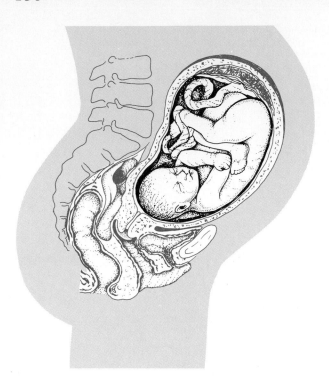

The baby's weight has about doubled since last month and it is about 3 inches longer. However, it still looks quite red, is covered with wrinkles which will eventually be erased by fat. At seven months the premature baby at this stage has a fair chance for survival in nurseries cared for by skilled physicians and nurses.

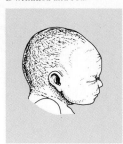

The seven month baby is wrinkled and red.

FIGURE 4.32

The fetus at seven months. Carnation Company.

The seventh month begins the third trimester of pregnancy (Fig. 4.32). Growth begins to slow down during this period. "At seven months or twenty-eight weeks the **age of viability** is reached . . . the baby is capable of independent life and is likely to survive if born then" (Annis, 1978, p. 41). Although a baby can survive if born during the seventh month, it is vulnerable to infection and needs a sheltered environment, such as an incubator (see Fig. 4.33). Babies born during the sixth month may also survive, although high amounts of oxygen may be required to keep them alive. The survival of infants born during the fifth month, or earlier, is unlikely because they are unable to sustain the necessary breathing movements.

During the eighth and ninth months of pregnancy, "the finishing touches" are added to the unborn infant (see Figs. 4.34 and 4.35). The wrinkled skin of the fetus—which makes it look like an elderly person—begins to fill out with fat. The

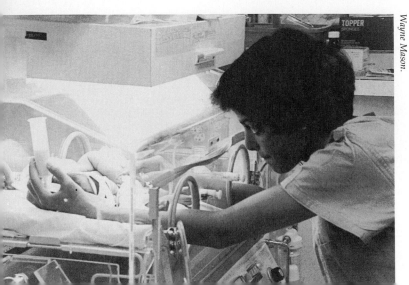

Wayne Mason.

FIGURE 4.33

Infants born prematurely usually require special care.

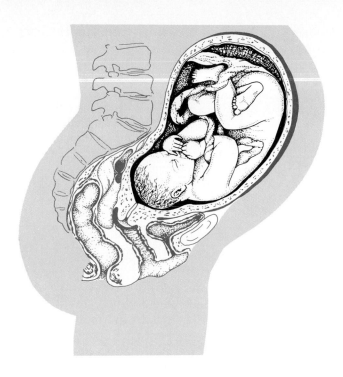

In the absence of premature labor the growth and maturation of the baby in the last two months are extremely valuable. From 2½ to 3 pounds at the beginning of the month, it will add 2–2½ more pounds and will lengthen to 16½–18 inches by the end of the eighth month. The bones of the head are soft and flexible. If born now, its chances for survival are much greater than those of a seven month fetus, although there is a popular fallacy to the contrary.

Ossification of all bones of the hand and wrist is not complete until the child is nearly 17 years old.

FIGURE 4.34

The fetus at eight months. Carnation Company.

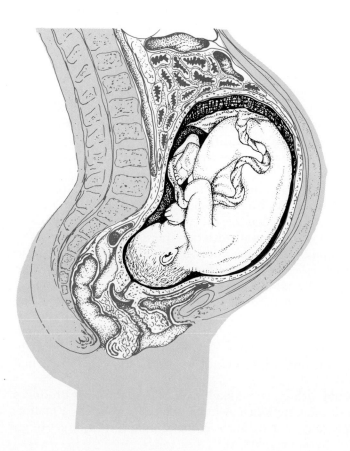

At birth or full term the baby weighs on an average about seven and a quarter pounds if a girl and seven and a half if a boy. Its length is about 20 inches. Its skin is coated with a creamy coating. The fine downy hair has largely disappeared. Fingernails may protrude beyond the ends of the fingers.

The size of the soft spot between the bones of the skull varies considerably from one child to another, but generally will close within 12 to 18 months.

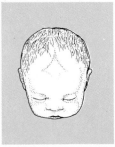

FIGURE 4.35

The fetus at nine months. Carnation Company.

baby gains about one-half pound per week from this time until birth. Annis (1978) described some of the major features of development during this period:

> the baby responds to light and sound, lifts its head, and appears to be pleased when caressed. The effects of cephalocaudal development direction (the sequence of growth from the head downward) are seen again in that at birth the fetal head is 60% of its adult size. The brain of a full-term infant is one-fourth of the adult human brain, which still makes it relatively large for the size of the infant when compared to the infant's other organs that are about ½₀ of the size and weight of adult organs. . . . By the end of the ninth month all intrauterine development has been completed. The baby is now ready to enter the world. (pp. 41–42)

Prenatal Environmental Influences

Ordinarily we think of the prenatal environment as fairly constant and rather simple compared with the more complex environments of childhood and beyond. The fact is that there are many variations in the prenatal environment, both throughout one pregnancy and from one pregnancy to another. Research on prenatal development indicates that both the mother's physical status and her emotional status may have an impact on the development of the fetus, as well as being an important influence on the future general health and adjustment of the child. The following sections describe some of the more important prenatal environmental factors that have been investigated to date.

Before we discuss these factors, however, several definitions of conditions that may accompany prenatal environmental influences will be useful.

DEFINITIONS

Premature infant. A baby with a short gestation period (born early—less than 37 weeks after conception). Premature infants may also have a low birth weight (less than 5½ pounds [2,500 grams]). Previously all low-birthweight babies were also considered premature. Birth weight is no longer a *necessary* criterion for prematurity. Prematurity may not, *in itself*, be harmful since such infants, if below normal weight, typically "catch up" to their normal weights.

Low-birthweight infant. A baby who weighs less than 5½ pounds (2,500 grams). Low birthweight may be due to prematurity (being born too early) or to a pathological condition, making the baby small for its actual age (even when born during a normal gestation period of 37–42 weeks). Whereas premature infants who have a low birthweight may catch up to normal weight, *normal-gestation babies* with a low birthweight of less than 5½ pounds and especially with a very low birthweight of less than 4 pounds, 7 ounces (2,000 grams) ordinarily do not catch up to normals. The fact that these newborns are at a low birthweight for full-term gestation suggests developmental problems possibly associated with maternal malnutrition, alcoholism, and so on. These infants may grow to become abnormally small children and adults with impaired physical and mental abilities.

Teratogen. An agent that increases the likelihood of deviations or produces malformations in a developing fetus. A teratogen that produces a malformation may be direct (e.g., a drug such as thalidomide) or indirect (e.g., a pregnant mother's thyroid condition).

Teratogens

During the course of prenatal development, many environmental factors or agents can increase the probability of fetal deviations or actually produce malformations. Such agents are called *teratogens.* Teratogens can include such factors as maternal diet, drugs, or blood disorders. In addition, such factors as maternal age, size, parity (number of previous children), and stress may influence the developing fetus (Moore, 1983).

Teratogens influence prenatal development in accordance with the following general principles (Moore, 1983):

Variation of teratogen effect in relation to the developmental stage of the unborn child (see Fig. 4.36 and Table 4.3). Teratogens have their strongest impact on newly differentiating and unformed organ systems. Generally, this critical period of sensitivity to teratogens begins the second week after conception and continues through the eighth week and beyond (Fig. 4.36). Since the various organ systems start and stop their development at differing times, their sensitivity to teratogens also varies in time. For example, the most vulnerable period for

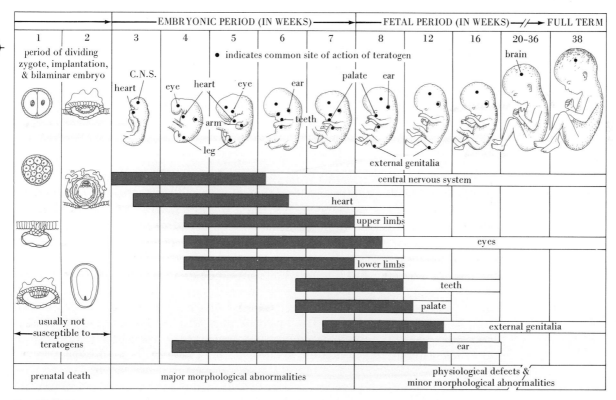

FIGURE 4.36

Teratogens and critical periods in development. The diagram shows the critical periods of development. Colored bars indicate less sensitive periods. Each organ or structure has a critical period during which its development may be deranged, and physiological defects, functional disturbances, and minor morphological changes may result from disturbances during the fetal period. Severe mental retardation may result from exposure of the fetus to high levels of radiation during the 8- to 16-week period. From Moore, 1983, p. 111.

the central nervous system is from weeks 3 through 5, and the most vulnerable time for the arms is from the middle of the fourth week through the seventh week.

- *Individual teratogens produce specific developmental deviations.* For example, rubella (German measles) typically affects the unborn child's eyes, heart, and brain. Likewise, the drug thalidomide (no longer used) mainly affects the limbs.
- *The genetic characteristics of both mother and unborn child influence the impact of teratogens.* For example, not all mothers who took thalidomide or who had rubella (during a critical period) had affected children.
- *The physiological status of the pregnant mother.* For example, the impact of a teratogen (e.g., the drug cortisone) may be adversely intensified by maternal nutritional deficiency. Likewise, the impact of maternal pathological conditions such as metabolic disorders or high blood pressure may intensify the negative impact of certain teratogens.

Maternal Diseases and Disorders

A wide range of maternal diseases and disorders can influence prenatal development in accordance with the principles of teratogenic influence discussed above. The time of onset of a disease during pregnancy may be more important than the degree to which the pregnant mother has the disease. For example, a mild case of rubella may be far more harmful to the unborn child during the first months of pregnancy than a more pronounced case during the end of pregnancy.

RUBELLA.   The threat of rubella to the unborn child is strongest during the first three months of pregnancy. The results of rubella can include congenital cataracts, deafness, heart disease, microcephaly, stunted growth, mental retardation, or even death.

VENEREAL DISEASE.   Other diseases that may have a disastrous effect on the newborn are maternal syphilis, herpes simplex, and gonorrhea. If the mother has syphilis, the chances of a spontaneous abortion or stillbirth increase drastically. In addition, the newborn may be deaf, blind, deformed, or mentally retarded. Fetuses under eighteen weeks of age are not susceptible to the disease. The disease can be cured by penicillin, and if it is given before the fetus is eighteen weeks old, the baby is unlikely to be affected.

In the case of both gonorrhea and herpes simplex, babies can become infected during the course of delivery. The result of such an infection can cause damage to the baby's central nervous system or blindness. Since many women may have gonorrhea without any noticeable symptoms, an antibiotic is routinely dropped into the eyes of newborns as a precautionary measure at all hospitals. In the case of herpes, if an active infection is detected in a pregnant woman, a Caesarean delivery may be used to prevent the newborn from contracting an infection in the birth canal. In infants under five weeks of age with an immature immune system, a herpes infection can cause blindness, motor problems, neurological disorders, or in some cases (38 percent) death (Babson et al., 1980).

The most common viral infection known to be teratogenic in humans is cyto-megalovirus (CMV). When it affects the embryo or young fetus during the first trimester, it can be fatal and probably cause the fetus to abort. When the virus affects a second- or third-trimester fetus, it causes abnormalities of the brain and eyes (Moore, 1983). To date there is no known cure for the disease (Truss, 1981).

DIABETES.   Diabetic mothers have an increased risk of toxemia. In addition, they are more likely to have abnormally large babies (weighing more than nine pounds), with resulting delivery complications and a higher-than-average infant mortality rate. Diabetic women are more likely than normal women to have spontaneous abortions and children with malformations.

> *DEFINITIONS*
>
> **Diabetes.** A deficiency in the ability to utilize insulin; there may be a high level of sugar in both blood and urine.
>
> **Insulin.** A hormone produced in the pancreas. The body uses insulin to metabolize carbohydrates (the basic source of energy). Insulin also affects the metabolism of fats and proteins.
>
> **Toxemia.** A condition during pregnancy in which the woman's blood pressure increases. She retains salt and water, she develops swelling (edema), she has albumin (a protein) in her urine, and she can develop seizure activity.

RH FACTOR INCOMPATIBILITY.   Another teratogenic problem involves an incompatibility between the blood types of the mother and child. The **Rh factor** is a genetically determined feature of the blood. About 85 percent of Caucasians are Rh positive (compared with 93 percent of blacks). The Rh factor can become a problem in the marriage of an Rh negative woman and an Rh positive man. This combination occurs in about 12 percent of American marriages (Annis, 1978). Perhaps 18 percent of the children born in these marriages have some form of Rh disease (26,000 children per year). It is possible to determine whether a person is Rh positive or Rh negative by means of a specially developed serum that causes Rh positive blood to agglutinate or clump and does not cause Rh negative blood to clump (March of Dimes, Rh Disease, 1984b).

Rh disease manifests itself in a predictable manner. The Rh positive fetus produces substances, called **antigens,** that pass through the semipermeable membrane of the placenta and enter the Rh negative mother's bloodstream. The mother's bloodstream, in turn, produces Rh antibodies in response to the Rh positive antigens of the fetus. These antibodies pass through the placenta from the mother to the unborn child and attack and destroy fetal red blood cells. The resulting disease, called **erythroblastosis fetalis,** produces severe fetal anemia. **Anemia** results because the level of red blood cells is reduced. The toxic substances produced by the destroyed red blood cells give the skin of the fetus a yellowish color.

Firstborn children are usually not affected by erythroblastosis because it takes the mother some time to develop a high enough level of antibodies. Subsequent children are therefore more likely to suffer the problem of Rh incompatibility. Fortunately, there are medical techniques for treating the problem when it occurs (March of Dimes, Rh Disease, 1984b).

> *DEFINITION*
>
> **Anemia.** A reduction in the number of red blood cells or in their hemoglobin (the oxygen-carrying protein of red blood cells) content, resulting in reduced transport of oxygen to the cells of the body.

Drugs

Both scientists and laypeople have become increasingly aware of the impact of chemicals (in our food and in our environment) on general health. There has been an accompanying awareness of the impact of drugs on the developing fetus (see

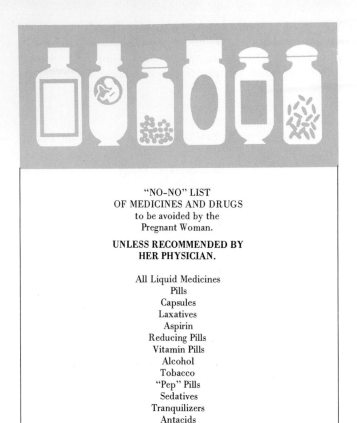

FIGURE 4.37
*"No-No" list of drugs for pregnant women. From
March of Dimes.*

Fig. 4.37). The idea that the fetus is completely insulated from the effects of the outside environment is no longer accepted. It is now recognized that although the placenta prevents the passage of some harmful large-molecule substances, it does act as a passageway for small-molecule substances, which may be either necessary for life (e.g., oxygen and antibodies) or harmful (e.g., thalidomide). In the case of drugs, the stage of development is more important than the strength of the drug in determining the extent or the type of damage that will occur (Moore, 1983). Much of the damage from drugs occurs during the first trimester (the first three months) of pregnancy. Sometimes damage occurs even before the doctor and the woman are certain about pregnancy.

THALIDOMIDE.   Thalidomide provides a tragic example of the effect of drugs on unborn children. The drug was widely available in Scandinavia, West Germany, and England in the early 1960s as a tranquilizer and sedative for "morning sickness." Unfortunately, morning sickness occurs during the critical first trimester of pregnancy, and some ten thousand children were affected. When thalidomide was taken from thirty-four to fifty days after conception (during the critical period), it interfered with the formation of arms, legs, ears (Carlson, 1984). When the drug was taken after this critical period, the arms, legs, and ears were already formed and there was no interference.

LABOR AND DELIVERY DRUGS.   There is also evidence of the influence of drugs taken prior to or during delivery: analgesics (painkillers) and anesthetics (sedatives). Although these drugs affect the newborn, it is not certain what the long-term effects might be. These drugs appear to slow the onset of newborn respiration, decrease the level of consciousness of the newborn, and reduce cerebral functioning (Murray et al., 1981). There is a critical cutoff level of use below which an infant is unaffected by obstetrical drugs. Below such a level (typically a low level) there appear to be no negative effects on the infant. However, such a cutoff level appears to vary with individual characteristics, including the following (Lester, Als, and Brazelton, 1982):

· The physiological condition of the mother.
· The length of labor.
· The size of the baby.
· Maternal attitudes toward a given childbirth experience.

Usually, the effects of drugs taken prior to or during delivery seem to be gone by the end of the first week of life. However, Yvonne Brackbill (1977) found that obstetrical medication may have more lasting effects on the newborn if administered in moderate to heavy dosage levels. She reported that in a group of apparently highly healthy infants and mothers, the infants of the more heavily medicated mothers showed developmental lags in sitting, standing, and moving about when tested at four, eight, and twelve months (in comparison to the less-medicated mothers). Because other factors might be related to levels of medication administered, further research is necessary to clarify the long-term consequences of obstetrical medication.

HEROIN.   The increase in the incidence of heroin addiction in the general population has resulted in an increasing number of infants who are born with an addiction to this drug. Mothers who are heroin addicts have infants who demonstrate withdrawal symptoms. During withdrawal, infants may vomit, become irritable, cry shrilly, become hyperactive, tremble, and have rapid respiration which can result, in some cases, in death during the first few days of life (Householder et al., 1982). Infants born to addicted mothers are frequently premature and have low birthweights. In addition, infant withdrawal symptoms may result in negative maternal reactions which, in turn, negatively influence mother-infant interactional patterns (Ostrea, Chavez, and Strauss, 1979). For example, addicted babies may not respond positively to caregiver cuddling or mother stimulation (as normal babies do) and would thus upset the mother. Furthermore, these mothers may have even more difficulty dealing with their infants because of the weight of their own problems. The result may be a parent-infant interactional system that is adversely affected over the long term. The problems of infants born to female addicts may be further complicated by other factors associated with heroin addiction, including infections, malnutrition, and the threat of Acquired Immune Deficiency Syndrome (AIDS).

NICOTINE.   Cigarette smoking by pregnant women has been found to be related to some serious consequences for the fetus and the newborn infant (Abel, 1984). Infants born to women who smoke are on average 200 grams (7.06 ounces) lighter than infants of nonsmokers. Maternal smoking also increases the risk of spontaneous abortion, fetal death, neonatal death, and other complications (Dwyer, 1984). In addition, there is evidence that SIDS (Sudden Infant Death Syndrome,

Smoking and Pregnancy

If you're pregnant or planning a family, here are three good reasons to quit smoking now.

1. *Smoking retards the growth of your baby in your womb.* Babies of women who smoke weigh, on average, less at birth than babies of women who do not smoke.

   This is caused by several factors. Nicotine restricts the blood vessels and breathing movements and carbon monoxide reduces the oxygen level in the baby's blood. Vitamin metabolism is also disturbed.

   Although the weight loss is quickly regained after birth, a follow-up study showed that the seven-year-old children of mothers who smoked during pregnancy were shorter in average stature, tended to have retarded reading ability, and rated lower in social adjustment than children of mothers who had not smoked during pregnancy.

2. *Smoking increases the incidence of infant mortality.* Statistics show a (positive) correlation between smoking during pregnancy and the incidence of spontaneous abortion and stillbirth. As the figure below shows, women who smoke a pack or more of cigarettes a day during pregnancy incur about a 50 percent greater risk of infant mortality.

   However, research also shows that the added risks of infant death are eliminated if the mother stops smoking before her fourth month of pregnancy.

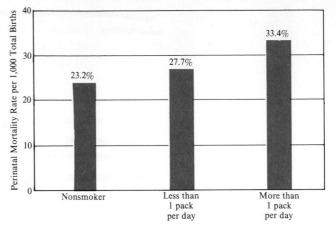

Perinatal mortality rate per 1,000 total births by cigarette smoking category.

From U.S. Dept. of Health, 1976.

3. *Families need healthy parents.* Most parents manage to stay healthy and alive until their children are grown and educated. Smokers, however, subject themselves to a much greater risk of death or disability at a younger age. It is estimated that 80 percent of lung cancers are caused by smoking, causing 101,000 deaths per year in the United States. Death rates from cancer of the pharynx, larynx, esophagus, tongue, and mouth are about six times as great for smokers as for nonsmokers, and death rates from heart disease are twice as high for smokers.

From American Cancer Society, 1982.

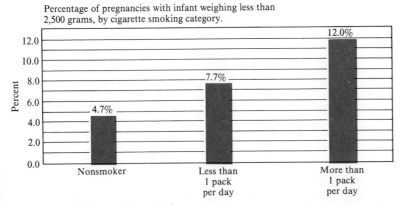

Percentage of pregnancies with infant weighing less than 2,500 grams, by cigarette smoking category.

From U.S. Dept. of Health, 1976.

in which infants under six months of age stop breathing and die) is more common for women who smoke, drink, or use narcotics (Stechler and Halton, 1982). Moreover, it has been shown that in 70 percent of cases of SIDS, mothers smoked during pregnancy (Germouty and Malauzat, 1984). Investigators have concluded that the chances for these unfortunate consequences are increased because maternal cigarette smoking may deprive the fetus of oxygen. This reduction in fetal oxygen may occur in two ways:

1. Cigarette smoking increases the levels of epinephrine and norepinephrine in the blood (which constrict blood vessels) and thus reduces the blood supply (and, therefore, the oxygen level) to the placenta.
2. Cigarette smoking results in a significant increase in the amount of carbon monoxide inhaled. This in turn reduces the amount of oxygen in the blood and, therefore, the amount of oxygen going to the placenta (Quigley et al., 1979).

There is some evidence that the effects of smoking are related to the degree of smoking (i.e., they are dose-related). That is, pregnant women who smoke more than ten cigarettes a day are more than twice as likely to have low-birthweight babies as mothers who do not smoke (U.S. Department of Health and Human Services, 1985b). As a result of these disturbing findings, an increasing number of physicians suggest that pregnant women do not smoke (see box).

ALCOHOL.   The impact of maternal alcohol consumption appears to be substantial. This is the case for both the babies of mothers who are chronic alcoholics and for the babies of mothers who are moderate social drinkers (Ashley, 1981; Streissguth, Barr, and Martin, 1983). A malformation syndrome called the **fetal alcohol syndrome** (FAS) has been found of the babies of mothers who are chronic alcoholics (Ashley, 1981) (see box). Infants who suffer from FAS may demonstrate such defects as prenatal and postnatal growth deficiencies, abnormal development of the heart, defects of the joints, mental retardation, and facial abnormalities. Generally, the damage to the fetus caused by alcohol appears to be the greatest during the *last* trimester of pregnancy (Rosett et al., 1980). There is reason to think that the mental retardation may be due to the cessation of fetal breathing movements caused by the intake of alcohol. For example, it has been found that fetal breathing movements ceased for more than one-half hour for many fetuses (in the last trimester of pregnancy) after their mother drank one ounce of 80-proof vodka (Fox et al., 1978).

In addition to these physical problems, infants of mothers who drink also exhibit behavioral irregularities such as hyperactivity and irritability (Streissguth, Barr, and Martin, 1983). Like infants born with a heroin addiction, infants of chronic alcoholics show withdrawal symptoms such as shaking and vomiting. Problematic infant behaviors were not confined to only infants of chronic or heavy alcohol users. In a study of 417 infants (under three days of age) who were the children of moderate or social drinkers (i.e., mothers who consumed the equivalent of three-fourths of a drink of wine or beer per day), a wide range of learning and behavioral problems were present in the infants (Streissguth, Barr, and Martin, 1983). Maternal alcohol use was related to lower levels of infant arousal, increased time spent in a nonalert awake state, and deficits in learned head-turning or sucking responses. Further research is necessary to determine the long-term impacts, if any, of the problems of infants of moderate drinkers.

Drinking During Pregnancy and Fetal Alcohol Syndrome

When you are pregnant, your unborn baby receives nourishment from you. What you eat, it eats. What you drink, it drinks.

So if you have a drink—beer, wine, or hard liquor—your unborn baby has a drink, too. And because it is so small, it is affected much faster than you are.

That's the immediate effect. But alcohol can also have serious long-lasting effects on an unborn baby.

Scientists have found that many children born to women who drink excessively while pregnant have a recognizable pattern of physical and mental birth defects. They call this the "fetal alcohol syndrome" (FAS).

Growth deficiency is one of the most prominent symptoms. Affected babies are abnormally small at birth, especially in head size. Unlike many small newborns, these youngsters never catch up to normal growth.

Most affected youngsters have small brains and show degrees of mental deficiency. Many are jittery and poorly coordinated and have short attention spans and behavioral problems. Evidence to date shows that their IQs do not improve with age.

FAS babies usually have narrow eyes and low nasal bridges with short upturned noses. These facial features make them look more like one another than like their parents or brothers and sisters. Almost half of them have heart defects, which in some cases require heart surgery.

Not every FAS baby has all of these defects, but there is a relationship between the severity of physical characteristics and the degree of mental impairment. The more severely retarded youngsters are those with the most noticeable physical defects.

Fetal alcohol syndrome is a very real problem in the United States today. It is estimated that there are more than 1 million alcoholic women of childbearing age. And the number is growing—particularly among teenagers.

Babies of adolescents who drink heavily are in double jeopardy. They are at increased risk of being born too small or too soon. If they also are subjected to excessive alcohol from their mothers, they may suffer some characteristics of fetal alcohol syndrome.

No one knows how little—or how much—alcohol may damage an unborn baby. Studies suggest that even moderate drinking is associated with retarded fetal growth. That is one of many questions for which researchers are trying to find answers.

Scientists know that, as with other things pregnant women eat and drink, alcohol passes through the placenta, the organ that nourishes the unborn baby. The drink the baby gets is as strong as the one the mother takes.

It is believed that alcohol adversely affects the baby's fast-growing tissues, either killing cells or slowing their growth. Because the brain develops throughout pregnancy, that is the organ most affected by maternal drinking.

From March of Dimes, 1980b.

Maternal Nutrition

Because food supply for the developing fetus comes from the mother's bloodstream by way of the placenta, there is good reason to be concerned about the expectant mother's diet. Poor or inadequate nutrition is probably the greatest potential threat to the normal development of the unborn child. Malnutrition during pregnancy has been associated with stillbirth, prematurity, low birthweight, and neonatal deaths.

In addition, improper maternal nutrition is also associated with a variety of problems after birth, including rickets, epilepsy, mental deficiency, general weakness, and susceptibility to disease (Annis, 1978). Because of the importance of nutrition, it is desirable for the woman to begin pregnancy with a history of good eating habits and in a healthy, well-nourished state. Even though expectant mothers ordinarily plan their diets carefully during pregnancy, it is difficult to quickly reverse the effects of a previously inadequate diet because of the increased nutritional demands made on the expectant mother by the unborn child.

There is consistent evidence that long-term cognitive deficits occur to children of mothers who were malnourished during pregnancy (Barrett, Radke-Yarrow, and Klein, 1982; Joos et al., 1983). A study of chronically malnourished mothers and children in Guatemala found that maternal caloric supplements during and after pregnancy and child caloric supplements during the first two years after birth were positively related to child development and behavior (e.g., improved social responsiveness) (Barrett, Radke-Yarrow, and Klein, 1982). The investigators concluded that the stress of malnutrition disrupts the infant-caregiver relationship since both mother and infant may lack the energy to reciprocally stimulate one another. The result is infant behavior characterized by withdrawal from potential interactions that support social and cognitive development (Barrett, Radke-Yarrow, and Klein, 1982).

Maternal Age and Size

Although the average female reproductive lifespan extends from about age twelve through forty-five or fifty, the recommended period for childbearing is between the ages of twenty and approximately thirty-five (Goodman, 1986), during which period the highest proportion of healthy children are born. Between twenty and thirty-five years of age, there are also fewer pregnancy complications, including spontaneous abortions, stillbirths, maternal deaths, and prematurity.

Women aged twenty to twenty-four are the most fertile. Fertility is reduced by approximately 6 percent for women aged twenty-five to twenty-nine, 14 percent for women aged thirty to thirty-four, 31 percent for women aged thirty-five to thirty-nine, and declines much more rapidly thereafter. Fertility rates also decline with marriage duration, possibly because of both decreased sexual activity and reproductive impairment connected with more pregnancies (Menken, Trussell, and Larsen, 1986).

More children with developmental problems tend to be born to mothers who are under twenty years of age or over thirty-five. Presumably the reason is that mothers under twenty may have inadequately developed reproductive systems and women over thirty-five may have aging and declining reproductive systems (Goodman, 1986). More specifically, mothers under twenty and over thirty-five or forty are more likely (than mothers between those ages) to experience irregular ovulation (egg production), which tends to be associated with problematic conceptions. The occurrence of such problems as miscarriages, hydrocephalus (water on the brain), and Down syndrome are associated with the advancing age of the mother (see Table 4.4). In approximately 80 percent of the cases, the mother contributes the extra chromosome; the father does so in the remaining 20 percent (Goodman, 1986).

About 2 percent of Down syndrome is inherited. In these families the parent has the twenty-first chromosome attached to another chromosome, so that it is carried into the wrong cell. A chromosome study of the parent will determine if this is the case (Goodman, 1986).

Two factors relative to maternal size may cause pregnancy difficulties for the mother. These are shortness (less than five feet in height) and obesity. Women under five feet tall are more likely to have difficult pregnancies, more difficult labors, and somewhat higher fetal mortality (death) rates. Obesity may be associated with more difficult labor, higher fetal mortality rates, and a higher incidence of toxemia.

TABLE 4.4
Risk of Down Syndrome and Maternal Age

MOTHER'S AGE	RATE	MOTHER'S AGE	RATE
20	1/1,923	35	1/365
21	1/1,695	36	1/287
22	1/1,538	37	1/225
23	1/1,408	38	1/177
24	1/1,299	39	1/139
25	1/1,205	40	1/109
26	1/1,124	41	1/85
27	1/1,053	42	1/67
28	1/990	43	1/53
29	1/935	44	1/41
30	1/885	45	1/32
31	1/826	46	1/25
32	1/725	47	1/20
33	1/592	48	1/16
34	1/465	49	1/12

From Goodman, 1986, p. 121.

Maternal Emotional State

Although the blood systems of the mother and the unborn child are separate, it is possible for the nervous system of the mother to affect the nervous system of the fetus (Standley, Soule, and Copans, 1979). When the mother experiences such emotions as rage, anger, and anxiety, her autonomic nervous system sends chemicals into the bloodstream. In addition to these chemicals (acetylcholine and epinephrine), the mother's endocrine glands secrete hormones that combine to modify cell metabolism. As a result, the composition of the mother's blood changes, and the change agents are passed through the placenta, in turn, producing changes in the fetal blood system and in fetal activity level. Furthermore, the production of epinephrine in the mother as a function of stress may cause the blood flow in her body to be diverted from the uterus to other organs in her body. Such a drop in blood to the uterus and placenta may result in a deficient supply of oxygen for the fetus (Stechler and Halton, 1982).

Although it is quite likely that the expectant mother will experience some stress during the course of the pregnancy, it is usually when stressful and emotional situations are prolonged that more serious consequences for the child may result (Revill and Dodge, 1978; Beck, Geden, and Brouder, 1986). A relationship has been uncovered between stressful life events, anxiety, and pregnancy abnormalities (Beck, Geden, and Brouder, 1986). Some factors that may contribute to prolonged emotional stress are the mother's attitude toward her pregnancy and her attitude toward her marriage. The woman who does not want her child, who is unhappy about being pregnant, or who is unhappily married may be emotionally distressed for extensive periods of time.

Generally speaking, the impact of emotional stress on the unborn child depends on the stage of pregnancy. Severe and prolonged emotional stress early in pregnancy may result in physical abnormalities, whereas such stress later in pregnancy is more likely to result in fetal behavioral changes (rather than physical deformities). There have been reports of severe emotional stress early in pregnancy by women who have had children with cleft lip and palate, Down syndrome, and infant stomach disorder (Reville and Dodge, 1978). On the other hand, mothers who have undergone stress during the latter phases of pregnancy have reported increased levels of general movement or hiccupping by the fetus (Revill and Dodge, 1978). Increased prenatal activity may also result in lower birthweight infants simply because the mother's food consumption may not have kept pace with fetal movement and energy expenditure.

Does maternal stress during pregnancy result in cranky, colicky, or hyperactive infants? Because stressful situations may not simply end with the birth of the child (that is, the stress may continue after birth), it is difficult to distinguish between prenatal and postnatal causes of infant irritability.

Summary

1. The science of genetics has made extraordinary gains in the last two decades. As a result, we are beginning to accumulate a great deal of information about the mechanisms of heredity.

2. The process of *conception* occurs when *fertilization* takes place. The question of an abortion of an embryo or fetus hinges, in part, on a definition of whether life begins at conception or sometime later in pregnancy when the full assortment of human systems becomes differentiated. The notion of when life begins remains controversial among both scientists and the lay public.

3. The elements of human heredity involve complex processes. Some of the characteristics that involve hereditary processes include physical traits (e.g., height, eye color), the timing of the onset of puberty, and susceptibility to diseases such as diabetes or heart disease. These inherited characteristics are subject to the influence of *genes* and their constituents including *DNA* and *RNA*. DNA is the "genetic code" or "genetic blueprint" for the transmission of inherited human characteristics. Since DNA is found within the nucleus of a given cell, it is necessary for the "message" of DNA to be transmitted outside the nucleus to the site of cell growth. This DNA information is carried by RNA.

4. After conception, the growth and development of the human being proceeds as a result of cell division (*mitosis*). There are two different types of cells in the human body—*body* cells and *sex* (germ) cells from which sperm and ova develop. Body cells are reproduced through the process of cell division called *mitosis*. Through mitosis, cells divide and make exact copies of themselves. The "directions" for the development of these new cells come from the DNA molecule in the genes. In contrast, sex or germ cells are produced by a process called *meiosis*.

5. The genetic transmission of most traits is dependent not on a single gene but on several genes. Important concepts for understanding genetic transmission are *dominant genes* and *recessive genes*. Where there is some genetic basis for a birth defect, it usually involves one of the following methods of transmission: dominant inheritance, recessive inheritance, sex-linked inheritance, or chromosomal abnormalities.

6. The months from conception to the birth of the child are marked by significant developments that have a profound effect on an individual's development. There are three stages of prenatal growth: the *germinal stage*, the *embryonic stage*, and the *fetal stage*.

7. During the course of prenatal development, many environmental factors or agents can increase the probability of fetal deviations or actually produce malformations. These agents are called *teratogens*. Some of the more important prenatal environmental factors that have been investigated to date include maternal diseases and disorders during pregnancy, drugs, maternal nutrition, maternal physical characteristics, and maternal emotional state.

Key Terms

Age of viability
Allele
Amniocentesis
Anemia
Antigens
Autosomes
Blastocyst (blastula)
Body (somatic) cells
Chromosomes
Complex genetic transmission
Conception
Congenital defects
Crossing over
Cytoplasm
Diabetes
DNA (deoxyribonucleic acid)
Dominant gene
Down syndrome
Ectoderm
Egg
Embryo
Embryonic stage
Endoderm
Enzyme
Erythroblastosis fetalis
Fertilization
Fetal alcohol syndrome
Fetal stage

Fetus
Gametes
Genes
Genotype
Germinal stage
Insulin
Low-birthweight infant
Meiosis
Mesoderm
Mitosis
Phenotype
PKU (phenylketonuria)
Premature infant
Protein
Recessive gene
Rh factor
Ribosome
RNA (ribonucleic acid)
Rubella
Sex chromosome
Sex (germ) cells
Teratogen
Thalidomide
Toxemia
Trimesters of pregnancy
Venereal disease
X-Linked inheritance
Zygote

Questions

1. Define the following terms: amniocentesis, gene, DNA, chromosome. Why is each important to prenatal development?
2. Where there is some genetic basis for birth defects, one of four methods of transmission is usually involved. Name and briefly describe all four.
3. What is the difference between a *genetic* defect and a *congenital* defect?
4. What are the three stages of prenatal growth? What are the four major developments in each stage?

5. What is Fetal Alcohol Syndrome (FAS)?
6. There are many important and controversial ethical questions relating to prenatal development. One of the most prominent and widely discussed issues is abortion. Carefully examine and summarize the arguments of two opposing groups on this issue.

Suggested Readings

ENGLAND, M. A. *Color Atlas of Life Before Birth: Normal Fetal Development*. Chicago: Yearbook Medical Publishers, 1983. An attractive and detailed photographic guide to prenatal development.

GOODMAN, R. M. *Planning for a Healthy Baby*. New York: Oxford University Press, 1986. An excellent and readable book on a broad range of timely questions and issues for planning pregnancy.

MOORE, K. L. *Before We Are Born* (2nd ed.). Philadelphia: Saunders, 1983. An excellent discussion of the detailed course of prenatal development.

STECHLER, G., and HALTON, A. "Prenatal influences on Human Development." In B. Wolman (ed.), *Handbook of Developmental Psychology*. Englewood Cliffs, N.J.: Prentice-Hall, 1982. An excellent review of research on major factors influencing prenatal development.

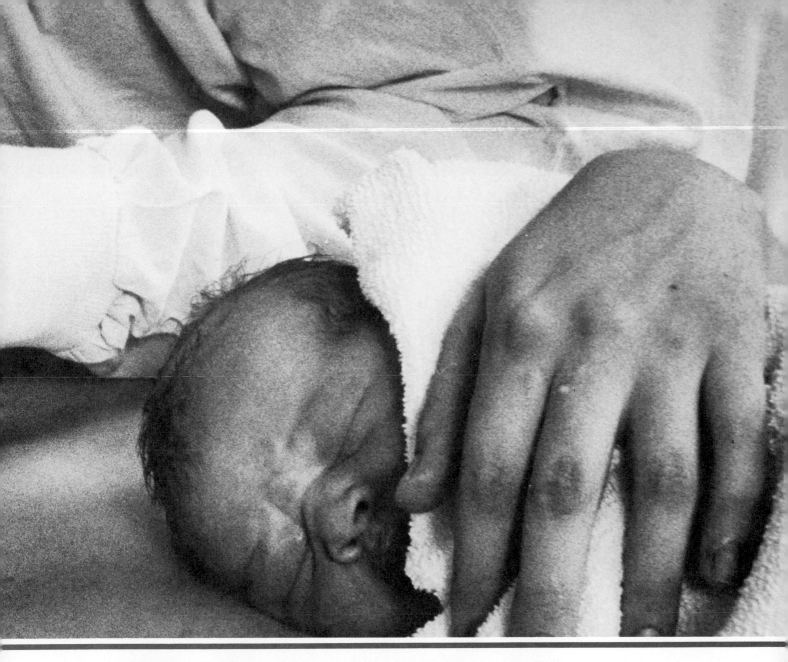

5 Birth: An Emerging Family Relationship

*For there is no king
   had any other first beginning
For all men have
   one entrance into life*
      —*The Wisdom of Solomon*
         in the Apocrypha

Pregnancy and the birth process are neither static nor brief experiences; rather, they are periods of human development filled with growth, change, and exciting enrichment. The birth process is both rewarding and challenging because, at the end, there is literally a new life both for the parents and for the child. Only recently has the period immediately before birth, during birth, and immediately after birth been studied by behavioral scientists with the same intensity and depth as other stages in the human life cycle. All too often, pregnancy and the birth process have been viewed as rather routine although somewhat unusual phenomena. Medical scientists, and particularly obstetrician-gynecologists, tend to describe most pregnancies and births as "routine" or "uncomplicated." Somehow this generalized evaluation conceals the anxieties, joys, frustrations, stresses, altered family relationships, and newly emerging relationships that many families experience during the course of a "routine" pregnancy.

The Birth Process in Context

In this chapter we examine the birth process from a systems, or ecological perspective. As indicated in Chapters 1 and 2, such a perspective emphasizes the *interaction* between the developing person and the contexts of development, which include the family, the neighborhood, the peer group, the schools, the world of work, and so on. The focus here is on the birth process as an emerging relationship between the newborn and the parents.

Before we discuss the birth process, however, it is important to place this process in context. Figure 5.1 illustrates some of the important factors in this context, including:

- The childbirth experiences of the father and the mother.
- The relationship of the mother and the father.
- Existing cultural and social attitudes toward pregnancy and childbirth (e.g., is childbirth an experience for the family or only for the mother, the newborn, and the physician?).
- Existing support systems (including hospital practices and available educational programs).

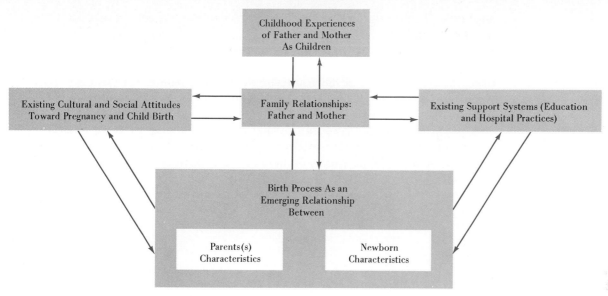

FIGURE 5.1
An ecosystems perspective of the birth process.

Development of a Parent-Newborn Relationship

In the following chapters we explore the development of maternal-infant bonding in greater detail. Here we sketch some of the factors that contribute to such bonding both prior to birth and immediately after birth. In discussing this most important issue, it is important to note that the event of childbirth is entering a period of dramatic change—both for the health care system and for the expecting families (Carter and Duriez, 1986). The elements of this transition include several factors (Young, 1982):

- *Changes in the structure and function of families*. Increasingly, families with young children and prospective new families lack the traditional support of extended family members such as grandparents, aunts, uncles, and cousins. In addition, such factors as the increase in divorce and parent absence tend to isolate children and families from traditional support systems.

    Many families have become more knowledgeable about childbirth. Consequently, they want their child born in an environment that is responsive to their specific needs and emphasizes the emotional and human aspect of childbirth. They want to participate in the management of their child's birth.
- *New birth settings*. An increased awareness of the needs of modern families has resulted in many new family-centered maternity care programs, both in and out of the hospital. Consequently, the choices available to childbearing families have increased substantially over the years. For example, within the hospital, many new programs that provide alternative birth arrangements for prospective parents have emerged, including birthing centers and special labor rooms (see below). Outside the hospital, home-birth programs may provide birthing centers and home delivery for low-risk families. Both within and outside the hospital,

alternative birth programs are continuing to evolve to meet the needs of the modern family.

New childbirth technology. In addition to an emphasis on "humanizing" maternity care in response to the needs of families, a second major development is a dramatically improved obstetrical technology. Specifically, for both low-risk families (e.g., healthy childbearing mothers) and high-risk families (e.g., mothers having diabetes or genital herpes, mother or father having had previous children with a genetic problem, or mother in her teens) there have been extraordinary technology advances such as ultrasound diagnosis, fetal-monitoring devices, and NICUs (neonatal intensive care units for high-risk infants). The challenge of modern maternity care is integrating or balancing both the improved childbirth technology *and* the "humanizing" emphasis on family needs (Young, 1982; Sagov et al., 1984).

Factors in the Relationship

The ability of both mother and father to develop a successful relationship with the newborn depends on a number of factors, including the parents' own personalities and temperaments, the response of the newborn infant to the parents, the history of interpersonal relationships of the mother and the father with their own families of origin (e.g., the way husband and wife were raised by their parents) and with each other, past experiences with pregnancy, and the assimilation of cultural values and practices by the parents (Klaus and Kennell, 1982).

Figure 5.2 is a diagram of some of the primary factors and potential disturbances that may affect initial parental behavior. At the time of the birth, some of these factors are unchangeable, including the mother's care by her own mother and her experiences with previous pregnancies. Other factors can change, for example, the behavior of attending physicians and the practices that result in newborn-parent separation. The figure also illustrates some potential disorders, such as disturbed mother–infant relations and the battered-child syndrome.

Before Pregnancy

Considerable research suggests that previous experiences of the parents (in particular, their experiences as children in the family of origin) are major determinants in developing parenting styles and care-giving roles (Klaus and Kennell, 1982). By observing their own parents, children learn and practice a repertoire of parenting

---

Klaus and Kennell (1982) identified the following events as being important to the formation of a mother's emerging relationship or attachment to her newborn:

BEFORE PREGNANCY
· Planning the pregnancy

DURING PREGNANCY
· Confirming pregnancy
· Accepting the pregnancy
· Fetal movement
· Accepting the fetus as an individual

AFTER BIRTH
· Birth
· Seeing the baby
· Touching the baby
· Giving care to the baby

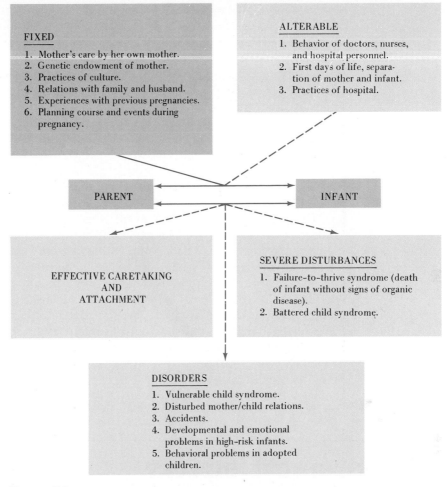

FIXED
1. Mother's care by her own mother.
2. Genetic endowment of mother.
3. Practices of culture.
4. Relations with family and husband.
5. Experiences with previous pregnancies.
6. Planning course and events during pregnancy.

ALTERABLE
1. Behavior of doctors, nurses, and hospital personnel.
2. First days of life, separation of mother and infant.
3. Practices of hospital.

PARENT ⟷ INFANT

EFFECTIVE CARETAKING AND ATTACHMENT

SEVERE DISTURBANCES
1. Failure-to-thrive syndrome (death of infant without signs of organic disease).
2. Battered child syndrome.

DISORDERS
1. Vulnerable child syndrome.
2. Disturbed mother/child relations.
3. Accidents.
4. Developmental and emotional problems in high-risk infants.
5. Behavioral problems in adopted children.

FIGURE 5.2

Major influences on parenting behavior and the newborn and resulting disturbances. Solid lines represent unchangeable determinants; dotted lines represent alterable determinants. Slightly modified from Marshall H. Klaus and John H. Kennell, Parent-Infant Bonding, *2nd ed., St. Louis: The C. V. Mosby Co. 1982.*

behaviors. Parents may be given a vivid example of this type of imitation when their young child "plays house" and acts out the parental roles. An interesting— and alarming—feature of the American nuclear family is that most young people are rarely exposed to any formal parenting training or education before they have their own children.

Furthermore, there is also considerable evidence that planning a pregnancy in advance is associated with acceptance of the infant by parents and, therefore, with positive developmental consequences. Such evidence comes primarily from studies of infants born to teenage mothers for whom pregnancy is an unplanned outcome (Lancaster and Hamburg, 1986).

During Pregnancy

ACCEPTANCE OF PREGNANCY.   During the first trimester (the first three months) of pregnancy, a major adjustment is the acceptance of pregnancy as a fact, a reality (Young, 1982; Abrams and Wexler, 1983). In many instances couples have previously thought of themselves as "expecting," only to be disappointed with the discovery that pregnancy has not occurred. When the pregnancy actually is confirmed, it takes some time to accept it as a reality (Galinsky, 1981).

In the second trimester (the second three-month period) the fetus becomes more of a reality to the parents (Young, 1982). During the first part of this trimester, fetal development is far enough along to allow prenatal testing (see Chapter 4). Typically the results of such tests will indicate that all is well. However, if the tests indicate a serious problem with the fetus, the parents may be faced with several choices: abortion, having the baby, or (when possible) fetal therapy or surgery (Harrison, Golbus, and Filly, 1984).

DIFFERENTIATION.   An important event of the second trimester is frequently called *differentiation,* or the maternal recognition of the fetus as a separate individual. The primary signal for this event is called "quickening" (the maternal sensation of fetal movement). The experience of quickening is thought to provide a basic foundation for the relationship with a newborn who will be physically separated from the mother (Kitzinger, 1983). In addition, parents (in particular the mother) may indicate further evidence of differentiation including fantasies about what the child will be like or behavioral signs such as considering children's names or purchasing cribs or toys. Preparation for childbirth continues into the third trimester (last three months) as both husband and wife become involved in the practical aspects of parenthood, including planning the new baby's living space as well as working through psychological and emotional preparation—"Will we be ready for the arrival?" "Do we have the requisite skills and temperamental characteristics to perform successfully as parents?" (Kitzinger, 1983).

Birth: Labor and Delivery

DEFINITIONS

Labor. The process by which the baby and placenta are expelled through the birth canal. Labor involves the muscular contraction of the uterus to aid the infant in moving through the birth canal. The primary purpose of labor is to permit the contractions of the uterus to open the cervix (the lower part of the uterus) wide enough (approximately four inches) to allow the widest part of the infant—the head—to pass. The baby then passes through the cervix and into the birth canal (the vagina).

Contractions. Contractions are the means through which labor and delivery occur. They are the movements of the uterus by means of which the cervix is opened and the baby is expelled or delivered.

There are several factors that characterize "real" labor (as distinguised from "false" labor):

• Real labor is characterized by the onset of contractions, which have a definite rhythm. For example, contractions may be fifteen or twenty minutes apart during the early phases of labor and may last about forty-five seconds. Over the next few hours, the contractions occur closer together, last longer, and become more intense. The muscles of the abdomen also harden because of the contractions.

- The beginning of real labor is characterized by the appearances of a discharge ("show"). This discharge is composed of a blood-tinged mucus that serves to seal the uterus during pregnancy; when labor begins, this plug is discharged.
- In most deliveries, real labor is characterized by the bursting of the "water bag" during the last hours of labor. The result is a discharge of clear amniotic fluid. In a small percentage of pregnancies, the membranes rupture before labor has begun. In some deliveries, the doctor ruptures the membranes. There is no pain involved in this procedure.

The Stages of Labor

DILATION.   The first stage of labor involves the thinning and widening of the cervix. The cervix is the opening of the uterus at the end of the vaginal canal and is composed of muscle and fibrous tissue. Before the onset of labor, the cervix is thick and narrow, measuring less than two centimeters (four-fifths of an inch) in diameter. With the onset of contractions, the cervix thins and widens to ten centimeters (about four inches), allowing the baby to pass through. Contractions come closer together as the cervix dilates (opens).

EXPULSION.   The second stage begins when the cervix is completely dilated at ten centimeters and ends when the child is born. At this time contractions are usually sixty to seventy seconds in duration and about two to three minutes apart. With each contraction, the baby moves further down the birth canal. Just prior to the delivery, the woman may be given an anesthetic (unless she is participating in a "natural" childbirth program) to ease her pain. Another common procedure at this time is an *episiotomy* (an incision to enlarge the vagina) (this is done to prevent the tearing of vaginal tissue during delivery).

   The actual birth of the baby occurs rather quickly after the widest part of the infant's head becomes visible ("crowning"). Once the baby's head is delivered, even before the infant is born, the physician begins the suction of mucus from the infant's mouth and nose. Sometimes the physician taps or rubs the soles of the infant's feet or its buttocks in order to get the infant to take oxygen in. As the baby exhales, it cries. (Crying forces the infant's breath through its lungs faster.)

   Once the baby is free of the birth canal, the cord is allowed to stop pulsating before it is clamped and cut so that the baby receives the remaining support in the cord. The vernix, a cheesy film covering the infant's skin, may be wiped off. Antibiotic drops are administered to each eye to prevent infection and possible blindness. The baby is then usually maintained in a slightly head-down position. This position aids in mucus drainage and respiration (see Figs. 5.3 and 5.4).

DELIVERY OF THE PLACENTA.   The third (and last) stage of labor is the delivery of the placenta. There is seldom any pain associated with the expulsion of the afterbirth. The episiotomy is repaired at this time. The new mother is allowed to see and hold her baby. She may even be able to nurse the child before leaving the delivery room. The new mother may experience mixed emotions. Even though she has carried and known this infant for nine months, the child may seem like a stranger to her. The development of mother-child and father-child bonds is now necessary to promote family roles.

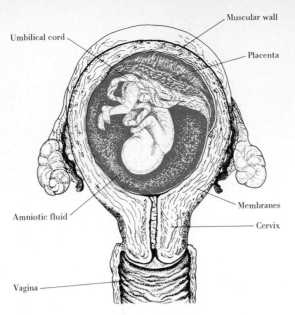

Muscular wall

Umbilical cord

Placenta

Membranes

Amniotic fluid

Cervix

Vagina

FIGURE 5.3

The fetus may develop within the uterus head down as shown or head up, and it may rotate completely before birth. It lives throughout its uterine life with the "bag of waters." The fluid filling this sac serves many purposes. It prevents the walls of the uterus from cramping the fetus and acts as an excellent shock absorber. At term, there is usually about a quart of amniotic fluid. This fluid is not stagnant. It is completely replaced about eight times daily. Carnation Company.

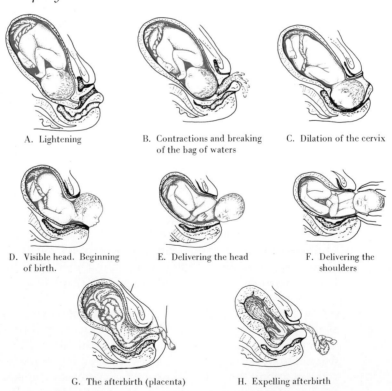

A. Lightening

B. Contractions and breaking of the bag of waters

C. Dilation of the cervix

D. Visible head. Beginning of birth.

E. Delivering the head

F. Delivering the shoulders

G. The afterbirth (placenta)

H. Expelling afterbirth

FIGURE 5.4

Labor and delivery. Labor is the process by which the fetus passes from its intrauterine environment to the outside world. Birth is the actual expulsion of the infant down the vaginal canal and through the vaginal opening. Carnation Company.

The Role of Fathers Before and After Delivery

Does the presence of the father enhance mother-infant or father-infant bonding? Contrary to some popular biases, it is apparent that fathers are capable

Shan Rucinski

of sensitive interaction with their infants from birth on (Lamb, 1981; Hanson and Bozett, 1985). In an extensive review of research on father-infant bonding, Parke and Tinsley (1981) described a study in which parents were observed in three different situations: (1) the mother alone with the infant (two or four days of age), (2) the father alone with the infant, and (3) the father, mother, and infant (triadic interaction) together in the mother's hospital room. Most of the fathers in the study had been present during labor and delivery. Results indicated that in the triadic situation the fathers tended to hold the infant almost twice as frequently as the mother and touched the infant more than the mother. In this situation the father clearly played a far more significant role than the cultural stereotype of the father would suggest.

There is some evidence that fathers who are present during delivery consider the experience to be a "peak" emotional event (May and Perrin, 1985). Although the presence of the father is perceived by many fathers as important, it is not a necessity for ensuring appropriate father-infant bonding and interaction. Fathers typically become involved with or even bond with their newborn infants even if they were not present during delivery (Palkovitz, 1985).

Methods of Childbirth

Babies may be delivered in a variety of ways. Historically, the concern in maternity care has been to find methods that are as safe and comfortable as possible for mothers and infants. In this section we discuss both the *traditional* deliveries (i.e., the delivery that occurs in the hospital, using all the available and necessary medical technology including drugs to ensure a safe and comfortable delivery) and alternative childbirth arrangements outside the hospital.

TRADITIONAL DELIVERY. The hospital delivery often involves the use of analgesics for pain relief during labor and delivery. This mode occurs in a relatively high percentage of Western middle-class childbirths. For example, medicated deliveries occurred in 95 percent of the childbirths in eighteen major teaching hospitals in the United States (Brackbill and Broman, 1979). In most hospitals women are given a regional anesthetic (e.g., a spinal or epidural block), which substantially reduces the sensation of pain, or an analgesic, which relaxes the individual (see Chapter 4 for a discussion of the impact of such drugs on the newborn).

In the United States, the traditional childbirth involves a doctor and nurses in attendance during the entire delivery. The expectant mother is admitted to the hospital and is prepared for the birth. When in the judgment of the nurses and/or physician she is ready to give birth, she is taken to the delivery room or, as is now often the case, she remains in the same room which becomes the "birthing

A Hospital Birth

6:00 A.M.   Six hours after the beginning of labor, Karen is admitted to the hospital. Her husband, Jerry, accompanies her. He is going to assist Karen by giving her support and coaching her during the entire birthing period.

6:30   Nurses check the baby's heartbeat. An examination indicates that Karen's cervix is dilated to 1½ centimeters. She has been experiencing regular contractions.

8:00   Karen's cervix has dilated to 4½ centimeters and her membranes have ruptured. Her contractions are now closer together in time and are stronger.

9:30   The doctor examines Karen. Her cervix is completely dilated. Karen is now ready to begin to push with her contractions to bring the baby down. Jerry coaches Karen and gives her comfort.

9:40   The baby's head is now visible in the vaginal canal.

9:45   Karen continues to push with each contraction. The baby's head is now outside the vaginal opening. The doctor tells Karen that she can momentarily stop pushing.

9:46   The doctor uses a suction syringe to remove mucus from the baby's mouth and nose to facilitate breathing. Karen pushes with the next contraction.

9:47   The rest of the baby's body glides easily through the vaginal canal. The doctor announces a baby girl and places the baby on Karen's stomach.

9:49   The cord has stopped pulsating. Jerry is allowed to cut the cord under the doctor's supervision. Karen and Jerry cuddle their new daughter.

9:52   The baby is placed in a warming crib.

---

room.'' The mother remains in the same bed, which "breaks away" and allows her, within reason, a choice of birthing positions—upright, sitting, or squatting. The physician or obstetrician then delivers the baby with assistance from nurses. In addition, it should be noted that the vast majority of hospitals (99 percent) allow fathers to be present during delivery (Wideman and Singer, 1984).

It is important to understand the origin of these practices. These procedures as used in contemporary hospitals have developed from efforts to make childbirth as safe as possible. Childbirth at the turn of the century was a notoriously dangerous experience for both mother and child. Standard hospital delivery procedures have all but eliminated the deaths of the mother or infant due to unsanitary conditions in the hospitals. It is important to keep in mind that even with such standard hospital cleanliness practices, some critics have argued that rates of maternal and **infant mortality** are still at unacceptably high rates in the United States due to health problems for mothers and infants *outside* the hospital.

Episiotomies have been routinely done in standard deliveries (especially for a first child) to prevent tearing of tissue as well as to facilitate the ease of delivery. In the United States they are done in almost 90 percent of all deliveries (Banta, 1981). They are considered to be a good preventive practice because the episiotomy cut is much easier to repair than a ragged tear, which can be dangerous if it extends to the anus (Thacker and Banta, 1980; Banta, 1981). Some women have objected to routine episiotomies for several reasons. They have argued that delivery techniques used (primarily in other countries) to reduce the likelihood of tearing (e.g., a vertical or semivertical delivery position or the application of warm compresses and oil with a massage) are not frequently used in the United States. In addition, episiotomies are, as might be expected, very uncomfortable after the anesthetic wears off and may interfere with intercourse for several weeks after birth.

THE LAMAZE METHOD. The Lamaze, or prepared-childbirth, technique involves the father-to-be as well as the mother-to-be. A woman and her husband are taught the Lamaze method with other couples in weekly sessions during the last months of pregnancy. By teaching what is involved in labor and delivery, the Lamaze method reduces the fear and tension associated with ignorance of these processes. Also taught are exercises and breathing techniques to be used throughout labor and delivery. The husband becomes his wife's coach and helps her learn and practice these procedures. During the birth process the husband is able to offer moral and physical support to his wife.

The basic principles of the Lamaze method are the following (Karmel, 1983; Carter and Duriez, 1986):

- *Instruction in the physiology and anatomy of childbirth.* This information is intended to relieve unnecessary anxiety and tension about childbirth.
- *Muscular relaxation.* The pregnant woman learns to relax body muscles as a way of improving body efficiency and reducing discomfort during labor and delivery.
- *Breathing techniques.* Active and varying techniques of breathing are taught as a method of reducing the inevitable pain and discomfort of childbirth. In other

---

The Lamaze Technique: The Husband as Coach

Bill stands right by her.

"That's right, Sandy, keep on panting, you're doing fine!"

Sandy smiles again, concentrating on her work and well in control, with Bill close and supporting her. The contraction is over. Bill holds a wet washcloth on Sandy's forehead as she waits for her next contraction. . . . As Bill supports Sandy with his right arm, his left hand seems to give her strength and courage.

"Push, Sandy, keep it up, you're doing fine!"

There is complete concentration on both Bill's and Sandy's faces. They are a team, working to give birth to their child.

At this moment it seems as if the world has shrunk into the tiny consciousness of two people pushing a baby out.

From Bing, 1983, pp. 107–116.

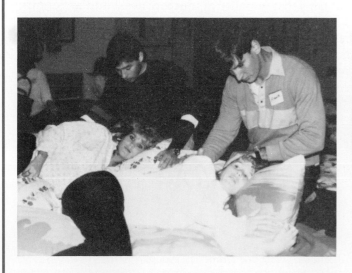

Marjorie Pyle

Marjorie Pyle

words, by concentrating heavily on breathing exercises, a woman may "displace" pain from a center of concentration (i.e., the uterus).

Use of a labor "coach." Typically, the husband or a friend helps the pregnant woman learn and practice the relaxation and breathing techniques. Ordinarily the coach attends childbirth-preparation classes with the mother. There is some evidence that the father's participation reduces maternal fears and improves the mother's sense of worth (Wideman and Singer, 1984).

THE LEBOYER METHOD: BIRTH WITHOUT VIOLENCE.   There is some concern that standard hospital delivery practices may create unnecessary discomfort or trauma for the infant. Frederick Leboyer (1975) proposed a new approach to reduce the pain and fear experienced by the newborn. Leboyer supports the view that birth is a sensory experience. Although the infant does not organize or integrate sensations, it does perceive its surroundings through sight, hearing, and touch. For example, the blinding lamps and floodlights used in the delivery room are thought to be unnecessary and may irritate the infant's eyes. Instead, Leboyer proposed utilizing minimal light in the delivery room. In addition, the newborn's ears are sensitive to the noises and voices during delivery. Lowered voices not only relax the mother but also protect the child's vulnerable ears.

The Leboyer method encourages patience during the delivery process, allowing the child to emerge from the birth canal slowly. So as to aid the baby in establishing respiration, this method also emphasizes refraining from immediately cutting the umbilical cord. The child's sensitivity to touch is also considered. The infant is placed on the mother's abdomen with its arms and legs folded under its stomach, a position that enables the child to straighten its posture at its own pace (see Fig. 5.5). The child is caressed by the hands of the physician or the mother; touching is the primary language by which the obstetrician and the mother communicate with the newborn. After the cord is cut, the child is submerged in warm water much like the fetal amniotic fluid (see Fig. 5.6). This procedure relaxes the infant, decreases fear, and allows the baby to explore its new environment. The similarity of the warm water to amniotic fluid minimizes the differences between the fetal environment and the new world.

Leboyer stresses that birth need not be frightening to either mother or newborn and that birth without violence creates children who are healthy, free, and without conflict. Furthermore, he maintains that impatience, nervousness, and anger may all be sensed by the infant. Those participating in the delivery need to be aware of the emotions they may be relaying to the newborn.

Although Leboyer's approach to childbirth has caused many parents and obstetricians to consider the infant's first moments of life more carefully, the eval-

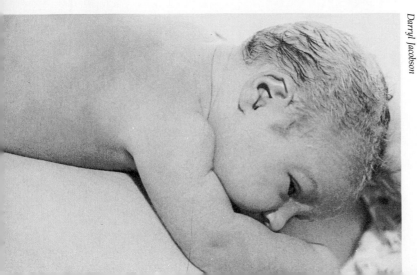

Darryl Jacobson

FIGURE 5.5

Leboyer method: infant is placed on the mother's abdomen.

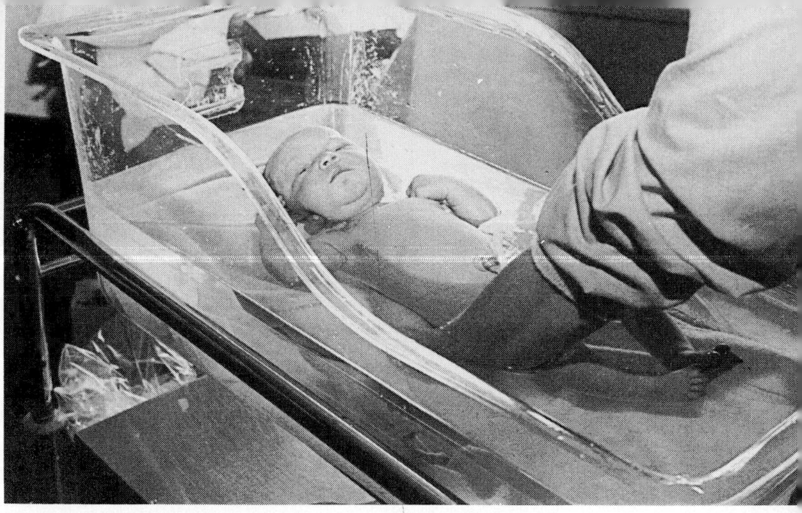

Darryl Jacobson

FIGURE 5.6
Leboyer method: child is submerged in warm water similar to amniotic fluid.

uative evidence on the approach is mixed. On one hand, there is some evidence that Leboyer babies are more alert during the first thirty hours after birth than conventionally delivered babies (Salter, 1978). On the other hand, there is evidence of no differences (advantages or disadvantages) between Leboyer-delivered babies and *gentle* conventional births (Nelson et al., 1980). For example, after birth (i.e., the first hour of life, at twenty-four and seventy-two hours, and at eight months) there were no differences in the health of the mothers or the infants nor were there any differences in maternal perception of childbirth or maternal perception of their infants.

Furthermore, there is no evidence that birth is perceived as a trauma by the newborn. However, evidence from the type of studies necessary to carefully evaluate the Leboyer method (i.e., controlled studies in which comparable families are randomly assigned to Leboyer and conventional delivery groups) are simply not available. The dimming of lights has now become a common practice in many hospitals. In addition, the presence of enjoyable background music appears to relax the mother. In light of these changes and others, strict adherence to the Leboyer method appears unnecessary.

Leboyer and Gentle Birth

Frederick Leboyer was born in 1918. He graduated from the University of Paris, School of Medicine and became its clinical chief in 1954. Since that time he has devoted most of his time to his clinical practice. Since 1953 he has delivered more than ten thousand babies. In 1975, his book *Birth Without Violence* described techniques of childbirth that lessen the pain, fear, and confusion of the newborn. In the passages below, Dr. Leboyer describes some of the features of his approach to birth. He argues against cutting the umbilical cord immediately after birth.

Cutting the Umbilical Cord

To sever the umbilicus when the child has scarcely left the mother's womb is an act of cruelty. . . . To conserve it intact while it still pulses is to transform the act of birth. . . .

[Nature] has arranged it so that during the dangerous passage of birth, the child is receiving oxygen from two sources rather than one: from the lungs and from the umbilicus.

Two systems [are] functioning simultaneously, one relieving the other: the old one, the umbilicus, continues to supply oxygen to the baby until the new one, the lungs, has fully taken its place. . . .

During this time, in parallel fashion, an orifice closes in the heart, which seals the old route forever.

In short, for an average of four or five minutes, the newborn straddles two worlds. Drawing oxygen from two sources, it switches gradually from one to the other, without a brutal transition. One scarcely hears a cry. What is required for this miracle to take place? Only a little patience. Only a refusal to rush things. Only knowing enough to wait, giving the child time to adjust. (Leboyer, 1975, pp. 44–50)

CESAREAN DELIVERY.   In a cesarean birth, the physician makes an incision through the abdominal wall and the uterus. The infant is removed, and then the incision is carefully sewn up. There are several reasons for this procedure: A fetus may be too large to emerge through the mother's pelvis; the mother might be experiencing toxemia or a hemorrhage; the mother may have a disease such as herpes, which can be contracted by the newborn passing through the birth canal; the mother may be about to deliver more than one baby; or the mother may be about to deliver her first baby but the baby is breech (fetus in such a position that it would cause the buttocks or feet to emerge before the head). This occurs in about 3 percent of all births (Queenan and Hobbins, 1982). From 1970 to 1983, cesarean deliveries for mothers of all ages increased from 5.5 per 100 deliveries to 20.3 per 100 deliveries (U.S. Department of Commerce, 1985d).

Although at one time cesarean births were somewhat hazardous, now they are only slightly riskier than normal births. The majority of cesarean births are arranged well in advance by the physician and the mother. Because delivery is scheduled for when the physician thinks the baby will be ready, there is some risk of infant prematurity (Placek, Taffel, and Keppel, 1983; Gleicher, 1984). New techniques, such as the use of ultrasound, have increased the accuracy of such predictions. Ultrasound is used to "see" or measure the approximate size of the fetus and thus to estimate its age, maturity, and readiness for birth. It used to be thought that once a woman had a cesarean delivery, the uterus and the abdominal walls were weakened. For this reason, it was believed that another pregnancy should be avoided. Today, however, a woman may have four or more cesarean deliveries satisfactorily. The belief that once a cesarean section is performed on a woman, all future deliveries must also be a cesarean section is no longer true. A vaginal delivery may follow a cesarean section depending on the reason for the previous cesarean section and where the incision had been made.

ALTERNATIVE CHILDBIRTH SETTINGS.   While most childbirths occur in a hospital, a relatively small but increasing number of families are electing to have childbirth in settings outside the hospital. The pregnant women in such families ordinarily have good medical histories and therefore are at low risk for pregnancy complications. There are many reasons for choosing out-of-hospital births, for example:

· It is a more natural or homelike setting.
· Reduced cost.

Childbirth at a free-standing birthing or maternity center includes both the comforts of home and the safety of a hospital setting. Such a birth may be attended by a nurse-midwife and a physician. Such centers are designed for low-risk pregnancies. However, maternity centers typically have emergency medical equipment available, as well as working arrangements with ambulances and nearby hospitals.

After the Birth

After the birth of the infant, there are many significant and exciting developments. In this section we discuss some of these events as they pertain to the mother, the father, the baby, and the relationship between parents and newborn.

The Parents

Typically, the birth of a first child initiates an experience that is new to the parents both as individuals and as a married couple. To adapt to this change requires a refocusing of their psychological worlds and their marital relationship. There no longer is an exclusively one-to-one relationship between husband and wife, with the possibilities of unlimited energy for shared activities, intimacy, and companionship. Ironically, the directions of these fundamental changes may not always be immediately apparent to the new parents, who are busy meeting the needs of the newborn.

In addition, there is evidence that how parents of the newborn were themselves reared as children (in their family of origin) and how well their own parents got along (as husband and wife) are predictive of changes in the quality of the newborn parents' relationship both during and following childbirth (Belsky and Isabella, 1985). In particular, when the relationships in one's family of origin have not been positive, it becomes more difficult to meet the demands created by the arrival of a newborn.

Following the birth, a mother's initial needs may include seeing, touching, and possibly holding and feeding the infant. She may wish to talk with her husband and relate her experience and feelings. She may request something to eat or may want to rest. The parent-newborn relationship begins immediately after delivery. Family-centered maternity care allows both parents to participate in the infant's care.

After the expectant parents' long months of watching the mother-to-be's abdomen gradually enlarge, their feeling the movements of the fetus, and their experiencing labor and delivery, what happens when the parents and the baby meet one another eye to eye? What are the feelings of the mother and the father when they see the child?

How do mothers respond to their infants? Observations indicate that there is an orderly and somewhat predictable pattern of behavior when the mother first examines her newborn infant (Klaus and Kennell, 1982). Marshall Klaus and John Kennell were able to determine this pattern by filming twelve mothers with their full-term infants between thirty minutes and thirteen hours after birth. The films lasted about ten minutes for each mother-infant pair and covered the first contact (except for the mother's brief look at the newborn during delivery). The films indicated the following pattern: (1) with her fingertips, the mother hesitatingly touched the newborn's hands and feet; (2) within four or five minutes, she caressed the newborn's body with the palms of her hands (as she caressed the newborn, the mother became increasingly excited); (3) there was a marked increase in the total time during which the mother positioned herself and her newborn so that they could look into one another's eyes. Klaus and Kennell indicated that the mothers showed great interest in waking their infants in order to get them to open their eyes. Nearly three-fourths of the mothers said something like "Open your eyes, oh come on now, open your eyes" or "If you open your eyes, I'll know you're alive." Many mothers indicated that they felt much "closer" to the infant once it looked at them.

The new mother may have feelings of depression during the early days or weeks following delivery. There are emotional as well as physical adjustments to be made. The woman realizes that she must fulfill the roles of both wife and mother. She may feel dependent and require more affection and appreciation from her spouse. In attempting to establish a satisfying relationship with her baby, the mother may need temporary help from someone when she returns home. The additional help is to enable the parents to be with the baby and to decrease the mother's feelings of inadequacy in not being able to cope with the household chores as well as mothering the infant.

There has been little research on the impact of childbirth on fathers. Generally, those who are present during delivery and afterwards report that childbirth is an important experience for them (May and Perrin, 1985). However, there is no evidence that simple presence of the father during delivery by itself makes a husband a better father (Palkovitz, 1985). That is, there is no conclusive relationship between the father's birth attendance and paternal involvement later in the child's life.

The Baby

Now let us discuss the baby during the first few hours after birth (see Fig. 5.7). The newborn's features and body are quite different from what they will be later on. The head is somewhat swollen and elongated from pushing against the cervix and from the passage through the bony pelvis and the birth canal. The infant's color is a bluish-purple, which gradually turns to pink. The nose is flattened and the chin recedes. There may be observable swelling of the sex organs because of maternal hormones.

Furthermore, the child may have white spots on the skin due to occluded sweat glands or visible capillaries because of the thinness of the skin.

The baby's appearance may be surprising to a couple who have not seen a newborn before. Reassurance is frequently necessary to allay anxieties and to assure the parents that these seemingly strange newborn characteristics are normal and are not permanent. Following is a detailed description of a healthy newborn:

> *The feet* look more complete than they are. X ray would show only one real bone of the heel. Other bones are now cartilage. Skin often loose and wrinkly. *The legs* are most often seen drawn up against the abdomen in prebirth position. Extended legs measure shorter than you'd expect compared to the arms. The knees stay slightly bent and legs are more or less bowed. *Genitals* of both sexes will seem large (especially scrotum) in comparison with the scale of, for example, the hands to adult size. *Weight*, unless well above the average of 6 or 7 pounds, will not prepare you for how really tiny the newborn is. Top to toe measure: anywhere between 18 to 21 inches. *The trunk* may startle you in some normal detail: short neck, small

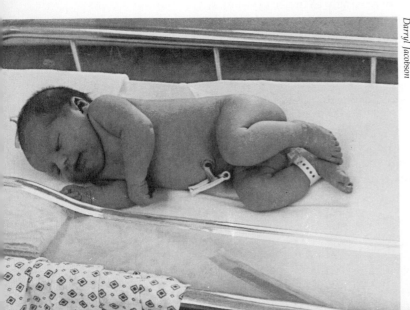

Darryl Jacobson

FIGURE 5.7
What a healthy week-old baby looks like.

sloping shoulders, swollen breasts, large rounded abdomen, umbilical stump (future navel), slender narrow pelvis and hips. *A deep flush* spreads over the entire body if baby cries hard. Veins on head swell and throb. You will notice no tears as tear ducts do not function as yet. *The skin* is thin and dry. You may see veins through it. Fair skin may be rosy-red temporarily. Downy hair is not unusual. *The hands,* if you open them out flat from their characteristic fist position, have: finely lined palms, tissue-paper thin nails, dry, loose fitting skin and deep bracelet creases at wrist. *The eyes* appear dark blue, have a blank stary gaze. You may catch one or both turning or turned to crossed or wall-eyed position. *The face* will disappoint you unless you expect to see: pudgy cheeks, a broad, flat nose with mere hint of a bridge, receding chin, undersized lower jaw. *The head* usually strikes you as being too big for the body. (Immediately after birth it may be temporarily out of shape—topsided or elongated—due to pressure before or during birth.) *On the skull* you will see or feel the two most obvious soft spots or *fontanels.* One is above the brow, the other close to crown of head in back. (Birch, 1980).

NERVOUS SYSTEM.   At birth, the infant's nervous system is relatively immature. Most of the bodily functions and responses are carried out by reflex action. The behavior of the newborn is controlled largely by processes in the human brain stem rather than by processes in the cerebral cortex. The *brain stem* is located below the cortex and is responsible for such basic biological processes as breathing and circulation in addition to basic reflexes. The *cerebral cortex* is primarily responsible for memory, thought, and perception. The cerebral cortex is not fully functional in the newborn and gradually begins to exercise control over infant behavior during the first few weeks of life. As the cerebral cortex gains control, it can influence or inhibit the brain stem activities responsible for reflexes. In addition to the impact of cortical control, more complex and purposeful behavior is also made possible by the gradual and continuing process of myelinization, which insulates nerve fibers. (Myelinization improves the efficiency, accuracy, and general effectiveness of nerve signals that initiate behavioral responses.)

A newborn possesses certain essential reflexes. These include the blinking, yawn, coughing, gagging, and sneezing reflexes. In addition, the so-called **rooting reflexes** are stimulated when one brushes the infant's cheek (see Fig. 5.8), and the infant turns its head in the direction of the stimulation as if to reach for food

FIGURE 5.8

The rooting responses. Stimulation: the adult touches the side of the infant's mouth with a finger. Head turning: the infant turns its head in the direction of the finger. Grasping with the mouth: the infant tries to suck the finger.

David Kostelnik

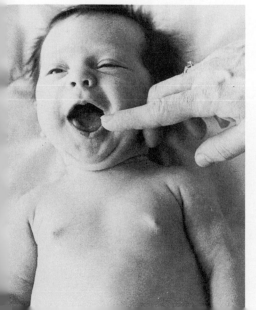
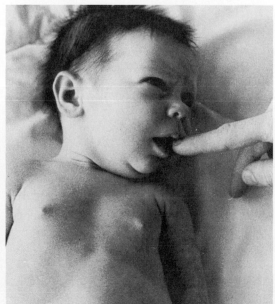
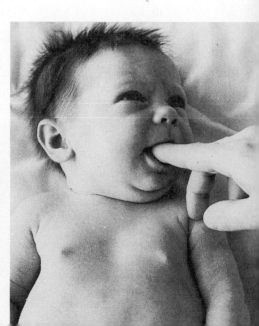

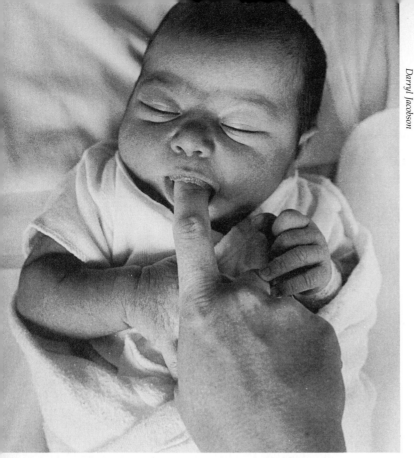

FIGURE 5.9
The sucking reflex. The infant sucks the finger placed in its mouth.

(Dubowitz and Dubowitz, 1981). The **sucking reflex** occurs when anything touches the infant's lips (see Fig. 5.9). The **withdrawal reflex** occurs when the infant cries and recoils from a pain-inducing stimulation (e.g., being accidentally stuck with a diaper pin) (see Fig. 5.10).

The **grasp (palmar) reflex** (Fig. 5.11) enables the infant to hold onto an object briefly and then release its grip. This reflex diminishes with maturity. If one holds the infant upright with its feet touching a solid surface, the legs will move as if in an attempt to walk or dance. This is the **walking reflex**. The **startle (Moro) reflex** is also present at birth (see Fig. 5.12). This reaction is stimulated by a sudden loud noise or loss of support; generalized, nonpurposeful muscular activity results.

FIGURE 5.10
The withdrawal reflex. Stimulation: the examiner pricks the infant's sole with a Q-tip *or pin. Response: the infant withdraws its foot.*

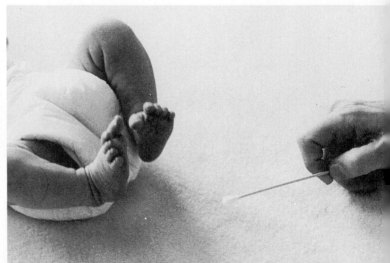

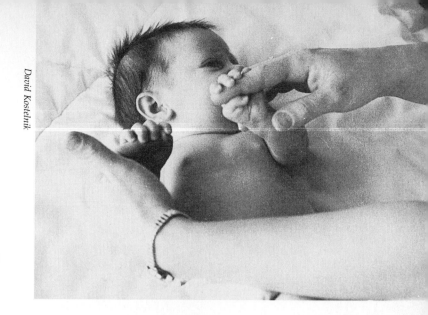

FIGURE 5.11

The palmar or grasping reflex. The adult presses a finger into the infant's palms, and the infant's fingers flex around the examiner's finger.

Another reflex which is present at birth and disappears by the sixth month is the **Babinski reflex** (Fig. 5.13). This reflex can be elicited by firmly pressing the sole of the infant's foot, which causes the toes to fan out and the foot to twist inward.

The infant's sense of equilibrium may be observed when, for example, a jarring of the infant causes it to draw up its legs and turn the soles of its feet inward. A postural reflex, the **tonic-neck reflex**, may be seen when the infant is laid on its back with its head turned to one side and its corresponding arm and leg extended at right angles to the body. The infant responds by flexing the other arm and leg and making fists with both hands.

These reflex mechanisms are important because they signify normal functioning of the nervous system (see Table 5.1). The relatively brief appearance of some reflexes (e.g., the startle reflex and the Babinski reflex) may reflect the emerging control of behavior by the cerebral cortex and, therefore, the maturation of the nervous system. Those reflexes that appear early in life and then cease to exist are sometimes referred to as the **primitive reflexes** because they are shared with lower

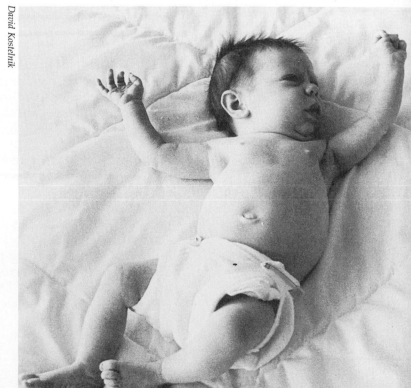

FIGURE 5.12

The Moro or startle reflex.

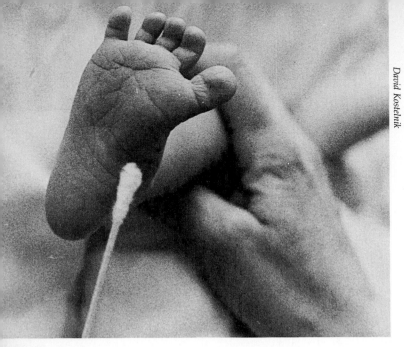

David Kostelnik

FIGURE 5.13
The Babinski reflex.

animals. For example, both the Moro and the grasping reflexes may well be evolutionary carryovers from primates that hang onto their mothers for survival and feeding.

NEWBORN ASSESSMENT.   One minute after delivery and again at five minutes after delivery, virtually all hospitals give the newborn a simple test developed by Dr. Virginia Apgar. The **Apgar test** is a standard measurement of the condition of the newborn, including its heart rate, breathing, body tone, reflexes, and circulation. A newborn is given a score of 0, 1, or 2 on each measurement. If the total score (for all infant characteristics) is 7 or above, the infant is in no danger. If the total score is 4 to 6, the infant is in fair condition. A total score of below 4 typically indicates critical condition. Newborn Apgar scores appear to be relatively good predictors of later abnormalities in such areas as motor development and neurological status.

Another test that can be used to evaluate the newborn's condition is the **Brazelton Neonatal Behavior Assessment Scale.** The Brazelton scale assesses the way newborns adapt to their environment. It measures four areas of infant behavior:

- Home-related adaptive behaviors (e.g., cuddliness, alertness, and so on).
- Motor behaviors (e.g., reflexes, hand-to-mouth behavior, and so on).
- Response to stress (e.g., the startle reaction).
- Control of physiological state (e.g., the ability of the infant to calm down after being upset).

The Brazelton test takes thirty minutes to administer. Some evidence suggests that it is a better predictor of newborns' future status than the Apgar test (Behrman and Vaughn, 1983).

INDIVIDUAL DIFFERENCES AND NEWBORN STATES.   Infants behave differently from the moment of birth. Parents and caretakers attest to the differences among individual babies. For example, some newborns seem to startle rather frequently during regular sleep, whereas others startle infrequently. Some newborns seem more irritable than others. Differences of this sort are important because they may affect the newborn's interactions with its parents. Parents react differently to a

TABLE 5.1
Some Newborn Reflexes

REFLEX	STIMULUS	DESCRIPTION	SIGNIFICANCE
Rooting (see Fig. 5.8)	An object touching the infant's cheek.	The head turns toward the source of stimulation, the mouth opens, and sucking actions begin. This reflex may appear within an hour after birth.	This reflex has survival value because it enables the infant to locate food.
Sucking (see Fig. 5.9)	An object touching the lips.	The infant makes sucking movements. This response becomes more efficient with time.	If absent, immaturity or possible brain damage may be indicated.
Withdrawal (see Fig. 5.10)	Heat (from a feeding bottle) or pinprick.	Crying and recoiling from pain.	Absence may indicate immaturity or damage to the nervous system.
Grasp or palmar (see Fig. 5.11)	An object placed on the palms.	The infant closes its hand around the object with a firm grip. The grasp may be secure enough to raise the infant to a standing position. This reflex disappears by about the first birthday.	Absence may indicate a nervous system problem.
Moro or startle (see Fig. 5.12)	Loud noise or a sudden change in body position.	The infant throws its arms and fingers out in full extension and arches its back and extends the legs. The hands are then returned to the midline of the body. The reflex disappears between the third and fifth months.	If this reflex is weak or absent, the central nervous system may be disturbed. If present, the newborn has an awareness of equilibrium.
Babinski (see Fig. 5.13)	Stimulation of the sole of the foot.	The toes fan out and the foot twists inward. After six months of age, this reflex disappears and the infant's toes curl inward when touched.	Absence may indicate immaturity of the central nervous system, defects of the spinal cord, or a lesion in the motor area of the brain.

baby who seems rather quiet than to one who is excitable and irritable. In addition, the parent's sense of being able to do something to calm an infant may contribute to a more positive attitude toward the infant.

In addition to the variations in infants' temperaments, there are also important variations within the daily behavior of each newborn infant. These variations—cycles of wakefulness, sleepiness, and activity—are called **newborn states.** A baby's reaction to its environment usually depends on its state.

DEFINITION

Newborn State. The continuum of alertness or consciousness ranging from regular sleep to vigorous activity.

The Apgar Test: An Evaluation of Newborn Life Processes

The Apgar test was developed by Dr. Virginia Apgar, an internationally recognized specialist in the study of neonates. The test is designed to assess the basic life processes of the infant. It is usually administered to the infant approximately one minute after birth and again five minutes later. The test is both quick and safe.

The tested infant receives a score that is based on five life signs (see Apgar chart). These signs, listed in order of importance, are

1. *Pulse or heart rate.* The infant's heart rate usually varies between 150 and 180 beats per minute during the first few moments of life and usually drops to about 135 beats per minute within an hour after birth. A heart rate less than 100 may indicate a difficulty.
2. *Respiration.* Regularity of respiration usually accompanies a healthy cry or follows shortly thereafter.
3. *Activity or muscle tone.* The newborn usually keeps its arms and legs in a fetal position. Muscle tone is evaluated by the degree of the infant's resistance when the examiner attempts to extend its limbs.
4. *Grimace or reflex irritability.* The newborn should respond vigorously to any test of reflex capability. *Grimace or irritability* is an indication of the general maturity of the nervous system. Little response could indicate impairment of the central nervous system.
5. *Appearance or color.* At first cyanosis, or blue coloring, is present in all newborns. After a few minutes, the operation of the heart and the lungs produces a rapid change to a pink coloration. The absence of the normally pink color may indicate respiratory or heart problems.

One easy way to remember these five signs is to use Dr. Apgar's name as an acronym: Appearance or coloring, Pulse or heart rate, Grimace or reflex irritability, Activity or muscle tone, and Respiration.

Apgar Scoring Chart for Evaluating Status of Newborn

SIGN	0 POINTS	1 POINT	2 POINTS
Activity or muscle tone	Limp	Some flexion of extremities	Extremities well flexed, active motion
Pulse or heart rate	Absent	Slow (less than 100)	Greater than 100
Grimace or reflex irritability (response to catheter in nostril)	No response	Grimace	Cough, sneeze or cry
Appearance or color	Blue, pale	Body pink, extremities blue	Completely pink
Respiratory effort	Absent	Slow, irregular	Good strong cry

(From Apgar, 1958, p. 1988).

The examiner takes all of the above vital signs into consideration when assigning the newborn an Apgar score. A total score of 7 to 10 points indicates that the newborn is in good condition. A score of 4 to 6 points indicates that the infant is in fair condition. In this case, the infant's air passages are further cleared and oxygen may be given. A score of 0 to 3 indicates either a stillbirth or a newborn in very poor condition requiring emergency procedures. It is important to note that an infant's Apgar may be affected by the drugs that the mother is given during birth (Apgar, 1958; Apgar and James, 1962).

When observing babies, researchers now commonly categorize the baby's behavior by the following states (Hutt, Lenard, and Prechtl, 1973):

Regular Sleep. The newborn's regular sleep is deep, and the breathing is regular. The infant makes no movements except for an occasional and generalized startle response. On an arousal continuum, this state is the low point.

Irregular Sleep. Irregular sleep is light, breathing is irregular, and the baby shows occasional restlessness. The muscles may twitch but ordinarily no major movements are made. The sounds and noises that the infant may have been oblivious to during regular sleep now bring such responses as a smile or a startle.

Drowsiness. The infant's state, both before and following sleep, is drowsiness. The eyes may be open, breathing is irregular, and the body is more active than during irregular sleep. The infant is sensitive to such stimuli as the sound of a television or the sight of its mother or father.

Alert Inactivity. The state of alert inactivity occurs after the baby has been fed and diapered or has just gotten up and remains awake with eyes open for a short period of time. The infant may move its head, trunk, or limbs while looking at something in the environment such as a swinging mobile.

Waking Activity and Crying. Waking and crying can begin with either intense internal stimulation (such as hunger or pain) or external stimulation (such as restraint of the newborn or removing its pacifier). This state may begin with rather quiet movements and turn into sustained thrashing and crying. The newborn seems to be "too busy" to respond to many things that would draw its attention in the states of drowsiness or alert activity.

THE OPERATION OF STATES.   How do states operate? What factors determine when newborn states occur? Newborn states are influenced by both internal timing mechanisms and external stimulation.

Sometimes the internal mechanisms are referred to metaphorically as *biological clocks*. These biological clocks appear to regulate human cycles of eating, sleeping, and elimination. These timing mechanisms also appear to regulate the pattern of movement from one state to another in the newborn.

Rhythms associated with the day-night cycle are called *circadian* (derived from the Latin words *circa*, which means "approximate," and *dies*, which means "day"). The most apparent human circadian rhythm is the sleep-wakefulness or activity cycle. Careful records kept of the temperature, the heart rate, and the sleeping habits of hundreds of infants showed that circadian rhythms are only slightly apparent at birth. Gradually, however, they develop during the first year of life. Figure 5.14 illustrates the development of circadian periodism in heart rate. Infants

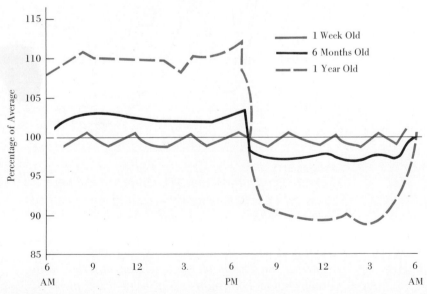

FIGURE 5.14

Development of circadian periodism in the heart rate of infants. From Beck, 1963.

who are one week old show only a slight fluctuation above and below the norm of 100 heartbeats per minute. However, a day-night rhythm becomes apparent at about six months. The cycle is very clear for the year-old child.

How are the states of the newborn distributed over a typical day? The newborn sleeps seventeen to twenty hours during a typical twenty-four-hour cycle. Of that sleeping time, approximately 75 percent is spent in irregular sleep. The newborn spends a total time of two to three hours in a state of alert inactivity and one to four hours in the state of waking activity and crying or fussing (Coons and Guilleminault, 1982).

From the perspective of the infant and parent or caretaker as an interacting system, newborn states both affect parental behavior and are, in turn, affected by parental activity (see Fig. 5.15). Of course, parents are interested in maintaining

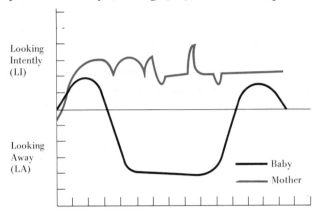

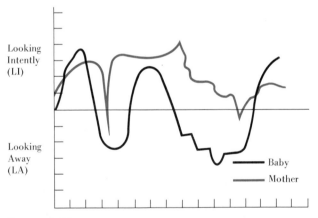

FIGURE 5.15

Parent-infant interaction. The figure at the top illustrates a relationship between a mother and baby in which there is limited synchrony (at the beginning and end) as the mother looks intently at the infant while the infant is looking away. The figure at the bottom shows a relationship that is in synchrony as both mother and baby spend most of the time in mutually supportive and similar behaviors. Adapted from Brazelton, Koslowski, and Main, 1974, p. 62.

an infant state that is pleasing and satisfying to them. Not unexpectedly, this normal desire results in a number of parental activities that both soothe the baby and preserve the "sanity" of the parents. Two of the more frequent methods used by parents to influence newborn states are feeding and rocking. Swaddling (snugly wrapping) a newborn baby in a blanket is soothing to the infant (Byrne and Horowitz, 1981).

To some extent, an infant is a self-soother and can move from one state to another without external influence. For example, infants can reduce distress by sucking (a response that is ready to operate at birth). Young infants are frequently observed in sucking movements during light sleep (Lipsitt, Crook, and Booth, 1985). Sucking on a pacifier is an effective way of reducing distress (Field and Goldson, 1984). There are wide variations in infants, not only in their activity levels and states, but also in their ability to be soothed (Bates, 1980).

In summary, the state of an infant influences how it responds to its world—including its parents. A drowsy or sleeping infant responds very differently than an infant that is awake and alert. Furthermore, the cyclical nature of the infant's states seems to promote *predictability* in the caregiving relationship. Because of the reduced level of communication between parent and newborn (i.e., compared with communication between parents and older children), parents need to rely more on a trial-and-error method of determining infant needs. Thus, the *regularity* of infant states helps guide caregivers in determining the category or type of infant need.

Complications of Childbirth

LOW-BIRTHWEIGHT BABIES.   Most infants weigh about 7½ pounds at birth; however, one American child in every twelve (about 8 percent) is born with a low birthweight (under 5½ pounds). All babies born small were traditionally considered *premature,* as were all babies with a gestation period of less than thirty-seven weeks.

Recently, physicians have begun to classify these babies into one of the following categories:

• *Preterm (or premature) babies.* These babies are born before the thirty-seventh gestational week. (Forty weeks is the normal gestation period.) These babies are typically low birthweight. In fact, preterm babies account for most low birthweight babies.
• *Low-birthweight babies.* These babies are born weighing less than 5½ pounds (2,500 grams). Such babies may or may not be preterm. If these babies weigh less than 90 percent of all babies at their gestational age, they are called small for gestation age. These babies are all low-birthweight babies, yet they are full term.

Because the distinction between preterm babies and low-birthweight babies has been made only in the past five to ten years, it is not always clear whether prior research deals with preterm babies or low-birthweight babies or both.

Generally speaking, the evidence suggests that babies born after a gestation period of thirty-six weeks will have few difficulties. However, babies born before that time tend to have problems, although the infant's physical maturity is more important than actual gestation time or birthweight. Likewise, infants who weigh less than three pounds at birth tend to be particularly at risk for death during the first month of life (U.S. Department of Health and Human Services, 1980). Babies that are small for gestational age usually have problems. They have not been gaining weight normally for one or more reasons including the following: The mother was malnourished, the umbilical cord and placenta did not function correctly, there were genetic problems, there were prenatal infections, and so on. In spite of these findings, there is nonetheless encouraging evidence of dramatic medical efforts that have enabled some babies born under two pounds or before the twenty-sixth gestation week to survive and become normal children (Buckwald, Zoren, and Egan, 1984). The results of another study indicated that although 80 percent of a sample of infants born under two pounds did not survive, thirteen of the sixteen survivors were doing reasonably well at three years of age (Bennett, Robinson, and Sells, 1983). The infants in the study showed no serious central nervous system problems or vision/learning difficulties, although one child was measured as subnormal in intelligence. Other evidence with surviving infants who were born under three pounds is also optimistic (Klein et al., 1985).

Standard care for preterm and low-birthweight babies includes placing them in an incubator or isolette. An isolette provides a temperature-regulated, antiseptic environment for the newborn under stress. Infant life for an extended time period in an isolette could lead to sensory deprivation and/or to a disturbed parent-infant relationship. Sensory impoverishment may occur because of the obvious isolation of the infant from environmental stimulation. A disturbed parent-infant relationship may be the result of several factors, including the following (Jeffcoate, Humphrey, and Lloyd, 1979):

· Parental reluctance to become attached to an infant who might die.
· Parental anxiety about the infant's health.

However, there is evidence that such low-birthweight infants can benefit from a variety of stimulating experiences (while still in the hospital) that support their individual development and the parent-infant relationship (Leib, Benfield, and Guidubaldi, 1980; Zeskind and Iacino, 1984). For example, low-birthweight infants who were given five minutes of soothing or rubbing during feeding and, when they grew bigger, were sung to in a rocking chair (also during feeding) performed considerably better on a measure of infant development (Bayley Scales of Infant Development) at six months (compared with a control group of low-birthweight infants who received no such stimulation) (Leib, Benfield, and Guidubaldi, 1980). In addition, there is evidence that frequent maternal visits to the isolette enhance the mother-infant relationship (Zeskind and Iacino, 1984).

ANOXIA.   Lack of oxygen, or **anoxia,** is a major problem that can occur with any long or stressful birth. During normal deliveries, periods of anoxia occur when contractions momentarily squeeze the umbilical cord. Only when anoxia occurs repeatedly and is prolonged can this be a problem for the fetus, with brain damage or even death resulting. Fetal monitoring today allows doctors to know when anoxia is a problem and the fetus is under too much stress. (Fetal monitors are sensing devices that measure the stress on the fetus. One type is attached to the fetus' scalp while the fetus is in the birth canal. Another type is placed around the mother's abdomen.) At this time, the delivery would be speeded up medically or a cesarean delivery would be performed (Scher and Dix, 1983).

HYALINE MEMBRANE DISEASE.   This problem is called respiratory distress syndrome. It occurs in 60 percent of infants born three months early and in 20 percent of infants born one month early. It causes about 50 percent of all newborn deaths in the United States (Behrman and Vaughn, 1983). Hyaline membrane disease is a critical problem for preterm babies. A substance called *surfactin*, which coats the lungs and aids in normal breathing, is produced in insufficient quantities and results in irregular breathing or cessation of breathing.

STILLBIRTH. Another complication of childbirth may be a **stillbirth,** or the delivery of a dead child. In some instances death is diagnosed by physicians several weeks or days prior to delivery. In other instances death is not discovered until labor or delivery. Regardless of when death is discovered, the parents typically experience four phases of grief (Kirkley-Best and Kellner, 1982):

- *Shock and numbness.* This phase of grief is characterized by disbelief. Most of the research evidence suggests that despite the emotional pain, the parents need to experience the reality of what has happened. Although many hospitals do not allow the parents to view or to hold the dead baby, such activities may be a normal part of the grieving process. In addition, having a funeral may help the parents deal with their feelings.
- *Searching for the lost child.* Some parents may try to "replace" the deceased child by immediately wanting to begin another pregnancy. However, this may not help them deal directly with their grief. It is important for the parents to face the reality of loss and not avoid such feelings.
- *Disorganization.* The period from about six months to a year following the stillbirth may be characterized, in part, by feelings of depression, self-devaluation, or apathy. If such feelings become unmanageable, counseling is particularly helpful.
- *Reorientation.* The final phase of grief involves an acceptance of loss coupled with a recognition that the focus of parental attention needs to be on life and the living.

Low-Birthweight Infants

Five and a half pounds is generally considered the dividing line between normal and low birthweight.

[Some 6.7 percent (246,105 annually) of American newborns weigh 5½ lb. (2,500 gm.) or less (U.S. Department of Health and Human Services, 1986).] Babies weighing less than 4 lb. 7 oz. (less than 2,000 gm.) are particularly susceptible to critical illness.

Structural defects occur in about 6 percent of babies weighing more than 5½ lb.; in 9 percent of those between 4 lb. 7 oz. and 5 lb. 8 oz.; and in more than 30 percent of those weighing 4 lb. 6 oz. or less.

Until recent years, many doctors restricted a woman's diet during pregnancy. They believed that little weight gain and a small baby were best for safe, easy delivery. Others felt that this was not best for healthy births. Indeed a recent study showed that a 24- to 30-pound weight gain for mother and a 7-pound,

Estimated Number of Liveborn Infants with and Without Birth Defects, by Birthweight, 1982

Condition of Newborn	More than 5 lbs. 8 oz.	4 lbs. 7 oz. to 5 lbs. 8 oz.	Less than 4 lbs. 7 oz.	Total, all birth weights
With structural or metabolic defects	188,900	13,700	30,400	233,000
Without structural or metabolic defects	2,908,100	138,500	53,700	3,100,300
Total	3,097,000	152,200	84,100	3,333,300

More than one-quarter million infants are born with structural or metabolic defects or markedly low birthweight in the United States each year.

(Continued)

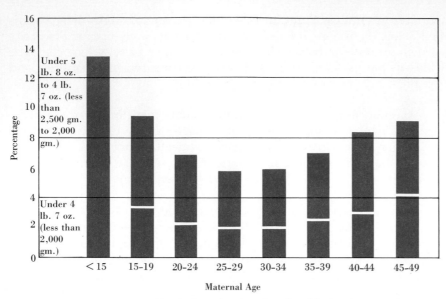

Percent of low-birth-weight infants (less than 5 lb. 8 oz.)
and very low-birth-weight infants (less than 4 lb. 7 oz.) by age of mother

Death rates for the newborn have declined sharply in recent years, but the rate of low birthweight has decreased only slightly. This reflects improved care of low-birthweight infants but relatively little progress in preventing prematurity and fetal growth retardation (small for gestational age). (U.S. Department of Health and Human Services, 1986)

4-ounce birthweight for baby were far healthier and safer for both.

Low birthweight now is considered the most common problem at birth, affecting one in every 12 babies born each year in the United States. It helps account for some 70 percent of our infant deaths.

What Causes Low Birthweight?

There are several known reasons why babies may be born too small, too soon, or both. Some are as yet unknown; others are suspected.

Earlier pregnancies that ended in miscarriage or a low-birthweight baby may be the result of conditions that could lead again to a low-birthweight baby. There may be an inherited disease in [the mother's] family that can cause fetal defects. Defects in an unborn baby, inherited or caused by an environmental factor, may keep it from growing to its normal birthweight.

Medical background of a mother influences birthweight, especially if she has high blood pressure, diabetes, heart, kidney, or breathing problems, hepati-

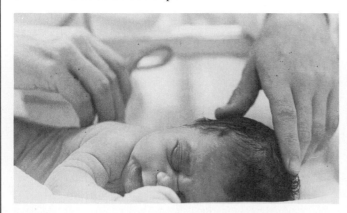

Newborn is examined by the physician in a nursery.

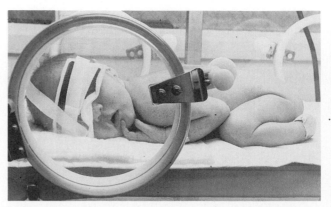

Baby in warming unit in Intermediate Intensive Care Nursery. Mask to protect eyes from light.

tis, viral or bacterial infections. Toxemia of pregnancy also may cause prematurity.

A mother's habits during pregnancy may affect birthweight. Among these are:

· Poor nutrition. An unborn baby is nourished by what its mother eats.
· Lack of early and regular prenatal care.
· Smoking, alcohol and drugs. Smokers tend to have smaller babies. Drug or alcohol use may stunt an unborn baby's growth.

Social factors, such as low income or little schooling, may place mothers at risk of having a low-birthweight baby. These mothers may be unable to afford good food and health care, or have never

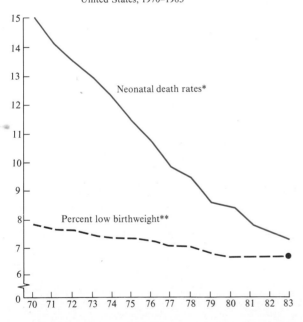

Neonatal Deaths and Low Birthweight
United States, 1970–1983

Neonatal death rates*

Percent low birthweight**

*Deaths under 28 days per 1,000 live births.
**Percent of live births weighing 2,500 grams (5½ lbs.) or less.

1983 Low Birthweight data not yet available.

Source: National Center for Health Statistics and state health departments.

Death rates for the newborn have declined sharply in recent years, but the rate of low birthweight has decreased only slightly. This reflects improved care of low-birthweight infants but relatively little progress in preventing prematurity and fetal growth retardation (small for gestational age).

(Figure taken from March of Dimes Birth Defects Foundation, Facts 1985, p. 29)

learned how to take care of themselves. Teenagers, especially, may not know or care about improving their health habits. Teenagers under 17 are among the mothers at greatest risk of having low-birthweight babies.

How Are Low Birthweight Problems Treated?

Special life saving equipment in intensive care nurseries helps to sustain small babies who otherwise might not survive. If a baby has trouble breathing, special cribs (isolettes), oxygen, and medication are right at hand. If the baby has low blood sugar, glucose can be fed through its veins.

If the infant is jaundiced, it may be treated with special lights in the nursery (phototherapy). If anemic, it may be treated with dietary supplements. In severe cases, it is given a blood transfusion.

Bleeding in the brain can't be corrected except in rare cases where vitamin K may help. Doctors watch for and treat the secondary effects of brain bleeding to help prevent possible brain damage. They examine normal spaces in the brain (ventricles) with such devices as ultrasound or CAT scanners. The spaces may begin to fill with fluid, which could be damaging. Doctors may put a tube inside to help drain the fluid off (shunting). In other cases, a hollow needle is put into the lower spine to drain off fluid. This is done every few days or so, until, as often happens, the excess fluid build up stops.

How Does Low Birthweight Affect a Baby?

Any of the complications that can happen to a newborn are more likely to happen to a low-birthweight baby than one of normal size.

The baby may have trouble breathing. Its lungs may not get enough oxygen to supply its blood system and body tissues. Some low-birthweight babies have low blood sugar (hypoglycemia), which may cause tremors, eye-rolling, poor appetite or brain damage. Jaundice (yellowish skin) may show that the baby's liver is slow to start working on its own. (During pregnancy, the mother's liver works for both of them.)

A premature baby may be anemic (have fewer red blood cells). Normally, the unborn baby stores iron during the later months of pregnancy and uses it in early infancy to make red blood cells. Born too soon, the infant may not have enough time to build up iron stores.

Low-birthweight babies may not have enough fat

(Continued)

under their skins to help keep a healthy body temperature. This can cause blood chemistry changes and slow growth.

One of the most severe results of low birthweight is bleeding in the brain. It happens to 40 to 45 percent of infants weighing less than 1,500 grams and may result in brain damage or death.

Later in childhood, nervous system and behavior problems may occur, as a result of the low birthweight.

Can Low Birthweight be Prevented?

Through public and professional health education, parents and health care workers can learn how to avoid or treat many factors that may contribute to low birthweight.

The first step is **early and regular prenatal care**. Health care professionals often can tell in advance which pregnant women or unborn babies may be at risk. Threatening medical conditions often can be safely treated and good health habits outlined. Weight gain can be carefully watched for unusual changes that might affect birthweight.

A recent San Francisco study showed that preterm delivery (birth before 37 weeks) could be prevented in a large number of cases when the start of preterm labor was noted early enough for drug treatment to be effective.

Through public health education and community programs, **good nutrition** can be taught and made available where needed, mothers can be motivated to take care of their health, and to avoid cigarette smoking, alcohol use, and taking unprescribed drugs.

From March of Dimes, 1982, 1983, 1985.

The Relationship Between Parent and Newborn

It is quite apparent to those who have observed the interaction of parent and newborn that an attachment relationship is developing. Why does this relationship seem to progress so rapidly? What are the features of the emerging relationship that bring parent and child together? Figure 5.16 indicates some of the maternal and child factors that contribute to this relationship. We first describe the interactions initiated by the mother and then discuss the interactions originating with the infant.

INTERACTIONS ORIGINATING WITH THE PARENT.   *Touch.* Although it is not perfectly clear which infant characteristics lead to touch by the mother, there is some

Wayne Mason

Mother ------------→ Infant		Mother ←------------ Infant	
1.	Touch	Eye to Eye	1.
2.	Eye to Eye	Cry	2.
3.	High-Pitched Voice	Entrainment	3.
4.	Entrainment		
5.	Time Giver		

FIGURE 5.16
The reciprocal interaction of mother and infant in the attachment process. Modified from Klaus and Kennel, 1982.

agreement on the characteristic touch patterns that mothers use when making their first contact with the newborn (Klaus and Kennell, 1982). Mothers appear to follow an orderly sequence of behavior after birth while they become acquainted with newborns. Klaus and Kennell observed that when nude infants were placed next to their mothers either a few minutes or a few hours after birth, the mothers touched them according to the following pattern: *fingertip contact* with the newborn's extremities; and *palm contact*, or massaging and stroking of the trunk. During the first three minutes of the observation period, fingertip contact occurred first and 52 percent of the time. Palm contact occurred only 28 percent of the time during the first three minutes. In the second three-minute period, the mothers used palm contact and stroking for 62 percent of the total time compared with 38 percent for fingertip contact. These results suggest that there is a sequence of tactile familiarity that mothers naturally follow. It is interesting to note that this sequence is modified and slowed down when babies are preterm or low birth-weight.

> *Eye-to-eye Contact.*
>
> Open your eyes. Oh, come on, open your eyes. If you open your eyes I'll know you're alive. (mother's comment reported in Klaus and Kennell, 1982, p. 74)

Eye-to-eye contact seems to serve the purposes of allowing the mother to give the newborn an identity and of providing exciting feedback to the mother. When mothers are given the opportunity of holding their newborns immediately after birth, there is a dramatic increase in the time spent in the face-to-face position during the first few minutes after birth (Klaus and Kennell, 1982; see Table 5.2).

While eye-to-eye contact may be a rewarding experience for mothers and fathers, the human eye and face also have visual characteristics that increase their "stimulus value" for the infant. Data on newborn vision suggest that infants prefer stimuli that are moving, moderately complex, and ovoid like the human face (Banks and Salapatek, 1983; Van Giffen and Haith, 1984). The eyes have extra stimulus features, such as shininess and black (pupil) and white (iris) contrast, that attract infant attention.

High-Pitched Voice. Mothers and fathers tend to speak to their newborns in a high-pitched voice (Aslin, Pisóni, and Jusczyk, 1983). Observations indicate that parents use a high-pitched voice for their infants and then switch to normal pitch for everyday conversation with adults. The parental use of a high-pitched voice fits with the newborn's sensitivity and attraction to high-frequency sounds.

Entrainment. When two people talk to one another, their communication is not simply verbal; it also involves movement. The analysis of sound films of human communication shows that both speaker and listener make body movements (sometimes imperceptible) "in time" to the words of the speaker (Condon and Sander, 1974a).

TABLE 5.2
Percentage of Total Observation Time in Face-to-Face Position

Initial Contact (Minutes)	Face to Face (Percentage)
0–3	10
3–6	17
6–9	23

Based on Klaus and Kennell, 1982.

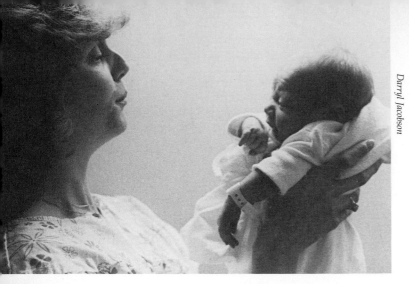

A mother and a newborn in face-to-face position.

Condon and Sander have also demonstrated that there is a complex interaction between newborn motor behavior and the organized speech patterns of adults. Specifically, the newborn's motor behavior is entrained by and synchronized with the speech of adults. An analysis of films of adults talking to newborns indicated that when the infant was already moving, changes in the organization of these movements were coordinated with changes in the sound patterns of adult speech. For example, as the adult paused for a breath or accented a syllable, the infant made body movements such as raising or lowering its arms and/or legs or raising its eyebrows. Thus, not only do the newborn and the parent or caretaker contribute to a shared relationship, but the shared rhythms of the relationship allow the infant to be introduced to many repetitions of linguistic forms long before it is capable of formal speech and communication.

Time Giver. The synchrony (mutual adaptation) of movement during speech is one part of a much larger picture of reciprocal interaction between parent and newborn. There seems to be a general synchrony of rhythms between the newborn and its mother that has its beginnings in the prenatal period (Klaus and Kennell, 1982). This synchrony of biological rhythms or biorhythmicity is thrown into a state of disequilibrium at birth. Prior to birth, the fetus is probably attuned to such intrauterine rhythms as the mother's sleep-wake cycle, the general pattern of the mother's day, the beat of the mother's heart, and the rhythmic contractions of the mother's uterus preceding birth (Klaus and Kennell, 1982). By following a routine after birth, the parent helps the newborn to reestablish biorhythmicity. This process is evident in the progressive increase of the co-occurrence of the mother's holding the newborn and the newborn's being in an alert state (Cassel and Sander, 1975). In addition, Cassel and Sander pointed out that mother-infant interaction allows the newborn to regulate its circadian rhythms. The newborn's apparent perception of this interaction was demonstrated by having a mother wear a mask and remain silent during one feeding when her newborn was seven days old. During the masked feeding, the infant took far less milk and its sleep patterns were significantly disrupted (following the masked feeding) compared with normal feedings. Thus, the mother serves as a time organizer or "time giver" for the reorganization of neonatal functions.

It is important to recognize that in the process of establishing the synchrony between infant and caregiver, it is typically the caregiver who is making the major adjustment. For example, there is evidence that many infants are rather rigid in their rhythms and that it is the mothers who quickly adapt to the patterns of their infants (Kaye, 1982).

INTERACTIONS ORIGINATING WITH THE NEWBORN.   *Eye-to-Eye Contact.*   Mutual gazing is an important affirmation of an emerging relationship for both parent and newborn. It is interesting to note that the ordinary distance between the mother or the father and the newborn during feeding is about twelve inches. Because the infant's visual system does not focus the eyes effectively beyond this distance, the feeding distance of twelve inches provides the ideal opportunity for mutual gazing. The significance of mutual gazing is reaffirmed in research with blind infants, whose mothers reported having difficulty "feeling close" to their newborns (Fraiberg, 1974). Infant-originated eye-to-eye contact may serve an important function as a releaser of caretaking responses (Fogel, 1982). The emotional meaning of mutual gazing may result in such responses as an increasing desire to hold the newborn and an increasing enthusiasm about "our baby."

Cry. The sound of an infant crying can affect parents in a number of ways. As any parent who has heard this sound during the middle of the night can testify, it is difficult to ignore. The cry of the newborn is, like mutual gazing, a way of influencing the interaction between parent and infant. Specifically, it reduces the distance between them, so that the infant's needs can be identified and satisfied (Lester, 1983).

In the case of mothers who breast-feed, there is some evidence that the newborn's cry may cause a physiological change that increases the likelihood of nursing (Lind, Vuorenkoski, and Wasz-Häckert, 1973). For example, some women who breast-feed their infants report feeling their milk "come in" (the "let-down" reflex) when they hear their hungry babies crying. Using thermal (heat-sensitive) photography, Lind et al. demonstrated that fifty-four (of sixty-three) mothers showed a substantial increase in the blood flow to their breasts after they heard their babies cry.

Entrainment.

You cannot fall in love with a dishrag. (mother's comment reported in Klaus and Kennell, 1982, p. 82)

Another basic feature of the emerging attachment relationship between the parent and the newborn is the necessity for mutual perception of responses or signals such as eye movement, body movement, and speech sounds. This process of mutual following or mutual entrainment is supported by both members in the relationship.

SUMMARY: PARENT-NEWBORN INTERACTIONS.   We have sketched some of the separate components of the interactional system between parent and newborn. This description has been useful in demonstrating that *both* parent and infant may originate an interaction. In addition, such a perspective may help us to appreciate the important contribution of the newborn as an active rather than a passive organism (Kaye, 1982).

Parent and newborn behaviors complement each other in various sensory systems. For example, infant crying helps to initiate the let-down reflex in nursing mothers. Parental use of a high-pitched voice complements the newborn's attraction to high-frequency sounds. Parental interest in the newborn's eyes fits the infant's interest in the parent's eyes and face:

Nature appears to have preferentially developed . . . the visual pathways so that these sensory and motor functions are ready for the newborn infant to receive stimulation from his mother and to interact with her. (Klaus and Kennell, 1982, p. 82)

Programs for Families

There is increasing evidence of a need to transfer the protection, warmth, and security of family support into the hospital setting, so that from the beginning, the emerging relationships between the family and their newborn are further enhanced and developed. If extended visiting of all immediate family members and "rooming-in" are encouraged, the family members can better learn to care for the baby. Confidence gained in the hospital during this postdelivery period provides a better base for child rearing.

TRENDS IN INFANT CARE.   Trends in infant care have gone through complete changes over the past fifty years. At the beginning of this century, babies were born in the home. Naturally the mother and the baby roomed together and the mother cared for the baby. The baby was breast-fed and allowed to eat when it wished to, and it was held and rocked when it appeared that it needed such attention. The father had an important part in the care of the mother and the baby.

Early in the twentieth century, infant care became increasingly strict, especially in the "scientific" 1920s, when everything was done according to schedule. Babies were fed on an inflexible schedule, were given artificial feedings according to the latest nutritional knowledge, and were allowed to cry for long periods of time, because picking them up would supposedly "spoil" them. All earlier methods of infant care were considered old-fashioned, and mothers were anxious to follow the latest scientific teachings. More and more babies were being born in hospitals, and the busy hospital staff made schedules seem even more important. There was little time to teach the mother about the care of her baby. She went home inexperienced but with a set of rules to follow. The father was considered relatively unimportant, especially during the hospitalization of the mother.

Then in the late 1930s, a change came about, with a return to many of the earlier practices. Schedules and routines became less important. The first organized effort to change infant care again began in 1942, when the Cornelian Corner was organized in Detroit, Michigan. This group was composed of a psychiatrist, a pediatrician, an obstetrician, a nurse, and workers in allied fields who planned to do research and education in child development and family life. They emphasized the importance of allowing each baby to follow its own individual schedule because it was often difficult for the baby to fit into a prearranged one. They stressed the value of such permissiveness in the development of a wholesome personality. Rooming-in, breast-feeding, and self-demand feeding schedules were given special emphasis by the Cornelians. They believed that the first step in the future development of a well-balanced, healthy adult was indulgent care for the baby.

ROOMING-IN.   **Rooming-in** is a hospital arrangement by which the mother and the baby are cared for in the same unit, and the father has the opportunity to care for the baby as much as he wishes, thus becoming closely acquainted with the infant. Rooming-in provides the mother with the advantages of hospital delivery and hospital care in as homelike an atmosphere as it is possible to provide. This program focuses on the family, providing for the interrelationship that comes from a close association of mother, father, family, and baby. Rooming-in usually involves having the baby in the mother's room for a part of each day and in a central nursery the remainder of the time. For rooming-in to be successful, the interest and cooperation of the parents and of the hospital personnel are essential, and an adequate staff for nursing care is necessary. Although all mothers do not wish to have this arrangement, it is possible to provide rooming-in when requested in most hospitals.

Summary

1. *Pregnancy* and the *birth process* are neither static nor brief experiences. Rather, they are periods of human development filled with growth, change, and exciting enrichment. This chapter examined the birth process from an interactional or systems perspective. The focus was on birth as an emerging relationship between the newborn and its parents.

2. The event of childbirth has entered a period of dramatic change—both for the health care system and for families. There have been changes in the structure and function of families, new birth settings, and new birth technology.

3. The ability of parents to develop a successful relationship with the newborn depends on a number of factors. These factors include the parents' own personalities and temperaments, the response of the newborn infant to the parents, the history of interpersonal relationships of the parents with their own families of origin and with each other, past experiences with pregnancy, and the assimilation of cultural values and practices by the parents (Klaus and Kennell, 1982).

4. During pregnancy a woman experiences two major changes. *Acceptance of pregnancy* occurs during the first trimester. During the second trimester, *differentiation* occurs. Differentiation is the maternal recognition of the fetus as a separate individual. The primary signal for this event is the maternal sensation of fetal movement.

5. *Labor* is the process by which the baby and placenta are expelled through the birth canal. It involves three stages—*dilation, expulsion,* and *delivery of the placenta.*

6. Babies may be delivered in a variety of ways. The *traditional hospital delivery* involves the use of all available and necessary medical technology including drugs to ensure a safe and comfortable delivery. In the United States, the traditional hospital childbirth involves a doctor and nurses in attendance during the entire delivery. While most childbirths occur in a hospital, a relatively small, but increasing number of families are electing to have childbirth in settings outside the hospital.

7. The *Lamaze* or prepared-childbirth technique involves instruction in the physiology and anatomy of childbirth, instruction in muscular relaxation, instruction in breathing techniques, and the use of a labor "coach" (typically the husband or a friend).

8. The *Leboyer* method is designed to create a soothing and relaxing birth experience for the infant. Although the Leboyer approach to childbirth has caused parents and obstetricians to more carefully consider the infant's first moments of life, the evaluative evidence on the approach is mixed. Practices such as the dimming of lights during delivery have become a common practice in many hospitals. Furthermore, there is no evidence that birth is a traumatic experience for the infant. Therefore, strict adherence to the Leboyer method appears unnecessary.

9. In *cesarean* births the physician makes an incision through the abdominal wall and the uterus, removes the infant, and then sews up the incision.

10. After the birth of the infant, many significant events happen to the mother, the father, the baby, and the relationship between parents and newborn. For parents, the birth of a first baby initiates an experience that is new to both husband and wife as individuals and as a marital pair. The newborn's features and body are quite different from what they will be later on. The baby's appearance may be surprising to a couple who have not seen a newborn before. At birth, the infant's nervous system is relatively immature. Most of the newborn's bodily functions and responses are carried out by reflex action. Newborn sensory capacities include vision, hearing, smell, taste, feeling pain, sensitivity to touch, sensitivity to rhythms, and imitative skills. Two tests that are used to assess the newborn's condition are the *Apgar test* and the *Brazelton Neonatal Behavioral Assessment Scale*.

11. Some complications of childbirth include *low-birthweight*, *anoxia*, *hyaline membrane disease*, and *stillbirth*.

12. In addition to the variations in infants' temperaments, there are also important variations in the daily behavior of each newborn infant. These variations in cycles of wakefulness, sleepiness, and activity are called *states*. A baby's reaction to its environment usually depends on its state. Newborn states are influenced by both internal timing mechanisms and external stimulation. The infant and parent/caretaker are an interacting system. Therefore, newborn states affect parental behavior and are, in turn, affected by parental activity.

13. The reciprocal interaction between parent and infant in the *attachment* process is based on interactions that originate with both parent and infant. Some of the components of this system include touch, eye-to-eye contact, infant crying, and parental voice pitch. The contribution of the newborn to the attachment system is as an active rather than a passive organism. Parent and newborn behaviors complement each other in various sensory systems. For example, the common practice of parents' using high-pitched voice tones when talking to newborns and infants complements the infants' attraction to high-frequency sounds.

   There is increasing evidence of a need to transfer the protection, warmth, and security of family support into the hospital setting. *Rooming-in* is a hospital arrangement by which the mother and the baby are cared for in the same unit and the father has the opportunity to care for the baby as much as he desires. The program focuses on the family as well as providing a homelike atmosphere in the hospital.

Questions

1. Briefly discuss both sides of the controversy of home births versus hospital births.
2. What are the factors that distinguish "real" labor from "false" labor?
3. Briefly summarize the three stages of labor.
4. What are the advantages of "prepared childbirth"?
5. Identify and briefly describe two newborn reflexes that illustrate the immaturity of the newborn's nervous system.
6. Briefly identify and describe three infant states. What is a "biological clock"?
7. Why is eye-to-eye contact important for the developing infant-caregiver relationship?

Key Terms

Anoxia	Lamaze method
Apgar test	Leboyer method
Babinski reflex	Low-birthweight babies
Brazelton Neonatal Behavioral Assessment Scale	Newborn states
	Primitive reflexes
Cesarean delivery	Rooming-in
Contractions	Rooting reflexes
Delivery of the placenta	Startle (Moro) reflex
Dilation	Stillbirth
Expulsion	Sucking reflex
Grasp (palmar) reflex	Tonic-neck reflex
Hyaline membrane disease	Traditional delivery
Infant mortality	Walking reflex
Labor	Withdrawal reflex

Suggested Readings

GOLDBERG, S., and DIVITTO, B. A. *Born Too Soon: Preterm Birth and Early Development.* San Francisco; Freeman, 1983. An excellent discussion of problems associated with preterm infants.

KITZINGER, S. *Birth over Thirty.* New York: Penguin, 1985. An excellent discussion of factors and risks associated with later pregnancy including Down syndrome, cesarean sections, and so on.

KLAUS, M. H., and KENNELL, J. H. *Parent-Infant Bonding,* 2nd ed. St. Louis: Mosby, 1982. A very timely book on the genesis of the earliest relationship that a baby has with its caregivers, including the factors that inhibit and enhance this relationship.

LEBOYER, F. *Birth Without Violence.* New York: Knopf, 1975. A discussion of a novel approach to childbirth by a French obstetrician—an interesting, well-illustrated, and poetic book.

SHAPIRO, H. *The Pregnancy Book for Today's Woman.* New York: Consumers Union, 1984. A readable book with practical suggestions on such topics as nutrition, exercise, prescription drugs, and environmental hazards.

6

Infancy and Toddlerhood: Contexts of Development

The beast and the bird their common charge attend
The mothers nurse it, and the sires defend;
The young dismissed, to wander earth or air,
There stops the instinct, and there the care.
A longer care man's helpless kind demands,
That longer care contracts more lasting bonds.
                    —*Alexander Pope,* Essay on Man

Although the reciprocal relationship or dyad between the infant and caretaker is a major focus of this chapter, the systems or ecological approach to infancy suggests something more: the mutual and dynamic relationship between the family of the infant and the social system in which that family exists. This social system includes at least (1) the *neighborhood and community* in which the family lives (including friendships, support networks, and services), (2) the parental work setting, and (3) the government structure and related social policies that affect families of infants (e.g., social policies that encourage or discourage the development of quality day-care programs for infants). As in the case of the relationship between infant and parent, the interaction between these contexts and the family of the infant is mutual and bidirectional (see Fig. 6.1).

The first major subdivision of this chapter explores the family system as the immediate context within which infants and toddlers develop, concentrating particularly on recent profound changes in the American family and on the form and function of the family. In the second portion of the chapter we turn to a broader but also very important context of child development—the family, the community/neighborhood, and the world of work from the point of view of the young adult (who is most often the infant's or toddler's parent)—and its impact on the young child. We look particularly at the subjects of marriage and parenthood, and then at child abuse as a breakdown in the family system. Our examination of the community/neighborhood deals especially with child-care programs, and we look at the world of work from the vantage of the working woman.

Development's Immediate Context: The Infant in the Family System

The reciprocal nature of parent-infant relationships means that the influence of the infant on the family (infant characteristics and behaviors such as crying or smiling, for example) is just as important for infant development as the influence of the family on the infant (parent characteristics and behaviors such as level of

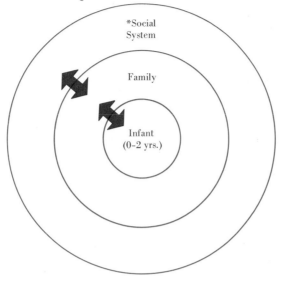

- Neighborhood/community
- Parental work setting
- Government structure
  and social policies
- Educational institutions

*Social
System

Family

Infant
(0–2 yrs.)

Infant System
(0–2 Years)

FIGURE 6.1
The system of infancy.

The infant in the context of the family.

Shan Rucinski

Garry Rowe

education or feeding practices). Traditional research and theory on infancy, however, have tended to emphasize infant development as the one-way result of parents' influencing their offspring (Bronfenbrenner, 1986).

Changes in the Family

The thought of family is often a stimulus for very strong emotion. Membership in a close-knit family can result in a sense of tremendous security, but it is also the framework within which rejection and conflict hurt more than in almost any other life situation. Furthermore, within the last generation many profound changes have occurred in American society that have had, in turn, a significant impact on the family. Some of these changes are a large increase in the number of working mothers (both full- and part-time), increasing numbers of single-parent families headed by women, and changing attitudes of women regarding their place in society. The results of these social changes on children and families include the following:

- In 1982, 32 million children, or 55 percent of all children under eighteen years of age, had a mother in the labor force (Fig. 6.2).
- The mothers of more than 45 percent of all youngsters age six and of nearly 60 percent of those six to seventeen years were in the labor force (Fig. 6.2).
- These proportions have grown rapidly in the last decade as it has become more acceptable for mothers to work (Fig. 6.2).
- In March 1982, 26 million wives, or 51 percent of all married women, were working or looking for work. Twenty years earlier, only a third were in the labor force (Fig. 6.3).
- Over half the growth in married women's labor force participation occurred during the 1970s, largely among those with school-age children. Between 1970

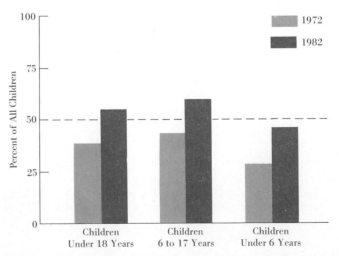

FIGURE 6.2
Children with mothers in the labor force as a proportion of all children by age of children, in 1972 and 1982. The proportion of children with mothers in the labor force has grown to more than half. From U.S. Department of Labor, Bureau of Labor Statistics.

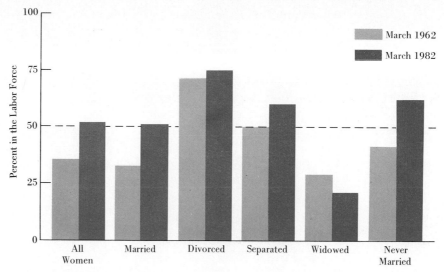

FIGURE 6.3

Labor force participation rates of women by marital status, 1962 and 1982. Half of all married women are now in the labor force. From U.S. Department of Labor, Bureau of Labor Statistics.

and 1980, the labor force participation rate of wives whose only children were six to seventeen years old rose from 49 percent to 62 percent. However, since 1980, most of the increase has been among those with preschool children.

· The proportions of divorced, separated, and never-married women in the labor force in 1982 were also greater than they had been twenty years earlier. Although the *increase* was smallest among divorced women, they remained far more likely to be in the labor force than women of any other marital status (Fig. 6.3).

· One of every six families was maintained by a woman in March 1982. During the past decade, the number of families in which no husband was present climbed steadily, reflecting the increased frequency of marital breakups and children born outside marriage (Fig. 6.4).

· The growth in the number of families maintained by women far outpaced that of other families. From 1972 to 1982, their number increased by 57 percent to a total of 9.7 million, compared with a 10 percent increase for other families (Fig. 6.4).

· Three out of five women maintaining families were in the labor force in 1982. On average, these women had completed fewer years of school than wives and were concentrated in lower skilled, lower paying jobs. (U.S. Department of Labor, 1983, pp. 20–25)

Why Look at the Family?

There are at least two major reasons for us to begin our discussion of infancy and toddlerhood with an analysis of the family.

In the first place, the family is *the* place in which early development largely occurs. Some have suggested that the social and cognitive level that preschool children possess on entering the formal school is largely influenced by their experiences in the family (Hess and Holloway, 1984). To a large degree the problems

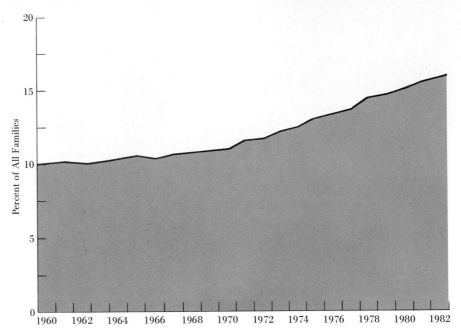

FIGURE 6.4

Families maintained by women as a proportion of all families, 1960–1982. The proportion of families maintained by a woman has increased markedly. From U.S. Department of Labor, Bureau of Labor Statistics, 1983.

and successes of children cannot be separated from the circumstances of those who are mainly responsible for their care. That is, the child and infant's environment is determined by the circumstances of significant adults, including but not restricted to parents. One cannot successfully intervene in the lives of infants or young children without, at the same time, influencing those adults (Bronfenbrenner, 1986).

In the second place, the changes in families that have resulted from broader social changes have affected the ability of the family to cope and function as a unit. Changes in the family directly affect the children.

What Is a Family?

The family has been defined in many ways, and its specific nature varies from one culture to another (Skolnick and Skolnick, 1986). Almost every known society has some type of family organization that is intermediate between the individual and the larger social community. Ordinarily, by *family* we mean a group of adults and children who live together for an extended period of time.

Most human beings belong to at least two types of family groups. The family that a child is born into is called the **family of orientation,** and the family formed by that child (usually through marriage) is called the **family of procreation**. Membership in the family of orientation is by birth, whereas membership in the family of procreation is by choice.

In addition to defining families by means of personal affiliation, one may also define families according to their structure.

THE NUCLEAR FAMILY. The **nuclear (or conjugal) family** consists of a married couple and their children (if any). In our society, the general expectation is that the husband, the wife, and their children will live in a household or home that is separate from the family of orientation. The nuclear family is more frequently a common family structure in industrialized or technologically advanced societies. The reason for the co-occurrence is the mobility of the nuclear family. In a society such as ours, where heads of households move about the country to different jobs (or to the same type of job in a different location), the mobility of the nuclear family is a valuable asset.

The nuclear family is not, however, without problems—or, at least, potential problems. The strength of the nuclear family—its independence and mobility—is also a potential source of difficulty. It has been suggested that the modern nuclear family tends to be isolated from the broad network of social support inherent in the extended family. The degree or nature of such isolation is controversial.

THE EXTENDED FAMILY.   The **extended family** includes the nuclear family and any number of other persons, related through marriage or birth, who share a single residence or live very close by. A typical extended family might include at least three generations: grandparents, two or more of their grown children and their spouses, and the sons and daughters of these children. In such extended families, it is common for the grandmother or the grandfather to serve as the head of the entire family group.

Such extended family arrangements are more commonly found in agricultural societies or preindustrial societies. Such family structures fit well with the needs of societies in which the family is the center of occupational and vocational effort. Where many hands are needed for the work of the family around the home or the farm, the extended family has been (and continues to be, in some societies and in some subcultures within our own society) an effective means of organizing the activities of family life and work. In the United States, extended families may be found, to some extent, among agricultural people as well as among the urban poor.

In some farm communities and urban neighborhoods mothers are more likely to have to work to support their children than elsewhere. Nearly two-thirds of mothers in single-parent families work, and another 20 percent are trying to find employment. Some social scientists refer to this situation, largely a result of the women's poor financial circumstances, as the "feminization of poverty" (Harrison, Serafica, and McAdoo, 1984). Almost 86 percent of black female-headed families and 38 percent of white female-headed families fall below the poverty level (Hill, 1983).

Alice Kandell

The extended family.

Strengths and Weaknesses of Six Family Forms

My appraisal of the strengths and weaknesses of each of six different family forms, based on a review of empirical studies, clinical reports and my own research activity, follows.

The Single Career Family

Intact nuclear family consisting of husband, wife and offspring living in a common household where one partner, usually the husband, is the provider. (Represents 13 percent of all households.)

STRENGTHS Maintains its position as the primary structure for potential socialization of members over the life cycle.

Is the primary unit for taking care of disabled, deviant and dependent members.

Is among the best adapted in terms of fitting the demands of the corporate economic structure.

WEAKNESSES Is easily broken, with increasing intervention of organizations and expenditures of monies to maintain individuals of broken marriages and new family forms.

The single breadwinner of the working class is unable to provide adequately for its maintenance. Among the middle classes, there is difficulty in providing an expected quality of life.

The Dual Career Family

Intact nuclear family consisting of husband, wife and offspring living in a common household where both partners work. (Represents 16 percent of all households.)

STRENGTHS Competent structure to provide maximal income for maintenance and to achieve quality of life aspirations.

Highly adequate form for effecting goals of gender equality. It provides work options for both marital partners and opportunity to share household tasks and marital responsibilities.

WEAKNESSES Dependence on kin and institutional support systems for effective maintenance and functioning.

Developing but still non-institutionalized values and means to harmonize the career activities and ambitions of both partners and the roles concerned with marital relationships and parenting.

The Single-Parent Household

With children under age 18. (Represents 16 percent of all households.)

Distribution of Adult Americans by Type of Household

HOUSEHOLD TYPE	PERCENTAGE OF ALL HOUSEHOLDS
Heading single-parent families	16
Other single, separated, divorced or widowed	21
Living in child-free or post-child-rearing marriages	23
Living in extended families	6
Living in experimental families or cohabiting	4
Living in dual-breadwinner nuclear families	16
Living in no wage-earner nuclear families	1
Living in single-breadwinner nuclear families	13

STRENGTHS Many adults who can function as socialization models for children are potentially available. Adults other than parents may be more effective in teaching and socializing children.

If supported appropriately, the single parent can achieve greater self-expression than a married counterpart; accountability is limited to children.

For a significant number of single-parent families, which result as a consequence of separation and divorce, the removal or absence of a violent parent results in a nurturant and liveable family form.

WEAKNESSES Need for support systems for parenting, economic and health maintenance and social relationships—often scarce or unavailable in particular communities.

The insufficiency of finances endemic to this family form often results in higher morbidity and expenditure of third party monies for maintenance and survival. Another consequence of economic deficiency is the pressure for some to remarry in order to obtain such support, with increased probability that the previous marriage experience will be repeated.

For some families, when the single parent is gainfully employed and substitute parents are unavailable or ineffective, the socialization is done by peers, and the behavior of children may be viewed as deviate and delinquent.

The Remarried Nuclear Family

Husband, wife and offspring living in a common household. (Represents 11 percent of all households.)

STRENGTHS Previous marital experiences may result in an increased number (actual incidence unknown) of stable marriages.

Parenting, which may formerly have been the function of a single adult, may be shared with the new partner and his or her older children.

For some, there is improved economic status as a consequence of shared income.

WEAKNESSES The difficulties in blending two formerly independent households into one functioning unit may result in extreme psychic stress for some members.

Formations consisting of two large-size families may require substantial economic help, counseling and other supports in order to survive.

Economic and social commitments to individuals of previous marriages may restrict the development of adequate, stable relationships in the new marriage.

The Kin Family

Consisting of bilateral or intergenerational-linked members living in the same household. (Represents six percent of all households.)

STRENGTHS Maintenance of familial values and transmission of accumulated knowledge and skill are likely occurrences.

Multiple adults are available for socialization and shared household and work responsibilities.

WEAKNESSES Demands for geographical mobility are not easily met.

From one perspective, the resistance to changes which threaten the maintenance of this family form can reduce the motivation of individuals to achieve in the society.

Experimental Families

Individuals in multi-adult households (communes) or cohabitating. (Represents four percent of all households.)

STRENGTHS In communal forms, a large number of individuals are available to form a support system to meet individual needs, a situation especially important to individuals in transition from one family form to another, such as recently divorced women with small children.

Individuals not ready or unwilling to make a commitment to a long-term partnership can experience economic and social sharing, psychic growth and open communication and interpersonal relationships.

WEAKNESSES Few of these forms have developed strategies, techniques or economic bases to sustain their activities or achieve their goals.

In a large number of experimental family forms, role responsibilities are not clearly delineated or articulated, with consequential difficulties in implementing parenting, economic, household and other functions.

From Sussman, 1978, pp. 32–37.

In later chapters, we return to detailed discussions of the impact of single-parent families on the development of children in terms of academic achievement, sex-role development, antisocial behavior, and so on. Here, we examine the stresses under which single-parent, mother-headed families operate. Such stresses include the following:

• Single-parent households tend to suffer from *task overload*. The single parent is trying to handle the tasks that are considered a full-time responsibility for a two-parent family (Hetherington, Cox, and Cox, 1982).
• Single-parent households tend to be under financial strain (Weinraub and Wolf, 1983).
• Mothers in single-parent families tend to be socially isolated and therefore lacking in emotional and social support (Hetherington, Cox, and Cox, 1982). (Part of this problem may be that there is not sufficient time to create or nurture such support relationships because of time required for work and child rearing by a single individual.)
• Single-parent mothers who do not have an adequate social support network may encounter problems in raising children. For example, there is some evidence that unless male participation emanates from the mother's support system, daughters

will adapt or develop better than sons (likewise, sons may develop better in father-headed single-parent families) (Santrock and Warshak, 1979).

• Single-parent families have no second spouse who can serve as a buffer between a child and the other parent. Such a situation may be particularly difficult if there is an incompatible relationship between the single parent and a child (Hetherington, Cox, and Cox, 1982).

Single-parent families, then, are at increased risk from the stresses and strains that may characterize their circumstances. At the same time, an exclusively negative picture need not inevitably characterize such families. The *functioning* of the family appears to be a more significant influence on the development of the child in the family than the simple factor of the *number* of parents in the home. Family functioning includes such features as the general family climate (i.e., the general circumstances or the environment of the family), the characteristics of individual family members (including the coping skills of the parent present in a single-parent family), and the interactions of family members.

What Do Families Do?

We have seen that the family is an important institution that may take different forms. Its major function is to *mediate,* or to be an intermediary, between the larger society or culture and the individual family member. Although this statement helps us to understand what families do *in general,* we can gain a better perspective of the significance of the family by examining six specific **family functions.**

FAMILY FUNCTIONS

1. *Economic cooperation and division of labor.* A basic problem that each family must deal with is the provision of food, shelter, and other amenities of life for its members. These economic responsibilities are accomplished in most societies through some sort of division of labor; that is, various family activities become the

Darryl Jacobson

What do families do?

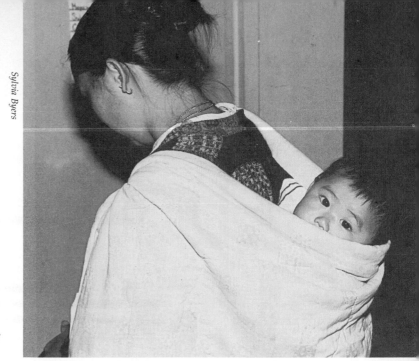

Sylvia Byers

The family is an important institution that may take different forms.

primary responsibility of certain members of the family unit. For example, a traditional division of labor in our society is that the husband is responsible for providing material goods for the family, and the woman keeps house and cares for the children. This is obviously not the *only* possible division of family labor. In fact, this "traditional" pattern is probably at the root of many of the changes—and the demands for change—that are taking place.

Because of single-parent status or the need for a career or the need to supplement family income, women in increasing numbers have entered the work force (Fig. 6.3). In many families, the husband's income may not be sufficient, so the wife may go to work to help the family maintain the desired standard of living or to help pay for a child's college expenses.

In a society where the "traditional" pattern of family organization has come under question, more women are free to pursue their own careers if they are so inclined. Such *dual-career* households may have such patterns of organization as sharing the homemaking and child-care responsibilities (in addition to sharing the income-maintenance functions). Another reason that some women work outside the home is personal preference. They would rather work outside the home than remain at home all day.

The newer options of family organization have at least two major consequences:

Stephen Dietrich

Where children are present, the family is the primary institution for their care and socialization.

· As a result of the sharing of the separated responsibilities inherent in the "traditional" division of labor, there is a shifting emphasis to shared decision-making power. When the wife works, the husband is less likely to control finances and financial decisions.

· As a result of the increasing number of women in the work force and the larger number of choices for these women, unmarried women may perceive more options for themselves. For example, an unmarried woman who has a good job is not dependent on marriage and raising children for her identity.

2. *Care for and socialization of children.* Where children are present, the family is the primary institution for their care and socialization. Human infants and children are dependent on their parents for physical care and psychological support for a considerable period after birth. A central function of the family is the *socialization* of its children. Socialization is the process of teaching the child what he or she needs to know to be a member of society. This knowledge includes facts, skills, values, and attitudes toward society, adults, and people in general. Over the last hundred years, the socialization function has come to be shared with the school, although the primary responsibility still resides with the family.

3. *Legitimizing sexual relations.* This function is perhaps one of the most controversial. To the extent that marriage and the family make legitimate and acceptable a sexual relationship only between married partners, this function comes into collision with the sexual norms of some other segments of society. For example, some people find it appropriate to engage in sex before marriage if they are in love, have made an emotional commitment to one another, and/or have plans to get married. The advent of contraceptives such as "the pill" has made it possible to prevent unwanted births.

According to tradition, however, husband and wife are expected to have sexual relations only with each other. Tradition and law also rule our sexual relationships between persons with certain degrees of kinship. In addition, homosexual and lesbian relationships are sometimes viewed as inappropriate or even "abnormal." These views have become highly controversial.

4. *Reproduction.* Regardless of the structure that the family takes and regardless of the rules that govern sexual relationships, a primary and undeniable function of the family has been reproduction. Throughout most of human history, many societies needed to produce a great number of babies. The reason, of course, was that the human lifespan was shorter than it now is, and infant mortality was higher. Because so many children died either in infancy or in early childhood, it made sense to have large families.

With improvements in modern medicine, better nutrition, and improved public health measures, the need for families to have many children has dramatically changed. In a world of overpopulation, families are being encouraged to have fewer children.

5. *Provision of status and role.* The family provides the child with an initial notion of who he or she is, as well as what his or her position is in the social system. What the family provides is only a beginning but, nonetheless, an important one. Social status is assigned on the basis of family attributes (e.g., where the family lives, parental income, parental occupation) over which the individual has no control. This initial status is called *ascribed status.* A child's status is based on the status of the family into which he or she is born. This notion of ascribed status is sometimes difficult to accept for people reared in a democratic society that values hard work and achievement.

There is, however, a second mode of gaining status—*achieved status*, which is accomplished through an individual's own efforts. Whereas ascribed status is largely beyond the control of the individual, achieved status is based on what the individual *does* with what he or she *can* control. Whereas ascribed status is conferred through the family, achieved status is ordinarily attained outside the family through peer, school, and work activities.

In addition to status, family membership usually provides the individual with one or more *roles*, or patterns of expected behavior. For example, there are certain kinds of behavior that are appropriate or expected (in a given family) of someone who fills the role of the father, the brother, the sister, the wife, the daughter, or the son. Most family roles are *ascribed* in the sense that family members are expected to behave in certain ways. In recent years, as we have seen, many people are moving away from "traditional" roles and are attempting to develop more flexible roles with a wider range of possible behavior. For example, fathers help with infant care and household chores, and mothers help earn a living.

6. *Emotional support and companionship.* Human beings need not only economic support—food, clothing, shelter—but also satisfying and meaningful relationships with other human beings. They need people with whom they can share their successes, their failures, their joys, their sorrows, and all that makes up the vast array of human emotional experiences. In a society that has become increasingly task-oriented, mobile, complex, and fragmented, such *primary* relationships have become increasingly difficult to attain. Because of the apparent predominance of impersonal relationships in the world of business, school, and work, many people consider the intimacy and permanence of family relationships the most important function of the family.

A Wider Developmental Context: Young-Adult Parent and Infant/Toddler

Although it is important to be aware of the family context of the infant, it is equally important to understand something of the typical life experiences or social contexts of the young adults who are most commonly the parents or the family of the infant. It is also important to understand the context of infant development as a function of the larger contexts in which young adults are involved (such as work and community/neighborhood).

The period of early adulthood usually brings the beginning of a commitment to a career, the beginning of marriage (or an alternate family form), and, sometimes, the beginning of parenthood. Figure 6.5 illustrates the place of these typical events of early adulthood in the total lifespan. Adolescence—as we will see in the final three chapters of this book—provides the foundation for early adulthood in the form of a relatively stable identity. The years of early adulthood are based on this beginning definition of selfhood. The development of the adult involves both activity in the significant contexts of adult life and the interpretation of this activity by the individual. In this section, we examine several important contexts: the family, the community, and the world of work (see Fig. 6.6).

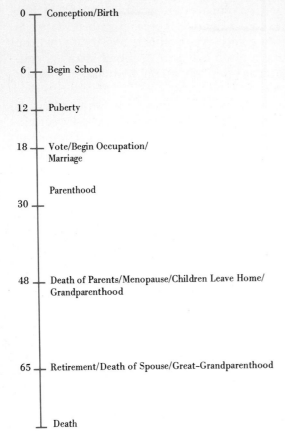

0 ┬ Conception/Birth

6 ┼ Begin School

12 ┼ Puberty

18 ┼ Vote/Begin Occupation/
       Marriage

       Parenthood

30 ┼

48 ┼ Death of Parents/Menopause/Children Leave Home/
       Grandparenthood

65 ┼ Retirement/Death of Spouse/Great-Grandparenthood

    ┴ Death

FIGURE 6.5

The human life line. The ages of important events are approximate because there are considerable individual and sex differences in the order of these milestones. From Kimmel, 1980, p. 4.

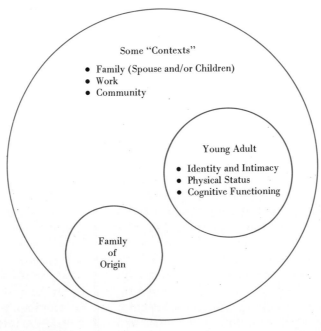

Some "Contexts"
- Family (Spouse and/or Children)
- Work
- Community

Young Adult
- Identity and Intimacy
- Physical Status
- Cognitive Functioning

Family
of
Origin

FIGURE 6.6

The system of young adulthood.

Family

Family life is a key factor in the development of children and adolescents. The family is a vital part of the system of childhood and adolescence, as well as a system in its own right. Children first learn about themselves—who they are, what they can and cannot do, who cares for and about them—in the family context.

The infant is almost totally dependent on the family as a source of nurture. Toddlers' and preschoolers' contexts of development include the peer group, the school, and the community/neighborhood. School-aged children's expanding horizons embrace sources of influence beyond the family. Older adolescents organize their experience in school, community/neighborhood, peer group, and family during an evolution from parent–child relationships to adult–adult relationships. Throughout childhood, adolescence, and maturity, the family nevertheless remains a vital framework for human development. Some experts contend that the survival of the family as we know it is threatened. Do you agree?

The Family

Of all the features of the world of young adulthood, the family is of prime importance because shifts in family-role performance affect all other aspects of life. Family-role changes, such as marriage, parenthood, and divorce affect self-concepts, work performance, and general life satisfaction.

MARRIAGE.   Marriage is a right of passage that signals the transition from the roles of singlehood to new roles that involve the couple's relationship, their relationship to their parents, their relationship to other couples, and their relationship to society as a whole.

For most couples, the first few years of marriage constitute a major transition in their lives—perhaps one of the most dramatic transitions in the family life cycle. During the early years of marriage, the couple attempts to establish its own family structure. Despite the "romantic" notions that prevail about marriage, the first few years may sometimes prove to be rocky. The major sources of marital problems in the early years are sex, living conditions and finances, general incompatibility, and parental interference (Skolnick, 1987). Disenchantment may also play a large role in the relatively high rate of divorce during the early years of marriage (Mace and Mace, 1985).

PARENTHOOD.   The next stage in the traditional family life cycle is parenthood. This stage begins with pregnancy and the birth of the first child. Many young couples have come to question the need for having children or may postpone beginning a family. In spite of these trends, approximately 94 percent of all ever-married women age forty to forty-four will have borne at least one child (U.S. Department of Commerce, 1983b).

Why do parents decide to have children? In traditional societies (including the United States prior to industrialization), parents need children as productive and economic contributors to the family. For example, if the parents own a farm, many "helping hands" are clearly an advantage. This is not to suggest, of course, that the only reason parents in a traditional society have children is economic.

In some industrialized societies, children (and the aged) are sometimes viewed as economic responsibilities or "burdens" because they cannot be, or are not allowed to be, economically productive. Therefore, parents in an industrialized society have children largely for psychological reasons: love, emotional gratification, companionship (Skolnick, 1987).

The major transition in this stage is a shift in roles from wife and husband to mother and father. This shift really represents the addition of new roles rather than the complete elimination of preparental roles. Furthermore, the couple needs to adjust to the presence of a third member. The birth of a first child is a significant transition in family life and brings with it some potential problems of adjustment (Cohler and Geyer, 1982; Weiss, 1985). As we will see in our discussion of infancy, the infant is a demanding creature that does not wait patiently for its needs to be satisfied.

There may be many reasons for unsatisfactory adjustment to parenthood. The following are three primary factors (Osofsky and Osofsky, 1984):

1. Negative attitudes toward pregnancy.
2. Feelings of parental inadequacy. Many parents are not prepared for the role

The Value of Children to a Marriage—Some Views

It's true in a technical sense, of course, that with all the contraceptive devices available today, people can decide not to have children. But in a deeper sense, one can only really make a free choice in an unprejudiced social context. And we don't have that today.

Everything in our society—from tax laws to television shows to women's magazines to the most casual conversation—is oriented toward parenthood. It's very difficult to even consider whether you shouldn't have children when everyone is pressuring you to "have kids and find out what you're missing."—A woman who decided not to have children (Katz, 1975, p. 162)

What people think they're missing, says NON (National Organization of Nonparents), is something that many of them are totally unsuited for—a child-centered life that fails to live up to the glorified picture usually painted of [parenthood]. NON believes that "the motherhood myth," as they call it, is a leftover from the early days of this country, when mortality rates were high, the vast wilderness needed settling, and large numbers of children were considered an important adjunct to a pioneering homestead. When that day passed, NON says, the idea that it was the duty and glory of every

woman to procreate was kept alive by "babysell"—the efforts of business and advertising to depict motherhood as chic, fun and glamorous, so that more and more consumer goods could be sold to an unsuspecting, continually expanding population. (Katz, 1975, p. 163)

Personal Experience. Among all the activities of life, parenthood is a unique experience. It is a part of life, of personal growth, that simply cannot be experienced in any other way, and hence is literally an indispensable element of the full life. (Berelson, 1975, p. 173)

Personal Pleasure . . . pleasure of having them, caring for them, watching them grow, shaping them, being with them, enjoying them. This reason . . . is typically the first one mentioned to the casual inquiry: "because I like children." Even this reason has its dark side, as with parents who live through their children, often to the latter's distaste and disadvantage. But that should not obscure a fundamental reason for wanting children: love. (Berelson, 1975, p. 173)

YOUR VIEW: Which of the above viewpoints would you be most likely to agree with? Why?

Darryl Jacobson

Darryl Jacobson

transition to parenthood, which requires attention and seemingly complete time involvement with the newcomer to the family. The lack of preparation and lack of experience with infants—particularly when the first child is born—can lead to feelings of inadequacy and being overwhelmed with things to do.
3. Unwillingness to accept role changes.

There is evidence that some reasons for having children are more likely to have maladaptive consequences than other reasons (Baruch, Barnett, and Rivers, 1983). In a study of women age thirty-five and fifty-five who already had children, Grace Baruch and her colleagues concluded that some reasons for parenthood were least beneficial to the women and to their families, including these:

• *"I can only be a complete woman if I have a baby."* The investigators found no significant differences in femininity between women who had children and those who did not.
• *"I can be a good daughter if I have children and therefore please my parents."* This was a particularly poor reason for having children since it led to the erroneous and counterproductive strategy of assuming that the mother's identity was defined primarily through pleasing others (in this case, her parents).
• *"A baby will fix my marriage."* Since the arrival of children is to some degree a strain even in the best of marriages, a child could make a troubled marriage even more difficult.
• *"A baby will give new meaning to my life."* Such motivation for having children transfers the responsibility for identity clarification from the parent to the child. This is an unreasonable expectation for an adult to have for a child.

According to Baruch and her associates, the reasons for having children that turned out to be the most adaptive over time involved decisions about these questions:

• *"Do I fully understand what children can and cannot do for my life?"* While a child may add variety or richness to one's life, having a child is by no means a guarantee of happiness.
• *"Do I like being with children?"* It is important to recognize whether one enjoys the company of children or would prefer to be alone or simply with a spouse.
• *"Would I be a reasonably competent parent?"* It is not necessary or even possible, for that matter, to be a "perfect parent." However, a prospective parent should honestly assess such factors as their personality characteristics in relation to child-rearing demands. For example, does a prospective parent have the patience or interest to comfortably "give of oneself" to others? It is, of course, best to be honest about oneself.
• *"Would I feel comfortable balancing the demands of career development (if relevant for me) and the demands of raising children?"* This is not an impossible task, but it is one that requires tolerance and flexibility for some imperfection in both domains.

CHILD ABUSE AS A BREAKDOWN IN THE FAMILY SYSTEM: AN ECOLOGICAL PERSPECTIVE. In some cases the family system breaks down and serious abuse of children occurs. The incidence of child abuse increased almost 84 percent from 1976 to 1983 (from 62,911 to 397,785 reported cases). Although this increase may reflect better reporting, it is still likely that numerous cases of child abuse go unreported (see Fig. 6.7). Many of those children have been beaten, starved, cut, burned, or sexually molested.

What factors produce such horrendous treatment of children? One way to understand the unfortunate problem of child abuse is from an ecological (or systems) perspective. Child abuse can be explained in terms of the interaction of the child/infant and its significant life contexts. Such contexts include the family (the characteristics of abusive parents) and the quality of the neighborhood/community in which the family resides (available support systems) (Bronfenbrenner, 1986).

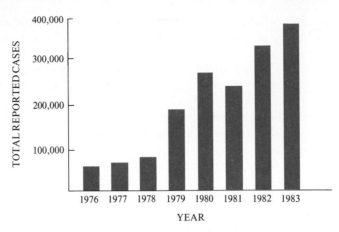

FIGURE 6.7

The increase in reported incidents of child abuse from 1976 to 1982. From American Humane Association.

The Abusive Family. Some characteristics of child and family are found to be commonly associated with child abuse. For example, child abuse is more likely to occur to children under three years of age, in large families. Furthermore, abused children tend to be more irritable, to have more physical and intellectual deviations, and to cry more (and to have a particularly irritating cry) than children who are not abused. These characteristics lead to antagonistic parental feelings toward the child (Reid, Patterson, and Loeber, 1982). As a result, abusive parents may feel that the child is abusing them by making their lives miserable.

Abusive parents also tend to have specific characteristics that distinguish them from nonabusive parents (Schmitt and Kempe, 1983; Reid, Patterson, and Loeber, 1982):

1. Abusive parents frequently dislike themselves for what they do. However, they feel powerless to control their violent behavior.
2. Abusive parents often have conflicts with each other.
3. Abusive parents tend to be social isolates who have few friends, neighbors, or relatives to turn to in stressful times.
4. Abusers tend to be mothers except in families where fathers are unemployed. (It may be that because mothers typically assume the major child-rearing responsibility in families, they are more often "locked into" stressful family situations.)
5. Abusers have unrealistic attitudes about child behaviors. Sometimes they expect their children to respond in a developmentally advanced way (e.g., exhibiting exceptional self-control). When their children fail to meet such unrealistic expectations, parents may become angry and abusive.
6. Abusive parents demonstrate more negative behaviors (e.g., threats, criticisms, and physical aggression) than positive behaviors compared with nonabusive parents.
7. The behavior of abusive parents tends to be unpredictable and unrelated to the type of behavior a child is exhibiting (Mash, Johnston, and Kovitz, 1983). For example, abusers are likely to respond to a happy, smiling baby in the same negative way they respond to a crying baby or to a child having a temper tantrum. The probability of abuse is increased when the parent responds adversely or angrily to all infant/child behaviors.

The Community/Neighborhood. There is some evidence that community/neighborhood characteristics are associated with child abuse. James Garbarino and Deborah Sherman (1980) examined two neighborhoods that were similar in socioeconomic and racial composition but with different rates of child abuse. (The high-risk neighborhood had a child abuse incidence of 130 cases per thousand families; the low-risk neighborhood has only 15 cases of child abuse per thousand families.) The investigators found that each neighborhood had characteristics that influenced the welfare of children and families. In the high-risk area there was less exchange of such things as child supervision or the use of neighborhood children as playmates, less self-sufficiency, and less adequate provision of child care. Also, in the high-risk neighborhood there was a higher number of "latchkey children" (who come home from school to no caretaker). In contrast, in 86 percent of the low-risk homes a parent was present when children returned home from school. Furthermore, families in high-risk neighborhoods used available community resources (recreational programs, health maintenance services, and the like) much less effectively than did parents in the low-risk neighborhoods. Therefore, the investigators concluded not only that family functioning is influenced by neighborhood factors, but that poorly functioning families also tend to be concentrated in high-risk neighborhoods.

The Community/Neighborhood

Although the most immediate context of infant development is the family, the impact of the broader social system in the form of other contexts is most relevant to a full understanding of infancy (see Fig. 6.1). Such contexts include the community/neighborhood, the parents' occupational experiences, and social/governmental policies toward infants and their families.

The major influence of these extrafamilial contexts of development on infancy occurs indirectly, through their impact on the lives of the parents of infants. The impact of the community context on the families of infants occurs in two primary ways (Bronfenbrenner, Moen, and Garbarino, 1984; Bronfenbrenner, 1986):

- *Effects of formal community structures* (health services, welfare and social services, day-care programs, and so on).
- *Effects of informal community structures* (social networks).

FORMAL COMMUNITY STRUCTURES. Many families have some contact with a broad range of community service organizations that to some extent influence the quality of family life. Such organizations include health, welfare, social services, and day-care programs.

1. *Health services.* Good health is a basic prerequisite and necessity for both child and adult development. However, access to the health care system is determined by the community in which a family resides and, likewise, by the socioeconomic status of the family (Bronfenbrenner, Moen, and Garbarino, 1984). Economically poorer families tend to have a lower quality of health care than more affluent families.

2. *Welfare and social services.* Welfare and social services are often provided to poor families. As with health services, there has been concern with the distribution of and access to social services. As a way of dealing with the accessibility problem, *neighborhood centers* have been designed as a resource for "connecting" or referring

poor people to needed services (Kamerman and Kahn, 1981). Unfortunately, many people who need social and welfare services are not using them because they continue to be unaware of them or of the neighborhood centers that can provide referrals.

Unfortunately, too, the problems of the social and welfare system extend beyond the questions of accessibility and utilization to the stigmatization of the people who use such services. Such attitudes and behaviors represent what has been called the "deficit model" of poor families:

> Our policies and practice, past and present, are based on what can be called a "deficit model." The model pervades all types of social services, but its distinctive properties are revealed in highest relief in our welfare system. To qualify for help, potential recipients must first prove that they and their families are inadequate—they must do so in writing, a dozen times over, with corroborating documentation, so that there can be little doubt that they, and their children, are in fact the inadequate persons they claim to be. (Bronfenbrenner and Weiss, 1983, p. 395).

Such a deficit model can have a destructive impact on the groups to whom it is addressed or aimed—in this case, the poor. Furthermore, it is possible that an image of incompetence may be communicated from parents (who are treated in a demeaning way by others) to children.

3. *Day-care programs*. An important indicator of both the quantity and quality of community support for families is the availability of day-care programs (Bronfenbrenner, Moen, and Garbarino, 1984). As already noted, there is some evidence that the provision of day care in a community is significantly correlated with a reduced incidence of child abuse and neglect (Garbarino and Sherman, 1980). In addition, there is good reason to believe that child development may be substantially affected, both directly and indirectly, through the contribution of day care as a parental support system (Belsky, 1984).

For the most part, it is generally agreed that working mothers with young children (and particularly mothers with infants) need substitute care for their children during working hours. However, in the United States it is not altogether clear who should provide for such services. Should it be the government (state or local) or private enterprise or the family or some combination of these institutions? It is of interest that every major European country has legislated extensive child support systems for working mothers. Although these efforts have not, in all instances, provided high-quality care for children, the existence of such programs indicates that the governments of these countries have, to some extent, assumed at least some responsibility for the welfare of children with working mothers (Feinstein, 1984).

Although the issue of responsibility for child care is complex, numerous studies have identified the forces that work against national child-care policies or programs in the United States (Greenblatt, 1978; Morgan, 1983; Feinstein, 1984):

- Philosophical disagreements over the purpose, scope, sponsorship, and program of a national effort.
- Resistance to subsidizing such a potentially costly service.
- Political disagreements over who would or should administer such a program.
- Lack of organizational clarity as to how best to deliver such a program.
- Fear of further stimulating maternal employment in an economy with already high levels of unemployment.

Child Care Services: A National Picture

In 1983, for the first time, half of all mothers with children under age 6 were in the labor force (Waldman, 1983). Out of a cohort of 19.0 million children under age 6, 47 percent had working mothers. In the near future, the *majority* of preschoolers will very likely have working mothers, as most school age children already do. How preschool children are cared for while their mothers work is something that relatively little is known about, although what is known suggests a quite complicated picture.

What is the picture today of child-care services for preschool aged children?

· Where are the children of working parents being cared for?
· What is known about the kinds of child-care services and arrangements that now exist?
· What are the current trends, developments, and emerging issues in the child-care services field? . . .

Child-care services include family day care and center care, public and private nursery school and prekindergartens, Head Start centers, all-day care, part-day care, and after-school care.

Types and Amounts of Available Child Care

Unfortunately, in addition to the child-care picture not being very clear, it is not very complete. National data are not collected in any systematic fashion on children in out-of-home care during the day, on child-care arrangements used while parents work, or on child-care service programs. To study what exists and who uses which type of care, one must piece together different, sometimes not fully comparable, data, collected by different sources at different times.

In providing an overview of child-care services for preschool-age children, the types of services can be distinguished by the following:

· The age of the child:
  —Infant and toddler care (birth to two years old)
  —Preschool care (three to five years old)
· The locus of care:
  —in own home
  —in a relative's home
  —in a nonrelative's home
  —in a group facility (center or school)
· The auspice of care:
  —education (nursery school, prekindergarten, kindergarten)

As more mothers hold jobs, the demand for child-care services continues to grow—especially for infant and toddler care—and is exacerbated by brief maternity leaves.

(Continued)

—social welfare (day-care center)
The source of funds:
—direct and indirect public subsidy (for example, public grants of monies to a provider or a tax benefit such as the child-care tax credit)
—employer-subsidized parent fees

Preschoolers. Although there are no precise figures concerning the numbers of children in out-of-home care by age of child and type of care, the most complete data to date are those on preschool children age three to five years. However, even here estimates must be used. . . . Almost two-thirds of *all* 3- to 5-year-olds and more than 70 percent of those with working mothers are in some form of group child-care program. . . .

Moreover, not only are children of working mothers more likely to be enrolled in preschool programs, but the enrollment rates are even higher when mothers have larger incomes and more education. Fifty-three percent of 3- to 4-year-old children in families with medium or higher incomes attended a preschool program in 1982, as contrasted with only 29 percent of those in lower income families. . . . Enrollment rates increase as mothers' education levels rise, and increase still more when those mothers are employed.

Given these data, one could argue that not only is there growing use of preschool as a child-care service for the 3-, 4-, and 5-year-olds with working mothers, but there is especially high use by affluent, educated, working families.

Infants and Toddlers. According to the 1977 Current Population Survey (CPS) (U.S. Department of Commerce, 1982b), the primary care arrangement for children under age three was family day care, usually in the home of a nonrelative.

Estimating from the CPS data, more than one-third of the children with working mothers were in either family day care or group care in 1977. More specifically, about one-third of these under age three with full-time working mothers and 17 percent of those with part-time working mothers were in family day care; and more than 9 percent of those with full-time working mothers and 5.5 percent of those whose mothers worked part time were in group care. Infant and toddler care has been growing rapidly since the mid-1970s; thus, the coverage data are undoubtedly higher today (U.S. Department of Commerce, 1982b).

The following rounds out this picture of how children are cared for while parents (especially mothers) are in the labor force:

· A small proportion of babies with working mothers are cared for, albeit briefly, by mothers on maternity leave. Fewer than 40 percent of working mothers are entitled to some paid leave at the time of childbirth, usually for about six to eight weeks, and a somewhat larger group may remain home on an unpaid but job-protected leave for three to four months (Kamerman, Kahn, and Kingston, 1983). [In January 1987 the U.S. Supreme Court ruled that states may order private firms to grant short unpaid disability leaves to new mothers.]
· Some parents, especially those with preschool-age children, work different shifts in order to manage child care. Although this method of care has received very little attention thus far, researchers using three different data sets (the Current Population Survey, the Panel Study of Income Dynamics, and the Quality of Employment Survey) have found that this may be a more significant pattern of work by parents with young children than suspected (Presser, 1982).
· A very few employers, largely hospitals, provide on-site child-care services (about 230 hospitals; about 50 employers), and a few others subsidize payment of care (Burud, Collins, and Divine-Hawkins, 1983).

Toward the Future

The major development in the field in recent years has been child-care information and referral services. These have burgeoned, especially in California, where they are publicly funded. This is an area in which more employers are considering involvement as well. Finally, concern with the quality of education is leading some states and localities to reexamine their preprimary programs. Some are now initiating full-day kindergarten; others are establishing pre-kindergarten, and still others are considering both.

The demand for child-care services continues to grow, and most parents of preschoolers want an educational program. Most such programs are private, particularly those below kindergarten level. Unfortunately, good programs very often are expensive. Moreover, there is still a scarcity of full-day programs, so many parents are "packaging" a group program with one or more other types of care with consequences not yet known. The cutbacks in funding group programs are especially significant in their impact on services for low- and middle-income children. Many of these children who were in publicly subsidized preschool programs are being transferred into informal and unregulated family day care as subsidies are cut back and programs close or parents lose their eligibility for a subsidy; the children must adapt to a new caregiver, and often to the loss of friends.

The biggest current demand for child-care services is for infants and toddlers, because it is among their mothers that the increase in labor force participation has been greatest, and the scarcity of services most severe. Paid maternity (disability) leaves are available only to a minority of working women and are usually brief. There is an urgent need to expand and improve maternity-related benefits provided at the workplace (Kamerman, Kahn, and Kingston, 1983). Data con-

cerning how babies and toddlers are being cared for and what types of care exist are largely inadequate. Most of these children are in informal facility day-care arrangements but, here again, little is known about these services.

Although the current child-care picture is hardly complete, all that is known suggests the likelihood of continuing demand. Accessibility, affordability, and quantity will remain central issues, but questions regarding *quality* will increasingly come to the forefront.

From Kamerman, 1984.

INFORMAL COMMUNITY STRUCTURES. In addition to the formal community structures such as health services, social/welfare services, and day-care programs, informal community structures such as social support networks also have a major impact on family functioning and child development (Bronfenbrenner, 1986) (see Fig. 6.8).

Although an ecological (or systems) perspective to child development includes a number of systems through which child behavior and development can be influenced (e.g., education, the mass media, parental employment, and so on), one system that has the potential to serve as a buffer between the family (including parent-child interaction) and external forces (e.g., unemployment) is the *personal social network* (Cochran and Brassard, 1979; Cochran and Henderson, 1986).

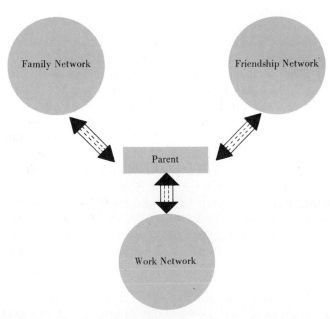

FIGURE 6.8
The social networks of parents provide a support system for effective family functioning and child rearing.

TABLE 6.1
Three Functions of Support Networks in Child Care

FUNCTION	EXAMPLES OF SUPPORT TO FAMILIES
Instrumental Support	Provision of child care Payments of child-care fees Health care Nutritional supplements
Emotional Support	Parenting skills to promote positive parent-child relations Stress relief
Information and Referral	Child-care location services Connections to other social services Child-care information

Adapted from Long, 1983, p. 199.

> *DEFINITION*
>
> **Personal Social Network.** The personal social network is a pattern of relationships that provide parents with social links to others outside the home who can provide a variety of supportive services (e.g., the provision of information, emotional support, or instrumental support) (see Table 6.1).

There is some evidence that the effectiveness of the child-rearing function of the family is enhanced by the existence of such personal social networks composed of friends, neighbors, relatives, and others outside the nuclear family (Crnic et al., 1983; Cochran and Henderson, 1986). In a program designed to enhance parents' personal social networks, Moncrieff Cochran and Charles R. Henderson found positive results for child performance in school and parents' perceptions of themselves as competent parents. Furthermore, in a study of mothers of premature and four-month-old infants, Keith A. Crnic and his associates found that *both* within-family support by the husband and extrafamilial (outside the family) support were significantly related to both maternal life satisfaction and the mother's satisfaction with her role as a parent.

The World of Work

In addition to the community/neighborhood, the parental work experience makes an indirect yet significant contribution to family functioning and child rearing (Bronfenbrenner, 1986). Work and family are clearly not separate systems; there is a two-way interaction between work and family, with "spillover" in the directions of both satisfactions and tensions (Piotrkowski, 1979; Crouter, 1984).

In comparison with previous generations of women, today more young women are employed out of the home and more of them are working when their children are young. Some young women prefer to devote most of their adult lives to being mothers, wives, and homemakers. Others have long-term career interests to which they wish to devote their primary attention without marrying or having children. Still others attempt to combine homemaking and career goals. Although some young adult women continue in the work force out of choice, others may do so out of necessity, that is, to help support the family.

The indirect impact of parental work experience on the developing infant or child can be examined in a number of ways, including how parents balance work and family responsibilities. Whatever the timing of parenthood (i.e., early or late in the life of the mother), the consequences for families and infants are played out primarily in the lives of women:

> Whatever else they do, whether they choose to be full-time mothers or to combine parenting with other work, it is women who see to the dailiness of family life. This is especially true in the early years of parenthood, but it remains true throughout . . . children's lives. (Daniels and Weingarten, 1982, p. 209)

Daniels and Weingarten interviewed a total of 72 women in three age groups (thirty-three, forty-four, or fifty-three years old at the time of the study). They found that whether women became mothers *early* or *late* in their lives, the birth of a first child changed their level of activity and their emotional involvement in both work and family. Most of the women in the sample "pulled back" from their outside (nonfamily) work with the birth of the first child. Although sixty-five of the seventy-two women were in the labor force prior to the birth of their first child, only eighteen remained in the labor force during the first year of parenthood.

After the first year of parenthood, two distinct patterns of motherhood emerged involving combinations of outside work and family life (Daniels and Weingarten, 1982):

- *A sequential pattern* in which a woman alternated between work and family life. In the sequential pattern, some period of parenthood after the first year of infancy was "cordoned off" or protected from the demands of outside work. The sequential pattern involved one of three possibilities: *employment followed by motherhood* (e.g., a woman started working, had her first child, and stopped work completely, with no intention of resuming work at a later date); *employment/motherhood/employment* (e.g., a woman started working, had a child, and then returned to work); or *motherhood followed by employment* (e.g., a woman first had a child and at some later time entered the work force). Approximately 70 percent of the sample (fifty-two women) followed one variation of the sequential pattern.
- *A simultaneous pattern* in which both nonfamily work and parenthood overlapped (the mother juggled the responsibilities of nonfamily work and parenthood at the same time). Unlike the sequential pattern, the simultaneous pattern did *not* involve a "protected" period of parenthood after the first year of infancy. Daniels and Weingarten (1982) describe the simultaneous pattern as potentially stressful for the mother:

> Logistically, she must coordinate child care and family work with the demands of her job or career; emotionally she stretches herself to incorporate and integrate both commitments. (p. 212)

Twenty-seven percent of the seventy-two women in the sample (twenty women) followed a simultaneous pattern.

With reference to infancy and the impact of mothers' work on infant development, the following conclusions of the study are pertinent:

- During the first year of infancy, the fact of becoming a parent resulted in a "pulling back" from outside work and other commitments (i.e., both the extent

TABLE 6.2

Sequential Pattern of Accommodating Parenting and Other Work

		MOTHER'S AVERAGE CURRENT AGE			
		33½ YEARS	44 YEARS	53½ YEARS	
Family-Timing Pattern	Early	(A): 9	(C):12	(E):11	32
	Late	(B): 5	(D): 7	(F): 8	20
		14	19	19	N = 52

From Daniels and Weingarten, 1982.

of participation and the emotional involvement were reduced). This was the case for most of the mothers regardless of the *timing of parenthood* (i.e., whether the birth of the first baby came early or late in the life of the woman).

• *During the second year of infancy* (and beyond), the timing of parenthood in the life of the woman was related to whether she followed a *sequential* or a *simultaneous* pattern. That is, late-timing mothers were fairly evenly divided between the sequential pattern (twenty) and the simultaneous pattern (sixteen) (see Table 6.2). However, early-timing mothers were more likely to adopt a sequential pattern than a simultaneous pattern by a ratio of 8 to 1 (see Table 6.3). One explanation for these results may be that early-timing mothers, for whatever reason, place more emphasis on parenthood than nonfamily work (at least in their early years). Therefore, they opt for the sequential pattern with a "protected" period of motherhood, allowing them the opportunity for nonfamily work sometime after childbirth. On the other hand, late-timing mothers include those who emphasize nonfamily work and would be more likely to choose the simultaneous pattern as well as a group of women who prefer the sequential pattern.

Furthermore, research on the impact of maternal employment on young children can be summarized as follows:

> By 1980 there had accumulated an appreciable body of evidence indicating that the mother's work outside the home tends to have a salutary effect on girls, but may exert a negative influence on boys. . . . The results indicate that daughters from families in which the mother worked tended to admire their mothers more, had a more positive conception of the female role, and were more likely to be independent. . . . None of these trends was apparent for boys. Instead, the pattern of findings, especially in recent investigations, suggests that the mother's working outside the home is associated with a lower academic achievement for sons in middle-class but not in low-income families. . . . A similar tendency for maternal

TABLE 6.3

Simultaneous Pattern of Accommodating Parenting and Other Work

		MOTHER'S AVERAGE CURRENT AGE			
		33½ YEARS	44 YEARS	53½ YEARS	
Family-Timing Pattern	Early	(A): 3	(C):0	(E):1	4
	Late	(B): 7	(D):5	(F):4	16
		10	5	5	N = 20

From Daniels and Weingarten, 1982.

employment to have a negative influence on the development of boys was apparent in investigation conducted as far back as the 1930s. (Bronfenbrenner and Crouter, 1982, pp. 51–52)

For example, in a study of parents' descriptions of their three-year-old children, highly flattering portraits of daughters were given by mothers who were employed full time and had some education beyond the high school level (Bronfenbrenner, Alvarez, and Henderson, 1984). However, sons were portrayed by these same mothers in less-favorable terms. The investigators offered the following interpretation: "The pattern brings to mind the picture of an aspiring professional woman who already sees her three-year-old daughter as an interesting and competent person potentially capable of following in her mother's footsteps" (p. 1366).

Our discussion of the indirect influence of work on infant and toddler development has focused largely on the impact of maternal employment on family functioning and child development. This is *not* to suggest that the full brunt of responsibility for successful infant/toddler development *should rest* on the shoulders of the mother. Certainly, fathers play an important role in child development as we shall see in our discussion of infant social and personality development (see Chapter 8) and throughout this book. Unfortunately, the reality of current sex-role divisions (however seemingly biased and unfair) places pressure on women for balancing the demands of parenthood and "family work" with the requirements of outside or "nonfamily" work. However, such pressure and the associated stress are *not* an inevitability. In fact, social policies toward working women with young children, including the availability of leave time for pregnant women and new mothers as well as flextime, are important considerations for healthy family contexts for infants/toddlers.

Summary

1. The most immediate and direct context of the infant is the family. The relationship between the infant and the family is reciprocal or bidirectional. Some relatively recent changes in the family include a large increase in the number of working mothers (both full- and part-time), increasing numbers of single-parent families headed by women, and changing attitudes of women regarding their place in society.

2. There are at least two primary reasons for us to begin a discussion of infancy and toddlerhood with an analysis of the family. First, the family is the place in which early development largely occurs. Second, changes in the family affect the ability of the family, as a unit, to cope and function in child rearing.

3. For our purposes, we define *family* as a group of adults and children who live together for an extended period of time. There are two types of family groups: the *family of orientation* (the family into which a child is born) and the *family of procreation* (which is formed later by that child by marriage). Membership in the family of orientation is by *birth*; membership in the family of procreation is by *choice*.

   In addition to mode of personal affiliation, families can also be defined according to their *structure*. Such structural forms or patterns include the *nuclear family*, the *extended family*, and a variety of others (the single-parent household, the remarried nuclear family, the kin family, and so on).

4. *Single-parent families* are at increased risk due to the stresses and strains that may characterize their situation (task overload, financial strain, and so on). However, an exclusively negative outcome is not an inevitability. That is, the *quality of family functioning* (general family climate, the nature of interactions between family members, and so on) appears to be a more important influence on the development of the child than the simple *number of parents* in the home.

5. The general function of the family is to mediate between the larger society or culture and the individual family members. More specific functions of the family include economic responsibilities, cooperation and division of labor, socialization of children, legitimization of sexual relations, reproduction of the species, and provision of status, roles, emotional support, and companionship.

6. Although it is important for us to be aware of the family context of the infant, it is equally important for us to understand something about the social contexts of the infant's parents. Such contexts include the *family experience*, the *community neighborhood*, and the *parents' work experience*.

7. The family experience of young adults involves two components: *marriage* and *parenthood*. Child abuse may be viewed as a breakdown in the family system.

8. The impact of the community/neighborhood on the developing infant is primarily through the medium of the family. There are two modes of influence: *formal community structures* (health services, welfare and social services, day-care programs, and so on) and *informal community structures* (personal social networks).

9. The impact of the world of work on the child also occurs through the medium of the family. Parent work experience makes an indirect yet significant contribution to child development. There is a "two-way" interaction between family and work, with a "spillover" of tensions and satisfactions in both directions.

Key Terms

Extended family   Formal community structures
Family functions   Informal community structures
Family of orientation   Nuclear (or Conjugal family)
Family of procreation   Personal social network

Questions

1. Give two reasons why it is critical to begin a description of the infant-toddler period with a discussion of the family.
2. Define and discuss the nuclear and the extended families.
3. Describe several alternate family forms (e.g., the single-parent family). What are their primary strengths and weaknesses?
4. In your opinion, are expectations for marriage unrealistic? What about reasons for having children? Why or why not?
5. Discuss why child abuse is a family problem.
6. Discuss the importance of quality day care for infants and parents.

Suggested Readings

BRONFENBRENNER, U., MOEN, P., and GARBARINO, J. "Child, Family and Community." In R. D. Parke (ed.), *Review of Child Development Research* (Vol. 7). *The Family*. Chicago: The University of Chicago Press, 1984. A well-written review of research on the influence of community factors and family functioning.

KAMERMAN, S. B., and HAYES, C. D. (eds.). *Families That Work: Children in a Changing World*. Washington, D.C.: National Academy Press, 1982. A collection of informative and scholarly articles on the relationship of families, children, and the world of work.

WHITTAKER, J. K., and GARBARINO, J. (eds.). *Social Support Networks: Informal Helping in the Human Services*. New York: Aldine, 1983. This is an excellent discussion of the role of social support networks in such areas as day care, mental health, health services, and programs for adolescents.

ZIEGLER, K., KAGAN, S. L., and KLUGMAN, E. (eds.). *Social Policy for Children and Their Families: A Primer*. Cambridge: Cambridge University Press, 1983. An excellent and readable discussion of relevant policy issues affecting children and their families.

7

Infancy and Toddlerhood: Physical and Cognitive Development

So runs my dream; but what am I?
An infant crying in the night;
An infant crying for the light,
And with no language but a cry.
  —*Tennyson*, In Memoriam

Physical, Perceptual, and Motor Development

Physical Growth

SIZE AND PROPORTIONS.   The physical growth of a baby is nothing short of remarkable. At birth, the average baby is about twenty inches long and weighs seven to seven and one-half pounds. During the first year of life, there is an astonishing growth spurt. Body length increases by almost a third and weight usually *triples.* Thus, at the end of the first year, the average baby boy is twenty-eight to thirty-two inches in length and weighs nineteen to twenty-six pounds while the average baby girl is twenty-eight to thirty-one inches long and is eighteen to twenty-five pounds. (See Figs. 7.1 and 7.2.) This increase is rather amazing if one were to imagine an adult, six feet tall and weighing 180 pounds, who increased his height by one-third and tripled his weight.

In addition to size, the proportions of the body change (see Fig. 7.3). For example, the size of the head appears to become proportionately smaller until full adult stature is attained. Newborns may seem top-heavy because their heads constitute virtually a fourth of their total length. However, at one year, their head makes up $\frac{1}{5}$ of their total length; at adulthood head size is approximately $\frac{1}{8}$ of total body length.

BRAIN MATURATION.   At birth, the newborn's brain is 25 percent of its adult weight. By age two the brain will be approximately 75 percent of its adult weight. In addition to these gross changes, there are significant developments in the maturing nervous system. (The nervous system includes the brain, the spinal cord, and nerves.) The nervous system is composed of thin nerve cells called **neurons**. At birth, the infant has the maximum number of neurons it will ever have. Further development of the nervous system involves the growth and branching of these neurons into dense, interconnecting networks. These connections between neurons are called **synaptic connections**. By adulthood, it has been estimated that there are about 1 quadrillion (10^{15}, or 1,000,000,000,000,000) synapses in the human brain (Lerner, 1984). Electrical impulses are transmitted along these connecting

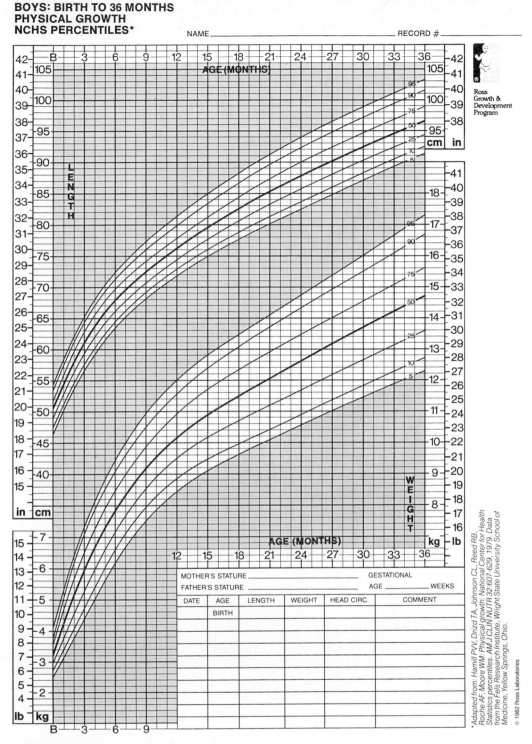

FIGURE 7.1

Iowa Growth Curves for Boys. The upper curves show average height gain in boys from birth to three years of age. The lower curves show the average increase in weight for boys. These graphs can be used to assess the growth of individual children. Copyright Ross Laboratories.

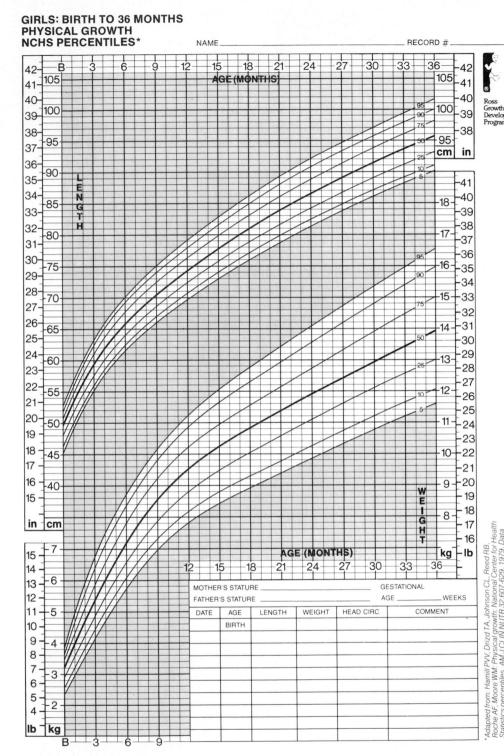

FIGURE 7.2

Iowa Growth Curves for Girls. The upper curves show average height gain for girls from birth to three years. The lower curves show the average increase in weight for girls. Copyright Ross Laboratories.

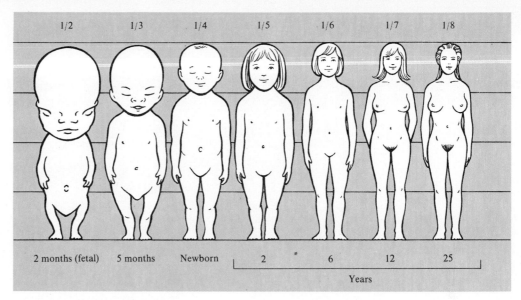

FIGURE 7.3

The proportions of the human body change as the individual grows into adulthood. The head becomes smaller in relation to the rest of body. Also, the legs become larger in proportion to the rest of the body. Based on data from Meredith, 1939, p. 141.

networks of neurons between the brain and other parts of the body. Every bodily function (breathing, seeing, hearing, and so on) is controlled through these brain processes.

The maturation of the brain during the first months of life is characterized by several important developments:

• Brain development is most pronounced in the **primary sensory areas** (hearing, vision, touch, and so on) and the **primary motor areas** (e.g., the areas responsible for simple body movements) (see Fig. 7.4).

• Although the basic brain structures that permit the development of specific brain functions (vision, movement, sensation of pain, and so on) appear to be genetically programmed and present at birth, the full and optimal expression of those capacities depends on experience during the early months of life (Parmelee and Sigman, 1983). Most normal infants will have such experiences during the course of their natural daily activity. The evidence for abnormal development derives largely from animal studies in which such animals have been deprived of sensory experiences very early in life, with consequent abnormalities (Lerner, 1984). For example, infant kittens and monkeys deprived of visual experience until several months after birth are never capable of vision (Hubel and Wiesel, 1970; Hubel, Wiesel, and LeVay, 1977).

• Early brain development regulates or controls infant states (see Chapter 5). As the infant's brain develops, its physiological states (quiet sleep, active sleep, alert wakefulness, and so on) become more regular (cyclical) and distinct. Each physiological state produces a specific pattern of electrical activity in the brain called a **brain wave.** Since these patterns of brain activity can be measured and recorded using a device that produces an **electroencephalogram (EEG)**, it is possible to graphically demonstrate the maturation of the infant's brain (see Fig. 7.5).

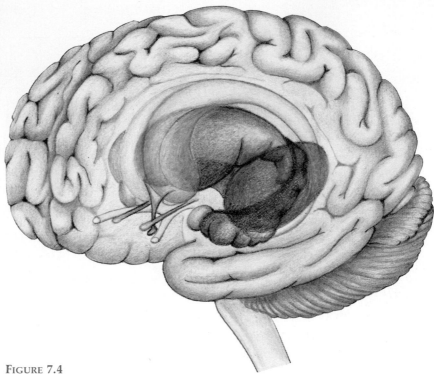

FIGURE 7.4
The human brain. From Benjamin, 1987. p. 45.

QUIET SLEEP

29 weeks conceptual age (3 months early)

40 weeks (= term)

3 months

FIGURE 7.5
EEG patterns of "quiet sleep" as indications of the maturation of the infant brain. An infant born three months early has a relatively immature EEG pattern as indicated by the frequent periods of absence of any brain activity (i.e., a straight line). Full-term infants have more mature EEG patterns (compared with preterm infants) as indicated by the greater differentiation and intensity of electrical signals. Finally, the three-month-old infant demonstrates even more mature brain development as the EEG pattern shows more frequent and more intense episodes of electrical activity. From Parmelee and Sigman, 1983, p. 116.

Sudden Infant Death Syndrome (SIDS) or Crib Death

The majority of infant deaths occur during the first few days of life and are typically related to maternal factors such as poor prenatal care, poor health, and malnutrition. After the first month of life, however, the majority of infant deaths are due to accidental or "unexpected" causes such as burns, suffocation, poisoning, or Sudden Infant Death Syndrome (SIDS). The most frequent cause of unexpected death in infants during the first year of life is SIDS, also known as crib death.

Causes of SIDS

There has been considerable speculation and some research on the cause(s) of SIDS. To date there are no conclusive answers and many hypotheses. Part of the problem is that the SIDS diagnosis is quite general and is applied when parents discover that their baby has died and there is no apparent or recognizable cause of death.

Since many SIDS deaths are frequently associated with mild respiratory difficulties or minor colds, some investigators have examined the relationship between respiratory/breathing processes and SIDS. It is a common observation that some infants may stop breathing for a very brief time during sleep. These pauses in breathing are called *apnea* (Baker and McGinty, 1979). In one study it was found that a high frequency of apneic episodes was associated with lower developmental test scores for sensorimotor activity at nine months (Black, Steinschneider, and Sheehe, 1979). This apparent connection between apnea and motor development has been expanded on by other investigators who have suggested that SIDS victims may suffer from a specific sensorimotor deficit which prevents their recovery from apneic pauses. That is, since almost all infants have some apneic pauses and manage to recover from them, some researchers have suggested that SIDS victims may be unable to make the appropriate motor movements and heart rate changes which would make recovery from apnea possible (Lipsitt, 1979; Lipsitt, Sturges, and Burke, 1979). There is some evidence that this motor deficit for control of breathing may be due to an inadequate perinatal (the period from one month before birth to about one month after birth) environment including a lack of oxygen or genetic factors which result in limited motor control over breathing (Naeye, 1980).

In addition to respiratory factors, several other possible causes for SIDS have been suggested. Infant *botulism* or food poisoning (to which infants are very susceptible) has been known to affect the nervous system and result in paralysis of vital functions including respiration (Marx, 1978). Infant botulism is caused by a poison from a spore that may be airborne or that may be found on raw vegetables and fruits. Typically, it is not recommended that infants under twelve months of age be given these foods (Marx, 1978).

Another possible cause of SIDS is heat. Some SIDS victims have been found dressed far too warmly at the time of death (Stanton, Scott, and Downhan, 1980). It is possible that these infants had symptoms similar to heat stroke.

While genetic factors and the lack of oxygen in the perinatal period have been implicated as possible systemic (affecting the entire body) explanations for limited motor control of breathing, it is also possible that these factors are related to the inability of SIDS victims to cope with toxicity in foods or with heat. Other systemic factors have also been suggested as underlying causes for the increased susceptibility of SIDS victims to breathing problems, heat, and mild toxicity. These factors are a deficiency in a B complex vitamin called *biotin* and a hormonal imbalance (Chacon and Tildon, 1981).

Prevention of SIDS

Currently, there is no sure method of preventing SIDS, nor is there any medical treatment for the problem. However, it is possible to identify some infants who may be at risk for SIDS for the following reasons: a high rate of apneic episodes, siblings who died of SIDS, a vitamin B deficiency, a hormonal imbalance, or perinatal oxygen deprivation.

If infants can be identified as being at risk for SIDS, it may be possible to do something. One approach to preventing SIDS deaths that has been tried with some success is the home use of an electronic monitoring unit. The unit is composed of a monitor about the size of a cigar box and a soft cloth belt which is placed around the infant's chest. The belt contains sensors which measure breathing and heartbeat, relaying this information to the monitor which then detects any potentially life-threatening breathing or heartbeat episodes. The monitor emits an alarm if the infant has

(Continued)

an irregular heart rate or stops breathing during sleep. The decision to implement such home monitoring is a complex one both for the medical staff, who carefully assess many tests to determine which infants may need such a procedure, and for the infant's family. Use of a home monitor requires training for parents in the use of the equipment, training in CPR (cardio-pulmonary resuscitation) techniques for reviving an infant, and information to help the parents understand their infant and SIDS. Research on the use of monitors in the home suggests that parents may have considerable anxiety during the first month about the use of the monitor and the resulting constriction it causes in their social life. However, once the family has adapted to the system, their recognition of its benefits far outweigh any added burdens (Cain, Kelly, and Shannon, 1980).

The Impact of SIDS Deaths on the Family

The grieving process for the SIDS victim is similar in many ways to such patterns for other infant deaths. For example, the family of the SIDS victim may express such common reactions as disbelief, anger, shock, and guilt. However, in other ways the family of the SIDS victim requires special support and understanding from the family physician and friends because of the unique factors surrounding a SIDS death. The unexpected nature of the death as well as the general uncertainty about the causes of the SIDS may lead to extreme guilt on the part of some parents that they were somehow at fault. For this reason, an autopsy is considered an essential process for relieving extreme parental guilt (Terjesen and Wilkins, 1979). In addition, there are several major organizations whose purpose is to provide support for the families of SIDS victims:

- Iowa Guild for Infant Survival
  P.O. Box 3586
  Davenport, Iowa 52808
- National Sudden Infant Death Syndrome
  Foundation
  8200 Professional Place
  Suite 104
  Landover, Md. 20785-2264

SKELETAL DEVELOPMENT. All of the bones of the body originate from soft cartilage which, over a period of time, becomes ossified or hardened into bone by the deposit of various minerals. The process of bone **ossification** begins during the prenatal period and extends, for some bones, into late adolescence. Because most infant bones are not ossified, they are softer, more pliable, and more reactive to pressure and sudden movements. Parents should be careful in handling children because bones can be pulled out of their sockets or deformed.

MUSCLE DEVELOPMENT. The neonate has all the muscle fibers it will ever have. These fibers are small in relation to the overall size of the infant. However, there is continuous growth in muscle length, breadth, and thickness until adulthood. At that time, the weight of the muscles is forty times what it was at birth. The striped or skeletal muscles (voluntary muscles) of the body are not completely under the infant's control during the first year of life. Therefore, the infant does not yet have efficient energy regulation and tires rapidly. As is true of the bones, different muscle groups grow at different rates. There is a general tendency for the muscles near the head and neck to develop earlier than the muscles of the torso, arms, and legs. This is an example of the *cephalocaudal principle* of development, from the head to the feet.

Sensory and Perceptual Development

During the past twenty years there has been a dramatic increase in research on how infants use their various senses (e.g., vision, hearing, taste, touch, and smell) to perceive their worlds. Techniques for understanding infant perception must, of necessity, be different from those used to study child or adult perception. For example, infants obviously cannot point or reach with much accuracy, or give verbal responses to investigators. Therefore, techniques that make use of the responses infants can make have been developed for studying infant perception. The basis of much infant perceptual research is that the infant's perception of unfamiliar objects or stimuli produces physiological responses including a change in heart rate, intensified gazing, intensified sucking (if a pacifier is in its mouth), and so on. When a new object or stimuli becomes familiar to the infant such that these physiological responses no longer occur, then the infant is *habituated* to that object or stimulus. Using this process of habituation, investigators can study infant perception. For example, an infant may repetitively be presented with a given stimulus (e.g., a solid white visual field) until habituation occurs. Then a new stimulus is presented (e.g., a white visual field with red dots). If the infant responds in some measurable way, the investigator may *infer* that the infant has perceived the difference between the new stimulus and the prior one.

VISION. We can begin our discussion of infant vision with visual sensitivity. Newborn infants can distinguish *movement* in a visual field, can *follow* or *track* a visual stimulus in a field, and can determine changes in *brightness* (Banks and Salapatek, 1983). Despite these visual capacities, newborn *visual acuity* is not completely developed at birth. A newborn's visual acuity is in the range of 20/150 to 20/190 (Lewis and Maurer, 1977). However, by six months to a year, the visual acuity of the newborn approximates normal adult vision (Banks and Salapatek, 1983).

> *DEFINITION*
>
> **Visual Acuity.** The ability to detect and recognize the separation in parts of a visual display such as the large "E" on the Snellen eye chart. If a person can only see this "E" at a distance of no greater than 20 feet away (and should be able to see it at 100 feet away) his or her visual acuity is said to be 20/100. Optimal visual acuity is 20/20.

Color Vision. Do infants see things in color or are they color-blind? There is evidence that newborns can distinguish between most colors (Teller and Bornstein, 1987). However, newborns are not as capable in perception of color as three- or four-month-old infants. For example, during the first three months of life, infants appear to have some difficulty distinguishing blues from grays (Adams and Maurer, 1983). The fact that newborns can perceive color is important because it suggests they can experience the full impact of a colorful, vivid environment quite early.

Pattern Preferences. Are there any particular patterns that infants prefer to look at? Generally, the evidence indicates that as infants develop, they appear to prefer increasingly complex visual stimuli (Banks and Salapatek, 1983; Olson and Sherman, 1983). For example, infants prefer the following patterns:

- Irregular rather than regular patterns.
- Curved rather than straight lines.
- Symmetrical rather than asymmetrical patterns.
- Concentric rather than nonconcentric patterns (Olson and Sherman, 1983).

In a series of classic studies, Fantz (1961, 1963) examined infant visual preferences by showing six types of disc patterns (three patterned discs and three nonpat-

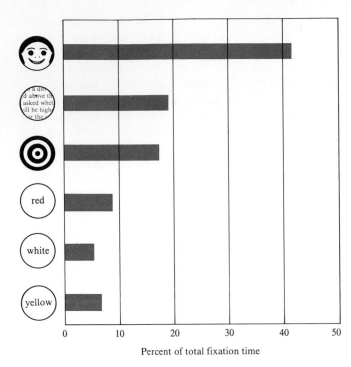

FIGURE 7.6

Infant visual preferences. Infants were presented with six different disc patterns: a face, newspaper print, a bull's eye, and solid red, solid white, and solid yellow circles. All the infants in the study preferred patterned discs to nonpatterned ones. (The dark bars indicate results for two-to-three-month-olds. From Fanz, 1963, pp. 296–297.

terned discs) to two-month-old infants and, in a later study, to forty-eight-hour-old newborns (see Fig. 7.6). The infants in both studies looked the longest at the three patterned discs (a face, newspaper print, and a bull's eye) compared with the nonpatterned discs (a solid white form, solid yellow form, and solid red form). The results of these studies support the suggestion that infants do indeed prefer complex visual patterns to plain ones.

Visual Scanning Patterns. Do infants scan in a particular way when visually inspecting their environments? According to Haith (1980), newborns do, in fact, follow a set of visual scanning "rules" which ensure that they see the world in an organized way:

Rule 1: If awake and alert and if light is not too bright, the newborn's eyes are opened.
Rule 2: If surroundings are dark, the newborn does a detailed search.
Rule 3: If in a lighted environment, the newborn looks for the edges of an object with broad visual sweeps.
Rule 4: If an edge can be found, the newborn stops the broad scan and concentrates on the vicinity of the edge. The newborn attempts eye movements that cross the edge.

Visual scanning improves with the age of the infant. Four- to six-week-old infants continue to fixate on angles or edges of visual objects, and two-month-olds can visually trace both the edge and the central areas of a given pattern (Olson and Sherman, 1983).

Face Perception. Infants appear to pay more attention to human faces than to other objects they encounter (e.g., face-shaped constructs of solid colors). The evidence suggests that infants find faces interesting, not because they recognize them as faces, but because of their visual appeal and unique patterns (white teeth, white eyeballs, hairlines, pink-colored lips, and so on) (Haaf, Smith, and Smitley,

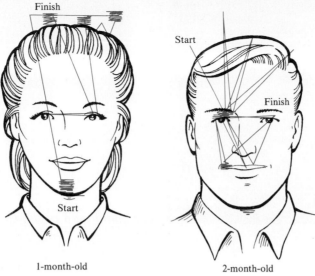

1-month-old   2-month-old

FIGURE 7.7

Visual scanning of the human face by one- and two-month-old infants. From Maurer and Salapatek, 1976, pp. 523–527.

1983). In the same way that one-month-old infants typically focus on the outermost edges or contours of a triangle, they follow a similar pattern in examining a drawing of the human face (see Fig. 7.7) (Maurer and Salapatek, 1976). Likewise, two-month-old infants that typically trace both the edge and the central areas of a given pattern do not stay fixated on the edges of the drawing of the face, but move to the center.

Furthermore, there appears to be a similar developmental pattern in the way infants visually scan *real human faces* (Haith, Bergman, and Moore, 1977). Older infants (seven to eleven weeks) spent more time fixating on central features of the face (e.g., eyes, nose, or mouth) than younger infants (three to five weeks), who focused on the outer edges of the face. In addition, between approximately three and six months of age, infants appear to develop a beginning concept of faces as *distinct patterns* (faces as people) rather than simply collections of curious parts (Cohen, DeLoache, and Strauss, 1979; Sherrod, 1981; Olson and Sherman, 1983).

Depth Perception. An important dimension of visual development in infancy is the ability to determine depth. Investigators who have studied the development of depth perception have debated how soon the infant demonstrates this ability. In order to examine this question, early investigators designed a special experimental apparatus or **visual cliff** (see Fig. 7.8). The device consists of an elevated glass platform divided into two parts: a "shallow" side in which the glass covers a checkerboard pattern just under the glass and a "deep" side in which the glass covers a checkerboard pattern that is several feet below the glass. The assumption was that if infants perceived depth, they would remain on the shallow side and avoid the deep end, or the "cliff" (i.e., since it had the appearance of a drop-off). The early evidence, in fact, indicated that infants six to fourteen months of age (who could crawl) excitedly moved toward their mothers who stood on the "shallow" side of the apparatus but refused to cross the visual cliff when their mothers stood on the "deep" side (Gibson and Walk, 1960).

More recent evidence suggests that infants do not develop a fear of heights or depth until they are able to crawl (Campos et al., 1978). That is, older infants who

FIGURE 7.8
An infant on a visual cliff.

could crawl showed accelerated heart-rate levels (an indication of fear) when they were placed on the "deep side." In contrast, younger infants (who could not crawl) showed no such increase in heart rate when they were placed on the "deep" end. In another study, infants who could not crawl and who were put in walkers (enabling them to experience heights) showed a distinct fear of high places (Campos et al., 1981). Taken together, these findings suggest that although infants may have the biological structures to learn to fear height, the activity of **locomotion** (or crawling) is often a necessary prerequisite to experience heights.

HEARING.   In comparison to infant vision, the hearing of the newborn is much more precise and completely developed (Aslin, Pisoni, and Jusczyk, 1983). Newborns and young infants exhibit several auditory skills, including the following:

· *Sound localization.* Research indicates that newborns can tell from which side a sound is coming by using head and eye movements (Muir and Field, 1979). Sounds coming from one side reach the nearest ear before they reach the other ear. The ability to turn toward or look toward the sound depends on these very small differences in timing and loudness as the sound strikes the two ears.

   At birth to one month of age, infants can turn their heads to locate a sound that is directly to one side (Field et al., 1980). By at least sixteen weeks of age the infant seems to be able to make more precise determinations of sounds that are only slightly to one side. This is done by differentiating the time and loudness cues that go to both ears (Bundy, 1980).

   An example of these infant sound-localization skills can be seen in everyday parent/caretaker–infant interactions. When the adult is out of the direct line of sight of the infant and begins to talk, infant head movements begin almost immediately and simultaneously with eye movements. The infant is using such head and eye movements to locate the sound of the human voice.

· *Discrimination of loudness and frequencies of sound.* Newborns and infants can distinguish between sounds of varying loudness. In addition, the sounds that appear to be most effective in eliciting infant responses were those that included the fundamental frequencies found in the human voice. There is evidence that infants are particularly sensitive to their own mother's voice. For example, sucking behaviors were found to increase more after infants heard their own mother's voice compared with the voice of another female (DeCasper and Fifer, 1980).

Of the human voice sound frequencies to which infants were sensitive, infants seemed to respond better to the higher frequencies than to the lower. It is a common observation that both parents "talk" to their babies in high-pitched voices and return to normal pitch when talking to one another or to other adults.

The development of an infant/parent prelanguage relationship. There is evidence of a precise interaction between newborn and adult during adult speech (Condon, 1974; Condon and Sander, 1974a, 1974b). William Condon and Louis Sander videotaped a series of infants age twelve hours to two days. They demonstrated that even at this very early age, the newborn babies were able to move in rather precise time to human speech. The authors stated, "The present study reveals a complex interactional 'system' in which the organization of the neonate's motor behavior is seen to be entrained by and synchronized with the organized speech behavior of adults in his environment" (1974a, p. 461).

Taken together, these findings suggest that not only are infant hearing skills highly organized from birth on, but they are particularly sensitive to human voice characteristics.

SMELL.   Newborns can distinguish among a variety of odors (Steiner, 1979). For example, newborns less than one day old indicated sensitivity to pleasant aromas of bananas and strawberries and to unpleasant odors such as rotten eggs. The sense of smell appears to be a built-in characteristic of newborns.

In addition, there is evidence that the newborn's sense of smell may play a role in parent-infant interaction. Aidan MacFarlane (1975) took a breast pad (a piece of gauze about four inches square) that had been inside the mother's bra between breast feedings (and had therefore absorbed some breast milk) and put it next to the baby's cheek. A clean (unused) breast pad was placed next to the other cheek. MacFarlane then filmed the baby's activities for one minute and then reversed the pads and filmed for another minute. Analysis of the films indicated that at five days of age, the babies spent more time with their heads turned toward the mother's used pad than toward the unused pad.

TASTE.   Newborns have the ability to discriminate various tastes. For example, there is evidence that changes in the sweetness of an infant's food have been shown to slow their rate of sucking and increase their heart rate (Werner and Lipsitt, 1981). In another study, newborns showed different facial expressions when sweet, sour, or bitter substances were placed on their tongues (Steiner, 1979). For example, newborns responded to a bitter-tasting substance by turning down the edges of their mouths, sticking out their tongues, or, in some cases, spitting out the substance.

Motor Development

The development of movement or motor skills goes hand in hand with the development of perceptual, cognitive, and social skills. In addition to beginning language (sounds and crying), motor development is a form of communication and interaction between the infant and the significant others in his or her life. Thus motor development and movement permeate virtually all domains of infant behavior. For example, most measures of so-called infant intelligence (e.g., the Cattell Measurement of Intelligence of Infants and Young Children, 1960; the Bayley Scales, 1969; the Brazelton Neonatal Assessment Scale, 1973) are really assessments of motor performance (e.g., visual following tasks, building towers of blocks, grasping cups).

THE ORDER OF INFANT MOTOR DEVELOPMENT.   Between birth and three years of age, infant motor development moves from very *general reflexes* to *differentiated* (and relatively skillful) *movements*. The so-called *gross* (large) *motor system* regulates movement of the head, body, arms, and legs. The *fine* (small) *motor system* governs the movement of hands, fingers, feet, toes, eyes, and lips. Both gross motor activity and small motor skills become more precisely regulated and controlled by the infant as it grows. Tables 7.1 and 7.2 and Figure 7.9 summarize the major features of infant motor development.

All of the stages of motor development follow the principles of cephalocaudal (from head downward) and proximodistal (from the center of the body to the outer areas) development. In this section, we give an overview of some of the milestones of motor development during the first three years.

The Four-Month-Old. By about four months of age, the average infant is usually sleeping through the night and has developed a somewhat regular schedule. The baby has organized the timing of its behavior to coincide more with family patterns of eating and sleeping. The infant can do a number of things, including being able to hold its head steady from a sitting position. This is an important behavioral attribute because it allows the infant to observe its surroundings carefully. Most four-month-olds can reach for and grasp an object (Frankenburg et al., 1981).

TABLE 7.1
Summary of the Major Stages of Infant Motor Development

AGE	STAGE	SOME BEHAVIORAL ACTIVITIES
0–1 months	Exercise of basic reflexes	Sucking, reflex grasp.
1–4 months	Perfection of visual control	Coordinates eye movement with head movements; develops differential viewpoints for moving and stationary objects; no prehensive (*prehension* is the ability to grasp objects between the fingers and opposable thumb) contact.
4–7 months	Head and arm control	Able to raise chin and chest while flat on stomach; raises head while on stomach; rudimentary reaching movements; sits alone (5–6 months).
7–10 months	Trunk and hand control; emerging prehension	Immature grasp.
10–13 months	Control of legs, feet, fingers, thumb; refine prehension	Stands alone; mature grasp; walks alone (approximately 13 months).
13 months to 2 years	Perfection of prehension, mobility skills	Walks sideways; walks backwards; walks up and down stairs; fast walk—run; emerging fundamental motor skills (e.g., throwing, catching); uses mature grasp.

TABLE 7.2
Development of Motor Skills

0.2 Months—crawling movements	7.6 Months—complete thumb opposition
0.5 Months—lifts head at shoulders	8.5 Months—sits alone with good coordination
1.7 Months—arm thrusts in play	9.2 Months—prewalking progression
1.9 Months—head erect—vertical	9.3 Months—fine prehension with pellet
2.6 Months—dorsal suspension—lifts head	9.4 Months—raises self to sitting position
2.9 Months—head erect and steady	10.5 Months—pulls self to standing position
3.4 Months—turns from side to back	10.6 Months—stands up
3.5 Months—sits with support	11.6 Months—walks with help
4.1 Months—beginning thumb opposition	12.5 Months—stands alone
5.0 Months—turns from back to side	13.0 Months—walks alone
5.4 Months—effort to sit	16.5 Months—walks sideways
5.7 Months—sits alone momentarily	16.9 Months—walks backward
6.2 Months—pulls to sitting position	20.3 Months—walks upstairs with help
6.2 Months—sits alone thirty seconds or more	24.3 Months—walks upstairs alone—marks time
7.0 Months—rolls from back to stomach	24.5 Months—walks downstairs alone—marks time

Abridged from Bayley, 1935.

Grasping objects is an important developmental milestone because it allows the infant to experience both the sensation of touching objects and the sensation of controlling and manipulating them.

The process of self-discovery seems to be well on its way during this period. The infant may look at its hands and fingers for several minutes. This experience of discovery may also be marked by various movements such as hand clasping or hand clapping. The infant may also discover its feet and toes during this period.

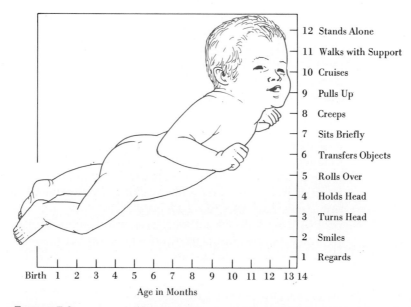

FIGURE 7.9
Developmental diagram for the first year of life. The infant's figure represents a diagonal line on which is plotted the progress of behavior (right of the diagram) against chronological age. The cephalocaudal pattern of behavior is diagrammatically illustrated by position of the figure. From Lowrey, 1978.

By about four months, the social relationship between the parent or caretaker and the infant may include mutual "games" involving touch, sights, and sound. For example, imitative sound-play games may occur in which the parent mimics the cooing or babbling sounds of the infant. The infant, in turn, may sustain these vocalizations in a fashion that amuses the parent. Tactual interactions might include simple social games in which the parent holds the infant and gently turns so as to swing the infant. The infant, of course, tactually follows the parent by grasping and holding onto the parent. Visual following games include such activities as peek-a-boo, patty-cake, and simple movement observation by parent and infant.

The Eight-Month-Old. Almost all babies at eight months can get themselves into a sitting position, and most infants can sit without support. About half of the eight-month-olds can pull themselves to a standing position. Once the eight-month-old is in a standing position, he or she can probably move about by holding onto fixed objects such as tables, chairs, and crib sides.

Most eight-month-old babies also are rather proficient crawlers and tend to rely on this mode of transportation as a major way of seeing the environment. Crawling is the primary means by which the infant gets *to* things and—sometimes to the amusement of parents—*into* things.

An eight-month-old uses his or her hands quite proficiently in grasping objects. Some are able to use the thumb and forefinger to grasp things, and almost all are able to pass objects from one hand to the other. Infants continue to enjoy playing interaction games such as peek-a-boo and patty-cake. Infants seem particularly to enjoy handing objects or toys to adults and then receiving them back. Another popular "game" seems to be for the infant to drop an object for the adult to pick up. This game may continue until one of the participants tires (usually the adult).

The Twelve-Month-Old. At twelve months of age, many babies are walking without any assistance. There is, however, a large range in months between infants as to when they start to walk. It is usually between eleven and thirteen months that infants walk (Frankenburg et al., 1981). Walking provides increased mobility, and mobility means that the infant is actively involved in many things. At twelve months, the child can open cabinets, climb stairs, climb on furniture, pull tablecloths (with or without dishes on them), bite lamp cords, feed themselves, and much more. The word *no* becomes an important part of the vocabulary for both parents and infants.

Eighteen Months and Beyond. The period that begins at about eighteen months and extends through two and one-half years is often called *toddlerhood* (see the detailed discussion of this period at the end of this chapter). Walking skills become refined, and the toddler is quite proficient at getting about. He or she may like to push or pull something while walking. By the age of two years, the child can not only walk but also run and jump. The child can also climb up steps and can probably walk down without assistance. The toddler can move things, push and pull objects, put things into containers, and stretch and bend objectives, to name only a few accomplishments.

TWO MAJOR DEVELOPMENTS: LOCOMOTION AND PREHENSION.　The two primary motor events of infancy are **locomotion** and **prehension** (reaching and grasping). The development of locomotion is described in Figure 7.10. Shown are several important phases in the process of learning to walk.

Walking is a monumental event for the child and the parents. The child is now capable of improved self-regulation by being able to move toward (or away from) objects and people.

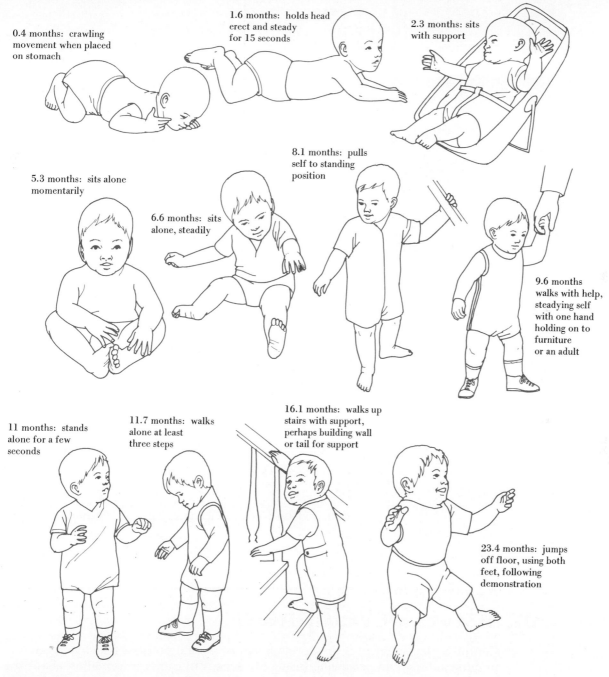

0.4 months: crawling movement when placed on stomach

1.6 months: holds head erect and steady for 15 seconds

2.3 months: sits with support

5.3 months: sits alone momentarily

6.6 months: sits alone, steadily

8.1 months: pulls self to standing position

9.6 months walks with help, steadying self with one hand holding on to furniture or an adult

11 months: stands alone for a few seconds

11.7 months: walks alone at least three steps

16.1 months: walks up stairs with support, perhaps building wall or tail for support

23.4 months: jumps off floor, using both feet, following demonstration

FIGURE 7.10

The sequence of motor development, with ages at which the average baby achieves each coordination. From Bayley, 1969.

Prehension constitutes one of the most important achievements in child development. Prehension is monumentally significant because it is the basis for a wide range of important infant/toddler skills. These skills include feeding oneself, block building, and scribbling with crayons.

*Prehension (grasping) is a monumentally significant
achievement because it is the basis for a wide range
of infant/toddler skills.*

When the baby extends its arm in a reaching movement after about three and
one-half months, parents or caretakers are witnessing a dramatic event.

For the first few months after the infant is born, it possesses a strong grasp,
which is a reflex action. This reflex disappears and is gradually replaced by grasping that is under voluntary control. Halverson (1931) identified ten stages in the
development of prehension (see Fig. 7.11). These stages appear in a sequence
ranging from "no contact" at sixteen weeks to a mature grasp ("superior forefinger" grasp) at fifty-two weeks.

Infant Cognitive Development

Cognitive development is the development of mental processes such as thinking,
understanding, and perceiving (using the senses to gather information about the
world). Mental development is a process that begins at least as early as the day
the infant is born and probably earlier. The motor and sensory skills already described serve as the basis for cognitive development. In this book, we will examine
cognitive development from three perspectives:

The Piagetian approach (see also the discussion of Piaget's theory of intelligence in
Chapter 2). This approach focuses on the qualitative changes in intellectual functioning as indicated in the stages of Piaget's theory of intelligence. The stage that
we discuss in this chapter is the **sensorimotor stage,** which covers the first two
years of life.

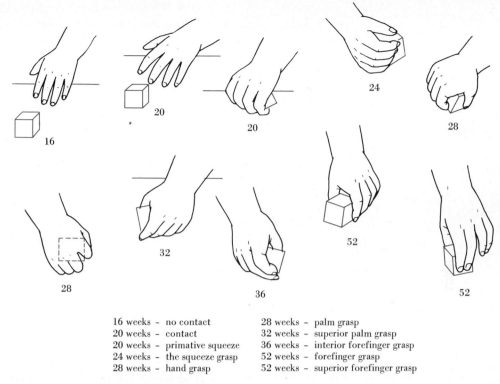

16 weeks – no contact	28 weeks – palm grasp
20 weeks – contact	32 weeks – superior palm grasp
20 weeks – primative squeeze	36 weeks – interior forefinger grasp
24 weeks – the squeeze grasp	52 weeks – forefinger grasp
28 weeks – hand grasp	52 weeks – superior forefinger grasp

FIGURE 7.11

Stages in the development of grasping. From Halverson, 1931.

The psychometric approach. Whereas the Piagetian view of intelligence deals with the qualitative or the structural dimensions of intelligence, the **psychometric** perspective examines intelligence from a *quantitative* perspective (see also the discussion of Lewis Terman and the development of intelligence testing in Chapter 2). Specifically, those who use the psychometric perspective attempt to identify the specific components or factors of intelligence and try to measure the amounts of these factors an individual has. Typically, this is done using an assessment instrument or intelligence test (Stanford-Binet, Wechsler Intelligence Scale for Children, and so on). Results of such assessments may be used to group individuals on the basis of intelligence or to predict future performance. (We discuss the development of intelligence tests and IQ scores in more detail in our discussion of the psychometric perspective in early and middle childhood in Chapters 10 and 13.)

• *The information-processing approach.* This approach to intelligence examines the processes that underly intelligent behavior, including *goal-oriented behavior* and *adaptive behavior*. Goal-oriented behavior refers to activities that are intentional and deliberately designed to attain specific objectives or goals. Adaptive behavior refers to the cognitive activities involved in problem solving, including defining the problem and developing a set of strategies for solving it.

The Piagetian Perspective

THE SENSORIMOTOR PERIOD.   Jean Piaget has observed and written extensively on the development of intelligence in infancy and throughout life. His research indicates that the processes of intelligence evolve from the sensorimotor activities of infancy. As the infant proceeds through the sensorimotor period, the changes in mental skills are dramatic. At birth, the infant has only a few patterns of action or reflexes including grasping, sucking, and crying. By the age of two, the child's repertoire of activities has become more sophisticated.

Jean Piaget Society.

Jean Piaget

AN INTERLUDE: PIAGET SAYS . . .

The period that extends from birth to the acquisition of language is marked by an extraordinary development of the mind. Its importance is sometimes underestimated because it is not accompanied by words that permit a step by step pursuit of the progress of intelligence and the emotions, as is the case later on. This early mental development nonetheless determines the entire course of psychological evolution. . . . At the starting point of this development, the neonate grasps everything . . . to his own body—whereas at the termination of the period, i.e., when language and thought begin, he is . . . in a universe that he has gradually constructed himself, and which hereafter he will experience as external to himself. (*From* Piaget, 1967, pp. 8–9)

Piaget has divided the stage of sensorimotor operations into six substages (Table 7.3 and Fig. 7.12 summarize the major characteristics of development during the sensorimotor period).

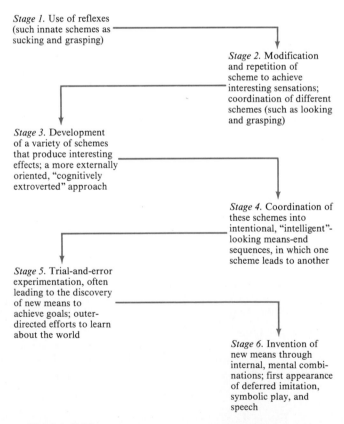

Stage 1. Use of reflexes (such innate schemes as sucking and grasping)

Stage 2. Modification and repetition of scheme to achieve interesting sensations; coordination of different schemes (such as looking and grasping)

Stage 3. Development of a variety of schemes that produce interesting effects; a more externally oriented, "cognitively extroverted" approach

Stage 4. Coordination of these schemes into intentional, "intelligent"-looking means-end sequences, in which one scheme leads to another

Stage 5. Trial-and-error experimentation, often leading to the discovery of new means to achieve goals; outer-directed efforts to learn about the world

Stage 6. Invention of new means through internal, mental combinations; first appearance of deferred imitation, symbolic play, and speech

FIGURE 7.12

The six substages of Piaget's sensorimotor period. From Flavell, 1985, p. 29.

TABLE 7.3

Characteristics of Development During the Sensorimotor Period

STAGE	GENERAL	OBJECT CONCEPT	SPACE	CAUSALITY
1 Reflex 0–1 mo.	Reflex activity	No differentiation of self from other objects	Egocentric	Egocentric
2 First differentiations 1–4 mos.	Hand-mouth coordination; differentiation via sucking, grasping	No special behavior re: vanished objects; no differentiation of movement of self and external objects	Changes in perspective seen as changes in objects	No differentiation of movement of self and external objects
3 Reproduction 4–8 mos.	Eye-hand coordination; reproduction of interesting events	Anticipates positions of moving objects	Space externalized; no spatial relationships of objects	Self seen as cause of all events
4 Coordination of schemas 8–12 mos.	Coordination of schemas; application of known means to new problems; anticipation	Object permanence; searches for vanished objects; reverses bottle to get nipple	Perceptual constancy of size and shape of objects	Elementary externalization of causality
5 Experimentation 12–18 mos.	Discovery of new means through experimentation	Considers sequential displacements while searching for vanished objects	Aware of relationships between objects in space, between objects and self	Self seen as object among objects and self as object of actions
6 Representation 18–24 mos.	Representation; invention of new means via internal combinations	Images of absent objects; representation of displacements	Aware of movements not perceived; representation of spatial relationships	Representative causality; causes and effects inferred

From Wadsworth, 1971, 1979.

Stage 1: Reflex Activity (Birth to One Month). Throughout most of Stage 1, the behavior of the infant is largely reflexive; that is, infants respond to the world largely in terms of the reflexes that they are born with (e.g., crying, grasping, sucking, and specific movements of head, trunk, legs, and arms). For example, whenever an object is placed in the mouth of an infant, the infant sucks it—regardless of what it is (bottle nipple, blanket, rattle). The infant's hand also grasps whatever comes into it.

During this stage, active groping or "searching" for objects begins to replace the simple exercise of reflexes. For example, an infant may begin to search actively for a nipple to suck on when the nipple is not present. Such searching behavior was not present at birth; therefore, it cannot be attributed to the simple exercise of reflexes.

By the end of this stage, the infant can distinguish between objects. When hungry, for example, the infant may actively suck a milk-producing nipple and repel other objects placed in its mouth. Such behavior was not present at birth.

Stage 2: Primary Circular Reactions (One to Four Months). The second stage begins with the alterations in reflexive behaviors. Several new behaviors appear that represent such changes.

- *Hand-mouth coordination* develops and is reflected in repeated thumbsucking.
- *Eye coordination* is the ability of the eyes to follow moving objects.
- *Eye-ear coordination* is reflected in the ability of the infant to move its head in the direction of sounds.

Stage 3: Secondary Circular Reactions (Four to Eight Months). Prior to Stage 3, the infant's behavior is oriented largely toward the self. In addition, the infant cannot distinguish itself from the objects of the environment, nor can it coordinate eye-hand movements. During Stage 3, however, all these things change.

1. The infant's behaviors are increasingly directed to events or objects beyond its own body.
2. The infant recognizes the difference between the self and other objects.
3. The infant grasps or manipulates objects that it can reach. This activity reflects the coordination of the eyes and the hands.

Another important characteristic of this period is that infants seem to *repeat events* that are interesting to them. When this occurs, the beginning of *intentional* action is evident. During Stage 2, behavior was random and was not designed to attain an object or goal.

Stage 4: Coordination of Secondary Schemas (Eight to Twelve Months). Prior to Stage 4, behavior has usually resulted in the *direct* action of the infant on objects. Inter-

Sylvia Byers

As the infant proceeds through the sensorimotor period, the changes in mental skills are dramatic.

esting phenomena may even have been repeated. During Stage 4, three very interesting and related things begin to happen:

1. The infant begins using *means* to attain *ends* that may not be attainable in a direct way. The infant *intentionally* selects appropriate or available means to achieve a goal. A significant difference between the intentionality of Stage 3 and the intentionality of Stage 4 is that both end and means in Stage 4 are chosen *prior* to behavior.

Piaget described this means-end relationship in the following example:

> Observation 121—At [8 months, 20 days] Jacqueline tries to grasp a cigarette case which I present to her. I then slide it between the crossed strings which attach her dolls to the hood [of her bassinet]. She tries to reach it directly. Not succeeding, she immediately looks for the strings which are not in her hands and of which she only saw the part in which the cigarette case is entangled. She looks in front of her, grasps the strings, pulls and shakes them, etc. The cigarette case then falls and she grasps it. (1952, p. 215)

2. The infant begins to *anticipate* events. Certain "signs" or "signals" seem to be associated with actions that follow.

> Observation 132—At [8 months, 6 days], Laurent recognizes by a certain noise caused by air that he is nearing the end of his feeding and instead of insisting on drinking to the last drop, he rejects his bottle. . . .
> At [1 year, 1 month, 10 days] he has a slight scratch which is disinfected with alcohol. He cries, chiefly from fear. Subsequently, as soon as he again sees the bottle of alcohol, he recommences to cry, knowing what is in store for him. Two days later, same reaction, as soon as he sees the bottle and even before it is opened. (1952, pp. 248–249)

3. For the first time, the infant recognizes that objects (besides itself) can *cause* things to happen. The infant is now aware that external objects can be the cause of actions.

Piaget described this change as follows:

> . . . the cause of a certain phenomenon is no longer identified by the child with the feeling he has of acting upon this phenomenon. The subject begins to discover that a spatial contact exists between cause and effect and so any object at all can be a source of activity (and not only his own body). (1952, p. 212)

> [8 months, 7 days] . . . [Laurent] . . . A moment later I lowered my hand very slowly, starting very high up and directing it toward his feet, finally tickling him for a moment. He bursts out laughing. When I stop midway, he grasps my hand or arm and pushes it toward his feet. (1954, p. 261)

Stage 5: Tertiary Circular Reactions (Twelve to Eighteen Months). In Stage 4, the infant was able to coordinate familiar behavior patterns to attain goals. In Stage 5, the infant is able to develop *new* means (through experimentation) to attain goals. When the infant is presented with a new problem that cannot be solved through existing behavior patterns, the infant experiments with new means. Through trial and error, new strategies of behavior are developed. During this period, the infant appears to be interested in how objects adapt to new situations.

The child playing in the bathtub may experiment by pushing objects underwater and splashing as if in a minor squall.

> Observation 167—At [1 year, 3 months, 12 days], Jacqueline throws a plush dog outside the bars of her playpen and she tries to catch it. Not succeeding, she then pushes the pen itself in the right direction! By holding onto the frame with one hand while with the other, she tried to grasp the dog, she observed that the frame was mobile. She had accordingly, without wishing to do so, moved it away from the dog. She at once tried to correct this movement and thus saw the pen approach its objective. These two fortuitous discoveries then led her to utilize movements of the playpen and to push it at first experimentally, then systematically. (Piaget, 1952, p. 315)

Stage 6: Invention of New Means Through Mental Combination (Eighteen to Twenty-four Months). Stage 6 provides evidence that the child has moved from a sensori-motor level of intelligence (as reflected in the five prior stages) to a *representational* level of thinking. By *representational* is meant the ability of the infant to symbolize objects or events mentally. This new development allows the infant to solve problems cognitively (by means of representations or symbols).

In Stage 5, the infant arrived at new means for problem solving through active experimentation. In Stage 6, the invention of means for problem solving is suddenly apparent, suggesting to Piaget that such invention occurs through representation and mental activity.

> Observation 181—At [1 year, 6 months, 23 days] for the first time Lucienne plays with a doll carriage whose handle comes to the height of her face. She rolls it over the carpet by pushing it. When she comes against a wall, she pulls, walking backward. But as this position is not convenient for her, she pauses and without hesitation, goes to the other side to push the carriage again. She therefore found the procedure in one attempt, apparently through analogy to other situations but without training, apprenticeship or chance. (1952, p. 338)

The infant's ability to represent objects and events internally also enhances its concept of *causality*. In Piaget's example, the infant was able to think of a "cause" (pushing the carriage in the opposite direction) without having to perceive or immediately experience its "effect" (freeing the carriage). Therefore true causality relationships had become understandable.

CONSTRUCTION OF THE PERMANENT OBJECT.   Piaget demonstrated that during the sensorimotor period, children begin to recognize that their environment is made up of objects and that they are part of the total environment in which they participate. The infant comes to recognize many objects, such as mother, father, food, toys, feeding bottle, brother, and sister. However, the infant does not seem to understand that these objects exist when they are out of sight. A prominent milestone in cognitive development comes when the infant recognizes that objects can be permanent (i.e., that objects can exist when they are not in view; see Fig. 7.13 and Table 7.4). The construction of the permanent object is significant because it signals the beginnings of the ability to "think" about what is not present or in immediate view. Much of cognitive functioning in later life involves the development and analysis of symbols regarding what is not immediately present or even abstracted from "real" objects.

Piaget observed and recorded the development of object permanence during the first three years of life. According to Piaget, object permanence occurs in six stages as follows (see Table 7.4).

FIGURE 7.13
Object permanency. By relating the sensory results of motor action, the infant learns to distinguish a world of permanent objects.

Stages 1 and 2: "Out of Sight, Out of Mind." The first two stages occur during the first four months of life. During these initial stages of object permanence, the infant's behavior indicates that an object that is out of sight is, in fact, out of mind or may not exist.

Stage 3 (Four to Eight Months of Age). Infants begin to indicate that they can maintain some contact with an object that is not present.

■ *Example:* Baby Elizabeth is sitting in her feeding chair. Her father places a cooked noodle before her. Baby Elizabeth grasps her noodle and is about to place it in her mouth when she accidentally drops it on the floor (to the dismay of her father). Instead of staring into space and forgetting about the noodle (as she might have done in Stages 1 and 2 when she dropped an object), Elizabeth leans over and looks down to the floor in the general area where the noodle now lies. She indicates that she can maintain some contact with an absent object.

In addition to contact-maintenance behavior, the Stage 3 infant can grasp and retrieve a partially hidden object if a large enough part remains visible.

■ *Example:* Baby Elizabeth is comfortably sitting at her feeding table. Elizabeth's father holds a toy next to one of her brother's books. When he has Elizabeth's attention, her father puts the toy behind the book so that a large part of the toy is visible to her. Elizabeth now reaches for the toy, at which point her father makes less and less of the toy visible. When the visible part becomes relatively small, Elizabeth's reaching hand seems to stop rather abruptly.

As illustrated by Elizabeth, Stage 3 infants usually make no attempt to recover objects that are barely visible or that have disappeared behind an obstruction.

TABLE 7.4
Stages in the Development of Object Permanence

APPROXIMATE AGE	SEARCH BEHAVIOR
0–4 months	Uses neither visual nor manual searching
4–8 months	May look for a partially hidden object
8–12 months	May search for a completely concealed object
12–18 months	May search after object has been visibly concealed or removed
18 months and older	May search after hidden concealment or removal of object

Stage 4 (Eight to Twelve Months of Age). During Stage 4, the infant will search for an object, but only in the *first* place where they saw the object. For example, if a toy is continually hidden behind one object (and the child repeatedly finds it there) and then (in full view of the child) is hidden behind a different object, the infant will probably continue to look for the toy behind the *first* object. The Stage 4 infant has made conspicuous progress because it realizes that objects continue to exist. However, it continues to indicate (by virtue of its searching behavior) that objects cannot exist in multiple places.

Stage 5 (Twelve to Eighteen Months). By Stage 5, the infant has clearly developed the idea that objects can exist in multiple places. The Stage 5 infant/toddler always looks for an object in the place in which it was *last* seen. In the Stage 4 example, for instance, even if a toy is continually hidden behind one object (and found there) and then is hidden behind a second object, the Stage 5 infant will always look behind the second, or last, object to find the toy. Thus, no matter where it was previously hidden, the infant will search for the toy where it was last seen.

Although the notion of object permanence has developed considerably during this stage, it is nonetheless not perfect or complete. For example, if an object (in full view) is moved behind one object and then (covered by the adult's hand) is moved behind another object, the child will look for the object where it was *last seen.* Stage 5 infants apparently do not *reason* that the toy must have been moved to another place under the cover of the adult's hand.

Stage 6 (Beginning at Eighteen Months). The Stage 6 infant/toddler has acquired the concept of object permanence with all of its subtle manifestations. The infant has the notion that an object continues to exist when it is moved from place to place and will continue to search for an object until it is found. The infant/toddler can understand the possibility that an object can be covered or hidden in an adult's hand and still exist. For example, if a small object is hidden in an adult's hand and is then placed behind one object after another, the toddler will search each hiding place (including the adult's hand) until the object is found.

SPACE AND TIME.   The construction of **object permanency** makes the world a more predictable and simpler place in which to live. Objects no longer have a dual existence in one space and then in another space or in one time period and then, several minutes or seconds later, in another time period. The discovery of object permanency helps the infant to separate the existence of the object from a particular or unique space and time, so that the object can exist in many different spaces and at different times. The ability of the infant to sort out the existence of an object from a particular time or place provides the foundation for the emerging concepts of space, time, and causality.

For the young child, the concept of space seems to derive primarily from the child's own movement experiences, rather than from an abstract notion of distance. For example, children under three years of age tend to think that the distance between two points (A and B) is increased when an object or obstacle (around which the child must walk) is placed between the two points. In other words, the infant/toddler's concept of distance is a *practical* one based on movement and motor experience rather than the *abstract* notion that (in plane geometry) the shortest distance between two stationary points is a straight line of constant length.

According to Piaget, the infant/toddler's concept of time is confounded with his or her notion of space. Piaget showed that young children who see a toy demonstration in which one man runs a distance of four feet in the same time that another man runs one foot usually report that the second man stopped before reaching the end. Young children report that the second man has stopped, even though they have seen both men running from beginning to end, without any evidence of stopping (Flavell, 1985). This example illustrates how the ideas of time and space are intertwined and are not yet, for infant/toddlers, separated and distinguished.

The concept of time, although not clearly distinguished from the notion of space, is an important dimension of comprehending simple causal relationships. By the time toddlerhood arrives (at about eighteen months), children have acquired simple notions of causality based on the close proximity, in *time*, of many events that occur on a daily basis in many families and households. For example, children see that a switch turns on a light, that a knob starts a television set, that pushing a doorbell produces a ringing noise, that putting a key in the car ignition starts the motor, and so on. Although there is a *physical distance* between the behavior that "causes" an activity and the activity itself (e.g., between the switch and the light), the infant/toddler appears to understand the simple, causal relationship as long as there is no extended *time* delay.

The Psychometric Perspective

THE MEASUREMENT OF INFANT/TODDLER INTELLIGENCE.   At about the same time that Piaget was developing his theories and research on the stages of infant cognitive development, American psychologists, such as Arnold Gesell (see Chapter 2) and Nancy Bayley, began to inquire about infant intelligence. Gesell established standards of scales of behavioral development that paralleled the physical development of infants, children, and adolescents. Bayley and her associates wanted to measure intellectual changes in infants over time and individual differences between infants. Both Bayley and Gesell were pioneering figures in the development of tests of infant intelligence.

There has always been some controversy surrounding the use of infant intelligence tests. Such controversy exists because intelligence tests for older children rely primarily on a child's response to written or verbal questions. Infants, of course, do not have the verbal facilities to communicate their thinking. Therefore, the only way to assess infant intelligence is by observing what they *do* (their motor behavior). For this reason, several questions have been posed regarding infant intelligence tests, including these:

- Do these behavioral measures assess the same cognitive or intellectual activities that are assessed in tests used for children?
- Can such behavioral measures be used to predict child intelligence at a later age?
- Can infant intelligence tests be used to diagnose developmental problems or mental retardation?

In order to answer these questions, we will discuss one of the most highly regarded and carefully studied tests of infant intelligence—**The Bayley Scales of Infant Development** (1969).

THE BAYLEY SCALES OF INFANT DEVELOPMENT.   The Bayley scales are organized into three parts:

- *The mental scale.* This section of the test assesses memory, perception, problem solving (the ability to find hidden objects), the ability to vocalize, the ability to respond to verbal instructions, and early indications of the infant's ability to classify objects.

• *The motor scale.* This scale is designed to assess the infant's control of its body and to coordinate its movements. The focus is on gross motor movements. The absence of such movements is sometimes associated with mental retardation.

• *The infant behavioral profile.* This section assesses the influence of such factors as infant motivation, sociability, and attention on the infant's overall performance.

Based on almost thirty years of experience working with infants, Bayley identified hundreds of potential test items. She administered these items to a representative sample of 1,300 infants, age two to thirty months. The items were "graded" at the age at which half of the infants successfully passed the item. For example, the item "turn pages of a book" (see Table 7.5) is graded at the twelfth month (12.0) because half of the twelve-month-old infants in Bayley's sample could pass the item. That is, *fewer* than half of the infants could pass the item at any age younger than twelve months (e.g., 11.5 months or 10 months) and *more* than half of the sample could pass the item at any age beyond twelve months (e.g., 12.2 months or 15 months).

The test items were then arranged in order of difficulty, from easiest to most difficult (Table 7.5). Bayley and her colleagues were concerned that infants would lose motivation to continue the examination if first presented with difficult items. Therefore, rather than mix the more difficult with the easier items, the infants are first given easy items (relative to their age). An infant's score on the Bayley scales is based on items successfully completed. An examiner can then compare such a score to that of other infants at the same age by consulting the appropriate table in the test manual for the Bayley scales.

TABLE 7.5

*Some Selected Items from the Bayley Scales
of Infant Development*

AGE IN MONTHS	ITEM
0.1	Responds to sound of bell
1.6	Turns eyes to light
2.0	Visually recognizes mother
2.8	Simple play with rattle
3.8	Inspects own hands
4.4	Eye-hand coordination in reaching
5.0	Reaches persistently
6.2	Playful response to mirror
7.9	Says "da-da" or equivalent
8.1	Uncovers toy
9.1	Responds to verbal request
9.7	Stirs with spoon in imitation
10.1	Inhibits on command
11.3	Pushes car along
12.0	Turns pages of a book
12.5	Imitates words
13.8	Builds tower of 2 cubes
14.3	Puts 9 cubes in cup
14.6	Uses gestures to make wants known

From Bayley, 1969.

EVALUATING INFANT INTELLIGENCE TESTS.   In relation to the questions posed earlier, to what extent are infant intelligence tests such as the Bayley scales useful in identifying infants with developmental problems or in predicting intelligence in childhood? There is some evidence that infant intelligence tests may be useful in diagnosing mental retardation or neurological deficits (Siegal, 1981). This may be the case even when such problems are mild and cannot be easily identified with standard pediatric or neurological tests. For example, Linda Siegal found that one could predict which children were likely to be developmentally delayed at age two from their scores on the Bayley Mental Development subtest at four, eight, twelve, or eighteen months.

However, infant intelligence tests compared with tests for older children have not been as successful in predicting the later performance or achievement of children in the normal range of intelligence. We have already indicated that infant intelligence tests (which tend to focus on motor behavior) may not be measuring the same type of intelligence as that measured by preschool or school-age tests (which include verbal or symbolic items). For example, the correlation between a child's IQ score at age six and later at adolescence is rather high. However, the correlation between infant intelligence scores and preschool intelligence measures (a much shorter span of time) is quite low (Honzik, 1983) (see Fig. 7.14).

The Information-Processing Perspective

WHAT IS INFORMATION PROCESSING?   The major difficulty with both the Piagetian and the psychometric approaches to intelligence is that they do not

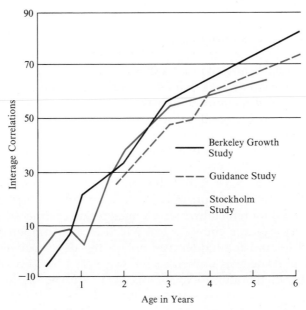

FIGURE 7.14

Predicting intelligence. Evidence from separate longitudinal studies of children indicated a negative correlation between infant intelligence scores and scores on the Stanford-Binet test at eight years of age. From Honzik, 1983.

discuss the specific processes that are involved in intelligent behavior (Siegler and Richards, 1982). An **information-processing** approach focuses on an analysis of the processes that are involved in cognitive or intellectual activity, including:

- *Acquiring information* (e.g., perception and attention).
- *Memory* (e.g., storing information).
- *Problem solving* (e.g., using information to resolve problems).

Earlier in this chapter we discussed one of the most basic forms of information processing—perception (see the discussion of infant perceptual processes). We discuss problem solving in our description of cognitive development in the pre-school and school-age child. In this section, we focus on memory as an information-processing activity of infancy.

MEMORY.   Infants become habituated (a simple type of learning in which infant familiarity with an object or stimulus no longer raises infants' responses such as heart rate or sucking rate) to a sound or an image because it is apparently familiar to them (Cohen, 1979); that is, they appear to *remember* it. The image or sound has now not only registered on the infants' senses, but has apparently remained in their mind.

Many people have thought of infant's and child's memory as a storehouse of past experiences but have failed to suggest how this storehouse is built. Memory is more than haphazard recall of past perceptions and activities. **Memory** is a process of *expecting* and *predicting* future events based on past events. What purpose would memory serve if it only recorded the past? By recording what he or she has done in the past, memory tells the infant what to expect in the next few minutes, in the next hour, and, perhaps, in the next day.

Piaget (1952) showed how memory develops in children below two years. The one-year-old baby who has just begun to crawl has a far more limited memory (yet memory it has) than a brother or sister of four. For example, the infant who watches its parent walk behind a screen and come out on the other side does not have the active memory to remember this sequence of behavior should the parent once again walk behind the screen. To find its mother, the baby will crawl to the side of the screen where the mother entered and disappeared. Or if a ball rolls behind a box, the baby will crawl to the side where the ball disappeared and will not go to the other side, where the ball would be expected to emerge.

Investigators have found that an infant's memory capacity advances in two primary ways after approximately eight months of age (Kagan, 1979). In the first place, an infant remembers for a longer period of time. In an experimental situation where an infant is shown a ball which is then hidden from view, eight-month-olds could find the hidden ball only if the delay between the time the ball was hidden and the start of their search was very brief (three seconds or less). On the other hand, ten-month-old infants would reach for the hidden ball even if the delay was seven seconds or more. This suggests an improvement in memory with age.

The second major development is the accumulation of a store of experiences in the infant's memory. Infants can begin to use their memory to anticipate the future (Kagan, 1979). For example, the infant's memory of a parent putting on a coat and leaving home may be activated at a future time when the parent again puts on a coat and the infant *anticipates* a departure.

Language Development

> All over the world the first sentences of small children are being as painstakingly taped, transcribed and analyzed as if they were the last sayings of great sages. Which is a surprising fate for the likes of "That doggie," "No more milk," and "Hit ball." (Brown, 1973)

Language represents one of the most mysterious events of biology and culture. Many who have studied language have marveled at its vast detail and organization. Although the most complex of all psychological and cultural adaptions, language is uniform in structure throughout the endless cultures of the world. The striking characteristic of language is that infants acquire all of the main forms of speech and language before the end of the second year—the end of infancy. This fact defines the theme of this section: speech and language are developed in a parallel fashion—on a moment-to-moment basis—with general behavior and adjustment, beginning early in life and continuing thereafter throughout all stages of development. People have wondered about the nature of language for thousands of years, but there are still major differences of opinion about its nature and how to study it. Psychologists and linguists have written at great length about language development.

Functions of Language

Language is used diversely throughout the human lifespan in various forms of communication, in thinking and problem solving, and in creative activity and writing. Although language therefore has many other specific functions that depend on the nature of the activity, three major functions are fundamental to language:

PRIMARY FUNCTIONS OF HUMAN LANGUAGE

- Language is a mechanism of self-stimulation and control of individual activity.
- Language is a self-guidance mechanism for predicting and thinking about future behavior.
- Language is a mechanism that organizes social behavior and interactions of people with each other.

What Is Language?

Although we customarily think of language and communication as the same thing, actually they are not. Language is only one form of communication (a verbal-symbolic form). As we have seen in our earlier discussions of the infant, there are many ways in which the infant (and people, in general) communicates its feelings, emotions, and thoughts. For example, a baby's social smile may convey to the parent general information about the infant's physical or emotional state. Such a mode of communication does not require verbal processes—speech or words—and, therefore is *nonverbal*. For our purposes, we use the term *language* to mean the transmission and reception of ideas and feelings by means of *verbal symbols* (Critchley, 1975).

Properties of Language

Language has several properties that are important for us to define if we are to understand the miraculous development of language in infants and young children:

- **Phonology.** The phonological component of language represents its sound structure. Every spoken language is composed of a limited number of primary sounds, or *phonemes,* usually three or four dozen (e.g., the sounds of the letters *p, t, d,* and *o* are phonemes). There are between forty-five and fifty phonemes represented by the twenty-six letters of the alphabet used in the three main dialects of English spoken in the United States (Darley and Spriestersbach, 1978). Vowel sounds (*a, e, i, o, u*) are produced first by infants because they are easier to utter than consonant sounds, which appear later as the infant develops better tongue control.
- **Semantics.** During the course of language development, children also learn how to combine the individual *phonemes* into the smallest meaningful units of language, called *morphemes.* Morphemes may be words or parts of words (e.g., *a, no, ma, play, s, ing*).

The **grammar** of a language is its "rules" or principles for organizing the sounds (phonemes) of the language into meaningful units (morphemes and words). For example, there are numerous words in the English language that begin with the morpheme *be* (e.g., *be, become, because*). We might say, then, that there is a grammatical "rule" in the English language that "allows" people to make these combinations. On the other hand, there is no word in the English language that begins with *zb.* In other words, there is no grammatical rule that allows for that letter combination to be combined with other morphemes or words. For example, there are no such words as *zbcome* or *zbcause.*

The **semantic** component of language constitutes its meaning. "The semantic system of a language is the knowledge that a speaker must have to understand sentences and relate them to his knowledge of the world. It includes both knowledge of individual lexical (vocabulary) items and knowledge of how the meaning of a sentence is determined by the meanings of individual lexical items and the structure of the sentence (Dale, 1976, p. 166).

- **Syntax.** *Syntax,* or the syntactical component of language, is made up of the rules that govern the organization of meaningful units (such as words) into meaningful utterances (such as phrases, clauses, and sentences). Each language has its own syntactical rules that define the function of words in a sentence and give meaning to the sentence. For example, the following two sentences have the same words but entirely different meanings because of syntactical rules:
  1. Jill ran past John.
  2. John ran past Jill.

In English there is a syntactical rule that in an active sentence, the noun that precedes the verb is the *agent* of the action and the noun following the verb is the *object* of the action.

- **Expressive Component.** The expressive component of language consists of the emotion, feeling, motivation, or action that accompanies the utterance of speech. It may be defined by emphasis, rhythm, loudness, and patterning of speech. Because the expressive factors in language denote the state and feeling of the speaker, they give additional meaning to particular phrases or sentences. The expressive component of speech is closely interlocked with the gestures, facial expression, and "body language" that accompany speech. The expressive components of vocal behavior are the first aspects of speech to develop in infancy and are seen in the varied patterns of crying, whimpering, cooing, gurgling, and babbling in the first year, before significant speech articulations emerge.

Theories of Language Acquisition

Although the significance of speech and language is certainly undeniable, the explanations of these processes differ and are controversial. In this section we examine three major theoretical perspectives to language development: learning theories, the nativist or psycholinguistic viewpoint, and the interactionist perspective.

LEARNING THEORIES.   There are two differing viewpoints among learning theorists as to how children learn to use language. The first approach, the *reinforcement model,* is an application of *traditional learning theory* to the development of language (see Chapter 2). The second learning theory approach involves the application of *social learning* theory to child language development (see also Chapter 2).

• *The reinforcement model (traditional learning theory).* The reinforcement perspective explains speech and language development as the products of reinforcement of infant responses. That is, language and speech are attained in much the same fashion as other behaviors, which are learned through the pairing of stimulus (S) and response (R) in the presence of appropriate reinforcement. According to this theory, the infant's production of sounds and words is the result of the caretaker's reinforcement of these activities by increased attention to the infant or by the provision of desired objects (e.g., milk, toys, cookies).

There are at least two major difficulties with this theory. First, the individual infant cannot possibly be reinforced for every utterance it makes. How do the infant and child "learn" to make utterances they have never heard before? Second, learning theory provides little or no insight into the development of the complex "rule" systems that govern languages. Where do these rules come from? Learning theory implies that these rules are attained through association and reinforcement. However, as we have indicated, infants generate speech and language that they have never heard before. Furthermore, observation of parent-child language interaction indicates that parents pay more attention to the ungrammatical but "cute" linguistic responses of their child than to "correct" responses.

• *Social learning theory.* Social learning theorists maintain that children learn language by listening, observing, and imitating models. This theory appears to explain language development as being the result of interactions between parent or caretaker and child. There is considerable evidence that mutual imitation does occur and is a factor in language learning (Price, Hess, and Dickson, 1981; Norman-Jackson, 1982; Sigel, Dreyer, and McGillicuddy-DeLisi, 1984). That is, parents and other companions appear to play a critical role in child language development. They introduce new linguistic principles in simplified sentences which are tailored to the child's level of understanding. For example, as we shall see later, parents may respond to a child's ungrammatical utterances with a modified statement that is grammatically correct.

On the other hand, imitation does not seem to be a sufficient explanation, by itself, for language development. Several studies suggest that imitation in the sense of children's attempts to reproduce the actual adult utterances they hear does not play an important role in the acquisition of syntax. Many of the very earliest utterances of children cannot be viewed as imitations or even reduced imitations of adult speech; for example, "Allgone sticky." Furthermore, even when children do imitate parental speech (which is not uncommon), they reformulate the sentences using their own grammar. Children can hardly acquire new grammatical features through imitation when it is precisely these new features that are omitted in imitations (Dale, 1976, p. 138).

THE NATIVIST OR PSYCHOLINGUISTIC PERSPECTIVE.   According to the nativist (or psycholinguistic) perspective, imitation or learning cannot be the primary or exclusive mechanisms of language development in children. If imitation or learning were the central or key factors, we would not hear children generate statements that do not appear in the speech of adults (but do appear to conform to a "rule" that the child has inferred). For example, a child who sees a picture of two birds in a book may say, "I see two gooses!"

> *DEFINITIONS*
>
> **Psycholinguistics.** Psycholinguistics is the study of the inborn cognitive and perceptual abilities that contribute to the development of language from the cooing and babbling of infants to the organized words and sentences of older children.
>
> **Language Acquisition Device (LAD).** An LAD is a set of language-processing skills that nativists or psycholinguists believe are innate and that accomplishes the following:
> · Enables a child to understand the rules governing others' speech.
> · Enables a child to use these inferred rules to produce language.
> For example, the child who hears others make a plural by adding a final *s* (e.g., "Do you want a toy? Here are some toys") may generate statements (based on "inferred rules") that do not appear in adult speech (e.g., "I will brush my tooths").

Furthermore, nativists (or psycholinguists) suggest that parents pay minimal attention to the grammatical correctness of child utterances (Slobin, 1979). Rather, psycholinguists such as Noam Chomsky (1975) argue that human beings have an inborn or innate capacity for language learning, which they call a *language acquisition device* (LAD). Presumably this innate language capacity enables the child to infer the phonological (sound) patterns, word meanings, and syntactical rules of adult speech which they hear. These inferences about language structure and function are then used to generate their own utterances.

As with learning theory, there are several difficulties with the psycholinguistic approach. First, it assumes that human beings are always capable of grammatical sentences whether or not they have anything meaningful to say. Psycholinguists tend to minimize the role of meaning in the development of language. A second difficulty is that psycholinguists attribute important functions of language generation to unverifiable structures of the mind. What exactly *is* an LAD? How do we know it exists except by *assuming* that it is the source of grammatical utterances? It is a fact that the child can generate a vast number of grammatical utterances without having heard them before. It is a matter of conjecture whether these utterances are generated by means of an LAD.

INTERACTIONIST PERSPECTIVE.   Piaget (1970a) has argued that *both* a linguistic environment (including reinforcement and imitation) *and* innate biological processes combine to produce language development in children. This position has been called an *interactionist perspective*. Although interactionists indicate that children are biologically programmed for language development, they argue that what is innate is not a language-processing device (e.g., LAD) but a *nervous system* that gradually matures. Piaget argues that this maturing nervous system provides the basis not only for language development but for all cognitive development as well (1970a). Therefore, it is to be expected that, since cognitive development is influenced by the maturation of the brain and nervous system, language development would also proceed in a series of stages akin to the stages of cognitive development (see Chapter 2).

Furthermore, Piaget (1970a) proposes that language development depends on the *interaction* of the maturing nervous system with a *linguistic environment*. The development of language patterns or schemas is facilitated by the child's linguistic interaction with adults and peers, who provide the input necessary for refining language schemas.

The Course of Early Language Development

Infants begin to make vocal sounds at birth. At first, their "language" is undifferentiated; however, they quickly develop a variety of cries. By six weeks, infants are also making a variety of cooing sounds. Two fundamental ideas underlie our notions of the child's language development (Dale, 1976):

1. The child does not simply speak a garbled form of adult language. Rather, infants and children speak a language of their own, with its own patterns and characteristics.
2. Infants and children act as their own "language specialists." That is, they are faced with an unlimited set of possible utterances from which they must somehow extract the underlying rules. The child is continually trying out hypotheses about these rules of the language. For example, if the child hears the parent make a plural noun by adding *s* (e.g., boys, dogs, cats), the child may extend the "rule" to *sheeps* and *peoples*.

■ *A SCENARIO: THE BABY ELIZABETH AS LANGUAGE SPECIALIST*

Most of the "hypotheses" of language usage that infants and young children develop are based on what they hear. Witness the following conversation between Elizabeth and her parents:

Father: (to Elizabeth's mother) By looking at the grass outside, I think it's time for me to mow the lawn.
Mother: This is a good time to do it.
Elizabeth: (repeating her mother) Daddy *do* it.

(Sometime later in the day).

Father: (wiping his brow) Well, I mow*ed* the lawn.
Mother: You complet*ed* your work.
Elizabeth: Daddy do*ed* it.

Elizabeth, on learning the past tense of such verbs as *mow* and *complete*, may have developed the following hypothesis: All past-tense forms are produced by adding *d* or *ed*. The application of this hypothesis led to her utterance—"*doed*" (in other words, to *overgeneralize*).

Biological and Maturational Factors

The interactional process by which the infant develops the use of speech and language in the family is based, in part, on biological and maturational features. The development of speech and language has a supporting basis, therefore, in the biological maturation of the infant. The sequence of speech development seems to be parallel to motor development (see Table 7.6). The human brain has many **association areas** that organize specific sensory functions such as touch, hearing, vision, and speech. The speech centers of the brain are generally located in the left brain hemisphere. The process by which the various brain centers mature and develop with regard to their functions is called **lateralization.** There is some evidence that where this process of lateralization of brain hemisphere functions is incomplete, interference with such activities as speech is possible (Kinsbourne and Hiscock, 1983). Thus biological maturation appears to be an important undergirding feature of speech and language.

TABLE 7.6

The Relationship Between Speech and Motor Development

AGE	LANGUAGE ACTIVITY	MOTOR ACTIVITY
Birth	Cries.	Limited voluntary control.
12 Weeks	Infant can smile and make cooing sounds.	Infant can support its head (when in a prone position).
16 Weeks	Infant can turn head in response to human voice.	When a rattle is placed in its hands, infant can play with it.
20 Weeks	Infant can make vowel-like and consonant-like cooing sounds.	Infant sits up when propped.
6 Months	Infant cooing changes to single-syllable babbling sounds (e.g., *ma, mu, di*).	Infant can grasp or reach toward people or objects.
8 Months	Infant can repeat many single-syllable sounds (e.g., *mama, gaga*).	Infant can stand by holding on to objects (e.g., crib sides, tables).
10 Months	Infant distinguishes between adult words by responding differently to them.	Infant creeps, pulls self to a standing position, and takes steps while holding on.
12 Months	Infant can utter words such as *ma-ma* or *da-da* and seems to understand other words.	Infant can sit on floor and can walk with assistance.
18 Months	Infant has vocabulary of 3–50 words and begins to use two-word combinations.	Infant can grasp and manipulate objects; infant can walk proficiently.
24 Months	Infant's vocabulary exceeds 50 words; infant uses two-word phrases.	Infant can run and walk up and down stairs.
30 Months	Variety of toddler's words increases dramatically; infant can use three- to five-word phrases.	Toddler refines walking behavior by being able to move on tiptoes and to stand on one foot alone.
3 Years	Toddler has clear pronunciation vocabulary of about 1,000 words.	Toddler can ride a tricycle.
4 Years	Language well established.	Preschooler can hop and jump over a rope.

Based on Lenneberg, 1967, pp. 128–130.

PRELIMINARIES TO LANGUAGE: CRYING, COOING, BABBLING. Psycholinguists have determined that the vocalization of prelinguistic children develops in a stepwise fashion during the first ten to twelve months of life. The following are the three stages of prelinguistic vocalization (Table 7.6 summarizes some of these developments):

· *Crying.* Infants are capable of initially producing at least three types of cries—a "hunger" cry, a "pain" cry, and a "mad" cry (Wolff, 1969a). These cries tend to be simple reactions to pain or discomfort rather than serving as a type of communication. However, one could argue that the "pain cry" serves as a signal to get the attention of a parent or caretaker.

By about the third week of life, some infants develop what Peter Wolff calls a "fake cry" ("cry of low pitch and intensity . . . consists of long drawn out moans which occasionally rise to more explicit cries . . ." [p. 98]). It is called a fake cry because it does not appear to be associated with any apparent pain or discomfort. Fake cries may be used to attract attention or simply for the pleasure of experimenting with sounds (Wolff, 1969a).

· *Cooing.* Sometime around three to five weeks, infants begin to make a variety of new sounds that appear to be related to comfortable states. These vocalizations are called **cooing** and are composed of vowel sounds such as *eeee, oooo,* and *iiii* (Menyuk, 1977).

· *Babbling.* At approximately three or four months of age, infants begin to add consonant sounds (*k, g,* and so on) to their repertoire of sounds. Shortly thereafter, they may combine consonants with vowels to produce *babbles* (e.g., *kaka, lala, papa,* and so on). Although such **babbling** may sound like real words, they are ordinarily not intended as such (deVilliers and deVilliers, 1979). It is usually not until ten to thirteen months that infants utter their first meaningful words.

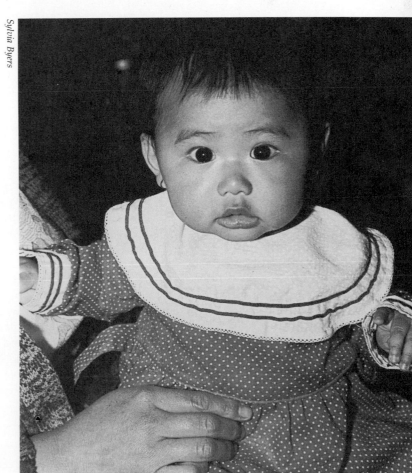

Sylvia Byers

By recording what she has done in the past, memory helps the infant learn what to expect in the future.

What is the relationship of these prelinguistic vocalizations to language development? Aside from the exercise of the mechanical skills ultimately necessary for meaningful speech and language, infants may be learning the bare rudiments of language as a two-way reciprocal communication process. For example, there is evidence that babies younger than six months are more likely to coo or babble while their caregivers are speaking (Rosenthal, 1982). It appears that such infants may be playing games in which they try to harmonize their cooing with adult speaking. Conversational-type turn taking where the infant is silent while the adult speaks does not ordinarily occur until the infant is seven to eight months old. Thus the prelinguistic infant may be learning the first rule of communication—language is a two-way process involving taking turns. Furthermore, there is some evidence that the infant may well be "preprogrammed" for language learning from as early as the first day of life. William Condon and Louis Sander (1974a, 1974b) demonstrated that long before the infant has any notion of the meaning of language, its physical movements can be matched or synchronized with the speech sounds of an adult speaker. This finding suggests that parents and caretakers can provide a supportive environment for the development of formal language well in advance of its emergence.

THE CHILD'S FIRST WORDS.   Sometime around the first birthday, the child achieves a milestone in language: the utterance of the first word. The range from ten to thirteen months includes most recorded observations of the first word (Nelson, 1973, 1981; Kuczaj and Barrett, 1986). The infant's first words are distinctive in several ways (Dale, 1976):

1. *Phonetically* (their pronunciation). Typically the words consist of one or two syllables. Each syllable is ordinarily of the form "consonant-vowel."
2. *Their meanings* or the *ways in which they are used*. Regardless of the type of first words used by the infant, most likely they do not *mean* the same thing to the infant that they mean to the parent.

The Meaning of First Words. There appears to be a great deal of similarity between children in the first fifty words or so that are acquired. Katherine Nelson (1973, 1981) used the following classification system to describe the infant's first words:

CATEGORIES OF FIRST WORDS
- *General nominals* (51 percent): doggie, ball, house.
- *Specific nominals* (14 percent): daddy, mommy, pet, names.
- *Action words* (14 percent): give, bye-bye, go.
- *Modifiers* (9 percent): dirty, mine, outside, nice.
- *Personal-social words* (8 percent): no, yes, please.
- *Function words* (4 percent): what, for.

The important individuals in the infant's life are commonly found in the infant's first words. Among the more common *general nominal* words are *juice, milk, cookie, shoes, ball,* and *car* (Nelson, 1981). An important factor in whether a word will be included among the first words is whether it is something that the *child can act on* fairly easily. For example, large objects that are simply "there" (e.g., stove, table, trees) are usually not found among the child's first words, whereas words such as *key, blanket, toy,* and *brush* (objects toward which the child acts) are common.

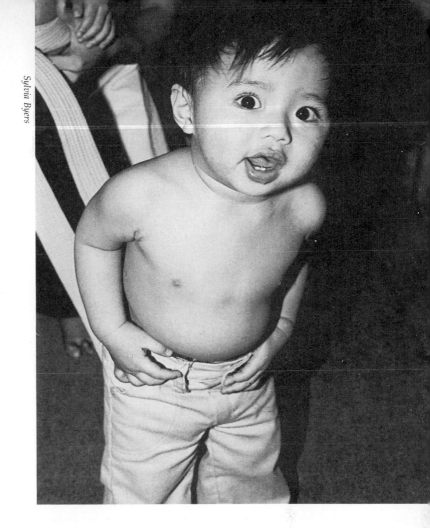

Sylvia Byers

Language represents one of the most mysterious events of biology and culture.

■ *A SCENARIO: THE BABY ELIZABETH (AT 1 YEAR)*

Our bouncing baby girl—Elizabeth—has been doing many things since we last saw her. Just the other day, she uttered what her parents thought was her first word: "Dada." Daddy, of course, was quite pleased because he assumed that he was clearly differentiated from Elizabeth's mother, her brother, and various neighbors or strangers. Daddy's relative state of euphoria lasted only until 6:00 P.M. that evening, when dinner guests arrived. At that time, Baby Elizabeth cheerfully greeted one of the male guests with a loud, booming "Dada!!"

A common phenomenon in almost every language is the child's *overextension* of the use of a word to refer to a broader category than appropriate in adult usage (Clark, 1973; Clark and Clark, 1977) (see Table 7.7). In the example, Elizabeth's word *dada* was extended to refer to adult males other than her father. Another example would be the word *ball*, which may sometimes be extended to include or "mean" other round objects, such as stones, gumballs, or radishes. Such overextensions appear to be most common during the period from thirteen to thirty months. It seems that the basis for overextensions (as well as for word meaning) is the *perceptual* attributes of objects (e.g., all round objects are "balls") or functional attributes (small round objects called *balls* are to play with).

Gradually the child narrows the meanings of words that have been overextended. One of the explanations for this process of limiting word meaning is the acquisition of new words. That is, new words take over parts of the broader,

TABLE 7.7
Some Perceptually Based Overextensions

SOURCE AND LANGUAGE	LEXICAL ITEM	FIRST REFERENT	EXTENSIONS IN ORDER OF OCCURRENCE
Shape			
Lewis (1951) English	tee (from name of cat)	cat	dogs; cows and sheep; horse
Pavlovitch (1920) French	bébé	reflection of self in mirror	photograph of self; all photographs; all pictures; all books with pictures; all books
Imedadze (1960) Russian	buti	ball	toy; radish; stone spheres at park entrance
Size			
Moore (1896) English	fly	fly	specks of dirt; dust; all small insects; his own toes; crumbs of bread; a toad
Taine (1877) French	bébé	baby	other babies; all small statues; figures in small pictures and prints
Sound			
Shvachkin (1948) Russian	dany	sound of bell	clock; telephone; doorbells
Leopold (1949) German-English	sch	noise of train	music; noise of movement; wheels; balls
Movement			
Moore (1896) English	bird	sparrows	cows and dogs; cats; any moving animal
Taste			
Leopold (1949) English	candy	candy	cherries; anything sweet
Texture			
Shvachkin (1948) Russian	kiki	cat	cotton; any soft material
Idelberger (1903) German	bow-wow	dog	toy dog; fur piece with animal head; fur piece without head

Adapted from Clark, 1973, Table 6.1.

overextended meanings (Kuczaj and Barrett, 1986). An example with Baby Elizabeth may help us:

■   The Baby Elizabeth who had been using the word *dada* rather freely for any adult male now begins to refine her meaning of the word (to the joy of her father). Let's look at the evolution of the word *dada* as she learns new words.

1. The first "meaning" apparently referred to her father, her grandfather, and other adult males.
2. When Elizabeth learns the word *papa* to refer to her grandfather, the word *dada* comes to be limited to her father and other males.
3. When Elizabeth learns the word *man* to refer to male adults other than her father and her grandfather, she limits her meaning of *dada* to her father alone.
4. Baby Elizabeth's "dada" is—to say the least—pleased.

Words That Are Sentences. The child's first words seem to be more than single words. They are used for more than description. They appear to express complex ideas (ideas that would be expressed in sentences by adults). The term **holophrase** is used to describe this use of words as sentences.

■ *SCENARIO*

Baby Elizabeth sees her father's pipe and says, "Daddy."

Baby Elizabeth is seated comfortably at her feeding table and is presented with some peas. She touches them and says, "Eat."

Baby Elizabeth is sitting on the grass and hears an airplane. She points to the airplane, follows it across the sky, and says, "Bye-bye."

In each of the examples, the infant's first words might be interpreted as comments on *experiences* or *actions* in the environment rather than simply as names for objects (Clark and Clark, 1977; Kuczaj and Barrett, 1986). First words are closely related to the child's experiences. In particular, they describe those experiences in which the child participates and over which he or she gains control (Dale, 1976).

Learning First Words: Family Contribution. Although there may be a pattern to the learning of first words, there may also be a contribution resulting from adult-child interaction. Nelson (1973, 1981) determined that the children in her experiment could be divided into two major groups: children who were talking more about *things* (referential or R group) and children who were talking more about *self and other people* (expressive or E group). She found that all of the *first-born children of parents with high educational achievement* were in the referential group (see Table 7.8). Nelson then examined the nature of adult-child interaction to see if there might be differences between R-group interactions and E-group interactions. In other words, did family behavior make a difference? The mothers of the R-group children did *not* name objects more frequently than the mothers of E-group children. Rather, R-group mothers did talk about objects more, whereas E-group mothers talked more about their children. Although the long-term implications of these family differences were not explored, there appears to be evidence that family interactional style may be a significant feature of language development.

FROM ONE WORD TO TWO.   Sometime around eighteen or twenty months of age, infants begin to make two-word combinations. These two-word combinations are significant for the following reasons (Dale, 1976):

1. Two-word phrases represent an important milestone in the expansion of language as a tool for expressing complex ideas.
2. Two-word phrases reflect the child's language-organization strategies. When the child first begins to use two-word phrases, there are no constraints on the order of the words. For example, Baby Elizabeth, on noticing an open door, is as likely to say, "Open, door," as "Door, open." In the two-word stage, observable patterns and emerging rules of organization become apparent.

TABLE 7.8

Distribution of Groups by Birth Order and Education of Parents

BIRTH ORDER	EDUCATION	REFERENTIAL	EXPRESSIVE
First	High	5	0
Later	High	2	2
First	Low	3	3
Later	Low	0	3

From Nelson, 1981.

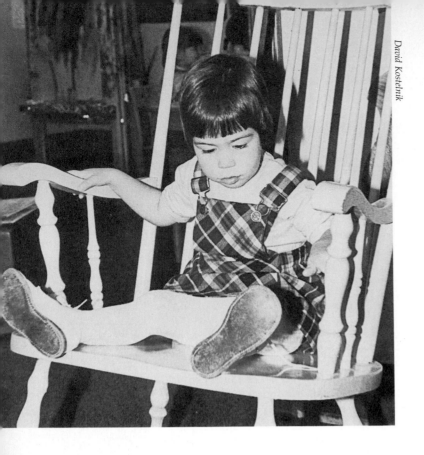

Telegraphic Speech. One of the primary characteristics of children's speech that is noted with the onset of two-word phrases is that it is **telegraphic.** In other words, there is a pattern to the words that are included and excluded in the child's utterances, compared with the "ideal" adult sentence for expressing a similar idea. Children's sentences or two-word utterances tend to omit the following types of words: prepositions (*to, for, be*); auxilliary verbs (*was, has, been*); and articles (*a, the*). It is as if the child were sending a telegram to those with whom he or she is trying to communicate (see Figs. 7.15 and 7.16).

The Meaning of Two-Word Utterances. The decade of the 1960s was marked by a consideration of the structure of two-word phrases (Braine, 1963; McNeil, 1970). Martin D. S. Braine (1963) suggested that two-word phrases were composed of two classes of words: **pivot words** and **open words.**

PIVOT WORDS

The *pivot* class is small, and each word in it is used with many different words from the much larger open class. For example, a child might say *bandage on, blanket on,* [and] *fix on . . . on* is a pivot word. It is always used in the second position, and many other words can occur with it. Or a child might say *allgone shoe, allgone lettuce, allgone outside,* and others. . . . A pivot word may be the first or the second in two-word utterances, but *each pivot word has its own position.* (Dale, 1976, p. 21)

Where pivot words come first, the Baby Elizabeth might say the following:

P	+	O
see		dog
see		cat
see		Bruce
see		Scott

262

Roger Brown on Telegraphic Speech

Roger Brown is currently Professor of Social Psychology at Harvard University. He has contributed numerous books and research articles to the study of child language development.

Brown and Bellugi described the child's use of telegraphic speech as follows:

When words cost money there is a premium on brevity or to put it otherwise, a constraint on length. The result is "telegraphic" English. . . . One does not send a cable reading: "My car has broken down and I have lost my wallet; send money to me at the American Express in Paris" but rather "Car broken down; wallet lost; send money American Express Paris." The telegram omits *my, has, and, I, have, my, to me, at, the, in*. All of these are *functors.* . . .

A telegraphic transformation of English generally communicates very well. It does so because it retains the high-information words (contentives) and drops the low-information words (functors). . . . If you say aloud sentences you will find that you place the heavier stresses . . . on contentives rather than on functors. In fact, the heavier stresses fall, for the most part, on the words the child retains (when the child repeats or tries to imitate adult utterances). We first realized that this was the case when we found that in transcribing tapes, the words of the mother that we could hear most clearly were usually the words that the child reproduced. We had trouble hearing the weakly stressed functors and, of course, the child usually failed to reproduce them. . . .

We are fairly sure that differential stress is one of the determinants of the child's telegraphic productions. For one thing stress will also account for the way in which children reproduce polysyllabic [many-syllable] words when the total is too much for them. Adam, for instance, gave us *'pression* for *expression* and Eve gave us *'raff* for *giraffe;* the more heavily stressed syllables were the ones retained.

From Brown and Bellugi, 1964, pp. 138–139.

FIGURE 7.15
Sample telegraphic utterances.

Adult Sentence	Child Utterance
Daddy will be gone.	Daddy gone.
Mommy can help us.	Mommy help.
Daddy's briefcase.	Daddy case.

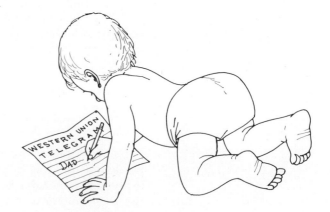

FIGURE 7.16
Children's speech is telegraphic.

In the example on the bottom of p. 262, *see* is the *pivot* word (P), and *dog, cat, Bruce,* and *Scott* are *open* (O) words.

Where pivot words come in second position, Elizabeth might say:

O	+	P
dog		all gone
cat		all gone
man		all gone
diaper		all gone

In the above examples, *all gone* is the *pivot* word, and *dog, cat, man,* and *diaper* are the *open* words. (Elizabeth's parents were particularly relieved to discover that, in fact, her diaper was not "all gone.")

Over the last decade, the accumulation of evidence has indicated that, as might have been expected, children's two-word phrases do not always conform to the structure described. In addition to *structural* descriptions (e.g., word classes and their combinations), children's sentences can also be described in terms of the *functions* that the words serve in the sentence (deVilliers and deVilliers, 1979). In the latter case, the *context* in which the child's utterance occurs and the child's *intentions* are critical factors in the organization of two-word phrases. For example, the child's utterance "Mommy hat" could mean "Mommy, put on a hat" or "Mommy, give me a hat."

■ *SCENARIO*

The irrepressible Baby Elizabeth is practicing her two-word phrases when she encounters an object on which she can act (an important criterion for language development): Daddy's shoe. Elizabeth promptly announces to her father (who is reading the newspaper in his easy chair), "Daddy shoe." She then hands the shoe to her father, who is only slightly startled when the shoe lands in his lap. Quickly recovering his dignity (an indispensable characteristic for the parent of a toddler), Elizabeth's father smiles at her and returns to his reading. Elizabeth again states— slightly louder this time—"Daddy shoe." At this point, Daddy concludes that if he wishes to finish the newspaper, perhaps he ought to put on his shoe. He does so. Elizabeth looks on with a rather astonished expression. She temporarily leaves the scene, circles the kitchen table, stares at her brother, and again spies her father quietly reading in his chair. She returns to her father's chair, where she indicates her presence by putting her hand against the back of the newspaper and gently shakes the paper. Her father lowers his newspaper to discover the smiling face of Elizabeth, who says, "Daddy shoe." Her father (wondering if there might not be a better time to read the newspaper) says to her, "Yes, Daddy shoe." Elizabeth seems pleased. She moves on to other adventures.

Comment. How do we explain why Elizabeth seemingly relented in her assault on her father? There are many possible answers, including the obvious fact that Elizabeth may simply have tired. Another explanation may involve the meaning or the *intent* of Elizabeth's statement: "Daddy shoe." There are at least two meanings: "Daddy's shoe" and "Daddy put on the shoe." It is quite possible that Elizabeth simply wished her father to acknowledge that the shoe belonged to him.

Some of the most common relationships that children use in their speech are presented in Table 7.9. One way of thinking about the semantic relationships expressed in the table is as a set of statements or propositions that verbally describe the sensorimotor world of the toddler as he or she emerges from infancy. You will remember from our discussion of infant cognitive development that the major

TABLE 7.9
Semantic Relations in Two-word Sentences

SEMANTIC RELATION	FORM	EXAMPLE
1. Nomination	that + N[1]	That book
2. Notice	hi + N	Hi belt
3. Recurrence	more + N	
	'nother + N	More milk
4. Nonexistence	all gone + N	
	no more + N	All-gone rattle
5. Attributive	adjective + N	Big train
6. Possessive	N + N	Mommy lunch
7. Locative	N + N	Sweater chair
8. Locative	V[2] + N	Walk street
9. Agent–action	N + V	Eve read
10. Agent–object	N + N	Mommy sock
11. Action–object	V + N	Put book

[1]N = noun.
[2]V = verb.

Adapted from Brown, 1970, p. 220.

achievements of infancy include the establishment of a stable world (object permanency), the distinction of the world from the self, and the ability to organize and self-regulate behavior directed at objects. Linguistic expression (and, in particular, the relationships in Table 7.9) can be viewed as the extension of action as a mode of self-regulation to include language as a technique for both self-control and object control (Brown, 1973; Smith and Schiamberg, 1973; Leung and Rheingold, 1981).

Out of the basic set of "rules" described in Table 7.9, the child generates three-word and four-word sentences. It is rather amazing that no new relationship rules beyond those for two-word phrases are required to generate more lengthy utterances that describe the exciting realities of toddler life (Anisfeld, 1984).

SOME PRACTICAL LESSONS OF COMMUNICATION. In addition to the semantic relationships described above, infants and toddlers learn several practical lessons of communication:

• In the first place, they learn to use language as a way of *gaining the attention* of parents/caretakers or other associates and of *sustaining such contacts*.
• They learn to *supplement their vocabularies* and use language production skills in order to generate more meaningful utterances. For example, infants learn to use point gestures as a way of increasing their communication and vocabulary skills. Eleanor Leung and Harriet Rheingold (1981) found that mothers respond to infant pointing by naming the object or event. In this way, the infant's vocabulary is increasingly enriched with the names of new objects and events.
• They become *good listeners* as a way of improving their communication skills. There is evidence that infants age twelve to twenty-four months are carefully listening for the responses of their conversation partners to determine if they have effectively communicated (Wilcox and Webster, 1980). For example, the infant (wanting a toy) who says "Toy" and finds that the parent simply restates the obvious ("Yes, that is a toy") may become more specific in his/her communication ("Give toy").

The Ecology of Language Development: The Role of the Family

As we will see in Chapter 10, there is a distinction between learning a language and the effective *use* of language in interpersonal communication. Even though the infant and the toddler may possess *competence* in such language activities as communicating needs, emotions, and various points of view, it is not until the school years that such complex "mutual following" skills which underlie effective adult communication begin to develop. For example, the ability to understand another person's point of view—and to design communication in line with this understanding—is not present in early language development. In fact, this mutual following skill does not ordinarily occur until the child is about ten years old. Language development occurs in a social system that involves *both* active, adult models and the creative, active child.

The verbal interchange between parent and child serves an important function in the development of language. The adult speaks to the child in language forms that are simpler than ordinary adult-adult speech. However, the adult's language is more effective as a language-teaching technique if it remains just above the level of the child's own language productions. In other words, the child is more likely to learn language through mutual verbal interaction if the parent's utterances are challenging rather than overwhelmingly new or simple repetitions of what the child can already say.

The problem for the language learner is that to develop competence in language, he or she can work only with the information available: the caretaker's or parent's speech heard by the child and the responses to the child's own speech. Because most of the language the young child hears is that of the parent or caretaker, we might ask, What kind of language environment do parents or caretakers provide for their children? As we have already indicated, the speech of the parent (usually the mother) is simpler than ordinary adult conversation. Maternal utterances are shorter in length, the rate of speech is slower, and there are fewer complex sentences. As the child acquires the patterns of language, maternal speech gradually increases in complexity (Dale, 1976).

Several interesting *types of verbal exchange* between parent and child have been observed (Kaye, 1982). These interchanges provide important opportunities for the infant and the toddler to refine language competence. The most interesting mode of exchange between parent and child is *expansion*. Expansion involves the mutual imitation of child by parent and parent by child. There are several types of expansion that a parent can initiate (see Table 7.10).

TABLE 7.10
Expansions of Child's Speech Produced by Mothers

CHILD	MOTHER
Baby highchair.	Baby is in the highchair.
Mommy eggnog.	Mommy had her eggnog.
Eve lunch.	Eve is having lunch.
Mommy sandwich.	Mommy'll have a sandwich.
Sat wall.	He sat on the wall.
Throw daddy.	Throw it to daddy.
Pick glove.	Pick the glove up.

From Brown and Bellugi, 1964, pp. 34, 141.

In the social system of language development, the child is an *active* autonomous investigator of the world. Mastering language is not a simple task. As we have indicated, the child constantly formulates hypotheses about the "rules" of language and tests them. Furthermore, it has been suggested that the child *actively* creates its own linguistic environment by the response it makes to adult and peer verbalizations. For example, as the infant and child matures, he or she will produce more sophisticated utterances that, in turn, prompt companions to increase the complexity of their own statements, and so on. The pattern of influence is clearly reciprocal, with the infant/child making a distinct contribution in *creating* its linguistic environment.

Summary

1. The physical growth of a baby is nothing short of remarkable. During the first year of life there is a dramatic growth spurt during which body length increases by almost a third and weight usually triples. At one year of age the brain is 25 percent of its adult weight. By two years the brain is 75 percent of its adult weight. At birth, the infant has the maximum number of neurons that it will ever have. Further development of the nervous system involves the growth and branching of these neurons into dense, interconnecting networks.

   The maturation of the brain during the first months of life is characterized by several important developments: (a) Brain development is most pronounced in the *primary sensory areas* and the *primary motor areas*; (b) the full or optimal expression of brain functions (genetically programmed and present at birth) depends on *experience* during the early months of life; (c) early brain development regulates infant states.

   All the bones of the body originate from soft cartilage which, over time, becomes hardened into bone (ossify). At birth, the neonate has all the muscle fibers it will ever have. However, there is continuous growth in muscle length, breadth, and thickness until adulthood.

2. Newborn infants can visually distinguish *movement*, can *follow* or *track* a given stimulus, and can determine changes in *brightness*. Newborn *visual acuity* is not fully developed at birth. Infants prefer to look at *complex visual stimuli* and appear to pay more attention to *human faces* than to other objects they may encounter. Infant *depth perception* is an important aspect of adaptation.

3. Newborn hearing is more precise and completely developed than newborn vision. Several important facets of newborn auditory activity include *sound localization, discrimination of loudness and frequencies of sound*, and the *development of an infant/parent prelanguage relationship*.

   Newborns can distinguish among a variety of odors and tastes.

4. The development of *movement* or *motor* skills goes hand in hand with the development of perceptual, cognitive, and social skills. Between birth and three years, infant motor development moves from *general reflexes* to *differentiated* (and skillful) *movements*. The two primary motor events of infancy are *locomotion* and *prehension* (reaching and grasping).

5. In this book we examine cognitive development from three perspectives: the *Piagetian* approach, the *psychometric* approach, and the *information-processing* perspective.

   Piaget's research indicated that the processes of intelligence evolved from the sensorimotor activities of infancy. As the infant proceeds through the sensorimotor period, the changes in mental skills are substantial. Piaget has divided the sensorimotor period into six substages.

The emerging understanding of *object permanency* in the infant makes the world a more predictable and simpler place in which to live. The discovery of object permanency helps the infant separate the existence of the object from a particular or unique space and time and, therefore, provides the foundation for the emerging concepts of space, time, and causality.

6. The *psychometric approach* to cognitive development involves the use of intelligence tests for infants. Several questions have been raised regarding infant intelligence tests, including the following: (a) Do they assess the same intellectual activities that are assessed in tests used for children? (b) Can infant intelligence tests be used to predict child intelligence at a later age? (c) Can infant intelligence tests be used to diagnose developmental problems?

7. The *information-processing* approach to cognitive development focuses on an analysis of the processes involved in cognitive activity, including acquiring information, memory, and problem solving.

8. Language represents one of the most mysterious events of biology and culture. The striking characteristic of language is that infants acquire all of the main forms of speech and language before the end of the second year— the end of infancy. Language serves several primary functions including self-stimulation, self-guidance, and organizing social behavior. For our purposes, we use the term *language* to mean the transmission and reception of ideas and feelings by means of *verbal symbols*. Language has several properties, including *phonology* (the sound structure), *semantics* (meaning of language), *syntax*, and *expressiveness*. There are three major perspectives to language development: *learning theories*, the *nativist* or *psycholinguistic viewpoint* and the *interactionist perspective*.

Two fundamental ideas underlie our notions of infant-child language development. (a) The child does not simply speak a garbled form of adult language. Rather, children speak a language of their own with unique patterns and characteristics. (b) Infants and children act as their own language specialists by continually experimenting with various utterances as a way of determining the "rules" of language.

9. The interactional process by which the infant develops the use of speech and language in the family is based, in part, on *biological* and *maturational* features. The development of speech and language has a supporting basis in the biological maturation of the infant. Psycholinguists have determined that the vocalization of prelinguistic children develops in a stepwise fashion during the first ten to twelve months of life. The three stages of prelinguistic vocalization are *crying*, *cooing*, and *babbling*.

Sometime around the first birthday, the infant achieves a milestone in language: the utterance of the first word. The infant's first words are distinctive in at least three ways: *phonetically*, *semantically* (their meanings), and in the way they are *used*.

Sometime around eighteen or twenty months of age, infants begin to make two-word combinations. A primary characteristic of such two-word utterances is that they are *telegraphic*.

10. Infants and toddlers learn several *practical lessons of communication*: (a) language is a *way of gaining attention*, (b) they learn to *supplement their vocabularies*, and (c) they *become good listeners*.

11. The *ecology* of language development includes the verbal interchange between parent and the infant/toddler.

Key Terms

Association areas
Babbling
The Bayley Scales of Infant
   Development
Brain waves
Cooing
Coordination of secondary schemas
Electroencephalogram (EEG)
Expressive component
Grammar
Holophrase
Information processing
Invention of new means
Language Acquisition Device (LAD)
Lateralization
Locomotion
Memory
Neurons
Object permanency
Open words

Ossification
Phonology
Pivot words
Prehension
Primary circular reactions
Primary motor areas
Primary sensory areas
Psycholinguistics
Psychometric
Reflex activity
Secondary circular reactions
Semantics
Sensorimotor stage
Sudden Infant Death Syndrome (SIDS)
Synaptic connections
Syntax
Telegraphic speech
Tertiary circular reactions
Visual acuity
Visual cliff

Questions

1. Discuss the general characteristics of brain maturation in infants.
2. Define the Piagetian, psychometric, and information-processing perspectives to infant cognitive development.
3. Briefly describe three properties of language.
4. Discuss the emergence of one- and two-word utterances.
5. How important is the role of the family in the early language development of infants?

Suggested Readings

FOGEL, A. *Infancy: Infant, Family and Society*. St. Paul, Minnesota: West, 1984. An excellent overview of infant development with up-to-date coverage of theory and research.

KAYE, K. *The Mental and Social Life of Babies—How Parents Create Persons*. Chicago: The University of Chicago Press, 1982. Kaye suggests that the behavior of infants depends on the universal interaction patterns of both infants and parents.

SMITH, K. U., and SCHIAMBERG, L. *The Infraschool: The Systems Approach of Parent-Child Interaction*. Madison: The University of Wisconsin, 1973. A readable book designed to provide an exami-

nation of feedback and social tracking skills, and their application to parent–infant/child interaction. Numerous activities involving tactual, visual, and auditory tracking are discussed.

WHITE, B. L. *The First Three Years of Life* (2nd ed.). Englewood Cliffs, N.J.: Prentice-Hall, 1985. A well-written and authoritative discussion of infant behavioral development during the first three years, accompanied by practical advice and techniques for parents.

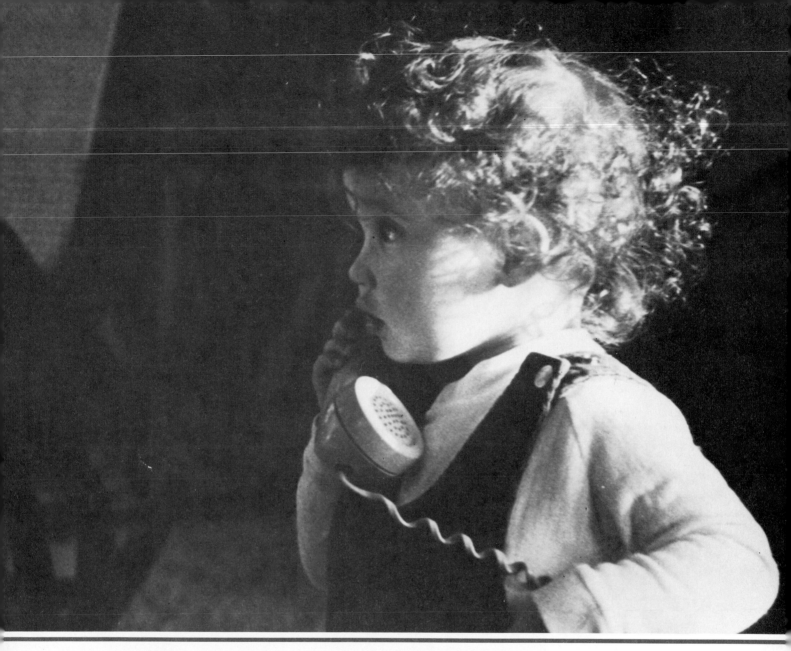

8 Infancy and Toddlerhood: Social and Personality Development

All our lives long, every day and every hour, we are engaged in the process of accommodating our changed and unchanged selves to our changed and unchanged surroundings; living, in fact, is nothing else than this process of accommodation; when we fail in it a little we are stupid, when we fail flagrantly we are mad. . . . A life will be successful or not according as the power of accommodation is equal to or unequal to the strain of fusing and adjusting internal and external changes.
—Samuel Butler, The Way of All Flesh, 1936

During the first three years of life, the child makes many important advances in development: learning to walk and to grasp objects and acquiring a language. Another extraordinarily important facet of development is the *sense of self* that the baby organizes. How does this sense of self develop? What are the factors that contribute to its evolution? What are the characteristics of self that emerge in the infant and the toddler? In this section, we examine these questions. To help us understand this evolution of selfhood, we discuss the following aspects of infant social and personality development:

· The *emotional development* of the infant. What emotions does the infant have? How do these emotions facilitate the development of selfhood?
· The *attachment relationships* between infants and their parents/caretakers.
· The emergence of the *sociable self.* How are early social development and attachment related?

Emotional Development

Children demonstrate a broad range of emotions. Even young infants express such emotions as surprise, joy, fear, sadness, interest, anger, and disgust (Campos et al., 1983). Emotions may serve a number of functions including the communication of infant feelings, needs, and desires. For example, an infant cry or frown indicates an unpleasurable experience, whereas an infant smile suggests the possibility that an event or object is pleasurable. In addition, the expression of infant emotions also serves to control social distance between the infant and its parents/caretakers. For example, the infant who cries or smiles is not only "sending a message" to its parents, but is regulating the social distance by bringing the parent/caretaker into close proximity.

The Emergence of Emotions

Studies by Carroll Izard and his colleagues suggest that infants have a wide range of emotions even during the early months of life (Izard et al., 1980; Trotter, 1983)

TABLE 8.1

The Emergence of Infant Emotions

EXPRESSION OF FUNDAMENTAL EMOTIONS*	APPROXIMATE TIME OF EMERGENCE
Interest	Present at birth
Neonatal smile (a sort of half smile that appears spontaneously for no apparent reason)	Present at birth
Startle response	Present at birth
Distress (in response to pain)	Present at birth
Disgust (in response to unpleasant taste or smell)	Present at birth
Social smile	4–6 weeks
Anger	3–4 months
Surprise	3–4 months
Sadness	3–4 months
Fear	5–7 months
Shame, shyness, self-awareness	6–8 months
Contempt	Second year of life
Guilt	Second year of life

From Trotter, 1983, pp. 14–20.

(see Table 8.1). Hundreds of infants were videotaped in a broad range of activities designed to elicit the full spectrum of emotional response (e.g., having a toy taken away, being reunited with a parent, and so on).

Furthermore, there is evidence that emotions appear in a progressive order (Izard and Dougherty, 1982; Trotter, 1983) (see Table 8.1).

- Some expressions such as *distress* (in response to pain), *disgust, startle,* and a *rudimentary or neonatal smile* appear to be present at birth. There is no conclusive evidence that these expressions (when they occur during the first few weeks of life) are related to inner feelings.
- The *social smile* appears at about four to six weeks. Unlike the neonatal smile, which seems unrelated to any specific events, the social smile appears to occur in the presence of such specific stimuli as faces or voices of parents/caretakers.
- *Anger, surprise,* and *sadness* appear at about three to four months.
- *Fear* appears at five to seven months.
- *Shame* and *shyness* appear at about six to eight months.
- *Contempt* and *guilt* do not appear in the infant's emotional repertoire until the second year.

Expressing Emotions

As we have seen, infants can exhibit a broad range of emotions. The expression of these emotions occurs in two primary ways: *facially* (smiling, frowning, and so on), and *vocally* (crying, laughing). Commonly, facial and vocal expressions of infant emotion are integrated. For example, infant cries are accompanied by distressed facial expressions and infant laughter occurs with a smiling face. In this section we examine three types of emotional expression and their significance—crying, smiling, and laughing.

CRYING.   In our discussion of infant language development in Chapter 7 we discussed some of the early research on types of infant cries (angry cry, pain cry, hunger cry, and so on) (Wolff, 1969b). Crying is clearly a powerful mode of infant emotional expression and an important means of communicating distress with the "slings and arrows of outrageous fortune" such as being undressed, being awakened, being chilled, being bathed, and so on. Despite the significance and frequency of the infant cry, there has been surprisingly little research evidence on this vocal expression of infant emotion (Campos et al., 1983).

SMILING.   The appearance of the social smile represents a milestone because it is a significant mode of attracting an adult to the infant. The development of the infant smile proceeds through the following phases (Campos et al., 1983):

- Smiling as a *reflex* (the neonatal smile).
- Smiling as a *response to stimulation*. Most two-month-olds will smile at almost

---

The Measurement of Infant Emotions

Measuring the emotions of an infant is not a simple activity. The basic reason is rather obvious—infants cannot tell researchers how they feel at any given time, in response to a given situation or object. However, recent research has challenged the previously widespread belief that facial expressions at all ages, including infancy, provide no reliable information about specific emotions (Campos et al., 1983). There is evidence, particularly from cross-cultural studies, that facial expressions for some common emotions (e.g., disgust, happiness, sadness, anger) are shared throughout the world. Furthermore, some facial expressions are not only universal but are significantly related to underlying physiological conditions (which are, in turn, the result of individual responses to given situations). Such cross-cultural and physiological evidence has provided a justifiable basis for the measurement of infant emotions.

A widely used approach to the measurement of emotions is the MAX system (Izard and Dougherty, 1980). The MAX approach involves the identification of twenty-six distinct patterns of facial muscle expression, which can be used to specify ten distinct infant emotions (see table). A photograph or a videotape of an infant is examined and a point value is then assigned for the position of brows, eyes/nose/cheeks, and mouth/lips (also see table). The total point value can then be compared with the formulas used to identify specific emotions (also see table). Some examples follow:

- FEAR = 22 (Brows) + 31 (Eyes/Nose/Cheeks) + 53 (Mouth/Lips)

- DISCOMFORT/PAIN = 25 (Brows) + 37 (Eyes/ Nose/Cheeks) + 54 (Mouth/Lips)

Table of Facial Expression Criteria and Illustrations

MAXIMALLY DISCRIMINATIVE FACIAL MOVEMENTS (MAX) CODES

BROWS (*B*); (FOREHEAD [*F*]; NASAL ROOT [*N*]	EYES/NOSE/CHEEKS	MOUTH/LIPS
20. *B*: Raised in arched or normal shape. (*F*: Long transverse furrows or thickening; *N*: Narrowed.) 21. *B*: One brow raised higher than other (other one may be slightly lowered). 22. *B*: Raised; drawn together, straight or normal shape. (*F*: Short transverse furrows or thickening in mid-region; *N*: Narrowed.) 23. *B*: Inner corners raised; shape under inner corner. (*F*: Bulge or furrows in center above brow corners; *N*: Narrowed.) 24. Drawn together, but neither raised nor lowered. (Vertical furrows or bulge between brows.) 25. *B*: Lowered and drawn together. (*F*: Vertical furrows or bulge between brows; *N*: Broadened, bulged.)	30. Enlarged, roundish appearance of eye region owing to tissue between upper lid and brow being stretched (upper eye furrow may be visible); upper eyelids not raised. 31. Eye fissure widened, upper lid raised (white shows more than normal). 33. Narrowed or squinted (by action of eye sphincters or brow depressors). 36. Gaze downward, askance. 37. Eye fissure scrouged, tightly closed. 38. Cheeks raised. 39. Gaze cast downward, head tilted back. 42. Nasal bridge furrowed (or shows lumpy ridge running diagonally upward from nasolabial fold). (42 need not be coded separately; it can be used as an additional cue in coding 54 and 59B.)	50. Opened, roundish, or oval. 51. Opened, relaxed. 52. Corners pulled back and slightly up (open or closed). 53. Opened, tense, corners retracted straight back. 54. Angular, squarish (open). 56. Corners drawn downward— outward (open or closed); chin may push up center of lower lip. 59A (= 51/66). Opened, relaxed; tongue forward (beyond gum line), may be moving. 59B (= 54/66). Opened, angular, upper lip pulled up; tongue forward (beyond gum line), may be moving. 61. Upper lip raised on one side. 63. Lower lip lowered (may be slightly forward). 64. Lower lip (or both lips) rolled inward (not illustrated and not observed in our video records of infants). 65. Lips pursed. 66. Tongue forward (beyond gum line), may be moving.

PARTIAL LIST OF FORMULAS USED TO IDENTIFY DISCRETE EMOTIONS AND THE INFANT PAIN EXPRESSION

Sadness-Dejection: SD
23 + 33,38 + 56

Fear: FT
22 + 31 + 53

Anger: AR
25 + (33, 38) + 54

Shame: SH
36 + 64 + 75 (head lowered)

Disgust: DR
25 + 33, 38 + 59B + 63

Discomfort/Pain: DP
25 + 37 + 54

Contempt: CS
21 + 61 + 39

Using techniques such as the MAX system, it is possible to investigate infant emotions reliably.

Source: From P.H. Mussen (Ed.) 1983, pp. 783–915.

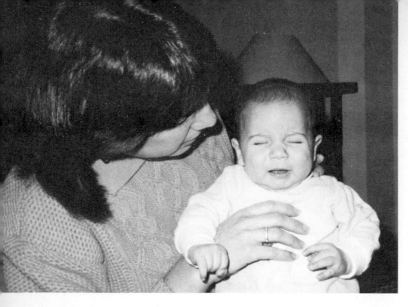

Crying is an early form of infant communication.

any event that captures their attention. They may show interest in people but are just as likely to be interested in bulls' eyes or other stimuli (see the discussion of infant vision in Chapter 7). In this phase, infant smiles are *indiscriminate*.

· At three or four months, infants begin to show a preference for human faces. However, any face, familiar or unfamiliar, may generate a smile.
· At five or six months, infants prefer to smile mainly at familiar faces.

LAUGHING. At four months of age, infants not only are accomplished smilers but also are beginning to laugh (Sroufe, 1979a). As in the case of smiling, there is reason to believe that infant laughter also serves an important adaptive function by attracting the parent/caretaker. In addition, there is evidence for a number of developmental changes in infant laughter (Sroufe and Wunsch, 1972) (see Fig. 8.1).

· There is an increase in the number of situations that produce laughter after its onset at approximately four months. (The increase is most dramatic from four to nine months of age.)
· As infants develop, there is a change in the type of events or stimuli that produce infant laughter. For example, at four to six months *tactile* stimuli (e.g., blowing in the infant's hair or bouncing the infant on the parent/caretaker's knee) or *social* events (e.g., games such as peek-a-boo) are more likely to evoke infant laughter than visual stimuli (e.g., adults wearing human masks, disappearing objects, and so on) or auditory stimuli (e.g., whispering, lip

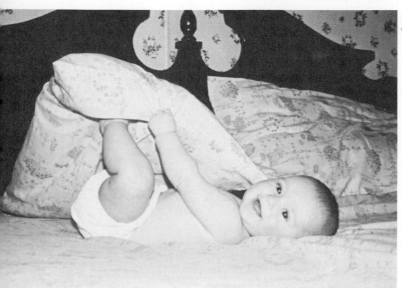

Garry Rowe

The appearance of the social smile is a developmental milestone; it attracts parents/caretakers to the infant.

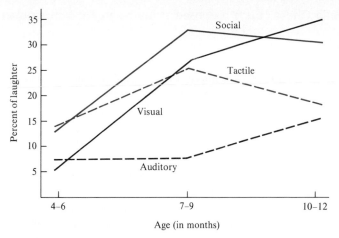

FIGURE 8.1

Developmental changes in infant laughter during the first year in response to auditory, visual, tactile (touch), and social stimuli. From Sroufe and Wunsch, 1972, pp. 1326–1344

popping, and so on). However, by ten to twelve months, *visual* spectacles and *social* events in which the infant actively participates are more likely to evoke laughter than either tactile or auditory events (Fig. 8.1).

· At the end of the first year and throughout the second year, there is evidence that infants are more likely to laugh at events that they *actively create* themselves (e.g., swatting at a suspended mobile crib display). Beyond the second year of life, laughter increasingly becomes a social experience that occurs in the presence of other children (Bainum, Lounsbury, and Pollio, 1984).

The progression in the development of infant laughter also reflects changes in infant sensory/perceptual and cognitive skills (see Chapter 7). As infants mature they are able to better appreciate the distinction between what is "expected" and what is not. Incongruities cause laughter.

Infant Temperament

Another important facet of the emotional development of infants is their *temperament* (an inborn style of approaching events and other people) (see the discussion in Chapter 3). That is, *individual differences in temperament* are as likely to influence the expression of infant emotions, such as laughter, as are the types of stimuli to which the infant is exposed (e.g., tactile, visual, social, or auditory) or the infant's level of cognitive development. In fact, differences in temperament among babies are apparent from birth. Some infants appear to be even-tempered and calm, and other infants may seem irritable and hard to manage. We have already discussed the question of the genetic and environmental contributions to temperament in Chapter 3. In this section we briefly review some of the research findings on temperament and infant personality organization.

THE NEW YORK LONGITUDINAL STUDY. One of the first empirical efforts to examine infant personality characteristics, including temperament, was the New York Longitudinal Study (NYLS). The NYLS was begun in the early 1950s and has continued into the 1980s (Thomas and Chess, 1977, 1980). Alexander Thomas and

Stella Chess (1977) proposed studying infant temperament in relation to nine dimensions, as follows:

- *Activity level* (general arousal level as expressed by motor reactions). Some infants squirm and move a good deal in their basinettes, whereas others are much more relaxed and calm.
- *Rhythmicity* (regularity in biological functions such as sleeping, eating, or defecating).
- *Approach/withdrawal* (the readiness of the infant to approach new situations and new people). Some infants appear to enjoy new situations, whereas others seem to recoil from every new experience.
- *Adaptability* (the extent to which the infant adjusts to changes in routine). Some infants adjust quickly to changes in their routine, but others appear unhappy at any minor disruption of their activities.
- *Threshold of responsiveness* (initial sensitivity to light, noise, or other sensory stimuli).
- *Mood* (unhappiness, cheerfulness, and so on).
- *Intensity of reactions* (strength of infant responses). For example, some infants cry loudly, and others have a more subdued cry.
- *Distractibility*. For example, some infants when hungry can be diverted and calmed with a pacifier, whereas other infants remain irate until they are given food.
- *Persistence* (duration of interest). For example, some infants are quite content to play with an object for a relatively long period of time compared with others, who move quickly from one toy to another.

On the basis of these nine patterns of temperament, Thomas and Chess (1977) derived three infant temperament types:

- **The easy child.** Approximately 40 percent of the infant sample was characterized by a positive mood, high approach, high adaptability, high rhythmicity, and low intensity.
- **The difficult child.** Approximately 10 percent of the infant sample was characterized by a temperament pattern opposite to that of the easy child.

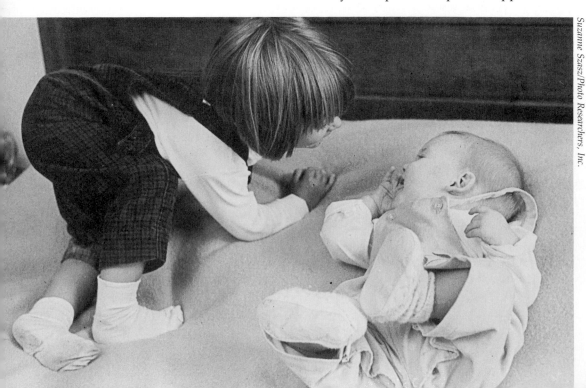

Suzanne Szasz/Photo Researchers, Inc.

Individual differences in temperament are apparent even among members of the same family.

· **The slow-to-warm-up child.** Approximately 15 percent of the sample was characterized by withdrawal, low adaptability, negative mood, low intensity, and high activity.

It is important to note, however, that there is considerable variety within each infant temperament type. Furthermore, the three types account for only 65 percent of the infants in the sample. Presumably, the other 35 percent could not be readily categorized into any specific category.

THE ECOLOGY OF TEMPERAMENT AND ENVIRONMENT.   Nonetheless, the findings of the NYLS challenged the prevailing views of infant social and emotional development during the 1950s. For example, earlier research and theory had been based on the assumption that infant social/emotional development was the result of environmental influence (Wachs and Gruen, 1982); that is, "good" or "bad" environments would have a uniformly similar impact on all infants. On the contrary, the findings of Thomas and Chess (1977, 1980) demonstrated that babies have different temperaments. Therefore, the key issue is the "fit" between infant temperament and environment (Lerner and Lerner, 1986). For example, parents who are themselves quiet, reserved, or inhibited might find an active baby a difficult challenge. On the other hand, outgoing parents might thoroughly enjoy a baby who mirrors their own activity level. Likewise, infants with different temperaments react differently to the same experience. For example, some infants respond to a stranger with an intense reaction of distress. On the other hand, another infant may respond to the same stranger with a less intense, easygoing look of surprise (Rothbart and Derryberry, 1982, 1984).

Is infant temperament continuous? For example, does a "slow-to-warm-up infant" become a "slow-to-warm-up" child? The evidence is not conclusive. For example, in one study 75 percent of infants judged to be extremely shy at twenty-one months of age were still extremely shy at four years of age (Kagan et al., 1984). On the other hand, other evidence suggests that infant temperament may change or fluctuate through childhood (Lewis and Starr, 1979).

Differences in infant temperament may be identified at birth. Although the question of the continuity of infant temperament is not settled, it is nonetheless clear that temperament does interact with the environment in the form of parents/caretakers, producing a variety of outcomes.

The Attachment Relationship: The Ecology of Selfhood

How does the infant's sense of self develop? It develops in the *context* of relationships with other people, including family members, peers, and adults outside of the family (e.g., teachers and neighbors). During infancy, the sense of self emerges from the affectional relationships between parents and infants that is called **attachment** (Bretherton and Waters, 1985; Thompson and Lamb, 1986).

Mary Ainsworth defined attachment as follows:

> An attachment is an affectional tie that one person forms to another specific person, binding them together in space and enduring over time. Attachment is discriminating

and specific. One may be attached to more than one person. . . . Attachment implies affect. . . . We usually think of attachment as implying affection or love. (1973, p. 1)

One way to view attachment is as a set of behaviors (by *both* parent and infant) that result in a *mutual* parent-infant relationship. This attachment relationship promotes the goal of parent-infant closeness or *proximity*. Proximity between parent and newborn is very important for human beings (and for many animals). Closeness between parents and infants allows for the satisfaction of infant and parent needs (e.g., feeding, looking, and affection). The sense of self is forged in this relationship.

Components of the Attachment System

The attachment relationship involves interaction in a number of areas (Ainsworth, 1979a) (see Fig. 8.2).

ROOTING AND SUCKING.   The behavior of the infant includes many responses that both facilitate feeding and provide "signals" to the mother to help her meet the infant's needs. The *rooting* reflex (see Chapter 7) is an infant behavior that makes it likely that the infant will find the nipple of the mother (if breast-fed) or the bottle (Ainsworth, 1979a). Rooting behavior is often a signal to the mother that

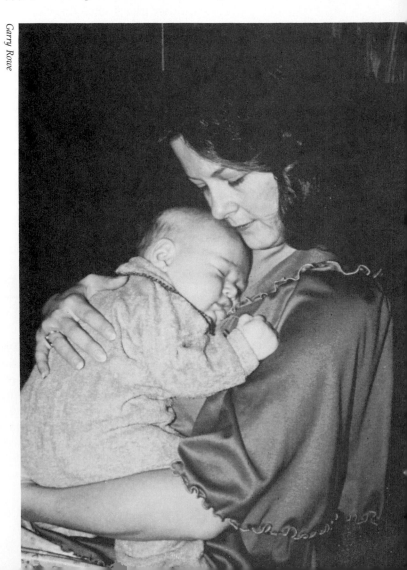

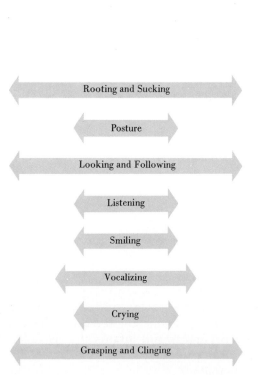

Rooting and Sucking

Posture

Looking and Following

Listening

Smiling

Vocalizing

Crying

Grasping and Clinging

FIGURE 8.2
Components of the attachment relationship.

The Beginnings of Love Between Parent and Child

The expectant mother, no less than the father, often finds it hard to imagine how she is going to feel about the unborn infant. But once the child arrives the mother love that so strongly shapes the infant's future unfolds in a complex and wonderful pattern. This mysterious process begins before birth. As our knowledge increases, all who bother to look at the process find themselves instilled with awe and respect.

The newborn, it turns out, is not the passive creature most people have assumed him to be. Recent research shows that the newborn comes well-endowed with charm and a full potential for social graces. His eyes are bright and equipped with surprisingly good vision. Shortly after birth, he likes to watch the human face. He looks at his mother and soon recognizes and prefers her. Dr. Robert Emde, of the University of Colorado Medical School, observes, "Little in life is more dramatic than the mother's moment of discovery that the baby is beaming at her with sparkling eyes." This is the time, mothers often say, when affection begins. The infant's cry alerts her and causes a biological as well as emotional reaction. Swedish studies using thermal photography have shown that the cry increases the flow of blood to her nipples, increasing milk secretion. The newborn hears the mother's or caretaker's voice and turns his head towards that person. The infant's ability to cling and cuddle communicates a pleasurable warmth to the mother. The infant's odor, too, is pleasant and uniquely his own. Although some experts say the smile is not "real" until some weeks after birth, the newborn does smile. Dr. Burton L. White of Harvard University says, "God or somebody has built into the human infant a collection of attributes that guarantee attractiveness." . . .

To get a close look at what happens between mother and the new infant, Dr. T. Berry Brazelton of Harvard has studied video-tapes of their interactions. Frame-by-frame "micro-analysis" of the pictures shows that the baby moves in smooth, circular "ballet-like" patterns as he looks up at the mother. The baby concentrates his attention on her whole body and limbs move in rhythm; the infant then withdraws briefly, but returns his attention, averaging several cycles a minute. The mother falls in step with the baby's cycles by talking and smiling, in a kind of "dance." If the mother falls out of step and disappoints the infant by presenting a still, unresponsive face when he gazes at her, the baby becomes "concerned" and keeps trying to get her attention. If he fails, the baby withdraws into a collapsed state of helplessness, face turned aside, and body curled up and motionless. If the mother becomes responsive again, the baby looks puzzled but returns to his cyclical motions. . . .

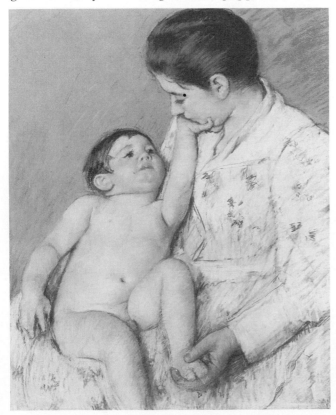

"First Caress" by the American artist Mary Cassatt. From the collection of the New Britain Museum of American Art, Harriet Russell Stanley Fund.

From Hersh and Levin 1978, pp. 2–6.

the infant is hungry. If the baby is being breast-fed, it moves its head in such a way that it will be likely to find the mother's nipple. The mother, in turn, adjusts her behavior so that the baby's search is likely to be successful (e.g., in the way in which she holds the baby or in the way she positions the breast). Once the breast or bottle nipple reaches the infant's mouth, the sensation of touch produces *sucking* movements. The presence of milk in the mouth, in turn, produces swallowing. This whole chain of events ensures that food will be taken in and, as an important by-product, that the infant and the parent will be brought together in an attachment relationship (Ainsworth, 1973, 1979a).

ADJUSTMENT OF POSTURE.   During the feeding process, there is a mutual or reciprocal adjustment of posture between infant and parent (Ainsworth, 1979a). This mutual adjustment also occurs when the infant is being held by the parent or the caretaker for reasons other than feeding. When being held in a feeding or "cuddling" position, the infant characteristically relaxes and "molds" its body against the adult (Ainsworth, 1979a). There is some limited evidence of the interaction between cuddling and attachment. Infants identified as "noncuddlers" had "less intense" attachments, as well as being somewhat slower to develop an attachment relationship (Ainsworth, 1979a).

LOOKING AND FOLLOWING.   The infant's looking behavior appears to be stimulated by certain properties of objects (see the discussion of vision in Chapter 7; Fantz, 1961, 1963). The objects that the infant encounters that are most likely to

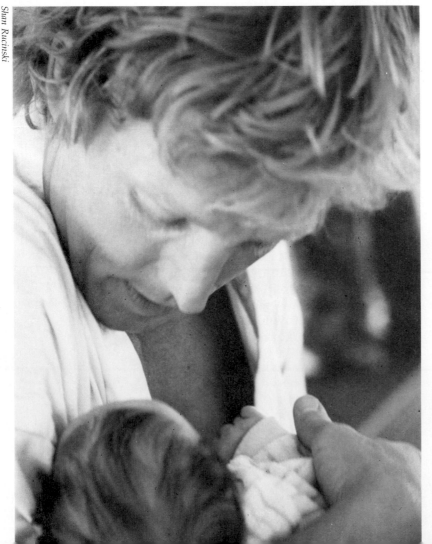

Shan Rucinski

Babies, like all human beings, can be close to many different people. Fathers can "bond" with their children.

possess these properties are *human faces* (Banks and Salapatek, 1983). As the infant develops increasing control over its visual responses, it is able to establish eye-to-eye contact. The *mutual process* in which the infant looks at an adult and the adult looks at the infant serves as a *signal* for both; the parent notes the attention of the infant, and the infant notes the attention of the parent (Peery, 1980). In the same way, the infant's ability to look away acts as a signal. Mutual gazing has affectional or emotional aspects, particularly when mutual social smiling occurs (see the discussion of smiling later in this chapter). Looking also enables the infant to supplement other mediums of attachment (e.g., touch) by helping the infant to discriminate between people while they are various distances away. All of these factors suggest the vital role that vision plays in the development of early social behavior and attachment.

LISTENING.   Although there has been considerably less research on infant hearing than on vision, there is reason to think that *mutual following* does occur (Bowlby, 1969; Aslin, Pisoni, and Jusczyk, 1983). For example, an infant's interest in its parent's voice is likely to lead the parent to talk more. This, in turn, will probably cause the infant to attend more to the sounds of the parent's voice (Bowlby, 1969).

In the development of attachment, the infant seems to show a progression in listening (Aslin, Pisoni, and Jusczyk, 1983):

1. By the second week of life, a soft sound (rather than a loud one) and especially a human voice are quite successful in causing the baby to smile. A high-pitched voice is most effective (see Chapter 7). Through about the fourth month of life, the *human voice alone* tends to calm the infant.
2. After the fourth month, the infant seems to want not only the sound but the sight of the parent as well.

SMILING.   There is reason to think that the motor ability to smile is probably "built into" the human being from birth (Campos et al., 1983). From birth on, some stimuli are more likely to cause a smile than others. These effective stimuli are more apt to come from a parent. Through learning, the *mutual interactions* that result in a sometimes irresistible infant smile come to be restricted to mutual following involving the human face and voice. Through further learning, smiles become more frequently elicited by one person, or a few specific persons, rather than by others. Finally, the baby's smile is itself a stimulus to reciprocal social behavior on the part of its parents and others. Therefore, the smile serves to increase the probability of interaction with, proximity to, and contact with the parents and potential attachment figures (Campos et al., 1983).

VOCALIZING.   The role of an infant's babbling in the formation of attachment has a similar function to that of smiling (Ainsworth, 1979a). According to Bowlby (1969, p. 11), "Both occur when a baby is awake and contented and both have as a predictable outcome that the baby's companion responds in a sociable way and engages with him in a chain of interaction." It is quite likely that an adult's vocal responses to an infant's vocalization strengthen the infant's tendency to vocalize in social transactions (Campos et al., 1983). Although language is significant throughout the lifespan as a mode of social communication, vocalizing is most important at the preverbal level of infancy as a source of attachment.

CRYING.   During the early phases of infancy, crying is usually activated by the infant. The causes of infant crying are fairly well known and include pain, hunger, and intestinal distress.

As a focus of attachment interaction, there appears to be a developmental progression for crying (Wolff, 1969b):

1. *Physical-physiological activation.* This phase extends from birth through about the first month. Crying is usually caused by stomach pains, general discomfort, or hunger.
2. *Psychological activation.* This phase begins at about one month with the onset of the "fake" cry (a low-pitched, nonrhythmical crying, without tears). Many parents feel that this cry usually means that the baby wants attention; often such crying stops when the baby gets attention.

   At about the sixth week, babies tended to stop crying when parent-infant eye-to-eye contact begins. By three months of age, thumb-sucking reduces crying. Of all the modes of reducing crying (including the above two), physical contact is the most effective.
3. *Differential crying.* Somewhere between two and twenty-two months of age, infants may protest the departure of a parent, although not of other adults. Thus different persons may activate and terminate crying. This differential crying suggests that the baby is becoming attached to specific people.

GRASPING AND CLINGING. Through its reflex responses, the human neonate grasps and clings to a figure with whom it is in close contact. Perhaps in the original environment of evolutionary adaptation, these reflexes gave way to voluntary grasping and clinging so that the infant could help to support itself while being transported. (There is no evidence that contemporary Western infants can do so in any voluntary way until considerably later in the first year of life, and perhaps only in special circumstances.) Nevertheless, it is reasonable to assume a genetic basis for clinging, and to consider clinging an attachment behavior.

The Development of Attachment in the Family: Four Phases

Attachment does not occur suddenly; rather, it is a process that takes place over many years of the child's early development. *Four major phases* have been identified in the development of attachment: a phase during which the infant's social behavior is undiscriminating; a phase of discriminating social behavior; a phase characterized by active infant initiative in seeking physical closeness and contact with the caregiver; and a final phase characterized by a finely tuned relationship guided by the mutual following skills of parent and child (Bowlby, 1969) (Table 8.2).

TABLE 8.2
Four Stages in the Development of Attachment

STAGE	AGE	CHARACTERISTICS
Stage 1	0–3 mos.	Infant uses sucking, rooting, grasping, smiling, gazing, cuddling, and visual tracking to maintain closeness with caregiver.
Stage 2	3–6 mos.	Infant is more responsive to familiar figures than to strangers.
Stage 3	7 mos. to 2 yrs.	Infant begins actively to seek proximity with the object of attachment.
Stage 4	Toddlerhood and beyond	Infant uses a variety of behaviors that influence behavior of object of attachment in order to satisfy the needs for closeness.

From Caldwell and Ricciuti, 1973, pp. 1–94.

Synchrony: The Dance of Development

Clov: What is there to keep me here?
Hamm: The dialogue.
                                    —Samuel Beckett, *Endgame,* 1958

One of the many aspects of parent-infant interaction that parents find so fascinating is the responsiveness of the infant to their behavior and their responsiveness to the infant's behavior. In Chapter 7 we discussed the way in which infants can organize their movements in response to or in synchrony with the adult voice. There is considerable evidence that infants are capable of engaging in mutual or synchronous relationships with their parents/caretakers (Smith and Schiamberg, 1973; Stern, 1977; Peery, 1980; Kaye, 1982; Meltzoff and Moore, 1983). For example, in a study of day-old infants, photographic analysis revealed a mutual syncrony of parent-newborn movement (Peery, 1980). That is, infants in face-to-face interaction with an adult withdrew (moved back) their heads when an adult (in close proximity) moved forward. Likewise, when the adult moved back, the infant moved forward. According to the investigator, a synchronized relationship between infant and caregiver had appeared as early as the first day of life.

Daniel Stern provides the following account of a parent-infant mutual interaction, or "dance."

A normal feeding, not a social interaction, was underway. Then a change began. When talking and looking at me, the mother turned her head and gazed at the infant's face. He was gazing at the ceiling, but out of the corner of his eye he saw her head turn toward him and he turned to gaze back at her . . . now he broke rhythm and stopped sucking. He let go of the nipple . . . as he eased into the faintest suggestion of a smile. The mother abruptly stopped talking and, as she watched his face begin to transform, her eyes opened a little wider and her eyebrows raised a bit. His eyes locked on to her, and together they held motionless for an instant. . . . This silent and almost motionless instant continued to hang until the mother suddenly shattered it by saying "Hey!" and simultaneously opened her eyes wider, raising her eyebrows further, and throwing her head up toward the infant. Almost simultaneously, the baby's eyes widened. His head tilted up and, as his smile broadened, the nipple fell out of his mouth. Now she said, "Well, Hello! . . . Heello . . . Heeelloo" so that her pitch rose and the "hellos" become longer and more emphatic on each successive repetition. With each phrase, the baby expressed more pleasure, and his body resonated almost like a balloon. . . . (1977, p. 3)

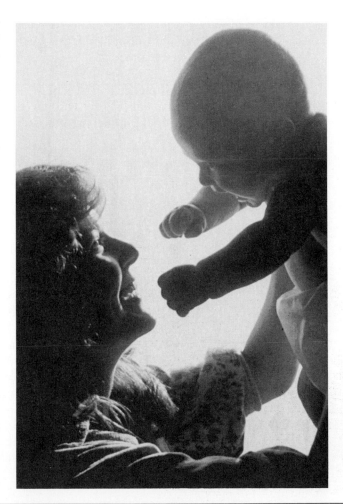

Garry Rowe

PHASE OF UNDISCRIMINATING SOCIAL RESPONSIVENESS (BIRTH TO TWO OR THREE MONTHS). Two primary activities occur in the first phase:
Infants begin to examine their environment, especially people. These activities include listening, visual following, and sucking. The infant's exploration of people may

be aided by crying, smiling, and vocalizing. These behaviors serve as "signals" by bringing adults closer to the infant.

Infants display their perceptual skills (e.g., vision and hearing) in distinguishing various stimuli. The infant seems to be most responsive to the sights and sounds of human adults (Ainsworth, 1979a). However, in spite of these skills, the infant cannot yet distinguish among the different persons who provide these stimuli.

PHASE OF DISCRIMINATING SOCIAL RESPONSIVENESS (THREE TO SIX MONTHS OF AGE).   The infant continues to explore the environment. However, during this phase, the infant can distinguish a few familiar figures (e.g., mother and father) from unfamiliar adults. Ainsworth (1979a) pointed out that this phase is divided into two parts:

1. *Responsiveness to people close at hand.* The infant distinguishes between familiar and unfamiliar adults by demonstrating different smiling or vocalizing patterns in their presence.

2. *Responsiveness to people at a distance.* The infant demonstrates its awareness of differences between people by showing different greeting behaviors when a familiar figure and an unfamiliar figure enter a room and different crying patterns when a familiar figure and an unfamiliar figure leave a room.

ACTIVE INITIATIVE IN SEEKING PROXIMITY AND CONTACT (SEVEN MONTHS TO TWO YEARS).   During this phase, there is a marked increase in the infant's ability to initiate behaviors that are likely to result in proximity or contact. Whereas in the previous phases the infant's signals were expressive, "fixed-action" signals, the baby's actions are now more carefully adjusted to the behavior of adults in order to promote proximity or contact. By this phase, infant locomotion and voluntary hand and arm movements are prominent techniques for initiating attachment. Also, parents may begin to notice that when they come into the infant's view, they may be "greeted" in a more active and affectionate way. Following, approaching, and clinging behaviors become significant in this phase.

"Goal-corrected" sequences of behavior also emerge during this phase (Bowlby, 1969, 1973, 1980). These are behavioral interactions that are mutual and are guided by a *constant stream of feedback.* In these sequences of behavior, the infant (as well as the parent) can guide and change the behavioral direction, speed, or motive in accordance with what the other is doing. In other words, this behavior is based on *mutual following.*

In addition, the onset of this phase of attachment coincides with the fourth phase of Piaget's first stage of intelligence—the stage of *sensorimotor development* (see the discussion of cognitive development). A major feature of this stage is the development of the *concept of object permanence.* In other words, the child's ability to search for a "missing" object may be a cognitive basis for attachment.

GOAL-CORRECTED PARTNERSHIP (TWO YEARS AND BEYOND).   In the third phase, the infant could, to some extent, predict its mother's movements and adjust its own movements in order to maintain the desired degree of proximity. The infant could not, however, understand the factors that infuenced its mother's movements and could not plan means to change her behavior. As the child begins to understand and "infer" the parent's set goals, it begins to attempt to alter them to fit better with its own needs for contact, proximity, and interaction. This relationship is characterized by Bowlby as a "partnership." In his or her early efforts to change the set goal (the degree to which the parent wants to maintain proximity) of the parent's behavior, a young child may have some difficulty because he or she cannot see things from the parent's point of view. The reciprocity of the partnership develops gradually.

■ SCENARIO: THE DAY BABY ELIZABETH ANTICIPATED HER PARENTS' EVENING OUT

Our Elizabeth is now a full-fledged toddler (two years, seven months). She has begun to anticipate separations from her parents. One evening, her parents were preparing to leave for an evening at another couple's home. Elizabeth became "suspicious" that something "unusual" was going on when her father began putting on his suit. As he was putting on his tie, Elizabeth marched into the bathroom and confronted him.

Elizabeth: Daddy, going away.
Daddy: Yes, your mother and I are going out to see Jeff, Brian, and Todd's mommy and daddy.
Elizabeth: Daddy, can stay with me and . . .

(At this moment, the bell rang. Elizabeth walked to the front door. Her mother opened the door. It was the baby-sitter, Mark. Elizabeth recognized him.)

Mark: Hi, Elizabeth.
Elizabeth: Mark . . . go home.

Sometimes you get discouraged
Because I am so small
And always leave my finger prints
On furniture and walls.
But every day I'm growing up
And soon I'll be so tall
That all those little hand prints
Will be hard to recall.
So here's a special hand print
Just so that you can say.
This is how my fingers looked
When I placed them here today.

Author Unknown
Artist: Elizabeth

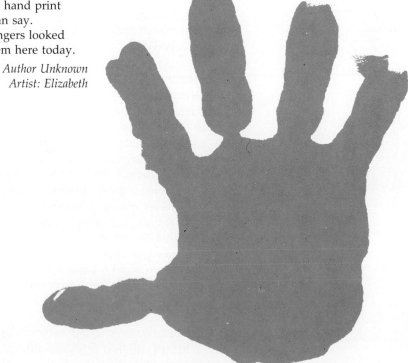

The Bonding Hypothesis: A Controversy

During the last decade, one of the most controversial dimensions of attachment has been the bonding hypothesis (Klaus and Kennell, 1982). The concept of bonding revolutionized childbirth practices in the United States by emphasizing the presumed importance of early contact between mothers and newborns on mother-infant attachment. Prior to the 1970s, mothers and newborns were rarely given more than a brief glimpse of one another immediately after birth. When mothers finally did see their infants, silver nitrate (currently, antibiotics are used) had been placed in their eyes (see the discussion of delivery practices in Chapter 5) which markedly hampered mother/newborn eye-to-eye contact (Butterfield et al., 1982). However, supporters of the bonding concept sensitized the medical profession to the potential importance of parent involvement very early in the newborn's life (Klaus and Kennell, 1982). In this section, we examine the evidence that both supports and calls into question this bonding hypothesis. Specifically, the question to be addressed is whether differences in practices of childbirth (e.g., early separation or allowing mother and infant to remain together immediately following birth) will affect the nature of the mother-infant bond and, therefore, affect the child. We discuss bonding for preterm infants (see Chapter 5) and full-term infants separately because hospital practices differ for each group.

> *DEFINITION*
>
> **Bonding Hypothesis.** The bonding hypothesis refers to the presumed establishment of an affectionate and long-lasting attachment of a mother toward her infant during a sensitive or critical period lasting for a few hours immediately after birth.

ATTACHMENT AND PRETERM INFANTS.   Evidence supporting the bonding hypothesis for preterm infants came initially from a study whose purpose was to demonstrate the effects of allowing parents to be present in a nursery for preterm infants (Barnett, Grobstein, and Seashore, 1982). The research was done to counter the assumption that parent visitation might spread viral or bacterial infections to the newborns. Although the study demonstrated that the assumption of increased infection was unwarranted, it also demonstrated some interesting differences in the way mothers of preterm infants and mothers of full-term infants responded to their newborns. Specifically, the mothers of full-term babies touched and explored their babies far more actively than did the mothers of preterm infants. It was not until their third visit to the nursery that the mothers of the preterm babies began to behave in a manner more similar to mothers of full-term infants. That is, they increased the number of times they touched the infant's body and the amount of time spent in face-to-face position with the infant. Despite these behavioral changes, the mothers of preterm infants were still well behind the mothers of full-term infants in terms of all measured behaviors.

In a long-term study done at Case Western Reserve University, additional support was found for the bonding hypothesis (Klaus et al., 1972; Klaus and Kennell, 1982). Mothers of preterm infants were assigned to one of two different treatment groups.

• *An early-contact group* which was allowed to freely visit their premature infants during the first few days after delivery.
• *A late-contact group* which was allowed only visual contact with the infant for several days after delivery.

Later in the study, movies were made of the mothers feeding their infants. These films were made at two points in time: (1) immediately before the infants were discharged from the hospital and (2) one month after the discharge, when the infants were brought back to the hospital by their mothers. In addition, the Bayley Developmental Scales were given to the infants at discharge and again when the infants were nine, fifteen, and twenty-one months of age. The Stanford-Binet I.Q. test was administered to the infants at forty-two months of age. Although there were not many differences between the early-contact and late-contact groups, there were a few differences of some interest. Early-contact mothers were more likely to look at their babies than late-contact mothers. I.Q. scores were higher for eighteen (out of a total of fifty-three) early-contact infants who were tested at four months compared with the available late contact infants. A problem in interpreting this finding is that it is not possible to determine the extent to which the eighteen early-contact infants were *representative* of the original sample of fifty-three.

In another independent study, Abby Rosenfield (1980) found that mothers of preterm infants in a special program involving extra stimulation for the infants increased their visits to the infants to a much greater extent than did mothers who did not participate in the stimulation program. It is probable that the stimulated babies became more appealing and interesting to their mothers, which, in turn, led to the increased frequency of visits.

On the other hand, several studies have raised questions about an assumption of the bonding hypothesis with reference to preterm infants. That is, the mothers of preterm infants should have more difficulty bonding with their infants than mothers of full-term infants because the preterm mothers are separated from their infants during the presumed critical or sensitive period after delivery. A number of studies suggest that preterm infants (as well as other "at-risk" infants) may, in fact, have many positive interactions (e.g., holding and affection) with their nurses as well as with their mothers (Crawford, 1982). Such results are not surprising in light of current medical/hospital practices that encourage interaction of parents and hospital personnel with preterm infants.

Other studies that do not support the bonding hypothesis have dealt with behaviors and outcomes of the preterm infants. The major conclusion of these studies was that infant experiences during the early birth or neonatal period were unrelated to infant behavior and development at later times (Bakeman and Brown, 1980; Brown and Bakeman, 1980; Rode et al., 1981). There was some evidence of some differences between the mothers of preterm infants compared with mothers of full-term infants in the nature and quality of interaction with the infant. However, these interactional differences had no effect on later measures of infant intelligence at one year, two years, and three years. This was the case for families who might be expected to have economic and family stresses, as well as for families without such strains.

In conclusion, the evidence for the bonding hypothesis with reference to preterm infants is not conclusive. Perhaps, one way to interpret these results is to suggest that early contact for *some mothers* of *some preterm* infants may be particularly helpful in developing a long-term attachment relationship, as well as supporting positive child behaviors and developmental outcomes. It may also be that particular mothers who have difficulty accepting the fact that they have a preterm infant may reduce their visits to the infant nurseries. This avoidance behavior may lead to later complications for the attachment relationship and for the child. For such mothers, early-contact programs might be particularly beneficial.

ATTACHMENT AND FULL-TERM INFANTS.   In order to test the bonding hypothesis for full-term infants, Marshall H. Klaus and John H. Kennell (1982) compared the development of two groups of infants and their mothers. One group (the control group) was subjected to the usual hospital routines after birth. In the second group (the experimental group), the mothers and infants were placed in a quiet, warm room where they could be together for an hour after birth. In addition, the experimental-group mothers and infants spent five hours together on each of the first three days after delivery. The investigators concluded that the contact that followed immediately after delivery was particularly important for bonding. The benefits of early and extended contact continued for several months after delivery and, according to Klaus and Kennell, were still apparent one year later. That is, the experimental-group mothers showed more physical affection during feeding, engaged in more eye-to-eye contact with their infants, and were more likely to soothe their infants in distressing situations than the control-group mothers. Other studies have also supported the bonding hypothesis in full-term infants (Hales et al., 1977; Carlsson et al., 1979; deChateau, 1980).

As with the bonding of premature infants, there are numerous findings that do not support the bonding hypothesis in full-term infants. Doris Entwisle and Susan Doering (1981) found that the amount of contact between mothers and infants during the first three days had no relationship to nurturant behavior even three to four weeks later. These investigations were particularly careful to take into account preexisting differences in maternal nurturance behavior and orientation. That is, if these initial nurturant behaviors and attitudes were statistically controlled (held constant), then the impact of the amount of contact between mother and infant made no contribution to later maternal nurturance behavior. Likewise, other studies have failed to confirm the bonding hypothesis for full-term infants and their mothers (Svedja, Campos, and Emde, 1980; Grossmann, Thane, and Grossmann, 1981; Lamb, 1982; McCall, 1982).

In conclusion, the findings for full-term infants, like those for premature infants, do not allow for strong conclusions of support or rejection for the bonding hypothesis. Rather, it appears that the strong form of the bonding hypothesis (i.e., that there is a universal critical or sensitive period immediately following birth during which mothers *must* have contact with their infants in order for an attachment relationship or bond to develop) is likely *not* the case. However, it would seem that early and extended contact might be particularly appropriate for some mothers in some contexts but not for all mothers. For example, mothers who experience considerable stress (financial, marital), personal instability, or a sense of inadequacy (due to their own inexperience or lack of knowledge about infants) may benefit from early and extended contact.

Secure and Insecure Attachments: Some Individual Differences

One of the important issues regarding attachment of infants to their mothers is the development of individual differences in attachment. That is, infants develop different styles of interacting with their caregivers, which reflect an underlying degree of *security* or *insecurity* (Ainsworth, 1979b; Thompson and Lamb, 1986).

On the basis of her observations using the Strange Situation Test, Mary Ainsworth has developed a set of standardized criteria for assessing the security or insecurity of attachment. Infants are categorized into one of three attachment types:

· **Secure infants.** These infants demonstrated active exploration of the environment prior to any separation from their mothers. Also, in the presence of their

Ainsworth's Strange Situation Test

A standardized laboratory technique for assessing attachment that has been widely used is the Strange Situation Test developed by Mary Ainsworth. The procedure for the test consists of a series of eight episodes that reflect a gradually increasing level of potential stress for the infant (see table). The assessment takes place in a laboratory room equipped with several chairs and a variety of toys for the infant. The test involves experiences that are similar to everyday experiences in that the parent is in the room with the infant. The test is also designed to assess the relationship of the infant to a stranger when the infant is alone in the room with the stranger. Sessions are usually videotaped and then analyzed by trained observers. The observers record such infant behaviors as proximity-seeking activities, contact-seeking activities, the use of the mother as a secure base for exploration, separation distress, and willingness to be comforted by a strange adult (Ainsworth and Wittig, 1969).

On the basis of her observations, Ainsworth has developed a set of standardized criteria for assessing the security or insecurity of infant attachment. Infants are categorized as having one of the following types of attachment:

1. Secure
2. Insecure
   - Anxious/avoidant
   - Anxious/resistant

These categorizations are made on the basis of the infant's cumulative performance on the Strange Situation Test. The test involves two separations from the mother and two subsequent reunions with her (see table). The first separation involves the child's being left with a stranger. In the second separation, the child is left entirely alone. Infant evaluation on the Strange Situation Test is heavily weighted by infant activity during the reunion episodes that follow each of these two separations. A securely attached infant will be able to resume exploration of the environment (using the mother as a secure base) much more quickly after a reunion episode than an insecurely attached infant.

Ainsworth's Strange Situation Test

EPISODE	TIME	CONTENT
1	1 min.	Mother and infant enter room; mother interests infant in toys.
2	3 min.	Mother sits and allows infant to explore and play freely.
3	3 min.	Stranger enters; sits silently for 1 min.; talks to the mother for 1 min.; engages infant in interaction or play for 1 min.
4	3 min.	Mother leaves; stranger allows infant to play alone, but is responsive to interaction bids; if the baby cries, the stranger tries to comfort him or her.
5	3 min.	Mother calls to infant from outside the door; steps in and pauses at doorway to greet infant and offer contact; stranger leaves; if necessary, mother comforts baby and reinterests baby in the toys; mother remains responsive to infant, but does not intrude on current activity.
6	3 min.	Mother leaves the infant alone.
7	3 min.	Stranger returns; sits, and, if the infant is distressed, offers comfort.
8	3 min.	Procedure for reunion Episode 5 is repeated.

From Ainsworth and Wittig, 1969.

mothers, these infants played easily with toys, used their mothers as a secure basis for exploration, and reacted positively to strangers. Furthermore, they appeared to be "in tune" with their mothers' smiling and vocalization (Waters, Wippman, and Sroufe, 1979). When their mothers left the room, these infants became visibly distressed and their play activity was noticeably reduced. However, during the reunion episodes these infants actively and enthusiastically greeted their mothers, typically seeking contact with them. The reunions reduced their stress and enabled the infants to resume their active play and exploration. According to Ainsworth (1979b), these infants have a healthy *balance* between attachment and exploration.

· **Anxious/avoidant infants (insecure).** For these infants, attachment and exploration were not in balance. Exploration appeared to be stronger and more prominent than attachment. During preseparation episodes, these infants did not appear to use their mothers as a secure base for exploration (that is, they did not check back with their mothers during exploration), either by looking, vocalizing, or touching. When their mothers left the room, these infants showed no apparent signs of distress. Their reunion with their mothers was marked by avoidance and turning away from them.

· **Anxious/resistant infants (insecure).** For these infants, attachment and exploration were also not in balance. Attachment was more prominent than exploration. These infants appeared to be anxious and fussy even prior to any separation from their mothers. They explored very little, stayed close to their mothers, and were extraordinarily distressed at separation. After reunion with their mothers, they had difficulty remaining calm and settling down. Although attachment behavior outweighed exploration, they nonetheless showed mixed feelings toward their mothers. For example, Ainsworth observed that some anxious/resistant infants would extend their arms to be picked up, squirm and cry to be put down again, and then seem to want to be picked up again. In summary, their anxious and intense attachment precluded successful exploration of the environment.

In most studies, approximately two-thirds of the infants are rated as secure, and the remaining one-third are divided between the two categories of insecure attachment. Although not all infants fit perfectly into one category of attachment, most investigators appear to agree on whether infants are either secure or insecure (Main and Weston, 1981). Furthermore, the type of attachment (secure or insecure) an infant has with one parent does not predict the type of attachment with a second parent. For example, the infant can be securely attached to both parents, securely attached to one parent and insecurely attached to the other, or insecurely attached to both parents.

Attachment types also appear to be reasonably stable over time. Studies that have examined attachment types at two different times (e.g., at twelve months and again at 18 months) indicate stability (Waters, 1978; Main and Weston, 1981). However, attachment types can change as a result of environmental changes. For

Garry Rowe

A secure attachment is a basis for infant exploration of the environment.

example, the transformation of a disorganized family situation to a more stable arrangement could change an insecure attachment to a secure attachment. Likewise, increased family stress (divorce, financial difficulties) could change a secure attachment to an insecure one (Vaughn et al., 1979; Thompson, Lamb, and Estes, 1982).

REASONS FOR SECURE OR INSECURE ATTACHMENTS.   Although changes in life circumstances can lead to changes in attachment, there are other, more direct causes of secure or insecure attachment. Specifically, the quality of child care and the infant's temperament are major determinants of attachment type. According to Ainsworth (1979b), mothers of secure infants differed from mothers of insecure infants in four primary characteristics of child care:

1. Mothers of secure infants responded more quickly and reliably to the infants' need for attention than did mothers of insecure infants (Ainsworth, 1979b).
2. Mothers of secure infants were more sensitive in interpreting and responding to their infants' behaviors and needs than were mothers of insecure infants (Blehar, Lieberman, and Ainsworth, 1977). Mothers of secure infants were careful to watch for responses from their infants that indicated that the interaction was progressing smoothly. If the infant indicated or signaled otherwise, then the parent was willing to alter her behavior to restore infant comfort. For example, mothers of secure infants were far more sensitive in starting, pacing, and terminating infant feeding (e.g., they did not force the infants to take food). This sensitivity continued throughout the toddler years as mothers of secure infants appeared to provide more supportive environments for problem-solving activities (Matas, Arend, and Sroufe, 1978).
3. The mothers of secure infants expressed their affection more consistently, and in a different manner, than mothers of insecure infants. For example, the mothers of secure infants more frequently used smiling, verbal communication, and affectionate touching than did mothers of insecure infants (Clarke-Stewart, 1973). On the other hand, mothers of insecure infants sometimes mingled expressed open rejection of their infants (for interfering with the mother's activities) with an unusually high frequency of kissing (Main, Tomasini, and Tolan, 1979). It was as if they were trying to compensate for their negative, rejecting feelings toward the infant. It is interesting to note that the potential pattern of inconsistent response to bids for attention is associated with anxious, attention-seeking behavior in preschool children (behavior that may "bug" parents or peers) (MacCoby, 1980). In addition, some mothers of insecure infants appeared to dislike close bodily contact with them. Since such body contact is a common technique for reducing infant distress, it is likely that such mothers were rather ineffective in soothing their infants (Tracy and Ainsworth, 1981).
4. Mothers of secure infants were more concerned about high standards of physical care for their infants. Infants whose parents were negligent in such activities as treating child wounds, changing diapers, or cleaning their homes were likely to be categorized as anxious/resistant (Egeland and Sroufe, 1981).

In addition to the quality of child care, infant temperament contributes to the type of attachment formed. Infants who are categorized as having "difficult" or irritable temperaments may "turn off" mothers. That is, their mothers may become less responsive and sensitive to them (Crockenberg, 1981). Research suggests that temperamentally difficult infants are more likely to make caregiving more difficult and, also, more likely to have an insecure attachment (Waters, Vaughn, and Egeland, 1980). However, *not all* temperamentally difficult infants develop an insecure attachment. Susan Crockenberg (1981) found that *only* when mothers lacked a social support system (i.e., a network of family and friends) did a temperamentally difficult infant reduce maternal sensitivity and, likewise, the likelihood of the infant's having a secure attachment. In other words, the mother's support network served as a buffer between the mother and the consequences of a difficult infant. In summary, we can conclude that three primary factors contribute to the formation of a secure or insecure attachment: changing life circumstances, maternal caregiving activities, and infant temperament.

RESULTS OF SECURE OR INSECURE ATTACHMENTS.   A secure attachment helps infants develop a positive concept of themselves as competent individuals, as well as a sense of trust in other people (Ainsworth, 1979b; Sroufe, 1979a). In a longitudinal study, children who had a secure attachment at fifteen months of age showed greater leadership and social interaction skills at three and one half years than did insecurely attached children. Generally, it appears that securely attached children develop patterns of positive and reciprocal interaction with their caregivers in the family setting and extend these patterns to peer relationships and to relationships with other adults (Arend, Gove, and Sroufe, 1979; Main and Weston, 1981; Pastor, 1981).

In addition, as securely attached infants mature, the need for physical contact with their mothers decreases and interest in peer interaction and exploring their environment increases (Clarke-Stewart and Hevey, 1981). Insecurely attached infants do not demonstrate this change (see Fig. 8.3). In fact, it appears that insecurely attached infants increase their physical contact with their mothers, perpetuating what may now be a developmentally inappropriate dependency need.

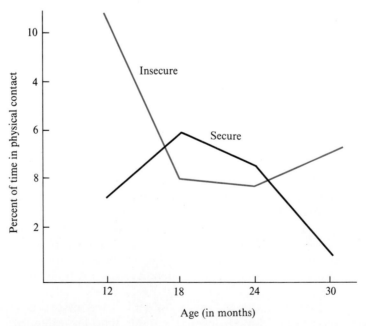

FIGURE 8.3

Changes with age in the percentage of time that secure and insecure infants spend in physical contact with their mothers. From Clarke-Stewart and Hevey, 1981.

Relationship Between Attachment and Other Infant Behaviors/Circumstances

The biological and cultural functions of attachment are fulfilled when the infant and the young child remain "close enough" to the parent(s) to survive and to learn valuable social skills. Attachment is also related to other behaviors that are important in human development. In this section, we explore the relationship between attachment behavior and exploration (and, therefore, cognitive development and competence) and behavior with strangers and in strange situations. The ability of the infant and the child to learn to extend social horizons and relationships using attachment as a base is significant in later development. The attachment relationship is the basis for more complex interaction in peer groups, school groups, and play relationships.

PLAY, EXPLORATION, AND ATTACHMENT. When a baby achieves locomotion, it is often eager to move away from its mother to explore the world around it (Ainsworth, 1979b). The parents seem to provide a secure base from which the baby can undertake explorations without anxiety. The baby keeps track of the parents' whereabouts, however, and will probably return to this base from time to time before venturing out again. The infant may explore objects and environments whose novelty might be frightening in the absence of the attachment figure. The smoothness and integration of the balance are affected by the characteristic interaction that has been built up between parent and infant. The infant's behavior in new situations can be a sign of the quality of infant-mother attachment (Ainsworth and Bell, 1969; Ainsworth, 1979b).

STRANGER ANXIETY. In contrast to smiling, cooing, and babbling, which are positive modes of greeting familiar or unfamiliar adults/caretakers, **stranger anxiety** is a cautious or frightened response to an unknown person. It was previously thought that the appearance of stranger anxiety in the infant was a milestone of development. That is, stranger anxiety was assumed to be an indicator of infant attachment to a caregiver, because it demonstrated wariness in the presence of unfamiliar company. More recent evidence suggests that infants may not always be afraid of strangers. In fact, some infants may react positively to unfamiliar people (Bretherton, Stolberg, and Kreye, 1981).

When Does Stranger Anxiety Occur? There is evidence that many infants react positively to a stranger (or, at least, not negatively) around six or seven months of age (Ainsworth, 1979b). Research on North American children suggests the pattern of development of stranger anxiety (Sroufe, 1977) on top of p. 296.

Interlude: M.D.S. Ainsworth on Attachment and Exploration

The dynamic balance between exploratory and attachment behavior has significance from an evolutionary point of view. Whereas attachment behaviors . . . serve a protective function during the long, helpless infancy of a species such as the human . . . exploratory behaviors reflect a genetic basis for an infant to be interested in novel features of the environment, to approach them, manipulate them . . . to play, and to learn more about the nature of his environment and the properties of the objects in it. It is an advantageous arrangement for an infant . . . to explore without straying too far from an adult who can protect him. (Ainsworth, Bell, and Stayton, 1974, p. 104)

- Cautious reactions to strangers emerge about six to seven months of age.
- Cautious reactions are at a peak from about seven to ten months of age.
- Stranger anxiety declines by ten months and throughout the second year of life.

However, there is some evidence that stranger anxiety does not completely disappear since two-, three-, or four-year-olds may show uneasiness with strangers in unfamiliar settings (Greenberg and Marvin, 1982).

Why Does Stranger Anxiety Occur? That is, why do many infants who are attached to a caregiver suddenly become uncomfortable in the presence of strangers? Several explanations have been proposed, including the following:

- *Cognitive/developmental perspective.* This viewpoint suggests that stranger anxiety is the natural result of infant cognitive and perceptual development. That is, the six-to-eight-month-old infant has developed stable schemas or mental representations (see the discussion of Piaget in Chapter 2) for faces of familiar people. Therefore, an unfamiliar face may be experienced as an inconsistent or fearful event. As infants mature, however, they are exposed to many unfamiliar faces. Therefore, their mental schemas for faces come to include a broader range of characteristics. As a result, they are much less likely to become upset at the sight of a strange face (stranger anxiety).

  What evidence is there for the cognitive interpretation of stranger anxiety? According to one study, infants who came from small families with few outside contacts (i.e., the infant has less opportunity to see strange faces) are more likely to be wary of strangers than infants who come from larger families with more outside contacts (i.e., with more opportunities to see strangers) (Schaffer, 1966).

- *The ethological or evolutionary perspective.* From an ethological or evolutionary perspective, stranger anxiety is one of a number of inborn or "biologically programmed" fears or avoidance responses (Bowlby, 1973). Apparently, as soon as the infant is able to perceive the difference between familiar companions and unfamiliar people, stranger anxiety automatically comes into play. However, according to ethological theory, stranger anxiety decreases during the second year of life as infants use their attachment figures as secure bases for exploration of their environment (Ainsworth, Bell, and Stayton, 1974). Stranger anxiety fades because the infant explores the environment and presumably discovers that heretofore strange objects and people are not so threatening. Such infant exploration is also considered to be a "biologically programmed" behavior.

  There is some evidence for the ethological perspective to fear of strangers. Specifically, several studies have suggested a genetic basis for the age of onset of fear of strangers (Freedman, 1974; Plomin and DeFries, 1985). According to Robert Plomin and John DeFries, identical twins are more similar in their reactions to strangers than fraternal twins.

Why Are Infants Afraid of Strangers? Whether an infant is frightened or alarmed by a stranger depends on many factors, including the following (Ainsworth, 1979b):

- The infant's developmental stage.
- The infant's previous experience with strangers or with people generally (Schaffer, 1966).
- The infant's temperament or predisposition to fearfulness.
- The behavior of the stranger, including how "close" he or she is or how "strange" he or she seems.

- Whether the parent is *present* or *absent* (and, if present, how close).
- The behavior of the mother (if present), including whether she herself is alarmed or anxious and whether she encourages or rebuffs the infant's attempt to cling.
- The *quality of the infant-mother attachment relationship*, including whether it is secure or has been disturbed in any way by special circumstances such as illness or extended separations.

Eventually, infants who initially may react with fear to a stranger can learn to establish a trusting and/or affectionate relationship with that person. The process may take several hours, several days, or, in some cases, several weeks. How do infants learn to transform a stranger into a friend?

Typically, a requirement for forming a friendship with a stranger is the presence of a secure base such as a parent. A study involving two-year-olds indicated that, in only a few minutes, they were able to play comfortably with a stranger in the presence of their mothers. Furthermore, these same infants continued to interact comfortably with their new friends after the mothers left the room (Greenberg and Marvin, 1982) (It should be noted that it would probably take one-year-olds longer than a few minutes to befriend and feel comfortable with a stranger.)

In addition, there is some evidence that infants will respond positively to strangers who allow them to control their initial interactions (Levitt, 1980). Ten-month-old infants were involved in a game of a peek-a-boo with a stranger, under two conditions:

- *Control or contingent-response condition.* The infant could control the stranger's peek-a-boo game. *Whenever* the infant touched a plastic cylinder in front of him, the stranger appeared from behind a curtain to smile and say "Hi (baby's name)."
- *No-control situation.* The appearance of the stranger (who made the same statement) was completely independent of the infant's actions.

Later in the sessions, children who participated in the control and the no-control situations were allowed to interact with the stranger in the presence of their mothers. The infants who had control over the appearance of the stranger (control or contingent-response condition) displayed much less fear when the stranger approached them than children who had no control over the situation (no-control or noncontingent response condition) (see Fig. 8.4). Infants in the control situation moved closer to the stranger, played more with the stranger, and imitated the stranger more than the infants who were in the no-control situation.

SEPARATION ANXIETY. **Separation anxiety** is produced when an attachment figure such as a parent or caretaker physically leaves the child and is no longer in view. Separation anxiety typically has the following developmental progression (Weinraub and Lewis, 1977):

- It appears during the latter half of the first year (approximately seven to twelve months).
- It peaks at fourteen to eighteen months.
- It declines after eighteen months and throughout the preschool years.

Why Does Separation Anxiety Occur? There are several explanations for infants who protest a separation from an attachment figure, including the following:

- *A cognitive-developmental perspective.* According to Jerome Kagan (1981) infants develop schemas or mental representations not only for the parent's/caretaker's

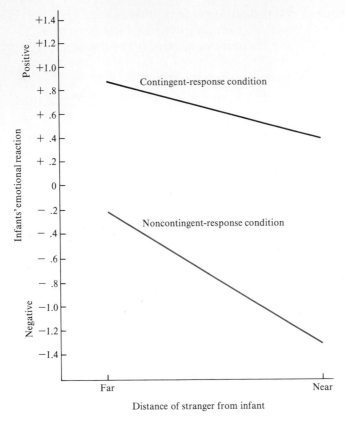

FIGURE 8.4
The emotional reactions of ten-month-old infants to a stranger. Infants in the contingent-response condition who had control over the stranger's peek-a-boo game responded favorably to the stranger. On the other hand, infants who had no such control (noncontingent-response condition) reacted negatively to the stranger. From Levitt, 1980, p. 429.

face but also for that person's whereabouts. That is, the infant develops schemas for "familiar faces in familiar places." Cognitive theorists suggest that infants are most likely to protest separations when they do not understand where their parents/caretakers have gone or when they will come back. Although infants are normally separated from their parents or caretakers during the course of daily activities (e.g., parents leave the child in the living room or den and move to the kitchen), the infants do *not* protest these brief separations. This is so because they probably understand where their mother has gone and that she will return fairly soon. However, if the infant's mother were to put on her coat and walk out the front door in front of the infant, such a departure would be accompanied by an infant protest.

Furthermore, there is reason to believe that an infant must have developed the concept of *object permanence* (see Chapter 7) in order to experience separation anxiety. That is, in order for infants to develop a mental schema of the location of a missing parent/caretaker, they must first understand that their parent/caretaker permanently exists. In fact, there is evidence that infants who have not developed the concept of object permanence do not protest when separated from their parents (Lester et al., 1974).

• *An ethological perspective.* Ethologists consider separation anxiety, like stranger anxiety, to be an inborn human characteristic. According to this view, separation anxiety is an infant response that serves to protect the young members of a species from harm by ensuring that they will remain with their parents (particularly if the parents heed infant protests). However, it is these same parents who provide the secure base for infants' exploration of their surroundings, leading to comfort with that environment. The end result is much less protest over separation.

Important evidence for the ethological perspective comes from cross-cultural studies that show a relatively high degree of similarity in the timing of infant fear reactions to being separated from their mothers (Kagan, Kearsley, and Zelazo, 1978; Kagan, 1981, 1983). As indicated in Figure 8.5, cultures as diverse as Guatamalan Indians, African Kalihari bushmen,and Israeli Kibbutzim show a markedly similar pattern in the peak period of stranger anxiety.

Can the Pain of Necessary Separation Be Reduced? Inevitably, there are unavoidable and necessary reasons for parents' being separated from their infants for a lengthy period of time. A case in point is when both parents work. Are there ways of easing or reducing the pain of such separations when infants are left with baby-sitters or in day-care centers for extended time periods? Some suggestions include the following:

- There is evidence that toddlers who were to be separated from their mother (e.g., by being taken to a day-care center) adapted constructively, with reduced crying, *if* the parent provided a brief explanation to the toddler (i.e., that the parent was leaving and would return) (Adams and Passman, 1981).
- While preparation of the toddler by means of an explanation is important, *brief* (yet clear and precise) explanations seem to work better for toddlers than for older preschool children (Adams and Passman, 1980). Preschoolers are typically more verbally advanced than toddlers and, therefore, better able to understand lengthy verbal messages and raise appropriate questions.
- Toddlers as well as nine-to-twelve-month-old infants (who may have limited understanding of verbal explanations) experience reduced separation anxiety if the substitute caregivers are able to show the infant/toddler a photograph of the absent parent(s) (Brooks-Gunn and Lewis, 1981; Passman and Longeway, 1982).

The issue of separation anxiety, discussed above, raises two important and related questions:

- What is the impact of the lack or loss of a caregiver/parent on infants (social deprivation)? For example, do institutionalized infants suffer from the absence of a single caregiver?

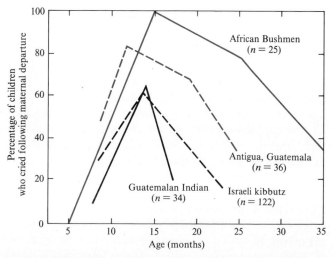

FIGURE 8.5

Separation anxiety shows a similar peaking pattern in a variety of cultures. From Kagan, Kearsley, and Zelazo, 1978, p. 107.

- Can multiple caregivers successfully assume a child-rearing function, not only for institutionalized infants but for other children? This is an issue because of the increasing number of parents whose children are in some form of day care.

SOCIAL DEPRIVATION.   Early studies of children reared in institutions showed that these children suffered devastating effects to their cognitive and social development (Dennis, 1960; Dennis and Sayegh, 1965). Some early interpretations of these studies attributed the disastrous results to the lack of mothering, or *maternal deprivation*. However, "maternal deprivation" is a catchall phrase that can refer to a broad range of early experiences (e.g., the lack of a single primary caregiver or the lack of stimulation for proper development) (Rutter, 1979). It is now apparent that the institutionalized infants in many of the early studies suffered from the lack of stimulating, enriching experiences in addition to the lack of a stable, concerned caregiver.

In a famous longitudinal study done by Harold Skeels (1966), it was found that the failure to develop an early attachment relationship with a single caregiver was not associated with irreversible negative outcomes. Skeels studied a group of children who had been discharged from a multiple-caregiver institution at nineteen months of age and were eventually adopted. As adults, these individuals could not be distinguished from the "normal" population in terms of education, intelligence, income, occupation, marriage, and number of children. The study suggests that being in an institution for the first nineteen months of life without an attachment figure does not lead to any serious maladjustment. However, a criticism of Skeel's research is that the infants in the study may have been the best-behaved, brightest, and most attractive who were adopted at nineteen months (Longstreth, 1981). There is some evidence that older infants (three years plus) transferred from institutions to adoptive homes may have much more difficulty adapting successfully to their new situations (Goldfarb, 1943).

Can infants and children recover from early social deprivation? There is considerable evidence that socially deprived infants can make dramatic recoveries from such initially handicapping experiences (Rutter, 1979). Several factors are involved, including the following:

- *The quality of the child's "new" home environment.* Children who are placed in enriched home environments may indicate substantial recoveries. In a study of twenty-five Asian children who were adopted by highly educated and affluent families, significant gains as well as above-average performance were obtained on standardized intelligence tests and assessments of social maturity (Clark and Hanisee, 1982). All the children had been adopted prior to three years of age and had been in their adoptive homes at least two years. The children had all been separated early in life from their natural parents and had lived in institutions, hospitals, or foster homes prior to coming to the United States. Furthermore, many of the children had experienced malnutrition or serious illnesses as infants. In spite of these difficulties, the Asian adoptees exhibited remarkable resilience in overcoming initial deprivation.
- *Time spent in sensory/social deprivation.* As we have already indicated, infants who spent their first three years in a deprived environment had more difficulty adjusting to new environments than infants who were moved at an earlier age (Goldfarb, 1943; Horn, 1983). These findings, however, do not necessarily paint a pessimistic picture of irreversible damage caused by early deprivation. In fact, the findings of the above study on Asian adoptees suggests the potential for positive outcomes (Clark and Hanisee, 1982).

Are such daily separations and contacts with alternate caregivers likely to have a harmful impact on the infant's/child's social-emotional development? Considerable evidence indicates that neither maternal employment nor alternative child-care arrangements are likely to have a negative impact on young children (Hoffman, 1979, 1984; Etaugh, 1980). For example, Lois Hoffman (1979, 1984) has concluded that maternal employment is unlikely to have a negative effect on the child because many working women tend to compensate for extended absences by spending more time with the child when they are together at home. In addition, children of working mothers continue to prefer their mothers to their substitute caregivers (when a choice is given), suggesting the continued vitality of their attachment (Cummings, 1980; Ragozin, 1980). Furthermore, there is evidence that excellent day care makes substantial contributions to the cognitive development of children from economically disadvantaged homes (O'Connell and Farran, 1982).

Despite this rather optimistic picture, not all the evidence is positive. For example, most of the research suggesting the absence of negative outcomes for children in day care have come from studies of *middle-class families* where the alternative child care was of high quality (Anderson et al., 1981). In a thorough review of the developmental effects and quality of day care, Jay Belsky (1984) concluded:

> These . . . data lead me to modify conclusions that have been arrived at in past reviews in order to underscore the potentially problematical nature of early entry into community-based, as opposed to university-based day care . . . . There seems to be cause for concern about early entry to the kind of day care that is available in most communities.

In addition, Ross Thompson, Michael Lamb, and David Estes (1982) reported data on a middle-class sample that showed that the stability of a secure attachment for twelve-to-nineteen-month-olds was lower for infants placed in day care.

Whether separation from both parents could be harmful to the child depends on a number of factors:

1. *Characteristics of the parents.* What are the parents' attitudes toward their child? How good is their attachment relationship to their child? What is the effect of parental personality and attitudes on the child's response to separation? Is it true that good parent-child interaction in the evening and on weekends can make up for long absences during the work week? Are the parents reasonably well adjusted to their work activities?

2. *Characteristics of the child.* Is the child "anxious" in his or her attachment to the parents? If the child is already insecure in the attachment relationship, separation from the parents may be irritating and disturbing. On the other hand, if the child is neglected, day care may be more beneficial.

One factor that may affect the adjustment of the infant/child to day care is the *age* of the child. Some investigators have found that infants from both lower-class and middle-class families are more likely to develop insecure attachments to their mothers under two conditions: (1) if their mothers return to work prior to their first birthday and (2) if that infant receives full-day alternative care (Vaughn, Gove, and Egeland, 1980; Schwartz, 1983). Other evidence suggests that three- and four-year-olds who began day care as infants were more aggressive than other three- and four-year-olds who began day care as toddlers (Etaugh, 1980).

3. *Characteristics of the substitute care.* What is the quality of the relationship between the child and the substitute caregiver? There is reason to think that the child can develop healthy multiple attachments to adults other than the parents

(e.g., caregivers). Is quality care available? Is substitute care provided by a caregiver who does not have to distribute his or her attention over too many children?

There is general agreement among child-care experts that an excellent or quality day-care program includes at least the following characteristics (Anderson et al. 1981):

· Caregivers who are warm and responsive to the needs of young children.
· Relatively stable staff with minimal turnover (so children can develop good relationships with staff).
· A reasonable staff-to-child ratio (approximately one adult to every four to twelve children, depending on the age of the children).
· Good staff-to-parent relationships.
· A curriculum that is appropriate for the ages and needs of the children.

Furthermore, there is evidence that children who have excellent alternative care are not likely to suffer any negative social or emotional consequences. Rather, they seem to develop secure attachments to their parents (Kagan, Kearsley, and Zelazo, 1978).

MULTIPLE CAREGIVING.   Does the absence of a single or primary caregiver *result in* harmful effects on children? Research evidence suggests that the most important feature of caregiving is its stability and responsiveness, rather than the number of caregivers (Rutter, 1979). Michael Rutter found that children who experience multiple caregiving demonstrate perfectly normal development.

Children raised in Israeli kibbutzim show normal development (Beit-Hallahmi and Rabin, 1977). In an Israeli kibbutz, young children are raised communally by several caregivers. While the parents are working, the children are cared for in residential nurseries. The parents see their children for only a few hours a day or on weekends. The conclusions of research on kibbutz children are that parents can, in fact, be away from their children for a significant time period without any adverse effects on the children. Nonetheless, it is important that children and infants in such multiple caregiving settings be with sensitive, responsive adults.

The Role of the Father

As we have discovered, attachment has an important role in the healthy development of human beings. Historically the research on attachment has focused largely on the relationship of the mother and the infant. This, of course, was no accident, as the "traditional" (sex-biased) cultural expectation has assured that the place of the mother was in the home—with her children. Over the last decade, this expectation has been called into question. Many women seek fulfillment in careers in the world of work, in addition to (and sometimes instead of) the roles of homemaking and child rearing. These changing values have generated research on the role of fathers in child development (Lamb, 1981). In other words, the historical or traditional expectation that the father's place will be in the world of work has also come into question.

FATHERS' PARTICIPATION IN CAREGIVING.   Despite the general recognition of the possibility of equal contributions to infant caregiving for both sexes, it is nonetheless the case that fathers still spend far less time caring for infants (feeding, bathing, changing diapers) than mothers (Lamb, 1981). It is possible that these lower levels of father interaction are due to obvious factors such as fathers' not being at home as much as mothers. However, when fathers and mothers are both home or even when they are in the same room, fathers still interact with infants less than mothers. It is interesting to note, however, that as infants get older, fathers and mothers are more equal in the amount of time they spend with them (Clarke-Stewart, 1978).

Although fathers may interact less with their infants, they are in no sense less sensitive or skilled than mothers when they do participate in caregiving. Fathers can—and do—become as attached to infants and young children as mothers. A common observation in middle-class families is that both father and mother interact with their newborn for about the same amount of time during the first few days after birth. When given the opportunity, working-class fathers also demonstrate responsive and nurturant behavior toward newborns (Parke and Sawin, 1980). Studies of fathers' attachment to infants show that fathers look and smile at their babies, kiss their babies, and give them their bottles. These behaviors are similar to those of the mothers.

DIFFERENCES IN MOTHER-INFANT AND FATHER-INFANT INTERACTION.   Even though fathers may interact less with their infants than do mothers, they typically spend a larger percentage of their total interaction time in play activities than mothers (Clarke-Stewart, 1978). This is likely due to the fact that the traditionally "difficult" chores of infancy (changing diapers, bathing, dressing, feeding) in many families may still be assumed to be the responsibility of the mother.

In addition, fathers and mothers may differ in the *styles* of play they use with their infants (Clarke-Stewart, 1978; Lamb, 1981; MacDonald and Parke, 1984). Fathers' play tends to much more vigorous and rough-and-tumble, whereas mothers are more gentle (Power and Parke, 1982). Furthermore, fathers typically do not use toys as a way of gaining an infant's attention. Instead, they appear to rely more on "social-physical" games, which seem to be made up on the spot. On the other hand, the play of mothers may be more cognitively or intellectually oriented.

Fathers' play tends to be more rough-and-tumble than mothers' play.

Beverly Austin

For example, mother-infant play interaction may involve verbalizations, such as nursery rhymes or standard games such as peek-a-boo or patty cake.

The Emergence of the Sociable Self

During the first two years of life, the infant "builds on" the attachment relationship. Infants expand their social horizons, refining their competence and autonomy in all relationships with people and things. They extend themselves to interact with new adults and with peers.

As we pointed out earlier, an important determinant of the infant's efforts to gain *competence* in exploring the environment and being "sociable" with others is the quality of the infant-parent attachment. Research has demonstrated that the infant is naturally a "sociable" person from birth on (Kagan, 1981). Detailed observations of parent-infant interactions indicate that the mother and the infant adjust mutually to each other's behavior (Kaye, 1982). Through this interaction, the baby learns to control its experiences and to develop a primitive sense of "me."

Who Am I?

When do infants recognize who they are? When can they distinguish between the "me" and the "not me"? Research evidence demonstrates that by twenty to twenty-four months, infants have developed a self-concept (Lewis and Brooks-Gunn, 1981). They recognize themselves as distinct from others, and they recognize differences between people (including height and facial differences).

One of the ways of studying the question of self-recognition has involved infant responses to their images in mirrors and to films or videotapes of their own behavior. Hanus Papousek (1967) found that younger infants (five months old) showed more interest in films or videotapes of their behavior than in looking at themselves in a mirror. Older infants became more interested in the behavior that they created and could observe in mirrors. Papousek suggested that as infants grow older, their concept of self expands to include what they are actively *doing* (i.e., the relationship between their behavior and that of the mirror image).

Beulah Amsterdam (1972) identified the time of mature self-recognition as occurring somewhere between twenty and twenty-four months. The experimenter put a rouge spot on the noses of children and watched their reaction to seeing the spot in the mirror. Amsterdam reasoned that mature self-recognition would occur when the infant used the mirror to identify and touch the rouge spot. Few babies under a year old seemed to recognize that the rouge spot and the nose belonged to them. It was not until twenty to twenty-four months that infants grabbed at the rouge spot, using the mirror as a guide.

Whom Do I Trust?

The development of an attachment relationship between the infant and his or her parents provides the stable basis for all further social and personality development. As we have suggested, the attachment relationship can be viewed as a *system* in which the infant and the caregiver *interact mutually* with one another. In this context, the infant develops a sense of trust.

*By twenty to twenty-four months of age infants have developed a
self-concept.*

Garry Rowe

Garry Rowe

The beginning of social and personality development occurs with the establishment of a sense of trust (Erikson, 1963). For the infant to "trust" the environment
and the people in it, he or she needs to feel that these "others" are in some sense
"predictable" or "controllable." This process of learning to *predict* and *control* one's
own behavior in relation to and in mutual interaction with others is what is meant
by the term *self-regulation*. A sense of trust emerges from this give-and-take relationship between the infant and its caregiver. The baby comes to learn that his or
her responses, in turn, generate the caregiver's responses, which, in turn, generate
more infant responses. For example, in the process of feeding, the baby learns
that its needs will be satisfied somewhat predictably. In turn, the caretaker also
learns that the infant needs to be fed on a generally predictable schedule. Through
such a process of *mutual accommodation,* a sense of trust is established.

THE INFANT SMILE.   One of the best "commonsense" indicators that a healthy,
trusting relationship is being established is the "dialogue" between the smiling
infant and the parent. Infants smile for many reasons, including as a response to
their recognition of familiar objects, as a simple response to internal physiological
changes, as a response to controlling objects by making them move, or as a response to surprises such as the game of peek-a-boo (Piaget, 1952; Watson, 1970;
Wolff, 1963). In addition to these reasons, the smile may develop into a social
means of communication between infant and caretaker.

The infant's smile appears to go through the following phases (Bowlby, 1969;
Sroufe and Waters, 1976):

1. *Spontaneous smiling.* This phase begins at birth and lasts until the age of about
   five weeks. These smiles seem to occur spontaneously and not as a response
   to any particular environmental event or stimulus; for example, the infant
   may smile during sleep.
2. *The transition from unselective to selective social smiling.* This phase begins at

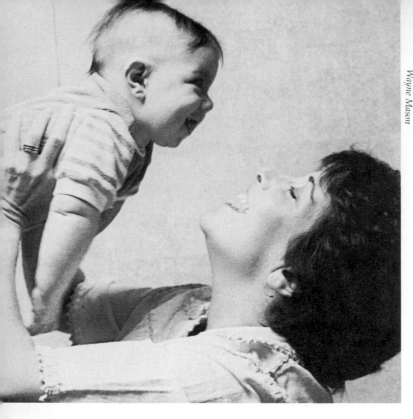

The emergence of the sociable self.

about the fifth week and extends to about the fourteenth week. The major characteristic of this phase is that at its onset, smiling can be produced by a rather broad range of moving and/or noise-making objects and by human faces, whereas at its conclusion, smiling is produced by a much narrower range of social stimuli (e.g., the stationary face).

3. *Differential social responsiveness.* This final phase, which begins at about six or seven months of age, has as its distinguishing characteristic the ability of the infant to use the social smile differently in response to different individuals. For example, the infant may smile more freely at familiar faces and may smile somewhat more cautiously at strangers.

Thus the smile is an important indicator of emerging attachment and trust. The emergence of the social smile (after the fifth week) and its refinement thereafter constitute a landmark in the development of the relationship between infant and caretaker. The change or transition from unselective smiling to social smiling is usually noted with some enthusiasm by the parent (Wolff, 1963). Such parental comments as "My baby seems more like a person" or "I'm beginning to enjoy my baby" are not uncommon responses to this change. Both the parent and the infant are beginning to gain a feeling of control in their mutual relationship.

What Can I Do?

By the end of the second year, the period of social development, including autonomy, or self-direction, emerges. As the child becomes aware of his or her competence in language, object manipulation, and interpersonal relationships, he or she wants to do things for himself or herself. Although two-year-olds possess the skills and the will to move out into the world, they are obviously not yet aware of the potential consequences of their behavior. For example, the child who recognizes that a lengthy cord is attached to a lamp and that the lamp can be pulled by the cord may not yet understand that the lamp could break in transit. This venturesome attitude on the part of toddlers has led to the toddler period's being humorously called the "terrible twos."

The development of autonomy may sometimes result in a clash of wills between the parent and the toddler. The parent may be all too aware of the consequences of pulling lamp cords, yet the child may be determined to establish a sense of control over the environment. The parent may say "no" to the child, and the child may offer a hearty "no" back to the parent.

There are several areas of behavior in which autonomy is developed and tested. Two of these are peer relationships and play. Competence with other people emerges in many forms, including peer relationships, during the toddler years. For many years, peer relationships between infants and toddlers were not often examined. The thought may have been that infants were too involved in their own world to relate successfully to peers. Mounting evidence has shown that this is not the case (Rubenstein and Howes, 1976; Becker, 1977). Infants and toddlers are, in fact, sociable creatures. It appears that infants and toddlers learn to expand their social skills in the presence of peers. Jacqueline M. Becker (1977) demonstrated that nine-month-old babies could relate to one another by reaching toward each other and handing toys to one another. By the end of the first year, these infant interactions also included occasional fights and screams over disputed toys. One-year-olds appeared to imitate one another's play activities. For example, when one child started playing with blocks, others wanted to participate. One-year-olds demonstrated the emergence of mutual excitement about play activity. Peer interaction continues to develop throughout the second year as infants and toddlers learn to relate mutually to one another in play situations with greater satisfaction and delight.

Summary

1. Children demonstrate a broad range of emotions. Even young infants express such emotions as surprise, joy, fear, sadness, interest, anger, and disgust. Emotions may serve a number of functions including the communication of infant feelings, needs, and desires. In addition, the expression of infant emotions also serves to control social distance between the infant and its parents/caretakers. There is evidence that emotions appear in a progressive order as follows: (a) expressions such as distress, disgust, and startle; (b) the social smile; (c) anger, surprise, and sadness; (d) fear; (e) shame and shyness; (f) and finally, contempt and guilt.

2. There are three types of emotional expression in infancy—*crying, smiling,* and *laughing.* Crying is a powerful mode of communicating distress. The appearance of the *social smile* and *laughter* represents milestones because they are significant modes of attracting an adult to the infant.

3. Infant temperament is an inborn style of approaching events and other people. *Individual differences* in temperament influence the expression of infant emotions. Such differences may be apparent at birth. The New York Longitudinal Study (NYLS) involved the study of infant temperament based on three temperament types: the *easy child,* the *difficult child,* and the *slow-to-warm-up child.*

4. The infant's organization of a sense of self is an extraordinary facet of social and personality development during the first three years of life. The sense of self develops in the context of relationships with other people including family members, peers, and adults outside the family. During infancy, the

sense of self emerges from the affectional relationship between parents and infants that is called *attachment*.

5. The attachment relationship involves several components including *rooting and sucking, posture, looking and following, listening, smiling, vocalizing, crying,* and *grasping/clinging*. The development of attachment in the family involves four phases: (a) the *phase of undiscriminating social responsiveness*, (b) the *phase of discriminating social responsiveness*, (c) the *phase of active initiative in seeking proximity and contact*, and (d) the *phase of goal-corrected partnership*.

6. One of the most controversial dimensions of attachment has been the *bonding hypothesis*. The evidence suggests that the strong form of the bonding hypothesis (i.e., that there is a universal critical or sensitive period, immediately following birth, during which mothers *must* have contact with their infants in order for any attachment relationship or bond to develop) is likely *not* the case.

7. Infants develop different styles of interacting with their caregivers that reflect an underlying degree of *security* and *insecurity*. Using Ainsworth's Strange Situation Test for assessing the security or insecurity of attachment, infants can be categorized into one of three attachment types: *secure infants, anxious/avoidant infants* (insecure), and *anxious/resistant infants* (insecure). While changes in life circumstances can lead to changes in the quality of attachment, the quality of child care and the infant's temperament are also major determinants of attachment type. A secure attachment helps infants develop a positive concept of themselves as competent individuals as well as a sense of trust in other people.

8. Attachment is also related to other infant behaviors such as play/exploration, stranger anxiety, and separation anxiety. The quality of parent-infant attachment appears to provide a secure base from which the infant can explore the environment without anxiety.

   Stranger anxiety is a cautious or frightened response to an unknown person. Explanations for stranger anxiety include the *cognitive/developmental* perspective and the *ethological* or *evolutionary* viewpoint. Whether an infant is frightened by a stranger depends on several factors, including the infant's developmental age, previous experience with strangers, infant temperament, and so on.

   Separation anxiety is produced when an attachment figure physically leaves the child and is no longer in view. Explanations for separation anxiety include a *cognitive-developmental* viewpoint and an *ethological* perspective. The issue of separation anxiety raises two important and related questions. What is the impact of the loss of an attachment relationship (i.e., social deprivation) on infant development? Can multiple caregivers successfully assume a child-rearing function? The latter issue assumes increasing importance as more parents place young children in some form of day care.

9. The role of the father in an attachment relationship with the infant has received increasing emphasis. Despite the general recognition of the possibility of equal contributions to infant caregiving for *both* sexes, fathers still spend far less time caring for infants than do mothers. Furthermore, there are differences in the ways that fathers and mothers interact with infants.

10. During the first two years of life, the infant "builds on" the attachment relationship. Infants expand their social horizons, refining their competence and autonomy in relationships with people and things. Research evidence suggests that by twenty to twenty-four months infants have developed a self-concept. They recognize themselves as distinct from others, and they recognize differences between people. Social and personality development

in infancy may be viewed as the emerging resolution to three questions: Who am I? Whom do I trust? What can I do?

Key Terms

Ainsworth's Strange Situation Test
Anxious/avoidant infants (insecure)
Anxious/resistant infants (insecure)
Attachment
Bonding Hypothesis
Crying
Difficult child
Easy child
Grasping/clinging
Listening
Looking/following
New York Longitudinal Study
Phase of activity initiative in seeking proximity and contact

Phase of discriminating social responsiveness
Phase of goal-corrected partnership
Phase of undiscriminating social responsiveness
Posture
Rooting/sucking
Secure infants
Separation anxiety
Slow-to-warm-up child
Smiling
Stranger anxiety
Vocalizing

Questions

1. Discuss the emotional development of infants. What emotions do infants have? In what sequence do these emotions occur? How are infant emotions measured?
2. Define infant temperament. Discuss the three types of temperament identified in the New York Longitudinal Study. Give examples, where possible, from your own experiences with infants of various temperamental types.
3. In what sense can attachment be thought of as a system? Discuss one component of that system with particular reference to the mutual relationship between infant and caregiver.
4. Describe the bonding hypothesis and discuss the evidence for it.
5. Discuss the meaning of secure and insecure attachments.
6. Discuss the impact of day care as an example of multiple caregiving on infant development.

Suggested Readings

BRETHERTON, I., and WATERS, E. (eds.). "Growing Points of Attachment Theory and Research," *Monographs of the Society for Research in Child Development*. Chicago: The University of Chicago Press, 1985, p. 50 (1–2, Serial No. 209). An excellent and current discussion of attachment, including theoretical perspectives, measurement issues, adaptation issues, and cross-national research.

LERNER, J. V., and LERNER, R. M. (eds.). *Temperament and Social Interaction in Infants and Children*. San Francisco: Jossey-Bass, 1986. An up-to-date examination of research on temperament in relation to such issues as attachment, infant cognitive development, differences in caregiving, maternal employment, schooling, and so on.

SCARR, S. *Mother Care—Other Care*. New York: Basic Books, 1984. An informative and readable book that provides a guide to child-care decisions. The needs of the child and working mothers are taken into consideration.

THOMPSON, R. A., and LAMB, M. E. "Infant-Mother Attachment: New Directions for Theory and Research." In P. B. Baltes, D. L. Featherman, and R. M. Lerner (eds.), *Life-Span Development and Behavior* (Vol. 7). Hillsdale, N.J.: Erlbaum, 1986, pp. 1–41. An excellent review of new directions in attachment research.

9 The Preschooler: Contexts of Development

CHILDREN LEARN WHAT THEY LIVE

If a child lives with criticism,
    He learns to condemn.
If a child lives with hostility,
    He learns to fight.
If a child lives with ridicule,
    He learns to be shy.
If a child lives with tolerance,
    He learns to be patient.
If a child lives with encouragement,
    He learns confidence.

If a child lives with praise,
    He learns to appreciate.
If a child lives with fairness,
    He learns justice.
If a child lives with security,
    He learns to have faith.
If a child lives with approval,
    He learns to like himself.
If a child lives with acceptance and friendship,
    He learns to find love in the world.

—Anonymous

In this book, we emphasize that the human being grows, develops, and functions in a *system* or set of contexts. This system, which includes the family, changes progressively as the individual matures from infancy through adulthood (see Fig. 9.1). The transition from the infant system to the preschool system is marked by a gradual movement of the child into the larger society. The social world of the infant is contained within the family. The preschooler begins to move out into a larger society, which becomes differentiated into neighborhood and peer group. This process of differentiation of the larger society continues throughout the life-span: The growing individual continually encounters "new" aspects of the social world, such as school and work, and integrates them with the family.

The Family

The family performs the primary function of socializing the child from birth through at least adolescence. This process of socialization is accomplished through mutual interactions between parent and child. These interactions include the transmission and interpretation of cultural standards of values and behavior. The family can be viewed as a dynamic system that changes over time, as do its members.

Two basic questions need be examined with reference to the family as a dynamic system:

1. What *intrafamilial* (inside the family) processes of interaction between family members constitute the basis of the family as a system?
2. What *extrafamilial* (outside the family) influences affect the *intrafamilial* processes of interaction between family members?

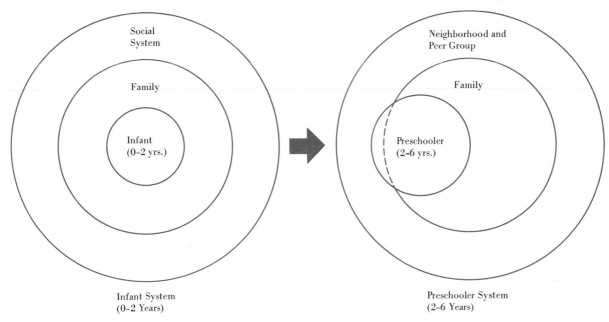

FIGURE 9.1

The transition from infancy to the preschool world.

The intrafamilial processes of family interaction are discussed first. The extrafamilial effects are examined next in the discussion of the other vital contexts of preschool development—the neighborhood/community, the peer group, and the preschool.

The Family as a System

The family can be viewed as a *system* in its own right. A system is a "set of objects together with relationships between the *objects* and between their *attributes* . . . *objects* are the components or parts of the system, *attributes* are the properties of the objects, and *relationships* tie the system together" (Hall and Fagen, 1956).

If we view the interpersonal relationships of the family as a system, then the *objects* of the system are the people (husband, wife, children, relatives). The *attributes* are the relevant characteristics of the family members, such as age, personality, and previous experiences. The *relationships* are the interactions or communications between the objects, or people.

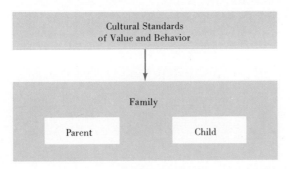

It is becoming increasingly apparent in the social sciences that any workable theory of family behavior is greatly advanced by this idea of the family as a system. The model suggested here views the activity of the family as "a complex interplay of systemic structures and forces which elaborate and change in response to both internal and external phenomena" (Kantor and Lehr, 1975).

David Kantor and William Lehr identified these characteristics of the family as a system:

1. **Organizational complexity.** Families evolve networks of interdependent relationships.

· These interactional networks involve relationships that are mutual in the sense that all parties contribute something to the relationship. That is, the components of family systems are *reciprocally influencing.*

· These interactional networks may be either *internal* (between members of the family, for example, parent, child, sibling, and grandparent) or *external* (between the family, as a unit, and other institutions or organizations, for example, school, other families, doctors, and health specialists).

· These interactional networks are rule-governed in the sense that either formal or informal "understandings" largely direct and influence the very nature of these relationships. For example, some family "rules" or organizational principles may result in an authoritarian, or *closed,* style of family functioning. Authoritarian parents may operate on the "rule" that the parent can simply hand down family decisions (including expectations about children's behavior) without consulting other family members. Other families may have "rules" that generate more democratic, or *open,* styles of family interaction and decision making (see Fig. 9.2).

2. **Openness.** The family is influenced by external (outside-the-family) forces, and it also influences these external forces. Therefore, the family is said to be an "open" system because it depends on mutual interaction with an environment to grow and develop. In order for the family to accomplish its many functions (child

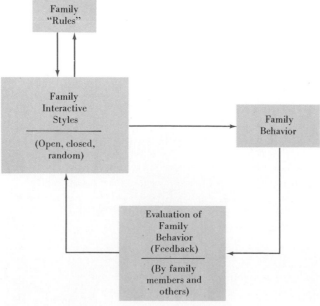

FIGURE 9.2
The family as a rule-governed system.

rearing, economic maintenance, and so on), it must interact with institutions such as the school and the world of work.

3. **Adaptiveness.** Open family systems develop and grow as a consequence of interaction with factors external to the family as well as adjustments to internal changes in the family system. Internal changes in the family or changes in one component of the family have an impact on all other parts of the family system. Such changes may promote adaptiveness. For example, when a father becomes ill or is permanently disabled, the mother and/or the older children may assume the father's role as economic provider. If a mother becomes ill or dies, then maternal responsibilities might be taken on by a grandmother, other relatives, and/or the father. In summary, the family as a system adapts in order to survive (1975, pp. 116–142).

Parenting Styles

One of the important components of the family system is the parenting style. By **styles of parenting,** we mean simply the attitudes and behaviors of parents. At least three dimensions of parenting style are related to the social and personality development of the preschool-age child.

PARENTAL MODELING.   Parents provide models with which the preschool child can interact and identify. Parents provide models of behavior that the child can adopt and use. If parents shout at one another, then it is possible that the child will use this behavioral technique.

Some of the most dramatic examples of the modeling of behavior by the preschooler often occur during free play time. It is during these moments that the child may imitate parental behaviors that were learned and observed at an earlier time.

   SCENARIO: THE DAY PRESCHOOLER BRUCE DISCIPLINED
   "CHARLIE McCARTHY"

Our irrepressible preschooler Bruce has many playmates. In addition to his friends Michael, Patrick, Susie, and Dana, Bruce also enjoys the company of "Charlie McCarthy," a toy "dummy" modeled after the one used by the famous ventriloquist Edgar Bergen.

   Yesterday, when Bruce was sitting at the dinner table, he reached for his fork and unintentionally knocked over his glass of milk. The milk spilled over Bruce's dinner plate, which now contained milky chicken and even milkier potatoes, over Bruce's trousers, and, of course, on the floor. Needless to say, Bruce's mother was not pleased with this turn of events. As she began the task of wiping up the milk, cleaning the floor, and replacing Bruce's trousers, the following dialogue occurred:

Mother: Bruce, you have to be more careful.
Bruce   (surprised expression):   Okay, Mom.
Mother: When you reach for something at the table, always look while you are
   reaching.
[A demonstration of reaching carefully immediately follows.]

   The next day, Bruce was seen playing with Charlie McCarthy. Charlie was seated at a small table with a small cup of water before him. Somehow the cup was knocked over, and the following dialogue occurred:

Bruce: Now Charlie, you just have to be careful not to spill the water.
Charlie (voice supplied by Bruce):   I'm sorry.
Bruce: See, this is how you do it.

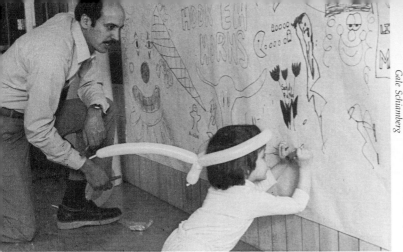

FIGURE 9.3
Children develop work habits largely in terms of the way in which parents work with them to develop their skills and talents.

Parenting behaviors are not confined to one-way modeling (i.e., the model or parent demonstrating a behavior that is then imitated by the child). A good deal of parent-child interaction involves *mutual following.* For example, parents and children engage in activities or play games in which the parents adjust their behavior to the child's movements in much the same way that the child observes the parents and organizes his or her behavior in relation to what the parents are doing (see Fig. 9.3).

PARENTAL EXPECTATIONS CONCERNING CHILDREN'S BEHAVIOR. Each family might be characterized to some extent by what parents expect of their children. Often these expectations are embedded in the "rule" structure or organizing principles of family behavior (Fig. 9.2). For example, some families might wish their children to participate in family decision making, whereas other families would find such involvement completely out of character with their expectations concerning child behavior ("Children should be seen and not heard."). Sometimes expectations about children's performance are so influential that they actively structure the way in which the parent or teacher acts toward the child, resulting in a self-fulfilling prophecy (if we believe something, our behavior may be altered in the direction of making the belief come true) (Minuchin, 1985). Parents usually control the entire area of discipline. For example, parents determine not only *what* the child is disciplined for, but *how* the child is disciplined; the parent may use rewards, punishments, verbal support, physical spanking, scolding, and so on.

Dimensions of Parent-Child Interaction

Parent-child relationships are *reciprocal*, or two-way. This is important to bear in mind because almost any episode of behavior between a parent and child could be interpreted as being one-way. For example, a sullen child could be viewed as a reaction to a rejecting parent. On the other hand, a rejecting parent could just as well be viewed as the reaction to a sullen, unresponsive child.

ONE-WAY RELATIONSHIP		
Parent influences	⟶	Child
	OR	
Child influences	⟶	Parent

"First, the *Good News* Dad! There'll be more
fresh air in the garage now!"
DENNIS THE MENACE® *used by permission of Hank Ketcham and* © *by
Field Enterprises, Inc.*

What is actually happening, however, is a *two-way* process of *mutual influence*
to which both parent and child contribute. In the remainder of this section, we
examine some of these mutual relationships as well as parental disciplinary patterns.

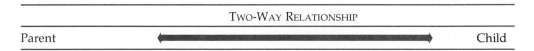

TWO-WAY RELATIONSHIP

Parent   Child

PARENT DISCIPLINARY PATTERNS.   Parents play an important role in their children's development—either by direct action or, in some cases, by inactive default.
Parent disciplinary strategies frequently have been conceptualized as the relationship between two dimensions (Maccoby and Martin, 1983):

• *Acceptance (warmth) or rejection (hostility).* This dimension deals with the
  emotional relationship between the parent and the child. Such a relationship
  can vary from *accepting and responsive* parent behavior (focused on the child's
  needs) on the one hand, to *rejecting and unresponsive* parent behavior (focused
  on the parent's needs) on the other hand.
• *Restrictive or permissive.* This dimension involves parental control and can vary
  from *demanding, controlling,* or *restrictive* parent behavior to laissez-faire,
  uncontrolling, or permissive parent behavior.

Table 9.1 describes the characteristics of the *four types of parents* that emerge from
the interaction of these two dimensions: *authoritative, authoritarian, indulgent, and
neglecting.* We will return to a more detailed discussion of each of these four parent
types. However, at this point it is important to emphasize that each parenting

TABLE 9.1
A Two-Dimensional Classification of Parenting Patterns

	ACCEPTING, RESPONSIVE, CHILD-CENTERED	REJECTING, UNRESPONSIVE, PARENT-CENTERED
DEMANDING CONTROLLING RESTRICTIVE	Authoritative-reciprocal High in bidirectional communication	Authoritarian Power-assertive
UNDEMANDING LOW IN CONTROL ATTEMPTS PERMISSIVE	Indulgent	Neglecting, ignoring, indifferent, uninvolved

Adapted from Maccoby and Martin, 1983, p. 39

type (authoritarian, indulgent, and so on) represents a type of **family system** with a set of "rules" governing the family relationships (Fig. 9.2). We now discuss the ways in which each of the two dimensions (acceptance-rejection and restrictiveness-permissiveness) influence the developing preschool child.

ACCEPTANCE-REJECTION.   Parental acceptance or warmth is considered an important determinant of positive child outcomes for several reasons (Maccoby and Martin, 1983):

· In the first place, warm parents who combine their acceptance with reasoned explanations are more likely to have children who follow parental rules.
· Warm and nurturing parents are more likely to have children who feel good about themselves. These children tend to have high self-esteem and low levels of anxiety. Parental warmth and acceptance are much more conducive to child learning and positive development than parent hostility or physical punishment.
· Children who are treated with warmth and acceptance are more likely to want to please parents than children treated with hostility. Such children are unlikely to require harsh or punitive forms of discipline since withdrawal or temporary loss of parental love is sufficient motivation to ensure positive socialization. In contrast, children of hostile parents are more likely to be the subject of harsh or punitive disciplinary tactics since parental withdrawal of love cannot work (love cannot be "withdrawn" if it has not been offered).
· Warm parents are also more effective than hostile parents in controlling child aggression (Patterson, 1982). Authoritarian or power-assertive parents who frequently use methods such as verbal or physical abuse to control child aggression arouse anger in the child as well as "modeling" the very aggressive behavior they are trying to control. In addition, children who receive punitive or harsh discipline are likely, in the future, to try to avoid the source of their frustration—the hostile parent. Such avoidance behavior substantially reduces the likelihood of parent socialization of the child. Furthermore, there is evidence that such children may, in fact, reduce their overt aggression at home (particularly in the presence of the punitive parent) while increasing aggression outside the home. Thus, unlike warm, accepting parents who are more likely to control child aggression through the positive motivation of the child to please parents, hostile parents may succeed only in displacing child aggression from the home to the school or the playground (Patterson, 1982).

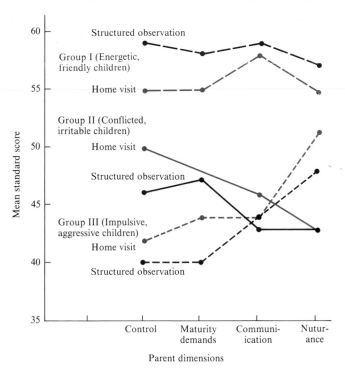

FIGURE 9.4

*Scores of parents on selected behavior for a home
visit and structured observation. From Baumrind,
1967, p. 73.*

RESTRICTIVENESS-PERMISSIVENESS.   Positive socialization of children requires not
only warmth or acceptance but also some level of parental control, restrictiveness,
or standards. Since the goal of child socialization is self-regulation (a subject we
discuss in more detail in Chapters 12 and 14) rather than control by external agents,
it is important to recognize that an overemphasis on extreme parental restrictiveness or on extreme parental permissiveness may be detrimental to the child.

    Diana Baumrind (1967, 1978, 1983) demonstrated the impact of variations in
parental control on preschoolers' behavior. Based on fourteen weeks of observations in a preschool, Baumrind identified three groups of children who differed
considerably in their behavior (see Fig. 9.4):

· Energetic-friendly children
· Conflicted-irritable children
· Impulsive-aggressive children

Baumrind then interviewed the parents of these children and observed them interacting with their children in the preschool. She found three distinctive patterns
of parenting which were associated with the three groups of children as follows
(see Table 9.2):

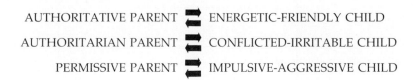

AUTHORITATIVE PARENT ⇌ ENERGETIC-FRIENDLY CHILD

AUTHORITARIAN PARENT ⇌ CONFLICTED-IRRITABLE CHILD

PERMISSIVE PARENT ⇌ IMPULSIVE-AGGRESSIVE CHILD

TABLE 9.2
Parenting Styles and Children's Behavior

PARENTAL TYPE	CHILDREN'S BEHAVIOR

Permissive-indulgent parent
  Rules not enforced
  Rules not clearly communicated
  Yields to coercion, whining, nagging,
    crying by the child
  Inconsistent discipline
  Few demands or expectations for
    mature, independent behavior
  Ignores or accepts bad behavior
  Hides impatience, anger, and
    annoyance
  Moderate warmth
  Glorification of importance of free
    expression of impulses and desires
	Impulsive-aggressive children
	  Resistive, noncompliant to adults
	  Low in self-reliance
	  Low in achievement orientation
	  Lacking in self-control
	  Aggressive
	  Quick to anger but fast to recover
	    cheerful mood
	  Impulsive
	  Aimless, low in goal-directed activities
	  Domineering

Authoritarian parent
  Rigid enforcement of rules
  Confronts and punishes bad behavior
  Shows anger and displeasure
  Rules not clearly explained
  View of child as dominated by
    uncontrolled antisocial impulses
  Child's desires and opinions not
    considered or solicited
  Persistent in enforcement of rules in
    the face of opposition and coercion
  Harsh, punitive discipline
  Low in warmth and positive
    involvement
  No cultural events or mutual activities
    planned
  No educational demands or standards
	Conflicted-irritable children
	  Fearful, apprehensive
	  Moody, unhappy
	  Easily annoyed
	  Passively hostile and guileful
	  Vulnerable to stress
	  Alternates between aggressive
	    unfriendly behavior and sulky
	    withdrawal
	  Aimless

Authoritative parent
  Firm enforcement of rules
  Does not yield to child coercion
  Confronts disobedient child
  Shows displeasure and annoyance in
    response to child's bad behavior
  Shows pleasure and support of child's
    constructive behavior
  Rules clearly communicated
  Considers child's wishes and solicits
    child's opinions
  Alternatives offered
  Warm, involved, responsive
  Expects mature, independent behavior
    appropriate for the child's age
  Cultural events and joint activities
    planned
  Educational standards set and enforced
	Energetic-friendly children
	  Self-reliant
	  Self-controlled
	  High-energy level
	  Cheerful
	  Friendly relations with peers
	  Copes well with stress
	  Interest and curiosity in novel situations
	  Cooperative with adults
	  Tractable
	  Purposive
	  Achievement-oriented

From Baumrind, 1967, pp. 43–88.

The characteristics of the authoritarian, permissive, and authoritative approaches to discipline were summarized by Baumrind (1978) as follows:

> (1) The **authoritarian** parent values obedience as a virtue and favors punitive, forceful measures to curb self-will at points where the child's actions or beliefs conflict with what the parent thinks is right. . . . The authoritarian parent believes in keeping the child in a subordinate role and in restricting his autonomy, and does not encourage verbal give and take, believing that the child should accept a parent's word for what is right. Authoritarian parents may be very concerned and protective or they may be neglecting.
>
> (2) The **permissive** prototype of adult control requires the parent to behave in an affirmative, acceptant, and benign manner towards the child's impulses and actions. The permissive parent sees him- or herself as a resource for the child to use as he wishes but not as an active agent responsible for shaping and altering the child's ongoing and future behavior. The immediate aim of the ideologically aware permissive parent is to free the child from restraint as much as is consistent with survival. Some permissive parents are very protective and loving, while others are self involved and offer freedom as a way of evading responsibility for the child's development.
>
> (3) The **authoritative** parent . . . attempts to direct the child's activities in a rational issue oriented manner. He or she encourages verbal give and take, shares with the child the reasoning behind parental policy, and solicits the child's objections when the child refuses to conform. Both autonomous self-will and discipline conformity are valued by the authoritative parent. Therefore, this parent exerts firm control when the young child disobeys, but does not hem the child in with restrictions. The authoritative parent enforces the adult perspective, but recognizes the child's individual interests and special ways. Such a parent affirms the child's present qualities, but also sets standards for future conduct, using reason as well as power and shaping by regimen and reinforcement to achieve parental objectives. . . .
>
> Authoritative discipline tends to foster in children a particular kind of social competence which is associated with success in Western society. This kind of social competence is called *instrumental competence*. (pp. 224–25)

What are the results of these models of discipline for preschool children? It appears that authoritative parents are most effective in controlling undesirable behavior such as aggression. Authoritarian parents tend to have children who are withdrawn, distrustful, less assertive, and less independent. Children of authoritative parents are more likely to be self-reliant, content, explorative, self-satisfied, and self-controlled. Children of permissive parents tended to be the least self-controlled, self-reliant, and explorative of all three groups (Baumrind, 1978) (see Table 9.2).

Was the impact of the parenting styles limited only to the preschool years or were there long-term effects? Baumrind (1983) followed her sample of families and their children in a longitudinal study through the adolescent years. Authoritarian child rearing had the most negative long-term outcomes for both girls and boys. The boys of authoritarian parents were low in academic performance, social competence, and self-confidence. Children of authoritative parents continued to fare the best, indicating the importance of warmth or responsiveness and firmness in parenting. Children of permissive (indulgent) parents fared somewhat between children of authoritative and authoritarian parents (Baumrind, 1983).

Baumrind's typology of parenting (authoritarian, authoritative, and permissive) includes only three of the four parenting types indicated in Table 9.1. She did not directly discuss the *indifferent-uninvolved pattern*. This type of parent is character-

Effective Ways of Communicating with Children

Dr. Thomas E. Gordon, a clinical psychologist, has developed communication techniques which can be taught to parents for the purpose of improving parent-child interaction. The techniques are described in detail in Dr. Gordon's book, *Parent Effectiveness Training* (1975). The success of the parent training is based, in part, on Gordon's observation that once parents become aware of the destructive power of "put-down" messages, they are eager to learn effective modes of confronting children. Gordon indicates that neither he nor any of his staff have ever encountered a parent who intentionally tried to damage a child's self-esteem.

"You-Messages" and "I-Messages"

One way for parents to understand the difference between effective and ineffective communication is to learn the distinction between "You-messages" and "I-messages." When Gordon and his staff ask parents to think carefully about "put-down" messages, the parents are frequently surprised to find that such messages begin with the word "You" or include that word. Examples of "You-messages" include the following:

"*You* had better stop doing that."
"Why didn't *you* do that?"
"*You* are behaving like a big baby."
"*You* are naughty."
"Why don't *you* try something else?"

In contrast, a parent can learn to simply and honestly tell a child how some unacceptable behavior is making the parent feel by using an "I" message. Such a communication is called an "I-message" because it typically begins with the word "I."

"*I* don't feel like playing with you when I am so tired."
"*I* can't say what I wish when you interrupt me like that."
"*I* can't rest when someone is climbing on my legs."

"*I* get very upset when someone puts their dirty shoes on the couch."

"I-Messages" Are More Effective Than "You-Messages"

According to Gordon, "I-messages" are more effective in parent-child interaction because they promote a healthy, open relationship. In so doing, they are much more successful in influencing the child to control behavior that may be unacceptable to the parent, maladaptive for the child, or both. "I-messages" are effective because they place the responsibility for changing or modifying behavior squarely on the shoulders of the child. For example, when a parent says to a child "I dislike your shouting," not only is the parent openly communicating a feeling but [he or she] is leaving the child with the responsibility for doing something about the situation.

An "I-message" tells a child that you are leaving the responsibility with him, trusting him to handle the situation constructively, trusting him to respect your needs, giving him a chance to start behaving constructively.

Because "I-messages" are honest, they tend to influence a child to send similar feelings *whenever he has a feeling.* "I-messages" from one person in a relationship promote "I-messages" from the other. (p. 118)

Unfortunately, "You-messages" from one person in a relationship tend to promote "You-messages" from the other. Typically, in deteriorating relationships between parents and children, conflicts degenerate into mutual blaming and name-calling.

This is typical of many conversations between parents and children when the parent starts his confrontation with a "You-message." Invariably, they end up in a struggle. . . . (p. 118)

Based on Gordon, 1975, pp. 115–19.

Training Parents to Be Authoritative

Gerald Patterson (1980, 1982, 1983) and his associates have, over the course of ten years of research, identified a number of family processes that they regard as central to family malfunctioning in the parenting role. Specifically, such families are more likely than better-functioning families to be involved in a vicious circle in which *parent* or *mother irritability* produces *both maladaptive child behavior* (such as aggression) and related "explosions" or *crises* in the family, both of which, in turn, create more mother irritability, and so on. Mother irritability leads to *disrupted problem solving*, which further aggravates the situation. Patterson (1983) refers to these processes that characterize poorly functioning families as the *irritability cycle.*

What can be done to alleviate such familial malfunctioning and to change patterns of family interaction? A central problem for malfunctioning families is child aggression and the failure to comply with parental requests. Patterson has designed family treatment programs for the purpose of helping parents overcome such problems. Such child management programs have the following characteristics:

• *Clear understandings of acceptable and unacceptable behavior are established.*
• *Child behavior is observed* so that the degree or amount of compliance and noncompliance with parent expectations can be readily determined (for a given time period).
• *Contingencies for such compliance or noncompliance are determined* (i.e., the situational circumstances or parent behaviors that appear to be associated with

or are contingent with child noncompliance or compliance). For example, some parents of aggressive children engage in what Patterson calls "sibling parenting." That is, parents respond to child aggression or other negative behaviors as if they were children themselves. They become drawn into bickering, yelling, or complaining behaviors that serve to create similar responses in the child and to divert parent attention away from their primary socialization responsibility. Patterson (1983) encourages parents to focus on their socialization role and adopt a more dispassionate or less emotional emphasis (e.g., withdrawal of privilege if children fail to comply).

• *The positive consequences of acceptable or prosocial child behavior* are stressed. Patterson emphasizes that in many distressed families parents praise their children or demonstrate affection more commonly as the result of the parent's *mood* than as the result of the child's behavior. That is, in such families positive parent behavior toward children is less associated with what the child does than with how the parent *feels* at a given moment in time. Patterson suggests that this may be one of the reasons that such children appear insensitive to social or parent approval. Therefore, a goal of the child management program is to re-establish the relationship between positive child behavior and parent affection, approval, and tangible rewards. Once the parents have learned how to establish a positive relationship with their children, they can much more effectively serve as positive socializing agents.

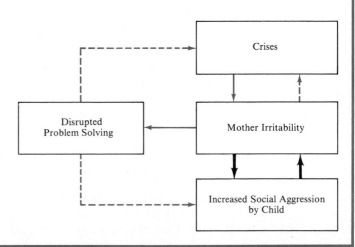

*A triad of variables for the coercion process. *Dotted lines refer to correlations of about .25 to .35, thin lines to correlations of about .36 to .50, and thick lines to correlations of over .51. From Patterson, 1983, p. 259.*

ized by being undemanding (low on attempts to control the child) and rejecting (unresponsive, uninvolved, parent-centered, and so on). Such parents appear motivated to minimize the effort and time involved in child rearing (Maccoby and Martin, 1983). With preschool and older children, indifferent-uninvolved parents may not monitor their children's activities sufficiently to know what they are doing or who they are with. Furthermore, there is some evidence that such parental detachment is associated with depression in the mother (Egeland and Stroufe, 1981). Depressed mothers may be incapable of effectively responding to their children's needs. Such parental detachment is associated with negative child behaviors such as low self-esteem, aggression, noncompliance, and moodiness (Martin, 1981; Maccoby and Martin, 1983).

THE EVOLUTION OF PARENT DISCIPLINARY STYLES.   Although parent disciplinary styles do appear to have consequences, it is not likely that this is a simple one-way effect. It is certainly likely that the parents of more competent and mature children have an easier time being democratic, authoritative, or moderate in their disciplinary practices than parents of less mature or difficult children. To be sure, the role of child temperament is an inevitable part of the success of parent disciplinary styles (Lewis, 1981a; Lerner and Lerner, 1986). In addition, there is evidence that as children get older, parents change their disciplinary techniques and, likewise, children also appear to change in their willingness to conform to parental requests. In a study by Barry McLaughlin (1983), it was found that parental ability to directly control child behavior diminished, whereas children's compliance with indirect suggestions increased as children moved from 1½ to 3½ years of age. That is, the 3½-year-olds in the study were more likely to comply with parents that were more *indirect* than *direct*. For example, the indirect request—"Why don't you pick up the toy?"—was much more successful in gaining the 3½-year-old's compliance than the direct statement, "Pick up the toy!"

CRITERIA FOR EFFECTIVE DISCIPLINE.   In light of the joint contribution of both parents and child to the success of preschool disciplinary practices, Ross D. Parke (1977) has suggested the following five criteria for effective discipline:

- *Promptness.* The less time between a child's act of misbehavior and the parent's response, the better.
- *Moderate punishment.* If punishment is necessary, it should be neither so lenient as to be insignificant to the child nor so severe as to be overwhelming to the child.
- *Discipline from a person on good terms with the child.* Discipline from a person who is typically warm and affectionate to the child will be more noticeable and meaningful to the child than discipline from someone who is typically grumpy or frequently scolds the child.
- *Explanation with discipline.* According to Parke, this may be the most important criterion of all. Through the explanation the child comes to realize that discipline is not a purely arbitrary or ill-conceived gesture. Rather, there are reasons for parental rules or requests. Furthermore, the explanations should be conveyed to children, as much as possible, at their level.
- *Consistent punishment.* According to Parke, inconsistency should be avoided. Children should realize that an appropriate punishment will be administered whenever a particular misbehavior occurs. Furthermore, Parke suggests that the most reasonable position for parents is to discipline on the important issues rather than trying to discipline for all possible child misbehavior.

Parental Control Techniques

In a study by Barry McLaughlin (1983), the mothers and fathers of twenty-four children age one and one half, two and one half, and three and one half were videotaped in a free-play situation in their home. The purpose of the study was to investigate differences in the way both parents achieved child compliance with the verbal requests of the parents. It is a common observation, as well as a verified finding, that adults are increasingly able to verbally regulate child behavior as the child grows older (Schaffer and Crook, 1980). The McLaughlin study tested this finding and observation in a more *ecologically valid* setting than previous studies (Schaffer and Crook, 1980). Whereas prior studies had usually examined parent control techniques in a laboratory setting in laboratory-directed circumstances, the McLaughlin study videotaped children and parents interacting together in a free-play situation in their own home. Furthermore, McLaughlin examined both mother-child and father-child interaction. (Schaffer and Crook had only looked at mother-child interaction.)

Using the videotape recordings and transcripts of parent-child interaction, an analysis was made of the *type* and *frequency* of parental control attempts aimed at the child and the *compliance* of the child. Parental control statements were those judged to be directed by the parent at modifying the child's ongoing behavior. For example, a parent's request to the child to "Please close the door" would be considered a control utterance. Parental control statements were divided on the basis of three categories:

1. *Grammatical structure controls* (parental *questions* such as "Why didn't you change the record?" or *imperative* statements or forceful commands such as "Open the toy box lid!").
2. *Directive or prohibitive controls* (directive statements that prescribe some behavior that should be performed by the child or a prohibitive statement designed to prevent or terminate a given child behavior, such as "Stop playing with the hammer or you will break the glass").
3. *Action or attention controls* (direct *action* by the parent to restrain, hold, or otherwise control the motor activity or movements of the child; parental attempts to gain or modify the *attention* or perceptual activity of the child, such as "Look at me" or "Listen to what I have to say").

The compliance of child-to-parental control attempts was measured in two ways: (1) *attention compliance*, or the success of the parent in directing the child's attention to a specific object or circumstance, and (2) *action compliance*, or the parent's success in getting the child to carry out a verbal request.

The results of the study follow:

1. There were *few differences between mothers and fathers in the type or the frequency of control directives.* There was no evidence that either fathers or mothers were more controlling than the other parent. Also, there was no evidence that parents were more controlling in interactions with either the same-sexed child or with the opposite-sexed child.
2. The majority of control statements by both parents were *directive* rather than *prohibitive*. In other words, most of the parents in the study regulated their child's behavior by explaining what they *should do* rather than telling them what they *should not do*. This was the case for both boys and girls and for all ages of children.
3. Children complied equally to both fathers and mothers. Thus, there was no evidence that children comply more with fathers than with mothers, as is sometimes believed.
4. All children shared greater compliance to *attention* controls ("Listen to me") than to parental *action* controls.
5. Direct imperative controls ("Move to the side immediately!") were more effective with one and one-half-year-olds than with three and one-half-year-olds. Likewise, indirect suggestions or questions ("If you moved to the side, maybe you could see the goldfish better") were more effective in gaining the compliance of three and one-half-year-olds than one and one-half-year-olds. This finding supports the contention that both the maturation of children and the change in parental disciplinary postures contribute to the success of discipline in young children.

Based on McLaughlin, 1983, pp. 667–73.

The Neighborhood/Community and Preschooler Development

Although the family is undoubtedly a vital context for the developing child, there is another, more global context in which the family and the child are merged—the neighborhood and the community. Every child develops, matures, and grows in some type of community and lives in some type of shelter. Children's understanding of their communities, neighborhoods, and housing spaces comes about gradually. Leon Pastalon (1977) described the emergence of this understanding as follows:

> as a child develops physically and intellectually his home range begins to expand. For instance, the child begins to make sense out of his surroundings. . . . He begins to sort out the various arrangements of objects and spaces that he can see and relate to. As soon as the child begins to develop his ability to walk, his home range expands even further, going beyond the crib, his nursery, out into the other rooms of the house, and soon the child is exploring not only spaces within the dwelling unit but outside as well and begins to sort out and respond to his immediate areas outside the dwelling unit. Then as he increases in age and development he continues to expand his home range until he reaches maturity where he has almost an unlimited home range in the sense that there can be a large number of spaces, objects, and people with sensed relationships that he experiences.

Community and Neighborhood: An Ecological Perspective

People use the term *community* in many ways including the development of a "sense of community" or fellowship. Our concern in the study of human development is, however, with the idea of a territory-based place in which such relationships might occur (Anderson and Carter, 1978).

A recent characterization of community is in terms of the following functions:

- Mutual support.
- The socialization of children.
- Economic production and consumption (Garbarino, 1982a, p. 23.).

According to this approach, a community has both social and economic functions.

DIRECT AND INDIRECT INFLUENCES.   Based on these functions and characteristics, the community can exert a strong influence on the quality of life for families living in it and, therefore, on the quality of child and human development. The ecological or systems perspective used in this book allows us to understand more fully the impact of the community on the family environment at both direct and indirect levels (Garbarino, 1982a; Bronfenbrenner, 1986; see also the discussion of systems theory in Chapter 2).

1. *Direct influence of community on the family and human development*. The community may have an effect on the **microsystem** of family dynamics and interaction. For example, a disturbance in the economic resources of a community, such as

the closing of a factory, could have an impact on the rate of violence in families (Strauss, Gelles, and Steinmetz, 1980; Steinberg, Catalano, and Dooley, 1981).

2. *Indirect influence of the community on the family and human development.* The ecological perspective helps us to appreciate the ways that the community indirectly influences families and development by influencing the *interaction between microsystems.* For example, the school and family as microsystems interact to influence the quality of the child's education. These relationship patterns between microsystems are called **mesosystems** (see Chapter 3). Mesosystems have an important role in influencing the daily lives of children and adults in families. That is, the quality or the richness of the mesosystems for the developing human being is indicated or measured by the *number* and *quality* of the connections or *linkages* between microsystems. If we use the example of the interaction of the home and school, then we can make some estimate about a child's likelihood of success or achievement in school based on the linkages between the school and the home. If the participation of people (e.g., parents/caretakers and teachers), other than the child, in both settings supports the similarity between the two settings, then the child's academic success is more likely.

> The central principle here is that the stronger and more diverse the links between settings, the more powerful the resulting mesosystem will be as an influence on the child's development (Garbarino, 1982a, p. 23).

EXOSYSTEMS AND PRESCHOOLER DEVELOPMENT. Another way of examining the indirect impact of the community is the consideration of **exosystems** (the formal and informal institutions such as political/governmental structures, neighborhood and community organization, transportation networks, and the informal communication networks within neighborhoods, communities, and workplaces) (see Chapter 3). That is, how is the family treated by the institutions of a community? For example, are employers aware of and responsive to the needs of families and children for day-care services (Garbarino, 1980)? Is the local government sensitive to the needs of families and children through tax policies and zoning regulations (Garbarino and Plantz, 1980)?

Still another source of indirect community effects on families and developing individuals is through the **macrosystem,** or the broad ideological or value patterns of a particular culture.

> Macrosystems are the "blueprints" for the ecology of human development. These blueprints reflect a people's shared assumptions about "how things should be done" (Garbarino, 1982a, p. 24).

The organization or institutional arrangements of a specific community can be viewed as the embodiment or the "carrying out" of the ideologies, beliefs, or values of the macrosystem. For example, communities having ethics or values that are opposed to child abuse or other forms of domestic violence are more likely to have reduced rates of such violence compared with communities that appear to allow or tolerate such violence (Garbarino, 1977).

Whereas the term *community* refers to a broad range of general and very specific relationships, the term *neighborhood* is used to refer to a part of the community. The *neighborhood* is the specific setting or place where parents interact with their children, as well as with other people. Children are also participants in the neighborhood and are typically given the freedom to interact with other people in the neighborhood (particularly with other children) independently of parents or caretakers. The quality of support and feedback given to the family through neighborhood relationships also has an influence on human development in the family context.

Examining Communities and Neighborhoods

Reasons to examine the neighborhood and the community as contexts of human development include these:

1. The neighborhood and community provide the major setting in which the child organizes free or unstructured time. Most outdoor play occurs in the neighborhood.
2. The neighborhood and community are a setting where certain activities are more likely or less likely to occur. For example, urban children can probably play with several age-mates in the immediate vicinity of their homes. A child in a rural setting might have to be driven several miles to play with the nearest peer.
3. The neighborhood may provide a broader or a more limited set of experiences for the child's socialization and development. For example, some neighborhoods contain a diverse range of people with varying occupations, income, social class, and racial or ethnic background. Other neighborhoods provide much less variety.

THE NEIGHBORHOOD.   In our discussion of the role of the neighborhood and the community in the development of the child, we focus on the urban environment. More than 70 percent of the population of the United States lives in cities or suburbs (compared with 6 percent in 1800). A number of features of city life affect child development.

Stress. The urban neighborhood (particularly the inner-city neighborhood) is thought to be contaminated by noise, polluted air, and various levels of congestion occasioned by many people. The density of inner-city neighborhoods has been blamed for creating special conditions that make it an unhealthy and stressful environment (Rutter, 1981a; Garmezy and Rutter, 1983).

Sociability and a Sense of Community. Although we may think of large cities as made up of large numbers of anonymous people, this stereotypical characterization is not always correct. On the contrary, sections of large cities provide inhabitants with a sense of identity based on territory or place. In fact, many of the satisfactions of living in an urban neighborhood or community have to do with the individual child's or adult's perception and use of both the social and the physical "spaces" provided in the neighborhood (Ittelson et al., 1974).

The Overloaded Environment. It has been suggested that one of the factors that may be at the root of the crowding problem is the *overloaded environment*. The large city is usually in a state of constant change. Much is happening and many people are congregating in a rather limited space. When the total amount of what is happening (including the number of people present) exceeds the individual's capacity to deal with all of it, the condition of overload exists. To conserve energy, the individual develops "priorities" that may force him or her to avoid all but superficial relationships. In other words, a "people overload" may result in a "turning off" or a withdrawal from social relationships.

The depersonalization and routinization of human relationships and activities in large cities affect the environment for families and for child rearing. This problem of depersonalization has been summarized as follows:

The concept of overload helps to explain a wide variety of contrasts between city and town behaviors: (1) The differences in "role enactment" (the urban tendency to deal with one another in highly segmented, functional terms; the constricted time and services offered customers by sales personnel); (2) The evolution of "urban norms" quite different from traditional town values (such as the acceptance of noninvolvement, impersonality and aloofness in urban life); (3) The adaptation of the urban-dweller's "cognitive processes" (his inability to identify most of the people seen daily; his screening of sensory stimuli; his development of blasé attitudes toward deviant or bizarre behavior; and his selectivity in responding to human demand); and (4) The far greater competition for scarce "facilities" in the city (the subway rush; the fight for taxis; traffic jams; standing in lines to await services). I would suggest that contrasts between city and rural behavior probably reflect the responses of similar people to very different situations, rather than intrinsic differences between rural personalities and city personalities. The city is a situation to which individuals respond adaptively. (Milgram, 1970, p. 1465)

▪ SCENARIO: THE PRIVILEGED POOR

I was raised in a section of New York that was called a slum by sightseeing guides and a depressed area by sociologists. Both were right. Our neighborhood fulfilled all the sordid requirements with honors. We were unquestionably above average in squalid tenements, putrid poolrooms, stenchy saloons, cold flats, hot roofs, dirty streets and flying garbage. Yet, paradoxically, I never felt depressed or deprived. My environment was miserable; I was not.

I was a fortunate child. Ours was a home rich enough in family harmony and love to immunize eight kids against the potentially toxic effects of the environment beyond our door. Since the social scientists do not, as far as I know, have a clinical name for the fortunate possessors of this kind of emotional security, I might suggest they label them "the privileged poor."

From Levenson, 1966, p. 12.

HOUSING AND SPACE.   Although the overall organization of neighborhoods and streets is an important aspect of the growing child's environment, the nature of the child's housing is also important in several ways. As in the case of crowding and social or physical ills, the relationship between housing and such factors as stress is again not a simple cause-effect relationship. Human beings have different levels of tolerance of stress as well as individualized strategies for handling it. Therefore, dilapidated slum dwellings are not necessarily more stressful than comfortable suburban homes. Stress in family members may result from coping with features of slum dwellings such as lack of sanitary facilities, inadequate space, lack of privacy, and the inadequacy of household design for raising children. On the other hand, the suburban home that has a large number of appliances and rooms to clean and organize could well be as stressful as a slum dwelling (Ittelson et al., 1974).

Again, the relationship between physical dilapidation and "social dilapidation" is not a simple one. It appears that subjective elements such as the kind of neighbors one has and the friendship relationships that have been developed are far more important than more objective measures of physical inconvenience or difficulty. People in slum areas tend to have many friends and to be involved in the social life of their neighborhoods. In an interesting study, Rossi (1955) found that of four urban areas, one area that rated very low on an objective assessment of physical quality, ranked the highest on subjective satisfaction.

In addition to the influence of housing space on child development, the spatial arrangements in the preschool need to be considered. In fact, most of the observational studies of the impact of crowding on preschool children have been done in the preschool setting. In a study of three- and four-year-old children, increases in the number of children present and reduction in the size of the classroom and number of toys available had little, if any, impact on undesirable types of behavior, such as aggression, up to a point (Smith and Connolly, 1981). Under conditions of extreme crowding (less than fifteen square feet for each child) or severely limited numbers of toys, aggression did increase. Other studies have found the critical point at which aggression begins is less than twenty-five square feet per child (Clarke-Stewart, 1982).

THE MEANING OF THE NEIGHBORHOOD.   As the preschool child ventures forth out of the house and into the immediate surroundings of the home, he or she begins to recognize the boundaries of the neighborhood in a very general sense. The preschooler comes to recognize such things as "my house," "my driveway," and "my street." Although he or she may recognize these general features, the preschooler also tends to estimate distances inaccurately. A distance of 200 miles to a grandmother's house may seem closer than it really is. The preschooler tends to view the things in the neighborhood as larger than they really are. Streets, alleys, houses, and fences seem much larger from the viewpoint of one who must look up to most people and things.

Play Settings. Play occupies a considerable amount of the preschooler's waking hours. The environments in which play occurs are of two major types: (1) planned play settings for children (e.g., playgrounds) and (2) unplanned play areas (neighborhood and household areas that promote play behavior although they were not originally designed for that purpose). Play in planned play areas usually accounts for a small part of the child's total play experience. Most play occurs during the unplanned daily agenda of the preschooler, for example, while walking in the house or running outside.

Two important criteria for evaluating play settings are availability and responsiveness. *Availability* refers to the relative ease with which the child can get to the play setting. *Responsiveness* refers to whether or not the play setting (and the objects or equipment located there) can engage or involve the child. Responsive play settings have the potential through diversity of design to meet a broad range of the needs of individual children. The opportunities available to children vary considerably in terms of geographic location (e.g., urban or rural) and family socioeconomic status. The child in an inner-city slum area has available a different kind of play environment than a preschooler from a suburban middle-class neighborhood or a child from a rural area. Each of these children has play settings that have limitations as well as strengths.

Although both availability and responsiveness are important characteristics for play settings, they are not always present. For example, although planned play spaces in urban areas may be more available in suburban middle-class neighborhoods, they may be somewhat less responsive than the informal collection of varied objects and assorted "junk" that might characterize inner-city slum areas. Children in suburban middle-class neighborhoods are often encouraged to stay in their nicely landscaped yards, which are usually supplied with toys and equipment. Unfortunately, much of this equipment may be unresponsive, thus discouraging exploration and creativity. On the other hand, inner-city neighborhoods may have a much larger collection of potentially "responsive" objects and materials and fewer organized and planned play areas. Unfortunately many of the responsive objects in inner-city neighborhoods may be potentially dangerous to the child (e.g., boards with exposed nails). Recognition by urban planners of the limitations of available and planned play spaces in urban areas has led to the creation of the so-called adventure or junk playground. Adventure playgrounds provide the opportunity for the child to deal with responsive play objects such as sand, scrap metal, wood, and rubber tires at the level of complexity that he or she is ready for. The adventure playground, in fact, simulates the elements of street play in the inner-city neighborhood and the "vacant lot" of previous generations.

How often do children really use planned playground facilities? Preschoolers appear to use planned play facilities more frequently than school-age children. However, most planned play facilities are largely unused, particularly after the child reaches the age of six or seven (Campbell and Frost, 1978). By the time children reach school age, they appear to blend their play into the adult world of the neighborhood. There is some evidence that the use of play areas varies as a function of the design of the play setting (Hayward, Rothenberg, and Beasley, 1974; Campbell and Frost, 1978). Three different types of play settings were studied (see Fig. 9.5) (Hayward, Rothenberg, and Beasley, 1974):

Darryl Jacobson

David Kostelnik

FIGURE 9.5
Three types of playground.

David Kostelnik

1. The **traditional play setting.** This setting includes equipment such as slides, swings, see-saws, or a sandbox.

2. The **designed play setting.** This setting includes traditional activities such as swings and slides that are integrated into a continuous sculptured pattern with sand commonly used as a base.

3. The **adventure (or "junk") play setting.** In this setting, children "create" their own play equipment from objects such as old tires, lumber and used packing crates, rocks, and bricks.

The general conclusion of the study is that the play environment was instrumental in determining the use of a play setting. In other words, the amount of time spent by a child in a given play area, as well as the type of activity that occurred, was a function of the *opportunities* provided in the play setting. Some play settings had more "potential" for generating creative and sustained interest than others.

Play Materials. In addition, play materials also appear to have effects on the types of activities in which young children engage. The following effects have been noted (Clarke-Stewart, 1982; Minuchin and Shapiro, 1983):

- Outdoor playground equipment frequently leads to large motor skill activities, such as rough-and-tumble play, running, and climbing.
- When children play outdoors, their games tend to be longer and more complex than indoor games.
- Outdoor play elicits more cooperative, more mature, and less aggressive activities than indoor play.
- Indoor play elicits more social and communicative interaction than outdoor play.
- Materials such as boards, blocks, sand, clay, and dress-up clothes promote more creative and experimental play than toys that have a clear function (guns, microscopes, telephones).
- Sandbox activities, books, and art projects appear to hold young children's attention longer than other play activities.
- The play activities that prompt the most child aggression include block play, playing house, and climbing. However, conflict and aggression can occur at any time when children can exclude one another from play activities.

The Peer Group and Preschooler Development

Increasingly, the important role of individuals outside the family in the development of children has been acknowledged. As more mothers of young children enter the work force and as more young children are placed in some type of daycare or preschool program, the role of peers in early child development is receiving increasing attention.

As we have seen, the family makes a substantial contribution to the developing child. The role of peers, however, is different from that of family members. Family relationships are more lasting and intense; peer relationships are less enduring and more egalitarian.

The Developmental Course of Peer Relationships

During the first two years of life the infant and the toddler usually play with family members. As the child matures, interaction expands to include other children in the neighborhood or, perhaps, in the setting of a preschool program. These early childhood years mark the beginnings of the first real peer group. The first signs of a shifting dependency pattern from parents to peers emerge during these years. The preschooler may seek approval from peers as well as asking them for assistance. This trend increases until adolescence, when dependence on peers is usually greater than dependence on parents.

INFANCY AND TODDLERHOOD. For many children, peer relationships begin as early as the first year of life. Evidence indicates that approximately 50 percent of American babies six to twelve months of age have contact with other babies at least once a week (Vandell and Mueller, 1980). Babies appear to be responsive to one another as early as the first year of life. With the onset of crawling, babies who are in close proximity may follow one another. Older infants may engage in mutual exploration of mouths, ears, and eyes (Vandell and Mueller, 1980). It is likely that these early infant behaviors are not truly social since there is no indication that one infant actually expects or seeks a response from the other infant. However, by the second half of the first year of life, what appear to be truly social interactions begin to emerge (Hay, Pedersen, and Nash, 1982). That is, interactive behavior between infants is more intentional and mutually responsive as they respond more to the signals of each other (Jacobson, 1981). Furthermore, there is some evidence that infants who interact more frequently with other infants tend to be more social than infants who have more limited interactive opportunities (Vandell and Wilson, 1982).

Throughout the first two years of life, there is evidence of a movement from solitary activity or **solitary play** (i.e., the infant playing alone with toys or objects) to social activity or **social play** (i.e., the infant and other people interacting with objects and/or with one another) (Eckerman, Whatley, and Kutz, 1975) (see Fig. 9.6).

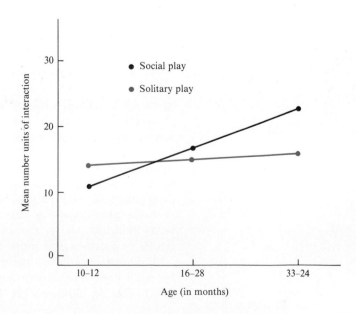

FIGURE 9.6

The movement from solitary play during the first two years of life. From Eckerman, Whatley, and Kutz, 1975, pp. 42–49.

As infants move into the second year of life, there is evidence that infant-infant interactions follow a pattern, as follows (Mueller and Vandell, 1979):

- *Object-center phase.* Infants interact together; however, the focus of attention is typically on an object or toy rather than each other.
- *Simple interactive phase.* Infants interact with one another while apparently trying to influence the behavior of the other (e.g., an infant who waves at another infant and evokes laughter repeats the action again getting a similar response).
- *Complementary interactive phase.* In this phase the social interactions become more complex. *Reciprocal* or *mutual interaction* becomes more common (Eckerman and Stein, 1982). In other words, infants attempt to influence one another's behaviors as they engage in a mutual activity (e.g., one infant handing a toy to another infant as both adjust their movements in such a way as to anticipate the response of the other). In addition, the infant interactions in this phase are more likely to be accompanied by demonstrations of emotional responses (laughing, smiling, crying, and so on). There is an increase in the expression of *both* positive and negative emotions accompanying interactive sequences (Mueller and Vandell, 1979). For example, fighting, biting, and hitting as well as smiling or laughing is not uncommonly associated with peer interactions in the second year.

Social interaction during this phase is also characterized by a preference for playing with peers over adults (even one's mother) (Eckerman, Whatley, and Kutz, 1975). Furthermore, infant-infant interactions are characterized by more equal participation of both parties (Vandell and Wilson, 1982). On the other hand, mother-infant interactions are longer in duration, but mothers tend to dominate the interaction (respond more than the infants and work harder to sustain the relationship).

Throughout the preschool years, peer interactions continue to increase. Furthermore, in a study of children (infancy to twelve years) in both the home and neighborhood settings, time spent with adults decreases and time spent with peers increases (Ellis, Rogoff, and Cromer, 1981) (see Fig. 9.7).

THE PRESCHOOL YEARS. For the most part, preschooler peer relationships have been examined in the context of nursery schools or day-care centers. Studies of relationships between preschoolers and their peers have rarely been done in the home setting. Several trends have been noted:

1. *Preschoolers tend to abandon the more immature or inefficient social behavior of toddlerhood while expanding their repertoire of more mature social actions.* For example, in nursery school settings, preschool children more frequently talk, play, and smile/laugh with peers than do younger children. On the other hand, toddlers more frequently cry, watch (rather than interact with) other children, and orient toward the teacher (Hartup, 1983). In addition, there is evidence that mutual social interactions are more complex for preschool than for younger children (Shatz, 1983). This is particularly seen in such behaviors as speaker-listener accommodations and collaborative problem solving.

2. *Increased sociability* appears to be a major accomplishment of the preschool years (Hartup, 1983). For example, bids for attention are directed less toward adults or teachers and more toward peers than is the case for toddlers.

3. *Even though more time is spent in peer interactions in the preschool years than in the toddler years, solitary or noninteractive contacts do not appear to diminish* (Hartup, 1983). That is, although preschool children may spend more time in social-inter-

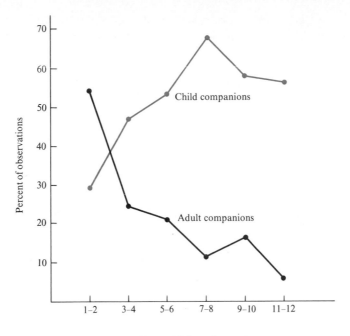

FIGURE 9.7

Changes in child interactions with adults and with peers. From Ellis, Rogoff, and Cromer, 1981, pp. 399–407.

Increased sociability appears to be a major accomplishment of the preschool years.

The preschooler begins to move into a larger world of interpersonal relationships.

active relationships (talking, communicative play) than toddlers, their level of solitary activity and noninteractive or parallel play (play in which two or more children simultaneously use similar toys but do not interact with each other) does not decline. These solitary or noninteractive contacts remain at relatively constant levels throughout the period from two to six years (Tieszen, 1979; Hartup, 1983). As Hartup suggests, "Preschool children spend considerable amounts of time by themselves or in noninteractive contact with other children" (1983, p. 117).

Play

One of the most important settings for the peer relationships described above is play. In fact, children spend more time playing with their peers outside of school than in any other activity.

WHAT IS PLAY? Play is not easy to define. As a matter of fact, it is probably easier to define what play is *not* than what it is. That is, play is not routine, nor is it work. For our purposes, we define **play** as a nonserious activity that is engaged in for itself or simply for the satisfaction that results. Other descriptive characteristics of play are often cited in a definition of play (Rubin, Fein, and Vandenberg, 1983; Yawkey and Pellegrini, 1984; Johnson, Christie, and Yawkey, 1987).

1. Play is enjoyable and pleasurable.
2. Play has no extrinsic purpose or external goals. (The motivation to play is intrinsic or internal and serves no particular end except, perhaps, enjoyment for its own sake.)
3. Play is undertaken *spontaneously* and *voluntarily*.
4. Play involves active participation on the part of the child.
5. Play is related in a coordinated way *to other aspects of development* (creativity, problem solving, language learning, motor activity, development of social roles).

In summary, play enlarges the child's understanding of the world in which he or she lives. Play allows the child to explore objects, social roles, language, and feelings without serious risk. In play situations, the child is free to choose an activity without regard to its consequences or to the achievement of a particular goal. Play is certainly behavior, but with two important qualifications (Rubin, Fein, and Vandenberg, 1983):

1. Play does not have any behavioral patterns that are unique to it; rather, the behaviors of play are all borrowed from other domains (e.g., movement or language).
2. Play behavior (e.g., simulated aggression in a play situation) is "buffered" from the normal consequences associated with the behavior.

THE FUNCTIONS OF PLAY.   What purposes does play serve in the development of the preschool child?

- In the first place, *play facilitates cognitive development* (Rubin, Fein, and Vandenberg, 1983). That is, play allows the preschool child to explore the environment, to become familiar with objects and people in their surroundings, and to solve problems.
- *Play facilitates social development.* Since play may involve people as well as objects or toys, it provides an opportunity for the preschooler to learn how to work with people. Furthermore, pretend play allows the child to learn about adult social and occupational roles.
- *Play allows children to deal with emotional concerns in a safe and nonthreatening way* (see box). For example, there is evidence that pretend or fantasy play may be used by children as a way of identifying, rehearsing, and managing fears. John Gottman (1985) cited one instance of a four-year-old girl who was afraid of the dark and required a nightlight. In a pretend game, the girl-as-mother calmed and reassured a fearful doll who represented the girl. "After a few months, she announced to her parents that she no longer needed the night light, and the theme of being afraid of the dark disappeared from her fantasy play . . . the girl and the doll were cured" (pp. 26–27).

THE DEVELOPMENTAL PROGRESSION OF PLAY.   The contributions of play to child development discussed above can be understood in relation to the developmental progression of play. According to Jean Piaget (1962), the development of play has three stages, as follows (see Fig. 9.8):

- **Sensorimotor (or practice) play.** Sensorimotor play extends from birth through the second year of life. The child acquires and exercises control over his or her movements and learns to coordinate these movements and their effects.

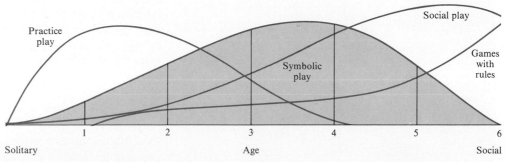

FIGURE 9.8
The developmental progression of play. Based on Piaget, 1962.

The Meaning of Dramatic Play

Dramatic play consists of activities that are imitative or representational, in which the child assumes the roles of people whom [he/she] knows as [he/she] understands their roles. It may also involve activities in which the child tries to communicate thoughts and feelings symbolically through the use of objects or actions. Dramatic play may be carried on by a child alone or by several children together, in which case it becomes sociodramatic play.

There are many reasons why children play. They play because it gives them pleasure. . . . They play because they have an urge to explore and discover. . . . The preschool child is absorbed as he pours water into the sand, watching how it runs down the channels he has dug. Children also play because of an urge to master a skill or solve a problem. A toddler will return again and again to a stairway, climbing up and coming down until he does it easily. Another child will persist in riding a tricycle until he rides with skill. Children play to make friends for it is one important way that young children form relationships with one another. Play also

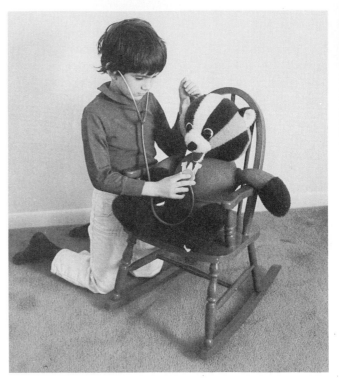

serves as a means of mastering the emotional problems that inevitably come with growth. It is essentially creative, involving all the child's capacities. Play leads to the integration of personality.

Dramatic play may occur as part of any activity. It is most likely to occur when children are playing together, trying to understand and make sense out of what they see and hear, and mastering feelings of fear, anxiety, or anger. . . . [E]very child has feelings which he needs to drain off. Children have many fears—the fear of being left or deserted, the fear of being little and helpless, or of being hurt, and sometimes the fear of their own violent impulses. As we watch children at play, we observe how often they take the role of the one who goes away and leaves or the one who punishes or controls. By reversing roles in play the child restores [his/her] own confidence.

In dramatic play children often act out aggressive, destructive feelings. It is important to accept them in play, being sure only that the children are safe and that the impulses are under control and kept on the pretend level.

From Read and Patterson, 1980, pp. 231–33.

An important step in socialization is learning to interact through play.

Play during this stage often takes the form of motor behaviors that are repeated and varied. According to Piaget, the infant derives pleasure simply from the experience of seeing, hearing, touching, and holding. In addition, the infant seems to enjoy making things happen.

- **Symbolic (or pretend) play.** This stage of play extends from two to six years of age. The child begins to organize play with symbols, and *pretending* becomes a common play mode (e.g., holding a stick against the back of a toy car and pretending that the car is at a gasoline station and is being filled with gasoline). By age six or seven, symbolic play declines as children become more interested in *games-with-rules*.
- **Games-with-rules.** These games ordinarily start at the beginning of the school years. The child becomes interested in structural games that involve the social concepts of cooperation and/or competition.

Over each of these three stages, there is an increase in *social play* (i.e., play involving interaction or cooperation between two or more children) (Fig. 9.8). Initially, in the sensorimotor (practice) stage, play is solitary (a child may play alone with an object or toy, or two children may each play with a toy in close proximity to one another with little or no interaction). However, by the time of symbolic play, the amount of social cooperation, turn taking, and give-and-take increases dramatically. At the stage of games-with-rules, most play is social (Fig. 9.8).

TYPES OF PLAY.   Another way to view play is to focus on the activities, materials, or resources involved in the various types of play (Rubin, Fein, and Vandenberg, 1983).

- *Play as Motion and Interaction.* Motion or the sensation of movement is probably the first play experience that adults provide for infants. As the infant learns to control its own movements, the joy and pleasure of play as body movement comes under the infant's own control.
- An important step in normal socialization is learning to interact—and play— with others, including adults and peers. Playing with other children is different from playing with adults and objects in two ways: (1) other children are less predictable, and (2) other children are less subject to control. As might be expected, a two-year-old child has much to learn about sustaining successful play interaction with peers. The social skills of the two-year-old are largely organized in terms of mutually *predictive relationships* with adults and/or objects (Eckerman, Whatley, and Kutz, 1975). Infants and toddlers appear to be more interested in objects and toys than in other children. Although they may be

attracted to other toddlers, they sometimes find these relationships erratic and threatening. About half of these peer encounters end in minor struggles (Rubin, Fein, and Vandenberg, 1983).

Another category of motion-interaction play is sometimes called *rough-and-tumble play,* a term that refers to a number of behavior or action patterns performed by a group at a high level of activity. For example, rough-and-tumble may include any of the following sample *cluster* behaviors: running, hopping, chasing, falling over one another, fleeing, wrestling, and laughing. These playful group interchanges are frequently observed among preschool children and, in particular, during outdoor free-play sessions in nursery schools. In nursery school settings, rough-and-tumble activities are usually organized according to sex. Toddlers probably spend more time watching than actually participating, a form of exploration that precedes actual involvement (Rubin, Fein, and Vandenberg, 1983).

- *Play with Objects.* Interaction with objects in the environment (e.g., toys), constitutes a large part of the play experiences of the toddler and the preschool child. Toys are objects designed by adults to elicit the interest of the child. As might be expected, most of the other objects in the home and the neighborhood are probably at least as interesting.

How does object play begin? The following pattern describes the progression of object play (Garvey, 1977):

■   *Nine months.* The child grasps objects that are close to him or her and brings them to his or her mouth. After the object has been brought to the mouth, the child may wave it about and bang the object. Action patterns are rather limited.

Twelve months. The child is likely to manipulate, investigate, or examine the object *before* doing anything with it.

Fifteen months. Investigative behaviors clearly occur before the child does anything else with an object. In addition, objects begin to be treated in accordance with their typical or conventional uses (e.g., a cup may be placed in a saucer, or the child may pick up a brush and put it in his or her hair).

Twenty-one months. The child now begins to search for objects that normally go with other things. For example, the child may look for a spoon or a fork to go with a cup and saucer with which he or she is playing.

Thirty to thirty-six months. The child's play has become considerably more realistic. For example, dolls sit at tables and are made to pick up and drink from glasses; dishes may be washed after the "dinner"; and the dolls may wipe their mouths with napkins.

Throughout childhood, objects provide a basis for the initiation of play and for promoting social contacts. For example, when a young child encounters a novel object for the first time, there is a progression of activity leading from discovery and exploration to imaginative and playful use of the object.

- *Play with Social Materials (Dramatic or Pretend Play).* The principal resources of play with social materials are social expectations and social roles. When recognizable roles or characters are involved, this type of play is referred to as *dramatic or pretend play.* This type of play is one of the most sophisticated forms of childhood play because it involves the *integration* of other play forms (motion and interaction, object play, and language games).

There are two primary modes for organizing such dramatic play (Garvey, 1977; Rubin, Fein, and Vandenberg, 1983):

1. An action play or the organized arrangements of events into a coherent episode.
2. A role assumed by the play participants.

It is thought that pretend play does not appear before about age three, and it seems to disappear sometime before adolescence. There are two explanations for the demise of dramatic play or pretend play:

1. Although overt make-believe play decreases, it is replaced by covert play, or fantasy. Fantasy, daydreaming, or "thinking" about make-believe situations becomes a part of the adolescent experience (e.g., concern about popularity, appearance, and vocation).
2. The beginning of games with rules and the onset of more realistic play serve as replacements for pretend play.

The Preschool and Preschooler Development

Types of Preschool Programs

There are many different types of early-childhood-education programs. These programs are designed to meet a wide range of needs among families and preschoolers (see Fig. 9.9). Verna Hildebrand has described the following programs:

- *Laboratory Prekindergarten and Kindergarten Programs.* . . . Laboratory schools are funded and operated by high schools, vocational technical centers, community colleges, and four-year colleges and universities. Laboratory schools may be organized to serve the needs of the college or secondary school curriculum. . . . Laboratory schools are organized to give practicum experiences to students. A well-educated, experienced lead teacher helps college students learn basic child development and early childhood education principles. . . . One problem with laboratory schools has been that they may demonstrate a program that is very ideal compared to the community programs. . . . Research is often connected with laboratory schools, especially in four-year colleges and universities. Such research strengthens educators' knowledge base for teaching about child development, early childhood education, discipline, parent education and the like. . . . Special experimental or innovative early childhood programs are often tried out in laboratory schools before being advocated for wider use.
- *Child Care Centers.* . . . These are centers that provide supplemental care for children from infancy through kindergarten ages during the typical working hours of parents. In some localities the hours are from 6:30 A.M. to 6:00 P.M. Occasionally centers provide 24-hour service. . . . Child care centers are organized by profit and nonprofit groups. Most charge parents a tuition for sending their child to the center even if they have a subsidy from a governmental agency, church or the like. Child care centers are regulated by an agency of your state government, typically the department of social services or health services.
- *Church-Sponsored Centers.* Churches are prime sponsors for both part-day and full-day early childhood education programs. The programs are held in the church-school facilities during the week. . . .
- *Employer-Sponsored Child Care.* Employer-sponsored child care is currently experiencing a revival, having been pioneered in the United Stated during

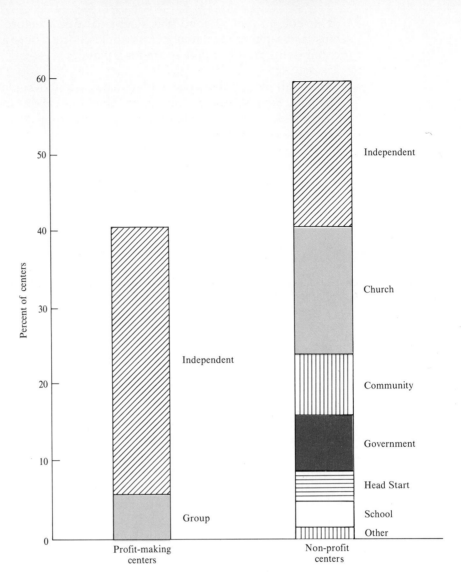

FIGURE 9.9
Legal status and sponsorship of day-care centers. From Dearman and Plisko, 1980.

World War II when mothers were needed to work in defense plants. Today
child care may be provided on the worksite for employees' children, or an
allowance for child care may be part of the employee benefit package, allowing
employees to select child care whenever they choose [Perry, 1982]. . . .
· *Family Day-Care Homes.* . . . Family day-care homes are regulated by a local or
state agency. Some states allow family group care which allows the mother
to hire an assistant and enroll more children. Family day care is the service of
choice for many families. It often allows care for school-age children who
attend after school.
· *Drop-In Child Care.* . . . These centers take young children on an hourly basis,
usually for an hourly fee, according to the number they are licensed to accept.
For instance, churches and community centers may organize "mother's day
out" to relieve mothers of child care for a time so they can shop or get medical
treatment. Drop-in centers are also located in places such as shopping centers,

amusement parks, or ski areas. Drop-in care is sometimes provided in medical centers giving noncontagious children waiting for tests or their siblings a child-appropriate environment in which to play while waiting. . . .

• *Prekindergartens for Three- and Four-Year Olds.* . . . These prekindergartens used to be called preschools or nursery schools, terms which [are] being phased out. The schools may be called early childhood education schools or centers or child development centers. Prekindergartens were generally credited with being more educational than child care centers. This difference is being eliminated with increased attention to higher quality in child care.

Many excellent prekindergartens are funded by tuition and have high standards of education. Some schools are operated by nonprofit agencies, while others are businesses for profit. The tuition expenses for these schools for some upper-income families can be very high.

• *Parent-Cooperative Schools.* Parent-cooperative nursery schools are typically organized by groups of middle-class families in order to provide a high-quality early childhood educational experience for their children at an affordable price. Because of the parents' (usually the mother's) participation as an assistant to the teacher about one-half day each month, the family pays lower tuition rates than they would pay in a typical for-profit school. Parents in cooperatives also contribute labor to build equipment, keep up the facility, and operate the program. One highly valued component of the parent-cooperative is the close link parents feel to their child's education and teacher. Parents learn a great deal about children by helping in their child's group.

• *Project Head Start.* Head Start early childhood centers were first organized under the joint sponsorship of the federal government and a local agency in many American communities in 1965. The program was begun as part of President Lyndon Johnson's War on Poverty. The program brought children of the poor together in groups for educational, medical, and nutritional assistance in hopes of reducing the observed handicap that such children experience when they enter elementary school. Some Head Start programs operated only in the summer, and others operated year round. Parent involvement has always been an important part of Head Start programs. . . .

• *Handicapped Prekindergartners.* The recent trend in education for the handicapped is away from segregated classrooms and toward integrating handicapped children in regular classrooms if their needs can be met there. This trend began in 1975 with the passage of Public Law 94-142. The federal law provides education for children and mandates an individualized program for each child. Head Start, using federal funds, initiated mainstreaming in Head Start groups. States have passed their own legislation and have provided services to young handicapped children in different ways.

• *Home Start Programs.* Home Start programs are usually arranged by the public schools and have [several] major objectives: to involve parents directly in the educational development of their children; to help strengthen parents' capacity for stimulating their children's development; and to demonstrate and evaluate methods of delivering services to the parents and children. The programs are federally funded. A trained visitor helps the parents develop an educational program for their children and helps them learn how to carry out the program. (Hildebrand, 1985a, pp. 15–20)

Project Head Start

The **Project Head Start** program was developed in the 1960s as an attempt to give poor preschoolers some of the advantages available to middle-class preschoolers.

It was thought that providing poor children with experiences they might be missing in their homes—being read to, playing with blocks, solving simple puzzles, drawing with crayons, or using scissors—would give them a head start toward formal learning in the school. The Head Start program began in 1965 as an eight-week summer program for children who were to enter school the following fall. By 1980, the program had become a full-year program with over 350,000 children participating (Zigler and Berman, 1983).

The typical Head Start center not only provides educational experiences for the children but also offers dental care and some medical services including immunizations. In addition, the children are served a snack and a hot meal. The centers also provide opportunities for parental involvement, including work at the centers on a volunteer or paid basis. Some centers offer courses for parents in child care,

The Montessori Preschool Program

The **Montessori** nursery schools are based on a philosophy of education in which children are assumed to be motivated by a natural curiosity for learning and a desire to participate in activities that utilize the senses and muscles. The program was developed in the early years of this century in Italy by Maria Montessori. The curriculum emphasizes individual work habits in the exploration of both academic skills and the senses. Montessori schools involve children in everyday tasks including cleaning up after themselves and using tools such as hammers, screwdrivers, and rulers. Some of the objectives of the program are to help children learn the important aspects of measurement, the alphabet, and other cultural skills by working with objects in a play experience. Children play with blocks of varying size and shape, simple musical instruments or keyboards with a range of musical tones, weights that fit into specific holes in a board, and other objects that help them develop the ability to make sensory discriminations. Another important objective of the Montessori school is to help children learn the value of individual work habits.

The program attempts to prepare the child to be a creative learner and to develop habits of initiative, persistence, curiosity, and concentration. The child is surrounded by a planned environment, composed largely of materials that can be manipulated or handled by the child. Experiences are designed to help children learn to do things for themselves and, in so doing, to encourage feelings of self-confidence and a positive self-image. The Montessori program involves a basic curriculum: practical life, sensorial materials, language, mathematics, science, geography, history, art, and music. Typically, the focus of the

Jerry Howard/Positive Images

preschool Montessori program is on the first four basic areas. As children approach five or six years of age, they may undertake the latter five areas.

Domain	Skills	Sample Activities
Practical Life	Muscle control and coordination, sense of order, completion of a task, independence	*Pouring:* water, rice, juice. *Polishing:* silver, shoes. *Dressing:* buttons, snaps, zippers, shoe lacing. *Watering plants. Feeding animals.*
Sensorial Material	Observation of likeness and difference, eye-hand coordination, pincer control, spatial orientation	Works with cylinder blocks (introduces graduations of size); red rods (introduces difference in size); touch board (introduces touch contrast—rough, smooth).
Language	Basic communication skill, phonetics, vocabulary, writing	Sandpaper letters (introduces alphabetical symbols, sound of letter, preparation for writing); classification cards (vocabulary building); sound games (exercises in using letter sounds).
Mathematics Materials	Logic, number concepts, quantity, number operations (addition, subtraction, multiplication, division)	Red and blue rods (counting 1 to 10); teen board (counting 11 to 19); ten board (counting by 10s); golden beads (addition, subtraction, and division); geometric solids (shape of geometric solids).

food preparation, food purchase, and home economics. Parental participation and involvement are considered an important goal of the Head Start program. Furthermore, Head Start centers may work with community social service agencies in helping to solve family or child problems in a coordinated fashion.

In the traditional Head Start program, children are involved in free play in an enriched environment for most of the day. That enriched environment includes books, puzzles, paints, a wide variety of toys, and other objects designed to stimulate child participation in daily activity. The curriculum is determined primarily by teacher goals. However, teachers are encouraged to engage children in conversation and to be warm and affectionate.

Not all Head Start centers offer only the more traditional nursery school programs involving social development and play activities. For example, some centers offer highly organized and formal instructional programs, such as the Distar curriculum (Bereiter and Englemann, 1966). In that program, groups of four- or five-year-old children may be drilled in rather fast-paced exercises designed to train them in reading, mathematics, or language skills. Of all the preschool or Head Start curricula we discuss, this one is based almost entirely on the principles of the behaviorist perspective to learning which was presented in Chapter 2. The entire curriculum is highly structured with drill sessions and workbook exercises, including frequent use of positive reinforcement, such as praise for working hard and getting the correct answers. Although the children are informed when they make an incorrect response, the primary focus of the program is to positively encourage their approximations to a correct answer, as well as the correct answer.

In contrast, other Head Start programs have used more low-key curricula, which focus on child "discovery." Such programs emphasize the child's freedom to explore a broad range of materials such as books, blocks, sandboxes, water, or science objects. The teacher has the option of responding to such child exploratory initiatives with prearranged lessons.

In addition, there are many other curricula that are used in Head Start centers, as well as in other preschool programs. The *Darcee* (Early Training Project) preschool program developed in Tennessee at the George Peabody College emphasizes the development of language skills which are typically taught in small-group sessions. Children are especially encouraged to develop listening skills, accurate speech skills, and good work habits. Other Head Start curricula vary in terms of both the content focus (language, emotional expression, prereading skills, and so on) and teaching approach (highly structured formal lessons, highly unstructured self-education programs).

Evaluating the Effects of Preschool Programs

Since the inception of Project Head Start and the increasing frequency of child participation in other preschool programs, there has been considerable interest in the evaluation of preschool programs. In this section, we examine the evaluations of Project Head Start and studies of the effects of day-care and nursery school programs.

EARLY EVALUATIONS OF HEAD START.   The early evaluations of Project Head Start conducted in the late 1960s and early 1970s suggested a mixed bag of outcomes (Klaus and Gray, 1968; Gray and Klaus, 1970; Bronfenbrenner, 1975). On the one hand, participants in Head Start were posting an average gain of 10 I.Q. points compared with the I.Q. scores of nonparticipants from similar social backgrounds, whose scores remained unchanged. On the other hand, when Head Start participants were again examined after a few years of elementary school, the earlier gains made on I.Q. test scores had largely disappeared. In other words, it appeared that Head Start participants made short-term intellectual gains, but these were seemingly lost over time.

These early evaluations prompted some investigators to suggest that "compensatory education has been tried and it apparently has failed" (Jensen, 1969). However, others argued that the impact of Project Head Start might be cumulative, such that its impact could not be fully appreciated or evaluated until many years later.

LONG-TERM EFFECTS OF HEAD START.   Irving Lazar and his colleagues (1982) examined the long-term effects of eleven Head Start programs that were begun in the 1960s. The children who participated in the programs were from several areas in the United States. Following the completion of these children's preschool progams in Project Head Start, the investigators examined the scholastic records and the scores on I.Q. and achievement tests as the children progressed through school. In addition, the children and their mothers were interviewed to determine changes in children's feelings of self-worth, children's attitudes about school and scholastic achievement, children's vocational aspirations, mothers' aspirations for their children, and their thoughts about children's progress in school. A very similar evaluative study of Project Head Start participants was conducted by Raymond C. Collins (1983). Both of these long-term follow-up studies of Project Head Start participants showed somewhat similar results:

· Children who participated in Project Head Start show *immediate* gains in I.Q. or in other measures of cognitive development. Although the cognitive gains persisted for some participants for as many as three or four years after the conclusion of the program, both participants and nonparticipants from similar social backgrounds show no apparent differences in I.Q. scores by junior high school.
· Head Start participants tend to score slightly higher than nonparticipants from

similar social backgrounds on achievement tests in mathematics, reading, and language at the grade school level. However, between the first and eighth grades, the gap between the achievement scores of the participants and nonparticipants widens, in favor of the Head Start participants.

· Head Start participants are less likely than nonparticipants from similar social backgrounds to be retained in a grade, to be assigned to special education, or to drop out of high school.

· The Head Start educational experience appears to have a long-term effect on achievement attitudes. For example, program participants were more likely than nonparticipants to mention (when asked in follow-up studies) their scholastic attainments or job-related successes as "something to be proud of."

· The Head Start experience influences the attitudes of the mothers of the participants. Mothers of participants were more likely than mothers of nonparticipants to have higher occupational aspirations for their children and to be more satisfied with their children's school performance.

In addition to these two follow-up evaluations, a more recent longitudinal evaluation of Head Start has supported many of the above findings (Berrueta-Clement et al., 1984). Furthermore, this study provided additional findings on the success of participants who, by age nineteen, had increased employment and enrollment in postsecondary education programs and reduced incidence of teenage pregnancy and delinquency. (See Fig. 9.10.)

HOME-BASED PROGRAMS.   Many of the most successful early childhood intervention efforts were those that began early in the target child's life and occurred in the home (Seitz, Rosenbaum, and Apfel, 1985). In these programs parents were an important part of the child's learning experiences. One very successful example of such a home-based intervention was the "toy demonstration" program developed by Phyllis Levenstein (1970). The program involves so-called disadvantaged two-year-olds and their mothers. About twice a week a member of the intervention team visited each home for a half-hour. During this time, the team members showed the parents how to use various educational books and toys. During the seven-month program, participant children gained an average of 17 I.Q. points, whereas nonparticipants showed no changes in I.Q. scores over the same time period. These gains were not simply short-term or temporary. Follow-up evaluations of the participants in the fourth, fifth, and sixth grades indicated that the participants still showed higher I.Q.s and were demonstrating higher academic achievement than nonparticipants (Lazar et al., 1982). A likely reason for the success of such home-based interventions is that parents of the children "learn" to be competent in stimulating intellectual development and *continue* to perform this way after the formal program ends. This may also help explain the frequent finding that younger siblings of the *target* children also benefit from the programs (Bronfenbrenner, 1975; Madden, Levenstein, and Levenstein, 1976). One of the most important lessons or conclusions to be derived from early intervention research is that it is important to involve parents and to involve them when their children are young (Bronfenbrenner, 1975).

EVALUATION OF PRESCHOOL PROGRAMS IN GENERAL.   Our discussion so far has focused almost exclusively on the evaluation of Project Head Start and other preschool programs for disadvantaged youngsters. What is the impact of preschool education on more advantaged children? Several thorough reviews of evaluative studies suggest that preschool education helps both disadvantaged and more advantaged children (Rutter, 1982a; Belsky, 1984; Clarke-Stewart, 1984; Scarr, 1984).

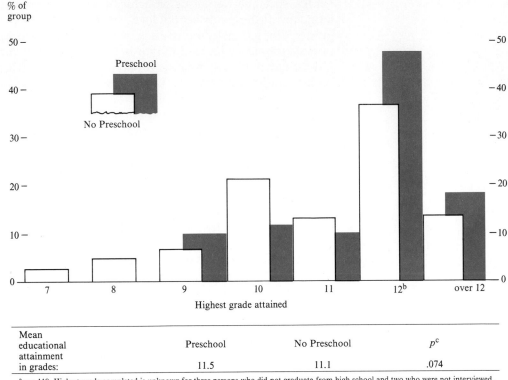

Mean educational attainment in grades:	Preschool	No Preschool	p^c
	11.5	11.1	.074

[a] $n = 118$. Highest grade completed is unknown for three persons who did not graduate from high school and two who were not interviewed.
[b] Attainment of grade 12 means high school graduation or G.E.D.
[c] The statistical test used was Student's t test.

FIGURE 9.10
The educational attainment of Head Start participants compared to non-participants.

Optimal Long-Term Intervention Programs

According to Urie Bronfenbrenner (1975), there are several guidelines that should be followed to promote successful preschool enrichment programs. These guidelines are, of course, based on the assessment of actual programs that have demonstrated relative success in promoting full academic and intellectual potential.

• *Preparation for parenthood.* Such preparation includes relevant information and skills in child care, medicine/health, and nutrition.
• *Setting the stage.* Before the beginning of any program, parents should have adequate income and housing.
• *The first three years of life.* The parent(s) should establish warm and responsive relationships with the child. These relationships should involve

reciprocal relationships which are focused on activities enjoyed by both parent(s) and child. Group meetings of parents and/or home visits should establish the role of the parent(s) as the central agent(s) in any enrichment or intervention program.
• *Ages four through six.* The child should be exposed to a cognitively oriented preschool program. Parents should be aware of the objectives of the program and, if possible, participate in the curriculum. This will help them to support the program. Parents should provide intellectually stimulating experiences for their child in the home setting.
• *Ages six through twelve.* Parents should continue to provide intellectually stimulating experiences in the home and to support the educational programs of the formal school.

However, virtually all of the studies reviewed involved high-quality programs (low teacher-child ratio, a curriculum geared toward cognitive growth and the needs of the child, a well-trained staff, excellent facilities). Such programs tend, of course, to be expensive.

Furthermore, it is important to recognize the difficulty—if not the impossibility—of doing rigorous, evaluative research of preschool education (Clarke-Stewart and Fein, 1983). The many variables that influence child learning in preschool programs (family background, family interaction, neighborhood/play experiences, preschool curriculum) are neither easy to separate nor easy to control in evaluation research. For example, it is not possible to assign some children to a given neighborhood environment and other children to another neighborhood environment. Nor is it possible randomly to have some children attend a preschool program and others not attend a program.

However, in one study of preschool education in Bermuda (where almost 85 percent of children age two to four years are in a preschool program), high-quality programs had a substantial impact on children's learning and development (McCartney, 1984). After the investigator controlled for parent socioeconomic status, these factors contributed to the child's intellectual development:

- Amount of teacher-child conversation.
- Programs where children were involved in a variety of activities (motor, language, social, and creative experiences).
- Programs where teachers spent more time teaching (usually in small groups) and less time managing child behavior problems.

Summary

1. The transition from the infant world to the preschool world is marked by a gradual movement of the child into the larger society. The social world of the infant is contained largely within the family. The preschooler begins to move out into the larger society, which becomes differentiated into neighborhood/community and peer contexts.

2. The role of the family in the preschool years can best be understood by viewing the *family as a system* in its own right. The characteristics of this system include the following: organizational complexity, openness, and adaptiveness. These characteristics govern the relationship of the people in a family as well as the interaction of the family unit with the larger society. The family as a system provides the framework for understanding the development of the preschool child.

3. One of the important components of this family system is parenting style (the attitudes and behaviors of parents or caretakers in child-rearing activities). There are at least two dimensions of parenting style that are related to the social and personality development of the preschool child: parent modeling and parent expectations.

4. Parent-child relationships are a *reciprocal* or two-way interaction. This is important to bear in mind because almost any episode of behavior between a parent and child could be interpreted as being one-way. For example, a sullen child can be viewed as the simple product of a rejecting parent. What is actually happening is a *two-way process of mutual influence* to which both parent and child contribute.

Parental disciplinary strategies frequently have been conceptualized as the relationship between two dimensions: (a) *acceptance* (warmth) or *rejection* (hostility and (b) *restrictiveness* or *permissiveness*. Four parent types emerge from the interaction of these two dimensions: *authoritative, authoritarian, indulgent,* and *neglecting.* Each of these four parent types represents a distinctive style of parenting with a differing impact on the developing child.

5. There is evidence that as children get older, parents change their disciplinary techniques and, likewise, children also appear to change in their willingness to conform to parental requests. There is evidence that several criteria are related to effective discipline: *promptness, moderate punishment, discipline from a person on good terms with the child, explanation with discipline,* and *consistent punishment.*

6. Although the family is undoubtedly a vital context for the developing child, there is another, more global context in which the family and the child are embedded—the neighborhood and community. There is evidence that the community performs three primary functions: mutual support, the socialization of children, and economic production/consumption.

   The ecological or systems perspective used in this book allows us to understand more fully the impact of the community on the family environment at both *direct* and *indirect* levels. There are many reasons for examining the neighborhood/community context. The neighborhood/community provides the major setting in which the child organizes free or unstructured time. The neighborhood/community is a setting where certain experiences or activities are likely to occur.

   Play occupies a considerable amount of the preschooler's waking hours. The environments in which play occurs are of two major types: *planned play settings* (e.g., playgrounds) and *unplanned play areas.*

7. As the preschool child matures, interaction expands to include other children in the neighborhood or, perhaps, in a preschool program. The first emergent signs of a beginning shift in dependence pattern from parents to peers emerges during these years.

   Throughout the first two years of life, there is evidence of a movement from *solitary activity* or *solitary play* to *social activity* or *social play.* Typically, preschooler peer relationships have been examined in the context of nursery schools or day-care centers.

8. One of the most important settings for peer relationships is *play.* In fact, children spend more time playing with their peers outside of school than in any other activity. Play enlarges the child's understanding of the world in which he or she lives. Play allows the child to explore objects, social roles, language, and feelings without regard to consequences or achievement of particular goals.

   According to Piaget, the development of play has three stages: *sensorimotor* (or *practice*) *play, symbolic* (or *pretend*), *play,* and *games-with-rules.* Another way of viewing play is to focus on the activities, materials, or resources of play: play as *motion* and *interaction,* play with *objects,* and play with *social materials* (dramatic and pretend play).

9. There are many different types of early-childhood-education programs, including laboratory prekindergarten and kindergarten programs, child-care centers, church-sponsored centers, employer-sponsored child care, family day-care homes, parent cooperative schools, Project Head Start, handicapped prekindergartners programs, and home start programs. Since the inception of Project Head Start and the increasing frequency of child participation in other preschool programs, there has been considerable interest in the evaluation of preschool programs.

Key Terms

Acceptance-rejection

Adaptiveness

Adventure (or "junk") play setting

Authoritarian (parent)

Authoritative (parent)

Child-care Centers

Conflicted-irritable children

Designed play setting

Energetic-friendly children

Exosystems

Family day-care homes

Family system

Games-with-rules

Impulsive-aggressive children

Indulgent-permissive (parent)

Laboratory schools

Macrosystem

Mesosystems

Microsystem

Montessori programs

Neglecting (parent)

Openness

Organizational complexity

Permissive (parent)

Personal social networks

Play

Project Head Start

Restrictiveness-permissiveness

Sensorimotor (or practice) play

Social play

Solitary play

Styles of parenting

Symbolic (or pretend) play

Traditional play setting

Questions

1. Discuss the family as a system. Indicate the three primary characteristics of such a family system.
2. Briefly identify the two dimensions that frequently have been used to conceptualize parent disciplinary strategies.
3. Describe the four types of parents that emerge from those two dimensions.
4. Can or should parents be trained to be authoritative?
5. Discuss the indirect influence of the community on the family and, therefore, on preschool child development. Give specific examples.
6. Briefly define social play, solitary play, and symbolic play.
7. Discuss three findings of the long-term evaluations of Project Head Start.

Suggested Readings

BELSKY, J. "Two Waves of Day Care Research: Developmental Effects and Conditions of Quality." In R. Ainslie (ed.), *The Child and the Day Care Setting*. New York: Praeger, 1984. An excellent review of the impact of day care on children.

BERRUETA-CLEMENT, J. R., SCHWEINHART, L. J., BARNETT, W. S., EPSTEIN, A. S., and WEIKART, D. P. *Changed Lives: The Effects of the Perry Preschool Program on Youths Through Age 19*. Ypsilanti, Mich.: The High/Scope Press, 1984. A well-written account of the long-term impact of preschool programs.

GOTTMAN, J. M., and PARKER, J. G. (eds.). *The Conversations of Friends*. New York: Cambridge University Press, 1985. An excellent and well-researched analysis of peer/friendship relationships.

HILDEBRAND, V. *Introduction to Early Childhood Education* (4th ed.). New York: Macmillan, 1985. A readable and thorough discussion of the practical issues involved in preschool education.

JOHNSON, J. E., CHRISTIE, J. F., and YAWKEY, T. D. *Play and Early Childhood Development*. Glenview, Ill.: Scott Foresman, 1987. An easy-to-read and authoritative discussion of both theoretical and practical issues relating to play.

10 The Preschooler: Physical, Cognitive, and Language Development

THE END

When I was One
I had just begun.

When I was Two,
I was nearly new.

When I was Three,
I was hardly me.

When I was Four,
I was not much more.

When I was Five,
I was just alive.

But now I am Six, I'm as clever as clever,
So I think I'll be six now for ever and ever.
  —*A. A. Milne,* Now We Are Six

Physical Characteristics and Motor Development

Physical Characteristics

In the physical growth of children, one activity comes after another. For example, the mature grasp (prehension) follows more primitive grasping efforts. This sequential pattern of development is again apparent at the preschool or early childhood ages (two to five years). Most of the physical skills developed during these years are built on the foundation of perceptual skills (e.g., vision, hearing, and touch) and motor skills (e.g., walking and grasping) of infancy and toddlerhood.

THE PATTERN OF GROWTH.   There is an overall pattern for the growth and maturation of physical characteristics. As indicated in Figure 10.1, there are four major types of organs and tissues that grow according to a predictable pattern. These are **lymphoid** (e.g., thymus and lymph nodes), brain and head (e.g., eyes and spinal cord), general (e.g., the body as a whole, muscles, and digestive organs), and reproductive (e.g., the testes and the ovaries).

General body growth increases rather rapidly during the first two years of life. During this time, dramatic growth in most bones and muscles can be observed. After the beginning of the third year, there is a slower and more gradual increase. At puberty, there is a distinct growth spurt (the adolescent growth spurt).

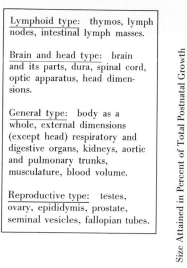

Lymphoid type: thymos, lymph nodes, intestinal lymph masses.

Brain and head type: brain and its parts, dura, spinal cord, optic apparatus, head dimensions.

General type: body as a whole, external dimensions (except head) respiratory and digestive organs, kidneys, aortic and pulmonary trunks, musculature, blood volume.

Reproductive type: testes, ovary, epididymis, prostate, seminal vesicles, fallopian tubes.

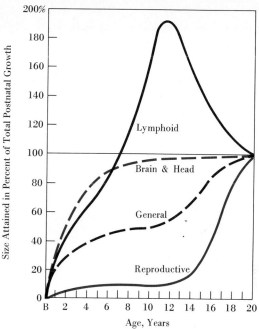

FIGURE 10.1

Growth curves of different parts and tissues of the body, showing the four chief types. All the curves are of the size attained (in percentage of the total gain from birth to maturity) and plotted so that size at age twenty is 100 on the vertical scale. From Harris et al., 1930.

Brain and head growth increase rapidly during infancy and the preschool years. The brain and the head grow the fastest. The lymphoid system has the second most rapid growth rate. By age six, about 80 percent of the lymphoid growth has occurred. The lymphatic system supports the immunity of the body to illness and helps to fight infections.

At age two, almost 60 percent of neurological development has occurred, and by age six, almost 90 percent has occurred. Development of the reproductive system occurs at a much slower pace. It is not until the onset of puberty that the reproductive organs are functionally mature.

From the early fetal period and beyond, the brain is nearer its adult size (in terms of weight) than any other organ of the body with the exception of the eyes. At two and one-half years the brain is about 75 percent of its adult weight; at five years, it is 90 percent of its adult weight, in contrast with the weight of the body as a whole, which is only about 50 percent of its adult weight at age ten (Tanner, 1978a).

NERVE CELLS AND BRAIN GROWTH. The nervous system is composed of a *central nervous system* and a *peripheral nervous system*. The **central nervous system** consists of the brain and the spinal cord. The **peripheral nervous system** consists of nerves that are connected to the brain and the spinal cord and extend to the exterior (or the periphery) of the body. These nerves carry impulses to and from the central nervous system. **Neurons** (nerve cells) are the building blocks of the nervous system. Neurons have a cell body and a nucleus, like all other cells, but unlike other cells, they also have special threadlike fibers that lead to and from the cell

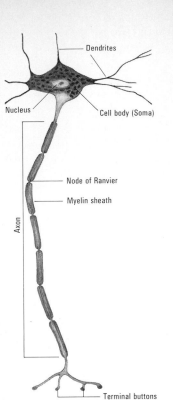

FIGURE 10.2
The structure of a neuron. From Benjamin, 1987, p. 30.

Dendrites

Nucleus

Cell body (Soma)

Node of Ranvier

Myelin sheath

Axon

Terminal buttons

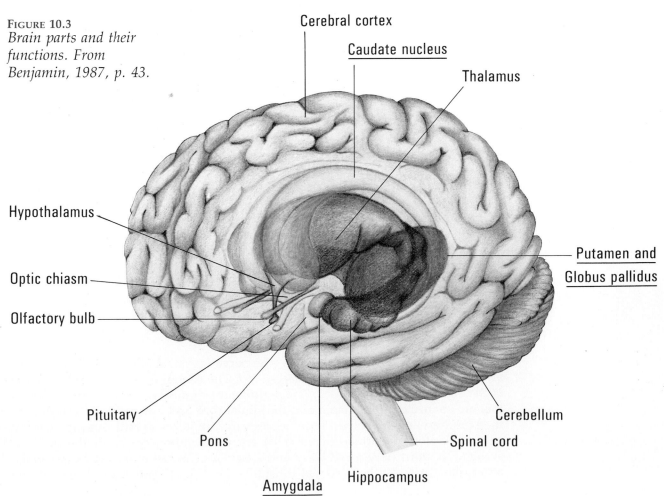

FIGURE 10.3
Brain parts and their functions. From Benjamin, 1987, p. 43.

Cerebral cortex

Caudate nucleus

Thalamus

Hypothalamus

Optic chiasm

Olfactory bulb

Putamen and
Globus pallidus

Pituitary

Pons

Cerebellum

Spinal cord

Amygdala

Hippocampus

body—an *axon* and several *dendrites*. The **axon** is a transmitter that carries impulses away from the cell body. It is a single long fiber transmitting messages away from the cell body to the next nerve cell body. The **dendrites** are receivers carrying impulses toward the cell body (see Fig. 10.2).

The development of new neurons as a result of mitosis occurs most frequently during the prenatal period and may continue for several months after birth (Rosenzweig and Leiman, 1982). It is important to note that if dietary protein is available, both the newer and older brain cells will increase in both weight and size. For this reason, the last trimester of the prenatal period and the first two years after birth constitute a growth spurt for the brain.

BRAIN DIFFERENTIATION.   Different parts of the human brain develop at different rates. At birth, the most developed area is the **brain stem** (composed, from top to bottom, of the midbrain, the pons, and the medulla) (see Fig. 10.3). This brain area controls such functions as inborn reflexes, states of consciousness, digestion, elimination, and respiration. The **cerebrum** (see Fig. 10.4) surrounds the brain stem. This area is involved in bodily movement, perception, and the higher cognitive activities such as language production, learning, and thinking. With reference to the cerebrum, the areas that are the first to mature are the **primary motor areas,** which control simple motor activities (e.g., moving the arms), and the **primary sensory areas,** which control perceptual activities such as hearing, taste, smell, and vision. Furthermore, development of nerve cells in the primary motor areas occurs first in the areas affecting control of the arms and the upper body trunk and only later in the areas affecting control of the lower body trunk. For

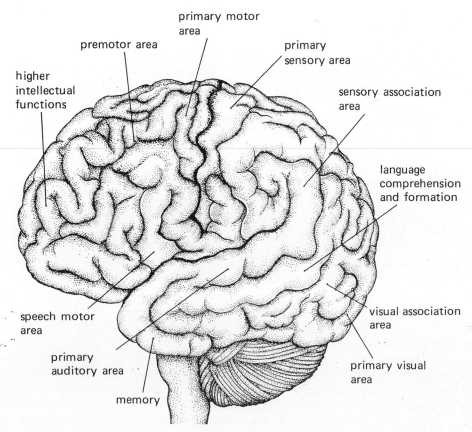

FIGURE 10.4

The cerebrum and its control areas. From Audesirk, 1986, p. 642.

this reason, infants are typically able to do things with their heads, arms, or hands before they can engage in such behaviors as crawling, sitting up, or walking. The primary motor areas of the cerebrum continue to develop, and by approximately six months of age they exert control over most infant physical activities. This control by the higher brain centers over the more primitive brain areas is evidenced by the disappearance of such inborn responses as the Babinski reflex and the Palmar grasp.

MYELINIZATION.   The neurons of most nerves are coated with a fatty substance called *myelin*. Myelin forms an insulating sheath around individual neurons which serves to increase the overall speed and efficiency of neural impulses. Most myelinization occurs prior to the first two years of life.

> *DEFINITIONS*
>
> **Myelin.** This is a white, fatty substance that covers many neural fibers. It serves to channel brain impulses along appropriate fibers and to reduce the random spread of brain signals.
>
> **Myelinization.** The process through which neural fibers acquire a myelin covering or sheath.

The pattern of myelinization follows a chronological order that is similar to the general maturation of the nervous system. At birth the neural pathways between the sensory organs (e.g., eyes and ears) and the brain are myelinated. Thus, the newborn is capable of efficient sensory functioning. However, the neural pathways between the skeletal muscles and the brain have not completed myelinization. Myelinization proceeds in a cephalocaudal/proximodistal pattern (from the head down to the feet and from the center of the body to the extremities). Therefore, the infant is capable of head, neck, and arm movements prior to being able to sit up, walk, or run (cephalocaudal direction) and is able to move his or her arms prior to skilled finger manipulation (proximodistal direction).

A number of areas in the brain have not completed myelinization until three or four years after birth. The **cerebellum** is the part of the brain concerned with the smooth and even performance of voluntary movements. In human beings, the **cerebral cortex** constitutes the major portion of the brain and occupies the upper part of the cranium. It contains the most highly developed functions of the nervous system, including intelligence and memory, and the centers for sight, hearing, smell, taste, and general body sensations. The neural fibers that connect the cerebellum and the cerebral cortex do not complete myelinization until about age four. These fibers are responsible for the fine control of voluntary movement. In addition, the **reticular formation** (the part of the brain concerned with the maintenance of attention and consciousness) does not complete myelinization until puberty or after (Tanner, 1978b). There is some reason, therefore, to suppose that the fine motor movements characteristic of such skills as writing and the attentional skills necessary to accomplish them are, in part, the result of brain maturation.

The critical importance of myelinization is further demonstrated when, for some unexplainable reason, myelin sheaths begin to deteriorate. This happens in the case of **multiple sclerosis,** a disease that is marked by such myelin disintegration and currently is incurable. Depending on the specific areas of the nervous system that are affected, multiple sclerosis usually results in loss of muscle control in affected areas and may eventually lead to paralysis or death. Reseachers have isolated a gene that may play a role in the disease (Roach et al., 1983). The gene produces myelin-basic protein, or MBP, one of the primary components of myelin.

BRAIN LATERALIZATION. The *cerebrum* (the highest brain center) is composed of two halves which are called **brain hemispheres** and are connected by a band of fibers called **corpus callosum.** Each cerebral hemisphere is covered by a *cerebral cortex*. Although each hemisphere of the brain looks similar, each performs different functions. The right cerebral hemisphere controls the left side of the body and the left cerebral hemisphere controls the right side of the body. The specialized functioning and control of each hemisphere is referred to as **brain lateralization.** The left cerebral hemisphere, which has been called the "logical brain," has centers that control such functions as hearing, speech, processing of verbal information (recognizing groups of letters as words and groups of words as sentences), and motor movements. Mathematicians and scientists use their left brain a great deal. The right cerebral hemisphere controls such functions as spatial and intuitive abilities. The right brain interprets the world through patterns, meanings, and emotions. The right brain is used frequently by artists and musicians. Lateralization of brain function does not mean that the hemispheres operate independently of each other. Rather, the corpus callosum integrates the functions of each hemisphere.

SPECIFIC CHARACTERISTICS: WHAT DOES A PRESCHOOLER LOOK LIKE? The typical two-year-old (see photographs) weighs somewhere between twenty-five and twenty-eight pounds and is from thirty-two to thirty-six inches tall. By age two, the arms have lengthened 60 to 75 percent over what they were at birth. The legs are about 40 percent longer than at birth. Soon the legs will catch up and eventually become longer than the arms. At the age of three, the average child weighs over

David Kostelnik

A two-year-old

thirty pounds and is over three feet tall. The average four-year-old weighs about thirty-six pounds and is about forty inches tall. The average five-year-old weighs about forty-three pounds and has grown to about forty-four inches in height (Corbin, 1980; Williams, 1983) (see Growth Charts in Chapter 7).

There are, of course, individual variations in the growth of children. Girls tend to be slightly shorter than boys, although they both develop at about the same rate throughout most of childhood. An important difference between boys and girls is that boys tend to have more muscle tissue per body weight than girls. Girls tend to have more fatty tissue than boys (Breckenridge and Murphy, 1969; Williams, 1983).

There are other important facets of preschool growth. Body proportions change during this period. By the time children are six years old, they have the body proportions of the adult; the child's legs are about half the length of the body, which is the adult proportion. Most of the weight gained by the preschool child is the result of muscle development.

Environmental Factors That Influence Growth

Human growth is the result of the interaction of hereditary and environmental factors. Any gene is dependent for its expression on two types of environment: (1) an internal environment composed of all other genes and (2) an external environment (Tanner, 1978a). It is difficult, if not impossible, to specify the precise relationship between heredity and environment. For example, a 10 percent increase in nutrition will not result in a similar increase in height for all individuals. Different genotypes respond differently to the same stimulus. In this section, we examine the effects of several environmental factors on growth, including nutrition, illness, exercise, and emotional stress.

NUTRITION.   Appropriate diet is necessary to the adequate growth of children. Such a diet includes the following (Williams and Caliendo, 1984):

Proteins provide the raw materials of growth.
Carbohydrates provide the energy necessary for activity.
Vitamins, fats, minerals, and water provide important support for growth.

What happens when children have too little to eat? In order to answer this question, we need to distinguish between two types of malnutrition: temporary and chronic. Considerable research and studies have been done on the effects of temporary malnutrition in children (Tanner, 1978a; Richardson, 1975). During short periods of malnutrition, children's growth may be delayed. When better times arrive and food is available, rapid growth occurs until the child "catches up." At the end of this catch-up phase, the child's growth is almost indistinguishable from what it would have been had no malnutrition occurred at all. On the other hand, when children experience chronic undernourishment, they may become smaller adults.

What happens when children have too much to eat? Although malnutrition is certainly an important problem in some parts of the world, "overnutrition" or overeating is probably more prevalent and no less dangerous in its potential outcomes. Recent research suggests that childhood obesity may have a strong family or genetic component. This puts some children who overeat at particular risk for obesity (Dietz, 1986; Epstein, 1986).

Montbeillard's Son (1759–1777)

The pattern of *general body growth* can be illustrated by the increase in height in human beings. The oldest published study of the physical growth of a child was made by Count Philibert Gueneau de Montbeillard from 1759 to 1777. Count de Montbeillard followed the growth in height of his son. The graphs provide a summary of the results of these observations. These data represent an accurate description of normal growth in height some two hundred years after they were initially recorded and described. (Of course people are taller today than they were in eighteenth-century France. However, the pattern of growth in terms of rate is similar to modern times.) The left diagram shows the pattern of increase in height. This pattern is similar to the "general" curve in Figure 10.1.

The graph on the right shows that the "velocity" or the rate of growth in height decreases from birth onward. This deceleration is interrupted briefly during the adolescent growth spurt. Count de Montbeillard's son experienced his adolescent growth spurt between thirteen and fifteen years of age. From birth through about age four or five years, the rate of growth in height declined quickly. The rate of decline is almost constant from about five or six years up to the adolescent growth spurt.

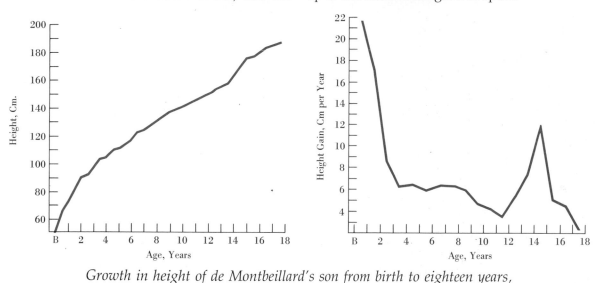

Growth in height of de Montbeillard's son from birth to eighteen years, 1759–1777. From Tanner, 1978a.

CHILDHOOD OBESITY.   In spite of the strong emphasis on thinness in our society, more children than ever before are obese. Using data from the Health and Nutrition Examination Surveys (HANES) (conducted every three to four years by the National Center for Health Statistics), Dietz (1986) concluded that the prevalence of obesity has increased by 54 percent for six-to-eleven-year-old American children and by 39 percent for twelve-to-seventeen-year-olds over the last twenty years. To further complicate the problem, it now appears that the conventional wisdom that overweight children outgrow their obesity is under serious question. According to Epstein (1986), approximately 40 percent of children who are obese at seven years of age will become obese adults. Also, 70 percent of obese adolescents will become obese adults (Epstein, 1986).

What causes a child to become obese? Answers to this question have been vigorously debated and have ranged from environmental factors such as simple overeating to genetic causes. According to Kretchmer (1986), children can become

Sylvia Byers

Appropriate diet is necessary for adequate growth of children.

obese by eating as few as fifty extra calories per day. This relatively small number of excess calories would itself then produce a weight gain of approximately five pounds per year. Since there is no evidence that supports the frequent assumptions that obese children dramatically overeat compared with normal-weight children or that obese children burn calories less efficiently than normal-weight children, what are the differences between obese and normal-weight children? More specifically, why do children who consume as few as fifty additional calories daily become obese? One common finding has been that obese children tend to be less active than normal-weight children. However, it is not clear whether this inactivity is a *cause of obesity* or whether obesity is a *cause of inactivity*. The direction of causation is uncertain in such studies because they are typically cross-sectional. Such studies have sought to explain the causes of childhood obesity by comparing populations of obese and normal children at one point in time rather than following children longitudinally to determine what makes them become obese. According to Klesges (1986), "virtually all of the studies are cross-sectional . . . there's a difference between the onset and maintenance of obesity."

Using longitudinal data, Dietz (1986) has offered the provocative hypothesis that the increased incidence of childhood obesity over the past twenty years is due, in part, to children's watching too much television. Dietz studied children who had originally been examined in a HANES survey in the early 1970s and followed them into the mid- and later 1970s. A striking result of this longitudinal assessment was that "next to prior obesity, television viewing is the strongest predictor of subsequent obesity" (1986). Dietz further comments on the relationship as follows:

> I argue that television viewing causes obesity. We have shown the relationship consistently in three studies, it is temporally related to the onset of obesity. . . .

Children eat more while they are watching TV and they eat more of the foods advertised on TV. The message that TV conveys is that you will be thin no matter what you eat. Nearly everyone on television is thin.

In addition, children who watch television are inactive. Dietz (1986) studied the metabolic rate of children as they watch television. In one case, a twelve-year-old boy's basal metabolic rate dropped at a rate of 200 calories per hour while watching a television cartoon show.

Although, as the discussion above indicates, there is evidence for environmental contributions to childhood obesity, there is also significant research that substantiates the hereditary or genetic factors. In other words, every child is not at equal risk to be obese. A recent study by Albert Stunkard and his colleagues (1986) at the University of Pennsylvania suggests that the tendency to be obese may be inherited and is not simply the result of poor eating habits. The study examined the contributions of genetic factors and the family environment of a sample of 540 adult Danish adoptees. The results indicated that the adoptees grew up to have the weight and body builds of their biological parents. Furthermore, there was no relationship between the weight and body build of the adoptees and their adoptive parents. The primary conclusion drawn from the study is that genetic influences have a significant role in determining obesity in adults, whereas family environment (e.g., eating habits) taken alone has no apparent effects.

Nonetheless, Stunkard is careful not to imply that individuals have no control over their weight or that excessive calories make no difference. Rather, Stunkard and his colleagues recognize that although there is a strong genetic factor in the expression of the obesity trait, the genetic expression of obesity nevertheless is made possible through the interaction of genetic potentials with an environment. Although the study clearly demonstrates the contribution of hereditary factors to obesity, it does not deal with an equally important consideration—what has society done to encourage or facilitate the maximum expression of the genetic potential for obesity? It could be argued that such environmental circumstances as fast-food restaurants and excessive inactivity or television watching have allowed the fullest impact of genetic traits for obesity, as never before.

Stunkard points out that the results of the study have implications for child rearing.

> Better understanding of the determinants of human obesity will be useful in preventing this disorder because it will help to restrict the size of the target population. Current efforts to prevent obesity are directed toward all children (and their parents) almost indiscriminately. Yet if family environment alone has no role in obesity, efforts now directed toward persons with little genetic risk of the disorder could be refocused on the smaller number who are more vulnerable. Such persons can already be identified with some assurance: 80 percent of the offspring to two obese parents become obese, as compared with no more than 14 percent of the offspring of two parents of normal weight. (Mayer, 1965) (Stunkard et al., 1986, p. 197).

ILLNESS.   Minor or short-term illnesses (e.g, influenza and measles) have rather little impact on the growth rate of well-nourished children. Preschool children catch a large number of such communicable diseases with no apparent effect on their growth.

Major illnesses that require extended periods of hospitalization may result in a marked slowing of children's growth. A "catch-up" phenomenon ordinarily occurs after such illnesses. However, depending on the severity of the disease, chronic illness can result in a reduction in size.

SOCIOECONOMIC STATUS.   There is evidence that children from families of differing socioeconomic levels differ in average body size. This difference is apparently true for all ages of childhood, with upper socioeconomic groups being larger (Tanner, 1978a). The British National Child Development Survey of 1958 showed differences between the height of children in relation to their family social status (Tanner, 1978a). Children of professional- and managerial-class families were found to be approximately three centimeters taller than children of unskilled laborers at age three and four or five centimeters taller at adolescence (Tanner, 1978a). This more rapid rate of growth may reflect better diet and health care (fewer illnesses). Some of this difference in height persists into adulthood.

EMOTIONAL STRESS AND GROWTH.   Some investigators have found a relationship between severe psychological stress and retardation of growth. Elsie M. Widdowson (1951) found that children living in a German orphanage in 1948 grew more slowly under the tutelage of a punitive matron than children in another orphanage who received food with fewer calories (see box). Furthermore, some children under severe stress appear actually to switch off the secretion of growth hormone. This condition has been identified as **deprivation dwarfism** (Gardner, 1972). When the severe stress is removed, the secretion of growth hormone resumes and a growth "catch-up" occurs.

Perceptual Development

Perceptual processes have to do with the reception or taking in of information about the environment. Various sensory systems are involved in providing this important information to the individual (touch, taste, sight, smell, and hearing). Perceptual information and the activity of the brain are important prerequisites to motor learning and development. Perceptual development has to do with age-related changes in the process of taking in information.

As children grow, there are at least three major changes in perceptual processes (Corbin, 1980; Williams, 1983):

1. A shift in the dominance of sensory systems.
2. An increase in communication between sensory systems.
3. An improvement in the functioning of individual sensory systems.

The earliest developmental change in perception is the *shift from primary reliance on* **tactual-kinesthetic** (*tactual* refers to the sense of touch; *kinesthetic* refers to the sense of one's body movement) *sensory systems to primary reliance on the visual system* for regulation of behavior. The visual system is the most advanced of all human perceptual processes in terms of the speed and the precision of information that it supplies to the individual (Kelso and Clark, 1982).

A second distinct change in perception is the improved *intersensory functioning* of the child. As children grow and mature, they are better able to interrelate information received from many sensory systems at the same time. For example, children can "match up" what they see with what they hear, what they see with what they smell, what they feel with what they see, and so on. Such multisensory functioning is important for several reasons; for example, it allows the child to make more precise judgments before action or movement is initiated. Multisensory functioning also indicates the appearance of integrative powers in the brain (Williams, 1983).

The third major change in perception is an increasing sharpness of discrimi-

The School

As a context of development, schools provide the central means of transferring cultural information from society to individual children and adolescents. From our systems or ecological perspective, the school reflects, in its curricular organization by a child's age or grade, the increasing complexity of necessary knowledge and technical skill. The middle-childhood years are marked and bounded by entrance into the formal school, which involves the development of such cultural skills as reading, writing, thinking, problem solving, and interpersonal skills.

From a historical and cross-cultural perspective, the school we know is both relatively recent in its inception and is a function of technologically complex societies. The educational transfer of cultural information and skills was historically the function of the family in societies where the level of cultural information was sufficiently simple to be known by virtually all adults. Examples are found in traditional Chinese and Indian societies, as well as in earlier historical periods in the Western Hemisphere. During the last hundred years in the United States, however, the school has become the primary medium for cultural transmission.

Emotional Stress and Physical Growth

"Better a dinner of herbs where love is than a stalled ox and hatred therein" (quoted in Widdowson, 1951).

Quality of care proved more important than quality of food in two postwar German orphanages studied by Elsie M. Widdowson. For six months during 1948 the fifty-odd war orphans in each home received nothing but basic rations yet the children in Orphanage A, supervised by a kindly matron, gained more weight than most of those in Orphanage B, whose matron was a stern disciplinarian. An exception was a group of favorites of the stern matron at B; they did better than their companions. After six months the matron at B was transferred to A and brought her favorites with her. Simultaneously the children at A were given extra rations, whereas the children at B remained on the same basic diet. (The transition is indicated by the vertical . . . line.) Relieved of the stern matron's discipline, the children at B began to show a sharp increase in weight; those at A showed a weight gain that averaged somewhat less than it had during the preceding six months in spite of the larger ration. Again matron's favorites were an exception; their gain was greatest of any. (Taken from L. I. Gardner, "Deprivation Dwarfism," p. 82. Copyright © July 1972 by Scientific American, Inc. All rights reserved.)

Lytt Gardner (1972) has suggested that serious deprivation of affection in the parent (caretaker)-child relationship may lead to a physical and emotional disturbance in the child called *deprivation dwarfism*. This disturbance is registered first in the *higher brain centers* where signals are sent to the *hypothalmus*. In turn, the hypothalmus regulates the pituitary gland (the "master gland" of the entire *endocrine system*). The pituitary gland, in turn, regulates the secretion of *somatotrophin* or *growth hormone*. Deprivation dwarfism results from reduced production of growth hormone (Gardner, 1972).

The emotional disturbance resulting from deprivation of affection, in turn, leads to disturbed sleeping modes. It is known that growth hormone is released during a mode of sleep when the higher brain centers are the least active. Deprivation dwarfism leads to irregular sleeping patterns which, in turn, result in reduced secretion of growth hormone. Normal growth is accompanied by a return to normal sleeping patterns (Gardner, 1972).

Although not as severe as deprivation dwarfism, the young child who is small and physically weak could possibly have diminished growth due to an emotionally disturbing family life. This assumes, of course, no nutritional deficiencies or diseases.

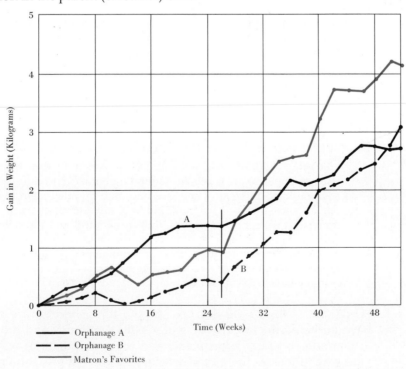

Orphanage A
Orphanage B
Matron's Favorites

natory skill of the individual sensory systems. Preschool children begin to make finer distinctions in what they see and hear. The child preparing to catch a thrown ball, for example, can now make a more precise determination of the location and speed of the ball than at an earlier age.

Motor Development

The period of early childhood (from two to five years of age) is a significant period of motor learning and development. Most of the fundamental motor patterns develop to a relatively high level of precision during this period, although many of the underlying motor skills, such as walking, have their beginnings prior to this period. Such basic activities as walking are the basis for such fundamental motor skills as jumping, climbing, hopping, skipping, and galloping. The number of activities that can be learned by a young child is almost unlimited. That is, the child at this age can learn almost any motor skill to some level of effectiveness. Catching, throwing, swimming, and bicycle riding are examples of motor skills (or combinations of motor skills) that can be learned by age six if the opportunity is given.

GENERAL CHARACTERISTICS: LEARNING AS PLAY AND PLAY AS LEARNING.   For preschoolers, it is important to have a good start at what will most likely be a lifelong process of learning, a start in which they are free to set their own pace. Such a situation encourages competence and the desire to learn, particularly as much of preschool learning occurs in the context of "play," whereas most learning beyond age six occurs in the context of school, or "work." Children who are two to six years old do not seem to want rules and regulations imposed on their play and motor games that are characteristic of such "play" beyond the age of six. In fact, preschoolers seem to be spontaneous in "inventing" their own play games (and the minimal rules that accompany them) using the "raw materials" of objects around the house or in the immediate neighborhood (pots, pans, tables, chairs, balls, sandboxes, ropes, wagons, puddles).

Use of toys in play is an important way in which the child learns to refine motor development and movement skills. On the whole, toys that effectively develop motor skills are sturdy, simple, and not overly realistic. In addition, objects and toys that can be moved and manipulated by the child seem to promote both motor skill and strength.

■   *SCENARIO: THE LOVE OF A MUD PUDDLE AND MOTOR DEVELOPMENT*
Like other children of her age, Elizabeth seems to be drawn to mud puddles. She appears to derive great delight from riding her bicycle (with training wheels) through such puddles. Little boys and girls and mud puddles seem to have an affinity for one another. It is as if the mud puddle is a world all its own, over which the child exercises total control. Coupled with this control and the delight of the water splashing on both sides of the bicycle, the child is, of course, refining and practicing a basic motor skill: bicycle riding. The situation is a natural play context in which motor development as well as development of self-confidence occurs as the child learns what she or he can do.

FUNDAMENTAL MOTOR SKILLS.   By the time children are four years old, they have mastered the underlying motor skills of infancy and toddlerhood, including locomotion, postural adjustment, and the manipulation or handling of objects. One way to look at the motor development of the preschooler is to look at those

Tricycles can be part of motor development.

motor activities that seem to be common in the experiences of most children from two or three to six years of age. We will call these common motor activities **fundamental motor skills.** This category includes such activities as throwing, catching, skipping, hopping, jumping, and balancing. In this section, we focus on fundamental motor skills that develop, to some degree of competency, during the preschool years and that are a basic part of childhood games and play activities.

Such fundamental skills as running, jumping, throwing, catching, and hitting are the basis for such recreational activities as sports and dance in middle childhood, adolescence, and adulthood. For this reason, the preschool period is a fundamentally significant period for motor development. Figure 10.5 shows the developmental pattern of motor skills ranging from the reflexes of early infancy to the advanced movement skills of older children, adolescents, and adults. It is important to note that there is a "proficiency barrier" that follows the preschool period of fundamental motor skills. This means the fundamental motor skills are the prerequisites for any advanced motor-skill performance. Table 10.1 summarizes the significant aspects of the developmental progression of these skills.

The following are some fundamental motor skills and their pattern of development:

Climbing. Climbing behavior emerges initially from infant crawling. In fact, many infants can climb steps before they can walk. Often, when infants reach the top of a staircase, they may try to descend in the same fashion in which they ascended: head first. After a few unsuccessful head-first attempts, the child discovers that it may be better to descend backwards. Studies of children's climbing ability suggest that there are several stages of climbing (Corbin, 1980; Kelso and Clark, 1982; Williams, 1983).

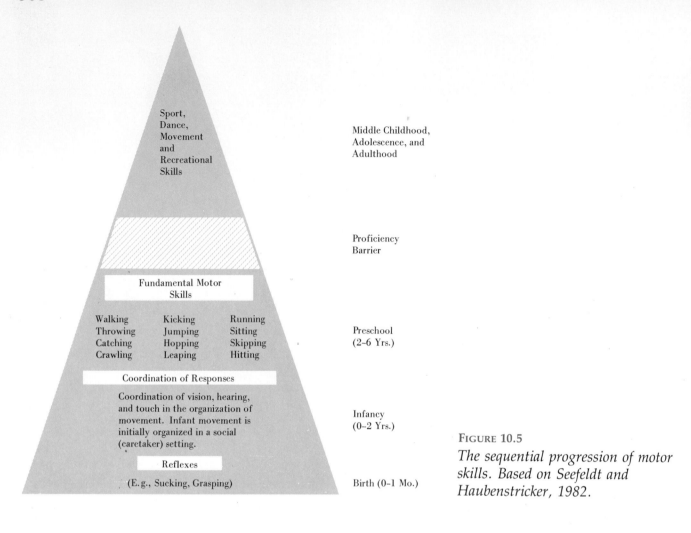

FIGURE 10.5
The sequential progression of motor skills. Based on Seefeldt and Haubenstricker, 1982.

TABLE 10.1
Motor Characteristics of Perceptual-Motor Development: The Preschool Child

MOTOR PATTERN	SKILL CHARACTERISTICS		
	The Three-Year-Old	*The Four-Year-Old*	*The Five-Year-Old*
Walking, running	Run is smoother and stride is more even than at two.	Run is improved in form and power.	Has effected adult manner of running.
	Cannot turn or stop suddenly or quickly.	More effective control over stopping, starting, and turning.	Can use this effectively in games.
	Can take walking and running steps on the toes.	In general, greater mobility than at three.	Runs 35-yard dash in less than 10 seconds.
	Can walk a straight line.	Coordinates body parts better in independent activities.	
	Can walk backwards long distances.	Walks 6-cm. board partway before stepping off.	
	Walks path (1 inch wide, 10 feet long) without stepping off.	Walks circle (1 inch wide, 4 feet in circumference) without stepping off.	
	Cannot walk circular path (1 nch wide, 4 feet in circumference).		

TABLE 10.1
(Continued)

MOTOR PATTERN	SKILL CHARACTERISTICS		
	The Three-Year-Old	*The Four-Year-Old*	*The Five-Year-Old*
Jumping	Jumps distance of 36–60 cm. 42% rated as jumping well.	Jumps distance of 60–85 cm. 72% skilled in jumping	80% have mastered the skill of jumping.
	Clears rope less than 20 cm. high.	Most show difficulty in executing jump over a barrier.	More adept at jumping over barriers.
	Can jump down from an 8-inch elevation. Leaps off floor with both feet. Jumps down from heights of 8, 12, and 18 inches *alone, feet together*. (This preceded at early stages of jumping with help followed by jumping alone, one foot in front of the other.)	umps down from 28-inch height with feet together. Crouches for a high jump of 2 inches. Standing broad jump 8–10 inches.	Makes running broad jump of 28–35 inches. Makes vertical jump and reach of 2½ inches.
		Running broad jump up to 23–33 inches.	
	Jumps down from a 28-inch height with help.	Jumps down from 28-inch height, alone with feet together.	
Hopping, galloping, skipping	Some attempt at hopping by 29 months.	Hops 2 meters on right foot.	22% skip well at end of fifth year.
	Hopping is largely an irregular series of jumps with some variation added.	Only 14% skip well. 43% are learning to gallop.	78% gallop but are not rated as skilled. Hops distance of 16 feet easily.
	Executes one to three consecutive hops with both feet: 38 months. Executes ten or more hops on both feet: 42 months (rapid skill development). Executes one to three consecutive hops 1 foot: 43 months. Performs a shuffle skip.	Hops four to six steps on one foot. Skips on one foot. Executes one to ten hops consecutively: one foot.	Ten or more consecutive hops: one foot. Alternates feet in skipping.
Climbing	50% rated as proficient in climbing on jungle gyms, packing boxes, inclined planks, etc. Ascends stairway unaided, alternating feet.	Further increase in proficiency.	Still further increase in proficiency.
	Ascends short stairway unaided, alternating feet: 31 months. Ascends long stairway unaided, alternating feet: 41 months.	Descends long stairway by alternating feet, if supported. With no support; marks time. Ascending skills mastered (stairways).	Descends long stairway or large ladder alternating feet. Descends long stairway, alternating feet, unaided. Ascending skills mastered (ladder).

(continued)

TABLE 10.1
(continued)

MOTOR PATTERN	SKILL CHARACTERISTICS		
	The Three-Year-Old	*The Four-Year-Old*	*The Five-Year-Old*
	Descends both short and long stairways, marking time; not supported. Ascends small ladder, alternating feet.	Descends long stairway, alternating feet if supported. Descends short stairway, alternating feet unaided. Ascends large ladder, alternating feet. Descends small ladder, alternating feet.	Descends large ladder, alternating feet.
Throwing	Frequently engaged in ball throwing, but does not throw well. Throws without losing balance. Throws approximately 3 feet; uses two-hand throw. Anteroposterior movement dominant in throwing. Body remains fixed during throw. Arm is initiating factor.	20% are proficient throwers. Beginning to assume adult stance in throwing. Can toss ring toss successfully at peg 4 feet 10½ inches away. Distance of throw increases. Horizontal-plane movements dominate. Whole body rotates right, then left. Feet remain together in place. Arm is the initiating factor.	74% are good throwers— great variation at each age level. Assumes adult posture in throwing. Some throw distances of 17 feet; use primarily unilateral throw. Introduction of weight transfer; right-foot-step-forward throw. At 6–6½ years: mature throw: left-foot-step-forward; trunk rotation, and horizontal adduction of arm in forward swing.
Catching	Attempts to stop rolling ball with hands or corrals it with legs. Gradually synchronized movements with speed of rolling ball and hands reach around object. Aerial ball: first attempts— hands and arms work as a single unit in an attempt to corral the ball against the body. Catches large ball with arms extended forward stiffly. Makes little or no adjustment of arms to receive ball. Catches large and small ball; arms straight.	29% are proficient in catching. Catches large ball tossed from 5 feet away with arms flexed at elbows. Moves arms in accordance with direction; definite efforts to judge position at which ball will land. Depends more on arms than hands in receiving ball. Catches both large and small balls; elbows in front of body.	56% are skilled at catching. Catches small ball; uses hands more than arms. Judges trajectory better than at four; not always successful. Attempts one-hand catches. Catches both large and small balls; elbows at side of body.
Bouncing	Bounces small ball distance of 1–5 feet; uses one hand. Cannot perform this task with a large ball.	Bounces large ball distance of 4–5 feet; uses two hands.	Bounces large ball 6–7 feet; uses two hands. One-hand bounce; large ball attempted at 72 months.

From Corbin, 1973, 1980, pp. 119-120.

1. *Mark-time pattern.* By the time children are about two years old, they can ascend steps using a mark-time pattern. This means they can go up one step at a time leading with the same foot each time.
2. *Alternating pattern.* By about forty-one months, children can climb stairs leading with each foot in an alternating pattern.

By age six, 92 percent of children are proficient climbers. There are no significant differences between boys and girls in climbing skills (Corbin, 1980).

Jumping. Jumping can occur shortly after the child has learned to walk. More strength is required for jumping than for running because the body must be lifted upward in jumping. The first attempt at jumping may appear as an emphatic step from an elevated level. At about twenty-eight months, children are able to jump with both feet simultaneously. About 81 percent of children are proficient jumpers by age five (Corbin, 1980; Kelso and Clark, 1982).

Hopping. Hopping skill is more difficult than jumping because it requires balancing on one foot. It is not until almost thirty months that children can balance themselves by standing on one foot. Most children can hop for short distances at around four years, but it is not until children are about six that they are proficient at hopping (Corbin, 1980).

Throwing. Throwing emerges through four stages (Milne, Seefeldt, and Reuschlein, 1975; Corbin, 1980). The last stage occurs at the end of the preschool period and into the school-age period (roughly six and one-half to seven years of age). We discuss all four stages in detail in Chapter 13.

Catching. The ability to catch a moving object such as a ball requires good eye-hand coordination as well as space-time perception. Toddlers are usually able to stop or gather in a rolling ball. First attempts at catching a ball in flight are somewhat awkward. The arms may be held out stiffly in anticipation of the ball. Eventually the preschooler learns to adjust arm movements in relation to the oncoming ball (Williams, 1983).

Cognitive Development

In Chapter 7 we considered the development of infant cognitive functioning from a threefold approach: the Piagetian perspective, an information-processing viewpoint, and a psychometric perspective. Here we follow a similar strategy as well as discuss an additional dimension of preschool cognitive development—children's drawings and art.

A Piagetian Perspective: The Preoperational Period

According to Piaget's theory of intelligence, early-childhood cognitive development includes the period of preoperational thinking (eighteen months to seven years). The preoperational period is sometimes subdivided into two parts: the preconceptual stage (two to four years of age) and the intuitive stage (five to seven years). Although the intuitive stage includes part of the preschool years and beyond, we discuss it here briefly because many preschool children may function at that level.

• The **preconceptual stage** (two to four years). The highlights of the preconceptual stage include the emergence of language, symbols, and symbolic play. The use of both symbols and symbolic play are significant because they indicate the emerging ability of the child to think about what is *not immediately* present. For example, the child may call a teddy bear a "baby," indicating that the teddy bear represents or symbolizes the idea "baby." The teddy bear is a "symbolic" baby. In the previous period of sensorimotor intelligence, cognitive functioning was limited to what was immediately present or before the infant. Furthermore, the development of language, or linguistic symbols, for action provides the opportunity to use verbal symbols as a way of extending the sensorimotor control of the environment (e.g., instead of walking toward the refrigerator and staring at it as a sensorimotor technique for getting some milk, the preschooler uses the word *milk*, or some facsimile thereof, to control the behavior of adults). The preconceptual child is able to use words to categorize objects; however, this process is limited by the *egocentrism* of the child's thinking (i.e., the inability to distinguish between one's own perceptions and the perceptions of others). Because their perception of the world is colored by their own relatively limited experiences, preschoolers cannot readily distinguish among mental, physical, and social realities. For example, if the child experiences living things as moving (dogs, cats, people, birds), he or she may extend this meaning to include the moon and the clouds as "living" because they also move.

• The **intuitive stage** (five to seven years). The intuitive stage begins at approximately age five. It is closer to adult thinking because the child is now able to separate mental from physical reality. The child is somewhat less egocentric than in the previous stage and therefore is able to distinguish between his or her own perceptions of the real world and the reality of physical and social behavior. For example, this ability to distinguish aspects of reality—and to categorize these features—helps the child differentiate between living objects that move and other objects (clouds, moon, stars) that also move but are not "alive." The child begins to grasp the force of other powers and can more readily appreciate multiple points of view. Thinking skills are improving; however at the intuitive level, children still depend on what they actually perceive (or think they perceive) as the basis of reality (see Fig. 10.6).

SYMBOLIC REPRESENTATION.   The most significant cognitive difference between the infant and the preschooler (two to five years of age) is the *use of symbols* by the preschooler. The preschooler's use of symbols includes a wide range of behavior, such as the use of action images or words to represent experience. For example, on being given a toy car, the twelve-month-old infant might do various things with it, including putting it in his or her mouth, banging it on the floor, throwing it, or simply looking at it. The two-year-old, however, on being presented with a similar car, will probably demonstrate by his or her use of the toy car that he or she knows what a car is or does. For example, the two-year-old may put the car down on the rug (as if the rug were a road) and move the car, making a sound like a running motor. In other words, the two-year-old uses movements and vocal sounds to imitate past events and roles with which he or she is familiar. Observation of the preschooler in play settings may indicate the development and acting out of extensive sequences of behavior relating to the use of the family car to go shopping or for other family activities.

When children first begin to use words, they may use them in idiosyncratic ways. As we saw in Chapter 7, Baby Elizabeth was somewhat general in her use of the word *father*. As symbol use becomes more effective and specific, more complex modes of thinking are possible. For example, the refined use of language

FIGURE 10.6
The intuitive stage of thinking (ages five to seven). Because the child's thinking is more a function of perception *(how things appear) than* logical *necessities, he or she solves problems in a "perceptual" manner. For example, the child is given a square piece of paper and asked to draw both the largest possible square and the smallest possible square on the paper. In order to solve this problem, the intuitive-stage child probably needs to draw many squares on the paper in order to compare them visually to see if each is larger or smaller than the previous one. This "perceptual" mode of problem solving can be contrasted with the "logical" or "abstract" mode of older children and adolescents (e.g. the largest possible square must "logically" be very near to the borders of the paper, whereas the smallest possible square must be very tiny).*

allows children to demonstrate to themselves (and to others) both the similarities and the differences of objects by assigning them labels. In addition, children can use words as a way of interpreting their past and predicting their future.

CLASSIFICATION.   The process of refining the idea of conservation during the preoperational phase of thinking is accompanied by other developments in the preschooler's thinking skills. In particular, the child's ability to organize and *classify* objects according to categories is also limited in certain ways. When asked to classify and organize objects, the preoperational child puts them in categories that reflect his or her egocentric perception of how the world is structured. In other words, the *basis* for classification arises out of the association of objects and perceptions.

■   *SCENARIO: THE CLOUDS IN THE SKY, GRAMPA'S PIPE,*
    AND A PREOPERATIONAL GRANDSON

Bruce's grandparents have come from Chicago to see their grandchildren. One evening, grandfather was smoking his pipe and pipe smoke began to rise over his head in a visible gray pattern. On noting this "cloud" of smoke, Bruce arose from his preoccupation with a small cardboard box and made the following observations to his grandfather:

1. "Grampa, your cloud is the same as the clouds outside in the sky."
2. "Grampa, did you make the clouds outside?"

"Now look what you've done! I had that trap all set for the tooth fairy!"

In this scenario, Bruce organizes his world according to a classification in which the clouds from his grandfather's pipe can be easily and seriously grouped with the clouds in the sky. The preoperational child who is given a collection of objects that vary along a number of dimensions, including size, shape, color, and texture, will probably not organize or *classify* the objects in the same fashion as an older child or an adult. As we pointed out, the preoperational child can usually focus on only one dimension or attribute of an object or a collection of objects. The preoperational child may have no difficulty grouping together objects on the basis of use, for example, plates, knives, forks, and spoons. The arrangement of objects on the basis of many characteristics at the same time is much more difficult.

CONSERVATION.   Several of the features (as well as limitations) of preschool children's thinking are illustrated in what Piaget and others have called **conservation** problems (see Figs. 10.7 and 10.8 and Table 10.2). According to Piaget, one of the most important cognitive achievements of child development is the construction of permanent concepts ("invariances") in the face of an environment that involves continuous changes. As we have mentioned before, around two years of age the child constructs the notion of the permanence of objects. Having acquired this idea, the preschool child is ready to refine the notion of the permanence of objects to include the *invariability* or conservation of object characteristics, such as weight, volume, number, or amount.

Piaget and others have studied the development of conservation using the following experimental arrangement:

1. The child is shown two amounts or quantities that are, in fact, equal. The child is then asked to affirm that the two amounts are equal. Most four-year-old children are able to recognize such equalities.

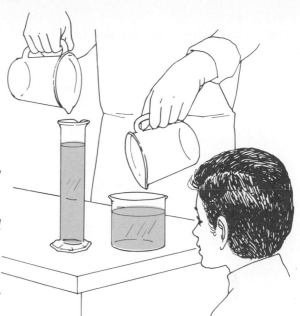

FIGURE 10.7
Conservation of liquid. Two beakers with equal amounts of water in them are presented to the child, and the child is asked to recognize the equality (most children can do this by the time they are four years of age). While the child watches, a transformation occurs: One beaker of water is poured into a tall, cylindrical beaker and the other is poured into a flat beaker. The child is now asked whether the amounts of water in the tall and the short beakers are the same or different. The preoperational child will say they are different and that the tall, cylindrical beaker has more water in it.

2. While the child watches, the equal objects are transformed so that they "appear" to be different.
3. The child is then asked whether the two amounts are now the same or different.

In the developmental pattern of conservation, the four-to-five-year-old child can usually recognize that the quantities presented in the first step of the conservation problem are equal. For example, when children are presented (as in Fig. 10.8) with

FIGURE 10.8
Conservation of number. When shown the arrangement of candy at the top, four-to-five-year-old children generally respond that both lines contain the same number of candies. In the configuration at the bottom, the lower line of candy has been spread out so that it appears to be wider and longer. When asked whether the candies in the lines of the bottom configuration are the same or different, the preoperational child insists that the line that appears longer has more candy in it, even if the child has counted the candies in each line. Based on J. Piaget, 1952.

TABLE 10.2

Some Tests of Child Conservation

Type of Conservation	Procedure	Average Age of Occurrence
Liquids:	Two identical beakers are filled to the same level, and the child agrees that they have the same amount to drink. → Contents of one beaker are poured into a different shaped beaker so that the two columns of water are of unequal height.	Conserving child recognizes that each beaker has the same amount to drink (on the average, conservation of liquids is attained at age 6–7 years).
Mass (continuous substance):	Two identical balls of playdough are presented. The child agrees that they have equal amounts of dough. → One ball is rolled into the shape of a sausage.	Conserving child recognizes that each object contains the same amount of dough (average age, 6–7).
Number:	Child sees two rows of beads and agrees that each row has the same number. → One row of beads is increased in length.	Conserving child recognizes that each row still contains the same number of beads (average age, 6–7).
Length:	Two sticks of equal length are presented, and the child agrees that they are of equal length. → One stick is moved (or bent to assume a different appearance).	Conserving child recognizes that the two sticks are still of equal length (average age, 6–7).
Area:	The child sees two identical sheets, each covered by the same number of blocks. The child agrees that each sheet has the same amount of uncovered area. → The blocks on one sheet are scattered.	Conserving child recognizes that the amount of uncovered area remains the same for each sheet (average age, 9–10).
Volume (water displacement):	Two identical balls of clay are placed in two identical beakers that has been judged to have the same amount to drink. The child sees the water level rise to the same point in each beaker. → One ball of clay is taken from the water, molded into a different shape, and placed above the beaker. Child is asked whether the water level will be higher than, lower than, or the same as in the other beaker when the clay is reinserted into the water.	Conserving child recognizes that the water levels will be the same because nothing except the shape of the clay has changed—that is, the pieces of clay displace the same amount of water (average age, 9–12).

From Shaffer, 1985, p. 348.

equal amounts of candy, they will say that both lines of candy are the same, probably because they "look" the same. In other words, the child's conclusion is based on his or her perception that the candy in both lines covers the same total distance. This reliance on perception becomes clear when a *transformation* is made in the perceptual characteristics of the candy arrangement (see bottom of Fig. 10.8), so that one line is longer than the other. When this happens, the child has difficulty understanding that there are still equal amounts of candy in both lines. The five-to-six-year-old child seems to be in a transitional phase and may respond inconsistently. At one time, the child will say that the transformed arrangements contain the same amounts and, at another time, will insist that the transformed arrangements are not equal. By the time the child reaches age seven, the concept of conservation of number seems to have been perfected. Furthermore, the average age for the attainment of some other types of conservation occurs, on the average between six and seven years of age (e.g., conservation of liquid, conservation of mass, and conservation of length) (see Table 10.2). On the other hand, conservation of area and conservation of volume (water displacement) usually occur at nine to ten years and nine to twelve years, respectively.

LIMITATIONS OF PREOPERATIONAL THINKING. Although the child at the preoperational level of thinking has made substantial improvements in thinking skills, preoperational thought has several *limitations*, according to Piaget.

- *Preoperational thinking is concrete.* That is, the child works best with the world of his or her immediate surroundings and his or her own perceptions of reality. The child is usually involved with the present and with objects or experiences that can be easily represented by images and simple words.
- *Preoperational thinking is not reversible.* **Reversibility** refers to the ability of mentally returning to an original circumstance or reversing one's thinking. For example, in the conservation of number problem (Fig. 10.7), the preoperational child is unable to recognize that if the longer line of candies in the lower configuration is shortened, it will, in fact, return to its prior equality with the shorter line of candies. In other words, the preoperational child is presumably incapable of mentally returning or "reversing" his or her thinking to a prior state of affairs.
- *Preoperational thinking tends to be egocentric.* The child focuses on the environment from the perspective of his or her own limited experience. (See the previous discussion of the preoperational child's classification skills and, in particular, the "scenario".)
- *Preoperational thinking may involve centration.* **Centration** is the tendency to focus on one dimension of a problem while overlooking other aspects that would be useful in developing a solution. For example, in the conservation-of-volume (liquid) problem in Figure 10.6, the preoperational child seems unable to correctly solve the problem because he or she cannot focus on *both* height and width. As a result, they fail to understand that an increase in width of a column of liquid *compensates* for the decreased height of that liquid (particularly, when compared to the height of the liquid in the tall narrow flask). Piaget refers to this ability to consider several dimensions of a problem simultaneously as *compensation*.
- *Preoperational thinking tends to involve "transductive reasoning."* The preschooler reasons from one specific and immediate (here-and-now) event to another equally specific and immediate event. Reasoning from particular to particular is a matter of thinking by association. For example, seeing the wind blowing leaves, trees, and paper about, the child might arrive at the conclusion that he or she, too, will be blown away, never to be seen again. Because the child reasons from particular

to particular, somewhat illogical and sometimes humorous conclusions are reached. Transductive reasoning differs from two types of reasoning employed by older children and adolescents:

a. *Inductive reasoning,* or moving from specific instances to generalities (e.g., a baseball, a golf ball, and a tennis ball are all examples of the general category *ball*).
b. *Deductive reasoning,* or reasoning from generalities to specifics (e.g., foods include cheese, tomatoes, meat, and cake).

HOW LIMITED IS PREOPERATIONAL THINKING?   To indicate that a child is at the preoperational level of thinking is to say more than that he or she simply has not attained concrete operations. That is, preoperational thinking is not described primarily in terms of its deficiencies with reference to concrete operations. For example, as we have indicated above, Piaget suggested that the preoperational child is egocentric, "centered" in his or her thinking, perception-bound, transductive, and unable to solve conservation problems.

Is it the case that preschoolers are actually preoperational in all ways? Numerous studies have, in fact, raised serious doubt about this characterization (Gelman and Baillargeon, 1983). For the most part, these studies demonstrate that young preschoolers, under certain conditions, can do such things as behave in a nonegocentric fashion, ignore misleading perceptual information, and so on.

With reference to egocentric behavior, the claim is frequently made that preschoolers are egocentric in their perspective-taking behavior. For example, Jean Piaget and Bärbel Inhelder (1956) suggest that preschoolers may be incapable of taking (or understanding) the perspective of another person. In Piaget and Inhelder's (1956) experiment, children were shown a model of three mountains. A doll was then placed at various positions around the model and the children were asked to tell the experimenter how the mountains would appear to the doll at each position. Children under six years of age responded to the question by choosing a picture or a small replica of the mountains which consistently reflected their own perspective rather than the doll's perspective. Piaget and Inhelder suggested that the young preschool child is involved "in his own viewpoint in the narrowest and most restricted fashion, so that he cannot imagine any perspective but his own" (p. 242).

Does this description of egocentrism accurately portray preschoolers' perspective taking? The findings of several studies contradict this Piagetian view (Masangkay et al., 1974; Borke, 1975; Lempers, Flavell, and Flavell, 1977; Flavell et al., 1981). Helene Borke (1975) demonstrated that the age at which nonegocentric perspective taking occurs is influenced by the nature of the display presented to the child and the type of response that is required from the child. Borke used three displays, two of which were of familiar toy objects and the third a replica of Piaget and Inhelder's (1956) three mountains. The children were asked to indicate the doll's perspective by rotating duplicates of the displays. On the two displays that involved familiar toy objects, Borke found that children as young as three and four years were able to correctly identify the doll's perspective between 79 percent and 93 percent of the time. However, on the display that was a replica of the one used by Piaget and Inhelder, Borke found that three-year-olds correctly identified the perspective of the doll only 42 percent of the time and four-year-olds were correct only 67 percent of the time. Borke suggested that her results call into question the Piaget and Inhelder findings:

> [These results] . . . raise considerable doubt about the validity of Piaget's conclusion that young children are primarily egocentric and incapable of taking the viewpoint of another person. When presented with tasks that are age appropriate, even very young subjects demonstrate perceptual perspective-taking ability. (p. 243)

With reference to the centration, what evidence is there that the preoperational child fails to solve conservation problems because of an inability to focus on more than one dimension of the problem? Several studies with young children provide strong evidence for questioning the notion of centration (Anderson and Cuneo, 1978; Cuneo, 1980). In the first study, children five years of age and older were shown cookies that varied systematically on two dimensions—height and width. The children were taught to rate the cookies using a long measuring rod that had a happy face at one end and a sad face at the other end. The task of the children was to point to the spot on the measuring rod—between the happy and the sad face—that indicated how happy or sad a child would feel if he ate a given-sized cookie. Results of the study indicated that the preschoolers used *both* height and weight in rating the projected reactions to the cookies. In another study, Cuneo found that three- and four-year-old children used a height and width rule to evaluate the size of cookies. In both studies, there was no indication of centration or fixation on one dimension.

What about the depiction of preschool children as perception-bound in their thinking? Evidence for the perception-bound hypothesis came not only from the work of Piaget, but from an early conservation experiment by the American psychologist Jerome Bruner and his associates (1966). In the latter experiment, two identical beakers filled with water were shown to the children. When the water from one of the beakers was poured into a third beaker, Bruner and his colleagues found that children were much less likely to give up their original idea of equivalence of beakers if the third beaker (whatever its dimensions) was hidden behind a screen, rather than visible to the child. In other words, the child's original perception of equivalence was more likely to continue if a screen prevented the perception of any cognitively unsettling information, such as a different-sized or different-shaped container.

However, other evidence has called into question both Piaget's and Bruner's contention of the perception-bound quality of preschooler thinking (Fein, 1979; Markman, 1979; Gelman, Spelke, and Meck, 1983; Flavell, Green, and Flavell, 1986). Greta Fein (1979) found that children were able to distinguish between appearance and reality and were, therefore, not limited by their perceptions. She found that children were able to distinguish between pretend activities involved in play and other play activities. In another experiment, three-year-olds demonstrated the ability to differentiate between real and apparent (perceptual) properties of objects (Flavell, Green, and Flavell, 1986). Children were shown a white piece of paper which was then placed behind a piece of pink plastic, making the paper appear pink. John Flavell and his associates found that over half of the children were able to distinguish between the perceptual appearance of pinkness and the reality of the white paper. Rochel Gelman, Elizabeth Spelke, and Elizabeth Mech (1983) found that three-year-olds recognized that dolls and persons were more similar than dolls and rocks. However, the three-year-olds also indicated that dolls could only *pretend* to do what people really do—walk, eat, sleep, play, and so on.

In addition, some investigators have had success with *training* preschool children to do conservation tasks (Gold, 1978; Beilin, 1980; Murray, 1981; Gelman,

1982). Such training has typically taken the form of teaching preschool children to recognize that even though an object has been *transformed* in some way (e.g., changing shape or position in space), it is still the *same* object. In other cases, nonconserving children have been taught to do conservation tasks by watching models (conserving children) (Murray, 1981). In a typical teaching paradigm, Gelman (1982) gave three- and four-year-olds a pretest or training experience in which the children counted the number of items in two groups of objects, displayed in rows. They were then asked which of the rows had more objects. Children worked with object set sizes of three or four items in the training phase. The children were then asked to perform standard conservation tasks, this time with object set sizes of five or ten items. Findings indicated that the training experience *transferred* successfully not only to the standard conservation experiences with smaller sets (five items), but to larger sets as well (ten items).

In summary, there is evidence from a number of studies that suggests that preschool preoperational children are not simply perception-bound, "centered," or egocentric in their thinking. The implication of these results is that the preschool child may be closer to the older or concrete operational child than Piagetian theory leads one to think (Gelman and Baillargeon, 1983). However, this is not to suggest that the cognitive limitations of the preoperational child, as discussed earlier, are totally inaccurate or inappropriate. It is the case that preoperational children still do not succeed as consistently as older, concrete operational children on standard conservation classification or serial ordering tasks.

Information Processing and Child Thinking

Although Piaget's observations and research provide a useful interpretation of children's thinking processes, many specific details remain to be filled. For example, when a preschool child is coping with a conservation problem or trying to serially organize a set of objects, how is his or her mind working during these activities? To provide an answer to this question, we can turn to an information-processing perspective.

The information-processing approach to the development of cognitive activity offers a detailed, step-wise description of thinking (Siegler and Richards, 1982; Siegler, 1983). The primary emphasis is on the following components:

· **Perception** *and* **Attention**—how human beings acquire information.
· **Memory**—how individuals store and retrieve information.
· **Problem Solving**—how human beings deal with present circumstances or make future plans.

The **information-processing** perspective is based on an analogy between the human mind and a computer. As in the case of computers, human beings can be said to have "programs" for receiving, organizing, storing, and retrieving information. The intent of the information-processing approach is to identify these programs and to determine how they operate. Such an analysis of children's thinking and learning raises several major issues about the differences between the thinking processes of young children compared with those of adults:

· Do children have a limited capacity for processing information?
· Do children handle information at a slower rate than adults?

Information Processing: Boy Meets Dog

Fishbein (1976) gives the following illuminating description of information processing:

Step 1 Receive information (e.g., patterns of light on the retina).

Step 2 Identification of information—"It's a dog."

Step 3 Information storage—some representation of the dog is transmitted and stored in memory.

Step 4 Manipulation of information— representation of dog is compared with other stored information about dogs—"This dog is bigger than any dog I've ever seen before!"

Step 5 Making a decision (which need not be conscious) about this information—"That dog is dangerous."

Step 6 Acts on the decisions made about the information—"Run like hell!"

Based on Fishbein, 1976.

· In what ways does the limited knowledge base of children affect their information processing?
· How are children's "programs" for learning different from those of adults?
· How do child perception, attention, memory, and problem solving develop or change over time?

The preschool child is able to perform the basic steps in information processing. These steps include the reception of information, the specific identification of the information (e.g., what is it?), simple operations on the information (e.g., comparisons with existing information in memory), decisions based on the information, and actions. However, as the child develops, the amount of information taken in, the speed of information processing, and the strategies or "programs" used by the child will change over time (Siegler, 1983). Two major dimensions of preschooler thinking which illustrate these developmental changes are attention and memory.

ATTENTION. The young child is typically in a situation where he or she is subject to a broad array and level of stimulation—including sights, sounds, smells, physical contact with people and objects, and so on. Since the child cannot efficiently give attention to all things, he or she has to select which objects, experiences, or people to investigate and which ones to ignore. Attention is the process of selecting what is worthy of exploration or further mental processing (Gibson and Spelke, 1983).

Over the preschool years, there appear to be three primary changes in attentional processes:

. The movement from *reactive* or environmentally determined attention to *investigative* or intention-directed attention. For example, the young child is more likely to attend to the loudest noise or to the brightest color, whereas the older child's attention is more a function of his or her own intentions or interest.
. The movement from *random* to *systematic* observations. The attention of preschoolers moves randomly from one situation or object to another situation or object. On the other hand, older children are typically more systematic and directed in their observations.
. The movement from *taking in all information* to the *selective screening* of irrelevant information. Older children can focus on the relevant features of an object or event better than younger children can.

The findings of a number of research studies have supported the above developmental transformations in attentional processes (Drozda and Flavell, 1975; Vurpillot, 1976; Vurpillot and Ball, 1979; Wellman, Somerville, and Haake, 1979; Anooshian and Prilop, 1980). As children grow older, the exploration of objects becomes more efficient and systematic. The studies by Elaine Vurpillot (Vurpillot, 1976; Vurpillot and Ball, 1979) provided children with the task of judging whether pairs of line drawings of houses were similar or different (see Fig. 10.9). Each house in a pair of houses had six windows (arranged in two columns of three windows each). The windows could be identical or they could vary on any number of details (e.g., curtains, plants, laundry on a line, and so on). Findings of the studies suggested that the children's scan paths (eye movements making comparisons) became more efficient from four to nine years of age. The most efficient comparative strategy involved eye scan movements from a window in one house to the same-positioned window in another house (homologous comparison). The number of children making such homologous comparisons ranged from zero (out of eighteen subjects) for the youngest group to eighteen (out of twenty subjects) for nine-year-olds. Once children reached six years of age, most of them made homologous comparisons. Furthermore, preschool children made their comparative judgments based on a limited sample of the total information available. On the other hand, the older children explored many differences between the windows in making their judgments. Similar findings with five-, eight-, and eleven-year-olds who were asked to compare mock-ups of houses indicated the following:

. Five-year-olds explored the differences in the houses in a haphazard
  fashion.
. Eight-year-olds searched more systematically for differences than five-year-olds; however, when asked to find one primary difference between the houses, they seemed unable to confine their attention to only one difference.
. Eleven-year-olds planned their search and comparison more carefully
  than either the five- or the eight-year-olds and were able to confine them
  to specific requests (e.g., "Find only one difference between the houses")
  (Vlietstra, 1982).

Although, as we have indicated, there is evidence of the inefficiency of preschooler comparative scanning, does this *necessarily* imply that such preschoolers

From Vurpillot, 1976.

FIGURE 10.9
These examples of line drawings of houses were used by Vurpillot (1976) to examine child attentional processes (i.e., visual scanning). From Vurpillot, 1976.

have inadequate attention spans? A common observation of parents and teachers is that preschoolers can indeed become so involved in their play activities as to be oblivious to the world around them. In a comparative study of preschoolers, first-graders, and second-graders who played with a box containing eighteen drawers (each drawer contained a different toy), it was the preschoolers who demonstrated the most curiosity, asked the most questions, and handled the toys the most (Henderson and Moore, 1979). On the other hand, it was the older children who moved the fastest from drawer to drawer, seemingly driven by a need to know about the box. It may well be that even *if* preschool children do understand minimal search strategies (e.g., one should look *first* at a *relevant* stimuli and then verbally *label* them, as a memory aid), they seem to be overwhelmed by the desire to explore all facets of objects/events—both relevant and irrelevant tasks (Miller and Weiss, 1982). Thus, although we would not suggest that preschoolers are incapable of sustained attention, it is typically the case that they do not translate even minimal scanning strategies into actual behavior until a later age. The assumption is that as they mature they will encounter numerous situations that will require them to exercise disciplined attention to specific stimuli in order to accomplish specific tasks.

MEMORY.   In addition to attentional processes, a second critical determinant of information processing is memory. If attention determines what information is processed, then memory determines the information that remains in the system and how that information is stored and retrieved at a later time. (Perlmutter 1986).

There is evidence that preschoolers have poorer memories than older children. For example, they have a more difficult time remembering pictures, words, or the order of items on a memory test (Pick, Frankel, and Hess, 1975). In addition, preschoolers have better **recognition memory** (the realization that an event or experience that one encounters has been experienced at a prior time) than **recall memory** (recollecting objects or events without having examples of them for comparison). For example, recognition, memory would be required to answer the following question—Did Roger Maris break Babe Ruth's home-run record of 60? On the other hand, recall memory would be necessary for the following question—Who broke Babe Ruth's home-run record?

Several reasons have frequently been given for the relatively poorer memory performance of preschoolers compared with older children (Pressley and Brainerd, 1985):

• *Preschooler memory is not as well organized as older-child or adult memory.* Older children and adults can use *concepts* to organize and identify information, but the preschooler's ability to use such concepts is quite limited. Concepts are particularly useful as guides or organizers for the retrieval of information. For example, it is far easier to remember the names Idaho, Oregon, and Washington if one uses the conceptual organizer "states of the Northwest" than to try to remember them simply as random names.
• *Preschoolers have limited information-processing ability.* Older children typically develop specific and more elaborate *rehearsal strategies* for remembering information compared with preschool children (Case, Kurlind, and Goldberg, 1982; Brown et al., 1983). For example, the older child has a plan for memorization that includes such strategies as grouping items together. On the other hand, preschoolers may resort to such precursors of organized rehearsal as sporadic attempts to remember information by naming, pointing, or eye fixation (Wellman, Ritter, and Flavell, 1975). By approximately five years of age, children demonstrate occasional labeling of some items. Typically, it is not until the early elementary-school years that labeling as well as rote repetition of single items of information become established memory rehearsal strategies (Brown et al., 1983).
• *Preschoolers have a limited knowledge base* (i.e., body of prior knowledge). It is a common observation that it is easier to both learn and remember new information if one already has, in memory, a set of ideas or concepts to which the new data can be related. Preschoolers are more likely to have less of a knowledge base than the older child and, therefore, to have more limited memories (Flavell, 1985).

Development of Attention in the Preschool Years

According to John C. Wright and Alice G. Vlietstra (1975), several changes in attentional processes occur over the preschool years:

• *Three-Year-Old Explorers.* They deal with their environment in a playful way. They may flit from one object/activity to another, primarily motivated by whatever attracts them. They are curious about their world although easily distracted.

• *Six-Year-Old Searchers.* In contrast to three-year-olds, six-year-olds explore their environment in a more organized and systematic fashion. They appear to be less impulsive than three-year-olds and may stop and reflect before dropping one activity in favor of another. They are less easily distracted since they appear to be motivated by a need to know about their experience.

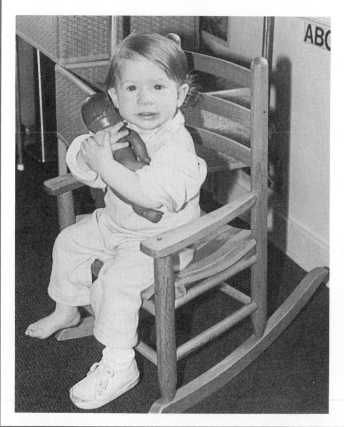

Sylvia Byers

Sylvia Byers

The Psychometric Approach

In addition to the Piagetian and information-processing perspectives, the psychometric viewpoint provides a useful way of understanding and measuring the intelligence of the preschool child. As we indicated in our discussion of measuring infant intelligence (see Chapter 7), scores on preschool measures of intelligence are more closely related to (or correlated with) measures of adolescent intelligence (a seven- or eight-year gap in time) than infant intelligence scores are related to preschool scores (a time gap of only two or three years) (Siegler and Richards, 1982; Honzik, 1983). One reason for such findings may be that infant intelligence measures tap or assess sensorimotor skills. Hence, it has been argued that infant intelligence (as measured using standard infant intelligence tests such as the Bayley scales) is qualitatively different from the more *verbal* measures that begin to be used in the preschool period and beyond. The predictability of adolescent intelligence increases during the preschool years, stabilizing around four to five years of age (Honzik, 1983) (see Chapter 7).

Two frequently used measures of preschool intelligence are the *Stanford-Binet Intelligence Scale* and the *Wechsler Preschool and Primary Scale of Intelligence* (WPPSI). The Stanford-Binet test is used for both preschoolers and older children, whereas the WPPSI is a test exclusively for the preschool age child. Since the Stanford-Binet is also used for older children and since the WPPSI is similar in design and format to the WISC (the Wechsler Intelligence Scale for Children, also used for older children), we discuss these tests in Chapter 13.

Children's Drawing: The Integration of Movement, Thinking, and Self-Perception

As we have pointed out before, human behavior involves the *integration* of many specific components into a unified whole or *system*. This integration is well illustrated by the development of children's drawing, which involves the integration of motor skills (e.g., eye-hand coordination), cognitive development, and expression of feelings about the self and the world. In its broadest context, children's drawing is the playful, nonserious representation of symbols on paper. In a nar-

Sylvia Byers

Children express creativity in drawing.

rower context, children's drawing has been interpreted (like adult artistic works of painting, sculpture, and design) as purposive and goal-oriented (and therefore, not really play). We will not try to resolve this issue. However, it is clear that children's drawing (whether or not an "official" mode of play) is an important indicator of child development. Children's drawing often occurs in the context of the family or the preschool.

From the very moment that he or she picks up a crayon, pencil, paintbrush, or other drawing implement, the child is taking significant steps toward the organization of his or her development. Children's drawing skills progress through several stages (Kellogg, 1970; Gardner, 1980):

· *The placement stage.* In the **placement stage,** the child is experimenting with various scribble marks. Much of the child's activity is exploratory as he or she tries different ways of holding the crayon as well as drawing on different places on the paper. Sometimes the child's drawing is confined to one small part of a paper, and at other times the child's drawing is composed of broad strokes that take up the entire paper (and sometimes beyond). By the time the child is two and one-half to three years of age, he or she has probably mastered most of the basic scribble movements (see Fig. 10.10).
· *The shape stage.* In the **shape stage,** children begin to draw actual forms. They can make the outline or the approximation of such shapes as circles, squares, Xs, and so on.
· *The design stage.* In the **design stage,** the child begins to make imaginative arrangements that combine the basic shapes and forms mastered in the previous stage.
· *The pictorial stage.* In the **pictorial stage,** by the time the child is four or five years old, he or she is able to combine the basic shapes and combinations (learned in earlier stages) to depict or represent familiar objects in the family, the neighborhood, or the preschool environment. For example, the child may draw reasonable facsimiles of houses, cars, dogs, cats, faces, and other people (see Fig. 10.11).

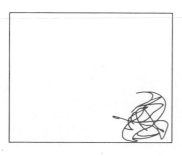

FIGURE 10.10

The placement stage of children's drawing. "The importance of the Placement Pattern lies in the developmental sequence that follows from them. The Patterns are the earliest evidence I have discerned of controlled shaping in children's work. The Basic Scribbles themselves suggest shapes, mainly circles, but also rectangles, and triangles." Based on Kellogg, 1970.

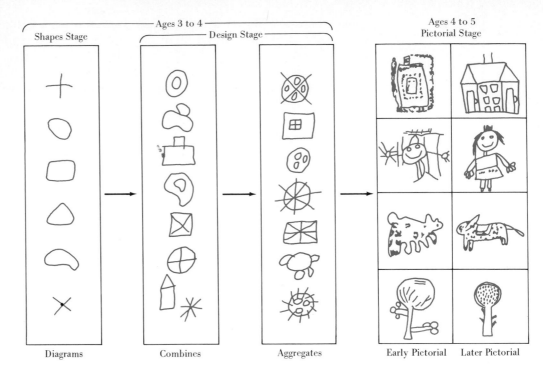

FIGURE 10.11
A chart depicting shape, design, and pictorial stages. From Kellogg, 1974.

Language and the Preschooler

Although infants and toddlers have developed rather remarkable language skills and can communicate with their companions (see the discussion of infant/toddler language development in Chapter 7), their language skills are quite modest in comparison to those of the preschooler (particularly four- and five-year-olds and some three-year-olds). For example, the preschool child's verbal utterances are different from those of the infant/toddler in two notable ways—*length* and *complexity*. In this section we examine how the preschooler is able to do this. First, however, we consider the more general issue of what a preschooler should be able to do with language.

General Language Skills

What should a preschooler be able to do with language? To fully understand the remarkable change that occurs in language from infancy to the preschool years, we need to know something about the general language skills of the preschooler. There is considerable evidence that by the age of five the child is able to use language in the following ways (Dale, 1976; Anisfeld, 1984; Kuczaj and Barrett, 1986):

. *Instrumental.* Children should understand that language is a tool for accomplishing things. The phrase "I want . . ." helps the child express needs.

* *Regulatory.* Children come to understand that language can be used to control their behavior. In turn, they can use language to influence the behavior of other children and adults. The regulatory function becomes elaborated into rules stated with language.
* *Interactional.* Language can be used to organize and define relationships with other people, for example, stating who can play a particular game or defining the make-believe roles to be assumed by playmates.
* *Personal.* Through the use of language, children become more aware of their individuality. The ability to label facets of the personality with words or phrases helps the child to develop a more objective sense of self in relation to other children.
* *Heuristic.* Children use language to discover the dimensions of reality. Asking questions is a common technique for accomplishing this goal.
* *Imaginative.* Language can be used in pretend play and games as well as in playing with combinations of real and "made-up" words.
* *Representational.* Children use language to represent aspects of reality. Language, then, becomes a system of mutually understood symbols that facilitate thinking and communication with others.

Another way to think about the changes in language skills that occur from infancy to the preschool years is to examine the *length* and *complexity* of the preschooler's language. For example, in the relatively brief period of time of eight to ten months, the preschooler has moved from the brief two-word telegraphic utterances of the infant/toddler (see the discussion of telegraphic speech in Chapter 7) to longer and more complex sentences. In Table 10.3 we see that children who are thirty-five to thirty-eight months of age are introducing *auxiliary verbs* (*have, has, had,* and so on), *word endings* (*-ed* or *-ing*), and *articles* (*the, a,* and so on) which are not present in the speech of younger children. In addition, the thirty-five- or thirty-eight-month-old may be *asking questions* as well as stating *negative sentences* ("No! I *don't* know").

TABLE 10.3
Samples of Speech at Three Ages

AGE		
28 MONTHS (TELEGRAPHIC SPEECH)	35 MONTHS	38 MONTHS
Somebody pencil	No—I don't know	I like a racing car
Floor	What dat feeled like?	I broke my racing car
Where birdie go?	Lemme do again	It's broked
Read dat	Don't—don't hold with me	You got some beads
Hit hammer, Mommy	I'm going to drop it—inne dump truck	Who put dust on my hair?
Yep, it fit	Why—cracker can't talk?	Mommy don't let me buy some
Have screw	Those are mines	Why it's not working?

Adapted from McNeil, 1970.

The Development of Grammatical Morphemes

Grammatical morphemes are word modifiers that give precision to the meaning of words (and, therefore, to sentences) and include the following:

- *Inflections* or word endings such as *-ed* for changing verbs from the present to the past tense (e.g., "I beg" to I beg*ged*), *-s* for changing singular nouns to the plural (e.g., boy to boy*s*), and so on.
- *Prepositions* (e.g., *in* or *on*)
- *Articles* (e.g., *the*, *a*, and so on)

Furthermore, there is evidence that children learn these grammatical morphemes in a specific order. That is, children appear to learn grammatical morphemes in the order presented in Table 10.4, beginning with the *-ing* endings. According to Roger Brown (1973), the reason for such a specific order has to do with the fact that simpler morphemes are learned before more complex ones. For example, *-ing* endings (e.g., he is sit*ting* down) are learned first because they describe an *ongoing process*, whereas *-ed* endings added to verbs (e.g., he jump*ed* the stream) are learned later because they describe something more complex—a process *earlier in time*.

The acquisition of grammatical morphemes demonstrates one of the most interesting characteristics of language development: *overregularization*. For example, **overregularization** occurs when children who are first learning language inflect the irregular (or strong) verbs of English for the past tense in the same way that regular (or weak verbs) are inflected. That is, they produce such verbs as *comed*, *breaked*, and *doed* by this process of overregularization. They use the inflection *d* or *ed*, which is appropriate for regular verbs such as *walk (walked)* or *talk (talked)*, and apply it to irregular verbs. Although the phenomenon of overregularization is interesting in its own right, it also demonstrates an important feature of early language development: *the child is searching for patterns of organizing words*. When a

TABLE 10.4
Development of Fourteen Grammatical Morphemes

MORPHEME	MEANING	EXAMPLE
1. Present progressive: *-ing*	Ongoing process	He is sit*ting* down
2. Preposition: *in*	Containment	The mouse is *in* the box
3. Preposition: *on*	Support	The book is *on* the table
4. Plural: *-s*	Number	The dog*s* ran away
5. Past irregular: for example, *went*	Earlier in time relative to time of speaking	The boy *went* home
6. Possessive: *-'s*	Possession	The girl*'s* dog is big
7. Uncontractible copula *be:* for example, *are*, *was*	Number; earlier in time	*Are* they boys or girls? *Was* that a dog?
8. Articles: *the*, *a*	Definite/indefinite	He has *a* book
9. Past regular: *-ed*	Earlier in time	He jump*ed* the stream
10. Third person regular: *-s*	Number; earlier in time	She run*s* fast
11. Third person irregular: for example, *has*, *does*	Number; earlier in time	*Does* the dog bark?
12. Uncontractible auxiliary *be:* for example, *is*, *were*	Number; earlier in time; ongoing process	*Is* he running? *Were* they at home?
13. Contractible copula *be:* for example, *-'s*, *-'re*	Number; earlier in time	That*'s* a spaniel
14. Contractible auxiliary *be:* for example, *-'s*, *-'re*	Number; earlier in time; ongoing process	They*'re* running very slowly

From Clark and Clark, 1977.

pattern is acquired, it will very likely be applied as broadly as possible (Slobin, 1985; Dale, 1976).

An interesting way in which the development of grammatical morphemes has been studied is by the use of nonsense nouns or verbs. This method ensures that the child has never heard the word before, and therefore it eliminates the possibility of rote memory. Jean Berko (1958) has used this technique (see Fig. 10.12). A typical language problem using this technique is the following: "This is a wug. Now we have another one. We have two of them. We have two ————." Results of this kind of experiment with toddlers and preschoolers indicate that children do overgeneralize by applying their known inflection patterns to all situations.

This extraordinary capacity for applying language patterns is illustrated by an interesting situation. One might expect that toddlers and young children begin their language development by using regular verb forms correctly (e.g., *walked* or *helped*) and then gradually extending these learned patterns to irregular verb forms (e.g., *come, do,* and *tear*). This commonsense expectation, however, is not what happens. Observations indicate that toddlers at first use the correct forms of the past tense for some irregular verbs *even before* they learn the correct inflections of regular verbs. Why should this be the case? It is probably not so surprising in light of two facts (Dale, 1976):

1. Irregular verbs (*come, do,* and so on) express *common actions* and are therefore used more often to describe simple behaviors.

This is a wug.

Now there is another one.
There are two of them.
There are two _____ .

FIGURE 10.12

Berko's experimental method for examining children's use of inflections. Nonsense verbs and nouns are used so that results will indicate generalized patterns of language rather than memory of spoken words. Adapted from Bellugi and Brown, 1964, p. 43–79.

2. Irregular verb forms are four times *more common in parental speech* than regular verb forms (Slobin, 1979, 1985).

Soon, the regular-verb past-tense inflection (*d* or *ed*) appears and is extended by the toddler to both regular and irregular verbs. The correct irregular past-tense forms that preceded may coexist with the regular and generalized pattern for a time, but they are ultimately abandoned. Later they are discovered again or re-learned as "exceptions" to the new-found inflection patterns (Dale, 1976).

Transformations of Simple Sentences

In addition to learning grammatical morphemes which modify and clarify the meaning of words, the preschool child also learns to transform or modify the basic declarative sentence. Such transformations include *asking questions, developing complex sentences,* and *making negative statements.*

THE DEVELOPMENT OF QUESTIONS. The development of questions illustrates the general development of complex transformations of simple sentences (Bloom, Merkin, and Wootten, 1982). Like most other languages, the English language has two types of questions:

· *Yes/no questions* are those that can be formed from almost any declarative sentence; they ask if the declarative statement is true or false. *Declarative statement:* "Johnny plays with his blocks." *Yes/no question:* "Does Johnny play with his blocks?"
· *"Wh" questions* are those that ask for specific information. They are called "wh" questions because they usually begin with "wh" words, such as *which, what, why,* and *who.*

The general pattern of development for question asking follows the same form as language development as a whole. That is, the toddler's questions are telegraphic at first, and then over time they approximate adult questions. Initially questions differ from their declarative equivalents only by a rising intonation (Dale, 1976):

Declarative statement: "See cat."
Question: "See cat?" (In this case, a rising intonation is symbolized by a question mark.)

COMPLEX SENTENCES. An important milestone in the development of language is the formation of *complex sentences.* These are formed by the joining of two simple sentences together by conjunction or by embedding. With the use of a conjunction, the two simple sentences *I can read* and *I can write* can be made into the complex sentence *I can read and write.* Using embedding, one can combine the two simple sentences *Where's a book?* and *I can read a book* into *Where's a book I can read?* Another example of two simple sentences combined by embedding would be *You can watch me* and *I can draw pictures,* formed into the simple sentence *You can watch me draw pictures.* The first complex sentences used by children are usually embedded in simple sentences (Hood and Bloom, 1979).

The appearance of these apparently embedded complex sentences seems to occur between two years and three and one-fourth years. At this point, it is not clear whether the child is really creating *complex* sentences or simply juxtaposing elements in a given context (Hood and Bloom, 1979).

NEGATIVE SENTENCES.   The earliest negative sentences are formed by adding a negative word, usually "no" (in English), at the beginning of an affirmative sentence. For example, a preschool child might say, "No eat cake" or "No go to school." Only later do children learn to put the negative word in the appropriate place in a sentence, such as "I not come here."

Growth of Communication Skills

During the preschool period, three-to-five-year-old children are learning to adjust their messages to their conversational partners in order to communicate effectively. For example, preschool children are often able to make adjustments to a listener in accordance with characteristics of the listener. Four-year-olds tend to generate simpler and shorter utterances when they are talking to five-year-olds than when talking to adults or older children (Shatz and Gelman, 1973; Shatz, 1983).

How effective are preschool-age children at communicating their messages? The answer seems to be that they are better communicators than younger children but not as good as school-age children. For example, there is evidence that four-year-olds are better than three-year-olds at *requesting a clarification* from a communication partner when such a clarification is necessary (Garvey, 1984; Revelle, Wellman,

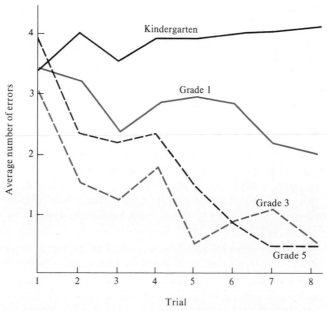

FIGURE 10.13

Errors in communication on a block-stacking task for kindergartners and for first, third, and fifth graders. From Krauss and Glucksberg, 1977.

and Karabenick, 1985). In one study, three- and four-year-olds were asked by an adult to do something that was impossible (e.g., "Bring me that refrigerator") (Revelle, Wellman, and Karabenick, 1985). Although both three- and four-year-olds could recognize when a request was problematic and both requested clarifications (e.g., "How heavy?" with reference to the refrigerator request), the four-year-olds were better able to tailor their requests to the specific type of ambiguity.

On the other hand, there is evidence that preschooler communication skills are not as effective as those of older children (Krauss and Glucksberg, 1977). In a study involving children four to ten years of age, two participants were seated at a table separated by an opaque screen. Each person had a set of six blocks on the table before him or her. Each block had an unfamiliar graphic design on it. The task of the speaker was to stack his or her blocks and tell the listener (the child on the other side of the opaque screen) how to stack the blocks so that the two stacks would be identical. The speaker and listener were given eight opportunities (or trials) to build identical stacks of blocks. As indicated in Figure 10.13 preschoolers (kindergartners), performed the poorest on the block stacking compared with older children (first, third, and fifth graders). Furthermore, the kindergartners tended to describe the unfamiliar block designs in such idiosyncratic ways that it was virtually impossible for the listener to identify it. For example, kindergarten speakers would identify a block by saying "this one" or even pointing to the appropriate block—even though there was an opaque screen separating the participants. In summary, the study provides evidence that communicated skills improve dramatically after the preschool years. The reasons for this improvement include the following:

· Although preschool-age children may *recognize* that a message is ambiguous or unclear, the school-age child is more likely to rate the message as inappropriate and to request a clarification (Beal and Flavell, 1983).
· School-age children are being trained in school to listen to and evaluate their own and other's speech (Pratt and Bates, 1982).

Summary

1. Growth and maturation of physical characteristics have an overall pattern. At least four major types of organs and tissues grow according to a predictable pattern: lymphoid, brain and head, general body, and reproductive. Although human growth is the result of the interaction of hereditary and environmental factors, it is difficult, if not impossible, to specify the precise relationship between both.

   The nervous system is composed of a *central nervous system* and a *peripheral nervous system*. Different parts of the human brain develop at different rates. Most nerve fibers are coated with a fatty substance called *myelin*. The pattern of myelinization follows a chronological order similar to the general maturation of the nervous system.

   Several environmental factors have an influence on growth: nutrition, illnesses, socioeconomic status, and emotional stress.
2. Perceptual processes involve the reception or taking in of information about the environment (e.g., touch, taste, sight, smell, and hearing). As preschool

children grow and develop there are at least three major changes in perceptual processes: a shift in the dominance of sensory systems, an increase in communication between sensory systems, and an improvement in the functioning of individual sensory systems.

3. Preschooler motor development is woven into the fabric of play activities. The primary task of motor development in the preschool years is the development of the *fundamental motor skills* (jumping, running, throwing, catching, climbing). These fundamental motor skills are the basis for all advanced motor skill and sport activities throughout childhood and adulthood.

4. According to Piaget, early-childhood cognitive development occurs in the period of *preoperational* thinking (eighteen months to seven years). This preoperational period is sometimes divided into two parts: the *preconceptual* stage (two to four years) and the *intuitive* stage (five to seven years). There are several important limitations of preoperational thinking. Several of the features of the preschool child's thinking (including limitations) are illustrated in what Piaget and others have called *conservation* problems. The process of refining conservation skills is accompanied by other developments in thinking including *classification* skills and better understanding of space, time, and sequence.

    Although the child at the preoperational level of thinking has made substantial improvements in thinking skills, preoperational thinking has several limitations: Preoperational thinking is *concrete*, it is *not reversible*, it tends to be *egocentric*, it may involve *centration*, and it may involve transductive reasoning. However, there is considerable research evidence that in all areas, the preoperational child may not be as limited as Piaget has indicated.

5. The *information-processing approach* to the development of cognitive activity offers a detailed, step-wise description of thinking. The primary emphasis is on the following components: *perception and attention, memory,* and *problem solving*. Over the preschool years, there appear to be three primary changes in attentional processes: the movement from *reactive* to *investigative attention*, the movement from *random* to *systematic observations*, and the movement from *taking in all information* to the *selective screening* of irrelevant information. In addition, preschoolers tend to have poorer memories than older children for several reasons: Preschooler memory is not as well organized as older-child or adult memory, preschoolers have limited information-processing ability, and preschoolers have a limited knowledge base.

6. In addition to the Piagetian and the information-processing perspectives, the *psychometric* viewpoint provides a useful way of understanding and measuring preschooler intelligence. Two frequently used measures of preschool intelligence are the *Stanford-Binet Intelligence Scale* and the *Wechsler Preschool and Primary Scale of Intelligence* (WPPSI).

7. Children's drawing involves the integration of motor skills, cognitive development, and the expression of feelings about the self and the world. There is some evidence that children's drawing skills progress through several stages: the *placement* stage, the *shape* stage, the *design* stage, and the *pictorial* stage.

8. The preschool child's verbal utterances are different from those of the infant/toddler in two notable ways—length and complexity. There is some evidence that children learn grammatical morphemes (e.g., inflections, prepositions, and articles) which modify and clarify the meaning of words in a specific order. The acquisition of grammatical morphemes demonstrates the principle of overregularization.

The preschool child also learns to transform or modify the basic declarative sentence. Such transformations include *asking questions, developing complex sentences,* and *making negative statements.*

During the preschool period, three-to-five-year-old children are learning to adjust their verbal messages to their conversational partners in order to communicate more effectively. Preschoolers are better communicators than younger children but not as good as school-age children.

Key Terms

Axon	Memory
Brain differentiation	Multiple sclerosis
Brain hemispheres	Myelin
Brain lateralization	Myelinization
Brain stem	Neurons
Central nervous system	Overregularization
Centration	Perception/Attention
Cerebellum	Peripheral nervous system
Cerebral cortex	Pictorial stage
Cerebrum	Placement stage
Conservation	Preconceptual stage
Corpus callosum	Primary motor areas
Deductive reasoning	Primary sensory areas
Dendrites	Problem solving
Deprivation dwarfism	Psychometric approach
Design stage	Recall memory
Egocentrism	Recognition memory
Fundamental motor skills	Reticular formation
Grammatical morphemes	Reversibility
Inductive reasoning	Shape stage
Information processing	Somatotrophin
Intuitive stage	Tactual-kinesthetic
Lymphoid organs	Transductive reasoning

Questions

1. Briefly describe the four major types of organs involved in physical growth.
2. Discuss the two hemispheres of the brain and how each influences different types of thinking activities.
3. Discuss the major determinants of childhood obesity. What measures can or should be taken to deal with or prevent the problem?
4. Preoperational thinking can best be described in terms of its deficiencies with reference to concrete operations. Do you agree or disagree? Why?
5. Briefly define each of the four stages of children's drawings.
6. How effective are preschool-age children at communicating their verbal messages?

Suggested Readings

AINSFELD, M. *Language Development from Birth to Three.* Hillsdale, N.J.: Erlbaum, 1984. An excellent review of theory and research on early language development.

CORBIN, C. *A Textbook of Motor Development* (2nd ed.). Dubuque, Iowa: W. C. Brown, 1980. A readable introduction to the basic facets of childhood motor development.

FLAVELL, J. H. *Cognitive Development* (2nd ed.). Englewood Cliffs, N.J.: Prentice-Hall, 1985. A well-written and thorough discussion of children's thinking processes.

GARDNER, H. *Artful Scribbles: The Significance of Children's Drawings.* New York: Basic Books, 1980. An interesting and well-documented discussion of children's drawings.

GARVEY, C. *Children's Talk.* Cambridge, Mass.: Harvard University Press, 1984. A readable discussion of the major aspects of children's langauge activities.

11 The Preschooler: Social and Personality Development

*The childhood shows the man
As morning shows the day.*
    —*John Milton,*
    Paradise Regained

*Respect the child.
Be not too much his parent.
Trespass not on his solitude.*
    —*Ralph Waldo Emerson*
    Education

The years from two to six are special primarily because so many new things happen. Children are gradually moving from exclusive relationships with parents or caretakers toward interaction with other adults and children. For the first time, children experience many new challenges as well as conflicts and anxieties. These challenges and anxieties result from the process of *socialization* (the ways in which a young child's behavior and attitudes are influenced by parents, other adults, and the institutions of society). Here we examine several aspects of personality that result from socialization: self-concept formation, sex-role identity, prosocial behavior, and aggressiveness.

The Sense of Self

In our discussion of infancy, we pointed out that the child has already begun the gradual process of self-definition. During infancy, cognitive developments occur that provide the basis for an emerging sense of self. In the first place, the infant learns to distinguish the self from other things in the environment. Although this distinction may appear to be rather basic, Jean Piaget and others have shown that the very young infant does not make this distinction. The separation of "self" from "nonself" develops as early as the first six months of life when the infant recognizes that objects other than itself exist in its world (caretakers, rattles, feeding nipples). In addition to recognizing the separation of self and objects, the infant comes to recognize the permanence of objects (and, by implication, the permanence of self). By age two or three, the infant has a view of the self as stable and organized. This view is enhanced by feelings of trust and autonomy.

■ *SCENARIO: CAN GRANDPARENTS BE PARENTS?—
AN ELIZABETHAN PERSPECTIVE*

Elizabeth (now four years old) is sitting at the dinner table with her family. The topic of discussion is the upcoming Thanksgiving holiday.

Elizabeth's father (announcing to all): Next week gramma and grampa will be coming for Thanksgiving. (Looking at Elizabeth) Your gramma and grampa are *also* my mother and father.

Elizabeth: *No* (pause), gramma and grampa are *not* your mother and father, they're *my* gramma and grampa.

Elizabeth's father (smiling at Elizabeth): My mother and father are *also* your . . .

Elizabeth (with a look of mild outrage, she forcefully and promptly replies): No! They're *my* gramma and grampa.

By about age four, a new extension of the self appears. Children begin to attach importance to their possessions. Commonly heard phrases include "my dolly," "my toy," "my book," and "my cereal." Objects seem to be extensions of the self and may be shared somewhat grudgingly. The possessiveness of the four-year-old may also be due to other factors. For example, it is quite likely that four-year-olds are involved in more frequent cooperative play situations in which competition over toys might occur. In addition, the four-year-old is still somewhat egocentric and, as a result, may not understand that grandparents can simultaneously be parents.

By the time children are five years old, they have been exposed to many evaluations of themselves by other people. These early evaluations influence the child's overall self-image. For example, the child may have developed a self-image that is largely positive or largely negative. The evaluations of others as well as the child's own evaluation (based on experiences of competence or inadequacy) contribute to the child's self-concept.

■ *WHAT DO CHILDREN HEAR ABOUT THEMSELVES?*

Throughout the early childhood years, young children are given many evaluations of themselves by parents. Based on your experiences with young children, you might be able to add to the list:

• "You're a good helper."
• "Why do you always spill your milk?"
• "You look handsome today."
• "Can't you ever stay out of the way when I'm doing something?"
• "You're a bad girl."
• "That's good! You can do that by yourself."

By the time children are five or six years old they begin to verbalize their self-concepts. Parents or caretakers may be pleased to hear such statements as "Let me help you—I'm a good helper." On the other hand, a negative self-concept is evident when the child says, "I can't do it—I can't do anything right." The family atmosphere and the parenting styles discussed in Chapter 9 contribute to the formulations of a child's self-concept.

The Self as a System

One approach to the study of self is the notion that individuals organize their thinking about themselves as a "theory" of themselves (Brim, 1976; Markus, 1980; Lynch, 1981). Although the analogy between the self and a "theory of self" has been primarily drawn for adults, it is useful to examine childhood self-concept in this fashion. According to this perspective, the self is really a "self-system" which is organized by the individual into a set of "core" and "peripheral" constructs.

(Core constructs relate to a person's basic existence and identity such as "I am a four-year-old girl" and peripheral constructs relate to aspects of personality that can be modified without serious consequences—"I enjoy collecting bottle caps.") Both of these self constructs serve as the basic axioms of a theory of self that guides human behavior:

> What humans learn during life are axioms, concepts and hypotheses—about themselves in relation to the world around them. We can think of the self as a personal epistemology, similar to theories in science in its components and its operations, but dealing with a specific person. (Harter, 1983, p. 242)

Recent developments in information-processing theory have been applied to self theory. For example, Hazel Markus (1980) suggests that whenever one attempts to explain or organize one's own behavior, the result is the development of **self schemas.**

> Self schema[s] are cognitive generalizations about the self, derived from past experience, that organize and guide the processing of self-related information contained in the individual's social experience. (p. 64)

Markus examined self schemas for such characteristics as independence, creativity, and body weight. Her findings include the following:

• It is possible to distinguish between individuals with clearly pronounced self-schemas (i.e., individuals for whom a given personality dimension is particularly relevant to their self-concepts) and aschematics (i.e., those for whom a given personality dimension is irrelevant to their self-concepts).
• Those individuals with clearly articulated self schemas for a given trait are better

Gale Schiamberg

The process of self-definition continues in the preschool years.

able, with reference to that trait, to process information about the self and to predict their future behavior.

The Categorical Self

What are the implications of the child as a "self theorist" for the developing self in the preschool years? When infants and young children recognize that they are separate and distinct from their environment and from their companions, they also begin to more fully understand the dimensions on which people differ from each other. They begin to think of themselves in relation to these dimensions (or categories). This activity leads to the emergence of the **categorical self** (the definition of self on such dimensions as age, gender, activity, preferences, and values).

AGE.   Age is one of the first dimensions that children recognize and integrate into their self-concepts. At the end of the first year, not only can infants distinguish a strange adult from a strange baby, but they also exhibit a preference for playing with the baby, rather than with the strange adult (Lewis and Brooks-Gunn, 1979). These distinctions between adults and babies are made on the basis of perceptual characteristics such as tone of voice, facial features, and, of course, size. Age as a *social category* is more precisely used by the preschool child. For example, children age three to five years who were shown photographs of people ranging in age from one to seventy were easily able to classify the photographs according to the categories "little boys and girls" (two- to six-year-olds), "mothers and fathers" (fourteen- to forty-nine-year-olds), and "grandmothers and grandfathers" (age fifty and older) (Edwards, 1984).

GENDER.   Another dimension of the categorical self that children appear to recognize rather early in life is gender. For example, nine-to-twelve-month-old infants are able to distinguish between photographs of strange men and strange women and smile more frequently at the photographs of the women (Brooks-Gunn and Lewis, 1981). By the time children are two to three years of age, they seem to have acquired accurate gender labels as measured by their ability to correctly identify photographs as either male or female (Brooks-Gunn and Lewis, 1982). Furthermore, three- and four-year-olds are clearly aware that they are either "boys" or "girls," although they may think they can change sex (Kohlberg, 1969; Brooks-Gunn and Lewis, 1982). However, by the time children are ready to enter the formal school (at middle childhood), they have already acquired many cultural stereotypes of "maleness" and "femaleness." They have also learned that their gender is constant or that they will always remain a male or female (Williams, Bennett, and Best, 1975; Brooks-Gunn and Lewis, 1982). In summary, gender identity is a significant part of the "categorical self"—a subject we treat in more detail later in this chapter as part of our discussion of sex-role development.

Preschooler Descriptions of Self

When they are asked to describe themselves, preschoolers tend to focus on actions that they can perform, physical characteristics, their possessions, and interpersonal relationships (Damon and Hart, 1982). When asked to complete the following statements "I am a boy/girl who _____ " and "I am a _____ ," approximately half of the three-to-five-year-old children in one study responded with action statements ("I am a tennis player," "I walk home") (Keller, Ford, and Meachum, 1978). Statements that involved psychological characteristics ("I am a sad person," "I like other people") were rare. The investigators concluded that the self-concepts of preschoolers seem to be centered on the ability to do things or to make things happen (Keller, Ford, and Meachum, 1978). These findings are consistent with Erik Erikson's psychosocial theory of development (see Chapter 2) in which two-to-three-year-olds try to become independent or *autonomous* and four-to-five-year-olds, who have attained some level of autonomy, are acquiring new skills and demonstrate *initiative* in new activities and in doing things (Erikson, 1963). From that perspective, preschoolers who define themselves primarily in terms of what they can do are perfectly normal.

THE PRIVATE SELF.   In addition to defining themselves primarily in terms of an activity-based self-concept, preschool children for the first time make a distinction that older children and adults may take for granted—the distinction between a **public self** (those parts of the self that others can perceive or infer about the person) and the **private self** (those parts of the self that are known only to the individual and are not public). In our discussion of infancy (Chapter 8), we indicated that a major development task with reference to social/personality development was the differentiation of the *bodily self* from significant others, such as parents. During the preschool years, the major task of self development is the differentiation of the *psychological self* from others. It appears that children begin to develop the idea of a private self between three and one-half and five years of age. For example, most children older than three and one-half years of age understand that another person cannot see their thoughts (Maccoby, 1980; Johnson and Wellman, 1982). In a much older study, Lev Vygotsky (1934) found that four- and five-year-olds were beginning to make a distinction between *speech for others* (or public communication) and *speech for the self* (or private communication).

Sylvia Byers

OWN EMOTIONS OR OTHERS' EMOTIONS.   Young children also learn to distinguish between their *own emotions* and those of others. Harter and Barnes (1981) found that three- and four-year-old children reported that the *causes* of parental emotions would be identical to the *causes* of their own emotions. For example, a child who had previously indicated sadness when he could not watch a particular television program attributed a similar emotion to his father—"Daddy would be sad if he couldn't stay up and watch cartoons on television." Eventually, children come to understand that their own emotions and feelings are not necessarily identical to those of others.

The Self and Social Competence

One of the important characteristics of the self that begins to crystallize during the preschool years as the child refines his or her "theory of self" is *social* competence. According to Everett Waters and L. Alan Sroufe (1983), **social competence** is the ability to use both personal and environmental resources for optimal adaptation. The competent child is one who can accommodate to new situations and adjust to new circumstances such as entering a preschool education program or accepting the birth of a new sibling.

PRINCIPLES OF SOCIAL COMPETENCE.   The developmental nature of social competence is based on the following principles (Sroufe, 1979a; Waters and Sroufe, 1983):

• *Adaptation.* The child is *actively* involved in both changing the environment and accommodating to the environment. That is, the child can be viewed as a *system* in his or her own right. Such a system does not simply *react* to environmental stimulation but organizes and selects its own behaviors in terms of its own goals.
• *The Child as a Coherent Whole.* There is a logic to individual personality that can best be understood when looking at the child's *total functioning.* That is, even though a child may not behave the same way in different situations, his or her behavior can still be viewed as a coherent whole across these situations. For example, the preschool child who can be expressive and spontaneous in free-play circumstances and who also can be goal-oriented and purposeful in structured learning situations is *not* viewed as inconsistent. Rather, such behavior reflects the expression of different personality characteristics as circumstances permit or require (Block and Block, 1980).
• *Emotion and Effect as Central to Personality.* Sroufe (1979b) suggests that an emotional/motivational duality in the form of security with familiar versus attraction to the unfamiliar is central to self development. For example, the preschool child needs to hold in balance a desire to explore and adapt to new circumstances on the one hand, and to watch for unknown hazards on the other hand.
• *Individual Differences.* Individual differences are expressed on a number of personality dimensions, including the balance between exploration/curiosity and awareness of potential danger. For example, some children may demonstrate little involvement in the environment, others may be unduly cautious or timid in the face of unfamiliar circumstances, and still others may be impulsive (i.e., showing little ability to control their behavior in the face of potentially ambiguous, novel, or complex situations).
• *Reorganization of Self as Development.* According to Sroufe (1979a), "development does not proceed in a linear, incremental manner" (p. 836). Rather, there are

Social competence is a developmental characteristic that changes with the level of child maturity.

changes in behavioral or cognitive organization (e.g., the movement from pre-operational to operational thinking) or the addition of new skills (e.g., advanced throwing skills; see Chapter 10) that transform the ways in which the preschooler interacts with his or her world. Each of these *periods of reorganization* constitutes the basis for a new series of developmental challenges.

THE DEVELOPMENT OF SOCIAL COMPETENCE.   In addition to these basic principles of self development, it is important to recognize that social competence is *developmental,* changing in relation to child maturity and differing environmental circumstances. For example, the dependency of the infant on its caregiver(s) is clearly an adaptive behavior in the earliest years of development. However, such dependency would obviously be maladaptive in middle childhood. Table 11.1 summarizes the major phases in the development of social competence (Sroufe, 1979a; Waters and Sroufe, 1983).

TABLE 11.1
The Phases in the Development of Social Competence

Phase	Age	Issue	Role for Caregiver
1	0–3 mos.	Physiological regulation	Smooth routines
2	3–6 mos.	Management of tension	Sensitive, cooperative interaction
3	6–12 mos.	Establishing an effective attachment relationship	Responsive availability
4	12–18 mos.	Exploration and mastery	Secure base
5	1½ to 2½ yrs.	Individuation (autonomy)	Firm support
6	2½ to 4½ yrs.	Management of impulses, sex-role identification, peer relations	Clear roles and values, flexible self-control

Based on Sroufe, 1979a.

• *Phases 1 and 2.* These phases apply to the young infant and have to do with *physiological regulation* (e.g., holding down food or focusing its eyes on the human face) and *management of tension* (e.g., learning to regulate emotional expression, such as crying or fussing, in relation to predictable caretaker response). Phases 1 and 2 are similar to Erikson's first stage of psychosocial development, trust versus mistrust (see Chapter 2 for the discussion of Erikson's psychosocial theory).

• *Phases 3 and 4.* These phases relate to the older infant who establishes an effective attachment relationship to one or more caregivers which serves as a secure base for exploration of the environment. Phases 3 and 4 are similar to Erikson's stage of autonomy versus shame and doubt (see Chapter 2).

• *Phase 5.* This phase involves the primary task of the toddler, which is mastering the environment by him- or herself. Whereas Erikson refers to this stage as the period of initiative versus guilt (e.g., the desire to do things competently *and* independently), Waters and Sroufe (1983) emphasize the development of skills in general problem solving in this phase rather than any specific skills. The competent toddler will approach such problem solving with confidence, enthusiasm, and persistence in finding solutions.

• *Phase 6.* In this phase the preschooler learns to manage his or her impulses in order to adjust to social roles such as sex roles and to functions within the peer group. One of the important areas for the demonstration of impulse control is in social play with peers. Such play requires that preschoolers be flexible in knowing how and when to express their feelings. In addition, social play becomes an indicator of preschooler competence in knowing how to respond to playmates, in knowing how to initiate play with others, and so on.

Dr. Mike Austin

One of the important arenas for the demonstration of impulse control is social play.

Sex-Role Development

An important dimension of self-concept is the development of the child's sex role. What does it mean to say, "I am a male" or "I am a female"? How do children come to think of themselves as sexual beings? How do children learn the "appropriate" behaviors for their sex? Are these "appropriate" behaviors useful guidelines for all children? Do they limit self-development for others?

At least as early as the delivery of the infant in the hospital, the male and female are subject to sex-role socialization. Parents viewing their newborns in the hospital nursery often describe their infant son in terms of the strength of his grasp, the power of his kicks, or the loudness of his cries. In contrast, the parents of newborn females are likely to describe their newborn daughter as adorable or cuddly, and might refer to her as "sugar" or "sweetie" (Maccoby, 1980). In addition, newborn infant girls may be immediately associated with the color pink (e.g., in pink clothing or pink hair bows), whereas infant boys may be associated with blue. This socialization process continues throughout the childhood years as parents may continue to behave differently toward children on the basis of gender, including purchasing "appropriate" toys and clothing and choosing hairstyles.

SEX-ROLE STANDARDS.   Virtually every human society has different expectations for the behavior of males and females. In order for the child to fulfill these expectations, he or she must eventually incorporate into his or her self-concept the *sex-role standards* that a given society views as appropriate for males or females. The entire process, which begins with the awareness of gender in early childhood and includes the child's acquisition of sex-role standards and the continued crystallization of a sex role throughout adolescence and young adulthood, is called *sex typing* or *sex-role development*.

> DEFINITIONS
>
> **Sex-Role Standard.** A value, motive, or behavior that a given society views as appropriate for a given sex.
>
> **Sex Typing (or Sex-Role Development).** The process in which the child becomes aware of his or her gender and acquires the values, motives, or behaviors that are considered appropriate by society for his or her sex.

TRADITIONAL STANDARDS.   Traditional sex-role standards have become very controversial over the past decade. The traditional female role has come under serious scrutiny as a result of the movement for equal rights among women. The female biological role as a childbearer has been the primary and determining factor of the traditional female role in many societies, including contemporary Western cultures. Females have historically been encouraged to assume an *expressive role*, which involves being a nurturant mother and wife. In order to accomplish that role, females have been expected to be cooperative, warm, and sensitive to the needs of other people (Parsons, 1955). On the other hand, males traditionally have been encouraged to adopt an *instrumental role*. That is, males have been expected to provide the funds to feed, clothe, and house the family. Therefore, young boys are expected to behave in a dominant, assertive, independent, and competitive fashion.

CONTROVERSIES. Obviously, these traditional role divisions leave much to be desired in terms of encouraging full and free development of human personality. Women's-rights groups have fought against the effects of these sex-role standards as they frequently appear in biased treatment of females in work settings and have, in fact, won major legal victories. For example, the Equal Opportunity Employment Act includes, among its provisions, the illegality of sex discrimination in hiring. Unfortunately, recent studies confirm that young adult males and females still support many traditional sex-role standards of femininity and masculinity (Shaffer and Johnson, 1980; Werner and LaRussa, 1983). For example, these young adults (primarily college students and mental health professionals) view "typical" men as reflecting an instrumental orientation and "typical" women as reflecting an expressive orientation. Furthermore, cross-cultural research suggests that many societies appear to endorse these traditional sex-role divisions (Best et al., 1977).

Dimensions of Sex Typing

As might be expected, sex typing involves many dimensions. One recent—and very useful—organization of these many dimensions of sex typing has been to divide them into *content areas* and *constructs* (Huston, 1983) (see Table 11.2).

CONTENT AREAS OF SEX TYPING. The five content areas of sex typing are:

- *Biological gender: male or female.*
- *Activities and interests:* include play activities, toys, household tasks, and measures of achievement in such areas as verbal, spatial, and mathematical abilities.
- *Personal-social attributes:* include traits or patterns of behavior such as dependence, aggression, and dominance.
- *Gender-based social relationships:* include the gender of those whom one imitates, associates with, "attaches" to, and/or identifies with. These individuals would include friends, parents, significant other adults, and so on.
- *Stylistic and symbolic contents:* include nonverbal behavior and speech patterns (Filmer and Haswell, 1977; Haas, 1979).

Even children's pets may be the subject of sex-role experimentation.

Gale Schiamberg

TABLE 11.2

Sex Typing—Content Areas and Constructs

CONTENT AREA	CONSTRUCT			
	A. CONCEPTS OR BELIEFS	B. IDENTITY OR SELF-PERCEPTION	C. PREFERENCES, ATTITUDES, VALUES (FOR SELF OR FOR OTHERS)	D. BEHAVIORAL ENACTMENT, ADOPTION
1. *Biological gender*	A1. Gender constancy.	B1. Gender identity as inner sense of maleness or femaleness. Sex role identity as perception of own masculinity or femininity.	C1. Wish to be male or female *or* gender bias defined as greater value attached to one gender than the other.	D1. Displaying bodily attributes of one gender (including clothing, body type, hair, etc.).
2. *Activities and interests:* Toys Play activities Occupations Household roles Tasks Achievement areas	A2. Knowledge of sex stereotypes *or* sex role concepts *or* attributions about others' success and failure.	B2. Self-perception of interests, abilities; *or* sex-typed attributions about own success and failure.	C2. Preference for toys, games, activities; attainment value for achievement areas; attitudes about sex-typed activities by others (e.g., about traditional or nontraditional roles for women).	D2. Engaging in games, toy play, activities, occupations, or achievement tasks that are sex-typed.
3. *Personal-social attributes:* Personality characteristics Social behavior	A3. Concepts about sex stereotypes *or* sex-appropriate social behavior.	B3. Perception of own personality (e.g., on self-rating questionnaires).	C3. Preference or wish to have personal-social attributes *or* attitudes about others' personality and behavior patterns.	D3. Displaying sex-typed personal-social behavior (e.g., aggression, dependence).
4. *Gender-based social relationships:* Gender of peers, friends, lovers, preferred parent, models, attachment figures	A4. Concepts about sex-typed norms for gender-based social relations.	B4. Self-perception of own patterns of friendship, relationship, or sexual orientation.	C4. Preference for male or female friends, lovers, attachment figures, or wish to be like male or female, or attitudes about others' patterns.	D4. Engaging in social or sexual activity with others on the basis of gender (e.g., same-sex peer choice).
5. *Stylistic and symbolic content:* Gestures Nonverbal behavior Speech and language patterns Styles of play Fantasy Drawing Tempo Loudness Size Pitch	A5. Awareness of sex-typed symbols or styles.	B5. Self-perception of nonverbal, stylistic characteristics.	C5. Preference for stylistic or symbolic objects or personal characteristics *or* attitudes about others' nonverbal and language patterns.	D5. Manifesting sex-typed verbal and nonverbal behavior, fantasy, drawing patterns.

From Huston, 1983, pp. 390-391.

CONSTRUCTS OF SEX TYPING.   There are four *constructs* that describe the relationship of the child to the five content areas:

· *Concepts or beliefs:* include social stereotypes of male and female characteristics, as well as the child's understanding of these stereotypes. In Table 11.2, concepts about the first content area—biological gender—include measures of *gender constancy,* or the extent to which children understand the stability and continuity of gender (Cell A1 in Table 11.2). Concepts for the four other content areas are typically assessed by examining sex stereotypes relating to interests, activities, toys, abilities, beliefs, and so on (Huston, 1983) (Cells A2–A5).

· *Identity or self-perception:* includes the perception to self as feminine or masculine. With reference to the first content area—biological gender—gender identity is typically measured as a psychological construct (e.g., a perception of oneself as feminine or masculine) (Storms, 1979) (Cell B1). Self-perception of activities and interests (Cell B2) may include self descriptions and expectations for success and failures. For self-perception of personal-social attributes (Cell B3), self-ratings of relevant adjectives or self-descriptions of personality traits have been used. With reference to the last two content areas (Cells B4 and B5), few measures have been done with children (Huston, 1983).

· *Preferences and attitudes:* include both sex-role preferences (e.g., the desire to have sex-typed characteristics) and positive attitudes or values about possessing such characteristics. Table 11.2 describes how these preferences and attitudes are measured for each of the five content areas.

· *Behavioral enactments:* include specific demonstrations of sex-typed activities that can be objectively assessed by others (Table 11.2).

Sex Differences: Myth or Reality?

There appear to be some obvious physical differences between adult males and females. For example, adult males are heavier, taller, and more muscular than adult females. On the other hand, females usually live longer than males and are less susceptible to many diseases. While such physical differences may seem obvious, differences in psychological behavior are not nearly as clear-cut (see Table 11.3).

In reviews of the research on sex differences in psychological functioning, Eleanor Maccoby and Carol Jacklin (1974) and Carol Tavris and Carole Wade (1984) found that few of the stereotyped or traditional views of male and female behavior were, in fact, true. They found that these traditional sex-role behaviors could be grouped into one of the following three categories:

· Sex-differences that are probably accurate.
· Sex differences for which there is some evidence but that remain open to question.
· Sex differences that are erroneous and have no basis in fact.

SEX DIFFERENCES THAT APPEAR TO BE REAL.   With reference to the sex differences that appear to be real, Maccoby and Jacklin (1974) and Tavris and Wade (1984) found only four such differences:

· *Verbal abilities.* Girls appear to have higher levels of verbal abilities than boys. Girls seem to develop their verbal skills at earlier ages than boys. A not-uncommon

TABLE 11.3
Sex Differences and Similarities

CATEGORY	FINDINGS	CATEGORY	FINDINGS
Physical Attributes		Emotionality	Self-reports and observations conflict; no convincing evidence that females feel more emotional, but they may express certain emotions more freely.
Strength	Males taller, heavier, more muscular after puberty.		
Health	Females less vulnerable to illness and disease, live longer.		
Activity level	Some evidence that preschool boys more active during play in same-sex groups; school-age boys and girls are active in different ways.	Dependence	Conflicting findings; dependence appears not to be a unitary concept or stable trait.
Manual dexterity	Women excel when speed is important; findings hard to interpret.	Susceptibility to influence	Preschool girls more obedient to parents; boys may be more susceptible to peer pressure; no overall difference in adult susceptibility to persuasion across different settings in laboratory studies.
Abilities			
General intelligence	No difference on most tests.		
Verbal ability	Some evidence that females acquire language slightly earlier; males more often diagnosed as having reading problems; females excel on various verbal tests after age 10 or 11.*	Self-esteem and confidence	No self-reported differences in self-esteem, but males more confident about task performance; males more likely to take credit for success, less likely to blame selves for failure.
Quantitative ability	Males excel on tests of mathematical reasoning from the start of adolescence.*	Nurturance	No overall differences in altruism; girls more helpful and responsive to infants, small children; some evidence that fathers as responsive to newborns as mothers are, but issue of maternal versus paternal behavior remains open.
Spatial-visual ability	Males excel starting in 10th grade, but not on all tests or in all studies.*		
Creativity	Females excel on verbal creativity tests, but otherwise no difference.		
Cognitive style	Males excel on spatial-visual disembedding tests starting at adolescence, but no general differences in cognitive style.	Aggressiveness	Males more aggressive from preschool age on; men more violent, more likely to be aggressive in public, more likely to be physically aggressive in situations not involving anger.
Personality Characteristics			
Sociability	No consistent findings on infants' responsiveness to social cues; school-age boys play in larger groups; women fantasize more about affiliation themes, but there is no evidence that one sex wants or needs friends more.	*Values and Moral Perceptions*	Some controversial evidence that males and females approach choice and conflict somewhat differently. Males seem more likely to emphasize abstract standards of justice, fairness, balancing of individual rights. Females seem more likely to emphasize the ethics of care, human attachments, balancing of conflicting responsibilities.
Empathy	Conflicting evidence; probably depends on situation and sex of participants in an interaction.		

*Differences statistically reliable but quite small.

Adapted from Tavris and Wade, 1984.

observation by early elementary-grade teachers is the greater frequency of girls in the higher reading groups than boys. However, on the *average*, the differences between girls and boys are rather small until adolescence. At that time, female superiority in verbal abilities becomes more pronounced.

• *Visual/spatial abilities.* Males seem to do better than females on such tasks as recognition of figures from different angles or recognition of block designs.

• *Arithmetic reasoning.* These differences favor males and may not become apparent until puberty.

• *Aggression.* Females appear to be less physically and verbally aggressive than males.

SEX DIFFERENCES WITH LIMITED SUPPORT.   With regard to sex differences for which there is limited or only suggestive evidence, several questionable generalizations have been suggested. For example, it is often assumed that females are more fearful or anxious than males. The evidence does not consistently support this point. Observation of children in a wide variety of situations does not indicate any differences in fearful or anxious behavior. However, other research using child self-report measures indicates that females are more likely to *say* that they are fearful or anxious. It is also commonly assumed that males are more dominant and competitive than females. The evidence is mixed on this point. Most studies find no differences between males and females in dominance or competitiveness; however, where differences are found, males are more dominant or competitive.

UNFOUNDED MYTHS.   With reference to the third category of sex-role stereotypes—those that are simply unfounded cultural myths—a number of curious assumptions of male/female differences occur. Some of these myths include the following (Maccoby and Jacklin, 1974; Tavris and Wade, 1984):

• *MYTH 1: Boys are more analytical than girls.* The evidence suggests that there are no differences between males and females on measures of logical reasoning or analytical thinking. The one exception, as indicated earlier, is that males appear to be better than females on tests of visual/spatial ability.

One unfounded myth is that girls are more sociable than boys.

• *MYTH 2: Boys have higher self-esteem than girls.* The evidence does not support any differences between boys and girls on self-confidence or self-esteem.

• *MYTH 3: Boys have higher achievement than girls.* The evidence suggests that in noncompetitive situations, girls exhibit higher levels of achievement motivation than boys. In competitive situations, boys do demonstrate higher levels of achievement motivation than girls, but only up to the level expressed by girls in noncompetitive circumstances.

• *MYTH 4: Girls are more sociable than boys.* The research evidence suggests that there are no differences in interest in social stimuli, in responsiveness to social experiences, or in the ability to imitate a social model.

• *MYTH 5: Girls are more conformist than boys.* Most studies report no differences on conformity behavior between boys and girls.

• *MYTH 6: Girls are better than boys at rote memory or repetitive tasks; boys are better than girls at higher-level cognitive activities.* The evidence does not support these findings. In fact, boys and girls are relatively similar in rote learning and concept formation.

Major Theories

Three major theories have been proposed to describe the acquisition of sex-role identity in young children. The major concepts of these theories have already been discussed in Chapter 2.

PSYCHOANALYTIC THEORY.   Freud used the concept of *identification* to describe the acquisition of sex-role identity. The process of identification is different for males and females.

For boys, identification occurs as a result of the *Oedipus complex* (the boy has fantasies of replacing his father and possessing his mother). The boy resolves the Oedipus complex by identifying with the father. According to Freud, such an identification represents an "If you can't beat 'em, join 'em' " approach. As a result, the male child takes on the sex-role behaviors of the father. Freud suggested that male sex-role development is largely the result of "identification with the aggressor," or more powerful figure (the father).

In the case of the female, identification with the mother is the result of the *Electra complex* (the girl has fantasies of possessing her father, whom she envies because he has something that she lacks: a penis). The girl fears that her mother will punish her for desiring her father by not loving her. Presumably because of her need to be loved, the girl tries to be like her mother.

What is the status of the psychoanalytic interpretation of sex-role identification? It is difficult—if not impossible—to arrange an experimental study to test Freud's conception of identification. Identification is a complex process that cannot easily be broken down into measurable parts. Where this has been done, experimenters have not been able to demonstrate the Freudian theory of identification. That is, there is no evidence that sex typing results from identification with a same-sex parent who is *thought by the child* to be a hostile rival for the opposite-sex parent's affection.

Although there is no evidence of this Freudian notion of identity, there is some evidence that child identification with the parent does influence sex typing. Unlike the Freudian explanation of identification based on "fear of an aggressor," considerable evidence suggests that the important factors in strengthening child imitation and identification with an adult are the adult's *warmth* and *perceived power* (Perry and Bussey, 1984). For example, there is considerable evidence that masculine boys have fathers who are perceived by their sons to be both affectionate and authoritative (Lamb, 1981; Snow, Jacklin, and Maccoby, 1983; Perry and Bussey, 1984). Apparently, these affectionate fathers are more likely to spend time interacting with their sons.

It is interesting to note that despite the substantial body of evidence for a strong relationship between fathers' personality characteristics and sons' masculinity, there is less evidence of a parallel relationship between mothers and daughters. The dramatic increase in maternal employment (see Chapter 6) has, in recent years, been suggested as an important factor in girls' sex typing. The evidence appears to suggest a significant relationship between maternal employment and girls' sex typing. For example, daughters of working mothers have more flexible ideas concerning sex roles than daughters of nonworking mothers. They believe that *both* men and women can work, make important decisions, raise children, do household chores, and so on. They think of women as capable of successful competition and not, as in stereotyped depictions, easily hurt emotionally. Of particular interest is the fact that these daughters were most likely to nominate their mothers as *the person they would most want to be* if they had their choice of being anyone in the world. Thus, daughters of working mothers appear to develop egalitarian notions of sex roles and are likely to emulate their mother's sense of independence (Perry and Bussey, 1984).

SOCIAL LEARNING THEORY.   Social learning theorists such as Walter Mischel (1970) and Albert Bandura (1977) suggest that children's sex-role development occurs in two ways:

• *Direct reinforcement* of sex-appropriate behaviors by parents, teachers, and significant others. For example, boys may be encouraged by their parents, in particular their fathers, to be physically strong and decisive and to exhibit "macho" behavior. Girls may be encouraged by the same socialization agents to play with dolls or dishes and to engage in nurturant behaviors.

There is evidence of parental encouragement of sex-appropriate behaviors during toddlerhood and the preschool years (Eccles and Hoffman, 1984; Jacklin, DiPietro, and Maccoby, 1984; Roopnarine, 1984; Ruble, 1984; Eccles, 1985). Children's earliest preferences for sex-typed toys and activities are, in part, the direct result of parental encouragment or nonencouragement. A striking example of such influence can be seen by comparing the bedrooms of boys and girls. Boys' rooms typically have sports equipment and aerospace, and automobile toys; girls' rooms may have dolls, flowers, and domestic toys (MacKinnon, Brody, and Stoneman, 1982).

• *Observational learning* of sex-appropriate behaviors by watching same-sex models including parents, siblings, teachers, or peers (Bandura, 1977). Children can learn about appropriate sex-role behaviors by observing live models, by watching television, or by reading (Liebert, Sprafkin, and Davidson, 1982).

What is the evidence for the observational learning of sex-appropriate behaviors? A problem with the observational learning hypothesis is that children may *not* pay more attention to a same-sex model until six or seven years of age (Ruble, Balaban, and Cooper, 1981). For example, there is evidence that four-to-five-year-old preschool boys will play with toys that have been labeled as "masculine" or "boy" toys even after they have observed girls playing with those same toys. On the other hand, the same preschoolers did not wish to play with toys that had been labeled as "girl toys" even after watching other boys play with them. In other

Feminist Psychoanalytic Theory—Turning the Tables

In the classical Freudian theory, both femininity and masculinity are sex-typed behaviors that are acquired through the process of identification. That is, such identification with the same-sexed parent occurs presumably because of the Oedipus complex in the male, and the Electra complex in the female. In traditional psychoanalytic thinking, "penis envy" was the dynamic force that led, ultimately, to identification with a girl's mother (see text for discussion of this process). However, in classical Freudian theory it is this penis envy that presumably leads females to feel inferior to males, to want to bear children (as a substitute for not having this organ), and to be generally submissive in relationships with males.

More recent psychoanalytic interpretations have rejected this classical position (Lerner, 1974, 1978).

rists, child fear and anger about her power. In the case of the male child, it is this sense of fear and anger, resulting from the child's sense of helplessness or powerlessness, that leads to a need to devalue the mother. As adults, this devaluation of the mother is extended to women in general, as men create paternalistic relationships with women that ensure their power and control. It is assumed that women ultimately cooperate in the development of these paternalistic relationships with males because they have "learned" to devalue their gender.

According to the theorists, this situation can be reversed with shared caretaking responsibilities for young children. With shared caretaking, both the positive outcomes of dependency and the negative outcomes (child anger and fear leading to parent de-

Sylvia Byers

Instead of female envy of males, these theorists have substituted male envy of females. In particular, the dynamic forces behind identification is the male envy of the female childbearing capacity and breast envy. The female breast symbolizes, to the young child, the seemingly all-powerful role of the mother as a source of gratification and punishment, as well as the bearer of life (Lerner, 1974, 1978). The major role of the mother in child caregiving leads to both positive forms of dependency and, according to these theo-

valuation) would not be directed at only the female parent. Such an arrangement would require much more involvement of males in caregiving responsibilities than is currently the case.

The feminist psychoanalytic theorists represent a refreshing and needed alternative to classical and traditional Freudian theory. However, it should be noted that the same limitations and shortcomings of the psychoanalytic theory apply to classical, traditional, and feminist orientations.

words, the sex-role behavior of the preschool boys appeared to be affected more by the *labels* given to the toys than by the *sex* of the observed model playing with those toys. However, once children come to understand that their gender is a permanent and unchanging part of their self-concept (at approximately six or seven years of age), they then selectively observe the behavior of same-sex models. They use these observations as a source of sex-role information. For example, six- and seven-year-old children are not likely to avoid playing with toys or engaging in activities that are of interest to the opposite sex (Ruble, Balaban, and Cooper, 1981).

COGNITIVE-DEVELOPMENTAL THEORY. Lawrence Kohlberg (1969) described the cognitive approach to sex-role development as being directed primarily by the development of the child's thinking skills. As indicated above, the social learning position is that sex typing is the *result* of direct reinforcement or observational learning which, in turn, leads the child to identify with (or habitually imitate) same-sex models. However, Kohlberg argues that gender identity is really a *cognitive judgment* about oneself which occurs *before* the child's attention to, and identification with, same-sex models.

Furthermore, Kohlberg believes that all children progress through the following *three stages* in acquiring an understanding of gender:

· **Basic gender identity.** By about three years, the child is able to *label* his or her own gender *correctly*. In other words, the child knows whether he or she is a boy or a girl. Correct labeling does not imply that the child understands the full meaning of sex-role identity. For example, a three-year-old does not yet understand that the gender of others is constant. The three-year-old typically classifies other children as "boy" or "girl" based on external characteristics such as clothes or hairstyle. Consequently, classifications are not always consistent.
· **Gender stability.** Gender is now perceived as a characteristic of the child that is permanent and stable *over time.*

The child recognizes that boys will eventually grow up to be men and girls will become women (Huston, 1983). However, the three- or four-year-old child may still be fooled by superficial changes in appearances (i.e., when girls wear "boy clothes").
· **Gender consistency or constancy.** In this stage, the six- or seven-year-old child realizes that an individual's gender is invariant over time *and* across situations, even with superficial changes in activity or appearance. For example, even when a boy plays with dolls he is still a boy, or when a girl wears a football helmet she is still a girl (Emmerich and Shepard, 1982).

What is the evidence for this developmental progression? The results of several studies indicate that child gender identity develops gradually and progresses through the three stages that Kohlberg (1969) describes (Slaby and Frey, 1975; Wehren and DeLisi, 1983; Munroe, Shimmin, and Munroe, 1984; Ruble, 1984). For example, there is evidence that children attain the basic gender identity stage by three years, the stage of gender stability at about age five, and gender consistency at approximately seven years. Furthermore, children in other cultures (Kenya, Nepal, Samoa, and so on) progressed through the same three stages (Munroe, Shimmin, and Munroe, 1984).

A major limitation with Kohlberg's cognitive approach is that sex-typing behavior is well under way *before* the attainment of a mature gender identity. In other words, although Kohlberg's theory suggests that *cognitive* development should *precede behavioral preferences* (in sex typing), the facts are that behavioral preferences occur so early (Fagot, 1985; Perry, White, and Perry, 1985) as to raise serious questions about Kohlberg's approach in the lives of children. Kohlberg's theory would *predict* that prior to five to seven years of age (i.e., prior to the third stage of gender consistency), there should be minimal child preferences for sex-appropriate activities. In fact, there is evidence that children prefer sex-appropriate toys and activities as early as two years of age (Faulkender, 1980; O'Brien, 1980; Ruble and Ruble, 1980; Schau et al., 1980; Huston, 1983). In a study in which masculine, feminine, and neutral toys were all equated in terms of primary attraction characteristics (e.g., size, number of moving parts, and number of pieces), it was found that toddlers continued to play with same-sex toys (O'Brien, Huston, and Risley, 1981). What, then, accounts for these early differences?

According to Aletha Huston (1983), what seems to be happening is that the child starts with a very global and general idea of gender (and only a very basic and limited understanding of gender consistency) which he or she gradually refines. Between three and eight years of age this general category of gender is reassessed such that those attributes that are essential for defining gender (masculinity and femininity) are distinguished from those that are not. According to Huston, "the developmental pattern, then, is to gain an increasingly refined awareness of societal sex stereotypes, while also learning that most of the activities and behaviors prescribed by stereotypes are *not* crucial to being male or female" (p. 407).

A speculative hypothesis for early behavioral preferences is that there may be subtle individual factors—over and above parental socialization—that contribute to the clear sex typing of play activities, social roles, and occupations, and the resulting segregation by sex of peer groups. Such an explanation cannot be entirely dismissed simply because there is not yet sufficient evidence for other explanations, as indicated above. The state of affairs is best described by Huston.

> . . . sex-typing of play activities and the resulting segregation of peer groups have often been dismissed as obvious (and therefore uninteresting) while investigators searched for more subtle personality traits and social behaviors or their antecedents in the process of socialization. . . . We have not paid enough attention to the most obvious, earliest, and most well-documented differences in expectations and experiences of young girls and boys. (1983, p. 407)

Current Perspectives on Sex Typing

In recent years there has been a reduced emphasis on the concept of identification. While observational learning and imitation continue to be viewed as important modes of sex typing, most theorists (social learning theorists and cognitive/development theorists) have de-emphasized identification with the parent (Huston, 1983). Parents are now viewed as one of many sex-role socialization influences.

Another important trend is the emphasis on a wider age range for sex typing. The traditional focus of psychoanalytic theory on the first five years of life with a secondary emphasis on puberty (see Chapter 2) has been replaced by the notion that developmental change can occur into adulthood. The reason for this lifespan emphasis has been the increasing focus of researchers and others on "becoming free" of biased or slanted (favoring one gender) sex-typing processes. There is now a greater emphasis on **androgyny** (a sex-role orientation that incorporates many masculine and feminine personality attributes and that reflects a freedom from traditional gender-based judgments, for organizing personality) than on the *acquisition* of conventional "sex-appropriate" roles (Bem, 1979, 1981; Martin and

Androgyny—A New Approach to Sex Roles

Androgyny refers to a sex-role orientation that includes many masculine and feminine attributes in one personality. Social scientists who have studied the process of sex typing have traditionally assumed that masculinity and femininity are at the opposite ends of a *single* dimension or continuum. In other words, the presence of masculinity means the absence of femininity, and vice versa. Bem (1978, 1979,

Sylvia Byers

1981) has challenged this viewpoint by suggesting that individuals can be both masculine and feminine (e.g., assertive and nonassertive, aggressive and nonagressive, competitive and noncompetitive, and so on) depending on the demands of a given situation. Bem (1981) suggests that masculinity and femininity are really *two separate dimensions*. From such a perspective a *masculine sex-typed individual* is one who has more masculine traits than feminine traits. Likewise, a *feminine sex-typed individual* is one who has more feminine traits than masculine traits. Finally, an androgynous individual has many of both masculine and feminine traits.

MASCULINE $\longleftrightarrow$ FEMININE

Do sex-typed individuals (whether masculine or feminine) differ from androgynous individuals in the way they organize or process gender-based information? According to Bem (1981), highly sex-typed individuals have shcemas (cognitive structures consisting of expectations or associations that guide a person's perception) in which *gender* is a dominant dimension, applied to most life circumstances. On the other hand, androgynous individuals have schemas in which gender dimensions are present but *not* dominant. Other bases for classifying and organizing experience are more potent and more frequently employed than is the case for sex-typed individuals. For example, on observing an individual receive some bad news, the sex-typed individual might ask "Did he take it like a man?" On the other hand, the androgynous individual might ask "Did he respond in a mature fashion?" Bem (1981) argues that androgyny is a relative freedom from gender-based judgments (Huston, 1983).

Halverson, 1981). In the words of Sandra Bem, the major purpose of doing research on sex roles is "to help free the human personality from the restrictive prison of sex-role stereotyping and to develop a conception of mental health that is free from culturally imposed definitions of masculinity and femininity" (1978).

Contexts of Sex Typing: An Ecological Perspective

The importance of socialization to the process of sex typing is illustrated by the fact that virtually all of the theories of sex typing recognize it as a major influence on children. Two processes of socialization as described by almost all of the theories are modeling or observational learning and direct teaching (primarily through reinforcement of desired child behaviors). The primary agents of socialization are parents, peers, siblings, teachers, and the mass media (Huston, 1983; Ruble, 1984; Eccles, 1985).

Do children actually observe sex-stereotyped behavior? Yes. The average American child sees women performing household tasks such as cleaning, sewing, and washing clothes, whereas men repair household items, mow the lawn, wash cars, and pursue "male" occupations. They typically see women as either unemployed or working in "female" occupations such as nursing, teaching, secretarial work, or much less frequently, in science, mathematics, or technical careers. Although there certainly are individual variations, most children are typically exposed to a steady experiential diet of sex-stereotyped roles and activities.

THE MEDIA.   The situation is typically aggravated by the sex-stereotyped content of mass media presentations. In particular, television assumes extraordinary importance in this regard because of its presence in the lives of children. The average child spends more time in front of the television set than any other activity with the exception of sleeping (Gross and Jeffries-Fox, 1978). Content analysis of virtually every type of television program suggests (Leary, Greer, and Huston, 1982; Liebert, Sprafkin, and Davidson, 1982; Huston, 1983):

· Adult males and females are frequently shown in sex-stereotyped household occupations and roles.
· In relation to their numbers in the population, males tend to be overrepresented and females underrepresented.
· Males and females are frequently shown using sex-stereotyped behaviors. According to Huston, "television 'communicates' attributes of dominance, aggression, autonomy, and activity as clearly sex-typed. In contrast, the image of femininity is largely a vacuum; females do very little except follow the lead of their active male companions" (1983, p. 421).

Have not these decidedly biased depictions of masculinity and femininity changed as a result of the women's movement and pressures for equality of op-

Janet Merchant

American television frequently portrays males and females in sex-stereotyped roles, although some programs—including "Sesame Street" and "Mr. Rogers' Neighborhood"—avoid such stereotypes and stress prosocial behavior.

portunity? Unfortunately, this has not been the case. Content analyses of television programs in recent years have shown little change in the depiction of male and female characters (Huston, 1983).

SOCIALIZATION OF SEX TYPING IN THE FAMILY.   The analysis of the contribution of the family to child acquisition of sex-typed behavior has frequently focused on the question of whether parents treat girls and boys differently. Evidence suggests that girls and boys are encouraged to pursue different types of play activity from the infant years on (Power and Parke, 1982; Jacklin, DiPietro, and Maccoby, 1984). Parents tend to promote sex-typed toy selection among their children, particularly doll play for girls (Huston-Stein and Higgins-Trenk, 1978). Likewise, parents encourage boys to engage in gross motor activity more than they encourage girls (Parke and Suomi, 1980; Block, 1983). Furthermore, there is evidence that household chores for school-age children are frequently assigned on the basis of sex-typed expectations (Duncan, Schuman, and Duncan, 1973).

With reference to the socialization of sex-typed personal and social behavior, the findings of several studies indicate that parents treat girls and boys differently. In several studies where the teaching behavior was directly observed, it was found that parents communicated higher expectations for independent functioning for boys than for girls (Block, 1979, 1983). In the case of girls, parents were more likely to provide assistance quickly and emphasize the interpersonal nature of the parent-child relationship. In a similar view, parents express higher expectations for the long-range academic achievement of boys than for the similar achievement of girls. Parents value achievement in mathematics less for their daughters than for their sons (Parsons, Adler, and Kaczala, 1982; Eccles and Hoffman, 1984; Eccles, 1985; Raymond and Benbow, 1986).

SEX TYPING IN SINGLE-PARENT FAMILIES.   As the composition and structure of the family has changed to include more single-parent families, it becomes important to examine the influence of such families on the sex-typing process. Theories of sex typing that emphasize the role of imitation, mutual parent-child interaction, or identification with the parent would predict problems without both parents available. On the other hand, sex-typing theories that emphasize cognitive/developmental processes and the influence of the broad culture (beyond the family) would predict no significant difference between dual-parent and single-parent families (Huston, 1983).

On the whole, the available evidence suggests that fathers play a significant but not an irreplaceable role in the development of sex typing for both boys and girls. In a longitudinal study, boys in divorced families exhibited little differences between boys in two-parent families for the first year after the divorce. However, after the second year of the divorce, the boys from the divorced families were less masculine in toy and activity preferences, played more with females and younger children, and were more dependent than boys from two-parent families (both sets of boys were six years old) (Hetherington, 1979; Hetherington, Cox, and Cox, 1978). In the case of girls, most of the evidence suggests few effects for father absence on sex-typed orientations or preferences (Hainline and Feig, 1978; Hetherington, Cox, and Cox, 1978).

For both boys and girls, the impact of the single-parent family on sex typing depends on both the *age* at which the father's absence occurred and the *influence of the mother*. For example, boys whose fathers left when they were preschool age or younger showed more effects than boys whose fathers left after the preschool period (Hetherington, 1972). In addition, when mothers in single-parent families encouraged the expression of such masculine behaviors as independence and assertiveness, boys exhibited more masculine behaviors than when the mothers were less encouraging. This finding is consistent with the general trend of increased importance of maternal behavior in father-absent families. Likewise, for girls, maternal behavior was a more important influence on sex typing in single-parent families than in dual-parent families. Girls in divorced families were more likely to display feminine behavior when mothers expressed warmth and encouragement. Generally speaking, these results suggest that both males and females can acquire sex-typed attributes through alternate paths. When the father is present, his personality can influence the son or daughter. When the father is absent, the mother's response becomes a primary influence. Both paths can achieve similar results. Unfortunately, there is little information from these studies on the impact of single-parent families on the development of androgynous sex typing. Nor is there much information on single-parent families where the mother is absent.

SEX TYPING AND MATERNAL EMPLOYMENT.   A potential influence on children's sex-typing behavior is the extent to which parents provide models of traditional sex-role behavior (in child rearing, in the performance of household tasks, in occupational tasks, and so on) for their children (Huston, 1983; Hoffman, 1984). One of the most significant social changes in this century has been the increase in maternal employment (see Chapter 6 for a discussion of this trend). Since child sex-typing preferences and behaviors are expressed as early as two or three years of age, it is important to note that, in addition to entering the labor markets, mothers are entering it at earlier stages of their child's development (see Chapter 6).
     How is maternal employment associated with changes in child sex typing?

• Children of employed mothers typically have *parental role models that are less traditional* than families where mothers are not employed. For example, when wives work, husbands tend to be involved more in traditionally female household chores, such as cleaning, child care, and preparing meals (Huston, 1983). Even though fathers help, *most* of these domestic chores are still performed by the mothers (Huston-Stein and Higgins-Trenk, 1978).
• *Child concepts of sex typing are less traditional and less stereotyped* when mothers are employed than when mothers are not employed (Huston, 1983). This generalization appears to be true for a wide age range of children, from three years through adolescence (Cordua, McGraw, and Drabman, 1979; Gold, Andres, and Glorieux, 1979; Urberg, 1979). In addition, a study of four-year-old preschool girls found a similar reduction in sex stereotypes when fathers assumed nontraditional roles (e.g., child care, cooking, and so on) in contrast to the girls whose fathers did not engage in such activities (Baruch and Barnett, 1981).
• *Maternal employment is associated with more dramatic changes in sex-typing behaviors for girls than for boys.* Girls with employed mothers have more androgynous interests, activities, and personal characteristics than girls with nonemployed mothers. Likewise, for girls, maternal employment is associated with higher educational aspirations, higher levels of achievement orientation, higher levels of self-esteem, and more engagement in physically active play (Gold and Andres, 1978a, 1978b; Gold, Andres, and Glorieux, 1979; Hoffman, 1979, 1984).
     For boys, however, maternal employment is not *consistently* related to sex-typed behavior (Huston, 1983; Hoffman, 1984). There is, however, some evidence that the potency of the father as a role model for boys may be reduced in working-class families with working mothers (Hoffman, 1979). According to Huston, "For

some children, maternal employment may signify paternal inadequacy in the male 'provider' role . . . '' (1983, p. 437).

Prosocial Behavior

■ SCENARIO

In the early 1970s a shocking event occurred in New York City. A night club manager named Kitty Genovese was returning home from work when she was attacked by a man with a knife in the courtyard of her apartment building. She screamed, and thirty-eight of her neighbors came to their windows and watched her being murdered. For one-half hour they watched, and not one of them even so much as called the police.

For what reasons do people help or not help one another? Why would thirty-eight people watch Kitty Genovese being attacked and ultimately murdered without providing some help or at least calling the police? Concerns about such issues have raised questions about the situational conditions that might influence helping behavior in children and adults and the developmental origins of prosocial behavior in children.

The simplest definition of prosocial behavior is ''action that aids or benefits another person'' (Radke-Yarrow, Zahn-Waxler, and Chapman, 1983). From this perspective many of the behaviors of children could be considered prosocial (helping friends, cooperative interaction with siblings, and so on). To this simple definition is sometimes added the qualification that aiding others is done *without* any expectation for *external reward*. Such behavior, which constitutes a variation of simple prosocial behavior, is called *altruism*.

> **Prosocial behavior.** Prosocial behavior is action intended to aid or benefit another person.
> **Altruism.** Altruism is a variation of prosocial behavior in which a person expects or anticipates no external reward.

Furthermore, it is of course possible for prosocial behavior to be *intrinsically* rewarding (i.e., internal satisfaction derived from the *performance* of an action rather than from the external consequences of the action). The research on prosocial behavior has focused on the study of the *broad* category of behaviors which includes actions motivated by the desire to help others. As such, our concern in this section is with such broadly defined behavior.

The Development of Prosocial Behavior in Infant and Preschooler

INFANCY. The focus of research on infant prosocial behavior has been on the development of sensitivity to the emotional activity of other infants (Radke-Yarrow, Zahn-Waxler, and Chapman, 1983). During the first two years of life, infants have been shown to demonstrate concerned attention to emotional distress of others (Dunn and Kendrick, 1979; Weston and Main, 1980; Zahn-Waxler and Radke-Yarrow, 1982). In a longitudinal study of ten-, fifteen-, and twenty-month-old infants that examined infant response to others' emotional distress, over a nine-month period, the following developmental sequence was proposed (Zahn-Waxler and Radke-Yarrow, 1982):

- Between ten and twelve months of age, infants demonstrate either no response or simple attending responses (e.g., frowning, crying, or visual checking with the parent) to incidents of emotional distress in other infants.
- Between thirteen and twenty months, positive initiations with others in distress began to appear (e.g., tentatively touching the person in distress).
- Between eighteen and twenty-four months, positive initiations become more frequent and differentiated. For example, children may respond to distress in others by expressing verbal sympathy, aggressively protecting the suffering person, or giving objects to the person to relieve the distress.

In addition, other studies suggest that infants also demonstrate prosocial behaviors through sharing, helping, and cooperation (Rheingold, 1982; Hay and Rheingold, 1983) (see Table 11.4). In one study involving two-year-olds and their mothers, helping behaviors were assessed in a laboratory setting which contained several uncompleted household chores (e.g., laundry to fold or scraps to sweep up). Mothers were instructed *not* to ask for help from their children. However,

TABLE 11.4
Markers of Early Prosocial Development

YEAR 1: BIRTH TO 6 MONTHS

Responds positively to others (smiles, laughs with others)
Participates in social games (peek-a-boo)
Reacts emotionally to distress (others' cries or upsets)

YEAR 1: 6 TO 12 MONTHS

Takes an active role in social games
Exhibits sharing behaviors
Displays affection to familiar persons

YEAR 2

Refines ability to point with index finger
Complies with simple requests
Indicates knowledge of rules of cooperative games
Shows knowledge of caregiving skills
Comforts persons in distress
Participates in the work of adults

YEAR 3

Draws person's attention to objects with words as well as gestures
Exhibits increasingly planful caregiving and helping sequences
Expresses own intentions to help and knowledge of task objectives

From Hay and Rheingold, 1983.

during a twenty-five-minute period of time, all of the two-year-olds helped their mothers (Rheingold, 1982).

PRESCHOOLER.   Our knowledge of prosocial behavior in preschool children is confined to the findings of research done mostly in nursery school settings (i.e., programs with abundant play materials and concerned adult teachers and supervisors). In other words, we know very little about the prosocial behavior of preschool children in other settings such as in playgrounds or in noninstructional peer gatherings (Radke-Yarrow, Zahn-Waxler, and Chapman, 1983). Nonetheless, several findings are of interest.

• The preschool child is capable of distinct prosocial behaviors that suggest that he or she is *"not* an overwhelmingly self-centered person" (Radke-Yarrow, Zahn-Waxler, and Chapman 1983, p. 482). In an observational study of the responses of three-to-seven-year-olds to a crying child, the majority of children demonstrated some level of prosocial sensitivity as follows (Sawin, 1980):
   —Almost half of the children showed an empathic or concerned facial expression.
   —Seventeen percent attempted to console the crying child.
   —Fifteen percent sought aid from an adult or tried talking to the child.
   —Twelve percent of the children withdrew from the situation.
   —Nine percent either showed no discernible response or a distinctly unsympathetic response.
• There is evidence that as children get older they are better able to respond to more subtle distress cues of another person (e.g., a slight frown rather than a loud cry) than younger children (Pearl, 1985). For example, eight-year-old children were better able to detect and respond to such subtle distress cues than were four-year-olds.
• The child's *motives* for engaging in prosocial behavior are not always clear (at least from the research perspective). There is limited evidence of caring and concern for the welfare of others. In a study of spontaneous sharing, helping, and comforting in a nursery school setting (over a twelve-week period), children were asked why they performed a specific prosocial behavior (Eisenberg-Berg and Neale, 1979). Reasons given included the following: meeting the needs of the other child ("He's hungry"), just "wanting" to help, friendship, mutual benefit, gaining approval, and so on. On the other hand, however, evidence suggests that sharing behavior may also have a self-serving quality or be done to attain a dominant position over a distressed child (Bar-Tal, Raviv, and Shavit, 1980; Bryant and Crockenberg, 1980).

Prosocial behavior appears early in life.

Cognitive Development and Prosocial Behavior

There are important relationships between prosocial behavior in children and their cognitive development (Perry and Bussey, 1984).

PROSOCIAL (MORAL) REASONING.   As children develop and mature, they become less egocentric in their reasoning about prosocial dilemmas or issues (Eisenberg, Lennon, and Roth, 1983) (see Table 11.5). Instead, they become more abstract in their reasoning about prosocial questions and more oriented toward and aware of others' needs. Children's prosocial reasoning becomes developmentally more sophisticated, moving from largely hedonistic motives (based primarily on what satisfies the self) to motives based on self-determined standards of "right" action. Furthermore, children who use more sophisticated moral reasoning methods are more likely to exhibit prosocial behaviors. For example, preschoolers who justify their behavior based on the "needs" of another child rather than on their own hedonistic desires are more likely to engage in the prosocial behavior of spontaneous sharing (Eisenberg-Berg and Hand, 1979).

SOCIAL NORMS.   The prevalence of prosocial behavior depends, in part, on the child's understanding and use of norms such as *social responsibility, deserving, reciprocity, equity,* and *equality.*

• *Norm of social responsibility.* This is the ideal that help should be given to others strictly on the basis of their need, regardless of the possibility of any reward to the giver. In the case of young children, the need of another person may not be clear enough to arouse helping behavior.
• *Norm of deserving.* This norm suggests that "people get what they deserve." Belief in this norm presumably causes people to try to ensure that help and resources are fairly distributed. Research suggests that children and adults are more helpful to those who do not deserve their plight than to those who appear to bring dire consequences on themselves. Likewise, there is some evidence that children who receive an unearned windfall gain (e.g., being overpaid for doing a task) often try to redistribute their gain by sharing it with other children. Also, children who think they have received less than their fair share on one occasion may react selfishly at a future time (Perry and Bussey, 1984).
• *Norm of reciprocity.* This is the principle that individuals should help those who have helped them. This norm develops during the preschool years but is more consistently understood and followed during the school years. Research suggests that both children and adults will return favors with some regularity (Peterson, 1980).
   Because the norm of reciprocity suggests that favors should be returned, child and adult helping behaviors may be motivated by the expectation of future reciprocity (rather than by an unselfish desire to give assistance or aid). Research evidence supports this possibility (Perry and Bussey, 1984).
• *Norms of distributive justice (equity vs. equality).* These are the norms used by individuals in order to determine rewards among members of a group in relation to their contribution to a given task. For example, how do children divide rewards on a group task when the contributions of the children are different? Do the children divide the rewards carefully in relation to the relative contribution of each child (the norm of *equity*)? Or do they simply give each child an equal amount (the

TABLE 11.5

The Developmental Progression in Prosocial Reasoning

LEVEL	ORIENTATION	DESCRIPTION	GROUP
1	Hedonistic, self-focused	The individual is concerned with self-oriented consequences rather than moral considerations. Reasons for assisting or not assisting another include consideration of direct gain to self, future, reciprocity, and concern for others whom the individual needs and/or likes (due to the affectional tie).	Preschoolers and younger elementary school children
2	Needs of others	The individual expresses concern for the physical, material, and psychological needs of others even though the others' needs conflict with one's own needs. This concern is expressed in the simplest terms, without clear evidence of self-reflective role taking, verbal expressions of sympathy, or reference to internalized effect such as guilt.	Preschoolers and elementary school children
3	Approval and interpersonal and/or stereotyped	Stereotyped images of good and bad persons and behaviors and/or considerations of others' approval and acceptance are used in justifying prosocial or nonhelping behaviors.	Elementary and high school students
4	(a) Empathic	The individual's judgments include evidence of sympathetic responding, self-reflective role taking, concern with the other's humanness, and/or guilt or positive effect related to the consequences of one's actions.	Older elementary school and high school students
	(b) Transitional (empathic and internalized)	Justifications for helping or not helping involve internalized values, norms, duties, or responsibilities, or refer to the necessity of protecting the rights and dignity of other persons; these ideas, however, are not clearly stated.	Minority of people high school age
5	Strongly internalized	Justifications for helping or not helping are based on internalized values, norms, or responsibilities; the desire to maintain individual and societal contractual obligations; and the belief in the dignity, rights, and equality of all individuals. Positive or negative effect related to the maintenance of self-respect for living up to one's own values and accepted norms also characterizes this stage.	Only a small minority of high school students and virtually no elementary school children

From Eisenberg, Lennon, and Roth, 1983.

norm of *equality*)? Do the norms of distributive justice used by children change with age and development?

Children under four or five years of age generally tend to operate without any norms of distributive justice. When asked to divide rewards on a group task, they simply take the largest share for themselves regardless of their actual contribution. By the first grade, children are capable of using both equity and equality norms (Enright, Franklin, and Manheim, 1980).

EMPATHY AND ROLE TAKING.   The development of *empathy* and *role taking* are also related to prosocial behavior. **Empathy** involves reacting to another individual's situation with the same emotion as that other individual. For example, the child who feels sad when another child is sad, happy when another child is happy, and so on, is exhibiting empathy. However, **role taking** involves the correct understanding of what another individual is thinking or feeling without having to feel the same way (We discuss role taking in more detail in Chapter 14).

The relationship between empathy and prosocial behavior becomes greater with age. Empathetic preschool children may or may not exhibit more prosocial behavior (Eisenberg-Berg and Lennon, 1980). Older children and adults who are empathetic are more consistently prosocial in their behavior (Hoffman, 1984).

From a rather early age, role-taking ability relates positively to prosocial behavior. Furthermore, there is evidence that children who are given practice in role taking can increase their level of prosocial behavior (Iannotti, 1985).

SELF-CONCEPT.   Although empathy and role taking are important in the development of prosocial behavior, the child's self-concept is an equally important ingredient. For example, children who learn to value prosocial behavior, to consider such behavior essential for their own self-esteem, and to have confidence in their ability to help another person will demonstrate more prosocial behaviors (Grusec and Redler, 1980).

Contexts of Prosocial Behavior: An Ecological Perspective

What types of family experiences lead to the development of prosocial behavior? How do specific dimensions of child rearing influence prosocial behavior? How important is it for parents to encourage or prompt prosocial behavior in children? Such questions can be answered, in part, by examining the *ecology* or the *contexts* of prosocial behavior.

MODELING: OBSERVING PARENTS AND WATCHING TELEVISION.   Helpful models affect the child's learning and performance of helpful behavior. When a child observes an adult or peer giving or helping, the likelihood of the child's imitating that behavior is increased (Hay and Murray, 1982; Hay and Rheingold, 1983). The effects of observation and imitation have been demonstrated with rescue acts, gift donations, and other prosocial acts (Bryan, 1975). Furthermore, there is evidence that the effects of prosocial models may be relatively longlasting (White, 1972).

In addition, what a parent or other model says is much less influential than what the model actually does (Bryan, 1975). For example, if parents or other models say things like "Giving is good" or "Helping other people will make them feel better," these statements are not motivating factors for child behavior unless they are coupled with appropriate actions. In other words, for young children the dictum "Do as I say, not as I do" does not work.

In addition, parents are not the only models of prosocial behavior for children. There is some evidence that television programs can provide another source of prosocial behavior (Freidrich and Stein, 1975). In one study, segments from the television program "Mr. Rogers' Neighborhood" (a program that focuses on understanding the feelings of others and helping people) were shown to five- and six-year-old children. In comparison with a control group of children who watched a "neutral" television program, the children who saw "Mr. Rogers' Neighborhood" not only learned more about specific prosocial behaviors but were more effective in applying that knowledge to situations involving other children (Freidrich and Stein, 1975).

PARENT CHARACTERISTICS.   The dimension of parental warmth–parental hostility is related to child behavior. Research indicates a positive relationship between parental warmth and prosocial behavior. Children who think of their parents as particularly loving and warm are more generous, supportive, and cooperative (M.L. Hoffman, 1975, 1984). However, parental warmth is most helpful in promoting prosocial behavior when it is given in response to the child's expressed need for attention (Bryant and Crockenberg, 1980). On the other hand, when adults offer warmth and rewards excessively and needlessly, they may foster an atmosphere of indulgence that restricts prosocial behavior (Weissbrod, 1980).

In addition, parents may play a vital role in encouraging prosocial behavior in children. It appears essential for parents to *actively* encourage the development of positive and desirable (prosocial) behaviors and *not limit* their disciplinary efforts only to the elimination of unwanted behavior. In other words, nurturing prosocial behavior in children appears to require parental support for positive behavior rather than parental indifference or only focusing on the elimination of undesirable behavior. Numerous studies support the conclusion that demanding prosocial behaviors, in fact, promotes future prosocial behaviors. For example, prosocially oriented toddlers tended to have mothers who forcefully stated to their children that socially responsible behavior was expected (Zahn-Waxler, Radke-Yarrow, and King, 1979). Furthermore, parents who use discipline as a means of promoting positive and prosocial behaviors in children (*prescriptive* parents) rather than only to eliminate undesirable behaviors (*proscriptive* parents) have children who are more generous (Olejnik and McKinney, 1973).

In a similar vein, parents who try to get their children to act prosocially (e.g., to share toys) by simply issuing warnings enforcing principles of social responsibility (e.g., "You ought to help others in need") are usually not very successful. In order to be effective, such statements of social norms must include some reasonable justification for such action. The use of *victim-centered reasoning* (i.e., spelling out to children the consequences of their behavior to other people) by parents is particularly helpful (M.L. Hoffman, 1975, 1984). For example, the parent might explain to the child how his or her behavior has emotionally or physically hurt another person and what corrective measures can be taken by the child. Research supports the conclusion that victim-centered reasoning promotes prosocial behavior for the following reasons (Perry and Bussey, 1984):

· It encourages empathy and role taking in the child.
· It helps children understand the rationale for parent discipline.
· It suggests how children can atone for their wrongdoing.

Perhaps one of the most obvious and most successful modes of encouraging prosocial behavior is through adult recognition and reinforcement. For example, if parents and other significant adults respond to child prosocial behavior with lavish praise and undivided attention, such behavior is more likely to occur again in the future (Grusec and Redler, 1980).

Aggression in Preschoolers

As in the case of prosocial behavior, aggression is learned in a context that includes the family, the neighborhood, peer groups, and in some cases television. Before we begin our discussion, it is important to keep in mind a distinction between *aggression* and *aggressive* or *assertive behavior*. **Aggression** means behavior *motivated* primarily by the desire to hurt another person. On the other hand, *aggressive behavior* means assertive responses that are not intended to hurt another person; for example, the preschooler who eagerly seeks to gain the attention of his or her parent or caretaker might be considered aggressive.

Developmental Patterns

There appears to be a developmental progression in the frequency and nature of aggression during the preschool years (Ferguson and Rule, 1980):

- Unfocused temper tantrums decrease during the preschool years and are replaced by acts of retaliation (revenge for a perceived injury). However, the *total* amount of aggression increases during the preschool years (see Fig. 11.1).
- Preschool children are more likely than school-age children to display physical aggression and to quarrel over toys or possessions.
- Older children (six-to-seven-year-olds) are more likely to replace physical aggression with more person-oriented hostile aggression (e.g., name calling, ridicule, tattling, verbal criticism, and so on).
- Preschool boys and girls exhibit differing patterns of aggression. Nursery school boys are more likely than nursery school girls to initiate and become involved in acts of aggression (Maccoby and Jacklin, 1980). Furthermore, nursery school boys are more likely to retaliate after being attacked than are nursery school girls (Darvill and Cheyne, 1981).

Contexts of Aggression: An Ecological Perspective

Aggression may be viewed as one type of response to a particular situation. Furthermore, aggression can be viewed as a *mutual interaction* in the context of family, neighborhood, and peers. In other words, aggression can be viewed as a characteristic of a *relationship* rather than as the characteristic of only one of the participants (e.g., parent or child).

Like prosocial behavior, the support or nonsupport of aggression is a characteristic of a complex, interacting system. The components of this system include the family, the neighborhood, and social-cultural values (as transmitted through

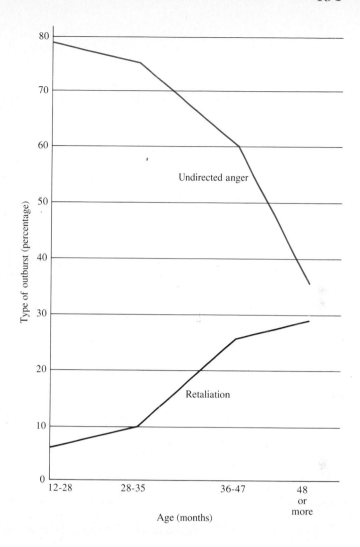

FIGURE 11.1

Unfocused temper tantrums decrease during the preschool years, although directed anger (acts of retaliation) increases. Based on Goodenough, 1931.

such media as the television). Family relationships have an impact on the occurrence of aggression in children. Children's temperaments and personalities (i.e., what they bring with them to a particular family encounter or activity) *interact* with the general "rule" structure of the family (e.g., closed, open, or random) and the characteristics or demands of the particular situation to produce many types of behavior (including, in some instances, aggression).

Whereas children bring with them a history of experience and a personal style of coping, the parents likewise bring their own experiential history and coping style. In addition, parents bring with them a specific mode of responding to aggression.

Figure 11.2 is a schematic depiction of the basic elements of an ecological perspective to child aggression (Parke and Lewis, 1981; Parke, 1982). Each component (family, child, community, and culture) has a two-way or bidirectional relationship with each of the other components. We use this approach as a basis for our discussion of the contexts of aggression.

ACQUISITION OF AGGRESSION IN THE FAMILY.   Explanations of the acquisition of behavior (including aggression) within the family have undergone a significant

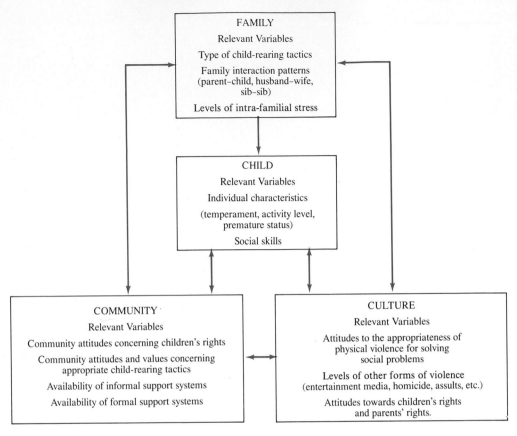

FIGURE 11.2

An ecological model of aggression. From Parke, 1982.

Intrafamilial Violence—Aggression in the Family

Reported Cases of Child Maltreatment Involving "Serious Injury" (1976–1983)

	NUMBER OF CASES INVOLVING "SERIOUS INJURY"	PERCENT OF TOTAL CASES	TOTAL REPORTED CASES
1976	1950	3.1%	62,911
1977	2538	3.7%	68,593
1978	2795	3.5%	79,871
1979	8536	4.5%	189,694
1980	10,471	3.9%	268,488
1981	9666	4.1%	235,768
1982	7957	2.4%	331,544
1983	12,729	3.2%	397,785

From American Humane Association, 1984.

One of the aspects of aggression that has received increasing attention as a problem of national propor- tions is *intrafamilial violence* (Gelles and Straus, 1979; Finkelhor et al., 1983; Gelles and Cornell, 1985; Lystad, 1986; Garbarino, 1986). Intrafamilial violence includes aggressive behavior by one family member against any other family member (child, wife, husband, parent, sibling, and so on). Such family violence includes physical abuse, sexual abuse, and neglect (physical, moral, or educational) as well as murder and assault. Although precise estimates are not available, a number of provocative statistics are worth noting. According to a report of the American Humane Association (1984), there were 397,785 children abused in 1983 in the United States. Of this total, about 40,000–80,000 are physically abused, 24,000–40,000 are sexually abused, and the remainder are neglected.

Furthermore, in a study of violence in the United States (Straus, Gelles, and Steinmetz, 1980), 3.8 percent of the subjects reported at least one wife-beating incident during the previous year. Applying this incidence rate to the approximately 47 million couples in the United States, in any one year about 1.8 million wives are beaten by their husbands. Among those couples in which violence occurred, the yearly frequency of such incidents was 2.4 (i.e., over two serious assaults per year). Moreover, the likelihood that couples underreported severe acts of violence makes it probable that the survey figures are underestimates of the true extent of wife beating. 11.6 percent of the husbands used violence against their wives compared with 12.1 percent of the wives who used violence against their husbands.

Furthermore, the analysis of intrafamilial violence supports the merit of considering the interaction patterns among all family members. For example, there is evidence that husband-wife violence may be closely associated with or may cause other types of family violence. Families who use physical or verbal abuse to resolve husband-wife disputes also use similar techniques in disciplining their children who, in turn, use these techniques to resolve sibling argu-

ments (Reid, Taplin, and Lorber, 1981). In summary, intrafamilial violence and aggression seem best understood from a family-systems perspective, which recognizes the need to consider the reciprocal interaction of all family members.

What accounts for the high rates of violence and aggression within families? Several explanations have been given for this unfortunate family phenomenon, including the following (Gelles and Straus, 1979; Finkelhor et al., 1983):

- *Time at risk* or the amount of time family members spend interacting with one another.
- *Diversity of family activities,* which means "that there are more events over which a dispute or failure to meet expectations can occur" (Gelles and Straus, 1979, p. 552).
- *The intensity of involvement* is greater in families than in comparison to other groups, which means, of course, that there is greater likelihood for strong disagreements and violence.
- The right of some family members (typically parents or older siblings) *to influence the behavior* of other family members may create potentially explosive situations.
- The *right to privacy* may insulate some family interactions from objective monitoring or from assistance in preventing or resolving conflicts.
- The *social expectation* that couples resolve their own problems and the *involuntary membership* in families, especially for children, may increase the potential for conflict.
- "The simple but important fact of . . . cultural norms legitimizing the use of violence between family members in situations which would make the use of physical force a serious moral or legal violation if it occurred between non-family members" (Gelles and Straus, 1979, p. 573).

transformation. They have moved beyond the limitations of only considering the *direct effects of one individual on another* (e.g., parental influence on the child) as inadequate explanations (Parke and Slaby, 1983). The complete family constellation, both parents and all children, needs to be considered (Parke, Power, and Gottman, 1979; Belsky, 1981; Lewis, 1982).

Typically, parents have been viewed as influencing the incidence of child aggression primarily through their specific child-rearing behaviors. Another perspective receiving increasing emphasis is the role of the *parent as manager of the child's environment* (Parke and Slaby, 1983). In such a role, parents can influence aggression in the ways they organize the home environment (particularly for infants and preschoolers) and the extent to which they monitor extrahome activities (particularly for school-age children and adolescents). The "management" function of parents becomes at least as important as the direct child-rearing role of parents when it is recognized that children spend more time interacting with inanimate objects than with socializing agents, such as parents (Hartup, 1979; Parke and Slaby, 1983). This is particularly the case in infancy and the preschool years, as evidenced by the following estimates based on home observations (White et al.):

> For 12-month old to 15-month old children, the figures were 89.7% for nonsocial tasks versus 10.3% for social tasks. By 18–21 months the figures are 83.8% nonsocial and 16.2% social; at 24–27 months 80.0% nonsocial and 20.0% social, and at 30–33 months they were 79.1% nonsocial and 20.9% social. (1976, p. 125)

In infancy and the preschool years, the management function of the parent may be particularly important since the child's access to aggressive toys (e.g., guns) or unmonitored television violence may influence the child's level of aggression.

AGGRESSION AND PARENTAL DISCIPLINARY STRATEGIES.   In addition to their managerial function, parents also exercise influence on the development of child aggression through their preferred disciplinary tactics. A number of parental factors have been shown to be individually related to aggression, including parental nonacceptance, permissiveness, inconsistent punishment (Sawin and Parke, 1979), disagreement about child-rearing values (Porter and O'Leary, 1980; Block, Block, and Morrison, 1981), and punitiveness (George and Main, 1979; Reid, Taplin, and Lorber, 1981).

• *Parental nonacceptance* has been shown to be associated with child aggression in a wide range of studies of preschoolers, school-age children, and adolescents.
• *Permissiveness* is frequently associated with aggressiveness, particularly when associated with parental inconsistency.
• *Parental inconsistency* is frequently associated with aggression. In one study, aggressive behavior during consistent verbal punishment from two people was greater following a period of inconsistent discipline than after either consistent approval or consistent ignoring (Sawin and Parke, 1979).
• *Parental disagreement over child-rearing values* has been shown to be related to the development of ego control which, in turn, influences the expression of aggression. In one study, parental disagreement measured when a child was three years old was releated to reduced ego control over a four-year period (to age seven) (Porter and O'Leary, 1980; Block, Block, and Morrison, 1981).
• *Parental punitiveness* has been linked to aggression in children. In a study of children one to three years of age who had either been physically abused or not abused (by their parents), the abused children physically attacked (e.g., hit, kicked, slapped, grabbed, and so on) other toddlers and preschoolers twice as often as the nonabused children (George and Main, 1979).

PARENTS AND CHILDREN AS RECIPROCAL INFLUENCES.   Although the examination of individual factors associated with childhood aggression provides useful and important information about the antecedents of aggression, a more complete picture can be gotten from an ecological perspective (Fig. 11.2). Specifically, an ecological or systems perspective recognizes the *reciprocal* influences that the parents, the child, and the siblings have on one another (Parke and Slaby, 1983).

One of the most detailed ecological examinations of the development of aggression in families is the research of Gerald Patterson (1982). According to Patterson, the *family is a system* of interacting components or members whose goal is to learn how to respond to one another. Through detailed home observations, Patterson has identified a specific *coercive pattern* that seems to produce and maintain aggression among family members. The coercive pattern operates as follows:

- One family member presents an *aversive stimulus* (e.g., an unkind or inconsiderate statement).
- A second family member counters with an *aversive stimulus, if* the first aversive stimulus seems alterable.
- The aversive interchange continues to escalate, and may involve additional family members, until one member finally withdraws.
- Usually the second family member also withdraws, momentarily disrupting the aversive cycle.
- The second family member *learns* that he or she has forced the withdrawal of the first family member, using tactics of aggression (e.g, verbal aggression). He or she will, in turn, be more likely to use aversive behavior in the future to control the behavior of family members.

As a result of such a pattern of coercive interaction, children can quickly become involved as either the *instigators* of aggression in families or the *victims* of family aggression (Parke and Slaby, 1983). Furthermore, such children can be "inadvertently *training* their parents to become highly punitive, since high-intensity aggressive responses by children may, in turn, elicit high-intensity disciplinary tactics from parents to suppress these behaviors" (Parke and Slaby, 1983, p. 586).

Although such coercive patterns of interaction can occur in all families, they are more likely to occur in families that already have problems with an aggressive child (Parke and Slaby, 1983). In such cases, as well as for all other families, *both* the parent child-rearing patterns *and* the characteristics of the child need to be considered. According to Patterson (1982), the parents of aggressive children tend to be ineffective as disciplinary agents. For example, aggressive children were found to be nearly twice as likely as nonaggressive children to respond to parental punishment by either continuing their aversive behavior or simply ignoring the parent (Patterson, 1982). Furthermore, the parents of aggressive children tend to be *inconsistent* disciplinarians and to use ineffective forms of discipline (e.g., nagging and scolding) (Patterson, 1982).

With reference to the child's contribution, there frequently are characteristics of the aggressive child that make him or her difficult for parents to handle. These children may have one or more of the following characteristics (Patterson, 1982):

- *Noncompliance.*
- *Arrested socialization.* They tend to be impulsive in seeking short-term satisfaction at the expense of long-term goals and satisfaction. In addition, they frequently use aversive means to get their way.
- *Less responsiveness to social circumstances and social reinforcers* (e.g., parental disciplinary strategies—approval or disapproval). There is some evidence, as suggested, that this reduced social responsiveness may be due, in part, to the indiscriminate and careless use of both positive and aversive social reinforcers

by parents (e.g., rewards that are not clearly associated, in time, with positive child behavior) (Patterson, 1980).
• *Skill limitations in peer relationships and academic achievement* (Patterson, 1982).

What happens when family members adopt coercive-aversive strategies for interacting and controlling family outcomes? As can well be imagined, the results are not positive.

> As more family members adopt aversive behaviors as a method of coping with each other, the entire family system may become disrupted. Indeed, the coercive pattern of family interaction has often been found to be accompanied by a wide variety of disruptions in family interaction including: (a) avoidance of interaction among family members; (b) cessation of family recreational activities; (c) disruption in communication and problem-solving; (d) loss of self-esteem, particularly for mothers; and (e) development of marital conflicts. (Parke and Slaby, 1983, p. 588)

AGGRESSION AND THE PEER GROUP.   Although families play a significant role in the development of child aggression, they are only one of several influences, including peers and the broad culture in which families live. Peers are important in the development of aggression in a number of significant ways. They can serve as models of aggression, they can bring out or elicit aggression in children, they can reinforce or actively support aggression, and they can serve as the targets of aggression. It is important to keep in mind that in each of these peer functions, aggression between peers is a *reciprocal process.* In other words, each participant or peer serves to elicit, model, or maintain aggressive responses in the other peer, and vice versa (Patterson, 1982).

In addition, peers can maintain, increase, or reduce the level of aggressive behavior, not only through their interaction but through the norms or rules they set regulating aggressive activity. For example, the violation of peer-group norms for the propriety of aggression (e.g., excessive aggression) can lead to rejection and dislike by peers. In one study, children who used physical and verbal aggression (e.g., excluding peers from play and insults) were rejected by peers, whereas children who engaged in more cooperative play were considered more popular by their peers (Dodge, 1981). It is not safe to generalize that aggression causes unpopularity since it could be the case that unpopular children behave aggressively because they are, in fact, rejected by their peers.

AGGRESSION AND CULTURE: TELEVISED VIOLENCE.   In addition to families and peers, the role of culture is extraordinarily important in the development of child aggression. In this section we focus on one dimension of culture that has been of continuing public concern in relation to aggression—the role of television. The majority of studies on the relationship of televised violence to child aggression establish a link between children's viewing violence on television and their performance of aggression (Parke and Slaby, 1983).

In light of this general consensus, it is important to recognize that virtually every child is exposed to a considerable amount of television violence, as indicated by the following facts:

• Television is accessible to virtually every child in the United States. Almost every household (98 percent) has at least one television.

"Don't you understand? This is life, *this is what is happening. We* can't *switch to another channel." Robert Day cartoon from The* New Yorker.

- American children, two to eighteen years of age, watch an average of three hours of television each day (Nielsen Television Index, 1982).
- Over 70 percent of prime-time dramatic fiction programs contained violence (sampled from 1967 through 1979). The highest amounts of violence were in children's cartoons and weekend morning programs (Gerbner et al., 1979; Gerbner et. al, 1980).
- Most children have few, if any, restrictions placed on the amount or the content of television viewing (Rossiter and Robertson, 1975).

Are there developmental changes in the ways children understand television programs and televised violence? Age-related differences have been found in several dimensions. Older children are better able than younger children to make discriminations in the following areas:

- Distinctions between fictional and real-life characters and events (Greenberg and Reeves, 1976).
- Distinctions between cartoon, puppet, and human characters (Quarfoth, 1979).
- Program content directly related to the plot or theme of a television program in contrast to tangential or peripheral material (Collins et al., 1978).
- The consequences of behavior portrayed in television programs (Collins, Berndt, and Hess, 1974).
- The motivations of characters in television programs (Collins, Berndt, and Hess, 1974).

• In addition, young children respond *more directly* to televised acts of violence than older children do. Younger children react to television violence as if it were unconnected to the context of the entire program or to the consequences of the violent behavior.

Considering these findings, an adult co-viewer may be particularly helpful for preschool children. This may be the case when the context of character motivations or the consequences of violence are not presented in close proximity (as is frequently the situation in television dramas). The adult co-viewer could lessen the effects of violence by explaining the context and consequences of aggressive behavior to the preschooler (Parke and Slaby, 1983).

Given the developmental differences in interpreting televised violence, it is important to examine in more detail the impact of televised violence on child aggression. What does the weight of the evidence suggest? The majority of studies point to two major behavioral effects of *heavy television watching* (Parke and Slaby, 1983).

• An increase in the level of child aggression.
• An increase in the passive acceptance of the use of aggression by, and against, others.

Support for viewing television violence as a source of increased child aggression comes from a wide variety of studies (using different-aged subjects, different materials, different methodologies, and so on), which all point to the credibility of this generalization. For example, viewed televised violence leads to increased child aggression in numerous situations, including:

• When violence is presented on a movie screen, on television, or by live models (Bandura, 1965; Parke et al., 1977).
• With cartoons or realistically portrayed violence (Bandura, 1965; Ellis and Sekyra, 1972).
• With children, adolescents, or adults viewing (Parke et al., 1977).
• When viewers have *not* experienced frustration prior to viewing violent program content *or* when the viewers have no previous history of aggressive behavior (Parke et al., 1977).
• With controlled experimental studies and in some naturalistic settings (Bandura, 1965; Freedman, 1984).
• When individuals are viewing the violence as individuals or in groups (Parke et al., 1977).
• In the case of single *or* repeated exposures to violence (Bandura, Ross, and Ross, 1963).
• When aggression is examined immediately after viewing the violence or with a long delay (Liebert and Baron, 1972).

Since the evidence for the link between viewed violence and aggression comes from a broad range of methodologies, we briefly consider that evidence here. For example, the large number of scholarly research articles (approximately 630 published articles) have been examined in groups to assess the overall direction of their findings. Several such studies (called meta-analyses) support the relationship between viewed violence and child aggression (Andison, 1977; Hearold, 1979; Glass, McGaw, and Smith, 1981). In addition to meta-analyses, studies utilizing a

Aggression in the Young Child

Infants occasionally hurt others by pushing too hard or striking another with a hard toy held in wobbly and uncertain grasp. The pushing is often a form of "Hello," a way of greeting for a child short on vocabulary. The striking is seldom done with any malice but more from lack of coordination. It isn't sensible

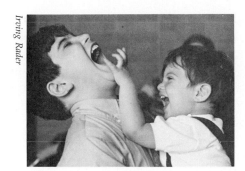

Irving Rader

to scold infants for these transgressions. We need only to keep them apart or free from toys or other objects that might be hurtful. . . .

Toddlers, too, are still short on vocabulary and on social skills. They learn to defend their space with shrieks, which may sound like they are badly hurt when they usually aren't. The shrill shriek serves a purpose. It causes adults to come running and scold anyone in sight, assuming the "poor baby" was the victim. This technique is successfully used on older siblings. . . .

Hitting and Kicking

Very seldom is a preschooler maliciously hitting and kicking. Rather these children strike out because of frustration or because of some interference or assumed interference from another child. . . . What can adults do about hitting or kicking? First, stop the behavior without blame or punishment—neither of these stops negative behavior except in a short-run sense. Second, make adjustments in indirect guidance, arranging the space, . . . routine, and so on in ways that more readily fit the children. Third, recognize the child for his strengths and good behavior. . . . In other words, give him attention for his "good" works, not for his "bad." Fourth, give him opportunities to talk out his feelings. Fifth, find a diversion for his energy.

(From Hildebrand, 1985b, pp. 311–13.)

---

variety of methodologies provide further insight into the relationship between childhood aggression and televised violence.

• *Laboratory studies* (provide the control necessary for examining the precise contribution of many factors, such as types of viewers, circumstances of viewing, types of program content, and so on). The weight of these studies supports the link between televised violence and aggression (Comstock, 1980). However, these studies have been criticized because they do not discuss the effects of television in the real world. For example, typical laboratory measures of aggression, such as hitting a Bobo doll, are unrelated to real-life aggression because there is no possibility of punishment or retaliation (Freedman, 1984).

• *Field experiments.* In response to the limitations of laboratory studies, field studies have examined the relationship of violence and aggression in *realistic* or *naturalistic* settings. Many of these field studies support the generalizations of the laboratory evidence (Parke and Slaby, 1983). However, not all of the studies supported the hypothesis that televised violence led to child aggression. Furthermore, where the hypothesis was supported, the effects were not strong (Freedman, 1984).

• *Correlational evidence.* These studies have demonstrated that a relationship (or correlation) between televised violence and aggression occurs in a wide variety of settings (in the United States, Great Britain, Australia, Poland, and so on) and with a variety of age groups (preschoolers, school-age children, adolescents, adults) (Greenberg, 1975; Eron, 1982). A limitation of these and of other correlational findings is of course, that causation cannot be imputed—only suggested.

• *Longitudinal evidence.* Such evidence suggests that there may be a long-term relationship between viewed violence and aggression (Granzberg and Steinberg, 1980; Singer and Singer, 1981). With particular reference to preschool children in a day-care setting, a relationship (between viewed violence and aggression) lasting longer than one year was found (Singer and Singer, 1981). For all age groups, other longitudinal studies have found relationships lasting as long as ten or even twenty years (Eron, 1982).

In addition to the relationship between televised violence and behavioral incidents of aggression, the second major conclusion from all studies, taken together, is the passive acceptance of the use of aggression by the viewer (Parke and Slaby, 1983). There is strong evidence that a steady diet of televised violence leads to *behavioral apathy* about the use of aggression. However, one may be particularly likely to passively accept aggression (or to *change* an existing position to acceptance) under the following conditions (Parke and Slaby, 1983):

• If violence is perceived as common, justified, effective, or rewarded.
• When the real-life world appears to conform to the television environment in which the violence occurs.
• When the child has little personal experience or awareness to compare against the world of television.

Summary

1. One approach to the study of self is the idea that an individual organizes thinking about the self into a "theory" of self. According to this perspective, the self is really a *self system* that is organized by the individual into a set of core and peripheral constructs. When they are asked to describe themselves, preschoolers tend to focus on actions they can perform, physical characteristics, their possessions, and interpersonal relations. In addition, preschool children for the first time make a distinction between a *public self* and a *private self.*

2. One of the most important characteristics of the self that begins to crystallize during the preschool years is *social competence.* Social competence develops in accordance with several basic principles: adaptation, the child as a coherent whole, the centrality of emotion and effect, individual differences, and the reorganization of self as development. In addition, social competence is *developmental,* changing in relation to child maturity and differing environmental circumstances.

3. Virtually every human society has different expectations for the behavior of males and females. The entire process, which begins with the awareness of gender in early childhood and which includes the child's acquisition of sex-role standards and the continued crystallization of a sex-role throughout adolescence and young adulthood, is called *sex typing* or *sex-role development.* Traditional sex-role standards have become very controversial over the past decade.

4. Sex typing involves many dimensions. One way to think about these dimensions is in terms of *content areas* and *constructs*.

   There is evidence that *few* of the *stereotyped* or *traditional* views of male and female behavior are, in fact, true. These traditional sex-role behaviors can be grouped into one of three categories: those few that are probably accurate, those for which there is some evidence but that remain open to question, and those that are erroneous.

   Three major theories have been proposed to describe the acquisition of sex-role identity in young children—*psychoanalytic theory*, *social learning theory*, and *cognitive developmental theory.*

   In recent years there has been a reduced emphasis on the concept of identification. Another important trend is the emphasis on a wider age range for sex typing.

5. Important contexts for sex typing include the *media* and the *family.* Content analysis of television programs indicates that male and female characters are typically presented in sex-stereotyped roles. With reference to the socialization of sex-typed behavior in families, there is evidence that girls and boys may be treated differently by parents. For both boys and girls, the impact of the single-parent family on sex typing depends on both the age at which parent absence (usually the father) occurred and the influence of the mother.

6. How is *maternal employment* associated with changes in sex typing? Children of employed mothers typically have parental role models who are less traditional than families where mothers are not employed. Child concepts of sex typing are less traditional and less stereotyped when mothers are employed compared with when mothers are not employed. Maternal employment is associated with more dramatic changes in sex-typing behaviors for girls than for boys.

7. The focus of research on infant prosocial behavior has been on the development of sensitivity to the emotional activity of other infants. Studies of the prosocial behavior of preschoolers have largely been confined to nursery school settings. The preschool child is capable of distinct prosocial behaviors that suggest that he or she is "not an overwhelmingly self-centered person." As children get older, they are better able to respond to more subtle distress cues of another person. The child's motives for engaging in prosocial behavior are not always clear.

8. There are important relationships between prosocial behavior in children and their cognitive development. As children develop and mature, they become less egocentric in their reasoning about prosocial dilemmas or issues. The prevalence of prosocial behavior depends, in part, on the child's understanding and use of norms such as *social responsibility, deserving, reciprocity, equity,* and *equality.* The development of *empathy* and *role taking* are also related to prosocial behavior.

   An ecological perspective to prosocial behavior involves an examination of the contexts of such behavior, including the role of parents and television.

9. There appears to be a developmental progression in the frequency and nature of aggression during the preschool years. The basic components of an ecological perspective to aggression include the child, the family, the community, and the culture. Explanations of the acquisition of aggression within the family have moved to a consideration of the complete family constellation. Parents exercise an influence on the development of child aggression as "managers" of the child's environment and through their preferred disciplinary tactics.

10. An ecological (or systems) perspective to childhood aggression recognizes the *reciprocal* influences that the parents, the child, and the siblings have on one another. The family can be viewed as a *system* of interacting components (or members) whose goal is to learn how to respond to one another. As a result of patterns of coercive interaction, children can become involved as either the *instigators* of aggression or the *victims* of family aggression.

     Although families may play a significant role in the development of child aggression, they are only one of several influences, including the peer group and the broad culture in which families live (e.g., televised violence). With reference to television violence, there are age-related or developmental differences in the ways younger and older children interpret the content of television programs.

11. The majority of studies on the relationships of childhood aggression and televised violence point to *two major behavioral effects* of *heavy* television watching: an *increase* in the *level of child aggression* and an *increase* in the *passive acceptance* of the use of aggression by, and against, others.

Key Terms

Aggression	Prosocial (moral) reasoning
Altruism	Public self
Androgyny	Role taking
Basic gender identity	Self schemas
Categorical self	Sex-role development
Empathy	Sex-role standards
Gender consistency or constancy	Sex typing
Gender stability	Social competence
Private self	Socialization
Prosocial behavior	Social norms

Questions

1. Briefly define each of the following: the self as a system, the categorical self, the private self, and social competence.
2. Discuss the controversies surrounding traditional sex-role standards. Discuss two unfounded myths of sex difference.
3. What is meant by the term *androgyny*?
4. Discuss the impact of maternal employment on sex-role development for boys and girls.
5. What are the relationships between cognitive development and prosocial behavior?
6. Discuss the ecological perspective to childhood aggression.

Suggested Readings

BROOKS-GUNN, J., and LEWIS, M. "The Development of Self-Knowledge. In C. B. Kopp and J. B. Krakow (eds.), *The Child in a Social Context*. Reading, Mass.: Addison-Wesley, 1982. An excellent review of research on the development of self-knowledge in children.

DAMON, W. *Social and Personality Development: Infancy Through Adolescence*. New York: Norton, 1983. A well-written analysis of the central theories and research on social and personality development.

ECCLES, J. S. "Sex Differences in Achievement Patterns." In T. Sonderegger (ed.), *Nebraska Symposium on Motivation*. Lincoln: University of Nebraska Press, 1985. A well-written and thorough analysis of sex differences in achievement.

GELLES, R. J., and CORNELL, C. P. *Intimate Violence*. Beverly Hills: Sage, 1985. An excellent discussion of violence in families.

LEWIS, M. "The Social Network Systems Model: Toward a Theory of Social Development." In T. M. Field, H. Huston, H. C. Quay, L. Troll, and G. E. Finley (eds.), *Review of Human Development*. New York: Wiley, 1982. A well-written analysis of the influence of social network systems on child social development.

TAVRIS, C., and WADE, C. *The Longest War: Sex Differences in Perspective*. New York: Harcourt Brace Jovanovich, 1984. A readable discussion of research on sex-role differences.

12 Middle Childhood: Contexts of Development

A Systems Overview of the Developing Self in Middle Childhood

Development during the years of middle childhood is an exciting phenomenon. The period of middle childhood begins at age five or six with entrance into the formal school, and it concludes with the onset of puberty, which heralds the arrival of adolescence. Development during the years of middle childhood is filled with many exciting and sometimes dramatic changes in the child. As children enter the formal school, the stage is set for developments in the way they think, learn, interact with others, and organize their behavior.

A good way to capture the total picture of what is happening during this period is to think of development in middle childhood from a *systems perspective*. This means that we look at the child as a self who is growing and developing in the contexts of middle-childhood experience. These contexts include the family, the neighborhood and the community, the school, and the peer group. You will remember that in Chapter 7 we examined the development of the preschooler in a similar manner. The major differences between the world of preschooler and the world of school-age child are summarized in Figure 12.1. During middle childhood, the child usually begins more extensive interactions outside of the family (e.g., in school and with peers) than in the preschool years. The relationship between child and family remains important but is now expanded to include the school, the peer group, and the neighborhood/community. In this chapter, we examine the contributions of each of these contexts to middle childhood in relation to the development of the child.

Before doing that, however, we present a brief overview of the development of self and the contributions of each context.

The Child as a Competent Person

During middle childhood, there is an increasing degree of "seriousness" about life as children begin to concentrate on what can be done and how well they can do it. This attitude contrasts with that of the preschool years, when learning to do things was more incidental to the total life activities of the child. We refer to the

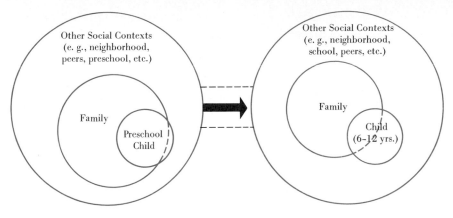

FIGURE 12.1

The transition figure from the preschool system (two to six years) to the middle childhood system (six to twelve years). The mutual relationship between family and child is expanded during the middle childhood years to include a larger society (school, neighborhood/community, and peers).

increasing seriousness of middle childhood as an emerging *sense of competence*. Two important elements relate to this sense of seriousness or **competence**: the refinement of the self-concept and skill learning.

REFINEMENT OF THE SELF-CONCEPT.   During middle childhood, there is an emphasis on the building of child skills such as reading, writing, interpersonal relationships, and game activities. For this reason, children may become occupied with the process of *self-evaluation*. Two primary sources of feedback for such self-evaluation are adults (e.g., parents, neighbors, relatives, and teachers), and peers. As a result of children's evaluations of themselves, two things happen:

In middle childhood there is curiosity about the world—and much to learn.

- Children refine their self-concepts in light of firsthand experiences.
- Children learn to approach the world with a sense of relative self-confidence or relative self-doubt.

In addition, children's sense of competence in relating to their world is based on the development of their personalities up to middle childhood. For example, Erik Erikson (1963) maintains that a sense of industry or competence is based on the prior development of trust (rather than mistrust), autonomy (rather than shame), and initiative (rather than guilt) (see Chapter 2).

As children develop standards for evaluating their performance, they begin to assess the extent to which they can readily learn skills. (Erikson referred to this stage as "industry versus inferiority.") In so doing, they develop a basic idea of how well they enjoy being "industrious," both in learning skills and in performing them, in comparison with others. This early sense of industriousness marks the beginning of vocational-occupational development—a process that will come to a head during adolescence.

SKILL LEARNING.   Learning skills is one of the most important and impressive facets of middle childhood. During this period, children develop many significant skills in thinking, interacting with others, body movement, writing and drawing, and reading, to name a few. Reading is one of the most important skills a child will learn. It is essential to success both in the school and, afterward, in the working world. In addition, reading skills allow the child to move beyond the world of immediate concrete experience to explore the past and the future and what others are thinking or feeling.

DEVELOPMENTAL CHANGES.   Developmental advances that occur in middle childhood provide the basis for the emergence of competence. In this section, we provide a brief overview of some of these changes.

> *DEFINITION*
>
> **Social Cognition.** The ability to understand the thoughts, emotions, intentions, and viewpoints of oneself and others, as well as the ability to think about social institutions and social relationships.

- *Social cognition and social competence.* From age six through twelve, the child's ability to understand the perspective of others increases (Selman and Byrne, 1974; Selman, 1980; Flavell, 1985). In turn, these changes in social cognition contribute to improved competence in social functioning. For example, the school-age child is better than the preschool child at communicating messages to others based on his or her understanding of a situation (Shatz, 1983; Garvey, 1984; Flavell, 1985). In addition, the school-age child presumably can interact with others better than the preschooler based on his or her increased understanding of social roles (e.g., sex rules or roles of pupil, teacher, parent, child, or friend).

Parent-child relationships and family interactions may be influenced by these changes in child conceptions of the roles of parent and child. In particular, there appears to be a transition in the child's concept of authority and the conceptualization of the right of parents to exercise authority (Damon, 1983). Preschoolers tend to believe that parental authority resides in the *power* of the parent to reward or punish. By middle childhood there is an emerging appreciation of the mutuality or interdependence of parent and child as the basis of parent authority. For example, school-age children may recognize that compliance with parental authority is justified because of all the things parents do for them (Maccoby, 1984a). Furthermore, there is evidence that by eight years of age children acknowledge the competence and expertise of parents as a basis for their authority (Damon, 1983). Throughout middle childhood, this increasing recognition of parents' experience and knowledge typically results in the reduced parental use of promises of rewards or threats of punishment as disciplinary techniques.

• *Self-concept*. Around six years of age, the child begins to develop the skill of viewing the self from the perspective of an outside observer (Maccoby, 1984a). In addition, the school-age child starts to define himself or herself in relation to characteristics or attributes such as appearance, activities, or possessions (Markus and Nurius, 1984). As a result of both of these changes, the school-age child is more likely to respond to parental requests that emphasize personal characteristics of the child. For example, in one study the generosity behavior of eight-year-old children was enhanced by a positive attributional statement such as "You are the type of person who likes to help others," whereas the generosity behavior of five-year-olds was not enhanced by such statements (Grusec and Redler, 1980). In other words, the eight-year-olds who heard such positive attributional statements were more likely to perform helpful acts in an unrelated situation several weeks later than five-year-olds who heard similar statements.

• *Impulsivity*. From early childhood through the school years, impulsive behavior declines in frequency. In a similar vein, there is a decline in the frequency of angry outbursts, which indicates the increasing ability of the child to tolerate frustration and delays in gratification (Maccoby, 1984a). Likewise, school-age children appear to be better able to control their bodily activities in relation to the demands of a given situation (i.e., as they grow older, there is less wild running or restless motion).

What is the impact of reduced child impulsivity on parents? In the first place, parents exhibit reduced need for and utilization of power techniques (e.g., physical punishment or verbal demands) for controlling child behavior. Thus, as children gain control of their own behavior, it becomes less necessary for parents to resort to physical restraint or raising their voices (Barkley, 1981; Maccoby, 1984a). In addition, parents are able to involve their children in problem-solving discussions that require sustained levels of attention from both parent and child. Finally, the school-age child's increased ability to control his or her impulses allows the child to pay more careful attention to the details of parental directions and advice,

During middle childhood, children begin to concentrate on what can be done and how well they can do it.

Christopher Morrow/Photo Researchers, Inc.

without distraction (Lane and Pearson, 1982). This reduces the likelihood of parental frustration due to the child's inattentiveness or daydreaming.

• *Cognitive processes.* There are many developmental changes in cognitive functioning that occur during the middle childhood years (discussed in detail in Chapter 13). Here, we only briefly describe changes in thinking activity that relate to child functioning in the family context. Most notably, the increasing ability of children to adopt goals or plans for their activities enables parents to reduce some of their monitoring activities (Sternberg and Powell, 1983). For example, as school-age children become increasingly skilled at monitoring their own activities, parents no longer need to supervise activities such as brushing teeth, bathing, or dressing.

The School: A Cultural Transfer Mechanism

When children enter the formal school at five or six years of age, they become involved with a primary institution for the transfer of cultural information and skills from one generation to the next. In the school, children are formally introduced to such cultural skills as reading, writing, thinking, problem solving, and interpersonal relations.

From a historical perspective, the formal public school is a relatively recent phenomenon. (Educational reformers such as Horace Mann supported free public education, which became a reality in the United States in the latter half of the nineteenth century.) In primarily agricultural societies (e.g., the United States prior to the Industrial Revolution of the latter nineteenth century), the transfer of cultural skills and information was traditionally a role of the family because the level of cultural knowledge and skills was sufficiently simple as to be known and communicated by most adults. In modern industrialized societies, such simplicity of cultural information and skills is no longer the case. Over the last hundred years

Sylvia Byers

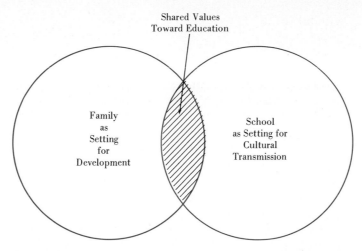

Shared Values
Toward Education

Family
as
Setting
for
Development

School
as Setting for
Cultural
Transmission

FIGURE 12.2
The family and the school as interacting contexts. Where the family and the school share similar values toward education, the success of the child in school will be enhanced.

in the United States, the school has come to serve as the primary means of cultural transmission.

For the most part, the formal school has succeeded fairly well in accomplishing this transfer of information and skills. One important factor that influences the success of the school is the relationship between the family and the school. For example, where there is some measure of agreement between school and family on the value and the purposes of education, the child's adaptation to the school will very likely be enhanced (see Fig. 12.2).

The Family

Although the child is making a major transition to the school, the family continues to act as a vital resource for development. The socializing function of the family continues to be significant, but it is now shared with the school. Several features of family life that are of vital concern to the child's development are the support and enhancement of the child's self-concept and self-esteem, the development of relationships between family members, the general quality of family life, and the development of relationships and linkages between the family and the other contexts of middle childhood (e.g., the school, the community and the neighborhood, and the peer group).

Jerry Bigner described the importance of the parents during the school years as follows:

> Parents remain a source of security and stability for the school-aged child during this relatively busy time in life. Children value their parents and other family members, although there is a gradual tendency not to admit this openly during the later years of this period.
>
> School-aged children generally view their parents in an idealistic way. Their dad is the greatest in every matter he undertakes and their mom is the very best in the whole world! . . . Relations with parents can become strained at the end of the middle childhood period because of the harsh unacceptance of parental imperfections. . . . (1979, pp. 177–78)

The Community and the Neighborhood

The community and the neighborhood provide support for the family in its child-rearing activities in several major ways, including the provision of resources such as playgrounds and community centers and the existence of informal communication and support networks between neighbors and friends.

In addition, the community/neighborhood is a place where the child learns to negotiate the challenges of the out-of-school environment. Because of the changes in children's thinking during middle childhood, they are able to "cognitively map" their neighborhoods. That is, the child's understanding of the spatial arrangement of neighborhood landmarks (e.g., home dwelling, friend's house, large tree) comes to include a more accurate and detailed representation than that of the preschooler.

Bigner discussed some of the community supports for families of school-aged children:

> Children of this age respond to more structured group activities. Communities respond to this need of school-aged children by providing programs that are peer group oriented.
>
> Larger communities and cities usually have extensive recreational programs for school-aged children. Arts and crafts programs are especially popular with children of this age as well as organized sports and game activities. . . . These programs are often held during after-school hours or on weekends.
>
> School-aged children have a particularly strong desire to belong to groups. As they progress through the years of middle childhood, children become eligible for . . . more formal groups [such as] Cub Scouts, Brownies, Camp Fire Girls, 4–H, and so on. . . . (1979, pp. 186–87)

The Peer Group

Children's interaction with their age-mates provides a major contribution to their development in both the school and the community. Peer interactions may occur in several settings including the school, organized group activities, and informal relationships in the neighborhood. As a result of peer relationships, children come to learn that some peers share their thoughts and feelings, although others may not. An awareness of these differences may have the positive effect of helping children to rethink their own perspectives. The peer group also provides a unique experience for sharing feelings and emotional experiences. Children come to realize that they are not the only ones in the world who feel a certain way. These unique emotional experiences are important because they provide an arena for handling many of the challenges and difficult feelings associated with self-evaluation and growing up. The friendship group offers a transitional allegiance between the family and the larger social system. By the time the individual reaches adolescence, the transition from reliance on family realtionships to commitment to a larger culture is much more prominent.

During the middle school years, a new feature is added to the quality of children's play. They develop a sense of the group and start to channel energy into team or group goals as well as into personal goals. Three significant characteristics of the group or peer experience are relevant to the child's development: (1) the subordination of personal goals to group goals; (2) the principle of division of labor; and (3) the principles of competition and cooperation.

The Middle Childhood System

The Family and the Emerging Self

In this section, we examine in more detail the contexts of development in middle childhood, through a look at the family, the community/neighborhood, the peer group, and the school. Children learn and discover much about themselves in the family context. Childhood is a period of *self-discovery* in which children learn about themselves in the course of engaging in activities and relating to other persons. Before beginning our discussion of the role of the family in the child's emerging self-concept, we need to stress two features of the total family system as they pertain to the developing child:

- In the first place, the relationship between children and their parents is marked by *inequality* in both power and authority. Many of the unpleasant aspects of child behavior seem to revolve around this imbalance of authority and power, which is a natural concern of children. It is not uncommon for children to act against it. The inequality of power and authority is a normal part of a healthy parent-child relationship.
- In the second place, whereas the problem of the child may be the inequality of the parent-child relationship, the problem of the parent is how best to use this power and authority. This problem leads to one of the major concerns of modern society: Specifically, how can people be prepared for the challenging role of parenthood? Indeed, there seem to be many parents who are quite unclear about how to handle their authority as parents.

THE FAMILY AS A CONTEXT.   Between the time the child first enters the formal school and the time adolescence begins, the family has a significant role in child development. Historically, this process of socialization of the child in the family context has focused almost entirely on *individual differences in children*, specifically, the sources of these differences in the family (Maccoby and Martin, 1983). This early work was *linear* in its orientation, based on the idea that the *direction of influence* was primarily from the parent to the child. For example, child outcomes such as competence or intelligence were studied in relation to the extent to which parents encouraged (e.g., directly by *rewarding* such behaviors or less directly through parental "warmth" or "acceptance") or discouraged such behaviors (Maccoby and Martin, 1983).

A significant modification of this perspective occurred with the recognition of *clusters* or *patterns of behaviors* in both children *and* parents as contributors to child or parent outcomes. In other words, a specific child or parent *outcome such as attachment* could be best described and understood not as a single behavior but as a cluster or pattern of behaviors (e.g., infant/toddler gazing, crying, or smiling, on the one hand, and parent visual attention, voice pitch, or facial expression, on the other). The major idea of this cluster- or pattern-of-behavior approach is that the effect of a given parental practice is dependent on the *content* (of other parenting behaviors) in which it occurs. A good example of this approach is the research by Diana Baumrind (1967, 1971, 1973, 1979) (discussed in Chapter 9) on the preschooler family. For example, the child outcome that Baumrind (1967, 1971) identifies as *social competence* is associated with a *cluster* or *pattern* of behavior called the *authoritative parent* (e.g., the parent who encourages verbal give-and-take, explains reasons for rules, asks for clarification of the child's objections, exerts firm control when the child disobeys but does not confine the child with restrictions, and so on).

The cluster approach has led to more interactive emphases which have focused on a *systems model* with the following parts (Maccoby, 1984a):

· The impact of parent contributions on children's behavior.
· The influence of child contributions on parent behavior.
· Changes in parent-child interaction as a result of changes in the developmental level of the child.

In the following sections, we examine the distinctive changes that occur in parent-child relationships as the child moves through middle childhood. In addition, we consider the impact of some variations in families—including single-parent families and working-mother families—on parent-child interaction in middle childhood.

DEVELOPMENTAL CHANGES AND CHILD REARING.   Several major changes occur in middle childhood with reference to parent-child interaction. The first has to do with the *amount of parent-child interaction* (Hill and Stafford, 1980).

· There is a significant reduction in the amount of time children spend in the immediate presence of their parents.
· In a related view, there is a decline in the amount of time parents devote to their children. In one study, it was found that there was a reported 50 percent drop in the amount of time parents spent teaching, talking, reading, and playing with children who were five to twelve years of age compared with preschoolers (Hill and Stafford, 1980).

Another important change has to do with the *type of day-to-day issues* of child rearing that parents and children encounter in middle childhood (Maccoby, 1984a). Typical issues parents deal with in the preschool years include child temper tantrums, fighting with siblings or other children, attention-getting behaviors, and so on (Newson and Newson, 1976, 1977). Some of these issues continue into middle childhood (e.g., fighting); however, other issues are new to middle childhood, including:

· Should children be required to do *household chores*? If so, should they be paid to do them?
· Should parents *monitor the friendship patterns of the school-age child* by encouraging or discouraging interaction with specific individuals?
· How should parents generally *monitor the away-from-home activities* of their children? Parents may encourage their children to keep them informed of their whereabouts and activities.
· How should parents handle any *child difficulties at school* (e.g., unhappiness with a teacher or a specific class activity)? Parents may consider to what extent they should become involved in their child's school activities (Newson and Newson, 1977).
· How should parents and children deal with *changes in affectional relationships*?

There is some limited evidence indicating a reduction in the amount of *physical affection* between parents and children (Newson and Newson, 1976). Furthermore, it appears to be the child who initiates this withdrawal from displays of physical affection. Although displays of physical affection may decline, there appears to be *no accompanying* decline in satisfaction with parenting or in appreciation of the child (Roberts, Block, and Block, 1984).

What is the status of displays of a negative nature (e.g., yelling, crying, whining, and so on) in middle childhood? The evidence suggests a decline in the number of angry child outbursts and in the frequency of child coercive behaviors directed at family members (Patterson, 1982).

Furthermore, there appears to be a decline in the number of disciplinary encounters (i.e., conflict over parents' insistence that a specific child activity either be begun or stopped) in middle childhood (Maccoby, 1983, 1984a). Likewise, there is a decline in the use of physical punishment accompanying such conflicts. This suggests that when such conflicts do occur, parents and children have alternative modes of conflict resolution (i.e., alternatives to child outbursts or to use of physical punishment by parents).

• *What changes occur in disciplinary techniques and control processes?* Parents indicate that school-age children may be somewhat easier to handle than preschool children because they can use reasoning with them. (Maccoby, 1984a). Consistent with that finding are the declining use of physical punishment coupled with the use of alternative disciplinary strategies (e.g., deprivation of privileges, appeals to the child's sense of humor, reminders of responsiblity for his or her actions, and so on) (Roberts, Block, and Block, 1984).

Coupled with the above changes in disciplinary technique, there also appears to be a *shift in power* from parent to child. For example, in a study of preadolescents and adolescents (12–17 years), the older individuals reported making decisions (how to dress, how to spend money, whom to associate with, and so on) by themselves (in contrast to having them made by parents alone) in increasing numbers (Dornbusch et al., 1985). One way to view this shift in power is in terms of a three-stage model (Maccoby, 1984a) (see Fig. 12.3):

   • STAGE I: *Parent Control* (child is six years or younger). The parent makes most of the important decisions for infants, toddlers, and preschoolers.

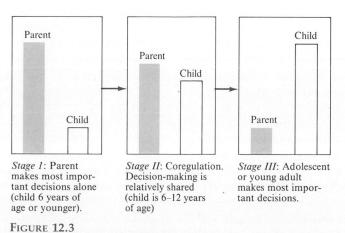

Stage 1: Parent makes most important decisions alone (child 6 years of age or younger).

Stage II: Coregulation. Decision-making is relatively shared (child is 6–12 years of age)

Stage III: Adolescent or young adult makes most important decisions.

FIGURE 12.3

The transition in power from parent to child. Based on Maccoby, 1984b.

· STAGE II: *Coregulation* (child is 6–12 years old). During this stage, parents have three primary activities:
    —Monitoring and guiding children's behavior, from a distance.
    —Effectively using time when direct contact occurs.
    —Strengthening *self-monitoring behaviors* in children (e.g., explaining acceptable standards of behavior and explaining how to avoid undue risks) and teaching children to know when to seek parental guidance.
· STAGE III: *Child/Adolescent Control* (child/adolescent is twelve years of age or older). The transition in power becomes more weighted in favor of the child/adolescent who now makes many important decisions himself or herself.

As indicated in the above discussion of the transition of power from parent to child, parents make distinctions between disciplinary techniques for direct or "face-to-face" control and indirect or "out-of-sight" control of children. The disciplinary methods employed by parents depend, in large part, on whether child infractions occur in or out of the presence of the parents (Grusec and Kuczynski, 1980). For example, for in-presence problems (throwing things at home, arguing with siblings) parents tend to use **power-assertion techniques** ("Unless you stop fighting with your brother, neither of you will watch television tonight!"). However, for out-of-presence infractions (playing in a forbidden area, stealing money), parents are more likely to use explanations and reasoning to gain future compliance ("It is important for you to learn the value of honesty so you will not take what does not belong to you.").

THE PARENT-CHILD RELATIONSHIP AND CHILD SELF-ESTEEM.   One of the most significant outcomes of the parent-child relationship is nurturance of the child's self-esteem (Harter, 1983; Abraham and Christopherson, 1984). The primary task of the school-age child is to develop a sense of self largely from experiences in the formal school and with peers. (We discuss the contributions of peers to the development of the child's self-concept later in this chapter.) Although there is a shift to peer interactions, the role of the parent is still vital. The school-age child lives in two worlds: the adult or family world and the world of her or his peers. The parent not only provides support for the child as a family member but also helps the child to manage the sometimes harsh judgments of the peer world.

There is evidence of a number of specific family experiences that are related to the development of the school-age child's self-esteem (Coopersmith, 1967; Harter, 1983; Abraham and Christopherson, 1984). According to Stanley Coopersmith (1967), the following family factors were important:

· *The imposition of limits.* Parents of children with high self-esteem were both concerned and attentive toward their children. These parents structured their children's world in ways that they believed to be both proper and appropriate and allowed their children a great deal of freedom within these limits.

The families of children with high self-esteem established a more extensive set of rules than families of children with low self-esteem. The former parents were more zealous in enforcing these rules. The pattern for the low-esteem group consisted of few and poorly defined limits and harsh control techniques. These parents either did not express their authority to their children or were so vague in their expression that it lacked clarity and force. These parents demanded absolute compliance without providing the guiding limits that would indicate what types of behavior they really valued. As a result of this lack of standards, the children in

The Self in Middle Childhood: "Don't Enter Without My Permishum"—

Baby Elizabeth, whom we have previously visited, has two older brothers, Scott and Bruce. Scott is now nine years old and in the fourth grade.

One day, Scott's father approached his son's bedroom only to find the door closed and a handwritten sign taped to it. The sign read as follows: "KEEP OUT—DON'T COME IN WITHOUT MY PERMISHUM." Well now, what is an innocent parent supposed to think about this?

This harsh notice bears happy tidings: Junior is bearing down on the "homework" of self; he is refining his separateness. . . .

The middle years of childhood are directed toward extending mastery and autonomy. . . .

. . . "Keep out" signs, secret drawers complete with lock and key and collections jealously hoarded accentuate autonomy.

What benefits come from collecting 376 rusty bottle caps, 208 green marbles, 452 unmatched playing cards and a string of 1,000 paper clips? They are "symbols"—psychological tools—that nourish self-esteem. They bring the joy of initiating, the excitement of the hunt, the comfort of status, the fascination of management, and the pride of ownership. The youngster gets experience in controlling, possessing, planning and trading. It is easier to treat junior-sized junk heaps with proper respect when you know the purpose they serve. If, in a fit of spring house cleaning, you dispose of them, you work against autonomy and control. You emphasize helplessness and nurture seething resentment.

Have you ever noticed that "big secrets" told to chums with all kinds of ceremonial flourish are later casually revealed to you? The "content" of the secret is unimportant: the process of shutting out a brother or friend (maybe even you!) is vital. Deciding whom he will let into his confidence accentuates a child's separateness. This bit of power gives control in a world where so much is still beyond his control. So, signs and secrets and locked diaries are not poor manners nor evidence of rejection. They are part of normal growth.

From Briggs, 1975, pp. 139–43.

these families were uncertain whether they were behaving appropriately. Feelings of insignificance or powerlessness often accompanied such uncertainty.

Coopersmith concluded that the imposition of limits was important to children. These limits serve to define the expectations of others, and their enforcement helps children to understand that such limits are real. The existence of limits contributes to the child's sense of reality that can be understood and successfully negotiated.

· *Acceptance*. Mothers of children with high self-esteem were more loving and had closer relationships with their children than mothers of children with less self-esteem. Greater acceptance of the child was demonstrated by interest in the child, concern about the child's companions, and the availability and willingness of the parent to participate in joint activities.

In families of children with low self-esteem, the parents were more likely to withdraw from their children. This isolation produced an environment for child self-esteem that was relatively deprived of meaningful contact with adults.

· *Success*. Favorable attitudes and treatment by persons significant to an individual, whether parents or peers, were likely to enhance self-judgments. The most favorable self-judgments were not associated with uncritical, unrestricted, and totally favorable attitudes and treatment. In families of children high in self-esteem, there were greater and more defined limits to behavior, parents were more apt to lead active lives outside their families, and there was a clear expression of parental authority.

· *Values*. Although individuals are theoretically free to select their values, the childhood years spent in home, school, and peer groups generally lead to acceptance of group standards and values. Furthermore, parents who had definite values, who had a clear idea of what they regarded as appropriate behavior, and who were able and willing to present and enforce their beliefs were more likely to rear children who valued themselves highly.

THE INFLUENCE OF SIBLINGS IN THE FAMILY.   Although the impact of the parents on the child is of primary importance, the child's relationship with his or her siblings, if any, exerts some influence on personality formation. The number of siblings a child has and his or her relationship to them are important components of the total system in which the child develops. For example, the social learning environment of the firstborn is different from that of younger siblings. The oldest child may have greater responsibilities placed on him or her and is the *only* child in the family to lose the "only-child" status. The impact of siblings on the development of the child is not a simple one and depends on the interaction of a number of factors, including the sex and age of the siblings, the spacing of siblings (proximity in age), the size of the family (the total number of children), and the mode of parent-child interaction.

Eighty percent of British and American children grow up in families with siblings. However, the United States is one of the few countries in which the sibling relationship is largely *recreational*. In contrast, the sibling relationship in most countries of the world involves *responsibilities* for the training or care of brothers and sisters.

As the size of families increases, the opportunities for exclusive contact between parents and a given child tend to decrease, but at the same time opportunities for a wide variety of interactions with siblings increase. As more children are added to a family, several changes may emerge with reference to the parent's attitude toward child rearing and the circumstances of the individual child's experience (Cicirelli, 1982):

· There is some evidence that in families with more than six children, family roles are defined more precisely, discipline becomes more severe and authoritarian, and household chores are assigned.
· In larger families, parents may feel that they cannot be indulgent, or confusion and sibling fighting may result.

Only-child status is the exception, not the rule.

• Older siblings in large families are frequently assigned the disciplinary and supervisory responsibilities that parents in smaller families do themselves.

• Girls in larger families are more likely than boys to be involved in active caretaking of younger siblings. For example, a ten- or eleven-year-old girl in a large family might be asked to perform such duties as changing diapers, feeding a baby, or soothing a crying infant.

One very significant role of siblings within the family context is as "teachers." Older siblings are likely to take an active role in instructing or teaching younger siblings about everyday play or household activities (Brody, Stoneman, and MacKinnon, 1982). When children enter the formal school (at the beginning of the middle childhood period), the teaching role of older siblings may become even more apparent. Some 70 percent of school-age children report getting assistance with their homework from older siblings, with older sisters being exceptionally

Sibling interactions provide a special context for social development.

The Impact of Birth Order

Birth Order and Parent-Child Interactions

Where differences in child behavior or personality appear to be related to the birth order of the child (e.g., some parents' observations that firstborn children seem to be more achievement oriented), such differences are frequently attributed to differences in parent-child interaction and sibling interaction associated with a particular birth order position (e.g., firstborn, second-born, youngest child, and so on). These apparent differences seem to be particularly common for firstborn children. Until another sibling is born, the first does not have to share the parents' attention with another child. Typically, the birth of a second child results in reduced interaction between the husband and wife as well as between the mother and the firstborn child (Dunn, 1983). Likewise, there is some evidence that some firstborns, especially boys, may have behavioral or emotional problems with the birth of a second child (Nadelman and Begun, 1982). These problems are frequently related to other factors in addition to the arrival of the new baby, including the following (Dunn and Kendrick, 1980, 1982a, 1982b; Dunn, 1983):

- *The temperament of the firstborn child* (e.g., firstborns who are more dependent on parents might be expected to have more problems adjusting to a new sibling than more independent children).
- *The emotional state of the mother* (e.g., children of depressed mothers are more likely to be distressed by the arrival of a new sibling).

Although there is a tendency for mothers to become more negative and to engage in fewer play activities with the firstborn at the arrival of a newborn, such an outcome is not inevitable (Lamb, 1979; Bryant and Crockenberg, 1980; Dunn and Kendrick, 1980, 1982a). That is, if mothers continue to be responsive to their firstborns or if fathers participate more in child-rearing activities (compensating for the mother's reduced involvement with the firstborn or by helping with the newborn while the mother interacts with the firstborn), then firstborn behavioral problems and emerging sibling rivalry can be minimized.

Birth Order and Variations in Sibling Characteristics

In addition to being associated with differences in parent-child relationships, birth order is also related to variations in sibling characteristics. Birth order appears to have some impact on personality development even when factors such as social class, the sex of siblings, and the size of the family are held constant. Research indicates that firstborn children are more adult-oriented, more achievement-oriented, more conscientious and prone to guilt feelings, more conforming to social pressures, and more concerned with being cooperative and responsible (Henderson, 1981). From an early age, it appears that the oldest child may be expected to take some responsibility for younger siblings.

In addition, when a firstborn child expresses hostility or jealousy toward a younger child, he or she is more likely to be either restrained or punished. On the other hand, when a younger child expresses such feelings toward the eldest child, he or she is more likely to be defended or protected (Abramovitch, Pepler, and Corter, 1982). However, since the firstborn is typically more dominant (i.e., more knowledgeable and experienced) than younger siblings, he or she can demonstrate *both* negative behaviors (e.g., anger, jealousy, or selfishness) toward the younger siblings *and* positive behaviors (e.g., sharing, helping, or nurturing). In fact, there is some evidence that older children exhibit more negative *and* positive behaviors toward their younger siblings than vice versa (Abramovitch, Pepler, and Corter, 1982). Furthermore, negative behaviors (aggression, cheating, and so on) are more likely to occur between same-sex siblings pairs than between opposite-sex pairs (Minnett, Vandell, and Santrock, 1983). Siblings appear to demonstrate an extraordinary sense of "how to annoy and how to console each other" (Dunn and Kendrick, 1982b, p. 42).

Typically, firstborn children tend to focus on parents as their primary source of social learning in the family context. On the other hand, younger siblings can utilize both parents and older siblings as models and sources of social information. There is some evidence that younger siblings watch, track, follow, or imitate their older siblings more than their older siblings watch, follow, or imitate them (Lamb, 1977; Samuels, 1977) (see Fig.). The fact that younger siblings imitate the behavior of their older siblings in such a thorough manner suggests the important role that older siblings play in helping a younger sibling learn about the environment (Lamb, 1977).

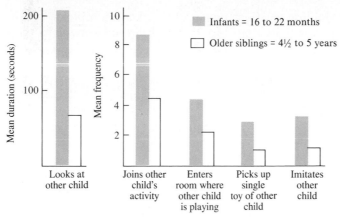

FIGURE 12.4

Younger siblings watch, follow, and imitate the behaviors of older siblings more than older siblings watch, follow, and imitate the behaviors of younger siblings. Based on Samuels, 1977.

well accepted by younger siblings as tutors (Cicirelli, 1982). Furthermore, younger siblings appear to benefit from this assistance as reflected in the finding that schoolchildren who learn to read with relative ease have older siblings who helped them with such activities as learning the alphabet or who played "school" with them (Norman-Jackson, 1982). Older siblings also benefit from such tutoring experiences. Older siblings who tutor younger children in academic lessons show greater gains in academic achievement than those who have no such opportunities (Feldman, Devin-Sheehan, and Allen, 1976). Other evidence suggests that first-borns who tutor younger siblings have both higher school achievement and higher I.Q. scores than only children who have no such opportunities to tutor siblings (Zajonc, Markus, and Markus, 1979).

How any individual child responds to the experience of being a sibling appears to be related to two important principles (Dunn, 1983):

• As a result of their behavior toward each other, siblings can create different environments for one another in the family context. This selection of different parts of the family environment by each sibling has been called "ecological niche picking" (Scarr and Grajek, 1982) (see discussion of "niche picking" in Chapter 3).

· Sibling relationships are part of the complexity of the total family context. This means that sibling relationships are influenced *by* parent-child relationships and, in turn, have an impact *on* those parent-child relationships.

Clinical psychologists have long suggested that the arrival of a new sibling can be a troubling experience for a child. Typically, they view the presence of a newborn as a basis for the development of rivalry and jealousy between siblings (Winnicott, 1977). Judy Dunn and Carol Kendrick (1982b) tested this assumption in a study of forty English families who were about to have a second child. (The older child was a two- or three-year-old preschooler at the time of the study.) Observations and interviews of the families occurred before the birth of the infant and for fourteen months after the birth. The assumptions were found to be only partially correct.

In some families the arrival of the newborn was associated with negative changes in the firstborn's behavior. Most of the mothers in the study reported that the child's behavior became "naughtier" or "more demanding." One mother described her child as follows: "She's so very selfish," "She won't do anything I ask" (p. 29). Other children had more frequent crying spells or were clinging to parents more often.

In other families the arrival of a newborn was a relatively positive event. The new baby produced a refocusing of conversation away from preoccupation with the older child's interests or feelings to a concern and interest in the infant. For example, conversation shifted to comparisons between the characteristics or developmental level of the newborn and those of the firstborn (e.g., comments about the similarities in appearance, ability, gender, or behavior). These discussions helped the firstborn to clarify and become more aware of his or her selfhood. On some occasions, the firstborn seemed particularly delighted that the newborn was able to accomplish a given feat ("Mom, listen, he called you 'mama'!"). At other times, the firstborn expressed particular appreciation of how he or she attained a developmental milestone before the newborn ("Mom, I learned to walk before the baby."). In addition, most firstborns expressed intense interest in the newborn's states and feelings, becoming upset when the baby cried and offering help with infant care (even when help was not needed).

A follow-up study of the original forty families was conducted when the firstborns were entering middle childhood (age six years). Findings suggested that the patterns of behavior and attitudes toward the newborn that were established earlier in the preschool years remained stable. Dunn and Kendrick (1982b) suggested that positive sibling relationships are more likely if (1) the mother involves the firstborn in infant care during the first months after the newborn arrives and (2) the child's immediate response to the baby's birth is positive.

The effect of ordinal position is not independent of such factors as the *sex* of the siblings and the *spacing* between them. Children with older brothers had more "masculine" traits than children with older sisters. For example, girls with older brothers, compared with girls with older sisters, were more ambitious and aggressive. Studies that have focused on boys only have had similar findings. That is, boys with older brothers demonstrated behavior that was more masculine, more aggressive, more independent and outgoing, and more achievement-oriented than boys with older sisters (Longstreth et al., 1975).

What is learned early in sibling relationships is likely to carry over into other situations including the elementary school years. Evidence suggests that inadequate sibling relationships during the preschool years are associated with maladaptive behavior toward peers and teachers in middle childhood (Richman, Graham, and Stevenson, 1982). Siblings' position is important because it duplicates many of the significant social interaction experiences of adolescence and adulthood (e.g., high or low power, siding with authority or rebelling against it).

GROUP DIFFERENCES IN CHILD REARING: SOCIOECONOMIC LEVEL AND ETHNIC-ITY. When families are compared on the basis of socioeconomic level or **social class** (i.e., income, education, occupation, or a combination of these factors), *group* differences in child rearing appear (Yankelovich, Clark, and Martire, 1977; Hill and Stafford, 1980; Laosa, 1981; Maccoby, 1984a). Typically, middle-class parents have been compared with lower-class or working-class parents. According to these studies, middle-class parents exhibit the following differences (Maccoby, 1984a):

- They *intereact more with their children* and are more responsive to the children's bids for attention. For example, middle-class parents are more likely than lower-class parents to give informative answers to their children's questions and to know the name(s) of their child's teacher(s) (Shipman, McKee, and Bridgeman, 1976).
- *They use more elaborative, descriptive, and precise language* in talking with their children.
- They are *more permissive* with respect to their children's sexual attitudes and behaviors.
- They are *more accepting* of child outbursts of anger directed at them.
- They are *less restrictive* then lower-class parents as to the variety of children's activities permitted.
- They tend to place *greater demands* on their children for independence, maturity, and achievement.
- They place more *emphasis on child creativity* and happiness rather than obedience to, or respect for, authority.
- They are *more democratic* and are, therefore, more likely to listen to their child's viewpoint and allow him or her a voice in family decision making.
- They are more likely to *use explanation and reasoning* rather than physical punishment as disciplinary techniques.
- They are *less likely to show an outwardly hostile or clearly rejecting attitude* toward their children.

It is important to keep in mind that all of the differences between middle-class and lower-class parents cited above are, in fact, *group* differences. That is, not every family conforms to the patterns described. In addition, *socioeconomic level or social class* is only a *convenient label* for the facts of parent educational level, occupation, or income. Social class does *not* tell us much about the *means* or *processes* through which characteristics of parent occupation, education, or income are *translated* into specific parent behaviors in family life. Specifically, how is child rearing linked to socioeconomic level or social class?

Several theoretical positions have been used to explain this linkage, including the following (Maccoby, 1984a):

- **Cultural lag model.** This theory comes primarily from cross-cultural studies of primitive societies. It has been observed that when preliterate societies are exposed to modernization, families will begin to teach their children new skills required for functioning in the changing society. However, since families are exposed to *differing pressures for modernization*, group differences will emerge in child rearing and other areas. According to this theory, it is assumed that there are sectors of our social system, primarily confined to the lower class, that resemble these simpler societies.

· **Role-status transmission model.** This theory suggests that parents (usually middle-class) who work in occupations that encourage or require initiative and self-regulation are likely to support and encourage self-direction and autonomy in their children. On the other hand, parents (primarily lower-class) who work in occupations that require and emphasize subordination to authority structures and rules are more likely to encourage obedience in their children (Kohn, 1977). In addition, since lower-class parents may experience a sense of powerlessness in several sectors of society (e.g., the community and the school, as well as the workplace), they may transmit this sense of powerlessness to their children (Sennett and Cobb, 1982). For example, lower-class parents may transmit such a sense of powerlessness through low mutuality (reduced negotiation) in communicating with their children.

· **Expanded functioning model.** According to this perspective, the *educational level* of parents leads to new and improved skills in thinking and communication in working with children. Specifically, education leads to a shift in parental communication techniques from *restricted modes* (general, vague, and nonspecific comments or advice) to *elaborative modes* (specific and precise use of words that are carefully tailored to the needs of a given child and to his or her level of thinking) (Hess and Holloway, 1984).

· **Stress-interference model.** From this viewpoint, all families, to some extent, are exposed to some external stressors (accidents, something stolen, car trouble, broken home appliances, and so on). These stressors may affect the child-rearing behaviors of some parents by reducing the frequency of interaction with children and causing them to be more irritable and impatient with their children. Unfortunately, such parent behavior may bring out irritable child behavior which, in turn, serves as a stressor to the parent and thus can lead to a vicious cycle of deteriorating parent-child relationships (Hetherington, Cox, and Cox, 1982; Patterson, 1982). However, many types of crises may be more common in lower-class families (something stolen, loss of a job, neighborhood physical violence, "bounced" checks, and so on). Maccoby (1984a) describes the circumstances of such families, as follows:

> In those families stressors may have a multiplicate, rather than an additive effect (Rutter, 1981, p. 209). Many, though not all, improverished families appear to live close to the point at which additional external stressors would produce disorganization of family functioning—loss of routines, abusiveness, or some degree of neglect or indifference toward children. Social-class differences in child-rearing, then, may be viewed as a reaction to the differential levels of stress impinging on parents in different social classes (Maccoby and Martin, 1983). (Maccoby, 1984a, p. 210).

All of the models discussed above appear to have some credibility for explaining how parent social class is translated into child-rearing practices that, in turn, lead to differences between middle-class and lower-class children. An interesting point to note is that the different patterns of child rearing employed by lower- and middle-class parents may help their children adapt to the social class circumstances of their parents. As a result, these children may be *maladapted* for life in other social classes. Thus, a *conservative cycle* may be developed that produces characteristics in children that will *keep them* in the social class level of their parents (Laosa, 1982b).

Many of the same issues involving parent social class and child rearing also apply to the **ethnicity** (for example, the ethnic classification or affiliation of an individual or a family) of the family and child rearing. Ethnic groups demonstrate great variation in the conditions of families (Laosa, 1982b; Hess and Holloway, 1984). Ethnic groups, which to outsiders appear to be almost totally homogeneous, are, in reality, not so. For example, Hispanic families comprise several subtypes which differ in life-style, including Mexican, Puerto Rican, Cuban, and Central American families (Laosa, 1982b).

In addition, some of the differences in child rearing that are due to social class are sometimes *incorrectly attributed* to ethnic differences (Harrison, Serafica, and McAdoo, 1984). This is a particular danger when comparisons are made between black and white families or between Hispanic and Anglo (English-speaking) families. On the average, both black and Hispanic families have low levels of income and parental education. It is these *social class* differences that can generate what appear to be ethnic differences. For example, in a study comparing the teaching styles of Mexican-American and Anglo mothers, it was found that, on the average (i.e., comparing all Mexican-American mothers, together, with all Anglo mothers, together), Mexican-American mothers tended to more frequently use directive statements ("Do it right!" or "Do it this way!") and demonstrations than Anglo mothers, who tended to use praise and carefully directed questions. However, when comparisons were made between subgroups of Mexican-American and Anglo mothers who were *matched on education* (had similar levels of education), there were *no differences* between ethnic groups on child-rearing practices (Laosa, 1982b). Thus, what mistakenly might have been thought to be *ethnic differences* turned out to be *social class differences*, in this case related to the *educational level* of the mother (Laosa, 1982b). However, the results of other studies have not always supported this conclusion.

When ethnic families were equated or matched on such social class variables as income or education, several studies have found *different* child-rearing strategies used compared with Anglo families. In the General Mills American family study (Yankelovich, Clark, and Martire, 1977) involving 1,230 families with children under thirteen years of age, it was found that black parents placed a higher value on achievement in both sports and school than white families did. In another national survey involving 2,301 children ages seven to eleven, the following results were obtained (Zill, in press):

- Hispanic families placed a greater emphasis on traditional values, such as respect for authority, than Anglo families and other ethnic groups.
- Black families are more likely to use physical punishment than white families.

Finally, in a third study which involved 764 sixth graders and their families in Oakland, California (most of the subjects were black, middle-class families and were comparatively well educated), the following differences were noted between black and white families (Medrich, Roizen, and Rubin, 1982):

- There were lower levels of interaction between parents and children in black families compared with white families (i.e., black families spent less time eating together, going to places together, or sharing hobbies).
- Black children spent more time watching television than white children did.

How can we best interpret these apparent ethnic-group differences? It should be noted that there are dangers in imposing middle-class white values on ethnic or minority cultures. For example, although the use of physical punishment may be associated with a number of negative outcomes in "mainstream" culture, it may not be so associated for black children (Baumrind, 1973; Peters, 1976). At this point in time, it is safe to say that there are not sufficient studies on this question for us to state any firm conclusions. Likewise, in the study of Oakland, California, families (Medrich, Roizen, and Rubin, 1982), the sample (both black and white) was from a large urban area and included educated, stable, middle-income families. Therefore, no inferences can be made about families—black or white—in inner-city or rural areas (Maccoby, 1984a). Although the results of the studies on ethnic differences are worth our consideration, care needs to be exercised in interpreting them.

SINGLE-PARENT FAMILIES.   So far we have been looking at characteristics of families—social class and ethnicity—and their relationship to development in middle childhood. In this and the following sections, we examine the impact of structural variations in families (e.g., single-parent families and working mothers) and related issues (e.g., the role and contribution of fathers) on development of the school-age child.

Currently, approximately 22 percent of American children ages six to fourteen live in single-parent households (U.S. Department of Commerce, 1985b). However, as many as 40 percent of children will live in single-parent families at some time during their childhood (Collins, 1984). Over the last 20 years, the number of single-parent households has nearly doubled, with approximately 91 percent of the children living with their mothers (U.S. Department of Commerce, 1985b). Almost 65 percent of single-parent families are the result of divorce or separation, 7.6 percent are single persons whose spouses have died, 24 percent have never married (including unwed teenage mothers), and 3.5 percent are married with one spouse absent (see Fig. 12.5). Furthermore, ethnic differences in single-parent families are pronounced. That is, in 1984, the percentages of children under eighteen years living in single-parent households by ethnic group were as follows (U.S. Department of Commerce, 1985b):

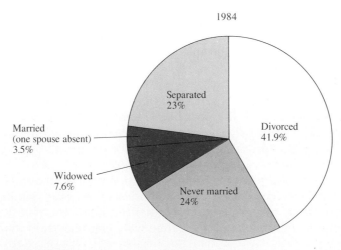

FIGURE 12.5

Children living with one parent, by marital status of parent: 1984. From U.S. Department of Commerce, Bureau of the Census, 1985b, p. 5.

- 17.2 percent for whites.
- 26.8 percent for Spanish origin.
- 53.1 percent for blacks.

In addition, the income level of single-parent households is considerably less than that of dual-parent families. The number of single-parent families that fall below the poverty level is as follows (U.S. Department of Commerce, 1985a):

- 47.5 percent of white female-headed households compared with 11.6 percent of white dual-parent families.
- 70.1 percent of black female-headed households compared with 21.9 percent of black dual-parent families.

Although single-parent families can be described, on the average, in terms of the broad characteristics described above, there is nonetheless considerable variety in such families (Hetherington and Camara, 1984; Maccoby, 1984a). For example, three distinct types of never-married single mothers have been identified (Eiduson et al., 1982):

- *Nest builders.* These women are relatively well educated and self-supporting who have children, of their own accord, to raise alone.
- *Post-hoc adapters.* These women are not as financially self-sufficient as the nest builders, although they have enough economic and personal resources to deal with their unplanned pregnancy.
- *Unwed mothers.* For these individuals pregnancy was both an unplanned and an unwelcomed event. They are typically poorly educated, have incomes below the poverty level, and lack job skills. As a result, they turn to their parents and/or welfare for economic support.

As a result of their differing circumstances, each of these types of women have different values and coping styles.

On the whole, all types of single-parent households, taken together, appear to suffer from "task overload" (Maccoby, 1984a). This means that they typically must accomplish *alone* the same family responsibilities that are *shared* in dual-parent households. Furthermore, most single-parent females are employed full-time and, in addition, must assume full responsibility for child rearing. The burden of this responsibility is further aggravated by the emotional difficulties that typically follow divorce or separation, the most common cause of single-parenthood. Marital disruption affects both the quality of parenting and the adaptation of children in several ways, as follows (Zill, 1978; Wallerstein and Kelly, 1980; Hetherington, Cox, and Cox, 1982; Hetherington and Camara, 1984).

• Marital separation involves serious emotional distress for children as well as a disruption of parent-child interaction (Maccoby, 1984a). For several years following a divorce or separation, single parents may demonstrate the following symptoms of a disturbed parent-child relationship: reduced attentiveness or responsiveness to children, increased irritability with children, a tendency for the parent to be preoccupied with the self, and a tendency to be less consistent in discipline (Maccoby, 1984a). Parenting functions may return to a more organized mode, for some single parents, as the time following the divorce or separation increases and levels of stress decrease. This is more likely to occur if the single parent either remarries or forms an intimate bond with another person (Maccoby, 1984a).

• The impact of separation or divorce on the child depends on the age of the child at the time of marital disruption.

—Children who are six to eight years old typically respond with grief, fear, and a strong desire for reconciliation of the parents. These feelings may continue well into middle childhood. For some children there may be a deterioration of behavior at home and at school, including increased aggressiveness, a decline in quality of schoolwork, or an increasing dependency on or resistance to teachers.

—Children who are nine to twelve years of age may express shame about the marital disruption and anger at the parent they think is most responsible for the dissolution of the marriage. Therefore, at this age children are most likely to take sides with one parent against the other. In addition, children are more likely to reject a stepparent at this age. As in the case of six-to-eight-year-olds, this age group may also show a deterioration of behavior at school and at home (Wallerstein and Kelly, 1980; Maccoby, 1984a).

• The impact of marital disruption on children over the long term is less clear than the relatively short-term effects described above. For example, some studies suggest that such long-term effects are minimal (Kulka and Weingarten, 1979), whereas other studies suggest that the impact may be important in young adulthood (Rutter, 1979; Fine, Moreland, and Schwebel, 1983). In a study of college students, individuals from intact families had closer relationships with parents than individuals from divorced families (Fine, Moreland, and Schwebel, 1983). Furthermore, there is some evidence for an "intergenerational transmission effect" in which children growing up in divorced families are more likely than children from intact families to have higher rates of marital disruption in their own marriages or to demonstrate parenting problems with their own children (Rutter, 1979b).

Perhaps the safest generalization that can be made is that single parents exhibit considerable variation in the ways they cope with their situations. Some function well, perhaps better than they did in unhappy marriages (Zill, 1978; Rutter, 1982). Other single parents function poorly. The burdens of single parents can be eased somewhat through the involvement of the former spouse in economic support and child care, through the formation of intimate relationships or remarriage, and through the support of relatives (Stack, 1974; Wallerstein and Kelly, 1980; Maccoby, 1984a).

WORKING MOTHERS.   In addition to single-parenthood, the significant increase in the number of working women represents a second major change in family structure (L. W. Hoffman, 1979, 1984; Lamb, 1981; Kamerman and Hayes, 1982; Moen, 1982; Hayes and Kamerman, 1983). Since we have already discussed the question of working mothers of infants and preschoolers (see Chapter 6), in this section we focus on the impact of working mothers on their school-age children. There is not a great deal of evidence to discuss here since the majority of studies deal with working mothers of infants and preschoolers.

One of the significant issues for parents of school-age children in general, and for working mothers of school-age children in particular, is the matter of parental monitoring of child activities (Patterson, 1982; Pulkkinen, 1982). Such parental monitoring is crucial for children who are at risk for delinquency or other antisocial activity (Maccoby, 1984a). Working parents of infants and preschoolers ordinarily accomplish such monitoring through formal or informal day care. However, the situation changes when children enter the formal school, since it becomes particularly difficult to monitor their after-school activities when they return to a home with no adult supervision. The situation is summarized by Eleanor Maccoby as follows:

> We know little about how parents monitor their children's activities during out-of-school-hours when parents are working and no adult is at home. Most schools

Latchkey Children

As the number of working mothers increases, the after-school care of school-age children has become a concern. In 1984 (the most recent date for which figures are available), approximately 1.4 million children (of the 10.6 million elementary-school children who had full-time working mothers) were reported to be unsupervised by an adult after school (U.S. Department of Commerce, 1985c). Such youngsters have been called "latchkey children" (because some of them may wear housekeys tied to strings around their necks).

What are the consequences of being a "latchkey" child? For example, are latchkey children more likely to get into trouble or to do worse in school than children who return from school to parent or other adult supervision? To date there has been very little research addressing these questions. Results of several recent investigations are mixed (Rodman, Pratto, and Nelson, 1985; Steinberg, 1986).

Hyman Rodman and his associates (1985) compared groups of self-care (latchkey) and adult-care children who were from the fourth through the seventh grades. The children in the self-care group were those children of working mothers who indicated that either no one or a younger sibling was at home when they returned from school. Children in the adult-care group were those children of working mothers who had a parent or grandparent at home when they returned from school. The investigators found no difference between the self-care (latchkey) and adult-care children on such measures as self-esteem and social/interpersonal competence.

However, in a study of 865 fifth-through-ninth-graders, Laurence Steinberg (1986) expanded the definition of self-care (latchkey) children used in the Rodman study to include youngsters who did not return home after school. In addition, Steinberg examined a dimension of psychosocial functioning that plays an important role in the child's involvement in dangerous or deviant activity—*susceptibility to peer*

Erika Stone

pressure. When the expanded group of latchkey children was compared with adult-care children, the following results were noted:

> Children who are more removed from adult supervision are found to be more susceptible to pressure from their friends to engage in antisocial activity. Children who are home alone are less susceptible to peer pressure than are youngsters who are at a friend's house after school, who are, in turn, less susceptible than youngsters who describe themselves as "hanging out." (Steinberg, 1986, p. 2)

do not provide after-school programs, and even when they do, children may choose not to attend. While a neighbor or relative may agree to "keep an eye" on a child after school and provide a place where the child can check in, we do not know whether these arrangements result in as effective monitoring of the child's activities as would be managed by the child's parents. We know that there are "latchkey" children (how many?) who are instructed to go home and remain at home until their parents return from work and whose mothers check on their whereabouts by phone. . . . We can only speculate that in some undetermined proportion of cases, supervision is loose and the children are allowed to drift toward activities and companions that parents would disapprove. (1984a, p. 222)

FATHERS' ROLES.   The increasing participation of females in the world of work has been accompanied by a rethinking of the role of fathers in child rearing (Parke and Tinsley, 1983; Maccoby, 1984a). One social indicator of the increasing importance and acceptance of fathers in child rearing is the increasing recognition of *joint custody* of children following divorce. (Joint custody presumes that both the father and the mother have a contribution to make to child development in contrast to the historical practice of granting exclusive custody to the mother.) In addition, there is evidence that among the current college generation, fathers are *expected* to take on a larger role in the daily activities of child rearing.

Although social attitudes toward paternal involvement in child rearing have changed, to what extent have these activities been translated into practice? The frequency of father participation seems to have been unaffected by changes in attitudes and expectations for fathers (Maccoby, 1984a). Studies that have compared father participation in families with working wives with families with non-employed wives indicate a very minimal increase (a few minutes a day) in father involvement when mothers worked (Lamb et al., 1982). Even when fathers do participate in child rearing, the traditional sex-based styles of interaction that characterize male and female parents remain unchanged (see the discussion of sex-typing in Chapter 11) (Lamb et al., 1982).

CHILD VULNERABILITY, LEARNED HELPLESSNESS, AND PARENTS: A SYSTEMS PERSPECTIVE.   Although it is undoubtedly important for parents to provide appropriate support and nurturance for the growing child, the contribution of the child to his or her own development is equally important. Put another way, why is it that children from apparently similar environments "turn out" so differently? How much influence do parents really have?

The Myth of Parental Determinism. Theoretical perspectives on parenting—and child care based on these perspectives—have frequently focused on two major ideas. The first is that children are *vulnerable* and sensitive beings who are easily damaged by traumatic events or, in some cases, by too much affection. This viewpoint has emerged from Freudian theories of childhood trauma as the root cause of adult problems (see the discussion of the theory in Chapter 2). Second, children have, with equal frequency, been viewed as completely *malleable* or capable of being shaped into any type of person by conscientious parents. This view has emerged from the traditional behaviorist perspective (see the discussion of this theory in Chapter 2). This viewpoint is well exemplified by the behaviorist J. B. Watson (1928) who once said, "Give me a dozen healthy infants, well-formed, and my own specified world to bring them up in and I'll guarantee to take any one at random and train him to be any type of specialist I might—doctor, lawyer, artist, merchant, chief, and yes, even beggarman and thief." Both the notions of vulnerability and malleability emphasize the power of the parent and the relative passivity of the child. *Only* if parents do the *right* things will their children turn out all right. The corollary to this is, of course, that if something goes wrong, then it is entirely the parent's fault (Skolnick, 1986; Runyan, 1982).

Current research provides a correction for such an overemphasis on parental power and control. It is now recognized that children are not passive receivers of information and, furthermore, that all children do not respond in the same way to what may seem to be similar environmental situations. Rather, children's needs, as well as their developing physical and mental qualities, influence their perceptions of external events (Lerner and Busch-Rossnagel, 1981; Lerner, 1984; Bronfenbrenner, 1986).

Furthermore, many studies that claim to demonstrate the impact of parents on children could just as easily be interpreted as demonstrating, instead, the impact of children on parents (Bell, 1968). For example, a study that indicates a correlation between severe parental punishment and child aggression might be interpreted as suggesting that punishment leads to aggression. However, such a study could just as well be interpreted as showing that aggressive children produce harsh disciplinary practices in their parents (Skolnick, 1986; Runyan, 1982).

In addition, the notion of parental determinism does not take into account the fact that parent-child interactions occur in the *context* of the complex reality of daily life. In *systems* terminology, this means that the quality of parent-child relationships is influenced by the significant contexts in which the family finds itself (e.g., community, neighborhood, and parent work arrangements).

The reciprocity of parent-child interaction, as well as the fact that parent-child interaction is imbedded within other contexts, should *not* be taken to imply that parents exercise no influence over or responsibility for the outcomes of child development. Rather, the distinction should be carefully made between *influence* and *control*. Parents exercise influence over their children, but so do other forces. Parents do not have complete control over their child's development, nor should they, as some would argue.

Research on the Consequences of Childhood Experience. The notion that childhood stress must inevitably result in an adult who is scarred for life is all too frequently accepted uncritically. Frequently, evidence for this notion is based on retrospective studies in the clinical literature that begin with adults who have problems and then trace these problems back to their childhood origins. It is true, of course, that when clinical psychologists, psychiatrists, or counselors examine the background experiences of delinquents or mental patients, they may indeed find that a substantial number came from "broken" homes or homes characterized by disturbed interactions. Frequently, the conclusion is that these conditions of childhood have *caused* the delinquency or emotional disturbances of adulthood. However, the fact remains that the majority of children who are exposed to such conditions in childhood still manage to emerge later as adequate, normal adults. In addition, studies of "normal" or "superior" people (e.g., scientists, professionals, executives, or well-known artists) also find "unhealthy" childhood environments in the same or greater proportion as that of troubled adults (Goertzel and Goertzel, 1978; Skolnick, 1986; Runyan, 1982).

Longitudinal research has, for the most part, failed to support the notion of inevitably troubled and scarred adults emerging from disturbed childhood backgrounds. Jean MacFarlane (1964) followed approximately 200 children from infancy through early adulthood (age thirty). Initial predictions were that children from troubled backgrounds would grow up to be troubled adults and those from good backgrounds would turn out to be well-adjusted adults. The researchers were *wrong* in approximately two-thirds of their predictions. They have overestimated the impact of *both* traumatic and seemingly positive environments on children. Surprisingly, many of the children who had come from apparently "good" childhood backgrounds turned out to be unhappy or immature adults. (This pattern was particularly the case for boys who had been athletic stars and girls who were popular and attractive in high school.) (Skolnick, 1986; Runyan, 1982)

Further support for the weak link between early traumatic or pathological conditions and later development comes from research on children who do well despite genetic or environmental disadvantage. Norman Garmezy studied children who were thought to be at high risk to develop schizophrenia as adults (because of possible genetic predisposition, environmental circumstances, or both) (Garmezy and Rutter, 1983). He found that only 10 to 12 percent actually became schizophrenic, whereas the vast majority did not. The British psychiatrist Michael Rutter has also done extensive research that suggests that a surprisingly large number of children turn out to be normal and successful adults despite disadvantaged or even brutalized childhoods (Garmezy and Rutter, 1983).

A Systems Perspective to Children's Vulnerability and Competence. If there is no perfectly clear or precise relationship between childhood background and adult status, then why are some children *vulnerable* to stress and others not? As we might expect, the answer is neither simple nor complete at this time. However, the application of the systems orientation that has been used in this book may help one to understand the issue more clearly.

In the first place, the fact that family relationships occur in the context of a neighborhood and a community suggests a possible relationship between the community and both family and child competence (i.e., a positive adaptive response to the environment). In fact, the local community may have a distinct role in modulating the impact of stressful home environments on the child (Cochran and Brassard, 1979). In a study of child rearing in six cultures, Beatrice Whiting and John Whiting (1975) found that parent behavior toward children was based less on the parent's principles or beliefs about child rearing than on a whole host of community or ecological factors. These factors included such things as the design of neighborhoods and housing, the social support networks within the community, work pressures, the pressures of daily household work, and the availability of alternate adults (other than parents) to help with the responsibilities of child care.

In addition to the fact that parent-child relationships do not occur in a vacuum, the apparent vulnerability (or invulnerability) of children to stress may be related to learned aspects of children's personalities. From time to time, various terms such as *resilience, competence,* and *coping skill* have been used to describe this positive and adaptive quality of child personality. More recently, the psychologist Martin Seligman has used the term *learned helplessness* to describe what makes a child vulnerable to stress (Seligman, 1975; Garber and Seligman, 1980). He suggests that people may "give up" in despair when faced with a potentially frustrating or traumatic situation *not* necessarily because of the actual severity of the experience but because they *feel* they have little or no *control* in changing it. According to Seligman, this sense of incompetence or helplessness is actually *learned* when people experience situations or events they cannot control or are led to believe they cannot control.

By applying the concept of *learned helplessness* to the findings of MacFarlane and others discussed above, we may be able to resolve some apparent contradictions. For example, why was it that children from apparently good or "ideal" homes in the MacFarlane study turned out to be somewhat discontented or poorly adapted adults? Or why was it that so many children from apparently troubled families turned out to be normal and stable adults? The theory of *learned helplessness* suggests that a child's sense of competence or self-esteem depends not on whether positive or negative things happen, but on whether the child perceives that he or she has some *control* over what happens. Is it possible, then, that in some "ideal" homes good things happened to the children completely *independent* of any effort or control by the child? Likewise, is it possible that some children from troubled families were able to actively adapt or "make the best" of a given situation? Thus, the principle of **learned helplessness** suggests that a sense of competence is more likely to emerge from a sense of "controlled stress" than from good or bad things happening without any contribution on the child's part. The late poet Dylan Thomas put it best when he said, "There's only one thing that's worse than having an unhappy childhood and that's having a too-happy childhood" (Ferris, 1977).

The roots of vulnerability, then, lie in the relationship of the child to the family and, in turn, in the relationship of the family to the community. We refer to these relationships as the *system* of childhood. Within this system, parents do not exercise unrestricted and absolute control; however, they make a valuable contribution to the development of child competence by both encouraging and modeling positive self-control and adaptation.

The Neighborhood/Community and the Emerging Self

DISCOVERY OF THE COMMUNITY/NEIGHBORHOOD.   The child's discovery of the various aspects of the self occurs in several settings, one of which is the community. On the whole, the child tends to have a rather limited perspective of the community and probably knows only the parts of the community with which he or she is familiar, such as stores, zoos, parks, police department, or fire department. Most children know little about the workings of government, nor are they familiar with public service agencies. In other words, the child's perception of the community is ordinarily fragmented. There is, of course, variation among children; for example, middle-class youngsters may be familiar with private physicians and dentists and may have little experience with social service agencies. Children whose families live in poverty may be less familiar with private doctors and more aware of public welfare or health agencies. It is not until the end of middle childhood or the beginning of adolescence that the individual can differentiate the various levels of government bodies—local, state, and national—and the related social service and administrative agencies. Most children's perceptions of the community are positive even though their knowledge is limited. Children are usually enthusiastic about visiting the firehouse, meeting police officers, and going on shopping trips with their parents. As the child moves into adolescence, some of this enthusiasm tends to disappear as the novelty of the situations wears off.

The child's changing attitude toward the community and the neighborhood is influenced by a changing conception of spatial relations. The preschooler's "cognitive map," or conception of the neighborhood, usually focuses on the largest, most noticeable elements of the neighborhood and on simple boundaries (e.g., between buildings and houses). These rather simple perceptions of preschoolers reflect their limited experience in the world. As their experiences and skills increase, so do their conceptions of their neighborhood.

Children's conception of space—including the neighborhood—is not a simple mirror image of what they see. Rather, it is a picture of the world that they develop as if they were actually acting, moving, or manipulating things in it (Ittelson et al., 1974; Poag, Goodnight, and Cohen, 1985). This skill of representing space was present in the preschool years (probably as early as age two). However, it is not until age seven or eight that children have become sufficiently "decentered" to be able to view their spatial environment in a coordinated way. **Decentering** means that children are able to explore many aspects and viewpoints in looking at objects and in thinking about them (Piaget, Inhelder, and Szeminska, 1960). The objects of the environment for the seven- or eight-year-old begin to acquire a quality of more "total" representation than for the preschooler.

In an interesting experiment conducted by Jean Piaget and his colleagues (1960), children between the ages of four and ten were asked to make a sandbox model of their school and its immediate environment. Piaget found that the children in the preoperational stage of thinking (usually preschoolers) used an "active-centered" organizational framework, in which the focus of the sand design was on the routes in and out of the school. Details of significant landmarks were added later, if at all. In contrast, the operational child tended to organize details into a whole pattern, including the routes in and out of the school.

Spatial concepts are influenced not only by cognitive development but also by experience in the environment and the "freedom" to explore. Both inside and outside the home, various adults (e.g., parent, teacher, playground supervisor, home owner, police officer) serve as "gatekeepers" to the environment by determining the accessibility and use of community/neighborhood spaces.

One indicator of the maturing spatial conceptualization of children is their **cognitive mapping skills.** There is considerable evidence that school-age children are capable of rather sophisticated mapping skills. When children are asked to draw a map of their neighborhood, the results indicate a good understanding of major features of the area. Figure 12.6 shows two cognitive maps of the same neighborhood—one by a preschooler, the other by an eight-year-old child.

Children learn about the environment in two ways (Ittelson et al., 1974; Poag, Goodnight, and Cohen, 1985):

1. First, children learn to orient themselves in an environment by relating to certain objects or reference points. This is a basic prerequisite for all future activity in the neighborhood—the knowledge of "what is where" and the resulting boost in self-esteem.
2. In the second place, the children learn the *social* features of the environment; specifically, they learn what spaces are accessible to them, what "rules" govern the use of those spaces, and *how well* they perform activities in those spaces. Some of these self-evaluative activities are discussed later when we examine children in the peer group and the school. As children move gradually "out" of the home and family and "into" the community, they become aware of relevant social factors that have an impact on self-evaluation or self-concept (e.g., the race, religion, and socioeconomic status of the family).

THE NATURE OF THE NEIGHBORHOOD CONTEXT IN MIDDLE CHILDHOOD.   As children move out into the neighborhood as a social context of development, it becomes important to understand the nature of this context of development and the sources of support within it. There is surprisingly little information on this significant matter in the child development literature. To what extent do children have access to neighborhood sources of support for their social and emotional development? To what extent does such access support and enhance their social and emotional development?

To answer these questions, Brenda Bryant (1985) examined the nature and sources of neighborhood support for 168 school-age children, ages seven and ten

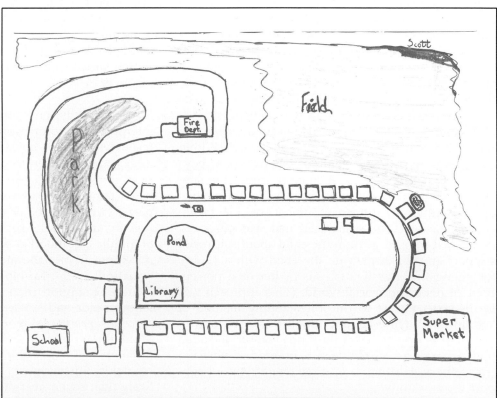

FIGURE 12.6
Cognitive maps of a neighborhood. (The top drawing is by a five-year-old preschooler; the bottom map is by an eight-year-old child.)

(see box). Each child was taken on a neighborhood walk and then given several measures that assessed his or her social and emotional functioning. Several interesting findings emerged from the study, as follows:

· A broad and varied network of neighborhood support (*other people* such as parents, peers, or grandparents; *intrapersonal sources* of support such as hobbies or skills; *environmental sources* of support such as informal meeting places or organizational activities) rather than a limited base of support contributes more to positive social and emotional development.
· Middle childhood is indeed a period of expansion and integration of the resources of the neighborhood as a social context of development (e.g., ten-year-

---

The Neighborhood Walk

One of the major recommendations of the Advisory Committee on Child Development (1976), a prominent group of scholars and policymakers, was that more information is needed on the "everyday" sources of support for children. Since that time, surprisingly little knowledge has emerged. In fact, one might argue that "nowhere in the existing research literature is there a reasonably complete description of the actual social context of the daily lives of American children" (Bryant, 1985, p. 1).

In a recent study, Bryant addressed this question as it pertains to the school-age child. Using a sample of 168 children, which included 72 seven-year-olds (first graders) and 96 ten-year-olds (fourth graders), each child was taken on a neighborhood walk to assess the available sources of social support. Within each age group, there were equal numbers of boys and girls, equal numbers of children from large families (three or more children) and small families (two or fewer children) and equal numbers of older brothers and sisters. The walk itself had two purposes: (1) to elicit reminders from the child about sources of support and (2) to provide the child with a vehicle for giving the investigators his or her own perceptions of his or her social world. (This approach was in distinct contrast to the longstanding method of learning about the child through verbal reports of parents.) For purposes of the study, *support* included both experiences of *relatedness* to others and *autonomy* from others. Furthermore, three major types of support were examined:

· *Others as resources* (peers, parents, grandparents, other adults, pets).

· *Intrapersonal sources of support* (hobbies, skills).
· *Environmental sources of support* (formal organizations, informal meeting places, and so on).

After the neighborhood walk, several measures of social and emotional functioning were administered to the children. The scores on these were then compared with the information provided by the children during the walk. The results of these comparisons indicated that the types of support reported by the children varied as a result of *sex, family size, and age*, as follows:

· *Sex.* Specifically, girls made more use of interpersonal (other people) and intrapersonal resources than the boys did.
· *Family size.* Children from smaller families were more involved with parents than children from larger families, who were more involved with peers, grandparents, or pets.
· *Age.* Bryant's results support the characterization of middle childhood as a time for the development of elaborate sources of support. Specifically, ten-year-olds had more elaborate sources of support than seven-year-olds. That is, ten-year-olds had *broader* and more *varied networks of social support* (i.e., more detailed combinations of the three types of social supports: other people, intrapersonal, and environmental) than seven-year-olds. Furthermore, ten-year-olds were more likely than seven-year-olds to make efficient and effective use of all types of social support.

Based on Bryant, 1985.

olds had more elaborate and detailed sources of social support than seven-year-olds; ten-year-olds made more effective use of all levels of neighborhood social support than seven-year-olds).

The School as a Context for Development

In addition to the family, another major force in the socialization of children is the school. Beginning with the child's enrollment in kindergarten and first grade, a large proportion of the child's daily time will be spent in school. In addition, the school has a marked impact on after-school time in several ways:

· Through homework assignments.
· Through school-related activities and social events.
· Through organization of children's peer and friendship networks (i.e., the peer and friendship patterns that occur in school also carry over to after-school hours).

HOW IMPORTANT IS THE SCHOOL?   In light of the considerable amount of time children spend in school, what is the evidence for the contribution of the school to the child's development?

· *The school experience as socialization.* There is considerable evidence for the role of the school as a socializing force. In conjunction with the family and the peer group, schools contribute significantly to political views, moral values, and occupational/achievement aspirations levels of children (Minuchin and Shapiro, 1983; Hess and Holloway, 1984).
· *The school and cognitive development.* Early critics of the schools argued that the schools were not the *most important* influence on school achievement or occupational attainment of the child (Coleman et al., 1966; Jencks et al., 1979). These investigators argued that child success in school achievement or occupational attainment was due primarily to such factors as family background or simple "luck" (being in the right place at the right time or knowing the "right" people). For some 600,000 students, James Coleman and his associates (1966) assessed the role of many factors in the academic success of the child, including the classroom (school characteristics), classmate-peer variables, and family background. He concluded that home environment (including parents' income and educational level) was the single most important factor in predicting the child's academic success. Next in importance were school characteristics (such as curriculum, quality of teachers, diversity and organization of instructional programs).

More recent studies have suggested that these early investigators were incorrect in minimizing the role of the school (Rogoff, 1981; Minuchin and Shapiro, 1983; Rutter, 1983; Hess et al., 1986). There is mounting evidence that the school has a substantial impact on student achievement and therefore makes a long-term contribution to occupational attainment. The school appears to exert a major influence in the acquisition of knowledge, as well as on how children organize their thoughts. For example, schooling teaches children to think in terms of abstract and general concepts and to reason about hypothetical events (Rogoff, 1981; Rutter, 1983).

THE FIRST TIME IN SCHOOL: SOME ADJUSTMENTS.   When the child enters the formal school for the first time, two major adjustments are made.

• *Learning to read and to write.* Once the child has mastered the basic structures of his or her language by developing speech and oral communication skills in the preschool years, the child has now to direct his or her efforts toward understanding the relationship between *oral* communication and *written* language.

• *Social adjustments.* When the child first enters the school, he or she is confronted with several social changes that require some adjustment.

In the first place, the child must adjust to a change of schedule. Instead of the freedom of doing almost whatever he or she wanted to do in the home setting, the child must adjust to a planned set of activities that may or may not be to her or his liking.

Second, the child is exposed to a new adult, known as the teacher. The teacher may not be like the child's parent(s), or like other adult figures whom the child may have been around.

Along with these differences of teacher personality and role, the child may, at first, feel lost in a crowd of children. Whereas the ratio of adults to children was much lower in the informal setting of the home, the child may now be one of fifteen or twenty children in a classroom with only one adult—the teacher.

THE ROLE OF TEACHERS.   The kinds of teachers that children have greatly influence whether their school experience will foster development or will simply increase difficulties and frustrations. The teacher's general attitudes and actions may appear to the child to be similar to those of the child's parents. This is particularly true if they are from the same social class. Many young children, therefore, react to the teacher as though he or she was a substitute parent. The motives, attitudes, fears, and overt behavior that children have developed in relation to their parents are likely to be generalized to the teacher. Because most elementary school teachers are women, children (especially boys) sometimes view school activities as more related to femininity than to masculinity (and, therefore, as more appropriate for girls than for boys) (Fagot, 1981; Huston, 1983). In this country, the teacher's values are usually middle-class. Neatness, obedience, cooperation, and cleanliness are rewarded; waste, lack of responsibility, lying, and aggression are punished. Many teachers feel that stealing, cheating, lying, and disobedience are the most serious offenses a young child can commit.

Most children respond to the beginning of school with favorable anticipation, and these feelings are usually maintained by most children, at least through the earliest school years. Young children exposed to warmer, more encouraging teachers were found to be more constructive when faced with possible failure and to be more involved in classroom activities (Rutter, 1983). Most children seem to do

Gale Schiamberg

Teachers can have a profound effect on students.

best under well-trained teachers who are *authoritative* but neither *authoritarian* or *permissive*. The *authoritative* teacher, unlike the *authoritarian* teacher, encourages individual initiative, self-esteem, and social responsibility. Unlike the *permissive* teacher, the *authoritative* teacher provides guidance and ultimate direction, and sets standards and goals.

Teacher Expectations and Student Behavior. Most educators are in fairly close agreement that a talented teacher is a vital force in influencing the child's performance in school. There is disagreement, however, on exactly why and how teachers influence students.

One of the most interesting ideas about the interaction of teachers and children is the so-called **Pygmalion hypothesis** (Rosenthal and Jacobson, 1968). The major idea is that teachers' expectations (whether high or low) may influence the level of student performance (high or low) independently of the child's actual ability (as measured by standardized tests). Robert Rosenthal and Lenore Jacobson arbitrarily divided a group of children from low-income families into two groups, which they labeled "potential bloomers" and "nonachievers." The children in each group were matched so that both groups were comparable in measured I.Q. The experimenters then informed the teachers of the "groups" to which each child belonged. At a later time, it was found that the children who were labled "potential bloomers" had done significantly better than the "nonachievers." Rosenthal and Jacobson concluded that the teachers' expectations of the children had been influenced by the arbitrary grouping and labeling of the children.

Although there has been some support for the Pygmalion hypothesis (Raudenbusch, 1984), there have been many criticisms. Specifically, the teacher's expectations are transmitted through his or her actual behavior and not in some general or unspecified manner. Furthermore, the teacher's expectations are a function of "realistic" indicators of performance, such as cumulative records and other teachers' recommendations, rather than general statements from "outside" sources, as in the Rosenthal and Jacobson research.

More recent formulations of the Pygmalion hypothesis suggest that teachers *treat* children differently because they *expect* certain behaviors from high achievers and somewhat different behaviors from low achievers, thereby sustaining those patterns of behavior (Cooper, 1979; Good, 1980). According to Harris Cooper, the teacher initiates more interaction with high-achieving students because their behavior is more predictable than the behavior of low achievers. In addition, students for whom the teacher has high expectations are criticized by the teacher when he or she thinks they are not trying (i.e., living up to teacher expectations) and praised when they make some effort to succeed. On the other hand, Bernard Weiner (1979) suggests that low achievers are treated much less logically or consistently. They are less frequently praised—even when they are trying. Furthermore, when they are praised or criticized, it is frequently for irrelevant reasons.

Given the significance of teachers' expectations in influencing children's success in the school, an important question concerns the *source* of these expectations. Where do teachers' expectations come from? Several factors appear to influence the development of teachers' expectations about children's academic and social behavior, including socioeconomic status and race, and social setting of the school.

· *Socioeconomic status and race.* As a result of many factors, including the transmission of values and attitudes toward people through child-rearing experiences and through such media as television, people (including teachers) develop expectations about many minority, ethnic, and social class groups. Attitudes about racial and socioeconomic group can be easily transmitted and, unless questioned or examined, can become part of one's belief system. Furthermore, the very organization of neighborhoods in some cities may make it less likely that individuals will know people from various socioeconomic, racial, or national backgrounds. Unfavorable and even untrue biases can easily be developed about those people with whom we have little direct contact. As a result of these and other influences, some teachers may come to expect middle-class students to perform better than lower-class students (Soar and Soar, 1979; Minuchin and Shapiro, 1983).

• *The social setting of the school.* The child gradually comes to develop both a cognitive map of the neighborhood of residence and an understanding of how others "evaluate" her or his neighborhood and general social background (e.g., parent's occupational and social standing). These evaluations are often transmitted to the child, for the first time, by the teacher. Such communications are usually not "direct," in the form of overt statements about the teacher's perceptions of the child's racial or socioeconomic background. Such evaluations are often communicated in an indirect form, through the teacher's perceptions and evaluations of the *social setting* of the school. It is not very surprising, therefore, to find middle-class teachers who neither empathize with nor understand children from lower socioeconomic neighborhoods or different racial groups. Michael Howe (1972) made an interesting study of novice teachers who had been warned to use a "firm" approach in dealing with ghetto youngsters. This approach led, unfortunately, to further defiance and low academic performance in the students that it was supposed to help. In many ghetto neighborhoods, the tendency for teachers to generate expectations based on social setting is even further aggravated by the tendency of most teachers to base their expectations of children on the performance of the children's older siblings (Seaver, 1973; Minuchin and Shapiro, 1983).

How Are Teachers' Expectations Transmitted? There are several ways in which teachers actively transmit their expectations of students' academic and social performance:

• Teachers tend to *spend more time* with students who are perceived to be high achievers (Good, 1980; Brophy, 1983).
• Teachers encourage more interaction and *generate more responsiveness* from chil-

Janet Merchant

Technological innovations such as computers can influence children's success in school.

dren from whom they have high expectations. For example, teachers call on students more often and pose harder and more challenging questions to them when the teachers have higher expectations (Good, 1980; Brophy, 1983).

· Teachers may differentially assign students to particular reading or study groups on the basis of expectations of student performance. In an interesting study, children who were placed in classes based on an overestimation of their abilities tended to perform better on standardized tests than children who had been placed in classes based on an underestimation of their talents (Good, 1980; Brophy, 1983).

The transmission of expectations can occur in several ways. The results may be good or bad, depending on what is transmitted. At any rate, it is usually a *self-perpetuating cycle.* Teachers develop expectations that are then transmitted to the child. The child (particularly the child in the early school grades) may internalize these expectations and may thus perform in accordance with these expectations. This performance, in turn, leads to confirmation of the expectations of both the student and the teacher, which, of course, leads to the same expectations, and so on. Where expectations are low, there is always the danger that children will become locked into a self-perpetuating cycle of poor performance or failure.

THE ROLE OF THE FAMILY IN EDUCATIONAL DEVELOPMENT.   Whatever the expectations that are encountered by the child in the school, it is the family that provides the cornerstone and the foundation of self-concept, self-esteem, and formal school skills. The role of the family in the educational development of the child is critical and sometimes goes unappreciated by both the school and the family itself. Although children may start their formal schooling as early as age five, it is the family that has been a dominant feature of their lives for many years before and that remains a vital force for many years after.

One of the most frequently studied aspects of family contribution to child school achievement is the *socioeconomic status* of the family. Typically, socioeconomic status has been defined as the educational level, income level, or occupational level of the parents (or some combination of these three factors). Research evidence consistently suggests that the higher the socioeconomic status of the family, the higher the child's school achievement and standardized achievement test scores (Maruyama, Rubin, and Kingsbury, 1981; White, 1982).

In addition to socioeconomic status, there is considerable evidence that *home environment* is related to measured levels of child intelligence and school achievement (Marjoribanks, 1979; White, 1982). *Home environment* typically refers to the *internal structure* of families (learning opportunity arrangements, communication patterns, personality characteristics of family members); socioeconomic factors (income, education, occupation of parents) may be thought of as the *surface structure* of families (Clark, 1982). Using this definition of home environment, Clark noted three types of home activities that were particularly related to school achievement:

· *Explicit literacy-nurturing activities* (e.g., child activities such as reading, studying, writing, and family discussions).
· *Cultural literacy-enhancing activities* (e.g., hobbies, watching television, or word games).
· *Home and personal health maintenance activities* (e.g., self-grooming, caring for children or other family members, and chores).

Home environment does not simply represent a one-way pattern of influence, moving from the parent to the child (Epps and Smith, 1984). For example, it is likely that bright children may encourage their parents to provide intellectually stimulating activities (Mercy and Steelman, 1982). In addition, parents' perceptions of their child's ability is likely to influence their aspirations for the child, including their desire to provide an appropriate home environment.

Research on the contributions of the family to child achievement also points to the important role of *maternal influence* (Epps and Smith, 1984). In fact, the evidence suggests that *maternal educational level* is the strongest predictor of child achievement (Hess and Shipman, 1967; Laosa, 1982b). Specifically, the greatest impact of maternal educational level appears to be on child language development (Carew, 1980; Slaughter, 1983). Furthermore, there is evidence of a relationship between the language that mothers use in working with their children and child success in problem-solving tasks (Bernstein, 1975; Epps and Smith, 1984). In a classic study, Robert Hess and Virginia Shipman (1967) found that parents of different social classes may use different "behavioral or language codes" in organizing their children's behavior. For example, lower-socioeconomic-group parents may rely more than other parents on gestures, facial expressions, vocal intonations, and a general collection of "unwritten rules" to communicate with their children. Middle-class parents may use much more elaborate verbal communication, complete with detailed descriptions of the features of problems and school-related tasks. Furthermore, Hess and Shipman (1967) found that these language differences were reflected in the manner in which parents interacted with children in both informal and formal problem-solving situations in the home. For example, middle-class parents tended to use language that was specific, instructive, varied, and tailored to the child's level of competency. On the other hand, lower-class parents tended to give very general and ambiguous directions, such as "Do it right!" or "Make sure it's good!"

In addition to problem-solving skills, maternal language behaviors serve as models for the acquisition of general cognitive strategies and for educability in the formal school (Hess and Shipman, 1967; Epps and Smith, 1984). In some ethnic group settings, such modeling may produce negative outcomes.

> The mother's strategies also have consequences for the cognitive structures (preferred response patterns) that emerge in the child and for his eventual educability in more formal, institutional instruction. . . . The styles of learning established at home interfere with subsequent learning and teaching processes in school. . . . (Hess and Shipman, 1967, pp. 58–60).

However, it is important to note that the differences in child academic achievement are not exclusively tied to social class differences. For example, there is evidence that when lower-class parents have high aspirations for their children and when they are familiar with the school system, child academic achievement improves (Laosa, 1982b; Hess and Holloway, 1984). Furthermore, a child from *any* social class can be actively *or* passively involved in school learning and be treated accordingly by a teacher (Kedar-Viovodas, 1983).

Furthermore, there is evidence that children whose parents are more *involved* in their children's education are more successful in school than children of less-involved parents (Epps and Smith, 1984; Hess and Holloway, 1984). However, not all forms of parental involvement contribute equally to child academic success. For example, although only relatively few parents can be involved in PTA programs or parent volunteer activities in the school, a much higher number can be involved in educational activities in the home. As it turns out, parent involvement in home-based educational activities probably makes the greatest contribution to child academic success than any other parent activity (Epstein and Becker, 1982). According to Joyce Epstein and Henry Becker, "of all types of parent involvement, supervision of learning activities at home may be the most educationally significant" (1982, p. 111). Furthermore, there is increasing evidence that intervention programs that are based totally, or in part, on parental involvement in education have been widely successful (Bronfenbrenner, 1986). Other supportive evidence for parental involvement includes the following:

· *Reading ability.* There is evidence that parental assistance with child reading improves reading ability (Hewison and Tizard, 1980; Hess and Holloway, 1984). Specifically, children of parents who listened to their children "read aloud" on a regular basis had higher reading achievement scores than children who did not have such a reading experience (Tizard, Schofield, and Hewison, 1982).
· *Mathematics.* Likewise, there is some evidence that parents who work with their children in mathematics and who convey positive expectations of success have children with high mathematics achievement (Hess and Holloway, 1984; Hess et al., 1986).
· *Achievement of low-income minority children.* Several modes of parent involvement have proved effective in enhancing the achievement of low-income, inner-city minority children (Comer, 1980). Such programs include *child-parent centers* that stress involvement of parents and include a supportive parental component such as in the Project Head Start program (Hess and Holloway, 1984).

ETHNIC FACTORS IN SCHOOL PERFORMANCE. The question of the contribution of racial and ethnic factors to school success was thrust into the limelight with the publication of *Equality of Educational Opportunity* (Coleman et al., 1966). Specifically, Coleman and his associates found that as the percentage of minority students in a school increased, the academic achievement of the students declined. In part, this finding may be the result of the fact that these minority students were from poverty-level families, with all the external and internal family stress associated with poverty (Epps and Smith, 1984; Maccoby, 1984a).

However, it is important to note that *not all* racial or ethnic minorities have low achievement and poor performance in American schools (Ogbu, 1978a). For example, minority groups such as the Chinese, Japanese, and Filipinos do not demonstrate school failure in the same way as other minorities (e.g., blacks, Puerto Ricans, Mexican Americans, or American Indians) (Ogbu, 1978a). The Coleman report (1966), cited above, also had a similar finding. Furthermore, research comparing minority student performance in six countries points to a similar pattern. That is, immigrant minorities (minorities entering a country) did relatively well in school, whereas nonimmigrant minorities had much higher levels of school failure (Epps and Smith, 1984; Ogbu, 1983). There is reason to believe that this high rate of failure is due, in part, to two primary factors (Ogbu, 1983):

· *Perceptions of limited opportunity* for success in school and, after, in the work force. (This may be more the case for high school students than for elementary-school-age children, who may have less well-formed opinions about the opportunity structure.)
· *Cultural inversion,* or the learning of cognitive, behavioral, or language patterns in the family that conflict with the expectations of school staff.

In addition, there is some evidence that *culturally different socialization goals* and *culturally specific styles of thinking* may contribute to the high failure rate of some minority groups:

> A review of the literature suggests that successful functioning within the current
> school context requires the cognitive strategies that are described as sequential,
> analytical, or object-oriented. An examination of the culture or lifestyle and world
> view of Afro-Americans, however, portrays strategies designed to foster survival
> and therefore tends to be rather universalistic, intuitive, and more than that, very
> person-oriented. (Shade, 1982, p. 238)

A key issue that emerges from our consideration of racial and ethnic differences is the need for a *workable interface* between the family and school environments (Epps and Smith, 1984). Where the school culture and the home/community culture do not interact in a productive fashion, the results are damaging for all children, and for minority children in particular. An interesting and enlightening approach to this problem occurs in the Kamehameha Early Education Program (KEEP) in Hawaii (Tharp and Gallimore, 1982). The working assumption of the KEEP program is that the two cultures of the home and the school need to be carefully integrated (in both the school and the home) in order to maximize child achievement.

THE ROLE OF CLASSROOM ORGANIZATION.   As we indicated in our discussion of the family, the role of the school and the classroom is clearly significant to the child's academic performance. The way the school or classroom is organized may go a long way toward supporting the child in the school. Although there have been numerous curricular and educational experiments—some more successful and some less—we examine here only one feature of classroom organization: classroom type, that is, *traditional* or *open*.

The **traditional classroom** is ordinarily characterized by a structured arrangement of lessons and discipline as the best ways to achieve student learning. In such a classroom, the teacher is the authority (in both subject areas and discipline). The desks are typically arranged in rows, each child has an assigned seat, and the activities of the day are organized by the teacher.

Although the so-called traditional classroom has worked rather well for some children, the general awareness that educational development involves self-regulated and self-determined mastery of subject areas has led to the development of the *open* classroom. Although the open-classroom movement received a large boost from the transplantation of the so-called British primary school in the United States and the "rediscovery" of Piaget in the 1960s, the origins and ideas of the open classroom can be traced back to the educational philosophy of John Dewey and the progressive education movement in the United States during the 1930s and 1940s (Dewey, 1943). The philosophy of the **open classroom** stresses the idea of the teacher and the student as cooperating partners in the learning process. The basic assumption is that children are naturally motivated to learn socially valued skills. Therefore, the function of education should be to tap this spontaneous interest in learning by providing the child with interesting choices of classroom activities. In other words, the classroom should be arranged so that each child moves at his or her own pace by making a choice of activities during the course of a school day. The child is viewed as an active "doer" and the teacher is considered a "facilitator" of learning. The child progresses in skill development by involvement with *concrete* materials and everyday problems and issues as the primary mode of developing competency in the formal school skills of reading, writing, mathematics, social studies, geography, and so on. Socially and emotionally, the emphasis of the open classroom is on the "here and now," as well as on the expression of the child's feelings and creativity.

Two different types of classrooms: on the lower right is a traditional classroom; in the upper right and left are two open classrooms.

Furthermore, in the open classroom, the meaning of "good behavior" is different from its counterpart in the traditional classroom. In the traditional classroom, being good means attending to the lessons of the day, adjusting to the established routines, and, of course, looking to the teacher for help in difficult situations. In an open classroom, good behavior consists of exploration and interaction with peers initiated by the student. Talking in the classroom—a sometimes forbidden behavior in the traditional classroom—is favorably viewed in the open classroom as a way of seeking out the help and resources of peers.

Which type of classroom is the best? Although this issue is important, we need to ask, "best for whom?" Although, there is a great deal of *diversity* in what are called traditional and open classrooms, there appears to be an emerging consensus that, like anything else in education, no single method is perfect for everyone. Attempts to compare the effects of the traditional and the open classroom have supported this position. For some children the open classroom was a stimulating experience; for others it was a source of tension and stress (Minuchin and Shapiro, 1983; Rutter, 1983). There was little difference between children in either type of classroom in cognitive skills, but there were differences in pupil self-perceptions.

Children from the open classrooms were more varied in their perceptions of themselves and seemed to be more open to variation in sex roles. On the other hand, children in traditional classrooms seemed to be more conventional in their perceptions of development and sex roles and to be more impersonal. Since the investigators were unable to control for the parents' reasons for selecting the classroom types for their children, it is possible that home influences might have been as likely an explanation for pupil differences as the classroom type (Minuchin and Shapiro, 1983).

Further evaluations of open education suggest that structured-direction instruction (the traditional classroom) contributes more than the open classroom to the learning of tasks requiring memorization or computational skills. However, problem-solving skills or conceptual learning is more effectively accomplished using activities that are more likely to occur in an open classroom (e.g., a peer-interaction approach to teaching problem-solving skills) (Cohen and DeAvila, 1983). Where open education instructional designs have been particularly successful, the following program characteristics are present (Giaconia and Hedges, 1982):

- An *active* role for the child in organizing and guiding his or her learning.
- *Diagnostic evaluation* of child performance (i.e., evaluation that focuses on the identification of the specific child behaviors that account for success or failure) rather than *norm-referenced evaluation* (e.g., standardized achievement or intelligence tests whose major function is to compare the performance of a given child to standards or "norms" for children at that age).
- A wide *variety of instructional materials* designed to *stimulate exploration and learning.*
- *Individualized instruction* (i.e., the teacher works with each student rather than exclusively teaching the entire group).

The Peer Group

The peer group in middle childhood is composed of same-sex individuals who all interact with one another to some extent. Its size is limited by the qualification that its members must interact with one another. Furthermore, its members usually share many common values as well as norms that govern the behavior of each child and the interaction between children. Usually there are status divisions in the peer group, so that some individuals assume a leadership role whereas others are followers. Peer groups are stable over time.

On the whole, evidence suggests that a substantial part of the average schoolchild's day is spent in peer interaction (Youniss, 1980; Medrich, Roizen, and Rubin, 1982). Furthermore, most of this interaction involves socialization and play. Other characteristics of peer relationships in middle childhood include the following (Hartup, 1984):

- Children become more skilled (than younger children) in sending and receiving messages (i.e., communication between one another).
- Children become more skilled in using information from a number of sources in determining their behavior toward other children.
- Children are better able to coordinate their activities with other children.

FUNCTIONS.   Children learn valuable things about themselves as a result of peer interaction. The peer group provides an opportunity for the following experiences.

"Man wishes to be confirmed in his being by man, and wishes to have a prescience in the being of another . . . secretly and bashfully he watches for a Yes which allows him to be and which can come to him only from one human person to another."—Martin Buber

• *The opportunity to learn how to interact with age-mates.* Mutual interaction skills that have been developing during the infant, toddler, and preschool years are now extended and refined in group activities. The ability to interact with parents, siblings, and a few playmates (the social skills of the preschool period) are extended to include relations between the self and numerous peer-group members. This total relationship has the characteristics of a *dynamic system* as individuals interact together in governing and organizing both individual and group behavior.

Included in the social skills that are learned are the ability to deal with hostility and dominance. How does the child learn to handle hostility in both herself or himself and other children? This skill is usually developed in the *context* of the peer group. Here the individual child learns to organize his or her responses in terms of peer-group norms that establish appropriate patterns of responding to hostility.

■ SCENARIO: "BAD DAY AT SANDBOX FLATS," OR THE RESOLUTION OF PEER CONFLICTS

Our two brothers, Scott and Bruce, have been playing in the neighborhood sandbox-playground area with several of Scott's eight-year-old age-mates. Things have been going fairly well, as everyone seems involved in "developing" what appears to be an interstate highway system complete with toy automobiles, rest areas, and several campers and recreational vehicles. Unbeknownst to our industrious road workers, a danger to their work is approaching. Baby Elizabeth (now one and a half years old) and her friend Todd the Toddler (who have been playing together in another area of the playground under the supervision of Elizabeth's mother) have spied what looks like something going on at the other end of the playground—beyond the swings and the monkey bars. With the direct speed of a tornado about to happen, Elizabeth and Todd make a beeline directly to the sandbox. Our brothers,

*Peer relationships in
mid-childhood.*

Scott and Bruce, and their friends (Jeffrey, Michael, Brian, and Johnny) have meanwhile gone to fetch some water for construction. While they are gone, the irrepressible Elizabeth and her assistant have traveled through the sandbox (after all, what is a highway system for, anyway?) when our boys return to find the remains of a once formidable development.

Hostility and conflict ensue. It turns out that during a debate prior to going for water, it was suggested by one faction that some of the group remain behind to guard the road construction. Jeffrey and Michael are upset with the others for not listening to them. "See, I told 'ya what would happen!" comes the refrain.

There are, of course, several possible resolutions to the conflict—some constructive and some not: (1) physical aggression, (2) verbal aggression, (3) leaving the scene, (4) crying, (5) pouting and tantrums, and (6) starting the project again. Although each child might prefer one or more of these solutions, it is the total group that arrives at a consensus as to what constitutes appropriate responses to the conflict. As the boys try to decide what to do, it is apparent that they are watching one another to determine mutually appropriate responses to the situation. Johnny starts to shout at Bruce and vice versa. Both boys are quickly told by the older boys that shouting isn't going to help matters. The solution that the boys finally decide on is to rebuild the road project.

Meanwhile the Baby Elizabeth and her friend Todd are looking for something to do. . . .

• *The opportunity to organize and evaluate one's self-concept.* The way in which peers react to the child and the bases on which he or she is accepted or rejected give the child a clearer and perhaps more realistic picture of personal assets and/or liabilities.

If we watch a group of children during a free-play period such as recess or lunchtime at school, it is apparent that a process of selection is going on. One child may appear to be surrounded by numerous children. Another may be alone in a corner of the lunchroom. Still another group of children may sit together in one area of the lunchroom almost every day, forming a tightly knit group.

One technique that psychologists and other social scientists use to study these group relationships is called the *sociogram*. The sociogram is a relatively simple map of the relationships within a group (see Fig. 12.7). Usually children are asked preference questions such as "Which three of your classmates do you like the best?" or "Which three of your classmates would you pick as your teammates for a game of tag?" The preference questions may refer to a number of tasks, for

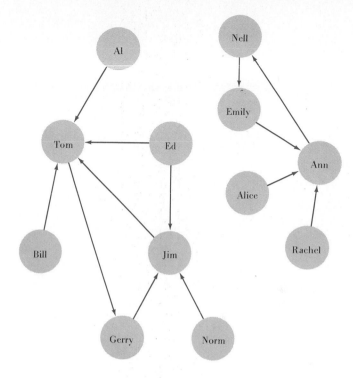

FIGURE 12.7

A sociogram is used to determine the network of relationships within a group. In this diagram, the members of a fifth-grade class have indicated their choice of classmates as best friends.

example, going on trips, working on a classroom project, or playing together on a sports team. As a result, a number of status skills can be tapped in addition to simple "popularity." Where a sociogram indicates a large number of arrows going toward a particular child, that child is sometimes called a *star*. Likewise, where a disproportionately small number of arrows are drawn toward an individual, that child may be called an *isolate*.

As indicated, sociometric techniques have been used to assess the characteristics of children that make them *attractive* to one another. Sociometric interviews are typically combined with personality and intelligence test scores and behavioral ratings by teachers, children, or other observers (Hartup, 1984). The following generalizations summarize our current knowledge of the basis for *social attractiveness*:

• *Social attractiveness is associated with social/cultural conditions.* For example, popularity among middle-class children is associated with verbal behavior in contrast to nonverbal interactions among working-class children (Gottman, Gonzo, and Rasmussen, 1975).

• *Positive child characteristics are related to social attraction.* For example, being liked by peers is associated with being socially outgoing, being supportive of others, being physically attractive, achieving well in school, and achieving well in sports. Rejection is associated with such characteristics as unattractiveness, immaturity, aggressiveness, and disruptiveness (Hartup, 1983).

• *Children's reputations reflect differences in social attraction.* Children who are popular or "average" in sociometric terms are regarded by their peers as accepting and having reputations that allow them flexibility in relating to their peers (Newcomb and Rogosch, 1982). They are considered to be attractive, cooperative, and supportive by their peers (Coie, Dodge, and Coppotelli, 1982). On the other hand, rejected children are restricted by the negative expectations of their peers (Coie, Dodge, and Coppotelli, 1982; Coie and Kupersmidt, 1983).

Furthermore, popular and rejected children belong to different social networks. Rejected children tend to socialize on the playground in small groups with other children who are younger or unpopular. Popular children associate in social networks that more likely are composed of mutual friends of the same age (Ladd, 1983).

FRIENDSHIP.   Given the conditions of social attractiveness or social rejection, how is it that children become friends? *Friendship formation* begins with the process of acquaintanceship (Hartup, 1984). It appears as two children become familiar with each other and discover mutually positive characteristics attraction increases (Hartup, 1983).

In one study of children ages six and thirteen, three questions were asked of each child in order to determine the process in which individuals become friends (Smollar and Youniss, 1982):

- "What do you think might happen to make X and Y [strangers] become friends?"
- "Not become friends?"
- "Become best friends?"

The results of the study showed that children's responses differed according to age, as follows:

- Younger children said that X and Y would become friends if one did something special for the other. The older children thought that X and Y would become friends only if they got to know one another (e.g., "talk and talk and find out if they like the same things").
- Younger children thought that X and Y would not become friends if they behaved in a negative or unfair manner toward one another. Older children equated not becoming friends with the mutual awareness that the two individuals are different.
- Younger children said that becoming best friends would be related to spending more time together, particularly after school. On the other hand, the older children said that to become best friends, two individuals need to discover commonalities between one another.
- Both younger and older children emphasized *reciprocity* as the basis for becoming friends. However, younger children emphasized *concrete reciprocities* (e.g., doing things together, spending time together, sharing a toy, and so on) while older children stressed *psychological reciprocities* (e.g., similarity of interests, attitudes, and so on).

On the average, school-age children say they have five best friends, a figure that is somewhat higher than for both preschoolers and adolescents (Hallinan, 1980). Furthermore, friendships in middle childhood tend to involve twosomes rather than large cliques or crowds as in adolescence (Hartup, 1984).

For both younger and older school-age children, the theme of friendship involves *reciprocity*. Development does not result in a change from the absence of reciprocity in younger school-age children to its presence in older children. Reciprocity is present among kindergartners (as *concrete reciprocities* [see the discussion of Youniss, 1980]) and among twelve-year-olds and adolescents (as *psychological reciprocities*). Brian Bigelow (1977) suggests a developmental progression of reciprocity in middle childhood, as follows:

- Second and third graders' expectations are based on common activities.
- Fourth graders' expectations are based on sharing rewards.
- Fifth and sixth graders' expectations are based on mutual understanding, self-disclosure (openness and honesty about the self), and sharing of interests.

DEVELOPMENTAL TRENDS IN THE FORMATION OF PEER GROUPS.   As we have indicated, the role of the peer group is important throughout middle childhood. Between ages six and eleven, there is a general shift in the overall structure and meaning of the peer group to the child.

During the early years of middle childhood, peer groups are largely *informal* and usually have the following characteristics:

- They are usually formed by the children themselves (as opposed to such organizational groupings as the Scouts or Campfire Girls, which are organized and supervised by adults).
- They have few formal rules for governing their operation or the interaction of the participants.
- There is a rapid turnover in membership. Children come and go with relatively little difficulty. Expediency and proximity appear to be the major criteria for membership.
- Groups are organized according to sex.

When children reach the age of about ten, the peer group takes on a more intense meaning for its members. The structure of the peer organization, such as special membership requirements and rituals for initiation, become common. Peer pressures become more apparent and assume a sometimes coercive influence.

PLAY: GAMES WITH RULES.   During the preschool years, play is characterized by make-believe games and the use of symbols or imagery. Such sociodramatic play reaches its peak during the period from four to six years. With the onset of middle

Huckleberry Finn, Tom Sawyer, and the Rules of the Peer Group

One of the important functions of the peer group is to familiarize the child with the nature of group goals, expectations, and rules. In this passage from *Huckleberry Finn*, Mark Twain describes what happens when Huck and Tom Sawyer try to help the slave Jim escape. At first Huck wants simply to open the shack door. However, Tom reminds him that it must be a "proper escape" in accordance with the unwritten rules of the peer group:

Well, if that ain't just like you, Huck Finn. You can get up the infant-schooliest ways of going at a thing. Why, hain't you ever read any books at all?—Baron Trenck, nor Casanova, nor Benvenuto Chelleeny, nor Henri IV, nor none of them heroes? Who ever heard of getting a prisoner the best authorities does is to saw the bed leg in two, and leave it just so, and swallow the sawdust, so it can't be found, and put some dirt and grease around the sawed place so the very keenest seneskal can't see no sight of its being sawed, and thinks the bed leg is perfectly sound. Then, the night you're ready, fetch the leg a kick, down she goes; slip off your chain, and there you are. Nothing to do but hitch your rope ladder to the battlements, skin down it, break your leg in the moat—because a rope ladder is nineteen foot too short you know—and there's your horses and your trusty vassles, and they scoop you up and fling you across a saddle, and away you go to your native Languadoc, or Navarre or wherever it is. It's gaudy, Huck. I wish there was a moat to this cabin. If we get time, the night of the escape, we'll dig one.

From Clemens, 1962.

During middle childhood, games, often competitive or team activities, become structured by rules.

childhood, games (often competitive or team activities) become structured by rules. These rules may specify such things as who may participate, how many participants may play, and what the participants can or cannot do. From a developmental perspective, the appearance of organized play with games at age five or six occurs at a time when children are now able to do things that they were unlikely to do at an earlier age. These new skills include the following (Garvey, 1984):

· The ability of the child to engage in sustained social interactions of a cooperative or competitive nature.
· The ability to plan and carry out purposeful activities over a longer period of time.
· The ability to use self-control and to submit voluntarily to the restrictions of game rules.

Games with rules appear to have a "natural history" that goes back to the infant's early social interactions with caretakers. Bruner and Sherwood (1976) observed how regularities or patterns of interaction evolve into rule-structured events in mother-infant interactions. Bruner found that most of the mother-infant pairs he studied played the game of peek-a-boo. Peek-a-boo is a game that depends on mutual interaction and the repetition of the same movements. Catherine Garvey (1984) described the rule structure of this *mutual following game* in this way:

INITIATOR'S TURN	RECIPIENT'S TURN
Round 1:	
Move 1 Attract R's attention	Give attention to I
Move 2 Hide object, self, or R, optional vocalization	Look for
Move 3 Reveal	Appreciate
Move 4 Reestablish contact	Reestablish contact
(simultaneous)	
Round 2:	
Optional repetition of the whole game, with or without permissible variations.	

Games in middle childhood require cooperation and rules. The rules are explicit and can be communicated and learned by the participants. The first peer games are usually cooperative ventures such as ring-around-the-rosy (Garvey, 1984). At age seven to nine, competitive games become popular.

Why Bother with Play?

The main reason is that life is generally dull. Often it is downright boring. Anything that makes life a little more interesting is an improvement; and if it makes life exciting, that is a special event. Play makes us enjoy being with each other a lot more. It makes us think life is a little more worth living. As such, play is a rare and life-giving feast. That is why we should bother with it. You may say that children first have to learn how to work; and furthermore, you may be too busy to show them how to play.

But work is not what it used to be. For most people work is not carpet weaving or cattle herding or road shoveling any longer. Work is going in to an advertising agency, a marketing research company, or a classroom and coming up with a new idea. To be successful in the modern world, to keep up with the enormous amounts of new information, and to try to handle the new ways of life thrown at you by a changing society, you have to be versatile. You have to be able to create, but you also must be able to adapt to other points of view. The word *versatile* means two things here: creative and flexible. If a person is creative but not flexible, he or she may put out the wrong product. If he or she is flexible but not creative, he or she may know what the smart thing to do is, but he or she may not be able to produce. A versatile person has both qualities.

What do we know about versatile people? We know they are more playful. Stated in another way, playful people are more versatile.

This is a staggering discovery. For centuries we have believed that playful people were wasting their time.

(Sutton-Smith and Sutton-Smith, 1974)

Summary

1. The period of middle childhood begins at age five or six with entrance into the formal school and concludes with the onset of puberty, heralding the arrival of adolescence. As children enter the formal school, the stage is set for changes in the way they think, learn, interact with others, and organize their behavior. The child now begins more extensive interactions outside the family than in the preschool years.

2. During middle childhood, there is an increasing degree of "seriousness" about life as children begin to concentrate on what can be done and how well they can do it. This attitude contrasts with that of the preschool years, when learning to do things was more incidental to the total life activities of the child. We refer to this increasing seriousness of middle childhood as an emerging *sense of competence.* Two important elements relate to this sense of seriousness or competence: the refinement of self-concept and skill learning.

3. Developmental changes that occur in middle childhood provide the basis for the emergence of a sense of competence. These changes include social cognition and social competence, changes in self-concept, a decline in impulsive behavior, and changes in cognitive functioning.

4. The contribution of the *family context* to development in middle childhood can be understood in terms of a *system* with the following features: the impact of parent contributions on child behavior, the influence of child contributions on parent behavior, and changes in parent-child interaction as a result of the child's developmental level.

Several major changes in parent-child interaction occur in middle childhood, including the *amount of interaction* and the *type of day-to-day issues* children and parents encounter in middle childhood.

5. Children learn and discover much about themselves in the family context. The school-age child lives in two worlds: the adult (or family) world and the world of peers. The parent not only provides support for the child as a family member but also helps the child to manage the sometimes harsh judgments of the peer world. Several major factors are associated with the development of child self-esteem.

6. The impact of siblings on the child's development is not a simple one and depends on the interaction of a number of factors including the sex and age of the siblings, the spacing of siblings (proximity in age), the size of the family (the total number of children), and the mode of parent-child interaction. As the size of families increases, the opportunities for exclusive contact between parents and a given child tend to decrease. Where differences in child behavior appear to be related to the *birth order* of that child, such differences are frequently attributed to differences in parent-child interaction and sibling interaction.

7. When families are compared on the basis of socioeconomic level, *group* differences appear in child rearing. However, socioeconomic level (or social class) does not tell us much about the *means* or processes through which characteristics of parent occupation, education, or income are *translated* into specific parent behaviors in family life. Several theoretical explanations have been used to describe this connection, including the *cultural lag model*, the *role-status transmission model*, the *expanded functioning model*, and the *stress-interference model*. Many of the same issues involving parent social class and child rearing also apply to the *ethnicity* of families. Some of the differences in child rearing that are due to social class are sometimes incorrectly attributed to ethnic differences.

In addition to social class and ethnicity, family structural variations (single-parent families, working mothers) may influence the development of the school-age child.

8. The school-age child's familiarity and participation in the community and neighborhood contexts depends, in part, on *cognitive mapping skills*. There is considerable evidence that school-age children are capable of rather sophisticated mapping skills. Children learn about the environment in two ways. First, they learn to orient themselves in an environment by relating to certain objects or reference points. Second, they learn the social features of the environment (i.e., what spaces are accessible to them, what "rules" govern the use of those spaces, and how well they perform activities in those spaces). As children move out into the neighborhood as a social context of development, it becomes important to understand the *nature* of this context of development and the *sources* of support within it.

9. The learning of school skills and the social changes in the child that the school fosters produce change in the child's self-concept. Several specific issues are of interest in assessing the child's adaptation to the elementary school. What challenges confront the child on entering the school? What are the characteristics of teacher-child relationships? How do teachers help the child develop a positive self-concept? What impact do family and peers have on the child's performance in school?

10. The peer group in middle childhood is composed of same-sex individuals who all interact with one another to some extent. Children learn valuable

things about themselves as a result of peer interaction. Between the ages of six and eleven, there is a general shift in the overall structure and meaning of the peer group to the child. The functions of the peer group include the opportunities to learn how to interact with age-mates and to organize and evaluate one's self-concept.

Friendship formation begins with the process of acquaintanceship. For both younger and older children, the theme of friendship involves *reciprocity*. During the early years of middle childhood, peer groups are largely *informal*.

During early childhood, play is characterized by make-believe games and the use of symbols or imagery. In middle childhood, games are often competitive or team activities that are structured by rules.

Key Terms

Cognitive mapping skills
Competence
Coregulation
Cultural lag model
Decentering
Ethnicity
Expanded functioning model
Latchkey children
Learned helplessness

Open classroom
Power-assertion techniques
Pygmalion hypothesis
Role-Status transmission model
Social class
Social cognition
Stress-interference model
Traditional classroom

Questions

1. What is meant by social competence?
2. Define *social cognition*. Explain its importance to social development.
3. Discuss three "day-to-day" issues that are characteristic of parent-child interaction in middle childhood.
4. Give an example of how differences in child rearing between families are incorrectly attributed to family ethnicity.
5. Discuss the consequences of being a "latchkey" child.
6. Describe the major characteristics of peer groups in middle childhood.

Suggested Readings

ELKIND, D. *The Hurried Child—Growing Up Too Fast Too Soon.* Reading, Mass.: Addison-Wesley, 1981. The book raises the provocative point that childhood as a phase of life may be disappearing.

JOHNSON, M. (ed.). *Toward Adolescence: The Middle School Years.* Chicago: The University of Chicago Press, 1980. An excellent, up-to-date collection of essays on important facets of middle childhood including significant context areas of intervention and approaches to research.

LAMB, M. E. (ed.). *Non-Traditional Families: Parenting and Child Development.* Hillsdale, N.J.: Erlbaum, 1982. A thorough and provocative discussion of nontraditional families.

WALLERSTEIN, J. S., and KELLY, J. B. *Surviving the Breakup: How Children and Parents Cope with Divorce.* New York: Basic Books, 1980. A readable and well-documented discussion of the impact of divorce on children and parents.

WILLIAMS, J., and SMITH, M. *Middle Childhood* (2nd ed.). New York: Macmillan, 1980. A readable discussion of key aspects of middle childhood with many practical suggestions.

WORELL, J. *Psychological Development in the Elementary Years.* New York: Academic Press, 1982. An excellent collection of reviews of research on important dimensions of middle childhood.

13 Middle Childhood: Physical and Cognitive Development

Growing is not the easy, plain sailing business that it is commonly supposed to be: it is hard work—harder than any but a growing [child] can understand. . . .
—Samuel Butler, The Way of All Flesh

Physical Development and Health

In most industrialized societies, school-age children are the healthiest age group in the population (Shonkoff, 1984). The reasons for this situation are that they are typically not exposed to the health problems common in many developing nations and they have not yet fully experienced the immediate risks for major diseases (e.g., cancer and heart disease) that adults face.

Poverty and the failure to use existing health care systems continue to pose problems for both the mental and physical health of children in this country. However, the most significant public health concern in middle childhood is *lifestyle*, because:

- *Accidents* were responsible for about half of the deaths of children, ages five to fourteen, in the United States in 1978 (U.S. Department of Commerce, Bureau of the Census, 1982a). More than half of these accidents were, in turn, related to motor vehicles.
- Many of the *specific risk factors* that are associated with the onset of major adult diseases have their beginnings in middle childhood. Life-style factors such as use of tobacco, coping with stress, alcohol abuse, and eating habits deserve preventive attention during middle childhood.

The Biological Bases of Growth

The general rate of increase in stature is fairly regular during middle childhood until the onset of puberty, when dramatic changes occur in the body. The best sign or general indicator of overall biological maturation is *skeletal maturity* as measured by *bone age*. The determination of **skeletal maturity** is predictable, based on the appearance of *ossification* in the growth regions or *epiphyses* of bones. Ossification of the epiphyses is determined primarily by genetic factors.

DEFINITIONS

Ossification. This process involves the deposit of calcium between bone cells, which makes the bone structure stronger. The skeletal system is composed of both *cartilage* (a semisoft substance) and *bone*. The skeleton of the infant is composed almost entirely of cartilage. Throughout childhood and adolescence and into adulthood, this cartilage is replaced with bone cells and minerals as bones become harder and capable of bearing more weight. *This process of the replacement of cartilage with bone is called ossification.*

Epiphyses. These are the growth centers of bone, located at the ends of each bone. When ossification occurs in the epiphyses, bone maturity is complete and bone growth can no longer occur.

498

Physical Health and the Emerging Life-Style of the School-Age Child

Increasingly, evidence supports the assertion that the way people live, in particular their patterns of behavior and adaptation, contributes significantly to individual health status throughout the lifespan. We refer to these behavioral and adaptation patterns as **life-style**. At a recent meeting of the Institute of Medicine, 400 leaders in the field of health reached the following conclusion:

> The heaviest burdens of illness in the United States today are related to aspects of individual behavior, especially long-term patterns of behavior often referred to as "lifestyle." As much as 50 percent of mortality from the 10 leading causes of death in the United States can be traced to lifestyle. (Hamburg, Elliott, Parron, 1982, p. 1)

How does the school-age child fit in with these significant health issues? Between the ages of six and twelve, the child is busy developing an emerging sense of self, which includes a wide variety of components, including the patterns of behavior and adaptation we have called *life-style*. Thus, the development of life-style patterns during middle childhood is particularly relevant to the *prevention* of the major diseases associated with adulthood (cancer and heart disease) as well as the major cause of death in childhood (accidents). In the next sections, we discuss the following critical dimensions of life-style (Shonkoff, 1984):

- Exercise.
- Dietary habits.
- Self-induced vulnerability (e.g., cigarette smoking).
- Chronic illness or disability (e.g., cystic fibrosis, asthma, or muscular dystrophy).

PHYSICAL EXERCISE.   For the most part, it has been well established that physical activity can have a health-enhancing effect (Shonkoff, 1984). In particular, exercise appears to reduce risk factors associated with atherosclerosis or heart disease (Dawber, 1980; Thomas et al., 1981).

For example, studies have shown a greater risk for coronary heart disease when so-called *low density lipoproteins* (LDLs) are at an elevated level in the blood and a protective effect when *high-density lipoproteins* (HDLs) are at an elevated level in the blood (U.S. Department of Health, Education and Welfare, 1981). Exercise has been shown to be associated with elevated levels of HDLs in both adults and children (Gilliam and Burke, 1978; Glomset, 1980). These results point to the importance of promoting exercise as a component of an emerging life-style in childhood (Shonkoff, 1984).

Concerns have been raised about such sendentary influences of modern life as television as contributing to the lack of physical fitness in middle childhood. In addition, only one third of all schoolchildren are involved in a daily physical education program (Select Panel for the Promotion of Child Health, 1981). On the other hand, interest in organized sports programs for children has increased substantially over the last decade, involving almost 8 million youngsters (Goldberg, Veras, and Nicholas, 1978). Presumably this growing popularity of informal and organized sports may reverse the traditional reduction in physical activity beyond childhood (Shonkoff, 1984).

Many critics have argued that the traditional school-based physical education programs have unduly emphasized programs for the athletically gifted in such

"AND NOW, AN IMPORTANT MESSAGE FROM YOUR SPONSOR: GO OUT AND PLAY!"

sports as basketball, football, or baseball (Pate and Blair, 1978). Such an emphasis leads to the following difficulties:

· Such sports as football, basketball, and baseball are not likely to be pursued in adulthood (Shonkoff, 1984).
· Unless they are played regularly (into adulthood), such sports have limited fitness benefits.
· An overemphasis on competitive sports ignores the vast majority of children.

DIETARY HABITS.   The eating habits of Americans have dramatically changed over the past quarter century (Shonkoff, 1984). There has been a dramatic drop in foods with high amounts of cholesterol (a risk factor for heart disease) such as eggs and butter with an accompanying increase in the use of margarine and vegetable oil (with much lower amounts of cholesterol) (Stamler, 1978; Rizek and Jackson, 1980). On the other hand, during this same period of time, the use of "processed" foods (foods prepared to be used at a later time such as frozen or canned items, which typically involve the use of preservative chemicals in their preparation) as well as sales by fast-food restaurants have increased (Select Panel for the Promotion of Child Health, 1981). Typically processed foods (including snacks) and fast foods are high in fats, calories, salt, sugar, and cholesterol. These foods are, of course, consumed in substantial quantities by both adults and children and may, therefore, serve a limited or negative nutritional function. An in-depth survey of the diet of children under age thirteen showed that consumption of foods high in salt, sugar, fats, and cholesterol constitute almost one-third of their total diet (Berenson et al., 1982).

When and how are eating habits developed? Dietary patterns are usually established in early childhood, with a strong influence from family and cultural factors (Lowenberg, 1977; Shonkoff, 1984). A particularly strong cultural force in shaping children's eating habits is television. Evidence suggests there is an excessive focus of television commercials on food products (National Science Foundation, 1977). In one study of children's programs, 68 percent of the commercial messages were for food products and of these, 25 percent were for cereal, 25 percent for candy and sweets, 8 percent were for snacks, and 10 percent were for fast-food restaurants (Barcus, 1975). There is some evidence for the impact of this heavy assault of commercials on children, since it has been found that five-to-ten-year-old children attend closely to commercials and are likely to ask parents to buy what is advertised (Blatt, Spencer, and Ward, 1972; Shonkoff, 1984).

The most serious problem related to the dietary habits of children is obesity (see the discussion in Chapter 10) (Merritt, 1982). Obesity is typically defined as weighing approximately 20 percent above the average weight for a given age, sex, and height (Van Itallie, 1979). In addition, obesity has been directly implicated in a number of diseases including high blood pressure (hypertension) and diabetes (Hamburg, Elliott, and Parron, 1982). In addition, obese children may be the subject of teasing or other discriminatory behavior, with potentially long-term psychological consequences (Shonkoff, 1984).

Although some individuals may be genetically predisposed to a lower energy utilization rate as a cause of their obesity (i.e., such individuals simply burn fewer calories in the course of an ordinary day than other, leaner individuals), the most common cause of obesity in children is excessive overeating (Weil, 1981; Shonkoff, 1984). A factor frequently associated with childhood obesity is a significantly reduced level of activity (Rowland, 1981). At this time, it is not clear whether the obesity results in reduced levels of inactivity or whether inactive children may be predisposed (perhaps, genetically) to obesity. In either case, a weight gain ordinarily results in lower energy needs, requiring fewer calories (in the face of excessive eating and increased caloric intake for obese children). Such a conclusion leads to a recognition of the importance of physical activity in dealing with childhood obesity.

To what extent does childhood obesity lead to adult obesity? Much more research evidence is necessary before a definitive answer can be given to this question or the question of the specific factors (e.g., overeating, reduced physical exercise, predisposed genetic factors, and so on) leading to adult obesity. However, one study that dealt with the medical records of a fairly large population in Rochester, New York (from infancy to age thirty years), found a 50 percent chance of an obese adult having been an obese child (Charney, Goodman, and McBride, 1976).

SELF-INDUCED VULNERABILITY. In addition to physical exercise and obesity as significant components of an emerging childhood life-style, **self-induced vulnerabilities** (e.g., smoking, alcoholism, or drug abuse) are of prime relevance to any discussion of middle childhood. Although the occurrence of such self-induced vulnerabilities is rather low in middle childhood, the school-age child is an important audience for early prevention activities. We focus our discussion here on cigarette smoking, which is a prime example. According to recent evidence from the U.S. Department of Health, Education and Welfare (1979), not only is cigarette smoking one of the most serious risk factors associated with disease, disability, and early death, but it is also one of the *most preventable* ones. According to health statistics, cigarette smoking is a primary contributor to lung cancer (Shonkoff, 1984). Although cigarette smoking by adolescents and adults has been the subject of numerous studies, there have been very few studies that have looked at cigarette smoking by the school-age child. This is unfortunate since we have little or no information on the transition from school-age nonsmokers to adolescent or young-adult smokers (Downey and O'Rouke, 1976; Banks et al., 1978).

> Obviously, reaching children before they begin smoking, or at least reaching young adolescents before they become addicted smokers, is the most logical way to reduce the health risks from smoking. Yet it is for this period of early smoking onset where data are most lacking. In other words, we cannot readily explain why children start to smoke or what means are most effective in preventing or reducing their smoking. (Blaney, 1981, p. 192)

CHRONIC ILLNESS OR DISABILITY. Although most school-age children are in rather good health, a significant minority have a *chronic disability* or *illness* (bronchial asthma, cystic fibrosis, muscular dystrophy).

> *DEFINITIONS*
>
> **Chronic illness or disability.** An illness or disability that significantly disables or limits the character and/or quality of a normal life-style. Certain disorders may limit the performance of an ordinary activity such as walking or breathing. Examples of chronic illnesses or disabilities include seizure disorders, bronchial asthma, cystic fibrosis, muscular dystrophy, cerebral palsy, and juvenile rheumatoid arthritis.
>
> **Juvenile rheumatoid arthritis.** A chronic joint problem that involves inflammation and pain and limits functioning.

March of Dimes

Successful adaptation occurs in many children with disabilities.

How many children have such chronic disorders? Estimates of prevalence indicate that "about one child in 10 will experience one or more chronic illnesses by the age of 15 and up to 30 percent of these children may be expected to be handicapped by secondary social and psychological maladjustments" (Pless and Roghmann, 1971, p. 357). Increasingly, the needs of chronically ill or disabled children and their families are being recognized as an important responsibility for healthcare professionals (Hobbs, Perrin, and Ireys, 1983; Task Force on Pediatric Education, 1978).

What is the impact of chronic illness or disability on the child? For a child who is judged by his or her peers, teachers, or other adults to be deficient or "different" academically, socially, or athletically, the impact of a chronic problem can be substantial. For example, perceived deficits in physical attractiveness or skill level can create problems of self-esteem in addition to excessive stress (Sperling, 1978). On

Development Models and Handicapped Children

Challenges to the use of so-called normative or standardized models of development have emerged from a number of sources. For example, in our discussion of language development (see Chapter 10)

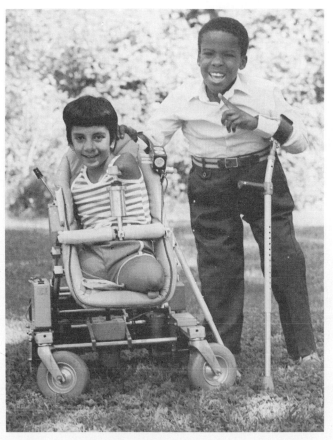

March of Dimes

we pointed out the concerns about "ethnic biases" in standard models and theories of language development. In addition, others have suggested that traditional theories of personality and moral development are too male-oriented and, therefore, dysfunctional when applied to females (Gilligan, 1979). Likewise, in the case of chronically impaired or disabled children, there is reason to consider alternative modes of adaptive development. Such a reconsideration of traditional developmental models is needed in light of the successful coping and positive adaptation of numerous handicapped children and their families.

Developmentalists have made a crucial oversight. They take it for granted that theories constructed for able-bodied children can correctly interpret the developmental significance of the handicapped child's behavior. The importance of this research shortcoming cannot be emphasized too much. Because of stigma and misunderstanding, handicapped children often live in a social world that is radically different from the one inhabited by their able-bodied peers, and their physical or mental disabilities often impose sharp constraints on the ways that they can obtain and analyze experience. These social and biological differences raise a fundamental . . . question for the field of child development: *do some handicapped children develop according to a healthy logic of their own?* By ignoring this question developmentalists more than imperil the value of their research; they run the risk of sometimes perpetuating the traditional deviance analysis of disability in a more subtle and more socially acceptable form. It is simply not enough to apply mainstream developmental theories to disability. Psychologists must first assess the applicability of these theories to each of the many groups of children with handicaps. (Gliedman and Roth, 1980, pp. 58–59).

the other hand, there is evidence of successful adaptation in a substantial number of children with chronic conditions (Pless and Pinkerton, 1975). Several factors have been associated with the level of adaptation of children with chronic conditions, including the following:

· Age of onset of the disease or disability.
· The course and severity of the disease or disabling condition.
· The visibility and consequences of any related handicaps.
· Child coping style.
· The quality of the parent-child relationship (Shonkoff, 1984).

As we have indicated throughout this book, the child grows and develops in several significant contexts—including the family. This is obviously no less true for the child with a chronic condition than it is for a child without one. What, then, is the impact of the chronically impaired child on the family? The evidence suggests that such a child is a stressor to which families adapt with different levels of success (Stein and Riessman, 1980). For example, there is evidence that in some families the stress associated with a chronically impaired child can lead to persistent parent anxiety or depression, lowered parental self-esteem, or marital discord (Marcus, 1977). On the other hand, there is evidence of more positive and adaptive outcomes in other families (Vance et al., 1980).

Motor Development and Athletic Skills

By the end of early childhood, children have almost completed the development of the fundamental motor skills that will allow them to accomplish the sport and dance skills of middle childhood, adolescence, and adulthood (see Chapter 10). Learning these fundamental motor skills represents a proficiency barrier; that is, the development of motor skills in middle childhood is extremely difficult unless foundational early-childhood skills are developed to a reasonable level. During middle childhood, fundamental motor skills are extended to simple games in play situations. For example, the child may begin to participate in such activities as street hockey or tag.

The types of activities in which children participate are very much related to the play activities common to middle childhood. Many of the games that are played involve the use of rules and the social understanding involved in coordinating one or more people in a mutual activity. For example, the game of tag requires the understanding of the rule that one child begins by trying to tag other children, who all join to try and tag the remaining children as they run within a bounded area. Such a game involves the fundamental motor skill of running coupled with more sophisticated dodging and balancing movements. As the child progresses through middle childhood, other fundamental motor skills such as catching, throwing, and hitting are coordinated in the performance of specific dance and sport skills such as baseball, football, volleyball, diving, and swimming. Relative competence in the performance of these skills is one part of the child's developing self-concept.

General Characteristics (Ages Six to Twelve)

On the whole, the period between six and twelve years is a period of skill learning. The range and depth of the child's motor learning are determined largely by at least two factors:

· The completion and refinement of fundamental motor skills.
· The child's opportunities for combining fundamental motor skills (throwing, hitting, running) into game skills (baseball, volleyball, Red Rover).

During this period, it is important that children engage in these motor activities, which will support their self-concepts and enhance their relationships with peers. Although much of this activity probably happens during free play, it is not always a certainty. The organization of neighborhoods and homes does not always ensure the development of motor skills.

Children who are six or seven years old are still perfecting fundamental motor skills and therefore may need more simple and less organized motor activities than older youngsters:

> The younger learners like rhythmic and dramatic activities, movement exploration, simple stunts and games of low organization. They progress best with individualized instruction and individualized challenges. Beginning with the younger learners and then continuing instruction throughout the six to twelve period, youngsters should be taught how to use force and space, how to improve timing and coordination; this means that they should be helped to gain "good form" in their movements for this makes possible the greatest amount of precision, force, ease and poise. (Corbin, 1973, p. 156)

By about the age of twelve, children have developed about 90 percent of their potential mobility and speed of reaction (Corbin, 1980; Williams, 1983). Balance, speed, strength, and coordination seem to improve with time and minimal practice. All of these prerequisites for motor skill can be improved through physical activity (see Fig. 13.1).

Specific Skills

RUNNING.   At the ages of four and five, there is continued improvement in the form and power used in running. This improvement results in the gradual devel-

Darryl Jacobson

PHYSICAL FITNESS

Definition: Physical fitness is composed of many different aspects including health-related physical fitness aspects and motor fitness (skill-related) aspects. To function effectively in our society without undue fatigue and to have reserve energy to enjoy leisure time require adequate development of both the health-related and skill-related aspects of physical fitness. The important aspects of physical fitness are:

HEALTH-RELATED ASPECTS

Cardiovascular Fitness. The ability to persist in numberous repetitions of an activity. Specifically, this aspect involves development of the respiratory and circulatory systems of the body.

Flexibility. The ability to move joints through a full range of motion.

Strength. The ability to exert force such as lifting a weight or lifting your own body.

Muscular Endurance. The ability to persist in numberous repetitions of an activity involving strength.

COMBINED ASPECT

Explosive Power. The ability to display strength explosively or with speed.

MOTOR-FITNESS ASPECTS

Agility. The ability to change directions quickly and to control body movements (total body).

Reaction Time. The ability to perceive a stimulus, begin movement, and finally complete a response.

Balance. The ability to maintain body position and equilbrium both in movement and in stationary body positions.

Coordination. The ability to perform hand-eye and foot-eye tasks such as kicking, throwing, striking, and the like.

Speed. The ability to move from one place to another in the shortest possible time.

FIGURE 13.1
The aspects of physical fitness.
From Corbin, 1976, p. 54.

opment of the necessary control for efficient stopping, turning, and starting. By the time the child reaches five or six, the adult manner of running is fairly well established. Furthermore, running skills are now effectively integrated into most play activities. The level of achievement of skill in running (see Fig. 13.2) is similar for both sexes and increases with age until adolescence, when the rate of girls' performance declines slightly and the performance of boys continues to improve. (We discuss the reasons for these apparent sex differences later.)

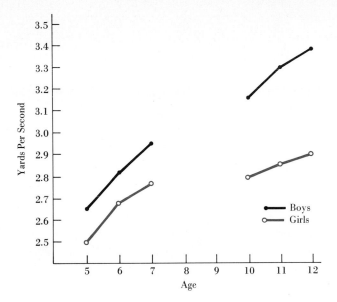

FIGURE 13.2
Endurance run performance in yards per second.
From Corbin, 1980, p. 80.

JUMPING.   Like running, jumping requires complex motor skills of form, balance, and maintenance of equilibrium. Because jumping requires the advanced skills of equilibrium and balance in negotiating an accelerated leap and a decelerated stop, the child usually does not undertake jumping until some degree of proficiency has been attained in more basic locomotion skills. About 80 percent of children usually have a good mastery of jumping skills at around five years of age (Williams, 1983). Like running, jumping proficiency increases in both sexes until around adolescence, when girls' performance begins to level off and boys' performance continues to increase (see Fig. 13.3).

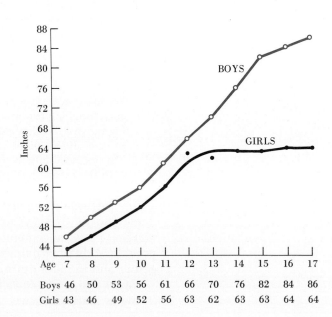

FIGURE 13.3
Standing long jump (based on data from seven studies
(Keogh, 1970). From Corbin, 1980.

Age	7	8	9	10	11	12	13	14	15	16	17
Boys	46	50	53	56	61	66	70	76	82	84	86
Girls	43	46	49	52	56	63	62	63	63	64	64

Stage I
Anterior–Posterior
Throw

Stage II
Horizontal Arm and
Body Movement
Throwing

Stage III
Weight Transfer
in Throwing

Stage IV
Mature
Overhead
Throw

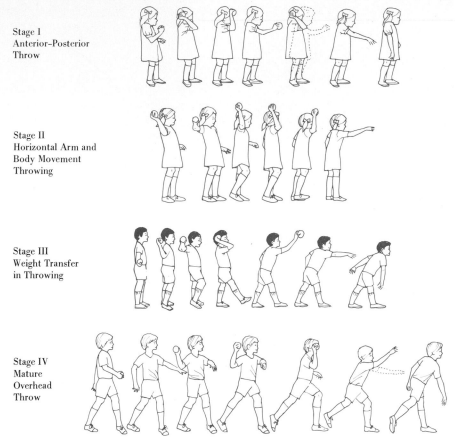

FIGURE 13.4
The developmental sequence of throwing. From Wickstrom, 1977.

THROWING.   Analysis of movies of youngsters' (two to seven years old) throwing indicates that there are four stages of throwing (Wickstrom, 1977) (see Fig. 13.4).

Anterior-Posterior Throw. The anterior-posterior throw is the least mature throw and is seen at two to three years of age. The major characteristic of this throw is that the movements of the arms and the body are confined to the anterior-posterior plane.

> For the preparatory phase, the arm is drawn up either obliquely or frontally with a corresponding extension of the trunk until the object to be thrown is at a point high above the shoulder. During delivery the trunk straightens with a forward carry of the shoulder as the arm comes through in a stiff, downward motion. Both feet remain firmly in place with the body facing in the direction of the throw during both the preparatory phase and delivery of the projectile. (Eckert, 1973, p. 166)

Throwing with Horizontal Arm and Body Movement. During the period of three and one-half to five or six years of age, there is a major shift to throwing with horizontal arm and body movements. The horizontal arm movements and the body rotation provide additional momentum for the object being thrown. The feet remain together and in place during throwing (Corbin, 1980; Williams, 1983).

Weight Transfer in Throwing. At five or six years of age, a dramatic change in the throwing pattern occurs. This change is marked by the transfer of weight from one foot to the other during throwing. For example, a right-handed child transfers his or her weight from the left foot to the leading right foot while throwing with the right hand. The transfer of weight coupled with the horizontal movement of arms and body produces greater power and distance in throwing than in the previous stage.

Mature Overhand Throw. The major characteristic of the mature overhand throw is a rearrangement of the foot patterning during the throw. For example, a right-handed child transfers body weight to the right rear foot during the preparatory phase of throwing and then takes a step forward onto the leading left foot as the object is thrown (Corbin, 1980; Williams, 1983).

By about the age of six, most children are proficient at the mature overhand throw. There appears to be a similar developmental pattern for throwing as for running and jumping, as the performance of boys continues to improve and girls' throwing tends to level off (Corbin, 1980; Williams, 1983) (see Fig. 13.5).

Sex Differences in Motor Skills

The preceding discussion of running, jumping, and throwing indicates a similar pattern of slightly higher performance levels for boys than for girls until the onset of adolescence, when the differences become more marked in favor of boys. We discuss the differences in adolescent physical growth that contribute, in part, to these sex-related performance differences in Chapter 16. Several factors—both physical and social—could contribute to the relatively slight performance differential between girls and boys six to eleven years of age.

In the first place, performance differences may be a reflection of the relationship between the greater height, weight, and limb length of boys from birth to adolescence. These factors give boys a slight mechanical and strength advantage in throwing objects. Averages in bone and muscle tissue favoring boys may also

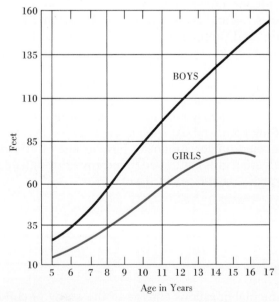

FIGURE 13.5

Distance throw. From Espenschade and Eckert, 1974.

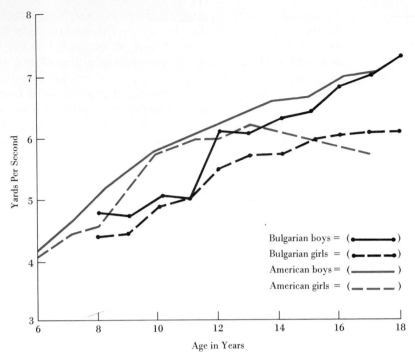

FIGURE 13.6
Curves of running performance for Bulgarian and American boys and girls.
From Espenschade and Eckert, 1974.

relate to the differential performance of boys and girls (Corbin, 1980; Espenschade and Eckert, 1980; Williams, 1983). However, it should be emphasized that although these differences in physical characteristics may account for a *slight* difference in performance between the sexes from six to eleven years, they are *not* great enough to account for the rather large sex differences at adolescence and beyond. It is possible that *social* and *cultural* factors influence the mean performance in throwing, jumping, and running so that performance differences are magnified at adolescence and beyond. In other words, it may be that the individual's efforts to consolidate and formulate an "identity" during the adolescent period may make him or her organize behavior in accordance with social-cultural sex-role expectations. Some evidence of the role of social-cultural factors in performance differences between sexes may be seen in cross-cultural comparisons. A comparison of scores of Bulgarian and American youngsters in running indicated that performance leveled off for American girls at ages thirteen to fifteen years of age, whereas Bulgarian girls continued to improve through age eighteen (Espenschade, 1960; Mangarov, 1964) (see Fig. 13.6).

Cognitive Skills

Two fundamental questions emerge in the study of children's congitive development:

· What is the nature of children's knowledge?
· How does knowledge change with development of the child?

The examination of each of these questions has, in turn, taken three primary directions. The *Piagetian* or *structuralist* tradition has been concerned primarily with how behavior is *organized* and how this organization changes with development. The *information processing* or *functionalist* perspective (see the discussion of information processing in Chapter 10) deals primarily with *processes* that are the basis for any cognitive change (Fischer and Bullock, 1984). And the *psychometric* tradition has been concerned with the measurement of individual differences using standardized tests. In this section, we examine research from the structural, functional, and psychometric perspectives in our discussion of the following dimensions of cognitive development:

- A detailed examination of the structuralist or Piagetian perspective to cognitive development in middle childhood. (It is important for us to look at this perspective in some detail because it is a most common reference point in the study of middle-childhood thinking activities.)
- The functionalist or information-processing perspective, including a discussion of basic processes such as perception, memory, and problem solving.
- The patterns of developmental change in cognitive functioning.
- The psychometric concept of intelligence and individual differences including how intelligence is measured in children.
- Some new directions in the study of school-age cognitive development, including the application of an ecological perspective.

The Piagetian/Structuralist Position

THE PIAGETIAN CONCEPT OF INTELLIGENCE.   While working in the laboratory of Alfred Binet, Jean Piaget became interested in the *incorrect* answers of the children on Binet's intelligence test. In order to understand what was happening, Piaget thought that two steps were necessary (Sternberg and Powell, 1983):

- Examine the child's performance (as had been done by Binet).
- Consider *why* a child performs as he or she does, including the cognitive structures that underlie such performance.

Through his observations of the errors in children's thinking, Piaget concluded that there were probably *cognitive structures*, which differ according to the stage of one's development.

According to Piaget, there are two related aspects of intelligence: *structure* and *function*. A biologist by training, Piaget considered that the function of intelligence was probably no different from the function of any other biological process—namely, intelligence was *adaptation*. According to Piaget, adaptation is, in turn, composed of two complementary processes: *assimiliation* (modifying current experience so that it is consistent with one's existing cognitive structures) and *accommodation* (changing one's cognitive structures in relation to the demand characteristics of the environment) (see Chapter 2 for a specific example). Piaget summarized these thoughts about intelligence as follows:

> A certain continuity exists . . . between intelligence and the purely biological process of . . . adaptation to the environment. (Piaget, 1952, p. 1)

> Intelligence is thus only a generic term to indicate the superior forms of organization or equilibrium of cognitive structuring. . . . Intelligence . . . is essentially a system of living and acting operations. (Piaget, 1976, p. 7).

Furthermore, Piaget proposed that the internal organization or structures of intelligence would vary according to the intellectual developmental level of each individual. He divided intellectual development into distinct stages. As the child moves from a given stage to the next one, the cognitive structures of the prior stage are reorganized through the adaptive behaviors (i.e., assimilation and accommodation) of the child. This reorganization results in a new level of **equilibrium**, which characterizes the next stage.

> At each new stage, the mechanisms provided by the factors already in existence make for an equilibrium which is still incomplete, and the balancing process itself leads to the next level. (Piaget, 1976, p. 49)

According to Piaget, this process of equilibrium formation or *equilibrium* is the *general mechanism*, which explains the transition from one developmental stage to the next one. The *specific* mechanism is the process of adaptation (assimilation and accommodation).

Piaget's theory of intelligence contains *three basic assumptions* about the developmental process:

1. The child is an *active participant in the development of his or her intelligence*. Four factors account for the development of the child:
   a. *Maturation*.
   b. *Experience in the physical environment*.
   c. *Experience in the social environment*.
   d. *Equilibration*, or the child's *self-regulatory processes*.
2. The development of intelligence is the result of the progression of stages that follow a sequential order and that incorporate and extend the achievements of a prior stage into the next stage.
3. Although there are individual differences in the rate of development, the stages and their invariant order are universal (Sternberg and Powell, 1983).

THE CONRETE OPERATIONAL PERIOD: GENERAL CHARACTERISTICS.   During the years from five to seven, a number of qualitative changes appear to take place in the child's thinking processes. These changes accompany the child's first years in the formal school. In our discussion of the preschool child's cognitive development, you will remember that Piaget characterized the four-to-seven-year-old child as being in the *intuitive period*. Children in the **intuitive period** rely primarily on their perceptions and their direct experiences rather than on logical operations. Two major characteristics of the intuitive level of thinking (from which the school-age child is emerging) are the following:

- *Centering*. This is the ability of the child to focus on only one dimension or feature of a configuration at a time.
- *Reversibility*. This is the ability of children to return in their thinking to the beginning of a sequence of behavior (e.g., when two equal beakers of water are poured into different-sized containers, the child can return, in his or her thinking, to the original condition of two equal amounts of water). The thinking of children in the intuitive period is *not* reversible.

As the intuitive period comes to an end, the child's thinking becomes more flexible, less dependent on perceptions, more dependent on logical operations, and more reversible.

How Come the Gerbil Doesn't Move? —Children's Understanding of Death

The title question has been known to strike terror into the heart of even the most experienced first grade teacher when the death of a classroom pet is discovered by a curious 6-year-old. The issues raised are more distressing when a classmate or a classmate's parent dies and questions are asked. The simplest path is that of silence, or of trying to dispose of the questions as swiftly and painlessly as possible. . . .

The conspiracy of silence that seems to exist among adults when it comes to discussing death with children has at least three basic roots. First, there is the adult's own emotional concern which may prevent him or her from confronting death-related issues. This may stem from actual experience or from fear of emotional losses. The second root is a general uncertainty about what to say or where to begin. It is hard to know what issues will be of immediate concern and which will be unimportant. Finally, there is the situation which combines the two mentioned above, when an emotional crisis such as the death of a parent or relative, for instance, forces an anxious adult into the awkward position of having to explain what has happened to a frightened child. . . .

Developmental Trends

Children's ideas about death develop along clear developmental lines and can be grouped by levels of mental functioning. A good example of this are the ideas children have about what causes living things to die. In the youngest group (under 6 or 7) the answers children tend to give to such questions are often magical and quite eccentric. Typically, they might include such causes of death as "Eating a dirty bug" or "Going swimming alone when your mother says no." In middle childhood (approximately ages 7 to 11) children tend to become more concrete in their reasoning, and they will typically cite as causes of death "cancer," "guns," "dope" or "poison." When children reach early adolescence (approximately age 12 and over), they become capable of more abstract formal reasoning and their explanations also take on a more abstract quality. Often they fall into such broad groups or general categories as "illness," "old age," "accidents," or "part of the body doesn't work right any more."

Large numbers of children under the age of seven may also fail to recognize the irreversibility of death. In answer to questions about how dead things can be brought back to life, such children might offer such answers as: "Take them to the emergency room," "Keep them warm and give them hot food" or "Take them to Grandma's house." In such cases the child has not yet developed the ability to break away from his own history of first-hand experiences . . . he cannot realize the permanence of death. When he reaches the more concrete level of mental operations he will be able to incorporate the experiences of others. He will then know that the gerbil in the title is not "asleep." . . . (From Keecher, 1975, pp. 18–21, 36)

"It was my turtle. It died." Doug, age 12.

"It's a bird that died of old age." Robert, age 12.

In the period of concrete operations, children use operations to solve problems and to reason.

Somewhere between five and seven years, the child begins to use what Piaget has called *operations*. **Operations** are mental activities that serve as the basis of thinking. This contrasts with the physical and perceptual activities that are primary features of thinking in infancy and the preschool years. During the period from approximately seven to eleven years of age, the child's reasoning is often called *logical* because of this newfound ability to use mental operations.

In the period of concrete operations, children use operations to solve problems and to reason. However, their thinking is tied to what is observable, or *concrete*. The child is able to think in terms of number, classes, and relationships. In order to do that, however, children need to be able to utilize two fundamental thinking procedures: *reversibility* and *conservation*. (We have already discussed reversibility; the meaning of conservation is discussed later.)

Piaget has described logical operations as the ability to do three things:

- *The ability to return to the original or starting point in a given thought process* (**reversibility**). Piaget (1973) considered reversibility a basic mechanism for the development of logical thinking as well as for the integration of cognitive structures at the stage of concrete operations and beyond.
- *The ability to organize objects into classes* (**classification**). Children at the preoperational level classify objects on the basis of one perceptual quality, such as shape or color, and may overlook other characteristics (Flavell, 1985). The concrete operational child can classify objects in terms of several dimensions simultaneously. Along with these sophisticated classification skills, the child learns to *center*, or to shift the focus from one attribute to another (you will recall that the preoperational child tends to *center* on only one attribute at a time). As the child's ability evolves and matures, he or she is able to organize objects into *hierarchies* that include superordinate classes (e.g., animal) and subclasses (e.g., dog, bird) (Flavell, 1985).
- *The ability to arrange objects along a continuum of increasing or decreasing value* (**seriation**). Ordinarily the child develops a relationship between objects in a descending or an ascending order (e.g., on such dimensions as length, width, or size). Initially children cannot do this, particularly preoperational children. For example, if the preoperational child is given a group of sticks varying in size, he or she will probably have no difficulty finding the longest and shortest sticks but may have some difficulty ordering the sticks in between (Flavell, 1985). The concrete operational child can make a total serial arrangement.

Once the seriation operation has been refined and perfected, the child can solve problems involving one-to-one correspondence. For example, given a group of dolls of varying size and a group of doll beds also of varied size, the concrete operational child can match both beds and dolls in a serial order, with bed sizes corresponding to doll sizes. This ability to make serial one-to-one correspondences is a prerequisite skill for understanding the formal school arithmetic functions as addition, subtraction, division, and multiplication (Flavell, 1985).

DEALING WITH CONCEPTS.   As a result of the acquisition of logical operations, the child is now able to deal with *concepts*. An example of the use of these three operations is the child's ability to reason and think in terms of *numbers*. In order to reason with numbers, the child must master the following prerequisite activities (Hunt, 1961; Flavell, 1985):

- *To perform reversible operations.*

$$\text{e.g., if } 2 + 2 = 4$$
$$\text{then } 4 - 2 = 2$$

In this case, the child knows that for a given manipulation of a number, there is another manipulation that "cancels" that one or returns the entire process to its original state.
- *To develop the logic of classes.* For example, 10, 20, 30, 40, and 50 are all units of 10.
- *To arrange items or quantities of items in order (seriation).* For example, if the child knows that object A weighes more than object B and that object B weighs more than object C, then the child can order the objects in a serial relationship.

$$\text{A B C}$$
$$\text{Heavy } - \text{ Light}$$

The mental operations described are used by the child to deal symbolically with many aspects of experience, including objects, numbers, and words. The child's mental operations are integrated into a total cognitive pattern that provides a way of generating concepts for representational thought (Piaget, 1950). The major differences between concrete operational thinking and adult (formal operational) thinking are twofold (Sigel and Cocking, 1977; Flavell, 1985):

- The child has limited experience and therefore limited knowledge.
- The child uses mental operations in the context of concrete things.

CONSERVATION.   As we pointed out in Chapter 7, Piaget emphasized that one of the most important milestones of the child's thinking is **conservation** (the ability to recognize that two equal quantities remain equal as long as nothing is added or taken away). Depending on the particular situation, conservation can refer to substance, weight, volume, length, number, or space. Children develop the various types of conservation at different ages. For example, conservation of substance occurs at age six or seven, conservation of weight at age nine or ten, and conservation of volume at age eleven or twelve.

Before mastering any type of conservation, children generally go through three stages (Flavell, 1985):

• *Stage I: No conservation present.* In Stage I, children fail to conserve. They may focus on only one aspect or dimension of a problem without recognizing relationships between such dimensions as height, weight, length, and width. Furthermore, they are probably fooled by general appearances and cannot recognize the reversible nature of a problem.

• *Stage II: Transitional period.* During Stage II, the child vacillates between being able to conserve and failing to conserve. Children seem to be able to focus on more than one dimension of a problem at a time but are very inconsistent in their understanding of the relationship between those dimensions.

• *Stage III: Conservation with logical explanations.* In Stage III, conservation occurs consistently whenever such problems arise. This consistency in all types of conservation problems usually does not occur until the child is ten or twelve. The logical explanations or justifications that accompany the solution of problems may take three forms (Sigel and Cocking, 1977; Flavell, 1985):

1. *Justification based on reversibility.* When confronted with a clay cylinder that has been shaped from a clay ball, the child might say, "Wait a minute—you could make the clay worm into a ball again if you wanted to."

2. *Justification or explanation of conservation based on the concept of identity.* When confronted with equal amounts of water poured into different-shaped containers, the child might say, "It's the same water; you haven't done anything to it."

3. *Justification based on the concept of compensation.* When presented with the clay cylinder formed from a clay ball, the child might say, "The cylinder is skinnier than the ball, but the ball was fatter and shorter than the cylinder—so they both have the same amount of clay."

Thus, conservation is a competency that develops over time and that reaches its completion as a result of maturation and experience.

UNDERSTANDING CAUSALITY.   One of the features of being around young children is hearing them ask "why" when they confront things that puzzle them. The question "why" is often posed to parents and may deal with many matters, such as "Why do people die?" "Why are you my daddy?" "Why do people go to school?" (to infinity, or so it may seem to weary parents). Many of the questions that children ask have to do with their developing conception of reality as well as their emerging notions of causality. In previous chapters, we discussed the development of causality as an outgrowth of sensorimotor activity. In this section, we examine **causality** as an instance of cognitive development in the six-to-twelve-year-old child.

At the concrete level, the child begins to apply rational judgments to causality although the process is not complete until the period of formal operations. An example of causal thinking is Piaget's experiment involving children's understanding of atomism. In the experiment, the child is shown a glass of water into which ice cubes are poured. Children are then asked what happens after the ice melts in the glass of water. Preoperational children tend to respond by saying that the ice simply disappears. Concrete operational children have varied responses depending on their level of conservation skill:

1. The seven-to-eight-year-old child thinks that the ice is still in the water; however, its weight and volume have *not* been added to or combined with the original water in the glass. Children at this age have not achieved conservation of weight or volume and, therefore, do not think that the ice has contributed to the weight or volume of the original water.

2. By the time children attain conservation of weight and volume, they recognize that several things have happened:

a. The ice has not disappeared but has been *transformed* in the melting process.

b. The weight and volume of the melted ice have been retained in a different form.

c. The transformed ice does not increase the water level of the container.

The understanding of causation is very much related to the operations used in conservation. Furthermore, causation in the six-to-twelve-year-old is also firmly rooted in the child's understanding of *object permanence* (see Chapter 7). In other words, because the ice disappears (in a simple perceptual sense) does not mean that the ice no longer exists. In the case of the melting ice, Piaget suggested that the concrete operational child comes to understand the *principle of atomism*. That is, objects are composed of particles (e.g., ice is composed of molecules and atoms) that, in that process of a physical change such as melting, change form and become smaller and thus invisible to the naked eye (Flavell, 1985). The understanding of causality by the child requires, among other things, that the child lessen his or her egocentric perspective of the world.

Piaget suggested that this happens through a gradual *socialization* of thinking in which the child comes to recognize that peers and others may have different viewpoints. This process of **sociocentrism** (Sigel and Cocking, 1977; Flavell, 1985) leads the child to reorganize his or her own thinking in general and his or her notions of causality in particular. Piaget described how this happens as a process of mutual interaction with other people: "[The child] makes the effort to adapt . . . he bows to the exigencies of . . . verification which are implied by discussion and argument, and this comes to replace egocentric logic with true logic created by social life" (1954, p. 302).

A CRITIQUE OF THE PIAGETIAN PERSPECTIVE.   Although Piaget's view of intelligence has made important contributions to the study of cognitive functioning in children and adults, strong criticisms have been presented (Siegel and Brainerd, 1978; Brown and Desforges, 1979). Four major criticisms have been put forth:

1. *Replicability.* Many of Piaget's critics argue that his experiments with children cannot always be replicated because of the extensive reliance on flexible language interaction between experimenter and child (i.e., too much reliance on the "way" Piaget poses a problem to the child and the interpretation of the child's verbal response).

2. *Interpretation of child success or failure on Piagetian tasks.* Specifically, it has been argued that for some tasks such as object permanence or conservation, Piaget's standards for success may be too high (Cornell, 1978). Much debate centers around whether a *correct response alone* is a sufficient criterion for success or whether the correct response must be accompanied by an *explanation/justification*. When Piaget advocates both criteria, then success in a Piagetian task may occur at a later age than if *only a correct response* (without a justification) is required.

3. *The relationship between Piagetian tasks and intelligence.* Criticisms have been focused on two primary questions (Sternberg and Powell, 1983): Do Piagetian tasks really measure what it is claimed they measure? Can one safely conclude that an individual is in a particular Piagetian stage of development based on performance on a specific task?

With reference to the first question, it has been shown that preschool children can perform a specific inferential operation that presumably should not occur (according to Piagetian theory) until much later in the concrete operational period (Riley and Trabasso, 1974). According to the investigators, the children were *not* using the inferential process which Piaget *assumed* to be required for the successful completion of the task. (Instead, they were using a mental spatial array to accomplish the task.) This, and other examples like it, suggest that in some cases the Piagetian tasks may not be measuring what it is presumed they measure.

With reference to the second question, Piaget has assumed that performance on specific tasks (e.g., conservation, object performance, and so on) are indicative of the child's stage of cognitive development. Unfortunately, the evidence does not support consistency of child performance on the various tasks that are proposed to reflect a given stage (Brown and Desforges, 1979).

4. *Usefulness of the theory.* With reference to usefulness of the theory, two basic criticisms have emerged. In the first place, it has been argued that Piagetians are only concerned with whether a given construct is present or not (Sternberg and Powell, 1982). Some investigators suggest that it would be more useful to practitioners to attend to the specific conditions (internal and external) that determine performance. Second, it has been argued that Piagetians pay too little attention to the determinants of individual differences. That is, aside from the simple recognition that individual differences exist, Piagetians do not consider the implications of inherent differences in ability (Sternberg and Powell, 1983).

Information Processing in Middle Childhood

INTELLIGENCE AS INFORMATION PROCESSING. Underlying all of the information-processing views is the idea that intelligence derives from the way people mentally organize or process information. Research on intelligence as information processing frequently uses the computer program as a metaphor or a model for developing descriptions of human intelligence.

An information-processing approach uses the computer program as a model or a metaphor for developing descriptions of human intelligence.

There have been many approaches to an information-processing perspective to intelligence. (For an excellent review of many of these, refer to Sternberg and Powell, 1983.) In this section, we briefly review one such recent attempt to incorporate many of the aspects of an information-processing viewpoint into a theory of intelligence. Specifically, we briefly examine the *triarchic theory of human intelligence* (Sternberg, 1985).

According to the triarchic theory, intelligence can be thought of as a type of "mental self-government" (Sternberg, 1985). Specifically, intelligence and government require an examination of *internal affairs* (the relationship of intelligence to the inner world of the individual), *external affairs* (the relationship of the individual to the external world of the individual), and *activities* over time (the relationship of intelligence to experience) (Sternberg, 1985). Using this analogy, there are three components of the triarchic theory:

- *Internal affairs.* Three types of information-processing activities are involved here:
  a. *Executive processes* including planning what to do (i.e., the steps involved).
  b. *Performance processes*, or carrying out plans.
  c. *Knowledge-acquisition* processes through which one learns how to solve problems in the first place. For example, sifting relevant from irrelevant information or comparing newly acquired information with what already exists in memory.

An example of the relationship of intelligence to the above "inner affairs" occurs in the solving of a simple analogy problem (see Fig. 13.7). The individual needs

---

QUESTION:

WASHINGTON IS TO ONE AS LINCOLN IS TO:

A. FIVE   B. TEN   C. FIFTEEN   D. FIFTY

The steps required to solve this analogy problem are:

1. *Encoding:* Identifying the terms in the analogy and retrieving from long-term memory information that might be relevant to a solution. (Washington was a president, a hero in the Revolutionary war; Lincoln was a president, a hero in the Civil War; both appear on currency.)
2. *Inferring:* Thinking about possible relationships between the first and second terms in the analogy. (Washington was our *first* president; his portrait appears on a *one*-dollar bill.)
3. *Mapping:* Tracing the higher-order relationship between the first and second halves of the analogy. (Washington and Lincoln were both presidents; both appear on currency; both provided the names for cities.)

4. *Applying:* Using inferences about the relationship between *Washington* and *one* to test relationships between *Lincoln* and the answer choices. (If the problem solver did not encode the presidents' protraits on the currency, he or she may guess that there are five Washingtons in the United States and ten Lincolns. Or the list of numbers may bring currency to mind.
5. *Justifying:* Explaining to oneself why this answer is better than the others. (Suppose the problem solver has not thought about currency. He or she may think that Lincoln was the sixteenth president, but conclude that his or her memory is wrong and that *Fifteen* must be the right answer.)
6. *Responding:* Supplying the answer that seems to be the best completion of the analogy.

ANSWER:

B. FIVE   (Washington appears on a one-dollar bill, Lincoln on a five-dollar bill.)

FIGURE 13.7

Analogy problem for solving with information-processing skills. Based on Sternberg, 1979, p. 13.

to decide on the steps required for a solution and a strategy for combining these steps (executive processes). The individual has to carry out the steps of the plan (performance processes). And initially, the individual has to learn the steps required for solving an analogy (knowledge-acquisition processes).

• *External affairs.* This component of intelligence involves three major functions in the external world:

   a. *Adaptation* to the existing environment.

   b. The *selection* of new environments.

   c. The *transformation* of existing environments into new ones. This perspective involves not only solving the practical problems of everyday life, but also solving abstract problems that may relate to hypothetical circumstances rather than to existing environments (Sternberg, 1985).

• *Activities over time (experience).* From this perspective, intelligence involves two distinct abilities that reflect the assessment of one's experience:

   a. The ability to cope with novel situations.

   b. The ability to cope with routine circumstances in a relatively automatic or effortless fashion (Sternberg, 1985).

INFORMATION PROCESSING AND MIDDLE CHILDHOOD. An information-processing approach to cognitive development in middle childhood presents a different picture than a Piagetian perspective. A Piagetian viewpoint suggests that the major basis for cognitive development is the changing *structures* of intelligence (the movement from one stage to the next one), including the differences in the type of logical skills in each stage. On the other hand, an information-processing perspective suggests that the major reason for changes in cognition are changes in the activities or *processes* that underlie thinking—perception, memory, and problem solving.

PERCEPTUAL PROCESSES. One of the major changes that occurs in attentional processes during middle childhood is the ability to *focus on information that is relevent* to a given task. This process is referred to as *central learning* (Hagen and Hale, 1973). In two similar studies of fourth, sixth, and eighth graders, children were shown a row of picture cards, each card having a picture of a common household item and an animal (see Fig. 13.8) (Hagen and Hale, 1973; Miller and Weiss, 1982). Before seeing the pictures the children were asked to try to remember the location of the animals. As a test of their *central learning* (ability to focus on task-relevant information), after seeing all of the cards, the children were then asked to recall the location of the animals. As indicated in Figure 13.8, they were able to attend to and to remember the location of the animals quite well. Their memory for relevent information increased with age (e.g., eighth graders remembered twice as much about the location of the animals as did fourth graders). On the other hand, when the children were asked about the household items (a measure of their irrelevant or *incidental* learning, because the children had not been initially asked to learn about those items), the results were the opposite of those for the location of the animals (relevant information). That is, there was a progressive decline in remembering with age. Younger children recalled more about the household items than did the older children. Taken together, these results suggest that school-age children are increasingly able to focus on task-relevant information and to screen out information that is incidental or irrelevant to a specific task. Similar results have been found for children's organization of information that they hear (Cherry, 1981). This perceptual skill of *central learning* is an important basis for many of the academic and social learning experiences that await the school-aged child.

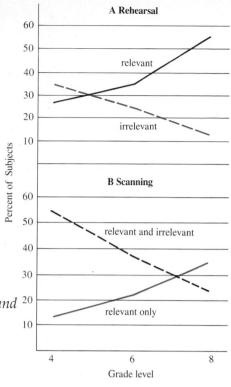

A Rehearsal

relevant

irrelevant

B Scanning

relevant and irrelevant

relevant only

Percent of Subjects

Grade level

FIGURE 13.8

The development of selective attention in middle childhood. Graph A (rehearsal) indicates the percentage of children who selected irrelevant and relevant figures as a memory aid. Graph B (scanning) indicates the percentage of children who usually scanned the relevant figures or both the relevant and irrelevant figures. Adapted from Drucker and Hagan, 1969, pp. 68–71.

THE MEMORY SYSTEM. The result of attentional processes is that information is placed in memory, or "remembered." In order to understand how this happens we need to know something about the human memory system (see Fig. 13.9).

Information first enters the *sensory register*. Presumably there is one such register for each of the senses (vision, hearing, touch, and so on), although only the visual and auditory registers have been studied in any detail. The sensory register has a large capacity for the initial storage of information. Typically, information enters just as it was presented and, unless coded, will rapidly be lost.

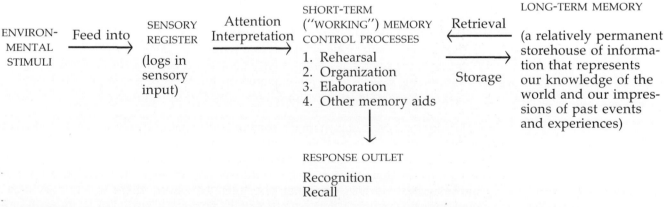

FIGURE 13.9

The memory system. Information flows from the environment to the sensory register and then to STM (short-term-memory) and LTM (long-term-memory), where it is stored and can be retrieved. Adapted from Atkinson and Shiffrin, 1968.

DEFINITIONS

Sensory Register. This is where memory information is initially stored. Information remains in the sensory register very briefly and, unless coded, will be lost in less than a second.

Short-term Memory (STM). The second stage in the memory system involving the reception of information from the sensory registers and the *storage* and *processing* of that information.

Long-term Memory (LTM). The relatively permanent store of information, including an individual's knowledge of the world.

Mnemonic Strategies. These are memory-aiding devices such as rehearsal, organization, and elaboration.

Rehearsal. This is a mnemonic device, involving the repetition of the items to be remembered.

Organization. This is a mnemonic device involving the categorization of items to be remembered (e.g., objects or words) by a common attribute (e.g., color, size, shape, or use).

Elaboration. This is a mnemonic device in which items to be remembered are linked in a meaningful order (e.g., memorizing the lines *Every Good Boy Does Fine*" helps one remember the treble clef in music, EGBDF).

Metamemory. This memory technique consists of the child's *knowledge* about his or her own memory capacity and the memory characteristics of various tasks (i.e., a child's estimate of how much he or she will remember given a specific memory task).

Knowledge Base. This is what children already know, which helps contribute to the new material they can learn and remember.

The next stage in the memory system is *short-term memory* (STM), which is also referred to as immediate memory, working memory, or primary memory. STM performs two functions:

· *Storage of information.* Information from the sensory registers may be held temporarily in STM; however, the storage capacity of STM is limited. Once its capacity is filled, incoming information must either displace already stored information or be lost to memory.

· *A central processing unit.* STM also may function as a central processor, in the following ways:

1. Selecting information from the sensory registers, which goes into STM.
2. Retrieving relevant information from long-term memory (LTM).
3. Performing operations and transformations on information in STM (i.e., organizing objects to be remembered on the basis of a category such as color, shape, size, or function).

The third stage in the memory system is *long-term memory* (*LTM*). LTM is a relatively permanent collection of individual knowledge, the contents of which are highly organized. As expected, adults know more than children and, therefore, the content of their LTM is larger. Little is known as to whether the LTM of children is less durable than that of adults. However, there is some evidence suggesting that children are less efficient in retrieval from LTM than adults are (House, 1982).

Given this three-stage memory system, an important question arises. Namely, how do school-age children influence their learning efficiency by processing information into memory? Three primary factors are involved:

- Memory strategies.
- Metamemory.
- Knowledge Base.

MEMORY STRATEGIES.   With reference to memory strategies, what *central processing* activities are performed on the contents of STM by the school-age child to transfer information from STM to LTM? Three such mnemonic (memory-aiding) devices are *rehearsal, organization,* and *elaboration.*

- *Rehearsal.* Rehearsal may be a mnemonic device involving the repetition of items to be remembered. In one study, children were shown an array of seven easily identifiable pictures. The experimenter then pointed to three of the pictures and asked two children to point to the same three, in order, after a fifteen-second delay. In order to assess the use of rehearsal, lip movements of the children were observed during the fifteen-second interval. Results indicated that only 10 percent of the kindergarten children used rehearsal, whereas 80 percent of the second graders and 100 percent of the fifth graders did so (Flavell, Beach, and Chinsky, 1966). However, additional studies have shown that younger children (kindergarten children and first graders) could be taught to use rehearsal techniques, although they frequently abandoned these techniques at a later time (Keeney, Cannizzo, and Flavell, 1967; Asarnow and Miechenbaum, 1979; Naus, 1982).

   In addition, it appears that the *method* of child rehearsal may change with age. In one study, eight-, eleven-, and thirteen-year-old children were asked to rehearse aloud a list of eight unrelated words. The older children systematically repeated a word until they knew it and then repeated the entire list each time, adding the newly learned word. The younger children simply repeated the last word learned (e.g., boy, boy, boy) and then proceeded to the next word. The younger children remembered fewer words than the older children did (Ornstein, 1978).

- *Organization.* A second mnemonic device that is used by school-age children is organization (Black and Rollins, 1982; Schmidt and Paris, 1983). This technique involves the categorization of the objects or words to be memorized according to a shared attribute (e.g., color, size, meaning of the word, and so on). For example, the following list of words can be "organized" in such a way as to be more easily remembered: hot dog, popcorn, potato chips, zebra, lion, ape, elephant. That is, the words can be more easily remembered if the first three (hot dog, popcorn, potato chips) are categorized as *foods* and the last four words (zebra, lion, ape, elephant) are categorized as *jungle animals.* Each of these category labels then serves as a cue for retrieval. Are there developmental differences in the way children organize information? Evidence suggests that younger children tend to organize items to be remembered according to *sound or rhyming patterns,* whereas older children use *concepts* or associations based on the *meaning of words.* Furthermore, younger children use simple associations (hat/coat; roof/floor) more often than older children, who tend to use specific categorizations (clothing: hat/coat, or building: roof/floor). In addition, older children are much more efficient in the use of organization than younger children are. Younger children divide lists of words or groups of objects into more categories than older children, thus making recall of the categories and items more difficult (Siegler and Richards, 1982).

ELABORATION.   A third memory device used by children is elaboration. Elaboration involves linking items to be remembered in some sort of meaningful order (McCarty, 1980; Pressley et al., 1982). For example, learning the names of the planets in our solar system (in order from the closest to the sun to the farthest) can be made much easier by remembering the following phrase: "Mary *very easily*

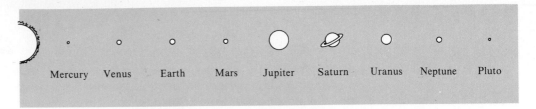

Mercury   Venus   Earth   Mars   Jupiter   Saturn   Uranus   Neptune   Pluto

Elaboration is a memory technique that involves connecting items to be remembered in some meaningful pattern. For example, recalling the names of planets (in order, from the closest to the sun to the farthest from the sun) is made much easier by first remembering the phrase "Mary very easily makes John sit up nights proposing." The first letter of each word stands for the name of a planet.

makes *J*ohn *s*it *u*p *n*ights *p*roposing" (the first letter of each word in the phrase stands for the name of a planet). The names of the planets are Mercury, Venus, Earth, Mars, Jupiter, Saturn, Uranus, Neptune, and Pluto.

Another example of an elaboration device is to spatially locate—and therefore remember—objects by recalling familiar places. For example, if you try to remember as many objects as you can in your bedroom, you may be more successful by first *visualizing* yourself walking through your bedroom door, to a desk, to a bed, to a phonograph, and so on. School-age children are more likely to use such spatially visualized elaboration than younger children (Paris and Lindauer, 1977).

METAMEMORY.   In addition to the three memory stategies discussed above, another major factor that can improve the learning and memory efficiency of the school-age child is *metamemory*. Metamemory refers to an an individual's knowledge of his or her memory capacity, as well as knowledge of the memory characteristics of various tasks (House, 1982). Metamemory develops during middle childhood and has been associated with efficiency in learning because it may lead to the use of appropriate learning strategies (Brown and DeLoache, 1978; Flavell, 1978, 1985). On the other hand, the relative absence of metamemory among preschool children may account for inefficient learning strategies. For example, the preschool child may not utilize rehearsal techniques because he or she does not recognize that forgetting will occur without some type of memory aid (House, 1982). In fact, there is evidence that children tend to be less aware of their memory limitations than adults (Flavell and Wellman, 1977). Elementary school children tend to overestimate their memory spans compared with adults. On the other hand, school-age children are much better able to evaluate how well they have learned something than younger children. For example, school-age children demonstrate increasing awareness, with age, of what makes information easy or difficult to remember (Cavanaugh and Perlmutter, 1982; Perlmutter, 1986). In one study, six- and seven-year-old children did not know that a list of words paired with opposites would be easier to learn than a list of randomly paired words. However, the nine- and eleven-year-olds in the study were well aware of this (Kreutzer, Leonard, and Flavell, 1975).

KNOWLEDGE BASE.   An additional factor that contributes to the improved memory of school-age children is that they know more things than younger children (Azmitia, Merriman, and Perlmutter, 1985). That is, as a result of more experience and learning opportunities, the *knowledge base* of the school-age child would likely be more extensive and elaborate than that of the preschool child (House, 1982).

The Peer Group

The peer group is a vital context of development for both child and adolescent. Children can experience some level of peer relationships as early as the preschool years or even in infancy. Peer interactions become more elaborate in middle childhood as children learn to appreciate diverse viewpoints, become sensitive to norms and pressures from the group, and experience the intimacy of friendship. In adolescence, the peer group becomes a source of feedback and self-validation, the significance of which rivals that of the family.

Peer relationships are a vital part of the system—the world—of the child and the adolescent. Families nurture self-esteem; the peer group is a crucible for self-evaluation. Children and adolescents learn more about who they are as their skills are appraised by others outside the family. Further, peer relationships are the foundation for the intimacy and friendship necessary for healthy adaptation and development.

Although one would *typically* expect increasing knowledge to be associated with increasing age, that is not *always* the case. In one study, a group of ten-year-old children competing in a chess tournament ("experts") and a group of college student chess amateurs ("nonexperts") were asked to reconstruct, from memory, the configuration of chess pieces on a chess board (Chi, 1978; Chi and Koeske, 1983). While one *might* assume that the age and cognitive maturity of the amateur chess players would override the knowledge and experience of the ten-year-old chess "experts," such was not the case. The results of the study showed that the young chess experts remembered the correct location of more chess pieces than the older college student amateurs did (see Fig. 13.10). In addition, the ten-year-olds were better able to predict how many trials they would need to reconstruct the arrangement of chess pieces (i.e., they demonstrated better *metamemory* than the college students). Thus, the contribution of *knowledge* or *expertise* to memory is significant, even more significant than simple age or general cognitive maturity. It is interesting to note that on simple digit recall (a "general" measure of cognitive maturity), the college students outperformed the ten-year-olds. This finding again reinforces the importance of *specific knowledge* (i.e., the child's *knowledge base*) and *experience* in memory.

PROBLEM SOLVING IN MIDDLE CHILDHOOD.   The dramatic cognitive changes that occur in middle childhood are the result not only of improvements in attentional skills and memory but also changes and improvements in problem-solving skills. Since problem solving involves attention and memory, it can be thought of as a higher level of information processing than either of those two processes. There appear to be two primary differences between the problem solving of adults and that of children (Klahr and Robinson, 1981):

· Children may possess *simpler forms of the same problem-solving processes* used by adults (e.g., children may use less rehearsal or repetition of words than adults in trying to memorize a list).

FIGURE 13.10

Knowledge base and memory. When asked to reconstruct, from memory, the arrangement of chess pieces on a chessboard, ten-year-old chess "experts" outperformed college student amateurs. However, on a simple test of digit recall (a measure of "general" cognitive maturity), the college students did better than the ten-year-olds. Based on Chi, 1978.

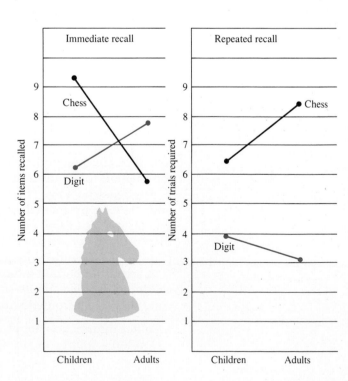

· Children may also use problem-solving strategies that are *different* from those of adults. For example, in one study where six- and seven-year-old children were asked to solve a seriation problem (e.g., putting sticks in order, by size), a common problem-solving strategy was to simply label each stick as "long" or "short" (Perner and Mansbridge, 1983). Such a strategy worked rather well when the task involved only a few sticks but proved inadequate when many sticks were involved. On the other hand, adults (and also older children) systematically arranged all the sticks in order of size.

In this section, we examine the development of problem-solving skills in two areas: (1) child understanding of daily routines (or *scripts*) and (2) child hypothesis testing.

One of the important indicators of the development of problem-solving skills is the development of competence in day-to-day routines, or **scripts**. These scripts provide a basic outline of activities to be accomplished, as well as problems to be solved (Schank and Abelson, 1977). For example, a school-age child might plan the following script for a given day: arise in the morning, shower, dress, eat breakfast, catch the bus to school, remember to bring money to buy lunch, and so on. The ability of the child to accomplish basic routines successfully—or almost without thinking—enables him or her to deal with more novel or complex problems. Furthermore, there is evidence that scripts become more complex throughout childhood (Nelson, 1978). Young children appear to depend more on an *expected sequence* of familiar events (e.g., first the table is set, then milk and sugar are put on the table, cereal is served, milk is poured, and so on), whereas older children are better able to accept *changes* (Wimmer, 1980).

Another indicator of the development of script complexity is the child's ability to develop successful strategies for finding lost or hidden objects (Heth and Cornell, 1980; Wellman and Somerville, 1982). Although younger children are able to maneuver their way through *familiar locations* (i.e., simple or well-understood scripts), it is not until middle childhood that they can develop complex and thorough search strategies for locating lost or hidden objects. For example, in one study children were told they would play a game at each designated location on a playground (see Fig. 13.11) (Wellman, Somerville and Haake, 1979; Wellman and Somerville, 1982). At the third location, the investigator used a camera to take a picture of a child. At the seventh location, the experimenter announced to the children that the camera was lost and asked them to help find it. Would they infer that if the camera was present at location three and reported lost at location seven, that it must be at locations four, five, or six? (Fig. 13.11). The children who were six years of age and older in fact looked first at these three locations. However, three- and four-year-olds looked at all locations. The investigators concluded that it is typically not until middle childhood that children are able to use relevant information to organize their search for missing items. Furthermore, there is evidence that school-age children are more skilled than preschoolers at constructing and drawing up mental and physical maps of familiar locations (neighborhood, school, home) (Siegel et al., 1979). Similarly, school-age children are better able than preschoolers to use drawn maps as a basis for traversing new environments (Curtis, Siegel, and Furlong, 1980; Hays and Siegel, 1981).

A second important indicator of emerging problem-solving capacities in middle childhood is child *hypothesis testing*. According to Robert Siegler (1978, 1981), a child who is confronted with a problem will do the following:

· Gather information about the problem.
· Develop a *strategy* or *rule* for solving the problem.

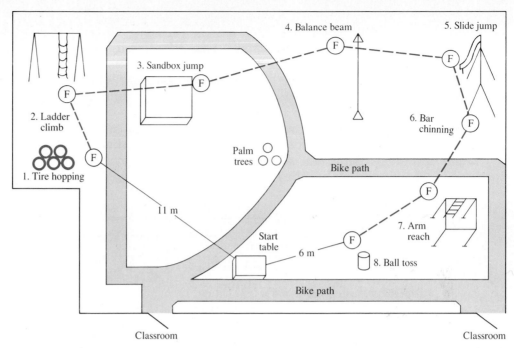

FIGURE 13.11

A diagram of the playground in the search for the lost camera. From Wellman, Somerville, and Haake, 1979.

It is assumed that the type of strategy developed to solve a problem depends on the type and quality of information that the child brings to the problem.

In one study, a set of balance-scale problems is presented to the child (see Fig. 13.12). The scale has four equally spaced pegs on each arm. When equal-sized weights are placed on the pegs, the child is asked to predict the result (i.e., will the right or left arm go down, or will the scale be in balance?). There are two significant aspects to the problem:

- The *number of weights* on each arm of the balance.
- The *distance* of the weights from the center (fulcrum) of the balance.

Siegler (1978, 1981) proposed that children will develop one of four possible strategies or rules based on the information of the *number* of weights and the *distance* of the weights from the fulcrum:

- *RULE 1*. The side of the balance beam with *more weights* is heavier. (The child attends only to the number of weights.)
- *RULE 2*. First apply Rule 1, but if weights are equal, the side with the weights farther from the fulcrum (the pivot point or the support on which the balance beam rests) is heavier.
- *RULE 3*. The child considers *both* weight and distance but does not fully understand the relationship between weight and distance (i.e., if one side has more weights whereas the other side has fewer weights but the weights are farther from the fulcrum, the child becomes confused and *guesses* what will happen).
- *RULE 4*. The child attends to *both* weight and distance and *understands* the rela-

Type of Problem	Rule Employed			
	I	II	III	IV
1. Balance problems. There are the same number and configuration of weights on each side of the fulcrum. 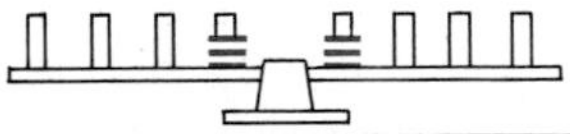	100	100	100	100
2. Weight problems. There are unequal amounts of weight at the same distance from the fulcrum on each side. 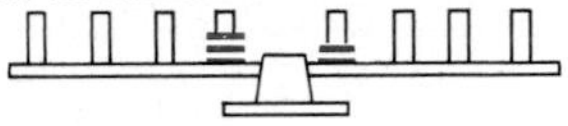	100	100	100	100
3. Distance problems. There are equal amounts of weight on each side but at different distances from the fulcrum. 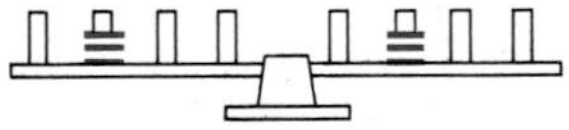	0 (Should say "balance")	100	100	100
4. Conflict-weight problems. One side has more weights; the other side has weights at a greater distance from the fulcrum. The side with more weights goes down. 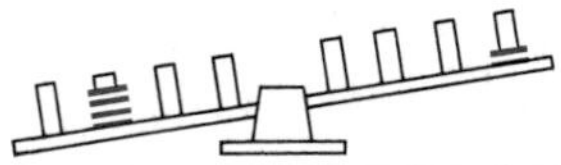	100	100	33 (Chance responding)	100
5. Conflict-distance problems. Same as 4, but the side having weights at a greater distance goes down. 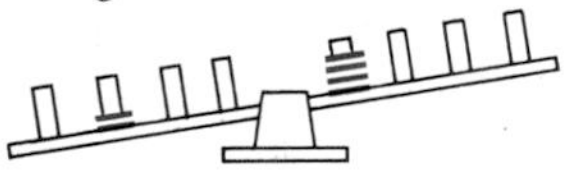	0 (Should say "right down")	0 (Should say "right down")	33 (Chance responding)	100
6. Conflict-equal problem. Like 4 and 5, but the two sides balance. 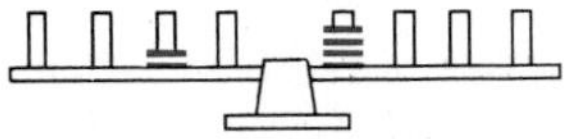	0 (Should say "right down")	0 (Should say "right down")	33 (Chance responding)	100

FIGURE 13.12
Six types of balance-beam problems and the percentage of correct answers expected. From Siegler, 1981.

tionship between the two (i.e., the *torque* or force of an arm is the result of *weight times distance*). For example, if there are four one-pound weights on the third peg three feet from the fulcrum of the left arm and there are three one-pound weights on the second peg two feet from the fulcrum of the right arm, then the force relationships are expressed as follows:

> TORQUE (FORCE) on an arm = Weight × Distance
>
> TORQUE (FORCE) on *left arm* = 4 (lbs.) × 3 (feet) = 12
> TORQUE (FORCE) on *right arm* = 3 (lbs.) × 2 (feet) = 6

Therefore, the left arm will drop.

In order to test children's level of sophistication using these four rules, Siegler (1978, 1981) developed six types of problems (Fig. 13.12). For example, in problem type 3 (distance problems), there are equal numbers of weights on each side of the fulcrum but at different distances from the fulcrum (the right side of the beam has three weights at one distance unit from the fulcrum and the left side has three weights at two distance units from the fulcrum). Therefore, the beam will tilt to the left. Children operating at the level of Rule 1 will say that the beam is in balance. However, children using Rules 2, 3, or 4 will all give the correct answer.

According to Siegler (1978, 1981), when individuals aged three to twenty years were presented with balance problems, the following results occurred:

- Ninety-one percent of the four-to-twenty-year-olds responded as if they were using one of the four hypotheses.
- None of the three-year-olds used any of the hypotheses.
- Eighty percent of the four-to-five-year-olds used hypothesis 1.
- At eight years, children were applying either hypothesis 2 or 3.
- Most of the twelve-year-olds were using hypothesis 3.
- Seventy percent of the twenty-years-olds continued to use hypothesis 3, whereas 30 percent used hypothesis 4.

In summary, hypothesis-generating skills improved throughout middle childhood, accompanied by improvement in problem solving.

A CRITIQUE OF THE INFORMATION-PROCESSING PERSPECTIVE. Information-processing models have not been immune to criticism. Three primary arguments have been presented:

1. It is unclear how similar human intelligence and computer programs (to which information-processing views are frequently compared) are. For example, some experts argue that human behavior is considerably more complex than computer programs.
2. The type of laboratory or test-like measures (for example, solving analogies) that are used in intelligence tests, which are the basis of most psychometric and information-processing views of intelligence, have *limited generalizability* to the so-called real world. For example, it is obvious that not all people who do well on such intelligence tests adapt equally well to life situations.
3. The information-processing model of intelligence is based, in part, on the assumption that computer program–like operations can be developed for efficient resolution of human problems or tasks. However, some experts argue that human problems and tasks differ from place to place (i.e., from one culture or society to another) and from one time in history to another time.

Therefore, it is argued that the meaning of "intelligent" behavior changes both over time and across cultures. Such cultural and historical variability in the meaning of intelligence puts a serious limitation on the applicability of computer analogies to intelligence (Sternberg, 1985).

Patterns of Developmental Change in Cognitive Functioning

Traditionally, there has been a controversy between the structuralist or Piagetian viewpoint and the functionalist or process-oriented perspective as to whether children really go through stages of cognitive development (Fischer and Bullock, 1984). In recent years, those who study the cognitive development of children have moved away from polarized or rigid positions on this controversy to the recognition that cognitive development can be stagelike in some ways and completely nonstagelike in other ways (Fischer and Bullock, 1981; McCall, 1983).

THE STATUS OF STAGES OF DEVELOPMENT.   Recent evidence suggests that children may develop cognitively in stages, but with the following correctives to traditional stage theories (Fischer and Bullock, 1984):

· In moving from one stage to another, behavior changes *gradually*, not abruptly.
· Children develop at varying rates in different domains of cognitive development rather than at the same rate for all domains (e.g., children may be performing seriation or the serial ordering of objects at a high level and solving various conservation tasks at a lower skill level).
· Children develop according to *individual* differences (Feldman, 1980; Flavell, 1982).

In addition, a number of characteristics of traditional stage theories appear to be generally supported, as follows:

· *Development occurs in an orderly pattern of steps*. This holds true for a specific domain of cognitive development (e.g., conservation of volume) and for a homogeneous or similar population of children (e.g., eleven-year-olds, inner-city Spanish-American children). For example, in Piaget's conservation tasks involving two balls of clay, there appears to be a specific sequence of steps, as follows (Fischer and Bullock, 1984):
    1. *Conservation of the amount of clay* (e.g., when the shapes of two equal balls of clay are changed, the amount of clay in each ball still remains the same).
    2. *Conservation of the weight of the clay balls* (e.g., when the shapes of two equal balls of clay are changed, the weight of the two balls of clay is still the same).
    3. *Conservation of volume of the clay balls* (e.g., when the shapes of two equal balls of clay are changed, each clay ball will still displace the same amount of water).
· *These orderly sequential steps are indicative of major qualitative changes in cognition*. In addition to improving and refining the cognitive skills already present, children appear to develop new cognitive activities that were not present earlier. For example, the conservation in the amount of clay (see the example above) seems to occur at a particular point in time (six to seven years of age) and not before (Fischer

and Bullock, 1984). In addition, there is evidence that such changes represent *large-scale reorganizations* of behavior that occur in child thinking (Fischer and Bullock, 1984). Furthermore, these changes appear to be rather *rapid* (Kenny, 1983; McCall, 1983).

LARGE-SCALE REORGANIZATIONS OF CHILD THINKING.   How can we describe the large-scale and rapid changes in childhood thinking? There appear to be *four* such major reorientations in thinking between the ages of four and eighteen (Fischer and Bullock, 1984), as follows:

• *The ability to deal with simple relations of symbols* (Case and Khanna, 1981; Biggs and Collis, 1982). This major reorganization occurs at approximately four years of age in Western cultures. At this time children appear to develop the ability to coordinate two or more symbolic concepts (Fischer and Bullock, 1984). For example, children are now able to relate and compare their own perspective toward an event with that of another person (i.e., elementary perspective taking) (Gelman, 1978).

• *Concrete operations.* This reorganization occurs in children from six to seven years of age (Piaget, 1970a). The distinguishing feature of this period is the ability of the child to go beyond the coordination of simple representations to the coordination of complexities of representations (Fischer, 1980; Biggs and Collis, 1982). For example, the conservation of the amount of clay first develops at this time. In the area of school relationships, the child is now able to *coordinate multiple perspectives* such as the fact that a man can simultaneously hold several social roles (e.g., doctor, husband, and father to a child who is his daughter and patient) (Watson, 1981). The child comes to understand what Piaget refers to as "the logic of concrete objects and events" (Fischer and Bullock, 1984).

• *Formal operations* This stage of thinking usually develops around ten to twelve years of age for middle-class children in Western cultures (Inhelder and Piaget, 1958; Fischer and Bullock, 1984). During this stage, children are able to function at a purely symbolic level (with symbols alone) rather than having to continually refer to concrete instances or examples of ideas (Case, 1980; Selman 1980; Richards and Commons, 1983). This enables the child to deal with the complexities of thinking about hypothetical situations. Children in this period can accomplish such tasks as using a definition of a concept (e.g., a noun or the process of division) in hypothetical situations (e.g., "If we have five bats and fifteen team members, then the most efficient number of batting practice groups will be three, or fifteen divided by five." Three groups will allow the maximum number of players the opportunity of batting an equal number of times.) or can solve complex problems such as demonstrating all possible combinations of four colored blocks (Martorano, 1977; Fischer, Hand, and Russell, 1983).

• *The ability to relate abstractions or hypotheses.* Research evidence suggests that cognitive development may continue beyond the level of formal operations (the last stage of cognitive development in Piaget's theory). Several theorists have indicated that a fourth large-scale reorganization occurs approximately at ages fourteen to sixteen years for middle-class children in Western cultures (Tomlinson-Keasey, 1982; Richards and Commons, 1983; Fischer, Pipp, and Bullock, 1984). In this phase, the adolescent is able to *generate new hypotheses* (i.e., originality and creativity) rather than simply dealing with old (i.e., already known or fully explored) hypotheses (Arlin, 1975).

Intelligence and Individual Differences: The Psychometric Perspective

In the previous sections we discussed the *common processes* or functions and the structures of intelligence that undergird cognitive development in middle childhood. In this section we take a different approach by examining *individual differences* in intellectual activity. The most common mode of assessing these individual differences is through the administration of a standardized intelligence test. Such tests produce scores that enable one to compare individual performance with the performance of others. Such tests and the ensuing individual comparisons are not without some measure of controversy.

In this section, we discuss the following matters relating to intelligence:

• What is intelligence? How is it defined?
• How is intelligence measured?

DEFINITIONS OF INTELLIGENCE.   There appears to be virtually unanimous agreement that intelligence develops. On the other hand, there is minimal agreement as to what intelligence is, or, more specifically, what it is that develops. In one study, a wide variety of people were asked to give their definition of intelligence. These people included college students, supermarket shoppers, and commuters waiting for a train (Sternberg, 1982; Sternberg and Davidson, 1982). As might be expected, the subjects had a wide variety of definitions of intelligence. However, they all agreed on three general characteristics of intelligence:

• *Verbal ability*—including reading often, being a good conversationalist, and speaking clearly.
• *Social competence*—including such behaviors as thinking before acting and being able to admit a mistake.
• *Practical problem solving*—including open-mindedness, seeing several sides to a problem, and relating ideas.

In the same study, the definitions of intelligence of these nonexperts were compared with those of authorities in the field of psychology and intelligence. In general, the definition of intelligence of both experts and nonexperts were remarkably similar, with the following exceptions (see Table 13.1):

• The experts considered *motivation* as a significant factor in intelligence; nonexperts did not.
• Nonexperts placed much more emphasis on *social competence* than did the experts.

In summary, it appears that, for the most part, what psychologists and nonexperts mean by intelligence are close but not entirely the same.

Formal or explicit definitions of intelligence generally include three major perspectives: the *psychometric* tradition, the *Piagetian* viewpoint, and the *information-processing* perspective. We have already discussed the Piagetian and information-processing perspectives.

PSYCHOMETRIC CONCEPTIONS OF INTELLIGENCE.   The psychometric tradition spawned two distinct camps: those who viewed intelligence as a *single general capacity* and those who held that intelligence was composed of *many separate abil-*

TABLE 13.1
Comparing Definitions of Intelligence: Experts and Nonexperts

CHARACTERISTICS OF INTELLIGENT INDIVIDUALS ACCORDING TO LAY PEOPLE	CHARACTERISTICS OF INTELLIGENT INDIVIDUALS ACCORDING TO EXPERTS
I. Practical problem-solving ability	I. Verbal intelligence
Reasons logically and well Identifies connections among ideas Sees all aspects of a problem Keeps an open mind Responds thoughtfully to others' ideas Sizes up situations well Gets to the heart of problems Interprets information accurately Makes good decisions Goes to original sources for basic information Poses problems in an optimal way Is a good source of ideas Perceives implied assumptions and conclusions Listens to all sides of an argument Deals with problems resourcefully	Displays a good vocabulary Reads with high comprehension Displays curiosity Is intellectually curious Sees all aspects of a problem Learns rapidly Appreciates knowledge for its own sake Is verbally fluent Listens to all sides of an argument before deciding Displays alertness Thinks deeply Shows creativity Converses easily on a variety of subjects Reads widely Likes to read Identifies connections among ideas
II. Verbal ability	II. Problem-solving ability
Speaks clearly and articulately Is verbally fluent Converses well Is knowledgeable about a particular field Studies hard Reads with high comprehension Reads widely Deals effectively with people Writes without difficulty Sets aside time for reading Displays a good vocabulary Accepts social norms Tries new things	Is able to apply knowledge to problems at hand Makes good decisions Poses problems in an optimal way Displays common sense Displays objectivity Solves problems well Plans ahead Has good intuition Gets to the heart of problems Appreciates truth Considers the result of actions Approaches problems thoughtfully
III. Social competence	III. Practical intelligence
Accepts others for what they are Admits mistakes Displays interest in the world at large Is on time for appointments Has social conscience Thinks before speaking and doing Displays curiosity Does not make snap judgments Makes fair judgments Assesses well the relevance of information to a problem at hand Is sensitive to other people's needs and desires Is frank and honest with self and others Displays interest in the immediate environment	Sizes up situations well Determines how to achieve goals Displays awareness to world around him or her Displays interest in the world at large

From Sternberg, 1982, p. 30.

ities. One of the leading proponents of the single-factor theory of intelligence was the American psychologist Charles Spearman. Spearman (1927) found that, as a rule, individuals who score high (or low) in one dimension of intelligence (e.g., mathematics) tended to score high (or low) in other areas also (e.g., vocabulary and spatial relations). Therefore, Spearman concluded that a single factor of intelligence accounted for whatever was common in intellectual performance. Spearman called this the "g" factor (the generalized ability to do well). As Spearman said: "All branches of intellectual activity have in common one fundamental function . . ." (1904).

In contrast to the single-factor approach to intelligence, another line of thinking developed in the psychometric tradition which proposed many *separate and independent abilities*. Louis Thurstone (1938) proposed a theory of intelligence that included seven primary abilities:

· Verbal comprehension.
· Number.
· Memory.
· Perceptual speed.
· Space.
· Verbal fluency.
· Inductive reasoning.

Thurstone used these mental abilities as the basis for the later development of a paper-and-pencil test of ability in children and adults (Thurstone and Thurstone, 1962). The American psychologist J. P. Guilford (1967) proposed an extension of Thurstone's theory incorporating the seven primary factors into a theory of intelligence with 120 mental abilities (see Fig. 13.13).

MEASUREMENT OF INTELLIGENCE.   As we have stated, intelligence is commonly measured with intelligence (I.Q.) tests. Such tests rank individuals in terms of their intellectual skills.

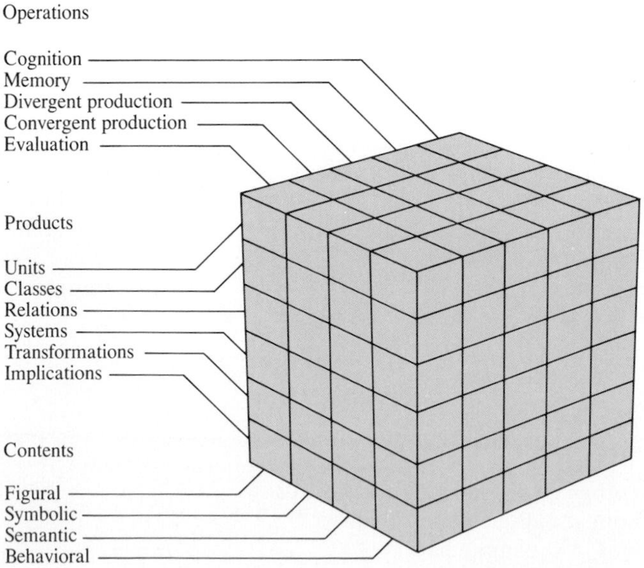

FIGURE 13.13
Guilford's theory of intelligence. From Guilford, 1967.

In order to accomplish the task of ranking and comparing individuals, the concept of *mental age* was developed. **Mental age** is a measure of the intelligence of an individual that reflects the number of age-graded test items he or she is able to solve. In 1908, the Binet-Simon test of intelligence was revised so that all items were age-graded, enabling the examiners to compare the performance of children. For example, test items that were passed by most five-year-olds and very few four-year-olds were assumed to reflect the average performance of five-year-olds. Likewise, those items that were passed by most thirteen-year-olds and few twelve-year-olds were assumed to measure the skills of an average thirteen-year-old. All the items of the Binet-Simon test (for ages three to thirteen) were age-graded in this fashion. However, it was not possible to compare the performance of children on intellectual functioning.

In order to make the comparison of child intelligence more accurate, the concept of intelligence quotient (I.Q.) was introduced. By itself, a *mental age* does not provide any information as to the comparative intelligence of a child. To be more meaningful, the mental age of a child needs to be compared with the chronological age of that same child. For example, if we know that a child has a mental age of ten without knowing the child's chronological age, we cannot determine whether he or she is average, below average, or above average. To make such determination possible, the intelligence quotient was developed. The **intelligence quotient** score is calculated by dividing the mental age by the chronological age and multiplying by 100, as follows:

$$IQ = MA/CA \times 100$$

An I.Q. score of 100 is average, which means that the child's mental age is equal to the child's chronological age. An I.Q. score greater than 100 indicates above average intelligence, and a score below 100 indicates below average intelligence.

Although an I.Q. score helps us to determine whether the score of a given child is average, below average, or above average, we still do not know *how* bright or slow a child is. In order to determine this, it is necessary to know how I.Q. scores are distributed in a population of children (see Fig. 13.14). For this purpose, a **normal distribution** (a bell-shaped, symmetrical curve that indicates the variability

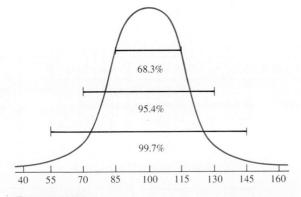

FIGURE 13.14

A normal distribution of I.Q. scores. Most scores are within 15 points of the average score of 100. (Two-thirds, or about 68.3 percent, of all I.Q. scores fall between 85 and 115.)

TABLE 13.2

*The Meaning of Stanford–Binet I.Q. Scores
Based on a Normal Distribution*

AN I.Q. SCORE OF	EQUALS OR EXCEEDS _____ % OF THE POPULATION
160	99.99
140	99.3
135	98
130	97
125	94
120	89
115	82
110	73
105	62
100	50
95	38
90	27
85	18
80	11
75	6
70	3
65	2
62	1

Based on Stanford–Binet, 1986.

of a given characteristic for a given population; most of the population falls near the average score, with fewer people at either extreme) is used. Using Figure 13.14 and Table 13.2, one can determine if an I.Q. score is above or below average.

Several modern intelligence tests use the concept of the I.Q. score, including the Stanford-Binet test (see Table 13.3) and the Wechsler Intelligence Scales (see Fig. 13.15). Generally speaking, these and similar tests have three major purposes:

• *Measuring the rate at which individuals learn.* Most I.Q. tests have sections that are timed to evaluate speed of learning. The justification for assessing speed is that

TABLE 13.3

*The Stanford–Binet Intelligence Scale: Area Scores**

VERBAL REASONING	QUANTITATIVE REASONING	ABSTRACT/VISUAL REASONING	SHORT-TERM MEMORY
Vocabulary: ages 2–18+ Comprehension: ages 2–18+ Absurdities: ages 2–14 Verbal Relations: ages 12–18+	Quantitative: ages 2–18+ Number Series: ages 7–18+ Equation Building: ages 12–18+	Pattern Analysis: ages 2–18+ Copying: ages 2–13 Matrices: ages 7–18+ Paper Folding and Cutting: ages 12–18+	Bead Memory: ages 2–18+ Memory for Sentences: ages 2–18+ Memory for Digits: ages 7–18+ Memory for Objects: ages 7–18+

*The 1985 edition of the Stanford–Binet Intelligence Scale makes maximum use of adaptive-testing concepts to determine four separate area scores within a manageable testing time. Area scores are provided for verbal reasoning, quantitative reasoning, abstract/visual reasoning, and short-term memory. . . . The test is organized into levels extending from 2-year-old to adult. Each examinee can be tested at the level that will provide the most information.

Reprinted with permission of the Riverside Publishing Company. *Stanford–Binet Intelligence Scale: Fourth Edition* by R. L. Thorndike, E. P. Hagen, and J. M. Sattler. The Riverside Publishing Company, 8420 W. Bryn Mawr Avenue, Chicago, Illinois 60631. Copyright 1985.

Information (30 questions)
How many legs do you have?
What must you do to make water freeze?
Who discovered the North Pole?
What is the capital of France?

Similarities (17 questions)
In what way are pencil and crayon alike?
In what way are tea and coffee alike?
In what way are inch and mile alike?
In what way are binoculars and microscope alike?

Arithmetic (18 questions)
If I have one piece of candy and get another one, how many pieces will I have?
At 12 cents each, how much will 4 bars of soap cost?
If a suit sells for 1/2 of the ticket price, what is the cost of a $120 suit?

Vocabulary (32 words)
ball   poem
summer   obstreperous

Comprehension (17 questions)
Why do we wear shoes?
What is the thing to do if you see someone dropped her packages?
In what two ways is a lamp better than a candle?
Why are we tried by a jury of our peers?

Digit Spin
Digits Forward contains seven series of digits, 3 to 9 digits in length (Example: 1–8–9).
Digits Backward contains seven series of digits, 2 to 8 digits in length (Example: 5–8–1–9).

Picture Completion
(26 items)
The task is to identify the essential missing part of the picture.
☐ A picture of a car without a wheel.
☐ A picture of a dog without a leg.
☐ A picture of a telephone without numbers on the dial…
An example of a Picture Completion task is shown here.

Picture Arrange (12 items)
The task is to arrange a series of pictures into a meaningful sequence. An example of a Picture Arrangement items is shown in the photograph of the WISC-R.

Block Design (11 items)
The task is to reproduce stimulus designs using four or nine blocks. An example of a block design item is shown here.

Object Assembly (4 items)
The task is to arrange pieces into a meaningful object. An example of an object assembly item is shown here.

Coding
The task is to copy symbols from a key. An example of the coding task is shown below.

Mazes
The task is to complete a series of mazes.

FIGURE 13.15

Sample items from the Wechsler Intelligence Scale for Children. From Sattler, J. M., 1982.

presumably all children have been exposed to and have well learned many tasks such as simple arithmetic computations. Since these tasks are "overlearned," individual differences will likely emerge in the rate of answering items.

• *Measuring the quantity of past learning.* In this case it is assumed that the intelligent person will have learned most of the information and concepts that other people have learned *in addition to* less commonly held ideas and information. Therefore, the focus of this objective is on *relatively rare* items (e.g., definitions of less commonly used words).

• *Measuring the quality of learning skills.* This objective is usually accomplished by assessing the child's skill in solving relatively *complex* problems. Again, the rationale for this is that the more intelligent person will be able to solve the "over-learned" or simpler problems that most people can do plus more complex ones.

USING INTELLIGENCE TESTS.   In using intelligence tests, it is important to keep in mind several characteristics of test construction and development. These qualities (or characteristics) of tests help us to assess the *quality of the test* and the *limitations of the results*. Following are four such characteristics of tests:

• *Item selection—the test as a sample.* When test makers design a test, they typically try out a large number of test items on a representative sample of people. The purpose is to find those items that best discriminate among people of different ages. This may mean that some items will be discarded simply because everyone gets them right or everyone gets them wrong. Or, if the items discriminate unfairly against various ethnic groups or against poor children, they will be discarded. The purpose is to build a test that is *fair* and adequately *represents* or *samples* human knowledge, experience, and learning.
• *Reliability.* In addition to being an adequate and fair sample of intelligent behaviors, a test must also be *reliable*. **Reliability** means that the score that a child receives on a test should be a reasonably *replicable* and *consistent* measure. For example, if a person takes a test twice over a relatively short interval (two years or less), his or her scores at both testing times should be quite similar. The reliability of the Stanford-Binet and the Wechsler tests is approximately +.90 (1.00 indicates perfect reliability and 0.00 indicates no reliability at all).
• *Validity.* The **validity** of a test is the extent to which it actually measures what it was constructed to measure. For example, I.Q. tests were originally designed and used for the purpose of *predicting* school achievement (*predictive validity*). In other words, children with high I.Q. scores presumably would do better in school than children with lower I.Q. scores. This is not, of course, always what happens.

Construct validity is another type of test validity that reflects the extent to which the test items actually represent the broad universe of possible test items. In this regard, it has been argued that a source of unfairness in testing is the *cultural content* of the test. Virtually all I.Q. tests reflect the experience and knowledge of a specific culture. Therefore, such tests are unfair to those who are not familiar with the content of that culture. For example, non-English-speaking children from other societies, or from within an English-speaking culture, would likely do rather poorly on an I.Q. test designed to reflect mainstream cultural content (see box on the Chitling test). Therefore, the I.Q. test may not reflect their actual ability.

A related criticism of I.Q. tests is that, in terms of *construct validity*, they reflect only a limited *sample* of the possible universe of intelligent behaviors. For example, such tests do not measure important interpersonal abilities and skills that enable individuals to successfully adapt to their various circumstances. A good example is the child who is able to "size up" feelings and needs of teachers, parents, and peers and to use that knowledge to resolve disputes. Is such interpersonal skill a valuable mode of intelligence for which there are individual differences? On the other hand, test makers may reply that the I.Q. tests are really designed to measure *school-related abilities* and not overall life-adaptation skills.

Some New Directions

TOWARD AN ECOLOGICAL PERSPECTIVE TO COGNITIVE DEVELOPMENT.   Although there has been some clarification of the concept of stages in childhood cognitive development, there still remains a serious historical problem in the study

The Chitling Test

Frequently, intelligence tests that are designed to measure logical thinking or other skills in children have a built-in cultural bias against some minority-group children. For example, black children growing up in the inner city may simply be unfamiliar with concepts that middle-class children may take for granted. Such children may not be as familiar with technological advances such as personal computers or in ways of handling money as middle-class children are.

To emphasize the fact that such children can operate perfectly intelligently in a world that may be unfamiliar to middle-class children, Adrian Dove, a black sociologist, designed his own intelligence test. It is called the Dove Counterbalanced General Intelligence Test, or the Chitling Test. The test is composed of thirty multiple-choice items, thirteen of which are presented below (answers at the end).

1. A "handkerchief head" is: (a) a cool cat, (b) a porter, (c) an Uncle Tom, (d) a hoddi, (e) a preacher.
2. Which word is most out of place here? (a) splib, (b) blood, (c) gray, (d) spook, (e) black.
3. A "gas head" is a person who has a: (a) fast-moving car, (b) stable of "lace," (c) "process," (d) habit of stealing cars, (e) long jail record for arson.
4. "Down-home" (the South) today, for the average "soul brother" who is picking cotton from sunup until sundown, what is the average earning (take-home) for one full day? (a) $.75, (b) $1.65, (c) $3.50, (d) $5, (e) $12.
5. "Bo Diddley" is a: (a) game for children, (b) down-home cheap wine, (c) down-home singer, (d) new dance, (e) Moejoe call.
6. If a pimp is up tight with a woman who gets state aid, what does he mean when he talks about "Mother's Day?" (a) second Sunday in May, (b) third Sunday in June, (c) first of every month, (d) none of these, (e) first and fifteenth of every month.
7. "Hully Gully" came from: (a) East Oakland, (b) Fillmore, (c) Watts, (d) Harlem, (e) Motor City.
8. If a man is called a "blood," then he is a (a) fighter, (b) Mexican-American, (c) Negro, (d) hungry hemophile, (e) Redman or Indian.
9. Cheap chitlings (not the kind you purchase at a frozen-food counter) will taste rubbery unless they are cooked long enough. How soon can you quit cooking them to eat and enjoy them? (a) 45 minutes, (b) two hours, (c) 24 hours, (d) one week (on low flame), (e) one hour.
10. What are the "Dixie Hummingbirds"? (a) part of the KKK, (b) a swamp disease, (c) a modern gospel group, (d) a Mississippi Negro paramilitary group, (e) Deacons.
11. If you throw the dice and seven is showing on the top, what is facing down? (a) seven, (b) snake eyes, (c) boxcars, (d) little Joes, (e) 11.
12. "Jet" is: (a) an East Oakland motorcycle club, (b) one of the gangs in "West Side Story," (c) a news and gossip magazine, (d) a way of life for the very rich.
13. T-Bone Walker got famous for playing what? (a) a trombone, (b) piano, (c) "T-flute," (d) guitar, (e) "Hambone."

Those who are not "culturally deprived" will recognize the correct answers are 1.(c), 2.(c), 3.(c), 4.(d), 5.(c), 6.(e), 7.(c), 8.(c), 9.(c), 10.(c), 11.(a), 12.(c), 13.(d).

(From Dove, 1968, pp. 51–52)

of cognitive development. That is, there has been a traditional tendency to attribute cognitive change to *either* the child *or* the environmental circumstances (Fischer and Bullock, 1984).

According to Kurt Fischer and Daniel Bullock (1984, pp. 86–87), one remedy for this difficulty is to introduce the concept of **collaboration** into the study of cognitive development.

Human beings are social creatures, who commonly work together for shared goals. That is, people collaborate. Often when two people collaborate to solve a problem, neither one possesses all the elements that will eventually appear in the solution. During their collaboration, a social system (Kaye, 1982) emerges in which each person's behavior supports the other's behavior and thought in directions that would not have been taken by the individuals alone. Eventually a solution—a new cognitive structure emerges. It bears some mark of each individual, yet it did not exist in either person prior to the collaboration, nor would it have developed in either one without the collaboration. . . . Of course, besides having the same two people collaborate again, it is also possible for one of them to collaborate with a different partner (Bereiter and Scardamalia, 1982; Brown, Bransford, Ferrara and Campione, 1983. . . .)

Figure 13.16 presents a diagrammatic depiction of the collaborative cycle. The two left circles in the diagram represent internal structures (child thinking processes) and external structures (environmental characteristics). For example, in the case of a boy working on a crossword puzzle with his father, the father would be providing the *external* structures for problem solving (advice, hints, obtaining a dictionary, and so on) (Brown, 1980; Wood, 1980; Kaye, 1982). The boy's skills in solving the crossword puzzle constitute the *internal* structures. The interaction (collaboration) of internal and external structures is indicated in the right circle in the diagram. As a result of the collaboration of father and son, a ''scaffolded'' mental structure (i.e., skill and knowledge that are continually updated, or ''scaffolded,'' through interaction of internal structures with external or environmental structures) develops. The arrows in the diagram illustrate the feedback characteristics of the model. For example, when the son collaborates with his father, his internal structures (problem-solving skills) improve to the point that he is no longer

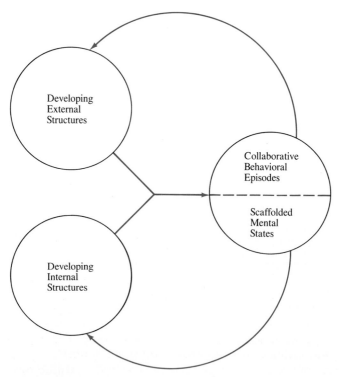

FIGURE 13.16
Development schematized as a collaborative cycle.
From Fischer and Bullock, 1984.

dependent on the initial advice and support of his father. In fact, the son may stimulate the father to provide additional support ("scaffolding") in keeping with the son's improved skill level (Fischer and Bullock, 1984).

Furthermore, it is important to keep in mind that even when children are involved alone in an activity, the nonpersonal environment still plays a significant role as a collaborator. That is, every environment is organized—whether by intent or not—to foster some behaviors over others. For example, a child's playground with swings and slides but no climbing bars obviously makes possible some motor behaviors rather than others. The same analogy can be extended to much of the human environment, which is *socially constructed* in such a way as to support or encourage some behaviors. This social construction is sometimes referred to as the *human factors* of a learning situation. Several examples of the human factors of a learning situation include the design of human tools and buildings to facilitate certain types of interaction.

RETHINKING ABILITY AND COMPETENCE IN A COLLABORATIVE CONTEXT. As we have seen in our discussion of child ability or competence and the measurement of these dimensions, child ability has frequently been *defined independently of any contexts of development* (Fischer and Bullock, 1984). That is, ability is sometimes conceived as a *static* set of characteristics which children have in varying degrees. For example, if a child "possesses" such characteristics, he or she can do a conservation task, whereas another child who is less "intelligent" cannot.

When the notion of collaboration is introduced into this discussion of ability or competence, there is need for a revision or rethinking of such trait-oriented definitions (Fischer and Bullock, 1984). Child ability and competence can now be considered as emerging characteristics of a child in a given context, rather than as fixed traits. For example, in certain contexts children may demonstrate the competence to function independently on a given task. In other contexts (perhaps more complex, or requiring the transfer of current skills to new circumstances), the child may demonstrate less competence to the point of needing a more knowledgeable and skillful collaborator (Overton and Newman, 1982).

> The collaboration orientation poses many new questions for the study of cognitive development. It is not enough to ask questions such as: How does the child's behavior change with age, or how does the child's behavior change as a function of experience? Instead, questions like the following need to be asked: Why do children often perform below capacity? How does context support or fail to support high-level performances that are known to be within the child's reach? How do specific collaborative systems support the acquisition of particular skills in different ways at different developmental levels? How is the nature of the child's experience jointly regulated by the child and by resources (human and other) available in the child's environment? (Fischer and Bullock, 1984, p. 93)

COGNITIVE DEVELOPMENT AND CHILD EMOTIONS. One of the important outcomes of considering child cognitive development in the context of a collaborative relationship is the increasing recognition that the development of children cannot be categorized into neat little boxes with labels such as thinking, emotions, social behavior, personality, and physical growth. Rather, these dimensions need to be integrated if one is to understand child development more completely (Selman, 1980; Harter, 1982, 1983).

Over the past ten years there has been a dramatic interest in the relationship of cognitive development to emotions (Fischer and Bullock, 1984). Susan Harter (1982) described the systematic changes that occur in how children think about their own emotions and the emotions of others. One of the primary developmental changes that emerged was the gradual ability of children to think of themselves as having two distinct emotions at the same time (e.g., when a child was happy about receiving a new toy but unhappy about the color of the toy). Preschoolers were unable to conceive of a child's simultaneously experiencing two emotions. Rather, they thought that one emotion must necessarily follow the other emotion (in time). Middle childhood was the watershed for the emergence of this skill, and it was not until age nine or older that the child could conceive of the simultaneity of emotional response with any consistency (Harter, 1982). Furthermore, a child's ability to conceive of emotional simultaneity is also related to the extent to which his or her collaborator is supportive and knowledgeable (Hand, 1982). In summary, a child's ability to think about emotions seems to follow the following sequence (Rosenberg, 1979; Harter, 1982; Fischer et al., 1986):

- Preschool children are able only to deal with one type of emotion at a time or with a simple relationship involving the same or closely related emotions (e.g., if you are nice to me, I will be nice to you).
- In middle childhood, the ability to understand the possibility of experiencing two or more emotions simultaneously emerges.
- During adolescence, children can understand the complexity of experience (i.e., experiencing two or more emotions) on a consistent basis and can use more specific and precise labels for these emotions than elementary school children.

Language Development

In addition to the general cognitive development of the school-age child, language skills also continue to be refined. Gains in linguistic competence are made as children use bigger words, use more complex statements, and use language in new ways. Furthermore, children's ability to meaningfully and effectively communicate with others increases substantially. (We have already discussed this in Chapter 10.)

Vocabulary

During middle childhood, children become more logical and analytic in the way they use words and less dependent on perceptual or action characteristics associated with words (Holtzman, 1983).

- When preschoolers are asked to respond to the word *orange*, they are likely to say things like "It's round," "It's orange-colored," or "I can eat it." In other words, the preschooler is bound by perceptual or action characteristics. On the other hand, the school-age child is more likely to respond by referring to logical categories such as "It's a fruit" or "It's a breakfast food."
- Preschoolers tend to define words by using examples. On the other hand, school-age children may define words by analyzing their relationships to other words.

For example, the preschooler may define *above* by saying "Place where the sun is," whereas a school-age child may say "Above is the opposite of below."
• School-age children are more likely than preschoolers to be able to understand and use words that may not have a direct experiential reference. For example, the word *vertebrate* (the class or phylum of animals having a spinal column) includes a broad range of animals including bony fish, crocodiles, birds, and human beings.

Grammar and Semantics

During the period of middle childhood, children are practicing current language skills, clarifying grammatical errors, and extending the meanings of words and sentences. Although most grammatical constructions are learned by age six, the refinement of grammar continues throughout middle childhood. For example, some preschool children have difficulty understanding the passive voice (e.g., "The ball was hit by the boy") (Chomsky, 1969; Romaine, 1984). They think that any noun that precedes a verb must be the source of the action in the sentence. However, school-age children understand that the sentence means that the boy is hitting the ball rather than vice versa. Likewise, there is evidence that school-age children use the passive voice more frequently in their speech than preschoolers (Romaine, 1984).

In addition, children's knowledge of semantics continues to develop throughout the grade-school years.

• By the time children are six years of age, they understand between 8,000 and 14,000 words (Carey, 1977). Their knowledge of words, of course, continues to grow.
• *School-age children* become more proficient than younger children at *making inferences* about meanings (Johnson and Smith, 1981; Ackerman, 1982). For example, if a talkative ten-year-old hears her teacher say, "You're being quiet today, aren't you," she will infer that this is a sarcastic statement rather than a statement of fact.
• As school-age children become more skillful at making inferences, they also come to appreciate jokes and humor based on subtleties of meanings (Reynolds and Ortony, 1980). For example, understanding the following joke requires an understanding of word meanings:

> **Question:** "When is a door not a door?"
> **Answer:** "When it's ajar."

Language and Culture

Most of us are aware that cultural features of our environment can enhance and support the development of both children and adults. Culture has an impact on how children learn to speak and develop language skills. A central question that emerges—and that has resulted in a great deal of heated controversy—is whether there is a "right" way to speak and use language. For example, in the United States, there are a variety of forms of spoken English. Some forms may differ in somewhat minor ways (e.g., differences in accent in various parts of the country). Other differences may include variations of standard spoken English such as so-called black English. Other problems arise when different languages (e.g., Spanish or American Indian languages) are spoken in neighborhoods or communities more frequently than the so-called standard English, which is taught in school. As a result of these concerns, the following important questions arise (McLaughlin, 1984; Diaz, 1985):

· Is "nonstandard" English necessarily "substandard" English?
· Should bilingualism (the use of two languages) be encouraged for some ethnic or cultural groups? Would a policy of bilingulism be a help or a severe handicap if and when a child grows up to live and work in the majority cultural and language system?
· Are cultural *differences* the same as cultural deficits?

Such issues become critical when one considers the important role of language skill as a basic tool for negotiating and controlling aspects of culture.

The Cultural Functions of Language

How is language related to a human being's functioning in a culture? There is considerable agreement that language plays an important role in guiding the thinking of human beings (Sapir, 1958; Bruner, 1966). Although language is undeniably an important component of the cultural environment of the growing, thinking, and developing child, there remains a controversy whether thinking is preeminent and therefore directs language or whether language conditions thinking.

DIFFERENCE OR DEFICIT? When we make comparisons between the language of middle-class children and children from economically poor situations, there are many obvious differences. When these differences are acknowledged, there are at least two interpretations:

1. The **deficit hypothesis**. Although we have rather little knowledge of language development among poor and, specifically, young black children, many psychologists, educators, and public servants have proceeded to develop the deficit hypothesis. In its simplest terms, this hypothesis suggests that the well-documented failure of many black children (particularly in school) is the result of an "impoverished" language. This hypothesis rests on some shaky assumptions.
2. The **difference hypothesis**. This hypothesis asserts that English, like other languages, has a number of forms (dialects), none of which is superior. Therefore, asserting that academic failure results simply from a different dialect may be a gross oversimplification of the child's total environment in contributing to "success" in school and in life.

"Black English": A Case Study. In order to put the language concepts we have been discussing in concrete terms, we have reproduced a sample of black English below.

■ *AN ANNOTATED TRANSCRIPTION OF A SAMPLE OF BLACK ENGLISH*

Calvin: One day I was walking. Then I met Lennie. Lennie say,[1,2] "Calvin, what happened to your lip?" I said, "Nothing." And then Lenn came over to me and he say,[1,2] "What you mean by nothing?" Like he always say[2] because he's always interested in me and me and him is[3] good friends. So I told him what happened. "This guy named Pierre, he about fifteen. . ."

Lennie: Yeah?
Calvin: He came over to me . . .
Lennie: Uh huh.
Calvin: And he hit me in my lip because . . .
Lennie: Yeah?
Calvin: I . . .
Lennie: Done[4] what?
Calvin: Had done copied[4] off his paper in school.

Annotations

1. Some verbs, like "come" and "say," are not marked for past tense in Black English narratives, even when the context is past time.
2. Black English lacks the -*s* suffix, which marks the present tense with third person singular subjects in Standard English.
3. Occasionally (and particularly with coordinate constructions), the singular conjugated forms of "be" ("is," "was") occur with the plural subject in Black English.
4. The use of "done" plus the past tense of a verb is a construction indicating completed action. Some speakers occasionally include a form of "have" as in "had done copied . . ."

Adapted from Wolfram and Fasold, 1969.

Black Children and Their Language Development. As indicated in the example, it would be wrong to infer that black English is without a meaningful structure or communication value. Although it is possible that some black children have problems learning and using standard English as taught in the public school, it is unlikely—as the deficit hypothesis suggests—that failure of black children could be attributed to language problems taken alone. Cognitive development may be slowed by poverty and other social factors. The following are some reasons to question the deficit hypothesis (Dale, 1976, p. 278):

1. In the first place, the deficit hypothesis assumes that language plays a determining role in thinking. It is, of course, possible to be a perfectly logical thinker using either standard English or black English.
2. Are black children inadequate in their mastery of standard English or in their inability to apply such a language system? The deficit hypothesis does not make this distinction.
3. The deficit hypothesis blurs the distinction between *race* and *social class* as contributing factors to language development. It is a fact of American life that blacks are overrepresented in the lower socioeconomic groups. It is certainly possible that differences between black children and white children are due more to social class factors than to some unspecified "racial" distinctions. Evidence suggests that the poor language performance of children from poverty settings appears to be limited primarily to vocabulary rather than to mastery of the total language system.

BLACK ENGLISH AND BLACK CULTURE. In keeping with our emphasis in this book on the total *system* of the child and the adolescent as the major arena for growth and development, we would point out that the black child and the black adolescent live in such a total ecosystem. The overall development of the child—and, in particular, the language development of the black child—can be profitably viewed from such a systems perspective.

Specifically, one of the major reasons that the language deficit hypothesis is on such shaky ground is that it tends to ignore these systems features of development.

One of the questions raised by those who have investigated black English is the *methods* of investigation used to assess such language development (Labov, 1970, 1972). Simply placing a black child in a room with a white adult (otherwise known as the "experimenter") may create defensive responses on the part of the black child, including withdrawal and nonfluent speech. Even placing the child in a room with a black adult may not eliminate the artificiality of the experimental situation.

The fact that some "experimental" situations are not "real" (*real* in the sense of representing or evoking behavior that would occur in the black child's ecosystem) is effectively demonstrated when the experimental situation is changed. William Labov (1970) reported the following change in the context or setting for a language development experiment for black children:

■   In the next interview with Leon, Clarence

1. brought along a supply of potato chips, changing the "interview" into something more in the nature of a party;
2. brought along Leon's best friend, 8-year-old Gregory;
3. reduced the height imbalance (when Clarence got down on the floor of Leon's room, he dropped from 6 ft. 2 in. to 3 ft. 6 in.);
4. introduced taboo words and taboo topics, and proved to Leon's surprise that one can say anything into our microphone without any fear of retaliation.

From Labov, 1970, p. 8.

This change in procedure resulted in much active, fluent, and argumentative speech from Leon (an eight-year-old) than had occurred outside of his ecosystem.

Furthermore, the so-called deficit hypothesis seems to be contradicted even further by observations of many social scientists that in the black culture, there is indeed an emphasis and importance placed on verbal fluency. There is considerable evidence that black children have a good knowledge of standard English. Furthermore, when the speech of black children is translated from black English to standard English, there are no differences in the overall language competency of lower-class black children and middle-class white children (Anastasiow and Hanes, 1974; Copple and Suci, 1974). It appears that once one understands the "rules" of black English, many instances of what seem to be illogical statements are really dialect differences. For example, in black English, the use of a double negative may be meaningful, particularly when one recognizes that other languages (e.g., Russian, Old English) may use not only two but three negatives (e.g., black English double-negative: "He don't know nothing").

One of the interesting features of black language development is the important role of peers in language formation. In some cases involving black families in which the parents speak standard English, the children's language is more similar to the black English of their peers. These children are approximately seven to eight years old when the dialect shifts from the parental dialect to the peer-group dialect. The dialect shift seems to be a function of interaction with a peer group in which the black English dialect is seen as normal. For both white and black children in the New York City area, dialect shifts have also been observed that are an apparent result of interaction with the child's peer group. This not-uncommon phenomenon raises some interesting questions about the relative role of parents and peers in language development. Do children learn more about language from their peers or from their family members? Would an educational emphasis on the quality of language in the home be misplaced? (Dale, 1976).

Summary

1. In most industrialized societies, school-age children are the healthiest age group in the population. The general rate of increase in stature is fairly regular during middle childhood, until the onset of puberty, when dramatic changes occur in the body. Increasingly, evidence supports the assertion that the way people live, or their *life-style*, contributes significantly to individual health status throughout the lifespan. The development of life-style patterns during middle childhood is particularly relevant to the *prevention* of the major diseases associated with adulthood. Important dimensions of life-style development include exercise, dietary habits, self-induced vulnerability (e.g., cigarette smoking), and chronic illness.

2. By the end of early childhood, children have almost completed the development of the fundamental motor skills that will allow them to accomplish the sport and dance skills of middle childhood and beyond. During middle childhood, fundamental motor skills are extended to simple games in play situations.

3. Piaget's theory of intelligence contains *three* basic assumptions about the developmental process. The child is an active participant in the development of his or her intelligence. The development of intelligence is the result of the progression of stages that follow a sequential order and that incorporate and extend the achievements of a prior stage into the next. Although there are individual differences in the *rate* of development, the stages and their invariant order are universal. During the years from five to seven, a number of qualitative changes occur in the child's thinking processes. These changes accompany the child's first years in the formal school. Two major characteristics of the *intuitive* level of thinking (four-to-seven-year-olds) are *centering* and *reversibility*. Somewhere between five and seven years, the child begins to use *operations* and, as a result, can now deal with concepts. An important milestone in child thinking is *conservation*. At least four major criticisms of Piagetian theory have been put forth.

4. Research on intelligence as information processing frequently uses the computer program as a model for developing descriptions of human intelligence. One recent attempt to incorporate many of the aspects of an information-processing viewpoint is Sternberg's *triarchic theory of human intelligence*. An information-processing perspective suggests that the primary reason for changes in cognition are changes in the activities (or *processes*) that underlie thinking—perception, memory, and problem solving. A major change that occurs in attentional processes is the ability to focus on information that is relevant to a given task.

    The memory system involves the flow of information from the environment to the *sensory register* and then to STM (short-term memory) and LTM (long-term memory), where it is stored and can be retrieved. School-age children increase the efficiency of processing information into memory using three factors—memory strategies, metamemory, and their knowledge base.

5. In recent years, those who study the cognitive development of children have suggested that cognitive development can be stagelike in some ways and nonstagelike in other ways.

6. The psychometric approach to the intelligence of school-age children involves

the assessment of individual differences through the administration of standardized intelligence tests. The psychometric tradition originally spawned two camps: those who viewed intelligence as a *single general capacity* and those who viewed intelligence as composed of *many separate abilities*. *Mental age* is a measure of intelligence that reflects the number of age-graded test items a child is able to solve. A child's *intelligence quotient* is calculated by dividing mental age by chronological age.

One way of integrating both the child and the environment in cognitive change is the concept of *collaboration*.

7. Language skills of school-age children continue to develop. Their vocabulary increases and they are able to use more complex statements. It is incorrect to assume that black English is without meaningful structure or communication value.

Key Terms

Causality
Centering
Chronic illness or disability
Classification
Collaboration
Concrete operational period
Conservation
Deficit hypothesis
Difference hypothesis
Elaboration
Epiphyses
Equilibrium
Intelligence Quotient
Intuitive period
Juvenile Rheumatoid Arthritis
Knowledge base
Life-style
Long-term memory (LTM)
Mental age

Metamemory
Mnemonic strategies
Normal distribution
Operations
Organization
Ossification
Physical fitness
Rehearsal
Reliability
Reversibility
Scripts
Self-induced vulnerabilities
Sensory register
Seriation
Short-term memory (STM)
Skeletal maturity
Sociocentrism
Validity

Questions

1. Why is life-style a significant health concern in middle childhood?
2. Discuss sex differences in motor skills in middle childhood.
3. Discuss the general characteristics of concrete operational thinking.
4. Briefly describe the triarchic theory of human intelligence.
5. Discuss the major features of the memory system.
6. Discuss the meaning of *collaboration* as an ecological perspective to cognitive development.
7. How is the cognitive development of school-age children related to their emotions?

Suggested Readings

COLLINS, W. A. (ed.). *Development During Middle Childhood: The Years from Six to Twelve*. Washington, D.C.: National Academy Press, 1984. An excellent discussion of the major aspects of middle childhood.

FLAVELL, J. H. *Cognitive Development* (2nd ed.). Englewood Cliffs, N.J.: Prentice-Hall, 1985. A well-written analysis of the central dimensions of cognitive development.

GLIEDMAN, J., and ROTH, W. *The Unexpected Minority: Handicapped Children in American Society*. New York: Harcourt, Brace, Jovanovich, 1980. A timely discussion of handicapped children in school and society.

STERNBERG, R. J. *Beyond I.Q.: A Triarchic Theory of Human Intelligence*. New York: Cambridge University Press, 1985. An excellent account of a recent information-processing theory of intelligence.

WILLIAMS, H. F. *Perceptual and Motor Development*. Englewood Cliffs, N.J.: Prentice-Hall, 1983. A readable and up-to-date discussion of perceptual and motor development.

14 Middle Childhood: Social and Personality Development

Train up a child in the way he should go: and when he is old, he will not depart from it.

—*Proverbs, 22:6*

Childhood has its own way of seeing, thinking and feeling, and nothing is more foolish than to try to substitute ours for theirs.

—*Rousseau*

In the preceding chapter we explored the changes in physical and cognitive development that occur in middle childhood. In much the same way that there are significant physical and intellectual changes in the lives of six-to-twelve-year-olds, there are also substantial changes in social and personality development. In this chapter we explore the following dimensions of social and personality development:

· The construction of the self as a *system* in middle childhood.
· Social cognition, or how the individual thinks about the self and others.
· Self-regulation, or how children learn to monitor, control, and evaluate their behavior.
· Moral development.
· Achievement motivation.

The Self as a System

As we have seen in earlier discussions, the self is an active ongoing construction of the individual that is continually undergoing developmental change. One can think of the self as being similar to a *theory* organized and constructed by the child (see Chapter 10). The differentiation of the self is a process that takes on new dimensions during middle childhood. In middle childhood, there are two significant dimensions of the self-concept that constitute the self as a system (Markus and Nurius, 1984) (see Fig. 14.1):

· The *content of self-concept*, or what children understand about themselves.
· The *function of self-concept*, or how the self-concept regulates, organizes, and controls child behavior.

There are *four aspects of middle childhood* that make this period have a particularly strong impact on the developing *content* and *function* of the self-concept.

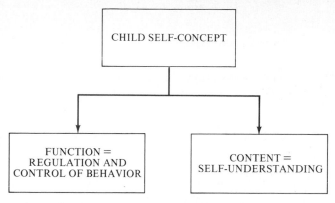

FIGURE 14.1
*The self-concept system in middle childhood is
composed of two primary dimensions: the* content
and the function *of the self-concept. Based on
Markus and Nurius, 1984.*

- School-age children have extensive contacts with their social environments (e.g., parents, teachers, and peers). Therefore, they must learn to
integrate their own needs and goals with those of others in their social
environment.
- School-age children tend to be less egocentric (self-centered) and, therefore,
better able to understand the perspective of others.
- In addition, the school-age child becomes more sensitive to social perspectives
and social rewards than to simple material rewards.
- The behavioral repertoire of the school-age child increases rapidly to include a
variety of social, recreational, artistic, and intellectual skills that serve as a basis
for self-definition.

The major theme of the development of self-concept in middle childhood is the
child's increasing appreciation of the *self as a social object* (Markus and Nurius,
1984). This theme is treated by most of the major theories of child development
(see Chapter 2).

- According to Sigmund Freud (1956), middle childhood is a period of *latency*,
during which the child is relatively free to develop the social self without the
domination of the emotions and feelings of the *id* (see the discussion in Chapter
2). Middle childhood is the time of the *ego* (or the self), during which the child
can rapidly become socialized (Markus and Nurius, 1984).
- According to Erik Erikson (1959), middle childhood is the stage of development
that can be characterized by the statement "I am what I learn" (Markus and Nurius, 1984). The child's interest in learning results in a "sense of industry." (A lack
of interest in learning may produce a "sense of inferiority.") A sense of industry
refers to the *competence* gained in mastering learning tasks and being able to cooperate with others.
- Jean Piaget (1952) characterized middle childhood as a period of cognitive development when thinking becomes less egocentric and the child is, therefore,
better able to respond to other people.

Self-concept regulates, organizes, and controls the child's behavior.

Self-Concept Tasks

The process of self-concept development in middle childhood is influenced by how well the school-age child negotiates several tasks of middle childhood. Child success in completing these tasks helps to shape the content and functioning of the self-concept (Markus and Nurius, 1984).

• *Developing a stable and comprehensive understanding of self.* In middle childhood, the child is exploring and refining his or her understanding of the "territories of the self" (Goffman, 1959). During the preschool years, much of the child's self-understanding is based on **ascribed characteristics** (e.g., sex, name, sibling relationship such as brother or sister) or on one's own interpretation of individual abilities and characteristics. In middle childhood, self-understanding is expanded to include the thoughts of other people about the self. Many of the school-age child's efforts at self-concept construction involve working at **achieved roles** (e.g., student, girl scout, soccer team member, and so on) and at *belongingness* in peer relationships (Markus and Nurius, 1984).

• *Refining one's understanding about the social world.* The school-age child is able to understand how several social roles can be coordinated in a complex fashion. For example, a child can understand how an adult can simultaneously be a parent and someone's child at the same time. This understanding of the complex organization of social roles facilitates the development of the child's self-concept by familiarizing the child with the potential complexity of his or her own roles.

In addition, the school-age child interacts more extensively than preschool children with peers who may not always share his or her values or perspectives. This peer experience enables children to understand the strengths and weaknesses of their own values. Recognition of such differences is important for the development of self-concept, including emotional and moral development (Markus and Nurius, 1984).

• *Development of standards for one's behavior.* The standards and expectations that are incorporated into the child's developing self-concept are the basis for self-evaluation. The overall level of child self-esteem depends on the results of this evaluation process.

The development of moral values and behavior is a particularly significant outcome of the acquisition of behavioral standards. Moral development in middle childhood hinges on the ability of the child to distinguish the viewpoint of the self

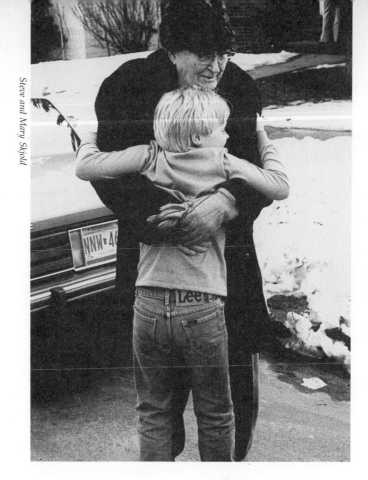

A child can understand how an adult can be a parent and someone else's child at the same time.

from the viewpoint of others and to carefully use his or her own viewpoint to reach conclusions about values (Higgins, 1981; Markus and Nurius, 1984; Flavell, 1985).

• *Development of strategies for controlling one's behavior.* As the school-age child increasingly experiences involvement in his or her social world, there is an accompanying need for the child to control his or her behavior. The school-age child who *now is exercising motives for mastery over the environment* must also demonstrate *impulse control.* In addition, the potentially conflicting expectations of parents, teachers, and peers require effective coping skills, including impulse control. In summary, school-age children need to develop self-control skills that enable them to monitor their behavior so it can conform to both personal and social expectations. One of the most common indicators of success in this area is the child's ability to realistically accept (and assign) responsibility or blame for specific actions (Markus and Nurius, 1984).

As school-age children progress through these various self-concept tasks, it is important to keep in mind that they do so at varying rates and in varying situations or contexts. Obviously, the school-age child who lives in the inner city experiences a situation that is different from the contexts experienced by the rural or suburban child. At any rate, the resulting knowledge that the school-age child accumulates from the activities associated with these self-concept tasks is extraordinarily important. Such self-knowledge includes information about self-capacities in relation to the characteristics of one's unique environment as well as proposed plans and strategies for meeting future personal and social needs. Thus, the development of the self-concept system reflects *both* the prior or *historical experience* of the child *and* a *future-oriented* component of plans and strategies (Markus and Nurius, 1984).

Regulation of Behavior

The regulation of behavior involves the interdependence or mutual coordination of both the *self system*, or personal factors (e.g., child's needs, desires, goals, skills, or knowledge), and the *social system*, or situational factors (e.g. the expectations, desires, or needs of others). According to Hazel Markus and Paula Nurius, such regulation is really **coregulation**.

> When . . . coregulation occurs, behavior does not seem to be regulated by the social situation, nor does it seem to be personally determined or completely controlled by individual needs and desires. Rather, coregulation stems from internalized norms and values—those that were originally imposed on the child by the social system but that have since been incorporated into the child's self-system and are now maintained by individual desires and goals. When this occurs, the self-system and the social system can be seen as interdependent. (1984, p. 150)

As children grow and mature, their socialization experience creates an increasing similarity or overlap between self-system factors and social system factors. As a consequence, children's own needs and goals become increasingly the same as those of society. For example, children begin to follow rules and to honor parental requests for sharing toys or doing homework because they themselves desire to do so. This increasing interdependence and similarity between the self system and the social system is the process of *coregulation*.

The Structure of the Self-Concept: Social Cognition

Social cognition is the way we form concepts about the social world (Flavell, 1985). Specifically, social cognition has to do with how we view ourselves *(self-knowledge)* and how we view the emotions, thoughts, and viewpoints of others *(role taking)*. Historically, studies of children's thinking focused largely on the child's understanding of the nonsocial world. This situation has changed as a considerable amount of interest and research have focused on children's understanding of their social world. The study of the development of social cognition is important because it helps us to understand how children view other people. These social conceptualizations, in turn, are an important influence on how children relate to others. In summary, social cognition is a kind of conceptual "system" that may organize and determine social relationships.

> *DEFINITIONS*
>
> **Social cognition.** Social cognition refers to the ability of the child to understand feelings, thoughts, or intentions of the self (self-knowledge) and others (role taking).
>
> **Role taking.** Role taking is the ability to assume the perspective of others and to understand their feelings and thoughts.

Self-Knowledge

The question "Who am I?" is one that human beings come to grips with throughout the lifespan. As we pointed out in our discussion of infancy and the preschool years (see Chapters 8 and 11), this important question of selfhood is addressed even in those early periods of development. The infant's recognition of the distinction between "self" and "other" and the young child's understanding of the permanence of self are examples of how the question "Who am I?" is resolved. For the most part, children have already developed an emerging "personality" with individual styles of coping with the world by about age two. The existence of such a personality pattern does not imply that the child is consciously aware of such a pattern (Flavell, 1985).

The development of conscious awareness of self seems to follow a pattern that is related to the child's level of cognitive development (Alschuler and Weinstein, 1976). Alschuler and Weinstein examined the conscious awareness of individuals ranging from preschoolers through adolescents. They asked their subjects to describe a memorable experience, including all relevant actions, thoughts, and feelings. Their analysis yielded four levels of self-knowledge (see Table 14.1):

- *Stage 1* (elemental)—includes the preschool years, with their emphasis on images of physical events, sometimes out of order.
- *Stage 2* (situational)—includes the beginning of the concrete operational stage of thinking as story images and symbols become more organized and more interpretive (less bound by the actual appearance of events).
- *Stage 3* (patterned)—involves more developed concrete operational thinking in which subjects see themselves as consistent across many situations.
- *Stage 4* (process)—requires the use of formal operations, which typically does not occur until adolescence.

SELF-DESCRIPTION. One way for us to get a better understanding of changes in the context of the self-concept is to examine how children describe themselves. The general pattern of development of self-description is that as a child grows older, his or her conception of the self moves from specific *concrete* descriptors (eye color, height, and so on) to increasingly *abstract* depictions (Lively and Bromley, 1973; Bannister and Agnew, 1977; Montemayor and Eisen, 1977; Rosenberg, 1979). For example, preschool children typically describe themselves in *concrete* terms by referring to their physical appearance, to their toys, to obvious characteristics of their home residence, and so on. A young child might say, "My name is Bruce, I have brown eyes, I'm 6 years old, I have 7 people in my family" (Montemayor and Eisen, 1977). On the other hand, an adolescent girl might describe herself as follows: "I am a human being, I am a girl, I am an individual" (Montemayor and Eisen, 1977). It is important to note, of course, that this transition from concrete to abstract thinking occurs during middle childhood (in particular, during later middle childhood).

It is not clear exactly how a child moves from the concrete self-concept of the preschooler to the abstract, more adult-like self-concept of the adolescent. However, some new patterns of thinking about the self appear to emerge as early as six or seven years of age. At that time, there is evidence that the child can make the distinction between a *subjective self* (how the child feels about himself or herself) and an *objective self* (how others feel about the child) (Selman, 1980). According to

TABLE 14.1
Alschuler and Weinstein's Levels of Self-Knowledge

STAGE 1: ELEMENTAL STAGE
Subjects in this stage recount the memorable experience in a fragmented, list-like fashion. Events are incomplete and show little continuity. They are overt, external, and observable rather than subjective. There are no metasituational statements—that is, no statements that summarize several situations. The self in this story has to be inferred by the listener instead of being disclosed by the speaker. For example, "I was bit by a dog. The dog was big. It was raining. I slipped down."

STAGE 2: SITUATIONAL STAGE
Subjects begin to describe subjective states, but the discussion seldom goes beyond the particular situation. The various parts of the recollected experience are connected in a causal chain. There are some attempts to define the general tone of the situation, but there is still no attempt to relate the situation to other situations. The subjects stay within one time frame rather than see consistency of self across past situations. The descriptions of internal states are rather global and lacking in nuances. For example, "I was bit by a dog. I screamed when he bit me. I think I was mad and afraid. It was a rather bad day. It upset me for a long time afterward."

STAGE 3: PATTERNED STAGE
Subjects begin to see themselves as consistent across situations. True hypotheses about self form and are tested against past experiences (for example, "I guess I must have problems with authority"). The person begins to see a pattern to his or her social behavior. The subject makes predictive statements about how he or she would probably react in a given situation, knowing what he or she knows about himself or herself. Situations are defined abstractly ("things that threaten me") rather than physically ("things that are hot"). Behavior is described dispositionally ("I have a tendency to get overly involved with members of the opposite sex") rather than overtly ("I try to kiss all the girls").

STAGE 4: PROCESS STAGE
Subjects do more than describe their personality patterns. They also have an awareness of how they deal with their internal states. Subjects can describe the process by which they control and modify their feelings and moods ("I try to make my guilt work positively by setting realistic deadlines and then feeling anxious if it looks like I'm not meeting those deadlines"). The awareness of how "self directs self" is explicit, conscious. In the previous stage generalized patterns are merely described, but there is no evidence that the self is seen as a possible agent in the change itself. In this stage the self is seen as proactive in influencing internal states ("I began to give myself permission to express my true feelings").[1]

[1]This view of self-awareness in terms of stage is supported by the research of Peevers and Secord (1973) and Livesley and Bromley (1973), who identified similar stages in the verbal descriptions subjects gave of friends, someone they disliked, and themselves.

From Alschuler and Weinstein, 1976.

Robert Selman (1980), one sign that the school-age child has made such a distinction is his or her understanding of the possibility of *self-deception*. By eight years of age, children understand that it is entirely possible to tell oneself (i.e., think to oneself) that one course of action is appropriate while in reality doing something quite different (Selman, 1980). An example is the child who tells himself that he shouldn't be having cookies before dinner and yet is somehow convinced by a sibling to have some cookies twenty minutes before dinner.

Furthermore, there is evidence that school-age children have a fairly well-organized system of self-understanding. This system of self-understanding includes four dimensions of self, as follows (Damon and Hart, 1982) (see Fig. 14.2):

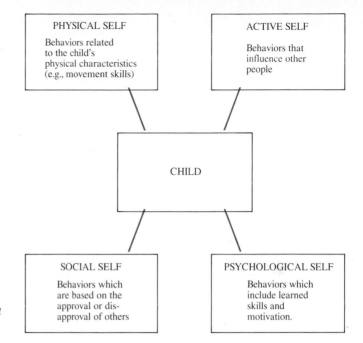

FIGURE 14.2

The system of self-understanding in middle childhood includes four dimensions of self. Based on Damon and Hart, 1982.

- *The physical self*, which includes behavior related to child physical characteristics (e.g., movement skills).
- *The active self*, which includes skills that influence other people.
- *The social self*, which includes activities based on the approval or disapproval of others.
- *The psychological self*, which includes knowledge, motivation, and learned skills.

It is commonly assumed that these four senses of self are the basis for school-age children's sense of competence. Furthermore, it is assumed that adult feelings of

One dimension of self-understanding is the physical self, *or behaviors related to the child's physical characteristics.*

self-confidence can be related to experiences of success or failure in middle childhood. For example, there is some evidence that one's enduring sense of academic self-confidence is related to elementary school experiences (Higgins and Eccles, 1983). Likewise, there is evidence that the school-age child's sense of self-esteem is related more to academic experiences than to nonacademic activities, such that success in the latter may not compensate for failure in the former (Epps and Smith, 1984).

Other general findings with reference to self-understanding in middle childhood include the following:

* By age eight, children appear to be quite capable of developing self-knowledge by making a wide variety of social comparisons (McGuire and McGuire, 1982). Children younger than seven years may describe their performance on a given task with an *absolute* judgment indicating how well they think they did (e.g., "I did it right"). On the other hand, older children are also able to evaluate their performance in relation to that of other children (Livesly and Bromley, 1973; Ruble, 1985).
* The school-age child becomes increasingly capable of *self-criticism*, which is linked to improved self-control and to a *temporary* drop in self-esteem (due to increasing use of self-criticism) (Markus and Nurius, 1984).

SELF-UNDERSTANDING AND INFORMATION PROCESSING.   Research on self-understanding suggests that the self-concept has several important characteristics, as follows (Markus, 1977, 1980; Markus and Nurius, 1984):

* The self-concept is an *organized set of cognitive structures* or *schemas*.
* The self-concept is *multifaceted* (not unitary).
* Many components of the self-concept are *continually changing*.
* The self-concept is an *active* and *dynamic* structure that relates the individual to his or her social environment.

> DEFINITION
>
> **Self schemas.** These are knowledge structures that are the result of prior experience. They guide and organize the individual's processing of information about the self and social experiences.

The self-concept characteristics are relevant to the relationship between self-understanding and information processing. For example, the child's processing of information is directly related to a type of cognitive structure or schema, called the *self schema*. Using these self-schemas, it is thought that children actively develop generalizations about themselves (e.g., "I am aggressive" or "I like most people") (Markus and Nurius, 1984). Ordinarily, self schemas develop in relation to those parts of the self-concept that become important to the individual as a result of his or her specific concerns, investment of time, and so on. When children use their self schemas for the processing of information in a specific area of concern, they display the following characteristics (Markus and Sentis, 1982; Markus and Nurius, 1984):

* They are *efficient information processors*, making self-evaluations with relative certainty.
* They have *better memory* for information relevant to the specific domain of concern than for other areas of lesser interest.

- They can *predict future behavior* or what they would like to do with reference to the specific domain of interest.
- They can effectively *evaluate new information* in terms of a specific domain of interest.

Self schemas and their related information-processing characteristics are of extraordinary importance in middle childhood. That is, many important self schemas are developed, including those relating to popularity with peers, athletic ability, and academic ability. These self schemas include not only a representation of self based on past experience, but a projection of a future/possible self, including goals and plans (Markus and Nurius, 1984).

Role Taking

Role taking refers to the development of the cognitive skills that are necessary for the child to take the perspective of others and to understand their thoughts and feelings (Flavell, 1985). There is evidence that important changes occur in role-taking ability during middle childhood. The four-to-six-year-old child does not fully realize that each person has his or her own thoughts and feelings, which serve as a basis for action (Flavell, 1985). Between six and eight years, the child's egocentric perspective lessens. By age six, the child usually can infer that another person may have different perceptions of the same event. In addition, the six-year-old realizes that other people may act on the basis of personal thoughts or feelings. Furthermore, by this age the child can understand whether another person's actions are accidental or intended (Shantz, 1983).

DEVELOPMENT OF ROLE-TAKING SKILLS. Selman (1980) has suggested that children gradually become more skillful at role taking. In order to study the progression of role taking, Selman asked children to respond to several interpersonal dilemmas including the following:

> Holly is an 8-year-old girl who likes to climb trees. She is the best tree climber in the neighborhood. One day while climbing down from a tall tree, she falls . . . but does not hurt herself. Her father sees her fall. He is upset and asks her to promise not to climb trees any more. Holly promises.
> Later that day, Holly and her friends meet Shawn. Shawn's kitten is caught in a tree and can't get down. Something has to be done right away or the kitten may fall. Holly is the only one who climbs trees well enough to reach the kitten and get it down but she remembers her promise to her father. (Selman, 1976, p. 302)

After the children had heard the dilemma, they were asked the following questions:

- Does Holly know how Shawn feels about the kitten?
- What will Holly's father think when he discovers that she has climbed the tree?
- What does Holly think will happen to her if her father finds out that she has climbed the tree?

Based on their answers to these questions, Selman suggested that children move through a progression of stages (Selman, 1980; Gurucharri and Selman, 1982) (see Table 14.2). Furthermore, these stages of role taking are closely related to Piaget's

Table 14.2
The Stages of Role Taking

Stage	Typical Responses to the "Holly" Dilemma
0. Egocentric or undifferentiated perspective (roughly 3 to 6 years) Children are unaware of any perspective other than their own. They assume that whatever they feel is right for Holly to do will be agreed on by others.	Children often assume that Holly will save the kitten. When asked how Holly's father will react to her transgression, these children think he will be "happy because he likes kittens." In other words, these children like kittens themselves, and they assume that Holly and her father also like kittens. They do not recognize that another person's viewpoint may differ from their own.
1. Social-informational role taking (roughly 6 to 8 years) Children now recognize that people can have perspectives that differ from their own but believe that this happens *only* because these individuals have received different information. The child is still unable to think about the thinking of others and know in advance how others will react to an event.	When asked whether Holly's father will be angry because she climbed the tree, the child may say, "If he didn't know why she climbed the tree, he would be angry. But if he knew why she did it, he would realize that she had a good reason." Thus, the child is saying that if both parties have exactly the same information, they will reach the same conclusion.
2. Self-reflective role taking (roughly 8 to 10 years) Children now know that their own and others' points of view may conflict even if they have received the same information. They are now able to consider the other person's viewpoint. They also recognize that the other person can put himself or herself in their shoes, so that they are now able to anticipate the person's reactions to their behavior. However, the child cannot consider his or her own perspective and that of another person at the same time.	If asked whether Holly will climb the tree, the child might say, "Yes. She knows that her father will understand why she did it." In so doing, the child is focusing on the father's consideration of Holly's perspective. But if asked whether the father would want Holly to climb the tree, the child usually says no, thereby indicating that he or she is now assuming the father's perspective and considering the father's concern for Holly's safety.
3. Mutual role taking (roughly 10 to 12 years) The child can now simultaneously consider his or her own and another person's points of view and recognize that the other person can do the same. At this point, each party can put the self in the other's place and view the self from that vantage point before deciding how to react. The child can also assume the perspective of a disinterested third party and anticipate how each participant (self and other) will react to the viewpoint of his or her partner.	At this stage, a child might describe the outcome of the "Holly" dilemma by taking the perspective of a disinterested third party and indicating that he or she knows that both Holly and her father are thinking about what each other is thinking. For example, one child remarked: "Holly wanted to get the kitten because she likes kittens, but she knew that she wasn't supposed to climb trees. Holly's father knew that Holly had been told not to climb trees, but he couldn't have known about [the kitten]. He'd probably punish her anyway just to enforce his rule."

TABLE 14.2
(Continued)

STAGE	TYPICAL RESPONSES TO THE "HOLLY" DILEMMA
4. Social and conventional system role taking (roughly 12 to 15 and older) The young adolescent now attempts to understand another person's perspective by comparing it with that of the social system in which he or she operates (that is, the view of the "generalized other"). In other words, the adolescent expects others to consider and typically assume perspectives on events that most people in their social group would take.	A Stage 4 adolescent might think that Holly's father would become angry and punish her for climbing the tree because fathers generally punish children who disobey. However, adolescents sometimes recognize that other people are nontraditional or may have a personal viewpoint quite discrepant from that of the "generalized other." If so, the subject might say the reaction of Holly's father will depend on the extent to which he is unlike other fathers and does not value absolute obedience.

Adapted from Selman, 1976.

stages of cognitive development (Keating and Clark, 1980) (see Table 14.3). This may be considered as additional evidence for the sequential nature of Selman's role-taking stages.

FAMILY INFLUENCE AS A ROLE-TAKING CONTEXT.   There is some evidence that parental child-rearing practices that stress the feelings or intentions of others and emphasize interpersonal relationships are related to role-taking skills (Maccoby and Martin, 1983). For example, parents who use such statements as "Your sister will feel unhappy if you don't stop teasing her" (rather than simply demanding that the child stop) are more likely to have children who can take the perspective of another and subsequently exhibit helping responses. Furthermore, there is evidence that children whose parents expect them to act in a mature fashion are more likely to demonstrate role-taking skills and empathy with others (Radke-Yarrow, Zahn-Waxler, and Chapman, 1983).

TABLE 14.3
Percentages of Children at Each Role-taking Stage in Relation to Their Piagetian Cognitive Stage

PIAGET'S STAGE	ROLE-TAKING STAGE				
	0 EGOCENTRIC	1 SOCIAL-INFORMATIONAL	2 SELF-REFLECTIVE	3 MUTUAL	4 SOCIAL SYSTEMS
Concrete operations	0	14	32	50	4
Transitional (late concrete)	1	3	42	43	10
Early formal operations	0	6	6	65	24
Consolidated formal operations	0	12[a]	0	38	50

[a]Since only eight consolidated formal operators were found in the sample, this figure of 12 percent represents only one subject.
From Keating and Clark, 1980, pp. 23–30.

The Function of the Self-Concept: Acquisition of Self-Control

In addition to self-understanding (or the *content* of self-concept), a second important feature of the development of the self in middle childhood includes *self-regulation* (or the *function* of the self-concept). One of the major responsibilities of both parents and teachers is to ensure that children are capable of controlling their own behavior. Children must be able to exercise control over their aggressive impulses, regulate the expression of emotions, delay immediate gratification (to facilitate attainment of long-term goals), and so on.

> *DEFINITION*
>
> **Self-regulation.** This is the *function* of the self-concept which includes several possible components such as self-control, self-monitoring, self-reinforcement, and self-evaluation. Self-regulation is a continuous or dynamic *process* rather than a single state or behavior (Markus and Nurius, 1984).

How do parents, teachers, and the other significant adults in a child's life accomplish the important responsibility of supporting the development of child self-control? In part, this is done through the broad process of socialization. That is, parents, teachers, and others instill in the child basic values, beliefs, and attitudes of society. This process of socialization is judged to be successful when the child internalizes these values, beliefs, and behavioral standards and demonstrates them independent of adult supervision.

A Sense of Control: Two Dimensions

The concept of control has two distinct aspects, as follows:

* **Self-control**, or control over one's own behavior.
* **Locus of control** (sometimes called a sense of personal efficacy or a sense of personal agency), which refers to one's control over the outside world. Those individuals who believe that their own actions primarily determine their fate (i.e., they feel personally responsible for their own success or failure) are said to have an *internal locus of control*. Those individuals who feel powerless in determining what happens to them (i.e., they do not feel personally responsible for their success or failure) are said to have an *external locus of control*.

Both types of control are related and both have been shown to be primary factors in the social and personal development of the child.

SELF-CONTROL. One of the most comprehensive studies of children's personality development and self-control was initiated in 1968 by Jeanne and Jack Block (1980). They began their study with 130 three-year-olds, who were followed until they were eleven years old. Each child was given a comprehensive battery of psychological tests at ages three, four, five, seven, and eleven. The findings of the study provide valuable information about individual differences and the stability of personality characteristics over time, including the *ego*. In psychoanalytic theory, the ego is the personality structure that orients the individual to reality by developing plans for the expression of feelings or emotions in a constructive way (i.e., in a way that will jeopardize neither society nor the individual). Using this concept of ego, the Blocks derived two constructs which they thought were at the heart of ego functioning: *ego control* and *ego resiliency*.

> *DEFINITIONS*
>
> **Ego.** According to psychoanalytic theory, the ego is the group of personality structures that help the individual relate to reality (i.e., what is happening in the person's actual experiential world). Specifically, the function of the ego is to evaluate the relationship between the *wishes* and the *feelings* of the individual and *social reality*. In practice, this means that the ego may control impulses, delay gratification, and/or develop socially acceptable modes of expressing feelings.
>
> **Ego control.** According to Block and Block (1980), ego control is "the operating characteristic of an individual with regard to the expression or containment of impulses, feelings, and desires". It can be viewed as a continuum going from *overcontrol* at one extreme to *undercontrol* at the other.
>
> **Ego resiliency.** According to Block and Block (1980), ego resiliency is a "resourceful adaptation to changing life situations". This means that the ego-resilient individual can be highly prepared or highly spontaneous, as a given situation requires.

Block and Block (1980) found that both ego control and ego resiliency when measured at age three were related to important aspects of social development at seven years of age. For example, children who were very low on ego control (undercontrollers) at age three were more likely at age seven to be highly active children who tended to be more assertive, more aggressive, less compliant, and less inhibited than children who were very high on ego control (overcontrollers) at age three. These differences appeared to be consistent from age three through seven years of age (Buss, Block, and Block, 1980). Other findings include the following (Block and Block, 1980):

• *Undercontrollers* (those low on ego control) at age three were later found to be more "energetic, curious, restless, expressive of impulse . . . less constricted and less relaxed" than *overcontrollers* (those high on ego control).
• Children who were undercontrollers were aware of their distinguishing personality characteristics by age seven.
• Three-year-old *undercontrollers* were more likely than *overcontrollers* to engage in later negative interpersonal behaviors such as aggression, teasing, or manipulativeness.
• Three-year-old *overcontrollers* were more likely than *undercontrollers* to be shy at later ages.
• Those three-year-olds who were assessed as *high in ego resiliency* were more likely than those *low in ego resiliency* to later display such positive interpersonal behaviors as empathy and responsiveness. Those children who were high in ego resiliency were later found to be "able to recoup after stress, . . . [and to be] less anxious, . . . [more] tolerant of ambiguity, and less likely . . . to withdraw under stress."
• The best combination at three years of age was to be high in *both* ego control and ego resiliency. According to Block and Block (1980), this combination was particularly adaptive, later producing individuals who demonstrated "a high de-

gree of socialization that fits well, a relative absence of anxiety and intimidation in reacting to and acting on the world".

These findings suggest that early differences in ego control and ego resiliency have long term consequences for children's personal and social development. These early differences in personality appear to derive from both early differences in child temperament and differences in home environment (Block and Block, 1980). According to Block and Block (1980), undercontrollers typically come from families that are conflict-ridden and make few demands of the child. On the other hand, overcontrollers tend to come from families that overemphasize order and structure. Ego-resilient children come from families that are loving, competent, communicative, and philosophically/morally oriented. Nonresilience is fostered in families that are marked by conflict and that have little philosophical/moral concerns (Block and Block, 1980).

LOCUS OF CONTROL.   In addition to learning to control one's feelings and emotions, a second important process is one's sense of control over external circumstances. This process is frequently called one's *locus of control.* As indicated above, there are two types of locus of control.

An internal locus of control in children is often associated with a high level of self-esteem, whereas a low level of self-esteem is often related to an external locus of control (Rosenberg, 1979). In addition, it has been suggested that a sense of personal control (i.e., an internal locus of control) is an essential aspect of a child's level of self-esteem (Damon and Hart, 1982). For example, there is evidence that the feelings of powerlessness that accompany an external locus of control may produce increased feelings of emotional depression and isolation (Rotter, 1966; Garber and Seligman, 1980).

Furthermore, an internal locus of control is based on the expectation that the world is responsive to one's actions. However, children who have experienced a lengthy history of nonresponsiveness from people and events may develop an external locus of control, or what has been called a sense of **learned helplessness** (Seligman, 1975; Garber and Seligman, 1980). (See Chapter 12.) In other words, they come to view themselves as incompetent or ineffectual in situations where they "believe" they have no power to influence outcomes. Unfortunately, these children learn to act helpless in situations where they could possibly affect an outcome. The world of the school-age child can appear nonresponsive for several reasons, including the following:

· The indifference of parents.
· The hostility of peers.
· The uncaring atmosphere of a school.
· The suppressive and deadening experience of poverty.

It is important to recognize that most parents, peers, and school officials are, to some extent, both sensitive and responsive to the behaviors of children.

Where children have previously developed an external locus of control, there is some evidence that this situation can be reversed. In one study, children who had failed on a school test were encouraged to think that their failures were *under their control* (Dweck et al., 1978). The study involved three similar groups of children who were given difficult mathematics problems. Each group failed to get the correct answers. However, the groups differed in the feedback they received about their problem solving:

• *Group 1—Induced helplessness.* This group was told that they did poorly, with the implication that their intellectual skills were not up to the task.
• *Group 2—Induced competence.* This group was told that they had not prepared sufficiently, that they had not paid enough attention in class, or that their papers were too messy. The *implication* of their feedback was that the reason for their failure was that *they had not tried hard enough.*
• *Group 3—Results only, no causal implications.* This group was simply given their results (i.e., number of problems wrong) with no suggestions or cues about the cause of their problem-solving outcomes.

When all three groups were again given the opportunity to solve mathematics problems (this time, the problems were only moderately difficult), children in Group 2 (induced competence) did the best of all the groups. Group 1 (induced helplessness) did the worst, becoming apathetic and losing interest in problem solving.

The results of this experiment suggest that children who continuously fail in the school setting may have *learned* to do so. In other words, they have learned to attribute their failures to factors outside their own abilities (Dweck et al., 1978). There is some evidence that teachers may contribute to this sense of learned helplessness through both their overt (explicit) and covert (implicit) communication to students (Dweck et al., 1978). For example, some teachers may assume that girls tend to apply themselves more to school tasks than boys do. Therefore, girls' failure might be attributed to their lack of intellectual skill or competence. On the other hand, boys' lack of success is, from this perspective, assumed to be the result of their lack of attention, sloppiness, fooling around, lack of interest, or other *motivational* rather than *intellectual* shortcomings. It is of course possible that such sexist treatment of female students—whether by male or female teachers—can lead to an unwarranted sense of learned helplessness.

Teaching Self-Control

Thus far in our discussion of self-control we have indicated the important role of significant adults (e.g., parents or teachers) in the child's development of self-control. In this section we examine some of the common modes of teaching self-control.

CONSEQUENCES OF BEHAVIOR.   One of the most common opportunities for the child to experience the consequences of his or her behavior is during a disciplinary encounter (between adult and child). Parents and teachers frequently rely on discouraging (or punishing) undesirable behaviors and encouraging desirable ones (reward).

Punishment as a technique of socialization has been criticized for several reasons, including the following:

• *Punishment may produce undesirable side effects.* While it may suppress certain undesirable child behaviors, its effects may broadly generalize to incorporate unintended outcomes. For example, the child who is harshly disciplined by a teacher for chewing gum in class *might* later avoid the teacher as well as avoid chewing gum in class.
• *The use of punishment by parents presents a potentially undesirable model for children.* Specifically, parents who use punishment exact compliance from the child based

on the *parent's superior power* (i.e., physical, psychological, or material power). The lesson taught to the child, then, may be that one gains compliance from others based on one's *greater strength or power* (and not necessarily on the intellectual or moral authority of one's case). There is evidence that children will use punitive techniques to gain the compliance of peers if, in fact, such punitive techniques have been used on them by significant adults (Grusec and Mills, 1982). For example, when young chldren were taught by an adult to play a game that included a rule that mistakes were subject to a monetary fine, the children treated their peers in the same punitive fashion when later playing the same game (Gelfand et al., 1974). In addition, there is consistent and shocking evidence that the children of abusive parents grow up to be abusive parents themselves (Grusec and Mills, 1982).

In spite of the negative evidence and concerns about punishment as a socialization technique, parents and others continue to rely rather extensively on its use for eliminating some undesirable child behaviors. For example, in one study of middle-class mothers of four-to seven-year-old children, 95 percent reported using some form of punishment (for example, withdrawing privileges, spanking, hitting, or verbal statements). However, there is some evidence that *moderate levels of punishment,* where the relationship between the undesirable behavior and the punishment is clear, do not lead to unwanted side effects (e.g., reduction in level of child self-esteem or the unwanted suppression of related behaviors). Children who are punished do not avoid the adult who does the punishing if that adult is *also* associated with positive experiences (Walters and Grusec, 1977). In addition to the use of punishment, parents and other adults also employ positive reinforcement or *reward* as a way of encouraging the development of self-control. This mode of parent discipline usually takes the form of ignoring undesirable child behaviors (rather than using punishment) and rewarding desirable or appropriate behaviors. Although there is considerable evidence that reward does indeed increase the later occurrence of such reinforced behavior, there are some limitations with the *exclusive* use of reward:

• There is no guarantee that undesirable behaviors (which are ignored by the adult) will disappear simply because they are ignored while other more desirable behaviors are rewarded. For example, if children practice some undesirable behaviors that are *inherently enjoyable or satisfying to them* (for example, eating cookies and candies beyond a stated limit, talking to friends in the classroom, and so on), simply ignoring undesirable behaviors and rewarding others may not eliminate the undesirable behaviors. Some form of mild or moderate punishment (with a clearly specified relationship between the undesirable behavior and the punishment) may be necessary.
• When a desirable behavior is no longer followed by a reward, it may cease, particularly if it is not inherently satisfying. Likewise, if an undesirable behavior is no longer followed by some punishment, it may continue (particularly if it is inherently enjoyable). Since it would be unrealistic or impossible for parents or other adults to be around to consistently administer rewards and punishments, there is a need for parents to look to other techniques for developing child self-control that can complement reward and punishment.

REASONING.   There is evidence that adults who reason with children are particularly successful in developing self-control in children (Grusec and Mills, 1982). Specifically, adults who use **other-oriented induction** (making children aware of the consequences of their behavior on others) sensitize their children to the impact of their behavior on others. The knowledge that a child has harmed—physically or psychologically—another person is an inescapable reality (i.e., the child cannot avoid the feelings of guilt and/or anxiety that result) and is, therefore, a strong motivator for proper behavior and self-control. In fact, it is argued that *other-oriented induction* is a stronger motivational force for self-control than punishment is because punishment can be avoided, whereas guilt (resulting from other-oriented induction) is unavoidable and difficult to handle emotionally.

There is evidence that mothers of children who are self-controlled, energetic, socially responsible, and achievement-oriented use *both reasoning* (for example, *other-oriented induction*) *and* **power assertion** (e.g., punishment such as withdrawal of privileges, spanking, or verbal censure) to gain compliance from their children (Baumrind, 1973). Furthermore, those adults who are successful in encouraging the development of self-control in children appear to rely on reasoning, backed up with power-assertion techniques (for example, moderate threats) (Zahn-Waxler, Radke-Yarrow, and King, 1979; Grusec and Kuczynski, 1980). There are several reasons that *successful socialization involves a combination of reasoning with moderate punishment:*

• Children are more likely to understand the fairness of appropriate levels of punishment *if* they are provided with the reasons (for example, other-oriented induction) that they should comply (Grusec and Mills, 1982).
• *Reasoning* provides the child with *general* rules for guiding future behavior (for example, "Be careful not to say anything insulting or you will hurt the feelings of others"), whereas *punishment* clarifies what will happen in a *specific* situation (for example, "If you go across the street without asking my permission, I will not take you to the movie"). This combination of *general rules* (reasoning) and *specificity* (punishment) allows the adult to stress reasoning as the most important basis for child self-control, thus providing the child with a more useful and acceptable *model* than punishment alone for gaining the compliance of others.

THE ATTRIBUTIONAL APPROACH.   In most episodes of human behavior, individuals search for or confirm the *reasons* for their behavior, as well as the behavior of others. At its most basic level, behavior can be attributed to *external* factors (e.g., "I did not talk in class because my teacher would have punished me if I did") or to *internal* factors (e.g., "I did not talk in the classroom because I am a good student"). School-age children who attribute their behavior to *internal* factors (considering themselves to be good students) are more likely (than those who attribute their behavior to external or situational factors) to exercise self-control in future circumstances on an independent basis, without adult surveillance. On the other hand, children who attribute their behavior to external factors (for example, threat of punishment) are much less likely (than internals) to exercise self-control independent of adult supervision and threat of punishment (Grusec and Mills, 1982). There is evidence that children who believe they have morally desirable characteristics (an internal locus of control) experience a high level of *self-criticism* when they do not live up to their own ideals. In order to *avoid* the pangs of this self-criticism, self-control and moral behavior may become a personal necessity (Perry et al., 1980).

Given the significant contribution of an internal locus of control to the child's development of self-control, the role of parents and other adults in helping the child develop internal attribution assumes considerable significance. Several parental/adult techniques have proved particularly useful:

• *Character attribution.* There is evidence that when parents or other adults attribute specific characteristics to a child, the child's behavior changes in accord with the attributions (Miller, Brickman, and Bolen, 1975; Jensen and Moore, 1977; Grusec and Mills, 1982; Grusec and Redler, 1980). The attribution of a given characteristic to a child by an adult appears to produce a change in the child's behavior. For example, when a parent uses an actual instance of polite behavior by a child as a basis for attributing that behavior to the child (e.g., "Johnny, you're really a polite person"), such an attribution may enhance that characteristic.

• *Assignment of responsibility.* Children who are made responsible for the training of other children appear to demonstrate improved self-control as well as positive changes in their moral perspective (Parke, 1974; Toner, Moore, and Ashley, 1978). In one study, six- and seven-year-old boys were told not to play with a set of toys. Some of the boys were videotaped as they avoided playing with the forbidden toys and were told that the videotape would be shown to other children as a training device (for teaching children appropriate behavior). In essence, this group was made to feel *responsible* for the later training of other children. A second group of boys was told that they would have been videotaped but the camera had "broken down" (the excuse given for not videotaping them) so that videotaping was not possible. At a later time, the boys in the responsibility-enhanced (videotaped) group demonstrated greater self-control in the face of temptation than the boys who had not been videotaped (Toner, Moore, and Ashley, 1978).

MODELING: ADULT EXAMPLES.   In addition to the consequences of behavior to the child—parent reasoning and the attribution of behavior—a powerful influence on the development of self-control is adult modeling. There is evidence that children will imitate models who exhibit self-control by also exhibiting self-control (Bussey and Perry, 1977; Grusec et al., 1979).

Moral Development

Moral development is one part of the total social development of the child. During the early years of childhood, it occurs, at first, in the family, and then the influences of the culture and the society are brought to bear as the child increasingly moves into peer and school circles. Throughout this transition, however, the family continues to be a primary influence. In this section, we examine the significant changes in moral development during the middle-childhood years.

What is meant by *moral development?* In simple terms, **morality** has been defined as "conscience," or a set of cultural-social rules for governing the appropriateness of social behavior that has been internalized by the individual (Kohlberg, 1976). Moral development, then, is the internalization and organization of these guiding principles over time. Moral development is directed toward the organization of priorities and values in social situations.

To be more specific, moral behavior is composed of four component parts (Rest, 1983):

1. *Interpreting the situation.* This means identifying the possible course of action in a given situation, as this potential behavior would affect the welfare of others.

With reference to this component, there is evidence for three important qualifications (Rest, 1983):

a. *Some people have difficulty interpreting what appear to be relatively simple situations* (in reality, the situations may be more complex than originally perceived). The well-publicized Kitty Genovese incident (see Chapter 11) in which a young girl was repeatedly assaulted and stabbed in the courtyard of her apartment building as 38 other residents looked on is a good example. Why didn't her fellow apartment dwellers help? Studies of the bystanders indicate that they had some difficulty interpreting the situation (Staub, 1978). For example, many thought that they were witnessing a simple lovers' quarrel and, therefore, they did not wish to become involved.

b. *There are striking differences among individuals in their awareness of the needs of other people.* According to Shalom Schwartz (1977), there are substantial differences in "the spontaneous tendency to attend to possible consequences of one's behavior for the welfare of others" (p. 243). For example, some people appear to be acutely aware of the moral implications of their own and others' behavior. On the other hand, some people become sensitive to the needs of others (or to the impact of their behavior on others) only with the most blatant or unmistakable signs of suffering.

c. *The ability to interpret situations increases with the child's age.* The ability to clarify a situation by making inferences about the motives, thoughts, or perceptions of others develops and improves throughout childhood (see the discussion of social cognition in this chapter). Therefore, the child's ability to understand the impact of his or her actions on the welfare of others would be *based* on such a knowledge of others (Rest, 1983; Shantz, 1983).

2. *Determining the appropriate moral course of action.* At this point, the individual is aware of several alternate courses of action, as well as how each of these potential actions will affect the welfare of others. The choice at hand is for the individual to determine what *ought* to be done in a given situation.

3. *Deciding what one will actually do.* The individual has already selected the morally appropriate course of action (i.e., what *ought* to be done) and must now decide what he or she will *actually* do. Typically, an individual will compare several possible outcomes of alternate courses of action (including what one *ought* to do). Each alternative could represent different underlying values and motives. Sometimes these choices not only are difficult but lead to infamous outcomes:

> Therefore, parallel to formulating a *moral* course of action, a person may be formulating courses of action oriented toward other values. Oftentimes, other values are so important to a person that they preempt or compromise moral values. For instance, John Dean writes in his book *Blind Ambition* that his activities as special counsel to President Nixon were motivated by his ambitions to succeed in the Nixon Administration and that questions of morality and justice were preempted by more pressing concerns. (Rest, 1983, p. 564)

There is evidence of similar phenomena operating in the lives of children. In one study, children were asked to determine in advance how ten candy bars *ought* to be divided up for other children as a reward for making bracelets (Damon, 1977). The children described various plans for candy distribution that were, in their judgment, fair and what *should* be done. However, when these children were actually given the ten candy bars to distribute, they did not follow their stated plans. Instead, they gave themselves an inordinately larger number of candy bars. Thus, in this specific study, it appears that the children's espoused moral positions did not take precedence over alternate positions of self-interest. Furthermore, there is additional evidence of this difference between determining what *ought* to be done and deciding what *actually* will be done (Sobesky, 1983).

4. *Implementing the chosen course of action.* This involves thinking through a plan of concrete behaviors for executing the chosen course of action, as well as having the perseverence, where necessary, to ensure accomplishment (Rest, 1983).

Piaget's Theory of Moral Development

Piaget believed that the child's progression in cognitive development (sensorimotor, preoperational, concrete operational, and formal operational stages) is *paralleled* by the child's moral development. Piaget suggested that mature morality involved both the child's *acceptance of social rules* and a concern for equality, reciprocity, and justice in human relationships. Piaget (1965) examined moral development in two ways:

- He investigated the change with age of children's conceptions of rules in such games as marbles.
- He examined children's judgments of transgressions by *telling them stories* and then asking them about the behavior of the characters in the stories.

THE STAGES OF MORAL DEVELOPMENT.   According to Piaget (1965) moral development evolves in an invariant sequence, as follows:

1. **Premoral period** *(birth to seven years of age).* The premoral period has two phases, which have their counterparts in the sensorimotor and the preoperational stages of cognitive development. The focus of the early phase of the premoral period is on the self—a highly egocentric self. For about the first one and a half to two years, the infant begins life fairly incapable of moral judgments or moral behavior. The child is bound by an eogcentrism of sensations, impulses, and generalized feelings. To a large extent, the sensorimotor infant is only beginning the process of differentiation between self and other. Therefore, all feeling (including moral emotion) is *centered* largely on the infant's body and actions.

The second, or later, phase of the premoral period is marked by a focus on the "permanent object" which the caretaker or the parent has come to be. The major characteristic of this phase is the shift from a focus on the *self* to a focus on the *authority* of that most prominent "permanent object," the parent or the caretaker. This emphasis on adult authority continues through the preoperational stage until about age seven. Much like the thinking during the preoperational period, this later phase of premoral thought is marked by moral feelings that are not "conserved" or generalized to all situations. For example, just as preoperational children cannot "conserve" in different situations, (e.g., when a quantity of water is poured into a different-shaped beaker), they cannot extend parental rules to new situations. For example, children may find it perfectly appropriate to tell the truth to their parents and lie to their peers (Piaget, 1965). Generally, however, Piaget refers to this second phase of the premoral period as a time of *moral absolutism.* Rules are ordinarily viewed as emanating from a parent or authority figure. Furthermore, any deviation from such rules will result in inevitable punishment or what Piaget called *immanent justice.* For example, young children may even think that accidents that befall them (getting a splinter in one's finger, falling down, and so on) after "lying to my father" are the punishments for a transgression.

Furthermore, Piaget suggests that children also evaluate actions in terms of their *consequences* rather than the intentions—good or bad—of the actor. Children entering middle childhood tend to judge actions and behavior (both their own and that of others) in terms of physical results, satisfaction of needs, or obedience to authority. For example, a child who breaks five cups while helping his father set the table may regard himself as having committed a greater offense than the child who breaks only one cup in the act of reaching for some forbidden candy. In other words, the greater the physical damage, the greater the crime. The child does not incorporate motivational or situational factors into moral decision making.

2. **Moral relationships based on mutual respect** *(ages eight to eleven)*. The obedience to authority of the previous period declines in favor of *autonomy* based on *mutual respect*. These moral feelings have their counterpart in the ability to conserve in the cognitive domain. In this period, the child moves from a focus on *authority* to a focus on *interactions* in *concrete* situations. For example, in the previous period, the child might share toys in the presence of his or her mother (in deference to the authority of his or her mother). In this new period, the child may note that other childen do not play with or like a child who does not share toys.

The child ultimately becomes able to "conserve" or generalize sharing behaviors to many situations. What has happened is that the child is now capable of *reversible operations.* In the toy-sharing example, the child who stops sharing and incurs the wrath of his or her playmate(s) can return (mentally) to the beginning of the play sequence, where sharing resulted in positive interaction. The ability to reverse thinking and return to a starting point helps the child to develop and extend the principle of reciprocity and sharing. Piaget suggested that such "reciprocal morality" is *autonomous*, primarily because it is no longer "dependent" on the relationship of the child to an authority figure (as in the previous stage). The morality of middle childhood depends on the *mental relationships* between peers on an equal, give-and-take basis in a *concrete situation* (Piaget, 1965).

Piaget refers to this stage as a period of developing or emerging **moral reciprocity.** In contrast to the period of moral absolutism (see the above discussion), the child's moral judgments are now characterized by the recognition of the following:

- Social rules are arbitrary arrangements that can be questioned, where necessary.
- Violations of rules are not always wrong.
- The feelings and viewpoints of others should be considered in evaluating their behavior.
- If there is to be punishment, the nature of the transgression (i.e., against people or property), the intentions of the actor, and the type of punishment (i.e., simple punitive retribution or requiring restitution on the part of the wrongdoer) all should be taken into account.

However, it is important to recognize that the focus on the *concrete* distinguishes the moral behavior of middle childhood from that of the adolescent and the adult. Because the child focuses on the real, the immediate, and the concrete, there is the possibility that the child may become *inflexible* in his or her moral judgments. Even though the individual in middle childhood is less egocentric than the premoral child, he or she is still dependent for both cognitive functioning and moral judgments on what he or she perceives. The "eye-for-an-eye" level of morality may still be popular in this stage. It is not until the later stages of moral development in adolescence and adulthood that the individual is able to take unique motivational and situational factors fully into account (e.g., "to temper justice with mercy").

3. **Moral relativity** (*ages eleven and twelve*). The relativity stage of moral development presumably begins sometime during the adolescent years, although, as we will see later, it is not certain that every human being attains this stage. With the attainment of *formal operational thinking*, the individual shifts from a focus on the *concrete* (centration) to a focus on the realistic application (taking all factors into account) of moral values and ideals to specific situations (a phase of moral development we discuss in more detail in Chapter 17).

AN EVALUATION OF PIAGET'S THEORY.   Although there is support for the general developmental order of Piaget's stages of moral development, recent research has raised several issues:

• There is some evidence that Piaget may have underestimated the cognitive skills of young children, particularly in judging the behavior and intentions of others (Nelson, 1980; Surber, 1982). For example, younger children may not have appre-

---

The Tale of the Babysitter

An example of the child's tendency to judge transgressions in terms of the unquestioned authority of the parent is the story of the babysitter. The following story also is an example of the research technique used by Piaget to assess levels of moral development in children. The story is told to two groups of children—a *premoral group* (birth to seven years of age) and a *transitional group* (eight to eleven years of age):

A baby-sitter arrives at the home of Mr. and Mrs. Walker. Mr. and Mrs. Walker say good-bye to their child, Jeffrey, and leave for a dinner engagement. Two hours later, the Walkers return home. Mr. Walker walks immediately through the front door and over to Jeffrey. He begins to spank his son.

So ends the story. These statements are the *only* facts given to the children. Piaget then asks the children in each experimental group to describe what happened. Specifically, why was the child spanked?
The responses of the children presumably indicate their level of moral development:

1. *The premoral children are rather sure that Jeffrey must have done something wrong.* Otherwise, why would he have been punished by his father? The implication, of course, is that parents are unerring authority figures who never make mistakes.
2. *The transitional children are much less certain about the appropriateness of the parental action.* Although some agree with the view of the premoral group,

a substantial number say that there just wasn't enough information given in the story for them to explain why Jeffrey was spanked. In other words, the transitional group is not as dependent on parental authority for defining moral behavior.

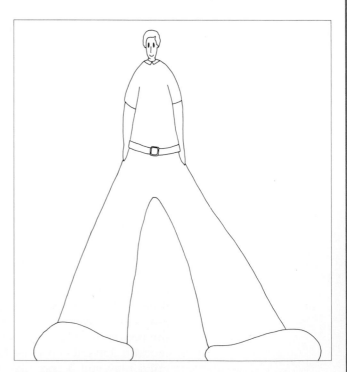

The All-Powerful, All-Knowing Authority Figure Known as the Parent.

ciated the intentions of the actors in the Piagetian stories simply because such information was not made clear or explicit to them while the consequences were (see box).

• Furthermore, there is emerging evidence with research using Piagetian stories that there is more to children's evaluation of others' behavior than simply the *intentions* of the actors or the *consequences* of their behavior (Grueneich, 1982). For example, many other factors may be involved including whether the consequences were physical or psychological, whether the actor was forced into doing something, whether the object of the action was a human being or an inanimate object, and so on.

Kohlberg's Theory of Moral Development

THE STAGES OF MORAL DEVELOPMENT.   Using Piaget's theories as a starting point, Lawrence Kohlberg (1968) described moral development in terms of three levels of moral thinking: *preconventional, conventional,* and *postconventional* (see Tables 14.4 and 14.5).

1. **Preconventional level.** The following are characteristic features of the preconventional level of moral thinking:

• The child defines wrong as "those things that I get punished for." Right is obeying the commands of authorities, such as teachers and parents.
• When moral judgment is fully developed at this level, the child defines right as whatever works out to his or her advantage.
• The criteria that a child uses to judge right and wrong are determined by his or her self-interest. Reasoning is concrete.
• Right, love, or kindness is something that one does.
• Rules are unchangeable commands from some higher authority. The understanding of rules is so limited that the application of them is very inconsistent.
• The child applies specific rules to specific situations.
• Right is what good people do.
• There are rules that govern the actions of the child's models.

During the first stage of this level (see Table 14.4), the child views adults as all-powerful and all-knowing authority figures and submits unquestioningly to them. During the second stage, "goodness" and "badness" refer to what does or does not satisfy one's needs. Although there may be some apparent instances of a morality based on mutual understanding, such events are almost always defined in a *self-satisfying* or egocentric way (e.g., "You do something for me, and I'll do it for you").

2. **Conventional level.** As the child moves into the conventional level, the rules of the society tend to be viewed as literal and rigid. In the third stage, the child sees "good" behavior as imperative. The *intent* of the child's actions becomes important because good behavior is what elicits the approval of significant others. In Stage 4 (see Table 14.4), the child becomes oriented toward authority and rules. Maintenance of rules and respect for authority become one's *duty*. Other characteristics of this level are that the child:

• Becomes aware of intentions and the personal differences that should be considered when judging actions.

TABLE 14.4
Kohlberg's Stages of Moral Development

LEVEL AND STAGE	CONTENT OF STAGE		SOCIAL PERSPECTIVE OF STAGE
	WHAT IS RIGHT	REASONS FOR DOING RIGHT	
LEVEL I— PRECONVENTIONAL Stage 1—Heteronomous Morality	To avoid breaking rules backed by punishment, obedience for its own sake, and avoiding physical damage to persons and property.	Avoidance of punishment, and the superior power of authorities.	*Egocentric point of view.* Doesn't consider the interests of others or recognize that they differ from the actor's; doesn't relate two points of view. Actions are considered physically rather than in terms of psychological interests of others. Confusion of authority's perspective with one's own.
Stage 2—Individualism, Instrumental Purpose, and Exchange	Following rules only when it is to someone's immediate interest; acting to meet one's own interests and needs and letting others do the same. Right is also what's fair, what's an equal exchange, a deal, an agreement.	To serve one's own needs or interests in a world where you have to recognize that other people have their interests too.	*Concrete individualistic perspective.* Aware that everybody has his own interest to pursue and these conflict so that right is relative (in the concrete individualistic sense).
LEVEL II— CONVENTIONAL Stage 3—Mutual Interpersonal Expectations, Relationships, and Interpersonal Conformity	Living up to what is expected by people close to you or what people generally expect of people in your role as son, brother, friend, etc. "Being good" is important and means having good motives, showing concern about others. It also means keeping mutual relationships, such as trust, loyalty, respect, and gratitude.	The need to be a good person in your own eyes and those of others. Your caring for others. Belief in the Golden Rule. Desire to maintain rules and authority which support stereotypical good behavior.	*Perspective of the individual in relationships with other individuals.* Aware of shared feelings, agreements, and expectations which take primacy over individual interests. Relates points of view through the concrete Golden Rule, putting yourself in the other guy's shoes. Does not yet consider generalized system perspective.
Stage 4—Social System and Conscience	Fulfilling the actual duties to which you have agreed. Laws are to be upheld except in extreme cases where they conflict with other fixed social duties. Right is also contributing to society, the group, or institution.	To keep the institution going as a whole, to avoid the breakdown in the system "if everyone did it," or the imperative of conscience to meet one's defined obligations (easily confused with Stage 3 belief in rules and authority).	*Differentiates societal point of view from interpersonal agreement or motives.* Takes the point of view of the system that defines roles and rules. Considers individual relations in terms of place in the system.

TABLE 14.4
(Continued)

| LEVEL AND STAGE | CONTENT OF STAGE | | SOCIAL PERSPECTIVE OF STAGE |
	WHAT IS RIGHT	REASONS FOR DOING RIGHT	
LEVEL III—POSTCONVENTIONAL or PRINCIPLED Stage 5—Social Contract or Utility and Individual Rights	Being aware that people hold a variety of values and opinions, that most values and rules are relative to your group. These relative rules should usually be upheld, however, in the interest of impartiality and because they are the social contract. Some nonrelative values and rights like *life* and *liberty*, however, must be upheld in any society and regardless of majority opinion.	A sense of obligation to law because of one's social contract to make and abide by laws for the welfare of all and for the protection of all people's rights. A feeling of contractual commitment, freely entered upon, to family, friendship, trust, and work obligations. Concern that laws and duties be based on rational calculation of overall utility, "the greatest good for the greatest number."	*Prior-to-society perspective.* Perspective of a rational individual aware of values and rights prior to social attachments and contracts. Integrates perspectives by formal mechanisms of agreement, contract, objective impartiality, and due process. Considers moral and legal points of view; recognizes that they sometimes conflict and finds it difficult to integrate them.
Stage 6—Universal Ethical Principles	Following self-chosen ethical principles. Particular laws or social agreements are usually valid because they rest on such principles. When laws violate these principles, one acts in accordance with the principle. Principles are universal principles of justice: the equality of human rights and respect for the dignity of human beings as individuals.	The belief as a rational person in the validity of universal moral principles and a sense of personal commitment to them.	*Perspective of a moral point of view from which social arrangements derive.* Perspective is that of any rational individual recognizing the nature of morality or the fact that persons are ends in themselves and must be treated as such.

From Kohlberg, 1976, pp. 34 and 35.

TABLE 14.5
A Comparison of Piaget and Kohlberg on Moral Development

PIAGET	KOHLBERG
Premoral period (birth–7 years)	Level I—Preconventional Stage 1: Obedience and punishment orientation Stage 2: Naively egoistic orientation
Concrete-transitional period (8–11 years)	Level II—Conventional Stage 3: Good-boy orientation Stage 4: Authority-and-social-order maintaining orientation
Moral relativity period (12 years and after)	Level III—Postconventional Stage 5: Contractual-legalistic orientation Stage 6: Conscience or principle orientation

. Becomes concerned about the way in which wrong actions and responses damage relationships between persons and in groups.
. Sees all laws as having equal importance.

3. **Postconventional level.** According to Kohlberg, the individual in the post-conventional level of moral development is no longer tied to the rules of authority or society but is able to organize and reanalyze moral principles in particular situations. In the fifth stage (Table 14.4), moral behavior is no longer governed by one's *duty* or by obedience to the *letter of the law* but by the *principles* that underlie the law. For example, the individual may support equal admission to professional schools not simply because "it's the law" but because of the underlying principle that all human beings are entitled to equality of opportunity. The individual operates in accordance with a "social contract." In the sixth stage, the individual is oriented toward moral decision based on a "personal" ethical system. Kohlberg suggested that this system is based on "universal principles of justice, reciprocity and equality of human rights and respect for the dignity of human beings as individual persons" (1968, p. 26). Whereas the Stage 5 individual was oriented toward a legalistic or social-contract approach, the Stage 6 individual attempts to develop a system that satisfies his or her own conscience. We discuss the post-conventional level of morality in greater detail in Chapter 17.

AN EVALUATION OF KOHLBERG'S THEORY. As in the case of Piaget's theory, there is general support for Kohlberg's general sequence of stages of moral development. However, several criticisms have been raised:

. Recent findings underscore the fact that few, if any, adults attain the Stage 5 level of moral reasoning and no adults were at Stage 6 level (Colby et al., 1983; Colby and Kohlberg, 1984) (Table 14.2). Does this mean that only very few people reach these stages?
. Feminist thinkers have argued that Kohlberg's stages of moral development are biased against women (Gilligan, 1982). For example, it has been argued that most women score lower than men on Kohlberg's stages (typically, women

---

Huck Finn's Conscience: Conventional Versus Postconventional Morality

Some of the most poignant descriptions of the development of conscience and moral judgment occur in literature. In the following passage, Mark Twain describes the thoughts of Huckleberry Finn as he argues with himself about the virtues of helping Jim— a runaway slave—to escape. Huck has learned that there is a reward for returning Jim. Both he and Jim are now escaping down the Mississippi River on a raft. The passage describes how Huck struggles with *conventional morality* (or the "conscience of the shore") and the as yet dimly perceived feeling of a *postconventional morality* (i.e., Jim is a human being and deserves to be free).

Jim said it made him all over trembly and feverish to be so close to freedom. Well, I can tell you it made me all over trembly and feverish, too, to hear him, because I begun to get it through my head that he was most free— and who was to blame for it? Why, me. I couldn't get that out of my conscience, no how nor no way. It got to troubling me so I couldn't rest; I couldn't stay still in one place. It hadn't even come home to me before what this thing was that I was doing. But now it did; and it stayed with me, and scorched me more and more. I tried to make out to myself that I warn't to blame, because I didn't run Jim off from his rightful owner; but it warn't no use, conscience up and says, every time, "But you knowed he was running for his freedom, and you could 'a' paddled ashore and told somebody."

are found at Stage 3 and men at Stage 4) because Stage 3 moral development is conceived of in interpersonal terms (i.e., pleasing others and maintaining good relations with them), whereas Stage 4 moral reasoning is seen as a more objective acceptance of social rules. As Carol Gilligan suggests, "The very traits that traditionally have defined the 'goodness' of women are those that mark them as deficient in moral development" (1982, p. 18).

Moral Thinking and Moral Behavior

Although Piaget and Kohlberg were primarily interested in **moral reasoning** (or *moral thinking*), it is important to recognize that *knowing* the difference between "right" and "wrong" and *doing* the right thing (behaving *morally*) are not necessarily the same (Blasi, 1983; Burton, 1984).

SELF-INTEREST.   There is evidence that the child's *self-interest* may play a considerable role in determining moral behavior, over and above moral reasoning (Carroll and Rest, 1981). For example, in a study by William Damon (1977), children were interviewed about the following *hypothetical* situation:

· You and your friends are given a job of making bracelets.
· You have one hour to work.
· One member of your group makes more bracelets than the others.
· After one hour you are given ten candy bars. How do you divide them up?

The experimenter then compared the children's verbal responses in the hypothetical situation with their behavioral responses in *a similar real-life* situation with real candy bars. The children's *actual behavior* was one or two levels below their *moral reasoning* (as measured in the hypothetical situation) as indicated by the following results:

· Children who *said* they would give *more candy* to the child who did the most work (in the hypothetical situation) distributed the candy bars *equally* in real life.
· Children who *said* they would distribute the candy *equally* (in the interview) in reality kept the most candy for themselves.

MORAL SOCIALIZATION.   As children get older, they spend increasingly more time away from parents and more time in the presence of peers. Likewise, the opportunities for breaking rules or giving in to temptation increase.
   What types of parental socialization are associated with children who *voluntarily* follow rules even when no one is watching? According to Martin Hoffman (1979), moral maturity can be enhanced by doing the following:

· *Reason* with children, point out the negative impact of misbehavior on others and, in particular, on other children. (Children are more likely to respond to reason if the parent emphasizes the effects of misbehavior on *peers*, rather than on adults.)
· *Point out the consequences* of misbehavior to others. This helps the child to develop role-taking skills and to empathize with others.
· Appeal to the child's desire and pride to be thought of as "grown up."
· Couple parental reasoning with affection. This enables the child to focus

primarily on the needs and feeling of others without undue stress about being punished.

Furthermore, there is evidence that parents who enhance their child's moral behavior need to combine reason/affection for achieving *long-term* moral development with *power-assertive discipline* (i.e., punishment, withdrawal of privileges, threats, and so on) to deal with some immediate situations (i.e., children's fighting, a child's breaking household furniture, and so on) (Grusec and Kuczynski, 1980).

The Role of Parent and Teacher in the Child's Moral Development

The following are some suggestions and clues for parents or teachers who deal with the child as a "moral" individual. Although each situation and each child is different, many parents and teachers want to provide an experience of justice in the home and in the school, and a variety of experiences to help the child see different viewpoints. In the home, an atmosphere of mutual respect of all persons is the most important starting point.

CLUES FOR PARENTS AND TEACHERS.   "Telling" is the least effective technique for teaching morality. Children can best "understand" moral reasoning at their own "level" or just one level above the level at which they are functioning.

One way to help children advance in their moral thinking is to involve them in trying to solve moral dilemmas. Kohlberg's research has shown that the children who reach the higher levels of moral development in their age group are those who have many associations and interactions with other children. Another factor that relates to higher levels of moral development is the amount of exposure that a child has to ways of life different from his or her own.

Moral judgment matures most rapidly in an atmosphere of mutual respect.

- Adults should admit mistakes when wrong.
- Adults should consider the opinions and feelings of children.
- Adults should encourage the children to consider the feelings of other family members when making decisions.
- Parents should be "growing" people themselves and serve as models for the child.

Achievement Motivation

As we have suggested in this chapter, one of the distinguishing features of middle childhood is the child's development of a sense of personal competence in dealing with the academic challenges of the school. An important determinant of this sense of competence is the ability of the school-age child to achieve. Because such importance is attached to achievement at an individual and a social level (i.e., social awards are commonly tied to achievement levels), there has been considerable interest in explaining the factors that contribute to achievement motivation.

In this section, after defining achievement motivation, we examine the following matters related to achievement:

* Factors that influence the development of achievement motivation.
* The development of achievement motivation.

Achievement refers to the idea of *competition with reference to a standard of excellence* (Solomon, 1982). This definition distinguishes achievement from undirected exploratory behavior, on the one hand, and infant/toddler mastery of such activities as speech and walking, on the other hand. It is assumed that infants/toddlers are not matching their behavior in speech or walking with some standard of excellence (Solomon, 1982). However, it is likely that infant/toddler attempts at mastery of the self and the environment are the forerunners of achievement in the formal academic skills of middle childhood (Veroff, 1969; Crandall, 1972). **Achievement motivation** refers to an "internal disposition to improve or maintain a high level of performance with respect to standards of excellence (this limits achievement to activities in which success or failure is possible)" (Solomon, 1982, p. 270).

Factors that Influence Achievement Motivation

This section examines some of the factors that contribute to the development of achievement motivation. It is necessary to view achievement motivation as a sense of related processes or components that can then be examined individually (see Figure 14.3). These processes, or components of achievement motivation, include the following (Dweck and Elliott, 1983):

* *Goal formation.* Specifically, what causes children to be oriented toward achievement goals?
* *Goal adoption.* What factors contribute to the selection of specific achievement goals (e.g., expectation of success)?
* *Task performance.* What effects do different levels of expectations (for success or failure) have on goal achievement?
* *Performance evaluation.* What types of questions do children ask themselves about their performance (e.g., How well have I done?) and how do these questions affect ongoing and future performance?

FIGURE 14.3

The process of achievement motivation. Based on Dweck and Elliott, 1983, p. 653.

GOAL FORMATION.   It is important to recognize that differences in achievement goals cause children to organize their achievement activities in different ways. For our purposes, we may think of achievement goals as falling into two broad categories: *learning goals* and *performance goals* (Dweck and Elliott, 1983). As indicated in Table 14.6, these two broad types of achievement goals can be distinguished in numerous ways. For example, the purpose of a *learning goal* is to increase one's competence ("What will I learn?"), whereas the purpose of a *performance goal* is to acquire the desired evaluations or judgments of competence, usually made by another person (the child may say to himself or herself, "Will I look like I know what I'm doing?").

Why do children select learning goals rather than performance goals, or vice versa? In addition to such specific factors as the requirements of a given task or achievement situation at home or school, school-age children may arrive at a task with their own "theories of intelligence." These theories of intelligence (Table 14.6) may orient children toward either learning or performance goals (Bandura and Dweck, 1981; Dweck and Elliott, 1981; Harari and Covington, 1981). Table 14.6 presents two very "different theories of intelligence" which represent differing views of intellectual competence, as follows (Dweck and Elliott, 1983):

• *Entity theory.* This theory involves the idea that intelligence is a *stable* and *global* characteristic. Such a trait or entity can be displayed in one's behavior and, as such, can be evaluated in terms of adequacy.

TABLE 14.6

Children's Theories of Intelligence and Achievement Goals

	THEORIES OF INTELLIGENCE	
	INCREMENTAL	ENTITY
Intelligence is:	A repertoire of skills that increases through effort.	A global, stable entity whose adequacy is judged through performance.
Effort is:	An investment that increases intelligence.	A risk that may reveal low intelligence.
	GOALS	
	LEARNING GOAL: COMPETENCE INCREASE	PERFORMANCE GOAL: COMPETENCE JUDGMENT
1. Entering Question:	How can I do it? What will I learn?	Can I do it? Will I look smart?
2. Focus on:	Process	Outcome
3. Errors:	Natural, useful	Failure
4. Uncertainty:	Challenging	Threatening
5. Optimal Task:	Maximizes learning (becoming smarter)	Maximizes looking smart
6. Seek:	Accurate information about ability	Flattering information
7. Standards:	Personal, long-term, flexible	Normative, immediate, rigid
8. Expectancy:	Emphasizes effort	Emphasizes present ability
9. Teacher:	Resource, guide	Judge, rewarder/punisher
10. Goal Value:	"Intrinsic": value of skill, activity, progress	"Extrinsic": value of judgment

Adapted from Dweck and Elliott, 1983, p. 655.

* *Incremental (instrumental) theory.* This theory involves the idea that intelligence is a collection of skills that can be increased and improved through individual effort. Unlike entity theory (where effort may be viewed as a compensation for low intelligence), effort in incremental theory is seen as an indicator of progress in developing one's intelligence.

Typically by the end of the elementary school years, most children appear to understand the meaning of both theories or types of intelligence (Heckhausen, 1981; Rholes and Ruble, 1981; Dweck and Elliott, 1983; Surber, 1984). However, by this time school-age children, *independent of their measured ability,* have developed a preference for one approach over another (Dweck and Elliott, 1981). As a result of these preferences, children may structure their school and home achievement situations in different ways (Nicholls, 1981). For example, *performance goals* would orient a child toward avoiding errors or mistakes (since an error can be viewed as a failure), whereas *learning goals* would orient a child toward a view of errors as a natural, necessary part of achievement (Table 14.6).

> Thus, children with learning goals would seek tasks that maximize learning, even if they are likely to make errors and thereby advertise their present lack of proficiency; children with performance goals would sacrifice learning tasks in favor of tasks that maximize competence judgements. (Dweck and Elliott, 1983, p. 655)

In addition to the *types* of goals to which a child is oriented, the *expectation of goal attainment* is a vital factor in the process of **goal formation** (Dweck and Elliott, 1983). There is considerable evidence that *high expectations for success* (which are typically associated with optimal performance) are the result of the following factors (Dweck and Elliott, 1983):

* *Realistic analysis of skills and task characteristics.* A realistic analysis of a task and the skills involved implies the avoidance of overestimating the difficulty of a new task or the tendency to be impulsively overoptimistic (Bandura, 1980; Meichenbaum and Asarnow, 1982).
* *High perceived ability and a high level of perceived control of the situation.* Research evidence suggests that it is important for the child to believe that he or she can affect an outcome (Covington, 1980; Bandura, 1981; Harter and Connell, 1981). Furthermore, it is important that the child perceive that his or her *effort* increases the possibility of success on a given task rather than being an indicator of low ability (i.e., because he or she must try harder). (Touhy and Villemez, 1980; Bandura and Dweck, 1981).
* *Personal, realistic, and flexible standards* (rather than normative/competitive standards). The child should define achievement as a continuous process, with errors and mistakes as a necessary component (Maehr and Stallings, 1972; Papert, 1980; Nicholls, 1981). This is in contrast to a situation where standards are rigid, creating a "sudden death" situation in which success or failure is evaluated on the basis of short-term results. Furthermore, productive achievement is more likely to occur when standards are *personal* (defined in terms of a child's prior or current level of functioning or defined in terms of an absolute standard) rather than *competitive* with others (Masters, Furman, and Barden, 1977; Nicholls, 1981). Competitive standards would prevent a large number of children from succeeding. In addition, standards should be *realistic,* which means that they should be challenging but reasonable in light of a child's skill level (Bandura and Schunk, 1981). Standards should also be *flexible,* or capable of change in terms of the child's actual performance, rather than fixed, creating an "all-or-nothing" situation.

Achievement Motivation and the Fear of Success in Females

In his early studies of the achievement motivation of men, the psychologist David McClelland (1961) divided the concept of achievement motivation into two parts: (1) the "hope of success" (or the motive to approach success) and (2) the "fear of failure" (or the motive to avoid failure). Although, such a division seemed perfectly logical, it did not completely describe the achievement motivation of women. Specifically, Matina Horner (1972) found that females tended to show more anxiety than did males in achievement situations. In the case of females, Horner identified a third category of achievement motivation, which she called the "fear of success." Specifically, females appeared to have difficulties with competitive achievement. The problem seemed to be the result of a perceived conflict between success or achievement and femininity.

> When success is likely or possible, threatened by the negative consequences they expect to follow success, young women become anxious and their positive achievement strivings become thwarted. (Horner, 1972, p. 171)

Furthermore, this fear of success exists because, for many women, the anticipation of success in competitive achievement situations with men "produce[s] anticipation of certain negative consequences, for example, threat of social rejection and loss of femininity" (Horner, 1972, p. 171).

The conflicts surrounding the fear of success might also be viewed in a different way. For example, Georgia Sassen (1980) suggested that these conflicts could indicate

> a heightened perception of the "other side" of competitive success, that is, the great emotional costs of success achieved through competition, or an understanding which, while confused, indicates an awareness that something is rotten in the state in which success is defined as having better grades than everyone else. (p. 171)

According to Sassen, fear of success appears to be present in women only when an achievement situation is directly competitive (i.e., where the success of one person is at the expense of another person's failure).

How, or in what ways, does this fear of success emerge in middle childhood? There is some evidence that girls tend to develop lower expectations for suc-

cess than boys, even in areas where they outperform boys (Dweck and Elliott, 1983). Furthermore, boys may be encouraged to attribute their successes to ability, whereas girls learn to attribute their failures to lack of ability (Dweck and Elliott, 1983). There is some evidence that boys and girls may learn these different attributions through different treatment by significant adults, particularly teachers (Dweck et al., 1978). Specifically, as a result of this differential treatment, girls may develop a sense of *learned helplessness* (a response to repeated failure in which an individual gives up trying), whereas boys develop a sense of *competence*. That is, when boys fail at a task, teachers may criticize them for their inattention, lack of effort, or sloppiness. On the other hand, when girls fail, teachers may simply indicate the error and praise them for turning in a neat paper or for trying hard. In other words, boys learn that they fail because of lack of effort (they have the ability), and girls learn that they fail because they lack the ability (they have made the effort).

Darryl Jacobson

In order to test this assumption, Carol Dweck and her associates (1978) placed both boys and girls in one of two groups and gave them a series of difficult word problems.

* *Group 1—Boy-type criticism.* When children in this group made errors, they were told to stop wasting time and to try harder.
* *Group 2—Girl-type criticism.* When the children in this group failed at a word problem, they were told something like "I know you tried hard but you got it wrong; too bad."

The results of the study indicate that the children's self-evaluations were the result of the teacher's criticism. The majority of children (both boys and girls) who had been treated "like boys" attributed their failure to a lack of effort (not to a lack of ability). Likewise, most of the boys and girls who had been treated "like girls" attributed their failure to a lack of ability.

GOAL ADOPTION.   Once the child has identified the type of goals (i.e., learning versus performance goals) and the expectation of success, he or she is ready to combine these conclusions with the *goal value* (i.e., the importance to the child of competence in a given goal) to select a given goal. Specifically, the desired goal is selected as the child weighs both the *value* assigned to the goal and his or her *expectation for success.* These expectancy value patterns are called *goal tendencies.*

TASK PERFORMANCE.   Once the child has made a choice of a goal, the task of implementing that goal is influenced by the nature of the child's goal tendencies. Specifically, certain goal tendency patterns may inhibit child achievement, including the following (Dweck and Elliott, 1983):

* *Unrealistically low or shaky expectations of success.* For example, some children have a tendency to focus too heavily on negative information in estimating their own skills. This may contribute to the setting of unreasonably low goals.
* *Unrealistically high expectations that are not adapted or revised on the basis of experience.* For example, a child who perseveres in a task for which there is a highly limited likelihood of success (Janoff-Bulman and Brickman, 1981).
* *A low value attached to whatever achievement goals are examined and selected.* For example, some children may attach little importance to evaluations made of their competence in the academic setting. Some minority group children find little need to succeed in school if they see adult or peer models for whom such success is irrelevant (Ogbu, 1978b).
* *Excessive focus on the negative consequences of goal attainment.* For example, the child who displays a "fear of success" as a way of denying his or her interest in a goal (Sigall and Gould, 1977). Such fear of success may take many forms, including fear of the interpersonal side effects of goal attainment (e.g., jealousies, rejection, social disapproval, and so on).

PERFORMANCE EVALUATION.   During the course of an achievement episode, children typically begin to assess or evaluate what they have done or accomplished. For example, the following questions (or versions thereof) might be asked: "What have I accomplished relative to the goals I have set?" "What do these results mean to me?" Such questions influence children's ongoing achievement activity (Dweck and Elliott, 1983).

The beginning step in the evaluation process is for the child to assess the basic data or results of the achievement activity (e.g., "How many problems have I solved? How does this compare with the results of other children?") There is evidence that children who have an orientation toward achievement inhibition (e.g., a sense of learned helplessness) have more negative perceptions of their achievement results than children with more positive achievement orientations (e.g., mastery or competence orientations) (Diener and Dweck, 1978; Lewinsohn et al., 1980). Specifically, the children with a sense of learned helplessness tended to overestimate their failures and underemphasize their successes.

Once the raw data of the achievement activity have been assessed, another step children typically engage in is *strategy analysis.* Specifically, as they engage in a task, they may evaluate the strategies they employ in light of the outcomes. There is evidence that when children focus, where necessary, on the modifying strategies or effort (time involved, trying harder, and so on), the result is more improved performance than if children focus on (as explanations of unsuccessful strategies) their ability or intelligence. In the former case, the child is concerned with future-oriented strategies for success. In the latter case, a preoccupation with self characteristics has limited benefit or utility for the child (Jennings, 1979; Anderson and Jennings, 1980; Licht and Dweck, 1981).

The Development of Achievement Motivation

In our discussion of the factors that influence achievement and achievement motivation, it is apparent that many changes are occurring as a result of both the growth and development of the school-age child and the experience of attending the formal school. In this section we examine the development of achievement motivation as a result of both of these factors—the changing child and the demands of the school experience.

CHANGING ACHIEVEMENT BELIEFS AND ACTIVITIES.   In the first place, there appears to be a change in the child's concept of ability during the years of middle childhood. Prior to age seven, children typically think of ability as the presence of a specific skill for doing an activity (e.g., the "ability" to count blocks) (Frieze, Francis, and Hanusa, 1981; Heckhausen, 1981). After age seven there is an increasing recognition of ability as a more global and stable characteristic of the person (Heckhausen, 1981; Rholes and Ruble, 1981). Furthermore, there is some reason to think that the large increase that occurs in the child's use of *social comparison* for self-evaluation (typically between seven and nine years of age) is related to this new development in looking for personal traits or global characteristics (Ruble et al., 1980; Ruble, 1985). Based on these changes, several investigators have proposed a stage theory of achievement motivation, as follows (Veroff, 1969; Solomon, 1982):

• *Autonomous achievement motivation.* This is the earliest stage of achievement, which evolves from infants'/toddlers' early attempts to exercise mastery or competence over themselves and their environments (e.g., walking, talking, grasping objects, and so on). This stage typically does *not* involve the evaluation of behavior in relation to an external standard of excellence. Rather, it appears that internal standards of child satisfaction are utilized (Solomon, 1982).
• *Social comparison achievement motivation.* This stage begins during the early school years and involves the child's comparison of his or her performance with that of other children. The standard of excellence against which children evaluate their performance is the performance of their peers. Furthermore, the child's mastery of experiences in the prior stage of autonomous achievement motivation sets the foundation for this stage.

• *The integration of autonomous and social comparison achievement motivation.* In this stage, the child can be guided by some combination of both types of achievement motivation. In other words, children can achieve on the basis of personal and flexible standards of achievement as well as the evaluative judgments of significant adults (typically based, in part, on comparison to the performance of peers) (Table 14.6). However, some children do not integrate or use both autonomous and social comparison modes and appear guided by only one or the other.

CHANGE FROM PHYSICAL ACTIONS TO INTELLECTUAL TASKS.   Before children enter school, most of their experiences center around activities that are primarily related to physical skills (e.g., riding bicycles, tying shoe laces, catching baseballs, and so on). With the advent of the formal school, the child begins for the first time to come to grips with a concentrated menu of intellectual skills, including reading, spelling, writing, and computation. The implications of this transition from physical to intellectual skills involves the following changes:

> on physical tasks compared with intellectual ones, children can more easily launch, monitor, and guide the acquisition process and judge their own successes. This is because physical tasks usually have observable execution processes and observable outcomes whose adequacy can be readily judged by inspection (e.g., the child has or has not caught the ball . . .). Moreover, children need not have a deliberate, advance plan of attack, since they can experiment with [process-outcome combinations]. In the intellectual domain (e.g., solving arithmetic problems) the problem-solving process requires a planned, covent sequence of skills. . . . In short, on intellectual tasks children may be less likely to know what they are aiming for, why they are aiming for it, how to get these and when they have gotten there. (Dweck and Elliott, 1983, pp. 676–677)

Summary

1. The self is an active, ongoing construction of the individual which is continually undergoing developmental change. In middle childhood there are two significant dimensions of the self-concept that constitute the self as a system: the *content* of self-concept (what children understand about themselves) and the *function* of self-concept (how the self-concept regulates and organizes child behavior). The major theme of development of self-concept in middle childhood is the child's increasing appreciation of the *self as a social object*. The process of self-concept development in middle childhood is influenced by how well the school-age child negotiates several tasks of middle childhood.
2. The regulation of behavior involves the interdependence or mutual coordination of both the *self system*, or personal factors (e.g., child's needs, desires, goals, skills, or knowledge), and the *social system*, or situational factors (e.g., the expectations, desires, or needs of others). As children grow and mature, their socialization experience creates an increasing similarity or overlap between the self system and the social system. This pattern of interdependence is called *coregulation*.
3. *Social cognition* refers to the way we view ourselves (self knowledge) and how we view the emotions, thoughts, and viewpoints of others (role taking). The general pattern of self description is that as children grow older, their conception of self moves from specific, concrete descriptors to increasingly abstract

depictions. There is evidence that school-age children have a fairly well-organized system of self-understanding, including the following dimensions: the physical self, the active self, the social self, and the psychological self.

4. *Role taking* refers to the development of the cognitive skills that are necessary for the child to take the perspective of others and to understand their thoughts and feelings. Role-taking skills improve as children progress through middle childhood.

5. *Self-regulation,* or the function of the self-concept, includes several possible components such as self-control and self-monitoring. Children must be able to exercise *self-control* over their aggressive impulses, regulate the expression of emotions, and so on. In addition to learning to control their feelings and emotions, a second important process is one's *locus of control* (i.e., the sense of control over external circumstances). There are two types of locus of control—*internal* and *external.*

   Some of the more common modes of teaching self-control include helping the child recognize the *consequences of behavior,* the use of *reasoning* by adults, the *attributional* approach, and modeling.

6. Moral behavior is composed of four component parts: interpreting the situation, determining the appropriate moral course of action, deciding what one will actually do, and implementing the chosen course of action. Piaget believed that the child's progression in cognitive development is *paralleled* by the child's moral development. According to Piaget, moral development has the following stages: the *premoral period* (birth to seven years), *moral relationships based on mutual respect* (eight to eleven years), and *moral relativity* (eleven to twelve years). Kohlberg described moral development in terms of three levels of moral thinking: *preconventional, conventional,* and *postconventional.*

7. Although Piaget and Kohlberg were primarily interested in moral reasoning or *moral thinking,* it is important to recognize that *knowing* the difference between "right" and "wrong" and *doing* the right thing are not necessarily the same. Such factors as the child's self-interest and moral socialization may influence moral behavior.

8. *Achievement motivation* refers to an "internal disposition to improve or maintain a high level of performance with respect to standards of excellence (this limits achievement to activities in which success or failure are possible)" (Solomon, 1982, p. 270). Components of achievement motivation include goal formation, goal adoption, task performance, and performance evaluation.

9. *Goal formation* is influenced by factors such as the *type of goals* (e.g., performance goals or learning goals) to which a child is oriented and the *expectation of goal attainment. Goal adoption* involves the selection of a desired goal based on both the *value* assigned to the goal and the child's *expectation for success. Task performance,* or the implementation of a goal, is influenced by a child's goal tendency patterns, including patterns that may inhibit achievement (e.g., excessive focus on the negative consequences of goal attainment). During the course of an achievement episode, children typically begin to assess or evaluate their performance.

Key Terms

Achieved roles
Achievement motivation
Ascribed characteristics
Conventional level
Coregulation
Ego
Ego control
Ego resiliency
Goal adoption
Goal formation
Learned helplessness
Locus of control
Morality
Moral reasoning
Moral reciprocity
Moral relationships based on mutual
  respect

Moral relativity
Other-oriented induction
Performance evaluation
Postconventional level
Power assertion
Preconventional level
Premoral period
Role taking
Self-control
Self-knowledge
Self-regulation
Self schemas
Social cognition
Task performance

Questions

1. Discuss the construction of the *self* as a system in middle childhood.
2. Define *social cognition, self-knowledge*, and *role-taking*.
3. Describe and compare Piaget's and Kohlberg's stages of moral development.
4. Define achievement motivation and discuss its role in middle childhood.

Suggested Readings

DWECK, C. S., and ELLIOTT, E. S. "Achievement Motivation." In P. H. Mussen (ed.), *Handbook of Child Psychology* (4th ed.) (Vol. 4, pp. 643–692). New York: Wiley, 1983. A thorough analysis of research on achievement motivation.

HIGGINS, E. T., RUBLE, D. N., and HARTUP, M. W. (eds.). *Social Cognition and Social Behavior: Developmental Issues*. New York: Cambridge University Press, 1983. An excellent discussion of research on social development and social cognition.

MARKUS, H., and NURIUS, P. "Self-Understanding and Self-Regulation in Middle Childhood." In W. A. Collins (ed.), *Development During Middle Childhood: The Years from Six to Twelve*. Washington, D.C.: National Academy Press, 1984. A well-written discussion of self-regulation and social development.

SELMAN, R. L. *The Growth of Interpersonal Understanding*. New York: Academic Press, 1980. An excellent analysis of social cognition.

15 Adolescence: Contexts of Development

Youth is not entirely a time of life, it is a state of mind. It is not wholly a matter of ripe cheeks, red lips, or supple knees. It is a temper of will, a quality of the imagination, a vigor of the emotions.

Nobody grows old by merely living a number of years. People grow old only by deserting their ideals. You are as young as your faith, as old as your doubt; as young as your self-confidence, as old as your fears; as young as your hope, as old as your despair.

In the central place of every heart, there is a recording chamber; so long as it receives messages of beauty, hope, cheer and courage, you are young.

When the wires are all down and your heart is covered with the snows of pessimism and the ice of cynicism, then and then only have you grown old.

—Anonymous

The period of middle childhood has introduced the child to elementary cultural skills (e.g., reading, writing, and social interaction skills). The period of adolescence requires the continued refinement and application of these skills to self-definition in relation to the culture. This process of self-definition in terms of a culture begins in early adolescence and culminates in later adolescence with the development of an identity that serves as the major mode of organizing individual behavior.

> DEFINITION
>
> **Puberty.** The period of time during which physical and physiological changes occur including the appearance of secondary sexual characteristics (e.g., the enlargement of the female breasts and the appearance of male facial hair) and the attainment of biological sexual maturity (We discuss puberty in more detail in Chapter 16).

The period of adolescence begins with the onset of puberty. Puberty is a series of *biological* events that signals the coming of other changes. The end of adolescence comes with entrance into the world of the adult—a *social and psychological* event. Although there is little dispute that adolescence begins with the biological events of puberty, the end of adolescence is much less clear. When, for example, does a person become an adult? (See Figure 15.1.) The answer to that question depends, of course, on the culture in which one lives. In many cultures, although not in ours, ceremonies called *rites of passage* are used to designate the arrival of adulthood.

There are many possible criteria for adulthood in our society. Some of these benchmarks are:

· Emotional independence from parents.
· Economic independence from parents (i.e., "making a living" at a job).

Soma Doran

"Who am I?" is an important question for the adolescent.

- Living away from one's childhood home.
- Graduation from high school or college.
- Commitment to a personal set of values or goals (i.e., a stance toward the world, an "identity").
- The minimum age for voting in public elections.
- Marriage and/or child rearing.

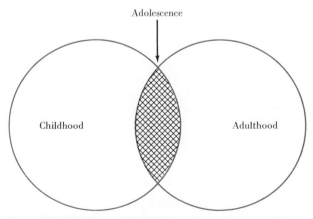

FIGURE 15.1
The world of the adolescent has sometimes been called a "no man's land" between childhood and adulthood.

593

It is possible for the later adolescent to have some of the above characteristics and still not be considered an adult.

Who Are Adolescents?

Because of the increasing length of the adolescent period, it has become increasingly difficult to define it; there are few characteristics that fit both a twelve-year-old and a twenty-six-year-old. Therefore, we adopt here a two-stage theory of adolescence: (1) **early adolescence** (twelve to sixteen years), or the high-school years, in which the major concern is with the development of the skills necessary for group interaction and group membership, and (2) **later adolescence, or youth** (seventeen to the middle or, in some instances, the late twenties), or the post-high school years, in which the major concern is with the development of skills that build on prior experiences of group interaction. These skills are necessary if the individual is to stand by himself or herself in relation to the social system and culture.

During the high school years the adolescent develops an identity in terms of the peer group. The process of identity formation continues into later adolescence with the development of the skills necessary to stand by oneself in the culture and the community. Having begun the process of identity crystallization through adaptation to physical changes in appearance, development of formal operations, and coping with peer pressures and values, the later adolescent is ready for a new phase of development. The lifelong process of identity development continues in later adolescence or youth with the establishment of several foundational components, including the organization of a career and a life-style, the evolution of a relatively mature value system, the acceptance of one's sexuality, and the development of autonomy from parents.

Youth, or later adolescence, is the stage that bridges the transition between adolescence and adulthood. Kenneth Keniston summarized the evolution of this "new" stage as follows:

> More than a decade's work with college and graduate students has convinced me that we have no psychology, apart from the work of Erik Erikson, adequate to understand the feelings and behavior of today's American youth. Millions of young people today are neither psychological adolescents nor sociological adults; they fall into a psychological no man's land. . . . I argue that the unprecedented prolongation of education has opened up opportunities for an extension of psychological development which in turn is creating a "new" stage of life. . . . I suggest that its central characteristic—the tension between selfhood and the existing social order—underlies many of the attitudes and behaviors of contemporary youth. (1975, p. 5)

For our purposes, the definition of the age span for this period is approximately seventeen to twenty-five years of age. It should be noted, however, that this range of years could be expanded to as low as fifteen years of age or to as high as twenty-seven or twenty-eight. In other words, some of the themes of the period we are calling *youth* are probably appropriate to some individuals whose chronological age would place them in early adolescence or young adulthood.

The primary factor that has created the stage of youth as a bona fide phase of development has been the extension of education (as a result of the increasing demands of a technological and industrialized society). It was this very same factor that produced the emergence of what we are calling *early adolescence* during the latter part of the nineteenth century. As a matter of fact, before the twentieth century, adolescence was rarely included as a stage of the life cycle. It was not until G. Stanley Hall's classic book (*Adolescence: Its Psychology and Its Relations to Physiology, Anthropology, Sociology, Sex, Crime, Religion and Education*) in 1904 that the period of adolescence was recognized as a prelude to adulthood. As Keniston pointed out, Hall's concept of adolescence was a reflection on what was really happening in America (and in other industrialized countries) at the turn of the century:

> Nonetheless, Hall was clearly reflecting a gradual change in the nature of human development, brought about by the massive transformations of American society in the decades after the Civil War. . . . America changed from a rural agrarian society to an urban industrial society, and this new industrial society demanded on a mass scale not only the rudimentary literacy taught in elementary schools, but higher skills that could be guaranteed only through secondary education. (1975, p. 5)

As a function of the demands of society for even better-educated young people, the stage of youth has evolved in much the same manner that its predecessor, adolescence, emerged. For example, in 1900 only about 6.4 percent of young people completed high school, whereas nearly 80 percent do so today, and half of them begin college. In 1900, there were only 238,000 college students, whereas approximately 12.5 million students attended college in 1983 (U.S. Department of Health and Human Services, 1985a). What seems to characterize these young people are two major features (Keniston, 1975):

1. They either have just formed or are working on a sense of identity. This emerging identity distinguishes youth or later adolescents from their younger, high school counterparts.
2. They have not decided major questions whose answers have historically defined adulthood: questions of lifestyle, questions of social role, matters of vocation, and questions of a general posture or stance toward the world.

The System of Adolescence

In this section, we provide a total picture of what happens during the adolescent years. In keeping with our perspective, we look at adolescence as a stage of life with two phases: early adolescence and later adolescence, or youth.

Early Adolescence: The Self in Context

The central feature of the early-adolescent world is the organization and evaluation of the adolescent's self-concept in terms of the high school and peer group (see Fig. 15.2). In a sense, it can be said that the individual is developing an identity in relation to the world of the high school and to the peer group (both in and out of school). This is a "group identity" as opposed to the identity formation of later adolescence, or a stance toward the world or the culture. The early adolescent is still very much influenced by his or her family. However, at this time, the discontinuities (as well as the continuities) between family values and the values of the peer group become apparent to the adolescent.

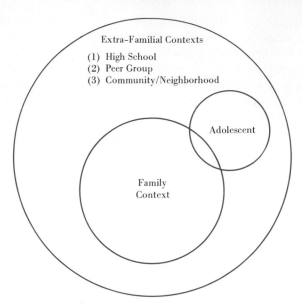

FIGURE 15.2
The system of the early adolescent.

GROUP IDENTITY VERSUS ALIENATION.   During early adolescence, the individual is usually pressured to affiliate with a group of peers. This pressure comes from many sources, including the family, the school, and age-mates. The world of the early adolescent is characterized by the *preeminence of the peer group* as a source of influence. The adolescent's circle of friends defines him or her in terms of a specific subgroup with a meaning in the neighborhood and the community. Parents sometimes become concerned about the groups that the adolescent is spending time with. Sometimes there is even pressure from parents for the adolescent to affiliate with the ''right'' group. Indirectly, high school teachers also exert pressure on adolescents to affiliate with groups by recognizing the *normality* of belonging to identifiable peer groups. Perhaps the most direct and intense pressure to identify with a peer group comes from the adolescent's age-mates, who support such affiliation as a standard norm of adolescence.

   Like the individual in middle childhood, the early adolescent is involved in a process of *self-evaluation* based on experiences in the school and with the peer group. There is, however, a major difference in the self-evaluation of these two periods. The pressure of the peer group during middle childhood is not nearly as strong as during early adolescence. During middle childhood, there is relatively little emphasis on ''belonging'' and ''affiliating'' as primary features of self-identity. Being good at game skills, or ''smart'' in school, or good-looking, or a good ''sport'' or having some other positively evaluated characteristic is probably more important than being a member of a particular group. This attitude changes during early adolescence.

GENERAL CHARACTERISTICS OF THE EARLY ADOLESCENT.   These are some general features of early adolescent development:

1. *General physical maturation.* During this stage, males and females have parallel periods of physical growth. There is usually a somewhat dramatic rate of

Early adolescence—"group" identity in the context of high school peers.

growth in the bones and muscles of the body. These changes have implications for participation in athletics or for sport skills.

2. *Changes in sexual factors and reproductive capability.* Closely related to changes in the skeletal and muscular dimensions of the body are changes in the reproductive systems. The psychological implications of these changes for the individual may include several reactions:
    - A greater concern about and attention to the self as a result of the rapidity of the physical changes.
    - Ambivalent feelings toward the self as a result of the recognition that changes have occurred. (The physical and sexual changes of early adolescence signal not only the beginning of a new phase of development but the end of a relatively comfortable and safe period—childhood. Early adolescents often resort to peers for support and approval at this time.)

3. *Cognitive development.* The changes in thinking skills that occur during early adolescence result in a more flexible and abstract view of the world and allow the early adolescent to understand logical sequences of action and to anticipate consequences of behavior. These skills lead to an ability to project action from the past and the present into a future dimension. The school-age child in concrete operations was somewhat limited to the real objects of the present or the past. Adolescents, however, are able to exert greater control over their behavior and their world because of their skill in anticipating a future.

4. *Social skills.* The early adolescent develops relationships with peers of both sexes that are more mature than those of the school-age child. Part of the reason is that adolescents' cognitive skills enable them to understand the perspectives of other people better.

THE CONTEXTS OF EARLY ADOLESCENCE.

- *The family.* The early adolescent is still very much involved in the family. The nature of family relationships, however, is changing as both parent and adolescent become aware of the needs of a maturing person. Increasingly, the evaluation of the self occurs more and more outside the family.
- *The neighborhood and the community.* In middle childhood, the individual began to develop "cognitive maps" of the major features of the neighborhood and a limited understanding of the general community, including the workings of government. In early adolescence, individuals begin to understand the community as a working organism. They may understand how resources are exchanged and how political organizations control them.
- *The peer group.* Toward the end of middle childhood, the peer group becomes more formally organized. In early adolescence, the peer group becomes a prominent source of feedback for self-evaluation and the individual is concerned with the opinions of others. It is not uncommon to find adolescents in a state of mild euphoria about being supported by the peer group. On the other hand, they may be in a state of mild depression when subjected to pressures for compliance or conformity. Usually individuals adjust fairly well to the differences of various peer-group members and provide mutual support for trying out the roles and the various life-styles of adulthood. Although most adults have perfected these skills of mutual interaction to a high level of efficiency, the early adolescent is exposed for the first time to the challenges of developing self-confidence in the face of pressures for conformity. Some individuals may be unable to affiliate with any existing group. In some instances, this inability results in a sense of alienation from the group, particularly if the individual *wants* to belong but does not possess the social or personality skills to do so. On the other hand, an individual who possesses these skills but who does not feel that the peer group can offer anything valuable may feel rather comfortable with a decision not to affiliate. Whether the early adolescent decides to affiliate with a particular group or not, the point is that the individual is confronted with an *affiliation choice.* It is safe to say that most adolescents become involved with some group. The peer group provides most adolescents with a needed *consensus* and *interpretation* of what is *real* and with *feedback* concerning the adolescent's self-image.
- *The high school.* The world of the high school, including the peer group, introduces the adolescent to the formal cognitive and social skills needed for independent living or for continued education in later adolescence and youth.

Later Adolescence or Youth: The Self in Context

Figure 15.3 illustrates the "world" or the "system" of later adolescence. The essential difference between early and later adolescence is the increased autonomy and independence of the later adolescent years (see Fig. 15.4). Several factors contribute to this emerging sense of independence.

- In some cases, living away from home.
- Thinking skills that allow independent problem solving and contribute to an emerging life-style.
- Relatively stable and self-determined peer relations and friendships.

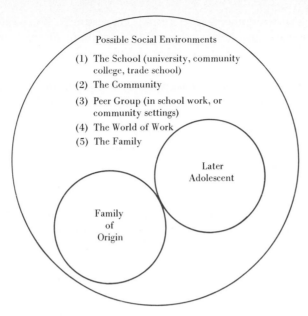

FIGURE 15.3
The system of later adolescence (youth). Youths
may, in some cases, still be living at home. Or they
may have started a "new" family relationship of
their own.

As the adolescent develops a more mature relationship with his or her parents, he or she also leaves the relatively stable world of the high school peer world for the uncharted seas of college or the world of work. These new experiences require the development of new self-regulatory skills. In the case of noncollege adolescents, career choice and vocational development may occur rather soon after high school. Although such individuals may, to some extent, experiment with various job roles or life-styles, they are in many ways similar to young adults. That is, they are confronted with the responsibility of supporting themselves, making a

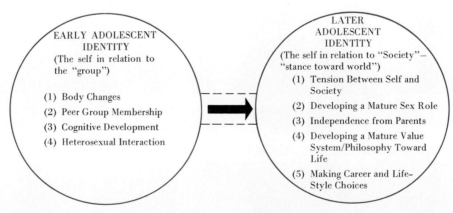

FIGURE 15.4
The evolution of identity from early to later adolescence.

living, and, in some cases, supporting a family. For college-bound adolescents, continued experimentation and thinking about alternative careers and life-styles is possible for a somewhat longer period of time.

As a result of either an initial job experience or continued role preparation and role experimentation in college, later adolescents usually become aware of the values and constraints of their society and culture. They may begin the *sorting* process of examining the options available to them. The idealism of the *desirable* may be transformed into the reality of the *possible*.

As the individual progresses through the period of later adolescence one might wonder what happens to the peer-group influence that has been so prominent since middle childhood. In early adolescence, the peer relationship usually occurs through group membership in the context of the high school world. Peer relationships and friendships are ordinarily with individuals of similar age because of the organization of the high school experience in terms of age. Peer relationships in later adolescence usually occur in the contexts of work and/or college. These relationships are usually not as rigidly organized around age as in early adolescence.

The skills of peer interaction and group membership acquired during the high school years may prepare the individual for later participation in a given career or life-style. Several *major themes* or *issues* organize development and behavior in later adolescence or youth (see Fig. 15.4).

THE TENSION BETWEEN THE SELF AND SOCIETY.   Whereas the early adolescent develops an identity in terms of the high school peer group, later adolescents or youth begin the process of determining who they are in relation to their culture and their society. This sense of identity may lead to the recognition of possible conflict between the self and the social order (Keniston, 1975).

Ambivalence toward both self and society and the attempt to make the two more congruent are central problems of youth. As Keniston suggested, "In youth, then, the potential and ambivalent conflicts between autonomous selfhood and social involvement—between the maintenance of personal integrity and the achievement of effectiveness in society—are fully experienced for the first time" (1975, p. 10).

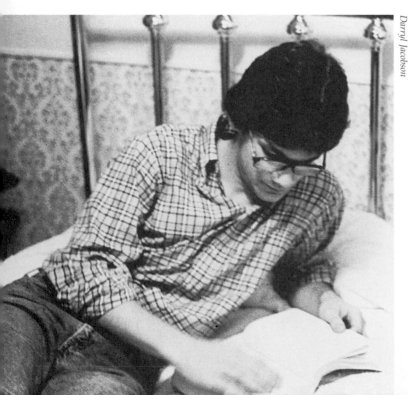

Darryl Jacobson

Later adolescence involves increased autonomy and independence.

The attempt to deal with the tension between the self and society leads to what Keniston called the "wary probe." Whereas the early adolescent experiments with various roles or life-styles with the aim of defining the self, later adolescents or youths attempt more serious and lasting ventures into the adult world. They can test aspects of the existing order more extensively and in a more precise fashion than early adolescents.

As later adolescents gain greater autonomy from the family, "probing" both the self and the society may become a central dimension of their lives. Through such "wary probing," each gradually comes to a "resolution" of the tension between himself or herself and society. This "resolution" is at the core of what is meant by *identity* (Erikson, 1965). A positive resolution of the tension between the self and society *does not eliminate* the tension but recognizes and accepts it as a real and perhaps necessary ingredient of continued development.

One way to understand the meaning of this resolution is to examine Erik Erikson's definition of **identity** as a "stance toward the world." (The polarities "identify versus self-diffusion" describe this process.) Identity involves a *balance* between the self and its relationship to or "stance" toward society. The meaning of this balance can be clarified further by a look at two extreme and inappropriate "resolutions" of the tension between the self and society:

- *Alienation from the self.* This resolution involves the affirmation of society but the denial of self. In other words, the individual resolves the tension between society and self by ignoring the self and "selling out" or joining the "rat race."
- *Alienation from society.* This resolution reduces tension by simply eliminating or blocking out the reality of society, which is not the same thing as a rejection of society; rather, it is a denial that society exists. "Here the integrity of the self is purchased at the price of a determined denial of social reality and the loss of social effectiveness" (Keniston, 1975, p. 16).

An appropriate identity involves a balanced recognition of *both* the self and society.

SEX-ROLE IDENTITY.   The continued development of sex-role identity during later adolescence involves the mature acceptance of one's sexuality and the choice of an occupation and a life pattern that reflect this acceptance. Several important experiences that occur before later adolescence contribute to sex-role identity. For example, same-sex peer relationships during middle childhood and early adolescence help the child learn about intimacy between equals and norms for behaving as a male or a female. As children enter later adolescence, they encounter further expectations from adults, as well as peers, regarding mature sex-role behavior. These expectations may include such things as holding a job and providing for a family for males and maternal-supportive behavior for females. (In Chapter 17 we will see that many of these traditional or sex-biased expectations have changed or are in the process of changing.) At the end of later adolescence, the young person has a sex-role identity that will serve as a basis for further growth in adulthood.

AUTONOMY AND UNDERSTANDING FROM PARENTS.   As the individual approaches the end of childhood, the period of early adolescence sets a foundation for separation from the parents and greater reliance on peer-group values. Although these values may not be totally different from parental values and beliefs, the fact that the individual is coming to rely more on extrafamilial sources for self-definition is the significant factor. Once this foundation is established, the indi-

vidual is prepared for the next major step of self-definition in terms of culture, society, and community. The development of autonomy from the family may be a gradual process in which both the adolescent and the family grow positively toward separation and independence, or it may be more difficult.

Although early adolescents may discover that their parents are not perfect and have weaknesses, in later adolescence the parents begin to be recognized as "persons" (human beings with strengths, weaknesses, concerns, problems, and products of their own historical situations). During early adolescence, the "hero worship" of parents (characteristic of middle childhood) begins to give way to a somewhat negative view. The early adolescent may become increasingly aware of parental weaknesses and shortcomings, and parents' "clay feet" may overshadow everything else. However, it is during youth that the parents may be rediscovered as "real" people (neither the "heroes" of childhood nor the "incompetents" of early adolescence). It is probably no accident that this understanding of parents as people begins during later adolescence, when youth are themselves probing the tensions between self and society.

AN INTERNAL MORAL CODE AND AN EMERGING PHILOSOPHY OF LIFE.   For the young child, many moral issues were resolved in terms of the parents' point of view; that is, morality for the very young child was determined by the satisfaction of the child's needs or by rewards or punishments given by the parents ("preconventional morality"). Morality for individuals in middle childhood is determined by the fulfillment of parental expectations of the "right" role behavior ("conventional morality"). Both the preconventional and the conventional levels of morality are based on the child's subordinate role to adult authority. As adolescents gain autonomy from their parents and are able to think about such abstract concepts as justice and freedom (we discuss the development of adolescent thinking in Chapter 16), they become capable of developing their own reasons for moral decisions. Not many adults reach this level of moral reasoning ("postconventional") (Colby et al., 1983; Colby and Kohlberg, 1984; and Kohlberg, 1985).

CAREER CHOICE AND A CONCEPT OF THE FUTURE.   The young person often has to make the choice of his or her life's work in the absence of actual experience in the world of work. However, there are some educational activities that can aid the individual in making an effective choice. Organized high school work experiences including career education programs can give a person insight into the climate, expectations, and rewards that exist in a particular occupational area. Such experiences may also provide information about how to gain access to a particular career (e.g., the necessary skills and training).

Contexts of the Adolescent System

To understand the adolescent experience fully, one needs to examine both the contexts in which they live and their perceptions of those contexts. In keeping with the emphasis throughout this book, the relationship between adolescents and their contexts of development is mutual and dynamic.

Adolescents' Perceptions of Their Contexts

What does the world of the adolescent look like to the adolescent? Before we discuss the contexts of adolescent development, it is important for us to understand how adolescents actually experience their environments. In a study of adolescents in a Chicago suburb Mihaly Csikszentmihalyi and Reed Larson (1984) examined the experiences of seventy-five adolescents. The adolescents were selected in a random manner in such a way that there would be equal numbers of males and females, equal numbers of adolescents from each of the four high school grade/year levels, and equal numbers from two different residential areas (a low-income area and an upper-middle-class area). The adolescents were asked to wear electronic pagers during a one-week period. The subjects were "beeped" at random intervals (2,700 random signals) and asked to fill out questionnaires on such matters as what they were doing, whom they were with, and what they were thinking and feeling at the time. According to the experimenters, it is this *subjective experience* of adolescents in their *daily interactions* with parents, friends, teachers, and other adults that constitutes a major (yet infrequently studied) aspect of the adolescent transition to adulthood.

THE EXTERNAL LANDSCAPE OF ADOLESCENCE.   One of the most revealing results of the study (Csikszentmihalyi and Larson, 1984) had to do with the external components (or landscape) of the adolescents' lives. The external component involved three factors:

- *Location*, or where they spend their time.
- *Activity*, or what they spend their time doing.
- *Companionship*, or with whom they spend their time.

Figure 15.5 summarizes the external landscape of the adolescents in the study. With reference to location, the adolescents spent most of their daily time in the home. The home experience appears to offer opportunities for interaction with family members as well as opportunities for relative solitude or time alone to deal with thoughts and feelings (12.9 percent of the adolescent's weekly time is spent in his or her bedroom).

> The [12.9 percent] of the time teens spend in their bedrooms may be used to read, reflect, and practice their skills, or it may be used to escape demands in hedonistic

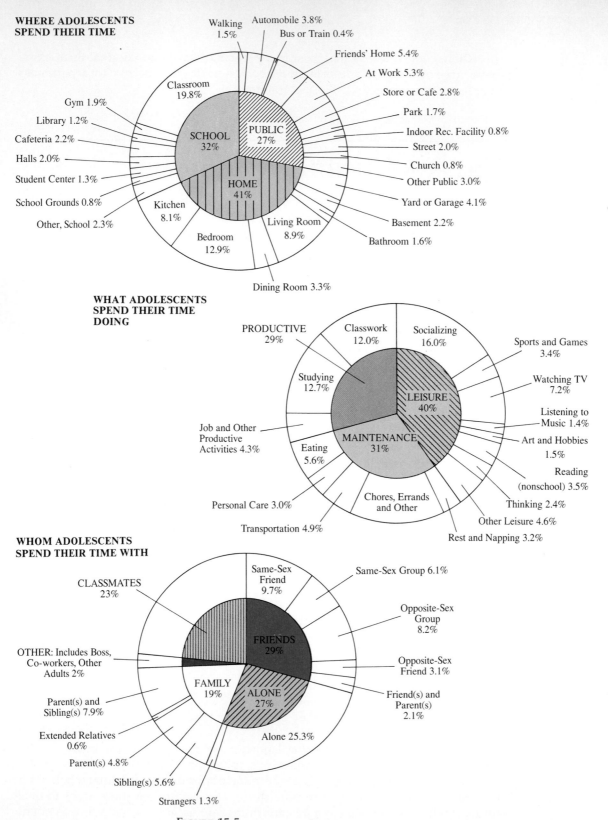

WHERE ADOLESCENTS SPEND THEIR TIME

Walking 1.5%
Automobile 3.8%
Bus or Train 0.4%
Friends' Home 5.4%
At Work 5.3%
Store or Cafe 2.8%
Park 1.7%
Indoor Rec. Facility 0.8%
Street 2.0%
Church 0.8%
Other Public 3.0%
Yard or Garage 4.1%
Basement 2.2%
Bathroom 1.6%
Living Room 8.9%
Dining Room 3.3%
Bedroom 12.9%
Kitchen 8.1%
Other, School 2.3%
School Grounds 0.8%
Student Center 1.3%
Halls 2.0%
Cafeteria 2.2%
Library 1.2%
Gym 1.9%
Classroom 19.8%
SCHOOL 32%
PUBLIC 27%
HOME 41%

WHAT ADOLESCENTS SPEND THEIR TIME DOING

PRODUCTIVE 29%
Classwork 12.0%
Socializing 16.0%
Sports and Games 3.4%
Watching TV 7.2%
Listening to Music 1.4%
Art and Hobbies 1.5%
Reading (nonschool) 3.5%
Thinking 2.4%
Other Leisure 4.6%
Rest and Napping 3.2%
Chores, Errands and Other
Personal Care 3.0%
Transportation 4.9%
Eating 5.6%
Job and Other Productive Activities 4.3%
Studying 12.7%
LEISURE 40%
MAINTENANCE 31%

WHOM ADOLESCENTS SPEND THEIR TIME WITH

CLASSMATES 23%
Same-Sex Friend 9.7%
Same-Sex Group 6.1%
Opposite-Sex Group 8.2%
Opposite-Sex Friend 3.1%
Friend(s) and Parent(s) 2.1%
Alone 25.3%
Strangers 1.3%
Sibling(s) 5.6%
Parent(s) 4.8%
Extended Relatives 0.6%
Parent(s) and Sibling(s) 7.9%
OTHER: Includes Boss, Co-workers, Other Adults 2%
FRIENDS 29%
ALONE 27%
FAMILY 19%

FIGURE 15.5

Profile of adolescent daily experience. The three diagrams show the percentage of self-reports in each location (N = 2734). For each diagram, one percentage point is the equivalent of approximately one hour a week spent in the given activity or location. From Csikszentmihalyi and Larson, 1984, pp. 59, 63, and 71.

or lethargic relaxation. . . . The bedroom provides a sanctuary for whatever a teenager wants to do—and can get away with. (Csikszentmihalyi and Larson, 1984, pp. 59–60)

In addition, these adolescents spent 32 percent of their daily time in the *high school*, where they were presumably exposed to the socializing influence of both teachers and peers. *Of that time in school*, 62 percent was spent in formal classrooms, and the remainder was spent in more informal areas such as hallways, cafeterias, or student centers. Furthermore, adolescents spent about 27 percent of their total weekly time in *public places* (stores, buses, parks, streets, friends' homes, work settings, and so on). Being in public places presumably offers the adolescent the opportunity to witness adult behavior, as well as the opportunity for unsupervised activities (Csikszentmihalyi and Larson, 1984). In summary, according to Csikszentmihalyi and Larson: "Much of their life space appears to be dominated by adult values; at the same time, there are numerous locations where a person can find a measure of freedom from all 'others' " (p. 61).

With reference to *activities*, the external language of adolescence was divided into three parts, as follows (Fig. 15.5):

- *Productive activities* (those primarily related to school work, such as classwork or studying, and jobs) account for 29 percent of the adolescent's time.
- *Maintenance activities* (eating, resting, bathing, dressing, and so on) account for 31 percent of the adolescent's time.
- *Leisure activities* (socializing, watching television, reading, hobbies, and so on) take up 40 percent of the adolescent's time.

Productive Activities. Csikszentmihalyi and Larson (1984) point out that the time their sample of teenagers spent studying is considerably less than is spent by adolescents in other technological societies. That is, the 12.7 percent time spent studying translates into approximately 13.3 hours per week of studying time (if one assumes an average waking day of 15 hours). Japanese students, however, spend about 59 hours per week studying (Japanese Finance Ministry, 1980). Furthermore, in the Soviet Union, boys study 50 hours per week and girls study 53 hours a week (Zuzanek, 1980). In addition, it should be remembered that the school year is longer in these countries than in the United States. For example, the Japanese school year is 243 days long, whereas the school year in the United States is, on the average, 174 days long (Stigler et al., 1982). Therefore, not only do Japanese adolescents spend 69 more days in school than do American adolescents, but they devote more hours to studying for every day that school is in session (Csikszentmihalyi and Larson, 1984).

Jerrold Jacobson

Productive activities such as those related to schoolwork account for 29 percent of the adolescent's time.

In addition to school work and studying, the seventy-five adolescents in the study spent, on the average (for all four grades), 4.3 percent of their time in work or other productive activities. This translates into an average of 7.4 hours per week of work for the entire sample (keeping in mind that the *range* of working hours per week was from 5 to 33 hours, with third- and fourth-year high school students reporting more working hours per week). When this average of 7.4 hours per week is compared with the rates of adolescent work and productive activities in other industrialized countries, it indicates a relatively heavy time investment (Csikszentmihalyi and Larson, 1984). For example, the average Japanese high school student works only 1.75 hours a week (Japanese Finance Ministry, 1980). On the one hand, this relatively heavy work involvement of American adolescents could be viewed as an asset, since work activity will likely be an important part of their adult lives. On the other hand (as we discuss in more detail later in this chapter), work experience does *not always* lead to prosocial or positive outcomes (Steinberg, Greenberger, Garduque, Ruggiero, and Vaux, 1982; Greenberger and Steinberg, 1986).

Maintenance Activities. Daily maintenance activities involve the necessities of life, including eating and resting, as well as doing chores and running errands. In terms of weekly allotments of time, the following pattern emerged for the seventy-five adolescents in the study:

· Approximately 6 percent of weekly time is spent eating. It is important to note that eating is not exclusively a physiological maintenance activity. For many people (including adolescents), it is not only a pleasurable activity but an opportunity for social interaction.
· Approximately 3 percent of weekly time is spent resting (including time alone in one's room).
· Approximately 5 percent of weekly time is spent walking, driving, and generally moving from one place to another.
· Another 16 hours involved various activities, such as doing household chores (cleaning bathrooms, mowing the lawn).
· Finally, about 3 percent of weekly time involved personal grooming, including bathing and dressing (Csikszentmihalyi and Larson, 1984).

Leisure Activities. The largest block of time for activities was for *leisure*—about 40 percent of weekly time (Csikszentmihalyi and Larson, 1984). Leisure activities are those that are not determined by either maintenance activities (e.g., eating or resting) or productive activities (e.g., studying or classwork). If we assume that adolescents typically have 12 waking hours each day, for a total of 84 waking hours each week, then leisure activities constitute 33.6 hours per week. This is more than that of adolescents in other technological societies. For example, Japanese adolescents have approximately 28 hours per week of leisure time (Japanese Finance Ministry, 1980), and Soviet youth have 26 hours (Zuzanek, 1980). Leisure activities for American adolescents are divided as follows:

· *Socializing* is both the most frequent *leisure* activity and the most frequent of *all* activities in which adolescents are involved. Typically, socializing means *talking* to others, including peers and adults (although adolescents converse with peers about three times as often as with adults). Such talking provides a significant opportunity for sharing ideas, feelings, and impressions with others.
· *Watching television* is the second most common leisure-time activity. Whereas socializing or talking involves communication between people, watching television

About 29 percent of the adolescent's time is spent with friends.

involves no such conversational exchange. Furthermore, adolescent television watching was characterized by a lack of involvement in the television programs, since most of the adolescents did not know the program being watched (Csikszentmihalyi and Larson, 1984).

COMPANIONSHIP.   Although it is commonly assumed that the United States is a child-oriented (including adolescents) society, it is interesting to note how little time parents and adolescents spend in each other's company (Fig. 15.5). The companions with whom an adolescent spends his or her time are divided as follows:

• About *29 percent* of the adolescent's time is spent with *friends* and another *23 percent* with *classmates or peers* (see Fig. 15.6). It is necessary to distinguish peers from friends. The time spent with peers includes relationships that may not be freely chosen, including associations based on age and assignment to similar classes. On the other hand, friendships are completely voluntary. Friends and peers constitute, by far, the largest presence in the lives of adolescents. Some 52 percent of the adolescent's time is spent with both peers (classmates) and friends.
• About *27 percent of the time*, the adolescent is *alone*. This appears not at all surprising or unusual since many activities are done alone, including studying, grooming, resting, and so on.
• About *19 percent* of the adolescent's time is spent with *family* members and *2 percent* is spent with *others* (e.g., other adults). According to Csikszentmihalyi and Larson this represents an astonishingly limited contact with prime sources of socialization.

> In all societies since the beginning of time, adolescents have learned to become adults by observing, imitating, and interacting with grown-ups around them. The self is shaped and honed by feedback from men and women who already know who they are, and can help the young person find out who he or she is going to be. It is, therefore, startling how little time these teenagers spend in the company of adults. (1984, p. 73)

THE INTERNAL LANDSCAPE OF ADOLESCENCE.   Having examined where adolescents spend their time, what they do, and with whom, we are now ready to ask another important question: How do they feel about all this? This is an important question because it relates to the *subjective experience* of adolescence or the routine, daily building blocks of adolescent identity formation. In which contexts or situations do adolescents feel "alive," and where or when do they feel unhappy?

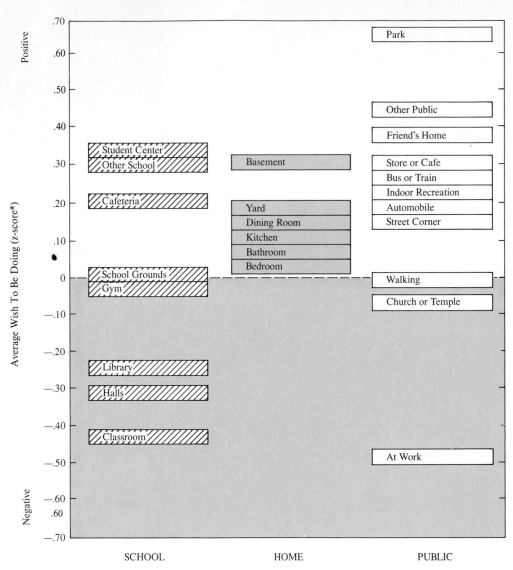

FIGURE 15.6
The relationship of intrinsic motivation to location. From Csikszentmihalyi and Larson, 1984, p. 90.

In order to capture the degree of self-sustained interest (intrinsic motivation) or satisfaction adolescents experienced, they were asked the following question: "Do you wish you had been doing something else?" This question was posed to the adolescents with reference to the *location* of their activities and the *activities* they were doing. The following results suggest where, when, and with whom adolescents feel active/motivated or passive/disinterested:

• *Motivation in locations.* The lowest level of motivation occurred in locations that were structured by adult standards (classroom, job, church, school library, and so on). The highest level of motivation occurred in settings that were the least organized by adult standards (parks, lunchroom, stores, friend's home, own dining room, and so on) (Fig. 15.6).
• *Motivation in different activities.* Teens appear to experience the lowest level of

motivation when they are involved in *productive activities* (classwork, job, studying, chores/errands, and so on). Maintenance activities (eating, resting, and personal care) and leisure activities (sports, socializing, watching television, hobbies, listening to music, and so on) produced higher levels of motivation.

Furthermore, it is interesting to note the activity the 75 adolescents found least enjoyable:

> Teenagers were most outraged when they had to do things simply "for show," such as straightening out their rooms or cleaning the blinds. "What f _____ g difference does it make if the tables are shiny?" a boy asked to [polish] the furniture grumbled. For most adults, order in the home is a very important sign of order in consciousness; but few teenagers see it that way. For them, concern with externalities is a hypocritical evasion of what is really important—namely, their inner feelings. (Csikszentmihalyi and Larson, 1984, pp. 93–94).

Culture and Society as Adolescent Context

In the world in which adolescents live, cultural and social values, norms, and expectations pervade their experience. The high school years are, in some sense, a preparation for living in a given culture and society. The specific skills learned in the high school as well as the social skills developed through peer interactions are a basis for social adaptation to the world of work, to interpersonal relationships, and, for many individuals, to family life.

Preparation for adult responsibilities has become more difficult as the rate of social change has increased. Adjusting to changes in society or personal circumstances is not easy for some people. Because of rapid social change, the future has become less predictable, complicating the role of adolescents attempting to make vocational choices and of schools attempting to prepare individuals with the skills necessary for the future (Schiamberg, 1973, 1986).

The Community

In middle childhood, the individual experiences the excitement of "discovering" people and things in the community. The firehouse, the police station, the city hall, and the supermarket are part of the "concrete" world of middle childhood. They are there, it seems, to be innocently experienced, to be visited, or to be talked about. But certainly they are not to be seriously criticized or thought about in too much detail. In adolescence, this changes.

By adolescence, the neighborhood/community boundaries are expanded, and the adolescent has increasing freedom to explore the neighborhood and community. By adolescence, most individuals have experienced numerous independent trips in and around the community with their friends. During early adolescence, the child consolidates a notion of himself or herself as a resident of a city and perhaps of a state. The concept of national affiliation, however, does not appear to develop until around twelve years of age or after (Piaget and Inhelder, 1969).

Although the early and later adolescents' ability to think about their social worlds may be enhanced, their ability to interact meaningfully with the broad social community may still be limited because there has been, and increasingly continues to be, a traditional pattern of segregating adolescents from adults (Coleman, 1974). There are both advantages and disadvantages to such enforced separation.

The Family

SOCIAL CHANGES IN THE ECOLOGY OF THE FAMILY.   The social changes that have influenced the families of adolescents include the same social changes that have influenced the families of infants, preschoolers, and school-age children (see Chapters 6, 9, and 12). These social changes include:

• *Urbanization and mobility of families.* This factor has had a dramatic impact on the role of the family in the lives of adolescents. Over the past fifty years, the movement to cities coupled with the geographic mobility between cities (about 16.6 percent of the population moved within the United States between 1982 and 1983) (U.S. Department of Commerce, 1984) has resulted in several changes influencing families. These changes have tended to weaken the very neighborhoods and communities that we have been talking about throughout this book in the following ways:

   1. The stability of communities, or organized entities of families with historical roots, has been seriously weakened.
   2. The relationship between the family, the community, and its institutions has become less effective.
   3. Finally, the accumulated results of these changes have made the family responsibilities of child rearing more difficult.

   The magnitude of the social changes that have occurred are often seen in the reminiscences of the parents of adolescents when they themselves were growing up. Urie Bronfenbrenner has made the following observations:

> Everybody in the neighborhood minded your business. . . . If you walked on the railroad tressle, the phone would ring at your home, and your parents would know what you had done before you got back home. People on the street would tell you to button your jacket, and ask why you were not in church last Sunday. Sometimes you liked it and sometimes you didn't—but at least people "cared." (1970, p. 96)

Adolescents in the past twenty years or so have probably been exposed to a much different concept of community and neighborhood.
• *Working mothers.* During the 1960s and 1970s a combination of changed attitudes toward women's roles (i.e., the women's movement) and economic changes necessitating full-time female employment brought on significant changes in the American family. Specifically, full-time employment became prevalent among women and, in particular, among women with young children. Although women had participated in the American work force before, their involvement was largely in part-time employment. It is generally acknowledged by economists and family specialists that full-time female employment can have a far more substantial impact on family life than part-time work (Masnick and Bane, 1980). A major change in family life was the modification of the historical family pattern—the man as sole wage earner and the women as full-time housewife.
• *Changing values.* One of the major changes in values in American society has been the increased tolerance for behavior and ideas that are different from past socially accepted norms (Conger, 1981). For family life, the impact of this value shift has meant a recognition and acceptance of a wide diversity of family structures including single-parent families, cohabitation, divorce, teenage pregnancy, and reconstituted families.

CHANGING FAMILIES AND ADOLESCENT DEVELOPMENT.   The social changes discussed above have had an impact on the structure of families. Generally, the result has been increased stress on many families as they attempt to negotiate new circumstances and demands brought on by such structural changes as divorce, single parenthood, absence of fathers, and maternal employment. Several factors appear to determine the impact of these family changes on adolescents:

• *Age of the child/adolescent.* The impact of a divorce or the absence of a father is greater if it occurs during childhood than during adolescence (Wallerstein and Kelley, 1980; Biller, 1981). There are several reasons for these differences, including the ability of the older child/adolescent to cope better with stress than the younger child and the greater access of the older child/adolescent to sources of emotional support outside the family (e.g., friends).
• *Sex of the child/adolescent.* Although children/adolescents of both sexes are affected, there is evidence that children/adolescents are more affected by changes in the status of the same-sex parent. For example, boys appear to be more influenced by father absence than girls (Biller, 1981). That is, boys from father-absent homes tend to have more school problems than girls from father-absent homes. Furthermore, girls are more influenced by maternal employment than boys (Hoffman, 1984). Specifically, girls with working mothers are more likely to indicate that they want a full-time career outside the home than girls whose mothers do not work. The work/career plans of boys appear to be unaffected by maternal employment (Hoffman, 1984).
• *Family stress and social support.* Structural changes in the family such as divorce or maternal employment are transitions for family members, which require some adaptation by all the family members to the new situations. A number of factors are related to the ability of family members, including the adolescent, to adapt to such transitions (e.g., maternal employment or divorce) (McCubbin, Sussman, and Patterson, 1983):

1. *Stressors and strains.* It is important to distinguish two types of demands that may be placed on families or individuals—stressors and strains. **Stressors** are events or experiences that occur at a moment in time, such as graduating from high school (a normative event) or having a car accident (a nonnormative event). **Strains** are unresolved problems due to prior stressors (e.g., financial hardship due to the loss of a job) or to the built-in tensions of ongoing role relationships (e.g., being a spouse in a failing marital relationship).

    The ability of family members to adapt to potential stressors, such as divorce or maternal employment, depends, in part, on whether that stressor is *transformed* into an unresolvable strain or whether there are ongoing strains that accompany a stressor. For example, if family members continue to maintain excessively negative attitudes toward a divorce, then the divorce (stressor) can be transformed into a continuous strain. That is, there is some evidence that children will adapt better to a divorce if both parents keep mutual conflict to a minimum, if both maintain a cooperative relationship during the separation, if both have adequate financial and emotional support, and if both continue involvement in the child's upbringing (Hetherington, 1981). Furthermore, there is evidence that children of working mothers who enjoy the combination of work and family responsibilities are more likely to benefit developmentally and to have a positive attitude toward maternal employment than are children of mothers who do not appreciate such a combination (Wallerstein and Kelly, 1980). Likewise, divorce may be much more difficult for children who have prior or ongoing psychological problems (Rutter, 1978).

2. *Adaptive resources. Family resources* are defined as the characteristics of the entire family system, individual family members, and the community that can be used to address the demands created by stressors and strains (McCubbin, Sussman, and Patterson, 1983). Family system resources are characteristics of the family unit that enable families to *protect* individual members from the impact of stressors and to *facilitate* the adaptation of individual family members during family crises. Two of the most important family resources for the management of family stress include *cohesion* (the bonds of unity between family members) and *adaptation* (the ability of family members to change their behavior or attitudes) (Olson, Russell, and Sprenkle, 1979, 1983). Other specific family resources that appear to be particularly helpful in dealing with stressful circumstances include the *ability to resolve conflicts,* family *communication skills* and a sense of *family pride* (Olson, Russell, and Sprenkle, 1983).

The resources of individual family members that contribute to stress management are numerous. Such resources include economic well-being, physical and emotional health, adequate education (which enables the individual to realistically and accurately understand a stressor and to develop adequate problem-solving skills), and psychological resources (George, 1980). Two particularly important psychological resources for managing stress include an adequate level of *self-esteem* (enabling the individual to be reasonably positive about himself or herself) and an *internal locus of control* (see discussion in Chapter 14) (Pearlin and Schooler, 1978).

Community resources are the characteristics of institutions or individuals outside the family that the family can utilize, including school programs, medical services, and so on. One of the most significant community resources for stress management is *social support* (Schiamberg and Abler, 1986). **Social support** can be defined as information that is shared for the purpose of facilitating problem solving and as the development of new social contacts (providing help and assistance). Social support can take several forms, including *emotional support,* which gives family members a feeling that they are loved and cared for; *esteem support,* which gives family members a feeling that they are important and valued; and finally, *network support,* which gives family members a feeling that they are part of a system of relationships involving mutual understanding and obligation (Cobb, 1982). There is considerable evidence that the availability and use of social support provide protection against the effects of stressful situations and help individuals recover from individual crises (Dohrenwend and Dohrenwend, 1980; Gottlieb, 1981; Cohen and Syme, 1985).

3. *Defining the situation.* Family members define stressful situations by assessing the demands of a given situation and the resources available to deal with it. Of course, these analyses are subjective and can vary considerably. That is, some family members may define a situation (e.g., divorce) as hopeless or unmanageable, whereas members of another family might define a similar situation as an opportunity for adaptation, change, or even growth. The success of family members in managing stressful situations depends, in part, on their ability to *redefine* a situation in a positive way in order to facilitate coping and adaptation. For example, if a family defines maternal employment as "being in the best interests of everyone, in the long run" (i.e., the mother has an opportunity to pursue an occupation outside the home and the family will have needed additional income), then such an attitude makes short-term problems more manageable and conducive to problem solving.

4. *Coping.* **Coping** is the behavioral and cognitive strategies one adopts in response to the demands of a given situation. Coping is "what you do" in that

situation. Coping efforts may take a number of forms, such as reducing or eliminating the demands in a situation (e.g., by actively working to solve a problem), organizing existing resources or developing new resources for dealing with the demands of a situation (e.g., contacting existing friends and making new acquaintances for social support), redefining the demands of a given situation to make it more manageable (e.g., saying "In the long-term, everything will work out for the best"), and managing the tension that results from a given situation (Pearlin and Schooler, 1978). Obviously, some coping strategies are more effective than others. For example, some family members and adolescents cope by *continually avoiding problems* (refusing to come to grips with the reality of a situation by denying its existence).

DIVORCE AND THE ADOLESCENT   In 1982, 1.18 million divorces affected more than a million children (Crosby, 1980; Kemper, 1983). Divorce affects a substantial number of adolescents—as many as one-third to one-half of all adolescents (Jurich and Jones, 1986).

Given the large proportion of adolescents affected by divorce, factors that determine the impact of divorce on adolescents are important. They include (Jurich and Jones, 1986):

• *Downward economic mobility.* The result of divorce is typically a single-parent family (usually with a female head of household) with diminished economic resources as the prime breadwinner (husband) withdraws (Blechman, 1982; Colletta, 1983). Adolescent response to this downward economic spiral depends on the age of the adolescent. Early adolescents (e.g., eleven- and twelve-year-olds) are more likely than older adolescents to feel the burden of reduced financial resources because younger adolescents tend to be influenced more than older adolescents by the pressures of peer-group membership and the related emphasis on clothes, hairstyles, and other items requiring reasonable spending money. On the other hand, older adolescents have, to some extent, moved beyond the simpler acceptance criteria of the larger peer group to the intimacy of smaller groups of friends (who are more concerned with the life changes brought on by puberty or with the personal attributes of friends).

• *Social support.* There is some evidence that the most important post-divorce support system for adolescents is friends (Visher and Visher, 1979; Saunders, 1983; Lutz, 1983). That is, the lack of supportive friends can be detrimental to adolescent adjustment after divorce, whereas the presence of supportive friends can speed the post-divorce recovery time (Haviland and Scarborough, 1981). Older adolescents, with more stable and intimate friendship patterns than younger adolescents, are more likely to benefit from the post-divorce support of adolescents (Jurich and Jones, 1986).

• *Absence of a parent.* In addition to friends, parents are also important parts of the adolescent's support system (Jurich, 1979). However, when divorce occurs, one parent frequently becomes the "custodial parent," and the other parent is physically absent. Furthermore, the situation is aggravated by the fact that divorce may really involve the emotional loss of *both* parents. Even though one parent may be physically absent, both parents may be lost to the adolescent as sources of support because of their emotional involvement in the divorce (Wallerstein and Kelly, 1975; Bloom, 1980).

Furthermore, there is some evidence that adolescents go through stages of separation from parents who divorce (Bloom, 1980):

1. *Stage of protest.* This first stage is characterized by highly emotional expressions of anger or outrage, sometimes designed by the adolescent as a last-ditch effort to bring the parents back together. This stage tends to last longer for early adolescents (approximately eleven to twelve years of age) than for middle adolescents (thirteen to fifteen years of age) or older adolescents (sixteen years and beyond).

2. *Stage of despair and detachment.* This stage is characterized by sadness and unresponsiveness as the adolescent recognizes his or her powerlessness in the face of an inevitable divorce. Middle adolescents spend most of their time in this stage:

> [Middle adolescents] focus on reality faster but have a difficult time accepting the fact that they are powerless to change such a major event in their lives. Consequently, they may consolidate their energies by isolating themselves and minimizing input from others. In the case of late adolescents, they are more mature and more capable of realizing that there are certain events over which they can have little or no control. Being less egocentric, late adolescents are also better able to distinguish the parent's decision to separate as distinct from any tacit separation from the parent-adolescent relationship. (Jurich and Jones, 1986, p. 317)

3. *Stage of reintegration.* This stage is characterized by the adolescent's feeling of relative security, having now accepted the divorce and the new family situation. Such acceptance is not, of course, a simple task, since it requires that the adolescent recognize the positive qualities of both parents, as well as establishing a sense of personal identity incorporating the new family arrangement (Kressel and Deutsch, 1977; Jurich and Jones, 1986).

Although it is ideal for both parents to be positively incorporated into the life of the adolescent, such a situation is not always possible. In the first place, the visits of the noncustodial parent tend to taper off over time, either because of barriers in the life of that parent (time constraints or the emotional pain of visitation) or barriers between the two parents (Whiteside, 1982; Peterson, Leigh, and Day, 1984; Jurich and Jones, 1986). In addition, some parents may try to win over the adolescent by actively competing against the other parent for the adolescent's loyalties (Wallerstein and Kelly, 1978; Whiteside, 1982; Abelsohn, 1983).

• *Discipline.* There is some evidence that a persistent source of difficulty for the adolescent is the quality of the disciplinary roles that occur both during and after the divorce (Jurich, 1979). Since it is generally acknowledged that adolescents need, at a minimum, reasonably consistent parental expectations or rules, a divorce that places disciplinary practices in a state of flux or confusion may be detrimental to the adolescent.

• *Emotional reactions of the adolescent to the divorce.* There is some evidence that the adolescent's emotional reaction to divorce may be similar to the mourning reactions to the death of a person. In this case, however, the adolescent is mourning the death of the parents' marriage (Theis, 1977; Jurich and Jones, 1986). Briefly, the stages of emotional reaction to divorce include the following:

1. *Denial.* Because adolescents' initial reaction to divorce is one of emotional upheaval, a first response to this situation is to *deny* that it is really happening. "There must be some mistake—it can't be my parents." The denial of the reality of divorce is more commonly found among early adolescents.

2. *Anger and guilt.* As the reality of the divorce sets in, adolescents experience feelings of anger and guilt. They experience anger that such a profound dis-

junction could be occurring in their lives and guilt that somehow they must be responsible for the divorce. This guilt appears to be the case for both younger and older adolescents (Wallerstein and Kelly, 1979).

3. *Bargaining.* Many adolescents attempt to bargain with their parents in an effort to reduce the conflict between parents and to reunite them. The adolescent may do such things as performing favors, doing household chores, and so on. Other adolescents (particularly middle and older adolescents) indicate disappointment in their parents' inability to effectively negotiate their marital relationship (Jurich and Jones, 1986).

4. *Depression.* When adolescents realize that nothing more can be done to save their parents' marriage, some level of depression is a common outcome. This depression may also lead to a reduced level of self-esteem. Most adolescents will eventually regain their normal level of feeling. However, those early adolescents who have had prior psychological problems may be at risk for a spiraling cycle of continued depression (Jurich and Jones, 1986).

5. *Acceptance.* In this final stage, the adolescent understands that the security and safety of his or her previous family life is gone. The emphasis is now on finding positive and creative ways of relating to his or her parents and others. This task of acceptance occurs during the same time that the adolescent is negotiating the task of identity development:

> Thus, acceptance of parental divorce, recognition of self-worth, and the establishment of a solid ego are difficult tasks to accomplish at the same time. After pain and struggle, however, these are tasks that most adolescents accomplish with varying degrees of difficulty. (Jurich and Jones, 1986, p. 325).

THE FAMILY WITH ADOLESCENT OFFSPRING.   The adolescent period may be a particularly difficult one for both adolescents and their parents. During this period, adolescents have a good deal of freedom and may spend most of the day away from home and away from the supervison of adults. It is during this period that many of the principles of moral behavior that parents have emphasized as important throughout childhood may be tested by the adolescent. During this phase of the family cycle, parents may be called on to balance their attempts to give the adolescent the freedom to make his or her own decisions with their attempts to provide appropriate limits and emotional support for the adolescent. Some of the issues that often occur in this period include career choices for the adolescent, the selection of a college, sexuality and dating, and the use of alcohol or drugs. Parents may sometimes feel that their adolescents resent their help.

Families with adolescent offspring.

Sylvia Byers

The adjustment of each adolescent to his or her own emerging sense of adulthood is unique. The adolescent on the verge of this transition often presents a special challenge to parents. The attempts of adolescents to attain a sense of identity may lead them to be assertive with their parents. This assertiveness, in turn, may contribute to increased intergenerational strife.

The general pattern of adolescent-parent relationships involves an increase in intergenerational conflict from the early to the later teens, with reduced conflict during young adulthood. During the period of adolescence, parents begin to accept—or rather, learn to accept—the growing independence of their adolescent offspring.

For many couples in this phase of the family life cycle, marriage no longer occupies the central position that it did earlier. Husbands may be heavily involved in occupational and community activities. Wives may be dissatisfied because they are "taken for granted" by both their husbands and their adolescent offspring. Communication between the parents of adolescents appears to occur even less frequently than between parents of younger children. A considerable amount of intellectual and emotional energy is apparently required to manage family affairs. Sometimes little energy is left for the husband-wife relationship. This stage involves the redefinition of the parents' roles in relation to their children. The parents are involved in "letting go of" their children and adjusting to their children's independence. Some conflict and upset may occur for parents, particularly for the mother if her center of interest and time involvement has been primarily the family. Furthermore, the husband may be in the midst of his career, highly involved in his work, and somewhat removed from the scene. On the other hand, the husband may be coming to grips with the "realities" of his occupational and life situation and, therefore, might be somewhat preoccupied with his own concerns. The interaction of these factors may well make this a particularly difficult time for parents. In fact, the role shifts and life concerns of the parents coupled with the typical life choices in adolescence may result in a co-occurrence of "identity" crises. Such a situation may not facilitate honest and open communication between generations (Steinberg, 1981).

ADOLESCENT-PARENT RELATIONSHIPS.   What does adolescence mean for family relationships or, more specifically, for adolescent-parent relationships?

> Studies where family interaction is directly observed suggest that there may be a period of temporary disequilibrium in early adolescence while the family adjusts to having a "new person" in the household—"new" in stature, "new" in approaching reproductive capability, "new" in cognitive competence—but this disequilibrium in no way approaches the shoot-out that many parents are led to expect from media reports. Instead, in most families, there appears to be a period of adaptation to the primary changes, a period when both parents and their newly adolescent children work out—often not consciously—what these changes mean for their relationship. (Hill, 1980, p. 33)

In order to fully appreciate the nature of the *adolescent*-parent relationship, it is important to understand how this relationship differs from the *child*-parent relationships (Garbarino and Gilliam, 1980; Garbarino, 1985):

• *The power of the child is much less than that of the adolescent.* For example, the adolescent typically has greater ability to actively participate in family interactions and, therefore, to directly influence and stimulate family decisions or family conflict.

"There's no pleasin' some people. . . . I got my hands nice an' clean . . . so now she's yellin' about the towel!"

• *The parent has to deal with significant others that have more influence over the adolescent than over the child.* Those significant others include other adults, peers, and intimate friends of the same and opposite sex.

• *The child's cognitive skills are usually not as advanced as the adolescent's.* This means, of course, that the parent-adolescent relationship should be evolving toward an adult-adult interaction (moving from a parent-child relationship). Furthermore, it has been suggested that parents of children can "get away with more" than can parents of adolescents (Garbarino and Gilliam, 1980; Garbarino, 1985). One reason for this is that adolescents are better able (due to their mental and social development) to perceive the flaws and inconsistencies in parental reasoning.

Given these differences between adolescents and children as well as the increased financial cost of raising adolescents, it is not surprising that many parents find the adolescent years both challenging and difficult (Pasley and Gecas, 1984). Specifically, evidence from one study indicated that ages fourteen to eighteen years were ranked by parents as the most difficult, followed by ages ten to thirteen years (Pasley and Gecas, 1984). As indicated previously, some of the vulnerability parents experience may be due to their own needs and issues in their own life histories, including their own mid-life crises (Pelcovitz et al., 1984). Such a situation is particularly unfortunate because this is just the time when adolescents need support from their parents in their movement toward autonomy and identity development (See box—Leaving Home and Adolescent Identity).

A useful approach to understanding how and why some families are able to manage the challenge of adolescence involves the two dimensions of *family cohesion*

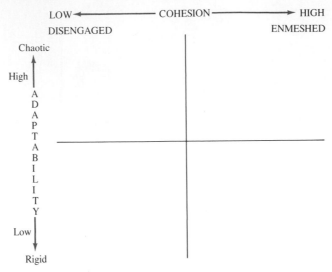

FIGURE 15.7
Family cohesion and family adaptibility in family functioning. Based on Barnes and Olson, 1985, pp. 438–447.

and *family adaptability* (Olson, Russell, and Sprenkle, 1979, 1983; Barnes and Olson, 1985):

- **Family cohesion** refers to the extent of emotional bonding occurring between family members. Family cohesion can be thought of as a single dimension or continuum going from *enmeshed* (*extreme connectedness* of family members) to *disengaged* (*extreme separateness* of family members) (see Fig. 15.7).
- **Family adaptability** refers to the general characteristics of the whole family system to reorganize (i.e., change the power structure, rules of interaction, and so on) in response to stress from specific situations or developmental changes in family members (e.g., adolescence). Family adaptability can be thought of as a single dimension moving from *chaotic* interaction at one extreme to *rigid* interaction at the other extreme (Fig. 15.7).

With regard to family cohesion, the terms *separateness* (recognition of the autonomy of the adolescent) and *connectedness* (recognition of the adolescent's need for intimacy and emotional support) are at the heart of the major challenge of adolescence. That is, both the adolescent and the parent must learn how to keep the need for both separateness and connectedness in proper balance. The term *cohesion* has been used by those in family research and family therapy to describe the nature of this separateness and/or connectedness (i.e., social bonding) in family relationships. Furthermore, cohesion can be thought of as a continuum with two extremes—*enmeshment* and *disengagement* (Olson, Russell, and Sprenkle, 1983; Grotevant and Cooper, 1985) (see Fig. 15.8):

- **Enmeshment.** Families that are highly cohesive are said to be *enmeshed*. This means that the life experiences and activities of members of such families are so closely connected and intertwined that there is little emphasis placed on individuality (or individual development) (Fig. 15.8). There is excessive emphasis placed on identification with family interests or goals, to the point that individual uniqueness or separateness is virtually ignored (Hoffman, 1981). Typically,

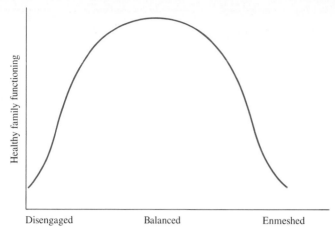

FIGURE 15.8
Cohesion between family members and healthy family functioning. From Galvin and Brommel, 1982.

extreme examples of family enmeshment are uncommon. Also, it does not follow that enmeshment characterizes *all* relationships in a family (i.e., some family relationships might be enmeshed, whereas others might not). In summary, enmeshed relationships offer a poor environment for development because they allow for little individuality, separateness, or identity. This is particularly significant for adolescents, who require reasonable levels of independence and separateness in order to continue the process of identity development.

· **Disengagement.** Family disengagement refers to families that have extremely low levels of cohesion (Fig. 15.8). In such a circumstance, there is little emotional attachment holding the family members together and, therefore, little basis for a relationship. As in the case of family enmeshment, family disengagement does not ordinarily characterize all the relationships in a family. Obviously, some amount of cohesion or "glue" is necessary to hold a family together (Hoffman, 1981). The concept of disengagement is particularly useful in describing the distance between specific family members. In extremely disengaged

Despite current concerns about the relevance of parental influence, parents are still vital in helping the adolescent.

Leaving Home and Adolescent Identity

Every year, virtually thousands of adolescents leave home for the first time to attend college or to work. Leaving home represents the beginning of adult status. Success in achieving full adult status as a psychologically autonomous individual may depend, to a large extent, on the impact of their departure on the *family system* (e.g., the attitudes of the parents toward their children and their own lives.)

Regardless of the timing or the manner of leaving home, many parents and young people are sometimes puzzled by the separation process. Is there a right or correct time for the adolescent to leave home? Our society offers few guidelines for assuring a smooth transition from adolescence to adulthood. How do parents know if they are pushing their children out of the nest too early or whether they are clinging too long to their offspring?

Several case studies will illustrate the variety of the timing of leaving home:

1. *Karen—Leaving Home Too Soon.* Some adolescents leave home before their parents think they are ready to do so. Karen was a seventeen-year-old who was living at home with her parents until two months before graduation from high school. At that time she had a violent argument with her mother about her right to stay out late at night, and she left home. Although she realized that her parents were upset about her departure, she felt she could no longer live at home, where she felt confined and unable to be anything more than a child.

2. *Brian—Leaving Home with "No Hassle."* Brian grew up in Fresno, California, and graduated from high school in 1979. In a scene that seemed to be right out of the movie *American Graffiti,* Brian boarded a plane and flew East to college. He returned home during summers and most vacations. After graduation Brian took a job with an advertising firm in Boston. Due to the requirements of his working activities, he was able to return home less and less regularly, usually only a few times a year. Brian's leaving home was a gradual process that seemed perfectly normal to both Brian and his parents.

3. *John—No Pressure to Leave Home.* John was twenty-eight years old, the son of a retired construction worker in Sioux City, Iowa. He was the second of five children. John's older brother was married

and lived nearby. His three younger sisters, age twelve, seventeen, and nineteen, also lived at home. John worked for a local radio station. He used part of his salary to help his family pay the bills. The family was always close and John never felt any pressure to leave home or, for that matter, to stay at home. Although he lived at home, John was treated as an adult and could come and go as he pleased.

Despite the variation in patterns of leaving home, there is evidence that, in both a psychological and a physical sense, leaving home is becoming more dif-

Gale Schiamberg

ficult. Since the late 1960s, the percentage of young Americans living at home has increased by 25 percent. One reason for this increase is economic. That is, young people are finding it harder to find jobs and to financially establish themselves. In addition, the average age of marriage for both males and females has risen. This means, of course, that young people are living at home for longer periods of time before marriage than previous generations of youth.

An emerging body of research has demonstrated the important relationship of the adolescent's success in leaving home to the *family system* (Stierlin, 1974, 1975; Haley, 1980; Sullivan and Sullivan, 1980). In a series of studies at the National Institutes of Mental Health, Helm Stierlin (1974) reported on the clinical profiles of thirty families who were referred to his group for family counseling because of a troubled adolescent child. Stierlin and his colleagues found that the adolescents' problems appeared to be linked to problems in the lives of their middle-aged parents.

The fathers of these adolescents appeared to be undergoing serious doubts about the direction of their own lives at the very moment their adolescent offspring seemed to have an array of options in love and work. These fathers were threatened by their child's movement toward adulthood. They responded to this situation with either total disengagement and lack of involvement or bickering criticism.

Stierlin and his colleagues found that the mothers of the adolescents were, like the father, involved in a crisis of their own at the time of adolescent separation. These mothers were confronted with the prospect of an "empty nest," or the loss of their child-rearing role. Many of these women responded by becoming overly involved in the lives of their children—to the point of meddling and intrusion of privacy—at the very time when these adolescents needed to be autonomous and independent.

A common result of this family profile of "resigned" fathers and "intrusive" mothers was an unhappy and frequently abrupt departure of the adolescent. In other instances, Stierlin found that when such adolescents remained at home, the relationship with their parents was characterized as a "running battle." Regardless of whether they left home or not, Stierlin found that these adolescents failed at the central tasks of adolescent identity formation—a beginning career orientation and meaningful interpersonal relationships outside the family.

The research of Stierlin and his colleagues has been supported by the findings of Jay Haley (1980). According to Haley, a family therapist, the time of greatest challenge or threat to a family system occurs when someone is entering the family (e.g., birth of a child) or leaving the family (e.g., the adolescent's leaving home or the death of a family member). Haley suggested that frequently when adolescents become involved in troublesome behaviors such as drug addiction, criminality, or school failure, the process of leaving home is *malfunctioning* for the *entire family system*. Haley frequently traced these adolescent problems to the need of some family members to preserve the stability of an unhealthy family system even at the price of damage to the psychological development of another family member. For example, the adolescent's problems often served to prevent the parents from addressing issues in their own relationship that might—when faced honestly and directly—result in divorce. Thus, if the adolescent's failures to successfully adapt in school, work, or intimate relationships regularly occupied parents' attention, then the family system could be saved. Unfortunately, the cost was high—the emotional growth of the adolescent.

Although most adolescents manage to leave home successfully, the question still remains—What is the significance of leaving home? The overall importance of leaving home lies in the challenge such a separation from parents poses to childhood identity (e.g., dependency on parents). However, it is important to distinguish between *physically* leaving home (simply living at a physical distance, apart from one's family of origin) and *symbolically* leaving home. Symbolically leaving home is the process of identity formation necessary for the attainment of independent adult status. It can be attained whether or not the adolescent physically leaves home. In other words, the real significance of leaving home is as an inner process, not an outer movement. Leaving home, then, is the capstone to adolescent identity that marks the beginning of adulthood.

relationships, adolescents would feel little of the emotional support and attachment that is *still* important for them in addition to independence and freedom (Garmezy and Rutter, 1983).

It is important to keep in mind that most families are in the "balanced" area of family cohesion (Fig. 15.8). Typically, it is this balance between recognizing needs for *both* separateness or individuality *and* connectedness that characterizes healthy family functioning (Grotevant and Cooper, 1983; Olson, Russell, and Sprenkle, 1983; Powers et al., 1983). There is considerable evidence that adolescents who demonstrate higher degrees of identity exploration are from families that provide an optimal or balanced environment in which *both* the individuality of the adolescent *and* his or her connectedness to the family are supported (Cooper, Grotevant, and Condon, 1983). In a similar view, there is evidence that positive adolescent ego development is more likely to occur in families where parents emphasize *enabling behaviors* (e.g., empathizing with the adolescent's general and specific circumstances, unconditionally accepting the adolescent as a person with strengths and weaknesses, and so on) rather than *constraining behaviors* (e.g., failing to understand or appreciate the adolescent's circumstances, not accepting or devaluing the adolescent as a person, withholding information, and so on) (Hauser et al., 1984).

ADOLESCENT-PARENT CONFLICTS.   A not-uncommon experience is the intensification of adolescent-parent conflict during the period of adolescence. It is important to note, however, that although there seems to be an increase in such conflict (at least for boys), parent-child relationships are generally more positive than negative during adolescence (Matteson, 1975). However, several reasons have been suggested for the apparent "conflict of generations" during the adolescent years (Burr et al., 1979; Ellis, 1986; Schiamberg, 1986):

• *The different content of experience.* The adolescents of any given era are likely to be living under a different set of historical circumstances than their parents when they were adolescents. For example, the content of experience for an adolescent during the American Depression of the 1930s was quite different from that of an adolescent during the more affluent 1960s. Differing adolescent experiences may lead to different expectations about appropriate adolescent values or behavior.

What Do Adolescents Expect from Parents?

The following is a composite (and by no means all-inclusive) list of some parental characteristics that seem beneficial to the adolescent.

Parental interest and help. One of the ways that adolescents know their parents care about them is by their interest and their willingness to back the ado-

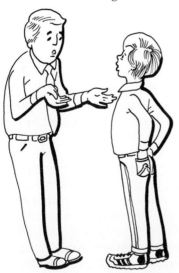

lescents up and help them when necessary. Adolescents want attention from their parents.

Listening, understanding, and talking. A frequent complaint of adolescents is that their parents do not listen to their ideas or accept their opinions as relevant or try to understand their feelings or point of view. Adolescents seem to value sympathetic, "understanding" parents who feel that their child has something important to say and are willing, therefore, to communicate with him or her.

Love and acceptance. One of the components of love is acceptance. One way that love is shown is by knowing, and then accepting, the adolescent as he or she is, faults and all.

Trust. Some parents have difficulty trusting their adolescents. These parents tend to project their own fears, anxieties, and guilt onto the adolescent.

Autonomy. One goal of every adolescent is to be accepted as an independent individual. As we have pointed out, such autonomy increases during adolescence. The adolescent wants and needs parents who will grant independence, but in slowly increasing amounts, rather than all at once.

Drawing by W. Miller; © 1971 The New Yorker Magazine, Inc.

"Could you redefine those commandments so as to make them more meaningful to the youth of today?"

• *The lack of clearly defined steps marking the recession of parental authority over children and adolescents.* As we pointed out, it is quite clear when adolescence begins (the onset of puberty). However, it is not nearly so clear when the period of adolescence is over. This lack of clarity or absence of formal ceremonies (rites of passage) to mark the beginning of adulthood makes it less certain when parental authority over the adolescent ends.

• *Psychological and social differences between adolescents and their parents.* On the psychological level, adolescents have often been described as "idealistic" (Schiamberg, 1969, 1973, 1986). On the other hand, adults are sometimes described as "realistic." This difference between the generations is often attributed to the "experience" of adults. Furthermore, this difference between the generations is not something new or recent. The ancient Greek philospher Aristotle felt that the youth of his day were not only idealistic but also naive and overconfident of their knowledge and abilities. He said, "They think they know everything and are always quite sure about it. This, in fact, is why they overdo everything."

On the social level, there are differences in the "roles" of parent and adolescent. For example, the parent's role during childhood and, to some degree, adolescence is to supervise or oversee the development of the young person. Adolescents, on the other hand, need independent experiences to establish themselves as persons in their own right. A reasonable level of adolescent-parent conflict or disagreement may be considered a normal activity in the process of adolescent self-determination.

The Peer Group

Peer groups and friends provide the adolescent with an arena for much of the learning that occurs in adolescence. In this section, we examine the following topics: (1) functions of the peer group; (2) structure of the peer group and how that structure changes over time; and finally, (3) stages of peer-group development and friendships.

FUNCTIONS OF THE PEER GROUP.   Peers play a vital role in the life of the adolescent as the adolescent's ties with parents become looser. Increasingly, relationships with peers of both the same and the opposite sex serve as an introduction and a prelude to later adult relationships in work and social relations. The functions of the peer group include the following (Hartup, 1984):

• *Providing primary status.* Primary status is the status that the individual earns through her or his own efforts and through the demonstration of her or his abilities and skills. It differs from attributed status, which comes from being a member of a given family. Peer groups help the adolescent form a self-image by conferring a primary status.
• *Providing norms for governing behavior.* By moving into and forming peer groups that establish their own norms and standards of behavior, the adolescent is able to deviate from parental norms while having the support of significant others. This support is particularly important to the adolescent because of the initial confusion the early adolescent must experience when confronted with the mass of possible values, life-styles, and vocations that make up our society. Peer-group norms are designed to provide both guidelines for behavior and a source of common evaluation for appraising activities.
• *Facilitating emancipation from the family.* We might begin by asking why it is necessary to be "emancipated" from the family. There are at least two good reasons. In the first place, as we pointed out earlier in our discussion of adolescent-parent relationships, healthy family relationships move naturally and normally in the direction of adolescent independence. The peer group builds on this trend. Second, because of the intensity of relationships in the modern nuclear family, the peer group serves a "distancing" function between parents and adolescents. That is, the peer group helps the parents "see" the adolescent as an independent individual. Furthermore, the adolescent begins to understand both the satisfaction and the pain of relating to others in an independent, adult fashion. These experiences help adolescents begin to appreciate their parents as people (Youniss, 1980).
• *The peer group as a testing ground.* The peer group allows adolescents to test themselves in a variety of roles. They can test abilities, emotions, feelings, values, and life-styles within an empathic group. By observing and talking about how peers react to his or her way of thinking or behaving, the adolescent is further able to extend and refine his or her self-concept and range of behaviors (Youniss, 1980; Smollar and Youniss, 1982).

STRUCTURE OF THE PEER GROUP.   How are peer groups organized? What types of peer groups are there? In one of the classic studies on the structure of adolescent peer groups and the organization of the "adolescent society," James Coleman (1961) found that the "leading crowds" in high schools throughout the United States were similarly composed. There was a relatively large emphasis on athletics and popularity and far less emphasis on academics or the brilliant student.

    Coleman's examination of the leading crowds in ten different high schools in Illinois led him to the conclusion that, for the most part, sports abilities for boys and success in social relationships for girls were the most important characteristics of membership in the leading crowd. In one part of his study he asked male adolescents the following question: "How would you most like to be remembered

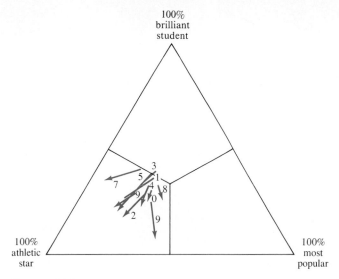

FIGURE 15.9

Adolescent boy's responses to the question "How would you most like to be remembered in school: as an athletic star, a brilliant student, or most popular?" From Adelson, 1980, p. 420.

in school: as an athletic star, a brilliant student, or most popular?" As indicated in Figure 15.9, athletic success was by far the most common choice.

A replication of this early research (Eitzen, 1975) indicated that the adolescent/ peer experience hadn't changed much over a fifteen to twenty-year period (at least, in terms of the support and prominence accorded various groups). Athletics were still of primary importance to male adolescents for attaining status in high school. To the question "What does it take to be important?" the answer "good grades, honor roll" ranked fourth out of six items for boys and fifth out of six items for girls. However, D. Stanley Eitzen (1975) qualified Coleman's findings in that the importance of athletics depended on several factors, including the adolescent, the community, and the school. For example, being a sports hero was more important to sophomores than to seniors and to boys who were highly involved in school than to those whose main friendship groups were elsewhere. For boys in smaller schools, athletics was more important than for those in larger schools. Likewise, athletics was more important in working-class communities than in upper-middle-class communities, where many parents were professionals. Thus, one could argue that the "adolescent society" really mirrors the values and behaviors of the larger community.

CLIQUES AND CROWDS.   The social structure of peer groups is composed of two basic subgroups: cliques and crowds (Dunphy, 1963). The **clique** (the small group-ing of two, three, or four friends) gives the adolescent the chance to establish some degree of companionship, security, and acceptance before moving out into the larger social scene, or **crowd.** The *crowd* is the larger unit.

Cliques and crowds have different functions. Most of the crowd, or large-group activities (dances, hayrides, parties, and so on), occur on weekends; cliques usually meet on weekdays. Crowd activities are more formally organized; cliques meet informally during school as well as before and after school. The predominant

Darryl Jacobson

Darryl Jacobson

Peer relationships involve both crowds and cliques.

activity of cliques is conversation. One function they perform is that of organizing, publicizing, and evaluating crowd activities.

STAGES OF PEER-GROUP DEVELOPMENT.   The development of the peer group in adolescence is marked by several distinct stages. Each of these stages serves to regulate and organize the adolescent's social development and particularly his or her heterosexual relationship (Dunphy, 1963) (see Fig. 15.10).

• *Stage 1: The precrowd stage.* Stage 1 includes the isolated unisexual peer groups of late childhood and early adolescence. There is little interaction *between* groups and almost no organized dating. What is learned occurs primarily within the group. At this stage, adolescents are not attending parties and their leisure activities may involve talking, playing sports, or just "hanging around" with a small group of same-sex friends.

• *Stage 2: The beginning of the crowd.* Stage 2 includes unisexual peer groups and the *beginnings* of group-to-group heterosexual interaction. Such interaction is considered "daring" and is undertaken only in the presence of other group members. For example, arranging a date requires the support of fellow group members to bolster the courage of the "asker." Boys and girls may attend the same party, but most of the time at the party is usually spent with same-sex peers. In this stage, both boys and girls may be relatively uncomfortable and uncertain about relating to members of the opposite sex. The mixed-sex social events at this stage provide the opportunity for adolescents to learn about the opposite sex, operating from the secure base of the same-sex peer group. For example, it is not uncommon to find young adolescent males and females observing each other from opposite ends of the same room.

• *Stage 3: The crowd in transition.* Stage 3 marks the beginning of the *heterosexual clique.* The upper-status members of the unisexual cliques begin to form an emergent heterosexual grouping. Those adolescents who belong to these emergent groupings still maintain membership in their unisexual groups. During this stage, dating begins to occur on a more frequent basis.

• *Stage 4: The fully developed crowd.* Stage 4 is marked by heterosexual cliques in

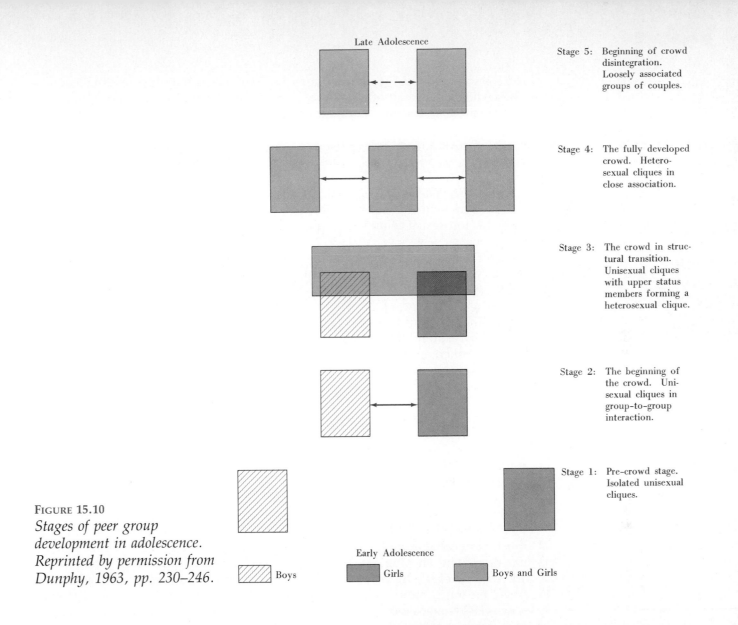

Late Adolescence

Stage 5: Beginning of crowd disintegration. Loosely associated groups of couples.

Stage 4: The fully developed crowd. Heterosexual cliques in close association.

Stage 3: The crowd in structural transition. Unisexual cliques with upper status members forming a heterosexual clique.

Stage 2: The beginning of the crowd. Unisexual cliques in group-to-group interaction.

Stage 1: Pre-crowd stage. Isolated unisexual cliques.

Early Adolescence

Boys   Girls   Boys and Girls

FIGURE 15.10
Stages of peer group development in adolescence. Reprinted by permission from Dunphy, 1963, pp. 230–246.

Darryl Jacobson

Stage 3, the crowd in transition, marks the beginning of the heterosexual clique.

close association. Soon the crowd comprises almost entirely heterosexual cliques. These cliques may pair off on the basis of common interests (e.g., yearbook staff, hall monitors, and so on). Furthermore, it may happen that some adolescents may drop out of the crowd if their interests do not coincide with those of the heterosexual cliques. In fact, one of the most frequent reasons for peer unpopularity or rejection is an adolescent's inability to successfully negotiate the transition from same-sex activities to heterosexual interests or dating (Savin-Williams, 1979).

• *Stage 5: Beginning of crowd disintegration.* With graduation from high school, the "glue" that held the heterosexual cliques together is no longer present. High school heterosexual cliques are replaced by loose associations of couples.

Clique Formation. The most important factor that influences the formation of cliques is *similarity* (of age, socioeconomic background, race, gender, and interests during early adolescence).

• *Age.* The high school experience is organized on the basis of age grades. The inevitable result of this age segregation is that clique membership and friendship are determined, in part, by an adolescent's age grade (e.g., freshman, sophomore, junior, and senior). It is interesting to note that when an adolescent's friends are from other schools, they are as likely to be younger or older than the adolescent (Blyth, Hill, and Thiel, 1982).

• *Social class level.* There is considerable evidence that adolescents associate primarily with peers, friends, and dating partners from the same or an adjacent social class. That is, adolescents in the upper middle class would ordinarily be with other upper-middle-class or middle-class adolescents, but rarely with lower-class adolescents (Hollingshead, 1975).

• *Race.* As a factor in clique formation, race appears to be a weaker determinant in childhood than in adolescence. Generally speaking, this finding is consistent with the fact that the formation of peer groups in middle childhood is subject to much more general and individual-based characteristics (e.g., being a nice person, not disrupting ongoing activities, being a "good sport," and so on) than in the adolescent years. On the other hand, participation in adolescent peer groups is based on much more specific and recognized requirements (e.g., specific skills, social class characteristics, particular interests, and so on). Race becomes a significant factor in adolescent clique formation for several reasons. In the first place, as indicated above, adolescent cliques tend to be structured on socioeconomic lines. A high number of minority-group adolescents are typically found in economically poor families. Second, adolescents tend to choose friends and associates with similar attitudes toward school and similar achievement levels (Schofield, 1981; Berndt, 1982). Unfortunately, the tendency is for minority youth to cluster at lower achievement levels. And, finally, racial prejudice may be a factor in the racial segregation of adolescent cliques. In one study of a recently desegregated high school, white students felt that the black students were hostile and aggressive. The black students thought the white students were prejudiced and unwilling to make friends with them. Unfortunately, these attitudes tended to reinforce each other and to prevent the formation of interracial cliques (Schofield, 1981). One of the constructive conclusions that emerged from this study was the recommendation that desegregation efforts are more likely to have positive outcomes (socially and academically) when they are begun in the early school years. When children grow up together and get to know one another over a longer period of time, they are less likely to develop misunderstandings.

• *Gender.* As indicated, during early adolescence cliques and crowds tend to be organized on the basis of sex. This same-sex organization precedes the transition to heterosexual cliques.

• *Common interests.* In addition to age, social class level, race, and gender, common interests are an important determinant of clique formation. Several factors are involved. In the first place, as indicated, adolescents organize cliques on the basis of attitudes toward school and school achievement (Berndt, 1982). Students who gravitate more toward school projects and homework may have less free or leisure time to spend with other adolescents who place less emphasis on school. Second, the nature of leisure or free-time activities strongly influences the organization of cliques. For example, their clothes, the music they listen to, where they congregate after (and during) school, and their activities all contribute to the formation of cliques.

Frequently, parents may become concerned when their adolescents associate with peers who, from the parents' perspective, have undesirable attitudes or behaviors. Of course, parents are concerned that their adolescents will become *similar* to these friends through the process of peer *socialization.* On the other hand, adolescents (and other people) *select* their friends on the basis of a series of real or perceived similarities (as discussed above in clique formation). Are the ultimate similarities between adolescent friends due to peer *socialization* or to *selecting* friends who are really similar to begin with? There is evidence that the similarity among adolescent friends on a broad range of dimensions (school attitudes, drug use, delinquency, and so on) is determined *almost equally* by *both socialization* and initial *selection* (Kandel, 1978).

Who's Popular and Who's Not? Within a given clique or peer group, what determines whether adolescents are accepted or rejected? What are the determinants of popularity in adolescence?

• *Popular* adolescents are those who have the requisite social skills, in the eyes of their peers, to perceive and meet the needs of peers and to have self-confidence (without being conceited). In addition, the popular adolescent is one who is cheerful, friendly, and intelligent (that is, intelligent enough to understand the requirements for popularity).

• *Unpopular* adolescents, for the most part, behave in ways opposite to that of popular adolescents (e.g., low levels of social skills, self-esteem, friendliness, and so on). Their behavior may interfere with group activities for any number of reasons, including a lack of enthusiasm, shyness, and being conceited. Another characteristic frequently associated with unpopularity or rejection (as mentioned before) is the inability to negotiate peer group/crowd transitions at the same time as one's peers. For example, the young adolescent who is quite popular in same-sex cliques but expresses little or no interest in dating or socializing with the opposite sex when heterosexual cliques emerge will experience rejection by peers (Dunphy, 1963; Savin-Williams, 1976, 1979).

FRIENDSHIPS. Whereas cliques and crowds operate as facilitators of social development in adolescence, intimate friendships (usually within peer groups) are important to self-development. The most important feature of adolescent friendship is the sharing of one's feelings and thoughts about important and everyday concerns.

As in the case of peer groups, there is a *developmental pattern of friendships* in adolescence (Douvan and Adelson, 1966; Gottman, 1985):

• *Superficial sharing.* Superficial sharing usually characterizes early adolescence. Friendship is based on the sharing of time, things, or mutual activity rather than on sharing of thoughts or feelings. Elizabeth Douvan and Joseph Adelson described this stage of friendship as follows:

> It is a busy age then [ages eleven to thirteen]; and the nature of friendship . . . reflects this business. . . . The friends focus more on activity—on what they are doing together—than they do on themselves. . . . We see this in the fact that girls at this period can tell us so little about friendship. When we ask what a friend ought to be like . . . the early adolescent mentions fewer qualities than older girls do. More important, the qualities she does mention are fairly superficial ones. For example, she wants a friend to do favors for her. She wants the friend to be . . . easy to get along with, cooperative and fair. (1966, p. 186)

• *Intense sharing.* Intense sharing occurs in early to middle adolescence. During this time of trying on roles, sampling life-styles, testing the limits of personal abilities, and acknowledging sexual changes, the adolescent requires the *continuous* and intense support of a friend. Friendship during this period may be marked by a *feverish* or desperate quality because of relative insecurity about self-concept, dating, or sexual changes.

   Douvan and Adelson described this stage of friendship in girls (fourteen, fifteen, and sixteen years old) as follows:

> What stands out . . . is the stress placed on security in friendships. They want the friend to be loyal, trustworthy and a reliable source of support. . . . Why so much emphasis on loyalty? We imagine that part of the reason is that friendship is less a

Darryl Jacobson

Superficial sharing usually characterizes early adolescence.

mutuality than it appears to be at first. The girl is less interested in the other than she thinks; what she seeks in the other is some response to, and mirroring of, the self. She needs the presence of someone who is undergoing the same trials, discoveries and despairs. . . . Through the sharing of knowledge and affects, she is relieved to some extent, of the anxiety and guilt which accompanies [sic] the emergence of sexuality. (1966, pp. 188–89)

• *Realistic sharing.* Realistic sharing is characteristic of late adolescence, youth, and adulthood. Friendship is based on what each partner brings to the relationship. Now there is a much greater stress on the *personality* of the friend.

Although these stages of friendship apply generally to boys and girls, there are some notable differences (Douvan and Adelson, 1966):

1. Girls may be socialized to place more emphasis on interpersonal relation-ships. Boys, on the other hand, may be socialized toward achievement, asser-tiveness, and activity. Therefore, girls may be disposed, more than boys, to use interpersonal, intimate methods of problem solving.

2. Boys are more concerned than girls with asserting and maintaining their independence from authority figures such as parents or teachers. Therefore, the boy develops a ganglike alliance:

> To this end he needs the gang . . . with whom he can confirm himself as autonomous and maintain a wall of resistance to authority. Even when the boys' close friendship group is small in number, they are apt to give it a ganglike definition, for example, calling themselves "The Three Musketeers" or "The Four Horsemen." Girls, . . . even when they are part of a large group of friends, tend to form centers of intimate two- and three-somes. (p. 194)

The best way to understand the friendship formation of children or adolescents is to examine it from a developmental perspective, from early childhood through the adolescent years. In one study, the play patterns of three-to-nine-year-old children were examined in terms of how children become more familiar and friend-lier with one another (Gottman, 1983). The investigator identified a set of social processes that distinguished between the play patterns of strangers and those of friends (see Table 15.1). Furthermore, friends self-disclosed more (revealed more about themselves to one another), had more positive exchanges, and were better able to resolve conflicts than strangers.

How did the friendship process identified in Table 15.1 change with the age of the child? John Gottman (1987) identified the following developmental pattern:

• For children three to seven years of age, the goal of peer interaction was *coor-dinated* play. All social processes were organized to promote this end result.
• For children eight to twelve years of age, the goal changed from play to being *accepted by* peers. At this stage children were primarily concerned with discovering what behaviors lead to inclusion or exclusion from the peer group.
• For adolescents thirteen to seventeen years of age, the goal of friendship shifted to *self-understanding.* According to Gottman, the most important vehicle or process for attaining this goal was *self-disclosure.* Adolescents shared much more infor-mation about themselves with one another than school-age children. Furthermore, this sharing was used as a primary way of gaining peer feedback and, therefore, self-understanding.

TABLE 15.1

The Social Processes of Friendship Formation

PROCESS	DEFINITION	EXAMPLE
1. Communication clarity and connectedness	Request for message clarification followed by appropriate clarification of the message.	**Child A:** Give it to me. **Child B:** Which one? **Child A:** The purple one with yellow ears.
2. Information exchange	Asking questions and eliciting relevant information.	Where do you live? What color is your crayon?
3. Establishing common ground	Finding something to do together and/or exploring their similarities and differences.	Let's play trucks. I like tea parties, do you?
4. Self-disclosure of feelings	Questions about feelings by one child are followed by expression of feeling by the partner.	I'm really scared of the dark and snakes, too.
5. Positive reciprocity	One partner responds to another's positive behavior or serves to extend or lengthen a positive exchange; usually involves joking, gossip, or fantasy.	**Child A:** Did you hear what happened to Mary's sister? **Child B:** No, tell me and then I'll tell you another thing about Mary.
6. Conflict resolution	The extent to which play partners resolve disputes and disagreements successfully.	**Child A:** I want the blue truck. **Child B:** No, I'm playing with it. **Child A:** I want it. **Child B:** O.K., let's play with it together.

From Gottman, 1983.

Education

Adolescents spend a considerable amount of their time in school. The school is the social mechanism for helping the adolescent to become a contributing member of society. There continues to be an important relationship between individual economic success and attending school. In addition, the school serves as a major socializing institution for the acquisition of interpersonal skills and socially responsible behavior.

HIGH SCHOOL. High school education in the United States has been dominated by one major type of organization: the comprehensive public school. This type of high school includes a wide variety of curricula and, to some extent, a variety of students from different social levels. Increasingly, American high school education has come to be characterized by large urban school districts with students assigned to schools on the basis of the neighborhood where they live. This trend toward

Adolescents spend a considerable amount of their time in school.

largeness has been stimulated by several factors, such as the urbanization of American society and the growth of the population (particularly through the 1950s) (Coleman, 1974).

There have been growing problems with the comprehensive public school in relation to the needs of adolescents. These problems include the multiplicity of bureaucratic devices needed to manage such institutions; the absence of consumer choice; the large size of single age-grade levels; the segregation of races, social classes, and ethnic groups; and institutional similarity or blandness.

Several major studies have revealed some of the critical problems in the modern American high school (DeCecco and Richards, 1975; National Panel on High School and Adolescent Education, 1976). John DeCecco and Arlene Richards examined 757 school districts and found the atmosphere of these schools to be one of tension and anger. Students expressed their unhappiness through defiance of authority, vandalism, absence, and disruption of classroom activities. Teachers showed their anger by using repressive disciplinary techniques and expelling students for relatively minor violations. School administrators often blamed both teachers and students for school problems. In addition, they aggravated tense situations by siding with one ethnic group against another and by making themselves unavailable to teachers or students.

The National Panel on High School and Adolescent Education (1976) found that many of the problems of the high school were due to "deficiencies" in the system. The panel found some of the following problems:

- High school education does not provide many students with experiences designed to develop adult responsibilities and values.
- High schools too often treat teenagers as immature children.
- The typical high school is too big to be managed effectively.
- The schools have been asked to take responsibility for the "total" education of children. In the past, the responsibility for such a vast undertaking was more broadly shared with the family, the community, and religious organizations.

The panel concluded that many teachers, administrators, and students were making sincere efforts to make the system work. However, the panel suggested that their efforts were not likely to meet with success unless the entire approach to secondary education is revamped. Some of the panel's suggestions were the following:

• *Comprehensive education (rather than the comprehensive high school)*. Adolescents should have the opportunity to learn through a variety of institutional arrangements. A good deal of the teenager's education should occur in the community (outside of the school).

• *Participatory education.* In order for adolescents to learn about adult roles and responsibilities, they need to be involved in the real world of the community. Adolescents should become involved in several types of community centers: a community career-education center, a community arts-and-crafts center, and a community center for government.

• *Reduction of compulsory attendance and all-day sessions.* The panel recommended that formal instruction be curtailed to about two to four hours a day. The rest of the day would be spent in "participatory" programs such as those discussed above.

• *Education of the "intellect."* The panel recommended that the primary focus of formal high school instruction be the cognitive or intellectual dimensions. Presumably this focus would be advisable—and possible—if the noncognitive goals were handled through the "participatory" programs outside the school.

During the 1980s there has been a strong emphasis on curricula that reflect the slogan "back to basics." Several studies have called for more demanding and rigorous programs (Adler, 1982; National Commission on Excellence in Education, 1983). This emphasis has been brought on by several factors, including the following:

• A documented drop in achievement test scores of American high school students.
• A recognition that the United States was losing its competitive edge in the world marketplace. In particular, the strong showing of the Japanese economy was a prod for increased academic rigor.

Unlike the National Panel (1976), the National Commission on Excellence in Education (1983) called for longer school days. In addition, the commission recommended that schools institute demanding academic requirements and tougher graduation standards. It is, of course, both interesting and important to note how high school curricula reflect contemporary social demands.

EDUCATION AND THE TRANSITION TO ADULTHOOD AND WORK.   As we indicated, the aims of education include some emphasis on preparation for an occupation as well as on the socialization of the young. Another way of putting this is that schools have traditionally fostered the development of two types of goals and skills:

1. *Cognitive or academic skills* (e.g., mathematics, writing, biology, chemistry), which have been the traditional responsibility of the school.
2. *Nonacademic content or skills,* which attempt to incorporate "real-life" situations into educational experiences (e.g., driver education) or which incorporate elements that are viewed as important to the development of the "whole" person.

Both of these types of skill are viewed as important for the transition to adulthood. However, over the course of the existence of the public school, there has always been some level of debate as to what should be taught in the school (see box).

What Should Be Taught in the High School?

One of the implications . . . of social changes . . . is that the nonschool portions of a youth's environment have dwindled in scope and force while the school portions have increased. One consequence has been to introduce into schools some things that were once outside in the form of extracurricular progams, work-related programs, community projects and other activities. This is one kind of solution: to bring into the school certain of those non-cognitive activities that are deemed valuable to the development of youth or at least those activities for which there is some demand on the part of youth or the community.

Another solution, however, is to take the opposite approach: to confine formal schooling to those cognitive skills that are traditional to it and to devise new organizational arrangements outside the formal structure of the school for those non-academic activities important to the movement into adulthood. Such an approach very likely implies a reduction in the time spent in formal educational settings, rather than the increase inherent in the first solution. An example of this solution is cooperative education programs in high school in which a young person typically spends half his day in school and half on the job working for an employer. . . .

The central defect of the school for activities other than transmission of academic knowledge and skills is that schools are not well organized for other activities. Schools are apart from society while the non-academic portions of becoming an adult, such as gaining the capacity to take responsibility and authority, learning to care for others who are dependent, acquiring the ability to take decisive action, learning how to work, achieving a sense of self respect, are directly part of society. . . .

The essential difficulty of schools in handling activity other than academic learning is the position of the child or youth within the school. He is a dependent, and the school is responsible for shepherding his development. Yet if youth is to develop in certain ways involving responsibility and decision-making, the responsibility and dependency are in the wrong place. To reorganize a school in such a way that young persons have responsibility and authority appears extremely difficult, because such reorganization is incompatible with the basic custodial function of the school.

Reprinted from J. S. Coleman, 1974, pp. 141–43.

YOUR VIEW What do you think? Do you agree with Coleman's argument? Why? Why not?

The comprehensive high school includes many educational experiences.

HIGH SCHOOLS THAT WORK.   Because adolescents spend a considerable amount of their time in high school, it is important for us to understand the characteristics of successful schools. That is, how can we describe successful schools in which adolescents are academically achieving and involved in the overall high school experience? In one of the most detailed and comprehensive assessments of the impact of high schools on adolescents, Michael Rutter and his colleagues examined students in twelve secondary schools in inner-city neighborhoods in London (Rutter et al., 1979). Specifically, Rutter and his associates wanted to know in what ways high school experience influenced performance of the London adolescents on national achievement tests (taken when the students completed secondary school). Rutter and his colleagues began their study by carefully assessing the characteristics of the students before they entered secondary school, as well as examining the operations of each school over a two and one-half-year period. They examined several school factors, including the following:

· The physical features of the school.
· The student composition.
· The typical interactions between students and teachers.
· Characteristics of the community.
· Abilities of the students who attended each school.

   Rutter and his colleagues found that secondary students' academic achievement was associated with the following school characteristics:

The *academic emphasis* of the *secondary school.* Academic emphasis refers to the *priority* placed on academic work in relation to other school-related activities. For example, was there an expectation that studying and academics were more important than extracurricular activities? Rutter and his colleagues found that an academic emphasis was present in some schools and not in others.
   Clear behavioral guidelines with an emphasis on positive support rather than punishment.

> The feedback that a child receives about what is and what is not acceptable at school will also constitute a powerful influence on his behavior. . . . Our findings show that the most immediate and direct feedback in terms of praise or approval had the strongest association with pupil behavior. (Rutter et al., 1979, pp. 189–90)

Furthermore, Rutter and his colleagues indicated the following regarding expectations:

> Exam successes were more frequent and delinquency less common in schools where discipline was based on general expectations set by the school . . . , rather than left to individual teachers to work out for themselves. (p. 192)

· *Response to physical conditions.* The age of the various school buildings was *not* related to significant academic outcomes, because the schools varied considerably in how they used or responded to the physical conditions that were made available to them. According to Rutter and his associates:

> It was striking how very different essentially similar buildings could be made to appear. Some of the older buildings had been made pleasant and attractive places through the imaginative and well planned use of decorations. They appeared smart and well-cared for; other schools, by contrast, had done little to transform their surroundings. (1979, p. 101)

• *Students' responsibility and participation.* Another dimension of school life that was significantly related to academic success and good behavior was the students' opportunities to take responsibility and be involved in the management of their school lives. For example, there was a higher incidence of academic achievement and good behavior when students had the opportunity to do such things as be homework monitors, take a special part in a class assembly, participate in lunch hour clubs, and so on.

• *School atmosphere.* Good student behavior and academic success were also related to what Rutter and his associates referred to as *school atmosphere*, or *school ethos*. For example, a school atmosphere variable that was associated with academic achievement was a highly organized staff that engaged in substantial planning of school programs. A highly organized staff was not one that was regimented or rigid. Rather, such a staff was one that operated with a sense of togetherness, working toward generally agreed-on school goals.

The World of Work

The choice of an occupational direction is a part of the overall process of identity formation in youth. Work and vocation set the tone for adult life and constitute integrating forces in determining what one's daily activities are, whom one associates with, where one lives, and how much physical and intellectual energy one expends.

Earlier in this century, most twenty-one-year-old adolescents were already involved in full-time employment or homemaking, that is, earning a living, organizing a marriage, and raising children. These now are common responsibilities of early adulthood. After World War II, this pattern of immediate involvement in work and adult activity changed substantially.

THE SEPARATION OF YOUTH FROM WORK.   With the historical changes in the working world, the young person has been less involved in the work environment. Parents' work becomes less visible to children, and there are fewer opportunities for children to watch their parents at work, to talk with them about their work, or to work with them in the work setting. An emotional detachment from work characterizes some young people. Many children shift from positive attitudes and images of work to negative ones. As they move through childhood and early adolescence, they appear to reject entire categories of work prematurely and irrationally. The phenomenon narrows the range of potential vocational choices (Greenberger and Steinberg, 1986). In addition, the trend toward more years of formal education (e.g., postsecondary education) has tended to isolate youth from firsthand job experience.

WORK DYSFUNCTIONS IN YOUTH.   For many youngsters from lower socioeconomic or minority backgrounds, negative experiences with neighborhood, school, and work have often created obstacles to vocational development and adjustment to work. Many of these youths hold negative self-images as potential workers and lack realistic pictures of the world of work. The widespread unemployment of such youths is a serious problem in the United States.

STUDENTS IN THE WORKPLACE.   Prior to World War II, adolescents who held jobs and those who attended school were in two almost distinct groups (Reubens,

Common adolescent work settings include retail stores and fast-food restaurants.

Harrison, and Rupp, 1981). Furthermore, in the early part of this century most adolescents were in the workplace rather than in schools. By the middle of the century, the situation had completely reversed—most adolescents were in school rather than in the workplace (Greenberger and Steinberg, 1986).

The movement of teenagers into the workplace (on a part-time basis) began to occur after 1950. For the most part, however, that movement did *not* result in a full *integration* of teenagers into adult work settings. Rather, what seems to have happened was the emergence of part-time work settings that were composed almost entirely of adolescents. Specifically, during the 1950s and afterward, certain sectors of the American economy expanded dramatically and required large numbers of part-time workers (Ginzberg, 1977). In particular, restaurants (including fast-food restaurants) and retail stores grew dramatically and began employing large numbers of workers who were willing to work part-time for relatively low wages, and for short periods of time (i.e., during peak hours or during peak seasons or holidays). Adolescents were often hired to fill these roles. By 1980, almost two-thirds of all high school seniors and almost one-half of all high school sophomores had held at least one part-time job (Lewin-Epstein, 1981).

In addition to the availability of part-time jobs as a result of a changing economy, other factors have also contributed to this increase in teenage employment (Greenberger and Steinberg, 1986).

• *The increasing cost of being an American teenager.* Particularly for middle-class adolescents, there has been an increase in both the number of items the "with-it" teenager might have (e.g., stereo equipment, designer clothes and shoes, records, tapes, tennis rackets, and so on) and the cost of those items over time (e.g., the dramatic increase in the cost of movie tickets). For example, there is evidence that the cost of being a teenager rose 20 percent from 1975 to 1979 (much more than

Unemployed Teenagers—A Time Bomb?

The jobless statistics among youths are among the more somber and gloomy statistics of national unemployment. The Economic Report of the President (1986) shows that youths (sixteen to nineteen years of age) had a jobless rate in 1985 that was over two and a half times as high as the national average for all workers (see figure below). The jobless rate among blacks and other minorities (sixteen to nineteen years old) was even more grim—more than double the rate for white youths. The implications of these high levels of youth unemployment are monumental in terms of the destruction of human beings and the frustration of human potential. The spillover of frustration could take the form of increased crime or riots.

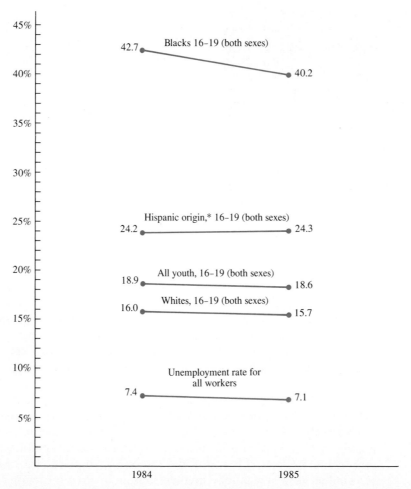

Youth unemployment. From U.S. Department of Labor, Bureau of Labor Statistics, January 1986, February, 1986.

the rate of inflation, which rose only 14 percent) (Rotbart, 1981). In order to deal with these costs, many adolescents have taken part-time jobs (Rotbart, 1981).

In the past, adolescent employment was associated with financial survival or simply helping one's family "make ends meet." However, it is now the case that working during high school is more common for middle- and upper-middle-class teenagers (Lewin-Epstein, 1981).

Well-designed work-experience programs provide adolescents opportunities to gain knowledge about occupations and to gain personal satisfaction.

• *Parent and adolescent expectations that work experience teaches important values.* Specifically, many parents and teenagers believe that work experience leads to many positive outcomes, including building character, preparing for the "real" world, and teaching responsibility. To what extent are these expectations and beliefs supported by facts and evidence? In order to answer this question it is important to distinguish at least two types of work. In the first place, there are *well-designed work-experience programs* (typically associated with high schools) that include a broad range of useful experiential activities (e.g., serving as an apprentice to a skilled craftsman or professional; providing services to the elderly, the disadvantaged, or the handicapped; and so on). The second type of work is the part-time employment typically found in the teenage workplace (e.g., fast-food restaurants or retail stores), which may involve routine or unstimulating jobs.

With reference to well-designed work-experience programs, there is some evidence that adolescents benefit from participation (Hamilton, 1981). Although such work experiences may not provide paid employment, those who participate report gains derived from personal satisfaction and increased knowledge about relevant occupations (those they might actually consider).

With reference to part-time employment in typical teenage jobs, some parent and adolescent assumptions about the value of work are supported by the evidence; others are not. For example, adolescents may gain in self-reliance by working. On the other hand, work experiences in such jobs as fast-food and retail stores do not enhance the adolescent's feelings of social obligation or concern for others (Greenberger and Steinberg, 1986; Steinberg et al., 1982).

Part-time Work in Adolescence: Costs and Benefits

Work has long been assumed to have positive outcomes for adolescents, including the development of responsibility (National Panel on High School and Adolescent Education, 1976; Carnegie Commission on Policy Studies in Higher Education, 1980; National Commission on Youth, 1980). Unfortunately, it has also been assumed that any and all types of work will produce such positive outcomes. In reality, however, the working world for many adolescents may not lead to only positive outcomes (Greenberger and Steinberg, 1986).

In a longitudinal study of 176 high school students in southern California, it was found that the part-time work in which adolescents are most commonly involved (e.g., fast-food restaurants or retail stores) produces a mixed bag of outcomes (Steinberg et al., 1982). Before discussing these findings, it is important to keep in mind that typical adolescent workplaces are primarily staffed by other adolescents. This can result in a limited learning environment in which adolescents have reduced opportunities to benefit from adult knowledge and adult models. At any rate, the mixed bag of outcomes was as follows:

· *Working contributes to the development of personal responsibility but not to the development of social responsibility.* Working adolescents learned important lessons in self-management skills. Specifically, they learned to be punctual and dependable and to be more self-reliant than nonworking adolescents.

On the other hand, *working did not increase adolescents' commitment to the welfare of others.* It did not foster greater tolerance of cultural or individual differences. Furthermore, some adolescents were negatively influenced, becoming more *cynical about the value of work and more willing to accept unethical practices.* For example, the type of jobs that adolescents typically have (repetitive or unstimulating) may teach them to do only the amount of work necessary to get by ("Anyone who works harder than they have to must be crazy"). Likewise, some adolescents learned to "call in sick" when they were not.

· *The benefits of working on the development of a sense of independence or autonomy were much greater for girls than for boys.* Laurence Steinberg and his associates (1982) suggested that this finding could be explained by the fact that taking an outside job might be a significant departure from the expectations of others for girls (rather than for boys). Thus, working could be viewed as an act of autonomy for girls and, in some cases, an act of conformity for boys.

· *Working reduces adolescent involvement in significant nonwork environments.* For example, working adolescents are less likely to be involved in school activities, in family relationships, and in friendship relationships. Steinberg and his colleagues raised the following issue:

We raise seriously the question of whether 15- and 16-year olds who commit 20 to 25 hours weekly to a part-time job may be missing out on important socialization and learning experiences that occur in other settings. This is especially important to ask in light of evidence that the nature of the learning, contact with adults, and social relationships with peers that occur within the context of the typical adolescent's part-time job are exceedingly limited. (1982, p. 394)

· *Working is related to increased use of marijuana and cigarettes.* Steinberg and his colleagues suggested that the additional requirement of time and energy in a part-time job (in addition to pressures of school, friends, parents, and so on) and working under stressful conditions (e.g., the busy time at a fast-food restaurant) might increase the likelihood of substance use or abuse.

Summary

1. Adolescence is a critical period in human development because it is during this period that the individual begins to develop a stance toward the world, or an *identity*. Adolescence begins with the onset of puberty and ends with

the entrance into the world of the adult—a social and psychological event. Although there is little dispute that adolescence begins with the biological event of puberty, the end of adolescence is much less clear.

2. Since there are few characteristics that uniformly apply to both twelve-year-olds and twenty-year-olds, we adopt a two-stage theory of adolescence: *early adolescence* and *later adolescence, or youth.* The central feature of early adolescence is the development of a *group identity* in relation to the world of the high school and peer group. The primary characteristic of later adolescence is the clarification of the self in relation to society as a whole (an identity that reflects a stance toward the world). Several major themes or issues of later adolescence or youth include the following: the tension between the self and society, developing a mature sex role, attaining independence from parents, developing a mature value system/philosophy of life, and making career and life-style choices.

3. An understanding of the *contexts* of the adolescent system involves a discussion of *adolescents' perception* of their environments or contexts as well as a specific description of those contexts. Adolescents' perception of their contexts includes an *external landscape* (e.g., where adolescents spend their time, what they do, and with whom) and an *internal landscape* (e.g., how adolescents subjectively feel about their experiences).

4. In adolescence, the neighborhood/community boundaries are expanded. The adolescent has increasing freedom to explore the neighborhood and community. However, the ability to interact with the broad social community may still be limited by traditional patterns of age segregation.

   The social changes that have influenced the families of adolescents include the same social changes that have influenced the families of infants, pre-schoolers, and school-age children. These social changes include the urbanization and mobility of families, working mothers, and changing values. Several factors appear to determine the impact of the structural changes in families (i.e., divorce and single parenthood) on the adolescent: the age of the child/adolescent, the sex of the child/adolescent, and the ability of the child/adolescent and family members to adapt to such experiences.

5. The adolescent-parent relationship differs from the child-parent relationship in several important ways. The power of the child is much less than that of the adolescent. The parent has to deal with significant others that have more influence over the adolescent than over the child. The child's cognitive skills are usually not as advanced as the adolescent's.

   A useful approach to understanding how and why some families are able to manage the challenge of adolescence involves the two dimensions of *family cohesion* and *family adaptability.*

6. Peer groups and friends provide the adolescent with an arena for much of the learning that occurs in early adolescence. Significant features of the peer context include the *functions of the peer group*, the *structure of the peer group* and how that structure changes over time, and the *stages of the peer-group development and friendship.*

   The *functions* of the peer group in adolescence include providing primary status, providing norms for governing behavior, facilitating emancipation from the family, and serving as a "testing ground." The social structure of peer groups is composed of *cliques* and *crowds.* The *stages of peer-group development* include the precrowd stage, the beginning of the crowd, the crowd in structural transition, the fully developed crowd, and the beginning of crowd disintegration. There is a developmental pattern of friendships including superficial sharing, intense sharing, and realistic sharing.

7. Adolescents spend a considerable amount of their time in schools. High school education in the United States has been dominated by one major type of organization—the comprehensive public school. Several major studies have revealed some of the critical problems in the modern American high school. Furthermore, it is important to understand the characteristics of successful schools.

Several factors have contributed to the increase in teenage employment, including a changing economy, the increasing financial costs of being an American teenager, and parent-adolescent expectations that work experience teaches important values.

Key Terms

Cliques	Family cohesion
Coping	Identity
Crowds	Later adolescence, or youth
Disengagement	Puberty
Early adolescence	Social support
Enmeshment	Stressors
Family adaptability	Strains

Questions

1. Define the period of adolescence. When does it begin? When does it end?
2. Discuss early adolescence and later adolescence.
3. Discuss the internal landscape of adolescence and the external landscape of adolescence.
4. Define *family cohesion* and *family adaptability*. How is each related to adolescent-parent relationships?
5. Discuss the factors involved in clique formation.
6. Discuss the value of work during adolescence.

Suggested Readings

ADELSON, J. (ed.) *Handbook of Adolescent Psychology*. New York: Wiley, 1980. A comprehensive review of research on adolescent development.

CSIKSZENTMIHALYI, M., and LARSON, R. *Being Adolescent*. New York: Basic Books, 1984. A well-written analysis of the subjective experience of adolescent life.

GARBARINO, J. *Adolescence: An Ecological Perspective*. Columbus, Ohio: Merrill, 1985. An excellent overview of adolescent development from an ecological viewpoint.

GARBARINO, J.; SCHELLENBACH, C. J.; SEBES, J. M.; and associates. *Troubled Youth, Troubled Families*. New York: Aldine Publishing Company, 1987. A well-written analysis of the relationship of adolescent difficulties and family factors.

GOTTMAN, J. M. and PARKER, J. G. (eds.). *The Conversations of*

Friends. New York: Cambridge University Press, 1987. An excellent examination of recent research on friendship formation.

GREENBERGER, E., and STEINBERG, L. *When Teenagers Work*. New York: Basic Books, 1986. A well-written book that examines the assumption that adolescent work experience is always beneficial.

GROTEVANT, H. D., and COOPER, C. R. *Adolescent Development in the Family*. San Francisco: Jossey-Bass, 1983. An excellent analysis of adolescent social and personality development in the family context.

RUTTER, M.; MAUGHAN, B.; MORTIMORE, P.; OUSTON, J.; and SMITH, A. *Fifteen Thousand Hours*. Cambridge, Mass.: Harvard University Press, 1979. A well-written analysis of the characteristics of successful secondary schools.

16 Adolescence: Physical and Cognitive Development

I remember my youth and the feeling that will never come back any more—the feeling that I could last forever, outlast the sea, the earth, and all men.
— *Joseph Conrad*, Youth

Although I'm only fourteen, I know quite well what I want, I know who is right and who is wrong, I have my opinions, my own ideas and principles, and although it may sound pretty mad from an adolescent, I feel more of a person than a child, I feel quite independent of anyone.
— *Anne Frank*, The Diary of a Young Girl

Our discussion in the preceding chapter of the significant contexts of adolescence has presupposed certain changes that are occurring in the life of the adolescent. Specifically, the relationships of adolescents to the family, the peer group, the school, and the community/neighborhood are strongly influenced by the following changes in the individual adolescent:

· Biological development: physical and sexual factors.
· Cognitive development.

The biological changes that occur are relatively rapid and dramatic. When these changes are coupled with changes in the ways adolescents think about their world and about themselves, the stage is set for the dynamic developments of adolescence.

Biological Development: Physical and Sexual Change

The term **puberty** technically refers to the series of physical and physiological changes that signal reproductive capability (maturation of the sex organs, testes, and ovaries, and the development of secondary sex characteristics). However, in a broader sense, the term *puberty* has also been used to refer to *both* these specific sexual changes that result in reproductive capability *and* other biological changes that lead up to reproductive capability (the adolescent growth spurt, and accompanying changes in respiration, circulation, and body composition). The period of time in which these latter changes occur is technically known as **pubescence.** For our purposes, *puberty* will refer to *all* the biological, physical, and sexual changes that occur as the individual moves from childhood to adulthood (including the "technical" definitions of both pubescence and puberty). From such a broad perspective, there are five primary manifestations of puberty (Marshall, 1978):

- *A growth spurt* or rapid acceleration in growth which results in dramatic changes in both weight and height.
- *Changes in body composition,* particularly in the distribution of muscle and body fat.
- *Changes in respiration and circulation,* resulting in increased physical strength and motor performance skills.
- *The continued development of the male and female sex organs* (e.g., male testes and female ovaries) leading to reproductive capability.
- *The development of secondary sex characteristics,* including changes in female breasts and male genitals, growth of facial hair, and so on.

General Physical Maturation

The general growth rate of body tissue slows down from birth through childhood. However, the onset of puberty is marked by a considerable increase in this growth rate. There are increases in body size, changes in body shape and composition, and a rapid development of reproductive organs and secondary sexual characteristics. Many of these changes are similar for both sexes, although most are sex-specific. Three facts about this adolescent growth activity have remained constant as accurate descriptors of the process (Tanner, 1981):

1. *Girls* usually develop *earlier* than *boys.*
2. For both girls and boys, the *rate* of development is different for individuals.
3. The *sequence* of biological changes has remained the same as in the past (see Table 16.1).

Although these three characteristics have remained an accurate general description of adolescent physical growth, some of the specific events of growth are now

TABLE 16.1
The Sequence of Physical Changes in Males and Females

FEMALES	MALES
Skeletal growth.	Skeletal growth.
Breast development.	Enlargement of testes.
Straight pigmented pubic hair.	Straight pigmented pubic hair.
Maximum adolescent growth spurt (speed or "tempo" of growth is the fastest).	Early voice changes (e.g., voice "cracks"). Ejaculations (e.g., nocturnal emissions or "wet dreams").
Kinky pigmented pubic hair.	Kinky pigmented pubic hair.
Menstruation (the first menstruation is called the *menarche*).	Maximum adolescent growth spurt. Appearance of downy facial hair.
Appearance of hair in underarms and on forearms.	Appearance of hair in underarms and on forearms. Late voice change. Appearance of coarse pigmented facial hair and chest hair.

Based on Tanner, 1962, 1978a.

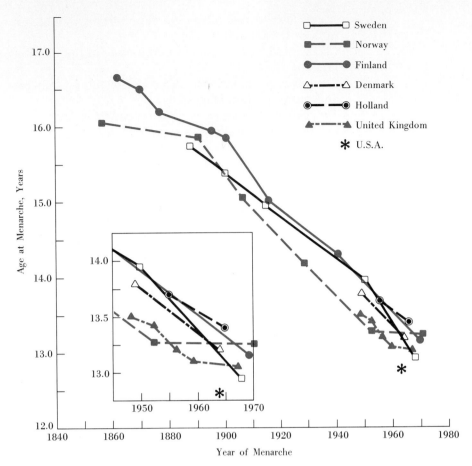

FIGURE 16.1
Secular trend in age of menarche, 1860–1970. From Tanner, 1962, 1973.

occurring *earlier* than in the past. For example, the onset of puberty in females (i.e., the menarche, or first menstruation) appears to be occurring at earlier ages (see Fig. 16.1). In addition, both children and adolescents appear to be taller now than at similar ages in the past (see Fig. 16.2). (Frisch, 1983). James Tanner (1978a) has pointed out that most of this trend toward greater size in adolescents and children is the result of *more rapid maturation rather than greater ultimate size*. In earlier historical periods, final adult height was not reached until about twenty-five years of age. Later adolescents now reach it at age eighteen or nineteen (Tanner, 1981). Therefore, we might conclude that the *sequence* of physiological changes (*see* Table 16.1) has remained the same; however, the *timing* is different for certain changes (Tanner, 1978a).

The Growth Spurt

The adolescent growth spurt may begin as early as eleven years of age for girls and thirteen years for boys (see Fig. 16.3). The physical changes of adolescence begin when the **hypothalmus** (an area of the lower brain stem that controls the functioning of the pituitary gland) stimulates the **pituitary gland** (a major gland regulating hormone levels in the body) to release specific hormones. In turn, these

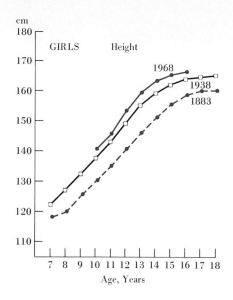

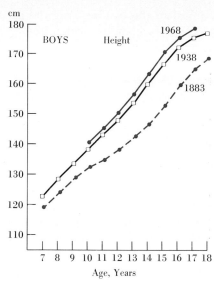

FIGURE 16.2

Secular trend in growth of height—Swedish boys and girls measured in 1883, 1938–1939, and 1965–1971. From Ljung, Bergsten-Brucefors, and Lindgren, 1974.

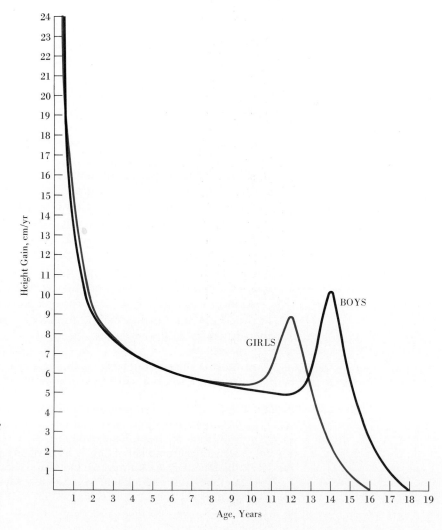

FIGURE 16.3

Typical individual velocity curves for height in boys and girls. The age at which the "peak" or maximal growth occurs is 14.0 years for boys and 12.0 years for girls. From Tanner, Whitehouse, and Takaishi, 1966, pp. 455–471.

hormones stimulate the ovaries (in girls) or the testes (in boys) and the adrenal glands (two ductless glands, located above the kidneys) to produce other hormones. These hormones act on the body to produce the rapid increase in physical growth (height and weight) called the **adolescent growth spurt**. (We discuss these hormonal activities in more detail later in this chapter. For now, we examine the specific changes in body size and physical capacity that constitute the growth spurt.)

The extent of the adolescent growth spurt during this period is quite remarkable. For a period of about a year, the *velocity* or *rate* of growth almost doubles. A boy grows at the same rate during this year as he did during the first two years of life. Tanner described this situation as follows:

> Admittedly during fetal life and the first year or two after birth developments occurred still faster, and a sympathetic environment was probably even more crucial, but the subject himself was not the fascinated, charmed, or horrified spectator that watches the developments or lack of developments of adolescence. (1971, p. 907)

The changes that occur in early adolescence are brought about by hormones that are secreted in larger amounts (Tanner, 1981). Hormones then act on specific *targets* or *receptors*, which are often not concentrated in a specific organ or tissue. For example, the hormone testosterone acts on several receptors located in the penis, in facial skin, in the cartilage of the shoulder joints, and in parts of the brain (Tanner, 1981). These hormonal activities result in the release of specific sexual *energy*, which can be channeled in numerous directions (Tanner, 1981). A good part of early adolescence is spent in learning both the meaning and the constructive channeling of this adolescent *energy*. It is probably no accident that only when the hormonal and physical changes in early adolescence have completed their course, are individuals able to direct their attention to other matters of self-development (Tanner, 1981).

HEIGHT.   Height changes dramatically as a result of the growth spurt. During this one-year period, boys usually grow between three and five inches (seven to twelve cm.) and girls grow between two and a half and four and a half inches (six to eleven cm.). The age at which the "peak" or maximal growth period occurs is approximately fourteen years for boys and twelve years for girls (Fig. 16.3). The two-year difference in peak growth appears to remain constant (i.e., if for a particular group of boys the average "peak" age is 13.5 years, then the average "peak" age for a comparable group of girls tends to be 11.5 years) (Tanner, 1981).

As hormones act on the various receptors in the body, changes begin to occur in practically all the skeletal and motor dimensions of the body. Tanner described the overall process as follows:

> Most of the spurt in height is due to acceleration of trunk length rather than length of legs. There is a fairly regular order in which the dimensions accelerate: leg length as a rule reaches its peak first, followed by the body breadths, with shoulder width last. Thus a boy stops growing out of his trousers (at least in length) a year before he stops growing out of his jackets. The earliest structures to reach their adult status are the head, hands and feet. At adolescence, children, particularly girls, sometimes complain of having large hands and feet. They can be reassured that by the time they are fully grown their hands and feet will be a little smaller in proportion to their arms and legs and considerably smaller in proportion to their trunk. (1971, p. 911)

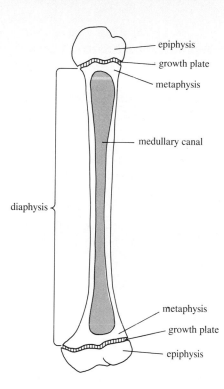

FIGURE 16.4

The location of the epiphyseal growth plates on a long bone. From Chumlea, 1982, pp. 471–485.

The dramatic increase in height (Fig. 16.3) comes as a result of the growth of the long bones in the body. For example, bones such as the *humerus* in the arms and the *femur* in the legs begin to grow rapidly at both ends (see Fig. 16.4). Growth continues until the open ends (or growth centers or plates at the end of each bone)—**epiphyses**—close. Long bones have growth plates composed of cartilage at their ends (Fig. 16.4). During adolescence there is a rapid increase in the amount of cartilage in these growth plates. These cartilage cells are transformed into bone cells, increasing the length of the bones. The rate of this growth of cartilage and bone declines toward the end of adolescence. Finally, the bones stop growing as the epiphyses at the ends of the bones close. This epiphyseal closing occurs after approximately eighteen years of age for girls and after approximately twenty years of age for boys (Chumlea, 1982). Once the bones close, growth can no longer occur.

It is important to keep in mind that although the growth spurt represents a dramatic change in height, most adolescents end up with the same relative height (compared with their peers) after their growth spurt as before it (Tanner, 1981). For example, the adolescent boy who was shorter than most of the boys in his class prior to his and their growth spurts is still likely to be shorter than most of the boys in his class after his and their growth spurts. Even though he may have recorded a substantial increase in height, so did all the other boys. One way to appreciate this fact is to examine the percentages of adult height that are attained from birth until the growth spurt ends at approximately nineteen years of age (see Table 16.2). If, for example, one assumes that the adolescent growth spurt begins as early as eleven years for girls and thirteen years for boys (Fig. 16.3), then 84 percent of adult height has been attained for girls prior to age eleven and 84 percent of adult height has been attained for boys prior to age thirteen.

TABLE 16.2

Percentages of Adult (Mature) Height Attained from Birth

CHRONOLOGICAL AGE, YEARS	PERCENTAGE OF AVERAGE MATURE HEIGHT		CHRONOLOGICAL AGE, YEARS	PERCENTAGE OF AVERAGE MATURE HEIGHT	
	BOYS	GIRLS		BOYS	GIRLS
Birth	28.6	30.9	10	78.0	84.4
1	42.2	44.7	11	81.1	88.4
2	49.5	52.8	12	84.2	92.9
3	53.8	57.0	13	87.3	96.5
4	58.0	61.8	14	91.5	98.3
5	61.8	66.2	15	96.1	99.1
6	65.2	70.3	16	98.3	99.6
7	69.0	74.0	17	99.3	100.0
8	72.0	77.5	18	99.8	100.0
9	75.0	80.7	19	100.0	100.0

From Bayley, 1956, pp. 187–194.

WEIGHT, MUSCLE, AND FAT.   As an adolescent's height increases, there is also a comparable increase in his or her weight as body mass increases (Chumlea, 1982). Specifically, tall boys and girls have greater lean body mass (LBM) (i.e., bones, muscles, and internal organs) than shorter children at comparable levels of maturity (Chumlea, 1982). During adolescence, the LBM of boys increases to anywhere from three to five times more than that of girls (see Fig. 16.5). Growth in LBM during the adolescent years is primarily due to the increase in muscle mass.

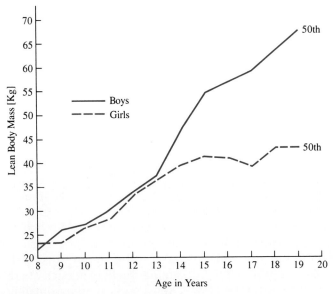

FIGURE 16.5

Changes in lean body mass (LBM) for boys and girls (based on changes in the 50th percentiles of LBM). Adapted from Forbes, 1972, pp. 325–338.

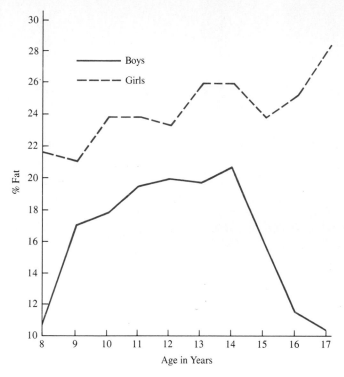

FIGURE 16.6

Changes in the average (mean) percentage of body fat in boys and girls with age. From Forbes, 1972.

Muscle mass increases as a result of increases in the *size* of muscle fibers. That is, the total *number* of muscle fibers is fixed at birth, so future increases in muscle mass are due to increases in the *length* or *diameter* of muscle fibers (Goldspink, 1972; Malina, 1978). The increase for muscle mass is slightly greater for boys than for girls up to the growth spurt years and substantially greater for boys after that time (Fig. 16.5) (Malina, 1978).

With reference to body fat (adipose tissue), there are alterations in amount during the adolescent years. Most of the body's stored fat is subcutaneous (under the skin) rather than throughout the body. Girls tend to have more subcutaneous fat than boys (Chumlea, 1982). This pattern holds true throughout the child and adolescent years. During adolescence, the average percentage of body fat for boys decreases from approximately 17–20 percent to about 10–12 percent (see Fig. 16.6). On the other hand, for girls the percentage of body fat increases from childhood levels of 19–23 percent to 25–28 percent.

In addition to sex differences in the amount of body fat, there are also differences in the distribution of body fat by sex. In the case of girls, fat is added to the thighs, the breasts, the buttocks, and the back of the arms (Sinclair, 1978). In the case of boys, subcutaneous fat declines on the arms and legs (while increasing in these same locations for girls) (Chumlea, 1982). These differences in fat distribution emphasize the sex differences in body form of males and females.

As weight, muscle, fat, and height change, the overall body shapes of males and females change. Male shoulders become broader in contrast to their hips, and their legs become relatively long compared with their trunk length. The typical

Development of muscles and physique is frequently a source of pride for adolescents.

female has narrower shoulders compared with her hips. In addition, the structure of the face changes in adolescence for both boys and girls. The shorter and typically wider face of childhood becomes longer and narrower, the nose projects more, and the jaw becomes more prominent (Cheek, 1968).

ADOLESCENT NUTRITIONAL NEEDS.   One of the major reasons for the problems that some teenage girls encounter with their nutritional status is the difference between the nutritional needs of males and females during adolescence. Female adolescents have an earlier maturational pattern as well as a social-cultural de-emphasis on physically vigorous activity. The general nutritional needs of girls reach a peak between the ages of eleven and fourteen and continue thereafter to decline gradually until they are physically mature. In contrast, the nutritional

needs of boys continue to rise throughout the period from the age of eleven to eighteen and remain at that level until about age twenty-two. Therefore, it is apparent that a boy consumes a much larger number of calories during the adolescent years than a girl. Because the female adolescent requires many fewer calories than the boy, she must get all the nutrients that she needs from a more restricted quantity of food:

> In order to provide the necessary calcium, iron and vitamins in her diet, it is necessary for her to concentrate on eating a well balanced diet with only a few additional frills permitted. The teenage boy, on the other hand, is confronted with the delightful responsibility of consuming a large number of calories, and it is likely that many boys will unconsciously meet their needs for the various nutrients simply by attempting to satisfy their ravenous appetites. (McWilliams, 1975, p. 298)

STRENGTH, PHYSICAL CAPACITY, AND MOTOR PERFORMANCE. Boys have a marked increase in muscle size at adolescence. Boys' muscle size or widths reach a "peak" velocity of growth that is considerably greater than that of females. This increase in muscle size leads to an increase in strength for boys (see Fig. 16.7). It should also be pointed out that boys are not only much stronger than girls at adolescence (probably, in part, because of larger muscles) but also have larger hearts, larger lungs, and a greater capacity for carrying oxygen in their blood (Tanner, 1981). Furthermore, girls have a considerably smaller increase in red blood cells and hemoglobin (see Fig. 16.8). It is possible that these biological and physical differences, as well as social stereotypes of femininity, produce the ap-

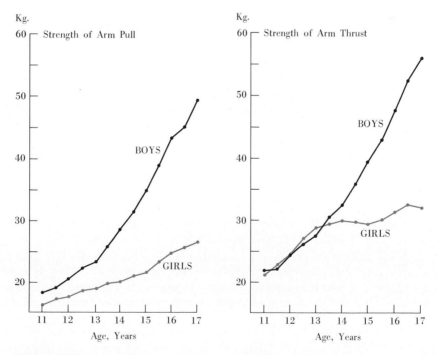

FIGURE 16.7
Strength of arm pull and arm thrust from ages eleven to seventeen years. Mixed longitudinal data for sixty-five to ninety-five boys and sixty-six to ninety-three girls in each age group. From Tanner, 1962; data from Jones, 1949.

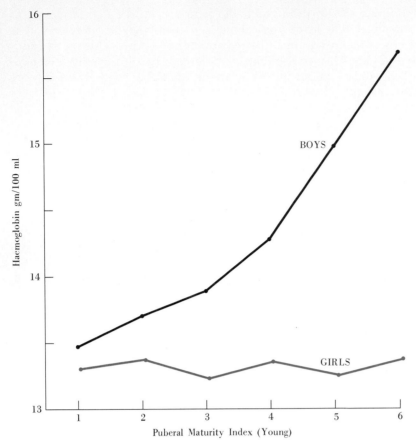

FIGURE 16.8
Blood hemoglobin level in girls and boys according to stage of puberty: cross-sectional data. Puberal maturity or "puberal age" describes the degree of maturity of an individual at puberty. Puberal age is measured as a scheme of six categories, which represent successive stages in transition from the degree of physical immaturity that exists before puberty through to maturity. From Tanner, 1969; data from Young, 1963, pp. 451–460.

parent athletic superiority of males over females during adolescence and beyond. Furthermore, these factors may also contribute to females' traditional lack of interest in sports and athletic skills. This situation is beginning to change. Sex differences in relation to motor activities begin to become apparent during the early adolescence years and are quite pronounced during middle and later adolescence and beyond. It should be emphasized that motor *learning* capabilities do *not* differ between the sexes; rather, physiological-anatomical differences, differential socialization, and related interest and motivation, taken together, probably account for sex-differentiated performance. Although it is not likely that the strongest females will ever equal the strongest males in activities involving sheer strength and power, two points are important here:

• Females are probably capable of both learning and performing motor skills at much higher levels than has generally been demonstrated in research to date.
• *Not all* athletic, sport, and general-movement skills require excessive strength and power to perform effectively. For example, the most productive home-run hitter in major league baseball history, Hank Aaron, was *not* the strongest man on his team. If anything, his sheer strength was probably average to slightly above average. However, the total *power* required to hit a baseball a considerable distance is a function of both the *strength* of the hitter and the *speed* or velocity at which the bat travels in meeting the ball. Aaron's superior bat-swinging speed (probably the result of superb coordination of wrists and arms) resulted in home-run production unequaled by "stronger" men.

Female Athletes

During adolescence, the bones and muscles of the arms, legs, and shoulders become considerably larger in boys than in girls. Furthermore, it is apparently the case that boys also become considerably stronger in these same areas (Malina, 1978). The end result is that presumably the maturing adolescent male is larger, taller, and stronger than his female counterpart. Is such a description completely true for female athletes, specifically world-class athletes?

Research on nationally prominent and world-class female athletes challenges the general picture of unqualified male athletic superiority (Wilmore, 1982).

records of world-class competition indicate that male athletes run a faster mile (approximately 14 percent faster) and a faster 100-yard dash (about 11 percent faster) than women athletes. In other sports, such as swimming, the gender gap is being reduced. For example, the female record holder in the 400-meter freestyle in the 1970s swam faster than the male champion in that same event in the 1956 Olympic Games (Wilmore, 1982).

In summary, the female athlete is approaching the male athlete in some but not all events. Furthermore, in many athletic activities the female athlete is sub-

In many athletic activities the female athlete is substantially better than the average male nonathlete.

Although the average female nonathlete may have as much as 25 percent body fat compared with 15 percent for the average male, the situation is different for female and male world-class athletes. That is, female athletes (particularly long-distance runners) have approximately 10 percent body fat compared with 8 percent for male runners. In addition, these same female runners have endurance levels (cardiovascular fitness) that are 25 percent better than that of the average male nonathlete (Wilmore, 1982).

After adolescence, males tend to do better than females in almost every sport activity. This is the case for both athletes and nonathletes. For example,

stantially better than the average male nonathlete. In addition one might argue that although *some* motor performance differences between males and females may continue, the *substantial* and *vast differences* between male and female nonathletes may be due largely to social and cultural factors. If it is the case that adolescent females are weaker and fatter than adolescent males, this situation may be due more to these social/cultural attitudes than to biological factors. According to Jack Wilmore, the average female may substitute "piano for climbing in the tree and sewing for chasing boys down the street" (1982, p. 115).

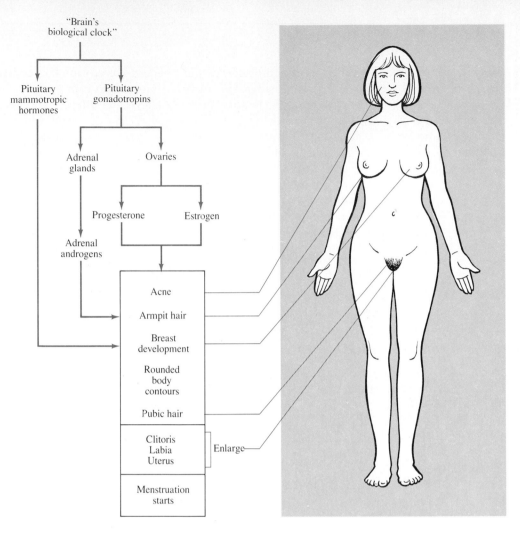

FIGURE 16.9

Hormones and the sexual maturation of females. From Allgeier and Allgeier, 1984.

Changes in Primary and Secondary Sex Characteristics

Despite the adolescent growth spurt and accompanying changes in body form, distribution of fat, and motor performance, it is the changes relating to sexual reproductive capability in males and females that are the hallmark of puberty. These specifically sexual characteristics are of two types:

· **Primary sex characteristics** refer to changes in the testes and ovaries that make reproduction possible.
· **Secondary sex characteristics** refer to aspects of appearance or function that distinguish between males and females. These changes include facial and body hair, female breast development, and male voice change. Secondary sex characteristics are the source of more concern to the adolescent than changes in primary sex characteristics because they are visible to both the adolescent and others.

THE HORMONAL BASIS OF PUBERTY.   Before we discuss the specific dimensions of primary and secondary sex characteristics in male and female adolescents, it is important for us to understand some basic facts about the human *endocrine system.*

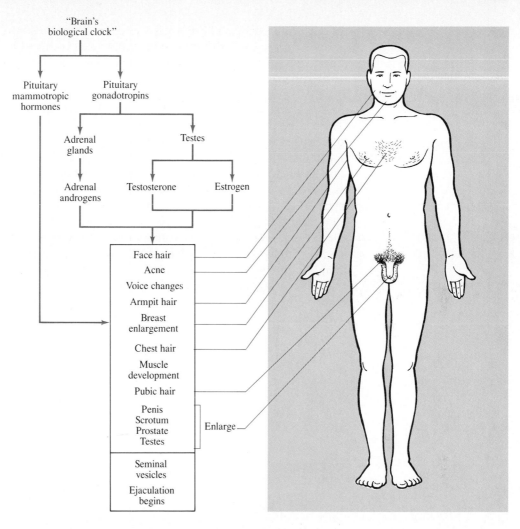

FIGURE 16.10

Hormones and the sexual maturation of males. From Allgeier and Allgeier, 1984.

> *DEFINITIONS*
>
> **Endocrine systems.** These are ductless hormone-producing glands that use the blood vessels of the body for transporting hormones. There are several endocrine systems, of which the gonadal (the glands of the reproductive system—male *testes* and female *ovaries*), the adrenal (the adrenal glands), and the hypothalmo-hypophyseal (the hypothalmus and pituitary glands) are particularly important to the processes of puberty.
>
> **Hormones** These are stong and highly specific chemical substances that interact with the cells of the human body. Cells are organized in such a way as to be receptive to (to "bind up" or to use) only certain hormones.

The onset of puberty begins in the brain (Dreyer, 1982). The hypothalmus gland sends nerve impulses to the pituitary gland which, in turn, secretes hormones that stimulate the development of the gonads (male testes and female ovaries). The maturing testes increase their production of male hormones, or **androgens.** The maturing ovaries increase their production of female hormones, or **estrogens.** Both androgens and estrogens interact or "bind" with cells in specific parts of the body to produce secondary sex characteristics (see Figs. 16.9 and 16.10). Although one typically thinks of androgens as male hormones and estrogens as female hormones, in reality both types of hormone are produced by both males and females. However, during adolescence the average male produces more androgens than estrogens. Likewise, the average female produces more estrogens than androgens.

SEXUAL MATURATION IN BOYS. The sequence of the development of secondary sex characteristics follows an orderly pattern (see Fig. 16.11 and Table 16.3). The onset of sexual maturation in boys usually occurs at about eleven to eleven and a half years of age. The first indicator in boys is the increased growth of the testes and the scrotum (the pouch of skin that contains the testes). Slightly later, there is a small growth of pubic hair, which proceeds gradually until the general growth spurt (Fig. 16.11). About a year after testicle growth begins, accelerations occur in height and in the size of the penis. Shortly after the height spurt, the adolescent's larynx enlarges. The voice begins to deepen when the growth of the penis is near completion. About two years after the beginning growth of pubic hair, axillary hair (under the arms) and facial hair appear (Tanner, 1978a).

The growth of facial hair follows a pattern. At first, there is an increase in length and pigmentation (coloring) at the corners of the upper lip. This increase in length and coloring spreads above the lips to complete the mustache. Hair then appears

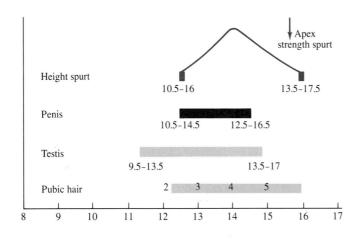

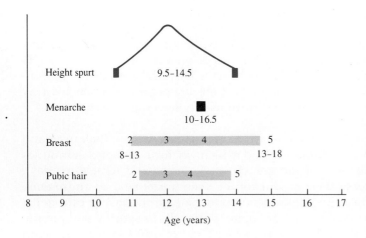

FIGURE 16.11

The sequence of the development of secondary sex characteristics in males and females. The numbers below the start and end of each bar in the diagram represent the variation among individuals in the ages when each dimension of sexual maturation begins and ends. For example, the growth of the testes may begin as early as 9½ or 13½ years and end at 13½ or 17 years of age. The numbers within bars refer to maturational ratings developed by the authors, for example, ratings for pubic hair and breast development. From Marshall and Tanner, 1969, 1970.

TABLE 16.3
Stages in Sexual Maturation

	CHARACTERISTIC		
STAGE	GENITAL DEVELOPMENT[a]	PUBIC-HAIR DEVELOPMENT[a,b]	BREAST DEVELOPMENT[b]
1	Testes, scrotum, and penis are about the same size and shape as in early childhood.	The vellus over the pubes is not further developed than over the abdominal wall, i.e., no pubic hair.	There is elevation of the papilla only.
2	Scrotum and testes are slightly enlarged. The skin of the scrotum is reddened and changed in texture. There is little or no enlargement of the penis at this stage.	There is sparse growth of long, slightly pigmented, tawny hair, straight or slightly curled, chiefly at the base of the penis or along the labia.	Breast bud stage. There is elevation of the breast and the papilla as a small mound. Areolar diameter is enlarged over that of stage 1.
3	Penis is slightly enlarged, at first mainly in length. Testes and scrotum are further enlarged than in stage 2.	The hair is considerably darker, coarser, and more curled. It spreads sparsely over the function of the pubes.	Breast and areola are both enlarged and elevated more than in stage 2 but with no separation of their contours.
4	Penis is further enlarged, with growth in breadth and development of glans. Testes and scrotum are further enlarged than in stage 3; scrotum skin is darker than in earlier stages.	Hair is now adult in type, but the area covered is still considerably smaller than in the adult. There is no spread to the medial surface of the thighs.	The areola and papilla form a secondary mound projecting above the contour of the breast.
5	Genitalia are adult in size and shape.	The hair is adult in quantity and type with distribution of the horizontal (or classically "feminine") pattern. Spread is to the medial surface of the thighs but not up the linea alba or elsewhere above the base of the inverse triangle.	Mature stage. The papilla only projects with the areola recessed to the general contour of the breast.

[a]For boys.
[b]For girls.
From Petersen and Taylor, 1980, p. 127.

on the upper part of the cheeks, below the lower lip, and finally along the sides of the chin (Tanner, 1981).

Also during puberty there are changes in the skin. It becomes somewhat rougher around the thighs and upper arms. In addition, **sebaceous** (oily) **glands** in the skin further develop, often producing acne or other skin eruptions. **Epocrine**

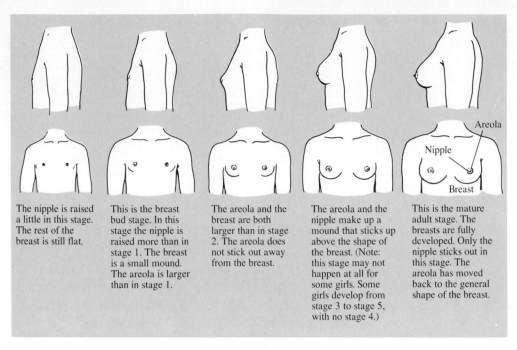

The nipple is raised a little in this stage. The rest of the breast is still flat.

This is the breast bud stage. In this stage the nipple is raised more than in stage 1. The breast is a small mound. The areola is larger than in stage 1.

The areola and the breast are both larger than in stage 2. The areola does not stick out away from the breast.

The areola and the nipple make up a mound that sticks up above the shape of the breast. (Note: this stage may not happen at all for some girls. Some girls develop from stage 3 to stage 5, with no stage 4.)

This is the mature adult stage. The breasts are fully developed. Only the nipple sticks out in this stage. The areola has moved back to the general shape of the breast.

FIGURE 16.12

Stages of breast development. From Morris and Udry, 1980, pp. 271–280.

(sweat) **glands** also continue to develop, producing a body odor that was not present before puberty.

SEXUAL MATURATION IN GIRLS. The sequence of the development of sexual maturity in girls also follows a regular pattern (Fig. 16.11 and Table 16.3). Typically, the first indicator of sexual maturity in girls is the increase in shape or elevation of the breast (the emergence of the "breast bud"). The stages in the development of breasts are described in Figure 16.12. (The number of each stage is the basis for the rating scale for breast development used in Figure 16.11.) In Stage 2 of breast development, or the "bud stage," the area around the nipple—the **areola**—widens and the nipple and breast become elevated as a small mound. In Stages 3 and 4, the nipple and the areola become distinct from the breast and extend beyond the contour of the breast. In the final stage, the areola becomes recessed to the contour of the breast, with only the nipple extending beyond the breast contour. It is important to recognize that these changes in breast development are primarily defined in terms of changes in the areola and nipple, without regard to the size of the breast. In other words, simple growth in breast size is not necessarily an accurate indicator of sexual maturation.

In some cases (about a third), the appearance of pubic hair occurs before the start of breast development. The development of female pubic hair follows a similar course of development to that of males (i.e., from sparse light-colored hair to densely curled and darker hair; this progression is the basis for the pubic hair rating scale in Figure 16.11).

The first menstruation or **menarche** is often regarded by adolescents and parents as a landmark event in female sexual maturity. Interestingly enough, it occurs relatively late in the pubertal sequence. Most American girls have their menarche

"Dear, this book says some rather profound things about adolescents."
"Well, between you and me, an adolescent is simply a person who can't pass a mirror without looking twice." From Shuttleworth, 1951.

at about age thirteen (Fig. 16.1). The occurrence of the menarche marks a relatively mature stage of female uterine growth. However, the menarche does *not* usually signify the attainment of complete reproductive functioning. For example, a female is less likely to become pregnant near her menarche than she is five or six years later. Full reproductive maturity is not attained until the early twenties (Tanner, 1981). It is important to bear in mind that full reproductive capacity (as with other dimensions of puberty) is a gradual process. This is true for both females and males. In the case of girls, full reproductive capacity means both *ovulation* and *menstruation*. This gradual acquisition of female reproductive capacity is sometimes manifested by irregular menstrual cycles after the first menarche (first bleeding) which are **anovulatory** (i.e., no egg or ovum is released by an ovary). Consequently, girls may not be fully fertile (ovulatory) with their first menstruation (Apter and Vihko, 1977).

DEFINITIONS

Menstruation. This refers to the periodic (approximately monthly) breakdown and discharge of uterine tissues and the unfertilized egg (if produced), which occurs in the absence of fertilization. (If an egg becomes fertilized and attaches itself to the uterine wall and a pregnancy has begun, menstruation does not occur.)

Ovulation. This refers to the release of an egg (ovum) from an ovary. (Typically, human ovaries produce one egg over the course of a twenty-eight-day cycle.) The egg travels through one of the fallopian tubes that connect the ovaries to the female uterus, where fertilization may occur.

Variations in the Timing and the Rate of Puberty

As we have discussed the adolescent growth spurt and the maturation of primary and secondary sex characteristics, it has become apparent that there is a wide variation in the ages at which pubertal events are supposed to occur (Fig. 16.11). There are considerable variations in the *timing* of puberty (when puberty begins) and the *rate* at which individuals proceed through puberty. For example, puberty can begin as early as eight years for girls and nine and a half years for boys or as late as thirteen years for girls and thirteen and a half years for boys (Fig. 16.11). In addition, the rate of puberty can vary considerably, taking as little as one and a half years for girls and two years for boys to as long as six years for girls and five years for boys. It is possible for an early-maturing boy or girl to start and complete puberty before a late-maturing girl or boy has even begun. Figures 16.13 and 16.14 provide an illustration of the differences between early-maturing (E) and late-maturing (L) children of the same chronological age.

GENETIC FACTORS.   There is evidence that the timing and rate of puberty are determined primarily by genetic factors (Katchadourian, 1977; Tanner, 1978b). For example, in one study identical twin girls (who share the same genetic inheritance) had their menarche within 2.8 months of each other, on the average. However, nonidentical (fraternal) twin girls (who are not as genetically similar) had their menarche, on the average, ten months apart. Furthermore, nontwin sibling girls had their menarches, on the average, thirteen months apart. (Tanner, 1978b, 1981).

ENVIRONMENTAL FACTORS.   The onset and rate of puberty are also influenced by environmental conditions. Although genetic factors may have a considerable impact on puberty, there are at least two significant environmental factors—*nu-*

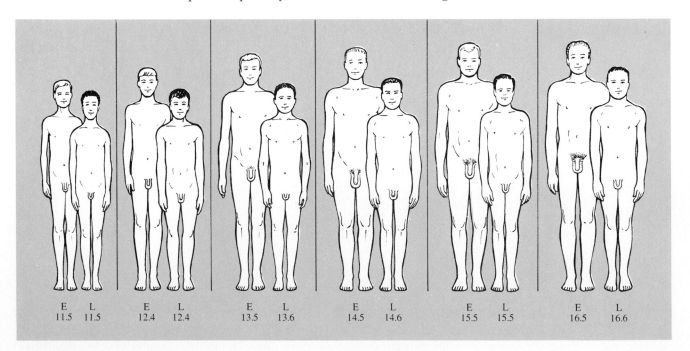

FIGURE 16.13

Adolescent boys who are the same chronological age but at different stages of puberty. From Shuttleworth, 1951.

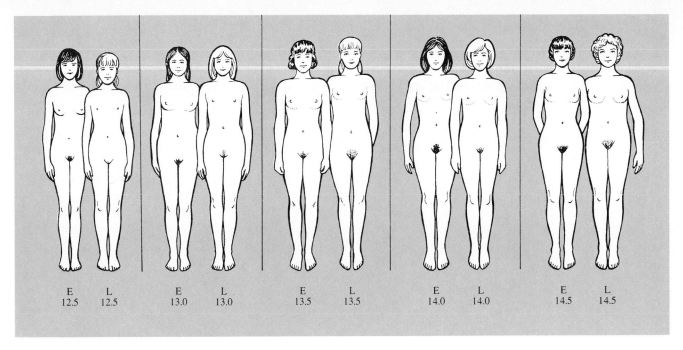

FIGURE 16.14

Adolescent girls who are the same chronological age but at different stages of puberty. From Shuttleworth, 1951.

trition and *health*. If adolescents are malnourished, the events of puberty can be markedly slowed down. This is particularly true in areas affected by severe poverty or famine. In one study that compared the age of menarche as a function of social class (a measure of income and nutrition), girls from more affluent homes reached menarche before girls from economically poorer families (Eveleth and Tanner, 1976; Tanner, 1981) (see Fig. 16.15). For example, Chinese adolescents in Hong

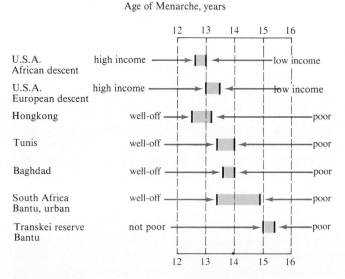

FIGURE 16.15

The average age of menarche varies across different social classes. From Eveleth and Tanner, 1976.

Kong had their menarche much earlier if they came from well-to-do families than if they came from poor families (and presumably had poor nutrition) (Eveleth and Tanner, 1976). In addition, poor health and chronic diseases have been shown to postpone the onset of pubertal events and to retard the rate of such events (Tanner, 1978b).

THE SECULAR TREND.   An excellent indicator of the impact of environmental factors on puberty is what has been called the *secular trend*. The **secular trend** refers to the tendency over historical time for the rate of some pubertal events to occur at a more rapid rate or at an earlier time. For example, the average age of the menarche has been declining over the past 200 years (Fig. 16.1) (Tanner, 1981; Frisch, 1983). In addition, there is some evidence that children have been growing taller at a more rapid rate (Fig. 16.2). Both of these secular trends can be attributed, in part, to improved nutrition and health over the past 150 years (including better sanitation and the control of many infectious diseases).

Is there a limit to these secular trends? That is, will the age of menarche continue to drop? Current evidence suggests that this secular trend has, in fact, leveled off. For example, there is no evidence of further drops in the average age of menarche over the past twenty-five years in Oslo, Norway, or London, England (Eveleth and Tanner, 1976).

The Psychological Impact of Puberty: An Ecological Perspective

The adolescent growth spurt and the changes in primary and secondary sex characteristics have far-reaching effects on the lives of adolescents. These biological and physical changes do not, however, account primarily for the psychological impact of puberty. Rather, these biological changes appear to influence the individual adolescent *indirectly*, in the following ways (Petersen, 1987; Boxer and Petersen, 1986) (see Fig. 16.16):

· Through the *subjective meanings* that the adolescent attaches to these changes.
· Through the reactions of the significant others in the life of the adolescent— peers and adults.

In summary, the impact of puberty on the self-esteem of the adolescent is the primary result of the adolescent's own and others' reactions to his or her maturation (Fig. 16.16).

EARLY AND LATE MATURATION.   Studies on early- and late-maturing adolescents provide important information on the psychological impact of puberty. These studies demonstrate the joint contribution of the adolescent's response to biological change, as well as the reactions of significant others (e.g., peers, parents, teachers, and so on) to the adolescent's self-esteem. For example, it may be that early-maturing adolescents find the challenges of adolescence easier because they are more easily accepted into the adult world (because they look more like adults). On the other hand, it could be argued that early-maturing adolescents may have a more difficult time negotiating adolescence because of the additional pressures placed on them by peers, parents, or other adults. For example, the high school boy who is exceptionally tall and poorly coordinated may be expected to be a good basketball player.

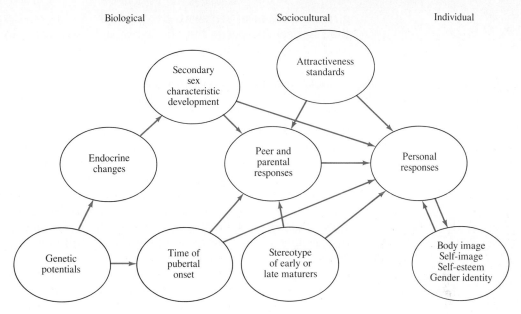

FIGURE 16.16

The impact of puberty: An ecological perspective. The impact of puberty on the adolescent's self-esteem is through the adolescent's own reactions and those of significant others—peers and adults. From Petersen and Taylor, 1980, p. 147.

Early studies of early- and late-maturing boys (Jones and Bayley, 1950) showed that the early maturers tended to be stronger, taller, and better coordinated than the later maturers. In addition, late maturers were found to be less well poised, more immoderate in their behavior, and more tense and anxious than early maturers. These findings were confirmed in later studies (Faust, 1960; Elkind, 1967a; Blos, 1970; Tobin-Richards, Boxer, and Petersen, 1983; Petersen, 1984). Some of these differences seemed to persist over time, even when the physical differences between early and later maturers were no longer present. For example, when early maturers reached their thirties, they tended to have higher occupational status and to be more socially active than late maturers (Jones, 1957). On the other hand, there is reason to think that there are some favorable results of relatively late maturation. Early maturers appear to achieve in a more conforming manner and to be more conventional in their thoughts and attitudes than late maturers. Late maturers seem to be more flexible and adaptive and are better able to tolerate ambiguity (Jones, 1965). Furthermore, it has been argued that early maturers may be "pushed" into adulthood too quickly without sufficient time to experiment with various life roles and identities. On the other hand, late maturers, unlike early maturers, do not experience early acceptance by the adult world. Therefore, they cannot rely on the conventions of the adult world for success in adolescence (Peskin, 1967).

The impact of early or late maturation on girls is not as clear-cut as it is for boys. Early research suggested that early-maturing girls, unlike early-maturing boys, were at a disadvantage. Specifically, early-maturing girls were less well-poised, more withdrawn, and more unsure of themselves than later-maturing girls (Jones, H., 1949; Jones and Mussen, 1958; Simmons, Blyth, and McKinney, 1983; Petersen, 1984). Late-maturing girls were higher in sociability, prestige, and popularity than early-maturing girls. The explanation for these findings is that the early-maturing girl may be out of step with her peers. Not only is she more physically mature than her female peers, but she is probably far more physically mature than her male classmates. (Recall that, on the average, girls are two years ahead of boys in physical development.)

However, more recent evidence suggests that early-maturing girls are more popular with boys and are more independent than later maturing girls (Simmons, Blyth, and McKinney, 1983). This later evidence also suggests that early maturers initially perform more poorly in school and have more self-esteem problems. An explanation for these findings may be that early maturation may make a girl somewhat conspicuous at first. She may appear older than the boys in her class. However, this disadvantage may be offset as she reaps some benefits of early maturation, including increased attention, dating opportunities, and expectations of more mature and socially responsible behavior (Faust, 1960; Crockett and Petersen, 1985). Furthermore, by the time most of the girls in a given group have physically matured, the early-maturing girls are frequently among the most popular in the group. There is some evidence that early-maturing girls (like late-maturing boys) may experience initial problems of self-esteem and adaptation that they may use to their advantage (Peskin, 1973; Petersen et al., 1984; Tobin-Richards et al., 1984). In other words, they may develop coping skills that make them more psychologically advanced than their cohorts in adulthood.

BODY IMAGE AND PUBERTY.   A second example of the interaction of adolescent perceptions of the physical changes of puberty with the reactions of others to those changes is the adolescent's satisfaction with the changes in his or her *body image*. The **body image** is the adolescent's perceptions of his or her physique and appearance. This body image is compared with the adolescent's own expectations for body type, the evaluations of relevant peers and adults, and the cultural norms and standards for male/female body types. As a result of these comparisons, adolescents may become somewhat self-conscious about their physical appearance. They may spend significant time and energy in assessing how their peers view these changes. It has been suggested that adolescents and their peers may be comparing themselves with a mythical **body ideal.** Through exposure to television, movies, and magazines, adolescents come to learn that there may be an ideal body type for males and females. Males, for example, may be expected to look relatively slim and to be slightly muscular. Female adolescents may perceive that boys prefer girls with a slender figure, well-developed breasts, and long legs. Deviations from such idealized norms of physical appearance may affect the way some adolescents are treated by others and how they view themselves (Petersen et al., 1984; Tobin-Richards et al., 1984).

One of the notorious problems of adolescent physical appearance is acne. During puberty the developing sebaceous (sweat) glands secrete an excess of skin oil, which causes a clogging and inflammation of skin pores. In addition, this situation is compounded by teenage eating habits and the normal anxieties of adolescent life. The result frequently is skin blemishes, which make the adolescent feel self-conscious and socially uncomfortable (Katchadourian, 1977). The situation may be further aggravated by the reactions of peers or adults, which may add to the adolescent's anxiety and self-consciousness.

In summary, both the general problem of adolescent body image and the specific example of skin acne illustrate how the basic biological changes of adolescence are subject to the interpretations of adolescents and to existing cultural/social norms and standards. Although most adolescents emerge from puberty with relative success and with their self-esteem intact, there are nevertheless some cases of

Anorexia Nervosa: A Problem of Body Image and Family

Because the period of adolescence is a time of dramatic change in physical appearance, there is always the possibility of disturbed reactions to these changes. Generally speaking, these biological and physical changes affect the adolescent's self-concept and level of self-esteem primarily, and indirectly, through the reactions of the adolescent and significant others to these changes. The boundaries for these reactions are set by cultural and social standards for approximate physical appearance or male/female body types. Consequently, the adolescent's self-esteem may be influenced by any perceived deviations from such "body ideals." *Anorexia nervosa* is a serious disorder that results from a disturbed and inaccurate body image (i.e., an *incorrectly* perceived deviation from a "body ideal").

Frequency of Occurrence. The frequency of anorexia nervosa appears to be increasing over the past twenty years. Whether this is due to an increase in the diagnosis of the disorder (i.e., case finding) or to an actual increase in occurrence is not clear. At any rate, the numbers who suffer from the disorder appear to have doubled over the past twenty years (Steiner, 1982).

Who Is Affected? Anorexia nervosa occurs most frequently among middle-class, white females who are between twelve and twenty years of age (Jones, Fox, and Babigian, 1980; Jeammet, 1981; Steiner, 1982). Furthermore, an adolescent female has the disorder an average of three to six years (Stein et al., 1982). The long-term prognosis is not good, with a mortality rate of between 5 and 15 percent (Steiner, 1982).

Defining Symptoms. Simply put, **anorexia nervosa** is an eating disorder resulting from an extremely disturbed *body image*. Anorectics (typically adolescent girls) see themselves as overweight, when they are really underweight. Consequently, they avoid food, sometimes to the extreme of starvation and death. The following are the primary symptoms of anorexia nervosa (Palmer, 1980; Rosen, 1980; Jeammet, 1981; Steiner, 1982; Bryant and Bates, 1985):

- *Behavior that leads to a marked loss of body weight* (e.g., a loss of 25 percent of body weight and/or being at least 15 percent below the standard weight for a given height and body build).
- *A studied avoidance of food accompanied by a morbid fear of becoming fat.* There is a phobic avoidance of

gaining weight brought on by a fear of "losing control" (i.e., being unable to stop eating).
- *One of several physical symptoms, including amenorrhea (the cessation of menstruation), extreme overactivity, regular vomiting, or hypothermia (abnormally low body temperature).* Although any of

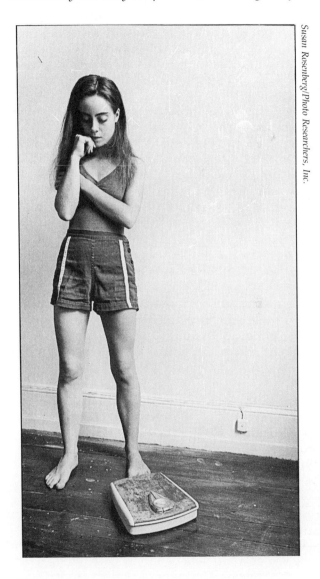

Susan Rosenberg/Photo Researchers, Inc.

these symptoms can occur, special mention should be made of *amenorrhea* because of its frequency among anorectics, as well as its association with weight. That is, there is much evidence that the pubertal event of menstruation is a *weight-related event* (Frisch, 1974). In other

(Continued)

words, the onset (and the cessation) of menstruation is associated with the individual's passing a given threshold body weight (for that individual). Thus, when an anorectic loses weight beyond a critical point, menstruation ceases. Thus, just as puberty may represent a "switching on" of hormones, anorexia nervosa can be viewed as a "switching off." According to Robert Palmer, "It is fair to describe the anorectic state as one of regression to a 'pre-pubertal' condition . . ." (1980, pp. 47–48). We return to this idea of "switching off" to a prepubertal state in our discussion of the psychological bases of anorexia nervosa.

The Social Basis for Anorexia Nervosa. There is a distinct emphasis in American society on fashion-model figures for females. In particular, the media and advertising encourage the pursuit of slimness and dieting as a way of life. Adolescents are literally bombarded with images of slenderness as the ideal for women. Unfortunately, such an emphasis is simply unrealistic from a biological/genetic perspective. Nonetheless, there may be considerable discussion among peers on clothes, beauty, and body weight, which affirms the ideal of slimness. Obviously, not everyone who talks about slimness or who diets becomes anorectic. The anorectic internalizes this body ideal to a self-destructive extreme.

Psychological Bases. A number of psychological factors have been implicated with anorectic behavior, including the following:

· *Low self-esteem.* There is evidence that anorectics have a generally low level of self-esteem, feeling particularly inadequate about sexual issues (Casper, Offer, and Ostrov, 1981; Boskind-White and White, 1983).
· *Difficulty coping with problems.* Adolescent girls who develop anorexia nervosa do so, with regularity, either just before or after the maturation of primary and secondary sex characteristics. Hence, anorectic behavior may be viewed as a problem of adolescence, brought on by the biological changes of puberty. In fact, one can view adolescence as the time of life requiring individual adaptation to the demands of growing,

demands that are initiated by puberty. Adolescents who become anorectic have typically been experiencing problems in making the transition from childhood to adulthood. Therefore, one explanation of the anorectic's need to lose weight is that it will produce a cessation of menstruation or a "prepubertal regression" (see the prior discussion). Presumably, this biological "switching off" of puberty is accompanied by a psychological "return" to childhood. As Palmer suggests, "the process of 'switching off' reduces the pressure upon them by, as it were, taking the steam out of their adolescent state" (1980, p. 48). The anorectic girl then becomes fearful of weight gain, with its implication of again "switching on" adolescence.

Family Factors. There is some evidence that certain family characteristics are associated with anorectic behavior in adolescence. *Family characteristics* that appear to encourage or maintain the development of anorexia nervosa in families include the following (Minuchin, Rosman, and Baker, 1978; White, 1983):

· *Enmeshed relationships,* such as when family members are so overly involved with one another to the extreme that members talk for one another with little recognition of separateness or individuality (see the discussion of enmeshment in Chapter 15).
· *Limited recognition of individual autonomy,* such as being so overly concerned with a family member's problems that he or she is not encouraged to solve problems himself or herself.
· *The unhealthy maintenance of a system of family relationships* such that change is neither discussed nor allowed.
· *Failure to develop family problem-solving techniques* such that conflicts are not handled properly and problems fester and remain unsolved. (Often such families refuse to allow open conflict while covert or concealed conflicts run rampant.)
· *The unhealthy involvement of children in parental issues* through such practices as *triangulation* (the parent puts the child in the position of having to take sides with one parent or the other).

serious disturbance. For example, adolescent females who suffer from an eating disorder called *anorexia nervosa* have an extremely disturbed body image. Some anorectics will starve themselves (leading to death in some cases, if untreated) to reduce their weight, even though they are *actually* underweight.

Cognitive Development

The maturational events we have described accompany the development of a new cognitive competence. Just as there is a spurt in physical and sexual development, there is also an intellectual and cognitive "spurt." The changes that take place in adolescent intellectual growth are both quantitative and qualitative.

> *DEFINITIONS*
>
> **Quantitative changes in thinking.** Alterations in the total "amount" of a particular skill or ability. For example, an increase in verbal skills during adolescence would represent a *quantitative* change in a skill that was present during middle childhood (e.g., an increasing precision in the use of words to label objects, people, or actions).
>
> **Qualitative changes in thinking.** Changes in the manner or process of cognitive functioning. For example, learning to use abstract labels (e.g., *justice, freedom*) without having to refer to concrete instances or examples of these abstractions is a *qualitative* change in thinking.

Quantitative Changes in Intelligence

In our discussion of quantitative issues in adolescent intelligence we refer primarily to research based on the *psychometric* measures of intelligence (e.g., intelligence tests such as the WISC and the Stanford-Binet; see the discussion of psychometric methods in Chapter 13). In this section we examine four basic questions: (1) How *stable* (reliable) are measurements of intelligence from childhood to adolescence? (2) Do children's measured abilities *improve* in adolescence? (3) Does intelligence become more *specialized* during adolescence? (4) And, finally, are there *sex differences* in intelligence that emerge in adolescence?

· *Stability of intelligence. Stability* refers to the continuity of mental skills from childhood to adolescence. Will the child who is first in his or her third-grade class in arithmetic continue to perform at a comparable level in high school algebra and

The changes that take place in adolescent intellectual growth are both qualitative and quantitative.

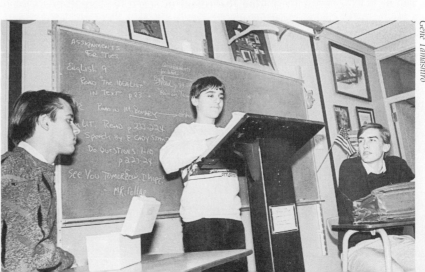

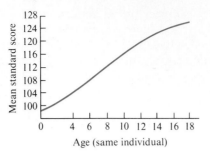

FIGURE 16.17
The improvement in measured ability from birth through age eighteen.

geometry classes? On the whole, a child's measured abilities and, therefore, his or her class standing, tend to remain stable from childhood through adolescence (McCall, Applebaum, and Hogarty, 1973). However, changes in the child's/adolescent's life circumstances sometimes result in dramatic changes in relative intellectual standing. For example, the adolescent who associates with a peer group that does not value or support school skills may show a decline in school performance.

• *Improvement in measured intelligence.* Although *each individual's* relative standing compared with his or her peers remains relatively stable, there is nonetheless a dramatic improvement for *all* children in measured ability from childhood through adolescence (see Fig. 16.17). On the average, intelligence scores increase throughout childhood and adolescence, leveling off during early adulthood.

• *The specialization of abilities.* During middle childhood, mental growth tends to be fairly even. During adolescence, however, some abilities and skills appear to develop more than others. It appears that intellectual skills tend to become more specialized during adolescence, and individuals may demonstrate what appears to be emerging special interests, such as an aptitude for science or verbal skills. Although there is a general improvement in all abilities (for all individuals) from childhood through adolescence, many high school students demonstrate specialized improvement in certain specific areas.

• *Sex differences in intelligence.* The differentiation and specialization of abilities is sometimes heavily weighted by social-cultural factors. Research on adolescent intelligence scores indicates that many sex differences emerge during the adolescent years. For example, it has been noted that adolescent girls may continue to develop verbal skills, whereas their scientific and mathematical abilities appear to languish. On the other hand, adolescence often marks a surge of interest and development for boys in science and mathematics. Some of this specialization might well be attributed to individual personality differences. However, it is also likely, in our culture, that males are expected to do well in science and mathematics, whereas females are expected to do well in verbal skills. These differences in ability may be the result of sex-role stereotypes that may be ingrained in our culture.

Qualitative Changes in Intelligence

So far we have only discussed the *quantitative* changes in adolescent intelligence. Table 16.4 describes some of the major *qualitative* differences between the *concrete operational* individual of middle childhood (see Chapter 13) and the *formal operational* adolescent. One way to think about these developments is to think of the adolescent as being a "scientific thinker." That is, the adolescent is capable of reasoning in abstract as well as concrete terms, can simultaneously consider several factors or variables in solving problems, can consider probabilities, and can de-

TABLE 16.4

A Comparison of Childhood and Adolescent Thought

CHILDHOOD	ADOLESCENT
Thought limited to here and now	Thought extended to possibilities
Problem solving dictated by details of the problem	Problem solving governed by planned hypothesis testing
Thought limited to concrete objects and situations	Thought expanded to ideas as well as concrete reality
Thought focused on one's own perspective	Thought enlarged to perspective of others

From Sprinthall and Collins, 1984, p. 93.

velop and test hypotheses. Jean Piaget (1970b) considered such abilities as characteristic of formal operations. From Piaget's perspective, the major difference between an adolescent who has attained formal operations and a professional scientist is the latter's experience. Both the professional scientist and the formal operational adolescent are scientific thinkers, whose qualitative characteristics of thinking are similar. Although formal operations may occur as early as eleven years of age, most adolescents are not fully into that stage until approximately fifteen years of age.

THE REAL AND THE POSSIBLE.   The most significant qualitative dimension of formal operational thinking is a new relationship between what is *real* and what is *possible*. Concrete operational children focus their thinking on *relations between objects that they can classify, categorize, and order* (see Chapter 13). In formal operational thinking, the adolescent or adult can think about the *possible* as well as the *real*. Instead of being limited to dealing with things as they *are*, the adolescent can now deal with things as they *might be* (and related hypotheses).

Furthermore, the formal operational adolescent begins with *possibilities* first and then moves to *reality*. For example, if asked to describe what would happen if the earth stopped revolving around the sun, the formal operational adolescent would be able to suggest many possible hypotheses (there would be no seasons, millions of people would have to move to warmer climates, farming outdoors would be impossible in many places). On the other hand, the concrete operational child would respond to such a query by first referring to *reality* and exploring possibilities only when encouraged to do so. For example, school-age children or younger might simply answer that it would "always be cold" or "always be warm." All such responses would reflect what the school-age child could *immediately* sense or experience. According to John Flavell:

> For the concrete operational thinker, the realm of abstract possibility is seen as an uncertain and only occasional extension of the safer and surer realm of palpable reality. For the formal-operational thinker, on the other hand, reality is seen as that particular portion of the much wider world of possibility which happens to exist or hold true in a given problem situation. Possibility is subordinated to reality in the former case, whereas reality is subordinated to possibility in the latter case. (1985, p. 98)

Adolescents tend to apply this newly acquired cognitive ability to many areas of their life including ethics, relationships with parents, identity development, careers, politics, religion, and so on. Piaget (1970b) suggested that the ability to contemplate the possible is the basis for what has been called (usually by adults) *adolescent idealism.* In other words, the ability to think about possibilities leads the adolescent to the creation of *ideals* and *ideal states.* This newfound ability to think in terms of ideals and absolutes sometimes brings criticism from adults that the adolescent is "living in a dream world," is "unrealistic," or is simply not "down-to-earth."

Thinking about ideals has another important facet for adolescents. It permits them to plan for the future by projecting possible situations into an approaching time period. The concept of *future orientation* becomes an important organizational feature of the adolescent's life process. It is a way of developing goals and organizing immediate activities in a meaningful way. Furthermore, the ability to organize activities meaningfully in terms of a future is an important skill in adulthood.

Another result of thinking about ideals is the inevitable—and sometimes painful—comparisons of "what is" with "what could be." These comparisons are often the basis for new perspectives on the family, the school, and the community. Sometimes the adolescent's recognition of the gap between the ideal and the real is the basis for minor or major conflicts between the adolescent and the parent.

Distinctions between the ideal and the real may come painfully close to home. The adolescent may come to realize the difference between what he or she is and what he or she would like to be. Such recognition can lead to many commonly observed adolescent behaviors, such as daydreaming, temporary stupors, or moodiness on the one hand, and to attempts to narrow the gap between reality and the ideal world (e.g., trying out roles or dressing "cool") on the other.

HYPOTHESES AND DEDUCTIONS.   Adolescents are able, in a *systematic fashion,* both to raise and to test hypotheses about the solution to a given problem. On the other hand, when a younger child is presented with a problem, he or she may not proceed systematically. A younger child may persevere with solutions (hypotheses) that do not work while failing to test alternatives. For example, such a child may persist with a hypothesis that does not fit the facts, perhaps even trying to make the facts fit the hypothesis. The adolescent is able to test one hypothesis after another systematically, until a correct solution is discovered.

Furthermore, adolescent problem solving is marked by the ability to *deal with many facts simultaneously.* For example, the adolescent recognizes that getting to the picnic on time depends on several factors, including the total distance, the speed of the automobile, and the total time needed to travel the distance. The child may be able to handle two factors but probably cannot understand how multiple determinants (distance, speed, and time) interrelate and contribute to a given solution.

THE USE OF ABSTRACT LOGIC.   Another important qualitative characteristic of the formal operational thinker is the ability to use *abstract reasoning.* Formal operations are logical manipulations of propositions, statements, or symbols that are *derived from* or based on concrete reality. (Formal operations are *not,* therefore, operations *directly* dealing with concrete reality.) Adolescents who are at the level of formal operational thinking can exercise logical reasoning involving such propositions and symbols based on concrete reality. On the other hand, a child in the period of concrete operations can reason about things or concrete objects but cannot reason about verbal propositions. For example, if a child is shown three objects of varying size, he or she will be able to see that if A is bigger than B, which in turn, is bigger than C, then A must be bigger than C. However, if he or she is presented with a verbal description of a solution, such as "Jeff is taller than Scott and Scott is taller than Bruce," the child will probably be unable to arrive at the logical conclusion that Jeff is taller than Bruce. The reason for this limitation with regard to verbal propositions is that the child is dependent on *concrete* objects for successful problem solving. Adolescents can solve word problems because they are able to think about and with symbols and words that transform concrete experience (Flavell, 1985).

In addition, the adolescent who has reached the level of formal operations has developed the ability to use a *second-order symbolic system*; that is, the adolescent has the ability to work with relationships between *symbols that represent other symbols*. For example, the early adolescent can learn algebra because he or she can now work with second-order symbols (e.g., X and Y) to represent first-order symbols (e.g., 5 and 10).

$$5 + X = 10$$
$$X = 5$$

The concrete operational child needs visual clues and props to be able to deal with complex symbolic relationships such as mathematical equations. On the other hand, adolescents can work exclusively with second-order symbols. Therefore, they can solve the boxed equation as well as many others without needing to refer to concrete examples or reference points.

INTROSPECTION AND EXAMINATION OF ONE'S OWN THINKING. In early adolescence a thinking process begins that will characterize both adolescence and adulthood: the ability to think introspectively about one's own thoughts. Adolescents can talk about their beliefs and thoughts on a wide range of subjects. They can articulate many experiences that were mainly at the level of feeling and emotion in middle childhood. However, they appear to be somewhat more tactful than children, who might simply state what is on their mind—no matter how potentially embarrassing. Adolescents seem to be more aware than children that their thoughts are private even though they are capable of discussing them (Flavell, 1985).

Darryl Jacobson

Early adolescence marks the beginning of introspection.

The Imaginary Audience and the Personal Fable

Self-consciousness—Another characteristic of the young teenager that results directly from thinking in a new key is self-consciousness. Formal operations make it possible for young people to think about thinking. . . . Because teenagers are caught up with

All of us retain some imaginary audience fantasies even when we are fully grown.

Self-centeredness. Perhaps because teenagers are so convinced that people are observing and thinking about them, they get an inflated opinion of their own

Jerrold Jacobson

Because some teenagers are intensely aware of the transformations in their lives, they become self-centered.

the transformations they are undergoing—in their bodies, in their facial structure, in their feelings and emotions, and in their thinking powers—they become self-centered. They assume that everyone around them is concerned about the same thing they are concerned with, namely, themselves. I call this assumption the *imaginary audience.* It is the imaginary audience that accounts for the teenager's extreme self-consciousness. Teenagers feel that they are always on stage and that everyone around them is as aware of and as concerned about their appearance and behavior as they themselves are.

importance. They begin to feel that they are special and unique. The teenage boy who is sure that the pretty girl at the party is looking at him in a special way reflects this kind of thinking. Like the imaginary audience, the personal fable, in a simplified form, stays with us for the rest of our lives. It is our legacy from adolescent thought. . . . The fable is much more prominent in adolescence than at any other stage in life. (From Elkind, 1984, pp. 33 and 36)

THE ABILITY TO UNDERSTAND METAPHOR AND HUMOR. Whereas the child almost always takes things literally, the adolescent is able to understand the symbolic meaning of metaphors, such as "stubborn as a mule." The child has difficulty understanding such metaphors and other symbolic expressions because he or she cannot "operate" on words without concrete examples. The child cannot sense the multiple meanings and levels of meaning in a metaphor, probably because his or her thinking is limited to the concrete, literal meaning (Elkind, 1984).

Differences in Early and Later Adolescent Thinking

In the discussion above we have presented the general dimensions of early-adolescent (ages twelve to sixteen) thinking. There are, however, important differences within the early adolescent period. David Elkind described these differences as follows:

> By and large the young adolescent [twelve to sixteen years] tends to be rather flighty as a consequence of the rapid changes that have been occurring in him. Because the changes are new he is more preoccupied with them than he will be later when he is more accustomed to his enlarged body, deeper voice, and awakened sexual interest and curiosity. The young person has to adjust not only to the new changes in his body, but also to new changes in his thinking abilities. Certain phenomena of early adolescence reflect this adjustment period. . . . the twelve- and thirteen-year-old can now deal with possibilities and consider many new alternatives in any given problem-solving situation. Initially this is a somewhat terrifying experience because while the young person can see the many possible alternatives, he does not have the background or experience upon which to make a choice. It often appears, as a consequence, that young adolescents are hopelessly dependent and indecisive. . . . By the age of fifteen and sixteen, however, young people have more experience in decision-making and have a better idea of the relative importance of things. (1971, p. 127)

The newfound cognitive skills of idealization are usually exercised first in the home. Parents are the first to feel the strength of these skills, as they may be compared with other parents or against an ideal and found wanting. As Elkind suggested, "In early adolescence not only is the grass greener in the other person's yard, but the house is bigger and more comfortable and the parents are nicer" (p. 128). After the family and the parents, the child's critical judgment may be turned toward the school and the teacher. Whereas young children are more concerned with the teacher's personality or how "nice" or "mean" the teacher is, the adolescent may become concerned about the teacher's competence in addition to his or her personality. By the time the individual reaches the middle to the latter part of adolescence, criticism shifts to more general social issues, social values, or social institutions, such as government and religion.

Thinking About Society

How do adolescents develop ideas about society and the political system? According to Judith Gallatin, this process occurs in the following way:

> Prior to adolescence, the child views government and law principally as coercive agencies. If asked, children will declare that the function of political institutions is to police people—to keep them in line and make sure that they are unable to get away with any wrong doing (Adelson and O'Neil, 1966; Adelson and Beall, 1970; Adelson, Green and O'Neil, 1969; Tapp, 1976; Tapp and Kohlberg, 1971; Tapp and Levine, 1972). As children reach adolescence, this perception begins to alter, and by the time they have reached their late teens, a substantial proportion of youngsters

have acquired a less forbidding image of the political system. The government is seen as a cooperative venture—an agency that provides services and insures that society functions smoothly rather than a glorified policeman. (1980, pp. 351–52)

The growth of political thinking appears to parallel the general pattern of the development of cognitive processes (from the concrete processes in childhood to the more abstract thinking in adolescence). Furthermore, there is some evidence for three levels in the development of political thinking (Gallatin, 1980). This progression in thinking can best be appreciated in the context of child/adolescent responses to a specific dilemma posed to them, as follows:

DILEMMA

There is a man who owns a home that he dearly enjoys. The state needs the land on which the home is built to construct a highway. Should the man be forced to sell his house to the state? Should the state detour the highway away from the man's house?

- *Level 1: A concrete and practical response focusing on the immediate or personal consequences of political decisions* (typically includes school-age children and early adolescents eleven to twelve years of age). Children and young adolescents at this level commonly favored the rights of the landowner because his case was concrete and personally immediate. For example, such a response might be "I don't think it's fair to make the man feel so bad."
- *Level 2: Transitional responses which include a mixture of immediate/personal consequences and vaguely defined political concepts* (typically includes early adolescents, thirteen to fourteen years). For example, a sample response might be "I think people should be able to do what they want to do most of the time. But I can't see how this guy can make everybody else go out of their way for him." Among other things, this response is based on *both* the personal consequences to the man and to other citizens *and* an emerging recognition of a political concept—public welfare.
- *Level 3: Conceptual responses* (typically includes middle and older adolescents, fifteen years and beyond). At this level, the adolescent's political thinking is based primarily on abstract ideas and political concepts. A sample response at this level might be "The rights of the entire community are more important than the property rights of one guy."

In summary, older adolescents formulated their political thinking in terms of general ethical or political concepts. They then applied these principles to specific situations, such as the dilemma posed above. Although the adolescent in Level 3 supported the concept of public welfare over individual property rights, it is, of course, possible and justifiable for Level 3 thinkers to support individual rights over the rights of the larger group. The main point, however, is that whatever the political position, it is based on general/abstract principles. Thus, the development of political thinking in adolescence reflects the general movement of cognitive development from concrete to formal operations.

A Critique of Piagetian Formal Operations

So far, much of our discussion on adolescent thinking has been based on Piaget's concept of formal operations. It is now appropriate to consider the criticisms that have been directed at this conception of adolescent thinking. In this section, we examine two specific questions that have been raised: (1) Do all adolescents attain formal operations? (2) Are there stages of thinking beyond formal operations?

• *Are formal operations attained by all adolescents?* Piaget (Piaget and Inhelder, 1969) originally hypothesized that the onset of formal operations occurred at about the age of eleven or twelve and stabilized at around fourteen or fifteen years of age. Subsequent research, however, has indicated a more complex situation (Neimark, 1975; Martorano, 1977; Moshman, 1979; Keating, 1980; Keating and Clark, 1980). Daniel Keating (1980) found that a third of his sample of college students and middle-age adults did not use formal operations to solve a new problem. Ann Higgins-Trenk and A. J. Gaite (1971) found that many adolescents do not attain formal operations until the late teen years or early twenties, if at all. About 50 percent of the subjects (mean age 17.7 years) were not performing at the level of formal operations. Similarly, Suzanne Martorano (1977) found, using a sample of females in sixth through twelfth grades, that not even the twelfth graders consistently performed at the level of concrete operations across all ten tasks in the experiment. These findings seem to suggest that all adolescents may not be grappling with the results of changing cognitive patterns; however, the vast majority *are* dealing with physical, sexual, hormonal, and emotional changes.

A related criticism is that formal operations depend, in part, on one's type or level of education and walk of life. That is, there is some evidence that some levels or types of formal education and life activities offer more practice and more reasons for using formal operations (Flavell, 1977). One study of college students found that physics, political science, and English majors were more likely to use formal operations than students in areas that did not require comparable levels of abstract thinking (DeLiss and Staudt, 1980). Likewise, abstract thinking may not be a necessity for competent adult performance in many work-related roles.

• *Are there stages of thinking beyond formal operations?* Although not all adolescents attain formal operations during early adolescence, there is evidence that some older adolescents may go beyond formal operations, or to a second phase of formal operations. This phase has been called *problem finding* in contrast to the *problem solving* that typically characterizes formal operations (Arlin, 1975). Thus, the thinking of some older adolescents fifteen to twenty years old might be characterized as "divergent" (moving toward new or creative solutions or the identification of problems) rather than "convergent" (moving toward known or accepted solutions to problems). This type of thinking characterizes the older adolescent, who raises questions about the social system and its institutions. This stage beyond formal operations (or the second phase of formal operations) is identified by the quality of the *questions asked* rather than the arrival at known conclusions. Parents or teachers may often respond to such thinking with comments like "That's a good question!"

Summary

1. For our purposes, the term *puberty* refers to all the biological, physical, and sexual changes that occur as the individual moves from childhood to adulthood. There are five primary manifestations of puberty: a growth spurt, changes in body composition, changes in respiration and circulation, the continued development of the male and female sex organs, and the development of secondary sex characteristics.
2. The onset of puberty is marked by a considerable increase in the rate of

growth. The adolescent growth spurt may begin as early as eleven years of age for girls and thirteen years for boys. The growth spurt may involve a doubling of the velocity or rate of growth. Increases in height and weight are accompanied by changes in body form, distribution of fat, and motor performance.

3. The changes relating to sexual reproductive capability are the hallmark of puberty. These sexual changes are of two types: changes in *primary sex characteristics* and changes in *secondary sex characteristics.* The sequence of the development of sexual maturity in boys and girls follows an orderly and sequential pattern.

4. There are considerable variations between individuals in the *timing* of puberty (when puberty begins) and the *rate* at which individuals proceed through puberty. Although there is evidence that the timing and rate of puberty are determined primarily by genetic factors, there are at least two significant environmental factors—*nutrition* and *health.* An excellent indicator of the impact of environmental factors on puberty is the *secular trend.*

5. The impact of puberty on the self-esteem of the adolescent is the primary result of the adolescent's own and others' reactions to his or her maturation. Studies of early- and late-maturing adolescents provide knowledge about the psychological impact of puberty. In addition, both the general problem of adolescent body image and the specific example of skin acne illustrate how the basic biological changes of adolescence are subject to the interpretations of adolescents and to existing cultural/social norms and standards.

6. Several factors are important for a consideration of the *quantitative changes* in intelligence in adolescence: the stability of intelligence, improvement in measured intelligence, the specialization of abilities, and sex differences in intelligence. The *qualitative* changes in adolescent thinking can be thought of in terms of the major differences between the *concrete operational* individual of middle childhood and the *formal operational* adolescent. The formal operational adolescent can think about the *possible* as well as the *real.* Adolescents are able, in a systematic fashion, to both raise and test hypotheses. In addition, the formal operational adolescent can use *abstract reasoning* and *introspection* and can understand metaphor and humor.

   Furthermore, there are important differences between early and later adolescent thinking. The growth of political thinking appears to parallel the general pattern of the development of cognitive development from concrete to more abstract thinking.

7. Criticisms of Piagetian formal operations include at least two issues. Are formal operations attained by all adolescents? Are there stages of thinking beyond formal operations?

Key Terms

Adolescent growth spurt	Body image
Androgens	Endocrine systems
Anorexia nervosa	Epiphyses
Anovulatory	Epocrine glands
Areola	Estrogens
Body ideal	Hormones

Hypothalmus
Menarche
Menstruation
Ovulation
Pituitary gland
Primary sex characteristics
Puberty

Pubescence
Qualitative changes in thinking
Quantitative changes in thinking
Sebaceous glands
Secondary sex characteristics
Secular trend

Questions

1. Discuss the meaning of puberty.
2. What happens during the adolescent growth spurt?
3. Discuss the secular trend with reference to the menarche.
4. Discuss three qualitative changes in intelligence that occur during adolescence.
5. Give a critique of Piagetian formal operations.

Suggested Readings

CHUMLEA, W. C. "Physical Growth in Adolescence." In B. Wolman (ed.), *Handbook of Developmental Psychology*. Englewood Cliffs, N.J.: Prentice-Hall, 1982, pp. 471–485. A detailed analysis of reserach on physical growth in adolescence.

ELKIND, D. *All Grown Up and No Place to Go*. Reading, Mass.: Addison-Wesley, 1984. A readable discussion of adolescent behavior including such curiosities as the imaginary audience.

LERNER, R. M., and ROCH, T. T. (eds.). *Biological-Psychosocial Interactions in Early Adolescence*. Hillsdale, N.J.: Erlbaum, 1985. A collection of articles on the interaction between the biological and physical changes of adolescence and psychosocial factors.

LERNER, R. M., and GALAMBOS, N. L. *Experiencing Adolescents: A Source-Book for Parents, Teachers, and Teens*. New York: Garland Press, 1984. An excellent book with lots of sound information based on research evidence.

TANNER, J. M. *Education and Physical Growth* (2nd ed.). New York: International Universities Press, 1978. A thorough discussion of the dynamics of the growth spurt preceding adolescence and the accompanying physiological changes.

17 Adolescence: Social and Personality Development

*The evidence in young lives of the search for something and somebody to be true
to is seen in a variety of pursuits more or less sanctioned by society. It is often
hidden in a bewildering combination of shifting devotion and sudden perversity,
sometimes more devotedly perverse, sometimes more perversely devoted. . . . Yet,
in all youth's seeming shiftiness, a seeking after some durability in change can
be detected, whether . . . in the sincerity of conviction . . . or in the genuineness
of personalities and the reliability of commitments.*

—*Erik Erikson*, Challenge of Youth

*. . . and blest are those
Whose blood and judgment are so well com-meddled
That they are not a pipe for Fortune's finger
To sound what stop she please. Give me that man
That is not passion's slave, and I will wear him
In my heart's core, ay, in my heart of heart, . . .*

—*Shakespeare*, Hamlet

So far, we have examined the contexts of adolescent development (the family, the school, the peer group, the world of work) and the physical and cognitive changes that accompany adolescence. Physical changes, such as the growth spurt and puberty, as well as changes in adolescent thinking are all intertwined with the adolescent's experiences in the significant contexts of his or her life. The question we address in this chapter is, How does the adolescent organize these varied experiences, feelings, and thoughts into a meaningful pattern? In short, we are talking about the continuing development of *personality* or, more specifically, the evolution of *identity*.

Identity

What is identity? One way to describe **identity** is as a *self-structure* or an *internal organization* of values, abilities, feelings, and prior experiences. This self-constructed entity is dynamic and changing, as elements are continually being added and subtracted. The more developed and organized this self-structure is, the more likely individuals are to be aware of their strengths and weaknesses—their uniqueness as persons. Likewise, the less developed one's sense of identity, the more confused and lacking in self-knowledge he or she is likely to be.

The internal structure or organization we are calling an identity is fairly stable over time and gives rise to characteristic behaviors. It is these behaviors or specific

The Community/Neighborhood

Children and adolescents usually experience the community/neighborhood context in two ways:

Indirectly, they experience it as a source of support for the child-rearing functions of the family, which is important as an enduring context of child development. The community/neighborhood is, in turn, the enduring context for families. Community/neighborhood resources for family support include such formal arrangements as social services, playgrounds, and community centers and informal or interpersonal relationships of friends, neighbors, and relatives.

Directly, children and adolescents experience the neighborhood/community as a place to be or as things to do outside the school and the home. There are fences or trees to climb and streets to ride bicycles on—and, of course, peers to do these things with. The child's mastery of the space of the neighborhood is a basis for an emerging sense of competency.

problem-solving responses to the varied circumstances of life and adolescence that tell us about identity. For example, the adolescent who is unusually intolerant of ambiguous or unclear situations may be telling us something about his or her personal need for certainty and order.

In this section, we explore several issues relating to identity in adolescence:

Why is *identity* an issue in adolescence?
What are the ways or patterns (these patterns are called *statuses*) of dealing with identity questions in adolescence?
What are the central *elements* in an identity or what are the primary types of identity (e.g., occupational identity, sexual identity, and moral/ideological identity)?

Identity in Adolescence

The way one's identity is structured or organized changes gradually as a result of both age and experience. There are several times in the lives of most individuals when the extent or amount of change in identity is likely to be greater. One such time is adolescence. Identity change during the adolescent years is intensified by the many significant transitions that occur in adolescence, including the following:

· A *cognitive transition* from the concrete operations of childhood to the formal operations of adulthood (see Chapter 16).

Gene Tamashiro

The way one's identity is structured changes gradually as a result of both age and experience.

- A *moral/value transition* from conventional moral reasoning (moral value is based on behavior in accordance with "law and order" or "duty") to postconventional moral reasoning (moral value derived from universal principles) (see the discussion later in this section).
- A *physical/biological transition* from the appearance and physical capabilities of the child, through a relatively dramatic growth spurt and change in primary and secondary sex characteristics, to the appearance and physical capabilities of an adult (see Chapter 16).
- *An autonomy transition* from the relative dependence of the child on parental expectations to the relative independence of the later adolescent (greater reliance on one's own abilities, skills, goals, and so on) (see the discussion of autonomy in this chapter).

Furthermore, it is important to keep in mind that identity formation neither begins nor ends in adolescence. For example, one could argue that the process of identity really begins in infancy, when the infant first recognizes the distinction between the self and external objects (see Chapter 8). Likewise, the development of identity does not actually end until later adulthood, when the individual deals with the final challenges of life (see the discussion of Erikson's eight stages of psychosocial development in Chapter 2). Adolescence, however, represents a significant milestone in the lifespan process of identity formation because of the adolescent's *intellectual awareness* of the major life transitions described above. There are numerous examples in literature of adolescents who are aware (or even painfully aware) of the developmental transitions in their lives (e.g. Holden Caulfield in J. D. Salinger's, *Catcher in the Rye*). Nonetheless, adolescence is only one point—albeit a significant one—in the ongoing lifework of identity development. According to James Marcia, "resolution of the identity issue at adolescence guarantees only that one will be faced with subsequent identity 'crises' " (1980, p. 160).

Drawing by Carl Rose; © 1971 The New Yorker Magazine, Inc.

"You think you're the only one around here with an identity crisis?"

IDENTITY DIFFUSION ⟶ IDENTITY

FIGURE 17.1
In Erikson's theory, the identity "crises" stage of adolescence involves identity *and* identity diffusion *as opposite ends of a single dimension.*

In addition, the development of identity is a gradual and continuous process.

> It gets done by bits and pieces. Decisions are not made once and for all, but have to be made again and again. And the decisions may seem trivial at the time: whom to date, whether or not to break up, . . . studying or playing, . . . and so on. Each of these decisions has identity-forming implications. (Marcia, 1980, p. 161)

The decisions the adolescent makes over time begin to take the form of a consistent organization or structure.

The danger in the process of identity development in adolescence is what Erik Erikson (1968) has called **identity diffusion.** Erikson's description of the identity development process involves *identity* and *identity diffusion* as the opposite ends of a single dimension or continuum (see Fig. 17.1). Identity diffusion characterizes an individual who seems unable to make decisions effectively and has no sense of direction or goals (Erikson, 1968).

Identity Status

As might be expected, individuals differ in the ways or styles through which they resolve identity questions. According to Marcia (1980), there are four *identity statuses* or modes of dealing with the identity questions of late adolescence:

- Identity achievement.
- Foreclosure.
- Identity diffusion.
- Moratorium.

Marcia (1966, 1980) derived these four statuses from his research on college students (male and female) in their late teens and early twenties. He defined the concept of identity in terms of two major characteristics:

Scott Schiamberg

· **Crisis,** or a decision-making period.
· **Commitment,** or the extent of personal investment in an occupation, a set of religious values, or a political position (1980).

In order to assess the presence of crisis and commitment in his subjects, Marcia designed and administered a questionnaire and interview (see Fig. 17.2). Based on results from these questionnaires and interviews, Marcia and his associates described the four identity statuses as follows (Marcia, Waterman, and Matteson, in press) (see Table 17.1):

· **Identity Achievement.** The adolescents in this status both have engaged in a period of decision making or crisis and have made a commitment to an occupation and a set of values/beliefs or an ideology. They have chosen their occupation and

FIGURE 17.2
The Marcia identity status interview.

INTRODUCTION

What year are you in?

Where are you from?

How did you decide to come to _____ ?

Had you considered any other schools?

What does your father do?

Did he go to college? Where?

What does your mother do?

Did she go to college? Where?

OCCUPATION

What are you majoring in? What do you plan to do with it?

When did you decide on this?
Had you considered anything else?

What seems attractive about _____ ?

Most parents have some plans for their children, things they'd like to see them do or go into. Did yours have any plans like that?

How do your parents feel about what you're going into now?

How willing do you think you'd be to change this if something better came along? (If *S* responds: "What do you mean by 'better'?") Well, what might be better in your terms?

RELIGION

Do you have any particular religious preference?

What about your parents?

Were you ever very active in your religion? How about now? Belong to any groups? Get into discussions?

Are your beliefs now different from those of your parents? How do they feel about your beliefs now?

Is there any time when you've come to doubt any of your religious beliefs? When? How did it happen? How did you resolve things?

POLITICS

Do you have any particular preferences?

How about your parents?

Have you ever taken any kind of political action— joined any groups, written letters, protested?

Are there any issues about which you feel strongly now?

Is there any particular time that you decided upon your political beliefs?

Do you have any questions you'd like to ask me?

(Based on a full-length interview in Marcia, J. E., Waterman, A. S., and Matteson, D. R. Ego Identity: A Handbook for Psychosocial Research. Hillsdale, N.J.: Erlbaum, in press).

TABLE 17.1
Criteria for the Four Identity Statuses

POSITION ON OCCUPATION AND IDEOLOGY	IDENTITY STATUS			
	IDENTITY ACHIEVEMENT	FORECLOSURE	IDENTITY DIFFUSION	MORATORIUM
Crisis	present	absent	present or absent	in crisis
Commitment	present	present	absent	present but vague

From Marcia, 1980, p. 162.

values/beliefs by themselves (and for themselves). As might be expected, identity-achievement adolescents have the highest level of self-esteem compared with the three other identity statuses (Breuer, 1973; Marcia, 1980). Furthermore, identity-achievement adolescents, compared with the three other statuses, were functioning at a higher level of moral reasoning (the postconventional level), had a higher level of autonomy (more inner-directed than externally directed), and were more likely to be reflective (rather than impulsive) problem solvers (Davidson, 1978; Marcia, 1980).

· **Foreclosure.** These are adolescents who demonstrate little or no evidence of a "crisis" (a decision-making period) but who are committed to an occupational role and an ideological position. The occupational/ideological choices have been made by parents rather than self-chosen (Marcia, 1980). Both male and female foreclosures are more authoritarian, rigid, and conforming than the other identity statuses. Furthermore, foreclosures showed the greatest susceptibility to changes in self-esteem (both positively and negatively) in response to external feedback (Marcia, 1980). This is consistent with the finding that foreclosures reveal the lowest level of autonomy (self-directness) of all four statuses (Marcia, 1980). Generally speaking, they appear to be at a serious loss in situations where their parents' values or rules do not apply. On measures of concept attainment in stressful situations, they performed the worst of all four statuses (Marcia, 1980).

· **Identity diffusion.** The adolescents in this identity status are primarily characterized by a lack of direction. They may or may not have undergone a "crisis" and have definitely made no commitment to an ideological or occupational direction. The evidence suggests that they are relatively unconcerned about occupational and ideological matters. As might be expected, identity diffusions are low on measures of autonomy and self-directedness (Orlofsky, Marcia, and Lesser, 1973; Marcia, 1980). Consistent with Erikson's description of identity diffusion, these adolescents were confused and disorganized.

· **Moratorium.** These are individuals who are currently in "crisis" and are dealing with questions of occupation and ideology. If they have made a commitment, it likely is vague and relatively unclear. Because they are in "crisis," moratoriums have the highest level of anxiety of all the identity statuses. Like identity achievements, moratoriums tend to function at the highest level of moral reasoning (postconventional level). They can be sensitive and open-minded. On the negative side, they can appear to be self-righteous and indecisive (Marcia, 1980).

The research on these identity statuses suggests that Erikson's identity crisis occurs in late adolescence (Marcia, 1980; Marcia, Waterman, and Matteson, in press). It is important to be aware that most of this research is based on college students. A frequent pattern is that many of these students become identity diffusions or moratoriums during their freshman year (Waterman and Waterman, 1972). On the other hand, some students are shaken out of a foreclosure status during their first year. However, the main point is that most freshmen college students and younger adolescents are just beginning their major identity work. The evidence suggests that the identity achievement status is not likely to occur before about eighteen to twenty-one years of age (Archer, 1982; Adams and Jones, 1983). By the end of the senior year, many students have attained the identity achievement status. This progression is not universal; some students begin and end their college careers as foreclosures or identity diffusions, and others end college as moratoriums. It is important to note, however, that it is not clear whether the college experience by itself contributes to the formulation and resolution of identity questions (Marcia, 1980).

In conclusion, the research on identity statuses appears to confirm Erikson's idea that the development of identity in adolescence can be viewed as a continuum moving from identity diffusion at one end to identity achievement at the other. There is, however, a serious omission that may call into question the validity of these identity statuses and also the Erikson model on which they are based. Historically, many (though not all) of the studies on identity statuses have focused primarily on male subjects. Furthermore, it has been argued that Erikson's eight stages of the life cycle and, in particular, the stage of adolescence are heavily directed at traditional male experiences (Gilligan, 1979). We take up this important question of sex differences in adolescent identity later in this chapter.

Elements of Identity

So far we have discussed why identity is an important concept for understanding adolescence and the common patterns (or statuses) for resolving identity questions. In this section, we raise an equally important question. What are the central elements or components of adolescent identity? There is some agreement that the minimal or basic ingredients of identity development in adolescence involve the following three components (Marcia, 1980) (see Fig. 17.3):

• Commitment to an *occupational/vocational direction.*
• Commitment to a *sexual orientation.*

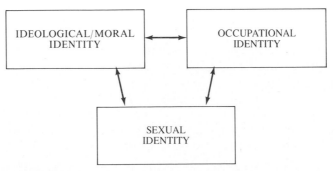

FIGURE 17.3

There is some agreement that identity development in adolescence involves three basic elements: occupational identity, sexual identity, and ideological/moral identity.

· Commitment to an *ideological stance* (i.e., a philosophy of life including a set of moral positions).

OCCUPATIONAL IDENTITY.   At a commonsense or experiential level, there is clear recognition that an important component of the adolescent's total identity and self-concept is his or her vocational or occupational identity. In our society, adolescents are expected to define themselves, in part, in terms of some vocation. Whereas society continues to change, moving from a larger number of jobs requiring only a high school education to fewer jobs requiring more advanced technical training, the question for the adolescent remains the same. "What are you going to do to make a living?" Although in prior generations this question may have been asked of—or asked by—the male adolescent, it is now a fully legitimate question for both sexes.

In addition to the commonsense or experiential recognition of the importance of an occupational/vocational identity, there is virtual agreement in the research literature that vocational career choice is a critical ingredient of both identity and optimal development beyond the adolescent years (Lerner and Shea, 1982; Vondracek and Lerner, 1982; Schiamberg and Chin, 1986; Lewko, 1987). Although we have discussed Piaget's theories and research primarily in terms of adolescent cognitive development (see Chapter 16), it is of more than a passing interest to recognize his comments on the importance of vocational identity.

> The focal point of the decentering process [the ability to focus on more than one concept such as height and length, simultaneously] is the entrance into the occupational world or the beginning of serious professional training. The adolescent becomes an adult when he undertakes a real job. (Inhelder and Piaget, 1958, p. 346)

> True adaptation to society comes automatically when the adolescent reformer attempts to put his ideas to work. Just as experience reconciles formal thought with the reality of things, so does effective and enduring work, undertaken in concrete and well-defined situations, cure dreams. (Piaget, 1967, pp. 68–69)

In order to fully understand the nature of occupational identity in adolescence, it is necessary for us to discuss two related perspectives:

· *The developmental perspective,* or the changes in the individual's vocational self-concept from childhood through adolescence.
· *The social context perspective,* or the historical and social changes in the world of work that shape the occupational/vocational choices made by adolescents.

The period of adolescence is a particularly critical time for the integration of *both* of these perspectives in the resolution of occupational/vocational identity. As the adolescent strives to reach the "identity achievement" status, he or she is, in part, integrating knowledge of self (what we are calling the developmental perspective) with the occupational/vocational demands of society (the social context perspective).

Developmental Perspective. From an individual perspective, how does the adolescent decide on an appropriate career direction or a specific job? Here we review several developmental theories in order to see the various features of development of vocation at each age level, from childhood through later adolescence and early adulthood. According to Eli Ginzberg (1972), the developing individual continually makes adjustments in aspirations and motivation that limit and refine vocational choices.

■ *GINZBERG'S STAGE THEORY (GINZBERG, 1972)*

Ginzberg suggested that individuals move through four major psychological periods as a part of the process of making vocational choices. Each stage represents a compromise between what is wished for and what is possible.

The fantasy period. The fantasy stage begins in early childhood and lasts until about age eleven to twelve. As early as age four or five, children are able to state vocational preferences. These are simply wishes that are usually based on a limited relationship with the working world. For example, when asked what they would like to be when they grow up, children may offer such responses as "I want to be a policeman" or "I want to be a fireman."

The tentative period (age eleven to about eighteen). This stage begins in later childhood and early adolescence, when the individual begins to take into account his or her own interests and capabilities when considering a vocation.

There are four substages during this period. In the *interest stage* (age eleven to twelve), the child begins to recognize the need to consider a vocation as well as identifying activities that are liked and disliked. These activities are generally similar to vocational activities.

The *capacity stage* (age twelve to fourteen) coincides with the onset of formal operations as the individual begins to assess and understand the prerequisite aptitudes, training, and education necessary for given professions.

The *value stage* (age fifteen to sixteen) involves the recognition of personal values, orientations, and goals as important dimensions of a vocational choice. The individual begins to recognize that given vocations have a particular relationship to his or her values, so that some vocations may be more suited to his or her value structure than others.

The *transition stage* (age seventeen to eighteen) is a period of consolidation during which aptitudes, interests, and values are focused on the necessity of making a realistic vocational decision.

The realistic period (eighteen to the early twenties). The realistic period is composed of two substages. In the *exploration stage*, the individual tests his or her tentative vocational choices against the demands of a vocation and personal values, aptitudes, and interests. During the *crystallization stage*, the individual develops a clear picture of a vocational goal, including specific occupations.

The specification period. The specification period is usually reached during the early twenties and occurs when the individual makes a commitment to a particular vocation. This happens when the individual begins to train for a particular vocation or actually enters that vocation.

In summary, Ginzberg's theory suggests that career decisions are made through a continual process of compromise between individual values, interests, and capabilities and vocational task demands.

Another theory of vocational development which is similar to Ginzberg's theory has focused, however, on a lifespan perspective. Specifically, the theory of Donald Super (1953) includes five major stages:

- *A growth stage* (from birth through approximately fourteen years of age), during which time the adolescent's self-concept grows primarily through identification with the significant others in the child's/adolescent's life.
- *An exploration stage* (from about age fifteen years through twenty-four), during which self-examination (i.e., assessment of individual skills and personality attributes) and investigation of various occupations occur (usually in relation to leisure and school activities). In this stage, the adolescent "tests out" the

In the exploration stage of vocational/occupational development, the adolescent tests out the "goodness of fit" between his or her characteristics and the requirements or demands of various occupations.

"goodness of fit" between his or her characteristics and the requirements of a given vocation.

- *An establishment stage* (from approximately age twenty-five through forty-four), during which time the individual consolidates his or her occupational choice and directs efforts toward enhancing his or her position in that occupation.
- *A maintenance stage* (from approximately age forty-five to sixty-four), during which time the individual sustains and elaborates his or her occupational position.
- *A decline stage* (age sixty-five and beyond), during which time occupational efforts ease or gradually diminish as a result of retirement.

In the developmental theories of both Ginzberg and Super, there appear to be two common factors that are of considerable importance in understanding adolescent vocational/occupational development—*vocational exploration* and *vocational maturity* (Vondracek and Lerner, 1982). Unfortunately, the concept of vocational exploration (as important as it is to adolescent occupational identity) has received almost no attention in the research literature (Vondracek and Lerner, 1982). Therefore, we focus our attention here on the role of vocational maturity.

DEFINITIONS

Vocational maturity. This refers to the adolescent's readiness to make the occupational choices that are required by both adolescent development and the demands of society.

Vocational exploration. This refers to the adolescent's investigation of the characteristics and requirements of various occupations, including limited role tryouts during leisure and school activities.

The most comprehensive examination of vocational maturity and occupational identity was a longitudinal study that was part of the Career Pattern Study (Jor-

Vocational maturity refers to the adolescent's readiness to make occupational choices.

daan and Heyde, 1979). Using interview data, the study examined the following elements of vocational maturity:

- *Crystallization of interests*—or the assumption that adolescent vocational interests should become more focused as adolescents gain knowledge and experience (e.g., one measure of crystallization of interests was the extent to which a primary interest pattern could be identified on standard interest tests such as the Strong Vocational Interest Blank).
- *Appropriateness of preferences*—refers to whether a given choice made by an adolescent is consistent with such factors as the adolescent's measured abilities and his or her measured interests (i.e., the "goodness of fit") between the individual and the job characteristics.
- *The nature of work experience*—refers to such factors as the adolescent's summer or vacation work activities, including the initiative the adolescent exercised in securing the job.
- *Occupational information*—refers to the accuracy and specificity of the adolescent's knowledge about jobs.
- *Acceptance of responsibility*— or the adolescent's willingness to make vocational choices and to be responsible, as appropriate, for meeting job-training requirements.
- *Planning*—refers to the adolescent's specificity of goals, the awareness of factors that might change one's goals (e.g., a dramatic drop in numbers of school-age children would reduce demands for teaching professionals) and the adolescent's willingness to consider alternative plans.
- *Implementation*—refers to the steps the adolescent has taken to carry out vocational plans.

The results of the study generally confirmed a developmental perspective to the growth of vocational maturity as follows (Jordaan and Heyde, 1979):

- The vocational preferences of children under eleven indicate that their choices are largely subjective. At this age, children have not assessed their own aptitudes or interests in relation to a proposed occupation. By the time they are sixteen years old, adolescents are much more realistic about what they are likely to achieve and more specific about what they want to do. For example, the high school senior is more likely to say that he or she would like to be a biologist rather than simply a scientist.
- Adolescents who were *consistently* assessed as *vocationally mature* (from ninth through twelfth grades) were generally brighter, were more likely to come from a higher socioeconomic level, and had a well-balanced self-concept.

Furthermore, additional analysis of the data from the study (Miller, 1978) identified important antecedent conditions of vocational maturity in adolescents. Specifically, *positive or facilitative parental behavior* was associated with vocational maturity when the adolescents reached college age. Likewise, negative or nonsupportive parental behavior (i.e., parental interference with normal/healthy psychological development) was associated with vocational immaturity. There is other compelling evidence of the critical role of families in the occupational and educational attainment of adolescents (Otto, 1986; Schiamberg and Chin, 1986). Such research supports the position taken throughout this book that development is the result of the dynamic interplay among the contexts of development (i.e., family, peers, school, and so on) and the individual.

Families and Career Development

Although it is commonly acknowledged that families play a significant role in the occupational and educational attainment of adolescents, limited research has been directed at the extent of this contribution (Schulenberg, Vondracek, and Crouter, 1984). For example, there is little or no information about the relative contribution of families to adolescent occupational and educational attainment compared with that of adolescent characteristics (I.Q., self-esteem) or school-related factors [individual achievement motivation, educational attainment] (Schiamberg and Chin, 1986; Stevenson, Lee, and Stigler, 1986).

One recent fourteen-year longitudinal study followed a group of rural low-income subjects in six Southern states (Schiamberg and Chin, 1986). In 1969, 1,202 fifth and sixth graders (black/white, male/female) and their mothers were assessed on the following factors: family background (e.g., parent occupation and educational levels), early socialization influences, and early socialization outcomes (e.g., child characteristics such as I.Q. and self-concept). In 1975, 945 of the children were reinterviewed when they were high school juniors and seniors. In 1979, 544 of the original sample were interviewed as young adults. The contribution of the following factors were examined in relation to young adult occupational attainment; family background (e.g., parent educational and occupational levels), child characteristics (e.g., I.Q. and self-concept), significant others—parent(s) (e.g., parent-adolescent communication and parenting practices), significant others—teachers (e.g., teacher-adolescent communications), achievement motivation (e.g., defined as adolescent occupational and educational aspirations/expectations), and educational attainment. These same variables (with the exception of educational attainment) were used in the analysis of educational attainment (total years of schooling). The total effect of family influence (family background and the influence of significant others, in the family) on occupational attainment exceeded the effect of both child characteristics and educational attainment. The total effect of family influence was second only to that of achievement motivation in predicting occupational attainment.

The family's influence on educational attainment was also found to be substantial. That is, the total effect of the family (i.e., *family background factors* such as parents' own occupational and educational levels *and* the *influence of parents as significant others*) on educational attainment was much stronger than the influence of achievement motivation or child characteristics (e.g., I.Q. and self-concept).

In summary, the role of the family in both educational and occupational attainment is substantial in comparison to the school or even individual characteristics. This finding is, however, in contrast to the historical situation in which family contributions to adolescent occupational and educational development are underestimated in relation to school and individual factors such as curriculum programs and child I.Q. scores. This is not to say that child characteristics, curricula, and teacher-training programs are unimportant. Rather, school and individual factors are further enhanced when the significant educational and occupational contributions of the family are supported.

An excellent example of this approach is the DAPCEP program (Detroit-Area Pre-College Engineering Program). The program involves middle school and high school students who work with engineers, visit their workplaces, and spend months or even years developing science fair projects. DAPCEP is notable in involving parents, the community, and schools in a joint educational development program. In particular, parents participate in school-organized workshops in which they learn how to monitor their child's homework, talk with teachers, and organize science-related field trips in the community. The success of the DAPCEP program is based on the partnership of schools and families.

(From Schiamberg, L. and Chin, C. H., The Influence of Family on Educational and Occupational Achievement. An invited address given at the Annual Meeting of the American Association for the Advancement of Science (AAAS). Philadelphia, May 1986.

Support for this research was provided by the Agricultural Experiment Station, Michigan State University (Projects S-63, S-126, and S-171). Appreciation is extended to the following project colleagues: Sarah Shoffner, University of North Carolina–Greensboro; Charles Proctor, North Carolina State University; Gary Peterson and Lois Southworth, University of Tennessee–Knoxville; William Kenkel, University of Kentucky; Shirley Farrier, Virginia Polytechnical Institute and State University; Charles Tillman, Alcorn State University; Virginia Caples, Alabama A&M University.)

Social Change and Social Context. In addition to developmental factors and cognitive maturity, adaptive vocational choices are those that are consistent with the demands of the social context. For example, there are significant changes in the lives of contemporary adolescents. These changes have created new demands that require variations from traditional ways of making career choices.

One example of a change in social and family arrangements, which has resulted in new variations of career choices, is maternal employment (see Chapter 12). More women than ever before now are combining both home roles (wife and mother) with working outside the home. What is the impact of maternal employment on the adolescent's vocational orientation? Specifically, maternal employment has contributed to a changed social context to which adolescents need to adaptively adjust. There is considerable evidence that the female children growing up in homes with working mothers were more likely to have vocational role orientations and behaviors that are nontraditional (Huston-Stein and Higgins-Trenk, 1978; Vondracek and Lerner, 1982). This influence is more clearly seen in girls of working mothers who (more than daughters of nonworking mothers) are likely to have:

· Less stereotyped perspectives toward female roles.
· A broader definition of the female role (including characteristics of traditional masculinity such as aggressiveness).
· A tendency to emulate their mothers (Huston-Stein and Higgins-Trenk, 1978).

Given the increasing number of children and adolescents growing up in families with such egalitarian views, the economic pressures on families to have dual wage earners, and the social pressures for greater sexual equality, adolescents must adjust their vocational choices.

Jerrold Jacobson

Adolescence is a time for the refinement of sexual identity.

If adolescents are to attain *adaptive development in relation to this changing context,* they should adopt vocational roles that transcend the traditionally sex-role stereotyped vocational distinctions extant in earlier historical eras. Adaptive development should be associated with more egalitarian development. . . . vocational orientations that are not [limited] by sex-traditional perspectives and an orientation to one's career activities which incorporates flexibility may be requisites for adaptive functioning in the current social context. (Vondracek and Lerner, 1982, p. 612)

SEXUAL IDENTITY.   In addition to an occupational identity, the adolescent also is involved in the refinement of a *sexual identity. Sexuality* is, of course, an area of great significance for both adolescents and their parents.

DEFINITIONS

Sexuality. Sexuality in adolescence refers to two primary dimensions:

1. *A cultural construct* involving the interplay of three components:
   - *Biological factors* refer to one's biological identity as a male or female (a process that occurs primarily in the early childhood years) and the incorporation of adolescent pubertal changes into that biological self-concept (see Chapters 11 and 14).
   - *Psychological factors* refer to one's cognitive/emotional or psychological identity as a male or female (this process has, likewise, been an on-going one since the childhood years) and the refinement of this psychological identity in adolescence.
   - *Social factors* refer to the socially defined sex-role behaviors and attitudes that pervade society.
2. *The specific behaviors* involved in learning about and integrating these biological, psychological, and social dimensions into a refined *sexual identity* (e.g., dating, sexual relationships, and so on).

Sexual identity. This refers to the definition of oneself as male or female, incorporating the biological, psychological, and social dimensions of sexuality.

By the onset of puberty they have already developed some clear-cut ideas about their sexual identities (see Chapters 11 and 14). For example, they have known since almost three years of age that they are biologically a male or a female. Furthermore, they are likely to understand that their sexual identity is permanent, that it does not change from one moment in time to another. Prior to adolescence, children are also likely to be familiar with the details of current sex-role stereotypes and expectations. In particular, they know rather well the social meanings of maleness and femaleness (Fox, 1986). The major challenge of adolescence is the *refinement* of these notions of sex roles and sex-role behaviors.

It has been suggested that adolescents are cognitively capable of examining current and emerging sex-role patterns and of making selections from these various alternatives (Scanzoni, 1975; Fox, 1986). The ability to make such choices is, however, not without some constraints (the adolescent's prior sex-role socialization, the current values of the adolescent's peer group, and so on). For example, whether an adolescent female decides to adopt an **androgynous** response (i.e., the traits, attitudes, and behaviors that include *both* traditional masculinity and feminity) to an emergency involving a friend by being *both decisive* (a *traditionally* masculine trait) *and compassionate/nurturant* (a traditionally feminine trait) may depend on her prior exposure to decisive and nurturant female models. In addition to her childhood socialization history, such an androgynous response might also be influenced by the specific context of peer and social attitudes in which the female adolescent finds herself (Fox, 1986).

Attitudes Toward Marriage. As a social institution marriage has been a traditional rite of passage from childhood or adolescence to adult independence and responsibility. Traditionally, males have developed active vocational commitments that allowed them to "provide for" a family. In the past, women presumably were socialized for marriage as the primary dimension of their identity. Appropriate sex-role behaviors learned in childhood and adolescence were *designed* to facilitate this ultimate goal: marriage and child rearing.

Marriage for many young people today is no longer a social institution necessary for the attainment of adult status and personal security. Rather, it is viewed more and more as an optional relationship, perhaps as a commitment to shared growth with a significant other person during the adult years. Sexual behavior is often viewed as a natural and acceptable part of life and many earlier restrictions are no longer appropriate (Dreyer, 1975, 1982). As changes have occurred in youth attitudes toward sexual relationships, in youth sexual behavior, and in traditional concepts of family functioning, the views of youths toward marriage have also changed. Youths are placing far less emphasis on the traditional notion of marriage as a social institution that provides stability and continuity. Instead, many see marriage as *one* source of personal growth and development (Dreyer, 1975, 1982). In such a marital relationship, each partner is free to play whatever roles are determined by mutual agreement rather than by the stereotypes of traditional masculine-feminine roles.

In one study, almost 90 percent of eighteen-year-olds expected eventually to get married; however, the pressure to marry was not felt to be very strong (Thornton and Freedman, 1982). In addition, the perceived benefits of marriage compared with singlehood were not seen as dramatically different. Furthermore, the teenagers in the study indicated ages of expected marriage that were considerably older than the actual marital ages of their mothers (Thornton and Freedman, 1982).

During the 1970s, the institution of marriage appeared to undergo some rather profound changes. Despite the continued and historical popularity of marriage, marriage rates have declined or at least leveled off during the last twenty years. For example, in 1965, 73.2 percent of the total population (persons eighteen and over) was married, whereas 63.2 percent were married in 1984. Meanwhile, divorce rates have dramatically increased from 2.9 percent in 1965 to 7.3 percent in 1984 (U.S. Department of Commerce, Table No. 43, 1985d).

Attitudes Toward Balancing Career and Family. The desire for females to be involved in both career and family is further supported by several studies (Herzog, Bachman, and Johnston, 1980; General Mills, 1981; Thornton and Freedman, 1982). In a survey of high school seniors, approximately 75 percent of the students of both sexes indicated that they planned to marry, although only 10 percent of the females indicated that they wished to be a homemaker exclusively (Herzog, Bachman, and Johnston, 1980). Furthermore, it is important to note that the overall evidence from these studies showed a *mixture* of egalitarianism (i.e., emphasis on equality of the sexes) and sex-role traditionalism. For example, the high school seniors in the Herzog study strongly preferred dual-wage-earning families when no children were present. However, when children were present (particularly young, preschool-age children), they reverted to a preference for the "traditional" family (i.e., working husband and nonworking wife).

When A. Regula Herzog and her colleagues asked the high school seniors about the division of family responsibilities (child care, home maintenance, family decision making), there was also a mixture of egalitarianism and traditionalism. For example, a majority of the seniors felt that family responsibilities should be shared between working husbands and wives (even when only one spouse worked). However, when there was a preference for unequal division of household labor, it was the *wife* who was expected to assume the major responsibility for performing the household labor (Herzog, Bachman, and Johnston, 1980). Furthermore, in another study, there was evidence that although a majority of three age groups (teenagers, 13–18 years; adults, 18–39 years; and adults, 40 and over) prefer egalitarian sharing of family responsibilities, it is the teenagers who tend to be the most conservative (see Table 17.2).

   Implications of Changes in Female Sex Roles. As a result of the changes in sex roles and the preferences of female youths, many interesting and important consequences have occurred.

TABLE 17.2

The Attitudes of Adolescents and Adults Toward the Division of Family Responsibilities

Question: As you know, there are a number of traditional assumptions about the ways of dividing up family responsibilities. Do you generally agree or disagree with the following statements?

| | TEENAGERS 13–18 YEARS | | BASE: ALL MARRIED AND LIVING WITH PARTNER | | | |
| | | | ADULTS 18–39 YEARS | | ADULTS 40 AND OVER | |
	MALE	FEMALE	MALE	FEMALE	MALE	FEMALE
	%	%	%	%	%	%
Raising children should be the responsibility of the mother, not the father, whether or not she works.						
Agree	28	20	7	7	12	12
Disagree	72	80	93	93	86	87
Not sure	—	—	*	—	1	1
The person whose salary or wages are most important to the family should make most of the big financial decisions.						
Agree	49	35	19	16	25	22
Disagree	51	64	80	84	74	78
Not sure	—	1	1	*	1	1
The person whose salary or wages are least important to the family should make most of the decisions about housework and family activities.						
Agree	41	23	15	17	20	18
Disagree	59	76	83	83	78	80
Not sure	—	1	2	*	2	2
Sample size:	116	119	299	291	321	280

*Less than 0.5%
From General Mills, 1981, p. 75.

Androgyny and Changes in Male Sex-Role Choices. One result of changing female sex roles has been an increasing flexibility in general sex-role behavior, so that traditional "male" and "female" roles are being incorporated into "human" sex roles (*androgyny*). This trend, in turn, has resulted in a long overdue recognition that the personality characteristics associated with the traditional roles of male and female represent an unrealistic division of human traits.

The Unsettling of Traditional Norms and Role Expectations. The changes described have created opportunities and choices that were not widely available in earlier times. In addition, these changes have placed men and women in positions of ambiguity, anxiety, and uncertainty. The role expectations that have historically organized the relationships between males and females in an industrial society have changed. When behavior becomes subject to choice, it also becomes subject to potential conflict, anxiety, uncertainty, and problems.

Ideological Stance. In addition to an occupational and sexual identity, one of the consequences of the adolescent search for identity is the clarification of values. Adolescents begin the process of organizing the set of values that will help them deal with life experiences. They are formulating a "philosophy of life." The changes in adolescent thinking that we have described lay the foundation for the development of this philosophy of life.

IDEOLOGICAL STANCE.   The school-age child is characterized by a level of moral reasoning in which concern for maintaining the rules or expectations of the family, school, or group is the primary focus. You may remember that Lawrence Kohlberg (1964; Kohlberg and Turiel, 1974) referred to this as the "conventional" level of moral reasoning. "Right" behavior for the school-age child is based on at least two central factors:

· The authority of parents, teachers, or other adults who hold these values.
· The child's identification with these adults (i.e., the child considers these adults important enough to try to please them).

According to Kohlberg (1981), adolescents may enter a stage of moral reasoning known as the *postconventional* level, at which "right" or "moral" behavior is determined by the *individuals themselves*. In contrast to the school-age child, the adolescent determines what is right independently of the expectations of other people (parents, teachers, other adults). The adolescent may still arrive at a moral principle that is similar or even identical to that of significant other adults or society at large; however, the critical factor is that these moral principles are self-developed. Right action is defined in terms of ethical principles that are based on what the individual thinks is right. These are usually universal principles of justice, equality, and respect for the dignity of human beings.

Adolescents' new cognitive tools (i.e., abstract reasoning) encourage them in their quest for a consistent set of principles or philosophy of life (Kaczkowski, 1962; Kohlberg, 1964; Kohlberg and Gilligan, 1972). Adolescents come to appreciate the fact that there may not be a single "correct" position or moral behavior. For example, are premarital sexual relations simply immoral and wrong in all cases? Or are they defensible for some adolescents who are presumably mature enough to avoid problems? The messages that the adolescent receives from family, peers, religious groups, and the school may indeed be conflicting. The adolescent's attempt to resolve or at least understand these inconsistencies is an important motivation for developing a philosophy of life. This process of developing such a moral stance toward the world has its *beginnings* during adolescence. However,

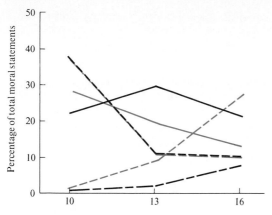

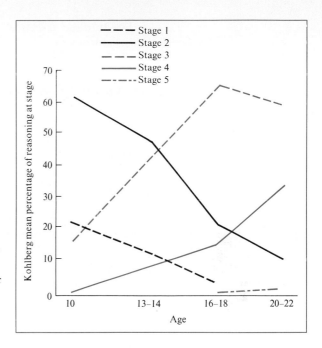

FIGURE 17.4

Moral judgments according to age trends. The diagram to the left was scored using Kohlberg's original scoring system. The diagram to the right represents a rescoring of the data using a more sophisticated technique. Left diagram from Kohlberg, 1969, pp. 384–385; right diagram from Kohlberg, 1979.

the process is not completed until at least the early twenties, if it is completed at all (Kohlberg, 1981). In some cases, the "conventional" morality of the school-age child may be the highest level of moral reasoning reached by some people (Kohlberg, 1981).

Moral Judgment Stages in Adolescence. It is important to keep in mind that although the adolescent is "entering" the postconventional level of thinking (Stages 5 and 6; see Table 14.2 for a detailed discussion of the levels and stages of Kohlberg's theory of moral development), the increase in postconventional thinking and the decrease in conventional thinking (Stages 3 and 4) are gradual (see Fig. 17.4). Generally speaking, the evidence supports the notion of an ordered progression through Kohlberg's six stages of moral development. However, Figure 17.4 suggests that with the rescoring of Kohlberg's original data, the postconventional level of moral reasoning (Stages 5 and 6) does not occur prior to eighteen years of age (see also Tables 17.3 and 17.4). In summary, as indicated following, several changes in moral development occur during early adolescence (from the onset of puberty through seventeen or eighteen years of age).

TABLE 17.3

Percentage of Moral Judgment Use for Ages 13–14 (longitudinal subjects rescored in 1979)

STAGE	PERCENTAGE
1	7
2	45
3	42
4	3
5	—

Note: The total does not equal 100 percent since some scores are too mixed to assign to a single stage.

From Kohlberg, 1979.

TABLE 17.4

Percentage of Moral Judgment Use for Ages 16–18 (longitudinal subjects rescored in 1979)

STAGE	PERCENTAGE
1	1
2	20
3	60
4	14
5	0

Note: The total does not equal 100 percent since some scores are too mixed for a single assignment to one stage.

From Kohlberg, 1979.

For thirteen-to-fourteen-year-olds the following changes occur (see Figure 17.4 and Table 17.3):

- A *decline* in *Stage 1* moral reasoning from 22 percent to 7 percent.
- A *decline* in *Stage 2* moral reasoning from 65 percent to 45 percent.
- An *increase* in *Stage 3* moral reasoning from 15 percent to 42 percent.
- *Stages 2 and 3* account for most of the moral reasoning at this age.
- For *Stage 3* moral reasoning in thirteen-to-fourteen-year-olds (compared with school-age children), the peer group replaces parents as the source of moral judgment (see Table 14.2 for a description of Stage 3).
- A small *increase* in *Stage 4* to 3 percent.

For sixteen-to-eighteen-year-olds the following changes in moral development occur (see Fig. 17.4 and Table 17.4):

- A *decline* in *Stage 3* moral reasoning from 45 percent to 22 percent.
- *Stage 3* moral reasoning accounts for approximately two-thirds of the moral judgment reasoning at these ages.
- An *increase* in *Stage 4* moral reasoning from 3 percent to 14 percent.

Educational Programs for Moral Development. Kohlberg (1981) suggested that during the teens and early twenties, educational programs can be developed that will stimulate higher stages of moral development. The relationship between experiential learning and moral development has been demonstrated for high school students (Sprinthall and Mosher, 1970), for college students (Gilligan, 1977), and for young adults in prison (Hickey, 1974). Richard Graham (1975) has suggested that there is a relationship between "action-learning" experiences and moral development (see Table 17.5). Various tasks and experiences (e.g., doing household chores, being a street crossing guard, performing secretarial activities, and so on) encourage the development of moral processes as well as an understanding of social roles.

Female Identity

Do males and females approach the identity question from different perspectives? Are there sex differences in the routes taken to attain identity? In our earlier discussion of identity statuses (identity achievements, foreclosures, identity diffusions, moratoriums) and Erikson's description of adolescent identity, we pointed out that there was some serious question about the validity of such perspectives for female identity development. Furthermore, in our discussion of sexual identity we indicated that social changes (e.g., working women) have created contexts in which sex-role alternatives (e.g., androgynous behavior) are now available to adolescents (who, as a result of their cognitive development, are now in a position to make choices). In this section, we examine two related questions:

- How applicable are the identity statuses (discussed earlier) to female identity development? (Our discussion focuses on the identity achievement status since most research has examined that status.)
- Do male and female adolescents resolve identity questions in different ways?

FEMALE IDENTITY AND IDENTITY STATUS.   The most thorough evidence relating to sex differences is focused on the identity-achievement status. Females who have

TABLE 17.5

Action-Learning Assignments Related to Moral Development and Role Taking

ACTION-LEARNING ASSIGNMENT

Stage 1

Carrying out orders in prescribed ways as in well defined, military assignments; some fixed rate production or assembly work. One's concern is for oneself, to receive reward or avoid punishment. Rules are to be obeyed.

Stage 2

Piece rate jobs, e.g., fruit picking at so much a basket, some sales clerk assignments, some assignments helping others. Pay or approbation is based on the quantity and quality of work performed. One's responsibilty is for self and, in part, for others. One's concern is to be fairly treated.

Stage 3

Group work as at some hamburger stands, secretaries in a pool, some kinds of sales work, some shared production work or group bench work, some responsibilities for helping others, e.g., child care. One's desire is to do one's share and be liked by peers, employers, or the persons served. Loyalty is to the "group" whether it is viewed as peers or employers. One's concern is for self and others.

Stage 4

Carrying out responsibilities in the absence of group support. Some supervisory or instructional assignments. Some kinds of legal or correctional work. Some sales work involving the influencing of others. Some assignments helping others. Work is according to rules or precedents which are to be maintained. Loyalty is to the company or the labor organization. Judgment is exercised but within prescribed limits. One's concern is for self and others, to do one's duty according to rules and convention.

Stage 5

Positions of decision-making in the presence of conflict. Some personnel work or counseling; some work involving responsibilities for others; negotiated policy formation and decision-making, some legislative work, negotiating goals and standards, cooperatively establishing or revising rules and procedures in light of underlying principles. One's concern is for Self and for Others according to fundamental principles of fairness and utility.

From Graham, 1975.

attained the identity achievement status (i.e., they have examined alternatives or engaged in a "crisis" and have made an occupational/ideological commitment) and males who have attained the same status are similar in some ways and different in others (Marcia, 1980). For example, both male and female identity achievements (compared with male and female peers with other identity statuses) are (Marcia, 1980):

- More likely to be at higher levels of moral reasoning.
- More likely to choose different college majors (i.e. to change majors).
- More likely to have intimate relationships with others (Kacerguis and Adams, 1980).
- More likely to resist pressures from peers.

However, the same identity-achieved individuals demonstrate the following differences (Marcia, 1980):

- *Sexual relationships* are more important for female identity than for male identity (e.g., having sexual relationships is much more likely to be an identity-related issue for females than for males).

Classroom Discussions of Moral Dilemmas

One of the most common methods for promoting growth in moral reasoning in the junior and senior high school is the presentation of open-ended moral dilemmas for classroom discussion. In one such program, English classes discussed ethical dilemmas from great works of literature (Carnegie-Mellon Civic Education English Curriculum, 1976). For example, in a high school English class the following format was used to discuss a moral dilemma in Mark Twain's *Huckleberry Finn:*

GUIDE FOR A MORAL DISCUSSION BASED ON MARK TWAIN'S NOVEL HUCKLEBERRY FINN

The climax of the novel comes in Chapter Thirty One. To identify the dilemma which Huck must deal with, it is suggested that the teacher read, or have the students read, or have the chapter reproduced as a handout, to just slightly past mid-chapter when Huck says, "I studied a minute, sort of holding my breath, and then says to myself. . . ."

Now have the books closed, or the reading stopped, or the handout put aside, and rehearse the dilemma. You might make students aware at this point, too, that in spite of Huck's lack of education, he is still able to think his way through to a solution.

The "duke" and the "king" are arguing, as the chapter gets moving, and Huck runs off to the raft to find Jim to escape them. No Jim. Instead, Huck encounters a boy who describes the capture of a runaway slave for whom there is a reward. Now Huck thinks about writing to Miss Watson to tell her where Jim is. Notice how he sets up the reasons why Jim should be returned:

1. Miss Watson's dependence on Jim (but also, on the negative side, that she might punish Jim and/or resell him);
2. Jim's own family back in St. Petersburg, Missouri;
3. Huck's own reputation: "It would get all around, that Huck Finn helped a nigger to get his freedom . . .";
4. The religious aspects of violating the law of slavery as "sinning." "I was stealing a poor old woman's nigger that hadn't (the woman) ever done me no harm, and now was showing me there's One that's always on the lookout . . . and something inside of me kept saying, 'There was the Sunday school . . . and if you'd a done

it they'd a learnt you, there, that people acts as I'd been acting about that nigger goes to ever-lasting fire.'"

So Huck writes the note revealing Jim's whereabouts to Miss Watson. Then the other side of the question pops up:

5. The friendship me and Jim have shared, and several examples of the friendship:
   a. "I'd see him standing my watch on top of his'n, stead of calling me, so I could go on sleeping;
   b. and see him how glad he was when I come back out of the fog;
   c. when I come to him again in the swamp . . . and such-like times;
   d. and would always call me honey and pet me, and do everything he could think of for me;
   e. and how good he always was;
   f. and at last I struck the time I saved him by telling the men we had small-pox aboard, and he was so grateful, and said I was the best friend old Jim ever had in the world, and the *only* one he's got now. . . ."

This is Huck's dilemma. Ask the class what Huck should do. Divide the class accordingly, and proceed with the discussion and the probe questions, if necessary.

PROBE QUESTIONS FOR HUCK FINN'S DILEMMA

1. Is it ever right to break a law? When? How do you decide?
2. Should Huck consider the fact that protecting his friend may make him an outcast in society?
3. Which is more important, an obligation to a friend or to the law? Why?
4. Does Huck have any obligation to Miss Watson who depends on Jim? Why or why not?
5. Would it make a difference if Huck were sure Miss Watson would punish or resell Jim? Why or why not?
6. From the point of view of Jim's own family back home, what should Huck do?
7. Should Huck violate religious teachings to make his choice about Jim? Why or why not?

From The Carnegie-Mellon Civic Education English Curriculum, 1976, p. 42.

• *Intimacy* influences the development of identity in different ways for males and for females. Specifically, males are expected to form an identity before they engage in intimate relationships. On the other hand, females are expected to develop intimate relationships prior to dealing with identity issues.

DIFFERENT ROUTES TO IDENTITY.   As we have indicated, one's gender appears to be an important criterion in the development of adolescent identity. Although sexual relationships and intimacy may have different emphasis in the identity-forming factors for females than for males, it is important for us to understand the pressures that may intensify or force such directions. For example, it has been suggested that during adolescence the pressure to behave in a "sex-appropriate" manner significantly increases, compared with pressures to do so in the childhood years (Hill and Lynch, 1983). This pressure becomes more intense for females than for males. According to this **gender-intensification hypothesis** (Hill and Lynch, 1983), sex identity (already a significant part of the school-age child's self-concept) becomes a more dominant factor in adolescence.

There is some evidence that this increased pressure to conform to "sex-appropriate" patterns may be associated with the emergence of certain sex-stereotyped behaviors during adolescence. For example, it may be reasonable to assume that the following sex differences (which emerge during adolescence) may be accounted for, in part, by intensified pressure (Hill and Lynch, 1983):

• Girls experience more disruption in their self-image and become more self-conscious than boys.
• Girls become more involved and competent in developing intimate relationships.
• Girls begin to excel in verbal skills, compared with boys, while boys begin to do better than girls in mathematical/spatial skills.

Furthermore, the dating arena, which expands during adolescence, may also increase the pressure on boys to act in a more stereotypically masculine fashion and, likewise, for girls "to be girls."

Although it is *generally* true that there is pressure to conform to "sex-appropriate" (sex-stereotyped) behaviors in adolescence (and that pressure is more intense for females), girls are more free to add masculine behaviors to a "feminine base" of behavior than boys are free to add occasional feminine behaviors to a repertoire of "male" behavior. In other words, it is easier for girls to be androgynous (combine male and female behavior) than for boys to be androgynous (Massad, 1981). This finding is consistent with the typical developmental experience of males, who are strongly socialized from their early years on not to demonstrate "feminine" characteristics. In contrast, girls, who are basically "feminine," can exercise the luxury of being a "tomboy" or an athlete, on occasion.

Do these differential pressures on male and female adolescents lead inevitably to differences in routes to identity? We have already suggested that sexual relationships and intimacy play a different role in female identity-forming experiences (Marcia, 1980). That position is best reflected by research carried out on adolescents in the 1960s and early 1970s. For example, Elizabeth Douvan and Joseph Adelson were among the first social scientists to note that "there is not one adolescent crisis, but two . . . clearly distinctive ones—the masculine and the feminine" (1966, p. 350) (i.e., the male identity crisis was linked to autonomy and independence, whereas the female crisis was linked to intimacy). Do such differences accurately reflect contemporary male and female identity processes? To some extent, the answer is "yes." However, there is more recent evidence of *similarities* between

Betsy Williamson/Photo Researchers, Inc.

It is easier for a female adolescent than a male adolescent to be androgynous.

male and female identity processes (Adams and Fitch, 1982; Grotevant and Thorbecke, 1982). That is, two separate identity crises may have been an accurate reflection of an earlier social context (which limited opportunities for females to do other than refine identity through intimacy first). Perhaps things have changed in the 1980s.

Psychosocial Factors in Personality Development

Personality development in adolescence is related to a number of psychosocial factors. Specifically, the development of identity is the result of several fundamental psychosocial processes that provide the arena in which the refinement of identity occurs. In this section we examine two such processes: autonomy and sexuality.

Autonomy

For most adolescents the establishment of a sense of independence or **autonomy** is an important prerequisite for building and refining identity. Because adolescents spend so much of their time away from the supervision of parents, it is important for them to learn to make decisions independently about a whole range of social and educational tasks. Furthermore, the physical and cognitive changes that occur during the adolescent years prompt the need to develop independence and autonomy.

· *The impact of puberty* creates physical changes that, in turn, spark a movement toward peers and away from parents. This movement toward peers is part of the process of developing independence from parents. The growth spurt and the changes in primary and secondary sexual characteristics may create a need for reassurance from peers. In addition, the physical changes of puberty cause the adolescent to look more like an adult, which may trigger a parental response of granting the adolescent more independence.

· *The impact of cognitive change* enables the adolescent to make better decisions, which is an important element of autonomous and independent functioning. For example, cognitive changes enable the adolescent to use abstract logic, to understand the perspective of others, and to think more effectively about the future. These changes are important bases for independent thinking and problem solving.

· *The impact of changing social roles* places the adolescent in new positions that require responsibility and independence. For example, the adolescent who can work, drive, or vote is involved in new experiences that may stimulate autonomy and independence.

In light of the changes that stimulate the development of autonomy, it is appropriate to ask what is meant by autonomy. For our purposes, we adopt a three-fold definition of autonomy (Steinberg and Silverberg, 1986):

· **Emotional autonomy** refers to the process of individuation, or the adolescent's relinquishing of childhood dependencies on parents as well as childhood conceptions of parental omnipotence.

· **Behavioral autonomy** refers to the adolescent's ability to make independent decisions and carry them out and to the susceptibility of the adolescent peer pressure.

· **Value autonomy** means having a set of principles that enable the adolescent to determine what is "right" or "correct" (moral behavior).

EMOTIONAL AUTONOMY.   The development of emotional autonomy has been viewed as a process of *individuation,* which refers to the continuous lifespan activity of the separation of children from parents. It is important to note here that separation refers primarily to the ongoing process of the development and the recognition (by significant others) of the child's *individuality* and uniqueness. We have already discussed in considerable detail the dynamics of this process of individuation (see Chapter 15). Here, we emphasize that adolescents who are the most likely to feel their parents have given them sufficient autonomy are those who maintain healthy nurturant relationships with their parents (not those who have separated themselves from parents by discontinuing the relationship) (Kandel and Lesser, 1972). That is, autonomous adolescents are more likely to be those who remain close to their parents in the sense of continuing to do things with them, asking them for advice, having fewer serious conflicts with them, and so on. Furthermore, there is evidence that more disturbed adolescent-parent relationships (e.g., extreme negativism on the part of the adolescent, excessive dependence on peers, and adolescent rebellion) are associated with adolescent psychological immaturity. In conclusion, the presence of autonomy is not associated with

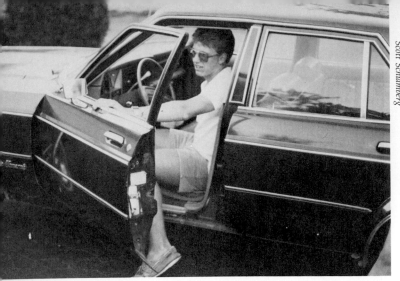

The adolescent who can work, drive, or vote is involved in activities that stimulate autonomy.

broken or strained parent-adolescent relationships (i.e., with adolescent rebellion or negativism) but, rather, with positive and nurturant family interactions.

BEHAVIORAL AUTONOMY.   Behavioral autonomy refers to two related factors:

- The *ability* of the adolescent *to make independent decisions* and to act on them.
- The *susceptibility* of the adolescent *to peer pressure*.

Each of these factors is an important ingredient in the development of adolescent identity.

   The changes in cognitive development described in Chapter 15 set the stage for the development of behavioral autonomy. That is, the adolescent's ability to use abstract logic, to consider future consequences of plans and goals, and to better understand the perspective of others (e.g., to understand the difference between good advice, freely given, and advice that protects or enhances the vested interests of the advice giver) facilitates improved decision making.

   In one study of adolescent decision-making skills, the subjects (100 adolescents, ages twelve to eighteen years) were asked to provide advice to another adolescent who had a "problem" (e.g., risk of cosmetic surgery, reconciling differing advice from experts, and so on) (Lewis, 1981b). The subjects listened to a tape recording of an adolescent describing his or her problem and were then asked to respond to the problem. The subjects' responses were assessed on five dimensions:

- Awareness of the potential risks involved (e.g., risks associated with surgery).
- Awareness of future consequences (e.g., offending one "expert" by following the advice of another "expert").
- Whether outside resources (technical specialists, medical doctors, and so on) were recommended.
- Whether the subjects were aware of the vested interests or biases of potential resources or advice givers (e.g., the surgeon might minimize the risk of an operation).
- Whether the subjects appropriately revised their recommendations based on the revelation of information and facts provided (e.g., the tape-recorded problem concludes with the following statement, "No matter what, I don't want to hurt my parents' feelings").

The results of the study indicated that on four of the five decision-making dimensions, older adolescents were superior to younger adolescents (Lewis, 1981b) (see

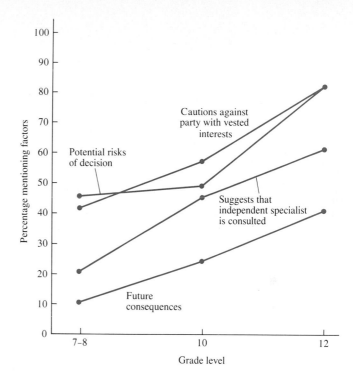

FIGURE 17.5

The improvement of decision-making skills over the adolescent years. From Lewis, 1981, pp. 538–544.

Fig. 17.5). Specifically, older adolescents were more likely than younger adolescents to be aware of potential risks, to be aware of future consequences, to suggest an outside consultant, and to caution against the vested interests of an advice giver. Furthermore, the results of the study indicate that adolescent decision-making skills improve through the adolescent years, providing a basis for behavioral autonomy.

In addition to improved decision-making skills in thinking about significant questions and issues, the adolescent is also faced with the task of carrying out those decisions. This raises an important question. Specifically, how does the adolescent take into account the views of parents and peers in both making and carrying out decisions? Put another way, how susceptible is the adolescent to peer pressure or to parent pressure? These questions are particularly pertinent for the adolescent who must consider and weigh advice given on positive goals, such as education, as well as advice given on antisocial behaviors, such as cheating, drug abuse, stealing, or vandalism. At stake is the behavioral autonomy of the adolescent, as well as the positive or negative outcomes of that process.

In addition to the improvement in decision-making skills through the adolescent years, are there any patterns of conformity to peers or parents in adolescence? The evidence suggests that conformity to the advice of peers (susceptibility to peer pressure) is higher during early and middle adolescence than during the preadolescent (middle childhood years) or during late adolescence (Berndt, 1979; Krosnick and Judd, 1982). This pattern appears to be particularly strong in the case of antisocial activities such as cheating or stealing. Furthermore, this finding is consistent with the evidence that many acts of juvenile delinquency are performed by groups of middle adolescents (Berndt, 1979). In addition, the evidence indicates that conformity to parents declines steadily from childhood through the adolescent years (Berndt, 1979).

With reference to both conformity to peers and conformity to parents, an overall

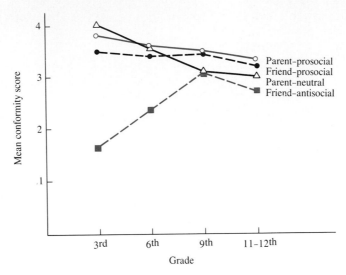

FIGURE 17.6
*Patterns of conformity to parents and peers from
childhood through adolescence. From Berndt, 1979,
pp. 608–616.*

pattern begins to develop (see Fig. 17.6). From middle childhood through early
adolescence (third through ninth grades) the influence of parents is stronger than
the influence of peers. However (as mentioned), conformity to parents decreases
(slightly on *prosocial matters* such as values and ethics and more dramatically on
neutral matters such as what to wear) and conformity to peers increases (dramatically on antisocial matters and slightly on prosocial matters). The *net effect* of this
pattern of declining parental influence and increasing peer influence is little, if
any, gain in behavioral autonomy (Fig. 17.6). In other words, as conformity to
parents declines, it is replaced almost completely by conformity to peers with *no
net decline in conformity.* It is not until middle or late adolescence (ninth grade and
after) that there is any gain in behavioral autonomy, as conformity to *both* parents
and peers declines (Berndt, 1979; Hill and Holmbeck, 1986).

VALUE AUTONOMY. The development of value autonomy refers to changes in
adolescent thinking about moral, religious, political, and ideological issues. We
have already discussed moral development earlier in this chapter. Here, we focus
on the general characteristics of value autonomy that enable the adolescent to
function at a more independent level on value-related matters.

• *Cognitive changes.* These include the ability to use abstractions in thinking activity.
For example, the older adolescent can now think about the social differences between the sexes and between minority and majority groups in terms of abstract
concepts such as *justice* and *equality.* Furthermore, the enhanced adolescent ability
to think in hypothetical terms (see Chapter 16) creates a heightened concern with
philosophical or ideological matters. In other words, hypothetical thinking, or the
consideration of alternatives, facilitates the exploration of different ethical perspectives, alternate political ideologies, and so on. For example, the adolescent
who develops a hypothesis for dealing with American poverty and welfare abuse
(e.g., providing all adults below the poverty line with a standard wage) is likely
to encounter opposing political ideologies (e.g., finding jobs for all able-bodied
adults below the poverty line).
• *Gains in emotional autonomy.* As the adolescent becomes less dependent on parents

as infallible authority figures, he or she can examine parental values and beliefs with greater objectivity.

• *Gains in behavioral autonomy.* As adolescents experience a number of situations where the advice of parents and peers is at odds, they begin to examine the alternatives critically. The result may be a clarification of their *own* values and beliefs.

Sexuality and Intimacy

In addition to the development of autonomy, sexuality is an important factor in the development of adolescent identity. In this section, our focus is on the behavioral component of sexuality and related issues such as contraceptive use, sex education, and teenage pregnancy.

ATTITUDES TOWARD SEX.   Attitudes toward sexual behavior between unmarried adolescents have been changing since the 1920s (Dreyer, 1982). The movement has been toward a greater acceptance of sexual expression for both males and females. Prior to World War I a *double standard* existed for the sexual behavior of men and women. This **double standard** meant that for women sex was acceptable only in marriage, whereas for men sex was acceptable *both* in marriage *and* in casual relationships before marriage. In other words, women were expected to remain virgins until marriage, yet men were given considerably more freedom to engage in premarital sexual relationships.

The Decline of the Double Standard. To a large extent, the changes in sexual attitudes since World War I have represented a significant decline in the popularity of this double standard (Dreyer, 1982). This change, however, has been a gradual one. For example, studies of sexual attitudes from the 1930s through the early 1960s indicated that the double standard still existed in the sexual attitudes of many adolescents (Terman, 1938; Kinsey et al., 1953; Ehrmann, 1959). Some females still felt that sexual relationships were appropriate only in marriage, although some males felt that sex was acceptable in both marital and casual relationships. By the end of the 1960s and throughout the 1970s, there was a marked reduction in the popularity of the double standard (Sorenson, 1973; Yankelovich, 1974; Hass, 1979). Both men and women felt that sex was acceptable in marriage and in premarital relationships characterized by love and affection. Through the mid-1980s, it is safe to say that a majority of adolescents and adults give qualified approval to premarital sexual relationships. This approval, however, is not to be confused with permissiveness. That is, the new norm is that premarital sex is acceptable *only* in what is deemed to be an affectionate and loving relationship (Dreyer, 1982). Furthermore, adolescents consider premarital sex to be unacceptable in the context of exploitation, promiscuity, and the failure to use birth control techniques (Dreyer, 1982).

The Relationship of Sexual Attitudes and Social Behavior. Although we have just indicated that *attitudes* toward premarital sex have changed (e.g., in the decline of the double standard), it is important for us to consider the *relationship of these changing attitudes to actual behavior.* In other words, is there evidence that adolescents, in fact, behave in accordance with the new norms for sexual behavior that have evolved to replace the double standard? The evidence since the 1970s points to a consistent pattern of *attitudinal acceptance of premarital sex exceeding actual participation in such behavior.* For example, in one study of fifteen-to-nineteen-year-olds, 95 percent of the boys and 83 percent of the girls approved of genital touching. However, only 55 percent of the boys and only 43 percent of the girls reported actually having experienced such behavior. The same general pattern of attitudes' exceeding practice held for other sexual behaviors as well (e.g., oral sex, sexual intercourse) (Hass, 1979).

How can we interpret this distinction between attitudes and behavior? Obviously not all adolescents who say that premarital sexual activity is acceptable are practicing such behavior. Why not? One interpretation is that on a *general attitudinal level* adolescents can agree with the newly emerging norms toward premarital sex (i.e., a continung positive value placed on chastity and virginity prior to marriage *without* negative sanctions or devaluation of premarital sex in an affectionate relationship between two people who are "in love"). However, on a *practical and more personal level* the adolescent must *decide for himself or herself* whether premarital behaviors are appropriate, often in the *context of conflicting values and norms*. For example, an adolescent from a sexually conservative and highly religious family may experience value conflict and personal stress when he or she joins a college peer group where premarital sexual activity occurs. Likewise, an adolescent from another subculture may experience value conflict between premarital sexual relationships that are accepted and practiced in his or her neighborhood yet are negatively valued by high school personnel and social service workers. Phillip Dreyer descibes the problematic circumstances of adolescents as follows:

> Thus, the issue for adolescents appears to be . . . that they are "marginal people" attempting to deal with a variety of adult reference groups which offer conflicting norms. The result of these conflicting subgroup norms is that youth are given very little consistent guidance for their sexual attitudes and behaviors which appears to result in adolescents being highly ambivalent about their own sexual attitudes and behaviors. (1982, p. 568)

The general ambivalence of the adolescent toward sexuality is reflected in the findings of several studies:

- Adolescents tend to express highly tolerant attitudes toward *other individuals* while being *conservative* about their own behavior (Hass, 1979).
- A major reason for adolescent failure to use contraceptive devices is their unwillingness or inability to accept themselves as sexual beings who can become sexually active and who, therefore, may need to protect themselves against unwanted pregnancy (Oskamp et al., 1978; Oskamp and Mindick, 1981).

In summary, adolescents' attitudes toward sex have changed. Although the double standard is no longer acceptable, it has been replaced by confusion and ambivalence. For most contemporary adolescents, sexual relationships are a source of confusion and conflict, with little guidance from their varied reference groups (Dreyer, 1982).

SEXUAL BEHAVIORS.   Historically, most of the information about adolescent sexual behaviors has come from studies on college-age youths (Dreyer, 1982). Over the past ten years this situation has changed as more information has accumulated on the sexual practices of high school adolescents. The findings of these latter studies may be summarized as follows (Zelnik and Kantner, 1980; Chilman, 1979; Hass, 1979; Pratt, 1984).

- Both male and female adolescents are practicing a *greater variety of sexual activities at earlier ages* than at prior times. Furthermore, the age of first experience and prevalence rates of sexual activities are similar for males and females (DeLamater and MacCorquodale, 1979) (see Table 17.6).

TABLE 17.6

The prevalence rates and the age of first experience for a variety of sexual behaviors are similar for males and females.

	MALE				FEMALE			
	STUDENT N = 509		NONSTUDENT N = 262		STUDENT N = 476		NONSTUDENT N = 401	
NINE SEXUAL BEHAVIORS	PERCENT OF RESPONDENTS AGE 18 TO 23 WHO HAVE DONE THIS	AGE AT FIRST EXPERIENCE	PERCENT OF RESPONDENTS AGE 18 TO 23 WHO HAVE DONE THIS	AGE AT FIRST EXPERIENCE	PERCENT OF RESPONDENTS AGE 18 TO 23 WHO HAVE DONE THIS	AGE AT FIRST EXPERIENCE	PERCENT OF RESPONDENTS AGE 18 TO 23 WHO HAVE DONE THIS	AGE AT FIRST EXPERIENCE
Necking	97	14.2	98	13.9	99	14.8	99	14.9
French kissing	93	15.3	95	15.1	95	15.8	95	16.0
Breast fondling	92	15.8	92	15.5	93	16.6	93	16.6
Male/female genitals	86	16.6	87	16.3	82	17.2	86	17.5
Female/male genitals	82	16.8	84	16.7	78	17.4	81	17.8
Genital apposition	77	17.1	81	16.8	72	17.6	78	17.9
Intercourse	75	17.5	79	17.2	60	17.9	72	18.3
Male oral/female genitals	60	18.2	68	17.7	59	18.1	67	18.6
Female oral/male genitals	61	18.1	70	17.8	54	18.1	63	18.8

From DeLamater and MacCorquodale, 1979.

• Adolescent *knowledge about sexual functioning* and *contraception is seriously inadequate*.

• *Increased adolescent sexuality has serious consequences for both adolescents and society.* In terms of numbers, there were 1 million pregnancies to adolescent girls in 1984. Of these pregnancies, approximately 400,000 were terminated by an abortion, 134,000 were terminated by a miscarriage, leaving 469,000 live births. Of these live births, approximately 230,000 were born to already married teenagers, 150,000 were born out of wedlock, and another 89,000 were born to mothers who had quickly gotten married (U.S. Department of Health and Human Services, 1984a; Forrest, 1986).

Stages of Sexual Activity. Is there a typical age at which adolescents begin to engage in sexual activities? Is there a particular order or sequence of such activities? Typically, adolescents begin sexual activity with hand holding and progress through a sequence of behaviors that may end in sexual intercourse. The regularity of this sequence of sexual behaviors for both boys and girls is indicated in Table 17.7. Furthermore, the level of experience is related to age, with older adolescents involved in more sexual behaviors than younger adolescents. In addition, there is

TABLE 17.7

Levels of Heterosexual Activity of Boys and Girls

	PERCENTAGE OF BOYS WHO HAVE PARTICIPATED IN AN ACTIVITY AT LEAST ONCE									
	13 AND YOUNGER		14		15		16		17 AND OLDER	
LEVELS OF SEXUAL ACTIVITY	1970	1973	1970	1973	1970	1973	1970	1973	1970	1973
I. Held hands	79	80	83	87	92	93	90	90	93	92
II. Held arm around or been held	60	67	79	78	83	87	90	87	90	90
III. Kissed or been kissed	63	65	72	78	76	84	86	85	86	87
IV. Necked (prolonged hugging and kissing)	46	48	54	56	64	70	76	69	77	78
V. Light petting (feeling above the waist)	37	40	49	55	59	66	70	65	71	71
VI. Heavy petting (feeling below the waist)	32	34	36	42	44	56	53	55	62	62
VII. Gone all the way (coitus)	24	28	21	32	26	38	31	38	38	34
VIII. Coitus with two or more partners	14	17	14	15	11	21	16	23	17	23
Number in sample	192	180	208	220	193	191	217	176	179	173

	PERCENTAGE OF GIRLS WHO HAVE PARTICIPATED IN AN ACTIVITY AT LEAST ONCE									
	13 AND YOUNGER		14		15		16		17 AND OLDER	
LEVELS OF SEXUAL ACTIVITY	1970	1973	1970	1973	1970	1973	1970	1973	1970	1973
I. Held hands	78	84	91	87	92	89	95	91	95	97
II. Held arm around or been held	68	72	85	81	88	87	94	90	92	96
III. Kissed or been kissed	66	68	80	75	82	82	92	89	90	96
IV. Necked (prolonged hugging and kissing)	46	43	64	56	69	65	81	77	82	84
V. Light petting (feeling above the waist)	27	31	41	40	49	55	66	65	71	71
VI. Heavy petting (feeling below the waist)	21	17	20	28	28	40	47	49	57	59
VII. Gone all the way (coitus)	10	10	10	17	13	24	23	31	27	35
VIII. Coitus with two or more partners	7	4	4	5	4	10	8	13	8	14
Number in sample	191	222	197	218	195	220	200	190	142	185

From Vener and Stewart, 1974, pp. 728–735.

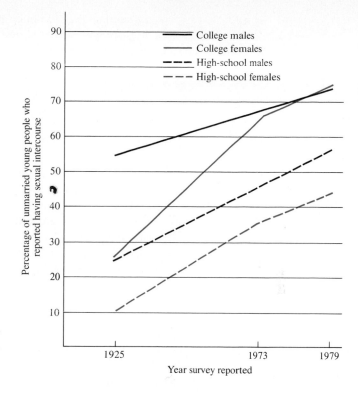

FIGURE 17.7
Changes in male and female sexual behavior, 1925–1980. Most of the increase in sexual activity is due to a decline in the double standard and to the dramatic increase in female sexual activity at earlier ages. From Dreyer, 1982, pp. 559–601.

evidence that adolescents' involvement in such sexual activities is related to a number of factors, including the values of the adolescent's peer group (i.e., peer support for sexual involvement is a strong inducement), the adolescent's "religiosity," and the adolescent's rate of physical maturation (as might be expected, earlier maturing adolescents are more likely to become involved in sexual activities than later maturing individuals) (Chilman, 1979).

Premarital Sexual Intercourse. Evidence indicates that over the past fifty years there has been a dramatic increase in the reported sexual intercourse for adolescents (Dreyer, 1982). Furthermore, the greatest increases have been reported by females. The primary reason for this differential increase is that males often had premarital sexual experiences in past generations (and, of course, males would be more likely to report these activities because of the double standard, which recognized the acceptance of casual male sex prior to marriage) (see Fig. 17.7). Most studies indicate that high school boys tend to be more sexually experienced than high school girls. However, in college, women have caught up with male levels of sexual experience (Dreyer, 1982).

What factors are associated with this dramatic increase in premarital sex? The early studies on psychological and social factors associated with premarital sexual intercourse painted profiles of males and females that have since come into question (Dreyer, 1982). For example, the early studies suggested that boys' sexual activity was part of a larger picture of rebellion, alienation from school, aggression, and flaunting masculinity. Sexually active girls were part of a pattern of feeling rejected by parents, having low self-esteem, alienation from school, and being passive (Dreyer, 1982). However, these profiles are likely to be very inaccurate in relation to contemporary adolescents.

As sexual activity becomes increasingly popular among teenagers, these large group images of the rebellious, aggressive boy and the passive, insecure girl, both of which perpetuate the old notion that sex is not part of the well-adjusted happy teenager's life, are generally inaccurate and misleading. To a greater and greater extent, as the percentages of sexually active youth indicate, sexual activity is becoming part of the teenage experience and is being experienced by all types of young people, not just those who use sex as a way to express personal frustrations or to meet dependency and security needs. (Dreyer, 1982, p. 575)

ADOLESCENT CONTRACEPTIVE USE.   Inadequate knowledge about birth control and contraceptive techniques constitutes a serious problem with widespread impact on adolescents and their families. The evidence indicates that only 44 percent of teenage boys and 48 percent of teenage girls used any type of contraceptive device at the time of their first sexual intercourse (Oskamp et al., 1978; Zelnik and Shah, 1983; Zelnick, Kantner, and Ford, 1981). Furthermore, among sexually active fifteen-to-nineteen-year-old adolescents, fewer than 27 percent reported consistently using some type of contraception and over 31 percent reported *never* using any type of contraception.

What forms of contraception are used by adolescents? By far the most popular form among adolescents who practice contraception is the birth control pill.. The pill is used by approximately half of all adolescent females using some form of contraception (Dreyer, 1982). Other methods used by teenagers who practice contraception include the condom and withdrawal.

Why do so few adolescents use contraceptive devices, even when they are readily available? The evidence suggests that nonuse of contraceptives is related to the following psychological factors (Oskamp and Mindick, 1981):

· *The inability or failure of adolescents to recognize themselves as sexual beings* who can become sexually active.
· *Poor socialization,* including inadequate acceptance of the norms of society.
· *Poor sense of personal efficiency,* or feelings of incompetence, passiveness, and external locus of control (i.e., the feeling that one is powerless in determining what happens to him or her; see Chapter 14) or a sense of learned helplessness (see Chapter 14).
· *Poor cognitive skills,* including the inability to solve problems, poor coping skills, and limited knowledge of reproduction and birth control.
· *Limited future orientation,* including the lack of, or failure to think about, plans or goals.
· *Poor social adjustment,* including the inability to communicate effectively with significant others (e.g., parents or one's sexual partner) or being unusually anxious or guilty about sex.
· *Poor attitudes about contraceptives,* including not intending to use them due to fear or ignorance.

In summary, the reasons for nonuse of contraceptive devices are numerous and varied. However, given these factors in failure to use contraception, there are some constructive suggestions that can be derived from the situation.

· If teenagers fail to use contraception because they cannot or will not think of themselves as sexual beings, then there is an obvious need for sex education. In particular, sex education at an *earlier time* (such as middle childhood) prior to the heightened sexual interests associated with puberty. Since sexual relationships may begin during the early teenage years, it is important to reach preadolescents with sex education.

Teenage Pregnancy: A Systems Perspective

Perhaps one of the most serious problems of adolescence is teenage pregnancy (girls who become pregnant during the high school years at approximately thirteen to seventeen years of age). Indeed, there appear to be few areas in the life of the adolescent that do not hold the potential to be negatively affected by a pregnancy.

1. *The adolescent mother as system: Blockage of the developmental tasks of adolescence.* Many of the developmental tasks of adolescence are omitted in order for the teenage mother to fulfill adult or parental responsibilities (Klein, 1978; Osofsky and Osofsky, 1978). For example, there is often a failure to remain in school, a failure to develop what might be considered a stable family, and a failure to enter a vocation and become relatively self-supporting. There is little doubt that these failures are heavy psychological burdens for both the adolescent and her family (Klein, 1978).

    These failures at the tasks of adolescence represent the closing of doors that typically serve as the transition from childhood to adulthood autonomy. Frequently, if these transitional tasks are not successfully managed during the adolescent years, the requirements and frustrations of being a teenage parent may prevent their completion at a later time.

2. *The crisis in the family system.* Sometimes the pregnant teenager may be viewed, particularly by other family members, as the individual who has caused a permanent crisis or strain in the family system.

    In spite of the fact that the adolescent's parents may move toward a posture of acceptance during the course of the pregnancy, Osofsky and Osofsky (1978) have determined that the most frequently occurring initial parental response is the traditionally anticipated one of anger. This anger is one mechanism of crisis generation and is often accompanied by a strong sense of shame and guilt. Through their work with parents, these two reseachers have observed family members to view the pregnancy event as the symbol of failed aspirations for the whole family. This view of the pregnancy as a pervasive failure may provoke guilt surrounding "what went wrong," as well as questioning within the parents themselves regarding any role they may have played that might have inadvertently contributed to the occurrence of this problem. The total picture of familial response to the pregnancy event spans the full range of positive and negative attitudes, but the situation is open throughout the entire process to the potential for crisis. (Bolton, 1980, p. 115).

3. *Prenatal care and the infant system.* For a number of reasons, the teenage mother is in a high-risk situation both for herself and her infant. These risks include the biological immaturity of the expectant mother and the frequent reluctance of the teenage mother to seek proper prenatal care. Infants born to teenage mothers have a greater risk of having a lower birthweight than infants born to mature women. This increased risk is

MOTHER'S AGE

Fetal-death ratios by age of mother (total of 41 reporting areas, 1981). From U.S. Department of Health and Human Services, 1981.

due to the association of teenage pregnancy with the absence of adequate prenatal care, poor maternal nutrition, and the poor socioeconomic status of the mother. Likewise, there is a greater risk for infant death among very young teenage mothers (Monkus and Bancalari, 1981). Furthermore, the relationship between teenage pregnancy and child abuse has raised serious concerns.

Does the age of parents have anything to do with child abuse? Professionals who work closely with

(Continued)

school-aged parents believe it is a serious problem. They feel that the dangerous age is when children are from one to three years old. During these years babies are able to move actively about and require constant attention but are still too young to understand why they should or shouldn't do things. DeLissovoy (1973) found that school-aged parents are apt to expect too much too soon of their babies. For example, mothers expected babies to sit up alone by 12 weeks, while records show that the average baby is not able to do so until 28 weeks. Young fathers expected even faster development. Very young parents showed a low tolerance for crying. DeLissovoy says, "This low tolerance (of crying), combined with unrealistic expectations of development, contributed to their impatience with their children—and to their sometimes cruel treatment of them." He reports babies as young as six or seven months being hit or spanked in his presence. (Nye, 1975)

. If failure to use contraceptives is associated with poor self-concepts and poor social adjustment, then sex education programs need to deal with *sexuality* in the broad sense of that term (see the definition earlier in this chapter). That is, in addition to the *biology* of conception and the mechanics of contraception (both important topics), effective sex education programs need to deal with the personal issues and questions adolescents are concerned about (What does it mean to be "in love"? What is the nature of physical and emotional intimacy? What is the relationship of the self-concept to sexual relationships? What are sexual ethics?) (Calderone, 1981; Scales, 1981). One of the reasons frequently given for the ineffectiveness of sex education programs is a preoccupation or exclusive emphasis on the "plumbing" of sexual relationships, with little or no attention given to the interpersonal nature of sexual intimacy (Calderone, 1981, Scales, 1981).

TEENAGE PREGNANCY.   The overall *birth rate* for teenagers declined during the 1970s and continued to decline into the 1980s (Eisen et al., 1983). Most of this decline has been attributed to the increase in abortions since 1973 (when the U.S. Supreme Court declared unconstitutional the existing ban on the abortion of first-trimester pregnancies). However, although the overall birth rate for teenagers declined, the *number* of teenagers who gave birth to children out of wedlock *increased* dramatically. There were two primary reasons for this dramatic increase:

. The actual *number* of adolescents (including the number of female teenage girls) increased dramatically (i.e., the so-called baby boom generation reached childbearing age during this time).
. The number of pregnant teenagers who decided to become single mothers increased. That is, fewer teenage mothers "legitimized" the birth of their child by getting married.

The *number* of out-of-wedlock births that occurred to teenagers more than doubled between 1960 and 1980. In 1980, almost half of the more than 100,000 births to teenagers were to unmarried girls.

Problems of Identity Development

Some adolescents have difficulties establishing a consistent identity and sense of who they are. These difficulties are frequently manifested in disruptions in the lives of adolescents and their families. It is important to recognize the distinction between such serious problems (e.g., delinquency or drug abuse) and the more normal adolescent struggles with occasional anxiety or identity diffusion (discussed earlier in this chapter). In this section we examine the following problems in identity development: delinquency, drug abuse, and suicide.

Delinquency

Delinquent behavior of all sorts ranging from occasional wrongdoing (e.g., using someone else's identification card to gain admission to a high school football game) to more serious crimes such as theft or robbery historically have been closely associated with the adolescent years. For example, one researcher has suggested that delinquency is often thought to be "as endemic to adolescence as acne." How accurate is such a depiction? Is there something about the stage of adolescence or the search for identity that leads some youngsters into delinquent behavior?

PREVALENCE.   According to results of the National Survey of Youth (eleven-to-eighteen-year-olds), delinquent behaviors (theft, assault, vandalism, "joyriding") increase throughout the adolescent years (Gold and Reimer, 1975). For example, eighteen-year-olds admitted to committing five times as many legal violations as eleven-year-olds (Gold and Petronio, 1980) (see Fig. 17.8). Although there is an increase in the number of incidents of delinquency through adolescence, there is

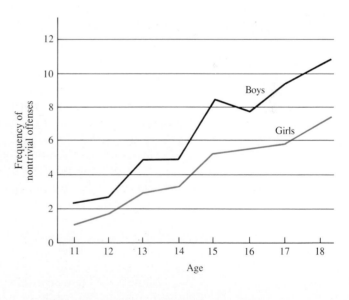

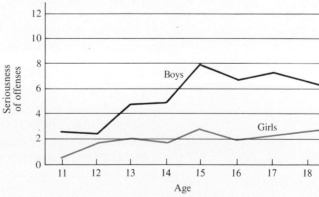

FIGURE 17.8

Crimes in adolescent years. Older adolescents confess to committing more crimes than do younger adolescents. Male adolescents commit more crimes than female adolescents. From Gold and Petronio, 1980, p. 504.

other evidence for a shift from overt antisocial incidents (e.g., fighting, taunting, and open confrontations) in childhood to covert antisocial behavior during the adolescent years (e.g., vandalism, drug use, truency, stealing, or other acts that are done behind the backs of adults).

Are there sex differences in the occurrence of adolescent delinquent behaviors? Ordinarily when one thinks of a delinquent adolescent, the image of a tough male comes to mind. In addition to the evidence of gender difference in delinquency as presented in Figure 17.8, there is other evidence that indicates that the rate of delinquent crimes committed by adolescent males climbs steadily, outnumbering delinquent acts by females (Loeber, 1982; Cairns and Cairns, 1983). There are almost ten times as many eighteen-year-old males arrested for murder as eighteen-year-old females (U.S. Department of Justice, 1982).

There is evidence that the gender gap in delinquent behavior is present in the early adolescent years (eleven to twelve years of age) and becomes more pronounced by later adolescence (e.g., eighteen years). Furthermore, there is evidence that this gender gap may begin to emerge toward the end of middle childhood. For example, one study which followed children from fourth (approximately nine to ten years of age) through the seventh grades (approximately twelve or thirteen years of age) demonstrated this trend (Cairns and Cairns, 1983). The experimenters asked the classmates and teachers of a group of fourth graders to identify the most aggressive and antisocial children in the group. An *equal number* of boys and girls were so identified. The experimenters followed twenty of these children (ten boys and ten girls) through the seventh grade. At the fifth- and sixth-grade levels, there were few discernible differences between the boys and the girls. For example, boys and girls were involved in almost the same number of fights, as well as other types of aggressive behaviors. However, by seventh grade a gender gap emerged. Girls became less aggressive than boys, who became increasingly aggressive and violent. This gender gap became more pronounced and distinct throughout the adolescent years, as indicated by the following sex differences in crime statistics (Gold and Petronio, 1980; Cairns and Cairns, 1983).

- Male adolescents more frequently commit crimes against property (e.g., stealing or vandalizing property) than females.
- When females are brought before the court system, it is more frequently (compared with males) for being "uncontrollable" (e.g., running away from home or being sexually overactive).
- Boys are arrested almost five times more frequently than girls. Because male crimes more often (compared with females) involve nonconsenting others (e.g., crimes against property), they are more likely to be arrested and jailed. On the other hand, female adolescents are more commonly involved in acts of delinquency in the family or with consenting males.

Why the difference at the seventh-grade level? Two primary factors appear to be important in explaining this delinquency gender gap:

- *Physical differences* between male and female adolescents begin to emerge during seventh grade (approximately twelve or thirteen years of age) as the impact of puberty begins to become apparent (see Chapter 16). Particularly in male-female confrontations, physical violence becomes a far-less-viable alternative for the adolescent female than for the adolescent male.
- *Peer support* for adolescent males who commit delinquent acts is far greater than for adolescent females (Gold and Petronio, 1980; Cairns and Cairns, 1983). For

example, aggression and dominance may enhance a male adolescent's sex appeal while serving the opposite function for females (Cairns and Cairns, 1983).

It is important to note that more recently the gender gap has been closing (although males still significantly outnumber females in crime statistics) as more females become involved in "male crimes" such as vandalism and burglary (U.S. Department of Justice, 1982).

TYPES.   One way to deal with the relationship of adolescent delinquency to the question of identity is to examine the types of delinquency and their developmental origins. What developmental characteristics separate "hard-core" delinquents from the adolescents who occasionally smoke marijuana or sneak into a high school football game without a ticket? The evidence indicates that there are a number of distinguishing traits (Loeber, 1982):

· Chronic delinquency *does not suddenly emerge full-blown* in adolescence. Rather, it appears that chronic adolescent delinquents engaged in antisocial behavior in middle childhood (Mitchell and Rosa, 1981). For example, early lying and stealing in childhood were more frequently associated with comparable behaviors in adolescence. Almost 67 percent of children whose parents reported that they had committed a theft later performed a crime in adolescence (compared with only 9 percent of the children whose parents reported no childhood crimes) (Mitchell and Rosa, 1981).
· Chronic adolescent delinquents were typically involved in *more than one type of antisocial behavior* in middle childhood (e.g., theft *and* property distribution *and* lying) and *in more than one setting* (e.g., in school *and* the home *and* the community) (Farrington, 1982).
· Once antisocial patterns are established in childhood, they are typically not relinquished later in adolescence (Loeber, 1982).

In addition to these more general patterns of behavior, psychologists and sociologists have identified two primary types of delinquents (Achenbach, 1982):

· *Socialized/subcultural delinquents.* These individuals are presumably normal adolescents who have grown up in or have been "socialized" in communities/neighborhoods where antisocial behaviors are tolerated and accepted. According to sociologists, identity development in socialized/subcultural delinquents is a *normal* process which is marred by the problem of *accessibility.* That is, these adolescents have the same hopes and dreams of other adolescents (e.g., developing a successful life-style, including a well-paying job and meaningful family relationships). However, they *lack access* to the legitimate opportunities for attaining their goals (e.g., they may not have appropriate educational experiences or "know the right people" to get a middle-class job). On the other hand, they *do have access to illegitimate opportunities* for success (e.g., drug dealing, gambling, prostitution, and so on).
· *Unsocialized/psychopathic (sociopathic) delinquents.* These are adolescents who appear to be incapable of long-term commitments to goals involving delay of immediate gratification. Furthermore, they are unable to sustain lasting relationships involving mutual goals or arrangements. In short, these individuals appear to have character disorders that make them appear casual or indifferent to inflicting pain on others.

DELINQUENCY AND EXPLOITATION OF ADOLESCENTS.   Although many adolescents do indeed fit into one of the two types of delinquency described above, there nonetheless remains a group of adolescents who do not easily fit into one of these two categories. Specifically, what about the incidence of delinquency in middle-class children and adolescents who appear to have every *material* advantage and opportunity? Some researchers have used the concept of *exploitation* to explain middle-class delinquency (Elkind, 1967b).

It is important to note, however, that such perceived exploitation can occur in the lives of both middle-class *and* lower-class adolescents. Among lower-class adolescents such perceived exploitation may happen when they become aware of their limited access to legitimate opportunities for success (poor housing, inadequate schools, poor opportunities for good jobs). Lower-class adolescents may then "get even" with society by performing delinquent acts that make full use of the illegitimate means of success at their disposal. In the case of middle-class adolescents, a sense of exploitation can occur for any one of several reasons (Elkind, 1967b):

- *Parents use the adolescent to vicariously meet their own needs,* for example, the socially frustrated mother who encourages her daughter to interact with many peers and join many high school social groups to satisfy the mother's unmet needs to be socially active. The mother then criticizes the adolescent for not devoting sufficient time to her studies.
- *Parents use the adolescent as slave labor,* for example, the parent who makes unreasonable demands on the adolescent to do too much household work too frequently. Of course, normal and reasonable chores do not constitute slave labor.
- *Parents who use the adolescent as a way of bolstering their own ego,* for example, the parent who puts pressure on a son or daughter to be a star athlete or an outstanding student, far beyond the child's actual capabilities.
- *Parents who use the adolescent to proclaim their own moral standards,* for example, parents who demand that their children maintain unreasonable standards of conduct (e.g., adolescent children of school principals, teachers, or religious officials may sometimes be expected to uphold virtually impossible behavioral codes).
- *Parents who use their children to absolve their own guilt,* for example, the parent who is in the process of a divorce may relieve guilt about his or her own behavior by forcing the child or adolescent to take sides against the other parent. If this happens, the parent may take some comfort that the divorce should be pursued.

How do middle-class adolescents respond to this exploitation? They may react in several ways including the following (Elkind, 1967b):

- *Quitting.* They may quit school, leave home and become runaways, or "psychologically quit" the family by misbehaving regularly (see box).
- *Going on strike.* The adolescent generally defies the authority of parents or teachers. For example, he or she may continue to attend school but refuse to perform or cooperate in any way. Or the adolescent may refuse to do his or her chores at home or may intentionally stay out late with peers who are not approved of by the parents.
- *Sabotaging parents.* These adolescents try to get even with parents by engaging in such behaviors as vandalism, alcoholism, taking drugs, becoming pregnant, and so on.
- *Submitting to parents.* Some adolescents passively submit to exploitation by parents, hoping to maintain a relationship with their parents.

The Adolescent Runaway

Yeah, I ran. I ran to get away from that house and the people in it. I wanted to be on my own without all the hassles. . . . Yeah, right, so I ended up on the street. No job because I was too young; no place to stay because I didn't have any money. So when this dude approached me I went with him. . . . You know the rest of the story.

—A 15-Year-Old Runaway (as quoted in Garbarino, Wilson, and Garbarino, 1986)

Who are runaways? Runaways are youths who leave home without permission, are absent for at least one night, and desire to remove themselves from parental control (Nye and Edelbrock, 1980). There is evidence that the majority of runaways are between fourteen and sixteen years of age (U.S. Department of Health, Education and Welfare, 1978). Some estimates of the total number of runaways range as high as 1 million children and adolescents (Garbarino, Wilson, and Garbarino, 1986). Other estimates indicate that one of every eight adolescents will run away before eighteen years of age (Nye and Edelbrock, 1980).

There is evidence that three primary problems of daily living contribute to or influence adolescent runaways: personal maladjustment, family conflict, and parental mistreatment (Garbarino, Wilson, and Garbarino, 1986):

• *Personal maladjustment*. Runaway behavior has been associated with various levels of dysfunctional or pathological behaviors (Adams and Gullotta, 1983). For example, there is evidence that runaways (compared with nonrunaways) have lower self-concept ratings, feel more rejected and inadequate, are more hostile, and are more anxious and impulsive (Wolk and Brandon, 1977; Jorgensen, Thornburg, and Williams, 1980; Jenkins, 1981). Furthermore, there is evidence that running away is part of a system of other "patterns of maladaptation" (Edelbrock, 1980). For example, runaways are more likely than nonrunaways to be involved in school truancy, theft, drug use, suicide threats, or vandalism.

Although running away is associated with psychological problems, not all adolescents who run away initially exhibit maladaptive behaviors. There are obviously many *more* "normal" adolescents than "disturbed" adolescents. Therefore, the *lower* rate of runaways for normals produces *more* runaways

(Continued)

Ed Lettau/Photo Researchers, Inc.

than the higher rate of runaways for disturbed adolescents. Social or family factors may contribute to running away among otherwise psychologically normal adolescents.

• *Family conflict.* There is evidence that approximately 80 percent of runaways leave home due to family problems (U.S. Department of Health, Education and Welfare, 1978, p. 90). Family problems can, of course, cover a wide range of difficulties from divorce to adolescent-parent behaviors. Generally, there is some evidence that the families of runaway adolescents are characterized by ineffective communication, poor parental supervision, and inadequate conflict resolution patterns (Garbarino, Wilson, and Garbarino, 1986). For example, these families often allow minor conflicts over issues such as clothes, hairstyles, or curfew hours to evolve into major disputes. Resolution of these conflicts is further hampered by poor communication patterns. Typically, youths who are involved in such family conflicts run away from home for a relatively short distance and return relatively quickly. This pattern ("short run" and relatively fast return home) is different from the pattern of "serious" runaways (running a greater distance and for a longer time), who leave home due to parental mistreatment (Garbarino, Wilson, and Garbarino, 1986).

• *Parental mistreatment.* There is evidence of several primary factors involved in serious runaways, who run for greater distances and for a longer period of time. Several studies have linked forms of parental mistreatment such as physical abuse, incest, or neglect to serious runaways (Garbarino and Gilliam, 1980; Gutierres and Reich, 1981; Silbert and Pines, 1981). In fact, according to one study, running away from home in response to such parental mistreat-

Program Information

1. Clearinghouse National Youth Work Alliance 1346 Connecticut Ave., N.W. Washington, D.C. 20036	For general information and information about aftercare (request *It's Me Again*)
2. National Network of Runaway and Youth Services 1705 DeSales St., N.W., 8th Floor Washington, D.C. 20036	For general information about runaway houses
3. New York City Runaway Coordinator 618 Avenue of the Americas New York, New York 10011	For information about community coordination of services
4. Youth Care Division Father Flanagan's Boys' Home Boys Town, Nebraska 68010	For information on social skills training for runaways via The Family Teaching Model
5. The Shelter Program Office Suite 509, Jones Building Seattle, Washington 98101	For information about dealing with runaways as part of the larger status offender population
6. D.C. Coalition for Youth P.O. Box 9035 Washington, D.C. 20003	For information about continuing care for runaways
7. GLIE Community Youth Program 2021 Grand Concourse 7th and 8th Floors Bronx, New York 10453	For information on their metropolitan programs for runaways
8. Youth Helping Youth Project Division of External Affairs Boys Town, Nebraska 68010	For information about setting up and running a youth self-help group

Table from Garbarino et al., 1986, p. 54.

ment may be "a healthy and adaptive response to an impossible situation" (Silbert and Pines, 1981). Furthermore, in another study, three-fourths of the runaways who were surveyed reported being subjected to harsh mistreatment in the year prior to running away (Farber and Kinast, 1984).

It is important to note that personal maladjustment, family conflict, and parental mistreatment may interact or combine to influence runaway behavior. Furthermore, these same factors that lead to running away from home may make the runaway adolescent more vulnerable to the risks and victimization that running away causes (Garbarino, Wilson, and Gar-

barino, 1986). For example, the lower levels of social competence and self-esteem associated with the runaway's personality make him or her vulnerable to such threats of street life as prostitution and drugs (Silbert and Pines, 1981). Most serious runaways who take to the streets (usually the streets of larger cities) find it difficult to meet basic needs for food, clothing, and shelter. "They eventually choose or fall into one of three courses: get off the street, steal what they need, or sell what they have" (Garbarino, Wilson, and Garbarino, 1986, pp. 47–48). Unfortunately, in many cases they are taken into the illicit economy of drugs or prostitution.

Many adolescent responses to parental exploitation are attempts to "make public" the exploitation that has remained, until the delinquent behavior, a private family affair. Unfortunately, these "cries for help" by the adolescent are injurious to the adolescent and his or her parents.

Drug Abuse

In negotiating the challenges of adolescence, young people undoubtedly will encounter peers who use drugs or may, themselves, experiment with drugs. For our purposes, a drug is defined as any substance (with the exception of food) that, when taken by an individual, alters one or more of the functions (e.g., excitation level, sensory perceptions, heart rate, blood pressure) of the individual. The health hazards resulting from adolescents' abuse of drugs constitutes a serious problem for adolescents and society. Table 17.8 shows several types of drugs that can be abused by adolescents as well as how the drug is taken into the body, the primary physical and behavioral signs associated with abuse, and the medical implications resulting from abuse.

PREVALENCE. Lloyd Johnston, Patrick O'Malley, and Jerald Bachman (1986), using national data on adolescent drug use (based on relatively large, representative surveys of high school seniors in public and private schools across the United States), established several key findings:

- *Alcohol use* has remained relatively stable since 1975, though at relatively high levels (Table 17.9). Nearly all young people have tried alcohol by the end of their senior year (92 percent) and the great majority (66 percent) have used it in the prior month (see Fig. 17.9, on p. 732).
- *Cigarette smoking* has declined since 1975 (Table 17.9). Nonetheless, 69 percent of all young people have smoked cigarettes by the end of their senior year. Of this number, approximately 30 percent have smoked in the prior month, a substantial proportion of whom are, or soon will be, daily smokers (Fig. 17.9). Cigarettes are used *daily* by more young people than any other category of drugs (20 percent). However, *daily* cigarette smoking decreased from a high in 1977 (29 percent) to 20 percent in 1985 and appears to have stabilized.

TABLE 17.8
Specific Drugs and Their Effects

CANNABIS

Effects

All forms of cannabis have negative physical and mental effects. Several regularly observed physical effects of cannabis are a substantial increase in the heart rate, bloodshot eyes, a dry mouth and throat, and increased appetite.

Use of cannabis may impair or reduce short-term memory and comprehension, alter sense of time, and reduce ability to perform tasks requiring concentration and co-ordination, such as driving a car. Research also shows that students do not retain knowledge when they are "high." Motivation and cognition may be altered, making the acquisition of new information difficult. Marijuana can also produce paranoia and psychosis.

Because users often inhale the unfiltered smoke deeply and then hold it in their lungs as long as possible, marijuana is damaging to the lungs and pulmonary system. Marijuana smoke contains more cancer-causing agents than tobacco.

Long-term users of cannabis may develop psychological dependence and require more of the drug to get the same effect. The drug can become the center of their lives.

Type	What is it called?	What does it look like?	How is it used?
Marijuana	Pot Grass Weed Reefer Dope Mary Jane Sinsemilla Acapulco Gold Thai Sticks	Dried parsley mixed with stems that may include seeds	Eaten Smoked
Tetrahydro-cannabinol	THC	Soft gelatin capsules	Taken orally Smoked
Hashish	Hash	Brown or black cakes or balls	Eaten Smoked
Hashish Oil	Hash Oil	Concentrated syrupy liquid varying in color from clear to black	Smoked—mixed with tobacco

INHALANTS

Effects

Immediate negative effects of inhalants include nausea, sneezing, coughing, nose-bleeds, fatigue, lack of coordination, and loss of appetite. Solvents and aerosol sprays also decrease the heart and respiratory rates, and impair judgment. Amyl and butyl nitrite cause rapid pulse, headaches, and involuntary passing of urine and fe-ces. Long-term use may result in hepatitis or brain hemorrhage.

Deeply inhaling the vapors, or using large amounts over a short period of time, may result in disorientation, violent behavior, unconsciousness, or death. High concentra-tions of inhalants can cause suffocation by displacing the oxygen in the lungs or by depressing the central nervous system to the point that breathing stops.

Long-term use can cause weight loss, fatigue, electrolyte imbalance, and muscle fa-tigue. Repeated sniffing of concentrated vapors over time can permanently damage the nervous system.

TABLE 17.8
Specific Drugs and Their Effects (Continued)

Type	What is it called?	What does it look like?	How is it used?
Nitrous Oxide	Laughing gas Whippets	Propellant for whipped cream in aerosol spray can Small 8-gram metal cylinder sold with a balloon or pipe (buzz bomb)	Vapors inhaled
Amyl Nitrite	Poppers Snappers	Clear yellowish liquid in ampules	Vapors inhaled
Butyl Nitrite	Rush Bolt Locker room Bullet Climax	Packaged in small bottles	Vapors inhaled
Chlorohydro-carbons	Aerosol sprays	Aerosol paint cans Containers of cleaning fluid	Vapors inhaled
Hydrocarbons	Solvents	Cans of aerosol propellants, gasoline, glue, paint thinner	Vapors inhaled

STIMULANT: COCAINE

Effects

Cocaine stimulates the central nervous system. Its immediate effects include dilated pupils and elevated blood pressure, heart rate, respiratory rate, and body temperature. Occasional use can cause a stuffy or runny nose, while chronic use can ulcerate the mucous membrane of the nose. Injecting cocaine with unsterile equipment can cause AIDS, hepatitis, and other diseases. Preparation of freebase, which involves the use of volatile solvents, can result in death or injury from fire or explosion. Cocaine can produce psychological and physical dependency, a feeling that the user cannot function without the drug. In addition, tolerance develops rapidly.

Crack or freebase rock is extremely addictive, and its effects are felt within 10 seconds. The physical effects include dilated pupils, increased pulse rate, elevated blood pressure, insomnia, loss of appetite, tactile hallucinations, paranoia, and seizures.

The use of cocaine can cause death by disrupting the brain's control of the heart and respiration.

Type	What is it called?	What does it look like?	How is it used?
Cocaine	Coke Snow Flake White Blow Nose Candy Big C Snowbirds Lady	White crystalline powder, often diluted with other ingredients	Inhaled through nasal passages Injected Smoked
Crack or cocaine	Crack Freebase rocks Rock	Light brown or beige pellets—or crystalline rocks that resemble coagulated soap; often packaged in small vials	Smoked

(Continued)

TABLE 17.8
Specific Drugs and Their Effects (Continued)

OTHER STIMULANTS

Effects

Stimulants can cause increased heart and respiratory rates, elevated blood pressure, dilated pupils, and decreased appetite. In addition, users may experience sweating, headache, blurred vision, dizziness, sleeplessness, and anxiety. Extremely high doses can cause a rapid or irregular heartbeat, tremors, loss of coordination, and even physical collapse. An amphetamine injection creates a sudden increase in blood pressure that can result in stroke, very high fever, or heart failure.

In addition to the physical effects, users report feeling restless, anxious, and moody. Higher doses intensify the effects. Persons who use large amounts of amphetamines over a long period of time can develop an amphetamine psychosis that includes hallucinations, delusions, and paranoia. These symptoms usually disappear when drug use ceases.

Type	What is it called?	What does it look like?	How is it used?

Amphetamines	Speed
	Uppers
	Ups
	Black Beauties
	Pep Pills
	Copilots
	Bumblebees
	Hearts
	Benzedrine
	Dexedrine
	Footballs
	Biphetamine
		Capsules
		Pills
		Tablets
			Taken orally
			Injected
			Inhaled through
			  nasal
			  passages

Methamphet-amines	Crank
	Crystal Meth
	Crystal
	Methedrine
	Speed
		White powder
		Pills
		A rock which resembles a
		  block of paraffin
			Taken orally
			Injected
			Inhaled through
			  nasal
			  passages

Additional Stimulants	Ritalin Cylert Preludin Didrex Pre-State Voranil Tenuate Tepanil Pondimin Sandrex Plegine Ionamin	Pills Capsules Tablets	Taken orally Injected

DEPRESSANTS

Effects

The effects of depressants are in many ways similar to the effects of alcohol. Small amounts can produce calmness and relaxed muscles, but somewhat larger doses can cause slurred speech, staggering gait, and altered perception. Very large doses can cause respiratory depression, coma, and death. The combination of depressants and alcohol can multiply the effects of the drugs, thereby multiplying the risks.

The use of depressants can cause both physical and psychological dependence. Regular use over time may result in a tolerance to the drug, leading the user to increase the quantity consumed. When regular users suddenly stop taking large doses,

TABLE 17.8
Specific Drugs and Their Effects (Continued)

they may develop withdrawal symptoms ranging from restlessness, insomnia, and anxiety to convulsions and death.

Babies born to mothers who abuse depressants during pregnancy may be physically dependent on the drugs and show withdrawal symptoms shortly after they are born. Birth defects and behavioral problems also may result.

Type	What is it called?	What does it look like?	How is it used?
Barbiturates	Downers Barbs Blue Devils Red Devils Yellow Jacket Yellows Nembutal Seconal Amytal Tuinals	Red, yellow, blue, or red and blue capsules	Taken orally
Methaqualone	Quaaludes Ludes Sopors	Tablets	Taken orally
Tranquilizers	Valium Librium Equanil Miltown Serax Tranxene	Tablets Capsules	Taken orally

HALLUCINOGENS

Effects

Phencylidine (PCP) interrupts the functions of the neocortex, the section of the brain that controls the intellect and keeps instincts in check. Because the drug blocks pain receptors, violent PCP episodes may result in self-inflicted injuries.

The effects of PCP vary, but users frequently report a sense of distance and estrangement. Time and body movement are slowed down. Muscular coordination worsens and senses are dulled. Speech is blocked and incoherent.

Chronic users of PCP report persistent memory problems and speech difficulties. Some of these effects may last 6 months to a year following prolonged daily use. Mood disorders—depression, anxiety, and violent behavior—also occur. In later stages of chronic use, users often exhibit paranoid and violent behavior and experience hallucinations.

Large doses may produce convulsions and coma, heart and lung failure, or ruptured blood vessels in the brain.

Lysergic acid (LSD), mescaline, and psilocybin cause illusions and hallucinations. The physical effects may include dilated pupils, elevated body temperature, increased heart rate and blood pressure, loss of appetite, sleeplessness, and tremors.

Sensations and feelings may change rapidly. It is common to have a bad psychological reaction to LSD, mescaline, and psilocybin. The user may experience panic, confusion, suspicion, anxiety, and loss of control. Delayed effects, or flashbacks, can occur even after use has ceased.

Type	What is it called?	What does it look like?	How is it used?
Phencyclidine	PCP Angel Dust Loveboat Lovely	Liquid Capsules White crystalline powder Pills	Taken orally Injected Smoked—can be sprayed

(Continued)

729

TABLE 17.8
Specific Drugs and Their Effects (Continued)

	Hog Killer Weed		on cigarettes, parsley, and marijuana
Lysergic Acid Diethylamide	LSD Acid Green or Red Dragon White Lightning Blue Heaven Sugar Cubes Microdot	Brightly colored tablets Impregnated blotter paper Thin squares of gelatin Clear liquid	Taken orally Licked off paper Gelatin and liquid can be put in the eyes
Mescaline and Peyote	Mesc Buttons Cactus	Hard brown discs Tablets Capsules	Discs—chewed, swallowed, or smoked Tablets and capsules— taken orally
Psilocybin	Magic mushrooms Mushrooms	Fresh or dried mushrooms	Chewed and swallowed

NARCOTICS

Effects

Narcotics initially produce a feeling of euphoria that often is followed by drowsiness, nausea, and vomiting. Users also may experience constricted pupils, watery eyes, and itching. An overdose may produce slow and shallow breathing, clammy skin, convulsions, coma, and possibly death.

Tolerance to narcotics develops rapidly and dependence is likely. The use of contaminated syringes may result in diseases such as AIDS, endocarditis, and hepatitis. Addiction in pregnant women can lead to premature, stillborn, or addicted infants who experience severe withdrawal symptoms.

Type	What is it called?	What does it look like?	How is it used?
Heroin	Smack Horse Brown Sugar Junk Mud Big H Black Tar	Powder, white to dark brown Tar-like substance	Injected Inhaled through nasal passages Smoked
Methadone	Dolophine Methadose Amidone	Solution	Taken orally Injected
Codeine	Empirin compound with Codeine Tylenol with Codeine Codeine Codeine in cough medicines	Dark liquid varying in thickness Capsules Tablets	Taken orally Injected
Morphine	Pectoral syrup	White crystals Hypodermic tablets Injectable solutions	Injected Taken orally Smoked

TABLE 17.8

Specific Drugs and Their Effects (Continued)

Meperidine	Pethidine Demerol Mepergan	White powder Solution Tablets	Taken orally Injected
Opium	Paregoric Dover's Powder Parepectolin	Dark brown chunks Powder	Smoked Eaten
Other Narcotics	Percocet Percodan Tussionex Fentanyl Darvon Talwin Lomotil	Tablets Capsules Liquid	Taken orally Injected

DESIGNER DRUGS

Effects

Illegal drugs are defined in terms of their chemical formulas. To circumvent these legal restrictions, underground chemists modify the molecular structure of certain illegal drugs to produce analogs known as designer drugs. These drugs can be several hundred times stronger than the drugs they are designed to imitate.

The narcotic analogs can cause symptoms such as those seen in Parkinson's disease—uncontrollable tremors, drooling, impaired speech, paralysis, and irreversible brain damage. Analogs of amphetamines and methamphetamines cause nausea, blurred vision, chills or sweating, and faintness. Psychological effects include anxiety, depression, and paranoia. As little as one dose can cause brain damage. The analogs of phencyclidine cause illusions, hallucinations, and impaired perception.

Type	What is it called?	What does it look like?	How is it used?
Analogs of Fentanyl (Narcotic)	Synthetic Heroin China White	White powder resembling heroin	Inhaled through nasal passages Injected
Analogs of Meperidine (Narcotic)	Synthetic Heroin MPTP (New Heroin) MPPP PEPAP	White powder	Inhaled through nasal passages Injected
Analogs of Amphet- amines and Methamphet- amines (Hallucino- gens)	MDMA (Ecstasy, XTC, Adam, Essence) MDM STP PMA 2, 5-DMA TMA DOM DOB	White powder Tablets Capsules	Taken orally Injected Inhaled through nasal passages
Analogs of Phencyclidine (PCP) (Hallucino- gens)	PCPy PCE TCP	White powder	Taken orally Injected Smoked

From U.S. Department of Education, 1986.

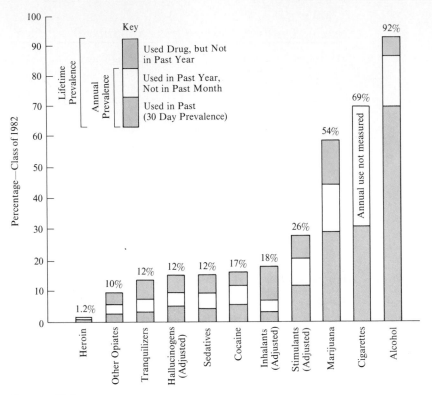

FIGURE 17.9

Prevalence and recency of use of 11 types of drugs, class of 1985. From Johnston, O'Malley, and Bachman, 1986, p. 17.

> What seems most noteworthy is the lack of appreciable decline in the smoking rates since 1981, despite (a) the general decline which has occurred for most other drugs (including alcohol), (b) some rise in the perceived harmfulness and personal disapproval associated with smoking, and (c) a considerable amount of restrictive legislation which has been debated and enacted at state and local levels in the past several years. (Johnston, O'Malley, and Bachman, 1986, p. 63)

- Sixty-one percent of all American young people try an illicit drug (e.g., marijuana, cocaine, or other drug that is illegal unless used under a physician's supervision) before they finish high school. (Alcohol and cigarettes are, of course, legal drugs.)
- "*Marijuana* is by far the most widely used illicit drug with 54% reporting some use in their lifetime, 41% reporting some use in the past year, and 26% reporting some use in the past month" (Johnston, O'Malley, and Bachman, 1986, p. 22).
- The most widely used class of other illicit drugs (other than marijuana) was *stimulants* (26 percent lifetime prevalance, adjusted). Next come *inhalants* (adjusted) at 18 percent and *cocaine* at 17 percent. These are followed closely by *hallucinogens* (adjusted) at 12 percent, *sedatives* at 12 percent, and *tranquilizers* at 12 percent.
- According to Johnston and his colleagues, these are alarming levels of substance use and abuse.

> Clearly this nation's high school students and other young adults still show a level of involvement with illicit drugs which is greater than can be found in any other

industrialized nation in the world. Even by historical standards in this country, these rates still remain extremely high. (1986, p. 20)

CAUSES. It is important to note that neither the heavy use of alcohol nor the use of marijuana in adolescence persists into adulthood (Blane, 1979). However, this does not mean that alcohol and drug use are unimportant concerns in adolescence. For example, the leading cause of death among adolescents is automobile accidents—many of which are believed to be alcohol-related. Furthermore, the incidence of delinquency behaviors such as vandalism, violent crimes, and family conflicts have also been related to alcohol/drug use (Blane, 1979).

There are no simple explanations for adolescent alcohol/drug abuse. Several factors are involved, including the adolescent's personality, the parents' role, and

TABLE 17.9
Trends in Lifetime Prevalence of Sixteen Types of Drugs

	PERCENT EVER-USED										
	CLASS OF 1975	CLASS OF 1976	CLASS OF 1977	CLASS OF 1978	CLASS OF 1979	CLASS OF 1980	CLASS OF 1981	CLASS OF 1982	CLASS OF 1983	CLASS OF 1984	CLASS OF 1985
APPROX. N =	(9400)	(15400)	(17100)	(17800)	(15500)	(15900)	(17500)	(17700)	(16300)	(15900)	(16000)
Marijuana/Hashish	47.3	52.8	56.4	59.2	60.4	60.3	59.5	58.7	57.0	54.9	54.2
Inhalants[a]	NA	10.3	11.1	12.0	12.7	11.9	12.3	12.8	13.6	14.4	15.4
Inhalants Adjusted[b]	NA	NA	NA	NA	18.7	17.6	17.4	18.0	18.6	19.0	17.9
Amyl & Butyl Nitrites[c]	NA	NA	NA	NA	11.1	11.1	10.1	9.8	8.4	8.1	7.9
Hallucinogens	16.3	15.1	13.9	14.3	14.1	13.3	13.3	12.5	11.9	10.7	10.3
Hallucinogens Adjusted[d]	NA	NA	NA	NA	18.6	15.7	15.7	15.0	14.7	13.3	12.2
LSD	11.3	11.0	9.8	9.7	9.5	9.3	9.8	9.6	8.9	8.0	7.5
PCP[c]	NA	NA	NA	NA	12.8	9.6	7.8	6.0	5.6	5.0	4.9
Cocaine	9.0	9.7	10.8	12.9	15.4	15.7	16.5	16.0	16.2	16.1	17.3
Heroin	2.2	1.8	1.8	1.6	1.1	1.1	1.1	1.2	1.2	1.3	1.2
Other opiates[e]	9.0	9.6	10.3	9.9	10.1	9.8	10.1	9.6	8.4	9.7	10.2
Stimulants[e]	22.3	22.6	23.0	22.9	24.2	26.4	32.2	35.6	35.4	NA	NA
Stimulants Adjusted[e,f]	NA	NA	NA	NA	NA	NA	NA	27.9	26.9	27.9	26.2
Sedatives[e]	18.2	17.7	17.4	16.0	14.6	14.9	16 0	15.2	14.4	13.3	11.8
Barbiturates[e]	16.9	16.2	15.6	13.7	11.8	11.0	11.3	10.3	9.9	9.9	9.2
Methaqualone[e]	8.1	7.8	8.5	7.9	8.3	9.5	10.6	10.7	10.1	8.3	6.7
Tranquilizers[e]	17.0	16.8	18.0	17.0	16.3	15.2	14.7	14.0	13.3	12.4	11.9
Alcohol	90.4	91.9	92.5	93.1	93.0	93.2	92.6	92.8	92.6	92.6	92.2
Cigarettes	73.6	75.4	75.7	75.3	74.0	71.0	71.0	70.1	70.6	69.7	68.8

NOTES: Level of significance of difference between the two most recent classes: s = .05, ss = .01, sss = .001.
NA indicates data not available.
[a]Data based on four questionnaire forms. N is four-fifths of N indicated.
[b]Adjusted for underreporting of amyl and butyl nitrites.
[c]Data based on a single questionnaire form. N is one-fifth of N indicated.
[d]Adjusted for underreporting of PCP.
[e]Only drug use which was not under a doctor's orders is included here.
[f]Adjusted for overreporting of the non-prescription stimulants. Data based on three questionnaire forms. N is three-fifths of N indicated.

From Johnston, O'Malley, and Bachman, 1986.

Adolescent Drug Abuse: Current Issues

"I felt depressed and hurt all the time. I hated myself for the way I hurt my parents and treated them so cruelly, and for the way I treated others. I hated myself the most, though, for the way I treated myself. I would take drugs until I overdosed, and fell further and further in school and work and relationships with others. I just didn't care anymore whether I lived or died. I stopped going to school altogether. . . . I felt constantly depressed and began having thoughts of suicide, which scared me a lot! I didn't know where to turn. . . ."

—"Stewart," a high school student

Extent of Drug Use
* *Drug use is widespread among American schoolchildren.* The United States has the highest rate of teenage drug use of any industrialized nation. The drug problem in this country is 10 times greater than in Japan, for example. Sixty-one percent of high school seniors have used drugs. Marijuana use remains at an unacceptably high level; 41 percent of 1985 seniors reported using it in the last year, and 26 percent said they had used it at least once in the previous month. Thirteen percent of seniors indicated that they had used cocaine in the past year. This is the highest level ever observed, more than twice the proportion in 1975.
* *Many students purchase and use drugs at school.* A recent study of teenagers contacting a cocaine hotline revealed that 57 percent of the respondents bought most of their drugs at school. Among 1985 high school seniors, one-third of the marijuana users reported that they had smoked marijuana at school. Of the seniors who used amphetamines during the past year, two thirds reported having taken them at school.
* *The drug problem affects all types of students.* All regions and all types of communities show high levels of drug use. Forty-three percent of 1985 high school seniors in nonmetropolitan areas reported illicit drug use in the previous year, while the rate for seniors in large metropolitan areas was 50 percent. Although higher proportions of males are involved in illicit drug use, especially heavy drug use, the gap between the sexes is lessening. The extent to which high school seniors reported having used marijuana is about the same for blacks and whites; for other types of drugs reported, use is slightly higher among whites.
* *Initial drug use occurs at an increasingly early age.*

The percentage of students using drugs by the sixth grade has tripled over the last decade. In the early 1960's, marijuana use was virtually nonexistent among 13-year-olds, but now about one in six 13-year-olds has used marijuana.

Cocaine use is the fastest growing drug problem in America. Most alarming is the recent availability of cocaine in a cheap but potent form called crack or rock. Crack is a purified form of cocaine that is smoked.

* *Crack is inexpensive to try.* Crack is available for as little as $10. As a result, the drug is affordable to many new users, including high school and even elementary school students.
* *Crack is easy to use.* It is sold in pieces resembling small white gravel or soap chips and is sometimes pressed into small pellets. Crack can be smoked in a pipe or put into a cigarette. Because the visible effects disappear within minutes after smoking, it can be used at almost any time during the day.
* *Crack is extremely addictive.* Crack is far more addictive than heroin or barbiturates. Because crack is smoked, it is quickly absorbed into the blood stream. It produces a feeling of extreme euphoria, peaking within seconds. The desire to repeat this sensation can cause addiction within a few days.
* *Crack leads to crime and severe psychological disorders.* Many youths, once addicted, have turned to stealing, prostitution, and drug dealing in order to support their habit. Continued use can produce violent behavior and psychotic states similar to schizophrenia.
* *Crack is deadly.* Cocaine in any form can cause cardiac arrest and death by interrupting the brain's control over the heart and respiratory system.

School and Community Resources
* ALCOHOL AND DRUG ABUSE EDUCATION PROGRAM, U.S. Department of Education. The "school team" approach offered in this program is designed to develop the capability of local schools to prevent and reduce drug and alcohol abuse and associated disruptive behaviors. Five regional centers now provide training and technical assistance to local school districts that apply. For information, write to the U.S. Department of Education, Alcohol and Drug Abuse Education

Program, 400 Maryland Avenue, SW, Washington, DC 20202-4101.

· AMERICAN COUNCIL ON DRUG EDUCATION (ACDE). ACDE organizes conferences; develops media campaigns; reviews scientific findings; publishes books, a quarterly newsletter, and education kits for physicians, schools, and libraries; and produces films. 5820 Hubbard Drive, Rockville, MD 20852. Telephone (301) 984-5700.

· COMMITTEES OF CORRESPONDENCE, INC. This organization provides a newsletter and emergency news flashes that give extensive information on issues, ideas, and contacts. Provides a resource list and sells many pamphlets. Membership is $15. 57 Conant Street, Room 113, Danvers, MA 09123. Telephone (617) 774-2641.

· FAMILIES IN ACTION. This organization maintains a drug information center with more than 100,000 documents. Publishes *Drug Abuse Update,* a 16-page newsletter containing abstracts of articles published in medical and academic journals and newspapers throughout the nation. $10 for 4 issues. 3845 North Druid Hills Road, Suite 300, Decatur, GA 30033. Telephone (404) 325-5799.

· NARCOTICS EDUCATION, INC. This organization publishes pamphlets, books, teaching aids, posters, audiovisual aids, and prevention magazines especially good for classroom use: WINNER for preteens and LISTEN for teens. 6830 Laurel Street, NW, Washington, DC 20012. Telephone 1-800-548-8700, or in the Washington, DC area, call 722-6740.

· NATIONAL FEDERATION OF PARENTS FOR DRUG-FREE YOUTH (NFP). This national umbrella organization helps parent groups get started and stay in contact. Publishes a newsletter, legislative updates, resource lists for individuals and libraries, brochures, kits, and a *Training Manual for Drug-Free Youth Groups.* It sells many books and offers discounts for group purchases. Conducts an annual conference. Membership: Individual $15, Group $35 (group membership offers tax-exemption). 8730 Georgia Avenue, Suite 200, Silver Spring, MD 20910.

Telephone: Washington, DC area 585-KIDS, or toll-free HOTLINE 1-800-554-KIDS.

· PARENTS' RESOURCE INSTITUTE FOR DRUG EDUCATION, INC. (PRIDE). This national resource and information center offers consultant services to parent groups, school personnel, and service. It conducts an annual conference; publishes a newsletter, youth group handbook, and many other publications; and sells and rents books, films, videos, and slide programs. Membership $8. Woodruff Bldg., Suite 1002, 100 Edgewood Avenue, Atlanta, GA 30303. Telephone 1-800-241-9746.

· TARGET. Conducted by the National Federation of State High School Associations, an organization of interscholastic activities associations. TARGET offers workshops, training seminars, and an information bank on chemical abuse and prevention. A computerized referral service to substance abuse literature and prevention programs [began] operating in 1987. National Federation of State High School Associations, 11724 Plaza Circle, P.O. Box 20626, Kansas City, MO 64195. Telephone (816) 464-5400.

· TOUGHLOVE. This national self-help group for parents, children, and communities emphasizes cooperation, personal initiative, avoidance of blame, and action. It publishes a newsletter and a number of brochures and books and holds workshops across the country each year. P.O. Box 1069, Doylestown, PA 18901. Telephone (215) 348-7090.

· U.S. CLEARINGHOUSES. (A publication list is available on request, along with placement on mailing list for new publications. Single copies are free).

National Institute on Alcoholism and Alcohol Abuse (NIAAA), P.O. Box 2345, Rockville, MD 20852. Telephone (301) 468-2600.

National Institute on Drug Abuse (NIDA), Room 10-A-43, 5600 Fishers Lane, Rockville, MD 20852. Telephone (301) 443-6500.

From U.S. Department of Education, 1986.

peer influence. There is evidence that some adolescents may be prone to drug abuse who place little trust or credence in adult-run institutions (e.g., they do poorly in school), place a high value on independence (in this case, no trusting relationships with adults), and spend considerable time away from home, including evenings (Jessor, Chase, and Donovan, 1980; Bachman, 1982). In addition, there is evidence that adolescents are more likely to drink or smoke if their peers and parents do so (Barnes, 1977; Kandel, 1978; Brook, Whiteman, and Gordon, 1983).

It is important to keep in mind that adolescent *personality factors* may interact with *socialization experiences* (in the family and with peers) to produce alcohol/drug abuse. For example, there is evidence that both peer and parental influences may overlap or interact to influence the adolescent's drug-related behaviors. Adolescents whose parents drink are more likely to associate with friends who also drink (Brook, Whiteman, and Gordon, 1983). Thus, it is not the simple situation (as many parents believe) that peers "force" unwilling and naive adolescents into alcohol or drug abuse. As we suggested in our earlier discussion of friendship development and clique formation (see Chapter 15), the adolescent's *predisposition* for certain values and behaviors (e.g., attitudes toward smoking or drinking) is an important determinant of friendship formation and influence by peers. However, once predisposed adolescents join peer groups in which drug use is a common and acceptable pattern of behavior, such peer activities can become powerful influences on their lives. In fact, there is evidence that by middle adolescence, the strength of this peer influence increases to the point where parental admonitions against drug use may be virtually ineffective compared with peer encouragement (Braucht, 1980; Adler and Kandel, 1982). As we have noted, this places adolescents in a particularly vulnerable position regarding automobile accidents or delinquent behaviors. However, there is a drop-off in alcohol/drug use by the time the adolescents reach (if they do) young adulthood (Zucker, 1979). Typically, this drop-off has been associated with the movement of adolescents into roles such as marriage or work, which encourage responsibility rather than alcohol or drug use.

The Suicidal Adolescent

Suicide is the third leading cause of death in adolescence (after automobile accidents and murder) (Santrock, 1984). As is the case for adult suicides, more females than males attempt suicide, but more males succeed in committing suicide (Weiner, 1982). In addition, most suicide attempters inform at least one person that they are considering suicide. Thus, it becomes particularly important for parents, teachers, and peers to "listen" carefully for such warnings and to take them seriously.

As with alcohol/drug abuse, there are no simple explanations for adolescent suicide. Typically, adolescents who attempt suicide have been struggling with problems. These problems may be generally referred to as serious identity concerns. For example, some suicide attempters have extreme problems relating to their parents (or have problems deriving from the parents' relationship with one another). Others may be described as alienated from peers, society, and, ultimately, from themselves (Schiamberg, 1986). Others have difficulty dealing with academic pressures at school (Weiner, 1982). Many such students believe they are not doing as well as they should, although, in fact, they are better-than-average students (Weiner, 1982). In the end, they become intensely involved in identity struggles with which they cannot cope.

The thought of a teenager's destroying his young life is so appalling that one tends to minimize the extent of this problem. However, the adolescent suicide rate has generally risen; the rate per 100,000 population for 15-to-24-year-olds was 13.9 for white males in 1970 and 21.2 in 1982, 10.5 for black males in 1970 and 11.0

in 1982. The rate for females per 100,000 population was 4.2 for white females in 1970 and 4.5 in 1982 and 3.8 for black females in 1970 and 2.2 in 1982. (U.S. Department of Commerce, Bureau of the Census, 1985d, p. 78).

These figures become even more alarming when we realize that many suicides are not recorded as suicides but may be recorded as accidents. For example, a physician may be reluctant to report a death as a suicide in order to "protect" a family he or she has served for a number of years. A death by suicide may be interpreted by the parents as a personal failure, whereas accidental death does not carry as heavy a burden of guilt.

POSSIBLE DANGER SIGNS.   Truancy from school and running away from home could be signs of a troubled teenager. Other signs to watch for are:

- Exaggerated or extended apathy, inactivity, or boredom.
- Subtle signs of self-destructive behavior, such as carelessness and accident-proneness.
- Loss of appetite or excessive eating.
- Decrease in verbal communication.
- Withdrawal from peer activities and from previously enjoyed activities.
- Substance abuse (drugs, alcohol).
- Sleep disturbance (nightmares, difficulty falling asleep, early morning awakening).
- Academic decline.
- Unusually long grief reaction following a loss (death, divorce, girlfriend/boyfriend relationship).
- Tearfulness.
- Depressive feelings such as sadness or discouragement, when they are more than transient, and especially if found in association with the breakdown of relationships with significant others.
- Recent hostile behavior (e.g., arguments with parents, unruly behavior in school).
- Recent increase in interpersonal conflict with significant others.
- A decrease in or inability to tolerate frustration.

Almost any sustained deviation from the normal pattern of behavior should be taken seriously and evaluated further (Hart and Keidel, 1979, p. 80).

Summary

1. One way to describe identity is as a *self-structure* or an *internal organization* of values, abilities, feelings, and prior experiences. Identity change during the adolescent years is intensified by the many significant transitions that occur in adolescence. It is important to keep in mind that identity formation neither begins nor ends in adolescence. The development of identity is a gradual and continuous process.
2. According to Marcia (1980), there are four *identity statuses* or modes of dealing with the identity questions of late adolescence. There is some agreement that the minimal or basic ingredients of identity development in adolescence

include a commitment to an *occupational/vocational* direction, a commitment to a *sexual orientation,* and a commitment to an *ideological stance.*

3. In order to fully understand the nature of occupational identity in adolescence, it is necessary to discuss two related perspectives: a *developmental perspective* (or the changes in the individual's vocational self-concept from childhood through adolescence) and a *social context perspective* (or the historical and social changes in the world of work that influence the adolescent's occupational/ vocational choices).

   In addition to an occupational identity, the adolescent also is involved in the refinement of a *sexual identity.* It has been suggested that adolescents are cognitively capable of examining current and emerging sex-role patterns and selecting from among these various alternatives.

   One of the consequences of the adolescent search for identity is the clarification of values. Changes in adolescent thinking provide the foundation for the development of a philosophy of life.

   An understanding of female identity involves an examination of at least two issues. How applicable are Marcia's *four identity statuses* to female identity development? Do male and female adolescents resolve identity questions in different ways?

4. Personality development in adolescence is related to a number of psychosocial factors including *autonomy* and *sexuality.* For most adolescents the establishment of a sense of independence or autonomy is an important prerequisite for building and refining identity. There is some evidence for a threefold definition of autonomy including emotional autonomy, behavioral autonomy, and value autonomy.

   Sexuality as an element of adolescent personality development includes the following dimensions: adolescent sexual values and attitudes, adolescent sexual behaviors, adolescent use of contraceptives, adolescent sex education, and teenage pregnancy.

5. Some adolescents have difficulty establishing a consistent identity. These difficulties are frequently manifested in behaviors that lead to serious disruptions in the lives of adolescents and their families. It is important to distinguish between such serious identity problems (e.g., drug abuse, delinquency, and suicide) and the more normal adolescent struggles including occasional anxiety or identity diffusion.

Key Terms

Androgynous	Identity
Autonomy	Identity achievement
Behavioral autonomy	Identity diffusion
Commitment	Moratorium
Crisis	Sexual identity
"Double standard"	Sexuality
Emotional autonomy	Value autonomy
Foreclosure	Vocational exploration
Gender-intensification hypothesis	Vocational maturity

Questions

1. Define and discuss the four identity statuses identified by Marcia.
2. Discuss occupational identity.
3. What is meant by value autonomy?
4. What is meant by the "double standard"?
5. Compare and contrast male and female identity.
6. What factors influence adolescent contraceptive use?
7. What developmental characteristics separate "hard-core" or chronic delinquents from adolescents who do such things as occasionally smoke marijuana?

Suggested Readings

ADAMS, G. R., and GULLOTTA, T. *Adolescent Life Experiences.* Monterey, Calif.: Brooks/Cole, 1983. A comprehensive and readable introduction to adolescent development and issues.

BYRNE, D., and FISHER, W. A. *Adolescents, Sex and Contraception.* Hillsdale, N.J.: Erlbaum, 1983. An excellent discussion of the factors affecting adolescent contraceptive use.

ELSTER, A. B., and LAMB, M. E. *Adolescent Fatherhood.* Hillsdale, N.J.: Erlbaum, 1986. A collection of well-written essays on research relating to adolescent fathers.

FOX, G. L. "The Family Context of Adolescent Sexuality and Sex Roles." In Leigh, G. K., and Peterson, G. W. (eds.), *Families in Adolescence.* Cincinnati, Ohio: South-Western, 1986, pp. 179–204.

GILLIGAN, C. *In a Different Voice: Psychological Theory and Women's Development.* Cambridge, Mass.: Harvard University Press, 1982. An excellent discussion of the place of female development in the study of human development.

HAYES, C. D. (ed.). *Risking the Future: Adolescent Sexuality, Pregnancy and Childbearing.* Washington, D.C.: National Academy Press, 1987. An excellent collection of essays on teenage pregnancy.

KIMMEL, D. C., and WEINER, I. B. *Adolescence: A Developmental Transition.* Hillsdale, N.J.: Erlbaum, 1985. This book presents theories, facts, and concepts relating to adolescent development.

MARCIA, J. E., WATERMAN, A. S., and MATTESON, D. R. *Ego Identity: A Handbook for Psychosocial Research.* Hillsdale, N.J.: Erlbaum, forthcoming. An excellent discussion of the factors influencing adolescent identity development.

SCHIAMBERG, L. *A Family Systems Perspective to Adolescent Alienation.* In Leigh, G. K., and Peterson, G. W. (eds.), *Adolescents in Families.* Cincinnati, Ohio: South-Western, 1986, pp. 277–307. A comprehensive discussion of adolescent alienation in the family context.

Epilogue

"The game ain't over 'til it's over."
—Yogi Berra

We have just completed a textbook journey from the very beginnings of life through the adolescent years, traveling from conception through the moment of birth, the infant/toddler's first steps and first words, the child's first day in school, and the onset of puberty to the adolescent's first steps toward autonomy and maturity. Our unique journey has:

- Examined child development from a lifespan perspective.
- Presented an ecological or systems perspective of child and adolescent growth and development.
- Attempted to capture the *reality* of children/adolescents and their families, teachers, and friends.

The Lifespan Perspective

We have emphasized the importance of a lifespan approach to child and adolescent development, although the time period on which we have focused (birth to the late teens or early twenties) is approximately 20 percent of the average life expectancy of almost 80 years. Many vital changes occur during childhood and adolescence, but development certainly does not grind to a halt during the remaining years of life. Human beings continue to develop and change throughout the adult years, and many such changes cannot be predicted simply from knowledge of a child's or adolescent's development. For example, there is evidence of considerable diversity in the pattern of intellectual change throughout adulthood and the aging years, with differences in individual intellectual performance becoming greater in the adult years (compared to the differences between the same individuals as children or adolescents).

Our lifespan perspective takes into account the facts that the development and behavior of human beings is not a simple result of chronological age and that individuals born at different times in history have probably experienced during childhood and adolescence unique historical circumstances that resulted in paths of development differing from those born at other times.

The lifespan perspective includes the influence of life events: both *normative* (that occur for most individuals at a specific time or range of times) and *nonnormative* events (that occur for some, but not all, individuals at almost any time) influence developmental change across the lifespan.

A Systems or Ecological Perspective

Our "systems" or "ecological" perspective of development emphasizes the mutual interaction of the individual and the significant contexts of development. Many of the important phases of the lifespan—including childhood and adolescence—are strongly influenced by the *reciprocal* and *dynamic interaction* between children and the enduring contexts of their lives (family, school, peer group, and community/neighborhood).

During our journey, we have seen many instances in which a systems or ecological viewpoint can be usefully applied to the study of child and adolescent development. Examples included:

- The *birth of the infant*, which can be viewed as a process involving the reciprocal interaction of the new parents (their individual characteristics or personal histories) and the organized environment for childbirth (type of hospital delivery practices, sensitivity of the hospital to the needs of families, and so on).
- The *attachment* of the infant to its caregiver, or the dynamic and reciprocal interaction of such infant characteristics as temperament, and such parent behaviors as visual gazing and touch.
- The *success of the child in the elementary school*, which can be viewed as a reciprocal and dynamic interaction and adaptation of the characteristics of the child to those of the school. Some children seem to do very well in traditional, teacher-structured classrooms, whereas others do better in less structured or open arrangements.
- The ability of the *later adolescent or young adult to leave home successfully* for work or schooling, which is in part a function of the reciprocal relationship between the characteristics of the adolescent and the functioning of the family as a system in its own right.

We have seen the role of such social contexts of development as family, work, school, and neighborhood in the development of the child and adolescent. This is a unique and necessary perspective, because the study of child development is certainly more than simply describing changes in children over time. A more complete understanding—and practical application—of the concepts of child and adolescent development requires serious attention to the *progressive interaction* and *mutual adaptation* of children and adolescents to their social contexts. Much as biologists and zoologists have successfully described and studied the *ecology* or mutual relationships between plant and animal life and their environments or habitats, the study of child development becomes much richer, more accurate, and more practically useful with the application of a systems perspective. However, unlike the ecological analysis of plant and animal life, the ecology of child development focuses on the widely diverse manmade or culturally evolved environment (including schools, computers, and television) that influences child and adolescent development.

The Reality of Child and Adolescent Development

One of our goals has been to capture some of the reality of child development, an objective best accomplished by emphasizing both the lifespan and systems/ecological perspectives. We are most likely to approach a complete and accurate understanding of the developing child insofar as we are able to more fully and accurately identify not only the changes in the developing child (the focus of most child-development textbooks) but also the *lifespan* dimensions and the *ecological* contexts of development.

Some New Directions in the Study of Child and Adolescent Development

The widening challenges of the lifespan and systems/ecological perspectives have created impetus for changes in the study of child and adolescent development. Here are a few themes that may be at the forefront of the field in future years.

• *Cognitive Development as Mutual Collaboration.* The study of cognitive development has traditionally attributed cognitive change either to the child or to environmental circumstances. However, a few cognitive theorists have introduced the concept of *collaboration*: that human beings are social creatures who work together (collaborate) on common goals. During such efforts, there emerges a social system characterized both by mutual following (of one another's behaviors) and by mutual support, so solutions to cognitive problems reflect the joint contributions of each individual.

Furthermore, even when individuals are involved alone in an activity, the non-personal environment plays a significant role as a collaborator. Every environment is organized—whether by intent or not—to foster some behaviors over others. For example, a child's playground that has swings and slides but no climbing bars obviously makes possible some motor behaviors and not others. The analogy can be extended to much of the human environment, which is socially constructed in such a way as to support or encourage some behaviors. Such social constructions are sometimes referred to as the *human factors* of a learning experience. Examples include the design of human tools and buildings to facilitate certain types of interaction. Although we have here mentioned only cognitive development as collaboration, many other aspects of child and adolescent development might also have been noted. For example, the attachment between caretaker and infant, friendship formation in childhood and adolescence (Gottman, 1985), and the adolescent leaving home.

• *The Contribution of the Family to Child and Adolescent Development.* As part of the focus on the ecology of child development, increasing attention has been given to the dynamic relationship between the developing child/adolescent and the family. We have explored this reciprocal relationship throughout this book in such areas as parent–child interaction, parent disciplinary practices, and adolescent–parent conflict. An understanding of these interactive relationships is further enhanced by the concept of the *family as a system* in its own right. This concept provides a fruitful basis for understanding, interpreting, and clarifying the role of the family as a context of development.

Several characteristics of such a family system that are pertinent here (Kantor and Lehr [1975]):

1. *Organizational Complexity.* Families develop networks of interdependent relationships that involve reciprocal interactions. These relationship networks may be *internal* (between members of a family) or *external* (between the family, as a unit, and such institutions as schools, health-care specialists, and other families). Such interactional networks are *rule-governed* in the sense that formal or informal "understandings" organize these relationships (some families may have authoritarian "rule" structures while others have democratic styles of family interaction and decision making).

2. *Openness.* The family is an "open" system because it depends on mutual interaction with external resources to develop maximally. The family is both influenced by external factors and influences those factors. However, in order for the family to accomplish its many functions (including childrearing, economic maintenance, and so on), interaction with external institutions is necessary.

3. *Adaptiveness.* Open family systems develop as a result of interaction with forces outside the family as well as adjustments within the family system (the need for both parents to adjust to requirements of work, for example, necessitates adaptation of roles within the family). The adaptiveness of the family ensures its survival.

Those who study and work with children and adolescents and their problems (runaways, drug abusers, delinquents, and so on) have become increasingly aware of the relationship between these problems and the viability of the child or adolescent's family. Some of the most revealing findings have come from investigators who have examined the process of adolescents leaving home (the successful development of adolescent autonomy, which is at the core of adolescent identity formation, competence in school and work, and the formation of intimate relationships outside the family). The success of the adolescent in leaving home seems to depend more on the positive characteristics of the adolescent's *family system* than on the unique characteristics of the adolescent's personality.

• *The Relationship between Knowledge of Child and Adolescent Development and Public Policy Decisions.* A third, but by no means final, theme of interest to current and future child development study is the relationship between research in child development and the development or modification of public policy. One of the enduring and significant contexts of child and adolescent development are public policies in the broad culture that influence the quality of development. Although we may consider ourselves a society that places priority on the welfare of children and families, many of our social policies suggest a subtle (although perhaps unintentional) bias against children and families. For example, many urban-renewal projects have resulted in the destruction of neighborhood social networks (which traditionally support family childrearing functions). Corporate or business policies still often require rigid and inflexible working hours, making it difficult for many parents to be at home when children need them. The limited range of choices in quality child care and the related absence of a formal social/government policy toward day care make working problematic for many parents of infants and young children. These and other policy issues will require the informed knowledge of those who understand how children grow and develop in the significant contexts of life—the ecology of child and adolescent development.

Appendix

Glossary

Acknowledgments

References

Author Index

Subject Index

Glossary

Acceptance-rejection A dimension of parent behavior that deals with the emotional relationships between the parent and the child. Such a relationship can vary from accepting and responsive (warm) parental behavior (focused on the child's needs) on the one hand to rejecting and unresponsive (hostile) parental behavior (focused on the parent's needs) on the other hand.

Accommodation In Piaget's theory of intelligence, the process of modifying existing schema in order to account for the novel properties of objects or events. See also *Assimilation.*

Achieved roles Roles that are characterized by individual attainment (outstanding student, popular group member, and so on).

Achievement motivation Refers to an "internal disposition to improve or maintain a high level of performance with respect to standards of excellence (this limits achievement to activities in which success or failure is possible)" (Solomon, 1982, p. 270).

Acuity (visual) The ability to see objects clearly and to resolve detail.

Adaptation In Piaget's cognitive theory, the adjustment of behavior to environmental circumstances. See also *Organization.*

Adaptiveness Changes and adjustments in family systems as a consequence of interaction with the external environment.

Adduction The action of drawing a body limb toward or past the median axis of the body.

Adolescence The period of development that begins with the onset of puberty and ends with the legal, social, and psychological status of adulthood.

Adolescent growth spurt A period of time marked by a substantial increase in the rate of growth. See also *Puberty.*

Adrenal glands Two ductless glands located one above each kidney. See also *Adrenal medulla* and *Epinephrine.*

Adrenal medulla The inner portion of the adrenal gland which secretes epinephrine. See also *Adrenal glands* and *Epinephrine.*

Adventure (or "junk") play setting In this setting, children create their own play equipment from objects such as old tires, lumber and used packing crates, rocks, and bricks.

Affect The emotion, feeling, or mood of a person.

Afterbirth This includes the placenta, its membranes, and the remainder of the umbilical cord, all of which are expelled in the final stage of labor.

Age of viability At seven months or twenty-eight weeks, the average fetus attains the age of viability. That is, the baby is capable of independent life and is likely to survive if born then.

Ainsworth's Strange Situation Test A standardized laboratory technique for assessing attachment.

Alimentary canal Those organs that compose the food tubes in man and animals.

Allele Any of several possible genes found at a given position or locus on a chromosome.

Alphafetoprotein assay The level of alphafetoprotein (AFP) in the mother's blood can be determined using a simple blood test. An elevated AFP level is frequently associated with neural-tube defects in the fetus (e.g., anencephaly, where part of the brain and skull is missing, and spina bifida, where the lower portion of the spine is not closed over). However, since elevated AFP levels are also related to the age of the fetus and the number of fetuses present, it is not a conclusive indicator of a problem.

Altruism Altruism is a variation of prosocial behavior in which a person expects or anticipates no external reward. See also *Prosocial behavior.*

Amino acids Substances from which organisms build proteins.

Amniocentesis A means of detecting fetal abnormalities by inserting a hollow needle through the abdomen of the pregnant women and withdrawing a sample of amniotic fluid for analysis.

Amnion The inner membrane of the sac that surrounds and protects the developing ovum and fetus.

Amniotic fluid A liquid in the amnion in which the developing fetus is suspended and protected from external jarring as well as from any pressure exerted by the mother's internal organs.

Anal stage In the psychoanalytical theory of Freud, the

second stage of psychosexual development during which the central features of development focus on elimination or toilet-training activities.

Androgens   Male hormones produced by the testes (in increased amounts during puberty).

Androgyny   Refers to a sex-role orientation that includes many traditionally masculine and traditionally feminine attributes in one personality.

Androgynous   See *Androgyny*.

Anemia   A reduction in the number of red blood cells or in their hemoglobin (the oxygen-carrying protein of red blood cells) content resulting in reduced transport of oxygen to the cells of the body.

Anorexia nervosa   A serious disorder that results from a disturbed and inaccurate body image (i.e., an incorrectly perceived deviation from a body ideal). See also *Body ideal*.

Anovulatory   Refers to menstrual cycles after the first menarche in which no egg or ovum is released by an ovary.

Anoxia   A lack of oxygen. It is a major problem that can occur for any long or stressful birth.

Antigens   A substance that causes the production of an antibody when introduced into the body.

Anxious/avoidant infants (insecure)   Using Ainsworth's Strange Situation Test, one of three attachment types characterized by infants for whom exploration is a stronger and more prominent response than attachment. See also *Ainsworth's Strange Situation Test*.

Anxious/resistant infants (insecure)   Using Ainsworth's Strange Situation Test, one of three attachment types characterized by infants for whom attachment is a stronger and more prominent response than exploration. See also *Ainsworth's Strange Situation Test*.

Apgar Test   A commonly used measure for assessing appearance, heart rate, activity, muscle tone, reflex irritability, and respiration in the newborn infant. The sum total of the score can vary from 0 to 10 points.

Areola   The area immediately around the female breast nipple.

Ascribed characteristics   Factors such as a child's sex, sibling relationship, name, and so on.

Assimilation   In Piaget's theory of cognitive development, the incorporation of the novel aspects of objects or events into existing schemata or structures of intelligence. See also *Accommodation*.

Association areas   Locations or sites in the brain that organize specific sensory functions such as touch, hearing, vision, and speech.

Attachment   The primary social bond that develops between the infant and its caretaker.

Authoritarian (parent)   A parenting style characterized by a high level of power assertiveness, rejecting, or unresponsive behaviors toward the child.

Authoritative (parent)   A parenting style characterized by a high level of reciprocity, bidirectional communication, and acceptance of the child.

Autonomic nervous system   A division of the nervous system which regulates vital internal organs. It operates involuntarily. See also *Central nervous system (CNS)* and *Sympathetic nervous system*.

Autonomy   The ability of the human being to self-regulate, or determine its own behavior.

Autonomy versus shame and doubt   The second of Erikson's stages of development (eighteen months to three years) in which the environment may encourage independence leading to a sense of pride.

Autosomes   All chromosomes with the exception of sex chromosomes.

Axon   A transmitter that carries impulses away from the neuron. It is a single long fiber transmitting messages away from the cell body to the next nerve cell body or neuron. See also *Neurons*.

Babbling   Infant vocalizations that occur at approximately three or four months of age and that are combinations of consonant and vowel sounds (kaka, dada, and so on).

Babinski reflex   A response of the newborn infant in which the toes extend or fan out when the sole of the foot is gently stroked. As the infant's nervous system matures, the toes will curl downward when the sole of the foot is stroked.

Basic gender identity   By about three years, the child is able to *label* his or her own gender *correctly*. In other words, the child knows whether he or she is a boy or a girl. Correct labeling does not imply that the child understands the full meaning of sex-role identity.

Bayley Scales of Infant Development   A test of infant intelligence that is divided into three parts: a mental scale, a motor scale, and a behavioral profile.

Behavior   Any human action or reaction in relation to internal, external, or self-generated stimulation (includes complex social and biological activities).

Behavioral autonomy   Refers to the adolescent's ability to make independent decisions and to carry them out and to the adolescent's susceptibility to peer pressure.

Behavioral stages   The concept of behavioral stages emerged from Gesell's notion that maturation represented the unfolding of interweaving growth forces.

Behavior and learning theories   In contrast to maturation theories, behavior and learning theories portray human behavior as primarily the result of environmental stimulation. Much of what an individual becomes is the result of what he or she has experienced or learned. See also *Maturation theories*.

Behaviorism   The school of psychology that emphasizes that an organism's behavior is largely the result of the learning produced by external factors such as reinforcement.

Behavior modification   The use of concepts from learning theory, in particular, reinforcement, association, and repetition to change behavior.

Blastocyst (blastula)   A hollow ball of a cells that has developed from the fertilized egg. This stage of development lasts for about a week after conception, until the sphere is implanted in the uterine wall. During the blastocyst period, cells begin to differentiate.

Body ideal The standard of comparison frequently used by adolescents to evaluate their body image. See also *Body image.*

Body image The adolescent's perceptions of his or her physique and appearance. See also *Body ideal.*

Body (somatic) cells Cells that are produced through the process of cell division called mitosis. See also *Mitosis* and *Sex (germ) cells.*

Bonding hypothesis Refers to the presumed establishment of an affectionate and long-lasting attachment of a mother toward her infant during a sensitive or critical period lasting for a few hours immediately after birth.

Brain differentiation Refers to the varying rates of development of the different parts of the brain.

Brain hemispheres The cerebrum (the highest brain center) is composed of two halves, called hemispheres, that are connected by a band of fibers called corpus callosum. See also *Cerebrum* and *Corpus callosum.*

Brain lateralization See *Lateralization.*

Brain stem At birth, the most developed area is the brain stem (composed, from top to bottom, of the midbrain, the pons, and the medulla). This brain area controls such functions as inborn reflexes, states of consciousness, digestion, elimination, and respiration.

Brain waves The specific pattern of electrical activity in the brain associated with a given physiological state (quiet sleep, active sleep, alert wakefulness, and so on).

Brazelton Neonatal Behavioral Assessment Scale The Brazelton scale assesses the way newborns adapt to their environment. It measures four areas of infant behavior: home-related adaptive behaviors, motor behaviors, response to stress, and control of physiological state.

Canalization A model for the development of genetic traits in which such traits can be thought of as a ball rolling down a canal. When the canals are fairly deep, the environment will have limited influence in changing the direction of the ball. At other times (sensitive periods) when the canals are shallow, the environment may play a significant role.

Case study An intensive study of one individual.

Categorical self The definition of self on dimensions such as age, gender, activity, preferences, and values.

Causality The child's cognitive ability to attribute a source, explanation, motive, or reason for a given event.

Centering The tendency in thinking to concentrate on some outstanding or prominent characteristics of an object to the exclusion of other characteristics.

Central nervous system (CNS) The brain, spinal cord, and the nerves arising from each. See also *Autonomic nervous system* and *Sympathetic nervous system.*

Centration The tendency to focus on one dimension of a problem while overlooking other aspects that would be useful in developing a solution.

Cephalocaudal development Physical growth and motor development that occurs from the head downward.

Cerebellum The part of the brain concerned with the smooth and even performance of voluntary movements.

Cerebral cortex The major portion of the brain that occupies the upper part of the cranium. It contains the most highly developed functions of the nervous system, including intelligence and memory, and the centers for sight, hearing, smell, taste, and general body sensations.

Cerebral dominance The fact that one hemisphere (half of the brain) prevails over the other in terms of the control of body movements or regulation of other behaviors.

Cerebrum The cerebrum surrounds the brain stem. This area is involved in bodily movement, perception, and the higher cognitive activities such as language production, learning, and thinking.

Cervix The narrow canal connecting the vagina and the uterus.

Cesarean delivery A surgical operation in which the walls of the abdomen and uterus are cut for the purpose of delivering a child.

Child-care centers Centers that provide supplemental care for children from infancy through kindergarten age during the typical working hours of parents.

Chorion The outer membrane of the sac that surrounds and protects the developing fertilized egg.

Chorion villus sampling In this relatively new procedure (used since 1983), a catheter or slender tube is inserted into the vagina. A tiny piece of tissue is then taken from the chorion (the membrane surrounding the embryo) and analyzed to determine if any fetal disorders are present.

Chromosomes The thin, rod-like strings of genes present in the nucleus of each cell of the human body which contain the genetic material necessary for directing cell activities.

Chronic illness or disability An illness or disability that significantly disables or limits the character and/or quality of a normal life-style. Certain disorders may limit the performance of an ordinary activity such as walking or breathing. Examples of chronic illnesses or disabilities include seizure disorders, bronchial asthma, cystic fibrosis, muscular dystrophy, cerebral palsy, and juvenile rheumatoid arthritis.

Classical conditioning Occurs with the formation of conditioned reflexes by associating a previously neutral stimulus (e.g., the sound of a bell) with an unconditioned stimulus (e.g., food). Because the conditioned stimulus (the sound of the bell) is repeatedly presented just before the unconditioned stimulus (food), an individual begins to respond to the conditioned stimulus just as it had originally responded to the unconditioned stimulus.

Classification The cognitive ability to organize objects into groups or classes according to their characteristics.

Clique A small grouping of two, three, or four friends that gives the adolescent the chance to establish some degree of companionship, security, and acceptance before moving out into the larger social scene or crowd. See also *Crowd.*

Cognitive development The qualitative and quantitative

changes throughout the lifespan in thinking, organizing perceptions, and problem solving.

Cognitive map   An internal mental representation of the environment.

Cognitive mapping skills   The child's spatial conception of the environment.

Cognitive theory   A cognitive approach to learning and human development emphasizes mental (or internal) factors as contrasted with the environment (or external factors) of the traditional behaviorists.

Cohort   In the design of research, a group of individuals born at the same time or during the same historical period.

Collaboration   With reference to cognitive development, the cooperation and mutual contributions of two or more people in problem solving.

Commitment   According to the identity formation theory of James Marcia, the extent of personal investment in an occupation, a set of religious values, or a political position. See also *Crisis*.

Competence   The feeling or sense that a person is capable of exercising mastery over the environment.

Complex genetic transmission   The interaction of many genes to produce human traits.

Conception   The union of sperm and egg signaling the beginning of life.

Concrete operational period   In Piaget's theory of cognitive development, the stage that begins when the child can use thought processes involving reversible transformations of actual or concrete objects or events in his or her immediate experience.

Conflicted-irritable children   Child behavior associated with authoritarian parent behavior and characterized by fearfulness, vulnerability to stress, irritability, and so on.

Congenital   Refers to the characteristics or defects acquired during the period of gestation and persisting after birth as distinguished from those characteristics acquired by heredity.

Congenital defects.   See *Congenital*.

Conservation   The realization that changes in perceptual characteristics of an object or objects do not change the real physical characteristics of that object or those objects. For example, rearranging one row of objects into two rows does not change the number of objects.

Contraception   The voluntary prevention of pregnancy.

Contractions   The means through which labor and delivery occur. They are the movements of the uterus by means of which the cervix is opened and the baby is expelled or delivered.

Control   The intentional manipulation of any condition of a research investigation such as the selection of participants or subjects.

Conventional level or stage   The stage or level of moral reasoning in which correct or moral behavior means the maintenance of the standard social order and expectations of others. See also *Postconventional level* and *Preconventional level*.

Cooing   Infant vocalizations that occur around three to five weeks; composed of vowel sounds such as "eeee" or "oooo."

Coordination of secondary schemas   The fourth substage of Piaget's sensori-motor stage of intelligence which involves the coordination or organization of existing schemas into intentional means-ends sequences such that one schema leads to another. See also *Schema*.

Coping   The behavioral and cognitive strategies one adopts in response to the demands of a given situation.

Coregulation   In Maccoby's three-stage model describing the shift in power from parent to child (adolescent), the second stage is called coregulation and occurs when the child is six to twelve years of age. During this stage, power is shared between parent and child.

Corpus callosum   A band of fiber that connects both halves or hemispheres of the brain. See also *Brain hemispheres*.

Correlational study   In situations where the use of experimental methods are difficult or impossible, experimenters can still examine the relationships between certain events or variables. The term *correlational study* is often used to describe such studies of factors that are not manipulated, per se.

Correlation coefficient   A statistical index for measuring the relationship or correspondence between changes in two variables. A perfect correspondence is $+1.00$; no correspondence is 0.00; a perfect correspondence in opposite directions is -1.00.

Crib death   This little-understood syndrome results in the death of approximately 7,000 to 10,000 young babies each year. The babies (usually six months of age or younger) typically die in their sleep with no clear or apparent cause for death (also called sudden infant death syndrome, or SIDS).

Crisis   According to the identity formation theory of James Marcia, a decision-making period involving the examination of alternatives. See also *Commitment*.

Critical periods   The critical period hypothesis suggests that there are specific time periods when the potential for growth and development (as well as damage from the environment) is maximal.

Crossing over   The tendency of chromosomes to exchange genes prior to cell division.

Cross-sectional design   Research that compares different age groups (e.g., eight-, ten-, and twelve-year-olds) at a specific point in time. See also *Longitudinal design*.

Cross-sequential design   This research design combines both the longitudinal and cross-sectional approaches by initially doing a cross-sectional sample of subjects and then following these same subjects longitudinally over time. See also *Cross-sectional design* and *Longitudinal design*.

Crowd   The larger unit of the peer group (compared with the clique). Most crowd activities are formally organized and occur on weekends.

Crying   A dimension of the caregiver-infant attachment system.

Cultural lag model   A theory of child rearing that posits that since families are exposed to differing pressure for modernization, group differences will emerge in child rearing and other areas.

Cytoplasm   Everything within the cell with the exception of the nucleus.

Decentering   Means that children are able to explore many aspects and viewpoints in looking at objects and in thinking about them.

Deductive reasoning   Reasoning from generalities to specifics.

Deficit hypothesis   In its simplest terms, this hypothesis suggests that the well-documented failure of many black children (particularly in school) is the result of an "impoverished" language.

Delivery of the placenta   The third stage of labor is the delivery of the placenta, or the expulsion of the afterbirth.

Dendrites   Receivers that carry nerve impulses toward the neuron. See also *Neurons*.

Dependence   The reliance on other people for assistance, nurturance, or comfort.

Dependent variable   The behavior resulting from the manipulation of the independent variable(s) which is of interest to a researcher. See also *Independent variables*.

Deprivation dwarfism   The reduction in the secretion of growth hormone and the accompanying decline in growth resulting from emotional stress in children. See also *Somatotrophin*.

Designed play setting   Includes traditional activities such as swings and slides that are integrated into a continuous sculptured pattern, with sand commonly used as a base.

Design stage   In this stage of children's drawing, the child begins to make imaginative arrangements that combine the basic shapes and forms mastered in the previous stage.

Developmental change   Change that meets three criteria: orderly or sequential, permanent, and adaptive.

Developmental task   Refers to a particular learning experience that tends to occur at a given stage of life and that individuals must successfully negotiate to meet cultural requirements.

Diabetes   A deficiency in the ability to utilize insulin so that there may be a high level of sugar in both blood and urine.

Difference hypothesis   This hypothesis asserts that English, like other languages, has a number of forms (dialects), none of which is superior.

Differentiation   This principle of growth suggests that the direction of growth and development is from gross to specific or from simple to complex.

Difficult child   In the New York Longitudinal Study of infant personality, approximately 10 percent of the infant sample was characterized by a temperament pattern opposite that of the easy child. See also *Easy child*.

Dilation   Being stretched or open beyond normal limits.

Disengagement   Family disengagement refers to families that have extremely low levels of cohesion. In such a circumstance, there is little emotional attachment holding the family members together and, therefore, little basis for a relationship. See also *Family cohesion*.

Dizygotic (DZ) twins   Refers to twins that develop from two separate fertilized eggs (fraternal twins). See also *Monozygotic (MZ) twins*.

DNA (deoxyribonucleic acid)   Complex chemical molecules that contain the genetic code or blueprint that determines the makeup of cells.

Dominant gene   A form of a gene that is always expressed in the phenotype when paired with the same or different gene.

"Double standard"   For women, sex is acceptable only in marriage, whereas for men sex is acceptable both in marriage and in casual relationships before marriage.

Down syndrome   A condition resulting from an extra chromosome in the fertilized egg; results in various physical abnormalities and mental retardation in the affected child.

Early adolescence   This period begins with the onset of puberty and extends through the high school years to about seventeen or eighteen years of age. The organizing feature of this stage is the development of a sense of group identity relative to the world of high school peer organization. Thus, the central task is to come to grips with the pressure to join groups.

Easy child   In the New York Longitudinal Study of infant personality, about 40 percent of the infant sample was characterized by a positive mood, high approach, high adaptability, high rhythmicity, and low intensity.

Ecological environment   Includes immediate settings (the home, school, work), interaction between immediate settings (the relationship between home and schools or home and workplace) and larger settings, including the culture (which influences specific settings). The ecological environment is composed of four structural layers. See also *Exosystem, Mesosystem, Macrosystem, and Microsystem*.

Ecological or systems theories   See *Ecology of human development*.

Ecological validity   Being able to generalize or apply the results of a research study to real-life circumstances.

Ecology of human development   As defined by Bronfenbrenner, the ecology of human development is the scientific study of the progressive and mutual accommodation between the human being and the significant contexts in which that person lives.

Ecosystem   Living organisms interacting with their environments.

Ectoderm   The outermost cell layer in the developing embryo from which structures such as the skin and nervous system develop.

Egg   See *Ovum*.

Ego   According to psychoanalytic theory, the ego is the group of personality structures that help the individual relate to reality (i.e., what is happening in the person's actual experiential world). Specifically, the function of the ego is to evaluate the relationship between the wishes and the feelings of the individual and social reality. In practice, this means the ego may control impulses, delay gratification, and/or develop socially acceptable modes of expressing feelings.

Egocentric Egocentric thinking is characterized by the child who focuses on the environment from the perspective of his or her own limited experience.

Egocentrism A self-centered style of thinking in which the individual is unable to consider the point of view of others. According to Piaget, egocentrism is characteristic of the preoperational child.

Ego control According to Block and Block (1980), ego control is "the operating characteristics of an individual with regard to the expression or containment of impulses, feelings and desires." It can be viewed as a continuum going from overcontrol at one extreme to undercontrol at the other. See also *Ego.*

Ego integrity versus despair The eighth of Erikson's psychosocial stages of development in which the older adult can develop a sense of acceptance of life and all that has happened.

Ego resiliency According to Block and Block (1980), ego resiliency is a "resourceful adaptation to changing life situations." This means that the ego-resilient individual can be highly prepared or highly spontaneous, as a given situation requires. See also *Ego control.*

Elaboration A mnemonic device in which items to be remembered are linked in a meaningful order (e.g., memorizing the lines *Every Good Boy Does Fine* helps one remember the treble clef in music, EGBDF).

Electroencephalogram (EEG) The device that measures brain waves; also refers to the graphical representation of such brain waves.

Embryo The period of prenatal life from the second to the eighth week; comes after the germinal period and is followed by the fetal period.

Embryonic stage This stage covers the six-week period from about the end of the second week until about the conclusion of the second month after conception. At the end of this period, the first bone cell is developed and the embryo appears to be a miniature human being. In other words, the embryo has all of its essential parts.

Emotional autonomy Refers to the process of individuation or the adolescent's relinquishing of childhood dependencies on parents as well as childhood conceptions of parental omnipotence.

Empathy Involves reacting to another individual's situation with the same emotion as that other individual. For example, the child who feels sad when another child is sad, happy when another child is happy, and so on, is exhibiting empathy.

Endocrine gland A ductless gland that secretes a hormone directly into the blood.

Endocrine systems Hormone-producing glands which are ductless and use the blood vessels of the body for transporting hormones. There are several endocrine systems, of which the gonads (the glands of the reproductive system—male testes and female ovaries), the adrenal (the adrenal glands), and the hypothalmo-hypophyseal (the hypothalmus and pituitary glands) are particularly important to the processes of puberty. See also *Endocrine gland, Hypothalmus,* and *Pituitary gland.*

Endoderm The innermost of the three cell layers of the embryo from which many visceral organs and the digestive tract develop.

Energetic-friendly children Child behavior associated with the authoritative style of parenting and characterized by self-reliance, cheerfulness, and so on.

Enmeshment Families that are highly cohesive are said to be enmeshed. This means that the life experiences and activities of members of such families are so closely connected and intertwined that there is little emphasis placed on individuality (or individual development.) See also *Family cohesion.*

Environment See *Ecological environment.*

Enzyme A protein that promotes reactions in a living system.

Epigenetic principle According to Erikson's theory, "this principle states that anything that grows has a ground plan and that out of this ground plan the parts arise, each having its time of special ascendancy, until all parts have arisen to form a functioning whole" (Erikson, 1959, p. 52).

Epinephrine A hormone secreted by the adrenal gland which can cause sudden bodily changes during anger or fright. Also called adrenalin. See also *Adrenal glands* and *Adrenal medulla.*

Epiphyses The growth centers of bone which are located at the ends of each bone. When ossification occurs in the epiphyses, bone maturity is complete and bone growth can no longer occur. See also *Ossification.*

Epistemology The branch of philosophy that deals with determining the nature of human knowledge.

Epocrine glands Sweat glands which continue to develop during adolescence and which produce a body odor not present before puberty.

Equilibrium According to Piaget, the process of equilibrium formation is the general mechanism that explains the transition from one developmental stage to the next one. The specific mechanism is the process of adaptation (i.e., assimilation and accommodation).

Erythroblastosis fetalis The disease that results from untreated Rh factor incompatibility.

Estrogens Female hormones produced by the ovaries (in increased amounts during puberty).

Ethnicity The characteristics of groups and individuals based on differences in such factors as language, customs, cultural background, and so on.

Exosystem This system includes the primary social structures that influence the developing person. The exosystem would be the formal and informal institutions such as political/governmental structures, neighborhood and community organizations, transportation networks, and the informal communication networks within neighborhoods, communities, and workplaces.

Expanded functioning model According to this perspective, the educational level of parents leads to new and improved skills in thinking and communication in working with children.

Experimental method Designed to provide an investigator with control over the subjects and the conditions in a study. A primary advantage of experimental research compared with naturalistic studies is that the standardized procedures of experiments ensure that the study can be repeated or replicated by other investigators. See also *Dependent variable* and *Independent variables.*

Expulsion (the stage of) The second stage of labor which begins when the cervix is completely dilated at ten centimeters and ends when the child is born. At this time, contractions are usually sixty to seventy seconds in duration.

Extended family The family that consists of three generations (parents, children, and grandparents) and, in some cases, other blood relatives all living under the same roof.

Eye-hand coordination The ability to integrate visual and motor activities for reaching and grasping.

Fallopian tube The tube that conveys eggs from the ovary to the uterus; fertilization occurs in the Fallopian tube.

Family adaptability Refers to the general characteristics of the whole family system to reorganize (i.e., change power structure, rules of interaction, and so on) in response to stress from specific situations or developmental changes in family members (e.g., adolescence). Family adaptability can be thought of as a single dimension moving from chaotic interaction at one extreme to rigid interaction at the other extreme.

Family cohesion Refers to the extent of emotional bonding occurring between family members. Family cohesion can be thought of as a single dimension or continuum going from enmeshment (extreme connectedness of family members) to disengagement (extreme separateness of family members). See also *Disengagement* and *Enmeshment.*

Family day-care homes Regulated by a local or state agency. Some states permit family group care, which allows the mother to hire an assistant and enroll more children. Family day care is the service of choice for many families. It often allows care for school-age children, who attend after school.

Family developmental tasks Growth responsibilities that must be accomplished by a family at a given stage of its development.

Family functions The typical responsibilities or activities of the family as a unit (e.g., care for and socialization of children, reproduction, and emotional support of family members).

Family of orientation The family to which one is born.

Family of procreation The family an individual starts as an adult.

Family system A set of components (family members) characterized by reciprocal interaction (within the family and between the family and an external environment) and a set of "rules" that govern or regulate those relationships.

Feedback The effects of activity that are sensed by a responding system and are used to regulate subsequent activity.

Fertilization The union of an egg cell with a sperm.

Fetal alcohol syndrome Infant malformation found in babies of mothers who are chronic alcoholics.

Fetal stage This period lasts from about the end of the second month of gestation until birth.

Fetoscopy A procedure in which a very narrow tube is inserted through a pregnant woman's abdomen into the uterus. A fetoscope (a fiber optic lighting instrument) is then inserted through the tube, allowing the physician to directly observe the entire fetus.

Fetus The prenatal organism from the eighth week after conception until birth.

Field study A study in which the investigator examines naturally occurring behavior and may control only some features of the situation.

Foreclosures Adolescents who demonstrate little or no evidence of a crisis (i.e., a decision-making period) but who are committed to an occupational role and an ideological position. The occupational/ideological choices have been made by parents rather than self-chosen. See also *Commitment* and *Crisis.*

Formal community structures One source of influence of the community context on families and child development involving a broad range of community service organizations (e.g., health, welfare, social services, and day-care programs). See also *Informal community structures.*

Formal operations In Piaget's theory of intelligence, this is the final stage of cognitive development characterized by the ability to think abstractly.

Fraternal twins See *Dizygotic (DZ) twins.*

Fundamental motor skills Basic patterns of movement skill (such as jumping, climbing, hopping, skipping, and so on) which develop from two to five years of age and which serve as the basis for more complex motor activities such as swimming or bicycle riding.

Games-with-rules These ordinarily start at the beginning of the school year. The child becomes interested in structural games that involve the social concepts of cooperation and/or competition.

Gamete A mature reproductive cell (e.g., egg or sperm).

Gender The sex of a person.

Gender consistency or constancy In this stage, the six- or seven-year-old child realizes that an individual's gender is invariant over time *and* across situations, even with superficial changes in an activity or appearance.

Gender-intensification hypothesis The hypothesis that during adolescence the pressure to behave in a sex-appropriate manner significantly increases, compared with pressures to do so in the childhood years. This pressure becomes more pronounced for females than for males.

Gender stability Gender is perceived as a characteristic of the child which is permanent and stable over time.

General hereditary code Includes those attributes that make any species, including human beings, similar to other members of that species.

Generativity versus stagnation The seventh of Erikson's psychosocial stages of development in which the middle-aged adult can develop a sense of concern and care for the next generation.

Genes The elements of heredity that are found in chromosomes and that contain the codes for transmitting inherited characteristics.

Genetic epistemology The science or study of the origins of knowledge (most frequently associated with Piaget).

Genital stage The fifth stage in Freud's theory of personality development (from the onset of puberty through the adolescent years). There is a concern with adult modes of sexual pleasure, barring fixations or regressions (movement to an earlier pattern of behavior).

Genotype The fundamental hereditary constitution (assortment of genes) or an individual contained in the cells of the body.

Germinal stage The first stage of prenatal development extending from conception through the first two weeks after conception during which time the fertilized egg is primarily engaged in cell division.

Gestation period The span of time between fertilization and birth.

Goal adoption The factors contributing to the selection of specific achievement goals (e.g., expectation of success).

Goal formation The factors that cause children to be oriented toward achievement goals.

Gonads The sex glands (testes in males and ovaries in females).

Grammar The rules or principles of a language for organizing the sounds or phonemes into meaningful units or morphemes. See also *Morphemes* and *Phonemes*.

Grammatical morphemes Word modifiers that give precision to the meaning of words (and, therefore, to sentences) and include inflections, prepositions, and articles.

Grasping/clinging A dimension of the caregiver-infant attachment system.

Grasp (Palmar) reflex The tendency of the newborn during the first few weeks of life to clutch at objects placed in its hands.

Growth gradients (or axes of growth) Refers to the various directions that physical and physiological changes take in the human body.

Handedness An individual's hand preference.

Hemoglobin An iron-containing protein compound that gives red blood corpuscles their color.

Heredity The total sum of all characteristics that are biologically transmitted from parents to offspring at conception.

Heritability An estimate of the relative contribution of genetics to a given trait or behavior. The estimate is based on a sample of individuals.

Heterosexual Attraction to and interaction with members of the opposite sex; seeking and finding gratification with a member of the opposite sex.

Holophrases One-word sentences that occur at about age one.

Hormones Strong and highly specific chemical substances that interact with the cells of the human body. Cells are organized in such a way as to be receptive to (to ''bind up'' or to use) only certain hormones.

Hyaline membrane disease Frequently called respiratory distress syndrome. A substance called surfactin, which coats the lungs and aids in normal breathing, is produced in insufficient quantities and results in irregular breathing or cessation of breathing. It is a critical problem for preterm babies.

Hypothalmus A part of the brain located at the base of the brain, above the pituitary gland. The hypothalmus controls body functions such as temperature, water balance, and the release of pituitary hormones. See also *Pituitary gland*.

Hypothesis A tentative interpretation of a given set of data based on supportive findings; a prediction of a solution to a given problem.

Icterus neonatorum See *Jaundice*.

Identical twins See *Monozygotic (MZ) twins*.

Identification The socialization process by which a person takes on the characteristics of a significant and/or admired other and incorporates these characteristics into his or her own personality.

Identity A self-structure or an internal organization of values, abilities, feelings, and prior experiences. This self-constructed structure is dynamic and changing (i.e., elements are continually being added and subtracted).

Identity achievement The adolescents in this status both have engaged in a period of decision making or crisis and have made a commitment to an occupation and a set of values/beliefs or an ideology. See also *Commitment* and *Crisis*.

Identity diffusion The adolescents in this identity status are characterized by a lack of direction. They may or may not have undergone a crisis (decision-making period) and have definitely made no commitment to an ideological or occupational direction. See also *Commitment* and *Crisis*.

Identity versus identity diffusion The fifth of Erikson's stages of development in which the adolescent can experiment with various roles in developing a mature sense of selfhood.

Imitation (modeling) The process of repeating or copying another person's (model's) words, gestures, or behaviors.

Impulsive-aggressive children   Child behavior associated with permissive-indulgent parental behavior and characterized by resistance, noncompliance to adults, aggressiveness, aimlessness, impulsiveness, and so on.

Independence   Self-reliance.

Independent variables   The factors in an experiment that the researcher can systematically control or change. See also *Dependent variable.*

Individual variation   Although individuals follow patterns of sequential change in dimensions of growth and development, there is considerable variation among individuals in the rate of growth and development.

Inductive reasoning   Moving from specific instances to generalities.

Indulgent-permissive (parent)   A parenting style characterized by acceptance and low levels of parental control of the child.

Industry versus inferiority   The fourth of Erikson's stages of development (six years to puberty) in which the individual can learn the value of work including acquiring the skills and tools of technology.

Infancy   The stage of human development that extends from birth through the development of relative independence in feeding, movement, and language at approximately two years of age.

Infant mortality   Death of an infant at or immediately following birth.

Informal community structures   One source of influence of the community context on families and child development such as the personal social network. See also *Personal social network.*

Information processing   A perspective to the study of intelligence that examines the processes that underlie intelligent behavior, including goal-oriented behavior and adaptive behavior.

Initiative versus guilt   The third of Erikson's stages of development (three to six years of age) in which the child may learn to begin activities and to enjoy a sense of competence and achievement.

Insulin   A hormone produced in the pancreas. The body uses insulin to metabolize carbohydrates, the basic source of energy. Insulin also affects the metabolism of fats and proteins.

Intelligence   A broad term that refers to an individual's abilities in a wide variety of cognitive areas including mathematical/number skills, language skills, and problem solving.

Intelligence quotient   The IQ score is calculated by dividing the mental age by the chronological age and multiplying by 100.

Intimacy versus isolation   The sixth of Erikson's psychosocial stages of development in which the young adult can develop a commitment to others.

Intuitive period   This stage begins at approximately age five. It is closer to adult thinking because the child is now able to separate mental from physical reality.

Intuitive thinking   The third stage of Piaget's theory of cognitive development in which the four-to-seven-year-old child's thinking is characterized by reliance on immediate perceptions and experiences rather than on flexible operations.

Invention of new means   The sixth substage of Piaget's sensori-motor stage of intelligence which involves the invention of new ways of problem solving.

Jaundice   A condition characterized by the yellowish pigmentation of the skin, tissues, and body fluids due to the deposit of bile pigments. Also called icterus neonatorum.

Juvenile   Relating to an older child or an adolescent.

Karotype   A chart in which photographs of chromosomes are arranged according to size and structure.

Kinesthetic   The perception or sense of one's body position or movement.

Knowledge base   This is what children already know, which facilitates the learning of new material.

Labor   The process by which the baby and placenta are expelled through the birth canal. Labor involves the muscular contraction of the uterus to aid the infant in moving through the birth canal.

Laboratory schools   Schools designed to give practical experiences to students. Research is often connected with laboratory schools, especially in four-year colleges and universities.

Lactation   The presence and secretion of milk that occurs automatically in the breasts of the mother of a newborn infant.

Lamaze method   A method of childbirth involving prechildbirth instruction as well as muscular relaxation and breathing techniques during labor.

Language acquisition device (LAD)   A set of language-processing skills that psycholinguists believe are innate and that enable a child to understand the rules governing others' speech and to use these inferred rules to produce language. See also *Psycholinguistics.*

Latchkey children   Children who are unsupervised after school, usually because both parents work.

Latency stage   The fourth stage in Freud's theory of personality development (six years to onset of puberty). There is a loss of interest in sexual gratification. Identification with like-sexed parent occurs.

Later adolescence, or youth   This period of development begins with completion of high school (seventeen to eighteen years of age) and extends until the person attains a sense of social status or social identity and a control of resources in the adult community (early twenties). In summary, this period deals with the post–high school years and the development of the skills that the individual now uses to develop a "stance toward the world."

Lateralization   The process by which the various brain centers mature and develop with regard to their functions.

Learned helplessness   The learned feeling or belief that one has little or no control in dealing with a given situation that may, in fact, be controllable.

Leboyer method A method of childbirth involving the creation of a soothing childbirth experience for the newborn.

Libido The driving force or sexual energy in Freud's psychoanalytic theory of personality development.

Lifespan The length of an individual's existence.

Lifespan perspective With reference to the study of child/adolescent development, the consideration of the child or adolescent in relation to his or her developmental history (past) as well as his or her developmental trajectory (potential future development).

Life-style The relatively permanent organization of individual activity including the balance between work and leisure and the general pattern of family and social relationships.

Listening A dimension of the caregiver-infant system involving mutual response to vocal sounds.

Locomotion Movement in space, particularly with reference to infants.

Locus of control (sometimes called a sense of personal efficacy or a sense of personal agency) Refers to one's control over the outside world.

Longitudinal design Research that examines the same subjects over a specified period of time.

Long-term memory (LTM) The relatively permanent store of information, including an individual's knowledge of the world.

Looking/following A dimension of the attachment relationship between infant and caregiver involving mutual gazing.

Low-birthweight infant A baby weighing less than 5½ pounds (2,500 grams) at birth. Low birthweight may be due to prematurity (being born too early) or to a pathological condition making the baby small for the actual age (even when born during a normal gestation period of thirty-seven to forty-two weeks).

Lymph This is a clear liquid part of blood that enters tissue spaces and tiny lymph vessels that come together to form enlargements called lymph nodes or lymph glands. Lymph is purified in these nodes before being returned to the blood. The entire lymph system helps fight infections and supports the immunity of the body to illness.

Lymph glands Lymph nodes.

Lymphoid organs Include the thymus, lymph nodes, and intestinal lymph masses.

Macrosystem According to Bronfenbrenner, this system is the overarching institutional patterns of culture (e.g., the economic, educational, legal, social, and political systems) of which the micro-, meso-, and exosystems are specific and concrete manifestations. The macrosystem consists of the most general values, beliefs, or ideologies that influence the ways in which special institutions are organized and, therefore, the way in which human development occurs.

Marijuana (or marihuana) A drug derived from *Cannabis sativa* containing tetrahydrocannabinal (THC). It has sedative-hypnotic effects and can reduce tension and induce the experience of a "high."

Maternal deprivation The lack of opportunities for interaction with a mother or primary caregiver.

Maturational readiness A given child has developed to an appropriate point where he or she could benefit from a specific type of experience.

Maturation rate The general tempo at which various biological, behavioral, and personal characteristics emerge and develop in the individual as a result of growth and development.

Maturation theories According to such theories (e.g., Gesell's maturation theory), human behavior and development are primarily the result of innate factors.

Meiosis The process of cellular division that results in daughter cells' each receiving half the number of chromosomes and thereby becoming gametes.

Memory The process of recalling or reproducing what has been learned in the past as a way of predicting and organizing present and future activities. See also *Long-term memory* and *Short-term memory*.

Menarche The beginning of regular menstrual periods for the female; occurs during adolescence.

Menstrual cycle The cyclical discharge of blood and discarded uterine tissue which occurs on a monthly basis in females from the menarch through the menopause (except during pregnancy).

Menstruation The periodic (approximately monthly) breakdown and discharge of uterine tissues and the unfertilized egg (if produced), which occurs in the absence of fertilization. (If an egg becomes fertilized and attaches itself to the uterine wall and a pregnancy has begun, menstruation does not occur.)

Mental age The concept of mental age is a measure of the intelligence of an individual that reflects the number of age-graded test items a child is able to solve.

Mesoderm The middle layer of the three basic layers of embryonic cells; it is the basis for the formation of the alimentary canal, digestive glands, muscle structure, and bones.

Mesosystem This system involves the relationship among the various settings or contexts in which the developing person finds himself or herself. For example, for a nine-year-old child, the mesosystem would involve the relationship between the school and the family or the relationship between the family and the peer group.

Metabolism The physical/chemical changes that occur in the human body for the purpose of building up, repairing, and supporting existing structures as well as for breaking down (as in digestion) and removing (as in elimination of) body wastes.

Metamemory This memory technique consists of the child's knowledge about his or her own memory capacity and the memory characteristics of various tasks (i.e., a child's estimate of how much he or she will remember given a specific memory task).

Microsystem This system involves the interaction between the developing person and his or her immediate setting or context. For example, the relationship between a child and teachers or peers in the school and the relationship between an adolescent and the employer in a work setting are topics of microsystem analysis.

Middle childhood This period begins with entrance into the formal school and continues to the beginning of adolescence with the onset of puberty (from about five or six years of age to approximately the age of twelve or thirteen).

Mitosis The process of cell division that results in two cells identical to the parent cell.

Mnemonic strategies Memory-aiding devices such as rehearsal, organization, and elaboration. See also *Elaboration, Organization,* and *Rehearsal.*

Model In social learning theory, the person who is imitated.

Mongolism See *Down syndrome.*

Monozygotic (MZ) twins Twins who develop from the same fertilized egg or ovum (identical twins). See also *Dizygotic (DZ) twins.*

Montessori programs The Montessori nursery schools are based on a philosophy of education in which children are assumed to be motivated by a natural curiosity for learning and a desire to participate in activities that utilize the senses and muscles. The program was developed in the early years of this century in Italy by Maria Montessori.

Moral conduct A complex form of behavior consisting of three primary components: thinking or cognition, feeling, and action.

Moral development The nature and the lifespan course of an individual's moral thoughts, feelings, and actions.

Morality The sense or judgment of what is right or wrong behavior.

Moral reasoning See *Prosocial (moral) reasoning.*

Moral reciprocity In this period, the child's moral judgments are characterized by the recognition of such factors as the consideration of the viewpoint of others in evaluating their behavior.

Moral relationships based on mutual respect In this phase of moral development, the child moves from a focus on authority to a focus on interactions in concrete situations. For example, in prior periods, the child might share toys in the presence of his or her mother (in deference to the authority of the mother). In this period, the child may note that other children do not play with or do not like a child who does not share toys.

Moral relativity This stage of moral development presumably begins sometime during the adolescent years. With the attainment of formal operational thinking, the individual shifts from a focus on the concrete to a focus on the realistic application (taking all factors into account) or moral values and ideas to specific situations.

Moratoriums Individuals who are currently in crisis (i.e., the decision-making period) and are dealing with questions of occupation and ideology. If they have made a commitment, it is likely vague and relatively unclear. See also *Commitment* and *Crisis.*

Moro reflex The startle reaction of the newborn, characterized by the extension of both arms to the sides of the body with fingers outstretched, closely followed by the retraction of the arms to the midline of the body.

Morphemes The smallest and most basic meaningful units of a language; composed of phonemes that are combined to produce basic words, suffixes, or prefixes. See also *Phonemes.*

Motor skill Body movement actions that require coordination of muscles (e.g., walking, jumping).

Multiple sclerosis A disease marked by myelin disintegration and currently incurable. Depending on the specific area of the nervous system that is affected, multiple sclerosis usually results in loss of muscle control in affected areas and may eventually lead to paralysis or death. See also *Myelin.*

Mutation Any change in a gene, usually from one allele to another, that results in the production of new forms.

Mutual following (adaptation) The changes in behavior that result from two or more people adjusting their movements or general behavior in response to the movement or behavior of others, and vice versa. See also *Social tracking.*

Myelin A white, fatty substance that coats some nerve fibers thereby channeling nerve signals along fibers and reducing random spread to other neurons.

Myelinization The process by which nerve fibers acquire a myelin sheath.

Nativism The belief that individual differences in children are due to genetic or constitutional factors.

Naturalistic observations The observation of behavior without any intervention or interference by the investigator.

Nature The genetic and biological factors that contribute to human development. See also *Nurture.*

Negative correlation When two variables are inversely related (i.e., when one variable increases, the other one decreases), the correlation is negative. For example, when the amount of calories consumed decreases, the number of pounds lost increases.

Neglecting (parent) A parenting style characterized by rejection and unresponsive behavior toward the child as well as parental indifference.

Neighborhood/community Children develop surrounded by various arrangements of buildings, people, open space, and streets or roads. This neighborhood/community provides both a setting for human growth and development and a potential resource and support system for developing human beings.

Neonate The technical term for a newborn infant up to about two to four weeks of age.

Neurons (nerve cells) The building blocks of the nervous system. Neurons have a cell body and a nucleus, like all other cells, but unlike other cells, they also have special threadlike fibers that lead to and from the cell body—an axon and several dendrites. See also *Axon* and *Dendrites.*

Newborn states   The continuum of alertness or consciousness ranging from regular sleep to vigorous activity. See also *State.*

New York Longitudinal Study (NYLS)   One of the first empirical efforts to examine infant personality characteristics including temperament.

Niche picking   According to this perspective individuals actively seek out environments, situations, or niches that are stimulating and compatible with their personal characteristics.

Nonnormative life events   Events that occur for some but not all individuals at almost any time, such as divorce, the death of a parent, or the onset of a serious illness or handicapping condition.

Norephinephrine   A crystalline compound occurring with epinephrine, which constricts the diameter of blood vessels and mediates the transmission of sympathetic nerve impulses. See also *Sympathetic nervous system.*

Norm   A brief description of the essential features of a skill or personal/social attribute as well as the approximate age(s) it appears in the average child.

Normal distribution   A bell-shaped, symmetrical curve that indicates the variability of a given characteristic for a given population; most of the population falls near the average score, with fewer people at either extreme.

Normative   Relating to or based on averages, standards, values, or established norms.

Normative life events   Events that occur for most individuals at a specific time or range of times and include the development of language in infancy, entering school at the beginning of middle childhood, the onset of puberty, and leaving home during adolescence.

Norm of reaction   The fact that the same genotype can give rise to a wide array of phenotypes depending on the environment in which it develops. See also *Genotype* and *Phenotype.*

Nuclear (or conjugal) family   A household grouping that includes a mother, a father, and their children. See also *Extended family.*

Nurture   The influence of environmental factors on human development. See also *Nature.*

Object permanency   A prominent milestone in infant cognitive development that indicates the beginning of the ability to think about what is not present or in immediate view.

Observation   Watching the behavior of others.

Observational learning   The changes in thinking and behavior that result from watching others.

Open classroom   A classroom arranged so that each child moves at his or her own pace by making a choice of activities during the course of a school day. The child is viewed as an active ''doer'' and the teacher is considered a facilitator of learning.

Openness   A characteristic of family systems characterized by mutual, reciprocal, and free-flowing interactions with an environment.

Open words   Part of two-word utterances of eighteen-to-twenty-month-olds that are combined with pivot words. See also *Pivot words.*

Operant conditioning   Conditioning or learning that occurs when an organism is reinforced for emitting a response.

Operations   According to Piaget, operations are mental activities that serve as the basis of thinking. (These operations contrast with the physical and perceptual activities that are primary features of thinking in infancy and the preschool years.)

Oral stage   In Freud's psychosexual theory of development, the first stage of life during which the mouth is the primary focus of interaction with primary caregivers.

Organization   In Piaget's theory of cognitive development, the changes in mental structures or schemas resulting from adaptation. See also *Adaptation* and *Schema.*

Organizational complexity   A characteristic of family systems characterized by the development of networks of interdependent relationships both internal and external to the family.

Ossification   The transformation or hardening of cartilage into bone.

Other-oriented induction   Making children aware of the consequences of their behavior for others.

Ovary   The female reproductive gland in which egg cells or ova are produced.

Overextension   A generalization in the apparent meaning of a word such that it is used to include or refer to dissimilar events or objects.

Overregularization   The exaggerated application of general language principles to specific experiences. For example, overregularization occurs when children who are first learning language inflect the irregular (or strong) verbs of English for the past tense in the same way that regular (or weak verbs) are inflected.

Overt behavior   Responses that are easily seen and recorded.

Ovulation   Refers to the release of an egg (ovum) from an ovary (typically, human ovaries produce one egg over the course of a twenty-eight-day cycle). The egg travels through one of the fallopian tubes that connect the ovaries to the uterus, where fertilization may occur.

Ovum   An egg or the female sex cell (gamete).

Parathyroid glands   The four small ductless glands embedded in the thyroid gland. See also *Thyroid gland.*

Parturition   Delivery of a baby.

Peer   Any individual at a comparable level of development, age, and/or social status.

Peer group   The collection of persons who constitute one's associates.

Perception   The recognition and organization of sensory behavior.

Perception/attention   A dimension of information processing involving how human beings acquire information.

Performance evaluation   The types of questions children ask themselves about their performance (e.g., How well have I done?) and how these questions affect ongoing and future performance.

Peripheral nervous system   Consists of nerves that are connected to the brain and the spinal cord and extend to the exterior or the periphery of the body. These nerves carry impulses to and from the central nervous system.

Personality   The characteristics and relatively stable pattern of thought, feeling, and action of an individual.

Personal social network   A pattern of relationships that provide parents with social links to others outside the home who can provide a variety of supportive services (e.g., the provision of information, emotional support, or instrumental support).

Phallic stage   The third stage in Freud's theory of personality development (three years to six years). The child becomes concerned with the genitals. The source of sexual pleasure involves manipulating genitals. (This is the period of the Oedipus or Electra complex.)

Pharynx   The muscular throat cavity extending from the soft palate to the nasal cavity.

Phase of active initiative in seeking proximity and contact   The third stage of caregiver-infant attachment (seven months to two years) in which the infant begins to actively seek closeness with the object(s) of attachment.

Phase of discriminating social responsiveness   The second stage of caregiver-infant attachment (three to six months) characterized by the infant's increased recognition of familiar persons.

Phase of goal-corrected partnership   The fourth stage of caregiver-infant attachment (two years and beyond) in which the infant uses a variety of behaviors that influence the behavior of the object(s) of attachment to satisfy needs for closeness.

Phase of undiscriminating social responsiveness   The first stage of caregiver-infant attachment (zero to three months) in which the infant uses such responses as sucking, rooting, grasping, smiling, and gazing to maintain closeness to a caregiver.

Phenotype   The observable characteristics that are the result of genetic and environmental contributions. See also *Genotype*.

Phonemes   The sounds of a given language that are the building blocks of morphemes. See also *Morphemes.*

Phonology   The sound structure of a language.

Physical fitness   Composed of several different dimensions including health-related physical fitness aspects and motor fitness (skill-related) aspects.

Pictorial stage   By the time the child is four or five years old, he or she is able to combine the basic shapes and combinations (learned in earlier stages of children's drawing) to depict or represent familiar objects in the family, the neighborhood, or the preschool environment. For example, the child may draw reasonable facsimiles of houses, cars, dogs, cats, faces, and other people.

Pituitary gland   A ductless gland located at the base of the brain and composed of two lobes. The anterior lobe secretes hormones such as growth hormones, *gonadotropic* hormones that influence the reproductive organs, and hormones that stimulate other endocrine glands. The posterior lobe secretes two hormones: *oxytocin* (regulates blood pressure and stimulates smooth muscles) and *vasopressin* (regulates water resorption in the kidneys). See also *Hypothalmus.*

Pivot words   With reference to the two-word combinations of eighteen-to-twenty-month-olds, these are words that are always in the same position (i.e., always first or second) and combined with many other words. See also *Open words.*

PKU (Phenylketonuria)   An inherited disease that, if untreated, causes mental retardation. About one baby in 8,000 is born with PKU in the United States each year.

Placement stage   In this stage of children's drawing, the child is experimenting with various scribble marks. Much of the child's activity is exploratory as he or she tries different ways of holding the crayon as well as drawing on different places on the paper. Sometimes the child's drawing is confined to one small part of a paper, and at other times the drawing is composed of broad strokes that take up the entire paper (and sometimes beyond). By the time the child is two and one-half to three years of age, he or she has probably mastered most of the basic scribble movements.

Placenta   The organ that conveys food and oxygen to the developing prenatal organism and discharges waste.

Positive correlation   Whenever two variables or factors change in the same direction, the correlation is positive. For example, when height increases, weight also increases.

Postconventional level   In Kohlberg's theory of moral development, the final and most-sophisticated level of moral development involving the organization of self-determined moral principles rather than simply conforming to the principles or expectations of others. See also *Conventional level or stage* and *Preconventional level.*

Postpartum   The time immediately following birth, usually the first week of life.

Posture   A dimension of the attachment relationship involving a mutual adjustment between infant and caretaker in which the infant "molds" its body against the adult when being held and the adult adapts to the infant.

Power-assertion techniques   Techniques involving parental use of authority and control of resources as the basis for disciplining the child.

Preconceptual stage   The highlights of this stage (two to four years) include the emergence of language, symbols, and symbolic play. The use of both symbols and symbolic play are significant because they indicate the emerging ability of the child to think about what is *not immediately* present.

Preconventional level   In Kohlberg's theory, the first level of moral development in which moral decisions are based on whether an action has positive or negative consequences or whether it is rewarded or punished by parents or caretakers. See also *Conventional level or stage* and *Postconventional level.*

Prehension   Grasping behavior that serves as a basis for a wide range of infant/toddler skills including feeding and object manipulation.

Premature infant   A baby having a short gestation period (i.e., born early, less than thirty-seven weeks after conception). Premature infants may also have a low birthweight (less than 5½ pounds, 2,500 grams). Previously all low-birthweight babies were also considered to be premature; birthweight is no longer a necessary criterion for prematurity. Prematurity may not in itself be harmful since such infants, if below normal weight, typically "catch up" to their normal weights. See also *Low-birthweight infant.*

Premoral period   According to Piaget, the premoral period occurs during the first seven years of life and is characterized by moral behavior evaluated and justified in terms of the needs of self, and later in terms of parental authority.

Prenatal   The stage of human development from conception to birth.

Preoperational thought   This period (two to seven years) is characterized by the development of symbolic functions such as language or imaginative play. During this stage, the child develops from an organism that functions primarily in a sensori-motor mode to one that functions primarily in a conceptual or symbolic mode. The child is increasingly able to internally represent events (to "think") while becoming less dependent on motor activities for the direction of behavior.

Prepared childbirth (Lamaze)   The method of childbirth where the woman acquires knowledge about the physiological processes in childbirth as well as learning exercises that make delivery somewhat easier.

Preschooler   This period extends from about three years of age until entrance into formal school at five or six years of age.

Primary circular reactions   The second substage of Piaget's sensori-motor stage of intelligence which involves the modification of reflexes to achieve several sensations such as hand-mouth coordination, eye coordination, and eye-ear coordination.

Primary motor areas   The locations in the brain that are responsible for simple body movements.

Primary sensory areas   The locations in the brain that are responsible for major perceptual functions such as hearing, vision, touch, and so on.

Primary sex characteristics   Refers to changes in the testes and ovaries that make reproduction possible.

Primitive reflexes   Reflexes that appear early in life and then cease to exist are sometimes referred to as the primitive reflexes because they are shared with lower animals. For example, both the Moro and the grasping reflexes may well be evolutionary carryovers from primates that hang onto their mothers for survival and feeding.

Private self   Those parts of the self that are known only to the individual and are not public.

Problem solving   A dimension of information processing involving how human beings deal with present circumstances or make future plans.

Project Head Start   Head Start early childhood centers were first organized in 1965 and brought children of the poor together in groups for educational, medical, and nutritional assistance in hopes of reducing the observed handicap that such children experience when they enter elementary school.

Prosocial behavior   Activity intended to help or assist others.

Prosocial (moral) reasoning   The thinking activity used in justifying prosocial action (or inaction).

Protein   A molecule containing amino acids.

Proximodistal development   The progressive growth of the human body from a central to an external direction. See also *Cephalocaudal development.*

Psychoanalytic theory   Focuses on emotional factors and personality development as the central forces in development.

Psycholinguistics   The study of the inborn cognitive and perceptual abilities that contribute to the development of language from the cooing and babbling of infants to the organized words and sentences of older children.

Psychometric approach   An approach to the study of intelligence focusing on the identification of quantitative factors or components of intelligence and the measurement of such factors typically using assessment instruments or tests.

Psychosexual stages   The stages of development in Freud's psychoanalytic theory (e.g., oral stage, anal stage, and so on).

Psychosocial stages   Freud was primarily concerned with the biologically based libido and the emerging feelings of gratification or frustration, whereas Erikson emphasized development of the self or ego in relation to the social environment. For this reason, it has been suggested that Freud's theory is psychosexual, and Erikson's theory is psychosocial.

Puberty   Refers to all the biological, physical, and sexual changes that occur as the individual moves from childhood to adulthood (i.e., including the technical definitions of both pubescence and puberty). From such a broad perspective, there are five primary manifestations of puberty. See also *Pubescence.*

Pubescence   The term used to describe the period of time leading up to changes in reproductive capability and including the growth spurt and changes in body composition. See also *Puberty*.

Public self Those parts of the self that others can perceive or infer about the person.

Pygmalion hypothesis The assumption that teachers' expectations (whether high or low) may influence the level of child performance (high or low) independently of the child's actual ability (as measured by standardized tests).

Qualitative change Refers to variations and modifications in functioning (e.g., the progression of locomotion skills, intellectual skills, and the development of grasping behavior).

Quantitative change Refers to the easily measurable and sometimes obvious aspects of development, including physical growth (height and weight) and years of education.

Quickening The first movements of the fetus that the pregnant woman can readily perceive.

Range of reaction The potential for development of a specific genetic endowment given variable environments.

Reaction time The time interval between the signal to make a response and the actual response.

Recall memory The recollection of objects or events without having examples of them for comparison.

Recessive gene The subordinate member of a pair of genes whose trait does not appear, unless paired with another recessive gene.

Reciprocal interaction A relationship in which the behavior of each participant is influenced by the responses of the other person.

Recognition memory The realization that an event, object, or experience that one encounters has been experienced at a prior time.

Reflex An unlearned behavior that occurs naturally in a given situation.

Reflex activity The first substage of Piaget's sensori-motor stage of intelligence, characterized by infants' response to their world primarily in terms of reflexes they are born with.

Rehearsal A mnemonic device, involving the repetition of the items to be remembered.

Reliability The extent to which a child's test score is replicable.

Restrictiveness-permissiveness A dimension of parental behavior that involves parental control. It can vary from demanding, controlling, or restrictive behavior to laissez-faire, uncontrolling, or permissive behavior.

Reticular formation The part of the brain concerned with the maintenance of attention and consciousness.

Reversibility In Piaget's theory, the awareness that an operation (mental thought process) can be restored or reversed to an original condition (e.g., a clay rod can be rolled into a ball and then back to a rod).

Rh factor (incompatibility) A problem involving an incompatibility between the blood types of the mother and the child. See also *Erythroblastosis fetalis*.

Ribosome Small spherical bodies in the cytoplasm; the site of protein synthesis; composed of protein and RNA.

RNA (ribonucleic acid) Molecules that convey the information in the DNA to the cytoplasm of the cell so that appropriate amino acids can be formed.

Role-status transmission model A theory that suggests that parents' experiences in their work roles may influence their child-rearing practices (e.g., parents, usually middle-class, who work in occupations that encourage or require initiative and self-regulation are likely to support and encourage self-direction and autonomy in their children).

Role taking Involves the correct understanding of what another individual is thinking or feeling without having to feel the same way.

Rooming-in A hospital arrangement by which the mother and the baby are cared for in the same unit, and the father has the opportunity to care for the baby.

Rooting reflex (rooting/sucking) An early reflex response of babies that includes head turning movements and attempts at sucking when the cheek is touched.

Rubella German measles.

Schema (*plural* schemata, schemas, or schemes) In Piaget's terminology, the organization of actions or thoughts into a unified whole or mental construct.

Scientific validity Refers to the clear and precise statement of objective procedures, methods of measurement, and findings such that other scientists can independently replicate these procedures, methods, and findings.

Scripts One of the important indicators of the development of problem-solving skills is the development of competence in day-to-day routines or scripts. These scripts provide a basic outline of activities to be accomplished, as well as problems to be solved.

Sebaceous (oily) glands Glands in the skin that further develop during adolescence and may contribute to acne and other skin eruptions.

Secondary circular reactions The third substage of Piaget's sensori-motor stage of intelligence which involves the development of a variety of schemas resulting in effects such as increasing attention to external events, differentiating between the self and other objects, and eye-hand coordination. See also *Schema*.

Secondary sex characteristics Physical characteristics that appear at the time of puberty including breast development, enlargement of the penis, deepening of the voice in males, and pubic hair in males and females. These characteristics are differentiated according to sex, but they are not necessary for sexual reproduction.

Secular trend Refers to the tendency over historical time for the rate of some pubertal events to occur at a more rapid rate or at an earlier time.

Secure infants Using Ainsworth's Strange Situation Test, one of three attachment types characterized by a balance between attachment behaviors and exploration (i.e., by active infant exploration of the environment prior to any separation from their mothers). See also *Ainsworth's Strange Situation Test*.

Self-concept   The characteristics and attributes one applies to oneself.

Self-control   Control over one's own behavior.

Self-induced vulnerabilities   Self-generated behavior that jeopardizes health (e.g., smoking, alcoholism, drug abuse, and so on).

Self-knowledge   The development of conscious awareness of self.

Self-regulation   The function of the self-concept that includes several possible components such as self-control, self-monitoring, self-reinforcement, and self-evaluation. Self-regulation is a continuous or dynamic process rather than a single stage or behavior (Markus and Nurius, 1984).

Self schemas   Cognitive generalizations about the self, derived from past experience, that organize and guide the processing of self-related information contained in the individual's social experience.

Semantics   The component of language that constitutes its meaning including knowledge of vocabulary and how the meaning of a sentence is determined by its structure.

Sensori-motor (or practice) play   Extends from birth through the second year of life. The child acquires and exercises control over his or her movements and learns to coordinate these movements and their effects. Play during this stage often takes the form of motor behaviors that are repeated and varied.

Sensori-motor intelligence   See *Sensori-motor stage*.

Sensori-motor stage   According to Piaget, the earliest phase of intelligence in infancy involving perceptual and movement activities and from which all later stages of intelligence evolve.

Sensory register   Where memory information is initially stored. Information remains in the sensory register very briefly and, unless coded, will be lost in less than a second. See also *Short-term memory (STM)*.

Separation anxiety   The negative reaction of some infants to the absence of the primary caregiver and the attempts made to regain contact with this object of attachment.

Seriation   The cognitive ability to arrange objects along a continuum of increasing or decreasing value according to a given characteristic (e.g., color, size, and so on).

Sex chromosomes   The single pair of chromosomes that determines the sex of the organism (XX = female; XY = male).

Sex (germ) cells   Cells that are produced by a process called meiosis. See also *Body (somatic) cells* and *Meiosis*.

Sex-role development   See *Sex typing*.

Sex-role identification   The integration of the awareness of social and cultural expectations associated with each sex, awareness of one's gender, preference for a sex role, and the close emotional association with the same-sex parent.

Sex-role preference   The positive value given to a set of expectations and standards held for a gender group.

Sex roles   The patterns of behavior that are considered appropriate for each sex.

Sex-role standard   A value, motive, or behavior that a given society views as appropriate for a given sex.

Sex typing   The process in which the child becomes aware of his or her gender and acquires the values, motives, or behaviors that are considered appropriate by society for his or her sex.

Sexual identity   The definition of oneself as male or female, incorporating the biological, psychological, and social dimensions of sexuality.

Sexuality   In adolescence, refers to two primary dimensions: a cultural construct (including one's biological/gender identity and one's psychological identity as male or female) and specific behaviors (e.g., dating, sexual relationships, and so on).

Shape stage   In this stage of children's drawing, children begin to draw actual forms. They can make the outline or the approximation of such shapes as circles, squares, X's, and so on.

Short-term memory (STM)   The second stage in the memory system involving the reception of information from the sensory register and the storage and processing of that information. The type of memory associated with the immediate perception of information (e.g., telephone numbers). See also *Sensory register*.

Sibling   A brother or sister.

Skeletal maturity   The determination of skeletal maturity is predictable, based on the appearance of ossification in the growth regions or epiphyses of bones. See also *Epiphyses* and *Ossification*.

Skeletal muscles   Voluntary muscles, such as the biceps in the arm.

Slow-to-warm-up child   In the New York Longitudinal Study, approximately 15 percent of the sample was characterized by withdrawal, low adaptability, negative mood, low intensity, and high activity.

Smiling   A dimension of the caregiver-infant attachment system.

Smooth muscles   The muscles that act involuntarily and are found lining the walls of the stomach, arteries, and intestines.

Social class   A social level that is differentiated from other social levels or strata by such characteristics as income, occupation, or education.

Social cognition   The ability to understand the thoughts, emotions, intentions, and viewpoints of oneself and others, as well as the ability to think about social institutions and social relationships.

Social competence   The ability to use both personal and environmental resources for optimal adaptation. The competent child is one who can accommodate to new situations and adjust to new circumstances such as entering a preschool education program or accepting the birth of a new sibling.

Socialization   The process of transmitting and enforcing social and cultural norms and values to the new members of a group.

Social learning theory   This approach examines the broad range of learning that is accomplished by means of observation and imitation (modeling). See also *Imitation (modeling)*.

Social norms   The prevalence of prosocial behavior depends, in part, on the child's understanding and use of behavioral guidelines or norms such as social responsibility, deserving, reciprocity, equity, and equality.

Social network   See *Personal social network*.

Social play   The infant or child and other individuals interacting with objects and/or with one another.

Social role   The set of expectations or standards associated with a given position.

Social support   Information shared for the purpose of facilitating problem solving and as the development of new social contacts (providing help and assistance).

Social tracking   Mutual following in which the actions of one participant serve as the basis of the response of another person, and vice versa. There are three primary modes of social tracking: tactual, visual, and auditory tracking. See *Mutual following (adaptation)*.

Sociocentrism   The gradual socialization of thinking in which the child comes to recognize that peers and others may have different viewpoints.

Sociogram   A graphic representation of preferences and rejections in social interaction.

Solitary play   An infant or child playing alone with toys or objects.

Somatotrophin   Growth hormone secreted by the anterior lobe of the pituitary gland. See also *Pituitary gland*.

Sonogram or ultrasound   A test involving the use of high-frequency sound waves to provide an outline of the shape of the fetus. See also *Amniocentesis*.

Specific hereditary code   Those attributes (including physical and psychological characteristics) that distinguish one member of a species from another member of the same species.

Sperm (spermatozoon; *plural* spermatazoa)   The male sex cell (gamete).

Startle (Moro) reflex   See *Moro reflex*.

State   The cyclical variation in an infant's wakefulness, sleep, and activity.

Stillbirth   The delivery of a dead child.

Strains   Unresolved problems due to prior stressors (e.g., financial hardship due to the loss of a job) or to the built-in tensions of ongoing role relationships (e.g, being a spouse in a failing marital relationship).

Stranger anxiety   The negative reactions that occur when infants are separated from primary caregivers and in the presence of unknown (strange) people. It usually occurs during the sixth or seventh month of infancy.

Stress-interference model   From this viewpoint, all families, to some extent, are exposed to some external stressors (e.g., accidents, something stolen, car trouble, broken home appliances, and so on). For some parents, these stressors may affect their child-rearing behaviors by reducing the frequency of interaction with children and causing them to be more irritable and impatient with their children.

Stressors   Events or experiences that occur at a specific time such as graduating from high school (a normative event) or having a car accident (a nonnormative event).

Styles of parenting   The attitudes and behaviors of parents.

Subjectivism   The belief that the main activity of psychologists and others interested in human development was a type of introspection that involved the study of the contents of the human mind, through self-analysis.

Sucking reflex   When an object touches the infant's lips, the infant makes sucking movements.

Sudden infant death syndrome (SIDS)   The most frequent cause of unexpected death in infants during the first year of life. Also called crib death.

Symbolic (or pretend) play   A stage of play that extends from two to six years of age. The child begins to organize play with symbols, and pretending becomes a common play mode (e.g., holding a stick against the back of a toy car and pretending that the car is at a gasoline station and being filled with gasoline). By age six or seven, symbolic play declines as children become more interested in games-with-rules.

Sympathetic nervous system   This nervous system is made up of two rows of nerve cords which lie on either side of the spinal column. The functions of the sympathetic nervous system include the regulation of the heart, the secretion of endocrine glands, and the action of smooth muscles.

Synaptic connections   The connections between neurons, over which electrical impulses are transmitted between the brain and other parts of the body.

Syntax   The rule structure of a language involving the organization of meaningful units (such as words) into meaningful utterances (such as phrases, clauses, or sentences).

System   A set of interrelated objects or components that are tied together by feedback relationships.

Systems (or ecological) perspective   See *Ecology of human development*.

Tactual-kinesthetic (perception)   The earliest mode of perception involving touch and a sense of one's body movement.

Tactual tracking Mutual following between two people using touch (e.g., as in a parent holding a clinging infant or in sexual intercourse).

Task performance The effects of different levels of expectations (for success or failure) on goal achievement.

Telegraphic speech With the onset of two-word phrases in infant speech, the pattern of words that are included and excluded in child utterances.

Temperament An individual style of relating to people and situations including behavioral style or characteristic mood.

Teratogen An agent that increases the likelihood of deviations or produces malformations in a developing fetus. A teratogen that produces a malformation may be direct (e.g., a drug such as thalidomide) or indirect (e.g., a pregnant mother's thyroid condition).

Teratogenic Capable of causing an organic malformation.

Tertiary circular reactions The fifth substage of Piaget's sensori-motor stage of intelligence which involves trial-and-error experimentation leading to the discovery of new means to achieve ends (goals) and increased attempts to interact with the external world.

Testis (*plural*** testes)** The male reproductive gland; also known as a testicle.

Thalidomide A drug that was used in the 1960s as a tranquilizer and sedative for "morning sickness" and that resulted in the birth of many deformed infants.

Thymus It is thought to be a ductless gland, located above the heart, whose function helps the body to fight diseases.

Thyroid gland The ductless gland, located on either side of the larynx, that regulates metabolism.

Toddlerhood The period of human development from about fifteen to thirty months.

Tonic-neck reflex A postural reflex that may be seen when the infant is laid on its back with its head turned to one side and its corresponding arm and leg extended at right angles to the body. The infant responds by flexing the other arm and leg and making fists with both hands.

Toxemia A condition during pregnancy in which the woman's blood pressure increases, she retains salt and water, develops swelling (edema), has albumin (a protein) in her urine, and can develop seizure activity.

Trachea The windpipe.

Traditional classroom Typically characterized by a structured arrangement of lessons and discipline as the best ways to achieve student learning. In such a classroom, the teacher is the authority (in both subject areas and discipline). The desks are typically arranged in rows, each child has an assigned seat, and the activities of the day are organized by the teacher.

Traditional delivery Delivery in the hospital under the care of physicians and frequently involving medication for relief of pain.

Traditional play setting A play setting that includes equipment such as slides, swings, sand boxes, and so on.

Transductive reasoning Characteristic of the preschooler, who reasons from one specific and immediate event to another immediate and specific event.

Trust versus mistrust The first of Erikson's stages of development (birth to eighteen months) in which reliance on a caregiver can lead to development of trust in the environment.

Umbilical cord The cord connecting the prenatal organism to the placenta through which the developing fetus receives nourishment.

Uterus The pear-shaped muscular organ in which the prenatal organism develops until birth.

Vagina The female genital canal or passage from the uterus to the external opening of the genital canal (vulva).

Validity The extent to which a given measure actually assesses what it purports to measure.

Value autonomy Having a set of principles that enable the adolescent to determine what is right or correct in moral behavior.

Venereal disease An infection transmitted by sexual intercourse.

Vernix The white greasy substance that covers the newborn and lubricates it for the passage through the birth canal.

Vernix caseosa The oily covering of the newborn secreted by its skin glands.

Visual acuity The ability to see objects, particularly small details. See also *Acuity (visual)*.

Visual cliff A special experimental apparatus designed to study infant depth perception.

Visual tracking The ability to follow an object with one's eyes and, as appropriate, to adjust body movements in accordance with visual feedback.

Vital capacity The air-holding capability of the lungs.

Vocalizing A dimension of the caregiver-infant attachment system.

Vocational exploration Refers to the adolescent's investigation of the characteristics and requirements of various occupations, including limited role tryouts during leisure and school activities.

Vocational maturity Refers to the adolescent's readiness to make the occupational choices that are required by both adolescent development and the demands of society.

Walking reflex If one holds a newborn infant upright with its feet touching a solid surface, the legs will move as if in an attempt to walk.

Wechsler Intelligence Scale for Children (WISC) A

standardized individual intelligence test for children that measures both verbal and performance abilities.

Withdrawal reflex   Occurs when the infant cries and recoils from a pain-inducing stimulation (e.g., being accidently stuck with a diaper pin).

X chromosome   A sex-determining chromosome of which the female has two (XX) and the male has only one (XY).

X-linked inheritance   The pattern of inheritance in which characteristics are conveyed on the X chromosome, transmitted by the female and expressed in the male.

Y chromosome   A sex-determining chromosome that when paired with the X chromosome produces a male (XY).

Zygote   The cell formed by the union of male and female gametes.

Acknowledgments

Figure and Table Credits

FIGURE (p. 10) From Meredith, H. V. "Length of Head and Neck, Trunk and Lower Extremities on Iowa City Children Aged 7–17 Years." Copyright © The Society for Research in Child Development, Inc., *Child Development* 10 (1939), p. 141.

TABLE (p. 25) Abridgement of Table on page 249 in *The First Five Years of Life* by Arnold Gesell, M.D. Copyright © 1940 by Arnold Gesell. Reprinted by permission of Harper & Row, Publishers, Inc.

FIGURE (p. 53) James Garbarino, from Kopp & Krakow, *The Child*. Copyright © 1982, Addison-Wesley Publishing Company, Inc., Reading, Massachusetts. P. 648 (chart). Reprinted with permission.

FIGURE (p. 73) From Erlenmeyer-Kimling, L., and Jarvik, L. F. "Genetics and Intelligence: A Research Review." Copyright © 1963 by the AAAS. *Science* 142 (1963), pp. 1477–1479.

FIGURE (p. 74) From Wilson, R. S. "Synchronies in Mental Development: An Epigenetic Perspective." Copyright © 1978 by the AAAS. *Science* 202 (1978), pp. 939–948.

FIGURE (p. 75) From Wilson, R. S. "The Louisville Twin Study: Developmental Synchronies in Behavior." Copyright © The Society for Research in Child Development, Inc. *Child Development* 54 (1983), pp. 298–316.

QUOTATION (p. 78) From Horn, J. M. "The Texas Adoption Project: Adopted Children and Their Intellectual Resemblance to Biological and Adoptive Parents." Copyright © The Society for Research in Child Development, Inc. *Child Development* 54 (1983), pp. 268–275.

FIGURE (p. 81) Table 2.1 from p. 28 in *Marriage and Family Development*, Sixth Edition by Evelyn Millis Duvall and Brent C. Miller. Copyright © 1985 by Harper & Row, Publishers, Inc. Reprinted by permission of Harper & Row, Publishers, Inc.

TABLE (p. 82) Table 3.5 from p. 62 in *Marriage and Family Development*, Sixth Edition by Evelyn Millis Duvall and Brent C. Miller. Copyright © 1985 by Harper & Row, Publishers, Inc. Reprinted by permission of Harper & Row, Publishers, Inc.

FIGURE (p. 84) From Rollins, B. C., and Feldman, H. "Marital Satisfaction over the Life Cycle." *Journal of Marriage and the Family* 32, No. 1 (February 1970), pp. 20–28. Copyright © 1970 by the National Council on Family Relations, 1910 West County Road B, Suite 147, St. Paul, Minnesota 55113. Reprinted by permission.

EXCERPT (p. 93) From Bronfenbrenner, U. "Developmental Research, Public Policy, and the Ecology of Childhood." Copyright © The Society for Research in Child Development, Inc. *Child Development* 45, No. 1 (March 1974), pp. 1–5.

FIGURE (p. 109) Reprinted with permission of Macmillan Publishing Company from *Biology*, 2/e by Joan E. Rahn. Copyright © 1980 by Joan E. Rahn.

FIGURE (p. 157) Reproduced and/or slightly modified by permission from Klaus, M. H., and Kennell, J. H., *Maternal-Infant Bonding*, St. Louis, 1976, The C. V. Mosby Co.

FIGURE (p. 182) Reproduced and/or slightly modified by permission from Klaus, M. H., and Kennell, J. H., *Parent-Infant Bonding*, St. Louis, 1982, The C. V. Mosby Co.

TABLE (p. 183) Reproduced and/or slightly modified by permission from Klaus, M. H., and Kennell, J. H., *Parent-Infant Bonding*, St. Louis, 1982, the C. V. Mosby Co.

TABLE (p. 214) From Long, F. "Social Support Networks in Day Care and Early Child Development." In J. Whittaker and J. Garbarino (eds.), *Social Support Networks: Informal Helping in the Human Services*. New York: Aldine, 1983, pp. 189–217.

FIGURE (p. 231) From Haith, M. M., Bergman, T., and Moore, M. J., "Eye Contact and Face Scanning in Early Infancy." University of Denver, 1977 (unpublished).

FIGURE (p. 235) Reproduced with permission from Lowrey, G. H.: *Growth and Development of Children*, 8th edition. Copyright © 1986 by Year Book Medical Publishers, Inc., Chicago. (After C. A. Aldrich and E. S. Hewitt, "Outlines for Well Baby Clinics: Development for the First Twelve Months," *American Journal of Diseases of Children*, 1946, pp. 71 and 131. Copyright © 1946, American Medical Association.)

TABLE (p. 235) From Bayley, N. "The Development of Motor Abilities During the First Three Years." Copyright © The Society for Research in Child Development, Monographs of the Society for Research in Child Development, No. 1 (1935), pp. 1–26, abridged.

TABLE (p. 237) From Frankenburg, W. K., Fandal, A. W., Sciarillo, W., and Burgess, D. "The Newly Abbreviated and Revised Denver Developmental Screening Test." Copyright © The Society for Research in Child Development, Inc. *The Journal of Pediatrics* 99 (1981), pp. 995–999.

FIGURE (p. 239) From "An Experimental Study of Prehension in Infants by Means of Systematic Cinema Records." *Genetic Psychology Monographs* 10, pp. 107–286, 1931. Reprinted with permission of the Helen Dwight Reid Educational Foundation. Published by Heldref Publications, 4000 Albemarle St., N.W., Washington, D. C. 20016. Copyright © 1931.

FIGURE (p. 240) The Six Substages of Piaget's Sensorimotor Period. John H. Flavell, *Cognitive Development*, 2/e. Copyright © 1985, p. 29. Adapted by permission of Prentice-Hall, Inc., Englewood Cliffs, New Jersey.

TABLE (p. 241) From *Piaget's Theory of Cognitive Development*, 2nd edition by Barry J. Wadsworth. Copyright © 1971 and 1979 by Longman Inc. Reprinted by permission of Longman Inc.

FIGURE (p. 277) From Sroufe, L. A., and Wunsch, J. "The Development of Laughter in the First Year of Life." Copyright © The Society for Research in Child Development, Inc. *Child Development* 43 (1972), pp. 1326–1344.

TABLE (p. 284) From Caldwell, B. M., and Ricciuti, H. N. (eds.). *Review of Child Development Research*, Vol. 3. Chicago: University of Chicago Press, 1973, pp. 1–94.

FIGURE (p. 294) From Clarke-Stewarte, K. A., and Hevey, C. M. "Longitudinal Relations in Repeated Observations of Mother-Child Interaction from 1 to 2 1/2 Years." *Developmental Psychology*

17 (1981), pp. 127–145. Copyright © 1981 by the American Psychological Association. Reprinted/adapted by permission of the author.

FIGURE (p. 298) From Levitt, M. J. "Contingent Feedback, Familiarization, and Infant Affect: How a Stranger Becomes a Friend." *Developmental Psychology* 16 (1980), pp. 425–432. Copyright © 1980 by the American Psychological Association. Reprinted/adapted by permission of the author.

FIGURE (p. 314) From *Genetic Psychology Monographs* 10, pp. 107–286, 1931. Reprinted with permission of the Helen Dwight Reid Educational Foundation. Published by Heldref Publications, 4000 Albermarle St., N. W., Washington, D.C. 20016. Copyright © 1931.

FIGURE (p. 319) From *Genetic Psychology Monographs* 10, pp. 107–286, 1931. Reprinted with permission of the Helen Dwight Reid Educational Foundation. Published by Heldref Publications, 4000 Albemarle St., N.W., Washington, D.C. 20016. Copyright © 1931.

FIGURE (p. 333) From Eckerman, C. O.; Whatley, J. L., and Kutz, S. L. "Growth of Social Play with Peers During the Second Year of Life." *Developmental Psychology* 11 (1975), pp. 42–49. Copyright © 1975 by the American Psychological Association. Reprinted/adapted by permission of the author.

FIGURE (p. 335) From Ellis, S., Rogoff, B., and Cromer, C. "Age Segregation in Children's Social Interactions." *Developmental Psychology* 17 (1981), pp. 399–407. Copyright © 1981 by the American Psychological Association. Reprinted/adapted by permission of the author.

FIGURE (p. 356) From *Modern Health* by James H. Otto, et al. Copyright © 1985 by Holt, Rinehart and Winston, Publishers. Reprinted by permission of the publisher.

FIGURE (p. 357) From *Modern Health* by James H. Otto et al. Copyright © 1985 by Holt, Rinehart and Winston, Publishers. Reprinted by permission of the publisher.

TABLE (p. 389) Adaptation and abridgment of table from pp. 16–19 in *The Acquisition of Language: The Study of Developmental Psycholinguistics* by David McNeill. Copyright © David McNeill. Reprinted by permission of Harper & Row, Publishers, Inc.

FIGURE (p. 391) From Berko, J. "The Child's Learning of English Morphology." Copyright © The Society for Research in Child Development, Inc. *Word* 14 (1958), pp. 150–177.

TABLE (p. 406) From Sroufe, L. A. "The Coherence of Individual Development: Early Care, Attachment, and Subsequent Developmental Issues." *American Psychologist* 34 (1979a), pp. 834–841. Copyright © 1979 by the American Psychological Association. Reprinted/adapted by permission of the author.

TABLE (p. 427) From Eisenberg, N., Lennon, R., and Roth, K. "Prosocial Development: A Longitudinal Study." *Developmental Psychology* 19 (1983), pp. 846–855. Copyright © 1983 by the American Psychological Association. Reprinted/adapted by permission of the author.

FIGURE (p. 506) From Corbin, C. B. *Becoming Physically Educated in Elementary School*, 2nd ed., p. 54, Philadelphia: Lea and Febiger Publishing Co., 1976.

FIGURE (p. 507) From Corbin, C. B. *A Textbook of Motor Development*, p. 80, Dubuque, Iowa: Brown, 1973; 2nd ed., 1980.

FIGURE (p. 507) From Corbin, C. B. *A Textbook of Motor Development*. Dubuque, Iowa: Brown, 1973; 2nd ed., 1980.

FIGURE (p. 508) From Wickstrom, R. L. *Fundamental Motor Patterns*, 2nd ed., Philadelphia: Lea and Febiger, 1977.

FIGURE (p. 509) Figure 24.6 p. 330 in "Motor Development" by Anna Espenschade and Helen Edkert from *Science and Medicine of Exercise and Sport*, Second Edition by Warren R. Johnson and Elsworth R. Buskirk. Copyright © 1974 by Warren R. Johnson and Elsworth R. Buskirk. Copyright © 1960 by Warren R. Johnson. Reprinted by permission of Harper & Row, Publishers, Inc.

FIGURE (p. 510) Figure 24.6, p. 330 in "Motor Development" by Anna Espenschade and Helen Edkert from *Science and Medicine of Exercise and Sport*, Second Edition by Warren R. Johnson and Elsworth R. Buskirk. Copyright © 1974 by Warren R. Johnson and Elsworth R. Buskirk. Copyright © 1960 by Warren R. Johnson. Reprinted by permission of Harper & Row, Publishers, Inc.

FIGURE (p. 519) From Sternberg, R. J. "Stalking the I.Q. Quark." *Psychology Today* 13 (September 1979), pp. 42–54. Copyright © 1979 by the American Psychological Association. Reprinted/adapted by permission of the author.

FIGURE (p. 527) From Welman, H. M., Somerville, S. C., and Haake, R. J. "Development of Search Procedures in Real-Life Spatial Environments." *Developmental Psychology* 15 (1979), pp. 530–542. Copyright © 1979 by the American Psychological Association. Reprinted/adapted by permission of the author.

FIGURE (p. 528) From Siegler, R. S. "Developmental Sequences Within and Between Concepts." Copyright © The Society for Research in Child Development, Inc. *Monographs of the Society for Research in Child Development* 46, No. 2, Serial No. 189, 1981.

TABLE (p. 533) From Sternberg, R. J. "Who's Intelligent?" *Psychology Today* (April 1982), pp. 30–39. Copyright © 1982 by the American Psychological Association. Reprinted/adapted by permission of the author.

TABLE (p. 563) From Keating, D. P., and Clark, L. V. "Development of Physical and Social Reasoning in Adolescents." *Developmental Psychology* 16 (1980), pp. 23–30. Copyright © 1980 by the American Psychological Association. Reprinted/adapted by permission of the author.

FIGURE (p. 604) From *Being Adolescent: Conflict and Growth in the Teenage Years*, by Mihaly Csikszentmihalyi and Reed Larson. Copyright © 1984 by Basic Books, Inc. Reprinted by permission of Basic Books, Inc., Publishers.

FIGURE (p. 608) From *Being Adolescent: Conflict and Growth in the Teenage Years*, by Mihaly Csikszentmihalyi and Reed Larson. Copyright © 1984 by Basic Books, Inc. Reprinted by permission of Basic Books, Inc., Publishers.

FIGURE (p. 618) From Barnes, H. L., and Olson, D. H. "Parent–Adolescent Communication and the Circumplex Model." Copyright © The Society for Research in Child Development, Inc. *Child Development* 56 (1985), pp. 438–447.

FIGURE (p. 625) From Adelson, J. (ed.). *Handbook of Adolescent Psychology*. Copyright © 1980 by John Wiley & Sons, Inc. Reprinted by permission of John Wiley & Sons, Inc.

TABLE (p. 632) From Gottman, J. M. "How Children Become Friends." Copyright © The Society for Research in Child Development, Inc. *Monographs of the Society for Research in Child Development* 48 Serial No. 201 (1983).

FIGURE (p. 651) From Chumlea, "Physical Growth in Adolescence" in *Handbook of Developmental Psychology*, by B. Wolman, ed. Copyright © 1982, p. 474. Reprinted by permission of Prentice-Hall, Inc., Englewood Cliffs, New Jersey.

FIGURE (p. 658) From *Sexual Interactions* by Elizabeth R. and Albert Richard Allgeier. Copyright © 1984 by D. C. Heath and Company. Reprinted by permission of the Publisher.

FIGURE (p. 659) From *Sexual Interactions* by Elizabeth R. and Albert Richard Allgeier. Copyright © 1984 by D. C. Heath and Company. Reprinted by permission of the Publisher.

TABLE (p. 661) From Adelson, J. (ed.). *Handbook of Adolescent Psychology*. Copyright © 1980 by John Wiley & Sons, Inc. Reprinted by permission of John Wiley & Sons, Inc.

FIGURE (p. 664) Copyright © The Society for Research in Child Development, Inc.

FIGURE (p. 665) Copyright © The Society for Research in Child Development, Inc.

FIGURE (p. 667) From Adelson, J. (ed.). *Handbook of Adolescent Psychology*. Copyright © 1980 by John Wiley & Sons, Inc. Reprinted by permission of John Wiley & Sons, Inc.

FIGURE (p. 672) From *Journal of Genetic Psychology* 75, pp. 165–196, (1949). Reprinted with permission of the Helen Dwight Reid Educational Foundation. Published by Heldref Publications, 4000 Albemarle St., N.W., Washington, D.C. 20016. Copyright © 1949.

TABLE (p. 689) From Marcia, J. E. "Identity in Adolescence." In J. Adelson (ed.), *Handbook of Adolescent Psychology*. New York: John Wiley & Sons, Inc. Copyright © 1980 John Wiley & Sons, Inc.

FIGURE (p. 709) From Lewis, C. C. "How Adolescents Approach Decisions: Changes over Grades Seven to Twelve and Policy Implications." Copyright © The Society for Research in Child Development. *Child Development* 52 (1981b), pp. 538–544.

FIGURE (p. 710) From Berndt, T. "Developmental Changes in Conformity to Peers and Parents." *Develomental Psychology* 15 (1979), pp. 608–616. Copyright © 1979 by the American Psychological Association. Reprinted/adapted by permission of the author.

FIGURE (p. 719) From Dreyer, "Sexuality During Adolescence" in *Handbook of Developmental Psychology*, by B. Wolman, ed. Copyright © 1982, p. 575. Adapted by permission of Prentice-Hall, Inc., Englewood Cliffs, New Jersey.

FIGURE (p. 732) From Adelson, J. (ed.). *Handbook of Adolescent Psychology*. Copyright © 1980 by John Wiley & Sons, Inc. Reprinted by permission of John Wiley & Sons, Inc.

TABLE (p. 724) Reprinted with permission from: James Garbarino, Cynthia J. Schellenbach, and Janet Sebes, *Troubled Youth, Troubled Families: Understanding Families At-Risk for Adolescent Maltreatment* (New York: Aldine de Gruyter). Copyright © 1986 by James Garbarino, Cynthia J. Schellenback, and Janet M. Sebes.

Chapter Opening Photo Credits

Chapter 1—Tim Davis/Photo Researchers, Inc.; 2—Ellan Young/Photo Researchers, Inc.; 3—Erika Stone; 4—Rosalie Herion Freese; 5—Mimi Cotter/International Stock Photo; 6—Roberta Hershenson/Photo Researchers, Inc.; 7—Maratea/International Stock Photo; 8—Jerry Howard/Positive Images; 9—Barbara Ries/Photo Researchers, Inc.; 10—Randy Masser/International Stock Photo; 11—Barbara Loudis/International Stock Photo; 12—Jerry Howard/Positive Images; 13—Robin Schwartz/International Stock Photo; 14—Susan McCartney/Photo Researchers, Inc.; 15—James Foote; 16—Doreen E. Pugh/Photo Researchers, Inc.; 17—Ellis Herwig.

Photo Essay Credits

FAMILY
First page: Jerry Howard *Second page*: Gary Mottau/Positive Images (top); Erika Stone (middle right); George Ancona/International Stock Photo (bottom left) *Third page*: Erika Stone (top); L. L. Smith/Photo Researchers, Inc. (middle); Larry Downing/Woodfin Camp and Associates (bottom) *Fourth page*: Gary Mottau/Positive Images (top left); Michal Heron/Woodfin Camp and Associates (top right); Michal Heron/Woodfin Camp and Associates (bottom).

SCHOOL
First page: Sepp Seitz *Second page*: R. S. Uzzell/Woodfin Camp and Associates (top); Jerry Howard/Positive Images (middle); Pellegrini/International Stock Photo (bottom) *Third page*: Louie Psihoyos/Contact Press Images (top); Pellegrini/International Stock Photo (middle); George Ancona/International Stock Photo (bottom); *Fourth page*: Erika Stone (top); Michal Heron/Woodfin Camp and Associates (middle); Bernard Gotfryd/Woodfin Camp and Associates (bottom).

PEERS/FRIENDS
First page: Michael O'Brien *Second page*: Erika Stone (top); George Ancona/International Stock Photo (middle); John Michael/International Stock Photo (bottom) *Third page*: Erika Stone (top); Mimi Cotter/International Stock Photo (middle); Erika Stone (bottom) *Fourth page*: Erika Stone (top); George Ancona/International Stock Photo (middle); Richard Hutchings/Photo Researchers, Inc. (bottom).

COMMUNITY
First page: Jeffrey D. Smith *Second page*: Lawrence Migdale/Photo Researchers, Inc. (top left); Erika Stone (top right); Jerry Howard/Positive Images (bottom) *Third page*: Sepp Seitz/Woodfin Camp and Associates (top); White/Pite/International Stock Photo (bottom left); Erika Stone (bottom right) *Fourth page*: Erika Stone (top); Erika Stone (middle); Jerry Howard/Positive Images (bottom).

References

ABEL, E. "Smoking and Pregnancy." *Journal of Psychoactive Drugs* 16 (1984), 327, 338.

ABELSOHN, D. "Dealing with the Abdication Dynamic in the Post-divorce Family: A Context for Adolescent Crises." *Family Relations* 22 (1983), 359–383.

ABRAHAM, K. G., and CHRISTOPHERSON, V. A. "Perceived Competence Among Rural Middle School Children: Parental Antecedents and Relation to Locus of Control." *Journal of Early Adolescence* 4 (1984), 343–351.

ABRAMOVITCH, R.; PEPLER, D.; and CORTER, C. "Patterns of Sibling Interaction Among Preschool-Age Children." In M. E. Lamb and B. Sutton-Smith (eds.), *Sibling Relationships*. Hillsdale, N.J.: Erlbaum, 1982.

ABRAMS, R. S., and WEXLER, P. *Medical Care of the Pregnant Patient.* Boston: Little, Brown and Company, 1983.

ACHENBACH, T. M. *Developmental Psychopathology*, 2d ed. New York: Wiley, 1982.

ACKERMAN, B. P. "Contextual Integration and Utterance Interpretation: The Ability of Children and Adults to Interpret Sarcastic Utterances." *Child Development* 53 (1982), 1075–1083.

ADAMS, C., and JONES, R. "Female Adolescents' Identity Development: Age Comparisons and Perceived Child-Rearing Experience." *Developmental Psychology* 19 (1983), 249–256.

ADAMS, G. R., and FITCH, S. "Ego Stage and Identity Status Development: A Cross-sequential Analysis." *Journal of Personality and Social Psychology* 43 (1982), 574–583.

ADAMS, G. R., and GULLOTTA, T. *Adolescent Life Experiences*. Monterey, Calif.: Brooks/Cole, 1983.

ADAMS, R. E., and PASSMAN, R. H. "The Effects of Advance Preparation upon Children's Behavior During Brief Separation from Their Mother." Paper presented at the annual meeting of the Southeastern Psychological Association, Washington, D.C. (March 1980).

———. "The Effects of Preparing Two-Year-Olds for Brief Separations from Their Mothers." *Child Development* 52 (1981), 1068–1070.

ADAMS, R. J., and MAURER, D. "A Demonstration of Color Perception in the Newborn." Paper presented at the meetings of the Society for Research in Child Development, Detroit, 1983.

ADELSON, J. (ed.). *Handbook of Adolescent Psychology*. New York: Wiley, 1980.

ADELSON, J., and BEALL, L. "Adolescent Perspectives on Law and Government." *Law Social Review* 4 (1970), 495–504.

ADELSON, J., and O'NEIL, R. P. "Growth of Political Ideas in Adolescence: The Sense of Community." *Journal of Personality and Social Psychology* (1966), 295–306.

ADELSON, J.; GREEN, B.; and O'NEIL, R. P. "Growth of the Idea of Law in Adolescence." *Developmental Psychology* (1969), 327–332.

ADLER, I., and KANDEL, D. "A Cross-Cultural Comparison of Sociopsychological Factors in Alcohol Use Among Adolescents in Israel, France and the United States." *Journal of Youth and Adolescence* 11 (1982), 89–113.

ADLER, M. *The Paideia Proposal: An Educational Manifesto*. New York: Macmillan, 1982.

Advisory Committee on Child Development. *Toward a National Policy for Children and Families*. Washington, D.C.: National Academy of Science, 1976.

AINSLIE, R. (ed.). *The Child and the Day Care Setting*. New York: Praeger, 1984.

AINSWORTH, M.D.S. "The Development of Infant-Mother Attachment." In B. Caldwell and H. Ricciuti (eds.), *Review of Child Development Research*, Vol. 3. Chicago: University of Chicago Press, 1973, 1–94.

———. "Attachment as Related to Mother-Infant Interaction." In J. S. Rosenblatt, et al. (eds.), *Advances in the Study of Behavior*, Vol. 9. New York: Academic Press, 1979a.

———. "Infant-Mother Attachment." *American Psychologist* 34 (1979b), 932–937.

AINSWORTH, M.D.S., and BELL, S.M.V. "Some Contemporary Patterns of Mother-Infant Interaction in the Feeding Situation." In J. A. Ambrose (ed.), *Stimulation in Early Infancy*. London: Academic Press, 1969, 133–170.

AINSWORTH, M.D.S., and WITTIG, B. A. "Attachment and Exploratory Behavior of One-Year-Olds in a Strange Situation." In B. M. Foss (ed.), *Determinants of Infant Behavior*, Vol. 4. London: Methuen, 1969, 111–136.

AINSWORTH, M.D.S., BELL, S. M., and STAYTON, D. J. "Infant-Mother Attachment and Social Development: Socialization as a Product of Reciprocal Responsiveness to Signals." In M.P.M. Richards (ed.), *The Integration of the Child into a Social World*. London: Cambridge University Press, 1974.

ALDOUS, J. "Birth Control Socialization: How to Avoid Discussing the Subject." *Population and Environment* 6 (1983), 27–38.

ALLAN, G. A. *Family Life: Domestic Roles and Social Organization*. New York: Basil Blackwell, 1985.

ALLGEIER, E. R., and ALLGEIER, A. R. *Sexual Interactions*. Lexington, Mass.: D. C. Heath, 1984.

ALSCHULER, A., and WEINSTEIN, G. "Self-Knowledge Development." Amherst, Mass.: School of Education. University of Massachusetts, 1976 (unpublished).

AMBROSE, A. "The Ecological Perspective in Developmental Psychology." In H. McGurk (ed.), *Ecological Factors in Human Development*. New York: Elsevier North-Holland Publishing Company, Inc., 1977, 3–10.

AMERICAN CANCER SOCIETY. "Why Start Life Under a Cloud?" New York, 1982.

AMERICAN HUMANE ASSOCIATION. "Trends in Child Abuse and Neglect: A National Perspective." 1984.

AMSTERDAM, B. "Mirror Self-Image Reactions Before Age Two." *Developmental Psychology* 5 (1972), 297–305.

ANASTASIOW, N. J., and HANES, M. L. "Cognitive Development and Acquisition of Language in Three Subcultural Groups." *Developmental Psychology* 10 (1974), 703–709.

ANDERSON, C. A., and JENNINGS, D. L. "When Experiences of Failure Promote Expectations of Success: The Impact of Attributing Failure to Ineffective Strategies." *Journal of Personality* 48 (1980), 393–407.

ANDERSON, C. W., NAGLE, R. J., ROBERTS, W. A., and SMITH, J. W. "Attachment to Substitute Caregivers as a Function of Center Quality and Caregiver Involvement." *Child Development* 52 (1981), 53–61.

ANDERSON, N. H., and CUNEO, D. O. "The Height + Width Rule in Children's Judgments of Quantity." *Journal of Experimental Psychology: General* 107 (1978), 335–378.

ANDERSON, R. E., and CARTER, I. *Human Behavior in the Social Environment: A Social Systems Approach,* 2d ed. New York: Aldine, 1978.

ANDISON, F. S. "T.V. Violence and Viewer Aggression: A Cumulation of Study Results 1956–1976." *Public Opinion Quarterly* 41 (1977), 314–331.

ANISFELD, M. *Language Development from Birth to Three.* Hillsdale, N.J.: Erlbaum, 1984.

ANNIS, L. *The Child Before Birth.* Ithaca, N.Y.: Cornell University Press, 1978.

ANOOSHIAN, L. J., and PRILOP, L. "Developmental Trends for Auditory Selective Attention: Dependence on Central-Incidental Word Relations." *Child Development* 51 (1980), 45–54.

APGAR, V. "Evaluation of Newborn Infant." *Journal of the American Medical Association* 168, no. 15 (1958), 1988.

APGAR, V., and JAMES, L. S. "Further Observations on the Newborn Scoring System." *American Journal of Diseases of Children* 104 (1962), 419–428.

APTER, D. and VIHKO, R. "Serum Pregnenolone, Progesterone, 17-Hydroxyprogesterone, Testosterone, and 5-Dehydrotestosterone During Female Puberty." *Journal of Clinical Endocrinology and Metabolism* 45 (1977), 1039–1048.

ARCHER, S. "The Lower Age Boundaries of Identity Development." *Child Development* 53 (1982), 1551–1556.

AREND, R.; GOVE, F. L.; and SROUFE, L. A. "Continuity of Individual Adaptation from Infancy to Kindergarten: A Predictive Study of Ego-resiliency and Curiosity in Preschoolers." *Child Development* 50 (1979), 950–959.

ARLIN, P. K. "Cognitive Development in Adulthood: A Fifth Stage?" *Developmental Psychology* 11, no. 5 (1975), 602–606.

ASARNOW, J. R., and MEICHENBAUM, D. "Verbal Rehearsal and Serial Recall: The Mediational Training of Kindergarten Children." *Child Development* 50 (1979), 1173–1177.

ASHLEY, M. J. "Alcohol Use During Pregnancy: A Challenge for the '80s." *Canadian Medical Association Journal* 125 (1981), 141–142.

ASLIN, R. N.; PISONI, D. B.; and JUSCZYK, P. W. "Auditory Development and Speech Perception in Infancy." In P. H. Mussen (ed.), *Handbook of Child Psychology,* 4th ed. Vol. 2, *Infancy and Developmental Psychobiology.* New York: Wiley, 1983, 573–688.

ATKINSON, R. C., and SHIFFRIN, R. M. "Human Memory: A Proposed System and Its Control Processes." In K. W. Spence and J. T. Spence (eds.), *The Psychology of Learning and Motivation,* Vol. 2. New York: Academic Press, (1968).

AZMITIA, M.; MERRIMAN, W. E.; and PERLMUTTER, M. "A Developmental Study of the Interaction of Selectivity and Knowledge in Memory." 1985 (unpublished).

BABSON, S. G.; PERNOLL, M. C.; BENDA, G. I.; and SIMPSON, K. *Diagnosis and Management of the Fetus and Neonate at Risk: A Guide for Team Care,* 4th ed. St. Louis: Mosby, 1980.

BACHMAN, J. G. "The American High School Student: A Profile Based on Survey Data." Paper presented in Berkeley, Calif., June 28, 1982.

BAILEY, C. A. *Loving Conspiracy.* London: Quartet Books, 1984.

BAINUM, C. K.; LOUNSBURY, K. R.; and POLLIO, H. R. "The Development of Laughing and Smiling in Nursery School Children." *Child Development,* 55 (1984), 1946–1957.

BAKEMAN, R., and BROWN, J. V. "Early Interaction: Consequences for Social and Mental Development at Three Years." *Child Development,* 51 (1980), 437–447.

BAKER, T. L., and McGINTY, D. J. "Sleep Apnea in Hypoxic and Normal Kittens." *Developmental Psychology* 12 (1979), 577–594.

BALTES, P. B., DITTMAN-KOHLI, F.; and DIXON, R. A. "New Perspectives on the Development of Intelligence in Adulthood: Toward a Dual Process Conception." In P. B. Baltes and O. G. Brim (eds.), *Lifespan Development and Behavior,* Vol. 6. Orlando, Fla.: Academic Press, 1984.

BANDURA, A. "Influence of Model's Reinforcement Contingencies on the Acquisition of Imitative Responses." *Journal of Personality and Social Psychology* (1965), 589–595.

———. *Aggression: A Social Learning Analysis.* Englewood Cliffs, N.J.: Prentice-Hall, 1973.

———. *Social Learning Theory.* Englewood Cliffs, N.J.: Prentice-Hall, 1977.

———. "The Self and Mechanisms of Agency." In J. Suls (ed.), *Social Psychological Perspectives on the Self.* Hillsdale, N.J.: Erlbaum, 1980.

———. "Self-referent Thought: The Development of Self-Efficacy." In J. H. Flavell and L. D. Ross (eds.), *Social Cognitive Development.* New York: Cambridge University Press, 1981.

BANDURA, A., ROSS, D., and ROSS, S. A. "Imitation of Film-Mediated Aggressive Models." *Journal of Abnormal and Social Psychology* 66 (1963), 3–11.

BANDURA, A., and SCHUNK, D. H. "Cultivating Competence, Self-Efficacy and Intrinsic Interest Through Proximal Self-Motivation." *Journal of Personality and Social Psychology* 41 (1981), 586–598.

BANDURA, A., and WALTERS, R. H. *Social Learning and Personality Development.* New York: Holt, 1963.

BANDURA, M., and DWECK, C. S. "Children's Theories of Intelligence as Predictors of Achievement Goals." Harvard University, 1981 (unpublished).

BANKS, M.; BEWLEY, B.; BLAND, J.; DEAN, J.; and POLLARD, V. "Long-term Study of Smoking by Secondary School Children." *Archives of Disease in Childhood* 53 (1978), 12–19.

BANKS, M. S., and SALAPATEK, P. "Infant Visual Perception." In P. H. Mussen (ed.), *Handbook of Child Psychology,* 4th ed. Vol. 2, *Infancy and Developmental Psychobiology.* New York: Wiley, 1983, 435–572.

BANNISTER, D., and AGNEW, J. "The Child's Construing of Self." In J. Cole (ed.), *Nebraska Symposium on Motivation.* Lincoln: University of Nebraska Press, 1977.

BANTA, H. D. "The Risks and Benefits of Episiotomy." Paper presented at the Conference on Obstetrical Management and Infant Outcome 1981: Implications for Future Mental and Physical Development. Sponsored by the American Foundation for Maternal and Child Health, Inc., New York, October 1981.

BARCUS, F. *Weekend Commercial Children's Television*—1975. Newtonville, MA: Action for Children's Television, 1975.

BARKER, R. G., and SCHOGGEN, P. *Qualities of Community Life: Methods of Measuring Environment and Behavior Applied to an American and an English Town.* San Francisco: Jossey-Bass, 1973.

BARKER, R. G., and WRIGHT, H. F. *Midwest and Its Children.* New York: Harper & Row, 1955.

BARKLEY, R. A. "The Use of Psychopharmacology to Study Reciprocal Influences in Parent-Child Interaction." *Journal of Abnormal Child Psychology* 9 (1981), 303–310.

BARNES, G. M. "The Development of Adolescent Drinking Behavior: An Evaluative Review of the Impact of the Socialization Process Within the Family." *Adolescence* 13 (1977), 571–595.

BARNES, H. L., and OLSON, D. H. "Parent-Adolescent Communication and the Circumplex Model." *Child Development* 56 (1985), 438–447.

BARNETT, C. R.; GROBSTEIN, R.; and SEASHORE, H. "Personal Communication to Klaus & Kennell." Cited in M. H. Klaus and J. H. Kennell (eds.), *Maternal-Infant Bonding.* St. Louis: Mosby, 1982.

BARRETT, D. E.; RADKE-YARROW, M.; and KLEIN, R. E. "Chronic

Malnutrition and Child Behavior: Effects of Early Caloric Supplementation on Social and Emotional Functioning at School Age." *Developmental Psychology* 18 (1982), 541–556.

BAR-TAL, D.; RAVIV, A.; and SHAVIT, N. "Motives for Helping Expressed by Kindergarten and School Children in Kibbutz and City." 1980 (unpublished).

BARUCH, G. K., and BARNETT, R. C. "Fathers' Participation in the Care of Their Preschool Children." *Sex Roles* 7 (1981), 1043–1056.

BARUCH, G. K.; BARNETT, R. C.; and RIVERS, C. *Lifeprints.* New York: McGraw-Hill, 1983.

BATES, J. E. "The Concept of Difficult Temperament." *Merrill Palmer Quarterly* 26 (1980), 299–320.

BAUMRIND, D. "Childcare Practices Anteceding 3 Patterns of Preschool Behavior." *Genetic Psychology Monographs* 75 (1967), 43–88.

———. "Current Patterns of Parental Authority." *Developmental Psychology Monographs* 4, no. 1 (1971), part 2.

———. "The Development of Instructional Competence Through Socialization." In A. D. Pick (ed.), *Minnesota Symposium on Child Psychology,* Vol. 7. Minneapolis: University of Minnesota, 1973.

———. "Parental Disciplinary Patterns." *Youth and Society* 9 (1978), 223–276.

———. "Sex-Related Socialization Effects." Paper presented at the meeting of the Society for Research in Child Development, San Francisco, 1979.

———. "Rejoinder to Lewis' Reinterpretation of Parental Firm Control Effects: Are Authoritative Families Really Harmonious?" *Psychology Bulletin* 94 (1983), 132–142.

BAYLEY, N. "The Development of Motor Abilities During the First Three Years." *The Society for Research in Child Development, Inc.* Monograph No. 1 (1935), 1–26, abridged.

———. "Consistency and Variability in the Growth of Intelligence from Birth to Eighteen Years." *Journal of Genetic Psychology* 75 (1949), 165–196.

———. "Growth Curves of Height and Weight by Age for Boys and Girls, Scaled According to Physical Maturity." *Journal of Pediatrics* 48 (1956), 187–194.

———. *Bayley Scales of Infant Development.* New York: The Psychological Corporation, 1969.

BEAL, C. R., and FLAVELL, J. H. "Young Speakers' Evaluations of Their Listener's Comprehension in a Referential Communication Task." *Child Development* 54 (1983), 148–153.

BECK, N. C.; GEDEN, E. A.; and BROUDER, G. T. "Techniques of Labor Preparation." In J. J. Sciarra, M. J. Daly, and G. I. Zatuchni (eds.), *Gynecology and Obstetrics,* Vol. 6. Rev. ed. Philadelphia: Harper and Row, 1986.

BECK, S. D. *Animal Photoperiodism.* New York: Holt, Rinehart and Winston, 1963.

BECKER, J. M. "A Learning Analysis of the Development of Peer-Oriented Behavior in Nine-Month Old Infants." *Developmental Psychology* 13 (1977), 481–491.

BECKETT, S. *Endgame, a Play in One Act, Followed by Act Without Words, a Mime for One Player.* New York: Grove Press, 1958.

BEHRMAN, R. E., and VAUGHN, V. C. (eds.). *Nelson Textbook of Pediatrics,* 12th ed. Philadelphia: Saunders, 1983.

BEILIN, H. "Piaget's Theory: Refinement, Revision, or Rejection?" In R. Kluwe and H. Spada (eds.), *Developmental Models of Thinking.* New York: Academic Press, 1980.

BEIT-HALLAHMI, B., and RABIN, A. I. "The Kibbutz as a Social Experiment and Child-Rearing Laboratory." *American Psychologist* 32 (1977), 532–541.

BELL, R. Q. "A Reinterpretation of the Direction of Effects in Studios of Socialization." *Psychological Review* 75 (1968), 81–95.

BELLUGI, U., and BROWN, R. (eds.). "The Acquisition of Language." *Monographs of the Society for Research in Child Development* 29, no. 1 (1964), 43–79.

BELSKY, J. "Child Maltreatment: An Ecological Integration." *American Psychologist* 35 (1980), 320–336.

———. "Early Human Experience: A Family Perspective." *Developmental Psychology* 17 (1981), 3–23.

———. "Two Waves of Day Care Research: Developmental Effects and Conditions of Quality." In R. Ainslie (ed.), *The Child and the Day Care Setting.* New York: Praeger, 1984, 1–34.

BELSKY, J., and ISABELLA, R. A. "Marital and Parent-Child Relationships in Family of Origin and Marital Change Following the Birth of a Baby: A Retrospective Analysis." *Child Development* 56 (1985), 342–349.

BELSKY, J.; LERNER, R. M.; and SPANIER, G. B. *The Child in the Family.* Reading, Mass.: Addison-Wesley, 1984.

BEM, S. L. "Beyond Androgyny: Some Presumptuous Prescriptions for a Liberated Sexual Identity." In J. A. Sherman and F. L. Denmark (eds.), *The Psychology of Women: Future Directions in Research.* New York: Psychological Dimensions, 1978.

———. "Theory and Measurement of Androgyny: A Reply to the Pedhazur-Tetenbaum and Locksley-Colten Critiques." *Journal of Personality and Social Psychology* 37 (1979), 1047–1054.

———. "Gender Schema Theory: A Cognitive Account of Sex Typing." *Psychological Review* 88 (1981), 354–364.

BENBOW, C. P., and STANLEY, J. C. "Sex Differences in Mathematical Ability: Fact or Artifact?" *Science* 210 (1980), 58–59ff.

BENNETT, F. C.; ROBINSON, N. M.; and SELLS, C. J. "Growth and Development of Infants Weighing Less Than 800 Grams at Birth." *Pediatrics* 71 (1983), 319–323.

BEREITER, C., and ENGLEMANN, S. *Teaching Disadvantaged Children in the Preschool.* Englewood Cliffs, N.J.: Prentice-Hall, 1966.

BEREITER, C., and SCARDAMALIA, M. "From Conservation to Composition: The Role of Instruction in a Developmental Process." In R. Glaser (ed.), *Advances in Instructional Psychology,* Vol. 2. Hillsdale, N.J.: Erlbaum, 1982.

BERELSON, B. "The Value of Children: A Taxonomical Essay." In J. G. Wells (ed.), *Current Issues in Marriage and Family.* New York: Macmillan. 1975, 168–176.

BERENSON, G.; FRANK, G.; HUNTER, S.; SRINIVASAN, S.; VOORS, A.; and WEBBER, L. "Cardiovascular Risk Factors in Children: Should They Concern the Pediatrician?" *American Journal of Diseases of Children* 136 (1982), 855–862.

BERKO, J. "The Child's Learning of English Morphology." *Word* 14 (1958), 150–177.

BERNDT, T. V. "Developmental Changes in Conformity to Peers and Parents." *Developmental Psychology* 15 (1979), 608–616.

———. "The Features and Effects of Friendship in Early Adolescence." *Child Development* (1982), 1447–1460.

BERNSTEIN, B. *Class, Codes and Control.* Vol. 3, *Towards a Theory of Educational Transmissions.* London: Routledge and Kegan Paul, 1975.

BERRUETA-CLEMENT, J. R.; SCHWEINHART, L. J.; BARNETT, W. S.; EPSTEIN, A. S.; and WEIKART, D. P. *Changed Lives: The Effects of the Perry Preschool Program on Youths Through Age 19.* Ypsilanti, Mich.: The High/Scope Press, 1984.

BEST, D. L.; WILLIAMS, J. E.; CLOUD, J. M.; DAVIS, S. W.; ROBERTSON, L. S.; EDWARDS, J. R.; GILES, H.; and FOWLES, J. "Development of Sex-Trait Stereotypes Among Young Children in the United States, England and Ireland." *Child Development* 48 (1977), 1375–1384.

BIGELOW, B. J. "Children's Friendship Expectations: A Cognitive-Developmental Study." *Child Development* (1977), 48, 246–253.

BIGGS, J. B., and COLLIS, K. F. *Evaluating the Quality of Learning: The SOLO Taxonomy (Structure of the Observed Learning Outcome).* New York: Academic Press, 1982.

BIGNER, J. J. *Parent-Child Relations.* New York: Macmillan, 1979.

BILLER, H. "Father Absence, Divorce and Personality Development." In M. Lamb (ed.), *The Role of the Father in Child Development,* 2d ed. New York: Wiley, 1981.

BINET, A., and SIMON, T. "Sur la necessite d'etablir un diagnostic scientific des etats inferieurs de l'intelligence." *L'Annee Psychologique* 11 (1905a), 162–190.

———. "Methodes nouvelles pour la diagnostic du niveau intellectual des anormaus." *L'Annee Psychologique* 11 (1905b), 191–244.

BING, E. D. *Dear Elizabeth Bing: We've Had Our Baby.* New York: Pocket Books, 1983.

BIRCH. W. G. *A Doctor Discusses Pregnancy.* Chicago: Budlong Press, 1980.

BLACK, L.; STEINSCHNEIDER, A.; and SHEEHE, P. R. "Neonatal Respiratory Instability and Infant Development." *Child Development* 50 (1979), 561–564.

BLACK, M. M., and ROLLINS, H. A. "The Effects of Instructional Variables on Young Children's Organization and Free Recall." *Journal of Experimental Child Psychology* 33 (1982), 1–19.

BLAIR, D. G.; COOPER, C. S.; OSKARSSON, M. K.; EATER, L. A.; and VANDEWOUDE, G. F. "New Methods for Detecting Cellular Transforming Genes." *Science* 218 (December 10, 1982), 1122–1125.

BLANE, H. "Middle Age Alcoholics and Young Drinkers." In H. Blane and M. Chafetz (eds.), *Youth, Alcohol and Social Policy.* New York: Plenum Press, 1979, 5–36.

BLANEY, N. "Cigarette Smoking in Children and Young Adolescents: Causes and Prevention." *Advances in Behavioral Pediatrics,* Vol. 2. Greenwich, Conn.: JAI Press, 1981.

BLASI, A. "Moral Cognition and Moral Action: A Theoretical Perspective." *Developmental Review* 3 (1983), 178–210.

BLATT, J.; SPENCER, L.; and WARD, S. "A Cognitive Developmental Study of Children's Reactions to Television Advertising." In E. Rubinstein, G. Comstock, and J. Murray (eds.), *Television and Social Behavior.* Vol. 4, *Television in Day to Day Life: Patterns of Use.* Washington, D.C.: U.S. Government Printing Office, 1972.

BLECHMAN, E. A. "Are Children with One Parent at Psychological Risk? A Methodological Review." *Journal of Marriage and the Family* 44, Vol. 1 (1982), 179–195.

BLEHAR, M. C.; LIEBERMAN, A. F.; and AINSWROTH, M.D.S. "Early Face-to-Face Interaction and Its Relation to Later Infant-Mother Attachment." *Child Development* 48 (1977), 182–194.

BLOCK, J. H. "Personality Development in Males and Females: The Influence of Differential Socialization." Paper presented as part of the Master Lecture Series at a meeting of the American Psychological Association, New York, September 1979.

————. "Differential Premises Arising from Differential Socialization of the Sexes: Some Conjectures." *Child Development* 54 (1983), 1335–1354.

BLOCK, J. H., and BLOCK, J. "The Role of Ego-Control and Ego-Resiliency in the Organization of Behavior." In W. A. Collins (ed.), *Development of Cognition, Affect, and Social Relations* (Minnesota Symposium on Child Psychology, Vol. 13). Hillsdale, N.J.: Erlbaum, 1980.

BLOCK, J. H.; BLOCK, J.; and MORRISON, A. "Parental Agreement—Disagreement on Child-Rearing Orientations and Gender-Related Personality Correlates in Children." *Child Development* 52 (1981), 965–974.

BLOOM, L.; MERKIN, S.; and WOOTTEN, J. "Wh-Questions: Linguistic Factors That Contribute to the Sequence of Acquisition." *Child Development* 53 (1982), 1084–1092.

BLOOM, M. V. *Adolescent-Parental Separation.* New York: Gardner Press, 1980.

BLOS, P. *The Young Adolescent: Clinical Studies.* New York: Free Press, 1970.

BLYTH, D.; HILL, J.; and THIEL, K. "Early Adolescents' Significant Others: Grade and Gender Differences in Perceived Relationships with Familial and Non-familial Adults and Young People. *Journal of Youth and Adolescence* 11 (1982), 425–450.

BOLTON, F. G. *The Pregnant Adolescent: Problems of Premature Parenthood.* Beverly Hills, Calif.: Sage, 1980.

BORKE, H. "Piaget's Mountains Revisited: Changes in the Egocentric Landscape." *Developmental Psychology* 11 (1975), 240–243.

————. "Piaget's Views of Social Interaction and the Theoretical Construct of Empathy." In L. Siegel and C. J. Brainerd (eds.), *Alternatives to Piaget: Critical Essays on the Theory.* New York: Academic Press, 1978.

BOSKIND-WHITE, M., and WHITE, W. J., JR. *Bulimerexia: The Binge/Purge Cycle.* New York: W. W. Norton, 1983.

BOUCHARD, T. J., and McGUE, M. "Familial Studies of Intelligence: A Review." *Science* 212 (1981), 1055–1059.

BOWLBY, J. "The Nature of the Child's Tie to His Mother." *International Journal of Psychoanalysis* 39 (1958), 350–373.

————. *Attachment and Loss.* Vol. 1, *Attachment.* London: Hogarth; New York: Basic Books, 1969.

————. *Attachment and Loss.* Vol. 2, *Separation.* London: Hogarth Press, 1973.

————. *Attachment and Loss.* Vol. 3, *Loss.* New York: Basic Books, 1980.

BOXER, A. M., and PETERSEN, A. C. "Pubertal Change in a Family Context." In G. K. Leigh and G. W. Petersen (eds.), *Adolescents in Families.* Cincinnati: South-Western, 1986, 73–103.

BRACKBILL, Y., "Long-term Effects of Obstetrical Anesthesia on Infant Autonomic Function." *Developmental Psychology* 10 (1977), 529–536.

BRACKBILL, Y., and BROMAN, S. H. "Obstetrical Medication and Development in the First Year of Life." 1979 (unpublished).

BRADLEY, R. H., and CALDWELL, B. M. "The Relation of Infant's Home Environments to Achievement Test Performance in First Grade: A Follow-Up Study. *Child Development* 55 (1984), 803–809.

BRAINE, M. D. S. "The Ontogeny of English Phrase Structure: The First Phrase." *Language* 39 (1963), 1–13.

BRAUCHT, G. "Psychosocial Research on Teenage Drinking: Past and Future." In F. Scarpitti and S. Datesman (eds.), *Drugs and the Youth Culture.* Beverly Hills, Calif.: Sage, 1980.

BRAZELTON, T. B. *Neonatal Behavioral Assessment Scale.* Philadelphia: Lippincott, 1973.

BRAZELTON, T. B.; KOSLOWSKI, B.; and MAIN, M. "The Origins of Reciprocity." In M. Lewis and L. A. Rosenblum (eds.), *The Effect of the Infant on Its Caregiver.* New York: Wiley, 1974.

BRECKENRIDGE, M. E., and MURPHY, M. N. *Growth and Development of the Young Child,* 8th ed. Philadelphia: Saunders, 1969.

BRETHERTON, I., and WATERS, E. (eds.). Growing Points of Attachment Theory and Research." *Monographs of the Society for Research in Child Development* 50, no. 1-2, Serial No. 209 (1985).

BRETHERTON, I.; STOLBERG, U.; and KREYE, M. "Engaging Strangers in Proximal Interaction: Infants' Social Initiative." *Developmental Psychology* 17 (1981), 746–755.

BREUER, H. "Ego Identity Status in Late-Adolescent College Males, as Measured by a Group-Administered Incomplete Sentences Blank and Related to Inferred Stance Toward Authority. Unpublished doctoral diss., New York University, 1973.

BRIGGS, D. C. *Your Child's Self-Esteem.* New York: Doubleday, 1975.

BRIM, O. G. "Life Span Development of the Theory of Oneself: Implications for Child Development." In H. W. Reese (ed.), *Advances in Child Development and Behavior,* Vol. 11. New York: Academic Press, 1976.

BRIM, O. G., AND KAGAN, J. (eds.), *Constancy and Change in Human Development.* Cambridge, Mass.: Harvard University Press, 1980.

BRODY, G. H.; STONEMAN, Z.; and MacKINNON, C. E. "Role Asymmetrics in Interactions Among School-Aged Children, Their Younger Siblings and Their Friends." *Child Development* 53 (1982), 1364–1370.

BRONFENBRENNER, U. *Two Worlds of Childhood: U.S. and U.S.S.R.* New York: Russell Sage Foundation, 1970.

————. "Developmental Research, Public Policy, and the Ecology of Childhood." *Child Development* 45, no. 1 (March 1974), 1–5.

————. "Is Early Intervention Effective? Some Studies of Early Education in Familiar and Extrafamiliar Settings." In A. Montagu (ed.), *Race and I.Q.* New York: Oxford University Press, 1975.

————. *The Ecology of Human Development.* Cambridge, Mass.: Harvard University Press, 1979.

————. "Ecology of the Family as a Context for Human Development: Research Perspectives." *Developmental Psychology* 22 (1986), 723–742.

BRONFENBRENNER, U.; ALVAREZ, W. F.; and HENDERSON, C. R. "Working and Watching: Maternal Employment Status and Parents' Perceptions of Their Three-Year-Old Children." *Child Development* 55 (1984), 1362–1378.

BRONFENBRENNER, U., and CROUTER, A. C. "Work and Family Through Time and Space." In S. B. Kamerman and C. D. Hayes (eds.), *Families That Work: Children in a Changing World*. Washington, D.C.: National Academy Press, 1982.

BRONFENBRENNER, U., and WEISS, H. B. "Beyond Policies Without People: An Ecological Perspective on Child and Family Policy." In E. Ziegler, S. L. Kagan, and E. Klugman (eds.), *Social Policy for Children and Their Families: A Primer*. Cambridge: Cambridge University Press, 1983.

BRONFENBRENNER, U.; MOEN, P.; and GARBARINO, J. "Child, Family and Community." In R. D. Parke (ed.), *Review of Child Development Research*, Vol. 7, *The Family*. Chicago: The University of Chicago Press, 1984.

BROOK, J. S.; WHITEMAN, M.; and GORDON, A. S. "Stages of Drug Use in Adolescence: Personality, Peer and Family Correlates. *Developmental Psychology* 19 (1983), 269–277.

BROOKS-GUNN, J., and LEWIS, M. "Infant Social Perception: Responses to Pictures of Parents and Strangers." *Developmental Psychology* 17 (1981), 647–649.

———. "The Development of Self-knowledge." In C. B. Kopp and J. B. Krako. (eds.), *The Child in a Social Context*. Reading, Mass.: Addison-Wesley, 1982.

BROPHY, J. E. "Research on the Self-Fulfilling Prophecy and Teacher Expectations." *Journal of Educational Psychology* 75 (1983), 631–661.

BROWN, A. L., and DeLOACHE, J. S. "Skills, Plans and Self-Regulation." In R. Siegler (ed.), *Children's Thinking: What Develops?* Hillsdale, N.J.: Erlbaum, 1978, 3–35.

BROWN, A. L.; BRANSFORD, J. D.; FERRARA, R. A.; and CAMPIONE, J. C. "Learning, Remembering, and Understanding." In P. H. Mussen (ed.), *Handbook of Child Psychology*, 4th ed. New York: Wiley, 1983, Vol. 3, pp. 77–166.

BROWN, G., and DESFORGES, C. *Piaget's Theory: A Psychological Critique*. Boston: Routledge and Kegan Paul, 1979.

BROWN, J. V., and BAKEMAN, R. "Relationships of Human Mothers with Their Infants During the First Year of Life." In R. W. Bell and W. P. Smotherman (eds.), *Maternal Influences and Early Behavior*. Jamaica, N.Y.: Spectrum, 1986.

BROWN, R. *Psycholinguistics*. New York: Free Press, 1970, 220.

———. *A First Language: The Early Stages*. Cambridge, Mass.: Harvard University Press, 1973.

———. "The Maintenance of Conversation." In D. R. Olson (ed.), *The Social Foundations of Language and Thought*. New York: Norton, 1980.

BROWN, R., and BELLUGI, U. "Three Processes in the Child's Acquisition of Syntax." *Harvard Educational Review* 34 (Spring 1964), 138–139, 141, 224. Copyright 1964 by the President and Fellows of Harvard College.

BRUNER, J. S. *Toward a Theory of Instruction*. Cambridge, Mass.: Belknap Press of Harvard University Press, 1966.

BRUNER, J. S., and SHERWOOD, V. "Peekaboo and the Learning of Rule Structures." In J. Bruner, A. Jolly, and K. Sylva (eds.), *Play: Its Role on Development and Evolution*. Hammondsworth, Eng.: Penguin, 1976.

BRUNER, J. S.; OLIVER, R. R.; GREENFIELD, P. M.; HORNSBY, J. R.; KENNEY, H. J.; MACCOBY, M.; MODIANO, N.; MOSHER, F. A.; OLSON, D. R.; POTTER, M. C.; REICH, L. C.; and McKINNON-SONSTROEM, A. *Studies in Cognitive Growth*. New York: Wiley, 1966.

BRYAN, J. H. "Children's Cooperation and Helping Behaviors." In E. M. Hetherington (ed.). *Review of Child Development Research*, Vol. 5. Chicago: University of Chicago Press, 1975.

BRYANT, B. K. "The Neighborhood Walk: Sources of Support in Middle Childhood." *Monographs of the Society for Research in Child Development* 50, no. 3, Serial No. 210 (1985).

BRYANT, B. K., and CROCKENBERG, S. B. "Correlates and Dimensions of Prosocial Behavior: A Study of Female Siblings with Their Mothers." *Child Development* 51 (1980), 529–544.

BRYANT, R., and BATES, B. "Anorexia Nervosa: Aetiological Theo-

ries and Treatment Methods." *Journal of Adolescence* 8 (1985), 93–103.

BUBER, M. *The Knowledge of Man*. New York: Harper & Row, 1965.

BUCKWALD, S.; ZOREN, W. A.; and EGAN, E. A. "Mortality and Follow-up Data for Neonates Weighing 500 to 800 g. at Birth." *American Journal of Diseases of Children* 138 (1984), 779–782.

BUNDY, R. S. "Discrimination of Sound Localization Cues in Young Infants." *Child Development* 51 (1980), 292–294.

BURR, W. R.; LEIGH, G. K.; DAY, R. D.; and CONSTANTINE, J. "Symbolic Interaction and the Family." In W. Burr et al. (eds.), *Contemporary Theories About the Family*, Vol. 2. New York: Free Press, 1979.

BURTON, R. V. "A Paradox in Theories and Research in Moral Development." In W. M. Kurtines and J. L. Gewirtz (eds.), *Morality, Moral Behavior and Moral Development*. New York: Wiley, 1984.

BURUD, S. L.; COLLINS, R. C.; and DIVINE-HAWKINS, P. "Employer-Supported Child Care: Everybody Benefits," *Children Today* (May-June 1983), 2–7.

BUSS, D.; BLOCK, J. H.; and BLOCK, J. "Preschool Activity Level: Personality Correlates and Developmental Implications." *Child Development* 51 (1980), 401–408.

BUSSEY, K., and PERRY, D. G. "The Imitation of Resistance to Deviation: Conclusive Evidence for an Elusive Effect." *Developmental Psychology* 13 (1977), 438–443.

BUTLER, N. R.; GOLDSTEIN, H.; and ROSS, E. M. "Cigarette Smoking in Pregnancy: Its Influence on Birth Weight and Prenatal Normality." *British Medical Journal* 2 (1972), 127–130.

BUTLER, S. *The Way of All Flesh*. New York: The Heritage Press, 1936.

BUTTERFIELD, P.; EMDE, R. N.; SVEJDA, M.; and NEIMAN, S. "Silver Nitrate and the Eyes of the Newborn: Effects on Parental Responsiveness During Initial Social Interaction." In R. N. Emde and R. J. Harmon (eds.), *The Development of Attachment and Affiliative Systems: Psychobiological Aspects*. New York: Plenum, 1982.

BYRNE, J. M., and HOROWITZ, F. D. "Rocking as a Soothing Intervention: The Influence of Direction and Type of Movement." *Infant Behavior and Development* 4 (1981), 207–218.

CAIN, L. P.; KELLY, D. H.; and SHANNON, D. C. "Parents' Perceptions of the Psychological and Social Impact of Home Monitoring." *Pediatrics* 66 (1980), 37–41.

CAIRNS, R. B., and CAIRNS, B. D. *Gender Similarities and Differences: A Developmental Perspective*. Paper presented at the Nag's Head Conference, October 11, 1983.

CALDERONE, M. "From Then to Now—And Where Next?" In L. Brown (ed.), *Sex Education in the Eighties*. New York: Plenum Press, 1981.

CALDWELL, B. M., and RICCIUTI, H. N. (eds.). *Review of Child Development Research*, Vol. 3. Chicago: University of Chicago Press, 1973, 1–94.

CAMPBELL, S. D., and FROST, J. L. *The Effects of Playground Type on the Cognitive and Social Play Behaviors of Grade Two Children*. Paper presented at the Seventh World Congress of the International Playground Association, Ottawa, Canada, August 1978.

CAMPOS, J. J.; BARRETT, K. C.; LAMB, M. E.; GOLDSMITH, H. H.; and STENBERG, C. "Socioemotional Development." In P. H. Mussen (ed.), *Handbook of Child Psychology*, (Vol. 2). 4th ed. New York: Wiley, 1983, 783–915.

CAMPOS, J.; HIATT, S.; RAMSAY, D.; HENDERSON, C.; and SVEJDA, M. "The Emergence of Fear on the Visual Cliff." In M. Lewis and L. Rosenblum (eds.), *The Origins of Affect*. New York: Plenum, 1978.

CAMPOS, J.; SVEJDA, M.; BERTENTHAL, B.; BENSON, N.; and SCHMID, D. "Self-Produced Locomotion and Wariness of Heights: New Evidence from Training Studies." Paper presented at the meetings of the Society for Research in Child Development, Boston, April 1981.

CAREW, J. "Experience and the Development of Intelligence in Young Children at Home and in Day Care." *Monographs of the Society for Research in Child Development* 45, no. 6–7, Serial No. 187 (1980).

CAREY, S. "The Child as a Word Learner." In M. Halle, J. Bresnan, and G. A. Miller (eds.), *Linguistic Theory and Psychological Reality*. Cambridge, Mass.: M.I.T. Press, 1977.

CARLSON, E. A. *Human Genetics*. Lexington, Mass.: D. C. Heath and Company, 1984.

CARLSSON, S. G.; FAGERBERG, H.; HORNEMAN, G.; HWANG, C. P.; LARSSON, K.; RODHOLM, M.; SCHALLER, J.; DANIELSSON, B.; and GUNDEWALL, C. "Effects of Various Amounts of Contact Between Mother and Child on the Mother's Nursing Behavior: A Follow Up Study." *Infant Behavior and Development* 2 (1979), 209–214.

CARNATION COMPANY. *Pregnancy in Anatomical Illustrations*. Los Angeles, 1962.

CARNEGIE COMMISSION ON POLICY STUDIES IN HIGHER EDUCATION. *Giving Youth a Better Chance*. San Francisco: Jossey-Bass, 1980.

CARNEGIE-MELLON CIVIC EDUCATION ENGLISH CURRICULUM. Pittsburgh: Carnegie-Mellon University, 1976.

CARROLL, J. L., and REST, J. R. "Development in Moral Judgment as Indicated by Rejection of Lower-Stage Statements." *Journal of Research in Personality* 15 (1981), 538–544.

CARTER, J., and DURIEZ, T. *With Child: Birth Through the Ages*. Edinburgh, Scotland: Mainstream Publishing Company, 1986.

CASE, R. "The Underlying Mechanism of Intellectual Development." In J. R. Kirby and J. B. Biggs (eds.), *Cognition, Development, and Instruction*. New York: Academic Press, 1980.

CASE, R., and KHANNA, F. "The Missing Links: Stages in Children's Progression from Sensorimotor to Logical Thought." In K. W. Fischer (ed.), *Cognitive Development*. New Directions for Child Development, No. 12. San Francisco: Jossey-Bass, 1981.

CASE, R.; KURLIND, D. M.; and GOLDBERG, J. "Operational Efficiency and the Growth of Short-Term Memory Span." *Journal of Experimental Child Psychology* 33, no. 3 (1982), 386–404.

CASPER, R. C.; OFFER, D.; and OSTROV, E. "The Self-Image of Adolescents with Acute Anorexia Nervosa." *The Journal of Pediatrics* 98 (1981), 656–661.

CASSEL, Z. K., and SANDER, L. W. "Neonatal Recognition Processes and Attachment: The Masking Experiment." Presented at the Society for Research in Child Development, Denver, 1975.

CATTELL, P. *The Measurement of Intelligence of Infants and Young Children*. New York: Psychological Corporation, 1960.

CAVANAUGH, J. C., and PERLMUTTER, M. "Metamemory: A Critical Examination." *Child Development* 53 (1982), 11–28.

CHACON, M. A., and TILDON, J. T. "Elevated Values of Triiodo-thyronine in Victims of Sudden Infant Death Syndrome." *Journal of Pediatrics* 99 (1981), 758–760.

CHARNEY, E.; GOODMAN, H.; and MCBRIDE, M. "Childhood Antecedents of Adult Obesity—Do Chubby Infants Become Obese Adults?" *New England Journal of Medicine* 295, no. 6 (1976).

CHEEK, D. B. *Human Growth*. Philadelphia: Lea and Febiger, 1968.

CHERRY, R. S. "Development of Selective Auditory Attention Skills in Children." *Perceptual and Motor Skills* 52 (1981), 379–385.

CHI, M.T.H. "Knowledge Structures and Memory Development." In R. S. Siegler (ed.), *Children's Thinking: What Develops*. Hillsdale, N.J.: Erlbaum, (1978), 73–96.

CHI, M.T.H., and KOESKE, R.D. "Network Representations of a Child's Dinosaur Knowledge." *Developmental Psychology* 19 (1983), 29–39.

CHILMAN, C. *Adolescent Sexuality in a Changing American Society: Social and Psychological Perspectives*. Washington, D.C.: U.S. Government Printing Office, 1979.

CHOMSKY, C. *The Acquisition of Syntax in Children from Five to Ten*. Cambridge, Mass.: MIT Press, 1969.

CHOMSKY, N. *Reflections on Language*. New York: Pantheon Books, 1975.

CHUMLEA, W. C. "Physical Growth in Adolescence." In B. Wolman (ed.), *Handbook of Developmental Psychology*. Englewood Cliffs, N.J.: Prentice-Hall, 1982, 471–485.

CICIRELLI, V. G. "Sibling Influence Throughout the Lifespan." In M. E. Lamb and B. Sutton-Smith (eds.), *Sibling Relationships*. Hillsdale, N.J.: Erlbaum, 1982.

CLARK, E. A., and HINISEE, J. "Intellectual and Adaptive Performance of Asian Children in Adoptive American Settings." *Developmental Psychology* 18 (1982), 595–599.

CLARK, E. V. "What's in a Word? On the Child's Acquisition of Semantics in His First Language." In T. E. Moore (ed.), *Cognitive Development and the Acquisition of Language*. New York: Academic Press, 1973.

CLARK, H. H., and CLARK, E. V. *Psychology and Language: An Introduction to Psycholinguists*. New York: Harcourt Brace Jovanovich, 1977.

CLARK, R. "The Quality of Family Pedagogic Life: What Is It?" Paper presented at the annual meeting of the American Educational Research Association, New York, 1982.

CLARKE-STEWART, K. A. "Interactions Between Mothers and Their Young Children." *Monographs of the Society for Research in Child Development* 38, no. 153 (1973), entire issue.

———. "And Daddy Makes Three: The Father's Impact on Mother and Young Child." *Child Development* 49 (1978), 466–478.

———. *Daycare*. Cambridge, Mass.: Harvard University Press, 1982.

———. "Day Care: A New Context for Research and Development." In M. Perlmutter (ed.), *Parent-Child Interactions and Parent-Child Relations in Child Development*. Vol. 17, *The Minnesota Symposia on Child Psychology*. Hillsdale, NJ: Erlbaum, 1984.

CLARKE-STEWART, K. A., and FEIN, G. G. "Early Childhood Programs." In Paul H. Mussen (ed), *Handbook of Child Psychology*. Vol. 2, *Infancy and Developmental Psychobiology*. New York: Wiley, 1983.

CLARKE-STEWART, K. A., and HEVEY, C. M. "Longitudinal Relations in Repeated Observations of Mother-Child Interaction from 1 to 2½ Years." *Developmental Psychology* 17 (1981), 127–145.

CLEMENS, S. *Huckleberry Finn*. New York: Macmillan, 1962.

COBB, S. "Social Support and Health Through the Life Course." In H. McCubbin, A. Cauble, and J. Patterson (eds.), *Family Stress, Coping and Social Support*. Springfield, Ill.: C. C. Thomas, 1982.

COCHRAN, M. M. "Cultural Boundaries and Developmentally Enhancing Relations Between Family and School." *Child Development* (1987).

COCHRAN, M. M. and BRASSARD, J. A. "Child Development and Personal Social Networks." *Child Development* 50, (1979), 601–616.

COCHRAN, M. M., and HENDERSON, C. R. "Family Matters: Evaluation of the Parental Empowerment Program. A Summary of a Final Report to the National Institute of Education" (NIE Contract #400-76-0150). Ithaca, N.Y.: Cornell University, February 1986.

COHEN, E., and DEAVILA, E. "Indirect Instruction and Conceptual Learning." Stanford University, 1983 (unpublished).

COHEN, L. B. "Our Developing Knowledge of Infant Perception and Cognition." *American Psychologist* 34 (1979), 894–899.

COHEN, L. B.; DELOACHE, J. S.; and STRAUSS, M. S. "Infant Visual Perception." In J. Osofsky (ed.), *Handbook of Infancy*. New York: Wiley, 1979.

COHEN, S., and SYME, S. L. (eds.), *Social Support and Health*. Orlando: Academic Press, 1985.

COHLER, B., and GEYER, S. "Psychological Autonomy and Interdependence Within the Family." In F. Walsh (ed.), *Normal Family Processes*. New York: Guilford Press, 1982.

COIE, J. D., and KUPERSMIDT, J. B. "A Behavioral Analysis of Emerging Status in Boys' Groups." *Child Development* 54 (1983), 1400–1416.

COIE, J. D.; DODGE, K. A.; and COPPOTELLI, H. "Dimensions and Types of Social Status: A Cross-Age Perspective." *Developmental Psychology* 18 (1982), 557–570.

COLBY, A., and KOHLBERG, L. "Invariant Sequence and Internal Consistency in Moral Judgment Stages." In M. W. Kurtines and J. L. Gewirtz (eds.), *Morality, Moral Behavior and Moral Development*. New York: Wiley, 1984.

COLBY, A.; KOHLBERG, L.; GIBBS, J.; and LIEBERMAN, M. "A Longitudinal Study of Moral Judgment." *Monographs of the Society for Research in Child Development* 48, Serial No. 200 (1983).

COLEMAN, J. S. *The Adolescent Society*. New York: Free Press. 1961.
———. *Youth: Transition to Adulthood*. Chicago: University of Chicago Press, 1974.

COLEMAN, J. S.; CAMPBELL, E. Q.; HOBSON, C. J.; McPARTLAND, J.; MOOD, A. M.; WEINFIELD, F. D.; and YORK, R. L. *Equality of Educational Opportunity*, U.S. Department of Health, Education, and Welfare. 2 vols. Washington, D.C.: U.S. Government Printing Office, 1966.

COLLETTA, N. D. "Stressful Lives: The Situation of Divorced Mothers and Their Children." *Journal of Divorce* 6 (1983) 19–31.

COLLINS, R. C. "Head Start: An Update on Program Effects." *Newsletter of the Society for Research in Child Development* (Summer 1983), 1–2.

COLLINS, W. A. (ed.). *Development During Middle Childhood: The Years from Six to Twelve*. Washington, D.C.: National Academy Press, 1984.

COLLINS, W. A.; BERNDT, T. V.; and HESS, V. L. "Observational Learning of Motives and Consequences for Television Aggression: A Developmental Study." *Child Development* 65 (1974), 799–802.

COLLINS, W. A.; WELLMAN, H.; KENISTON, A. H.; and WESTBY, S. D. "Age-Related Aspects of Comprehension and Inference from a Televised Dramatic Narrative." *Child Development* 49 (1978), 389–399.

COMER, J. P. *School Power*. New York: Free Press, 1980.

COMSTOCK, G. "New Emphases in Research on the Effects of Television and Film Violence." In E. L. Palmer and A. Dorr (eds.), *Children and the Faces of Television: Teaching, Violence, Selling*. New York: Academic Press, 1980.

CONDON, W. S. "Speech Makes Baby Move." *New Scientist* 6 (June 1974), 624–627.

CONDON, W. S., and SANDER, L. W. "Neonate Movement Is Synchronized with Adult Speech: Interactional Participation and Language Acquisition." *Science* 183 (1974a), 99–101.
———. "Synchrony Demonstrated Between Movements of the Neonate and Adult Speech." *Child Development* 45 (1974b), 456–462.

CONGER, J. J. "Freedom and Commitment: Families, Youth, and Social Change." *American Psychologist* 36 (1981), 1475–1484.

CONSUMERS UNION OF UNITED STATES, INC., Mount Vernon, N.Y., 1979.

COONS, S., and GUILLEMINAULT, C. "Development of Sleep-Wake Patterns and Non-rapid Eye Movement Stages During the First Six Months of Life in Normal Infants." *Pediatrics* 69 (1982), 793–798.

COOPER, C. R.; GROTEVANT, H. D.; and CONDON, S. M. "Individuality and Connectedness in the Family as a Context for Adolescent Identity Formation and Role-Taking Skill." In H. D. Grotevant and C. Cooper (eds.), *Adolescent Development in the Family*. San Francisco: Jossey-Bass, 1983, 43–60.

COOPER, H. M. "Pygmalion Grows Up: A Model for Teacher Expectation, Communication and Performance Influence." *Review of Educational Research* 49 (1979), 389–410.

COOPERSMITH, S. *The Antecedents of Self-esteem*. San Francisco: Freeman, 1967.

COPPLE, C. E., and SUCI, G. J. "The Comparative Ease of Processing Standard English and Black Nonstandard English by Lower-Class Black Children. *Child Development*, 45 (December 1974), 1048–1053.

CORBIN, C. B. *Becoming Physically Educated in Elementary School*, 2d ed., Philadelphia: Lea and Febiger Publishing Co., 1976.
———. *A Textbook of Motor Development*. Dubuque, Iowa: Brown, 1973; 2d ed., 1980.

CORDUA, G. D.; McGRAW, K. O.; and DRABMAN, R. S. "Doctor or Nurse: Children's Perceptions of Sex-Typed Occupations." *Child Development* 50 (1979), 590–593.

CORNELL, E. H. "Learning to Find Things: A Reinterpretation of Object Permanence Studies." In L. S. Siegel and C. J. Brainerd (eds.), *Alternatives to Piaget: Critical Essays on the Theory*. New York: Academic Press, 1978.

COSTELLO, J. "The First Grader's Rites of Passage." *Parents Magazine* (November 1978).

COVINGTON, M. V. "Strategic Thinking and Fear of Failure." Chapter for NIE-LRDC Proceedings, October 1980.

CRANDALL, V. C. "The Fels Study: Some Contributions to Personality Development and Achievement in Childhood and Adulthood." *Seminars in Psychiatry* 4, (1972), 383–397.

CRAWFORD, J. W. "Mother-Infant Interaction in Premature and Full-Term Infants." *Child Development* 53 (1982), 957–962.

CREAGER, J. G.; JANTZEN, P. G.; and MARINER, J. L. *Biology*. New York: Macmillan, 1981.

CRITCHLEY, M. "Language." In E. H. Lenneberg and E. Lenneberg (eds.), *Foundations of Language Development: A Multidisciplinary Approach*, Vol. 1. New York: Academic Press, 1975.

CRNIC, K. A.; GREENBERG, M. C.; RAGOZIN, A. A.; ROBINSON, N. M.; and BASHAM, R. "Effects of Stress and Social Supports on Mothers of Premature and Full-term Infants." *Child Development*, 54 (1983), 209–217.

CROCKENBERG, S. B. "Infant Irritability, Mother Responsiveness, and Social Support Influences on the Security of Infant-Mother Attachment." *Child Development* 52 (1981), 857–865.

CROCKETT, L. J., and A. C. PETERSEN. "Pubertal Status and Psychosocial Development: Findings from the Early Adolescent Study." In R. H. Lerner and T. T. Foch (eds.), *Biological-Psychosocial Interactions in Early Adolescence: A Life-span Perspective*. Hillsdale, N.J.: Erlbaum, 1985.

CROSBY, J. F. "A Critique of Divorce Statistics and Their Interpretation." *Family Relations* 29, (1980), 51–58.

CROUTER, A. C. "Participative Work as an Influence on Human Development." *Journal of Applied Development Psychology* 5 (1984), 71–90.

CSIKSZENTMIHALYI, M., and LARSON, R. *Being Adolescent*. New York: Basic Books, 1984.

CUMMINGS, E. M. "Caregiver Stability and Day Care." *Developmental Psychology* 16 (1980), 31–37.

CUNEO, D. O. "A General Strategy for Quantity Judgments: The Height and Width Rule." *Child Development* 51 (1980), 299–301.

CURTIS, L. E.; SIEGEL, A. W.; and FURLONG, N. E. "Developmental Differences in Cognitive Mapping: Configural Knowledge of Familiar Large-scale Environments." Unpublished manuscript, University of Pittsburg, 1980.

CVETKOVICH, G., and GROTE, B. "Psychological Factors Associated with Adolescent Premarital Coitus." Paper presented at the National Institute of Child Health and Human Development, Bethesda, Maryland, May 1976.

DALE, P. S. *Language Development: Structure and Function*, 2d ed. New York: Holt, Rinehart, and Winston, 1976.

DAMON, W. *The Social World of the Child*. San Francisco: Jossey-Bass, 1977.
———. "Social and Personality Development." New York: Norton, 1983.

DAMON, W., and HART, D. "The Development of Self-Understanding from Infancy Through Adolescence." *Child Development* 53, (1982), 841–869.

D'ANDRADE, R. G. "Sex Differences and Cultural Institutions." In

E. E. Maccoby (ed.), *The Development of Sex Differences*. Stanford, Calif.: Stanford University Press, 1966.

DANHOFF, J. "Children's Art: The Creative Process." *Children Today*. Washington, D.C.: July-August 1975, 7–10.

DANIELS, P., and WEINGARTEN, K. *Sooner or Later: The Timing of Parenthood in Adult Lives*. New York: Norton, 1982.

DARLEY, F. L., and SPRIESTERBACH, D. C. *Diagnostic Methods in Speech Pathology*. New York: Harper and Row, 1978, 222.

DARVILL, D., and CHEYNE, J. A. "Sequential Analysis of Response to Aggression: Age and Sex Effects." Paper presented at the Biennial Meeting of the Society for Research in Child Development, Boston, 1981.

DARWIN, C. *On the Origin of Species*. London: J. Murray, 1859.

———. "A Biographical Sketch of an Infant." *Mind* 2 (1877), 286–294.

DAVIDSON, S. "The Level of Differentiation of Ego-Functioning in the Identity-Achieved and Identity-Foreclosed Statuses. Unpublished doctoral diss., Boston University, 1978.

DAWBER, T. *The Framingham Study: Epidemiology of Artherosclerotic Disease*. Cambridge, Mass.: Harvard University Press, 1980.

DEARMAN, N. B., and PLISKO, V. W. *The Condition of Education*. Washington, D.C.: National Center for Educational Statistics, 1980.

DECASPER, A., and FIFER, W. "Of Human Bonding: Newborns Prefer Their Mothers' Voices." *Science* 208 (1980), 1174–1176.

DECECCO, J. P., and RICHARDS, I. K. "Civil War in the High Schools." *Psychology Today* 9, no. 6 (1975), 51–52, 120.

deCHATEAU, P. "Effects of Hospital Practices on Synchrony in the Development of the Infant-Parent Relationship." In P. M. Taylor (ed.), *Parent-Infant Relationships*. New York and London: Grune and Stratton, 1980.

DeLAMATER, J., and MacCORQUODALE, P. *Premarital Sexuality: Attitudes, Relationships, Behavior*. Madison: University of Wisconsin Press, 1979.

DeLISS, R., and STAUDT, J. "Individual Differences in College Students' Performance on Formal Operational Tasks." *Journal of Applied Developmental Psychology* 1 (1980), 201–208.

DeLISSOVOY, V. "Child Care by Adolescent Parents." *Children Today* (July-August 1973), 22–25.

DENNIS, W. "Causes of Retardation Among Institutional Children: Iran." *Journal of Genetic Psychology*, 96 (1960), 47–59.

DENNIS, W., and SAYEGH, Y. "The Effect of Supplementary Experiences upon the Behavioral Development of Infants in Institutions." *Child Development*, 36 (1965), 81–90.

deVILLIERS, P. A., and deVILLIERS, J. G. *Early Language*. Cambridge, Mass.: Harvard University Press, 1979.

DEWEY, J. "The Reflex Arc Concept in Psychology." *Psychological Review*, 3, (1896), 357–370.

———. *The School and Society*. Chicago: University of Chicago Press, 1943.

DIAMOND, N. "Cognitive Theory." In B. Wolman (ed.), *Handbook of Developmental Psychology*. Englewood Cliffs, N.J.: Prentice Hall, 1982, 3–22.

DIAZ, R. M. "Bilingual Cognitive Development: Addressing Three Gaps in Current Research." *Child Development*, 56, (1985), 1376–1388.

DICKIE, J. R.; VanGENT, E.; HOOGERWERF, K.; MARTINEZ, I.; and DIETERMAN, L. "Mother-Father-Infant Triad: Who Affects Whose Satisfaction." Paper presented at the biennial meeting of the Society for Research in Child Development, Boston, April 1981.

DIENER, C. I., and DWECK, C. S. "An Analysis of Learned Helplessness: Continuous Changes in Performance, Strategy, and Achievement Cognitions Following Failure." *Journal of Personality and Social Psychology*, 36,(1978), 451–462.

DIETZ, W. Comments at the Workshop on Childhood Obesity, National Institutes of Health, Washington, D.C., March 10–11, 1986.

DODGE, K. A. "Behavioral Antecedents of Peer Rejection and

Isolation." Paper presented at the meeting of the Society for Research in Child Development, Boston, April 1981.

DOHRENWEND, B. S., and DOHRENWEND, B. P. (eds.) *Life Stress and Illness*. New York: Neale Watson, 1980.

DORNBUSCH, S. M.; CARLSMITH, J. M.; BUSHWALL, S. J.; RITTER, P. L.; LEIDERMAN, H.; HASTORF, A. H.; and GROSS, R. T. "Single Parents, Extended Households and the Control of Adolescents." *Child Development* 56 (1985) 326–341.

DOUVEN, E. "Sex Differences in the Opportunities, Demands and Development of Youth." In R. L. Havighurst and P. H. Dreyer (eds.), *Youth*. Chicago: University of Chicago Press, 1975, 27–45.

DOUVAN, E., and ADELSON, J. *The Adolescent Experience*. New York: Wiley, 1966.

DOVE, A. "Taking the Chitling Test." *Newsweek* 72 (July 1968), 51–52.

DOWNEY, A., and O'ROUKE, T. "The Utilization of Attitudes and Beliefs as Indicators of Future Smoking Behavior." *Journal of Drug Education* 6 (1976), 283–295.

DREYER, P. H. "Sex, Sex Roles and Marriage Among Youth in the 1970's." In R. J. Havighurst and P. H. Dreyer (eds.), *Youth*. Chicago: University of Chicago Press, 1975, 194–223.

———. "Sexuality During Adolescence." In B. Wolman (ed.), *Handbook of Developmental Psychology*. Englewood Cliffs, N.J.: Prentice-Hall, 1982.

DROZDA, J. G., and FLAVELL, J. H. "A Developmental Study of Logical Search Behavior." *Child Development 46*, (1975), 389–393.

DRUKER, J. F., and HAGEN, J. W. "Developmental Trends in the Processing of Task-Relevant and Task-Irrelevant Information." *Child Development* 40, (1969), 371–382.

DUBOWITZ, L., and DUBOWITZ, V. *The Neurological Assessment of the Preterm and Full-Term Infant*. Philadelphia: Lippincott, 1981.

DUNCAN, O. D.; SCHUMAN, H.; and DUNCAN, B. *Social Change in a Metropolitan Community*. New York: Russell Sage, 1973.

DUNN, J. "Sibling Relationships in Early Childhood." *Child Development* 54, (1983), 787–811.

DUNN, J., and KENDRICK, C. "Interaction Between Young Siblings in the Context of Family Relationships." In M. Lewis and L. A. Rosenblum (eds.), *The Child and Its Family*. New York: Plenum, 1979.

———. "The Arrival of a Sibling: Changes in Patterns of Interaction Between Mother and Firstborn Child." *Journal of Child Psychology and Psychiatry* 21 (1980), 119–132.

———. "Interactions Between Young Siblings: Association with the Interaction Between Mother and Firstborn." *Developmental Psychology* 17 (1982a), 336–343.

———. *Siblings: Love, Envy, and Understanding*. Cambridge, Mass.: Harvard University Press, 1982b.

DUNPHY, D. "The Social Structure of Urban Adolescent Peer Groups." *Sociometry* 26, no. 2 (1963), 230–246.

DUVALL, E. M., and MILLER B. C. *Marriage and Family Development*, 6th ed. New York: Harper and Row, 1985.

DWECK, C. S., and ELLIOTT, E. S. "A Model of Achievement Motivation, a Theory of Its Origins and a Framework for Motivational Development." Harvard University, 1981 (unpublished).

———. "Achievement Motivation." In P. H. Mussen (ed.), *Handbook of Child Psychology*, Vol. 4. 4th ed. New York: Wiley, 1983, 643–692.

DWECK, C. S.; DAVIDSON, W.; NELSON, S.; and ENNA, B. "Sex Differences in Learned Helplessness: II. The Contingencies of Evaluative Feedback in the Classroom, and III. An Experimental Analysis." *Developmental Psychology* 14, (1978), 268–276.

DWYER, J. "Impact of Maternal Nutrition on Infant Health." *Resident and Staff Physician* 30, no. 8 (August 1984), 19PC–23PC, 26PC–28PC, 30 PC.

EAGLE, M. *Recent Developments in Psychoanalysis*. New York: McGraw-Hill, 1984.

ECCLES, J. S. "Sex Differences in Achievement Patterns." In T. Sonderegger (ed.), *Nebraska Symposium on Motivation*. Lincoln: University of Nebraska Press, 1985.

ECCLES, J. S.; and HOFFMAN, L. W. "Sex Roles, Socialization and Occupational Behavior." In H. W. Stevenson and A. E. Siegel (eds.), *Research in Child Development and Social Policy*, Vol. 1. Chicago: University of Chicago Press, 1984.

ECKERMAN, C. O., and STEIN, M. R. "The Toddler's Emerging Social Skills." In K. H. Rubin and H. S. Ross (eds.), *Peer Relationship and Social Skills in Childhood*. New York: Springer-Verlag, 1982.

ECKERMAN, C. O.; WHATLEY, J. L.; and KUTZ, S.L. "Growth of Social Play with Peers During the Second Year of Life." *Developmental Psychology* 11 (1975), 42–49.

ECKERT, H. M. "Age Changes in Motor Skills." In G. L. Rarick (ed.), *Physical Activity—Human Growth and Development*. New York: Academic Press, 1973.

"Economic Report of the President." Washington, D.C.: U.S. Government Printing Office, February 1986.

EDELBROCK, C. "Running Away from Home: Incidence and Correlates Among Children and Youth Referred for Mental Health Services." *Journal of Family Issues* 1, no. 2 (1980), 210–228.

EDWARDS, C. P. "The Age Group Labels and Categories of Preschool Children." *Child Development* 55, (1984), 440–452.

EGELAND, B. and SROUFE, L. A. "Attachment and Early Maltreatment." *Child Development* 52 (1981), 44–52.

EHRMANN, W. *Premarital Dating Behavior*. New York: Holt, Rinehart, and Winston, 1959.

EIDUSON, B.; KORNFEIN, M.; ZIMMERMAN, I.; and WEISNER, T. "Comparative Socialization Practices in Traditional and Alternative Families." In M. E. Lamb (ed.), *Non-traditional Families: Parenting and Child Development*. Hillsdale, N.J.: Erlbaum, 1982.

EISEN, M.; ZELLMAN, G. L.; LEIBOWITZ, A.; CHOW, W. K.; and EVANS, J. R. "Factors Discriminating Pregnancy Resolution Decision of Unmarried Adolescents." *Genetic Psychology Monographs* 108, (1983), 69–95.

EISENBERG, N.; LENNON, R.; and ROTH, K. "Prosocial Development: A Longitudinal Study." *Developmental Psychology* 19 (1983), 846–855.

EISENBERG-BERG, N., and HAND, M. "The Relationship of Preschoolers' Reasoning About Prosocial Moral Conflicts to Prosocial Behavior." *Child Development* 50 (1979), 356–363.

EISENBERG-BERG, N., and LENNON, R. "Altruism and the Assessment of Empathy in the Preschool Years." *Child Development* 51, (1980), 552–557.

EISENBERG-BERG, N., and NEALE, C. "Children's Moral Reasoning About Their Own Spontaneous Prosocial Behavior." *Developmental Psychology* 15 (1979), 228–229.

EITZEN, D. S. "Athletics in the Status System of Male Adolescents: A Replication of Coleman's *The Adolescent Society*." *Adolescence* 38, no. 10 (1975), 267–276.

ELDER, G. H.; NGUYEN, T. V.; and CASPI, A. "Linking Family Hardship to Children's Lives." *Child Development* 56 (1985), 361–375.

ELKIND, D. "Egocentrism in Adolescence." *Child Development* 38 (1967a), 1025–1034.

———. "Middle-Class Delinquency." *Mental Hygiene* 51 (1967b), 80–84.

———. *A Sympathetic Understanding of the Child Six to Sixteen*. Boston: Allyn and Bacon, 1971.

———. *The Hurried Child*. Reading, Mass.: Addison-Wesley, 1981.

———. *All Grown Up and No Place to Go*. Reading, Mass.: Addison-Wesley, 1984.

ELLIS, G. J. "Societal and Parental Predictors of Parent-Adolescent Conflict." In G. K. Leigh and G. W. Peterson (eds.), *Adolescents in Families*. Cincinnati: South-Western, 1986, 155–178.

ELLIS, G. T., and SEKYRA, F. "The Effect of Aggressive Cartoons on the Behavior of First Grade Children." *Journal of Psychology* 81 (1972), 37–43.

ELLIS, S.; ROGOFF, B.; and CROMER, C. "Age Segregation in Children's Social Interactions." *Developmental Psychology* 17 (1981), 399–407.

EMMERICH, W., and SHEPARD, K. "Development of Sex-Differentiated Preferences During Late Childhood and Adolescence." *Developmental Psychology* 18 (1982), 406–417.

ENGLAND, M. *Color Atlas of Life Before Birth*. Chicago: Year Book Medical Publishers, 1983.

ENRIGHT, R. D.; FRANKLIN, C. C.; and MANHEIM, L. A. "Children's Distributive Justice Reasoning: A Standardized and Objective Scale." *Developmental Psychology* 16 (1980), 193–202.

ENTWISLE, D. R., and DOERING, S. G. *The First Birth: A Family Turning Point*. Baltimore: Johns Hopkins University Press, 1981.

EPPS, E., and SMITH, S. F. "School and Children: The Middle Childhood Years." In W. A. Collins (ed.), *Development During Middle Childhood: The Years from Six to Twelve*. Washington, D.C.: National Academy Press, 1984, 283–334.

EPSTEIN, J. L. "Longitudinal Effects of Family-School-Person Interactions on Students' Outcomes. *Research in Sociology of Education and Socialization* 4 (1983), 101–127.

EPSTEIN, J. L., and BECKER, H. J. "Teachers' Reported Practices of Parental Involvement: Problems and Possibilities." *Elementary School Journal* 83 (1982), 103–113.

EPSTEIN, L. Comments at the Workshop on Childhood Obesity, National Institutes of Health, Washington, D.C., March 10–11, 1986.

ERIKSON, E. H. *Childhood and Society*. New York: Norton, 1950.

———. *Young Man Luther: A Study in Psychoanalysis and History*. New York: Norton, 1958.

———. *Identity and the Life Cycle*. New York: International Universities Press, 1959.

———. *Childhood and Society*, 2d ed. New York: Norton, 1963.

———. *Challenge of Youth*. New York: Doubleday, 1965.

———. *Identity: Youth and Crisis*. New York: Norton, 1968.

———. *Dimensions of a New Identity*. New York: Norton, 1974.

ERLENMEYER-KIMLING L., and JARVIK, L. F. "Genetics and Intelligence: A Research Review." *Science* 142 (1963), 1477–1479.

ERON, L. D. "Parent-Child Interaction, Television Violence, and Aggression of Children." *American Psychologist* 37 (1982), 197–211.

ESPENSCHADE, A. S. *Monographs of the Society for Research in Child Development* 5, no. 1 (1960), entire issue.

ESPENSCHADE, A. S., and ECKERT, H. M. "Motor Development." In W. R. Johnson and E. R. Buskirk (eds.), *Science and Medicine of Exercise and Sport*, 2d ed. New York: Harper, 1974, 419–439.

———. *Motor Development*, 2d ed. Columbus, Ohio: Merrill, 1980.

ETAUGH, C. "Effects of Nonmaterial Care on Children: Research Evidence and Popular Views." *American Psychologist* 35 (1980), 309–319.

EVELETH, P., and TANNER, J. M. *Worldwide Variation in Human Growth*. New York: Cambridge University Press, 1976.

FAGOT, B. I. "Male and Female Teachers: Do They Treat Boys and Girls Differently?" *Sex Roles* 7 (1981), 263–272.

———. "Changes in Thinking About Early Sex Role Development." *Developmental Review* (1985).

FAMILY ECONOMICS RESEARCH GROUP. "Updated Estimates of the Cost of Raising a Child." *Family Economics Review* 4 (1983), 30–31.

FANTZ, R. L. "The Origin of Form Perception." *Scientific American* 204 (1961), 66–72.

———. "Pattern Vision in Newborn Infants." *Science* 140 (1963), 296–297.

FARBER, E. D., and KINAST, C. "Violence in Families of Adolescent Runaways." *Child Abuse and Neglect* 8 (1984), 295–299.

FARRINGTON, D. P. "Delinquency from 10 to 25." In S. A. Mednick (ed.), *Antecedents of Aggression and Antisocial Behavior*. Hingham, Mass.: Kluwer Boston, 1982.

FAULKENDER, P. J. "Categorical Habituation with Sex-Typed Toy Stimuli in Older and Younger Preschoolers." *Child Development* 51 (1980), 515–519.

FAUST, M. S. "Developmental Maturity as a Determinant in Prestige of Adolescent Girls." *Child Development* 31 (1960), 173–184.

FEIN, G. G. "Play and the Acquisition of Symbols." In L. Katz (ed.),

Current Topics in Early Childhood Education. Norwood, N.J.: Ablex, 1979.

FEINSTEIN, K. W. "Directions for Day Care." In P. Voyandoff (ed.), *Work and Family*. Palo Alto: Mayfield Publishing Company, 1984, 298–309.

FELDMAN, D. H. *Beyond Universals in Cognitive Development*. Norwood, N.J.: Ablex, 1980.

FELDMAN, R. S.; DEVIN-SHEEHAN, L.; and ALLEN, V. L. "Children Tutoring Children: A Critical Review of Research." In V. L. Allen (ed.), *Children as Teachers: Theory and Research on Tutoring*. New York: Academic Press, 1976.

FELDMAN, S. S.; BIRINGER, Z. C.; and NASH, S. C. "Fluctuations of Sex Related Self-Attributions as a Function of Stage of Family Life Cycle." *Developmental Psychology* 17 (1981), 24–35.

FENNEMA, E., and SHERMAN, J. "Sex-Related Differences in Mathematics Achievement, Spatial Visualization and Affective Factors." *American Educational Research Journal* 14 (1977), 51–71.

FERGUSON, T. J., and RULE, B. G. "Effects of Inferential Sex, Outcome Severity and Basis of Responsibility on Children's Evaluations of Aggressive Acts." *Developmental Psychology* 16 (1980), 141–146.

FERRIS, P. *Dylan Thomas*. London: Hadley and Stoughton, 1977.

FIELD, J.; MUIR, D.; PILON, R.; SINCLAIR, M.; and DODWELL, P. "Infants' Orientation to Lateral Sounds from Birth to Three Months." *Child Development* 51 (1980), 295–298.

FIELD, T., and GOLDSON, E. "Pacifying Effects of Nonnutritive Sucking on Term and Preterm Neonates During Heelstick Procedures." *Pediatrics* 74 (1984), 1012–1015.

FILMER, H. T., and HASWELL, L. "Sex-Role Stereotyping in English Usage." *Sex-Roles* 3 (1977), 257–263.

FINE, M. A.; MORELAND, J. R.; and SCHWEBEL, A. I. "Long-Term Effects of Divorce on Parent-Child Relationships." *Developmental Psychology* 19 (1983), 703–713.

FINKELHOR, D.; GELLES, R. J.; HOTALING, G. T.; and STRAUS, M. A. (eds.), *The Dark Side of Families: Current Family Violence Research*. Beverly Hills, Calif.: Sage, 1983.

FISCHER, K. W. "A Theory of Cognitive Development: The Control and Construction of Hierarchies of Skills." *Psychological Review* 87 (1980), 477–531.

FISCHER, K. W., and BULLOCK, D. "Patterns of Data: Sequence, Synchrony, and Constraint in Cognitive Development." In K. W. Fischer (ed.), *Cognitive Development*. New Directions for Child Development, No. 12. San Francisco: Jossey-Bass, 1981.

———. "Cognitive Development in School-Age Children: Conclusions and New Directions." In W. A. Collins (ed.), *Development During Middle Childhood: The Years from Six to Twelve*. Washington, D.C.: National Academy Press, 1984, 70–146.

FISCHER, K. W.; HAND, H. H.; and RUSSELL, S. "The Development of Abstractions in Adolescence and Adulthood." In M. L. Commons, F. A. Richards, and C. Armon (eds.), *Beyond Formal Operations*. New York: Praeger, 1983.

FISCHER, K. W.; HAND, H. H.; WATSON, M. W.; VAN PARYS, M.; and TUCKER, J. "Putting the Child into Socialization: The Development of Social Categories in the Preschool Years." In R. L. G. Katz (ed.), *Current Topics in Early Childhood Education*, Vol. 6. Norwood, N.J.: Ablex, 1986.

FISCHER, K. W.; PIPP, S. L.; and BULLOCK, D. "Detecting Discontinuities in Development: Method and Measurement." In R. N. Emde and R. Harmon (eds.), *Continuities and Discontinuities in Development*. Norwood, N.J.: Ablex, 1984.

FISHBEIN, H. D. *Evolution, Development, and Children's Learning*. Pacific Palisades, Calif.: Goodyear, 1976.

———. *The Psychology of Infancy and Childhood: Evolutionary and Cross-Cultural Perspectives*. Hillsdale, N.J.: Erlbaum, 1984.

FLAVELL, J. H. *The Development of Role-Taking and Communication Skills in Children*. Huntington, N.Y.: Krieger, 1975. Originally published by Wiley in 1968.

———. "Comments." In R. S. Siegler (ed.), *Children's Thinking: What Develops?* Hillsdale, N.J.: Erlbaum, 1978, 97–105.

———. "Structures, Stages, and Sequences in Cognitive Development." In W. A. Collins (ed.), *Minnesota Symposium on Child Psychology*. Hillsdale, N.J.: Erlbaum, 1982.

———. *Cognitive Development*, 2d ed. Englewood Cliffs, N.J.: Prentice-Hall, 1985.

FLAVELL, J. H., and WELLMAN, H. M. "Metamemory." In R. V. Kail, Jr., and J. W. Hagen (eds.), *Perspective on the Development of Memory and Cognition*. Hillsdale, N.J.: Erlbaum, 1977, 3–33.

FLAVELL, J. H.; BEACH, D. R.; and CHINSKY, J. M. "Spontaneous Verbal Rehearsal in a Memory Task as a Function of Age." *Child Development* 37 (1966), 283–299.

FLAVELL, J. H.; FLAVELL, E. R.; GREEN, F. L.; and WILCOX, S. A. "The Development of Three Spatial Perspective-Taking Rules." *Child Development* 52 (1981), 356–358.

FLAVELL, J. H.; GREEN, F. L.; and FLAVELL, E. R. "Development of Knowledge About the Appearance-Reality Distinction." *Monographs of the Society for Research in Child Development* 51, no. 1 Serial No. 212 (1986), entire issue.

FOGEL, A. "Early Adult-Infant Face-to-Face Interaction: Expectable Sequences of Behavior." *Journal of Pediatric Psychology* 7 (1982), 1–22.

FORBES, G. B. "Growth of the Lean Body Mass in Man." *Growth* 36 (1972), 325–338.

FORREST, J. D. "Proportion of U.S. Women Ever Pregnant Before Age 20: A Research Note." New York: Alan Guttmacher Institute, 1986 (unpublished).

FOX, G. L. "The Family's Role in Adolescent Sexual Behavior." In T. Ooms (ed.), *Teenage Pregnancy in a Family Context*. Philadelphia: Temple University Press, 1981.

———. "The Parents' Role in Teens' Sexuality Education." *Grosberg Journal* 2 (1984), 25–34.

———. "The Family Context of Adolescent Sexuality and Sex Roles." In G. K. Leigh and G. W. Peterson (eds.), *Families in Adolescence*. Cincinnati: South-Western, 1986, 179–204.

FOX, G. L., and INAZU, J. K. "Patterns and Outcomes of Mother-Daughter Communication About Sexuality." *Journal of Social Issues* 36 (1980), 7–29.

FOX, H. E.; STEINBRECHER, M.; PESSEL, D.; INGLIS, J.; MEDVID, L.; and ANGEL, E. "Maternal Ethanol Ingestion and the Occurrence of Human Fetal Breathing Movements." *American Journal of Obstetrics and Gynecology* 132 (1978), 354–358.

FOX, L. H.; BRODY, L.; and TOBIN, D. (eds.). *Women and the Mathematical Mystique*. Baltimore: Johns Hopkins University Press, 1980.

FRAIBERG, S. "Blind Infants and Their Mothers: An Examination of the Sign System." In M. Lewis and L. A. Rosenblum (eds.), *The Effect of the Infant on Its Caregiver*. New York: Wiley, 1974.

FRANKENBURG, W. K.; FANDAL, A. W.; SCIARILLO, W.; and BURGESS, D. "The Newly Abbreviated and Revised Denver Developmental Screening Test." *The Journal of Pediatrics* 99 (1981), 995–999.

FREEDMAN, D. *Human Infancy: An Evolutionary Perspective*. Hillsdale, N.J.: Erlbaum, 1974.

FREEDMAN, J. L. "Effect of Television Violence on Aggression." *Psychological Bulletin* 96, no. 2 (1984), 227–246.

FREIDRICH, L. K., and STEIN, A. H. "Prosocial Television and Young Children: The Effects of Verbal Labeling and Role Playing on Learning and Behavior." *Child Development* 16 (1975), 27–36.

FREUD, S. "Formulations in the Two Frames of Mental Functioning." In J. Strachy and A. Freud (eds.), *The Standard Edition of the Complete Psychological Works of Sigmund Freud*, Vol. 12. London: Hogarth, 1956. Originally published in 1911.

FREIDMAN, T. "Prenatal Diagnosis of Genetic Disease." *Scientific American* 225, no. 5 (November 1971), 34–42.

FRIEZE, I. H.; FRANCIS, W. D.; and HANUSA, B. H. "Defining Success in Classroom Settings." In J. Levine and M. Wang (eds.), *Teacher and Student Perceptions: Implications for Learning*. Hillsdale, N.J.: Erlbaum, 1981.

FRISCH, R. E. "Critical Weight at Menarche, Initiation of the Adolescent Growth Spurt, and Control of Puberty." In M. M. Grumbach, G. D. Grave, and F. E. Mayer (eds.), *Control of the Onset of Puberty*. New York: Wiley, 1974.

———. "Fatness, Puberty, and Fertility: The Effects of Nutrition and Physical Training on Menarche and Ovulation." In J. Brooks-Gunn and A. C. Petersen (eds.), *Girls at Puberty: Biological and Psychosocial Perspectives*. New York: Plenum Press, 1983.

FROST, R. *The Collected Poems of Robert Frost*. New York: Holt, 1939.

FURSTENBERG, F. *Unplanned Parenthood: The Social Consequences of Teenage Parenthood*. New York: Free Press, 1976.

FURSTENBERG, F. F., JR.; LINCOLN, R.; and MENKEN, J. "Locating the Problem/Defining the Solution." In F. Furstenberg, F. Lincoln, and J. Menken (eds.), *Teenage Sexuality, Pregnancy and Childbearing*. Philadelphia: University of Pennsylvania Press, 1981.

GAGE, N. L. "Paradigms for Research on Teaching." In N. L. Gage (ed.), *Handbook of Research on Teaching*. Chicago: Rand McNally, 1963.

GALINSKY, E. *Between Generations: The Six Stages of Parenthood*. New York: Berkley, 1981.

GALLATIN, J. E. *Adolescence and Individuality*. New York: Harper & Row, 1975.

———. "Political Thinking in Adolescence." In J. Adelson (ed.), *Handbook of Adolescent Psychology*. New York: Wiley, 1980, 344–382.

GALVIN, K. M., and BROMMEL, B. J. *Family Communication: Cohesion and Change*. Glenview, Ill.: Scott, Foresman, 1982.

GARBARINO, J. "The Human Ecology of Child Maltreatment: A Conceptual Model for Research." *Journal of Marriage and the Family* 39 (1977), 721–736.

———. "Latchkey Children: Getting the Short End of the Stick?" *Vital Issues* 30, no. 3 (1980).

———. *Children and Families in the Social Environment*. New York: Aldine Publishing Company, 1982a.

———. "Sociocultural Risk: Dangers to Competence." In C. Kopp and J. Krakow (eds.), *Child Development in a Social Context*. Reading, Mass.: Addison-Wesley, 1982b, 648.

———. *Adolescence: An Ecological Perspective*. Columbus, Ohio: Merrill, 1985.

———. "Can We Measure Success in Preventing Child Abuse? Issues in Policy, Programming and Research." *Child Abuse and Neglect* 10 (1986), 143–156.

GARBARINO, J., and GILLIAM, C. *Understanding Abusive Families*. Lexington, Mass.: Lexington Books, 1980.

GARBARINO, J., and PLANTZ, M. C. *Urban Environments and Urban Children*. ERIC/CUE Urban Diversity Series, #69. New York: ERIC Clearinghouse on Urban Education, 1980.

GARBARINO, J., and SHERMAN, D. "High-Risk Neighborhoods and High-Risk Families: The Human Ecology of Child Maltreatment." *Child Development* 51 (1980), 188–198.

GARBARINO, J.; SCHELLENBACH, C. J.; SEBES, J. M.; and ASSOCIATES (eds.). *Troubled Youth, Troubled Families*. New York: Aldine, 1986.

GARBARINO, J.; WILSON, J.; and GARBARINO, A. "The Adolescent Runaway." In J. Garbarino, C. J. Schellenbach, J. M. Sebes, and Associates (eds.), *Troubled Youth, Troubled Families*. New York: Aldine, 1986, 41–54.

GARBER, J., and SELIGMAN, M. E. P. *Human Helplessness: Theory and Applications*. New York: Academic Press, 1980.

GARDNER, H. *Artful Scribbles: The Significance of Children's Drawings*. New York: Basic Books, Inc., 1980.

GARDNER, L. I. "Deprivation Dwarfism." *Scientific American* (1972).

GARMEZY, N., and RUTTER, M. (eds.). *Stress, Coping and Development in Children*. New York: McGraw-Hill, 1983.

GARVEY, C. *Play*. Cambridge, Mass.: Harvard University Press, 1977.

———. *Children's Talk*. Cambridge, Mass.: Harvard University Press, 1984.

GELFAND, D. M.; HARTMANN, D. P.; LAMB, A. K.; SMITH, C. L.; MAHAN, M. A.; and PAUL, S. C. "The Effects of Adult Models and Described Alternatives on Children's Choice of Behavior Management Techniques." *Child Development* 45 (1974), 585–593.

GELLES, R. J. and CORNELL, C. P. *Intimate Violence*. Beverly Hills: Sage, 1985.

GELLES, R. J., and STRAUS, M. A. "Determinants of Violence in the Family: Toward a Theoretical Integration." In W. Burr, R. Hill, F. I. Nye, and I. Reiss (eds.), *Contemporary Theories About the Family*. New York: Free Press, 1979.

GELMAN, R. "Cognitive Development." *Annual Review of Psychology* 29 (1978), 297–332.

———. "Assessing One-to-One Correspondence: Still Another Paper on Conservation." *British Journal of Psychology* 73 (1982), 209–220.

GELMAN, R., and BAILLARGEON, R. "A Review of Some Piagetian Concepts." In P. H. Mussen (ed.), *Handbook of Child Psychology*, Vol. 3. 4th ed. New York: Wiley, 1983, 167–262.

GELMAN, R.; SPELKE, E. S.; and MECK, E. "What Preschoolers Know About Animate and Inanimate Objects." In J. Sloboda, D. Rogers, P. Bryant, and R. Kramer (eds.), *Acquisition of Symbolic Skills*. London: Plenum, 1983.

GENERAL MILLS AMERICAN FAMILY REPORT. *Families at Work: Strengths and Strains*. Minneapolis: General Mills, 1981 (9200 Wayzata Blvd., Minneapolis, Minn. 55440).

GEORGE, C., and MAIN, M. "Social Interactions of Young Abused Children: Approach, Avoidance, and Aggression." *Child Development* 50 (1979), 306–318.

GEORGE, L. "Role Transitions in Later Life." Belmont, Calif.: Brooks/Cole, 1980.

GERBNER, G.; GROSS, L.; MORGAN, M.; and SIGNORIELLI, N. "The Mainstreaming of America." *Journal of Communication* 30 (1980), 12–29.

GERBNER, G.; GROSS, L.; SIGNORIELLI, N.; MORGAN, M.; and JACKSON-BEECK, M. "The Demonstration of Power: Violence Profile No. 10." *Journal of Communication* 29 (1979), 177–196.

GERMOUTY, J., and MALAUZAT, C. Les victimes innocentes du tabac [The Innocent Victims of Tobacco]. *Journal de medecine et de chirurgic pratiques* 155, no. 6–7 (June-July 1984), 293–298.

GESELL, A. *Infancy and Human Growth*. New York: Macmillan, 1928.

———. *The First Five Years of Life: The Preschool Years*. New York: Harper & Row, 1940.

GESELL, A., and AMATRUDA, C. *Developmental Diagnosis*, 2d ed. New York: Harper & Row, 1947.

GIACONIA, R. M., and HEDGES, L. V. "Identifying Features of Effective Open Education." *Review of Educational Research* 52 (1982) 579–602.

GIBSON, E. J., and SPELKE, E. S. "The Development of Perception." In P. H. Mussen (ed.), *Handbook of Child Psychology*, Vol. 3. 4th ed. New York: Wiley, 1983, 1–76.

GIBSON, E. J., and WALK, R. D. "The 'Visual Cliff.'" *Scientific American* 202 (1960), 64.

GILLIAM, T. B., and BURKE, M. "Effects of Exercise on Serum Lipids and Lipoproteins in Girls, Ages 8 to 10 Years." *Artery* 4 (1978), 203.

GILLIAM, T. B.; KATCH, V. L.; THORLAND, W.; and WELTMAN, A. "Prevalence of Coronary Heart Disease Risk Factors in Active Children, 7 to 12 Years of Age." *Medicine and Science in Sports* 9 (1977), 21–25.

GILLIGAN, C. "In a Different Voice: Women's Conceptions of Self and of Morality." *Harvard Educational Review* 47 (1977), 481–517.

———. "Woman's Place in Man's Life Cycle." *Harvard Education Review* 49 (1979), 431–446.

———. *In a Different Voice*. Cambridge, Mass.: Harvard University Press, 1982.

GINZBERG, E. "Toward a Theory of Occupational Choice: A Restatement." *Vocational Guidance Quarterly* 20 (1972), 169–176.

———. "The Job Problem." *Scientific American* 237 (1977), 43–51.

GLASS, G. V.; McGAW, B.; and SMITH, M. L. *Meta-Analysis of Social Research*. Beverly Hills, Calif.: Sage, 1981.

GLEICHER, N. "Cesarean Section Rates in the United States." *Journal of the American Medical Association* 252 (1984), 3273–3276.

GLENN, N. D., and McLANAHAN, S. "Children and Marital Happiness: A Further Specification of the Relationship." *Journal of Marriage and the Family* 44 (1982), 63–72.

GLICK, P. C. "The Children of Divorced Parents in Demographic Perspective." *Journal of Social Issues* 35 (1979), 170–182.

GLIEDMAN, J., and ROTH, W. *The Unexpected Minority: Handicapped Children in American Society.* New York: Harcourt Brace Jovanovich, 1980.

GLOMSET, J. "High-Density Lipoproteins in Human Health and Disease." *Advances in Internal Medicine* 25 (1980), 91.

GOERTZEL, V., and GOERTZEL, M. G. *Cradles of Eminence.* Boston: Little Brown, 1978.

GOFFMAN, E. *The Presentation of Self in Everyday Life.* Garden City, N.Y.: Doubleday, 1959.

GOLD, D., and ANDRES, D. "Comparisons of Adolescent Children with Employed and Nonemployed Mothers." *Merrill-Palmer Quarterly* 24 (1978a), 243–254.

———. "Developmental Comparisons Between Ten-Year-Old Children with Employed and Nonemployed Mothers." *Child Development* 49 (1978b), 75–84.

GOLD, M., and PETRONIO, R. J. "Delinquent Behavior in Adolescence." In J. Adelson (ed.), *Handbook of Adolescence Psychology.* New York: Wiley, 1980.

GOLD, M., and REIMER, D. J. "Changing Patterns of Delinquent Behavior Among Americans 13–16 Years Old, 1967–1972." *Crime and Delinquency Literature* 7 (1975), 483–517.

GOLD, D.; ANDRES, D.; and GLORIEUX, J. "The Development of Francophone Nursery—School Children with Employed and Nonemployed Mothers. *Canadian Journal of Behavioral Science* 11 (1979), 169–173.

GOLD, R. "On the Meaning of Nonconservation." In A. M. Lesgold, J. W. Pellegrino, S. D. Fokkema, and R. Glaser (eds.), *Cognitive Psychology and Instruction.* New York and London: Plenum, 1978.

GOLDBERG, B.; VERAS, G.; and NICHOLAS, J. "Sports Medicine: Pediatric Perspective." *New York State Journal of Medicine* 78 (1978), 1406.

GOLDBERG, S., and DiVITTO, B. A. *Born Too Soon.* San Francisco; Freeman, 1983.

GOLDFARB, W. "Effects of Early Institutional Care on Adolescent Personality." *Journal of Experimental Education* 12 (1943), 106–129.

GOLDSMITH, H. H., and GOTTESMAN, I. I. "Origins of Variation in Behavioral Style: A Longitudinal Study of Temperament in Young Twins." *Child Development* 52 (1981), 99–103.

GOLDSPINK, G. "Postembryonic Growth and Differentiation of Striated Muscle." In G. H. Bourne (ed.), *The Structure and Function of Muscle*, Vol. 1. 2d ed. New York: Academic Press, 1972.

GOOD, T. L. "Teacher Expectations, Teacher Behavior, Student Perceptions and Student Behavior: A Decade of Research." Paper presented at the meeting of the American Educational Research Association, Boston, 1980.

GOODENOUGH, F. L. *Anger in Young Children.* Minneapolis: University of Minnesota Press, 1931.

GOODMAN, R. M. *Planning for a Healthy Baby.* New York: Oxford University Press, 1986.

GORDON, T. E. *P.E.T.—Parent Effectiveness Training.* New York: Peter H. Wyden, Inc., 1975.

GOTTESMAN, I. I. "Developmental Genetics and Ontogenetic Psychology: Overdue Détente and Propositions from a Matchmaker. In Ann Pick (ed.), *Minnesota Symposia on Child Psychology*, Vol. 8. Minneapolis: The University of Minnesota Press, 1974, 60.

GOTTLIEB, B. H. "The Primary Group as a Supportive Milieu: Applications to Community Psychology." *American Journal of Community Psychology* (1979).

———. "Social Networks and Social Support in Community Mental Health." In B. H. Gottlieb (ed.), *Social Networks and Social Support.* Beverly Hills, Calif.: Sage Publications, 1981.

GOTTMAN, J. M. "How Children Become Friends." *Monographs of the Society for Research in Child Development* 48, Serial No. 201 (1983).

———. "The World of Coordinated Play: Same and Cross-Sex Friendship in Young Children." In J. M. Gottman and J. G. Parker (eds.), *The Conversations of Friends.* New York: Cambridge University Press, 1985.

GOTTMAN, J. M.; GONZO, J.; and RASMUSSEN, B. "Social Interaction, Social Competence, and Friendship in Children." *Child Development* 45 (1975), 709–718.

GRAHAM, R. "Youth and Experimental Learning." In R. J. Havighurst and P. H. Dreyer (eds.), *Youth.* Chicago: University of Chicago Press, 1975.

GRANZBERG, G., and STEINBERG, J. "Television and the Canadian Indian (Tech. Rep.)." Manitoba, Canada: University of Winnipeg, Department of Anthropology, 1980.

GRAVES, Z., and GLICK, J. "The Effects of Context on Mother-Child Intervention: A Progress Report." *Quarterly Newsletter of the Institute of Comparative Human Development* 2 (1978), 41–46.

GRAY, S., and KLAUS, R. "The Early Training Project: A Seventh Year Report." *Child Development* 41 (1970), 909–924.

GREENBERG, B. S. "British Children and Televised Violence." *Public Opinion Quarterly* 38 (1975), 531–547.

GREENBERG, B. S., and REEVES, B. "Children and Perceived Reality of Television." *Journal of Social Issues* 32, no. 4 (1976), 86–97.

GREENBERG, J. R., and MITCHELL, S. A. *Object Relations in Psychoanalytic Theory.* Cambridge, Mass.: Harvard University Press, 1983.

GREENBERG, M. T. and MARVIN, R. S. "Reactions of Preschool Children to an Adult Stranger: A Behavioral Systems Approach." *Child Development* 53 (1982), 481–490.

GREENBERGER, E., and STEINBERG, L. *When Teenagers Work: The Psychological and Social Costs of Adolescent Employment.* New York: Basic Books, 1986.

GREENBLATT, B. *Responsibility for Child Care.* San Francisco: Jossey-Bass, 1978.

GREENWALD, A. G. "The Totalitarian Ego: Fabrication and Revision of Personal History." *American Psychologist* 7 (1980), 603–618.

GRINDER, R. *The Psychology of Adolescence.* New York: Macmillan, 1975.

GROSS, L., and JEFFRIES-FOX, S. "What Do You Want to Be When You Grow Up, Little Girl?" In G. Tuchman, A. K. Daniels, and J. Benet (eds.), *Hearth and Home: Images of Women in the Mass Media.* New York: Oxford University Press, 1978, 240–265.

GROSSMANN, K.; THANE, K.; and GROSSMANN, K. E. "Maternal Tactual Contact of the Newborn After Various Postpartum Conditions of Mother-Infant Contact." *Developmental Psychology* 17 (1981), 158–169.

GROTEVANT, H. D., and COOPER, C. R. *Adolescent Development in the Family.* San Francisco: Jossey-Bass, 1983.

———. "Patterns of Interaction in Family Relationships and the Development of Identity Exploration in Adolescence." *Child Development* 56 (1985), 415–428.

GROTEVANT, H. D., and THORBECKE, W. "Sex Differences in Styles of Occupational Identity Formation in Late Adolescence." *Developmental Psychology* 18 (1982), 396–405.

GRUENEICH, R. "The Development of Children's Integration Rules for Making Moral Judgments." *Child Development* 53 (1982), 887–894.

GRUSEC, J. E., and KUCZYNSKI, L. "Direction of Effect in Socialization: A Comparison of the Parents' *vs.* the Child's Behavior as Determinants of Disciplinary Techniques." *Developmental Psychology* 16 (1980), 1–9.

GRUSEC, J. E.; KUCZYNSKI, L.; RUSHTON, J. P.; and SIMUTIS, Z. M. "Learning Resistance to Temptation Through Observation." *Developmental Psychology* 15 (1979), 233–240.

GRUSEC, J. E., and MILLS, R. "The Acquisition of Self-Control." In J. Worrell (ed.), *Psychological Development in the Elementary Years.* New York: Academic Press, 1982, 151–186.

GRUSEC, J. E., and REDLER, E. "Attribution, Reinforcement, and Altruism: A Developmental Analysis." *Developmental Psychology* 16 (1980), 525–534.

GUILFORD, J. P. *The Nature of Human Intelligence*. New York: McGraw-Hill, 1967.

GURUCHARRI, C., and SELMAN, R. L. "The Development of Interpersonal Understanding During Childhood, Preadolescence, and Adolescence: A Longitudinal Follow-up Study." *Child Development* 53 (1982), 924–927.

GUTIERRES, S. E., and REICH, J. W. "A Developmental Perspective on Runaway Behavior: Its Relationship to Child Abuse." *Child Welfare* 60 (1981), 89–94.

HAAF, R. A.; SMITH, P. H.; and SMITLEY, S. "Infant Response to Facelike Patterns Under Fixed Trial and Infant Control Procedures." *Child Development* 54 (1983), 172–177.

HAAS, A. "Male and Female Spoken Language Differences: Stereotypes and Evidence." *Psychological Bulletin* 86 (1979), 616–626.

HAGEN, J. W., and HALE, G. H. "The Development of Attention in Children." In A. D. Pick (ed.), *Minnesota Symposium on Child Psychology*, Vol. 7. Minneapolis: University of Minnesota Press, 1973, 117–140.

HAINLINE, L., and FEIG, E. "The Correlates of Childhood: Father Absence in College-Aged Women." *Child Development* 49 (1978), 37–42.

HAITH, M. M. *Rules That Babies Look By: The Organization of Newborn Visual Activity*. Hillsdale, N.J.: Erlbaum, 1980.

HAITH, M. M.; BERGMAN, T.; and MOORE, M. J. "Eye Contact and Face Scanning in Early Infancy." University of Denver, 1977 (unpublished).

HALES, D.; LOZOFF, B.; SOSA, R.; and KENNELL, J. "Defining the Limits of the Maternal Sensitive Period. *Developmental Medicine and Child Neurology* 19 (1977), 454–461.

HALEY, J. *Leaving Home*. New York: McGraw-Hill, 1980.

HALL, A. D., and FAGEN, R. E. "Definition of Systems." Revised introductory chapter of *Systems Engineering*. New York: Bell Telephone Laboratories, 1956.

HALL, C. S. *A Primer of Freudian Psychology*. New York: World, 1954.

HALL, G. S. *Adolescence: Its Psychology and Its Relations to Physiology, Anthropology, Sociology, Sex, Crime, Religion and Education*. 2 vols. New York: Appleton, 1904.

HALLINAN, M. T. "Patterns of 'Cliquing' Among Youth." In H. C. Foot, A. J. Chapman, and J. R. Smith (eds.), *Friendship and Peer Relations in Children*. New York: Wiley, 1980.

HALVERSON, H. M. "An Experimental Study of Prehension in Infants by Means of Systematic Cinema Records." *Genetic Psychology Monographs* 10 (1931), 107–286.

HAMBURG, D.; ELLIOTT, G.; and PARRON, D. (eds.). *Health and Behavior: Frontiers of Research in the Biobehavioral Sciences*. Report of a study from the Institute of Medicine. Washington, D.C.: National Academy Press, 1982.

HAMILTON, S. "Adolescents in Community Settings: What Is to Be Learned?" *Theory and Research in Social Education* 9 (1981), 23–38.

HAND, H. H. "The Development of Concepts of Social Interaction: Children's Understanding of Nice and Mean." Unpublished doctoral diss., University of Denver. Available from Dissertation Abstracts International, 1981.

HANSON, S. M. H., and BOZETT, F. W. (eds.), *Dimensions of Fatherhood*. Beverly Hills, Calif.: Sage, 1985.

HARARI, O., and COVINGTON, M. V. "Reactions to Achievement Behavior from a Teacher and Student Perspective: A Developmental Analysis." *American Educational Research Journal* 18 (1981), 15–28.

HARRIS, J. A.; JACKSON, C. M.; PATTERSON, D. G.; and SCAMMON, R. E. *The Measurement of Man*. Minneapolis: University of Minnesota Press, 1930.

HARRISON, A.; SERAFICA, F.; and McADOO, H. "Ethnic Families of Color." In R. D. Parke (ed.), *Review of Child Development Research*. Vol. 7, *The Family*. Chicago: The University of Chicago Press, 1984, 329–371.

HARRISON, M.; GOLBUS, M. S.; and FILLY, R. A. *The Unborn Patient: Prenatal Diagnosis and Treatment*. Orlando, Fla.: Grune and Stratton, 1984.

HART, N. A., and KEIDEL, G. C. "The Suicidal Adolescent." *American Journal of Nursing* (1979), 80–84.

HARTER, S. "A Cognitive-Developmental Approach to Children's Use of Affect and Trait Labels." In F. Serafico (ed.), *Socio-Cognitive Development in Context*. New York: Guilford Press, 1982.

———. "Developmental Perspectives on the Self-System." In E. M. Hetherington (ed.), *Handbook of Child Psychology*. Vol. 4, *Socialization, Personality, and Social Development*. New York: John Wiley & Sons, 1983, 275–385.

HARTER, S., and BARNES, R. *Children's Understanding of Parental Emotions: A Developmental Study*. University of Denver, 1981 (unpublished).

HARTER, S., and CONNELL, J. P. "A Structural Model of Children's Self Perceptions of Competence, Control, and Motivation Orientation in the Cognitive Domain." Paper presented at the meeting of the International Society for the Study of Behavioral Development, Toronto, August 1981.

HARTUP, W. W. "The Social Worlds of Childhood." *American Psychologist* 34 (1979), 944–950.

———. "Peer Relations." In P. H. Mussen (ed.), *Handbook of Child Psychology*, Vol. 4. New York: Wiley, 1983, 103–196.

———. "The Peer Context in Middle Childhood." In W. A. Collins (ed.), *Development During Middle Childhood: The Years from Six to Twelve*. Washington, D.C.: National Academy Press, 1984, 240–282.

HASS, A. *Teenage Sexuality, a Survey of Teenage Sexual Behavior*. New York: Macmillan, 1979.

HAUSER, S. T.; POWERS, S.; NOAM, G. G.; JACOBSON, A. M.; WEISS, B.; and FOLLANSBEE, D. J. "Familial Contexts of Adolescent Ego Development." *Child Development* 55 (1984), 195–213.

HAVILAND, J. M., and SCARBOROUGH, H. S. *Adolescent Development in Contemporary Society*. New York: Van Nostrand, 1981.

HAY, D. F., and MURRAY, P. "Giving and Requesting: Social Facilitation of Infants' Offers to Adults." *Infant Behavior and Development* 5 (1982), 301–310.

HAY, D. F., and RHEINGOLD, H. L. "The Early Appearance of Some Valued Social Behaviors." State University of New York at Stony Brook, 1983 (unpublished).

HAY, D. F.; PEDERSEN, J.; and NASH, A. "Dyadic Interaction in the First Year of Life." In K. H. Rubin and H. S. Ross (eds.), *Peer Relationships and Social Skills in Childhood*. New York: Springer-Verlag, 1982.

HAYES, C. D., and KAMERMAN, S. B. (eds.), *Children of Working Parents: Experiences and Outcomes*. Panel on Work, Family, and Community, Committee on Child Development Research and Public Policy. Washington, D.C.: National Academy Press, 1983.

HAYS, J. D., and SIEGEL, A. W. "Way Finding and Spatial Representation: A Test of a Developmental Model of Cognitive Mapping of Large Scale Environments." Paper presented at the meeting of the Society for Research in Child Development, Boston, April 1981.

HAYWARD, D. G.; ROTHENBERG, M.; and BEASLEY, R. R. "Children's Play in Urban Playground Environments: A Comparison of Traditional, Contemporary and Adventure Playground Types." *Environment and Behavior* 6, no. 2 (1974), 131–168.

HEAROLD, S. L. "Meta-Analysis of the Effects of Television of Social Behavior." Doctoral diss., University of Colorado, 1979.

HECKHAUSEN, H. "The Development of Achievement Motivation." In W. W. Hartup (ed.), *Review of Child Development Research*, Vol. 6. Chicago: University of Chicago Press, 1981.

HENDERSON, B., and MOORE, S. G. "Measuring Exploratory Behavior in Young Children: A Factor-Analysis Study." *Developmental Psychology* 15, no. 2 (1979), 113–119.

HENDERSON, R. W. "Home Environment and Intellectual Performance." In R. W. Henderson (ed.), *Parent-Child Interaction: Theory, Research, and Prospects*. New York: Academic Press, 1981.

HERSH, S. P., and LEVIN, K. "How Love Begins Between Parent and Child." *Children Today* 47, Washington, D.C. (March-April 1978), 2–6.

HERZOG, A. R.; BACHMAN, J. C.; and JOHNSTON, L. D. "High School Seniors' Preferences for Division of Labor in the Family—1977." In D. G. McGuigan (ed.), *Changing Family/Changing Workplace*. Ann Arbor: University of Michigan, Center for Continuing Education of Women, 1980.

HESS, R. D., and HOLLOWAY, S. D. "Family and School as Educational Institutions." In R. D. Parke (ed.), *Review of Child Development Research*. Vol. 7, *The Family*. Chicago: The University of Chicago Press, 1984, 179–222.

HESS, R. D., and MCDEVITT, T. M. "Some Cognitive Consequences of Maternal Intervention Techniques: A Longitudinal Study." *Child Development* 55 (1984), 2017–2030.

HESS, R. D., and SHIPMAN, V. C. "Cognitive Elements in Maternal Behavior." In J. P. Hill (ed.), *Minnesota Symposium on Child Psychology*, Vol. I. Minneapolis: University of Minnesota Press, 1967.

HESS, R. D.; HOLLOWAY, S. D.; AZUMA, H.; and KASHIWAGI, K. "Causal Attributions by Japanese and American Mothers and Children About Performance in Mathematics." *International Journal of Psychology* 21, no. 3 (1986), 269–286.

HESS, R. D.; HOLLOWAY, S. D.; DICKSON, W. P.; and PRICE, G. G. "Maternal Variables as Predictors of Children's School Readiness and Later Achievement in Vocabulary and Mathematics in Sixth Grade." *Child Development* 55 (1984), 1902–1912.

HETH, C. D., and CORNELL, E. H. "Three Experiences Affecting Spatial Discrimination Learning in Ambulatory Children." *Journal of Experimental Child Psychology* 30 (1980), 246–264.

HETHERINGTON, E. M. "Effects of Father Absence on Personality Development in Adolescent Daughters." *Developmental Psychology* 7 (1972), 313–326.

———. "Divorce: A Child's Perspective." *American Psychologist* 34 (1979), 851–858.

———. "Children and Divorce." In R. Henderson (ed.), *Parent-Child Interaction: Theory, Research and Prospects*. New York: Academic Press, 1981.

HETHERINGTON, E. M.; and CAMARA, K. A. "Families in Transition: The Processes of Dissolution and Reconstitution." In R. D. Parke (ed.), *Review of Child Development Research*. Vol. 7, *The Family*. Chicago: The University of Chicago Press, 1984, 398–440.

HETHERINGTON, E. M.; COX, M.; and COX, R. "Family Interaction and Social, Emotional and Cognitive Development of Children Following Divorce." Paper presented at the Symposium on the Family: Setting Priorities, sponsored by the Institute for Pediatric Service of the Johnson and Johnson Baby Company, Washington, D.C., May 1978.

———. "Effects of Divorce on Parents and Children." In M. Lamb (ed.), *Nontraditional Families: Parenting and Child Development*. Hillsdale, N.J.: Erlbaum, 1982.

HEWISON, J., and TIZARD, J. "Parental Involvement and Reading Attainment." *British Journal of Educational Psychology* 50 (1980), 209–215.

HICKEY, J. "Stimulation of Moral Reasoning in Delinquents." In L. Kohlberg and E. Turiel (eds.), *Recent Research in Moral Development*. New York: Holt, 1974.

HIGGINS, E. T. "Role-Taking and Social Judgments: Alternative Developmental Perspectives and Processes." In J. H. Flavell and L. Ross (eds.), *Social Cognitive Development: Frontiers and Possible Futures*. New York: Cambridge University Press, 1981.

HIGGINS, E. T., and ECCLES, J. "Social Cognition and the Social Life of the Child: States and Subcultures." In E. T. Higgins, D. N. Ruble, and M. W. Hartup (eds.), *Social Cognition and Social Behavior: Development Issues*. New York: Cambridge University Press, 1983.

HIGGINS-TRENK, A., and GAITE, A. "Elusiveness of Formal Operational Thought in Adolescence." *Proceedings of the 79th Annual Convention of the American Psychological Association*, 1971.

HILDEBRAND, V. *Introduction to Early Childhood Education*, 4th ed. New York: Macmillan, 1985a.

———. *Guiding Young Children*, 3d ed. New York: Macmillan, 1985b.

HILL, C. R., and STAFFORD, F. P. "Parental Care of Children: Time Diary Estimate of Quantity, Predictability and Variety." *Journal of Human Resources* 15 (1980), 219–239.

HILL, J. P. "The Family." In M. Johnson (ed.), *Seventy-ninth Yearbook of the National Society for the Study of Education*. Chicago: University of Chicago Press, 1980.

HILL, J. P., and HOLMBECK, G. "Attachment and Autonomy During Adolescence." In G. Whitehurst (ed.), *Annals of Child Development*, Vol. 3. Greenwich, Conn.: JAI Press, 1986.

HILL, J. P., and LYNCH, M. "The Intensification of Gender-Related Role Expectations During Early Adolescence." In J. Brooks-Gunn and A. Petersen (eds.), *Female Puberty*. New York: Plenum Press, 1983.

HILL, M. S. "Trends in the Economic Situation of U.S. Families and Children." In R. Nelson and F. Skidmore (eds.), *American Families and the Economy*. Committee on Child Development Research and Public Policy. Washington, D.C.: National Academy Press, 1983, 9–58.

HIRSCH, J. "Behavior-genetic Analysis and Its Biosocial Consequences." *Seminars in Psychiatry* 2 (1970), 69–105.

HOBBS, N.; PERRIN, J.; and IREYS, H. *Summary of Findings and Recommendations: Public Policies Affecting Chronically Ill Children and Their Families*. Nashville: Center for the Study of Families and Children, Institute for Public Policy Studies, Vanderbilt University, 1983.

HOFFMAN, L. W. "Maternal Employment." *American Psychologist* 34 (1979), 859–865.

———. *Foundations of Family Therapy: A Conceptual Framework for Systems Change*. New York: Basic Books, 1981.

———. "Work, Family and the Socialization of the Child." In R. D. Parke (ed.), *Review of Child Development Research*. Vol. 7, *The Family*. Chicago: The University of Chicago Press, 1984, 223–281.

HOFFMAN, M. L. "Altruistic Behavior and the Parent-Child Relationship." *Journal of Personality and Social Psychology* 31 (1975), 937–943.

———. "Development of Moral Thought, Feeling, and Behavior." *American Psychologist* 34 (October 1979), 958–966.

———. "Empathy, Its Limitations, and Its Role in a Comprehensive Moral Theory." In W. M. Kurtines and J. L. Gewirtz (eds.), *Morality, Moral Behavior and Moral Development*. New York: Wiley, 1984.

HOGGE, W. A.; SCHONBERG, S. A.; and GOLBUS, M. S. "Chronic Villus Sampling: Experience of the First 1000 Cases." *American Journal of Obstetrics and Gynecology* 154 (1986), 1249–1252.

HOLLINGSHEAD, A. *Elmtown's Youth and Elmtown Revisited*. New York: Wiley, 1975. (Originally published 1949.)

HOLZMAN, M. "The Language of Children: Development in Home and in School." Englewood Cliffs, N.J.: Prentice-Hall, 1983.

HOMEL, R.; BURNS, A.; and GOODNOW, J. J. "Parental Social Networks and Aspects of Child Development." 1984 (unpublished).

HONZIK, M. P. "The Values and Limitations of Measurement." In M. Lewis (ed.), *Origins of Intelligence: Infancy and Early Childhood*, 2d ed. New York: Plenum, 1983.

HOOD, L., and BLOOM, L. "What, When and How About Why: A Longitudinal Study of Early Expressions of Causality." *Monographs of the Society for Research in Child Development* 44, Serial No. 181 (1979).

HORN, J. M. "Duration of Preschool Effects on Later School Competence." *Science* 213 (1981), 1145.

———. "The Texas Adoption Project: Adopted Children and Their Intellectual Resemblance to Biological and Adoptive Parents." *Child Development* 54 (1983), 268–275.

HORN, J. M.; LOEHLIN, J. C.; and WILLERMAN, L. "Intellectual Resemblance Among Adoptive and Biological Relatives: The Texas Adoption Project." *Behavior Genetics* 9 (1979), 177–208.

HORNER, M. "Toward an Understanding of Achievement-Related Conflicts in Women." *Journal of Social Issues* 28, no. 2 (1972), 157–174.

HOUSE, B. J. "Learning Processes: Developmental Trends." In J. Worell (ed.), *Psychological Development in the Elementary Years.* New York: Academic Press, 1982, 187–232.

HOUSEHOLDER, J.; HATCHER, R.; BURNS, W.; and CHASNOFF, I. "Infants Born to Narcotic-Addicted Mothers." *Psychological Bulletin* 92 (1982), 453–468.

HOWE, M. J. *Understanding School Learning: A New Look at Educational Psychology.* New York: Harper & Row, 1972.

HUBEL, D. H., and WIESEL, T. N. "Receptive Fields of Cells in Striate Cortex of Very Young, Visually Inexperienced Kittens." *Journal of Neurophysiology* 26 (1963) 996–1002.

———. "The Period of Susceptibility to the Physiological Effects of Unilateral Eye Closure in Kittens." *Journal of Physiology* 206 (1970), 419–436.

HUBEL, D. H.; WIESEL, T. N.; and LeVAY, S. "Plasticity of Ocular Dominance Columns in Monkey Striate Cortex." *Philosophical Transactions of the Royal Society of London.* Series B: *Biological Sciences* 278 (1977), 377–409.

HUNT, J. McV. *Intelligence and Experience.* New York: Ronald, 1961.

HUSTON, A. C. "Sex-typing." In P. H. Mussen (ed.), *Handbook of Child Psychology,* Vol. 4. 4th ed. New York: Wiley, 1983, 387–468.

HUSTON-STEIN, A., and HIGGINS-TRENK, A. "Development of Females from Childhood Through Adulthood: Career and Feminine Role Orientations." In P. B. Baltes (ed.), *Life-span Development and Behavior,* Vol. 1. New York: Academic Press, 1978, 258–296.

HUTT, S. J.; LENARD, H. G.; and PRECHTL, H. F. R. "Influence of 'State' upon Responsivity to Stimulation." In S. J. Hutt and C. Hutt (eds.), *Early Human Development.* Oxford: Oxford University Press, 1973.

IANNOTTI, R. J. "Naturalistic and Structured Assessments of Prosocial Behavior in Preschool Children: The Influence of Empathy and Perspective Taking." *Developmental Psychology* 21 (1985), 46–55.

IDELBERGER, H. "Hauptproblemen der kindlichen sprachentwicklung." *Zeitschrift fur Pedagogische Psychologie* 5 (1903), 241–297.

IMEDADZE, N. V. K. "Psikhologicheskoy prirode rannego dvuya-zychiya." *Voprosy Tsikhologii* 6 (1960), 60–68.

IMMELMANN, K. *Introduction to Ethology.* New York: Plenum Press, 1980.

INHELDER, B., and PIAGET, J. *The Growth of Logical Thinking from Childhood to Adolescence.* New York: Basic Books, 1958.

ITTELSON, W. H.; PROSHANSKY, H. M.; RIVLIN, L. G.; and WINKEL, G. H. *An Introduction to Environmental Psychology.* New York: Holt, 1974.

IZARD, C. E.; HUEBNER, R.; RISSER, D.; McGINNESS, G.; and DOUGHERTY, L. "The Young Infant's Ability to Produce Discrete Emotion Expressions." *Developmental Psychology* 16 (1980), 132–140.

IZARD, C. E., and DOUGHERTY, L. "A System for Identifying Affect Expressions by Holistic Judgments (Affex)." University of Delaware, 1980 (unpublished).

———. "Two Complementary Systems for Measuring Facial Expressions in Infants and Children." In C. E. Izard (ed.), *Measuring Emotions in Infants and Children.* New York: Cambridge University Press, 1982.

JACKLIN, C. N.; DiPIETRO, J. A.; and MACCOBY, E. E. "Sex-Typing Behavior and Typing Pressure in Child-Parent Interaction." *Sex Roles* 13 (1984), 413–425.

JACKSON, A. S., and COLEMAN, E. "Validation of Distance Run Tests for Elementary School Children." *Research Quarterly* 47 (1975), 86.

JACOBSON, J. L. "The Role of Inanimate Objects in Early Peer Interaction." *Child Development* 52 (1981), 618–626.

JANOFF-BULMAN, R., and BRICKMAN, P. "Expectations and What People Learn from Failure." In N. T. Feather (ed.), *Expectancy, Incentive and Action.* Hillsdale, N.J.: Erlbaum, 1981.

JAPANESE FINANCE MINISTRY. White paper on adolescence, 10–91. Tokyo: Printing Office, 1980.

JEAMMET, P. "The Anorexic Stance." *Journal of Adolescence* (1981) 113–129.

JEFFCOATE, J. A.; HUMPHREY, M. E.; and LLOYD, J. K. "Disturbance in the Parent-Child Relationship Following Preterm Delivery." *Developmental Medicine and Child Neurology* 21 (1979), 344–352.

JENCKS, C.; BARTLETT, S.; CORCORAN, M.; CROUSE, J.; EAGLESFIELD, D.; JACKSON, G.; McCLELLAND, K.; MUESER, P.; OLNECK, M.; SCHWARTZ, J.; WARD, S.; and WILLIAMS, J. *Who Gets Ahead? The Determinants of Economic Success in America.* New York: Basic Books, 1979.

JENKINS, R. L. "The Runaway Reaction." *American Journal of Psychiatry* 128 (1981), 168–173.

JENNINGS, D. L. "Effects of Attributing Failure to Ineffective Strategies." Unpublished doctoral diss., Stanford University, 1979.

JENSEN, A. M., and MOORE, S. G. "The Effect of Attribute Statements on Cooperativeness and Competitiveness in School-Aged Boys." *Child Development* 48 (1977), 305–307.

JENSEN, A. R. "How Much Can We Boost I.Q. and Scholastic Achievement?" *Harvard Educational Review* 39 (1969), 1–123.

JESSOR, R.; CHASE, J. A.; and DONOVAN, J. E. "Psychosocial Correlates of Marijuana Use and Problem Drinking in a National Sample of Adolescents." *American Journal of Public Health* 70 (1980), 604–613.

JOHNSON, C. N., and WELLMAN, H. M. "Children's Developing Conceptions of the Mind and Brain." *Child Development* 53 (1982), 222–234.

JOHNSON, H., and SMITH, L. B. "Children's Inferential Abilities in the Context of Reading to Understand." *Child Devleopment* 52 (1981), 1216–1223.

JOHNSON, J. E.; CHRISTIE, J. F.; and YAWKEY, T. D. *Play and Early Childhood Development.* Glenview, Ill.: Scott Foresman, 1987.

JOHNSTON, L. D.; O'MALLEY, P. M.; and BACHMAN, J. G. "Drug Use Among American High School Students, College Students, and Other Young Adults." *National Trends Through 1985.* National Institute of Drug Abuse, Department of Health and Human Services. Washington, D.C.: U.S. Government Printing Office, 1986.

JONES, D. J.; FOX, M. M.; and BABIGIAN, H. M. "Epidemiology of Anorexia Nervosa in Monroe County, New York, 1960–1976." *Psychosomatic Medicine* 42 (1980), 551–554.

JONES, H. "Adolescence in Our Society." In *The Family in a Democratic Society* (anniversary papers of the Community Service Society of New York). New York: Columbia University, 1949.

JONES, H. E. *Motor Performance and Growth.* Berkeley: University of California Press, 1949.

JONES, M. C. "The Later Careers of Boys Who Were Early—or Late—Maturing. *Child Development* 28 (1957), 113–128.

———. "Psychological Correlates of Somatic Development." *Child Development* 36 (1965), 899–911.

JONES, M. C., and BAYLEY, N. "Physical Maturing Among Boys as Related to Behavior." *Journal of Educational Psychology* 41 (1950), 129–248.

JONES, M. C., and MUSSEN, P. "Self-Conceptions, Motivations and Inter-Personal Attitudes of Early- and Late-Maturing Girls." *Child Development* 29 (1958), 491–501.

JOOS, S.K.; POLLITT, E.; MUELLER, W. H.; and ALBRIGHT, D. L. "The Bacon Chow Study: Maternal Nutritional Supplementation and Infant Behavioral Development." *Child Development* 54 (1983), 669–676.

JORDAAN, J. P., and HEYDE, M. B. *Vocational Maturity During the High School Years.* New York: Teacher's College Press, 1979.

JORGENSEN, S. R. "Sex Education and the Reduction of Adolescent Pregnancies: Prospects for the 1980s." *Journal of Early Adolescence* 1 (1981), 38–52.

JORGENSEN, S. R.; THORNBURG, H. D.; and WILLIAMS, J. K. "The Experience of Running Away: Perception of Adolescents Seeking Help in a Shelter Care Facility." *High School Journal* 64 (1980), 87–96.

JURICH, A. P. "Parenting Adolescents." *Family Perspective* 13 (1979), 137–149.

JURICH, A. P., and JONES, W. "Divorce and the Experience of Adolescents." In G. K. Leigh and G. W. Peterson (eds.), *Adolescents in Families*. Cincinnati: South-Western Publishing Co., 1986, 308–336.

KACERGUIS, M. A., and ADAMS, G. R. "Erikson Stage Resolution: The Relationship Between Identity and Intimacy." *Journal of Youth and Adolescence* 9 (1980), 117–126.

KACH, J., and MCGHEE, P. "Adjustment to Early Parenthood: The Role of Accuracy of Pre-parenthood Expectations." *Journal of Family Issues* 3 (1982), 375–388.

KACZKOWSKI, H. "Sex and Age Differences in the Life Problems of Adolescents." *Journal of Psychological Studies* 13 (1962), 165–169.

KAGAN, J. "Structure and Process in the Human Infant: The Ontogeny of Mental Representation." In M. H. Bornstein and W. Kessen (eds.), *Psychological Development from Infancy: Image to Retention*. Hillsdale, N.J.: Erlbaum, 1979.

———. *The Second Year*. Cambridge, Mass.: Harvard University Press, 1981.

———. "Stress and Coping in Early Development." In N. Garmezy and M. Rutter (eds.), *Stress, Coping and Development in Children*. New York: McGraw-Hill, 1983.

———. *The Nature of the Child*. New York: Basic Books, 1984.

KAGAN, J., and MOSS, H. A. *Birth to Maturity*. New York: Wiley, 1983.

KAGAN, J.; KEARSLEY, R. B.; and ZELAZO, P. R. *Infancy: Its Place in Human Development*. Cambridge, Mass.: Harvard University Press, 1978.

KAGAN, J. and MOSS, H.A. *Birth to Maturity*. New York: Wiley, 1983.

KAGAN, J.; REZNICK, R. J.; CLARKE, C.; SNIDMAN, N.; and GARCIA-COLL, C. "Behavioral Inhibition to the Unfamiliar." *Child Development* 55 (1984), 2212–2225.

KALISH, R. A. *The Psychology of Human Behavior*, 4th ed. Belmont, Calif.: Wadsworth Publishing Co., Inc., 1966, 1973.

KAMERMAN, S. B. "Child-Care Services: A National Picture." In U.S. Department of Labor, Bureau of Labor Statistics, *Families at Work: The Jobs and the Pay*. Special Labor Force Report, Bulletin 2209. Washington, D.C.: U.S. Government Printing Office, August 1984.

KAMERMAN, S. B., and HAYES, C. D. (eds.), *Families That Work: Children in a Changing World*. Panel on Work, Family and Community. Committee on Child Development Research and Public Policy. Washington, D.C.: National Academy Press, 1982.

KAMERMAN, S. B., and KAHN, A. J. *Child Care, Family Benefits and Working Parents: A Study in Comparative Policy*. New York: Columbia University Press, 1981.

KAMERMAN, S. B.; KAHN, A. J.; and KINGSTON, P. W. *Maternity Policies and Working Women*. New York: Columbia University Press, 1983.

KANDEL, D. "Homophily, Selection, and Socialization in Adolescent Friendships." *American Journal of Sociology* 84 (1978), 427–436.

KANDEL, D., and LESSER, G. S. *Youth in Two Worlds*. San Francisco: Jossey-Bass, 1972.

KANTER, R. M. "Jobs and Families: Impact of Working Roles on Family Life." *Children Today* 45, Washington, D. C. (March-April 1978), 11–15.

———. "Job and Families: Impact of Working Roles on Family Life." In P. Voydanoff (ed.), *Work and Family*. Palo Alto, Calif.: Mayfield Publishing Company, 1984, 111–119.

KANTOR, D., and LEHR, W. *Inside the Family*. San Francisco: Jossey-Bass, 1975.

KARMEL, M. *Thank You, Dr. Lamaze: A Mother's Experience in Painless Childbirth*. Philadelphia: Lippincott, 1983.

KATCHADOURIAN, H. *The Biology of Adolescence*. San Francisco: Freeman, 1977.

KATZ, B. J. "Cooling Motherhood." In J. G. Wells (ed.), *Current Issues in Marriage and the Family*. New York: Macmillan, 1975, 161–164.

KAYE, K. *The Mental and Social Life of Babies: How Parents Create Persons*. Chicago: The University of Chicago Press, 1982.

KEATING, D. P. "Thinking Processes in Adolescence." In J. Adelson (ed.), *Handbook of Adolescent Psychology*. New York: Wiley, 1980.

KEATING, D. P., and CLARK, L. V. "Development of Physical and Social Reasoning in Adolescents." *Developmental Psychology* 16 (1980), 23–30.

KEDAR-VIOVODAS, G. "The Impact of Elementary Children's Roles and Sex Roles on Teacher Attitudes: An Interactional Analysis." *Review of Educational Research* 53 (1983), 414–437.

KEECHER, G. P. "Why Isn't the Gerbil Moving Anymore?" *Children Today*. Washington, D.C. (January-February, 1975).

KEENEY, T. J.; CANNIZZO, S. R.; and FLAVELL, J. H. "Spontaneous and Induced Verbal Rehearsal in a Recall Task." *Child Development* 38 (1967), 953–966.

KELLER, A.; FORD, L. H., JR.; and MEACHUM, J. A. "Dimensions of Self-Concept in Preschool Children." *Developmental Psychology* 14 (1978), 483–489.

KELLOGG, R. *Analyzing Children's Art*. Palo Alto, Calif.: Mayfield Publishing Co., 1970.

———. *Child Art Collection*. San Francisco, 1974.

KELSO, J. A., and CLARK, J. E. *The Development of Movement Control and Co-ordination*. New York: Wiley, 1982.

KEMPE, R. S., and KEMPE, C. H. *Child Abuse*. Cambridge, Mass.: Harvard University Press, 1978.

KEMPER, T. D. "Predicting the Divorce Rate Down?" *Journal of Family Issues* 4 (1983), 507–524.

KENISTON, K. "Prologue: Youth as a Stage of Life." In P. H. Dreyer and R. J. Havighurst (eds.), *Youth*. Chicago: University of Chicago Press, 1975.

KENNY, S. L. "Developmental Discontinuities in Childhood and Adolescence." In K. W. Fischer (ed.), *Levels and Transitions in Children's Development*. New Directions for Child Development, No. 12. San Francisco: Jossey-Bass, 1983.

KEOGH, J. F. "Motor Performance Test Data for Elementary School Children." *Research Quarterly* 40 (1970), 600–602.

KIMMEL, D. C. *Adulthood and Aging*, 2d ed. New York: Wiley, 1980.

KINSBOURNE, M., and HISCOCK, M. "The Normal and Deviant Development of Functional Lateralization of the Brain." In P. H. Mussen (ed.), *Handbook of Child Psychology*, 4th ed. Vol. 2, *Infancy and Developmental Psychobiology*. New York: Wiley, 1983, 157–280.

KINSEY, A. C.; POMEROY, W. B.; MARTIN, C. E.; and GEBHARD, P. H. *Sexual Behavior in the Human Female*. Philadelphia: W. B. Saunders, 1953.

KIRKLEY-BEST, E., and KELLNER, K. R. "The Forgotten Grief: A Review of the Psychology of Stillbirth." *American Journal of Orthopsychiatry* 52 (1982), 420–429.

KITZINGER, S. *The Complete Book of Pregnancy and Childbirth*. New York: Knopf, 1983.

KLAHR, D., and ROBINSON, M. "Formal Assessment of Problem-Solving and Planning Processes in Preschool Children." *Cognitive Psychology* 13 (1981), 113–148.

KLAUS, M. H., and KENNELL, J. H. *Maternal-Infant Bonding*. St. Louis: Mosby, 1976.

———. *Parent-Infant Bonding*, 2d ed. St. Louis: Mosby, 1982.

KLAUS, M. H.; JERAULD, R.; KREGER, N. C.; McALPINE, W.; STEFFA, M.; and KENNELL, J. H. "Maternal Attachment: Importance of the First Post-Partum Days." *New England Journal of Medicine* 286 (1972), 460–463.

KLAUS, R., and GRAY, S. "The Early Training Project for Disadvantaged Children: A Report After Five Years." *Monographs of the Society for Research in Child Development* 4, Serial No. 120 (1968), 33.

KLEIN, L. "Antecedents to Teenage Pregnancy." *Clinical Obstetrics and Gynecology* 32 (1978), 1151–1159.

KLEIN, N.; HACK, M.; GALLAGHER, J.; and FARANOFF, A. A. "Preschool Performance of Children with Normal Intelligence Who Were Very Low-Birth Weight Infants." *Pediatrics* 75 (1985), 531–537.

KLESGES, R. "Comments at the Workshop on Childhood Obesity." National Institutes of Health, Washington, D.C., March 10–11, 1986.

KLOOSTERMANN, G. J. "The Dutch System of Home Births." In S. Kitzinger and J. A. Davis (eds.), *The Place of Birth*. New York: Oxford University Press, 1978, 85–92.

KOHLBERG, L. "Development of Moral Character and Moral Ideology." In M. L. Hoffman and L. W. Hoffman (eds.), *Review of Child Development Research*. Vol. 1. New York: Russell Sage Foundation, 1964.

———. "The Child as a Moral Philosopher." *Psychology Today* (September 1968), 25–30.

———. "Stage and Sequence: The Cognitive-Developmental Approach to Socialization." In D. A. Goslin (ed.), *Handbook of Socialization Theory and Research*. Chicago; Rand McNally, 1969, 384–385.

———. "Moral Stages and Moralization: The Cognitive-Developmental Approach." In T. Lickona (ed.), *Moral Development and Behavior: Theory Research and Social Issues*. New York: Holt, Rinehart, and Winston, 1976.

———. *Measuring Moral Judgment*. Worcester, Mass.: Clark University Press, 1979.

———. *The Philosophy of Moral Development*. New York: Harper & Row, 1981.

———. *The Psychology of Moral Development*. San Francisco: Harper & Row, 1985.

KOHLBERG, L., and GILLIGAN, C. "The Adolescent as a Philosopher: The Discovery of the Self in a Post-conventional World." In J. Kagan and R. Coles (eds.), *12 to 16: Early Adolescence*. New York: Norton, 1972, 144–179.

KOHLBERG, L., and TURIEL, E. (eds.). *Recent Research in Moral Development*. New York: Holt, 1974.

KOHLBERG, L.; LACROSSE, J.; and RICKS, D. F. "The Predictability of Adult Mental Health from Childhood Behavior." In B. Wolman (ed.), *Manual of Child Psychopathology*. New York: McGraw-Hill, 1972.

KOHN, M. L. *Class and Conformity: A Study in Values*, 2d ed. Chicago: University of Chicago Press, 1977.

KOLARS, J. C.; LEVITT, M. D.; AOUJI, M.; and SAVAIANO, D. A. "Yogurt: An Auto-Digesting Source of Lactose." *New England Journal of Medicine* 310 (January 5, 1984), 1.

KOLATA, G. B. "First Trimester Prenatal Diagnosis." *Science* 221 (1983), 1031–1032.

KOPP, C. B., and McCALL, R. "Predicting Later Mental Performance for Normal, At-Risk, and Handicapped Infants." In P. B. Baltes and O. G. Brim (eds.)., *Lifespan Development and Behavior*, Vol. 4. New York: Academic Press, 1982.

KRAUSS, R. M., and GLUCKSBERG, S. "Social and Nonsocial Speech." *Scientific American* 236 (1977), 100–105.

KRESSEL, K., and DEUTSCH, M. "Divorce Therapy: An In-Depth Survey of Therapists' Views." *Family Process* 16 (1977), 413–444.

KRETCHMER, N. Comments at the Workshop on Childhood Obesity, National Institutes of Health, Washington, D.C., March 10–11, 1986.

KREUTZER, M. A.; LEONARD, C.; and FLAVELL, J. H. "An Interview Study of Children's Knowledge About Memory." *Monographs of the Society for Research in Child Development* 40 (no. 1, Whole No. 159), 1975.

KROSNICK, J., and JUDD, C. "Transitions in Social Influence at Adolescence: Who Induces Cigarette Smoking?" *Developmental Psychology* 18 (1982), 359–368.

KUCZAJ, S. A., and BARRETT, M. D. (eds.). *The Development of Word Meaning*. New York: Springer-Verlag, 1986.

KULKA, R. A., and WEINGARTEN, H. "The Long-Term Effects of Parental Divorce in Children on Adult Adjustment." *Journal of Social Issues* 35 (1979), 50–78.

LABOV, W. "The Logic of Nonstandard English." In J. E. Alatis (ed.), *Twentieth Annual Roundtable*. Washington, D.C.: Georgetown University Press, 1970.

———. *Language in the Inner City: Studies in the Black English Vernacular*. Philadelphia: University of Pennsylvania Press, 1972.

Lact Aid. *Why Lact Aid? The Problem with Milk and the Answer*. New Jersey, 1985.

LADD, G. W. "Social Networks of Popular, Average, and Rejected Children in School Settings." *Merrill-Palmer Quarterly* 29 (1983), 283–308.

LAMB, M. E. "The Relationships Between Mothers, Fathers, Infants, and Siblings in the First Two Years of Life." Paper presented at the biennial conference of the International Society for the Study of Behavioral Development, Pavia, Italy, 1977.

———. "Paternal Influences and the Father's Role." *American Psychologist* 34 (1979a), 938–943.

———. "Influence of the Child on Marital Quality and Family Interaction During the Prenatal, Perinatal and Infancy Period." In R. M. Lerner and G. D. Spanier (eds.), *Contributions of the Child to Marital Quality and Family Interaction Through the Lifespan*. New York: Academic Press, 1979b.

———. "Early Contact and Maternal-Infant Bonding: One Decade Later." *Pediatrics* 70 (1972), 763–768.

———. *The Role of the Father in Child Development*, 2d ed. New York: Wiley, 1981.

LAMB, M. E.; FRODI, A. M.; HWANG, C. P.; and FRODI, M. "Varying Degrees of Parental Involvement in Infant Care: Attitudinal and Behavioral Correlates." In M. E. Lamb (ed.), *Non-traditional Families: Parenting and Child Development*. Hillsdale, N.J.: Erlbaum, 1982.

LANCASTER, J. B., and HAMBURG, B. A. (eds.). *School-Age Pregnancy and Parenthood*. New York: Aldine, 1986.

LANE, D. M., and Pearson, D. A. "The Development of Selective Attention." *Merrill-Palmer Quarterly* 28 (1982), 317–337.

LAOSA, L. M. "Maternal Behavior: Sociocultural Diversity in Modes of Family Interaction." In R. W. Henderson (ed.), *Parent-Child Interaction: Theory, Research and Prospects*. New York: Academic Press, 1981.

———. "Families as Facilitators of Children's Intellectual Development at 3 Years of Age: A Causal Analysis. In L. M. Laosa and I. E. Sigel (eds.), *Families as Learning Environments for Children*. New York: Plenum, 1982a.

———. "School, Occupation, Culture and Family: The Impact of Parental Schooling on the Parent-Child Relationship." *Journal of Educational Psychology* 74 (1982b), 791–827.

LAOSA, L. M., and SIGEL, I. E. (eds.), *Families as Learning Environments for Children*. New York: Plenum, 1982.

LAZAR, I., and DARLINGTON, R. "Lasting Effects of Early Education: A Report from the Consortium of Longitudinal Studies." *Monographs of the Society for Research in Child Development* 47, no. 2–3, Serial No. 195 (1982).

LAZAR, I.; DARLINGTON, R. B.; MURRAY, H.; ROYCE J.; and SNIPPER, A. "Lasting Effects of Early Education: A Report from the Consortium for Longitudinal Studies." *Monographs of the Society for Research in Child Development* 47, no. 2–3, Serial No. 195 (1982).

LAZARUS, R. *Psychological Stress and the Coping Process*. New York: McGraw-Hill, 1966.

LEARY, M. A.; GREER, D.; and HUSTON, A. C. "The Relation Between TV Viewing and Gender Roles." Paper presented at the meeting of the Southwestern Society for Research in Human Development, Galveston, Texas, April 1982.

LEBOYER, F. *Birth Without Violence*. New York: Knopf, 1975.

LEIB, S.; BENFIELD, G.; and GUIDUBALDI, J. "Effects of Early Intervention and Stimulation on the Preterm Infant." *Pediatrics* 66 (1980), 83–90.

LEIFER, M. *Psychological Effects of Motherhood: A Study of First Pregnancy*. New York: Praeger, 1980.

LEMPERS, J. D.; FLAVELL, E. R.; and FLAVELL, J. H. "The Development in Very Young Children of Tacit Knowledge Concerning Visual Perception." *Genetic Psychology Monographs* 95 (1977), 3–53.

LENNEBERG, E. H. *Biological Foundations of Language*. New York: Wiley, 1967.

LEOPOLD, W. F. *Speech Development of a Bilingual Child*. Evanston, Ill.: Northwestern University Press, 1949.

LERNER, H. E. "Early Origins of Envy and Devaluation of Women: Implications for Sex Role Stereotypes." *Bulletin of the Menninger Clinic* 38 (1974), 538–553.

———. "Adaptive and Pathogenic Aspects of Sex-Role Stereotypes: Implications for Parenting and Psychotherapy." *American Journal of Psychiatry* 135 (1978), 48–52.

LERNER, J. V, and LERNER, R. M. (eds.), *Temperament and Social Interaction in Infants and Children*. San Francisco: Jossey-Bass, 1986.

LERNER, R. M. *On the Nature of Human Plasticity*. Cambridge, England: Cambridge University Press, 1984.

———. *Concepts and Theories of Human Development*, 2d ed. Reading, Mass.: Addison-Wesley, 1986.

LERNER, R. M., and BUSCH-ROSSNAGEL, N. A. (eds.). *Individuals as Producers of Their Development: A Life-span Perspective*. New York: Academic Press, 1981.

LERNER, R. M., and SHEA, J. A. "Social Behavior in Adolescence." In B. Wolman (ed.), *Handbook of Developmental Psychology*. Englewood Cliffs, N.J.: Prentice-Hall, 1982, 503–525.

LESTER, B. M. "A Biosocial Model of Infant Crying." In L. P. Lipsitt (ed.), *Advances in Infant Behavior and Development*. New York: Ablex, 1983.

LESTER, B. M., ALS, H.; and BRAZELTON, T. B. "Regional Obstetric Anesthesia and Newborn Behavior: A Reanalysis Toward Synergistic Effects." *Child Development* 53 (1982), 687–692.,

LESTER, B. M.; KOTELCHUCK, M.; SPELKE, E.; SELLERS, M. J.; and KLEIN, R. E. "Separation Protest in Guatemalan Infants: Cross-Cultural and Cognitive Findings." *Developmental Psychology* 10 (1974), 79–85.

LEUNG, E. H. L., and RHEINGOLD, H. L. "Development of Pointing as a Social Gesture." *Developmental Psychology* 17 (1981), 215–220.

LEVENSON, S. *Everything But Money*. New York: Simon and Schuster, 1966.

LEVENSTEIN, P. "Cognitive Growth in Preschoolers Through Verbal Interaction with Mothers." *American Journal of Orthopsychiatry* 40 (1970), 426–432.

LEVITT, M. J. "Contingent Feedback, Familiarization, and Infant Affect: How a Stranger Becomes a Friend." *Developmental Psychology* 16 (1980), 425–432.

LEWIN-EPSTEIN, N. *Youth Employment During High School*. Washington, D.C.: National Center for Education Statistics, 1981.

LEWINSOHN, P. M.; MISCHEL W.; CHAPLAIN, W.; and BARTON R. "Social Competence and Depression: The Role of Illusory Self-Perceptions." *Journal of Abnormal Psychology* 89 (1980), 203–212.

LEWIS, C. C. "The Effects of Parental Firm Control: A Reinterpretation of Findings." *Psychological Bulletin* 90 (1981a), 547–563.

———. "How Adolescents Approach Decisions: Changes over Grades Seven to Twelve and Policy Implications." *Child Development* 52 (1981b), 538–544.

LEWIS, M. "The Social Network Systems Model: Toward a Theory of Social Development." In T. M. Field, A. Huston, H. C. Quay, L. Troll, and G. E. Finley (eds.), *Review of Human Development*. New York: Wiley, 1982.

LEWIS, M., and BROOKS-GUNN, J. *Social Cognition and the Acquisition of Self*. New York: Plenum Press, 1979.

———. "The Self as Social Knowledge." In M. D. Lynch, A. A. Norem-Hebeisen, and K. J. Gergen (eds.), *Self-Concept: Advances in Theory and Research*. Cambridge, Mass.: Ballinger, 1981, 101–118.

LEWIS, M., and STARR, M. "Developmental Continuity." In J. Osofsky (ed.), *Handbook of Infant Development*. New York: Wiley, 1979.

LEWIS, M. M. *Infant Speech*. London: Routledge and Kegan Paul, 1951.

LEWIS, T. L., and MAURER, D. "Newborns' Central Vision: Whole or Hole?" Paper presented at the meeting of the Society for Research in Child Development, New Orleans, 1977.

LEWKO, J. H. (ed.). *How Children and Adolescents View the World of Work*. San Francisco: Jossey-Bass, 1987.

LEWONTIN, R. C. *Human Diversity*. San Francisco: W. H. Freeman, 1982.

LEWONTIN, R. C.; ROSE, S.; and KAMIN, L. J. *Not in Our Genes: Biology, Ideology and Human Nature*. New York: Pantheon, 1984.

LICHT, B. G., and DWECK, C. S. "Determinants of Academic Achievement." The interaction of children's achievement orientations with skill area, 1981.

LIEBERT, R. M., and BARON, R. A. "Short-Term Effects of Televised Aggression on Children's Aggressive Behavior." In J. P. Murray, E. A. Rubinstein, and G. A. Comstock (eds.), *Television and Social Behavior: II. Television and Social Learning*. Washington, D.C.: U.S. Government Printing Office, 1972.

LIEBERT, R. M.; SPRAFKIN, J. N.; and DAVIDSON, E. S. *The Early Window: Effects of Television on Children and Youth*. New York: Pergamon Press, 1982.

LIND, J.; VUORENKOSKI, V.; and WASZ-HACKERT, O. "The Effect of Cry Stimulus on the Temperature of the Lactating Breast Primipara. A Thermographic Study." In N. Morris (ed.), *Psychosomatic Medicine in Obstetrics and Gynecology: Proceedings of the International Congress of Psychosomatic Medicine in Obstetrics and Gynecology, London, 1971*. Basel: S. Karger, 1973.

LIPSITT, L. P. "Infants at Risk: Perinatal and Neonatal Factors." *International Journal of Behavioral Development* 2 (1979), 23–42.

LIPSITT, L. P.; CROOK, C.; and BOOTH, C. A. "The Transitional Infant, Behavioral Development and Feeding." *American Journal of Clinical Nutrition* 41 (1985), 485–496.

LIPSITT, L. P.; STURGES, W. Q.; and BURKE, P. "Perinatal Indicators and Subsequent Crib Death." *Infant Behavior and Development* 2 (1979), 325–328.

LIVESLEY, W. J., and BROMLEY, D. B. *Person Perception in Childhood and Adolescence*. London: John Wiley and Sons, 1973.

LJUNG, B. O.; BERGSTEN-BRUCEFORS, A.; and LINDGREN, G. "The Secular Trend in Physical Growth in Sweden." *Annals of Human Biology* 1 (1974), 245–256.

LOEBER, R. "The Stability of Antisocial and Delinquent Child Behavior: A Review." *Child Development* 53 (1982), 1431–1446.

LONG, F. "Social Support Networks in Day Care and Early Child Development." In J. Whittaker and J. Garbarino (eds.), *Social Support Networks: Informal Helping in the Human Services*. New York: Aldine, 1983, 189–217.

LONGSTRETH, L. E.; LONGSTRETH, G. V.; RAMIREZ, C.; and FERNANDEZ, G. "The Ubiquity of Big Brother." *Child Development* 46 (1975), 769–772.

———. "Revisiting Skeels' Final Study: A Critique." *Developmental Psychology* 17 (1981), 620–626.

LOWENBERG, M. "The Development of Food Patterns in Young Children." In P. Pipes (ed.) *Nutrition in Infancy and Childhood*. St. Louis: Mosby, 1977.

LOWREY, G. H. *Growth and Development of Children*, 7th ed. Copyright © 1978 by Year Book Medical Publishers, Inc., Chicago. After C. A. Aldrich and E. S. Hewitt. "Outlines for Well Baby Clinics: Development for the First Twelve Months." *American Journal of Diseases of Children* 71 (1946), 131. Copyright © 1946, American Medical Association.

LUTZ, P. "The Stepfamily: An Adolescent Perspective." *Family Relations* 22 (1983), 367–375.

LYNCH, M. D. "Self-Concept Development in Childhood." In M. D. Lynch, A. A. Norem-Hebeisen, and K. Gergen (eds.), *Self-Concept: Advances in Theory and Research.* Cambridge, Mass.: Ballinger, 1981.

LYSTAD, M. *Violence in the Home.* New York: Brunner/Mazel, 1986.

McCALL, R. B. "The Development of Intellectual Functioning in Infancy and the Prediction of Later I.Q." In J. D. Osofsky (ed.), *Handbook of Infant Development.* New York: Wiley, 1979.

————. "A Hard Look at Stimulating and Predicting Development: The Cases of Bonding and Screening." *Pediatrics in Review* 3 (1982), 205–212.

————. "Exploring Developmental Transitions in Mental Performance." In K. W. Fischer (ed.), *Levels and Transitions in Children's Development.* New Directions for Child Development, No. 12. San Francisco: Jossey-Bass, 1983.

McCALL, R. B.; APPLEBAUM, M.; and HOGARTY, P. "Developmental Changes in Mental Performance." *Monographs of the Society for Research in Child Development* 38, Serial No. 150 (1973).

McCARTNEY, K. "Effect of Quality of Day Care Environment on Children's Language Development." *Developmental Psychology* 20 (1984), 244–260.

McCARTY, D. L. "Investigation of a Visual Imagery Mnemonic Device for Acquiring Face-Name Associations." *Journal of Experimental Psychology: Human Learning and Memory* 6 (1980), 145–155.

McCLELLAND, D. C. *The Achieving Society.* Princeton, N.J.: Van Nostrand, 1961.

————. *Power: The Inner Experience.* New York: Irvington, 1975.

MACCOBY, E. E. *Social Development: Psychological Growth and the Parent-Child Relationship.* New York: Harcourt Brace Jovanovich, 1980.

————. "Social-emotional Development and Response to Stressors." In N. Garmezy and M. Rutter (eds.), *Stress, Coping and Development in Children.* New York: McGraw-Hill, 1983.

————. "Context of the Family." In W. A. Collins (ed.), *Development During Middle Childhood: The Years from Six to Twelve.* Washington, D.C.: National Academy Press, 1984a, 184–239.

————. "Socialization and Developmental Change." *Child Development* 55 (1984b), 317–328.

MACCOBY, E. E., and JACKLIN, C. N. *The Psychology of Sex Differences.* Stanford, Calif.: Stanford University Press, 1974.

————. "Sex Differences in Aggression: A Rejoinder and Reprise." *Child Development* 51 (1980), 964–980.

MACCOBY, E. E., and MARTIN, J. A. "Socialization in the Context of the Family: Parent-Child Interaction." In P. H. Mussen (ed.), *Handbook of Child Psychology,* Vol. 4. 4th ed. New York: Wiley, 1983, 1–102.

McCUBBIN, H.; NEEDLE, R.; and WILSON, M. "Adolescent Health Risk Behaviors: Family Stress and Adolescent Coping as Critical Factors." *Family Relations* 34 (1985), 51.

McCUBBIN, H.; SUSSMAN, M.; and PATTERSON, J. (eds.). *Social Stress and the Family: Advances and Developments in Family Stress Theory and Research.* New York: Haworth, 1983.

MACDONALD, K., and PARKE, R. D. "Bridging the Gap: The Relationship Between Parent-Child Play and Peer Interactive Competence." *Child Development* 55 (1984), 1265–1277.

MACE, D., and MACE, V. "Lifetime Monogamy Is the Preferred Form of Marital Relationship." In H. Feldman and M. Feldman (eds.), *Current Controversies in Marriage and Family.* Beverly Hills, Calif.: Sage, 1985.

MACFARLANE, A. "Olfaction in the Development of Social Preferences in the Human Neonate." In M. A. Hofer (ed.), *Parent-Infant Interaction.* Amsterdam: Elsevier, 1975.

MACFARLANE, J. "Perspectives on Personality Consistency and Change from the Guidance Study." *Vita Humana* 7 (1964), 115–126.

McGUINNESS, D. *When Children Don't Learn: Understanding the Biology and Psychology of Learning Disabilities.* New York: Basic Books, 1985.

McGUIRE, T. R., and HIRSCH, J. *Behavior-Genetic Analysis.* Stroudsburg, Penna.: Hutchinson Ross Publishing Co., 1982.

McGUIRE, W. J., and McGUIRE, C. V. "Significant Others in Self-Space. Sex Differences and Developmental Trends in the Social Self." In J. Suls (ed.), *Psychological Perspectives on the Self,* Vol. 1. Hillsdale, N.J.: Erlbaum, 1982.

McGURK, H. (ed.). *An Ecological Approach to Human Development.* Amsterdam: North Holland, 1977.

MacKINNON, C. E.; BRODY, G. H.; and STONEMAN, Z. "The Effects of Divorce and Maternal Employment on the Home Environments of Preschool Children." *Child Development* 53 (1982), 1392–1399.

McLAUGHLIN, B. "Child Compliance to Parental Control Techniques." *Developmental Psychology* 19 (1983), 667–673.

————. *Second Language Acquisition in Childhood.* Vol. 1, *Preschool Children,* 2d ed. Hillsdale, N.J.: Erlbaum, 1984.

McNEIL, D. *The Acquisition of Language: The Study of Developmental Psycholinguistics.* New York: Harper & Row, 1970.

MacPHEE, D.; RAMEY, C. T.; and YEATES, K. "Home Environment and Early Cognitive Development: Implications for Intervention." In A. W. Gottfried (ed.), *Home Environment and Early Cognitive Development.* New York: Academic Press, 1984.

McWILLILAMS, M. *Nutrition for the Growing Years,* 2d ed. New York: Wiley, 1975.

MADDEN, J.; LEVENSTEIN, P.; and LEVENSTEIN, S. "Longitudinal I. Q. Outcomes of the Mother-Child Home Program." *Child Development* 47 (1976), 1015–1025.

MAEHR, M. L., and STALLINGS, W. M. "Freedom from External Evaluation." *Child Development* 43 (1972), 177–185.

MAIER, H. W. *Three Theories of Child Development.* New York: Harper & Row, 1969.

MAIN, M., and WESTON, D. R. "The Quality of the Toddler's Relationship to Mother and to Father. Related to Conflict Behavior and the Readiness to Establish New Relationships." *Child Development* 52 (1981), 932–940.

MAIN, M.; TOMASINI, L.; and TOLAN, W. "Differences Among Mothers of Infants Judged to Differ in Security." *Developmental Psychology* 15 (1979), 472–473.

MALINA, R. M. "Growth of Muscle Tissue and Muscle Mass." In F. Falkner and J. M. Tanner (eds.), *Human Growth.* Vol. 2, *Postnatal Growth.* New York: Plenum, 1978.

MANASTER, G. *Adolescent Development and the Life Tasks.* New York: Allyn and Bacon, 1977.

MANGAROV, I. "Bulletin Information." *Bulgarian Olympic Committee, Year IX,* 5 (1964), 22.

MARCH OF DIMES BIRTH DEFECTS FOUNDATION. "Birth Defects: Original Article Series." White Plains, N.Y. Vol. 16, No. 6. December 1980a.

————. "Pregnant? Before You Drink, Think. . . . White Plains, N.Y., 1980b.

————. "Facts/1982." Statistical tables and charts, Fig. 1, 1982a, 31.

————. "Your Special Child." White Plains, N.Y., 1982b.

————. "Be Good to Your Baby Before It Is Born." White Plains, N.Y., 1983a.

————. "Genetic Series: PKU." Public Health Information Sheet. White Plains, N.Y., 1983b.

————. "Low Birthweight." Public Health Education Information Sheet. White Plains, N.Y., 1985b.

————. "Facts." White Plains, N.Y., 1984a, 5.

————. "Genetic Series: Rh Disease." Public Health Education Information Sheet. White Plains, N.Y., 1984b.

————. "Genetic Series: Tay-Sachs." Public Health Education Information Sheet. White Plains, N.Y., 1984c.

————. "The Same Inside." White Plains, N.Y., 1984d.

————. "Facts/1985." White Plains, N.Y., 1985a.

————. "Genetic Counseling." White Plains, N.Y., 1987.

————. "Genetic Series: Down Syndrome." Public Health Education Information Sheet. White Plains, N.Y., 1985c.

————. "Genetic Series: Sickle Cell Anemia." Public Health Education Information Sheet. White Plains, N.Y., 1985d.

————. "Rubella." Public Health Education Information Sheet. White Plains, N.Y., 1985e.

MARCIA, J. E. "Development and Validation of Ego Identity Status." *Journal of Personality and Social Psychology* 3, no. 5 (1966), 551–558.

————. "Identity in Adolescence." In J. Adelson (ed.), *Handbook of Adolescent Psychology*. New York: Wiley, 1980.

MARCIA, J. E.; WATERMAN, A. S.; and MATTESON, D. R. *Ego Identity: A Handbook for Psychosocial Research*. Hillsdale, N.J.: Erlbaum, in press.

MARCUS, L. "Patterns of Coping in Families of Psychotic Children." *American Journal of Orthopsychiatry* 47 (1977), 388–395.

MARJORIBANKS, K. "Family Environments." In H. Walberg (ed.), *Educational Environments and Effects*. Berkeley, Calif.: McCutchan, 1979.

————. *Ethnic Families and Children's Achievements*. Sydney: Allen and Unwin, 1980.

MARKMAN, E. M. "Classes and Collections: Conceptual Organization and Numerical Abilities." *Cognitive Psychology* 11 (1979), 395–411.

MARKUS, H. J. "Self-Schemata and Processing Information About the Self." *Journal of Personality and Social Psychology* 35 (1977), 63–78.

————. "The Self in Thought and Memory." In D. M. Wegner and R. R. Vallacher (eds.), *The Self in Social Psychology*. New York: Oxford University Press, 1980.

MARKUS, H. J., and NURIUS, P. S. "Self-Understanding and Self-Regulation in Middle Childhood." In W. A. Collins (ed.), *Development During Middle Childhood: The Years from Six to Twelve*. Washington, D.C.: National Academy Press, 1984, 147–183.

MARKUS, H. J., and SENTIS, D. "The Self in Social Information Processing." In J. Suls (ed.), *Psychological Perspectives on the Self*. Hillsdale, N.J.: Erlbaum, 1982.

MARSHALL, W. A. "Puberty." In F. Falkner and J. Tanner (eds.), *Human Growth*, Vol. 2. New York: Plenum, 1978.

MARSHALL, W. A., and TANNER, J. M. "Variations in the Pattern of Pubertal Changes in Girls." *Archives of Disease in Childhood* 44 (1969), 291–303.

————. "Variations in the Pattern of Pubertal Changes in Boys." *Archives of Disease in Childhood* 45 (1970), 13–23.

MARTIN, B. "Parent-Child Relations." In F. D. Horowitz (ed.), *Review of Child Development Research*, Vol. 4. Chicago: University of Chicago Press, 1975.

MARTIN, C. L., and HALVERSON, C. F., JR. "A Schematic Processing Model of Sex Typing and Stereotyping in Children." *Child Development* 52 (1981), 1119–1134.

MARTIN, J. A. "A Longitudinal Study of the Consequences of Early Mother-Infant Interaction: A Microanalytic Approach." *Monographs of the Society for Research in Child Development* 46, no. 3, Serial No. 190 (1981).

MARTORANO, S. C. "A Developmental Analysis of Performance on Piaget's Formal Operations Tasks." *Developmental Psychology* 13 (1977), 666–672.

MARUYAMA, G.; RUBIN, R.; and KINGSBURY, G. "Self-Esteem and Educational Achievement: Independent Constructs with a Common Cause." *Journal of Personality and Social Psychology* 40 (1981), 962–975.

MARX, J. L. "Botulism in Infants: A Cause of Sudden Death?" *Science* (September 1, 1978), 799–801.

————. "The Case of the Misplaced Gene (Translocations of Viral Oncogenic Genes)." *Science* 218 (December 3, 1982), 983–985.

MASANGKAY, Z. S.; McCLUSKEY, K. A.; McINTYRE, C. W.; SIMS-KNIGHT, J.; VAUGHN, B. E.; and FLAVELL, J. H. "The Early Development of Inferences About Visual Percepts of Others." *Child Development* 45 (1974), 357–366.

MASH, E. J.; JOHNSTON, J. L.; and KOVITZ, K. A. "A Comparison of the Mother-Child Interactions of Physically Abused and Nonabused Children During Play and Task Situations." *Journal of Clinical Child Psychology* 12, no. 3 (Winter 1983), 337–346.

MASNICK, G., and BANE, M. *The Nation's Families: 1960–1990*. Boston: Auburn House, 1980.

MASSAD, C. "Sex Role Identity and Adjustment During Adolescence." *Child Development* 52 (1981), 1290–1298.

MASTERS, J. C.; FURMAN, W.; and BARDEN, R. C. "Effects of Achievement Standards, Tangible Rewards, and Self-Dispensed Achievement Evaluations on Children's Task Mastery." *Child Development* 48 (1977), 217–224.

MATAS, L.; AREND, R. A.; and SROUFE, L. A. "Continuity of Adaptation in the Second Year: The Relationship Between Quality of Attachment and Later Competence." *Child Development* 49 (1978), 547–556.

MATERNITY CENTER ASSOCIATION. *A Baby Is Born*. New York: Maternity Center Association, 1964.

MATTESON, D. R. *Adolescence Today*. Homewood, Ill.: Dorsey, 1975.

MAURER, D., and SALAPATEK, P. "Developmental Changes in the Scanning of Faces by Young Infants." *Child Development* 47 (1976), 523–527.

MAY, K. A., and PERRIN, S. P. "Prelude: Pregnancy and Birth." In S. M. H. Hanson and F. W. Bozett (eds.), *Dimensions of Fatherhood*. Beverly Hills, Calif.: Sage, 1985.

MAYER, J. "Genetic Factors in Human Obesity." *Annals of the New York Academy of Science* 131 (1965), 412–421.

MEDRICH, E. A.; ROIZEN, J.; and RUBIN, V. *The Serious Business of Growing Up*. Berkeley: University of California Press, 1982.

MEICHENBAUM, D., and ASARNOW, J. R. "Cognitive-Behavior Modification and Metacognitive Development: Implications for the Classroom." In P. C. Kendall and S. D. Hollon (eds.), *Cognitive-Behavioral Interventions: Theory, Research, and Procedures*. New York: Academic Press, 1982.

MELTZOFF, A. N., and MOORE, M. K. "Newborn Infants Imitate Adult Facial Gestures." *Child Development* 54 (1983), 702–709.

MENKEN, J.; TRUSSELL, J.; and LARSEN, U. "Age and Infertility." *Science* 233 (1986), 1389–1394.

MENYUK, P. *Language and Maturation*. Cambridge, Mass.: M.I.T. Press, 1977.

MERCY, J. A., and STEELMAN, L. C. "Familial Influence on the Intellectual Attainment of Children." *American Sociological Review* 47 (1982), 532–542.

MEREDITH, H. V. "Length of Head and Neck, Trunk and Lower Extremities on Iowa City Children Aged 7–17 Years." *Child Development* 10 (1939), 141.

MERRITT, R. "Obesity." *Current Problems in Pediatrics* 12, no. 11 (1982).

MILGRAM, S. "The Experience of Living in Cities." *Science* 167 (1970), 1461–1468.

MILLER, A. *The Death of a Salesman*. New York: Viking, 1967.

MILLER, M. I. "Childhood Experience Antecedents of Career Maturity Attitudes." *The Vocational Guidance Quarterly* 27, no. 1 (1978), 137–143.

MILLER, P. H., and WEISS, M. G. "Children's and Adults' Knowledge About What Variables Affect Selective Attention." *Child Development* 53 (1982), 543–549.

MILLER, R. L.; BRICKMAN, P.; and BOLEN, D. "Attribution Versus Presuasion as a Means for Modifying Behavior." *Journal of Personality and Social Psychology* 31 (1975), 430–441.

MILNE, C.; SEEFELDT, V.; and REUSCHLEIN, P. "Relationship Between Grade, Sex, Race, and Motor Performance in Young Children." *Research Quarterly* 47 (1975), 726.

MINNETT, A. M.; VANDELL, D. L.; and SANTROCK, J. W. "The Effects of Sibling Status on Sibling Interaction: Influences of Birth Order, Age Spacing, Sex of Child and Sex of Sibling." *Child Development* 54 (1983), 1064–1072.

MINUCHIN, P. P., and SHAPIRO, E. K. "The School as a Context for

Social Development." In P. H. Mussen (ed.), *Handbook of Child Psychology*, Vol. 4. New York: Wiley, 1983, 197–274.

————. "Families and Individual Development: Provocations from the Field of Family Therapy." *Child Development* 56 (1985), 289–302.

MINUCHIN, S.; ROSMAN, B. L.; and BAKER, L. *Psychosomatic Families*. Cambridge, Mass.: Harvard University Press, 1978.

MISCHEL, W. "Sex-Typing and Socialization." In P. H. Mussen (ed.), *Carmichael's Manual of Child Psychology*, Vol. 2. New York: Wiley, 1970.

MITCHELL, G., and SHIVELY, C. "Naturalistic and Experimental Studies of Nonhuman Primate and Other Animal Families." In R. D. Parke (ed.), *Review of Child Development Research*. Vol. 7, *The Family*. Chicago: The University of Chicago Press, 1984.

MITCHELL, S., and ROSA, P. "Boyhood Behavior Problems as Precursors of Criminality: A Fifteen-Year Follow-up Study." *Journal of Child Psychology and Psychiatry* 22 (1981), 19–33.

MOEN, P. "The Two-Provider Family: Problems and Potentials." In M. E. Lamb (ed.), *Non-traditional Families: Parenting and Child Development*. Hillsdale, N.J.: Erlbaum, 1982.

MONKUS, E., and BANCALARI, E. "Neonatal Outcome." In K. G. Scott, T. Field, and E. Robertson (eds.), *Teenage Parents and Their Offspring*. New York: Grune and Stratton, 1981, 131–144.

MONTEMAYOR, R., and EISEN, M. "The Development of Self-Conception from Childhood to Adolescence." *Developmental Psychology* 13 (1977), 314–319.

MOON, T. J.; OTTO, J.; and TOWLE, A. *Modern Biology*. New York: Holt, Rinehart, and Winston, 1963, 616.

MOORE, K. C. "The Mental Development of a Child." *Psychological Review, Monograph Supplements* 1, no. 3 (1896).

MOORE, K. L. *The Developing Human: Clinically Oriented Embryology*, 3d ed. Philadelphia: W. B. Saunders, 1982.

————. *Before We Are Born*, 2d ed. Philadelphia: W. B. Saunders, 1983, 111.

MORGAN, G. "Child Day Care Policy in Chaos." In E. F. Zigler, S. L. Kagon, and E. Klugman (eds.), *Children, Families and Government: Perspectives on American Social Policy*. Cambridge: Cambridge University Press, 1983, 249–265.

MORRIS, N. M., and UDRY, J. R. "Validation of a Self-Administered Instrument to Assess Stage of Adolescent Development." *Journal of Youth and Adolescence* 9 (1980), 271–280.

MOSHMAN, D. "Development of Formal Hypothesis-Testing Ability." *Developmental Psychology* 15 (1979), 104–112.

MOSS, H. A., and SUSMAN, E. J. "Longitudinal Study of Personality Development." In O. Brim and J. Kagan (eds.), *Constancy and Change in Human Development*. Cambridge, Mass.: Harvard University Press, 1980, 530–595.

MUELLER, E., and VANDELL, D. "Infant-Infant Interaction." In J. Osofsky (ed.), *Handbook of Infant Development*. New York: Wiley, 1979.

MUIR, D., and FIELD, J. "Newborn Infants Orient to Sounds." *Child Development* 50 (1979), 431–436.

MUNROE, R. H.; SHIMMIN, H. S.; and MUNROE, R. L. "Gender Understanding and Sex-Role Preferences in Four Cultures." *Developmental Psychology* 20 (1984), 673–682.

MURPHY, L. B. *The Widening World of Childhood*. New York: Basic Books, 1962.

MURRAY, A. D.; DOLBY, R. M.; NATION, R. L.; AND THOMAS D. B. "Effects of Epidural Anesthesia on Newborns and Their Mothers." *Child Development* 52 (1981), 71–82.

MURRAY, F. B. "The Conservation Paradigm." In D. Brodzinsky, I. Siegel, and R. Golinkoff (eds.), *New Directions in Piagetian Research and Theory*. Hillsdale, N.J.: Erlbaum, 1981.

NADELMAN, L., and BEGUN, A. "The Effect of the Newborn on the Older Sibling: Mothers' Questionnaires." In M. E. Lamb and B. Sutton-Smith (eds.), *Sibling Relationships*. Hillsdale, N.J.: Erlbaum, 1982.

NAEYE, R. "Sudden Infant Death." *Scientific American* 242 (1980), 56–62.

NATIONAL CENTER FOR HEALTH STATISTICS. "United States Life Tables. U.S. Decennial Life Tables for 1979–81," Vol. 1, no. 1. DHHS Pub. No. (PHS) 85-1150-1, Table 2, p. 8 and Table 3, p. 10, Public Health Service. Washington, D.C.: U.S. Government Printing Office, August 1985.

NATIONAL COMMISSION ON EXCELLENCE IN EDUCATION. *A Nation at Risk: The Imperative for Educational Reform*. Washington, D.C.: U.S. Department of Education, 1983.

NATIONAL COMMISSION ON YOUTH. *The Transition of Youth to Adulthood: A Bridge Too Long*. Boulder, Colo.: Westview Press, 1980.

NATIONAL PANEL ON HIGH SCHOOL AND ADOLESCENT EDUCATION. *The Education of Adolescents*. Washington, D.C.: U.S. Department of Health, Education, and Welfare, 1976.

NATIONAL SCIENCE FOUNDATION. *Research on the Effects of Television Advertising in Children: A Review of the Literature and Recommendations for Future Research*. Washington, D.C.: National Science Foundation, 1977.

NAUS, M. J. "Memory Development in the Young Reader: The Combined Effects of Knowledge Base and Memory Processing." In W. Otto and S. White (eds.), *Reading Expository Text*. New York: Academic Press, 1982.

NEFF, W. S. *Work and Human Behavior*. New York: Aldine, 1985.

NEIMARK, E. D. "Intellectual Development During Adolescence." In F. D. Horowitz (ed.), *Review of Child Development Research*, Vol. 4. Chicago: University of Chicago Press, 1975.

NELSON K. "Pre-syntactic Strategies for Learning to Talk." Paper delivered to the Society for Research in Child Development, Minneapolis, March 1971.

————. "Structure and Strategy in Learning to Talk." *Monographs of the Society for Research in Child Development*, 38, no. 149 (1973), entire issue.

————. "How Children Represent Knowledge of Their World in and out of Language: A Preliminary Report." In R. S. Siegler (ed.), *Children's Thinking: What Develops?* Hillsdale, N.J.: Erlbaum, 1978.

————. "Individual Differences in Language Development: Implications for Development and Language." *Developmental Psychology* 17 (1981), 170–187.

NELSON, N.; ENKIN, M.; SAIGAL, S.; BENNETT K.; MILNER, R.; and SACKETT, D. "A Randomized Clinical Study of the Leboyer Approach to Childbirth." *The New England Journal of Medicine* 302 (1980), 655–660.

NELSON, S. A. "Factors Influencing Young Children's Use of Motives and Outcomes as Moral Criteria." *Child Development* 51 (1980), 823–829.

NEMY, E. "Women Speak Out Against Sexual Harassment at Work." *The New York Times* (August 19, 1975), 38.

NESSELROADE, J. R., and BALTES, P. B. "Adolescent Personality Development and Historical Change: 1970–72." *Monographs of the Society for Research in Child Development* 39 (1974), 1–80.

NEWCOMB, A. F., and ROGOSCH, F. "The Influence of Social Reputation on the Social Relations of Rejected and Isolated Children." Michigan State University, 1982 (unpublished).

NEWSON, J., and NEWSON, E. *Seven Years Old in the Home Environment*. New York: Wiley, 1976.

————. *Perspectives on School at Seven Years Old*. Winchester, Md.: Allen and Unwin, 1977.

NICHOLLS, J. G. "Striving to Demonstrate and Develop Ability: A Theory of Achievement Motivation." Purdue University, 1981 (unpublished).

NIELSEN TELEVISION INDEX. "National Audience Demograp Report, 1982." Northbrook, Ill.: A. C. Nielsen, 1982.

NOFZ, M. P. "Fantasy-Testing Assessment: A Proposed Model for the Investigation of Mate Selection." *Family Relations* 33 (1984), 273–281.

NORMAN-JACKSON, J. "Family Interactions, Language Development and Primary Reading Achievements of Black Children in Families of Low Income." *Child Development* 53 (1982), 349–358.

NYE, F. I. *School-Age Parenthood.* Extension Bulletin 667. Pullman, Wash.: Cooperative Extension Service, 1975.

NYE, F. I., and EDELBROCK, C. "Introduction: Some Social Characteristics of Runaways." *Journal of Family Issues* 1 (1980), 147–150.

O'BRIEN, M. "Sex Differences in Toy and Activity Preferences of Toddlers." Unpublished master's thesis, University of Kansas, Department of Human Development, 1980.

O'BRIEN, M.; HUSTON, A. C.; and RISLEY, T. "Emergence and Stability of Sex-Typed Toy Preferences in Toddlers." Paper presented at the meeting of the Association for Behavioral Analysis, Milwaukee, May 1981.

O'CONNELL, J. C., and FARRAN, D. C. "Effects of Day-Care Experience on the Use of Intentional Communicative Behaviors in a Sample of Socioeconomically Depressed Infants." *Developmental Psychology* 18 (1982), 22–29.

OGBU, J. U. *Minority Education and Caste: The American School System in Cross-Cultural Perspective.* New York: Academic Press, 1978a.

———. *Minority Education and Caste.* New York: Academic Press, 1978b.

———. "Crossing Cultural Boundaries: A Comparative Perspective on Minority Education." Paper for a Symposium on Race, Class, Socialization, and the Life Cycle, University of Chicago, October 21–22, 1983 (unpublished).

OLEJNIK, A. B., and MCKINNEY, J. P. "Parental Value Orientation and Generosity in Children." *Developmental Psychology* 8 (1973), 311.

OLSON, D. H.; RUSSELL, C. S.; and SPRENKLE, D. H. "Circumplex Model of Marital and Family System. II: Empirical Studies and Clinical Intervention." In J. Vincent (ed.), *Advances in Family Intervention, Assessment and Theory.* Greenwich, Conn.: JAI Press, 1979.

———. "Circumplex Model of Marital and Family Systems. VI: Theoretical Update." *Family Process* 22 (1983), 69–83.

OLSON, G. M., and SHERMAN, T. "Attention, Learning and Memory in Infants." In P. H. Mussen (ed.), *Handbook of Child Psychology.* Vol. 2, *Infancy and Developmental Psychobiology,* 4th ed. New York: Wiley, 1983, 1001–1081.

OLSON, L. *Cost of Children.* Lexington, Mass.: Lexington Books, 1983.

OLWEUS, D. "Stability in Aggressive, Inhibited and Withdrawn Behavior Patterns." Paper presented at the meeting of the Society for Research in Child Development, Boston, April 1981.

ORAM, R. F.; HUMMER, P. J., JR.; and SMOOT, R. C. *Biology,* 3d ed. Columbus, Ohio: Charles E. Merrill, 1979, 510.

ORLOFSKY, J. L.; MARCIA, J. E.; and LESSER, I. M. "Ego Identity Status and the Intimacy vs. Isolation Crisis of Young Adulthood." *Journal of Personality and Social Psychology* 27, no. 2 (1973), 211–219.

ORNSTEIN, P. A. *Memory Development in Children.* Hillsdale, N.J.: Erlbaum, 1978.

ORR, M. T. "Sex Education and Contraceptive Education in U.S. Public High Schools." *Family Planning Perspectives* 14 (1982), 304–313.

ORTHO DIAGNOSTICS SYSTEMS INC., Raritan, N.J.

OSKAMP, S., and MINDICK, B. "Personality and Attitudinal Barriers to Contraception." In D. Byrne and W. A. Fisher (eds.), *Adolescents, Sex, and Contraception.* New York: McGraw-Hill, 1981.

OSKAMP, S.; MINDICK, B.; BERGER, D.; and MOTTA, E. A. "Longitudinal Study of Success Versus Failure in Contraceptive Planning." *Journal of Population* 1 (1978), 69–93.

OSOFSKY, J. D., and OSOFSKY, H. S. "Teenage Pregnancy: Psychosocial Considerations." *Clinical Obstetrics and Gynecology* 21 (1978), 1161–1173.

———. "Psychological and Developmental Perspectives on Expectant and New Parenthood." In R. D. Parke (ed.), *Review of Child Development Research.* Vol. 7, *The Family.* Chicago: The University of Chicago Press, 1984, 372–397.

OSTREA, E. M.; CHAVEZ, C. J.; and STRAUSS, M. E. "A Study of

Factors That Influence the Severity of Neonatal Narcotic Withdrawal." *Journal of Addictive Diseases* 56 (1979), 74–89.

O'TOOLE, J. *Senate Subcommittee on Children and Youth, American Families: Trends and Pressures.* Washington, D.C.: U.S. Government Printing Office, 1973, 98–109.

OTTO, J. H., and TOWLE, A. *Modern Biology.* New York: Holt, Rinehart, and Winston, 1977, 627–628.

OTTO, J. H.; JULIAN, C. J.; TETHER, J. E.; and NASSIF, J. Z. *Modern Health.* New York: Holt, Rinehart, and Winston, 1985.

OTTO, L. "Family Influences on Youth Occupational Aspirations and Achievements." In G. K. Leigh and G. W. Peterson (eds.), *Adolescents in Families.* Cincinnati: South-Western, 1986, 226–255.

OVERTON, W. F., and NEWMAN, J. L. "Cognitive Development. A Competence-Activation/Utilization Approach." In T. M. Field, A. Huston, H. C. Quay, L. Troll, and G. E. Finley, (eds.), *Review of Human Development.* New York: John Wiley and Sons, 1982.

PALKOVITZ, R. "Fathers' Birth Attendance, Early Contact and Extended Contact with Their Newborns: A Critical Review." *Child Development* 56 (1985), 392–406.

PALMER, R. L. *Anorexia Nervosa: A Guide for Sufferers and Their Families.* New York: Penguin, 1980.

PAPERT, S. *Mindstorms: Children, Computers and Powerful Ideas.* New York: Basic Books, 1980.

PAPOUSEK, H. "Experimental Studies of Appetitional Behavior in Human Newborns and Infants." In H. W. Stevenson, E. H. Hess, and H. L. Rheingold (eds.), *Early Behavior: Comparative and Developmental Approaches.* New York: Wiley, 1967; Huntington, N.Y.: Krieger, 1975, 249–278.

PARIS, S. G., and LINDAUER, B. K. "Constructive Aspects of Children's Comprehension and Memory." In R. V. Kail, Jr., and J. W. Hagen (eds.), *Perspectives on the Development of Memory and Cognition.* Hillsdale, N.J.: Erlbaum, 1977.

PARKE, R. D. "Rules, Roles and Resistance to Deviation: Recent Advances in Punishment, Discipline and Self-Control." In A. Pick (ed.), *Minnesota Symposium on Child Psychology,* Vol. 8. Minneapolis: University of Minnesota Press, 1974.

———. "Punishment in Children: Effects, Side Effects, and Alternative Strategies." In H. Hom and P. Robinson (eds.), *Psychological Processes in Early Education.* New York: Academic Press, 1977.

———. "Perspectives on Father-Infant Interaction." In J. D. Osofsky (ed.), *Handbook of Infancy.* New York: Wiley, 1978.

———. "On Prediction of Child Abuse: Theoretical Considerations." In R. Starr (ed.), *Prediction of Abuse.* Philadelphia: Ballinger, 1982.

———. *Review of Child Development Research.* Vol. 7, *The Family.* Chicago: The University of Chicago Press, 1984.

PARKE, R. D., and LEWIS, N. G. "The Family in Context: A Multi-Level Interactional Analysis of Child Abuse." In R. Henderson (ed.), *Parent-Child Interaction.* New York: Academic Press, 1981.

PARKE, R. D., and SAWIN, D. B. "Fathering: It's a Major Role." *Psychology Today* (November 1977).

———. "The Family in Early Infancy: Social Interaction and Attitudinal Analyses." In F. A. Pederson (ed.), *The Father-Infant Relationship: Observational Studies in a Family Context.* New York: Praeger, 1980.

PARKE, R. D., and SLABY, R. G. "The Development of Aggression." In P. H. Mussen (ed.), *Handbook of Child Psychology,* Vol. 6. 4th ed. New York: Wiley, 1983, 548–641.

PARKE, R. D., and SUOMI, S. J. "Adult Male-Infant Relationships: Human and Nonprimate Evidence." In K. Immelmann, G. Barlow, M. Mann, and L. Petrinovitch (eds.), *Behavioral Development: The Bielefeld Interdisciplinary Project:* New York: Cambridge University Press, 1980.

PARKE, R. D., and TINSLEY, B. R. "The Father's Role in Infancy: Determinants of Involvement in Caregiving and Play." In M. E. Lamb (ed.), *The Role of the Father in Child Development,* New York: Interscience, Wiley, 1981.

———. "Fatherhood: Historical and Contemporary Perspectives."

In K. A. McCluskey and H. W. Reese (eds.), *Life-span Developmental Psychology: Historical and Cohort Effects.* New York: Academic Press, 1983.

PARKE, R. D.; BERKOWITZ, L.; LEYENS, J. P.; WEST, S. G.; and SEBASTIAN, R. J. "Some Effects of Violent and Nonviolent Movies on the Behavior of Juvenile Delinquents." In L. Berkowitz (ed.), *Advances in Experimental Social Psychology,* Vol. 10. New York: Academic Press, 1977.

PARKE, R. D.; POWER, T. G.; and GOTTMAN, J. M. "Conceptualizing and Quantifying Influence Patterns in the Family Triad." In M. E. Lamb, S. J. Suomi, and G. R. Stephenson (eds.), *The Study of Social Interaction: Methodological Issues.* Madison: University of Wisconsin Press, 1979.

PARMELEE, A. H., and SIGMAN, M. D. "Perinatal Brain Development and Behavior." In P. H. Mussen (ed.), *Handbook of Child Psychology.* Vol. 2, *Infancy and Developmental Psychology.* New York: Wiley, 1983, 95–156.

PARSONS, J. E.; ADLER, T. F.; and KACZALA, C. M. "Socialization of Achievement Attitudes and Beliefs: Parental Influences." *Child Development* 53 (1982), 310–339.

PARSONS, T. "Family Structure and the Socialization of the Child." In T. Parsons and R. F. Bales (eds.), *Family Socialization and Interaction Processes.* Glencoe, Ill.: Free Press, 1955.

PASLEY, K., and GECAS, V. "Stresses and Satisfactions of the Parental Role." *Personnel and Guidance Journal* 62 (1984), 400–404.

PASSMAN, R. H., and LONGEWAY, K. P. "The Role of Vision in Maternal Attachment: Giving 2-Year-Olds a Photograph of Their Mother During Separation." *Developmental Psychology* 18 (1982), 530–533.

PASTALON, L. "The Empathic Model." *Journal of Architectural Education* (1977), 10.

PASTOR, D. L. "The Quality of Mother-Infant Attachment and Its Relationship to Toddlers' Initial Sociability with Peers." *Developmental Psychology* 17 (1981), 326–335.

PATE, R., and BLAIR, S. "Exercise and the Prevention of Atherosclerosis: Pediatric Implications." In W. Strong (ed.), *Atherosclerosis: Its Pediatric Aspects.* New York: Grune and Stratton, 1978.

PATTERSON, G. R. "Mothers: The Unacknowledged Victims." *Monographs of the Society for Research in Child Development* 45, no. 5, Serial No. 186 (1980).

———. *Coercive Family Process.* Eugene, Ore.: Castalia Press, 1982.

———. "Stress: A Change Agent for Family Process." In N. Garmezy and M. Rutter (eds.), *Stress, Coping and Development.* New York: McGraw-Hill, 1983.

PATTERSON, J., and McCUBBIN. H. *A-COPE: Adolescent Coping Orientation for Problem Experiences* (research instrument). St. Paul: University of Minnesota, Family Social Science, 1982.

PAVLOVITCH, M. *Le language enfantin: Acquisition du Serbe et du Francais par un enfant Serbe.* Paris: Champion, 1920.

PEARL, R. "Children's Understanding of Others' Need for Help: Effects of Problem Explicitness and Type." *Child Development* 56 (1985), 735–745.

PEARLIN, L. I., and SCHOOLER, C. "The Structure of Coping." *Journal of Health and Social Behavior* 19 (1978), 2–21.

PEERY, J. C. "Neonate and Adult Head Movement: No and Yes Revisited." *Developmental Psychology* (1980), 245–250.

PEEVERS, B. H., and SECORD, P. F. "Developmental Changes in Attribution of Descriptive Concepts to Person." *Journal of Personality and Social Psychology* 27 (1973), 120–128.

PELCOVITZ, D.; KAPLAN, S.; SAMIT, C.; KRIEGER, R.; and CORNELIUS, P. "Adolescent Abuse: Family Structure and Implications for Treatment." *Journal of Child Psychology* 23 (1984), 85–90.

PERLMUTTER, M. "A Life-span View of Memory." In P. B. Baltes, D. L. Featherman, and R. M. Lerner (eds.), *Life-Span Development and Behavior,* Vol. 7. Hillsdale, N.J. Erlbaum, 1986, 271–313.

PERNER, J., and MANSBRIDGE, D. G. "Developmental Differences in Encoding Length Series." *Child Development* 54 (1983), 710–719.

PERRY, D. G., and BUSSEY, K. *Social Development.* Englewood Cliffs, N.J.: Prentice-Hall, 1984.

PERRY, D. G.; PERRY, L. C.; BUSSEY, K.; ENGLISH, D.; and ARNOLD, G. "Processes of Attribution and Children's Self-Punishment Following Misbehavior." *Child Development* 51 (1980), 545–552.

PERRY, D. G.; WHITE, A. J.; and Perry, L. C. "Does Early Sex Typing Result from Children's Attempts to Match Their Behavior to Sex-Role Stereotypes?" *Child Development* (1985).

PERRY, K. S. *Employers and Child Care: Establishing Services Through the Workplace.* Washington, D.C.: U.S. Department of Labor, Women's Bureau, 1982.

PESKIN, H. "Pubertal Onset and Ego Functioning: A Psychoanalytic Approach." *Journal of Abnormal Psychology* 72 (1967), 1–15.

———. "Influence of the Developmental Schedule of Puberty on Learning and Ego Functioning." *Journal of Youth and Adolescence* 2 (1973), 273–290.

PETERS, M. F. "Nine Black Families: A Study of Household Management and Child-Rearing in Black Families with Working Mothers." Doctoral diss., Harvard University, 1976.

PETERSEN, A. C. "Differential Cognitive Development in Adolescent Girls." In M. Sugar (ed.), *Female Adolescent Development.* New York: Brunner/Mazel, 1979.

———. "The Early Adolescence Study: An Overview." *Journal of Early Adolescence* 40 (1984), 103–106.

———. "The Nature of Biological-Psychosocial Interactions: The Sample Case of Early Adolescence." In R. M. Lerner and T. T. Fochs (eds.), *Biological-Psychosocial Interactions in Early Adolescence.* Hillsdale, N.J.: Erlbaum, 1987, 35–62.

PETERSEN, A. C., and TAYLOR, B. "The Biological Approach to Adolescence: Biological Change and Psychological Adaptation." In J. Adelson (ed.), *Handbook of Adolescent Psychology.* New York: Wiley, 1980.

PETERSEN, A. C.; SCHULENBERG, J. E.; ABRAMOWITZ, R. H.; OFFER, D.; and JARCHO, H. "A Self-Image Questionnaire for Young Adolescents (SIQYA): Reliability and Validity Studies." *Journal of Youth and Adolescence* 13 (1984), 93–111.

PETERSEN, A. C.; TOBIN-RICHARDS, M. H.; and BOXER, A. M. "Puberty: Its Measurement and Its Meaning." *Journal of Early Adolescence* 3 (1983), 47–62.

PETERSON, G. W.; LEIGH, G. K.; and DAY, R. "Family Stress Theory and the Impact of Divorce on Children." *Journal of Divorce* 7 (1984), 1–20.

PETERSON, L. "Developmental Changes in Verbal and Behavioral Sensitivity to Cues of Social Norms of Altruism." *Child Development* 51 (1980), 830–838.

PIAGET, J. *The Psychology of Intelligence.* London: Routledge and Kegan Paul, 1950.

———. *The Origins of Intelligence in Children,* 2d ed. New York: International Universities Press, 1952.

———. *The Construction of Reality in the Child.* New York: Basic Books, 1954.

———. *Play Dreams and Imitation in Childhood.* New York: Norton, 1962.

———. *The Origins of Intelligence in Children,* 3d ed. New York: International Universities Press, 1963.

———. *The Moral Judgement of the Child.* New York: Free Press, 1965.

———. *Six Psychological Studies.* New York: Random House, 1967.

———. *Genetic Epistemology.* New York: Columbia University Press, 1970a.

———. "Piaget's Theory." In P. H. Mussen (ed.), *Carmichael's Manual of Child Psychology,* Vol. 1. New York: Wiley, 1970b.

———. *Child and Reality.* New York: Grossman, 1973.

———. *The Psychology of Intelligence.* Totowa, N.J.: Littlefield, Adams, 1976.

PIAGET, J., and INHELDER, B. *The Child's Conception of Space.* London: Routledge and Kegan Paul, 1956.

———. *The Psychology of the Child.* New York: Basic Books, 1969.

PIAGET, J.; INHELDER, B.; and SZEMINSKA, A. *The Child's Conception of Geometry.* New York: Basic Books, 1960.

PICK, A. D.; FRANKEL, D. G.; and HESS, V. L. "Children's Attention:

The Development of Selectivity." In E. M. Hetherington (ed.), *Review of Child Development Research*, Vol. 5. Chicago: University of Chicago Press, 1975.

PIOTRKOWSKI, C. S. *Work and the Family System: A Naturalistic Study of the Working Class and Lower Middle Class Families*. New York: The Free Press, 1979.

PLACEK, P. J.; TAFFEL, S. M.; and KEPPEL, K. G. "Maternal and Infant Characteristics Associated with Cesarean Delivery." DHS Publication No. PHS 84-1232. Washington, D.C.: Government Printing Office, 1983.

PLESS, I. B., and PINKERTON, P. *Chronic Childhood Disorder: Promoting Patterns of Adjustment*. London: Henry Klimpton Publishers, 1975.

PLESS, I. B., and ROGHMANN, K. "Chronic Illness and Its Consequences: Observations Based on Three Epidemiologic Surveys." *Journal of Pediatrics* 79 (1971), 351–359.

PLOMIN, R., and DE FRIES, J. C. "The Colorado Adoption Project." *Child Development* 54 (1983), 276–289.

———. *Origins of Individual Differences in Infancy*. New York: Academic Press, 1985.

POAG, C. K.; GOODNIGHT, J. A.; and COHEN, R. "The Environments of Children: From Home to School." In R. Cohen (ed.), *The Development of Spatial Cognition*. Hillsdale, N.J.: Erlbaum, 1985, 71–114.

PORTER, G., and O'LEARY, D. K. "Marital Discord and Child Behavior Problems." *Journal of Abnormal Psychology* 8 (1980), 287–295.

POWER, T. G., and PARKE, R. D. "Play as a Context for Early Learning: Lab and Home Analyses." In L. M. Laosa and I. E. Sigel (eds.), *The Family as a Learning Environment*. New York: Plenum, 1982.

POWERS, S.; HAUSER, S. T.; SCHWARTZ, J. M.; NOAM, G. C.; and JACOBSON, A. M. "Adolescent Ego Development and Family Interaction: A Structural-Developmental Perspective." In H. D. Grotevant and C. Cooper (eds.), *Adolescent Development in the Family*. San Francisco: Jossey-Bass, 1983, 5–26.

PRATT, M. W., and BATES, K. R. "Young Editors: Preschoolers' Evaluation of Ambiguous Messages." *Developmental Psychology* 18 (1982), 30–42.

PRATT, W. F. "National Survey of Family Growth, 1982." Cycle III. National Center for Health Statistics, 1984.

PRESSER, H. B. "Guessing and Misinformation About Pregnancy Risk Among Urban Mothers." In F. Furstenberg, R. Lincoln, and J. Menken (eds.), *Teenage Sexuality, Pregnancy, and Childbearing*. Philadelphia: University of Pennsylvania Press, 1981.

———. "Working Women and Child Care" In P. W. Berman and E. R. Ramey (eds.), *Women: A Developmental Perspective*. Washington, D.C.: U.S. Government Printing Office, 1982.

PRESSLEY, M., and BRAINERD, C. J. (eds.). *Cognitive Learning and Memory in Children*. New York: Springer-Verlag, 1985.

PRESSLEY, M.; HEISEL, B. E.; McCORMICK, C. B.; and NAKAMURA, G. U. "Memory Strategy Instruction with Children." In C. Brainerd and M. Pressley (eds.), *Progress in Cognitive Development Research*. Vol. 2, *Verbal Processes in Children*. New York: Springer-Verlag, 1982.

PRICE, G. C.; HESS, R. D.; and DICKSON, W. P. "Processes by Which Verbal-Educational Abilities Are Affected When Mothers Encourage Preschool Children to Verbalize." *Developmental Psychology* 17 (1981), 554–564.

PULKKINEN, L. "Self-Control and Continuity from Childhood to Adolescence." In P. B. Baltes and O. G. Brim (eds.), *Life-Span Development and Behavior*, Vol. 4. New York: Academic Press, 1982.

QUARFOTH, J. M. "Children's Understanding of the Nature of Television Characters." *Journal of Communication* 29 (1979), 210–218.

QUEENAN, J. T., and HOBBINS, C. J. (eds.). *Protocols for High-Risk Pregnancies*. Oradell, N.J.: Medical Economics Books, 1982.

QUIGLEY, M. E.; SHEEHAN, K. L.; WILKES, M. M.; and YEN, S.S.C. "Effects of Maternal Smoking on Circulating Catecholamine Levels and Fetal Heart Rates." *American Journal of Obstetrics and Gynecology* 133 (1979), 685–690.

RACKI, G. "The Effects of the Flexible Working Hours." Doctoral diss., University of Lousanne, 1975.

RADKE-YARROW, M.; ZAHN-WAXLER, C.; and CHAPMAN, C. "Children's Prosocial Dispositions and Behavior." In P. H. Mussen (ed.), *Handbook of Child Psychology*, Vol. 4. 4th ed. New York: Wiley, 1983, 470–545.

RAGOZIN, A. S. "Attachment Behavior of Day-Care Children: Naturalistic and Laboratory Observations." *Child Development* 51 (1980), 409–415.

RAHN, J. E. *Biology*. New York: Macmillan, 1980.

RAMEY, C. T.; BRYANT, D.; SPARLING, J. T.; and WASIK, B. H. "Educational Interventions to Enhance Intellectual Development." In S. Harel and N. Anastasiow (eds.), *The At-Risk Infant: Psycho/ Social/Medical Aspects*. Baltimore, Md.: Paul H. Brooks, 1985.

RAUDENBUSCH, S. W. "Magnitude of Teacher Expectancy Effects on Pupil IQ as a Function of Credibility of Expectancy Induction: A Synthesis from 18 Experiments." *Journal of Experimental Psychology* 76 (1984), 85–97.

RAYMOND, C. L., and BENBOW, C. P. "Gender Differences in Mathematics: A Function of Parental Support and Student Sex Typing." *Developmental Psychology* 22 (1986), 808–819.

READ, K. *The Nursery School*. Philadelphia: Saunders, 1971.

REICHERT, P. A., and WERLEY, H. H. "Contraception, Abortion, and Venereal Disease: Teenagers' Knowledge and the Effect of Education." In F. Furstenberg, R. Lincoln, and J. Menken (eds.), *Teenage Sexuality, Pregnancy, and Childbearing*. Philadelphia: University of Pennsylvania Press, 1981.

REID, J. B.; PATTERSON, G. R.; and LOEBER, R. "The Abused Child: Victim, Instigator or Innocent Bystander?" In D. J. Bernstein (eds.), *Response Structure and Organization*. Lincoln: University of Nebraska Press, 1982.

REID, J. B.; TAPLIN, P. S.; and LORBER, R. A. "A Social Interactional Approach to the Treatment of Abusive Families." In R. B. Stuart (ed.), *Violent Behavior: Social Learning Approaches to Prediction, Management and Treatment*. New York: Bruner/Mazel, 1981.

REISTER, A. E., and ZUCKER, R. A. "Adolescent Social Structure and Drinking Behavior." *Personnel and Guidance Journal* 46 (1968), 304–312.

REST, J. R. "Morality." In P. H. Mussen (ed.), *Handbook of Child Psychology*, Vol. 3. 4th ed. New York: Wiley, 1983, 556–629.

REUBENS, B.; HARRISON, J.; and RUPP, K. *The Youth Labor Force, 1945–1995: A Cross-National Analysis*. Totowa, N.J.: Allanheld, Osmun, and Co., 1981.

REVELLE, G. L.; WELLMAN, H. M.; and KARABENICK, J. D. "Comprehension Monitoring in Preschool Children." *Child Development* 56 (1985), 654–663.

REVILL, S. I., and DODGE, J. A. "Psychological Determinants of Infantile Pyloric Stenosis." *Archives of the Diseases in Childhood* 53 (1978), 66–68.

REYNOLDS, R. E., and ORTONY, A. "Some Issues in the Measurement of Children's Comprehension of Metaphorical Language." *Child Development* 51 (1980), 1110–1119.

RHEINGOLD, H. L. "Little Children's Participation in the Work of Adults: A Nascent Prosocial Behavior." *Child Development* 53 (1982), 114–125.

RHOLES, W. S., and RUBLE, D. N. "Children's Understanding of Dispositional Characteristics of Others." 1981.

RICHARDS, F. A., and COMMONS, M. L. "Systematic and Metasystematic Reasoning: A Case for Stages of Reasoning Beyond Formal Operations." In M. L. Commons, F. A. Richards, and C. Armon (eds.), *Beyond Formal Operations: Late Adolescent and Adult Cognitive Development*. New York: Praeger, 1983.

RICHARDSON, S. A. "Physical Growth of Jamaican School Children Who Were Severely Malnourished Before 2 Years of Age." *Journal of Biosocial Science* 7 (1975), 445–462.

RICHMAN, N.; GRAHAM, P.; and STEVENSON, J. *Preschool to School: A Behavioral Study*. London: Academic Press, 1982.

RICKLEFS, R. E. *Ecology*. London: Nelson, 1973.

RILEY, C. A., and TRABASSO, T. "Comparatives, Logical Structures and Encoding in a Transitive Inference Task." *Journal of Experimental Child Psychology* 17 (1974), 197–203.

RIZEK, R., and JACKSON, E. *Current Food Consumption Practices and Nutrient Sources in the American Diet*. Hyattsville, Md.: Consumer Nutrition Center, Human Nutrition Science and Education Administration, U.S. Department of Agriculture, 1980.

ROACH, A.; BOYLAN, K.; HORVATH, S.; PRUSINER, S. B.; and HOOD, L. E. "Characterization of Cloned Complementary DNA Representing Rat Myelin Basic Protein Absence of Expression in Brain of Shiverer Mutant Mice." *Cell* 34 (1983), 799–806.

ROBERTS, E. J.; KLINE, D.; and GAGNON, J. *Family Life and Sexual Learning*. Cambridge, Mass.: Population Education, 1978.

ROBERTS, F. "The Little Backseat Driver." *Parents Magazine* (November 1978).

ROBERTS, G. C.; BLOCK J. H.; and BLOCK, J. "Continuity and Change in Parents' Child-Rearing Practices." *Child Development* 55 (1984), 586–597.

RODE, S. S.; CHANG, P.; FISCH, R. O.; and SROUFE, L. A. "Attachment Patterns of Infants Separated at Birth." *Developmental Psychology* 17 (1981) 188–191.

RODMAN, H.; PRATTO, D.; and NELSON, R. "Child Care Arrangements and Children's Functioning: A Comparison of Self-Care and Adult-Care Children." *Developmental Psychology* 21 (1985), 413–418.

ROGOFF, B. "Schooling and the Development of Cognitive Skills." In H. C. Triandis and A. Heron (eds.), *Handbook of Cross-Cultural Psychology: Developmental Psychology*, Vol. 4. Boston: Allyn and Bacon, 1981.

ROLLINS, B. C., and FELDMAN, H. "Marital Satisfaction over the Life Cycle." *Journal of Marriage and the Family* 32, no. 1 (February 1970), 20–28.

ROMAINE, S. *The Language of Children and Adolescents: The Acquisition of Communication Competence*. Oxford: Blackwell, 1984.

ROOPNARINE, J. L. "Sex-Typed Socialization in Mixed Aged Preschool Classrooms." *Child Development* 55 (1984), 1078–1084.

ROSEN, L. W. "Modification of Secretive or Ritualized Eating Behavior in Anorexia Nervosa." *Journal of Behavior Therapy and Experimental Psychiatry* 11 (1980), 101–104.

ROSENBERG, M. *Conceiving the Self*. New York: Basic Books, 1979.

ROSENFELD, A. "Visiting the Intensive Care Nursery." *Child Development* 51 (1980), 939–941.

ROSENTHAL, M. K. "Vocal Dialogues in the Neonatal Period." *Developmental Psychology* 18 (1982), 17–21.

ROSENTHAL, R., and JACOBSON, L. *Pygmalion in the Classroom: Teacher Expectation and Pupils' Intellectual Development*. New York: Holt, 1968.

ROSENZWEIG, M. R., and LEIMAN, A. L. *Physiological Psychology*. Lexington, Mass.: Heath, 1982.

ROSETT, H. L.; WEINER, L.; ZUCKERMAN, B.; McKINLEY, S.; and EDELIN, K. C. "Reduction of Alcohol Consumption During Pregnancy with Benefits to the Newborn." *Alcoholism: Clinical and Experimental Research* 4 (1980), 178–184.

ROSSI, P. H. *Why Families Move: A Study in the Social Psychology of Urban Residential Living*. New York: Free Press, 1955.

ROSSITER, J. R., and ROBERTSON, T. S. "Children's Television Viewing: An Examination of Parent-Child Consensus." *Sociometry* 38 (1975), 308–326.

ROTBART, D. "Allowances Stay Flat, Candy Rises—And Kids Lose Their Innocence." *Wall Street Journal* (March 2, 1981), 1ff.

ROTHBART, M. K., and DERRYBERRY, D. "Development of Individual Differences in Temperament." In M. E. Lamb and A. L. Brown (eds.), *Advances in Developmental Psychology*, Vol. 1. Hillsdale, N.J.: Erlbaum, 1982.

———. "Emotion, Attention, and Temperament." In C. E. Izard, J. Kagan, and R. Zajonc (eds.), *Emotion, Cognition, and Behavior*. New York: Cambridge University Press, 1984.

ROTHBART, M. K., and ROTHBART, M. "Birth Order, Sex of Child, and Maternal Helpgiving." *Sex Roles* 2 (1976), 39–46.

ROTTER, J. B. "Generalized Expectancies for Internal Versus External Control of Reinforcement." *Psychological Monographs* (1966), 80.

ROWLAND, T. "Physical Fitness in Children: Implications for the Prevention of Coronary Artery Disease." *Current Problems in Pediatrics* 9 (1981).

RUBENSTEIN, J., and HOWES, C. "The Effects of Peers on Toddler Interaction with Mother and Toys." *Child Development* 47 (1976), 597–605.

RUBIN, K. H., FEIN, G. G., and VANDENBERG, B. "Play." In P. H. Mussen (ed.), *Handbook of Child Psychology*, Vol. 4. New York: Wiley, 1983.

RUBLE, D. N. "Sex Role Development." In M. C. Bornstein and M. E. Lamb (eds.), *Developmental Psychology: An Advanced Textbook*. Hillsdale, N.J.: Erlbaum, 1984.

———. "The Development of Social Comparison Processes and Their Role in Achievement-Related Self-Socialization." In E. T. Higgins, D. N. Ruble, and W. W. Hartup (eds.), *Social Cognition and Social Development: Developmental Issues*. New York: Cambridge University Press, 1985.

RUBLE, D. N., and RUBLE, T. L. "Sex Stereotypes." In A. G. Miller (ed.), *In the Eye of the Beholder: Contemporary Issues in Stereotyping*. New York: Holt, Rinehart, and Winston, 1980.

RUBLE, D. N.; BALABAN, T.; and COOPER, J. "Gender Constancy and the Effects of Sex-Typed Televised Toy Commercials." *Child Development* 52 (1981), 667–673.

RUBLE, D. N.; BOGGIANO, A. K.; FELDMAN, N. S.; and LOEBL, J. H. "A Developmental Analysis of the Role of Social Comparison in Self-Evaluation." *Developmental Psychology* 16 (1980), 105–115.

RUNYAN, W. M. *Life Histories and Psychobiography*. New York: Oxford University Press, 1982.

RUTTER, M. "Protective Factors in Children's Responses to Stress and Disadvantage." In M. Kent and J. Rolf (eds.), *Primary Prevention of Psychopathology*. Vol. 3, *Promoting Social Competence and Coping in Children*. Hanover, N.J.: University Press of New England, 1978.

———. "Maternal Deprivation, 1972–1978: New Findings, New Concepts, New Approaches." *Child Development* 50 (1979), 283–305.

———. "The City and the Child." *American Journal of Orthopsychiatry* 51 (1981a), 610–625.

———. *Maternal Deprivation Reassessed*, 2d ed. Harmonsworth, England and New York: Penguin Books, 1981b.

———. "Epidemiological-Longitudinal Approaches to the Study of Development." In W. A. Collins (ed.), *The Concept of Development*. Vol. 15, *Minnesota Symposium on Child Psychology*. Hillsdale, N.J.: Erlbaum, 1982a.

———. "Socio-Emotional Consequences of Day Care for Preschool Children." In E. F. Zigler and E. W. Gordon (eds.), *Day Care: Scientific and Social Policy Issues*. Boston: Auburn House, 1982b.

———. "School Effects on Pupil Progress: Research Findings and Policy Implications." *Child Development* 54 (1983), 1–29.

RUTTER, M.; MAUGHAN, B.; MORTIMORE, P.; OUSTON, J.; and SMITH, A. *Fifteen Thousand Hours*. Cambridge, Mass.: Harvard University Press, 1979.

RYTINA, N. F. "Earnings of Men and Women: A Look at Specific Occupations." U.S. Department of Labor, *Monthly Labor Review* 105. Washington, D.C.: U.S. Government Printing Office, April 1982, 25–31.

SAGOV, S.; FEINBLOOM, R.; SPINDEL, P.; and BRODSKY, A. *Home Birth: A Practitioner's Guide to Birth Outside the Hospital*. Rockville, Md.: Aspen Publications, 1984.

SALTER, A. "Birth Without Violence: A Medical Controversy." *Nursing Research* 27 (1978), 84–88.

SAMUELS, H. R. "The Role of the Sibling in the Infants' Social Environment." Paper presented at the biennial meeting of the Society for Research in Child Development, New Orleans, 1977.

SANTROCK, J. W. *Adolescence: An Introduction*, 2d ed. Dubuque, Iowa: William C. Brown, 1984.

SANTROCK, J. W., and WARSHAK, R. A. "Father Custody and Social Development in Boys and Girls." *Journal of Social Issues* 35 (1979), 112–125.

SAPIR, E. "Language and Environment." In D. G. Mandelbaum (ed.), *Selected Writings of Edward Sapir in Language, Culture, and Personality*. Berkeley: University of California Press, 1958, 89–103.

SASSEN, G. "Success-Anxiety in Women: A Constructivist Theory of Its Significance." *Harvard Educational Review* 50, no. 1 (February 1980), 13–24.

SATTLER, J. M. *Assessment of Children's Intelligence and Special Abilities*, 2d ed. Boston: Allyn and Bacon, 1982.

SAUNDERS, B. E. "The Social Consequences of Divorce: Implications for Family Policy." *Journal of Divorce* 6 (1983), 1–17.

SAVIN-WILLIAMS, R. "An Ethological Study of Dominance Formation and Maintenance in a Group of Human Adolescents." *Child Development* 47 (1976), 972–979.

SAVIN-WILLIAMS, R. "Dominance Hierarchies in Groups of Adolescents." *Child Development* 50 (1979), 923–935.

SAWIN, D. B. A Field Study of Children's Reactions to Distress in Their Peers. Unpublished manuscript, University of Texas at Austin, 1980.

SAWIN, D. B. and PARKE, R. D. "The Effects of Interagent Inconsistent Discipline on Children's Aggressive Behavior." *Journal of Experimental Child Psychology* 28 (1979), 525–538.

SCALES, P. "Sex Education and the Prevention of Teenage Pregnancy: An Overview of Policies and Programs in the United States." In T. Ooms (ed.), *Teenage Pregnancy in a Family Context: Implications for Policy*. Philadelphia: Temple University Press, 1981.

SCANZONI, J. *Sex Roles, Life-styles and Childbearing*. New York: Free Press, 1975.

SCARR, S. "Constructing Psychology: Facts and Fables for Our Times." *American Psychologist* 40 (1985), 499–512.

SCARR, S. *Mother Care/Other Care*. New York Basic Books, 1984.

SCARR, S. "On Quantifying the Intended Effects of Interventions: Or a Proposed Theory of the Environment." In L. A. Bond and J. M. Joffe (eds.), *Facilitating Infant and Early Childhood Development*. Hanover, N.H.: University Press of New England, 1982.

SCARR, S., and GRAJAK, S. "Similarities and Differences Among Siblings." In M. E. Lamb and B. Sutton-Smith (eds.), *Sibling Relationships: Their Nature and Significance Across the Lifespan*. Hillsdale, N.J.: Erlbaum, 1982.

SCARR, S., and McCARTNEY, K. "How People Make Their Own Environments: A Theory of Genotype-Environment Effects." *Child Development* 54 (1983), 424–435.

SCARR, S., and WEINBERG, R. A. "Intellectual Similarities Within Families of Both Adopted and Biological Children." *Intelligence* 1 (1980), 170–191.

———. "The Minnesota Adoption Studies: Genetic Differences and Malleability." *Child Development* 54 (1983), 260–267.

SCHAFFER, H. R. "Activity Level as a Constitutional Determinant of Infantile Reaction." *Child Development* 37 (1966), 595–602.

SCHAFFER, H. R., and CROOK, C. K. "Child Compliance and Maternal Control Techniques." *Developmental Psychology* 16 (1980), 54–61.

SCHAIE, K. W. "The Seattle Longitudinal Study: A Twenty-one Year Exploration of Psychometric Intelligence in Adulthood." In K. W. Schaie (ed.), *Longitudinal Studies of Adult Psychological Development*. New York: Guilford Press, 1983, 64–135.

SCHAIE, K. W.; LABOUVIE, G. V.; and BUECH, B. V. "Generational and Cohort Specific Differences in Adult Cognitive Functioning: A Fourteen-Year Study of Independent Samples." *Developmental Psychology* 9 (1973), 156–166.

SCHANK, R. C., and ABELSON, R. P. *Scripts, Plans, Goals and Understanding*. Hillsdale, N.J.: Erlbaum, 1977.

SCHAU, C. G.; KAHN, L.; DIEPOLD, J. H.; and CHERRY, F. "The Re-lationships of Parental Expectations and Preschool Children's Verbal Sex Typing to Their Sex-Typed Toy Play Behavior." *Child Development* 51 (1980), 266–270.

SCHER, J., and DIX, C. *Will My Baby Be Normal? Everything You Need to Know About Pregnancy*. New York: Dial Press, 1983.

SCHIAMBERG, L. "Some Sociocultural Factors in Adolescent-Parent Conflict: A Cross-Cultural Comparison of Selected Cultures." *Adolescence* 4 (1969), 333–360.

———. *Adolescent Alienation*. Columbus, Ohio: Merrill, 1973.

———. *Human Development*, 2d ed. New York: Macmillan, 1985.

———. "A Family Systems Perspective to Adolescent Alienation." In G. K. Leigh and G. W. Peterson (eds.), *Adolescents in Families*. Cincinnati: South-Western, 1986, 277–307.

SCHIAMBERG, L., and ABLER, W. "The Ecology of Social Support and Older Adult Adaptation." Paper presented at the meeting of the American Educational Research Association, San Francisco, 1986.

SCHIAMBERG, L., and CHIN, C. H. "The Influence of Family on Educational and Occupational Achievement." Address presented at the annual meeting of the American Association for the Advancement of Science (AAAS), Philadelphia, May 1986.

SCHMIDT, C. R., and PARIS, S. G. "Children's Use of Successive Clues to Generate and Monitor Inferences." *Child Development* 54 (1983), 742–759.

SCHMITT, B. D., and KEMPE, C. H. "Abusing Neglected Children." In R. E. Behrman and V. C. Vaughn (eds.), *Nelson Textbook of Pediatrics*, 12th ed. Philadelphia: Saunders, 1983.

SCHOFIELD, J. "Complementary and Conflicting Identities: Images and Interaction in an Interracial School." In S. Asher and J. Gottman (eds.), *The Development of Children's Friendships*. Cambridge: Cambridge University Press, 1981.

SCHOGGEN, P. "Behavior Settings and the Quality of Life." *Journal of Community Psychology* 11 (1983), 144–157.

SCHOONMAKER, A. N. *A Student's Survival Manual*. New York: Harper & Row, 1971.

SCHULENBERG, J. E.; VONDRACEK, F. W.; and CROUTER, A. C. "The Influence of the Family on Vocational Development." *Journal of Marriage and the Family* (1984), 129–143.

SCHWARTZ, P. "Length of Day-Care Attendance and Attachment Behavior in Eighteen-Month-Old Infants." *Child Development* 54 (1983), 1073–1078.

SCHWARTZ, S. H. "Normative Influences on Altruism." In L. Berkowitz (ed.), *Advances in Experimental Social Psychology*, Vol. 10. New York: Academic Press, 1977.

SEARS, R. R. "Your Ancients Revisited." In E. M. Hetherington, J. W. Hagen, R. Kron, and A. H. Stein (eds.), *Review of Child Development Research*, Vol. 5. Chicago: University of Chicago Press, 1975, 1–73.

SEAVER, W. B. "Effects of Naturally Induced Teacher Expectancies." *Journal of Personality and Social Psychology* 28 (1973), 333–342.

SEEFELDT, V., and HAUBENSTRICKER, J. "Pattern, Phases or Stages: An Analytical Model for the Study of Developmental Movement." Michigan State University, Department of Health, Physical Education and Recreation, 1982.

SEGINER, R. "Parents' Educational Expectations and Children's Academic Achievements: A Literature Review." *Merrill-Palmer Quarterly* 29 (1983), 1–23.

SEITZ, V.; ROSENBAUM, L. K.; and APFEL, N. H. "Effects of Family Support Intervention: A Ten Year Follow-up." *Child Development* 56 (1985), 376–391.

SELECT PANEL FOR THE PROMOTION OF CHILD HEALTH. *Better Health for Our Children: A National Strategy*. DHHS (PHS) Publication No. 79-55071. Washington, D.C.: U.S. Department of Health and Human Services, 1981.

SELIGMAN, M. E. P. *Helplessness: On Depression, Development and Death*. San Francisco: W. H. Freeman, 1975.

SELMAN, R. L. "Social-Cognitive Understanding: A Guide to Educational and Clinical Practice." In T. Lickona (ed.), *Moral Devel-*

opment and Behavior: Theory, Research and Social Issues. New York: Holt, Rinehart, and Winston, 1976.

———. *The Growth of Interpersonal Understanding: Developmental and Clinical Analyses.* New York: Academic Press, 1980.

SELMAN, R. L., and BYRNE, D. F. "A Structural Developmental Analysis of Levels of Role-Taking in Middle Childhood." *Child Development* 45 (1974), 803–806.

SENDAK, M. *Where the Wild Things Are.* New York: Harper & Row, 1972.

SENNETT, R., and COBB, J. *The Hidden Injuries of Class.* New York: Random House, 1982.

SHADE, B. "Afro-American Cognitive Style: A Variable in School Success." *Review of Educational Research* 52 (1982), 219–244.

SHAFFER, D. R. *Developmental Psychology.* Monterey, Calif.: Brooks/Cole, 1985.

SHAFFER, D. R., and JOHNSON, R. D. "Effects of Occupational Choice and Sex-Role Preferences on the Attractiveness of Competent Men and Women." *Journal of Personality* 48 (1980), 505–519.

SHANTZ, C. U. "Social Cognition." In P. H. Mussen (ed.), *Handbook of Child Psychology,* Vol. 3. 4th ed. New York: Wiley, 1983, 495–555.

SHATZ, M. "Communication." In P. H. Mussen (ed.), *Handbook of Child Psychology,* Vol. 3. New York: Wiley, 1983, 841–889.

SHATZ, M., and GELMAN, R. "The Development of Communication Skills: Modification in the Speech of Young Children as a Function of Listener." *Monographs of the Society for Research in Child Development* 38, no. 152 (1973).

SHERROD, L. R. "Issues of Cognitive-Perceptual Development: The Special Case of Social Stimuli." In M. E. Lamb and L. R. Sherrod (eds.), *Infant Social Cognition.* Hillsdale, N.J.: Erlbaum, 1981.

SHIPMAN, V. C.; McKEE, J. D.; and BRIDGEMAN, P. *Stability and Change in Family Status, Situational and Process Variables and Their Relation to Children's Cognitive Performance.* Princeton, N. J.: Educational Testing Service, 1976.

SHONKOFF, J. P. "The Biological Substrate and Physical Health in Middle Childhood." In W. A. Collins (ed.), *Development During Middle Childhood: The Years from Six to Twelve.* Washington, D.C.: National Academy Press, 1984, 24–69.

SHUTTLEWORTH, F. H. "The Adolescent Period: A Pictorial Atlas." *Monographs of the Society for Research in Child Development* 14, Serial No. 50 (1951), 13–14.

SHVACHKIN, N. KH. "Razvitye fouematichekogo vospriyatiya rechi v rannem vozraste (Development of Phonemic Speech Perception in Early Childhood)." *Izv. Akad. Pedagog. Nauk RSFSR* 13 (1948), 101–132.

SIEGAL, L. S. "Infant Tests as Predictors of Cognitive Development at Two Years." *Child Development* 52 (1981), 545–557.

SIEGEL, A. W.; HERMAN, J. F.; ALLEN, G. F.; and KIRASIC, K. C. "The Development of Cognitive Maps of Large- and Small-Scale Spaces." *Child Development* 50 (1979), 582–585.

SIEGEL, L. S., and BRAINERD, C. J. (eds.), *Alternatives to Piaget: Critical Essays on the Theory.* New York: Academic Press, 1978.

SIEGLER, R. S. "The Origins of Scientific Reasoning." In R. S. Siegler (ed.), *Children's Thinking: What Develops?* Hillsdale, N.J.: Erlbaum, 1978.

———. "Developmental Sequences Within and Between Concepts." *Monographs of the Society for Research in Child Development* 46, no. 2, Serial No. 189 (1981).

———. "Information Processing Approach to Development." In P. H. Mussen (ed.), *Handbook of Child Psychology,* Vol. 1. New York: Wiley, 1983, 129–212.

SIEGLER, R. S., and RICHARDS, D. D. "The Development of Intelligence." In R. J. Sternberg (ed.), *Handbook of Human Intelligence.* Cambridge: Cambridge University Press, 1982, 897–971.

SIGALL, H., and GOULD, R. "The Effects of Self-Esteem and Evaluator Demandingness on Effort Expenditure." *Journal of Personality and Social Psychology* 35 (1977), 12–20.

SIGEL, I. E. "The Relationship Between Parental Distancing Strate-

gies and the Child's Cognitive Behavior." In L. M. Laosa and I. E. Sigel (eds.), *Families as Learning Environments for Children.* New York: Plenum, 1982.

SIGEL, I. E., and COCKING, R. *Cognitive Development from Childhood to Adolescence: A Constructivist Perspective.* New York: Holt, 1977.

SIGEL, I. E.; DREYER, A. S.; and McGILLICUDDY-DeLISI, A. V. "Psychological Perspectives of the Family." In R. D. Parke (ed.), *Review of Child Development Research.* Vol. 7, *The Family.* Chicago: The University of Chicago Press, 1984, 42–79.

SILBERT, M., and PINES, A. *Runaway Prostitutes.* San Francisco: Delancey Street Foundation, 1981 (unpublished).

SIMMONS, R. G.; BLYTH, D. A.; and McKINNEY, K. L. "The Social and Psychological Effects of Puberty on White Females." In J. Brooks-Gunn and A. C. Petersen (eds.), *Girls at Puberty: Biological and Psychosocial Perspectives.* New York: Plenum Press, 1983, 229–257.

SINCLAIR, D. *Human Growth After Birth.* London: Oxford University Press, 1978.

SINGER, J. L., and SINGER, D. G. *Television Imagination and Aggression: A Study of Preschoolers' Play.* Hillsdale, N.J.: Erlbaum, 1981.

SKEELS, H. "Adult Status of Children with Contrasting Early Life Experiences." *Monographs of the Society for Research in Child Development* 31, no. 3 (1966).

SKINNER, B. F. *The Behavior of Organisms: An Experimental Analysis.* New York: Appleton, 1938.

———. *Beyond Freedom and Dignity.* New York: Knopf, 1971.

SKODAK, M., and SKEELS, H. M. "A Final Follow-up on One Hundred Adopted Children." *Journal of Genetic Psychology* 75 (1949), 85–125.

SKOLNICK, A. "Married Lives: Longitudinal Perspective on Marriage." In D. H. Eichorn, J. A. Clausen, N. Haan, M. P. Honzik, and P. H. Mussen (eds.), *Present and Past in Middle Life.* New York: Academic Press, 1981, 269–298.

———. "Early Attachment and Personal Relationships Across the Life Course." *Life-span Development and Behavior* 7 (1986) 173–206.

———. *The Intimate Environment: Exploring Marriage and the Family,* 4th ed. Boston: Little, Brown, 1987.

SKOLNICK, A., and SKOLNICK, J. *Family in Transition.* Boston: Little, Brown, 1986.

SLABY, R. G., and FREY, K. S. "Development of Gender Constancy and Selective Attention to Same-Sex Models." *Child Development* 46 (1975), 849–856.

SLAUGHTER, D. "Education and Family." In B. Bloom and C. Mathis (eds.), *The Schools, Schools of Education and Major Changes Affecting Education: The Crises of Our Time.* 1983 (unpublished).

SLOBIN, D. I. *Psycholinguistics.* Glenview, Ill.: Scott Foresman, 1979.

———. *The Crosslinguistic Study of Language Acquisition.* Vol. 1, *The Data.* Hillsdale, N.J.: Erlbaum, 1985.

SMITH, G. *Statistical Reasoning.* Boston: Allyn and Bacon, 1985.

SMITH, K. U., and SCHIAMBERG, L. "The Infraschool: The Systems Approach to Parent-Child Education." Madison: Behavioral Cybernetics Laboratory, University of Wisconsin, 1973.

SMITH, P. K., and CONNOLLY, K. *The Behavioral Ecology of the Preschool.* Cambridge: Cambridge University Press, 1981.

SMOLLAR, J., and YOUNISS, J. "Social Development Through Friendship." In K. H. Rubin and H. S. Ross (eds.), *Peer Relationships and Social Skills in Childhood.* New York: Springer-Verlag, 1982.

SNOW, M. E.; JACKLIN, C. N.; and MACCOBY, E. E. "Sex-of-child Differences in Father-Child Interaction at One Year of Age." *Child Development* 54 (1983), 227–232.

SOAR, R. S., and SOAR, R. M. "Emotional Climate and Management." In P. L. Peterson and H. J. Walberg (eds.), *Research on Teaching: Concepts, Findings and Implications.* Berkeley, Calif.: McCutchan, 1979.

SOBESKY, W. E. "The Effects of Situational Factors on Moral Judgments." *Child Development* 54, no. 3 (June 1983), 575–584.

SOLLIE, D. L., and MILLER, B. C. "The Transition to Parenthood as a Critical Time for Building Family Strengths." In N. Stinnett, B. Chesser, J. Defain, and P. Kraul (eds.), *Family Strengths: Posi-*

tive Models of Family Life. Lincoln: University of Nebraska Press, 1980.

SOLOMON, D. "Theory and Research on Children's Achievement." In J. Worrell (ed.), *Psychological Development in the Elementary Years*. New York: Academic Press, 1982, 269–320.

SORENSON, R. *Adolescent Sexuality in Contemporary America*. New York: Collins, 1973.

SPEARMAN, C. "General Intelligence, Objectively Determined and Measured." *American Journal of Psychology* 15 (1904), 201–293.

———. *The Abilities of Man*. New York: Macmillan, 1927.

SPERLING, E. "Psychological Issues in Chronic Illness and Handicap." In E. Gellert (ed.), *Psychosocial Aspects of Pediatric Care*. New York: Grune and Stratton, 1978.

SPRINTHALL, N. A., and COLLINS, W. A. *Adolescent Psychology*. Reading, Mass.: Addison-Wesley, 1984.

SPRINTHALL, N. A., and MOSHER, R. "Psychological Education in Secondary Schools." *American Psychologist* 25 (October 1970), 911–924.

SROUFE, L. A. "Wariness of Strangers and the Study of Infant Development." *Child Development* 48 (1977), 1184–1199.

———. "The Coherence of Individual Development: Early Care, Attachment, and Subsequent Developmental Issues." *American Psychologist* 34 (1979a), 834–841.

———. "Socioemotional Development." In J. Osofsky (ed.), *Handbook of Infant Development*. New York: Wiley, 1979b.

SROUFE, L. A., and WATERS, E. "The Ontogenesis of Smiling and Laughter: A Perspective on the Organization of Development in Infancy." *Psychological Review* 83 (1976), 173–189.

SROUFE, L. A., and WUNSCH, J. "The Development of Laughter in the First Year of Life. *Child Development* 43 (1972), 1326–1344.

STACK, C. B. "Sex Roles and Survival Strategies in an Urban Black Community." In M. Z. Risaldo and L. Lamphere (eds.), *Women, culture and Society*. Stanford, Calif.: Stanford University Press, 1974.

STAMIER, J. "Introduction to Risk Factors in Coronary Artery Disease." In H. McIntosh (ed.), *Baylor College of Medicine Cardiology Series* (3). Northfield: Medical Communications, 1978.

STANDLEY, K.; SOULE, B.; and COPANS, S. A. "Dimensions of Prenatal Anxiety and Their Influence on Pregnancy Outcome." *American Journal of Obstetrics and Gynecology* 135 (1979), 22–26.

STANJEK, K. "Das uberreichen von Gaben: Funkton und Entwicklung in den ersten Lebensjahren." *Zeitschrift für Entwicklungspsychologie und Padagogische Psychologie* 10 (1978), 103–113.

STANTON, A. N.; SCOTT, D. J.; and DOWNHAN, M. A. "Is Overheating a Factor in Some Unexpected Infant Deaths?" *Lancet* (1980), 1054–1057.

STAUB, E. *Positive Social Behavior and Morality*. Vol. 1, *Social and Personal Influences*. New York: Academic Press, 1978.

STECHLER, G., and HALTON, A. "Prenatal Influences on Human Development." In B. Wolman (ed.), *Handbook of Developmental Psychology*. Englewood Cliffs, N.J.: Prentice-Hall, 1982, 175–189.

STEIN, G. S.; HARTSHORN, S.; JONES, J.; and STEINBERG, D. "Lithium in a Case of Severe Anorexia Nervosa." *British Journal of Psychiatry* 140 (1982), 526–528.

STEIN, R., and RIESSMAN, C. "The Development of an Impact-on-Family Scale: Preliminary Findings." *Medical Care* 18 (1980), 465–472.

STEINBERG, L. D. "Transformations in Family Relations at Puberty." *Developmental Psychology* 17 (1981), 833–840.

———. "Latchkey Children and Susceptibility to Peer Pressure: An Ecological Analysis." *Developmental Psychology* 22 (1986), 433–439.

STEINBERG, L. D., and SILVERBERG, S. B. "The Vicissitudes of Autonomy in Early Adolescence." *Child Development* 57 (1986), 841–851.

STEINBERG, L. D.; CATALANO, R.; and DOOLEY, D. "Economic Antecedents of Child Abuse and Neglect." *Child Development* 52 (1981), 975–985.

STEINBERG, L. D.; GREENBERGER, E.; GARDUQUE, L.; RUGGIERO, M.; and VAUX, A. "Effects of Working on Adolescent Development." *Developmental Psychology* 18 (1982), 385–395.

STEINER, H. "Anorexia Nervosa." *Pediatrics in Review* 4 (1982), 123–129.

STEINER, J. E. "Human Facial Expressions in Response to Taste and Smell Stimulation." In H. W. Reese and L. P. Lipsett (eds.), *Advances in Child Development and Behavior*, Vol. 13. New York: Academic Press, 1979.

STEINMETZ, S. K. *The Cycle of Violence: Assertive, Aggressive, and Abusive Family Interaction*. New York: Praeger, 1977.

STERN, D. *The First Relationship: Infant and Mother*. Cambridge, Mass.: Harvard University Press, 1977.

STERNBERG, R. J. "Stalking the I.Q. Quark." *Psychology Today* 13 (September 1979), 42–54.

———. "Who's Intelligent?" *Psychology Today* (April 1982), 30–39.

———. *Beyond I.Q.: A Triarchic Theory of Human Intelligence*. New York: Cambridge University Press, 1985.

STERNBERG, R. J., and DAVIDSON, J. E. "The Mind of the Puzzler." *Psychology Today* (June 1982), 37–44.

STERNBERG, R. J., and POWELL, J. S. "Theories of Intelligence." In R. J. Sternberg (ed.), *Handbook of Human Intelligence*. New York: Cambridge University Press, 1982.

———. "The Development of Intelligence." In P. H. Mussen (ed.), *Handbook of Child Psychology*, Vol. 3. 4th ed. New York: Wiley, 1983, 341–419.

STEVENSON, H. W., and SIEGEL, A. (eds.). *Child Development Research and Social Policy*. Chicago: The University of Chicago Press, 1984.

STEVENSON, H. W.; LEE, S-Y; and STIGLER, J. W. "Mathematics Achievement of Chinese, Japanese, and American Children." *Science* 231 (1986), 693–699.

STIERLIN, H. *Separating Parents and Adolescents: A Perspective on Running Away, Schizophrenia, and Waywardness*. New York: New York Times Book Company, 1974.

———. "The Adolescent as Delegate of His Parents." *Adolescent Psychiatry* 4 (1975).

STIGLER, J. W.; LEE, S.; LUCKER, G. W.; and STEVENSON, H. W. "Curriculum and Achievement in Mathematics: A Study of Elementary School Children in Japan, Taiwan and the U.S." *Journal of Educational Psychology* 74 (1982), 315–322.

STORMS, M. D. "Sex-Role Identity and Its Relationships to Sex-Role Attributes and Sex-Role Stereotypes." *Journal of Personality and Social Psychology* 37 (1979), 1779–1789.

STRAUS, M. A.; GELLES, R.; and STEINMETZ, S. *Behind Closed Doors*. New York: Doubleday, 1980.

STREISSGUTH, A. P.; BARR, H. M.; and MARTIN, D. C. "Maternal Alcohol Use and Neonatal Habituation Assessed with the Brazelton Scale." *Child Development* 54 (1983), 1109–1118.

STUNKARD, A.; THORKILD, M. D.; SORENSON, I. A.; HANIS, C.; TEASDALE, T. W.; CHAKRABORTY, R.; SCHULL, W. J.; and SCHULSINGER, F. "An Adoption Study of Human Obesity." *The New England Journal of Medicine* 314 (1986), 193–198.

SULLIVAN, K., and SULLIVAN, A. "Adolescent-Parent Separation." *Developmental Psychology* 16, no. 2 (1980), 93–99.

SUPER, D. E. "A Theory of Vocational Development." *American Psychologist* 8 (1953), 185–190.

SURBER, C. F. "Separable Effects of Motives, Consequences, and Presentation Order on Children's Moral Judgments." *Developmental Psychology* 18 (1982), 257–266.

———. "The Development of Achievement Related Judgment Processes." In J. Nicholls (ed.), *The Development of Achievement Motivation*. Greenwich, Conn.: JAI Press, 1984.

SUSSMAN, M. B. "The Family Today—Is It an Endangered Species?" *Children Today* 45. Washington, D.C.: U.S. Government Printing Office, March-April 1978, 32–37.

SUTTON-SMITH, B., and SUTTON-SMITH, S. *How to Play with Your Children (and When Not To)*. New York: Hawthorne Books, 1974.

SVEDJA, M. J.; CAMPOS, J. J.; and EMDE, R. N. "Mother-Infant 'Bonding': Failure to Generalize." *Child Development* 51 (1980), 775–779.

TAINE, H. "Acquisition of Language by Children." *Mind* 2 (1877), 252–259.

TANNER, J. M. *Growth at Adolescence*, 2d ed. Oxford: Blackwell, 1962.

———. "Growth and Endocrinology of the Adolescent." In L. I. Gardner (ed.), *Endocrine and Genetic Diseases of Childhood and Adolescence*. Philadelphia: Saunders, 1969.

———. "Sequence, Tempo and Individual Variation of the Growth and Development of Boys and Girls Aged Twelve to Sixteen." *Journal of the American Academy of Arts and Sciences* 100 (Fall 1971) 907–930.

———. "Trends Towards Earlier Menarche in London, Oslo, Copenhagen, the Netherlands and Hungary." *Nature* 243 (1973), 95–96.

———. *Education and Physical Growth*, 2d ed. New York: International Universities Press, 1978a.

———. *Fetus into Man: Physical Growth from Conception to Maturity.* Cambridge, Mass.: Harvard University Press, 1978b.

———. *A History of the Study of Human Growth.* Cambridge, Mass.: Harvard University Press, 1981.

TANNER, J. M.; WHITEHOUSE, R. H.; and TAKAISHI, M. "Standards from Birth to Maturity for Height, Weight, Height Velocity and Weight Velocity; British Children, 1965." *Archives of the Diseases of Childhood* 41 (1966), 455–471.

TAPP, J. L. "Psychology and the Law: An Overture." *Annual Review of Psychology* 27 (1976), 359–404.

TAPP, J. L., and KOHLBERG, L. "Developing Senses of Law and Legal Justice." *Journal of Social Issues* 27 (1971), 65–93.

TAPP, J. L., and LEVINE, F. J. "Compliance from Kindergarten to College: A Speculative Research Note." *Journal of Youth and Adolescence* 1 (1972), 233–249.

TASK FORCE ON PEDIATRIC EDUCATION. *The Future of Pediatric Education.* Evanston, Ill.: American Academy of Pediatrics, 1978.

TAVRIS, C., and WADE, C. *The Longest War: Sex Differences in Perspective*, 2d ed. San Diego: Harcourt Brace Jovanovich, 1984.

TELLER, D. Y., and BORNSTEIN, M. H. "Infant Color Vision and Color Perception." In P. Salapatek and L. B. Cohen (eds.), *Handbook of Infant Perception*. Vol. 1, *From Sensation to Perception*. Orlando, Fla.: Academic Press, 1987, 185–236.

TERJESEN, N. C.; and WILKINS, L. P. "A Proposal for a Model of Sudden Infant Death Syndrome Act: Help for the 'Other' Victims of SIDS." *Family Law Quarterly* 12 (1979), 285–308.

TERKEL, S. *Working.* New York: Pantheon, 1974.

TERMAN, L. M. (ed.). *Genetic Studies of Genius. I: Mental and Physical Traits of a Thousand Gifted Children.* Stanford, Calif.: Stanford University Press, 1925.

TERMAN, L. M. *Psychological Factors in Marital Happiness.* New York: McGraw-Hill, 1938.

TERMAN, L. M., and ODEN, M. H. *Genetic Studies of Genius. V: The Gifted Group at Mid-Life.* Palo Alto, Calif.: Stanford University Press, 1959.

THACKER, S. B., and BANTA, H. D. "Benefits and Risks of Episiotomy: An Interpretive Review of the English-Language Literature, 1860–1980." *Obstetrical and Gynecological Survey* 34 (1980), 627–642.

THARP, R., and GALLIMORE, R. "Inquiry Process in Program Development." *Journal of Community Psychology* 10 (1982), 103–118.

THEIS, J. M. "Beyond Divorce: The Impact of Remarriage on Children." *Journal of Clinical Child Psychology* 6 (1977), 59–61.

THOMAS, A., and CHESS, S. *Temperament and Development.* New York: Brunner/Mazel, 1977.

———. *The Dynamics of Psychological Development.* New York: Brunner/Mazel, 1980.

THOMAS, A.; CHESS, S.; and KORN, S. C. "The Reality of Difficult Temperament." *Merrill-Palmer Quarterly* 28 (1982), 1–20.

THOMAS, A.; CHESS, S.; BIRCH, H. G.; HERTZIG, M. E.; and KORN, S. *Behavioral Individuality in Early Childhood.* New York: New York University Press, 1983.

THOMAS, G.; LEE, P.; FRANKS, P.; and PAFFENBARGER, R. (eds.). *Exercise and Health: The Evidence and the Implications.* Cambridge: Oelgeschlager, Gunn and Hain, 1981.

THOMPSON, R. A., and LAMB, M. E. "Infant-Mother Attachment: New Directions for Theory and Research." In P. B. Baltes, D. L. Featherman, and R. M. Lerner (eds.), *Life-span Development and Behavior*, Vol. 7. Hillsdale, N.J.: Erlbaum, 1986, 1–41.

THOMPSON, R. A.; LAMB, M. E., and ESTES, D. "Stability of Infant-Mother Attachment and Its Relationship to Changing Life Circumstances in an Unselected Middle-Class Sample." *Child Development* 53 (1982), 144–148.

THORNDIKE, E. L. *Animal Intelligence.* New York: Macmillan, 1911.

———. *Educational Psychology.* 3 vols. New York: Teachers College Columbia University, 1913–1914.

THORNDIKE, R. L.; HAGEN, E. P.; and SATTLER, J. M. *The Stanford-Binet Intelligence Scale: Fourth Edition. Guide for Administering and Scoring.* Chicago: The Riverside Publishing Company, 1986.

THORNTON, A., and FREEDMAN, D. "Changing Attitudes Toward Marriage and Single Life." *Family Planning Perspectives* 14 (1982), 297–303.

THURSTONE, L. L. *Primary Mental Abilities.* Chicago: University of Chicago Press, 1938.

THURSTONE, L. L., and THURSTONE, T. G. *SRA Primary Mental Abilities.* Chicago: Science Research Associates, 1962.

TIESZEN, H. R. "Children's Social Behavior in a Korean Preschool." *Journal of Korean Home Economics Association* 17 (1979), 71–84.

TIZARD, J.; SCHOFIELD, W. N.; and HEWISON, J. "Collaboration Between Teachers and Parents Assisting Children's Reading." *British Journal of Educational Psychology* 52 (1982), 1–15.

TOBIN-RICHARDS, M. H.; BOXER, A. M.; and PETERSEN, A. C. "The Psychological Significance of Pubertal Change: Sex Differences in Perceptions of Self During Early Adolescence." In J. Brooks-Gunn and A. C. Petersen (eds.), *Girls at Puberty: Biological and Psychosocial Perspectives*. New York: Plenum, 1983.

TOBIN-RICHARDS, M. H.; BOXER, A. M.; KAVRELL, S. M.; and PETERSEN, A. C. "Puberty and Its Social and Psychological Significance." In R. M. Lerner and N. L. Galambos (eds.), *Experiencing Adolescents: A Sourcebook for Parents, Teachers, and Teens*. New York: Garland Press, 1984.

TOFFLER, A. *Future Shock.* New York: Random House, 1972.

TOMLINSON, KEASEY, C. "Structures, Functions and Stages: A Trio of Unresolved Issues in Formal Operations." In S. Modgil and C. Modgil (eds.), *Piaget 1896–1980: Consensus and Controversy*. New York: Praeger, 1982.

TONER, I. J.; MOORE, L. P.; and ASHLEY, P. K. "The Effect of Serving as a Model of Self-Control on Subsequent Resistance to Deviation in Children." *Journal of Experimental Child Psychology* 26 (1978), 85–91.

TOUHY, J. C., and VILLEMEZ, W. J. "Ability Attribution as a Result of Variable Effort and Achievement Motivation." *Journal of Personality and Social Psychology* 38 (1980), 211–216.

TRACY, R. L.; and AINSWORTH, M. D. S. "Maternal Affectionate Behavior and Infant-Mother Attachment Patterns." *Child Development* 52 (1981), 1341–1343.

TROTTER, R. J. "Baby Face." *Psychology Today* 17, no. 8 (1983), 14–20.

TRUSS, T. J. (ed.). *Child Health and Human Development: An Evaluation and Assessment of the State of the Science.* NIH Publication No. 82-2304. U.S. Department of Health and Human Services, October 1981.

TUCHMANN-DUPLESSIS, H.; DAVID G.; and HAEGEL, P. *Illustrated Human Embryology.* Vol. 1, *Embryogenesis*. Springer-Verlag, New York, 1972; Masson S. A., Paris, 1975.

UNITED NATIONS CHILDREN'S FUND. *The State of the World's Children.* New York: Oxford University Press, 1983.

URBERG, K. A. "The Development of Androgynous Sex-Role Concepts in Young Children." Paper presented at the meeting of the Society for Research in Child Development, San Francisco, March 1979.

U.S. DEPARTMENT OF COMMERCE. Bureau of the Census. "Characteristics of American Children and Youth: 1980." *Current Popu-*

lation Reports. P-23, No. 114. Washington, D.C.: U.S. Government Printing Office, 1982a.

———. "Trends in Child Care Arrangements of Working Mothers." *Current Population Reports*. Population Characteristics, Series 9-23, No. 117. Washington, D.C.: U.S. Government Printing Office, 1982b.

———. "Child Care Arrangements of Working Mothers: June 1982." *Current Population Reports*. Series P23, No. 129, Table 2, Parts A and B, November 1983a, p. 404.

———. Special Demographic Analyses. *American Women: Three Decades of Change*. CDS-80-8. Washington, D.C.: U.S. Government Printing Office, 1983b, 5.

———. "Geographical Mobility: March 1982 to March 1983." *Current Population Reports*. Population Characteristics, Series P-20, No. 393. Washington, D.C.: U.S. Government Printing Office, 1984.

———. "Characteristics of the Population Below the Poverty Level, 1983." *Current Population Reports*. Series P-60, No. 147. U.S. Government Printing Office, 1985a, Table 30, pp. 118–121.

———. "Marital Status and Living Arrangements: March 1984." *Current Population Reports*, Series P-20, No. 399. Washington, D.C.: U.S. Government Printing Office, 1985b, Table D, p. 4; Fig. 2, p. 5; and Table 4, p. 29.

———. *Statistical Abstract of the United States: 1986*, 106th ed. Washington,D.C., 1985c, No. 83, p. 57 and no. 110, p. 70.

———. *Statistical Abstract of the United States: 1986*, 106th ed. Washington, D.C.: U.S. Government Printing Office, 1985d, Table No. 43, p. 35 and Table No. 122, p. 78.

U.S. DEPARTMENT OF EDUCATION. *What Works: Schools Without Drugs*. Washington, D.C.: U.S. Government Printing Office, 1986.

U.S. DEPARTMENT OF HEALTH AND HUMAN SERVICES. Public Health Services. *Preterm Babies*. DHSS Pub. No. (ADM) 80-972. Washington, D.C.: U.S. Government Printing Office, 1980.

———. Public Health Services, National Center for Health Statistics. *Vital Statistics of the United States*. Vol. 2, *Mortality. Part A*. Washington, D.C.: U.S. Government Printing Office, 1981.

———. Public Health Services. "Births: National Center for Health Statistics." *Monthly Vital Statistics Report* 33, no. 6 (1984a).

———. Public Health Services. *Health, United States, 1984*. DHSS Pub. No. (PHS) 85-1232. Washington, D.C.: U.S. Government Printing Office, December 1984b.

———. National Center for Educational Statistics. *Condition of Education, 1985 Edition*. Washington, D.C.: U.S. Government Printing Office, 1985a.

———. Public Health Services, National Center for Health Statistics. *Health. United States, 1985*. DHSS Pub. No. (PHS) 86-1232. Washington, D.C.: U.S. Government Printing Office, 1985b.

———. Public Health Services, National Center for Health Statistics. "Advance Report on Final Natality Statistics, 1984." *Monthly Vital Statistics Report* 35, no. 4. Table 5, Supplement. U.S. Government Printing Office, July 18, 1986.

U.S. DEPARTMENT OF HEALTH, EDUCATION, AND WELFARE. *Annual Report on the Runaway Youth Act*. Washington, D.C.: U.S. Government Printing Office, 1978.

———. Public Health Service. *Smoking and Health: A Report of the Surgeon General*. DHEW Pub. No. (PHS) 79-50066. Washington D.C.: U.S. Government Printing Office, 1979.

———. National Heart, Lung, and Blood Institute. *Arteriosclerosis, 1981*. DHHS Pub. No. (NIH) 81-2034. Washington, D.C.: U.S. Government Printing Office, 1981.

U.S. DEPARTMENT OF JUSTICE. *Crime in the U.S.: Uniform Crime Reports*. Published annually by the FBI, Washington, D.C., 1982.

U.S. DEPARTMENT OF LABOR. Bureau of Labor Statistics. *Women at Work: A Chartbook*. Bulletin 2168. Washington, D.C.: Department of Labor, April 1983, 20–25, 29.

———. Bureau of Labor Statistics. *Employment and Earnings*. Vol. 33, no. 1. Washington, D.C.: U.S. Government Printing Office, January 1986.

U.S. HOUSE OF REPRESENTATIVES SUBCOMMITTEE ON DOMESTIC AND INTERNATIONAL SCIENTIFIC PLANNING, ANALYSIS AND COOPERATION. *Research into Violent Behavior: Domestic Violence*. Washington, D.C.: U.S. Government Printing Office, 1978.

VANCE, J.; FAZAN, L.; SATTERWHITE, B.; and PLESS, I. B. "Effects of Nephrotic Syndrome on the Family: A Controlled Study." *Pediatrics* 65 (1980), 948–955.

VANDELL, D. L., and MUELLER, E. C. "Peer Play and Friendships During the First Two Years." In H. C. Foot, A. J. Chapman, and J. R. Smith (eds.), *Friendship and Social Relations in Children*. London: Wiley, 1980.

VANDELL, D. L., and WILSON, K. S. "Social Interaction in the First Year." In K. Rubin and H. S. Ross (eds.), *Peer Relationships and Social Skills in Childhood*. New York: Springer-Verlag, 1982.

VAN GIFFEN, K., and HAITH, M. "Infant Visual Response to Gestalt Geometric Forms." *Infant Behavior and Development* 1 (1984), 335–346.

VAN ITALLIE, T. "Obesity: Adverse Effects on Health and Longevity." *American Journal of Clinical Nutrition* 32 (1979), 2723–2733.

VAUGHAN, V. C., and MCKAY, R. J. (eds.). *Textbook of Pediatrics*, 10th ed. Philadelphia: Saunders, 1975.

VAUGHN, B. E.; EGELAND, B.; SROUFE, L. A.; and WATERS, E. "Individual Differences in Infant-Mother Attachment at Twelve and Eighteen Months: Stability and Change in Families under Stress." *Child Development* 50 (1979), 971–975.

VAUGHN, B. E.; GOVE, F. L.; and EGELAND, B. R. "The Relationship Between Out-of-Home Care and the Quality of Infant-Mother Attachment in an Economically Disadvantaged Population." *Child Development* (1950), 1203–1214.

VENER, A., and STEWART, C. "Adolescent Sexual Behavior in Middle America Revisited: 1970–1973." *Journal of Marriage and the Family* 36 (1974), 728–735.

VEROFF, J. "Social Comparison and the Development of Achievement Motivation." In C. P. Smith (ed.), *Achievement-Related Motives in Children*. New York: Russell Sage Foundation, 1969, 46–101.

VISHER, E., and VISHER, J. *Stepfamilies: A Guide to Working with Stepparents and Stepchildren*. New York: Brunner/Mazel, 1979.

VLIETSTRA, A. G. "Children's Responses to Task Instructions: Age Changes and Training Effects." *Child Development* 53 (1982), 534–542.

VOLPE, E. P. *Understanding Evolution*, 4th ed. Dubuque, Iowa: W. C. Brown, 1981.

VONDRACEK, F. W., and LERNER, R. M. "Vocational Role Development in Adolescence." In B. Wolman (ed.), *Handbook of Developmental Psychology*. Englewood Cliffs, N.J.: Prentice-Hall, 1982, 602–614.

VOYDANOFF, P. *Work and Family*. Palo Alto, Calif.: Mayfield, 1984.

VURPILLOT, E. *The Visual World of the Child* (W.E.C. Gillham, trans.) New York: International Universities Press, 1976. (Originally published 1972).

VURPILLOT, E., and BALL, W. A. "The Concept of Identity and Children's Selective Attention." In G. A. Hale and M. Lewis (eds.), *Attention and Cognitive Development*. New York: Plenum, 1979.

VYGOTSKY, L. S. *Thought and Language*. Cambridge, Mass.: MIT Press, 1934.

WACHS, T. D., and GRUEN, G. E. *Early Experience and Human Development*. New York: Plenum, 1982.

WADDINGTON, C. H. *The Strategy of the Genes*. London: Allen and Unwin, 1957.

———. *Principles of Development and Differentiation*. New York: Macmillan, 1966.

WADSWORTH, B. J. *Piaget's Theory of Cognitive Development*, 2d ed. Copyright © 1971. New York: McKay and Longman, 1971, 1979.

WALDMAN, E. "Labor Force Statistics from a Family Perspective." *Monthly Labor Review*. Washington, D.C.: U.S. Government Printing Office, December 1983, 14–18.

WALLERSTEIN, J. S., and KELLY, J. B. "The Effects of Parental Divorce: The Adolescent Experience." In E. Anthony and A. Koupernik (eds.), *The Child in His Family: Children as a Psychiatric Risk,* Vol. 3. New York: Wiley, 1974.

———. "The Effects of Parental Divorce: Experiences of the Preschool Child." *Journal of the American Academy of Child Psychiatry* 14 (1975), 600–616.

———. "The Effects of Divorce on Visiting Father-Child Relationships." *American Journal of Psychiatry* 137 (1978), 1534–1538.

———. "Children and Divorce: A Review." *Social Work* 24 (1979), 468–475.

———. *Surviving the Breakup: How Children and Parents Cope with Divorce.* New York: Basic Books, 1980.

WALTER, H. *Region and Socialization,* Vol. 1. Stuttgart: Fromman-Holzboog, 1981.

———. *Region and Socialization,* Vol. 2. Stuttgart: Fromman-Holzboog, 1982.

WALTERS, G. C., and GRUSEC, J. E. *Punishment.* San Francisco: Freeman, 1977.

WATERMAN, A. S., and WATERMAN, C. K. "The Relationship Between Freshman Ego Identity Status and Subsequent Academic Behavior: A Test of the Predictive Validity of Marcia's Categorization System for Identity Status." *Developmental Psychology* 6, no. 1 (1972), 179.

WATERS, E. "The Reliability and Stability of Individual Differences in Infant-Mother Attachment." *Child Development* 49 (1978), 483–494.

WATERS, E., and SROUFE, L. A. "Social Competence as a Developmental Construct." *Developmental Review* 3 (1983), 79–87.

WATERS, E.; VAUGHN, B. E.; and EGELAND, R. R. "Individual Differences in Infant-Mother Attachment Relationships at Age One: Antecedents in Neonatal Behavior in an Urban, Economically Disadvantaged Sample." *Child Development* 51 (1980), 208–216.

WATERS, E.; WIPPMAN, J.; and SROUFE, L. A. "Attachment, Positive Affect, and Competence in the Peer Group: Two Studies in Construct Validation." *Child Development* 50 (1979), 821–829.

WATSON, J. B. *Behaviorism.* New York: Norton, 1924.

———. *Psychological Care of Infant and Child.* New York: Norton, 1928.

———. "Smiling, Cooing and 'the Game.' " Paper presented at the annual meeting of the American Psychological Association, Miami Beach, 1970.

WATSON, M. W. "The Development of Social Roles: A Sequence of Social-Cognitive Development." In K. W. Fischer (ed.), *Cognitive Development.* New Directions for Child Development, No. 12. San Francisco: Jossey-Bass, 1981.

WEHREN, A., and DeLISI, R. "The Development of Gender Understanding: Judgments and Explanations." *Child Development* 54 (1983), 1568–1578.

WEIKERT, D. A. *Changed Lives: The Effects of the Perry Preschool Program on Youths Through Age 19.* Ypsilanti, Mich.: High/Scope Educational Research Foundation, 1984.

WEIL, W. "Obesity in Children." *Pediatrics in Review* 3 (1981), 180–189.

WEINER, B. "A Theory of Motivation for Some Classroom Experiences." *Journal of Educational Psychology* 7 (1979), 3–25.

WEINER, I. B. *Child and Adolescent Psychopathology.* New York: Wiley, 1982.

WEINRAUB, M., and LEWIS, M. "The Determinants of Children's Responses to Separation." *Monographs of the Society for Research in Child Development* 42, no. 4, Serial No. 172 (1977).

WEINRAUB, M., and WOLF, B. M. "Effects of Stress and Social Supports on Mother-Child Interactions in Single and Two-Parent Families." *Child Development* 54 (1983), 1297–1311.

WEISS, R. "Men and the Family." *Family Processes* 24 (1985), 49–58.

WEISSBROD, C. S. "The Impact of Warmth and Instructions on Donation." *Child Development* 51 (1980), 279–281.

WELLMAN, H. M., and SOMERVILLE, S. C. "The Development of Human Search Ability." In M. E. Lamb and A. L. Brown (eds.), *Advances in Developmental Psychology,* Vol. 2. Hillsdale, N.J.: Erlbaum, 1982.

WELLMAN, H. M., RITTER, K.; and FLAVELL, J. H. "Deliberate Memory Behavior in the Delayed Reactions of Very Young Children." *Developmental Psychology* 11 (1975), 780–787.

WELLMAN, H. M.; SOMERVILLE, S. C.; and HAAKE, R. J. "Development of Search Procedures in Real-Life Spatial Environments." *Developmental Psychology* 15 (1979), 530–542.

WERNER, E. E. *Cross-Cultural Child Development: A View from the Planet Earth.* Monterey, Calif.: Brooks/Cole, 1979.

WERNER, E. E., and SMITH, R. S. *Vulnerable but Invincible: A Longitudinal Study of Resilient Children and Youth.* New York: McGraw-Hill, 1982.

WERNER, J. S., and LIPSITT, L. P. "The Infancy of Human Sensory Systems." In E. S. Gollin (ed.), *Developmental Plasticity.* New York: Academic Press, 1981, 35–68.

WERNER, P. D., and LaRUSSA, G. W. "Persistence and Change in Sex-Role Stereotypes." California School of Professional Psychology, 1983 (unpublished).

WESTON, D., and MAIN, M. "Infant Responses to the Crying of an Adult Actor in the Laboratory: Stability and Correlates of 'Concerned Attention.' " Paper presented at the meeting of the International Conference on Infant Studies, New Haven, Connecticut, April 1980.

WHALEY, L. F. *Understanding Inherited Disorders.* St. Louis: Mosby, 1974.

WHITE, B. L. "Human Infants: Experience and Psychological Development." Englewood Cliffs, N.J.: Prentice-Hall, 1971.

WHITE, B. L.; KABAN, B.; SHAPIRO, B.; and ATTONUCCI, J. "Competence and Experience." In I. C. Uzgiris and F. Weizmann (eds.), *The Structuring of Experience.* New York: Plenum Press, 1976.

WHITE, G. M. "Immediate and Deferred Effects of Model Observation and Guided and Unguided Rehearsal on Donating and Stealing." *Journal of Personality and Social Psychology* 21 (1972), 139–148.

WHITE, K. R. "The Relation Between Socioeconomic Status and Academic Achievement." *Psychological Bulletin* 91 (1982), 461–481.

WHITE, M. "Anorexia Nervosa: A Transgenerational System Perspective." *Family Process* 22 (1983), 255–273.

WHITE, R. W. "Motivation Reconsidered: The Concept of Competence." *Psychological Review* 66 (1959), 297–333.

WHITE, S. "The Learning Theory Approach." In P. H. Mussen (ed.), *Charmichael's Manual of Child Psychology,* Vol. 1. New York: Wiley, 1970.

WHITESIDE, M. F. "Remarriage, A Family Developmental Process." *Journal of Marital and Family Therapy* 8 (1982), 59–68.

WHITING, B. B., and WHITING, J. W. M. *Children of Six Cultures: A Psychocultural Analysis.* Cambridge, Mass.: Harvard University Press, 1975.

WICKSTROM, R. L. *Fundamental Motor Patterns,* 2d ed. Philadelphia: Lea and Febiger, 1977.

WIDDOWSON, E. M. "Mental Contentment and Physical Growth." *Lancet* 1 (1951), 1316–1318.

WIDEMAN, M. V., and SINGER, J. F. "The Role of Psychological Mechanisms in Preparation for Childbirth." *American Psychologist* 34 (1984), 1357–1371.

WILCOX, M. I., and WEBSTER, E. J. "Early Discourse Behavior: An Analysis of Children's Responses to Listener Feedback." *Child Development* 51 (1980), 1120–1125.

WILLIAMS, E. R., and CALIENDO, M. A. *Nutrition: Principles, Issues and Applications.* New York: McGraw-Hill, 1984.

WILLIAMS, H. G. *Perceptual and Motor Development.* Englewood Cliffs, N.J.: Prentice-Hall, 1983.

WILLIAMS, J. E.; BENNETT, S. M.; and BEST, D. L. "Awareness and Expression of Sex Stereotypes in Young Children." *Developmental Psychology* 11 (1975), 635–642.

WILMORE, J. H. "The Female Athlete." In R. S. Magill, M. J. Ash, and F. L. Smoll (eds.), *Children in Sports,* 2d ed. Champaign, Ill.: Human Kinetics, 1982, 106–117.

WILSON, R. S. "Synchronies in Mental Development: An Epigenetic Perspective." *Science* 202 (1978), 939–948.

———. "The Louisville Twin Study: Developmental Synchronies in Behavior." *Child Development* 54 (1983), 298–316.

WIMMER, H. "Children's Understanding of Stories: Assimilation by a General Schema for Actions or Coordination of Temporal Relations." In F. Wilkening, J. Becker, and T. Trabasso (eds.), *Information Integration by Children*. Hillsdale, N.J.: Erlbaum, 1980.

WINNICOTT, D. W. *The Piggle*. London: Hogarth/Institute of Psychoanalysis, 1977.

WOLFF, P. H. "Observations on the Early Development of Smiling." In B. M. Foss (ed.), *Determinants of Infant Behavior*, Vol. 2. New York: Wiley, 1963, 113–138.

———. "Crying and Vocalization in Early Infancy." In B. M. Foss (ed.), *Determinants of Infant Behavior*, Vol. 4. London: Methuen; New York: Wiley, 1969a, 81–110.

———. "The Natural History of Crying and Other Vocalizations in Early Infancy." In B. M. Foss (ed.), *Determinants of Infant Behavior*, Vol. 4. London: Methuen, 1969b.

WOLFRAM, W., and FASOLD, R. "Toward Reading Materials for Speakers of Black English: Three Linguistically Appropriate Passages." In J. C. Baratz and R. W. Shuy (eds.), *Teaching Black Children to Read*. Washington, D.C.: Center for Applied Linguistics, 1969, 144–147, 152–154.

WOLF, S., and J. BRANDON. "Runaway Adolescents' Perceptions of Parents and Self." *Adolescence* 12 (1977), 175–888.

WOOD, D. J. "Teaching the Young Child: Some Relationships Between Social Interaction, Language, and Thought." In D. R. Olson, (ed.), *The Social Foundations of Language and Thought*. New York: Norton, 1980.

WRIGHT, J. C., and VLIETSTRA, A. G. "The Development of Selective Attention: From Perceptual Exploration to Logical Search." In H. W. Reese (ed.), *Advances in Child Development*, Vol. 10. New York: Academic Press, 1975, 195–239.

YANKELOVICH, D. *The New Morality: A Profile of American Youth in the 1970's*. New York: McGraw-Hill, 1974.

YANKELOVICH, D.; CLARK, R.; and MARTIRE, G. *General Mills American Family Report*. Minneapolis; General Mills, Inc., 1977.

YAWKEY, T., and PELLEGRINI, A. D. (eds.). *Children's Play*. Hillsdale, N.J.: Erlbaum, 1984.

YOUNG, D. *Changing Childbirth: Family Birth in the Hospital*. Rochester, N.Y.: Childbirth Graphics, Ltd., 1982.

YOUNG, H. B. "Aging and Adolescence." *Developmental Medicine and Child Neurology* 5 (1963), 451–460.

YOUNISS, J. *Parents and Peers in Social Development: A Sullivan-Piaget Perspective*. Chicago: University of Chicago Press, 1980.

ZAHN-WAXLER, C., and RADKE-YARROW, M. "The Development of Altruism: Alternative Research Strategies." In N. Eisenberg-Berg (ed.), *The Development of Prosocial Behavior*. New York: Academic Press, 1982.

ZAHN-WAXLER, C. Z.; RADKE-YARROW, M. R.; and KING, R. A. "Child-Rearing and Children's Prosocial Initiations Toward Victims of Distress." *Child Development* 50 (1979), 319–330.

ZAJONC, R. B.; MARKUS, H.; and MARKUS, G. B. "The Birth Order Puzzle." *Journal of Personality and Social Psychology* 37 (1979), 1325–1341.

ZELNIK, M. "Sex Education and Knowledge of Pregnancy Risk Among U.S. Teenage Women." *Family Planning Perspectives* 11 (1979), 355–357.

ZELNIK, M., and KANTNER, J. F. "First Pregnancies to Women Aged 15–19: 1976 and 1971." *Family Planning Perspectives* 10 (1978), 11–20.

———. "Sexual Activity, Contraceptive Use, and Pregnancy Among Metropolitan-Area Teenagers." *Family Planning Perspectives* 12, no. 5 (September-October 1980).

ZELNIK, M., and SHAH, F. "First Intercourse Among Young Americans." *Family Planning Perspectives* 15, no. 2 (1983).

ZELNIK, M.; KANTNER, J. F.; and FORD, K. *Sex and Pregnancy in Adolescence*. Beverly Hills, Calif.: Sage, 1981.

ZESKIND, P. S., and IACINO, R. "Effects of Maternal Visitation to Preterm Infants in the Neonatal Intensive Care Unit." *Child Development* 55 (1984), 1887–1893.

ZIGLER, E., and BERMAN, W. "Discerning the Future of Early Childhood Intervention." *American Psychologist* 38 (1983), 894–906.

ZIGLER, E.; KAGAN, S.; and KLUGMAN, E. (eds.). *Children, Families and Government*. Cambridge; Cambridge University Press, 1983.

ZILL, N. "Divorce, Marital Happiness and the Mental Health of Children: Findings." FCD National Survey of Children. Paper presented for NIMH Workshop on Divorce and Children, Bethesda, Md., February 1978.

———. *Happy, Healthy and Insecure: A Portrait of Middle Childhood in the United States*. New York: Cambridge University Press, in press.

ZUCKER, R. "Developmental Aspects of Drinking Through the Young Adult Years." In H. Blane and M. Chafetz (eds.), *Youth, Alcohol and Social Policy*. New York: Plenum Press, 1979.

ZUZANEK, J. *Work and Leisure in the Soviet Union: A Time-Budget Analysis*. New York: Praeger, 1980.

Author Index

D

Dale, P.S., 252, 254, 255, 258, 261, 262, 266, 388, 391, 392, 545, 546
Damon, W., 403, 448, 449, 558, 566, 571, 579
Daniels, P., 215, 216
Danielsson, B., 290
Darley, F.L., 252
Darlington, R.B., 28, 78, 346, 347
Darvill, D., 430
Darwin, C., 22, 23, 94, 95
Davidson, E.S., 415, 420
Davidson, J.E., 532
Davidson, S., 689
Davidson, W., 567, 584, 585
Davis, S.W., 409
Dawber, T., 499
Day, R., 61
DeAvila, E., 486
DeCasper, A., 232
DeCecco, J.P., 633
deChateau, P., 290
DeFries, J.C., 76, 296
DeLamater, J., 712, 713
DeLisi, R., 417
DeLiss, R., 679
DeLissovoy, V., 718
DeLoache, J.S., 231, 524
deMontbeillard, 361
Dennis, W., 300
Derryberry, D., 279
Desforges, C., 517, 518
Detroit-Area Pre-College Engineering Program, 695
Deutsch, M., 614
deVilliers, J.G., 257, 264
deVilliers, P.A., 257, 264
Devin-Sheehan, L., 461
Dewey, J., 33, 484
Di Vitto, B.A., 58
Diamond, N., 41
Diaz, R.M., 544
Dickie, J.R., 84
Dickson, W.P., 253
Diener, C.I., 586
Diepold, J.H., 418
Dietz, W., 360, 361, 362, 363
DiPietro, J.A., 415, 421
Dittman-Kohli, 5
Divine-Hawkins, P., 212
Dix, C., 178
Dixon, R.A., 5
Dodge, J.A., 148, 149
Dodge, K.A., 436, 489
Dodwell, P., 232
Doering, S., 290
Dohrenwend, B.P., 612
Dohrenwend, S., 612
Dolby, R.M., 143
Donovan, J.E., 735
Dooley, D., 327
Dornbusch, S.M., 455
Dougherty, L., 272, 273, 274
Douvan, E., 630, 631, 705
Dove, A., 539
Downey, A., 502
Downhan, M.A., 227
Drabman, R.S., 422
Dreyer, A.S., 253

Dreyer, P.H., 659, 698, 711, 712, 715, 716
Drozda, J.G., 382
Dubowitz, L., 170
Dubowitz, V., 170
Duncan, B., 421
Duncan, O.D., 421
Dunn, J., 424, 460, 461, 462
Dunphy, D., 625, 626, 628, 629
Duriez, T., 155, 163
Duvall, E.M., 81, 82, 103
Dweck, C.S., 566, 567, 581, 582, 583, 584, 585, 586, 587
Dwyer, J., 143

E

Eagle, M., 44
Eater, L.A., 70
Eccles, J.S., 415, 420, 421, 560
Eckerman, C.O., 333, 334, 339
Eckert, H.M., 508, 510
Edelbrock, C., 723
Edelin, K.C., 145
Edwards, C.P., 403
Edwards, J.R., 409
Egan, E.A., 178
Egeland, B.R., 293, 301, 324
Ehrmann, W., 711
Eiduson, B., 467
Eisen, M., 557
Eisenberg, N., 426, 427
Eisenberg-Berg, N., 425, 426, 428
Eitzen, D.S., 625
Elder, G.H., 5
Elkind, D., 15, 667, 676, 677, 722
Elliott, E.S., 581, 582, 583, 584, 585, 586, 587
Elliott, G., 499, 501
Ellis, G.J., 622
Ellis, G.T., 438
Ellis, S., 334
Emde, R.N., 281, 290
Emmerich, W., 417
Englemann, S., 345
Enkin, M., 165
Enna, B., 567, 584, 585
Enright, R.D., 428
Entwisle, D., 290
Epps, E., 481, 482, 483, 484, 560
Epstein, A.S., 347
Epstein, J.L., 87, 360, 361, 483
Erikson, E., 41, 43, 44, 45, 46, 47, 48, 50, 59, 82, 92, 305, 404, 407, 448, 553, 601, 686, 687, 689, 690, 702
Erlenmeyer-Kimling, L., 73
Eron, L.D., 440
Espenschade, A.S., 510
Estes, D., 293, 301
Etaugh, C., 301
Eveleth, P., 665, 666

F

Fagen, R.E., 313
Fagerberg, H., 290
Fagot, B.I., 418, 478
Fandal, A.W., 234, 236
Fantz, R.L., 229, 282
Faranoff, A.A., 178
Farber, E.D., 725
Farran, D.C., 301

Farrington, D.P., 721
Fasold, R., 545
Faulkender, P.J., 418
Faust, M.S., 667, 668
Feig, E., 421
Fein, G.G., 336, 337, 339, 340, 349, 379
Feinbloom, R., 156
Feinstein, K.W., 210
Feldman, D.H., 530
Feldman, H., 84
Feldman, R.S., 461
Feldman, S.S., 84
Ferguson, T.J., 430
Fernandez, G., 462
Ferrara, R.A., 384, 540
Ferris, P., 473
Field, J., 232
Field, T., 177
Fifer, W., 232
Filly, R.A., 158
Filmer, H.T., 409
Fine, M.A., 468
Finkelhor, D., 432, 433
Fisch, R.O., 289
Fischer, K.W., 511, 530, 531, 539, 541, 542
Fishbein, H.D., 66, 381
Fitch, S., 706
Flavell, E.R., 378, 379
Flavell, J.H., 247, 378, 379, 382, 384, 394, 448, 514, 515, 516, 517, 523, 524, 530, 555, 556, 557, 561, 673, 675, 679
Fogel, A., 185
Ford, A.J., Jr., 404
Ford, K., 716
Forrest, J.D., 714
Fox, G.L., 697, 698
Fox, H.E., 145
Fox, M.M., 669
Fraiberg, S., 185
Francis, W.D., 586
Frankel, D.G., 384
Frankenburg, W.K., 234, 236
Franklin, C.C., 428
Freedman, D., 296, 698
Freedman, J.L., 438, 439
Freidrich, L.K., 429
Freud, S., 41, 42, 43, 44, 45, 46, 48, 49, 50, 59, 416, 553
Frey, K.S., 417
Frieze, I.H., 586
Frisch, R.E., 648, 666, 669
Frodi, M., 470
Frost, J.L., 331
Furlong, N.E., 526
Furman, W., 583, 585

G

Gaite, A.J., 679
Galinsky, E., 158
Gallagher, J., 178
Gallatin, J., 23, 677, 678
Gallimore, R., 484
Garbarino, A., 723, 724, 725
Garbarino, J., 6, 7, 58, 79, 85, 86, 209, 210, 326, 327, 433, 616, 617, 723, 724, 725
Garber, J., 472, 566
Garcia-Coll, C., 79, 279
Gardner, H., 387

Subject Index